THE
PRACTICAL
IMAGINATION

THE PRACTICAL IMAGINATION

STORIES, POEMS, PLAYS

REVISED COMPACT EDITION

NORTHROP FRYE
Massey College, University of Toronto

SHERIDAN BAKER
The University of Michigan

GEORGE PERKINS
Eastern Michigan University

BARBARA PERKINS
Eastern Michigan University

📖 HarperCollins*Publishers*

For permission to use copyrighted materials, grateful acknowledgment is made to copyright holders listed on pages 1425–1432.

Sponsoring Editor: Phillip Leininger
Project Editor: Joan C. Gregory
Text Design: Rafael H. Hernandez
Cover Design: Lucy Zakarian
Production Manager: Jeanie Berke
Production Assistant: Brenda DeMartini
Compositor: ComCom Division of Haddon Craftsmen, Inc.
Printer and Binder: R. R. Donnelley & Sons Company
Cover Illustration: Georges Pierre Seurat (1859-1891), *Invitation to the Sideshow (La Parade)*. Oil on canvas. H. 39¼ × 59 W. The Metropolitan Museum of Art, Bequest of Stephen C. Clark, 1960.

The Practical Imagination:
Stories, Poems, Plays
Revised Compact Edition

Library of Congress Cataloging-in-Publication Data

The Practical imagination.

   Rev. ed. of: The practical imagination/Northrop Frye, Sheridan Baker, George Perkins. c1983.
   Includes index.
   1. Literature—Collections. I. Frye, Northrop. II. Frye, Northrop. Practical imagination.
PN6014.P68   1986   808   86-22788
ISBN 0-06-042223-8
      91 9 8 7 6 5 4

CONTENTS

CHAPTER 3
LANGUAGE   **473**

CHAPTER 10
POEMS FOR STUDY   703

PREFACE

In revising *The Practical Imagination* for this new and compact edition, we have kept most of the original features and added others. The new anthology is lighter, more attractive, and easier to handle—and at the same time more effective as a tool for teaching, both because of our own second thoughts and the helpful suggestions of users.

As we observe recent trends toward "practical" education in our colleges and universities—which means, more often than not, narrowly vocational education —it seems to us more important than ever to introduce students to the idea that the imagination is practical, and that literature is uniquely valuable in its capacity to widen vision and clarify perspectives. To support this point, we have made this book both an anthology and an introduction to literature. As an anthology, it includes many forms and varieties of fiction, poetry, and drama. As an introduction to literary study, it moves from simple to more subtle and complex elements. At each step of the way, explanations, discussions, and questions inform students of the principles under consideration and help them to engage in imaginative and intellectual dialogue with the literary texts. Each section begins with an introduction to the genre, broadly surveying the ground to be covered. At the end of the first chapter of the fiction section, we provide students with a few brief suggestions to help them frame their thoughts into essays. At the end of the book, we provide a glossary as a ready reference to terminology.

Our generic survey introducing fiction emphasizes the relationship between oral and written traditions. In Chapter 1, "The Narrative Impulse," we begin with the oral tale—"Rumpelstiltskin" and "Stone Soup"—and examine the ways the ancient theme of wish-fulfillment has been shaped by three sophisticated modern storytellers, ending with the narrative complexities of Lawrence's "The Rocking-Horse Winner." In the next three chapters, we explore narrative perspective, discussing concepts much more fully in this edition than in the earlier one, and enriching the discussion with four newly selected stories: Alice Munro's "An Ounce of Cure," George Garrett's "King of the Mountain," Gail Godwin's "A Sorrowful Woman," and Ernest Hemingway's "Hills Like White Elephants." Chapters 5 and 6, divisions new to this edition, treat "Character" and "Setting," with Cynthia Ozick's "The Shawl," E. L. Doctorow's "The Hunter," and John Cheever's "The Swimmer" newly selected as examples for discussion. Chapter 7 discusses "Metaphor, Symbol, Allegory," and includes for the first time Ann Beattie's "Janus." In Chapter 8, "Theme," we now begin with Margaret Atwood's "When It Happens" and end with Thomas Pynchon's "Entropy." As before, the last chapter, "Longer Fiction," includes Tolstoy's *The Death of Ivan Ilych* and Conrad's "The Secret Sharer," but with questions newly added to each and diagrams supplied to assist students toward understanding the Conrad story.

Poetry follows fiction because beginning students generally do best when armed with a confidence, a vocabulary, and a strategy of criticism won through successful study of short stories. Nevertheless, because poetry still strikes some as an alien form, we begin slowly, with assistance in definition, discussion, and footnotes. After the introductory overview, we divide the field into "lyric" and "narrative," before considering the elements of dramatic situation and character fundamental to poetry. Then comes a chapter on language, followed by one on images, metaphors, and symbols. In Chapter 5, we explore sound patterns, including rhyme and meter, and in Chapter 6 the traditional forms of ballad, sonnet, villanelle, and sestina. Chapter 7, much expanded from the earlier edition, introduces the forms of free verse, with examples newly added from Walt Whitman, Lawrence Ferlinghetti, Margaret Atwood, and A. R. Ammons. In Chapter 8, our discussion of time and place includes two new poems, Walt Whitman's "Crossing Brooklyn Ferry" and Emma Lazarus's "The New Colossus." In Chapter 9, poems are grouped according to timeless human themes. The last chapter, "Poems for Study," presents chronologically some valuable poems not otherwise represented.

Our plays represent the Western tradition, from the Greeks to the present. We begin with tragedy and comedy, with Sophocles, Shakespeare, Aristophanes, and Congreve as examples against which students may measure the plays from later times. A chapter on "Social Drama" directs attention to theme. In "Plays for Study," we print and discuss Beckett's *Not I* as a paradigm of how difficulties in interpretation may be met and surmounted. We conclude our consideration of drama with two modern masterpieces, Tennessee Williams's *The Glass Menagerie* and Arthur Miller's *Death of a Salesman*. Of the eleven plays that now constitute our introduction to drama, four are new to this edition: *Hamlet, The Way of the World, Suppressed Desires,* and *The Glass Menagerie*.

FICTION

ON FICTION

THE ORAL TRADITION

Stories were told orally long before they came to depend on reading and writing. Many such stories have survived as folk tales preserved in a community's memory, and a few examples of such tales are given here. As a rule folk tales have simple characterization, seldom going beyond, say, a contrast between a clever and a stupid person. The story line is what is important, and it usually drives straight to the end, with few if any surprises. As there is little dependence on local or specific allusion, folk tales can travel through the world past all barriers of language and culture. In *The Pardoner's Tale* Chaucer tells a story that had probably reached him from a French source, but the story itself can be traced to India, where, five centuries later, Rudyard Kipling heard it and put it into his *Second Jungle Book.* Kipling's story is recognizably the "same" story as Chaucer's, even though all the details are different.

Similarly, the motif of the impossible task that is somehow accomplished, in "Rumpelstiltskin," can be found in a famous Classical myth, the story of Cupid and Psyche, and the story of the soup made of stones forms the subject of a play by W. B. Yeats. In W. W. Jacobs's "The Monkey's Paw," the three wishes remind us of folk tale again, as does the sardonic treatment of the love potion in John Collier's "The Chaser."

The oral story with its linear drive can be, like many simple structures, a very powerful one, and we can see its influence in, for example, Jack London's "To Build a Fire." Here there is only one character (except for the dog), and the only suspense is that of inevitability. We know what will happen: the story seems to exist in only one dimension, that of time, and we are anxious to reach the end, not because we are bored, but because the end

3

gives us the sense of resolution, of a pattern completing itself. The man in the story is not a sympathetic character, and the workings of his imagination are kept to a minimum. No identification with him is wanted: our attention is wholly absorbed in the sequence of movements he makes to keep alive. The smallest details become gigantic: the spark of life in his body depends on the tiny flame of his match, and as some snow slides off a branch it carries his death sentence with it. Such urgency of narrative movement, even in a story written to be read, still derives from the sense of listening to a speaking voice. Even a story as long and complex as Tolstoy's "The Death of Ivan Ilych" preserves the same feeling of inexorable advance. The emphasis on narrative pacing reaches an extreme in Poe's "The Tell-Tale Heart," where the movement of time, represented by the ticking of a watch and the heartbeat associated with it, enters the story as, in a way, its chief character.

THE WRITTEN TRADITION

Most stories now, however, are written to be read, and a printed page gives a second dimension, a sense of space as well as time. When the whole story is visually before us, a number of things can go on simultaneously, and the plot may twist unexpectedly. If we read Ambrose Bierce's "The Boarded Window" or Faulkner's "A Rose for Emily" quickly, concentrating on the narrative movement, the last sentence may come as a puzzling surprise, but we can always look back to see what clues the author gave us that we missed. The nightmarish experiences of the young man in Hawthorne's "My Kinsman, Major Molineux" may also impel us to see whether the opening paragraph, about political upsets in pre-Revolutionary America, was really as irrelevant as it may have seemed on first reading. In a written story a sense of the difference between appearance and reality makes itself felt, so that we feel that we are discovering something behind the narrative movement.

NARRATIVE TECHNIQUES

Naturally, most writers will look for some way of preserving both the driving energy of the oral tale and the sense of discovery in the written one. The most common way of doing this is to tell the story through one of the main characters, in contrast to the so-called "omniscient" narrator who is not tied to a single point of view. The urgency of a speaking voice still dominates our attention, but the speaking character is not the whole story, and the interactions with the other characters provide the second or spatial dimension. The narrator is often not aware of all the implications in the story he or she is telling. When the narrator of Ring Lardner's "Haircut" says at the end, "it probably served Jim right, what he got," the reader agrees verbally, but the agreement is on different levels of comprehension. In John Updike's "A & P" the narrator tells us his side of a confrontation of two attitudes that are both quixotic, though for different reasons. The narrator, however, has enough self-knowledge to say "it seems to me that once you begin a gesture it's fatal not to go through with it," so he also understands that he is only part of the story.

There are two limitations, not necessarily hampering ones, in telling a story through a major character. One is that the author is restricted to that character's speech, and in modern times standard literary English and colloquial speech are often almost different languages. In Faulkner's "A Rose for Emily" the story is told by a minor character whom we never really see, hence a full vocabulary can be used, with such phrases as "stubborn and coquettish decay" in describing Emily's house. But in Sherwood Anderson's "I'm a Fool" the inarticulateness of the boy narrator is part of the point of the story: he knows what has happened to him, but cannot break out of his immature framework of language with its recurrent "gee whiz." The reader has to supply an understanding that makes up for this. On the other hand inarticulateness has its own eloquence, as a failure of expression increases pathos. Elsewhere we can see reasons for not using a narrator. Fitzgerald's "Babylon Revisited," though focused on Charles Wales, is not told by him, and the different technique makes it easier for the author to present the two points of view about the custody of Honoria as equally strong, and, for those who hold them, equally justifiable.

The other limitation is one of positive sympathy: we do not need to "identify" with, or even like, the teller of a story, but we have to accept the narrator sufficiently to be willing to see the story through his or her eyes. The narrator in Charlotte Perkins Gilman's "The Yellow Wall-Paper" is mad, but madness is not alienating: we have reservations about the reality of what she sees, but a mad world can have both a logic of its own and a logical reason for deviating from the "normal," besides being related to our own phobias. But in Flannery O'Connor's "Good Country People," where the Bible salesman first appears to us as naive and innocent, we realize, as he gradually turns nastier with every paragraph, how difficult, perhaps impossible, it would be to make him a narrator. We prefer to look at such people objectively: there is something about real evil that has to remain inscrutable.

There is a corresponding limitation in the "omniscient" technique. In D. H. Lawrence's "Mother and Daughter" the author tells us a good deal about the motivation of his characters, and he has opinions about many other subjects as well, such as the difference between male and female attitudes to holding jobs. We may feel that we are free to disagree with Lawrence, if we like: he gives the impression of "omniscience" only to the extent that he is telling his story. Once he starts commenting on it, he has no more authority than we have. A good story, apparently, has a life of its own, and its author does not so much make it up as release it. Lawrence himself remarked, in fact, that we are not to trust an author, only the story.

MEANING

If these observations have any validity, we seem to be led to some such principle as this: story writers do not moralize, or if they do they are apt to weaken their creative authority, but they keep us in touch with moral realities. What we get from the story, therefore, is not a "message" or any concept to be inferred from the story, but the vision presented by the story itself. In modern stories this vision is normally ironic, in a special sense of seeing more of the whole situation than the characters in the story do. Irony does not, in this context, mean any lack of sympathy, but it excludes the sentimental sympathy that refuses to see the whole picture. In James Joyce's "A Little Cloud" we can understand Little Chandler's provincial wistfulness and his envy for the glamorous life of Gallaher, but we can also see that Gallaher's real life is not likely to be glamorous at all.

Even here, however, we are still in a moral and human area, and irony is not confined to that. In Katherine Mansfield's "Bliss" the long dammed-up sexual feelings of the heroine are suddenly released in an enveloping sense of euphoria. The euphoria enables her, while feeling complacent about the rather foolish babble of her guests, to find her real affinity with a blossoming pear tree. This latter is what T. S. Eliot calls an objective correlative, a natural image symbolizing, and corresponding to, a human emotion. But it appears that while pear trees usually blossom on schedule, human emotions often do not. There is no moral factor directly involved here: only the irony of a humanity imprisoned in a world that it so often feels it does not belong to.

Such a perspective, in which we struggle to see the whole story as the characters in it ordinarily cannot, brings us closer to the universality of what is presented. The story expands from being that particular story to being a story about human life as a whole. The characters at the opening of "The Death of Ivan Ilych" are very unsure of their most trivial actions and gestures, because they are trying to pretend that they are not thinking only of their own lives and of the fact that at least they are not dead. As the story goes on, we see how utterly unique every person's death is for that individual, and thus how even the unique can be the universal. When the pilot in Ralph Ellison's "Flying Home" remarks that "jimcrows" is an appropriate name for buzzards, hardly knowing at that moment what he is saying, we begin to see that Ellison's story is not simply a story about an injured pilot, but about the outlook of black people in a society dominated by hostile whites. Literature, then, may be among other things a technique for training us to look at life with an enlarged vision.

But we can hardly stop here, enlarging our vision at the expense of the illusions and frustrations of imaginary characters. In Eudora Welty's "A Memory" a vision from waking life moves across the dreamworld of a young woman, threatening her emotional security with a reality that she struggles to keep within her picture-frame of reverie. But we suspect that she has really grown beyond that point and is now ready to deal with reality on its own terms. Similarly, at any moment our ironic perspective may go into reverse and show us that we have illusions too that protect us from reality, and that the story we are reading may be part of that reality. Thus as we read Doris Lessing's account of how a shy white child fails to make any human contact with Africans, the appalling callousness of the white attitude to the blacks looms out of the background of the story and confronts us directly.

But it is not only social and outward realities that literature presents; the conflict of reality and illusion goes on inside our minds too. In John Barth's "Lost in the Funhouse" we eavesdrop on the inner debate in an author's mind about how he is to write his story. The uncertainty in the "funhouse" itself about what is real is a projection of that inner debate. In Conrad's "The Secret Sharer" the story of how an inexperienced sea captain tries to get rid of a stowaway is given a new dimension by the unexplained mystery of the stowaway's resemblance to the captain, "my double," as the captain calls him. The story is told with a psychological resonance that gives it the universal theme of separating from a self that we do not want and yet is a part of ourselves.

This twofold focus of reality, inside and outside the mind at once, is particularly important when we are reading what is called fantasy. Stanislaw Lem's story of a kingdom created from robots, "The Seventh Sally," raises questions that have tormented us for centuries, about the relation of God or the gods to humanity, about the distinction between an organism and a mechanism, about the difference between what is created and what has come into existence by itself. And in Ursula Le Guin's story, "The Ones Who Walk Away from Omelas," the science-fiction setting does not make the central situation less relevant to our own lives; we have all asked ourselves how far it is possible to be happy in a society based on making other people miserable. It is these fantastic stories in particular that lead us to another critical principle. A story presents us with what is technically an illusion, something that did not happen or could not happen. But whatever reality may be, one of the most direct and intense ways that we can grasp it is through the deliberate illusions of literature.

We began with the folk tales that can travel through the world past all social and linguistic barriers, and we end with the suggestion that when a story presents a form of universal experience, there are no limits to its communicating power. In Borges's little story, "The Gospel According to Mark," we are in a remote part of South America, as far as we can get from all our normal cultural habits and references. Yet the story which is familiar to us in the Gospels makes its way there, too, in a most disconcerting form. Such a tale reminds us that the vision described in the biblical story of the fall of man has a permanent place in our own minds. This is not a religious doctrine: it is a statement about the intelligibility of great stories, which may come to us from immense distances of time and space, and yet are stories that we recognize because we have lived through them.

CHAPTER 1

THE NARRATIVE IMPULSE

"Once upon a time, long long ago." We are already flying on the storyteller's carpet to some magical otherwhere and otherwhen, eager to find out what happened. In an instant, we are in another reality that yet seems intensely real, no matter how indistinct its setting. We follow the happenstances of some character as if they were our own, no matter how different from us and how thinly outlined. *Mutato nomine, de te fabula narratur*—with name changed, the story tells of you—as Horace observed some years before psychologists invented "identification."

This is the story's magical appeal, even when realism focuses on the here and now and the love next door. We observe people other than ourselves. We experience their fears and triumphs, because they tell us something about ourselves, about how we are all alike, and they do this at the very time we are feeling how it is in another apartment, in another sex or age, in another country. The story illustrates something about this life we share. Something in us craves and enjoys this vicarious excursion, unscathed, into another reality that yet reflects and illuminates our own.

All stories are really wish-fulfilling, some more obviously than others. We wish we may; we wish we might. And for a few minutes or hours our wishes come true. We adventure on the Malayan archipelago; we sigh on the Left Bank of Paris. Even the most squalid realism satisfies our wish to know and rewards us in safety. The fairy tale dreams our wishes more directly into being. We start with the simple narrative urge to find out what happened. We soon discover that we are involved, satisfying that even deeper psychological urge to come out on top. We identify our interests with those of the central character. We want the miller's innocent daughter to be queen and stay happy. We want the old soldier to win his feast. We are responding to the child's essential need to believe that he or she can overcome the adversities and giants on all sides, thereby contributing to the safety and stability of the big world—the deep wish fulfillment we seem never to outgrow. We need to believe, at least while the enchantment lasts, that life has a moral order rewarding the good and triumphing over evil. We secretly believe ourselves to be, like those in the story, the best of the good, no matter how unlucky and misunderstood. Our noble unselfishness rises resplendent from the cinders as the cruel and selfish stepsisters get their due.

All the stories in this section reveal the two basic narrative impulses: the first and most simple, to find out what happened; the second and deeper, to hope for the best for our secret selves—even when the realities turn against our unrealistic hopes. All illustrate the moral dimension. In "Rumpelstiltskin" and "Stone Soup," the impossible task is finally accomplished. In all, greediness, the wish to outwit fate and our natural doom is punished, or at least twitted. The appeal of magic, with its magical three wishes, tempts us always, because we always know it cannot really be.

That magical three suggests how deeply these narratives are rooted in our psychological being. Throughout our imaginative fairyland, the bell rings thrice —three wishes, three sons, three daughters. Three is a part of our narrative expectation and satisfaction, a basic fact of our psychology. Three dots, psychologists tell us, are the largest number everyone automatically sees as a unit. Add another dot, and many see two units of two. Three is built into our perceptions and our thinking. Our ideal family is just Mother, Father, and us. All life has a beginning, middle, and end. The world we live in has three dimensions.

So these simple narratives meet basic psychological needs, as do the more realistic ones that follow, and in the same basic way. Above all, we need to see ourselves in the world outside ourselves, to expand our sense of what life means, to confirm that we are not alone, that we share the hopes and frustrations of our human lot.

"Rumpelstiltskin" starts with what is wrong. It begins with the miller's showing off and thrives on the king's greed. Both impose on the innocent girl. Rumpelstiltskin, the diabolically attractive imp, apparently embodies these vices, and the gruesome ending has delighted generations of listeners. Why? In what ways does "the story tell of you"?

RUMPELSTILTSKIN

*Anonymous**

There was once upon a time a poor miller who had a very beautiful daughter. Now it happened one day that he had an audience with the King, and in order to appear a person of some importance he told him that he had a daughter who could spin straw into gold.

'Now that's a talent worth having,' said the King to the miller. 'If your

*One of the many fairy tales collected by the brothers Jacob (1785–1863) and Wilhelm (1786–1859) Grimm. The version presented here was first printed by Andrew Lang in *The Blue Fairy Book* (1889).

daughter is as clever as you say, bring her to my palace tomorrow, and I'll put her to the test.'

When the girl was brought to him he led her into a room full of straw, gave her a spinning-wheel and spindle, and said, 'Now set to work and spin all night till early dawn, and if by that time you haven't spun the straw into gold you shall die.' Then he closed the door behind him and left her alone inside.

So the poor miller's daughter sat down, and didn't know what in the world she was to do. She hadn't the least idea of how to spin straw into gold, and became at last so miserable that she began to cry.

Suddenly the door opened, and in stepped a tiny little man and said, 'Good evening, Miss Miller-maid; why are you crying so bitterly?'

'Oh!' answered the girl, 'I have to spin straw into gold, and haven't a notion how it's done.'

'What will you give me if I spin it for you?' asked the manikin.

'My necklace,' replied the girl.

The little man took the necklace, sat himself down at the wheel, and whir, whir, whir, the wheel went round three times, and the bobbin was full. Then he put on another, and whir, whir, whir, the wheel went round three times, and the second too was full; and so it went on till the morning, when all the straw was spun away, and all the bobbins were full of gold.

As soon as the sun rose the King came, and when he perceived the gold he was astonished and delighted, but his heart was only the more filled with greed. He had the miller's daughter put into another room, much bigger than the first, and full of straw. He bade her, if she valued her life, spin it all into gold before the following morning.

The girl didn't know what to do, and began to cry; then the door opened as before, and the tiny little man appeared and said, 'What'll you give me if I spin the straw into gold for you?'

'The ring from my finger,' answered the girl.

The manikin took the ring, and whir! round went the spinning wheel again, and when morning broke he had spun all the straw into glittering gold.

The King was pleased beyond measure at the sight, but his greed for gold was still not satisfied, and he had the miller's daughter brought into a yet bigger room full of straw, and said, 'You must spin all this away in the night; but if you succeed this time you shall become my wife.'

'She's only a miller's daughter, it's true,' he thought; 'but I couldn't find a richer wife if I were to search the whole world over.'

When the girl was alone the little man appeared for the third time, and said, 'What'll you give me if I spin the straw for you once again?'

'I've nothing more to give,' answered the girl.

'Then promise me when you are Queen to give me your first child.'

'Who knows what mayn't happen before that?' thought the miller's daughter; and besides, she saw no other way out of it, so she promised the manikin what he demanded, and he set to work once more and spun the straw into gold. When the King came in the morning, and found everything as he had desired, he straightaway made her his wife, and the miller's daughter became a Queen.

When a year had passed a beautiful little son was born to her, and she thought no more of the little man, till all of a sudden one day he stepped into her room and said, 'Now give me what you promised.'

The Queen was in a great state, and offered the little man all the riches in her kingdom if he would only leave her the child. But the manikin said, 'No, a living creature is dearer to me than all the treasures in the world.'

Then the Queen began to cry and sob so bitterly that the little man was sorry for her, and said, 'I'll give you three days to guess my name, and if you find out in that time you may keep your child.'

Then the Queen pondered the whole night over all the names she had ever heard, and sent a messenger to scour the land, and to pick up far and near all the names he should come across. When the little man arrived on the following day she began with Kasper, Melchior, Belshazzar, and all the other names she knew, in a string, but at each one the manikin called out, 'That's not my name.'

The next day she sent to inquire of all the names of all the people in the neighborhood, and had a long list of the most uncommon and extraordinary for the little man when he made his appearance. 'Is your name, perhaps Sheepshanks, Cruickshanks, Spindleshanks?' but he always replied, 'That's not my name.'

On the third day the messenger returned and announced, 'I have not been able to find any new names, but as I came upon a high hill round the corner of the wood, where the foxes and hares bid each other good night, I saw a little house, and in front of the house burned a fire, and round the fire danced the most grotesque little man, hopping on one leg and crying:

> "Tomorrow I brew, today I bake,
> And then the child away I'll take;
> For little deems my royal dame
> That Rumpelstiltskin is my name!" '

You may imagine the Queen's delight at hearing the name, and when the little man stepped in shortly afterwards and asked, 'Now my lady Queen, what's my name?' she asked first, 'Is your name Conrad?'

'No.'

'Is your name Harry?'

'No.'

'Is your name, perhaps, Rumpelstiltskin?'

'Some demon has told you that, some demon has told you that,' screamed the little man, and in his rage drove his right foot so far into the ground that it sank in up to his waist; then in a passion he seized the left foot with both hands and tore himself in two.

QUESTIONS

1. What expectations does the first sentence arouse?
2. How many series of three can you find? How do they support the basic narrative impulse, satisfying our wish to know what happened?
3. In the original German, *Rumpelstilzchen,* the term for a noisy little

goblin, suggests disorder both in its meaning and its lengthy comic sound (*rumpel:* to rumble, jumble, jolt). What things are disorderly in this story? How does the end symbolize that disorder? What does the story suggest about how we should act?

The next sophisticated little tale is one of many in which we enjoy seeing the deceivers deceived. We enjoy, too, its *dramatic irony* in our knowing, with the author and the old soldier, what the villagers do not know and never understand. We will see more of dramatic irony—so fundamental to the stage and indeed to all narrative literature—when we consider first-person narrative in Chapters 2 and 3. Indeed, we have already enjoyed dramatic irony in "Rumpelstiltskin" when the imp sings his song not knowing the messenger is listening. Dramatic irony deepens amusingly with the very concept of "stone soup," which the peasants understand as a great discovery while we (and the soldiers) enjoy our superior knowledge of its impossibility. The old soldier's every declaration is a dramatic irony that we perceive as amusingly false and psychologically shrewd while the peasants take it as true and candid. All is climaxed in the peasants' concluding statement, which they understand simply and we understand in a broader and different sense.

STONE SOUP

A Folk Tale

*Anonymous**

Once three soldiers were coming home from the wars. They had eaten nothing since early morning when they had brushed themselves free from a haystack and finished the last crusts of their rations. Suddenly, the youngest soldier said, "Ah, at last, a village. Now for a good hot meal and a bed."

"Something to eat and a haystack will do for me," said the second soldier.

"We'll see," said the old soldier.

In the village, a boy ran into the marketplace. "The soldiers are coming," he shouted.

"Quick," said the elder, "hide everything. They'll clean us out of house and home."

When the soldiers came into the village square, they marched in good order up to the little group of men sitting in the shade by the well.

"Good evening," said the old soldier, saluting, "We are three weary soldiers coming home from the wars. We would be most grateful for a bite to eat and a place to rest for the night."

"I am sorry," said the elder, "but there is nothing to eat in this village. You soldiers have gone back and forth over us all year, first one side then the other, picking our bones clean every time. We ourselves have nothing to eat. You had better go on to the next village."

*Retold by Sheridan Baker.

"Nothing to eat at all?" said the old soldier.

"Nothing at all," said the elder.

"Well," said the old soldier, "in that case we must make some stone soup."

"Stone soup!" the villagers exclaimed.

"Yes," said the old soldier, "it's a trick we learned in the wars, when every-thing else ran out. I suppose you have a big iron kettle."

"Oh, yes," said the villagers.

"Well," said the old soldier, "bring it here to the marketplace, and fill it full of good clear water, and get a good fire going under it, and in the meantime find me three big round stones, all of a size."

The village began to hum with life. Four came up with the village's biggest kettle. They set up a tripod and filled the kettle with buckets from the well as others brought armloads of wood and started the fire. Still others came carrying stones from the fields, each wanting his to be chosen. The soldier examined them all carefully, finding one, matching another, carefully matching a third, three big oval stones as smooth as ostrich eggs or loaves of bread. He dropped these carefully into the water, which soon began to simmer.

The soldier took out his sword, nudged the stones a little, and stirred the water as the boiling increased. The villagers watched him breathlessly.

He nodded in satisfaction. "These are some of the finest soup stones I have ever seen," he said. "Your village is very fortunate. This will be a fine stone soup, though it will take a while. Too bad we don't have some salt and pepper, and perhaps a cup of barley."

"Well," said one of the women, "I think I could find some salt and pepper the last troops overlooked." And another ran off and came back redfaced with a bag of barley.

"Ah," said the soldier as he sprinkled and stirred. "I can smell the stones already, and now we will really have a soup. Too bad we don't have a few carrots, or an onion, or perhaps a small cabbage."

"Well," said the women, "perhaps . . . ," and soon came back with aprons filled, some with carrots, some with onions, some with cabbage.

"Now," said the soldier, lopping the vegetables in with his sword, lopping and stirring, "this will be a stone soup fit for a general. A little more water to give it time. With a soup like this, it's a shame we don't have some bacon for a finishing touch."

"Well," said an old villager, "I might just possibly. . . . ," and soon the soldier was chopping a side of bacon into the soup. "More pepper," he cried, "more water, the stones are just beginning to work." And the rich aroma and the soldier's own pleasure as he stirred with his sword made everyone happy. "Now we'll have a stone soup fit for the king himself," the soldier cried. "A soup like this calls for a feast and a festival and a roasted ox and plenty of wine. Ah, well. Too bad. But it would be fine."

"Well," said the elder himself, "I think perhaps I have a small side of beef under my bed which the last troops may have overlooked."

And soon a whole ox was spitted and turning over a new blazing fire, and as the soldier hummed, and stirred in new loppings of this and that, the women set

tables in the square, and brought out flowers and bunting and jugs of wine, and the whole village feasted on the most delicious soup and roast they had ever tasted, and the three soldiers enjoyed it most of all. And then they all danced in the square to the accordion and violin.

Then the elder said to the three soldiers, "This has been a day and a night to remember. You, sir, shall sleep in my own bed itself, the best in the village, and the middle soldier shall sleep in the miller's bed, and the young one in the priest's." And the villagers all escorted the soldiers to their beds, where they sank to sleep between clean sheets smelling of fresh air and sun.

In the morning, after baths and breakfast, when the soldiers were ready to leave, all the village gathered to see them off.

"We want to thank you for your splendid hospitality," said the old soldier. "Of all the villages we have ever seen, yours is the best. You have treated us like kings."

"You well deserve it," said the elder, "for you have taught us a priceless secret, how to make soup from stones."

"Yes," said the old soldier, "it's all in knowing how."

The villagers waved as the three soldiers marched bravely off. They shook their heads and sighed. "Such men don't grow on every bush," they said.

QUESTIONS

1. How does the traditional narrative "three" operate in this story?
2. What aspects of this story are in the fairyland of "Rumpelstiltskin" and what aspects suggest the real world?
3. Explain the dramatic irony in the elder's remark about a small side of beef.
4. Explain the dramatic ironies in the concluding speeches, beginning with that of the old soldier.
5. To what things in the story do "you-of-the-fable" respond?

"The Monkey's Paw" rationalizes the magical three as coming from India, the mysterious East colonized by practical whisky-drinking Britishers. Modern skepticism ends in horror to suggest the impossibility in man's persistent wish to outwit the natural order. What are some of the elements Jacobs includes to make the basic fairy tale realistic?

THE MONKEY'S PAW
W. W. Jacobs   (1863–1943)

I

Without, the night was cold and wet, but in the small parlour of Laburnam Villa the blinds were drawn and the fire burned brightly. Father and son were at chess, the former, who possessed ideas about the game involving radical changes, putting his king into such sharp and unnecessary perils that it even provoked comment from the white-haired lady knitting placidly by the fire.

"Hark at the wind," said Mr. White, who, having seen a fatal mistake after it was too late, was amiably desirous of preventing his son from seeing it.

"I'm listening," said the latter, grimly surveying the board as he stretched out his hand. "Check."

"I should hardly think that he'd come tonight," said his father, with his hand poised over the board.

"Mate," replied the son.

"That's the worst of living so far out," bawled Mr. White, with sudden and unlooked-for violence; "of all the beastly, slushy, out-of-the-way places to live in, this is the worst. Pathway's a bog, and the road's a torrent. I don't know what people are thinking about. I suppose because only two houses in the road are let, they think it doesn't matter."

"Never mind, dear," said his wife, soothingly; "perhaps you'll win the next one."

Mr. White looked up sharply, just in time to intercept a knowing glance between mother and son. The words died away on his lips, and he hid a guilty grin in his thin grey beard.

"There he is," said Herbert White, as the gate banged to loudly and heavy footsteps came toward the door.

The old man rose with hospitable haste, and opening the door, was heard condoling with the new arrival. The new arrival also condoled with himself, so that Mrs. White said, "Tut, tut!" and coughed gently as her husband entered the room, followed by a tall, burly man, beady of eye and rubicund of visage.

"Sergeant-Major Morris," he said, introducing him.

The sergeant-major shook hands, and taking the proffered seat by the fire, watched contentedly while his host got out whiskey and tumblers and stood a small copper kettle on the fire.

At the third glass his eyes got brighter, and he began to talk, the little family circle regarding with eager interest this visitor from distant parts, as he squared his broad shoulders in the chair and spoke of wild scenes and doughty deeds; of wars and plagues and strange peoples.

"Twenty-one years of it," said Mr. White, nodding at his wife and son. "When he went away he was a slip of a youth in the warehouse. Now look at him."

"He don't look to have taken much harm," said Mrs. White, politely.

"I'd like to go to India myself," said the old man, "just to look round a bit, you know."

"Better where you are," said the sergeant-major, shaking his head. He put down the empty glass, and sighing softly, shook it again.

"I should like to see those old temples and fakirs and jugglers," said the old man. "What was that you started telling me the other day about a monkey's paw or something, Morris?"

"Nothing," said the soldier, hastily. "Leastways nothing worth hearing."

"Monkey's paw?" said Mrs. White, curiously.

"Well, it's just a bit of what you might call magic, perhaps," said the sergeant-major, off-handedly.

His three listeners leaned forward eagerly. The visitor absent-mindedly put his empty glass to his lips and then set it down again. His host filled it for him.

"To look at," said the sergeant-major, fumbling in his pocket, "it's just an ordinary little paw, dried like a mummy."

He took something out of his pocket and proffered it. Mrs. White drew back with a grimace, but her son, taking it, examined it curiously.

"And what is there special about it?" inquired Mr. White as he took it from his son, and having examined it, placed it upon the table.

"It had a spell put on it by an old fakir," said the sergeant-major, "a very holy man. He wanted to show that fate ruled people's lives, and that those who interfered with it did so to their sorrow. He put a spell on it so that three separate men could each have three wishes from it."

His manner was so impressive that his hearers were conscious that their light laughter jarred somewhat.

"Well, why don't you have three, sir?" said Herbert White, cleverly.

The soldier regarded him in the way that middle age is wont to regard presumptuous youth. "I have," he said, quietly, and his blotchy face whitened.

"And did you really have the three wishes granted?" asked Mrs. White.

"I did," said the sergeant-major, and his glass tapped against his strong teeth.

"And has anybody else wished?" persisted the old lady.

"The first man had his three wishes. Yes," was the reply; "I don't know what the first two were, but the third was for death. That's how I got the paw."

His tones were so grave that a hush fell upon the group.

"If you've had your three wishes, it's no good to you now, then, Morris," said the old man at last. "What do you keep it for?"

The soldier shook his head. "Fancy, I suppose," he said slowly. "I did have some idea of selling it, but I don't think I will. It has caused enough mischief already. Besides, people won't buy. They think it's a fairy tale; some of them, and those who do think anything of it want to try it first and pay me afterward."

"If you could have another three wishes," said the old man, eyeing him keenly, "would you have them?"

"I don't know," said the other. "I don't know."

He took the paw, and dangling it between his forefinger and thumb, suddenly threw it upon the fire. White, with a slight cry, stooped down and snatched it off.

"Better let it burn," said the soldier, solemnly.

"If you don't want it, Morris," said the other, "give it to me."

"I won't," said his friend, doggedly. "I threw it on the fire. If you keep it, don't blame me for what happens. Pitch it on the fire again like a sensible man."

The other shook his head and examined his new possession closely. "How do you do it?" he inquired.

"Hold it up in your right hand and wish aloud," said the sergeant-major, "but I warn you of the consequences."

"Sounds like the *Arabian Nights,*" said Mrs. White, as she rose and began to set the supper. "Don't you think you might wish for four pairs of hands for me?"

Her husband drew the talisman from his pocket, and then all three burst into laughter as the sergeant-major, with a look of alarm on his face, caught him by the arm.

"If you must wish," he said, gruffly, "wish for something sensible."

Mr. White dropped it back in his pocket, and placing chairs, motioned his friend to the table. In the business of supper the talisman was partly forgotten, and afterward the three sat listening in an enthralled fashion to a second instalment of the soldier's adventures in India.

"If the tale about the monkey's paw is not more truthful than those he has been telling us," said Herbert, as the door closed behind their guest, just in time for him to catch the last train, "we sha'nt make much out of it."

"Did you give him anything for it, father?" inquired Mrs. White, regarding her husband closely.

"A trifle," said he, colouring slightly. "He didn't want it, but I made him take it. And he pressed me again to throw it away."

"Likely," said Herbert, with pretended horror. "Why, we're going to be rich, and famous and happy. Wish to be an emperor, father, to begin with; then you can't be henpecked."

He darted round the table, pursued by the maligned Mrs. White armed with an antimacassar.

Mr. White took the paw from his pocket and eyed it dubiously. "I don't know what to wish for, and that's a fact," he said, slowly. "It seems to me I've got all I want."

"If you only cleared the house, you'd be quite happy, wouldn't you?" said Herbert, with his hand on his shoulder. "Well, wish for two hundred pounds, then; that'll just do it."

His father, smiling shamefacedly at his own credulity, held up the talisman, as his son, with a solemn face, somewhat marred by a wink at his mother, sat down at the piano and struck a few impressive chords.

"I wish for two hundred pounds," said the old man distinctly.

A fine crash from the piano greeted the words, interrupted by a shuddering cry from the old man. His wife and son ran toward him.

"It moved," he cried, with a glance of disgust at the object as it lay on the floor. "As I wished, it twisted in my hand like a snake."

"Well, I don't see the money," said his son as he picked it up and placed it on the table, "and I bet I never shall."

"It must have been your fancy, father," said his wife, regarding him anxiously.

He shook his head. "Never mind, though; there's no harm done, but it gave me a shock all the same."

They sat down by the fire again while the two men finished their pipes. Outside, the wind was higher than ever, and the old man started nervously at the sound of a door banging upstairs. A silence unusual and depressing settled upon all three, which lasted until the old couple rose to retire for the night.

"I expect you'll find the cash tied up in a big bag in the middle of your bed," said Herbert, as he bade them good-night, "and something horrible squatting up on top of the wardrobe watching you as you pocket your ill-gotten gains."

He sat alone in the darkness, gazing at the dying fire, and seeing faces in it. The last face was so horrible and so simian that he gazed at it in amazement. It got so vivid that, with a little uneasy laugh, he felt on the table for a glass containing a little water to throw over it. His hand grasped the monkey's paw, and with a little shiver he wiped his hand on his coat and went up to bed.

II

In the brightness of the wintry sun next morning as it streamed over the breakfast table he laughed at his fears. There was an air of prosaic wholesomeness about the room which it had lacked on the previous night, and the dirty, shrivelled little paw was pitched on the sideboard with a carelessness which betokened no great belief in its virtues.

"I suppose all old soldiers are the same," said Mrs. White. "The idea of our listening to such nonsense! How could wishes be granted in these days? And if they could, how could two hundred pounds hurt you, father?"

"Might drop on his head from the sky," said the frivolous Herbert.

"Morris said the things happened so naturally," said his father, "that you might if you so wished attribute it to coincidence."

"Well, don't break into the money before I come back," said Herbert as he rose from the table. "I'm afraid it'll turn you into a mean, avaricious man, and we shall have to disown you."

His mother laughed, and followed him to the door, watched him down the road; and returning to the breakfast table, was very happy at the expense of her husband's credulity. All of which did not prevent her from scurrying to the door at the postman's knock, nor prevent her from referring somewhat shortly to retired sergeant-majors of bibulous habits when she found that the post brought a tailor's bill.

"Herbert will have some more of his funny remarks, I expect, when he comes home," she said, as they sat at dinner.

"I dare say," said Mr. White, pouring himself out some beer; "but for all that, the thing moved in my hand; that I'll swear to."

"You thought it did," said the old lady soothingly.

"I say it did," replied the other. "There was no thought about it; I had just —What's the matter?"

His wife made no reply. She was watching the mysterious movements of a man outside, who, peering in an undecided fashion at the house, appeared to be trying to make up his mind to enter. In mental connection with the two hundred pounds, she noticed that the stranger was well dressed, and wore a silk hat of glossy newness. Three times he paused at the gate, and then walked on again. The fourth time he stood with his hand upon it, and then with sudden resolution flung it open and walked up the path. Mrs. White at the same moment placed her hands behind her, and hurriedly unfastening the strings of her apron, put that useful article of apparel beneath the cushion of her chair.

She brought the stranger, who seemed ill at ease, into the room. He gazed at her furtively, and listened in a preoccupied fashion as the old lady apologized for the appearance of the room, and her husband's coat, a garment which he usually reserved for the garden. She then waited as patiently as her sex would permit, for him to broach his business, but he was at first strangely silent.

"I—was asked to call," he said at last, and stooped and picked a piece of cotton from his trousers. "I come from 'Maw and Meggins.' "

The old lady started. "Is anything the matter?" she asked, breathlessly. "Has anything happened to Herbert? What is it? What is it?"

Her husband interposed. "There, there, mother," he said, hastily. "Sit down, and don't jump to conclusions. You've not brought bad news, I'm sure, sir;" and he eyed the other wistfully.

"I'm sorry—" began the visitor.

"Is he hurt?" demanded the mother, wildly.

The visitor bowed in assent. "Badly hurt," he said, quietly, "but he is not in any pain."

"Oh, thank God!" said the old woman, clasping her hands. "Thank God for that! Thank—"

She broke off suddenly as the sinister meaning of the assurance dawned upon her and she saw the awful confirmation of her fears in the other's perverted face. She caught her breath, and turning to her slower-witted husband, laid her trembling old hand upon his. There was a long silence.

"He was caught in the machinery," said the visitor at length in a low voice.

"Caught in the machinery," repeated Mr. White, in a dazed fashion, "yes."

He sat staring blankly out the window, and taking his wife's hand between his own, pressed it as he had been wont to do in their old courting-days nearly forty years before.

"He was the only one left to us," he said, turning gently to the visitor. "It is hard."

The other coughed, and rising, walked slowly to the window. "The firm wished me to convey their sincere sympathy with you in your great loss," he said, without looking around. "I beg that you will understand I am only their servant and merely obeying orders."

There was no reply; the old woman's face was white, her eyes staring, and her breath inaudible; on the husband's face was a look such as his friend the sergeant might have carried into his first action.

"I was to say that Maw and Meggins disclaim all responsibility," continued the other. "They admit no liability at all, but in consideration of your son's services, they wish to present you with a certain sum as compensation."

Mr. White dropped his wife's hand, and rising to his feet, gazed with a look of horror at his visitor. His dry lips shaped the words, "How much?"

"Two hundred pounds," was the answer.

Unconscious of his wife's shriek, the old man smiled faintly, put out his hands like a sightless man, and dropped, a senseless heap, to the floor.

III

In the huge new cemetery, some two miles distant, the old people buried their dead, and came back to a house steeped in shadow and silence. It was all over so quickly that at first they could hardly realize it, and remained in a state of expectation as though of something else to happen—something else which was to lighten this load, too heavy for their old hearts to bear.

But the days passed, and expectation gave place to resignation—the hopeless resignation of the old, sometimes miscalled, apathy. Sometimes they hardly exchanged a word, for now they had nothing to talk about, and their days were long to weariness.

It was about a week after that the old man, waking suddenly in the night, stretched out his hand and found himself alone. The room was in darkness, and the sound of subdued weeping came from the window. He raised himself in bed and listened.

"Come back," he said, tenderly. "You will be cold."

"It is colder for my son," said the old woman, and wept afresh.

The sound of her sobs died away on his ears. The bed was warm, and his eyes heavy with sleep. He dozed fitfully, and then slept until a sudden wild cry from his wife awoke him with a start.

"*The paw!*" she cried wildly. "The monkey's paw!"

He started up in alarm. "Where? Where is it? What's the matter?"

She came stumbling across the room toward him. "I want it," she said, quietly. "You've not destroyed it?"

"It's in the parlour, on the bracket," he replied, marvelling. "Why?"

She cried and laughed together, and bending over, kissed his cheek.

"I only just thought of it," she said, hysterically. "Why didn't I think of it before? Why didn't *you* think of it?"

"Think of what?" he questioned.

"The other two wishes," she replied, rapidly. "We've only had one."

"Was not that enough?" he demanded, fiercely.

"No," she cried triumphantly; "we'll have one more. Go down and get it quickly, and wish our boy alive again."

The man sat up in bed and flung the bedclothes from his quaking limbs. "Good God, you are mad!" he cried, aghast.

"Get it," she panted; "get it quickly, and wish—Oh, my boy, my boy!"

Her husband struck a match and lit the candle. "Get back to bed," he said, unsteadily. "You don't know what you are saying."

"We had the first wish granted," said the old woman, feverishly; "why not the second?"

"A coincidence," stammered the old man.

"Go and get it and wish," cried his wife, quivering with excitement.

The old man turned and regarded her, and his voice shook. "He has been dead ten days, and besides he—I would not tell you else, but—I could only recognize him by his clothing. If he was too terrible for you to see then, how now?"

"Bring him back," cried the old woman, and dragged him toward the door. "Do you think I fear the child I have nursed."

He went down in the darkness, and felt his way to the parlour, and then to the mantelpiece. The talisman was in its place, and a horrible fear that the unspoken wish might bring his mutilated son before him ere he could escape from the room seized upon him, and he caught his breath as he found that he had lost the direction of the door. His brow cold with sweat, he felt his way round the table, and groped along the wall until he found himself in the small passage with the unwholesome thing in his hand.

Even his wife's face seemed changed as he entered the room. It was white and expectant, and to his fears seemed to have an unnatural look upon it. He was afraid of her.

"*Wish!*" she cried, in a strong voice.

"It is foolish and wicked," he faltered.

"*Wish!*" repeated his wife.

He raised his hand. "I wish my son alive again."

The talisman fell to the floor, and he regarded it fearfully. Then he sank trembling into a chair as the old woman, with burning eyes, walked to the window and raised the blind.

He sat until he was chilled with the cold, glancing occasionally at the figure of the old woman peering through the window. The candle-end, which had burned below the rim of the china candlestick, was throwing pulsating shadows on the ceiling and walls, until, with a flicker larger than the rest, it expired. The old man, with an unspeakable sense of relief at the failure of the talisman, crept back to his bed, and a minute or two afterward the old woman came silently and apathetically beside him.

Neither spoke, but lay silently listening to the ticking of the clock. A stair creaked, and the squeaky mouse scurried noisily through the wall. The darkness was oppressive, and after lying for some time screwing up his courage, he took the box of matches, and striking one, went downstairs for a candle.

At the foot of the stairs the match went out, and he paused to strike another; and at the same moment a knock, so quiet and stealthy as to be scarcely audible, sounded on the front door.

The matches fell from his hand and spilled in the passage. He stood motionless, his breath suspended until the knock was repeated. Then he turned and fled swiftly back to his room, and closed the door behind him. A third knock sounded through the house.

"*What's that?*" cried the old woman, starting up.

"A rat," said the old man in shaking tones—"a rat. It passed me on the stairs."

His wife sat up in bed listening. A loud knock resounded through the house.

"It's Herbert!" she screamed. "It's Herbert!"

She ran to the door, but her husband was before her, and catching her by the arm, held her tightly.

"What are you going to do?" he whispered hoarsely.

"It's my boy; it's Herbert!" she cried, struggling mechanically. "I forgot it was two miles away. What are you holding me for? Let me go. I must open the door.

"For God's sake don't let it in," cried the old man, trembling.

"You're afraid of your own son," she cried, struggling. "Let me go. I'm coming, Herbert; I'm coming."

There was another knock, and another. The old woman with a sudden wrench broke free and ran from the room. Her husband followed to the landing, and called after her appealingly as she hurried downstairs. He heard the chain rattle back and the bottom bolt drawn slowly and stiffly from the socket. Then the old woman's voice, strained and panting.

"The bolt," she cried, loudly. "Come down. I can't reach it."

But her husband was on his hands and knees groping wildly on the floor in search of the paw. If he could only find it before the thing outside got in. A perfect fusillade of knocks reverberated through the house, and he heard the scraping of a chair as his wife put it down in the passage against the door. He heard the creaking of the bolt as it came slowly back, and at the same moment he found the monkey's paw, and frantically breathed his third and last wish.

The knocking ceased suddenly, although the echoes of it were still in the house. He heard the chair drawn back, and the door opened. A cold wind rushed up the staircase, and a long loud wail of disappointment and misery from his wife gave him courage to run down to her side, and then to the gate beyond. The street lamp flickering opposite shone on a quiet and deserted road.

QUESTIONS

1. What does Jacobs achieve with his realistic detail? How would the story come across if it were still "once upon a time" in some unspecified somewhere?
2. What is the effect of setting—weather, time of day, the house, the fire? What effect does the game of chess have? What do the details of "living so far out" (in England a street is a "road"), imply about the Whites's home and circumstances?
3. What is the significance, and effect, of the paw's previous owner's wishing for death?
4. How does Jacobs use and vary the traditional threes?
5. What does the allusion to the *Arabian Nights* do for the story? Have you noticed this kind of allusion in other fiction or in plays?
6. What are the facts implied but not described in the ending? What is the effect of this indirection?
7. What does Jacobs, an Englishman writing in the 1880s and '90s, mean by "the other's *perverted* face" as he breaks the awful news? Check your dictionary for the word's etymology. How would you translate "It's in the parlour, on the bracket"?
8. How does the ending differ from the traditional fairy tale?

9. What does the story imply about "oughts" and "ought nots"—its significance, message, or theme?

In "The Chaser," the magical wish to conquer nature moves into another modern fairyland—on Pell Street, only two blocks long, in New York City's Chinatown, lower Manhattan. Notice the deft touches of realism. Again, as in "Stone Soup," dramatic irony energizes the whole. We, with the old man, enjoy our superior and secret knowledge. Indeed, we encounter *verbal irony* for the first time, and in an unusual kind laid on top of the dramatic irony, as it were, to increase the savor. Usually verbal irony conveys something by saying its opposite, to increase the punch: "What a beautiful day" (raining cats and dogs); "You're a fine one" (what a stinker). Both speaker and listener know exactly what is what, whereas dramatic irony springs from a character's ignorance of the ironic implications that other characters, or the audience alone, perceive.

In this story, when the old man calls his potion a cleaning fluid or spot remover, both he and Alan understand exactly what he means, in a brand of verbal irony known as *understatement.* But the old man also perceives a good deal more, which we too suspect and fully perceive as the story unfolds, as Alan does not. Furthermore, we can glimpse here the third and last category of irony: *situational* (also called irony of fate or irony of circumstance). Situational irony arises when the opposite of what ought to be happens—"life's little ironies" we call them when we smash our dreamed-of new car while driving it out of the dealer's, or spatter our brand-new outfit, or it rains on the weather bureau's picnic. We find it in comedy when the young lovers run into the worst possible luck, and in tragedy when the most noble spirit goes to his death while the featherheads survive. Situational irony usually prompts the other two (verbal, dramatic). What ironic situation supports the verbal and dramatic ironies in this little story?

THE CHASER
John Collier   (1901–1980)

Alan Austen, as nervous as a kitten, went up certain dark and creaky stairs in the neighborhood of Pell Street, and peered about for a long time on the dim landing before he found the name he wanted written obscurely on one of the doors.

He pushed open this door, as he had been told to do, and found himself in a tiny room, which contained no furniture but a plain kitchen table, a rocking chair, and an ordinary chair. On one of the dirty buff-colored walls were a couple of shelves, containing in all perhaps a dozen bottles and jars.

An old man sat in the rocking chair, reading a newspaper. Alan, without a word, handed him the card he had been given. "Sit down, Mr. Austen," said the old man very politely. "I am glad to make your acquaintance."

"Is it true," asked Alan, "that you have a certain mixture that has—er—quite extraordinary effects?"

"My dear sir," replied the old man, "my stock in trade is not very large—I don't deal in laxatives and teething mixtures—but, such as it is, it is varied. I think nothing I sell has effects which could be precisely described as ordinary."

"Well, the fact is—" began Alan.

"Here, for example," interrupted the old man, reaching for a bottle from the shelf. "Here is a liquid as colorless as water, almost tasteless, quite imperceptible in coffee, milk, wine, or any other beverage. It is also quite imperceptible to any known method of autopsy."

"Do you mean it is a poison?" cried Alan, very much horrified.

"Call it cleaning fluid if you like," said the old man indifferently. "Lives need cleaning. Call it a spot-remover. 'Out, damned spot!' Eh? 'Out, brief candle!' "

"I want nothing of that sort," said Alan.

"Probably it is just as well," said the old man. "Do you know the price of this? For one teaspoonful, which is sufficient, I ask five thousand dollars. Never less. Not a penny less."

"I hope all your mixtures are not as expensive," said Alan apprehensively.

"Oh, dear, no," said the old man. "It would be no good charging that sort of price for a love-potion, for example. Young people who need a love-potion very seldom have five thousand dollars. If they had they would not need a love-potion."

"I'm glad to hear you say so," said Alan.

"I look at it like this," said the old man. "Please a customer with one article, and he will come back when he needs another. Even if it *is* more costly. He will save up for it, if necessary."

"So," said Alan, "you really do sell love-potions?"

"If I did not sell love-potions," said the old man, reaching for another bottle, "I should not have mentioned the other matter to you. It is only when one is in a position to oblige that one can afford to be so confidential."

"And these potions," said Alan. "They are not just—just—er—"

"Oh, no," said the old man. "Their effects are permanent and extend far beyond the mere carnal impulse. But they include it. Oh, yes, they include it. Bountifully. Insistently. Everlastingly."

"Dear me!" said Alan, attempting a look of scientific detachment. "How very interesting!"

"But consider the spiritual side," said the old man.

"I do, indeed," said Alan.

"For indifference," said the old man, "they substitute devotion. For scorn, adoration. Give one tiny measure of this to the young lady—its flavor is imperceptible in orange juice, soup, or cocktails—and however gay and giddy she is, she will change altogether. She'll want nothing but solitude, and you."

"I can hardly believe it," said Alan. "She is so fond of parties."

"She will not like them anymore," said the old man. "She'll be afraid of the pretty girls you may meet."

"She'll actually be jealous?" cried Alan in a rapture. "Of me?"

"Yes, she will want to be everything to you."

"She is, already. Only she doesn't care about it."

"She will, when she has taken this. She will care intensely. You'll be her sole interest in life."

"Wonderful!" cried Alan.

"She'll want to know all you do," said the old man. "All that has happened to you during the day. Every word of it. She'll want to know what you are thinking about, why you smile suddenly, why you are looking sad."

"That is love!" cried Alan.

"Yes," said the old man. "How carefully she'll look after you! She'll never allow you to be tired, to sit in a draft, to neglect your food. If you are an hour late, she'll be terrified. She'll think you are killed, or that some siren has caught you."

"I can hardly imagine Diana like that!" cried Alan, overwhelmed with joy.

"You will not have to use your imagination," said the old man. "And by the way, since there are always sirens, if by any chance you *should,* later on, slip a little, you need not worry. She will forgive you, in the end. She'll be terribly hurt, of course, but she'll forgive you—in the end."

"That will not happen," said Alan fervently.

"Of course not," said the old man. "But, if it does, you need not worry. She'll never divorce you. Oh, no! And, of course, she herself will never give you the least, the very least, grounds for—not divorce, of course—but even uneasiness."

"And how much," said Alan, "how much is this wonderful mixture?"

"It is not so dear," said the old man, "as the spot-remover, as I think we agreed to call it. No. That is five thousand dollars; never a penny less. One has to be older than you are to indulge in that sort of thing. One has to save up for it."

"But the love-potion?" said Alan.

"Oh, that," said the old man, opening the drawer in the kitchen table and taking out a tiny, rather dirty-looking phial. "That is just a dollar."

"I can't tell you how grateful I am," said Alan, watching him fill it.

"I like to oblige," said the old man. "Then customers come back, later in life, when they are rather better-off, and want more expensive things. Here you are. You will find it very effective."

"Thank you again," said Alan. "Good-bye."

"*Au revoir,*" said the old man.

QUESTIONS

1. What does the title mean? Which details in the story explain the title?
2. What details in the first sentence set the mood for the story?
3. What details throughout the story create its air of actuality?
4. Explain " 'Out, damned spot!' Eh? 'Out, brief candle!' "
5. Point out some of the dramatic ironies.
6. Explain the last two lines.
7. What is the underlying ironic situation?

Thus far we have not mentioned *plot:* the events of the story arranged in the order we meet them, an arrangement often very different from the chronological sequence in which they supposedly happened. A major part of narration is the desire to make the telling most effective. So the teller creates a plot: selecting a beginning to interest the audience, adding details to keep their interest, and omitting others to keep them guessing until the end.

Since different people narrate in different ways, we may usefully describe a plot by examining the events selected. The narration begins with one event, rather than another, catching interest and setting the plot in motion. It may continue in a straight *chronological order,* or with mixed chronology, as an occasional *flashback* into the past helps to illuminate the present action. A *unified plot* follows an unbroken chain of cause and effect from beginning to end; an *episodic plot* includes scenes outside the causal chain, though they may help to define a character or clarify a theme.

The plot of "The Chaser" is chronological and unified (one episode, really), restricted to a conversation between two men in one room within the span of a few minutes. The plots of "Rumpelstiltskin," "Stone Soup," and "The Monkey's Paw" cover more time and space and involve more people, but are relatively uncomplicated. The next story, "The Rocking-Horse Winner," is more complexly plotted. After setting his theme of "luck" in the first sentence, D. H. Lawrence gives us considerable background in a fairy-tale sort of way. His opening event is the mother's attempt to "make something," but the plot really begins with the boy's question about not having a car. Then events follow chronologically until the flashback, nicely contrived through conversations, which begins when the sister remarks that the boy is always talking about horse races. Watch for the point where the flashback ends, and events again move chronologically.

"The Rocking-Horse Winner" is perhaps the best realistic fairy tale ever written—a carefully plotted story in which the essential wish-fulfilling psychology of the fairy tale combines with the Oedipal urge; the boy supplants the father to please the mother, a pattern not infrequent in fairyland, as in *Jack and the Beanstalk.* What elements does this story share with the preceding stories? How does Lawrence's language evoke the spellbinding effect? Some of it directs our attention to a *symbol,* the rocking horse, as Lawrence asks us to respond to the ancient power of an object made to stand for an idea. From Hebrew and Greek times the dove has symbolized love and peace because of its soft and peaceful nature. From the Roman and Austrian empires to the American confederation, the eagle has symbolized power. What does the rocking horse symbolize?

THE ROCKING-HORSE WINNER

D. H. Lawrence   (1885–1930)

There was a woman who was beautiful, who started with all the advantages, yet she had no luck. She married for love, and the love turned to dust. She had bonny children, yet she felt they had been thrust upon her, and she could not love them. They looked at her coldly, as if they were finding fault with her. And hurriedly she felt she must cover up some fault in herself. Yet what it was that she must cover up she never knew. Nevertheless, when her children were present, she always felt the centre of her heart go hard. This troubled her, and in her manner she was all the more gentle and anxious for her children, as if she loved them very much. Only she herself knew that at the centre of her heart was a hard little place that could not feel love, no, not for anybody. Everybody else said of her: "She is such a good mother. She adores her children." Only she herself, and her children themselves, knew it was not so. They read it in each other's eyes.

There were a boy and two little girls. They lived in a pleasant house, with a garden, and they had discreet servants, and felt themselves superior to anyone in the neighbourhood.

Although they lived in style, they felt always an anxiety in the house. There was never enough money. The mother had a small income, and the father had a small income, but not nearly enough for the social position which they had to keep up. The father went in to town to some office. But though he had good prospects, these prospects never materialized. There was always the grinding sense of the shortage of money, though the style was always kept up.

At last the mother said: "I will see if *I* can't make something." But she did not know where to begin. She racked her brains, and tried this thing and the other, but could not find anything successful. The failure made deep lines come into her face. Her children were growing up, they would have to go to school. There must be more money, there must be more money. The father, who was always very handsome and expensive in his tastes, seemed as if he never *would* be able to do anything worth doing. And the mother, who had a great belief in herself, did not succeed any better, and her tastes were just as expensive.

And so the house came to be haunted by the unspoken phrase: *There must be more money! There must be more money!* The children could hear it all the time, though nobody said it aloud. They heard it at Christmas, when the expensive and splendid toys filled the nursery. Behind the shining modern rocking-horse, behind the smart doll's-house, a voice would start whispering: "There *must* be more money! There *must* be more money!" And the children would stop playing, to listen for a moment. They would look into each other's eyes, to see if they had all heard. And each one saw in the eyes of the other two that they too had heard. "There *must* be more money! There *must* be more money!"

It came whispering from the springs of the still-swaying rocking-horse, and even the horse, bending his wooden, champing head, heard it. The big doll, sitting so pink and smirking in her new pram,[1] could hear it quite plainly, and seemed to be smirking all the more self-consciously because of it. The foolish puppy, too, that took the place of the teddy-bear, he was looking so extraordinarily foolish for no other reason but that he heard the secret whisper all over the house: "There *must* be more money!"

Yet nobody ever said it aloud. The whisper was everywhere, and therefore no one spoke it. Just as no one ever says: "We are breathing!" in spite of the fact that breath is coming and going all the time.

[1]Doll carriage.

"Mother," said the boy Paul one day, "why don't we keep a car of our own? Why do we always use uncle's, or else a taxi?"

"Because we're the poor members of the family," said the mother.

"But why *are* we, mother?"

"Well—I suppose," she said slowly and bitterly, "it's because your father has no luck."

The boy was silent for some time.

"Is luck money, mother?" he asked rather timidly.

"No, Paul. Not quite. It's what causes you to have money."

"Oh!" said Paul vaguely. "I thought when Uncle Oscar said *filthy lucker,* it meant money."

"*Filthy lucre* does mean money," said the mother. "But it's lucre, not luck."

"Oh!" said the boy. "Then what *is* luck, mother?"

"It's what causes you to have money. If you're lucky you have money. That's why it's better to be born lucky than rich. If you're rich, you may lose your money. But if you're lucky, you will always get more money."

"Oh! Will you? And is father not lucky?"

"Very unlucky, I should say," she said bitterly.

The boy watched her with unsure eyes.

"Why?" he asked.

"I don't know. Nobody ever knows why one person is lucky and another unlucky."

"Don't they? Nobody at all? Does *nobody* know?"

"Perhaps God. But He never tells."

"He ought to, then. And aren't you lucky either, mother?"

"I can't be, if I married an unlucky husband."

"But by yourself, aren't you?"

"I used to think I was, before I married. Now I think I am very unlucky indeed."

"Why?"

"Well—never mind! Perhaps I'm not really," she said.

The child looked at her, to see if she meant it. But he saw, by the lines of her mouth, that she was only trying to hide something from him.

"Well, anyhow," he said stoutly, "I'm a lucky person."

"Why?" said his mother, with a sudden laugh.

He stared at her. He didn't even know why he had said it.

"God told me," he asserted, brazening it out.

"I hope He did, dear!" she said, again with a laugh, but rather bitter.

"He did, mother!"

"Excellent!" said the mother, using one of her husband's exclamations.

The boy saw she did not believe him; or, rather, that she paid no attention to his assertion. This angered him somewhat, and made him want to compel her attention.

He went off by himself, vaguely, in a childish way, seeking for the clue to "luck." Absorbed, taking no heed of other people, he went about with a sort of stealth, seeking inwardly for luck. He wanted luck, he wanted it, he wanted it. When the two girls were playing dolls in the nursery, he would sit on his big rocking-horse, charging madly into space, with a frenzy that made the little girls peer at him uneasily. Wildly the horse careered, the waving dark hair of the boy tossed, his eyes had a strange glare in them. The little girls dared not speak to him.

When he had ridden to the end of his mad little journey, he climbed down and stood in front of his rocking-horse, staring fixedly into its lowered face. Its red mouth was slightly open, its big eye was wide and glassy-bright.

"Now!" he would silently command the snorting steed. "Now, take me to where there is luck! Now take me!"

And he would slash the horse on the neck with the little whip he had asked Uncle Oscar for. He *knew* the horse could take him to where there was luck, if only he forced it. So he would mount again, and start on his furious ride, hoping at last to get there. He knew he could get there.

"You'll break your horse, Paul!" said the nurse.

"He's always riding like that! I wish he'd leave off!" said his elder sister Joan.

But he only glared down on them in silence. Nurse gave him up. She could make nothing of him. Anyhow he was growing beyond her.

One day his mother and his Uncle Oscar came in when he was on one of his furious rides. He did not speak to them.

"Hallo, you young jockey! Riding a winner?" said his uncle.

"Aren't you growing too big for a rocking-horse? You're not a very little boy any longer, you know," said his mother.

But Paul only gave a blue glare from his big, rather close-set eyes. He would speak to nobody when he was in full tilt. His mother watched him with an anxious expression on her face.

At last he suddenly stopped forcing his horse into the mechanical gallop, and slid down.

"Well, I got there!" he announced fiercely, his blue eyes still flaring, and his sturdy long legs straddling apart.

"Where did you get to?" asked his mother.

"Where I wanted to go," he flared back at her.

"That's right, son!" said Uncle Oscar. "Don't you stop till you get there. What's the horse's name?"

"He doesn't have a name," said the boy.

"Gets on without all right?" asked the uncle.

"Well, he has different names. He was called Sansovino last week."

"Sansovino, eh? Won the Ascot. How did you know his name?"

"He always talks about horse-races with Bassett," said Joan.

The uncle was delighted to find that his small nephew was posted with all the racing news. Bassett, the young gardener, who had been wounded in the left foot in the war and had got his present job through Oscar Cresswell, whose batman[2] he had been, was a perfect blade of the "turf." He lived in the racing events, and the small boy lived with him.

[2]Officer's servant.

Oscar Cresswell got it all from Bassett.

"Master Paul comes and asks me, so I can't do more than tell him, sir," said Bassett, his face terribly serious, as if he were speaking of religious matters.

"And does he ever put anything on a horse he fancies?"

"Well—I don't want to give him away—he's a young sport, a fine sport, sir. Would you mind asking him himself? He sort of takes a pleasure in it, and perhaps he'd feel I was giving him away, sir, if you don't mind."

Bassett was serious as a church.

The uncle went back to his nephew and took him off for a ride in the car.

"Say, Paul, old man, do you ever put anything on a horse?" the uncle asked.

The boy watched the handsome man closely.

"Why, do you think I oughtn't to?" he parried.

"Not a bit of it! I thought perhaps you might give me a tip for the Lincoln."

The car sped on into the country, going down to Uncle Oscar's place in Hampshire.

"Honour bright?" said the nephew.

"Honour bright, son!" said the uncle.

"Well, then, Daffodil."

"Daffodil! I doubt it, sonny. What about Mirza?"

"I only know the winner," said the boy. "That's Daffodil."

"Daffodil, eh?"

There was a pause. Daffodil was an obscure horse comparatively.

"Uncle!"

"Yes, son?"

"You won't let it go any further, will you? I promised Bassett."

"Bassett be damned, old man! What's he got to do with it?"

"We're partners. We've been partners from the first. Uncle, he lent me my first five shillings, which I lost. I promised him, honour bright, it was only between me and him; only you gave me that ten-shilling note I started winning with, so I thought you were lucky. You won't let it go any further, will you?"

The boy gazed at his uncle from those big, hot, blue eyes, set rather close together. The uncle stirred and laughed uneasily.

"Right you are, son! I'll keep your tip private. Daffodil, eh? How much are you putting on him?"

"All except twenty pounds," said the boy. "I keep that in reserve."

The uncle thought it a good joke.

"You keep twenty pounds in reserve, do you, you young romancer? What are you betting, then?"

"I'm betting three hundred," said the boy gravely. "But it's between you and me, Uncle Oscar! Honour bright?"

The uncle burst into a roar of laughter.

"It's between you and me all right, you young Nat Gould,"[3] he said, laughing. "But where's your three hundred?"

---

[3]British sportswriter.

"Bassett keeps it for me. We're partners."

"You are, are you! And what is Bassett putting on Daffodil?"

"He won't go quite as high as I do, I expect. Perhaps he'll go a hundred and fifty."

"What, pennies?" laughed the uncle.

"Pounds," said the child, with a surprised look at his uncle. "Bassett keeps a bigger reserve than I do."

Between wonder and amusement Uncle Oscar was silent. He pursued the matter no further, but he determined to take his nephew with him to the Lincoln races.

"Now, son," he said, "I'm putting twenty on Mirza, and I'll put five for you on any horse you fancy. What's your pick?"

"Daffodil, uncle."

"No, not the fiver on Daffodil!"

"I should if it was my own fiver," said the child.

"Good! Good! Right you are! A fiver for me and a fiver for you on Daffodil."

The child had never been to a race-meeting before, and his eyes were blue fire. He pursed his mouth tight, and watched. A Frenchman just in front had put his money on Lancelot. Wild with excitement, he flayed his arms up and down, yelling *Lancelot! Lancelot!* in his French accent.

Daffodil came in first, Lancelot second, Mirza third. The child, flushed and with eyes blazing, was curiously serene. His uncle brought him four five-pound notes, four to one.

"What am I to do with these?" he cried, waving them before the boy's eyes.

"I suppose we'll talk to Bassett," said the boy. "I expect I have fifteen hundred now; and twenty in reserve; and this twenty."

His uncle studied him for some moments.

"Look here, son!" he said. "You're not serious about Bassett and that fifteen hundred, are you?"

"Yes, I am. But it's between you and me, uncle. Honour bright!"

"Honour bright all right, son! But I must talk to Bassett."

"If you'd like to be a partner, uncle, with Bassett and me, we could all be partners. Only, you'd have to promise, honour bright, uncle, not to let it go beyond us three. Bassett and I are lucky, and you must be lucky, because it was your ten shillings I started winning with. . . ."

Uncle Oscar took both Bassett and Paul into Richmond Park for an afternoon, and there they talked.

"It's like this, you see, sir," Bassett said. "Master Paul would get me talking about racing events, spinning yarns, you know, sir. And he was always keen on knowing if I'd made or if I'd lost. It's about a year since, now, that I put five shilling on Blush of Dawn for him—and we lost. Then the luck turned, with that ten shillings he had from you, that we put on Singhalese. And since that time, it's been pretty steady, all things considering. What do you say, Master Paul?"

"We're all right when we're sure," said Paul. "It's when we're not quite sure that we go down."

"Oh, but we're careful then," said Bassett.

"But when are you *sure?*" smiled Uncle Oscar.

"It's Master Paul, sir," said Bassett, in a secret, religious voice. "It's as if he had it from heaven. Like Daffodil, now, for the Lincoln. That was as sure as eggs."

"Did you put anything on Daffodil?" asked Oscar Cresswell.

"Yes, sir. I made my bit."

"And my nephew?"

Bassett was obstinately silent, looking at Paul.

"I made twelve hundred, didn't I, Bassett? I told uncle I was putting three hundred on Daffodil."

"That's right," said Bassett, nodding.

"But where's the money?" asked the uncle.

"I keep it safe locked up, sir. Master Paul he can have it any minute he likes to ask for it."

"What, fifteen hundred pounds?"

"And twenty! And *forty,* that is, with the twenty he made on the course."

"It's amazing!" said the uncle.

"If Master Paul offers you to be partners, sir, I would, if I were you; if you'll excuse me," said Bassett.

Oscar Cresswell thought about it.

"I'll see the money," he said.

They drove home again, and sure enough, Bassett came round to the garden-house with fifteen hundred pounds in notes. The twenty pounds reserve was left with Joe Glee, in the Turf Commission deposit.

"You see, it's all right, uncle, when I'm *sure!* Then we go strong, for all we're worth. Don't we, Bassett?"

"We do that, Master Paul."

"And when are you sure?" said the uncle, laughing.

"Oh, well, sometimes I'm *absolutely* sure, like about Daffodil," said the boy; "and sometimes I have an idea; and sometimes I haven't even an idea, have I, Bassett? Then we're careful, because we mostly go down."

"You do, do you! And when you're sure, like about Daffodil, what makes you sure, sonny?"

"Oh, well, I don't know," said the boy uneasily. "I'm sure, you know, uncle; that's all."

"It's as if he had it from heaven, sir," Bassett reiterated.

"I should say so!" said the uncle.

But he became a partner. And when the Leger was coming on, Paul was "sure" about Lively Spark, which was a quite inconsiderable horse. The boy insisted on putting a thousand on the horse, Bassett went for five hundred, and Oscar Cresswell two hundred. Lively Spark came in first, and the betting had been ten to one against him. Paul had made ten thousand.

"You see," he said, "I was absolutely sure of him."

Even Oscar Cresswell had cleared two thousand.

"Look here, son," he said, "this sort of thing makes me nervous."

"It needn't, uncle! Perhaps I shan't be sure again for a long time."

"But what are you going to do with your money?" asked the uncle.

"Of course," said the boy, "I started it for mother. She said she had no luck, because father is unlucky, so I thought if *I* was lucky, it might stop whispering."

"What might stop whispering?"

"Our house. I *hate* our house for whispering."

"What does it whisper?"

"Why—why"—the boy fidgeted—"why, I don't know. But it's always short of money, you know, uncle."

"I know it, son, I know it."

"You know people send mother writs,[4] don't you, uncle?"

"I'm afraid I do," said the uncle.

"And then the house whispers, like people laughing at you behind your back. It's awful, that is! I thought if I was lucky . . ."

"You might stop it," added the uncle.

The boy watched him with big blue eyes, that had an uncanny cold fire in them, and he said never a word.

"Well, then!" said the uncle. "What are we doing?"

"I shouldn't like mother to know I was lucky," said the boy.

"Why not, son?"

"She'd stop me."

"I don't think she would."

"Oh!"—and the boy writhed in an odd way—"I *don't* want her to know, uncle."

"All right, son! We'll manage it without her knowing."

They managed it very easily. Paul, at the other's suggestion, handed over five thousand pounds to his uncle, who deposited it with the family lawyer, who was then to inform Paul's mother that a relative had put five thousand pounds into his hands, which sum was to be paid out a thousand pounds at a time, on the mother's birthday, for the next five years.

"So she'll have a birthday present of a thousand pounds for five successive years," said Uncle Oscar. "I hope it won't make it all the harder for her later."

Paul's mother had her birthday in November. The house had been "whispering" worse than ever lately, and, even in spite of his luck, Paul could not bear up against it. He was very anxious to see the effect of the birthday letter, telling his mother about the thousand pounds.

When there were no visitors, Paul now took his meals with his parents, as he was beyond the nursery control. His mother went into town nearly every day. She had discovered that she had an odd knack of sketching furs and dress materials, so she worked secretly in the studio of a friend who was the chief "artist" for the leading drapers. She drew the figures of ladies in furs and ladies in silk and sequins for the newspaper advertisements. This young woman artist earned several thousand pounds a year, but Paul's mother only made several hundreds, and she was again dissatisfied. She so wanted to be first in something, and she did not succeed, even in making sketches for drapery advertisements.

[4]Demands for payment.

She was down to breakfast on the morning of her birthday. Paul watched her face as she read her letters. He knew the lawyer's letter. As his mother read it, her face hardened and became more expressionless. Then a cold, determined look came on her mouth. She hid the letter under the pile of others, and said not a word about it.

"Didn't you have anything nice in the post for your birthday, mother?" said Paul.

"Quite moderately nice," she said, her voice cold and absent.

She went away to town without saying more.

But in the afternoon Uncle Oscar appeared. He said Paul's mother had had a long interview with the lawyer, asking if the whole five thousand could not be advanced at once, as she was in debt.

"What do you think, uncle?" said the boy.

"I leave it to you, son."

"Oh, let her have it, then! We can get some more with the other," said the boy.

"A bird in the hand is worth two in the bush, laddie!" said Uncle Oscar.

"But I'm sure to *know* for the Grand National; or the Lincolnshire; or else the Derby. I'm sure to know for *one* of them," said Paul.

So Uncle Oscar signed the agreement, and Paul's mother touched the whole five thousand. Then something very curious happened. The voices in the house suddenly went mad, like a chorus of frogs on a spring evening. There were certain new furnishings, and Paul had a tutor. He was *really* going to Eton, his father's school, in the following autumn. There were flowers in the winter, and a blossoming of the luxury Paul's mother had been used to. And yet the voices in the house, behind the sprays of mimosa and almond blossom, and from under the piles of iridescent cushions, simply trilled and screamed in a sort of ecstasy: "There *must* be more money! Oh-h-h; there *must* be more money. Oh, now, now-w! Now-w-w —there *must* be more money!—more than ever! More than ever!"

It frightened Paul terribly. He studied away at his Latin and Greek with his tutors. But his intense hours were spent with Bassett. The Grand National had gone by: he had not "known," and had lost a hundred pounds. Summer was at hand. He was in agony for the Lincoln. But even for the Lincoln he didn't "know," and he lost fifty pounds. He became wild-eyed and strange, as if something were going to explode in him.

"Let it alone, son! Don't you bother about it!" urged Uncle Oscar. But it was as if the boy couldn't really hear what his uncle was saying.

"I've got to know for the Derby! I've got to know for the Derby!" the child reiterated, his big blue eyes blazing with a sort of madness.

His mother noticed how overwrought he was.

"You'd better go to the seaside. Wouldn't you like to go now to the seaside, instead of waiting? I think you'd better," she said, looking down at him anxiously, her heart curiously heavy because of him.

But the child lifted his uncanny blue eyes.

"I couldn't possibly go before the Derby, mother!" he said. "I couldn't possibly!"

"Why not?" she said, her voice becoming heavy when she was opposed. "Why not? You can still go from the seaside to see the Derby with your Uncle Oscar, if that's what you wish. No need for you to wait here. Besides, I think you care too much about these races. It's a bad sign. My family has been a gambling family, and you won't know till you grow up how much damage it has done. But it has done damage. I shall have to send Bassett away, and ask Uncle Oscar not to talk racing to you, unless you promise to be reasonable about it; go away to the seaside and forget it. You're all nerves!"

"I'll do what you like, mother, so long as you don't send me away till after the Derby," the boy said.

"Send you away from where? Just from this house?"

"Yes," he said, gazing at her.

"Why, you curious child, what makes you care about this house so much, suddenly? I never knew you loved it."

He gazed at her without speaking. He had a secret within a secret, something he had not divulged, even to Bassett or to his Uncle Oscar.

But his mother, after standing undecided and a little bit sullen for some moments, said:

"Very well, then! Don't go to the seaside till after the Derby, if you don't wish it. But promise me you won't let your nerves go to pieces. Promise you won't think so much about horse-racing and *events,* as you call them!"

"Oh, no," said the boy casually. "I won't think much about them, mother. You needn't worry. I wouldn't worry, mother, if I were you."

"If you were me and I were you," said his mother, "I wonder what we *should* do!"

"But you know you needn't worry, mother, don't you?" the boy repeated.

"I should be awfully glad to know it," she said wearily.

"Oh, well, you *can,* you know. I mean, you *ought* to know you needn't worry," he insisted.

"Ought I? Then I'll see about it," she said.

Paul's secret of secrets was his wooden horse, that which had no name. Since he was emancipated from a nurse and a nursery-governess, he had had his rocking-horse removed to his own bedroom at the top of the house.

"Surely, you're too big for a rocking-horse!" his mother had remonstrated.

"Well, you see, mother, till I can have a *real* horse, I like to have *some* sort of animal about," had been his quaint answer.

"Do you feel he keeps you company?" she laughed.

"Oh, yes! He's very good, he always keeps me company, when I'm there," said Paul.

So the horse, rather shabby, stood in an arrested prance in the boy's bedroom.

The Derby was drawing near, and the boy grew more and more tense. He hardly heard what was spoken to him, he was very frail, and his eyes were really uncanny. His mother had sudden strange seizures of uneasiness about him. Sometimes, for half-an-hour, she would feel a sudden anxiety about him that was almost anguish. She wanted to rush to him at once, and know he was safe.

Two nights before the Derby, she was at a big party in town, when one of her rushes of anxiety about her boy, her first-born, gripped her heart till she could hardly speak. She fought with the feeling, might and main, for she believed in common-sense. But it was too strong. She had to leave the dance and go downstairs to telephone to the country. The children's nursery-governess was terribly surprised and startled at being rung up in the night.

"Are the children all right, Miss Wilmot?"

"Oh, yes, they are quite all right."

"Master Paul? Is he all right?"

"He went to bed as right as a trivet. Shall I run up and look at him?"

"No," said Paul's mother reluctantly. "No! Don't trouble. It's all right. Don't sit up. We shall be home fairly soon." She did not want her son's privacy intruded upon.

"Very good," said the governess.

It was about one o'clock when Paul's mother and father drove up to their house. All was still. Paul's mother went to her room and slipped off her white fur cloak. She had told her maid not to wait up for her. She heard her husband downstairs, mixing a whisky-and-soda.

And then, because of the strange anxiety at her heart, she stole upstairs to her son's room. Noiselessly she went along the upper corridor. Was there a faint noise? What was it?

She stood, with arrested muscles, outside his door, listening. There was a strange, heavy, and yet not loud noise. Her heart stood still. It was a soundless noise, yet rushing and powerful. Something huge, in violent, hushed motion. What was it? What in God's name was it? She ought to know. She felt that she knew the noise. She knew what it was.

Yet she could not place it. She couldn't say what it was. And on and on it went, like a madness.

Softly, frozen with anxiety and fear, she turned the door-handle.

The room was dark. Yet in the space near the window, she heard and saw something plunging to and fro. She gazed in fear and amazement.

Then suddenly she switched on the light, and saw her son, in his green pyjamas, madly surging on the rocking-horse. The blaze of light suddenly lit him up, as he urged the wooden horse, and lit her up, as she stood, blonde, in her dress of pale green and crystal, in the doorway.

"Paul!" she cried. "Whatever are you doing?"

"It's Malabar!" he screamed, in a powerful, strange voice. "It's Malabar!"

His eyes blazed at her for one strange and senseless second, as he ceased urging his wooden horse. Then he fell with a crash to the ground, and she, all her tormented motherhood flooding upon her, rushed to gather him up.

But he was unconscious, and unconscious he remained, with some brain-fever. He talked and tossed, and his mother sat stonily by his side.

"Malabar! It's Malabar! Bassett, Bassett, I *know!* It's Malabar!"

So the child cried, trying to get up and urge the rocking-horse that gave him his inspiration.

"What does he mean by Malabar?" asked the heart-frozen mother.

"I don't know," said the father stonily.

"What does he mean by Malabar?" she asked her brother Oscar.

"It's one of the horses running for the Derby," was the answer.

And, in spite of himself, Oscar Cresswell spoke to Bassett, and himself put a thousand on Malabar: at fourteen to one.

The third day of the illness was critical: they were waiting for a change. The boy, with his rather long, curly hair, was tossing ceaselessly on the pillow. He neither slept nor regained consciousness, and his eyes were like blue stones. His mother sat, feeling her heart had gone, turned actually into a stone.

In the evening, Oscar Cresswell did not come, but Bassett sent a message, saying could he come up for one moment, just one moment? Paul's mother was very angry at the intrusion, but on second thought she agreed. The boy was the same. Perhaps Bassett might bring him to consciousness.

The gardener, a shortish fellow with a little brown moustache, and sharp little brown eyes, tip-toed into the room, touched his imaginary cap to Paul's mother, and stole to the bedside, staring with glittering, smallish eyes, at the tossing, dying child.

"Master Paul!" he whispered. "Master Paul! Malabar came in first all right, a clean win. I did as you told me. You've made over seventy thousand pounds, you have; you've got over eighty thousand. Malabar came in all right, Master Paul."

"Malabar! Malabar! Did I say Malabar, mother? Did I say Malabar? Do you think I'm lucky, mother? I knew Malabar, didn't I? Over eighty thousand pounds! I call that lucky, don't you, mother? Over eighty thousand pounds! I knew, didn't I know I knew? Malabar came in all right. If I ride my horse till I'm sure, then I tell you, Bassett, you can go as high as you like. Did you go for all you were worth, Bassett?"

"I went a thousand on it, Master Paul."

"I never told you, mother, that if I can ride my horse, and *get there*, then I'm absolutely sure—oh, absolutely! Mother, did I ever tell you? I *am* lucky!"

"No, you never did," said the mother.

But the boy died in the night.

And even as he lay dead, his mother heard her brother's voice saying to her: "My God, Hester, you're eighty-odd thousand to the good, and a poor devil of a son to the bad. But, poor devil, poor devil, he's best gone out of a life where he rides his rocking-horse to find a winner."

QUESTIONS

1. Beginning with the first sentence, point out some of Lawrence's phrases that evoke his fairy-tale context.

2. How do the uncle and Bassett function in this fairyland context?

3. In one of Freud's primal theories, the "Oedipus complex," the son wishes to murder and supplant the father to possess the mother. How does this story reflect that Freudian concept? What does the secret rocking on the rocking horse suggest?

4. In what sense is the house "whispering" and "haunted"?
5. Explain "heard her brother's voice saying to her . . ." in the last paragraph.
6. How does this story condemn the traditional fairy-tale wish for status, riches, and happiness?

ON WRITING ABOUT LITERATURE

All the questions after each reading have stirred up things to write about. Consider such details as straw or disorder in "Rumpelstiltskin," food or psychology in "Stone Soup," money or love in "The Rocking-Horse Winner." You might like to explain the kinds of irony, or the importance of a metaphor or a minor character in a story—or in a poem or a play. Since literature implies its meanings without stating them, it is tailor-made for an essay. You simply state the work's implied point as the thesis of your essay, perhaps:

> The real point of "The Rocking-Horse Winner" is the danger of wanting something for nothing.

In short, you make yourself a thesis asserting the importance of one detail or another, or asserting what all the work's details and questions add up to: the work's implied point.

Whatever you choose to write about, the procedure is the same. You open your paper with some introductory remarks to situate your reader:

> Lawrence's "The Rocking-Horse Winner" opens with a woman who has everything except love. She has a heart of stone, and never enough money. . . .

Give your readers a few more details, then set your thesis:

> The story, in a magical way, shows the real cost of materialism.

You will now have introduced your paper, usually in a paragraph ending with your thesis. Now start a new paragraph and describe and quote and explain until you feel that you have fully shown your reader what you mean. Your story will have been in the past tense: "There *was* a woman who *was* beautiful. . . ." But your description will be in the present tense:

> The story opens with a woman who *is* beautiful, who *has* all the advantages, including a husband, a nice house, servants, and two "bonny children."

Your quotations will come from the story exactly as you find them, including the past tense. In dialogue, you will usually find a shift from the present of the spoken words to the past of the narrative: " 'Because we're the poor members of the family,' *said* the mother." Your description of this will be in the present: "The mother *replies* that they are the poor members of the family," or " 'Because we're the poor members of the family,' *says* the mother"—since here you are quoting only the mother's words and not Lawrence's "said the mother."

When you have put all your evidence before your reader, write a concluding paragraph to sum up your point and drive it home, and your paper is done. But don't forget a title that will direct your reader toward what you are going to show: "Sex and the Rocking-Horse Loser."

CHAPTER 2

THE NARRATOR AS PARTICIPANT

Every story has a teller, a *narrator*. When stories are told orally—to children at bedtime, to friends around a camp fire, to lunchroom companions—the narrator is physically present, talking to the listeners. Stories written and printed in books imitate this fundamental narrative situation. As readers, we turn the words on the page into the voice of a narrator. Someone is telling us something.

The story can have happened to the narrator, to someone the narrator knows, or to someone else. These three possibilities may be called:

1. The narrator as participant
2. The narrator as observer
3. The omniscient narrator

In this chapter, we consider the narrator as participant. In Chapters 3 and 4, we discuss the other two kinds.

When you tell a personal experience, you become a narrator as participant. You adopt the grammatical first person; the pronoun "I" is your focal point. "I came, I saw, I conquered," wrote Julius Caesar to begin the history of his *Gallic War*. In first-person fiction, a writer invents a narrating "I," appropriating for make-believe the authority you command when you narrate your true experience or Caesar commanded when he narrated his. "I was there, I saw it happen"; the *first-person perspective* helps the fiction work its magic. The "I" thus created may be a *participant* in the action of the story, or merely an *observer*. If the I is a participant, it is often the *protagonist,* the hero or main character. If the I is an observer, it stands aside, recording the actions of the protagonist, the *antagonist* (or opposing character) if there is one, and the other people of the story.

First-person narration limits the reader's understanding of the story. We know only what the narrator knows or has chosen to tell. But we must be wary of accepting everything we are told. Caesar's report may not be in all respects the story the Gauls would tell. A fictional narrator, too, shapes and interprets according to a personal vision; the story may be different from another viewpoint. For most stories, this difference seems not to matter. Occasionally, however, a story will derive much of its effect from a teller that Wayne Booth, in his *Rhetoric of Fiction,* conveniently designated an *unreliable narrator:* a narrator whose account is significantly different from the story that would be told by a neutral observer in command of all the facts. An unreliable narrator reports inaccurately or interprets incorrectly. The other kind of a teller, one who reports accurately and interprets correctly, is a *reliable narrator.*

As readers we stand back from a story, hearing what we are told, but also judging it. When we recognize that the narrator's understanding or behavior is different from ours, we see the story from two perspectives—the story being told and the story that might be told. The result is a pervasive *dramatic irony;* we perceive a distinction between the words and actions of the narrator and the words and actions of a wiser or more prudent person if placed in the same situation.

The *time of narration* may also be important. Many first-person narrations occur not long after the events described, but if the narration comes much later, the narrator may have changed in understanding or attitude, matured as a result of experience. There then may be a dramatic tension between the feelings of the narrator during the events and the feelings with which he or she now tells them.

In each of the following stories the first-person narrator is a participant, but the effects are shaded in different ways. We begin with Poe's story of a man who says he is not mad, but whose words soon convince us, in dramatic irony, that he is.

THE TELL-TALE HEART

Edgar Allan Poe   (1809–1849)

True!—nervous—very, very dreadfully nervous I had been and am; but why *will* you say that I am mad? The disease had sharpened my senses—not destroyed—not dulled them. Above all was the sense of hearing acute. I heard all things in the heaven and in the earth. I heard many things in hell. How, then, am I mad? Hearken! and observe how healthily—how calmly I can tell you the whole story.

It is impossible to say how first the idea entered my brain; but once conceived, it haunted me day and night. Object there was none. Passion there was none. I loved the old man. He had never wronged me. He had never given me insult. For his gold I had no desire. I think it was his eye! yes, it was this! He had the eye of a vulture—a pale blue eye, with a film over it. Whenever it fell upon me, my blood ran cold; and so by degrees—very gradually—I made up my mind to take the life of the old man, and thus rid myself of the eye forever.

Now this is the point. You fancy me mad. Madmen know nothing. But you should have seen *me*. You should have seen how wisely I proceeded—with what caution—with what foresight—with what dissimulation I went to work! I was never kinder to the old man than during the whole week before I killed him. And every night, about midnight, I turned the latch of his door and opened it—oh so gently! And then, when I had made an opening sufficient for my head, I put in a dark lantern, all closed, closed, so that no light shone out, and then I thrust in my head. Oh, you would have laughed to see how cunningly I thrust it in! I moved it slowly—very, very slowly, so that I might not disturb the old man's sleep. It took me an hour to place my whole head within the opening so far that I could see him as he lay upon his bed. Ha!—would a madman have been so wise as this? And then, when my head was well within the room, I undid the lantern cautiously—oh, so cautiously—cautiously (for the hinges creaked)—I undid it just so much that a single thin ray fell upon the vulture eye. And this I did for seven long nights—every night just at midnight—but I found the eye always closed; and so it was impossible to do the work; for it was not the old man who vexed me, but his Evil Eye. And every morning, when the day broke, I went boldly into the chamber, and spoke courageously to him, calling him by name in a hearty tone, and inquiring how he had passed the night. So you see he would have been a very profound old man indeed, to suspect that every night, just at twelve, I looked in upon him while he slept.

Upon the eighth night I was more than usually cautious in opening the door. A watch's minute hand moves more quickly than did mine. Never before that night, had I *felt* the extent of my own powers—of my sagacity. I could scarcely contain my feelings of triumph. To think that there I was, opening the door, little by little, and he not even to dream of my secret deeds or thoughts. I fairly chuckled at the idea; and perhaps he heard me; for he moved on the bed suddenly, as if startled. Now you may think that I drew back—but no. His room was black as pitch with the thick darkness, (for the shutters were close fastened, through fear of robbers,) and so I knew that he could not see the opening of the door, and I kept pushing it on steadily, steadily.

I had my head in, and was about to open the lantern, when my thumb slipped upon the tin fastening, and the old man sprang up in bed, crying out—"Who's there?"

I kept quite still and said nothing. For a whole hour I did not move a muscle, and in the meantime I did not hear him lie down. He was still sitting up in the bed listening;—just as I have done, night after night, hearkening to the death watches in the wall.

Presently I heard a slight groan, and I knew it was the groan of mortal terror. It was not a groan of pain or of grief—oh, no!—it was the low stifled sound that arises from the bottom of the soul when overcharged with awe. I knew the sound well. Many a night, just at midnight, when all the world slept, it has welled up from my own bosom, deepening, with its dreadful echo, the terrors that distracted me. I say I knew it well. I knew what the old man felt, and pitied him, although I chuckled at heart. I knew that he had been lying awake ever since the first slight noise, when he had turned in the bed. His fears had been ever since growing upon him. He had been trying to fancy them causeless, but could not. He had been saying to himself—"It is nothing but the wind in the chimney—it is only a mouse crossing the floor," or "it is merely a cricket which has made a single chirp." Yes, he had been trying to comfort himself with these suppositions: but he had found all in vain. *All in vain;* because Death, in approaching him, had stalked with his black shadow before him, and enveloped the victim. And it was the mournful influence of the unperceived shadow that caused him to feel—although he neither saw nor heard—to *feel* the presence of my head within the room.

When I had waited a long time, very patiently, without hearing him lie down, I resolved to open a little—a very, very little crevice in the lantern. So I opened it—you cannot imagine how stealthily, stealthily—until, at length, a simple dim ray, like the thread of the spider, shot from out the crevice and fell full upon the vulture eye.

It was open—wide, wide open—and I grew furious as I gazed upon it. I saw it with perfect distinctness—all dull blue, with a hideous veil over it that chilled the very marrow in my bones; but I could see nothing else of the old man's face or person: for I had directed the ray as if by instinct, precisely upon the damned spot.

And have I not told you that what you mistake for madness is but over acuteness of the senses?—now, I say, there came to my ears a low, dull, quick sound, such as a watch makes when enveloped in cotton. I knew *that* sound well, too. It was the beating of the old man's heart. It increased my fury, as the beating of a drum stimulates the soldier into courage.

But even yet I refrained and kept still. I scarcely breathed. I held the lantern motionless. I tried how steadily I could maintain the ray upon the eye. Meantime the hellish tattoo of the heart increased. It grew quicker and quicker, and louder and louder every instant. The old man's terror *must* have been extreme! It grew louder, I say, louder every moment!—do you mark me well? I have told you that I am nervous: so I am. And now at the dead hour of the night, amid the dreadful silence of that old house, so strange a noise as this excited me to uncontrollable terror. Yet, for some minutes longer I refrained and stood still. But the beating grew louder, louder! I thought the heart must burst. And now a new anxiety seized me—the sound would be heard by a neighbour! The old man's hour had come! With a loud yell, I threw open the lantern and leaped into the room. He shrieked once—once only. In an instant I dragged him to the floor, and pulled the heavy bed over him. I then smiled gaily, to find the deed so far done. But, for many minutes, the heart beat on with a muffled sound. This, however, did not vex me; it would not be heard through the wall. At length it ceased. The old man was dead. I removed the bed and examined the corpse. Yes, he was stone, stone dead. I placed my hand upon the heart and held it there many minutes. There was no pulsation. He was stone dead. His eye would trouble me no more.

If still you think me mad, you will think so no longer when I describe the wise precautions I took for the concealment of the body. The night waned, and I worked hastily, but in silence. First of all I dismembered the corpse. I cut off the head and the arms and the legs.

I then took up three planks from the flooring of the chamber, and deposited all between the scantlings. I then replaced the boards so cleverly, so cunningly, that no human eye—not even *his*—could have detected any thing wrong. There was nothing to wash out—no stain of any kind—no blood-spot whatever. I had been too wary for that. A tub had caught all—ha! ha!

When I had made an end of these labors, it was four o'clock—still dark as midnight. As the bell sounded the hour, there came a knocking at the street door. I went down to open it with a light heart,—for what had I *now* to fear? There entered three men, who introduced themselves, with perfect suavity, as officers of the police. A shriek had been heard by a neighbor during the night; suspicion of foul play had been aroused; information had been lodged at the police office, and they (the officers) had been deputed to search the premises.

I smiled,—for *what* had I to fear? I bade the gentlemen welcome. The shriek, I said, was my own in a dream. The old man, I mentioned, was absent in the country. I took my visitors all over the house. I bade them search—search *well*. I led them, at length, to *his* chamber. I showed them his treasures, secure, undisturbed. In the enthusiasm of my confidence, I brought chairs into the room, and desired them *here* to rest from their fatigues, while I myself, in the wild audacity of my perfect triumph, placed my own seat upon the very spot beneath which reposed the corpse of the victim.

The officers were satisfied. My *manner* had convinced them. I was singularly at ease. They sat, and while I answered cheerily, they chatted of familiar things. But, ere long, I felt myself getting pale and wished them gone. My head ached, and I fancied a ringing in my ears: but still they sat and still chatted. The ringing became more distinct:—it continued and became more distinct: I talked more freely to get rid of the feeling: but it continued and gained definiteness—until, at length, I found that the noise was *not* within my ears.

No doubt I now grew *very* pale;—but I talked more fluently, and with a heightened voice. Yet the sound increased—and what could I do? It was *a low, dull, quick sound—much such a sound as a watch makes when enveloped in cotton.* I gasped for breath—and yet the officers heard it not. I talked more quickly—more vehemently; but the noise steadily increased. I arose and argued about trifles, in a high key and with violent gesticulations; but the noise steadily increased. Why *would* they not be gone? I paced the floor to and fro with heavy strides, as if excited to fury by the observations of the men—but the noise steadily increased. Oh God! what *could* I do? I foamed—I raved—I swore! I swung the chair upon which I had been sitting, and grated it upon the boards, but the noise arose over all and continually increased. It grew louder —louder—*louder!* And still the men chatted pleasantly, and smiled. Was it possible they heard not? Almighty God!—no, no! They heard!—they suspected! —they *knew!*—they were making a mockery out of my horror—this I thought, and this I think. But anything was better than this agony! Anything was more tolerable than this derision! I could bear those hypocritical smiles no longer! I felt that I must scream or die! and now—again!—hark! louder! louder! louder! *louder!*

"Villains!" I shrieked, "dissemble no more. I admit the deed!—tear up the planks! here, here!—it is the beating of his hideous heart!"

QUESTIONS

1. We have only the narrator's words to go by. Even so, what evidence do you find within the story to suggest that the old man's heart is at the end as silent as any other dead man's?
2. Perhaps the dead man's heart does beat, as the narrator says, "loud —louder—*louder!,*" animated by a supernatural power. Perhaps the officers are indeed "making a mockery" of the teller's horror by ignoring the sound, just as he suggests they are. What makes this interpretation unlikely?
3. The narrator insists he is not mad. What makes us think he is?
4. What are the facts of the story, those elements that we can be sure any neutral observer would accept as true?
5. What details does the narrator ask us to accept that we must believe untrue?
6. What has Poe gained by telling the story in the first person, from the narrative perspective of a murderer?
7. How would the story be changed if it were told by one of the officers?

"The Tell-Tale Heart" presents an extreme example of an unreliable narrator, a teller whose facts and interpretations we cannot trust. If Poe had told the story in his own voice, as an author, instead of as a character in the story, he would almost certainly have told us the killer is mad, the eye is not evil, and the dead heart makes no sound—and he would have ruined the story, or at least he would have told a quite different one.

In "The Yellow Wall-Paper" we again have a protagonist who narrates, and again there is a question of madness.

THE YELLOW WALL-PAPER

Charlotte Perkins Gilman   *(1860–1935)*

It is very seldom that mere ordinary people like John and myself secure ancestral halls for the summer.

A colonial mansion, a hereditary estate, I would say a haunted house, and reach the height of romantic felicity—but that would be asking too much of fate!

Still I will proudly declare that there is something queer about it.

Else, why should it be let so cheaply? And why have stood so long untenanted?

John laughs at me, of course, but one expects that in marriage.

John is practical in the extreme. He has no patience with faith, an intense horror of superstition, and he scoffs openly at any talk of things not to be felt and seen and put down in figures.

John is a physician, and *perhaps*—(I would not say it to a living soul, of course, but this is dead paper and a great relief to my mind)—*perhaps* that is one reason I do not get well faster.

You see he does not believe I am sick! And what can one do?

If a physician of high standing, and one's own husband, assures friends and relatives that there is really nothing the matter with one but temporary nervous depression—a slight hysterical tendency—what is one to do?

My brother is also a physician, and also of high standing, and he says the same thing.

So I take phosphates or phosphites—whichever it is—and tonics, and journeys, and air, and exercise, and am absolutely forbidden to "work" until I am well again.

Personally, I disagree with their ideas.

Personally, I believe that congenial work, with excitement and change, would do me good.

But what is one to do?

I did write for a while in spite of them; but it *does* exhaust me a good deal —having to play so sly about it, or else meet with heavy opposition.

I sometimes fancy that in my condition if I had less opposition and more society and stimulus—but John says the very worst thing I can do is to think about my condition, and I confess it always makes me feel bad.

So I will let it alone and talk about the house.

The most beautiful place! It is quite alone, standing well back from the road, quite three miles from the village. It makes me think of English places that you read about, for there are hedges and walls and gates that lock, and lots of separate little houses for the gardeners and people.

There is a *delicious* garden! I never saw such a garden—large and shady, full of box-bordered paths, and lined with long grape-covered arbors with seats under them.

There were greenhouses, too, but they are all broken now.

There was some legal trouble, I believe, something about the heirs and coheirs; anyhow, the place has been empty for years.

That spoils my ghostliness, I am afraid, but I don't care—there is something strange about the house—I can feel it.

I even said so to John one moonlight evening, but he said what I felt was a draught, and shut the window.

I get unreasonably angry with John sometimes. I'm sure I never used to be so sensitive. I think it is due to this nervous condition.

But John says if I feel so I shall neglect proper self-control; so I take pains to control myself—before him, at least, and that makes me very tired.

I don't like our room a bit. I wanted one downstairs that opened on the piazza and had roses all over the window, and such pretty old-fashioned chintz hangings! But John would not hear of it.

He said there was only one window and not room for two beds, and no near room for him if he took another.

He is very careful and loving, and hardly lets me stir without special direction.

I have a schedule prescription for each hour in the day; he takes all care from me, and so I feel basely ungrateful not to value it more.

He said we came here solely on my account, that I was to have perfect rest and all the air I could get. "Your exercise depends on your strength, my dear," said he, "and your food somewhat on your appetite; but air you can absorb all the time." So we took the nursery at the top of the house.

It is a big, airy room, the whole floor nearly, with windows that look all ways, and air and sunshine galore. It was nursery first and then playroom and gymnasium, I should judge; for the windows are barred for little children, and there are rings and things in the walls.

The paint and paper look as if a boys' school had used it. It is stripped off— the paper—in great patches all around the head of my bed, about as far as I can reach, and in a great place on the other side of the room low down. I never saw a worse paper in my life.

One of those sprawling flamboyant patterns committing every artistic sin.

It is dull enough to confuse the eye in following, pronounced enough constantly to irritate and provoke study, and when you follow the lame certain curves for a little distance they suddenly commit suicide—plunge off at outrageous angles, destroy themselves in unheard of contradictions.

The color is repellant, almost revolting; a smouldering unclean yellow, strangely faded by the slow-turning sunlight.

It is a dull yet lurid orange in some places, a sickly sulphur tint in others.

No wonder the children hated it! I should hate it myself if I had to live in this room long.

There comes John, and I must put this away—he hates to have me write a word.

• • •

We have been here two weeks, and I haven't felt like writing before, since that first day.

I am sitting by the window now, up in this atrocious nursery, and there is nothing to hinder my writing as much as I please, save lack of strength.

John is away all day, and even some nights when his cases are serious.

I am glad my case is not serious!

But these nervous troubles are dreadfully depressing.

John does not know how much I really suffer. He knows there is no *reason* to suffer, and that satisfies him.

Of course it is only nervousness. It does weigh on me so not to do my duty in any way!

I meant to be such a help to John, such a real rest and comfort, and here I am a comparative burden already!

Nobody would believe what an effort it is to do what little I am able—to dress and entertain, and order things.

It is fortunate that Mary is so good with the baby. Such a dear baby!

And yet I *cannot* be with him, it makes me so nervous.

I suppose John never was nervous in his life. He laughs at me so about this wall-paper!

At first he meant to repaper the room, but afterwards he said that I was letting it get the better of me, and that nothing was worse for a nervous patient than to give way to such fancies.

He said that after the wall-paper was changed it would be the heavy bedstead, and then the barred windows, and then the gate at the head of the stairs, and so on.

"You know the place is doing you good," he said, "and really, dear, I don't care to renovate the house just for a three months' rental."

"Then do let me go downstairs," I said, "there are such pretty rooms there."

Then he took me in his arms and called me a blessed little goose, and said he would go down cellar, if I wished, and have it whitewashed into the bargain.

But he is right enough about the beds and windows and things.

It is an airy and comfortable room as any one need wish, and, of course, I would not be so silly as to make him uncomfortable just for a whim.

I'm really getting quite fond of the big room, all but that horrid paper.

Out of one window I can see the garden, those mysterious deep-shaded arbors, the riotous old-fashioned flowers, and bushes and gnarly trees.

Out of another I get a lovely view of the bay and a little private wharf belonging to the estate. There is a beautiful shaded lane that runs down there from the house. I always fancy I see people walking these numerous paths and arbors, but John has cautioned me not to give way to fancy in the least. He says that with my imaginative power and habit of story-making, a nervous weakness like mine is sure to lead to all manner of excited fancies, and that I ought to try to use my will and good sense to check the tendency. So I try.

I think sometimes that if I were only well enough to write a little it would relieve the press of ideas and rest me.

But I find I get pretty tired when I try.

It is so discouraging not to have any advice and companionship about my work. When I get really well, John says, we will ask Cousin Henry and Julia down for a long visit; but he says he would as soon put fireworks in my pillowcase as to let me have those stimulating people about now.

I wish I could get well faster.

But I must not think about that. This paper looks to me as if it *knew* what a vicious influence it had!

There is a recurrent spot where the pattern lolls like a broken neck and two bulbous eyes stare at you upside down.

I get positively angry with the impertinence of it and the everlastingness. Up and down and sideways they crawl, and those absurd, unblinking eyes are everywhere. There is one place where two breadths didn't match, and the eyes go all up and down the line, one a little higher than the other.

I never saw so much expression in an inanimate thing before, and we all know how much expression they have! I used to lie awake as a child and get more entertainment and terror out of blank walls and plain furniture than most children could find in a toy-store.

I remember what a kindly wink the knobs of our big, old bureau used to have, and there was one chair that always seemed like a strong friend.

I used to feel that if any of the other things looked too fierce I could always hop into that chair and be safe.

The furniture in this room is no worse than unharmonious, however, for we had to bring it all from downstairs. I suppose when this was used as a playroom they had to take the nursery things out, and no wonder! I never saw such ravages as the children have made here.

The wall-paper, as I said before, is torn off in spots, and it sticketh closer than a brother—they must have had perseverance as well as hatred.

Then the floor is scratched and gouged and splintered, the plaster itself is dug out here and there, and this great heavy bed which is all we found in the room, looks as if it had been through the wars.

But I don't mind it a bit—only the paper.

There comes John's sister. Such a dear girl she is, and so careful of me! I must not let her find me writing.

She is a perfect and enthusiastic housekeeper, and hopes for no better profession. I verily believe she thinks it is the writing which made me sick!

But I can write when she is out, and see her a long way off from these windows.

There is one that commands the road, a lovely shaded winding road, and one that just looks off over the country. A lovely country, too, full of great elms and velvet meadows.

This wall-paper has a kind of sub-pattern in a different shade, a particularly irritating one, for you can only see it in certain lights, and not clearly then.

But in the places where it isn't faded and where the sun is just so—I can see a strange, provoking, formless sort of figure, that seems to skulk about behind that silly and conspicuous front design.

There's sister on the stairs!

• • •

Well, the Fourth of July is over! The people are all gone and I am tired out. John thought it might do me good to see a little company, so we just had mother and Nellie and the children down for a week.

Of course I didn't do a thing. Jennie sees to everything now.

But it tired me all the same.

John says if I don't pick up faster he shall send me to Weir Mitchell[1] in the fall.

---

[1] Silas Weir Mitchell (1829–1914), an internationally known neurologist who was also a well-known novelist.

But I don't want to go there at all. I had a friend who was in his hands once, and she says he is just like John and my brother, only more so!

Besides, it is such an undertaking to go so far.

I don't feel as if it was worth while to turn my hand over for anything, and I'm getting dreadfully fretful and querulous.

I cry at nothing, and cry most of the time.

Of course I don't when John is here, or anybody else, but when I am alone.

And I am alone a good deal now. John is kept in town very often by serious cases, and Jennie is good and lets me alone when I want her to.

So I walk a little in the garden or down that lovely lane, sit on the porch under the roses, and lie down up here a good deal.

I'm getting really fond of the room in spite of the wall-paper. Perhaps *because* of the wall-paper.

It dwells in my mind so!

I lie here on this great immovable bed—it is nailed down, I believe—and follow that pattern about by the hour. It is as good as gymnastics, I assure you. I start, we'll say, at the bottom, down in the corner over there where it has not been touched, and I determine for the thousandth time that I *will* follow that pointless pattern to some sort of a conclusion.

I know a little of the principle of design, and I know this thing is not arranged on any laws of radiation, or alternation, or repetition, or symmetry, or anything else that I ever heard of.

It is repeated, of course, by the breadths, but not otherwise.

Looked at in one way each breadth stands alone, the bloated curves and flourishes—a kind of "debased Romanesque" with delirium tremens—go waddling up and down in isolated columns of fatuity.

But, on the other hand, they connect diagonally, and the sprawling outlines run off in great slanting waves of optic horror, like a lot of wallowing sea-weeds in full chase.

The whole thing goes horizontally, too, at least it seems so, and I exhaust myself trying to distinguish the order of its going in that direction.

They have used a horizontal breadth for a frieze, and that adds wonderfully to the confusion.

There is one end of the room where it is almost intact, and there, when the crosslights fade and the low sun shines directly upon it, I can almost fancy radiation after all,—the interminable grotesques seem to form around a common centre and rush off in headlong plunges of equal distraction.

It makes me tired to follow it. I will take a nap I guess.

• • •

I don't know why I should write this.

I don't want to.

I don't feel able.

And I know John would think it absurd. But I *must* say what I feel and think in some way—it is such a relief!

But the effort is getting to be greater than the relief.

Half the time now I am awfully lazy, and lie down ever so much.

John says I mustn't lose my strength, and has me take cod liver oil and lots of tonics and things, to say nothing of ale and wine and rare meat.

Dear John! He loves me very dearly, and hates to have me sick. I tried to have a real earnest reasonable talk with him the other day, and tell him how I wish he would let me go and make a visit to Cousin Henry and Julia.

But he said I wasn't able to go, nor able to stand it after I got there; and I did not make out a very good case for myself, for I was crying before I had finished.

It is getting to be a great effort for me to think straight. Just this nervous weakness I suppose.

And dear John gathered me up in his arms, and just carried me upstairs and laid me on the bed, and sat by me and read to me till it tired my head.

He said I was his darling and his comfort and all he had, and that I must take care of myself for his sake, and keep well.

He says no one but myself can help me out of it, that I must use my will and self-control and not let any silly fancies run away with me.

There's one comfort, the baby is well and happy, and does not have to occupy this nursery with the horrid wall-paper.

If we had not used it, that blessed child would have! What a fortunate escape! Why, I wouldn't have a child of mine, an impressionable little thing, live in such a room for worlds.

I never thought of it before, but it is lucky that John kept me here after all, I can stand it so much easier than a baby, you see.

Of course I never mention it to them any more—I am too wise—but I keep watch for it all the same.

There are things in that paper that nobody knows but me, or ever will.

Behind that outside pattern the dim shapes get clearer every day.

It is always the same shape, only very numerous.

And it is like a woman stooping down and creeping about behind that pattern. I don't like it a bit. I wonder—I begin to think—I wish John would take me away from here!

· · ·

It is so hard to talk with John about my case, because he is so wise, and because he loves me so.

But I tried it last night.

It was moonlight. The moon shines in all around just as the sun does.

I hate to see it sometimes, it creeps so slowly, and always comes in by one window or another.

John was asleep and I hated to waken him, so I kept still and watched the moonlight on that undulating wall-paper till I felt creepy.

The faint figure behind seemed to shake the pattern, just as if she wanted to get out.

I got up softly and went to feel and see if the paper *did* move, and when I came back John was awake.

"What is it, little girl?" he said. "Don't go walking about like that—you'll get cold."

I thought it was a good time to talk so I told him that I really was not gaining here, and that I wished he would take me away.

"Why darling!" said he, "our lease will be up in three weeks, and I can't see how to leave before.

"The repairs are not done at home, and I cannot possibly leave town just now. Of course if you were in any danger, I could and would, but you really are better, dear, whether you can see it or not. I am a doctor, dear, and I know. You are gaining flesh and color, your appetite is better, I feel really much easier about you."

"I don't weigh a bit more," said I, "nor as much; and my appetite may be better in the evening when you are here, but it is worse in the morning when you are away!"

"Bless her little heart!" said he with a big hug, "she shall be as sick as she pleases! But now let's improve the shining hours by going to sleep, and talk about it in the morning!"

"And you won't go away?" I asked gloomily.

"Why, how can I, dear? It is only three weeks more and then we will take a nice little trip of a few days while Jennie is getting the house ready. Really, dear, you are better!"

"Better in body perhaps—" I began, and stopped short, for he sat up straight and looked at me with such a stern, reproachful look that I could not say another word.

"My darling," said he, "I beg of you, for my sake and for our child's sake, as well as for your own, that you will never for one instant let that idea enter your mind! There is nothing so dangerous, so fascinating, to a temperament like yours. It is a false and foolish fancy. Can you not trust me as a physician when I tell you so?"

So of course I said no more on that score, and we went to sleep before long. He thought I was asleep first, but I wasn't, and lay there for hours trying to decide whether that front pattern and the back pattern really did move together or separately.

· · ·

On a pattern like this, by daylight, there is a lack of sequence, a defiance of law, that is a constant irritant to a normal mind.

The color is hideous enough, and unreliable enough, and infuriating enough, but the pattern is torturing.

You think you have mastered it, but just as you get well underway in following, it turns a back-somersault and there you are. It slaps you in the face, knocks you down, and tramples upon you. It is like a bad dream.

The outside pattern is a florid arabesque, reminding one of a fungus. If you can imagine a toadstool in joints, an interminable string of toadstools, budding and sprouting in endless convolutions—why, that is something like it.

That is, sometimes!

There is one marked peculiarity about this paper, a thing nobody seems to notice but myself, and that is that it changes as the light changes.

When the sun shoots in through the east window—I always watch for that first, long, straight ray—it changes so quickly that I never can quite believe it.

That is why I watch it always.

By moonlight—the moon shines in all night when there is a moon—I wouldn't know it was the same paper.

At night in any kind of light, in twilight, candlelight, lamplight, and worst of all by moonlight, it becomes bars! The outside pattern I mean, and the woman behind it is as plain as can be.

I didn't realize for a long time what the thing was that showed behind, that dim sub-pattern, but now I am quite sure it is a woman.

By daylight she is subdued, quiet. I fancy it is the pattern that keeps her so still. It is so puzzling. It keeps me quiet by the hour.

I lie down ever so much now. John says it is good for me, and to sleep all I can.

Indeed he started the habit by making me lie down for an hour after each meal.

It is a very bad habit I am convinced, for you see I don't sleep.

And that cultivates deceit, for I don't tell them I'm awake—O, no!

The fact is I am getting a little afraid of John.

He seems very queer sometimes, and even Jennie has an inexplicable look.

It strikes me occasionally, just as a scientific hypothesis, that perhaps it is the paper!

I have watched John when he did not know I was looking, and come into the room suddenly on the most innocent excuses, and I've caught him several times *looking at the paper!* And Jennie too. I caught Jennie with her hand on it once.

She didn't know I was in the room, and when I asked her in a quiet, a very quiet voice, with the most restrained manner possible, what she was doing with the paper—she turned around as if she had been caught stealing, and looked quite angry—asked me why I should frighten her so!

Then she said that the paper stained everything it touched, that she had found yellow smooches on all my clothes and John's, and she wished we would be more careful!

Did not that sound innocent? But I know she was studying that pattern, and I am determined that nobody shall find it out but myself!

· · ·

Life is very much more exciting now than it used to be. You see I have something more to expect, to look forward to, to watch. I really do eat better, and am more quiet than I was.

John is so pleased to see me improve! He laughed a little the other day, and said I seemed to be flourishing in spite of my wall-paper.

I turned it off with a laugh. I had no intention of telling him it was *because* of the wall-paper—he would make fun of me. He might even want to take me away.

I don't want to leave now until I have found it out. There is a week more, and I think that will be enough.

· · ·

I'm feeling ever so much better! I don't sleep much at night, for it is so interesting to watch developments; but I sleep a good deal in the daytime.

In the daytime it is tiresome and perplexing.

There are always new shoots on the fungus, and new shades of yellow all over it. I cannot keep count of them, though I have tried conscientiously.

It is the strangest yellow, that wall-paper! It makes me think of all the yellow things I ever saw—not beautiful ones like buttercups, but old foul, bad yellow things.

But there is something else about that paper—the smell! I noticed it the moment we came into the room, but with so much air and sun it was not bad. Now we have had a week of fog and rain, and whether the windows are open or not, the smell is here.

It creeps all over the house.

I find it hovering in the dining-room, skulking in the parlor, hiding in the hall, lying in wait for me on the stairs.

It gets into my hair.

Even when I go to ride, if I turn my head suddenly and surprise it—there is that smell!

Such a peculiar odor, too! I have spent hours in trying to analyze it, to find what it smelled like.

It is not bad—at first, and very gentle, but quite the subtlest, most enduring odor I ever met.

In this damp weather it is awful, I wake up in the night and find it hanging over me.

It used to disturb me at first. I thought seriously of burning the house—to reach the smell.

But now I am used to it. The only thing I can think of that it is like is the *color* of the paper! A yellow smell.

There is a very funny mark on this wall, low down, near the mopboard. A streak that runs round the room. It goes behind every piece of furniture, except the bed, a long, straight, even *smooch,* as if it had been rubbed over and over.

I wonder how it was done and who did it, and what they did it for. Round and round and round—round and round and round—it makes me dizzy!

· · ·

I really have discovered something at last.

Through watching so much at night, when it changes so, I have finally found out.

The front pattern *does* move—and no wonder! The woman behind it shakes it!

Sometimes I think there are a great many women behind, and sometimes only one, and she crawls around fast, and her crawling shakes it all over.

Then in the very bright spots she keeps still, and in the very shady spots she just takes hold of the bars and shakes them hard.

And she is all the time trying to climb through. But nobody could climb through that pattern—it strangles so; I think that is why it has so many heads.

They get through, and then the pattern strangles them off and turns them upside down, and makes their eyes white!

If those heads were covered or taken off it would not be half so bad.

• • •

I think that woman gets out in the daytime!

And I'll tell you why—privately—I've seen her!

I can see her out of every one of my windows!

It is the same woman, I know, for she is always creeping, and most women do not creep by daylight.

I see her in that long shaded lane, creeping up and down. I see her in those dark grape arbors, creeping all around the garden.

I see her on that long road under the trees, creeping along, and when a carriage comes she hides under the blackberry vines.

I don't blame her a bit. It must be very humiliating to be caught creeping by daylight!

I always lock the door when I creep by daylight. I can't do it at night, for I know John would suspect something at once.

And John is so queer now, that I don't want to irritate him. I wish he would take another room! Besides, I don't want anybody to get that woman out at night but myself.

I often wonder if I could see her out of all the windows at once.

But, turn as fast as I can, I can only see out of one at one time.

And though I always see her, she *may* be able to creep faster than I can turn!

I have watched her sometimes away off in the open country, creeping as fast as a cloud shadow in a high wind.

• • •

If only that top pattern could be gotten off from the under one! I mean to try it, little by little.

I have found out another funny thing, but I shan't tell it this time! It does not do to trust people too much.

There are only two more days to get this paper off, and I believe John is beginning to notice. I don't like the look in his eyes.

And I heard him ask Jennie a lot of professional questions about me. She had a very good report to give.

She said I slept a good deal in the daytime.

John knows I don't sleep very well at night, for all I'm so quiet!

He asked me all sorts of questions, too, and pretended to be very loving and kind.

As if I couldn't see through him!

Still, I don't wonder he acts so, sleeping under this paper for three months.

It only interests me, but I feel sure John and Jennie are secretly affected by it.

• • •

Hurrah! This is the last day, but it is enough. John has to stay in town over night, and won't be out this evening.

Jennie wanted to sleep with me—the sly thing! but I told her I should undoubtedly rest better for a night alone.

That was clever, for really I wasn't alone a bit! As soon as it was moonlight and that poor thing began to crawl and shake the pattern, I got up and ran to help her.

I pulled and she shook, I shook and she pulled, and before morning we had peeled off yards of that paper.

A strip about as high as my head and half around the room.

And then when the sun came and that awful pattern began to laugh at me, I declared I would finish it to-day!

We go away to-morrow, and they are moving all my furniture down again to leave things as they were before.

Jennie looked at the wall in amazement, but I told her merrily that I did it out of pure spite at the vicious thing.

She laughed and said she wouldn't mind doing it herself, but I must not get tired.

How she betrayed herself that time!

But I am here, and no person touches this paper but Me—not *alive!*

She tried to get me out of the room—it was too patent! But I said it was so quiet and empty and clean now that I believed I would lie down again and sleep all I could; and not to wake me even for dinner—I would call when I woke.

So now she is gone, and the servants are gone, and the things are gone, and there is nothing left but that great bedstead nailed down, with the canvas mattress we found on it.

We shall sleep downstairs to-night, and take the boat home to-morrow.

I quite enjoy the room, now it is bare again.

How those children did tear about here!

This bedstead is fairly gnawed!

But I must get to work.

I have locked the door and thrown the key down into the front path.

I don't want to go out, and I don't want to have anybody come in, till John comes.

I want to astonish him.

I've got a rope up here that even Jennie did not find. If that woman does get out, and tries to get away, I can tie her.

But I forgot I could not reach far without anything to stand on!

This bed will *not* move!

I tried to lift and push it until I was lame, and then I got so angry I bit off a little piece at one corner—but it hurt my teeth.

Then I peeled off all the paper I could reach standing on the floor. It sticks horribly and the pattern just enjoys it! All those strangled heads and bulbous eyes and waddling fungus growths just shriek with derision!

I am getting angry enough to do something desperate. To jump out of the window would be admirable exercise, but the bars are too strong even to try.

Besides I wouldn't do it. Of course not. I know well enough that a step like that is improper and might be misconstrued.

I don't like to *look* out of the windows even—there are so many of those creeping women, and they creep so fast.

I wonder if they all come out of that wall-paper as I did?

But I am securely fastened now by my well-hidden rope—you don't get *me* out in the road there!

I suppose I shall have to get back behind the pattern when it comes night, and that is hard!

It is so pleasant to be out in this great room and creep around as I please!

I don't want to go outside. I won't, even if Jennie asks me to.

For outside you have to creep on the ground, and everything is green instead of yellow.

But here I can creep smoothly on the floor, and my shoulder just fits in that long smooch around the wall, so I cannot lose my way.

Why there's John at the door!

It is no use, young man, you can't open it!

How he does call and pound!

Now he's crying for an axe.

It would be a shame to break down that beautiful door!

"John dear!" said I in the gentlest voice, "the key is down by the front steps, under a plantain leaf!"

That silenced him for a few moments.

Then he said, very quietly indeed, "Open the door, my darling!"

"I can't," said I. "The key is down by the front door under a plantain leaf!"

And then I said it again, several times, very gently and slowly, and said it so often that he had to go and see, and he got it of course, and came in. He stopped short by the door.

"What is the matter?" he cried. "For God's sake, what are you doing!"

I kept on creeping just the same, but I looked at him over my shoulder.

"I've got out at last," said I, "in spite of you and Jane. And I've pulled off most of the paper, so you can't put me back!"

Now why should that man have fainted? But he did, and right across my path by the wall, so that I had to creep over him every time!

QUESTIONS

1. "John is a physician," the narrator tells us, "and *perhaps*—(I would not say it to a living soul, of course, but this is dead paper and a great relief to my mind)—*perhaps* that is one reason I do not get well faster." What does she mean? Is there any evidence that her observation is accurate?

2. Characterize John as he is seen by the narrator. How does her attitude toward him change? Can we tell whether her characterization of him is fair?

3. Some of what the narrator reports is fantasy (the women behind the wallpaper, for instance). How can we tell which details possess objective reality and which do not?

4. One subject of the story is madness. What would you suggest is the underlying *thematic idea* (central thought) about madness?

5. How would you relate your statement of theme to the subject of madness in women?

6. How might you support the idea that the story has more important things to say about women and men than about madness? What things?

In "The Tell-Tale Heart" and "The Yellow Wall-Paper," we know that madness has distorted the narrators' perceptions. We believe some of what they say, but not all. Other first-person narrators, although sane, may still be unreliable in some respects, as they color the telling with personal attitudes and emotions.

In "I'm a Fool" the narrator is sane, but has acted foolishly. He tells what happened as honestly as he knows how, giving us no reason to doubt his story. But do we fully share his attitudes? Do we understand his story the way that he does?

I'M A FOOL

Sherwood Anderson   *(1876–1941)*

It was a hard jolt for me, one of the most bitterest I ever had to face. And it all came about through my own foolishness, too. Even yet sometimes, when I think of it, I want to cry or swear or kick myself. Perhaps, even now, after all this time, there will be a kind of satisfaction in making myself look cheap by telling of it.

It began at three o'clock one October afternoon as I sat in the grandstand at the fall trotting and pacing meet at Sandusky, Ohio.

To tell the truth, I felt a little foolish that I should be sitting in the grandstand at all. During the summer before I had left my home town with Harry Whitehead and, with a nigger named Burt, had taken a job as swipe with one of the two horses Harry was campaigning through the fall race meets that year. Mother cried and my sister Mildred, who wanted to get a job as a school teacher in our town that fall, stormed and scolded about the house all during the week before I left. They both thought it something disgraceful that one of our family should take a place as a swipe with race horses. I've an idea Mildred thought my taking the place would stand in the way of her getting the job she'd been working so long for.

But after all I had to work, and there was no other work to be got. A big lumbering fellow of nineteen couldn't just hang around the house and I had got too big to mow people's lawns and sell newspapers. Little chaps who could get next to people's sympathies by their sizes were always getting jobs away from me. There was one fellow who kept saying to everyone who wanted a lawn mowed or a cistern cleaned, that he was saving money to work his way through college, and I used to lay awake nights thinking up ways to injure him without being found out. I kept thinking of wagons running over him and bricks falling on his head as he walked along the street. But never mind him.

I got the place with Harry and I liked Burt fine. We got along splendid together. He was a big nigger with a lazy sprawling body and soft, kind eyes, and when it came to a fight he could hit like Jack Johnson. He had Bucephalus, a big black pacing stallion that could do 2.09 or 2.10, if he had to, and I had a little gelding named Doctor Fritz that never lost a race all fall when Harry wanted him to win.

We set out from home late in July in a box car with the two horses and after that, until late November, we kept moving along to the race meets and the fairs. It was a peachy time for me, I'll say that. Sometimes now I think that boys who are raised regular in houses, and never have a fine nigger like Burt for a best friend, and go to high schools and college, and never steal anything, or get drunk a little, or learn to swear from fellows who know how, or come walking up in front of a grandstand in their shirt sleeves and with dirty horsey pants on when the races are going on and the grandstand is full of people all dressed up—What's the use of talking about it? Such fellows don't know nothing at all. They've never had the opportunity.

But I did. Burt taught me how to rub down a horse and put the bandages on after a race and steam a horse out and a lot of valuable things for any man to know. He could wrap a bandage on a horse's leg so smooth that if it had been the same color you would think it was his skin, and I guess he'd have been a big driver, too, and got to the top like Murphy and Walter Cox and the others if he hadn't been black.

Gee whizz, it was fun. You got to a county seat town, maybe say on a Saturday or Sunday, and the fair began the next Tuesday and lasted until Friday afternoon.

Doctor Fritz would be, say in the 2.25 trot on Tuesday afternoon and on Thursday afternoon Bucephalus would knock 'em cold in the "free-for-all" pace. It left you a lot of time to hang around and listen to horse talk, and see Burt knock some yap cold that got too gay, and you'd find out about horses and men and pick up a lot of stuff you could use all the rest of your life, if you had some sense and salted down what you heard and felt and saw.

And then at the end of the week when the race meet was over, and Harry had run home to tend up to his livery stable business, you and Burt hitched the two horses to carts and drove slow and steady across country, to the place for the next meeting, so as to not overheat the horses, etc., etc., you know.

Gee whizz, Gosh amighty, the nice hickorynut and beechnut and oaks and other kinds of trees along the roads, all brown and red, and the good smells, and Burt singing a song that was called Deep River, and the country girls at the windows of houses and everything. You can stick your colleges up your nose for all me. I guess I know where I got my education.

Why, one of those little burgs of towns you come to on the way, say now on a Saturday afternoon, and Burt says, "let's lay up here." And you did.

And you took the horses to a livery stable and fed them, and you got your good clothes out of a box and put them on.

And the town was full of farmers gaping, because they could see you were race-horse people, and the kids maybe never see a nigger before and was afraid and run away when the two of us walked down their main street.

And that was before prohibition and all that foolishness, and so you went into a saloon, the two of you, and all the yaps came and stood around, and there was always someone pretended he was horsey and knew things and spoke up and began asking questions, and all you did was to lie and lie all you could about what horses you had, and I said I owned them, and then some fellow said, "Will you have a drink of whisky" and Burt knocked his eye out the way he could say, offhandlike, "Oh well, all right, I'm agreeable to a little nip. I'll split a quart with you." Gee whizz.

But that isn't what I want to tell my story about. We got home late in November and I promised mother I'd quit the race horses for good. There's a lot of things you've got to promise a mother because she don't know any better.

And so, there not being any work in our town any more than when I left there to go to the races, I went off to Sandusky and got a pretty good place taking care of horses for a man who owned a teaming and delivery and storage and coal and real estate business there. It was a pretty good place with good eats, and a day off each week, and sleeping on a cot in a big barn, and mostly just shoveling in hay and oats to a lot of big good-enough skates of horses, that couldn't have trotted a race with a toad. I wasn't dissatisfied and I could send money home.

And then, as I started to tell you, the fall races came to Sandusky and I got the day off and I went. I left the job at noon and had on my good clothes and my new brown derby hat, I'd just bought the Saturday before, and a stand-up collar.

First of all I went downtown and walked about with the dudes. I've always thought to myself, "put up a good front" and so I did it. I had forty dollars in my pocket and so I went into the West House, a big hotel, and walked up to the cigar stand. "Give me three twenty-five cent cigars," I said. There was a lot of horsemen and strangers and dressed-up people from other towns standing around in the lobby and in the bar, and I mingled amongst them. In the bar there was a fellow with a cane and a Windsor tie on, that it made me sick to look at him. I like a man to be a man and dress up, but not to go put on that kind of airs. So I pushed him aside, kind of rough, and had me a drink of whisky. And then he looked at me, as though he thought maybe he'd get gay, but he changed his mind and didn't say anything. And then I had another drink of whisky, just to show him something, and went out and had a hack out to the races, all to myself, and when I got there I bought myself the best seat I could get up in the grandstand, but didn't go in for any of these boxes. That's putting on too many airs.

And so there I was, sitting up in the grandstand as gay as you please and looking down on the swipes coming out with their horses, and with their dirty horsey pants on and the horse blankets swung over their shoulders, same as I had been doing all the year before. I liked one thing about the same as the other, sitting up there and feeling grand and being down there and looking up at the yaps and feeling grander and more important, too. One thing's about as good as another, if you take it just right. I've often said that.

Well, right in front of me, in the grandstand that day, there was a fellow with a couple of girls and they was about my age. The young fellow was a nice guy all right. He was the kind maybe that goes to college and then comes to be a lawyer or maybe a newspaper editor or something like that, but he wasn't stuck on himself. There are some of that kind all right and he was one of the ones.

He had his sister with him and another girl and the sister looked around over his shoulder, accidental at first, not intending to start anything—she wasn't that kind—and her eyes and mine happened to meet.

You know how it is. Gee, she was a peach! She had on a soft dress, kind of a blue stuff and it looked carelessly made, but was well sewed and made and everything. I knew that much. I blushed when she looked right at me and so did she. She was the nicest girl I've ever seen in my life. She wasn't stuck on herself and she could talk proper grammar without being like a school teacher or something like that. What I mean is, she was O.K. I think maybe her father was well-to-do, but not rich to make her chesty because she was his daughter, as some are. Maybe he owned a drugstore or a drygoods store in their home town, or something like that. She never told me and I never asked.

My own people are all O.K. too, when you come to that. My grandfather was Welsh and over in the old country, in Wales he was—But never mind that.

The first heat of the first race come off and the young fellow setting there with the two girls left them and went down to make a bet. I knew what he was up to, but he didn't talk big and noisy and let everyone around know he was a sport, as some do. He wasn't that kind. Well, he come back and I heard him tell the two girls what horse he'd bet on, and when the heat was trotted they all half got to their feet and acted in the excited, sweaty way people do when they've got money down on a race, and the horse they bet on is up there pretty close at the end, and they think maybe he'll come on with a rush, but he never does because he hasn't got the old juice in him, come right down to it.

And then, pretty soon, the horses came out for the 2.18 pace and there was a horse in it I knew. He was a horse Bob French had in his string but Bob didn't own him. He was a horse owned by a Mr. Mathers down at Marietta, Ohio.

This Mr. Mathers had a lot of money and owned some coal mines or something, and he had a swell place out in the country, and he was stuck on race horses, but was a Presbyterian or something, and I think more than likely his wife was one, too, maybe a stiffer one than himself. So he never raced his horses hisself, and the story round the Ohio race tracks was that when one of his horses got ready to go to the races he turned him over to Bob French and pretended to his wife he was sold.

So Bob had the horses and he did pretty much as he pleased and you can't blame Bob, at least, I never did. Sometimes he was out to win and sometimes he wasn't. I never cared much about that when I was swiping a horse. What I did want to know was that my horse had the speed and could go out in front, if you wanted him to.

And, as I'm telling you, there was Bob in this race with one of Mr. Mather's horses, was named "About Ben Ahem" or something like that, and was fast as a streak. He was a gelding and had a mark of 2.21, but could step in .08 or .09.

Because when Burt and I were out, as I've told you, the year before, there was a nigger, Burt knew, worked for Mr. Mathers and we went out there one day when we didn't have no race on at the Marietta Fair and our boss Harry was gone home.

And so everyone was gone to the fair but just this one nigger and he took us all through Mr. Mather's swell house and he and Burt tapped a bottle of wine Mr. Mathers had hid in his bedroom, back in a closet, without his wife knowing, and he showed us this Ahem horse. Burt was always stuck on being a driver but didn't have much chance to get to the top, being a nigger, and he and the other nigger gulped that whole bottle of wine and Burt got a little lit up.

So the nigger let Burt take this About Ben Ahem and step him a mile in a track Mr. Mathers had all to himself, right there on the farm. And Mr. Mathers had one child, a daughter, kinda sick and not very good-looking, and she came home and we had to hustle and get About Ben Ahem stuck back in the barn.

I'm only telling you to get everything straight. At Sandusky, that afternoon I was at the fair, this young fellow with the two girls was fussed, being with the girls and losing his bet. You know how a fellow is that way. One of them was his girl and the other his sister. I had figured that out.

"Gee whizz," I says to myself, "I'm going to give him the dope."

He was mighty nice when I touched him on the shoulder. He and the girls were nice to me right from the start and clear to the end. I'm not blaming them.

And so he leaned back and I give him the dope on About Ben Ahem. "Don't bet a cent on this first heat because he'll go like an oxen hitched to a plow, but when the first heat is over go right down and lay on your pile." That's what I told him.

Well, I never saw a fellow treat anyone sweller. There was a fat man sitting beside the little girl, that had looked at me twice by this time, and I at her, and both blushing, and what did he do but have the nerve to turn and ask the fat man to get up and change places with me so I could set with his crowd.

Gee whizz, craps amighty. There I was. What a chump I was to go and get gay up there in the West House bar, and just because that dude was standing there with a cane and that kind of a necktie on, to go and get all balled up and drink that whisky, just to show off.

Of course she would know, me setting right beside her and letting her smell of my breath. I could have kicked myself right down out of that grandstand and all around that race track and made a faster record than most of the skates of horses they had there that year.

Because that girl wasn't any mutt of a girl. What wouldn't I have give right then for a stick of chewing gum to chew, or a lozenger, or some liquorice, or most anything. I was glad I had those twenty-five cent cigars in my pocket and right away I give that fellow one and lit one myself. Then that fat man got up and we changed places and there I was, plunked right down beside her.

They introduced themselves and the fellow's best girl, he had with him, was named Miss Elinor Woodbury, and her father was a manufacturer of barrels from a place called Tiffin, Ohio. And the fellow himself was named Wilbur Wessen and his sister was Miss Lucy Wessen.

I suppose it was their having such swell names got me off my trolley. A fellow, just because he has been a swipe with a race horse, and works taking care of horses for a man in the teaming, delivery, and storage business, isn't any better or worse than anyone else. I've often thought that, and said it too.

But you know how a fellow is. There's something in that kind of nice clothes, and the kind of nice eyes she had, and the way she had looked at me, awhile before, over her brother's shoulder, and me looking back at her, and both of us blushing.

I couldn't show her up for a boob, could I?

I made a fool of myself, that's what I did. I said my name was Walter Mathers from Marietta, Ohio, and then I told all three of them the smashingest lie you ever heard. What I said was that my father owned the horse About Ben Ahem and that he had let him out to this Bob French for racing purposes, because our family was proud and had never gone into racing that way, in our own name, I mean. Then I had got started and they were all leaning over and listening, and Miss Lucy Wessen's eyes were shining, and I went the whole hog.

I told about our place down at Marietta, and about the big stables and the grand brick house we had on a hill, up above the Ohio River, but I knew enough not to do it in no bragging way. What I did was to start things and then let them drag the rest out of me. I acted just as reluctant to tell as I could. Our family hasn't got any barrel factory, and, since I've known us, we've always been pretty poor, but not asking anything of anyone at that, and my grandfather, over in Wales—But never mind that.

We sat there talking like we had known each other for years and years, and I went and told them that my father had been expecting maybe this Bob French wasn't on the square, and had sent me up to Sandusky on the sly to find out what I could.

And I bluffed it through I had found out all about the 2.18 pace, in which About Ben Ahem was to start.

I said he would lose the first heat by pacing like a lame cow and then he would come back and skin 'em alive after that. And to back up what I said I took thirty dollars out of my pocket and handed it to Mr. Wilbur Wessen and asked him, would he mind, after the first heat, to go down and place it on About Ben Ahem for whatever odds he could get. What I said was that I didn't want Bob French to see me and none of the swipes.

Sure enough the first heat come off and About Ben Ahem went off his stride, up the back stretch, and looked like a wooden horse or a sick one, and come in to be last. Then this Wilbur Wessen went down to the betting place under the grandstand and there I was with the two girls, and when that Miss Woodbury was looking the other way once, Lucy Wessen kinda, with her shoulder you know, kinda touched me. Not just tucking down, I don't mean. You know how a woman can do. They get close, but not getting gay either. You know what they do. Gee whizz.

And then they give me a jolt. What they had done, when I didn't know, was to get together, and they had decided Wilbur Wessen would bet fifty dollars, and the two girls had gone and put in ten dollars each, of their own money, too. I was sick then, but I was sicker later.

About the gelding, About Ben Ahem, and their winning their money, I wasn't worried a lot about that. It come out O.K. Ahem stepped the next three heats like a bushel of spoiled eggs going to market before they could be found out, and Wilbur Wessen had got nine to two for the money. There was something else eating at me.

Because Wilbur come back, after he had bet the money, and after that he spent most of his time talking to that Miss Woodbury, and Lucy Wessen and I was left alone together like on a desert island. Gee, if I'd only been on the square or if there had been any way of getting myself on the square. There ain't any Walter Mathers, like I said to her and them, and there hasn't ever been one, but if there was, I bet I'd go to Marietta, Ohio, and shoot him tomorrow.

There I was, big boob that I am. Pretty soon the race was over, and Wilbur had gone down and collected our money, and we had a hack downtown, and he stood us a swell supper at the West House, and a bottle of champagne beside.

And I was with that girl and she wasn't saying much, and I wasn't saying much either. One thing I know. She wasn't stuck on me because of the lie about my father being rich and all that. There's a way you know. . . . Craps amighty. There's a kind of girl, you see just once in your life, and if you don't get busy and make hay, then you're gone for good and all, and might as well go jump off a bridge. They give you a look from inside of them somewhere, and it ain't no vamping, and what it means is—you want that girl to be your wife, and you want nice things around her like flowers and swell clothes, and you want her to have the kids you're going to have, and you want good music played and no ragtime. Gee whizz.

There's a place over near Sandusky, across a kind of bay, and it's called Cedar Point. And after we had supper we went over to it in a launch, all by ourselves. Wilbur and Miss Lucy and that Miss Woodbury had to catch a ten o'clock train back to Tiffin, Ohio, because, when you're out with girls like that you can't get careless and miss any trains and stay out all night, like you can with some kinds of Janes.

And Wilbur blowed himself to the launch and it cost him fifteen cold plunks, but I wouldn't never have knew if I hadn't listened. He wasn't no tin horn kind of a sport.

Over at the Cedar Point place, we didn't stay around where there was a gang of common kind of cattle at all.

There was big dance halls and dining places for yaps, and there was a beach you could walk along and get where it was dark, and we went there.

She didn't talk hardly at all and neither did I, and I was thinking how glad I was my mother was all right, and always made us kids learn to eat with a fork at table, and not swill soup, and not be noisy and rough like a gang you see around a race track that way.

Then Wilbur and his girl went away up the beach and Lucy and I sat down in a dark place, where there was some roots of old trees, the water had washed up, and after that the time, till we had to go back in the launch and they had to catch their trains, wasn't nothing at all. It went like winking your eye.

Here's how it was. The place we were setting in was dark, like I said, and there was the roots from that old stump sticking up like arms, and there was a watery smell, and the night was like—as if you could put your hand out and feel it— so warm and soft and dark and sweet like an orange.

I most cried and I most swore and I most jumped up and danced, I was so mad and happy and sad.

When Wilbur come back from being alone with his girl, and she saw him coming, Lucy she says, "we got to go to the train now," and she was most crying too, but she never knew nothing I knew, and she couldn't be so all busted up. And then, before Wilbur and Miss Woodbury got up to where we was, she put her face up and kissed me quick and put her head up against me and she was all quivering and—Gee whizz.

Sometimes I hope I have cancer and die. I guess you know what I mean. We went in the launch across the bay to the train like that, and it was dark, too. She whispered and said it was like she and I could get out of the boat and walk on the water, and it sounded foolish, but I knew what she meant.

And then quick we were right at the depot, and there was a big gang of yaps, the kind that goes to the fairs, and crowded and milling around like cattle, and

how could I tell her? "It won't be long because you'll write and I'll write to you."
That's all she said.

I got a chance like a hay barn afire. A swell chance I got.

And maybe she would write me, down at Marietta that way, and the letter
would come back, and stamped on the front of it by the U.S.A. "there ain't any
such guy," or something like that, whatever they stamp on a letter that way.

And me trying to pass myself off for a bigbug and a swell—to her, as decent
a little body as God ever made. Craps amighty—a swell chance I got!

And then the train come in, and she got on it, and Wilbur Wessen he come
and shook hands with me, and that Miss Woodbury was nice too and bowed to
me, and I at her, and the train went and I busted out and cried like a kid.

Gee, I could have run after that train and made Dan Patch look like a freight
train after a wreck but, socks amighty, what was the use? Did you ever see such
a fool?

I'll bet you what—if I had an arm broke right now or a train had run over
my foot—I wouldn't go to no doctor at all. I'd go set down and let her hurt and
hurt—that's what I'd do.

I'll bet you what—if I hadn't a drunk that booze I'd a never been such a boob
as to go tell such a lie—that couldn't never be made straight to a lady like her.

I wish I had that fellow right here that had on a Windsor tie and carried a
cane. I'd smash him for fair. Gosh darn his eyes. He's a big fool—that's what he
is.

And if I'm not another you just go find me one and I'll quit working and be
a bum and give him my job. I don't care nothing for working, and earning money,
and saving it for no such boob as myself.

QUESTIONS

1. What has Anderson gained by adopting the narrative perspective of
   the boy?
2. In what ways might the story be different if Anderson were to tell it
   in his own voice as an author?
3. Characterize the narrator. What has caused him to behave foolishly?
   Would he make the same mistake again?
4. Why does he make so much of the man with the cane and the
   Windsor tie?
5. The narrator says of "boys who are raised regular in houses" that they
   "don't know nothing at all. They've never had no opportunity." Later
   he says: "You can stick your colleges up your nose for all me. I guess
   I know where I got my education." He calls his friend Burt "a nigger."
   Sharing the narrator's perspective on the story, do we also share his
   opinions or his way of expressing himself?

"I'm a Fool" owes much of its effect to the distance established between the
narrator's understanding of his situation and the reader's greater knowledge and

sophistication. The running dramatic irony of his statements tells us more than he knows. Like many good stories, this one has ironies upon ironies. Ironically, the narrator's attempt to impress the girl has led to his permanent separation from her. This much he understands when it is too late. But he appears to think that he could have won her if only he had been honest, creating a final dramatic irony when measured against the reader's sense that the social gap is so great that he would not have won her in any case.

In the next story, the narrator who remembers the events is no longer the child who experienced them.

A MEMORY

Eudora Welty *(1909–)*

One summer morning when I was a child I lay on the sand after swimming in the small lake in the park. The sun beat down—it was almost noon. The water shone like steel, motionless except for the feathery curl behind a distant swimmer. From my position I was looking at a rectangle brightly lit, actually glaring at me, with sun, sand, water, a little pavilion, a few solitary people in fixed attitudes, and around it all a border of dark rounded oak trees, like the engraved thunderclouds surrounding illustrations in the Bible. Ever since I had begun taking painting lessons, I had made small frames with my fingers, to look out at everything.

Since this was a weekday morning, the only persons who were at liberty to be in the park were either children, who had nothing to occupy them, or those older people whose lives are obscure, irregular, and consciously of no worth to anything: this I put down as my observation at that time. I was at an age when I formed a judgment upon every person and every event which came under my eye, although I was easily frightened. When a person, or a happening, seemed to me not in keeping with my opinion, or even my hope or expectation, I was terrified by a vision of abandonment and wildness which tore my heart with a kind of sorrow. My father and mother, who believed that I saw nothing in the world which was not strictly coaxed into place like a vine on our garden trellis to be presented to my eyes, would have been badly concerned if they had guessed how frequently the weak and inferior and strangely turned examples of what was to come showed themselves to me.

I do not know even now what it was that I was waiting to see; but in those days I was convinced that I almost saw it at every turn. To watch everything about me I regarded grimly and possessively as a *need*. All through this summer I had lain on the sand beside the small lake, with my hands squared over my eyes, finger tips touching, looking out by this device to see everything: which appeared as a kind of projection. It did not matter to me what I looked at; from any observation I would conclude that a secret of life had been nearly revealed to me —for I was obsessed with notions about concealment, and from the smallest gesture of a stranger I would wrest what was to me a communication or a presentiment.

This state of exaltation was heightened, or even brought about, by the fact that I was in love then for the first time: I had identified love at once. The truth is that never since has any passion I have felt remained so hopelessly unexpressed within me or appeared so grotesquely altered in the outward world. It is strange that sometimes, even now, I remember unadulteratedly a certain morning when I touched my friend's wrist (as if by accident, and he pretended not to notice) as we passed on the stairs in school. I must add, and this is not so strange, that the child was not actually my friend. We had never exchanged a word or even a nod of recognition; but it was possible during the entire year for me to think endlessly on this minute and brief encounter which we endured on the stairs, until it would swell with a sudden and overwhelming beauty, like a rose forced into premature bloom for a great occasion.

My love had somehow made me doubly austere in my observations of what went on about me. Through some intensity I had come almost into a dual life, as observer and dreamer. I felt a necessity for absolute conformity to my ideas in any happening I witnessed. As a result, all day long in school I sat perpetually alert, fearing for the untoward to happen. The dreariness and regularity of the school day were a protection for me, but I remember with exact clarity the day in Latin class when the boy I loved (whom I watch constantly) bent suddenly over and brought his handkerchief to his face. I saw red—vermilion—blood flow over the handkerchief and his square-shaped hand; his nose had begun to bleed. I remember the very moment: several of the older girls laughed at the confusion and distraction; the boy rushed from the room; the teacher spoke sharply in warning. But this small happening which had closed in upon my friend was a tremendous shock to me; it was unforeseen, but at the same time dreaded; I recognized it, and suddenly I leaned heavily on my arm and fainted. Does this explain why, ever since that day, I have been unable to bear the sight of blood?

I never knew where this boy lived, or who his parents were. This occasioned during the year of my love a constant uneasiness in me. It was unbearable to think that his house might be slovenly and unpainted, hidden by tall trees, that his mother and father might be shabby—dishonest—crippled—dead. I speculated endlessly on the dangers of his home. Sometimes I imagined that his house might catch on fire in the night and that he might die. When he would walk into the schoolroom the next morning, a look of unconcern and even stupidity on his face would dissipate my dream; but my fears were increased through his unconsciousness of them, for I felt a mystery deeper than danger which hung about him. I watched everything he did, trying to learn and translate and verify. I could reproduce for you now the clumsy weave, the exact shade of faded blue in his sweater. I remember how he used to swing his foot as he sat at his desk—softly, barely not touching the floor. Even now it does not seem trivial.

As I lay on the beach that sunny morning, I was thinking of my friend and remembering in a retarded, dilated, timeless fashion the incident of my hand brushing his wrist. It made a very long story. But like a needle going in and out among my thoughts were the children running on the sand, the upthrust oak trees growing over the clean pointed roof of the white pavilion, and the slowly changing attitudes of the grown-up people who had avoided the city and were lying prone and laughing on the water's edge. I still would not care to say which was more real—the dream I could make blossom at will, or the sight of the bathers. I am presenting them, you see, only as simultaneous.

I did not notice how the bathers got there, so close to me. Perhaps I actually fell asleep, and they came out then. Sprawled close to where I was lying, at any rate, appeared a group of loud, squirming, ill-assorted people who seemed thrown together only by the most confused accident, and who seemed driven by foolish intent to insult each other, all of which they enjoyed with a hilarity which astonished my heart. There were a man, two women, two young boys. They were brown and roughened, but not foreigners; when I was a child such people were called "common." They wore old and faded bathing suits which did not hide either the energy or the fatigue of their bodies, but showed it exactly.

The boys must have been brothers, because they both had very white straight hair, which shone like thistles in the red sunlight. The older boy was greatly overgrown—he protruded from his costume at every turn. His cheeks were ballooned outward and hid his eyes, but it was easy for me to follow his darting sly glances as he ran clumsily around the others, inflicting pinches, kicks, and idiotic sounds upon them. The smaller boy was thin and defiant; his white bangs were plastered down where he had thrown himself time after time headfirst into the lake when the older child chased him to persecute him.

Lying in leglike confusion together were the rest of the group, the man and the two women. The man seemed completely given over to the heat and glare of the sun; his relaxed eyes sometimes squinted with faint amusement over the brilliant water and the hot sand. His arms were flabby and at rest. He lay turned on his side, now and then scooping sand in a loose pile about the legs of the older woman.

She herself stared fixedly at his slow, undeliberate movements, and held her body perfectly still. She was unnaturally white and fatly aware, in a bathing suit which had no relation to the shape of her body. Fat hung upon her upper arms like an arrested earthslide on a hill. With the first motion she might make, I was afraid that she would slide down upon herself into a terrifying heap. Her breasts hung heavy and widening like pears into her bathing suit. Her legs lay prone one on the other like shadowed bulwarks, uneven and deserted, upon which, from the man's hand, the sand piled higher like the teasing threat of oblivion. A slow, repetitious sound I had been hearing for a long time unconsciously, I identified as a continuous laugh which came through the motionless open pouched mouth of the woman.

The younger girl, who was lying at the man's feet, was curled tensely upon herself. She wore a bright green bathing suit like a bottle from which she might, I felt, burst in a rage of churning smoke. I could feel the genie-like rage in her narrowed figure as she seemed both to crawl and to lie still, watching the man heap the sand in his careless way about the larger legs of the older woman. The two little boys were running in wobbly ellipses about the others, pinching them indiscriminately and pitching sand into the man's roughened hair as though they were not afraid of him. The woman continued to laugh, almost as she would hum an annoying song. I saw that they were all resigned to each other's daring and ugliness.

There had been no words spoken among these people, but I began to comprehend a progression, a circle of answers, which they were flinging toward one another in their own way, in the confusion of vulgarity and hatred which twined among them all like a wreath of steam rising from the wet sand. I saw the man lift his hand filled with crumbling sand, shaking it as the woman laughed, and pour it down inside her bathing suit between her bulbous descending breasts. There it hung, brown and shapeless, making them all laugh. Even the angry girl laughed, with an insistent hilarity which flung her to her feet and tossed her about the beach, her stiff, cramped legs jumping and tottering. The little boys pointed and howled. The man smiled, the way panting dogs seem to be smiling, and gazed about carelessly at them all and out over the water. He even looked at me, and included me. Looking back, stunned, I wished that they all were dead.

But at that moment the girl in the green bathing suit suddenly whirled all the way around. She reached rigid arms toward the screaming children and joined them in a senseless chase. The small boy dashed headfirst into the water, and the larger boy churned his overgrown body through the blue air onto a little bench, which I had not even known was there! Jeeringly he called to the others, who laughed as he jumped, heavy and ridiculous, over the back of the bench and tumbled exaggeratedly in the sand below. The fat woman leaned over the man to smirk, and the child pointed at her, screaming. The girl in green then came running toward the bench as though she would destroy it, and with a fierceness which took my breath away, she dragged herself through the air and jumped over the bench. But no one seemed to notice, except the smaller boy, who flew out of the water to dig his fingers into her side, in mixed congratulation and derision; she pushed him angrily down into the sand.

I closed my eyes upon them and their struggles but I could see them still, large and almost metallic, with painted smiles, in the sun. I lay there with my eyes pressed shut, listening to their moans and their frantic squeals. It seemed to me that I could hear also the thud and the fat impact of all their ugly bodies upon one another. I tried to withdraw to my most inner dream, that of touching the wrist of the boy I loved on the stair; I felt the shudder of my wish shaking the darkness like leaves where I had closed my eyes; I felt the heavy weight of sweetness which always accompanied this memory; but the memory itself did not come to me.

I lay there, opening and closing my eyes. The brilliance and then the blackness were like some alternate experiences of night and day. The sweetness of my love seemed to bring the dark and to swing me gently in its suspended wind; I sank into familiarity; but the story of my love, the long narrative of the incident on the stairs, had vanished. I did not know, any longer, the meaning of my happiness; it held me unexplained.

Once when I looked up, the fat woman was standing opposite the smiling man. She bent over and in a condescending way pulled down the front of her bathing suit, turning it outward, so that the lumps of mashed and folded sand came emptying out. I felt a peak of horror, as though her breasts themselves had turned to sand, as though they were of no importance at all and she did not care.

When finally I emerged again from the protection of my dream, the undefined austerity of my love, I opened my eyes onto the blur of an empty beach. The group of strangers had gone. Still I lay there, feeling victimized by the sight of the unfinished bulwark where they had piled and shaped the wet sand around their bodies, which changed the appearance of the beach like the ravages of a storm. I looked away, and for the object which met my eye, the small worn white pavilion, I felt pity suddenly overtake me, and I burst into tears.

That was my last morning on the beach. I remember continuing to lie there, squaring my vision with my hands, trying to think ahead to the time of my return to school in winter. I could imagine the boy I loved walking into a classroom, where I would watch him with this hour on the beach accompanying my recovered dream and added to my love. I could even foresee the way he would stare back, speechless and innocent, a medium-sized boy with blond hair, his unconscious eyes looking beyond me and out the window, solitary and unprotected.

QUESTIONS

1. How much time do you think has passed between the events and the telling? Where is the evidence?
2. Characterize the girl as she appears in the story. Can we tell whether she is different now from what she was? What is the significance of the line: "Even now it does not seem trivial"? (end of paragraph six).
3. Why does the girl make frames with her fingers, "to look out at everything"? Does the habit suggest anything about her attitude toward life?
4. Why is she so upset by the "common" people?

Here is another story of young people and bathing suits, but this time in an A & P. Updike's narrator is a boy, but like the girl of "A Memory" he is a keen observer. Do they share other characteristics?

A & P

John Updike   (1932–)

In walks these three girls in nothing but bathing suits. I'm in the third checkout slot, with my back to the door, so I don't see them until they're over by the bread. The one that caught my eye first was the one in the plaid green two-piece. She was a chunky kid, with a good tan and a sweet broad soft-looking can with those two crescents of white just under it, where the sun never seems to hit, at the top of the backs of her legs. I stood there with my hand on a box of HiHo crackers trying to remember if I rang it up or not. I ring it up again and the customer starts giving me hell. She's one of these cash-register-watchers, a witch about fifty with rouge on her cheekbones and no eyebrows, and I know it made her day to trip me up. She'd been watching cash registers for fifty years and probably never seen a mistake before.

By the time I got her feathers smoothed and her goodies into a bag—she gives me a little snort in passing, if she'd been born at the right time they would have burned her over in Salem—by the time I get her on her way the girls had circled around the bread and were coming back, without a pushcart, back my way along the counters, in the aisle between the checkouts and the Special bins. They didn't even have shoes on. There was this chunky one, with the two-piece—it was bright green and the seams on the bra were still sharp and her belly was still pretty pale so I guessed she just got it (the suit)—there was this one, with one of those chubby berry-faces, the lips all bunched together under her nose, this one, and a tall one, with black hair that hadn't quite frizzed right, and one of these sunburns right across under the eyes, and a chin that was too long—you know, the kind of girl other girls think is very "striking" and "attractive" but never quite makes it, as they very well know, which is why they like her so much—and then the third one, that wasn't quite so tall. She was the queen. She kind of led them, the other two peeking around and making their shoulders round. She didn't look around, not this queen, she just walked straight on slowly, on these long white prima-donna legs. She came down a little hard on her heels, as if she didn't walk in her bare feet that much, putting down her heels and then letting the weight move along to her toes as if she was testing the floor with every step, putting a little deliberate extra action into it. You never know for sure how girls' minds work (do you really think it's a mind in there or just a little buzz like a bee in a glass jar?) but you got the idea she had talked the other two into coming in here with her, and now she was showing them how to do it, walk slow and hold yourself straight.

She had on a kind of dirty-pink—beige maybe, I don't know—bathing suit with a little nubble all over it and, what got me, the straps were down. They were off her shoulders looped loose around the cool tops of her arms, and I guess as a result the suit had slipped a little on her, so all around the top of the cloth there was this shining rim. If it hadn't been there you wouldn't have known there could have been anything whiter than those shoulders. With the straps pushed off, there was nothing between the top of the suit and top of her head except just *her,* this clean bare plane of the top of her chest down from the shoulder bones like a dented sheet of metal tilted in the light. I mean, it was more than pretty.

She had sort of oaky hair that the sun and salt had bleached, done up in a bun that was unravelling, and a kind of prim face. Walking into the A & P with your straps down, I suppose it's the only kind of face you *can* have. She held her head so high her neck, coming up out of those white shoulders, looked kind of stretched, but I didn't mind. The longer her neck was, the more of her there was.

She must have felt in the corner of her eye me and over my shoulder Stokesie in the second slot watching, but she didn't tip. Not this queen. She kept her eyes moving across the racks, and stopped, and turned so slow it made my stomach rub the inside of my apron, and buzzed to the other two, who kind of huddled against her for relief, and then they all three of them went up the cat-and-dog-food-breakfast-cereal-macaroni-rice-raisins-seasonings-spreads-spaghetti-soft-drinks-crackers-and-cookies aisle. From the third slot I look straight up this aisle to the meat counter, and I watched them all the way. The fat one with the tan sort of fumbled with the cookies, but on second thought she put the package back. The sheep pushing their carts down the aisle—the girls were walking against the usual traffic (not that we have one-way signs or anything)—were pretty hilarious. You could see them, when Queenie's white shoulders dawned on them, kind of jerk, or hop, or hiccup, but their eyes snapped back to their own baskets and on they pushed. I bet you could set off dynamite in an A & P and the people would by and large keep reaching and checking oatmeal off their lists and muttering "Let me see, there was a third thing, began with A, asparagus, no, ah, yes, applesauce!" or whatever it is they do mutter. But there was no doubt, this jiggled them. A few houseslaves in pin curlers even looked around after pushing their carts past to make sure what they had seen was correct.

You know, it's one thing to have a girl in a bathing suit down on the beach, where what with the glare nobody can look at each other much anyway, and another thing in the cool of the A & P, under the fluorescent lights, against all those stacked packages, with her feet paddling along naked over our checkerboard green-and-cream rubber-tile floor.

"Oh Daddy," Stokesie said beside me. "I feel so faint."

"Darling," I said. "Hold me tight." Stokesie's married, with two babies chalked up on his fuselage already, but as far as I can tell that's the only difference. He's twenty-two, and I was nineteen this April.

"Is it done?" he asks, the responsible married man finding his voice. I forgot to say he thinks he's going to be manager some sunny day, maybe in 1990 when it's called the Great Alexandrov and Petrooshki Tea Company or something.

What he meant was, our town is five miles from a beach, with a big summer colony out on the Point, but we're right in the middle of town, and the women generally put on a shirt or shorts or something before they get out of the car into the street. And anyway these are usually women with six children and varicose veins mapping their legs and nobody, including them, could care less. As I say, we're right in the middle of town, and if you stand at our front doors you can see two banks and the Congregational church and the newspaper store and three real-estate offices and about twenty-seven old freeloaders tearing up Central Street because the sewer broke again. It's not as if we're on the Cape; we're north of Boston and there's people in this town haven't seen the ocean for twenty years.

The girls had reached the meat counter and were asking McMahon something. He pointed, they pointed, and they shuffled out of sight behind a pyramid of Diet Delight peaches. All that was left for us to see was old McMahon patting his mouth and looking after them sizing up their joints. Poor kids, I began to feel sorry for them, they couldn't help it.

Now here comes the sad part of the story, at least my family says it's sad, but I don't think it's so sad myself. The store's pretty empty, it being Thursday afternoon, so there was nothing much to do except lean on the register and wait for the girls to show up again. The whole store was like a pinball machine and I didn't know which tunnel they'd come out of. After a while they come around out of the far aisle, around the light bulbs, records at discount of the Caribbean Six or Tony Martin Sings or some such gunk you wonder they waste the wax on, sixpacks of candy bars, and plastic toys done up in cellophane that fall apart when a kid looks at them anyway. Around they come, Queenie still leading the way, and holding a little gray jar in her hand. Slots Three through Seven are unmanned and I could see her wondering between Stokes and me, but Stokesie with his usual luck draws an old party in baggy gray pants who stumbles up with four giant cans of pineapple juice (what do these bums *do* with all that pineapple juice? I've often asked myself) so the girls come to me. Queenie puts down the jar and I take it into my fingers icy cold. Kingfish Fancy Herring Snacks in Pure Sour Cream: 49¢. Now her hands are empty, not a ring or a bracelet, bare as God made them, and I wonder where the money's coming from. Still with that prim look she lifts a folded dollar bill out of the hollow at the center of her nubbled pink top. The jar went heavy in my hand. Really, I thought that was so cute.

Then everybody's luck begins to run out. Lengel comes in from haggling with a truck full of cabbages on the lot and is about to scuttle into that door marked MANAGER behind which he hides all day when the girls touch his eye. Lengel's pretty dreary, teaches Sunday school and the rest, but he doesn't miss that much. He comes over and says, "Girls, this isn't the beach."

Queenie blushes, though maybe it's just a brush of sunburn I was noticing for the first time, now that she was so close. "My mother asked me to pick up a jar of herring snacks." Her voice kind of startled me, the way voices do when you see the people first, coming out so flat and dumb yet kind of tony, too, the way it ticked over "pick up" and "snacks." All of a sudden I slid right down her voice into her living room. Her father and the other men were standing around in ice-cream coats and bow ties and the women were in sandals picking up herring snacks on toothpicks off a big glass plate and they were all holding drinks the color of water with olives and sprigs of mint in them. When my parents have somebody over they get lemonade and if it's a real racy affair Schlitz in tall glasses with "They'll Do It Every Time" cartoons stencilled on.

"That's all right," Lengel said. "But this isn't the beach." His repeating this struck me as funny, as if it had just occurred to him, and he had been thinking all these years the A & P was a great big dune and he was the head lifeguard. He didn't like my smiling—as I say he doesn't miss much—but he concentrates on giving the girls that sad Sunday-school-superintendent stare.

Queenie's blush is no sunburn now, and the plump one in plaid, that I liked better from the back—a really sweet can—pipes up. "We weren't doing any shopping. We just came in for the one thing."

"That makes no difference," Lengel tells her, and I could see from the way his eyes went that he hadn't noticed she was wearing a two-piece before. "We want you decently dressed when you come in here."

"We *are* decent," Queenie says suddenly, her lower lip pushing, getting sore now that she remembers her place, a place from which the crowd that runs the A & P must look pretty crummy. Fancy Herring Snacks flashed in her very blue eyes.

"Girls, I don't want to argue with you. After this come in here with your shoulders covered. It's our policy." He turns his back. That's policy for you. Policy is what the kingpins want. What the others want is juvenile delinquency.

All this while, the customers had been showing up with their carts but, you know, sheep, seeing a scene, they had all bunched up on Stokesie, who shook open a paper bag as gently as peeling a peach, not wanting to miss a word. I could feel in the silence everybody getting nervous, most of all Lengel, who asks me, "Sammy, have you rung up their purchase?"

I thought and said "No" but it wasn't about that I was thinking. I go through the punches, 4, 9. GROC, TOT—it's more complicated than you think, and after you do it often enough, it begins to make a little song, that you hear words to, in my case "Hello *(bing)* there, you *(gung)* hap-py *pee*-pul *(splat)*!"—the *splat* being the drawer flying out. I uncrease the bill, tenderly as you may imagine, it just having come from between the two smoothest scoops of vanilla I had ever known were there, and pass a half and a penny into her narrow pink palm, and nestle the herrings in a bag and twist its neck and hand it over, all the time thinking.

The girls, and who'd blame them, are in a hurry to get out, so I say "I quit" to Lengel quick enough for them to hear, hoping they'll stop and watch me, their unsuspected hero. They keep right on going, into the electric eye; the door flies open and they flicker across the lot to their car, Queenie and Plaid and Big Tall Goony-Goony (not that as raw material she was so bad), leaving me with Lengel and a kink in his eyebrow.

"Did you say something, Sammy?"

"I said I quit."

"I thought you did."

"You didn't have to embarrass them."

"It was they who were embarrassing us."

I started to say something that came out "Fiddle-de-doo." It's a saying of my grandmother's, and I know she would have been pleased.

"I don't think you know what you're saying," Lengel said.

"I know you don't," I said, "But I do." I pull the bow at the back of my apron and start shrugging it off my shoulders. A couple customers that had been heading for my slot begin to knock against each other, like scared pigs in a chute. Lengel sighs and begins to look very patient and old and gray. He's been a friend of my parents for years. "Sammy, you don't want to do this to your Mom and Dad," he tells me. It's true, I don't. But it seems to me that once you begin a gesture it's fatal not to go through with it. I fold the apron, "Sammy" stitched in red on the pocket, and put it on the counter, and drop the bow tie on top of it. The bow tie is theirs, if you've ever wondered. "You'll feel this for the rest of your life," Lengel says, and I know that's true, too, but remembering how he made that pretty girl blush makes me so scrunchy inside I punch the No Sale tab and the machine whirs "pee-pul" and the drawer splats out. One advantage to this scene taking place in summer, I can follow this up with a clean exit, there's no fumbling around getting your coat and galoshes, I just saunter into the electric eye in my white shirt that my mother ironed the night before, and the door heaves itself open, and outside the sunshine is skating around on the asphalt.

I look around for my girls, but they're gone, of course. There wasn't anybody but some young married screaming with her children about some candy they didn't get by the door of a powder-blue Falcon station wagon. Looking back in the big windows, over the bags of peat moss and aluminum lawn furniture stacked on the pavement, I could see Lengel in my place in the slot, checking the sheep through. His face was dark gray and his back stiff, as if he'd just had an injection of iron, and my stomach kind of fell as I felt how hard the world was going to be to me hereafter.

QUESTIONS

1.   What can we tell about the narrator just from his manner of speaking?
2.   Near the end of the second paragraph, the narrator says "You never know for sure how girls' minds work (do you really think it's a mind in there or just a little buzz like a bee in a glass jar?)." What does this tell us of his attitude toward women? Is the attitude conveyed here consistent with his actions later in the story?
3.   Which words and phrases most clearly convey the narrator's attitudes toward the other customers (apart from the three girls) and toward the store manager?
4.   When Sammy quits his job, we know his action is precipitated by the manager's treatment of the three girls, but can we see evidence of other reasons as well?
5.   What is the meaning of the final words: "I felt how hard the world was going to be to me hereafter"?

As you begin the next story, compare its first few sentences with the first few sentences of "A & P." What are the obvious differences in style? To what do you attribute these differences?

AN OUNCE OF CURE

Alice Munro   (1931–   )

My parents didn't drink. They weren't rabid about it, and in fact I remember that when I signed the pledge in grade seven, with the rest of that superbly if impermanently indoctrinated class, my mother said, "It's just nonsense and fanaticism, children of that age." My father would drink a beer on a hot day, but my mother did not join him, and—whether accidentally or symbolically—this drink was always consumed *outside* the house. Most of the people we knew were the same way, in the small town where we lived. I ought not to say that it was this which got me into difficulties, because the difficulties I got into were a faithful expression of my own incommodious nature—the same nature that caused my mother to look at me, on any occasion which traditionally calls for feelings of pride and maternal accomplishment (my departure for my first formal dance, I mean, or my hellbent preparations for a descent on college) with an expression of brooding and fascinated despair, as if she could not possibly expect, did not ask, that it should go with me as it did with other girls; the dreamed-of spoils of daughters —orchids, nice boys, diamond rings—would be borne home in due course by the daughters of her friends, but not by me; all she could do was hope for a lesser rather than a greater disaster—an elopement, say, with a boy who could never earn his living, rather than an abduction into the White Slave trade.

But ignorance, my mother said, ignorance, or innocence if you like, is not always such a fine thing as people think and I am not sure it may not be dangerous for a girl like you; then she emphasized her point, as she had a habit of doing, with some quotation which had an innocent pomposity and odour of mothballs. I didn't even wince at it, knowing full well how it must have worked wonders with Mr. Berryman.

The evening I baby-sat for the Berrymans must have been in April. I had been in love all year, or at least since the first week in September, when a boy named Martin Collingwood had given me a surprised, appreciative, and rather ominously complacent smile in the school assembly. I never knew what surprised him; I was not looking like anybody but me; I had an old blouse on and my home-permanent had turned out badly. A few weeks after that he took me out for the first time, and kissed me on the dark side of the porch—also, I ought to say, on the mouth; I am sure it was the first time anybody had ever kissed me effectively, and I know that I did not wash my face that night or the next morning, in order to keep the imprint of those kisses intact. (I showed the most painful banality in the conduct of this whole affair, as you will see.) Two months, and a few amatory stages later, he dropped me. He had fallen for the girl who played opposite him in the Christmas production of *Pride and Prejudice*.

I said I was not going to have anything to do with that play, and I got another girl to work on Makeup in my place, but of course I went to it after all, and sat down in front with my girl friend Joyce, who pressed my hand when I was overcome with pain and delight at the sight of Mr. Darcy in white breeches, silk waistcoat, and sideburns. It was surely seeing Martin as Darcy that did it for me; every girl is in love with Darcy anyway, and the part gave Martin an arrogance and male splendour in my eyes which made it impossible to remember that he was simply a high-school senior, passably good-looking and of medium intelligence (and with a reputation slightly tainted, at that, by such preferences as the Drama Club and the Cadet *Band*) who happened to be the first boy, the first really presentable boy, to take an interest in me. In the last act they gave him a chance to embrace Elizabeth (Mary Bishop, with a sallow complexion and no figure, but big vivacious eyes) and during this realistic encounter I dug my nails bitterly into Joyce's sympathetic palm.

That night was the beginning of months of real, if more or less self-inflicted, misery for me. Why is it a temptation to refer to this sort of thing lightly, with irony, with amazement even, at finding oneself involved with such preposterous emotions in the unaccountable past? That is what we are apt to do, speaking of love; with adolescent love, of course, it's practically obligatory; you would think we sat around, dull afternoons, amusing ourselves with these tidbit recollections of pain. But it really doesn't make me feel very gay—worse still, it doesn't really surprise me—to remember all the stupid, sad, half-ashamed things I did, that people in love always do. I hung around the places where he might be seen, and then pretended not to see him; I made absurdly roundabout approaches, in conversation, to the bitter pleasure of casually mentioning his name. I day-dreamed endlessly; in fact if you want to put it mathematically, I spent perhaps ten times as many hours thinking about Martin Collingwood—yes, pining and weeping for him—as I ever spent with him; the idea of him dominated my mind relentlessly and, after a while, against my will. For if at first I had dramatized my feelings, the time came when I would have been glad to escape them; my well-worn daydreams had become depressing and not even temporarily consoling. As I worked my math problems I would torture myself, quite mechanically and helplessly, with an exact recollection of Martin kissing my throat. I had an exact recollection of *everything*. One night I had an impulse to swallow all the aspirins in the bathroom cabinet, but stopped after I had taken six.

My mother noticed that something was wrong and got me some iron pills. She said, "Are you sure everything is going all right at school?" *School!* When I told her that Martin and I had broken up all she said was, "Well so much the better for that. I never saw a boy so stuck on himself." "Martin has enough conceit to sink a battleship," I said morosely and went upstairs and cried.

The night I went to the Berrymans was a Saturday night. I baby-sat for them quite often on Saturday nights because they liked to drive over to Baileyville, a much bigger, livelier town about twenty miles away, and perhaps have supper and go to a show. They had been living in our town only two or three years—Mr. Berryman had been brought in as plant manager of the new door-factory—and they remained, I suppose by choice, on the fringes of its society; most of their friends were youngish couples like themselves, born in other places, who lived in new ranch-style houses on a hill outside town where we used to go tobogganing. This Saturday night they had two other couples in for drinks before they all drove over to Baileyville for the opening of a new supper-club; they were all rather festive. I sat in the kitchen and pretended to do Latin. Last night had been the Spring Dance at the High School. I had not gone, since the only boy who had asked me was Millerd Crompton, who asked so many girls that he was suspected of working his way through the whole class alphabetically. But the dance was held in the Armouries, which was only half a block away from our house; I had been able to see the boys in dark suits, the girls in long pale formals under their coats, passing gravely under the street-lights, stepping around the last patches of snow. I could even hear the music and I have not forgotten to this day that they played

"Ballerina," and—oh, song of my aching heart—"Slow Boat to China." Joyce had phoned me up this morning and told me in her hushed way (we might have been discussing an incurable disease I had) that yes, M.C. *had* been there with M.B., and she had on a formal that must have been made out of somebody's old lace tablecloth, it just *hung*.

When the Berrymans and their friends had gone I went into the living room and read a magazine. I was mortally depressed. The big softly lit room, with its green and leaf-brown colours, made an uncluttered setting for the development of the emotions, such as you would get on a stage. At home the life of the emotions went on all right, but it always seemed to get buried under the piles of mending to be done, the ironing, the children's jigsaw puzzles and rock collections. It was the sort of house where people were always colliding with one another on the stairs and listening to hockey games and Superman on the radio.

I got up and found the Berrymans' "Danse Macabre" and put it on the record player and turned out the living-room lights. The curtains were only partly drawn. A street light shone obliquely on the windowpane, making a rectangle of thin dusty gold, in which the shadows of bare branches moved, caught in the huge sweet winds of spring. It was a mild black night when the last snow was melting. A year ago all this—the music, the wind and darkness, the shadows of the branches—would have given me tremendous happiness; when they did not do so now, but only called up tediously familiar, somehow humiliatingly personal thoughts, I gave up my soul for dead and walked into the kitchen and decided to get drunk.

No, it was not like that. I walked into the kitchen to look for a coke or something in the refrigerator, and there on the front of the counter were three tall beautiful bottles, all about half full of gold. But even after I had looked at them and lifted them to feel their weight I had not decided to get drunk; I had decided to have a drink.

Now here is where my ignorance, my disastrous innocence, comes in. It is true that I had seen the Berrymans and their friends drinking their highballs as casually as I would drink a coke, but I did not apply this attitude to myself. No; I thought of hard liquor as something to be taken in extremities, and relied upon for extravagant results, one way or another. My approach could not have been less casual if I had been the Little Mermaid[1] drinking the witch's crystal potion. Gravely, with a glance at my set face in the black window above the sink, I poured a little whisky from each of the bottles (I think now there were two brands of rye and an expensive Scotch) until I had my glass full. For I had never in my life seen anyone pour a drink and I had no idea that people frequently diluted their liquor with water, soda, et cetera, and I had seen that the glasses the Berrymans' guests were holding when I came through the living room were nearly full.

I drank it off as quickly as possible. I set the glass down and stood looking at my face in the window, half expecting to see it altered. My throat was burning,

[1]In the fairy tale "The Little Mermaid," by Hans Christian Andersen (1805–1875).

but I felt nothing else. It was very disappointing, when I had worked myself up to it. But I was not going to let it go at that. I poured another full glass, then filled each of the bottles with water to approximately the level I had seen when I came in. I drank the second glass only a little more slowly than the first. I put the empty glass down on the counter with care, perhaps feeling in my head a rustle of things to come, and went and sat down on a chair in the living room. I reached up and turned on a floor lamp beside the chair, and the room jumped on me.

When I say that I was expecting extravagant results I do not mean that I was expecting this. I had thought of some sweeping emotional change, an upsurge of gaiety and irresponsibility, a feeling of lawlessness and escape, accompanied by a little dizziness and perhaps a tendency to giggle out loud. I did not have in mind the ceiling spinning like a great plate somebody had thrown at me, nor the pale green blobs of the chairs swelling, converging, disintegrating, playing with me a game full of enormous senseless inanimate malice. My head sank back; I closed my eyes. And at once opened them, opened them wide, threw myself out of the chair and down the hall and reached—thank God, thank God!—the Berrymans' bathroom, where I was sick everywhere, everywhere, and dropped like a stone.

From this point on I have no continuous picture of what happened; my memories of the next hour or two are split into vivid and improbable segments, with nothing but murk and uncertainty between. I do remember lying on the bathroom floor looking sideways at the little six-sided white tiles, which lay together in such an admirable and logical pattern, seeing them with the brief broken gratitude and sanity of one who has just been torn to pieces with vomiting. Then I remember sitting on the stool in front of the hall phone, asking weakly for Joyce's number. Joyce was not home. I was told by her mother (a rather rattlebrained woman, who didn't seem to notice a thing the matter—for which I felt weakly, mechanically grateful) that she was at Kay Stringer's house. I didn't know Kay's number so I just asked the operator; I felt I couldn't risk looking down at the telephone book.

Kay Stringer was not a friend of mine but a new friend of Joyce's. She had a vague reputation for wildness and a long switch of hair, very oddly, though naturally, coloured—from soap-yellow to caramel-brown. She knew a lot of boys more exciting than Martin Collingwood, boys who had quit school or been imported into town to play on the hockey team. She and Joyce rode around in these boys' cars, and sometimes went with them—having lied of course to their mothers—to the Gay-la dance hall on the highway north of town.

I got Joyce on the phone. She was very keyed-up, as she always was with boys around, and she hardly seemed to hear what I was saying.

"Oh, I can't tonight," she said. "Some kids are here. We're going to play cards. You know Bill Kline? He's here. Ross Armour—"

"I'm *sick*," I said trying to speak distinctly; it came out an inhuman croak. "I'm *drunk*. Joyce!" Then I fell off the stool and the receiver dropped out of my hand and banged for a while dismally against the wall.

I had not told Joyce where I was, so after thinking about it for a moment she phoned my mother, and using the elaborate and unnecessary subterfuge that young girls delight in, she found out. She and Kay and the boys—there were three of them—told some story about where they were going to Kay's mother, and got into the car and drove out. They found me still lying on the broadloom carpet in the hall; I had been sick again, and this time I had not made it to the bathroom.

It turned out that Kay Stringer, who arrived on this scene only by accident, was exactly the person I needed. She loved a crisis, particularly one like this, which had a shady and scandalous aspect and which must be kept secret from the adult world. She became excited, aggressive, efficient; that energy which was termed wildness was simply the overflow of a great female instinct to manage, comfort and control. I could hear her voice coming at me from all directions, telling me not to worry, telling Joyce to find the biggest coffeepot they had and make it full of coffee (*strong* coffee, she said), telling the boys to pick me up and carry me to the sofa. Later, in the fog beyond my reach, she was calling for a scrub-brush.

Then I was lying on the sofa, covered with some kind of crocheted throw they had found in the bedroom. I didn't want to lift my head. The house was full of the smell of coffee. Joyce came in, looking very pale; she said that the Berryman kids had wakened up but she had given them a cookie and told them to go back to bed, it was all right; she hadn't let them out of their room and she didn't believe they'd remember. She said that she and Kay had cleaned up the bathroom and the hall though she was afraid there was still a spot on the rug. The coffee was ready. I didn't understand anything very well. The boys had turned on the radio and were going through the Berryman's record collection; they had it out on the floor. I felt there was something odd about this but I could not think what it was.

Kay brought me a huge breakfast mug full of coffee.

"I don't know if I can," I said. "Thanks."

"Sit up," she said briskly, as if dealing with drunks was an everyday business for her, I had no need to feel myself important. (I met, and recognized, that tone of voice years later, in the maternity ward.) "Now drink," she said. I drank, and at the same time realized that I was wearing only my slip. Joyce and Kay had taken off my blouse and skirt. They had brushed off the skirt and washed out the blouse, since it was nylon; it was hanging in the bathroom. I pulled the throw up under my arms and Kay laughed. She got everybody coffee. Joyce brought in the coffeepot and on Kay's instructions she kept filling my cup whenever I drank from it. Somebody said to me with interest. "You must have really wanted to tie one one."

"No," I said rather sulkily, obediently drinking my coffee. "I only had two drinks."

Kay laughed, "Well it certainly gets to you, I'll say that. What time do you expect *they*'ll be back?" she said.

"Late. After one I think."

"You should be all right by that time. Have some more coffee."

Kay and one of the boys began dancing to the radio. Kay danced very sexily, but her face had the gently superior and indulgent, rather cold look it had when she was lifting me up to drink the coffee. The boy was whispering to her and she was smiling, shaking her head. Joyce said she was hungry, and she went out to the kitchen to see what there was—potato chips or crackers, or something like that, that you could eat without making too noticeable a dint. Bill Kline came over and sat on the sofa beside me and patted my legs through the crocheted throw. He didn't say anything to me, just patted my legs and looked at me with what seemed to me a very stupid, half-sick, absurd and alarming expression. I felt very uncomfortable; I wondered how it had ever got around that Bill Kline was so good looking, with an expression like that. I moved my legs nervously and he gave me a look of contempt, not ceasing to pat me. Then I scrambled off the sofa, pulling the throw around me, with the idea of going to the bathroom to see if my blouse was dry. I lurched a little when I started to walk, and for some reason—probably to show Bill Kline that he had not panicked me—I immediately exaggerated this, and calling out, "Watch me walk a straight line!" I lurched and stumbled, to the accompaniment of everyone's laughter, towards the hall. I was standing in the archway between the hall and the living room when the knob of the front door turned with a small matter-of-fact click and everything became silent behind me except the radio of course and the crocheted throw inspired by some delicate malice of its own slithered down around my feet and there—oh, delicious moment in a well-organized farce!—there stood the Berrymans, Mr. and Mrs., with expressions on their faces as appropriate to the occasion as any old-fashioned director of farces could wish. They must have been preparing those expressions, of course; they could not have produced them in the first moment of shock; with the noise we were making, they had no doubt heard us as soon as they got out of the car; for the same reason, we had not heard them. I don't think I ever knew what brought them home so early—a headache, an argument—and I was not really in a position to ask.

Mr. Berryman drove me home. I don't remember how I got into that car, or how I found my clothes and put them on, or what kind of a good-night, if any, I said to Mrs. Berryman. I don't remember what happened to my friends, though I imagine they gathered up their coats and fled, covering up the ignominy of their departure with a mechanical roar of defiance. I remember Joyce with a box of crackers in her hand, saying that I had become terribly sick from eating—I think she said *sauerkraut*—for supper, and that I had called them for help. (When I asked her later what they made of this she said, "It wasn't any use. You *reeked.*") I remember also her saying, "Oh, no, Mr. Berryman I beg of you, my mother is a terribly nervous person I don't know what the shock might do to her. I will go down on my knees to you if you like but *you must not phone my mother.*" I have no picture of her down on her knees—and she would have done it in a minute—so it seems this threat was not carried out.

Mr. Berryman said to me, "Well I guess you know your behavior tonight is a pretty serious thing." He made it sound as if I might be charged with criminal negligence or something worse. "It would be very wrong of me to overlook it," he said. I suppose that besides being angry and disgusted with *me,* he was worried about taking me home in this condition to my strait-laced parents, who could always say I got the liquor in his house. Plenty of Temperance people would think that enough to hold him responsible, and the town was full of Temperance people. Good relations with the town were very important to him from a business point of view.

"I have an idea it wasn't the first time," he said. "If it was the first time, would a girl be smart enough to fill three bottles up with water? No. Well in this case, she *was* smart enough, but not smart enough to know I could spot it. What do you say to that?" I opened my mouth to answer and although I was feeling quite sober the only sound that came out was a loud, desolate-sounding giggle. He stopped in front of our house. "Light's on," he said. "Now go in and tell your parents the straight truth. And if you don't, remember I will." He did not mention paying me for my baby-sitting services of the evening and the subject did not occur to me either.

I went into the house and tried to go straight upstairs but my mother called to me. She came into the front hall, where I had not turned on the light, and she must have smelled me at once for she ran forward with a cry of pure amazement, as if she had seen somebody falling, and caught me by the shoulders as I did indeed fall down against the bannister, overwhelmed by my fantastic lucklessness, and I told her everything from the start, not omitting even the name of Martin Collingwood and my flirtation with the aspirin bottle, which was a mistake.

On Monday morning my mother took the bus over to Baileyville and found the liquor store and bought a bottle of Scotch whisky. Then she had to wait for a bus back, and she met some people she knew and she was not quite able to hide the bottle in her bag; she was furious with herself for not bringing a proper shopping-bag. As soon as she got back she walked out to the Berrymans'; she had not even had lunch. Mr. Berryman had not gone back to the factory. My mother went in and had a talk with both of them and made an excellent impression and then Mr. Berryman drove her home. She talked to them in the forthright and unemotional way she had, which was always agreeably surprising to people prepared to deal with a mother, and she told them that although I seemed to do well enough at school I was extremely backward—or perhaps eccentric—in my emotional development. I imagine that this analysis of my behavior was especially effective with Mrs. Berryman, a great reader of Child Guidance books. Relations between them warmed to the point where my mother brought up a specific instance of my difficulties, and disarmingly related the whole story of Martin Collingwood.

Within a few days it was all over town and the school that I had tried to commit suicide over Martin Collingwood. But it was already all over school and the town that the Berrymans had come home on Saturday night to find me drunk, staggering, wearing nothing but my slip, in a room with three boys, one of whom was Bill Kline. My mother had said that I was to pay for the bottle she had taken the Berrymans out of my baby-sitting earnings, but my clients melted away like the last April snow, and it would not be paid for yet if newcomers to town had not moved in across the street in July, and needed a baby sitter before they talked to any of their neighbours.

My mother also said that it had been a great mistake to let me go out with boys and that I would not be going out again until well after my sixteenth birthday, if then. This did not prove to be a concrete hardship at all, because it was at least that long before anybody asked me. If you think that news of the Berrymans adventure would put me in demand for whatever gambols and orgies were going on in and around that town, you could not be more mistaken. The extraordinary publicity which attended my first debauch may have made me seemed marked for a special kind of ill luck, like the girl whose illegitimate baby turns out to be triplets: nobody wants to have anything to do with her. At any rate I had at the same time one of the most silent telephones and positively the most sinful reputation in the whole High School. I had to put up with this until the next fall, when a fat blonde girl in Grade Ten ran away with a married man and was picked up two months later, living in sin—though not with the same man—in the city of Sault Ste. Marie. Then everybody forgot about me.

But there was a positive, a splendidly unexpected, result of this affair: I got completely over Martin Collingwood. It was not only that he at once said, publicly, that he had always thought I was a nut; where he was concerned I had no pride, and my tender fancy could have found a way around that, a month, a week, before. What was it that brought me back into the world again? It was the terrible and fascinating reality of my disaster; it was *the way things happened.* Not that I enjoyed it; I was a self-conscious girl and I suffered a good deal from all this exposure. But the development of events on that Saturday night—that fascinated me; I felt that I had had a glimpse of the shameless, marvelous, shattering absurdity with which the plots of life, though not of fiction, are improvised. I could not take my eyes off it.

And of course Martin Collingwood wrote his Senior Matric that June, and went away to the city to take a course at a school for Morticians, as I think it is called, and when he came back he went into his uncle's undertaking business. We lived in the same town and we would hear most things that happened to each other but I do not think we met face to face or saw one another, except at a distance, for years. I went to a shower for the girl he married, but then everybody went to everybody else's showers. No, I do not think I really saw him again until I came home after I had been married several years, to attend a relative's funeral. Then I saw him; not quite Mr. Darcy but still very nice-looking in those black clothes. And I saw him looking over at me with an expression as close to a reminiscent smile as the occasion would permit, and I knew that he had been surprised by a memory either of my devotion or my little buried catastrophe. I gave him a gentle uncomprehending look in return. I am a grown-up woman now; let him unbury his own catastrophes.

QUESTIONS

1. How much time has passed since the events narrated? How do you know?
2. Would the story have been as effective if told not long after it happened, by a girl who was still a teenager? Why or why not?
3. "But ignorance, my mother said, ignorance, or innocence if you like, is not always such a fine thing as people think and I am not sure it may not be dangerous for a girl like you": Is the mother right? What is cured in this story?

CHAPTER 3

THE NARRATOR AS OBSERVER

Sometimes the first-person narrator is less participant than observer. The story happens to someone else. The narrator may be a friend, a relative, a member of the community at the time of the event, or one who heard a story that happened long ago and now repeats it. As readers, we are interested in the story. What happened to the protagonist? But we are also interested in the narrator. Who tells the story? The narrator's voice and personality color the story even when the narrator is not a major participant.

In creating the story, the author had a choice. The events might have been told by one of the people most directly involved, the narrator as participant. Shifting from the narrative perspective of a participant to that of an observer forces a shift in the reader's focus. Experiencing the story at one remove from the understanding and emotions of the primary participants, we now have to consider the understanding and emotions of an onlooker. Again we may enjoy a continuous dramatic irony as the observer's report reveals more than he or she understands or intends to convey.

Reading Ring Lardner's "Haircut," we do not see Jim Kendall the way the narrator does. What does the narrator reveal about himself as he tells his story about Jim?

HAIRCUT

Ring Lardner   (1885–1933)

I got another barber that comes over from Carterville and helps me out Saturdays, but the rest of the time I can get along all right alone. You can see for yourself that this ain't no New York City and besides that, the most of the boys works all day and don't have no leisure to drop in here and get themselves prettied up.

You're a newcomer, ain't you? I thought I hadn't seen you round before. I hope you like it good enough to stay. As I say, we ain't no New York City or Chicago, but we have pretty good times. Not as good, though, since Jim Kendall got killed. When he was alive, him and Hod Meyers used to keep this town in an uproar. I bet they was more laughin' done here than any town its size in America.

Jim was comical, and Hod was pretty near a match for him. Since Jim's gone, Hod tries to hold his end up just the same as ever, but it's tough goin' when you ain't got nobody to kind of work with.

They used to be plenty fun in here Saturdays. This place is jam-packed Saturdays, from four o'clock on. Jim and Hod would show up right after their supper, round six o'clock. Jim would set himself down in that big chair, nearest the blue spittoon. Whoever had been settin' in that chair, why they'd get up when Jim come in and give it to him.

You'd of thought it was a reserved seat like they have sometimes in a theayter. Hod would generally always stand or walk up and down, or some Saturdays, of course, he'd be settin' in this chair part of the time, gettin' a haircut.

Well, Jim would set there a w'ile without openin' his mouth only to spit, and then finally he'd say to me, "Whitey,"—my right name, that is, my right first name, is Dick, but everybody round here calls me Whitey—Jim would say, "Whitey, your nose looks like a rosebud tonight. You must of been drinkin' some of your aw de cologne."

So I'd say, "No, Jim, but you look like you'd been drinkin' somethin' of that kind or somethin' worse."

Jim would have to laugh at that, but then he'd speak up and say, "No, I ain't had nothin' to drink, but that ain't sayin' I wouldn't like somethin'. I wouldn't even mind if it was wood alcohol."

Then Hod Meyers would say, "Neither would your wife." That would set everybody to laughin' because Jim and his wife wasn't on very good terms. She'd of divorced him only they wasn't no chance to get alimony and she didn't have no way to take care of herself and the kids. She couldn't never understand Jim. He *was* kind of rough, but a good fella at heart.

Him and Hod had all kinds of sport with Milt Sheppard. I don't suppose you've seen Milt. Well, he's got an Adam's apple that looks more like a mushmelon. So I'd be shavin' Milt and when I'd start to shave down here on his neck, Hod would holler, "Hey, Whitey, wait a minute! Before you cut into it, let's make up a pool and see who can guess closest to the number of seeds."

And Jim would say, "If Milt hadn't of been so hoggish, he'd of ordered a half a cantaloupe instead of a whole one and it might not of stuck in his throat."

All the boys would roar at this and Milt himself would force a smile, though the joke was on him. Jim certainly was a card!

There's his shavin' mug, settin' on the shelf, right next to Charley Vail's. "Charles M. Vail." That's the druggist. He comes in regular for his shave, three times a week. And Jim's is the cup next to Charley's. "James H. Kendall." Jim won't need no shavin' mug no more, but I'll leave it there just the same for old time's sake. Jim certainly was a character!

Years ago, Jim used to travel for a canned goods concern over in Carterville. They sold canned goods. Jim had the whole northern half of the State and was on the road five days out of every week. He'd drop in here Saturdays and tell his experiences for that week. It was rich.

I guess he paid more attention to playin' jokes than makin' sales. Finally the concern let him out and he come right home here and told everybody he'd been fired instead of sayin' he'd resigned like most fellas would of.

It was a Saturday and the shop was full and Jim got up out of that chair and says, "Gentlemen, I got an important announcement to make. I been fired from my job."

Well, they asked him if he was in earnest and he said he was and nobody could think of nothin' to say till Jim finally broke the ice himself. He says, "I been sellin' canned goods and now I'm canned goods myself."

You see, the concern he'd been workin' for was a factory that made canned goods. Over in Carterville. And now Jim said he was canned himself. He was certainly a card!

Jim had a great trick that he used to play w'ile he was travelin'. For instance, he'd be ridin' on a train and they'd come to some little town like, well, like, we'll say, like Benton. Jim would look out the train window and read the signs on the stores.

For instance, they'd be a sign, "Henry Smith, Dry Goods." Well, Jim would write down the name and the name of the town and when he got to wherever he was goin' he'd mail back a postal card to Henry Smith at Benton and not sign no name to it, but he'd write on the card, well, somethin' like "Ask your wife about that book agent that spent the afternoon last week," or "Ask your Missus who kept her from gettin' lonesome the last time you was in Carterville." And he'd sign the card, "A Friend."

Of course, he never knew what really come of none of these jokes, but he could picture what *probably* happened and that was enough.

Jim didn't work very steady after he lost his position with the Carterville people. What he did earn, doin' odd jobs round town, why he spent pretty near all of it on gin and his family might of starved if the stores hadn't of carried them along. Jim's wife tried her hand at dressmakin', but they ain't nobody goin' to get rich makin' dresses in this town.

As I say, she'd of divorced Jim, only she seen that she couldn't support herself and the kids and she was always hopin' that some day Jim would cut out his habits and give her more than two or three dollars a week.

They was a time when she would go to whoever he was workin' for and ask them to give her his wages, but after she done this once or twice, he beat her to it by borrowin' most of his pay in advance. He told it all round town, how he had outfoxed his Missus. He certainly was a caution!

But he wasn't satisfied with just outwittin' her. He was sore the way she had acted, tryin' to grab off his pay. And he made up his mind he'd get even. Well, he waited till Evans's Circus was advertised to come to town. Then he told his wife and two kiddies that he was goin' to take them to the circus. The day of the circus, he told them he would get the tickets and meet them outside the entrance to the tent.

Well, he didn't have no intentions of bein' there or buyin' tickets or nothin'. He got full of gin and laid round Wright's poolroom all day. His wife and the kids waited and waited and of course he didn't show up. His wife didn't have a dime with her, or nowhere else, I guess. So she finally had to tell the kids it was all off and they cried like they wasn't never goin' to stop.

Well, it seems, w'ile they was cryin', Doc Stair came along and he asked what was the matter, but Mrs. Kendall was stubborn and wouldn't tell him, but the kids told him and he insisted on takin' them and their mother in the show. Jim found this out afterwards and it was one reason why he had it in for Doc Stair.

Doc Stair come here about a year and a half ago. He's a mighty handsome young fella and his clothes always look like he has them made to order. He goes to Detroit two or three times a year and w'ile he's there he must have a tailor take his measure and then make him a suit to order. They cost pretty near twice as much, but they fit a whole lot better than if you just bought them in a store.

For a w'ile everybody was wonderin' why a young doctor like Doc Stair should come to a town like this where we already got old Doc Gamble and Doc Foote that's both been here for years and all the practice in town was always divided between the two of them.

Then they was a story got round that Doc Stair's gal had throwed him over, a gal up in the Northern Peninsula somewheres, and the reason he come here was to hide himself away and forget it. He said himself that he thought they wasn't nothin' like general practice in a place like ours to fit a man to be a good all round doctor. And that's why he'd came.

Anyways, it wasn't long before he was makin' enough to live on, though they tell me that he never dunned nobody for what they owed him, and the folks here certainly has got the owin' habit, even in my business. If I had all that was comin' to me for just shaves alone, I could go to Carterville and put up at the Mercer for a week and see a different picture every night. For instance, they's old George Purdy—but I guess I shouldn't ought to be gossipin'.

Well, last year, our coroner died, died of the flu. Ken Beatty, that was his name. He was the coroner. So they had to choose another man to be coroner in his place and they picked Doc Stair. He laughed at first and said he didn't want it, but they made him take it. It ain't no job that anybody would fight for and what a man makes out of it in a year would just about buy seeds for their garden. Doc's the kind, though, that can't say no to nothin' if you keep at him long enough.

But I was goin' to tell you about a poor boy we got here in town—Paul Dickson. He fell out of a tree when he was about ten years old. Lit on his head and it done somethin' to him and he ain't never been right. No harm in him, but just silly. Jim Kendall used to call him cuckoo; that's a name Jim had for anybody that was off their head, only he called people's head their bean. That was another of his gags, callin' head bean and callin' crazy people cuckoo. Only poor Paul ain't crazy, but just silly.

You can imagine that Jim used to have all kinds of fun with Paul. He'd send him to the White Front Garage for a left-handed monkey wrench. Of course they ain't no such a thing as a left-handed monkey wrench.

And once we had a kind of a fair here and they was a baseball game between the fats and the leans and before the game started Jim called Paul over and sent him way down to Schrader's hardware store to get a key for the pitcher's box.

They wasn't nothin' in the way of gags that Jim couldn't think up, when he put his mind to it.

Poor Paul was always kind of suspicious of people, maybe on account of how Jim had kept foolin' him. Paul wouldn't have much to do with anybody only his own mother and Doc Stair and a girl here in town named Julie Gregg. That is, she ain't a girl no more, but pretty near thirty or over.

When Doc first come to town, Paul seemed to feel like here was a real friend and he hung round Doc's office most of the w'ile; the only time he wasn't there was when he'd go home to eat or sleep or when he seen Julie Gregg doin' her shoppin'.

When he looked out Doc's window and seen her, he'd run downstairs and join her and tag along with her to the different stores. The poor boy was crazy about Julie and she always treated him mighty nice and made him feel like he was welcome, though of course it wasn't nothin' but pity on her side.

Doc done all he could to improve Paul's mind and he told me once that he really thought the boy was gettin' better, that they was times when he was as bright and sensible as anybody else.

But I was goin' to tell you about Julie Gregg. Old Man Gregg was in the lumber business, but got to drinkin' and lost the most of his money and when he died, he didn't leave nothin' but the house and just enough insurance for the girl to skimp along on.

Her mother was a kind of a half invalid and didn't hardly ever leave the house. Julie wanted to sell the place and move somewheres else after the old man died, but the mother said she was born here and would die here. It was tough on Julie, as the young people round this town—well, she's too good for them.

She's been away to school and Chicago and New York and different places and they ain't no subject she can't talk on, where you take the rest of the young folks here and you mention anything to them outside of Gloria Swanson or Tommy Meighan and they think you're delirious. Did you see Gloria in Wages of Virtue? You missed somethin'!

Well, Doc Stair hadn't been here more than a week when he come in one day to get shaved and I recognized who he was as he had been pointed out to me, so I told him about my old lady. She's been ailin' for a couple of years and either Doc Gamble or Doc Foote, neither one, seemed to be helpin' her. So he said he would come out and see her, but if she was able to get out herself, it would be better to bring her to his office where he could make a completer examination.

So I took her to his office and w'ile I was waitin' for her in the reception room, in come Julie Gregg. When somebody comes in Doc Stair's office, they's a bell that rings in his inside office so as he can tell they's somebody to see him.

So he left my old lady inside and come out to the front office and that's the first time him and Julie met and I guess it was what they call love at first sight. But it wasn't fifty-fifty. This young fella was the slickest lookin' fella she'd ever seen in this town and she went wild over him. To him she was just a young lady that wanted to see the doctor.

She'd came on about the same business I had. Her mother had been doctorin' for years with Doc Gamble and Doc Foote and without no results. So she'd heard they was a new doc in town and decided to give him a try. He promised to call and see her mother that same day.

I said a minute ago that it was love at first sight on her part. I'm not only judgin' by how she acted afterwards but how she looked at him that first day in his office. I ain't no mind reader, but it was wrote all over her face that she was gone.

Now Jim Kendall, besides bein' a jokesmith and a pretty good drinker, well, Jim was quite a lady-killer. I guess he run pretty wild durin' the time he was on the road for them Carterville people, and besides that, he'd had a couple little affairs of the heart right here in town. As I say, his wife could of divorced him, only she couldn't.

But Jim was like the majority of men, and women, too, I guess. He wanted what he couldn't get. He wanted Julie Gregg and worked his head off tryin' to land her. Only he'd of said bean instead of head.

Well, Jim's habits and his jokes didn't appeal to Julie and of course he was a married man, so he didn't have no more chance than, well, than a rabbit. That's an expression of Jim's himself. When somebody didn't have no chance to get elected or somethin', Jim would always say they didn't have no more chance than a rabbit.

He didn't make no bones about how he felt. Right in here, more than once, in front of the whole crowd, he said he was stuck on Julie and anybody that could get her for him was welcome to his house and his wife and kids included. But she wouldn't have nothin' to do with him; wouldn't even speak to him on the street. He finally seen he wasn't gettin' nowheres with his usual line so he decided to try the rough stuff. He went right up to her house one evenin' and when she opened the door he forced his way in and grabbed her. But she broke loose and before he could stop her, she run in the next room and locked the door and phoned to Joe Barnes. Joe's the marshal. Jim could hear who she was phonin' to and he beat it before Joe got there.

Joe was an old friend of Julie's pa. Joe went to Jim the next day and told him what would happen if he ever done it again.

I don't know how the news of this little affair leaked out. Chances is that Joe Barnes told his wife and she told somebody else's wife and they told their husband. Anyways, it did leak out and Hod Meyers had the nerve to kid Jim about it, right here in this shop. Jim didn't deny nothin' and kind of laughed it off and said for us all to wait, that lots of people had tried to make a monkey out of him, but he always got even.

Meanw'ile everybody in town was wise to Julie's bein' wild mad over the Doc. I don't suppose she had any idear how her face changed when him and her was together; of course she couldn't of, or she'd of kept away from him. And she didn't know that we was all noticin' how many times she made excuses to go up to his office or pass it on the other side of the street and look up in his window to see if he was there. I felt sorry for her and so did most other people.

Hod Meyers kept rubbin' it into Jim about how the Doc had cut him out. Jim didn't pay no attention to the kiddin' and you could see he was plannin' one of his jokes.

One trick Jim had was the knack of changin' his voice. He could make you think he was a girl talkin' and he could mimic any man's voice. To show you how good he was along this line, I'll tell you the joke he played on me once.

You know, in most towns of any size, when a man is dead and needs a shave, why the barber that shaves him soaks him five dollars for the job; that is, he don't soak *him,* but whoever ordered the shave. I just charge three dollars because personally I don't mind much shavin' a dead person. They lay a whole lot stiller than live customers. The only thing is that you don't feel like talkin' to them and you get kind of lonesome.

Well, about the coldest day we ever had here, two years ago last winter, the phone rung at the house w'ile I was home to dinner and I answered the phone and it was a woman's voice and she said she was Mrs. John Scott and her husband was dead and would I come out and shave him.

Old John had always been a good customer of mine. But they live seven miles out in the country, on the Streeter road. Still I didn't see how I could say no.

So I said I would be there, but would have to come in a jitney and it might cost three or four dollars besides the price of the shave. So she, or the voice, it said that was all right, so I got Frank Abbott to drive me out to the place and when I got there, who should open the door but old John himself! He wasn't no more dead than, well, than a rabbit.

It didn't take no private detective to figure out who had played me this little joke. Nobody could of thought it up but Jim Kendall. He certainly was a card!

I tell you this incident just to show you how he could disguise his voice and make you believe it was somebody else talkin'. I'd of swore it was Mrs. Scott had called me. Anyways, some woman.

Well, Jim waited till he had Doc Stair's voice down pat; then he went after revenge.

He called Julie up on a night when he knew Doc was over in Carterville. She never questioned but what it was Doc's voice. Jim said he must see her that night; he couldn't wait no longer to tell her somethin'. She was all excited and told him to come to the house. But he said he was expectin' an important long distance call and wouldn't she please forget her manners for once and come to his office. He said they couldn't nothin' hurt her and nobody would see her and he just *must* talk to her a little w'ile. Well, poor Julie fell for it.

Doc always keeps a night light in his office, so it looked to Julie like they was somebody there.

Meanw'ile Jim Kendall had went to Wright's poolroom, where they was a whole gang amusin' themselves. The most of them had drank plenty of gin, and they was a rough bunch even when sober. They was always strong for Jim's jokes and when he told them to come with him and see some fun they give up their card games and pool games and followed along.

Doc's office is on the second floor. Right outside his door they's a flight of stairs leadin' to the floor above. Jim and his gang hid in the dark behind these stairs.

Well, Julie come up to Doc's door and rung the bell and they was nothin' doin'. She rung it again and she rung it seven or eight times. Then she tried the door and found it locked. Then Jim made some kind of a noise and she heard it and waited a minute, and then she says, "Is that you, Ralph?" Ralph is Doc's first name.

They was no answer and it must of came to her all of a sudden that she'd been bunked. She pretty near fell downstairs and the whole gang after her. They chased her all the way home, hollerin', "Is that you, Ralph?" and "Oh, Ralphie, dear, is that you?" Jim says he couldn't holler it himself, as he was laughin' too hard.

Poor Julie! She didn't show up here on Main Street for a long, long time afterward.

And of course Jim and his gang told everybody in town, everybody but Doc Stair. They was scared to tell him, and he might of never knowed only for Paul Dickson. The poor cuckoo, as Jim called him, he was here in the shop one night when Jim was still gloatin' yet over what he'd done to Julie. And Paul took in as much of it as he could understand and he run to Doc with the story.

It's a cinch Doc went up in the air and swore he'd make Jim suffer. But it was a kind of a delicate thing, because if it got out that he had beat Jim up, Julie was bound to hear of it and then she'd know that Doc knew and of course knowin' that he knew would make it worse for her than ever. He was goin' to do somethin', but it took a lot of figurin'.

Well, it was a couple days later when Jim was here in the shop again, and so was the cuckoo. Jim was goin' duck-shootin' the next day and had come in lookin' for Hod Meyers to go with him. I happened to know that Hod had went over to Carterville and wouldn't be home till the end of the week. So Jim said he hated to go alone and he guessed he would call it off. Then poor Paul spoke up and said if Jim would take him he would go along. Jim thought a w'ile and then he said, well, he guessed a half-wit was better than nothin'.

I suppose he was plottin' to get Paul out in the boat and play some joke on him, like pushin' him in the water. Anyways, he said Paul could go. He asked him had he ever shot a duck and Paul said no, he'd never even had a gun in his hands. So Jim said he could set in the boat and watch him and if he behaved himself, he might lend him his gun for a couple of shots. They made a date to meet in the mornin' and that's the last I seen of Jim alive.

Next mornin', I hadn't been open more than ten minutes when Doc Stair come in. He looked kind of nervous. He asked me had I seen Paul Dickson. I said no, but I knew where he was, out duck-shootin' with Jim Kendall. So Doc says that's what he had heard, and he couldn't understand it because Paul had told him he wouldn't never have no more to do with Jim as long as he lived.

He said Paul had told him about the joke Jim had played on Julie. He said Paul had asked him what he thought of the joke and the Doc had told him that anybody that would do a thing like that ought not to be let live.

I said it had been a kind of a raw thing, but Jim just couldn't resist no kind of a joke, no matter how raw. I said I thought he was all right at heart, but just bubblin' over with mischief. Doc turned and walked out.

At noon he got a phone call from old John Scott. The lake where Jim and Paul had went shootin' is on John's place. Paul had came runnin' up to the house a few minutes before and said they'd been an accident. Jim had shot a few ducks and then give the gun to Paul and told him to try his luck. Paul hadn't never handled a gun and he was nervous. He was shakin' so hard that he couldn't control the gun. He let fire and Jim sunk back in the boat, dead.

Doc Stair, bein' the coroner, jumped in Frank Abbott's flivver and rushed out to Scott's farm. Paul and old John was down on the shore of the lake. Paul had rowed the boat to shore, but they'd left the body in it, waitin' for Doc to come.

Doc examined the body and said they might as well fetch it back to town. They was no use leavin' it there or callin' a jury, as it was a plain case of accidental shootin'.

Personally I wouldn't never leave a person shoot a gun in the same boat I was in unless I was sure they knew somethin' about guns. Jim was a sucker to leave a new beginner have his gun, let alone a half-wit. It probably served Jim right, what he got. But still we miss him round here. He certainly was a card!

Comb it wet or dry?

QUESTIONS

1. What does the narrator mean by calling Jim Kendall a "card"?
2. How is the reader's attitude toward Jim different from the narrator's?
3. How does the attitude of Ring Lardner, the author, toward Jim Kendall differ from the attitude of the barber who narrates? Which passages best demonstrate this difference?
4. In what respects is the barber an unreliable narrator?
5. Was Jim's death an accident? Can we be sure?
6. What ironies in the story seem most important to you?
7. How important to this story is the voice of the narrator, his characteristic ways of speaking? How much can we say about him with only his speech mannerisms as evidence?

The events in Miss Emily's story take place at different times over many years. Indeed, because of the manner of telling, we may experience difficulty relating the events to one another in their proper chronological order. Watch for clues.

A ROSE FOR EMILY

William Faulkner   *(1897–1962)*

I

When Miss Emily Grierson died, our whole town went to her funeral: the men through a sort of respectful affection for a fallen monument, the women mostly out of curiosity to see the inside of her house, which no one save an old manservant—a combined gardener and cook—had seen in at least ten years.

It was a big, squarish frame house that had once been white, decorated with cupolas and spires and scrolled balconies in the heavily lightsome style of the seventies, set on what had once been our most select street. But garages and cotton gins had encroached and obliterated even the august names of that neighborhood; only Miss Emily's house was left, lifting its stubborn and coquettish decay above the cotton wagons and the gasoline pumps—an eyesore among eyesores. And now Miss Emily had gone to join the representatives of those august names where they lay in the cedar-bemused cemetery among the ranked and anonymous graves of Union and Confederate soldiers who fell at the battle of Jefferson.

Alive, Miss Emily had been a tradition, a duty, and a care; a sort of hereditary obligation upon the town, dating from that day in 1894 when Colonel Sartoris, the mayor—he who fathered the edict that no Negro woman should appear on the streets without an apron—remitted her taxes, the dispensation dating from the death of her father on into perpetuity. Not that Miss Emily would have accepted charity. Colonel Sartoris invented an involved tale to the effect that Miss Emily's father had loaned money to the town, which the town, as a matter of business, preferred this way of repaying. Only a man of Colonel Sartoris' generation and thought could have invented it, and only a woman could have believed it.

When the next generation, with its more modern ideas, became mayors and aldermen, this arrangement created some little dissatisfaction. On the first of the year they mailed her a tax notice. February came, and there was no reply. They wrote her a formal letter, asking her to call at the sheriff's office at her convenience. A week later the mayor wrote her himself, offering to call or to send his car for her, and received in reply a note on paper of an archaic shape, in a thin, flowing calligraphy in faded ink, to the effect that she no longer went out at all. The tax notice was also enclosed, without comment.

They called a special meeting of the Board of Aldermen. A deputation waited upon her, knocked at the door through which no visitor had passed since she ceased giving china-painting lessons eight or ten years earlier. They were admitted by the old Negro into a dim hall from which a stairway mounted into still more shadow. It smelled of dust and disuse—a close, dank smell. The Negro led them into the parlor. It was furnished in heavy, leather-covered furniture. When the Negro opened the blinds of one window, they could see that the leather was cracked; and when they sat down, a faint dust rose sluggishly about their thighs, spinning with slow motes in the single sun-ray. On a tarnished gilt easel before the fireplace stood a crayon portrait of Miss Emily's father.

They rose when she entered—a small, fat woman in black, with a thin gold chain descending to her waist and vanishing into her belt, leaning on an ebony cane with a tarnished gold head. Her skeleton was small and spare; perhaps that was why what would have been merely plumpness in another was obesity in her. She looked bloated, like a body long submerged in motionless water, and of that pallid hue. Her eyes, lost in the fatty ridges of her face, looked like two small pieces of coal pressed into a lump of dough as they moved from one face to another while the visitors stated their errand.

She did not ask them to sit. She just stood in the door and listened quietly until the spokesman came to a stumbling halt. Then they could hear the invisible watch ticking at the end of the gold chain.

Her voice was dry and cold. "I have no taxes in Jefferson. Colonel Sartoris explained it to me. Perhaps one of you can gain access to the city records and satisfy yourselves."

"But we have. We are the city authorities, Miss Emily. Didn't you get a notice from the sheriff, signed by him?"

"I received a paper, yes," Miss Emily said. "Perhaps he considers himself the sheriff . . . I have no taxes in Jefferson."

"But there is nothing on the books to show that, you see. We must go by the—"

"See Colonel Sartoris. I have no taxes in Jefferson."

"But, Miss Emily—"

"See Colonel Sartoris." (Colonel Sartoris had been dead almost ten years.) "I have no taxes in Jefferson. Tobe!" The Negro appeared. "Show these gentlemen out."

II

So she vanquished them, horse and foot, just as she had vanquished their fathers thirty years before about the smell. That was two years after her father's death and a short time after her sweetheart—the one we believed would marry her—had deserted her. After her father's death she went out very little; after her sweetheart went away, people hardly saw her at all. A few of the ladies had the temerity to call, but were not received, and the only sign of life about the place was the Negro man—a young man then—going in and out with a market basket.

"Just as if a man—any man—could keep a kitchen properly," the ladies said; so they were not surprised when the smell developed. It was another link between the gross, teeming world and the high and mighty Griersons.

A neighbor, a woman, complained to the mayor, Judge Stevens, eighty years old.

"But what will you have me do about it, madam?" he said.

"Why, send her word to stop it," the woman said. "Isn't there a law?"

"I'm sure that won't be necessary," Judge Stevens said. "It's probably just a snake or a rat that nigger of hers killed in the yard. I'll speak to him about it."

The next day he received two more complaints, one from a man who came in diffident deprecation. "We really must do something about it, Judge. I'd be the last one in the world to bother Miss Emily, but we've got to do something." That night the Board of Aldermen met—three graybeards and one younger man, a member of the rising generation.

"It's simple enough," he said. "Send her word to have her place cleaned up. Give her a certain time to do it in, and if she don't . . ."

"Dammit, sir," Judge Stevens said, "will you accuse a lady to her face of smelling bad?"

So the next night, after midnight, four men crossed Miss Emily's lawn and slunk about the house like burglars, sniffing along the base of the brickwork and at the cellar openings while one of them performed a regular sowing motion with his hand out of a sack slung from his shoulder. They broke open the cellar door and sprinkled lime there, and in all the outbuildings. As they recrossed the lawn, a window that had been dark was lighted and Miss Emily sat in it, the light behind her, and her upright torso motionless as that of an idol. They crept quietly across the lawn and into the shadow of the locusts that lined the street. After a week or two the smell went away.

That was when people had begun to feel really sorry for her. People in our town, remembering how old lady Wyatt, her great-aunt, had gone completely crazy at last, believed that the Griersons held themselves a little too high for what they really were. None of the young men were quite good enough for Miss Emily and such. We had long thought of them as a tableau, Miss Emily a slender figure in white in the background, her father a spraddled silhouette in the foreground, his back to her and clutching a horsewhip, the two of them framed by the back-flung front door. So when she got to be thirty and was still single, we were not pleased exactly, but vindicated; even with insanity in the family she wouldn't have turned down all of her chances if they had really materialized.

When her father died, it got about that the house was all that was left to her; and in a way, people were glad. At last they could pity Miss Emily. Being left alone, and a pauper, she had become humanized. Now she too would know the old thrill and the old despair of a penny more or less.

The day after his death all the ladies prepared to call at the house and offer condolence and aid, as is our custom. Miss Emily met them at the door, dressed as usual and with no trace of grief on her face. She told them that her father was not dead. She did that for three days, with the ministers calling on her, and the doctors, trying to persuade her to let them dispose of the body. Just as they were about to resort to law and force, she broke down, and they buried her father quickly.

We did not say she was crazy then. We believed she had to do that. We remembered all the young men her father had driven away, and we knew that with nothing left, she would have to cling to that which had robbed her, as people will.

III

She was sick for a long time. When we saw her again, her hair was cut short, making her look like a girl, with a vague resemblance to those angels in colored church windows—sort of tragic and serene.

The town had just let the contracts for paving the sidewalks, and in the summer after her father's death they began the work. The construction company came with niggers and mules and machinery, and a foreman named Homer Barron, a Yankee—a big, dark, ready man, with a big voice and eyes lighter than his face. The little boys would follow in groups to hear him cuss the niggers, and the niggers singing in time to the rise and fall of picks. Pretty soon he knew everybody in town. Whenever you heard a lot of laughing anywhere about the square, Homer Barron would be in the center of the group. Presently we began to see him and Miss Emily on Sunday afternoons driving in the yellow-wheeled buggy and the matched team of bays from the livery stable.

At first we were glad that Miss Emily would have an interest, because the ladies all said, "Of course a Grierson would not think seriously of a Northerner, a day laborer." But there were still others, older people, who said that even grief could not cause a real lady to forget *noblesse oblige*—without calling it *noblesse oblige.* They just said, "Poor Emily. Her kinsfolk should come to her." She had some kin in Alabama; but years ago her father had fallen out with them over the estate of old lady Wyatt, the crazy woman, and there was no communication between the two families. They had not even been represented at the funeral.

And as soon as the old people said, "Poor Emily," the whispering began. "Do you suppose it's really so?" they said to one another. "Of course it is. What else could . . ." This behind their hands; rustling of craned silk and satin behind jalousies closed upon the sun of Sunday afternoon as the thin, swift clop-clop-clop of the matched team passed: "Poor Emily."

She carried her head high enough—even when we believed that she was fallen. It was as if she demanded more than ever the recognition of her dignity as the last Grierson; as if it had wanted that touch of earthiness to reaffirm her imperviousness. Like when she bought the rat poison, the arsenic. That was over a year after they had begun to say "Poor Emily," and while the two female cousins were visiting her.

"I want some poison," she said to the druggist. She was over thirty then, still a slight woman, though thinner than usual, with cold, haughty black eyes in a face the flesh of which was strained across the temples and about the eyesockets as you imagine a lighthouse-keeper's face ought to look. "I want some poison," she said.

"Yes, Miss Emily. What kind? For rats and such? I'd recom—"

"I want the best you have. I don't care what kind."

The druggist named several. "They'll kill anything up to an elephant. But what you want is—"

"Arsenic," Miss Emily said. "Is that a good one?"

"Is . . . arsenic? Yes, ma'am. But what you want—"

"I want arsenic."

The druggist looked down at her. She looked back at him, erect, her face like a strained flag. "Why, of course," the druggist said. "If that's what you want. But the law requires you to tell what you are going to use it for."

Miss Emily just stared at him, her head tilted back in order to look him eye for eye, until he looked away and went and got the arsenic and wrapped it up. The Negro delivery boy brought her the package; the druggist didn't come back. When she opened the package at home there was written on the box, under the skull and bones: "For rats."

IV

So the next day we all said, "She will kill herself"; and we said it would be the best thing. When she had first begun to be seen with Homer Barron, we had said, "She will marry him." Then we said, "She will persuade him yet," because Homer himself had remarked—he liked men, and it was known that he drank with the younger men in the Elks' Club—that he was not a marrying man. Later we said, "Poor Emily" behind the jalousies as they passed on Sunday afternoon in the glittering buggy, Miss Emily with her head high and Homer Barron with his hat cocked and a cigar in his teeth, reins and whip in a yellow glove.

Then some of the ladies began to say that it was a disgrace to the town and a bad example to the young people. The men did not want to interfere, but at last the ladies forced the Baptist minister—Miss Emily's people were Episcopal—to call upon her. He would never divulge what happened during that interview, but he refused to go back again. The next Sunday they again drove about the streets, and the following day the minister's wife wrote to Miss Emily's relations in Alabama.

So she had blood-kin under her roof again and we sat back to watch developments. At first nothing happened. Then we were sure that they were to be married. We learned that Miss Emily had been to the jeweler's and ordered a man's toilet set in silver, with the letters H. B. on each piece. Two days later we learned that she had bought a complete outfit of men's clothing, including a nightshirt, and we said, "They are married." We were really glad. We were glad because the two female cousins were even more Grierson than Miss Emily had ever been.

So we were not surprised when Homer Barron—the streets had been finished some time since—was gone. We were a little disappointed that there was not a public blowing-off, but we believed that he had gone on to prepare for Miss Emily's coming, or to give her a chance to get rid of the cousins. (By that time it was a cabal, and we were all Miss Emily's allies to help circumvent the cousins.) Sure enough, after another week they departed. And, as we had expected all along, within three days Homer Barron was back in town. A neighbor saw the Negro man admit him at the kitchen door at dusk one evening.

And that was the last we saw of Homer Barron. And of Miss Emily for some time. The Negro man went in and out with the market basket, but the front door remained closed. Now and then we would see her at a window for a moment, as the men did that night when they sprinkled the lime, but for almost six months she did not appear on the streets. Then we knew that this was to be expected too; as if that quality of her father which had thwarted her woman's life so many times had been too virulent and too furious to die.

When we next saw Miss Emily, she had grown fat and her hair was turning gray. During the next few years it grew grayer and grayer until it attained an even pepper-and-salt iron-gray, when it ceased turning. Up to the day of her death at seventy-four it was still that vigorous iron-gray, like the hair of an active man.

From that time on her front door remained closed, save for a period of six or seven years, when she was about forty, during which she gave lessons in china-painting. She fitted up a studio in one of the downstairs rooms, where the daughters and granddaughters of Colonel Sartoris' contemporaries were sent to her with the same regularity and in the same spirit that they were sent to church on Sundays with a twenty-five-cent piece for the collection plate. Meanwhile her taxes had been remitted.

Then the newer generation became the backbone and the spirit of the town, and the painting pupils grew up and fell away and did not send their children to her with boxes of color and tedious brushes and pictures cut from the ladies' magazines. The front door closed upon the last one and remained closed for good. When the town got free postal delivery, Miss Emily alone refused to let them fasten the metal numbers above her door and attach a mailbox to it. She would not listen to them.

Daily, monthly, yearly we watched the Negro grow grayer and more stooped, going in and out with the market basket. Each December we sent her a tax notice, which would be returned by the post office a week later, unclaimed. Now and then we would see her in one of the downstairs windows—she had evidently shut up the top floor of the house—like the carven torso of an idol in a niche, looking or not looking at us, we could never tell which. Thus she passed from generation to generation—dear, inescapable, impervious, tranquil, and perverse.

And so she died. Fell ill in the house filled with dust and shadows, with only a doddering Negro man to wait on her. We did not even know she was sick; we had long since given up trying to get any information from the Negro. He talked to no one, probably not even to her, for his voice had grown harsh and rusty, as if from disuse.

She died in one of the downstairs rooms, in a heavy walnut bed with a curtain, her gray head propped on a pillow yellow and moldy with age and lack of sunlight.

V

The Negro met the first of the ladies at the front door and let them in, with their hushed, sibilant voices and their quick, curious glances, and then he disappeared. He walked right through the house and out the back and was not seen again.

The two female cousins came at once. They held the funeral on the second day, with the town coming to look at Miss Emily beneath a mass of bought flowers, with the crayon face of her father musing profoundly above the bier and the ladies sibilant and macabre; and the very old men—some in their brushed Confederate uniforms—on the porch and the lawn, talking of Miss Emily as if she had been a contemporary of theirs, believing that they had danced with her and courted her perhaps, confusing time with its mathematical progression, as the old do, to whom all the past is not a diminishing road but, instead, a huge meadow which no winter ever quite touches, divided from them now by the narrow bottle-neck of the most recent decade of years.

Already we knew that there was one room in that region above stairs which no one had seen in forty years, and which would have to be forced. They waited until Miss Emily was decently in the ground before they opened it.

The violence of breaking down the door seemed to fill this room with pervading dust. A thin, acrid pall as of the tomb seemed to lie everywhere upon this room decked and furnished as for a bridal: upon the valance curtains of faded rose color, upon the rose-shaded lights, upon the dressing table, upon the delicate array of crystal and the man's toilet things backed with tarnished silver, silver so tarnished that the monogram was obscured. Among them lay a collar and tie, as if they had just been removed, which, lifted, left upon the surface a pale crescent in the dust. Upon a chair hung the suit, carefully folded; beneath it the two mute shoes and the discarded socks.

The man himself lay in the bed.

For a long while we just stood there, looking down at the profound and fleshless grin. The body had apparently once lain in the attitude of an embrace, but now the long sleep that outlasts love, that conquers even the grimace of love, had cuckolded him. What was left of him, rotted beneath what was left of the nightshirt, had become inextricable from the bed in which he lay; and upon him and upon the pillow beside him lay that even coating of the patient and biding dust.

Then we noticed that in the second pillow was the indentation of a head. One of us lifted something from it, and leaning forward, that faint and invisible dust dry and acrid in the nostrils, we saw a long strand of iron-gray hair.

QUESTIONS

1. Why does the narrator always speak of "we," never of "I"? Who are the "we"?
2. Since the teller is indistinct as a character, why did Faulkner choose to create a teller at all?
3. In the fifth paragraph of the story, the narrator describes the interior of Miss Emily's house when it was once visited by "a deputation." Should we assume the narrator was one of the visitors that day? If not, how does he (or she) know what they saw?
4. In the last sentence of the story, "One of us lifted something from" the pillow. Why does the narrator not say who?

5. List the major events of the story in their chronological order, from first to last in time. Why are they not told that way?

6. How much are we told about Emily that helps explain her behavior toward Homer Barron? For example, does her reaction to her father's death, narrated at the end of section II, help? What does the story tell of the society in which she lives that proves useful as we try to understand the reasons for her actions?

The narrator of "The Boarded Window" tells a story that he heard from his grandfather, rather than one observed at first hand, but he has been close enough to the events to have thrown a stone at the cabin where they occurred. He fills out the details with an imaginative grasp akin to that of the omniscient storyteller.

THE BOARDED WINDOW

Ambrose Bierce   *(1842–1914?)*

In 1830, only a few miles away from what is now the great city of Cincinnati, lay an immense and almost unbroken forest. The whole region was sparsely settled by people of the frontier—restless souls who no sooner had hewn fairly habitable homes out of the wilderness and attained to that degree of prosperity which today we should call indigence than impelled by some mysterious impulse of their nature they abandoned all and pushed farther westward, to encounter new perils and privations in the effort to regain the meagre comforts which they had voluntarily renounced. Many of them had already forsaken that region for the remoter settlements, but among those remaining was one who had been of those first arriving. He lived alone in a house of logs surrounded on all sides by the great forest, of whose gloom and silence he seemed a part, for no one had ever known him to smile nor speak a needless word. His simple wants were supplied by the sale or barter of skins of wild animals in the river town, for not a thing did he grow upon the land which, if needful, he might have claimed by right of undisturbed possession. There were evidences of "improvement"—a few acres of ground immediately about the house had once been cleared of its trees, the decayed stumps of which were half concealed by the new growth that had been suffered to repair the ravage wrought by the ax. Apparently the man's zeal for agriculture had burned with a failing flame, expiring in penitential ashes.

The little log house, with its chimney of sticks, its roof of warping clapboards weighted with traversing poles and its "chinking" of clay, had a single door and, directly opposite, a window. The latter, however, was boarded up—nobody could remember a time when it was not. And none knew why it was so closed; certainly not because of the occupant's dislike of light and air, for on those rare occasions when a hunter had passed that lonely spot the recluse had commonly been seen sunning himself on his doorstep if heaven had provided sunshine for his need. I fancy there are few persons living today who ever knew the secret of that window, but I am one, as you shall see.

The man's name was said to be Murlock. He was apparently seventy years old, actually about fifty. Something besides years had had a hand in his aging. His hair and long, full beard were white, his gray, lustreless eyes sunken, his face singularly seamed with wrinkles which appeared to belong to two intersecting systems. In figure he was tall and spare, with a stoop of the shoulders—a burden bearer. I never saw him; these particulars I learned from my grandfather, from whom also I got the man's story when I was a lad. He had known him when living near by in that early day.

One day Murlock was found in his cabin, dead. It was not a time and place for coroners and newspapers, and I suppose it was agreed that he had died from natural causes or I should have been told, and should remember. I know only that with what was probably a sense of the fitness of things the body was buried near the cabin, alongside the grave of his wife, who had preceded him by so many years that local tradition had retained hardly a hint of her existence. That closes the final chapter of this true story—excepting, indeed, the circumstances that many years afterward, in company with an equally intrepid spirit, I penetrated to the place and ventured near enough to the ruined cabin to throw a stone against it, and ran away to avoid the ghost which every well-informed boy thereabout knew haunted the spot. But there is an earlier chapter—that supplied by my grandfather.

When Murlock built his cabin and began laying sturdily about with his ax to hew out a farm—the rifle, meanwhile, his means of support—he was young, strong and full of hope. In that eastern country whence he came he had married, as was the fashion, a young woman in all ways worthy of his honest devotion, who shared the dangers and privations of his lot with a willing spirit and light heart. There is no known record of her name; of her charms of mind and person tradition is silent and the doubter is at liberty to entertain his doubt; but God forbid that I should share it! Of their affection and happiness there is abundant assurance in every added day of the man's widowed life; for what but the magnetism of a blessed memory could have chained that venturesome spirit to a lot like that?

One day Murlock returned from gunning in a distant part of the forest to find his wife prostrate with fever, and delirious. There was no physician within miles, no neighbor; nor was she in a condition to be left, to summon help. So he set about the task of nursing her back to health, but at the end of the third day she fell into unconsciousness and so passed away, apparently, with never a gleam of returning reason.

From what we know of a nature like his we may venture to sketch in some of the details of the outline picture drawn by my grandfather. When convinced that she was dead, Murlock had sense enough to remember that the dead must be prepared for burial. In performance of this sacred duty he blundered now and again, did certain things incorrectly, and others which he did correctly were done over and over. His occasional failures to accomplish some simple and ordinary act filled him with astonishment, like that of a drunken man who wonders at the suspension of familiar natural laws. He was surprised, too, that he did not weep —surprised and a little ashamed; surely it is unkind not to weep for the dead. "Tomorrow," he said aloud, "I shall have to make the coffin and dig the grave; and then I shall miss her, when she is no longer in sight; but now—she is dead, of course, but it is all right—it *must* be all right, somehow. Things cannot be so bad as they seem."

He stood over the body in the fading light, adjusting the hair and putting the finishing touches to the simple toilet, doing all mechanically, with soulless care. And still through his consciousness ran an undersense of conviction that all was right—that he should have her again as before, and everything explained. He had had no experience in grief; his capacity had not been enlarged by use. His heart could not contain it all, nor his imagination rightly conceive it. He did not know he was so hard struck; *that* knowledge would come later, and never go. Grief is an artist of powers as various as the instruments upon which he plays his dirges for the dead, evoking from some the sharpest, shrillest notes, from others the low, grave chords that throb recurrent like the slow beating of a distant drum. Some natures it startles; some it stupefies. To one it comes like the stroke of an arrow, stinging all the sensibilities to a keener life; to another as the blow of a bludgeon, which in crushing benumbs. We may conceive Murlock to have been that way affected, for (and here we are upon surer ground than that of conjecture) no sooner had he finished his pious work than, sinking into a chair by the side of the table upon which the body lay, and noting how white the profile showed in the deepening gloom, he laid his arms upon the table's edge, and dropped his face into them, tearless yet and unutterably weary. At that moment came in through the open window a long, wailing sound like the cry of a lost child in the far deeps of the darkening wood! But the man did not move. Again, and nearer than before, sounded that unearthly cry upon his failing sense. Perhaps it was a wild beast; perhaps it was a dream. For Murlock was asleep.

Some hours later, as it afterward appeared, this unfaithful watcher awoke and lifting his head from his arms intently listened—he knew not why. There in the black darkness by the side of the dead, recalling all without a shock, he strained his eyes to see—he knew not what. His senses were all alert, his breath was suspended, his blood had stilled its tides as if to assist the silence. Who—what had waked him, and where was it?

Suddenly the table shook beneath his arms, and at the same moment he heard, or fancied that he heard, a light, soft step—sounds as of bare feet upon the floor!

He was terrified beyond the power to cry out or move. Perforce he waited— waited there in the darkness through seeming centuries of such dread as one may know, yet live to tell. He tried vainly to speak the dead woman's name, vainly to stretch forth his hand across the table to learn if she were there. His throat was powerless, his arms and hands were like lead. Then occurred something most frightful. Some heavy body seemed hurled against the table with an impetus that pushed it against his breast so sharply as nearly to overthrow him, and at the same instant he heard and felt the fall of something upon the floor with so violent a thump that the whole house was shaken by the impact. A scuffling ensued, and a confusion of sounds impossible to describe. Murlock had risen to his feet. Fear had by excess forfeited control of his faculties. He flung his hands upon the table. Nothing was there!

There is a point at which terror may turn to madness; and madness incites to action. With no definite intent, from no motive but the wayward impulse of a madman, Murlock sprang to the wall, with a little groping seized his loaded rifle, and without aim discharged it. By the flash which lit up the room with a vivid illumination, he saw an enormous panther dragging the dead woman toward the window, its teeth fixed in her throat! Then there were darkness blacker than before, and silence; and when he returned to consciousness the sun was high and the wood vocal with songs of birds.

The body lay near the window, where the beast had left it when frightened away by the flash and report of the rifle. The clothing was deranged, the long hair in disorder, the limbs lay anyhow. From the throat, dreadfully lacerated, had issued a pool of blood not yet entirely coagulated. The ribbon with which he had bound the wrists was broken; the hands were tightly clenched. Between the teeth was a fragment of the animal's ear.

QUESTIONS

1. Since the narrator of Bierce's "The Boarded Window" says he "never saw" Murlock, whose story he tells, how does he know the story?
2. The narrator has seen the cabin with the boarded window and once "ventured near enough . . . to throw a stone against it." What is the effect of his telling us these things?
3. What effects result from Bierce's choice of a narrator whose observations depend upon such limited personal knowledge of the events?
4. From what other perspectives could this story be told? What are the possible effects?

The narrator of "The Boarded Window" tells in detail things he has not witnessed, placing words in Murlock's mouth, revealing the man's inner feelings. In the next story, "King of the Mountain," we encounter a narrator also distanced from the story he tells, as he was a child at the time it happened.

KING OF THE MOUNTAIN

George Garrett   (1929–)

The time is the heart of the Depression and the place is Florida. Not the one you know about with white beaches and palm trees, orange-juice stands and motels, shuffleboards and striptease, amateur and professional, for young and old, all the neon glare and gilt of a carnival. This is at the center of the state where you might as well be a thousand miles from the unlikely ocean in long hot summer days, where in those days truck farmers and small-time ranchers grubbed for a living from the sandy earth or maybe planted and tended orange trees and hoped and sweated through the year for enough rain and, especially in winter, for warm weather, no frost.

Ask me why I pick that time and I'll tell you. There's a whole generation of us now, conceived in that anxious time, and if we're fat now, flash wide advertisement grins at the cockeyed careless world, we know still, deeply as you know the struggles of blood on the long pilgrimage of flesh, the old feel and smell of fear, the gray dimensions of despair, and, too, some of us, the memory of the tug and gnaw of being hungry.

As for the place, it's a place I know. I know the weather, the sights and smells. I have a child's view of it. I know what's happening down at the roots of the grass among the worms and crawlers and I know how a jaybird looks flying in a feathered flash of blue and white like a swift piece of the sky. Thinking about it, time and place, over years and miles, I can still wince with being there. I can see the faces of people who are dead. I know what some of them loved. And I love it still, that time and place, believe it or not, because where you suffered first, acquired your first wounds and scars, is where you've hung your heart once and for all and called it home. . . .

They beat the hell out of him. It was the Fourth of July and the band was playing to the crowd in the heat-stricken park; so loud and near it blared that it drowned out the fury of white shirtsleeves around him. The boy's mother screamed, but he could only see her mouth open and her whole face and lips quivering tautly as if her flesh were elastic. He couldn't hear a sound of her anguish. Some women held her back, but nobody was holding the boy. He saw his father go down amid that flailing of white like a man thrashing in the surf and bobbing under. He came up gasping for air, scattering them every which way, his own white shirt shredded now and his crude, powerful body tense with heavy muscles, using his fists like hammers, his great bald head shining like a polished stone. He went down in the middle of them again, surged up bloody and terrible, roaring above the sound of the band. And, as if in a dance, they came in closer around him, forcing him to earth by the sheer weight of them. Then they kicked and beat him almost to death. When he had stopped moving, twitching, they stepped back in a ragged circle and looked at him silently like a ring of hunters around a fallen beast. Then they scattered into the crowd and the band still played march music.

The women released his mother, and she ran and bent over his fallen father in the long bright curve of her summer holiday dress, fanning him with one of those paper fans that undertakers put out for the ladies on public occasions, for advertising. She just bent over him fanning and nobody paid any attention. He was too big a man for her to move out of the sun by herself. After a little while a Negro came from across the street and together they dragged him under a shade tree. The Negro had a tin cup in his lunch pail and he got some water from the old stone horse trough at the edge of the park and sloshed it over the boy's father.

GEORGE GARRETT / KING OF THE MOUNTAIN   **107**

When the water hit him he shook his head and tried to sit up. He tried to say something through the bloody bubbles of his mouth, couldn't, laid his head back on the ground gently, slowly, like a man settling on a soft pillow to sleep. Then the woman saw her son. She called to the policeman who had been watching from a little distance.

"Take the boy home, Ernie," she said. "At least you can do that."

The policeman took the boy's hand in his own, as if the boy were a little child, and the boy felt the strange sweaty chill of it, but clung to his hand, wouldn't turn loose. He clung to the policeman and kept looking at his mother fanning the fallen man.

"You want a ice-cream cone?" the policeman said. "Sure you do, boy. And I'm going to buy you one."

That sounded like a fine idea, and they turned and walked away from the park together, hand in hand.

Those were bad times then with so little money and people having to claw and wrestle each other for the little there was. It was the time of the Ku Klux Klan in that place. Not those men in sheets, crackpot fanatics, you can joke about now or piously deplore, but a ruthless political machine, a club for the lost and lonely, the embittered and the discontented. They had the county and a lot of the state and they meant to keep what they had. They didn't hate the man. Nothing personal. They were afraid of him. They knew him. He was one of their own, a hard farm boy who had read the law and now was a lawyer in the town, and, being self-educated, he believed in some few things with an unsophisticated tenacity. He had said in public that they were going to have law and order in the county and that the Klan must be swept out of office and authority. He had said they are few and we are the many and we have the vote. So when he went to say it again in a formal speech on the Fourth of July, they met him at the edge of the park and they made a cripple of him. Always after that he had a limp and a cane and the hurt face of a prizefighter.

When he finally came home from the hospital, still bandaged, using his cane, the boy stood shy in the living room next to the upright piano his mother played and watched his father move awkwardly among familiar objects like a stranger.

"What's this?" his father hollered. He was bent over the desk, looking through the drawers.

"What is it?" his mother said from the kitchen.

"I say what's this you've got in the desk drawer?"

And he pulled out of the drawer a shiny pistol and held it loosely in his left hand like a dead thing. His mother came from the kitchen wiping her hands on her apron. As soon as she saw his father standing there with the pistol in his hand she started to cry.

"They almost killed you," she said. "They're liable to kill you next time."

He started to stamp out of the room past her but she snatched at the gun. He pushed her away.

"It's mine," she said. "Let the blame fall on me. I bought it with my own money. I have the right. They might try to do something to me or the boy."

"You know I don't allow no firearms in this house," his father said. "If it wasn't for the boy I'd beat you with my cane."

His mother turned away, hiding her face in the crook of her arm, and he heard his father stamping through the kitchen and, slowly, down the back steps and he heard the banging lid of the garbage can. After that it was very quiet for a moment, so quiet the boy could hear a mockingbird in the backyard, probably in the mulberry tree, making a sound like a cat, and even behind that sound, the hum, not much louder than the sound of a bumblebee, of the colored washwoman in the house next door who always sang and hummed when she ironed. He heard his father then begin to mount the back stairs like a clumsy creature on three legs. When his father spoke in the kitchen his voice was so soft and controlled he might have been the Episcopal minister giving the benediction.

"You don't have to worry," he said. "I'm home now and you don't have to be afraid anymore."

And she saying, "It's too much to ask. I can't go through it again. The women held me and I could have scratched my eyes out of my head rather than to watch anymore."

"And what am I supposed to do? What am I supposed to be? God knows I am not a little boy anymore."

"They hurt you," she said. "My God, how they hurt you."

"They only *confirmed* me," he said. "You could call it the laying on of hands."

"We can go," she said. "Let's move up to Jacksonville. You can practice law there. You can make a good living in Jacksonville and we'll be safe there."

"We're not going anywhere," he said. "I'm going upstairs and lie down for a few days and get a hold of myself. Then I'm going back out on the street and hold up my head."

"I believe in you," she said. "I know you have the strength. But it's so futile, like Samson pulling the roof down on the Philistines."

"If I have to I'll pull the house down on their heads," he answered, laughing the big outdoor laugh that sounded like a wild animal in the dark. "Whoever heard," he said, still laughing, "whoever heard of a baldheaded Samson?"

After his father went up to the bedroom, climbed the flight of stairs painfully, his mother came in from the kitchen and sat down at the piano. She played a couple of little waltz tunes. He knew them, but he liked "The Washington and Lee March" better. She was in the mood for little waltz tunes. She had never liked it in this raw town. She was a lady and her people were different. They had been to Waycross, Georgia, to visit; and he remembered his grandfather, a kind man with a soft voice who always smelled warmly of whiskey and cigars. He stayed in the house, padding about as light-footed as a cat in his bedroom slippers, and he had opened his leather-bound history books and showed the pictures to the boy. He knew how ashamed his mother must feel in this town, remembering the big house and the people there, especially his grandfather.

"All right," he remembered his father shouting at her one night after they had returned. "Make a hero out of him. But just remember this. They would all be in the poorhouse if it wasn't for me. There wouldn't be any big house for you to go and visit and show off to the boy. Oh, he's a fine old gentleman and I do dearly love him, but bear in mind sometimes when he's sitting in his armchair by the fire and talking so well behind the smoke of a twenty-five-cent cigar, so gracefully, that it's my cigar he's smoking. He's a fine old gentleman by grace of me."

"What's the matter, honey?" his mother said, looking away from the bright slick piano keys, stopping in the middle of a tune. "You look so sad, honey boy. Don't you be sad. Everything is going to be all right."

Then she lay her face on the piano keys and started to cry, noiselessly, only her body shaking as if she had fever and chills, and the tears rolling down her cheeks. The boy went outside in the backyard and picked up a stone to make that mockingbird be quiet, but the mockingbird was gone. He climbed up into the mulberry tree and looked all around, as high and proud and lonely as the king of the mountain, and nobody, nobody would dare to come and pull him from his perch.

They had a little dog in those days, a Boston bull, as cute as he was ugly, and smart. He could do all the ordinary tricks like begging, rolling over, and playing dead, but they had taught him a very special one. In the afternoon they'd turn him loose and he'd run all the way downtown to the post office. The clerk would put the mail in his mouth and he'd run straight home to stand at the screen door scratching with his paw until somebody let him in. He never messed up one of the letters. It was called a mighty fine trick and the people around town knew all about it and talked about it. You might find it hard to believe a dog could learn a trick like that. Don't doubt it; I know myself of a dog that a grocer uses to deliver packages in a dogcart.

It hadn't been long after his father came home from the hospital, on a Friday afternoon, when the boy noticed that the dog didn't come back from the post office. He took it for a sign and kept quiet about it. Around suppertime the clerk from the post office came and brought the mail to the house. His father limped out on the front step and took it from him.

"Thanks for the special delivery," his father said. "Did you see my little old dog today?"

"No, sir," the clerk said. "It's the first time I can remember that dog didn't show up."

"That's a remarkable thing," his father said. "How would you account for it?"

The boy stood inside the door, his face pressed against the screen, watching. He could see that the clerk was embarrassed. He wanted to do right but he was scared. And the boy could also tell that his father knew this and he would get the truth out of the man easy. He would have the truth even if the man went down on his knees and begged not to tell.

"I don't know, sir. I don't have any idea. Maybe he just run off."

"Ha! Ha!" his father laughed like a big wind in the man's face. "Oh! Ho! That's funny. After five years all of a sudden the dog gets sick and tired and runs off."

"Well," the man said, "it could have happened."

The boy watched the bulked muscles in his father's body tighten under his shirt and saw him jut his neck forward, thrust his bald, battered head so close to the

man's face they could have kissed. When he spoke now, the boy knew, he would
be staring into the depths of the man's eyes, so deep the man would feel naked,
and when he spoke it would be hardly more than a whisper, but with the tone
of a growl in it, like a dog guarding a bone.

"Now you listen to me," his father said. "I know what happened. They killed
him. I know that much. Now what I want out of you is the truth. That's what
I'm going to get. I'll have the truth from you if I have to gut you like a catfish
from your jaw to your crotch. You understand me?"

"Yes, sir," the man said. "They killed him. Chief of Police shot him right
outside the post office."

"They had a big laugh? That produced a great big laugh?"

"Yes, sir. Chief of Police said he don't allow no mad dogs running loose in
this town. . . ."

"He's a real good shot? He can shoot that pistol like a marksman?"

"Yes, sir."

"Will they give him the distinguished dog-killing medal? Will he cut a big
notch in that .38 and strut his fat ass up and down the sidewalk like a bad man?"

"I don't know, sir. I really don't know what he's going to do."

All of a sudden his father broke into a wide bright smile and slapped the clerk
on the back. The clerk jumped as if he thought he was going to be struck down,
but when he felt the hand soft on his back and the arm around his shoulders he
relaxed. He leaned back on that arm and let it hold him up, like a girl in a man's
arm.

"Well," his father said, "you done right to come here and tell me. It took some
doing what with people waving pistols around and shooting dogs and things.
Come on in and have a cup of coffee. You want a cup of coffee, don't you?"

"Yes, sir," the clerk said. "That would be very nice."

In the morning, Saturday morning, his father was up early, singing in the
bathroom while he shaved. It had been a long time since he had been singing in
the morning. The boy went into the bathroom and stood beside his naked father
watching him shave. Keeping his eyes on the mirror, his father popped a white-
lather beard on the boy's chin with the shaving brush. His father laughed while
the boy wiped his chin with the back of his hand.

"You better watch. You better study," his father said. "One of these days
you'll have a beard to shave. You want to know how to do it right."

"How come you still got hair growing on your face and none on the top of
your head?"

"That, boy, is a mystery," his father said, tipping himself a wink in the mirror.
"If I knew the answer to that question I'd be a millionaire."

"Would you like to be a millionaire?"

"Well, I don't know. I don't have any idea what it's like to be a millionaire.
You might just as well ask me if I'd like to be a jaybird."

"I know what it's like to be a jaybird."

"You do?"

"You got to be mean to be a jaybird."

"But maybe the jaybird don't think he's mean. Maybe he don't know what mean is."

"I never thought of that," the boy said. "A jaybird is smart, though."

"Oh, you can be smart, real smart, and you still can't tell how you're doing something. You can tell most of the time *what* you're doing, but you can't always tell *how* you're doing it or why."

"I always know why I'm doing something."

"You're lucky," his father said.

"It's not so lucky," the boy said. "Sometimes it worries me so much I don't feel like doing anything."

His father laughed and splashed himself with water, rubbed his face hard with a towel until it flushed pink, and then patted some sweet-smelling lotion on his cheeks.

"Looka there, boy," his father said. "I'm as pink as a baby."

The boy went with him into the bedroom to watch his father dress. He dressed as if he were going to the courthouse or the church, the Episcopal church of his mother where people dressed better and walked more softly than the Baptist church where his father's family had always gone. His father put on a dark suit and a white shirt with a gleaming starched collar and a necktie. He wore his best shoes, black ones shined up like patent leather. When he had finished and inspected himself in the mirror, the two of them went downstairs to breakfast.

"Where in the world are you going?" the boy's mother said.

"I thought the boy and I would take a stroll down to the post office and pick up the mail. It comes in the morning on Saturday."

His mother stood by the table like a statue of a woman with a coffeepot in her hand.

"Don't take the boy," she said. "You don't want to do that."

"We're just going to stroll downtown."

"You know what I mean," she said. "Keep the boy out of it."

"No, I don't know what you mean. I just got an idea I'd like to go down and get the mail."

"He don't have to go along. If you have to go downtown, just looking for trouble, let him stay here."

"Ask the boy. Ask him if he want to go or not. You want to go with me?"

He thought about it before he said yes. His mother looked angry but she must have known there was nothing to say, so she poured the coffee and sat down. When they had finished, the boy's father rose from the table and picked up his cane.

"It might be a waste of time," his mother said at the door. "There might not be any mail."

"We'll see about that."

Saturday was the day for county people to come to town, the farmers, the ranchers, the citrus growers, the hired hands and the Negroes from the sawmills and turpentine camps. They came, clogging the highway with trucks and wagons, on foot, the women to pass their time window-shopping and gossiping, the men to lounge in knots and clusters at public places. They leaned against the walls and posts, squatted on their heels, smoked and chewed and spat and studied each other, friends and enemies. Saturday used to be a strutting day, but now there wasn't much to buy in town and no money to buy it with anyway. His father could not have been more conspicuous that day, his shaved face shining in the light, his Sunday clothes vividly crisp. They had started to mount the stairs to the post office.

"Hey, lawyer!"

His father stopped and turned slowly, glanced along the line of farmers who were sitting on the fence by the walk until he found the face that went with the voice, a tall thin long-legged farmer, his clean khaki trousers flapping loosely above high-topped mail-order shoes, his eyes keen and uncommitted.

"What you going to do now, lawyer?"

"Nothing," his father said. "It's up to them. They got to think up something else to do. They tried to kill me with their hands and they couldn't. The best they could do was to cripple me up a little bit."

He let his voice rise as the man swung down from his perch and came forward to the edge of the steps. Others came, one by one, from the fence and the curb and the sidewalk and grouped close to listen. The boy stood in his father's shadow and listened, noticing as he assumed the old pattern of the country speech, the rhythm and tone of it.

"Why, a whole army of them jumped me and tried to kill me but they couldn't. Know why? They forgot something you and I know. They forgot I was a man, a farmer's boy raised here, a real cracker. They thought maybe reading a lawbook had changed my flesh and bones and blood to something soft. You can't kill a man that easy. You can stomp and beat and make a cripple out of him. You can cut and shred him in little pieces and scatter the parts of him like the chaff in the wind, but when you turn your back and wipe your hands all those parts come together and he's standing there ready for a fight."

"Tell them about it!" somebody yelled. "Tell them about it!"

"That's what I'm doing. I'm telling them all about it. Those boys forgot that a man in truth has got nine lives like a cat. I got eight more coming to me. Oh my! Oh my! They found out though. Oh my, didn't they find out?"

"Didn't they?"

"They know now I got blood like turpentine in my veins and two big fists like knotty pine, like cypress knees, and I got a head like a cannon ball. Oh, they found out. They know about it now. And what do you think they done? They was so mad I wouldn't just lay down and curl up and die for them. They was as mad, as all around frustrated as the preacher comes for Sunday dinner and don't get nothing on his plate but the tough old neck of the chicken. They wanted breast and soft meat."

"Keep talking. Tell 'em about it!"

"Why, they just didn't know what to do with theirselves. They didn't know whether to shit or get off the pot. And then, and then, and then an idea come to one of them. They got a plan. Down come the Chief of Po-lice and hid hisself behind that oak tree over there, laying for my dog. There he is trying to hide his fat ass behind a tree and along comes my little old Boston bulldog to pick up the mail, and out pops the Chief of Po-lice. A bang! bang! Shooting at a little old dog. It made him feel good. It made him feel so much better. Oh, yes, none of them could kill a man, but they was brave enough to rise up in righteous indignation and shoot down a puppy dog. Well now, my friends, I'll tell you the honest truth, when I got over being mad about it, I was glad they done it. It showed them up for what they are. What do you think a dog is?"

He leveled his cane and jabbed out with it at the crowd.

"Know what that dog was? He wasn't nothing but a poor little old son of a bitch. And any man that would shoot a dog is lower than a son of a bitch. He's lower than anything in all of God's whole wide creation except a diamondback rattler. And I got my doubts about that. I'll let a diamondback come a-wiggling on his belly in the dust of my backyard before I'll let their Chief of Po-lice come a-hanging around."

The boy stood tense beside his father, looking out into the crowd of faces. It was a big crowd now, out into the street, and his father was shouting out to them. They were bunched together and they swayed with his voice, were moved by the rhythm of his waving cane, as if they were dancing to a tune.

"Man back here says we're blocking the street," a voice called from the street.

"Tell the man to go and get a policeman. I'm going to stay right here. I'm disturbing the peace and I'm going to keep right on disturbing the so-called peace."

His father flung off his hat. It sailed in a wild arc, fell in a flutter like a wounded bird into the crowd. He tore the coat off his shoulders and his white shirt shone in the sunlight when he spread his arms wide.

"I'm bigger than a dog," he yelled. "Ask the policeman can he hit me from the street. Let them kill me now if they're going to because if they don't they must reckon with me. I'll come on and I'll be tearing flesh off of bones and I'll be scattering brains and innards from here to kingdom come!"

"Tell 'em! Tell 'em about it!"

"Ain't nobody going to shoot at you. Keep talking."

"I'm going to tell you all about your Ku Klux Klan. Oh they're a brave bunch, they are, noble shooters of dogs. They come out at night, like thieves in the night, dressed in white sheets like children on Halloween and they spend their time harassing the poor niggers and the poor folks. Poor folks . . . that's all of us, ain't it?"

"Amen. Amen."

"Oh, they're waxing fat and sassy on taxes and who's paying for it? Your sweat, brothers, and mine put every hole in the Chief of Po-lice's belt. And, brothers, that's a mighty big piece of leather goods."

(Laughter)

"You could rope a calf with it!"

(Laughter)

"You could hang a man with it!"

"Let him be careful he don't trip up and hang hisself," a voice hollered.

"Now when they go out in their costumes they burn the fiery cross. Burn it! That's what they do with the holy cross of our Almighty Lord and Savior, Jesus Christ!"

"Amen! Amen!"

"Let them take heed! Let them heed my words. We're not going to pluck them out and run them out of town. We ain't going to run them out of the state or the United States of America. Let them take heed lest we purge the last trace of them off the face of the earth. They can't hurt us. We ain't afraid. We ain't dogs, by God!"

His father kept talking, shouting at them, and the boy saw that he was leading the crowd now like a bandmaster. When he wanted to he had them growling and snarling like animals in the zoo. His father put his arm around the boy and leaned over close to his ear.

"Let's quiet them down a little," he said.

Then he began to talk softly, so soft they had to strain to hear. He told them what the law was and he told them what he had been planning to say on the Fourth of July about the vote and the elections in the fall. They yelled at him to run for county judge, but he shook his head and smiled. That seemed to rile them up and they kept yelling for him to run for office until at last he held his hands wide apart and they got quiet. He told them if that's what they wanted he guessed he would have to do it and if he lived to take office he would throw the whole bunch of public enemies in the jail and throw the key away.

"Now I've said my piece," he said. "I'm going across the street and celebrate our victory, going to buy my little boy a bottle of soda pop and smoke myself a rich man's ten-cent cigar."

The crowd fell back in front of them, making a path. They walked all the way across the street through the dense Saturday crowd, his father dripping sweat, smiling at everyone and calling out to people he knew. Afterwards, as they strolled home, people, friends and strangers, stepped up and shook his father's hand and looked into his eyes. And now the boy knew for the first time how close is violence to love. If you rubbed the lamp and said the right words you could call up a giant.

When they entered the house, his mother was playing the piano.

"Was there any mail?" she asked. "Did you get a letter?"

"Isn't that remarkable?" his father said. "I got to talking to some fellows and completely forgot about the mail."

After that the conclusion was foregone; everything was quiet. His father went back to work every day at the law office, the summer ended, and the boy started school again. It might never have happened. He might have dreamed it all in the long, breathless, heat-humming days of midsummer, except that there was a car parked right across the street from the house night and day, and always a man in it, sitting on the front seat with a high-powered deer rifle sticking out of the window.

In November they held the elections and then one midnight the telephone rang and they woke the boy. As they walked to the courthouse the band was playing in the street and there were fireworks and men fired rifles and pistols in the air. They climbed the flight of steps in front of the courthouse and stood there while the people cheered and hollered, his father laughing, tears of joy running down his cheeks, shaking his big cane at the people while they cheered him. His mother smiled and smiled, looking right through the swirl of faces, smiling and not seeing any of them, like a queen from another country. . . .

I know the place and I know the time, the rich, sweaty, bootleg liquor smell of that night, the brass band sound of it, the once-in-a-blue-moon flavor of the celebration that follows the slaying of a dragon.

I could tell you the rest of the story about the man, how he became a public man, a senator, a governor. I know the anecdotes of his terrible temper and his inconsistencies. Years later I saw him beat a man to his knees with his cane for talking sassy to him on the street; yet I've also seen him have an Air Force officer jailed for browbeating the Negro bootblack in the barbershop. I know the rest of the story, how the boy grew up and went away to college and, as he grew and changed, came to see those days in a different and a sadder light.

"It's a pity," he told me once, "that it took a narrow-minded, petty demagogue with a wild desire to be a martyr to stand up for law and order at that time."

"Somebody had to do it," I said. "Your old families with their fine names and fine silver wouldn't lift a finger to do it. Who was going to take responsibility if he didn't?"

"You may be right," he said. "But it's a pity."

"Why do you hate him?"

"Wouldn't you?" he said quickly.

"I don't know," I said.

"I'll tell you the truth," he said, smiling. "I don't know either."

QUESTIONS

1. After a brief introduction, the narrator begins his story: "They beat the hell out of him." What is the relationship between the "I" who narrates and the man who gets beaten?

2. Who is the boy of the story? What is his relationship to the narrator?

3. How much of what he tells has the narrator directly observed? Point to details he could not have known. What justifies his inclusion of these things?

4. The "I" Narrator appears only at the beginning and end. He tells the major portion in the third person, like the omniscient narrations that follow in the next chapter. What did the author gain by introducing an "I" narrator here? What would be lost if the beginning and ending passages were deleted?

CHAPTER 4

THE OMNISCIENT NARRATOR

The first-person narrator is an "I" who tells a story as a participant or observer. The story happened to me or it happened to someone near me. As first-person narrator, I tell you what I know, shaping it in the way I think will make it most interesting or best suit my purpose in telling. If I leave things out, it is because I don't want them known, don't know them myself, or don't think they will interest you. If I am a madman, or dishonest, or ignorant, you cannot fully trust my story, though you may find it even more interesting than the stories told by sane people, or those who are more honest than I, or more intelligent. You may be fascinated by my character. Perhaps I am like you in some way, as you are or might be. My "I" draws us together, one person to another. At the same time, I may give you reasons to draw back as my unreliability puts you on your guard. Through dramatic irony, I may reveal more than I am aware of concerning my story or myself.

For many stories, however, the "I" perspective has serious limitations:

1. In some stories, the direct connection between the "I" narrator and the events told is unnecessary or inappropriate.

2. The first-person narrator is limited in narrative powers by the level of sophistication appropriate to the character.

3. The first-person narrator can tell only what he or she has seen, heard, or guessed. In many stories, much important information lies outside the knowledge of a single person.

4. The first-person narrator can tell what people say or do, but cannot easily report their thoughts.

5. The first-person narrator can never speak with the authority of complete objectivity. A witness or participant always bears some subjective relationship, however slight, to the events narrated.

The *omniscient narrator* tells the story but is not a character in it. Appearing in the story only as a disembodied voice, the teller pretends no immediate relationship to the events narrated, either as participant or observer. This is the traditional storyteller, all-knowing, all-powerful, and ever present, taking us at times into the minds of protagonist and antagonist alike, exposing their most secret desires and hidden motives. The voice of such a teller transcends time and crosses seas, unhindered by any pretense of personal involvement or observation. Although we are told of the miller's daughter and the king and Rumpelstiltskin, we have no illusion we are listening to a person who was there. Instead, we move invisibly with the voice of the storyteller from hut to palace to forest as no single participant or observer can do.

But though the name translates as "all-knowing," the omniscient narrator is first of all a storyteller, a hider of secrets, a revealer of consequences in their own good time. The magic of the tale comes from its withholding, as the teller unfolds the details in the order that makes the telling most effective. As readers, we will want to observe the way the narrator constructs this scene and then that, skips from this location to another far away, moves ahead or back in time, summarizes in one passage, develops at length in another. Sometimes we will observe that a scene another teller might have thought important is omitted entirely in the craft of this particular narrator.

The omniscient narrator tells the story in the grammatical third person: the characters are "he," "she," or "they." For this reason, the teller is sometimes called a *third-person narrator* or a *third-person omniscient narrator*. No "I" intrudes. As we follow the ways of this kind of teller, we percieve that the concept of *narrative perspective* becomes important: from what standpoint is the narrative presented? An *external narrative perspective* witnesses events from outside, with the narrator standing apart, invisible, and telling us what is seen and heard from that vantage point. An *internal narrative perspective* witnesses things as though from within a character, sharing, perhaps, some of that character's personality. Many omniscient narrators shift about, presenting external views in some portions of a story, internal views in others, as though a camera were focused from afar, moving in for a close-up and then seeing through the eyes of a character.

When the powers of the third-person narrator are limited in systematic ways, we have a *limited omniscient* narrative perspective or a *limited third-person* narration. Common among limited perspectives are narrations entirely external, narrations entirely internal, narrations that follow the actions of one character only (omitting scenes without that character), or narrations that enter into the unspoken thoughts of one character only (presenting the thoughts of others only when they speak them out loud), but other forms of limitation are also possible. Sometimes we communicate much about a story when we describe the limitations of the narrator's omniscience.

In presenting a character's thoughts, the omniscient narrator generally signals the reader that a mind has been entered and then proceeds much as with a *direct* or *indirect* quotation of speech: " 'I have lost my way,' he thought," or else "He thought he had lost his way." In some stories, however, the narrator places an unusual emphasis on the thoughts of the characters, and for these the following descriptive terms prove useful.

An *interior monologue* presents a character's thoughts at length, as though they were spoken in *soliloquy,* as on a stage, or as though we were able to tune in electronically on what is passing through the brain but is not said aloud. *Direct interior monologue* presents thoughts in the words the omniscient narrator finds in the character's mind, quoting directly. *Indirect interior monologue* presents the character's thoughts in the narrator's words, quoting indirectly. In *stream of consciousness,* the narrator tries to reproduce the contents of a mind—including conscious thoughts, unconscious associations, immediate sensory perceptions, and memories—stringing all together in a continual, streamlike, mental flow.

One specialized form of third-person limitation removes thoughts entirely, deletes much else common in most omniscient narrations, and results in the *dramatic method* of writing fiction. A writer using this method presents the story much as though it were a play performed before the reader's imagination. The narrator provides only the information that would be available to an invisible viewer of the action, or to a strategically placed camera and microphone, describing characters and settings and reporting action and dialogue, but eliminating all other evidence of a storyteller. No moral is given, no authorial summary intrudes, and no thoughts of the characters appear (unless they speak them aloud).

In reading Fitzgerald's "Babylon Revisited," observe how the omniscient narrator focuses attention on a man named Charlie Wales.

BABYLON REVISITED

F. Scott Fitzgerald   (1896–1940)

I

"And where's Mr. Campbell?" Charlie asked.

"Gone to Switzerland. Mr. Campbell's a pretty sick man, Mr. Wales."

"I'm sorry to hear that. And George Hardt?" Charlie inquired.

"Back in America, gone to work."

"And where is the Snow Bird?"

"He was in here last week. Anyway, his friend, Mr. Schaeffer, is in Paris."

Two familiar names from the long list of a year and a half ago. Charlie scribbled an address in his notebook and tore out the page.

"If you see Mr. Schaeffer, give him this," he said. "It's my brother-in-law's address. I haven't settled on a hotel yet."

He was not really disappointed to find Paris was so empty. But the stillness in the Ritz bar was strange and portentous. It was not an American bar any more —he felt polite in it, and not as if he owned it. It had gone back into France. He felt the stillness from the moment he got out of the taxi and saw the doorman, usually in a frenzy of activity at this hour, gossiping with a *chausseur*[1] by the servants' entrance.

Passing through the corridor, he heard only a single, bored voice in the once-clamorous women's room. When he turned into the bar he traveled the twenty feet of green carpet with his eyes fixed straight ahead by old habit; and then, with his foot firmly on the rail, he turned and surveyed the room, encountering only a single pair of eyes that fluttered up from a newspaper in the corner. Charlie asked for the head barman, Paul, who in the latter days of the bull market had come to work in his own custom-built car—disembarking, however, with due nicety at the nearest corner. But Paul was at his country house today and Alix giving him information.

"No, no more," Charlie said, "I'm going slow these days."

Alix congratulated him: "You were going pretty strong a couple of years ago."

"I'll stick to it all right," Charlie assured him. "I've stuck to it for over a year and a half now."

"How do you find conditions in America?"

"I haven't been to America for months. I'm in business in Prague, representing a couple of concerns there. They don't know about me down there."

Alix smiled.

"Remember the night of George Hardt's bachelor dinner here?" said Charlie. "By the way, what's become of Claude Fessenden?"

Alix lowered his voice confidentially: "He's in Paris, but he doesn't come here any more. Paul doesn't allow it. He ran up a bill of thirty thousand francs, charging all his drinks and his lunches, and usually his dinner, for more than a year. And when Paul finally told him he had to pay, he gave him a bad check."

Alix shook his head sadly.

"I don't understand it, such a dandy fellow. Now he's all bloated up—" He made a plump apple of his hands.

Charlie watched a group of strident queens installing themselves in a corner.

"Nothing affects them," he thought. "Stocks rise and fall, people loaf or work, but they go on forever." The place oppressed him. He called for the dice and shook with Alix for the drink.

"Here for long, Mr. Wales?"

"I'm here for four or five days to see my little girl."

"Oh-h! You have a little girl?"

Outside, the fire-red, gas-blue, ghost-green signs shone smokily through the tranquil rain. It was late afternoon and the streets were in movement; the *bistros* gleamed. At the corner of the Boulevard des Capucines he took a taxi. The Place de la Concorde moved by in pink majesty; they crossed the logical Seine, and Charlie felt the sudden provincial quality of the left bank.

Charlie directed his taxi to the Avenue de l'Opera, which was out of his way. But he wanted to see the blue hour spread over the magnificent façade, and imagine that the cab horns, playing endlessly the first few bars of *Le Plus que*

[1]Footman.

Lent, were the trumpets of the Second Empire. They were closing the iron grill in front of Brentano's Book-store, and people were already at dinner behind the trim little bourgeois hedge of Duval's. He had never eaten at a really cheap restaurant in Paris. Five-course dinner, four francs fifty, eighteen cents, wine included. For some odd reason he wished that he had.

As they rolled on to the Left Bank and he felt its sudden provincialism, he thought, "I spoiled this city for myself. I didn't realize it, but the days came along one after another, and then two years were gone, and everything was gone, and I was gone."

He was thirty-five, and good to look at. The Irish mobility of his face was sobered by a deep wrinkle between his eyes. As he rang his brother-in-law's bell in the Rue Palatine, the wrinkle deepened till it pulled down his brows; he felt a cramping sensation in his belly. From behind the maid who opened the door darted a lovely little girl of nine who shrieked "Daddy!" and flew up, struggling like a fish, into his arms. She pulled his head around by one ear and set her cheek against his.

"My old pie," he said.

"Oh, daddy, daddy, daddy, daddy, dads, dads, dads!"

She drew him into the salon, where the family waited, a boy and a girl his daughter's age, his sister-in-law and her husband. He greeted Marion with his voice pitched carefully to avoid either feigned enthusiasm or dislike, but her response was more frankly tepid, though she minimized her expression of unalterable distrust by directing her regard toward his child. The two men clasped hands in a friendly way and Lincoln Peters rested his for a moment on Charlie's shoulder.

The room was warm and comfortably American. The three children moved intimately about, playing through the yellow oblongs that led to other rooms; the cheer of six o'clock spoke in the eager smacks of the fire and the sounds of French activity in the kitchen. But Charlie did not relax; his heart sat up rigidly in his body and he drew confidence from his daughter, who from time to time came close to him, holding in her arms the doll he had brought.

"Really extremely well," he declared in answer to Lincoln's question. "There's a lot of business there that isn't moving at all, but we're doing even better than ever. In fact, damn well. I'm bringing my sister over from America next month to keep house for me. My income last year was bigger than it was when I had money. You see, the Czechs——"

His boasting was for a specific purpose; but after a moment, seeing a faint restiveness in Lincoln's eye, he changed the subject:

"Those are fine children of yours, well brought up, good manners."

"We think Honoria's a great little girl too."

Marion Peters came back from the kitchen. She was a tall woman with worried eyes, who had once possessed a fresh American loveliness. Charlie had never been sensitive to it and was always surprised when people spoke of how pretty she had been. From the first there had been an instinctive antipathy between them.

"Well, how do you find Honoria?" she asked.

"Wonderful, I was astonished how much she's grown in ten months. All the children are looking well."

"We haven't had a doctor for a year. How do you like being back in Paris?"

"It seems very funny to see so few Americans around."

"I'm delighted," Marion said vehemently. "Now at least you can go into a store without their assuming you're a millionaire. We've suffered like everybody, but on the whole it's a good deal pleasanter."

"But it was nice while it lasted," Charlie said. "We were a sort of royalty, almost infallible, with a sort of magic around us. In the bar this afternoon"—he stumbled, seeing his mistake—"there wasn't a man I knew."

She looked at him keenly. "I should think you'd have had enough of bars."

"I only stayed a minute. I take one drink every afternoon, and no more."

"Don't you want a cocktail before dinner?" Lincoln asked.

"I take only one drink every afternoon, and I've had that."

"I hope you keep to it," said Marion.

Her dislike was evident in the coldness with which she spoke, but Charlie only smiled; he had larger plans. Her very aggressiveness gave him an advantage, and he knew enough to wait. He wanted them to initiate the discussion of what they knew had brought him to Paris.

At dinner he couldn't decide whether Honoria was most like him or her mother. Fortunate if she didn't combine the traits of both that had brought them to disaster. A great wave of protectiveness went over him. He thought he knew what to do for her. He believed in character; he wanted to jump back a whole generation and trust in character again as the eternally valuable element. Everything else wore out.

He left soon after dinner, but not to go home. He was curious to see Paris by night with clearer and more judicious eyes than those of other days. He bought a *strapontin*[2] for the Casino and watched Josephine Baker[3] go through her chocolate arabesques.

After an hour he left and strolled toward Montmartre, up the Rue Pigalle into the Place Blanche. The rain had stopped and there were a few people in evening clothes disembarking from taxis in front of cabarets, and *cocottes*[4] prowling singly or in pairs, and many Negroes. He passed a lighted door from which issued music, and stopped with the sense of familiarity; it was Bricktop's, where he had parted with so many hours and so much money. A few doors farther on he found another ancient rendezvous and incautiously put his head inside. Immediately an eager orchestra burst into sound, a pair of professional dancers leaped to their feet and a maître d'hôtel swooped toward him, crying, "Crowd just arriving, sir!" But he withdrew quickly.

"You have to be damn drunk," he thought.

Zelli's was closed, the bleak and sinister cheap hotels surrounding it were dark; up in the Rue Blanche there was more light and a local, colloquial French crowd.

[2]A type of theater seat.   [3]American entertainer.   [4]Prostitutes.

The Poet's Cave had disappeared, but the two great mouths of the Café of Heaven and the Café of Hell still yawned—even devoured, as he watched, the meager contents of a tourist bus—a German, a Japanese, and an American couple who glanced at him with frightened eyes.

So much for the effort and ingenuity of Montmartre. All the catering to vice and waste was on an utterly childish scale, and he suddenly realized the meaning of the word "dissipate"—to dissipate into thin air; to make nothing out of something. In the little hours of the night every move from place to place was an enormous human jump, an increase of paying for the privilege of slower and slower motion.

He remembered thousand-franc notes given to an orchestra for playing a single number, hundred-franc notes tossed to a doorman for calling a cab.

But it hadn't been given for nothing.

It had been given, even the most wildly squandered sum, as an offering to destiny that he might not remember the things most worth remembering, the things that now he would always remember—his child taken from his control, his wife escaped to a grave in Vermont.

In the glare of a *brasserie*[5] a woman spoke to him. He bought her some eggs and coffee, and then, eluding her encouraging stare, gave her a twenty-franc note and took a taxi to his hotel.

II

He woke upon a fine fall day—football weather. The depression of yesterday was gone and he liked the people on the streets. At noon he sat opposite Honoria at Le Grand Vatel, the only restaurant he could think of not reminiscent of champagne dinners and long luncheons that began at two and ended in a blurred and vague twilight.

"Now, how about vegetables? Oughtn't you to have some vegetables?"

"Well, yes."

"Here's *épinards* and *chou-fleur* and carrots and *haricots.*"[6]

"I'd like *chou-fleur.*"

"Wouldn't you like to have two vegetables?"

"I usually only have one at lunch."

The waiter was pretending to be inordinately fond of children. *"Qu'elle est mignonne la petite! Elle parle exactement comme une Française."*[7]

"How about dessert? Shall we wait and see?"

The waiter disappeared. Honoria looked at her father expectantly.

"What are we going to do?"

"First, we're going to that toy store in the Rue Saint-Honoré and buy you anything you like. And then, we're going to the vaudeville at the Empire."

She hesitated. "I like it about the vaudeville, but not the toy store."

"Why not?"

[5]Tavern.   [6]Spinach, cauliflower, beans.   [7]"What a darling little girl! She speaks exactly like a French girl."

"Well, you brought me this doll." She had it with her. "And I've got lots of things. And we're not rich any more, are we?"

"We never were. But today you are to have anything you want."

"All right," she agreed resignedly.

When there had been her mother and a French nurse he had been inclined to be strict; now he extended himself, reached out for a new tolerance; he must be both parents to her and not shut any of her out of communication.

"I want to get to know you," he said gravely. "First let me introduce myself. My name is Charles J. Wales, of Prague."

"Oh, daddy!" her voice cracked with laughter.

"And who are you, please?" he persisted, and she accepted a role immediately: "Honoria Wales, Rue Palatine, Paris."

"Married or single?"

"No, not married. Single."

He indicated the doll. "But I see you have a child, madame."

Unwilling to disinherit it, she took it to her heart and thought quickly: "Yes, I've been married, but I'm not married now. My husband is dead."

He went on quickly, "And the child's name?"

"Simone. That's after my best friend at school."

"I'm very pleased that you're doing so well at school."

"I'm third this month," she boasted. "Elsie"—that was her cousin—"is only about eighteenth, and Richard is about at the bottom."

"You like Richard and Elsie, don't you?"

"Oh, yes. I like Richard quite well and I like her all right."

Cautiously and casually he asked: "And Aunt Marion and Uncle Lincoln— which do you like best?"

"Oh, Uncle Lincoln, I guess."

He was increasingly aware of her presence. As they came in, a murmur of ". . . adorable" followed them, and now the people at the next table bent all their silences upon her, staring as if she were something no more conscious than a flower.

"Why don't I live with you?" she asked suddenly. "Because mamma's dead?"

"You must stay here and learn more French. It would have been hard for daddy to take care of you so well."

"I don't really need much taking care of any more. I do everything for myself."

Going out of the restaurant, a man and a woman unexpectedly hailed him.

"Well, the old Wales!"

"Hello there, Lorraine. . . . Dunc."

Sudden ghosts out of the past: Duncan Schaeffer, a friend from college. Lorraine Quarrles, a lovely, pale blonde of thirty; one of a crowd who had helped them make months into days in the lavish times of three years ago.

"My husband couldn't come this year," she said, in answer to his question. "We're poor as hell. So he gave me two hundred a month and told me I could do my worst on that. . . . This your little girl?"

"What about coming back and sitting down?" Duncan asked.

"Can't do it." He was glad for an excuse. As always, he felt Lorraine's passionate, provocative attraction, but his own rhythm was different now.

"Well, how about dinner?" she asked.

"I'm not free. Give me your address and let me call you."

"Charlie, I believe you're sober," she said judicially. "I honestly believe he's sober, Dunc. Pinch him and see if he's sober."

Charlie indicated Honoria with his head. They both laughed.

"What's your address?" said Duncan skeptically.

He hesitated, unwilling to give the name of his hotel.

"I'm not settled yet. I'd better call you. We're going to see the vaudeville at the Empire."

"There! That's what I want to do," Lorraine said. "I want to see some clowns and acrobats and jugglers. That's just what we'll do, Dunc."

"We've got to do an errand first," said Charlie. "Perhaps we'll see you there."

"All right, you snob. . . . Good-by beautiful little girl."

"Good-by."

Honoria bobbed politely.

Somehow, an unwelcome encounter. They liked him because he was functioning, because he was serious; they wanted to see him, because he was stronger than they were now, because they wanted to draw a certain sustenance from his strength.

At the Empire, Honoria proudly refused to sit upon her father's folded coat. She was already an individual with a code of her own, and Charlie was more and more absorbed by the desire of putting a little of himself into her before she crystallized utterly. It was hopeless to try to know her in so short a time.

Between the acts they came upon Duncan and Lorraine in the lobby where the band was playing.

"Have a drink?"

"All right, but not up at the bar. We'll take a table."

"The perfect father."

Listening abstractedly to Lorraine, Charlie watched Honoria's eyes leave their table, and he followed them wistfully about the room, wondering what they saw. He met her glance and she smiled.

"I liked that lemonade," she said.

What had she said? What had he expected? Going home in a taxi afterward, he pulled her over until her head rested against his chest.

"Darling, do you ever think about your mother?"

"Yes, sometimes," she answered vaguely.

"I don't want you to forget her. Have you got a picture of her?"

"Yes, I think so. Anyhow, Aunt Marion has. Why don't you want me to forget her?"

"She loved you very much."

"I loved her too."

They were silent for a moment.

"Daddy, I want to come and live with you," she said suddenly.

His heart leaped; he had wanted it to come like this.

"Aren't you perfectly happy?"

"Yes, but I love you better than anybody. And you love me better than anybody, don't you, now that mummy's dead?"

"Of course I do. But you won't always like me best, honey. You'll grow up and meet somebody your own age and go marry him and forget you ever had a daddy."

"Yes, that's true," she agreed tranquilly.

He didn't go in. He was coming back at nine o'clock and he wanted to keep himself fresh and new for the thing he must say then.

"When you're safe inside, just show yourself in that window."

"All right. Good-by, dads, dads, dads, dads."

He waited in the dark street until she appeared, all warm and glowing, in the window above and kissed her fingers out into the night.

III

They were waiting. Marion sat behind the coffee service in a dignified black dinner dress that just faintly suggested mourning. Lincoln was walking up and down with the animation of one who had already been talking. They were as anxious as he was to get into the question. He opened it almost immediately:

"I suppose you know what I want to see you about—why I really came to Paris."

Marion played with the black stars on her necklace and frowned.

"I'm awfully anxious to have a home," he continued. "And I'm awfully anxious to have Honoria in it. I appreciate your taking in Honoria for her mother's sake, but things have changed now"—he hesitated and then continued more forcibly—"changed radically with me, and I want to ask you to reconsider the matter. It would be silly for me to deny that about three years ago I was acting badly—"

Marion looked up at him with hard eyes.

"—but all that's over. As I told you, I haven't had more than a drink a day for over a year, and I take that drink deliberately, so that the idea of alcohol won't get too big in my imagination. You see the idea?"

"No," said Marion succintly.

"It's a sort of stunt I set myself. It keeps the matter in proportion."

"I get you," said Lincoln. "You don't want to admit it's got any attraction for you."

"Something like that. Sometimes I forget and don't take it. But I try to take it. Anyhow, I couldn't afford to drink in my position. The people I represent are more than satisfied with what I've done, and I'm bringing my sister over from Burlington to keep house for me, and I want awfully to have Honoria too. You know that even when her mother and I weren't getting along well we never let anything that happened touch Honoria. I know she's fond of me and I know I'm able to take care of her and—well, there you are. How do you feel about it?"

He knew that now he would have to take a beating. It would last an hour or two hours, and it would be difficult, but if he modulated his inevitable resentment to the chastened attitude of the reformed sinner, he might win his point in the end.

Keep your temper, he told himself. You don't want to be justified. You want Honoria.

Lincoln spoke first: "We've been talking it over ever since we got your letter last month. We're happy to have Honoria here. She's a dear little thing, and we're glad to be able to help her, but of course that isn't the question—"

Marion interrupted suddenly. "How long are you going to stay sober, Charlie?" she asked.

"Permanently, I hope."

"How can anybody count on that?"

"You know I never did drink heavily until I gave up business and came over here with nothing to do. Then Helen and I began to run around with—"

"Please leave Helen out of it. I can't bear to hear you talk about her like that."

He stared at her grimly; he had never been certain how fond of each other the sisters were in life.

"My drinking only lasted about a year and a half—from the time we came over until I—collapsed."

"It was time enough."

"It was time enough," he agreed.

"My duty is entirely to Helen," she said. "I try to think what she would have wanted me to do. Frankly, from the night you did that terrible thing you haven't really existed for me. I can't help that. She was my sister."

"Yes."

"When she was dying she asked me to look out for Honoria. If you hadn't been in a sanitarium then, it might have helped matters."

He had no answer.

"I'll never in my life be able to forget the morning when Helen knocked at my door, soaked to the skin and shivering and said you'd locked her out."

Charlie gripped the sides of the chair. This was more difficult than he expected; he wanted to launch out into a long expostulation and explanation, but he only said: "The night I locked her out—" and she interrupted, "I don't feel up to going over that again."

After a moment's silence Lincoln said: "We're getting off the subject. You want Marion to set aside her legal guardianship and give you Honoria. I think the main point for her is whether she has confidence in you or not."

"I don't blame Marion," Charlie said slowly, "but I think she can have entire confidence in me. I had a good record up to three years ago. Of course, it's within human possibilities I might go wrong any time. But if we wait much longer I'll lose Honoria's childhood and my chance for a home." He shook his head. "I'll simply lose her, don't you see?"

"Yes, I see," said Lincoln.

"Why didn't you think of all this before?" Marion asked.

"I suppose I did, from time to time, but Helen and I were getting along badly.

When I consented to the guardianship, I was flat on my back in a sanitarium and the market had cleaned me out. I knew I'd acted badly, and I thought if it would bring any peace to Helen, I'd agree to anything. But now it's different. I'm functioning, I'm behaving damn well, so far as—"

"Please don't swear at me," Marion said.

He looked at her, startled. With each remark the force of her dislike became more and more apparent. She had built up all her fear of life into one wall and faced it toward him. This trivial reproof was possibly the result of some trouble with the cook several hours before. Charlie became increasingly alarmed at leaving Honoria in this atmosphere of hostility against himself; sooner or later it would come out, in a word here, a shake of the head there, and some of that distrust would be irrevocably implanted in Honoria. But he pulled his temper down out of his face and shut it up inside him; he had won a point, for Lincoln realized the absurdity of Marion's remark and asked her lightly since when she had objected to the word "damn."

"Another thing," Charlie said: "I'm able to give her certain advantages now. I'm going to take a French governess to Prague with me. I've got a lease on a new apartment—"

He stopped, realizing that he was blundering. They couldn't be expected to accept with equanimity the fact that his income was again twice as large as their own.

"I suppose you can give her more luxuries than we can," said Marion. "When you were throwing away money we were living along watching every ten francs. . . . I suppose you'll start doing it again."

"Oh, no," he said. "I've learned. I worked hard for ten years, you know—until I got lucky in the market, like so many people. Terribly lucky. It won't happen again."

There was a long silence. All of them felt their nerves straining, and for the first time in a year Charlie wanted a drink. He was sure now that Lincoln Peters wanted him to have his child.

Marion shuddered suddenly; part of her saw that Charlie's feet were planted on the earth now, and her own maternal feeling recognized the naturalness of his desire; but she had lived for a long time with prejudice—a prejudice founded on a disbelief in her sister's happiness, and which, in the shock of one terrible night, had turned to hatred for him. It had all happened at a point in her life where the discouragement of ill health and adverse circumstances made it necessary for her to believe in tangible villainy and a tangible villain.

"I can't help what I think!" she cried out suddenly. "How much you were responsible for Helen's death, I don't know. It's something you'll have to square with your own conscience."

An electric current of agony surged through him; for a moment he was almost on his feet, an unuttered sound echoing in his throat. He hung on to himself for a moment, another moment.

"Hold on there," said Lincoln uncomfortably. "I never thought you were responsible for that."

"Helen died of heart trouble," Charlie said dully.

"Yes, heart trouble." Marion spoke as if the phrase had another meaning for her.

Then, in the flatness that followed her outburst, she saw him plainly and she knew he had somehow arrived at control over the situation. Glancing at her husband, she found no help from him, and as abruptly as if it were a matter of no importance, she threw up the sponge.

"Do what you like!" she cried, springing up from her chair. "She's your child. I'm not the person to stand in your way. I think if it were my child I'd rather see her—" She managed to check herself. "You two decide it. I can't stand this. I'm sick. I'm going to bed."

She hurried from the room; after a moment Lincoln said:

"This has been a hard day for her. You know how strongly she feels—" His voice was almost apologetic: "Where a woman gets an idea in her head."

"Of course."

"It's going to be all right. I think she sees now that you—can provide for the child, and so we can't very well stand in your way or Honoria's way."

"Thank you, Lincoln."

"I'd better go along and see how she is."

"I'm going."

He was still trembling when he reached the street, but a walk down the Rue Bonaparte to the *quais*[8] set him up, and as he crossed the Seine, fresh and new by the *quai* lamps, he felt exultant. But back in his room he couldn't sleep. The image of Helen haunted him. Helen whom he had loved so until they had senselessly begun to abuse each other's love, tear it into shreds. On that terrible February night that Marion remembered so vividly, a slow quarrel had gone on for hours. There was a scene at the Florida, and then he attempted to take her home, and then she kissed young Webb at a table; after that there was what she had hysterically said. When he arrived home alone he turned the key in the lock in wild anger. How could he know she would arrive an hour later alone, that there would be a snowstorm in which she wandered about in slippers, too confused to find a taxi? Then the aftermath, her escaping pneumonia by a miracle, and all the attendant horror. They were "reconciled," but that was the beginning of the end, and Marion, who had seen with her own eyes and who imagined it to be one of many scenes from her sister's martyrdom, never forgot.

Going over it again brought Helen nearer, and in the white, soft light that steals upon half sleep near morning he found himself talking to her again. She said that he was perfectly right about Honoria and that she wanted Honoria to be with him. She said she was glad he was being good and doing better. She said a lot of other things—very friendly things—but she was in a swing in a white dress, and swinging faster and faster all the time, so that at the end he could not hear clearly all that she said.

[8]Wharfs.

IV

He woke up feeling happy. The door of the world was open again. He made plans, vistas, futures for Honoria and himself, but suddenly he grew sad, remembering all the plans he and Helen had made. She had not planned to die. The present was the thing—work to do and someone to love. But not to love too much, for he knew the injury that a father can do to a daughter or a mother to a son by attaching them too closely: afterward, out in the world, the child would seek in the marriage partner the same blind tenderness and, failing probably to find it, turn against love and life.

It was another bright, crisp day. He called Lincoln Peters at the bank where he worked and asked if he could count on taking Honoria when he left for Prague. Lincoln agreed that there was no reason for delay. One thing—the legal guardianship. Marion wanted to retain that a while longer. She was upset by the whole matter, and it would oil things if she felt that the situation was still in her control for another year. Charlie agreed, wanting only the tangible, visible child.

Then the question of a governess. Charles sat in a gloomy agency and talked to a cross Béarnaise and to a buxom Breton peasant, neither of whom he could have endured. There were others whom he would see tomorrow.

He lunched with Lincoln Peters at Griffons, trying to keep down his exultation.

"There's nothing quite like your own child," Lincoln said. "But you understand how Marion feels too."

"She's forgotten how hard I worked for seven years there," Charlie said. "She just remembers one night."

"There's another thing." Lincoln hesitated. "While you and Helen were tearing around Europe throwing money away, we were just getting along. I didn't touch any of the prosperity because I never got ahead enough to carry anything but my insurance. I think Marion felt there was some kind of injustice in it—you not even working toward the end, and getting richer and richer."

"It went just as quick as it came," said Charlie.

"Yes, a lot of it stayed in the hands of *chasseurs* and saxophone players and maitres d'hôtel—well, the big party's over now. I just said that to explain Marion's feeling about those crazy years. If you drop in about six o'clock tonight before Marion's too tired, we'll settle the details on the spot."

Back at his hotel, Charlie found a *pneumatique*[9] that had been redirected from the Ritz bar where Charlie had left his address for the purpose of finding a certain man.

DEAR CHARLIE: You were so strange when we saw you the other day that I wondered if I did something to offend you. If so, I'm not conscious of it. In fact, I have thought about you too much for the last year, and it's always been in the back of my mind that I might see you if I came over here. We *did* have such good times that crazy spring, like the night you and I stole the butcher's tricycle, and the time we tried to call on

[9]Special-delivery letter.

the president and you had the old derby rim and the wire cane. Everybody seems so old lately, but I don't feel old a bit. Couldn't we get together some time today for old time's sake? I've got a vile hang-over for the moment, but will be feeling better this afternoon and will look for you about five in the sweat-shop at the Ritz.

"Always devotedly,

"LORRAINE."

His first feeling was one of awe that he had actually, in his mature years, stolen a tricycle and pedaled Lorraine all over the Etoile between the small hours and dawn. In retrospect it was a nightmare. Locking out Helen didn't fit in with any other act of his life, but the tricycle incident did—it was one of many. How many weeks or months of dissipation to arrive at that condition of utter irresponsibility?

He tried to picture how Lorraine had appeared to him then—very attractive; Helen was unhappy about it, though she said nothing. Yesterday, in the restaurant, Lorraine had seemed trite, blurred, worn away. He emphatically did not want to see her, and he was glad Alix had not given away his hotel address. It was a relief to think, instead, of Honoria, to think of Sundays spent with her and of saying good morning to her and of knowing she was there in his house at night, drawing her breath in the darkness.

At five he took a taxi and bought presents for all the Peters—a piquant cloth doll, a box of Roman soldiers, flowers for Marion, big linen handkerchiefs for Lincoln.

He saw, when he arrived in the apartment, that Marion had accepted the inevitable. She greeted him now as though he were a recalcitrant member of the family, rather than a menacing outsider. Honoria had been told she was going; Charlie was glad to see that her tact made her conceal her excessive happiness. Only on his lap did she whisper her delight and the question "When?" before she slipped away with the other children.

He and Marion were alone for a minute in the room, and on an impulse he spoke out boldly:

"Family quarrels are bitter things. They don't go according to any rules. They're not like aches or wounds; they're more like splits in the skin that won't heal because there's not enough material. I wish you and I could be on better terms."

"Some things are hard to forget," she answered. "It's a question of confidence." There was no answer to this and presently she asked, "When do you propose to take her?"

"As soon as I can get a governess. I hoped the day after tomorrow."

"That's impossible. I've got to get her things in shape. Not before Saturday."

He yielded. Coming back into the room, Lincoln offered him a drink.

"I'll take my daily whisky," he said.

It was warm here, it was a home, people together by a fire. The children felt very safe and important; the mother and father were serious, watchful. They had things to do for the children more important than his visit here. A spoonful of medicine was, after all, more important than the strained relations between

Marion and himself. They were not dull people, but they were very much in the grip of life and circumstances. He wondered if he couldn't do something to get Lincoln out of his rut at the bank.

A long peal at the door-bell; the *bonne à tout faire*[10] passed through and went down the corridor. The door opened upon another long ring, and then voices, and the three in the salon looked up expectantly; Richard moved to bring the corridor within his range of vision, and Marion rose. Then the maid came back along the corridor, closely followed by the voices, which developed under the light into Duncan Schaeffer and Lorraine Quarrles.

They were gay, they were hilarious, they were roaring with laughter. For a moment Charlie was astounded; unable to understand how they ferreted out the Peters' address.

"Ah-h-h!" Duncan wagged his finger roguishly at Charlie. "Ah-h-h!"

They both slid down another cascade of laughter. Anxious and at a loss, Charlie shook hands with them quickly and presented them to Lincoln and Marion. Marion nodded, scarcely speaking. She had drawn back a step toward the fire; her little girl stood beside her, and Marion put an arm about her shoulder.

With growing annoyance at the intrusion, Charlie waited for them to explain themselves. After some concentration Duncan said:

"We came to invite you out to dinner. Lorraine and I insist that all this shishi, cagy business 'bout your address got to stop."

Charlie came closer to them, as if to force them backward down the corridor.

"Sorry, but I can't. Tell me where you'll be and I'll phone you in half an hour."

This made no impression. Lorraine sat down suddenly on the side of a chair, and focusing her eyes on Richard, cried, "Oh, what a nice little boy! Come here, little boy." Richard glanced at his mother, but did not move. With a perceptible shrug of her shoulders, Lorraine turned back to Charlie:

"Come and dine. Sure your cousins won' mine. See you so sel'om. Or solemn."

"I can't," said Charlie sharply. "You two have dinner and I'll phone you."

Her voice became suddenly unpleasant. "All right, we'll go. But I remember once when you hammered on my door at four A.M. I was enough of a good sport to give you a drink. Come on, Dunc."

Still in slow motion, with blurred, angry faces, with uncertain feet, they retired along the corridor.

"Good night," Charlie said.

"Good night!" responded Lorraine emphatically.

When he went back into the salon Marion had not moved, only now her son was standing in the circle of her other arm. Lincoln was still swinging Honoria back and forth like a pendulum from side to side.

"What an outrage!" Charlie broke out. "What an absolute outrage!"

Neither of them answered. Charlie dropped into an armchair, picked up his drink, set it down again and said:

[10]Maid of all work.

"People I haven't seen for two years having the colossal nerve—"

He broke off. Marion had made the sound "Oh!" in one swift, furious breath, turned her body from him with a jerk and left the room.

Lincoln set down Honoria carefully.

"You children go in and start your soup," he said, and when they obeyed, he said to Charlie.

"Marion's not well and she can't stand shocks. That kind of people make her really physically sick."

"I didn't tell them to come here. They wormed your name out of somebody. They deliberately—"

"Well, it's too bad. It doesn't help matters. Excuse me a minute."

Left alone, Charlie sat tense in his chair. In the next room he could hear the children eating, talking in monosyllables, already oblivious to the scene between their elders. He heard a murmur of conversation from a farther room and then the ticking bell of a telephone receiver picked up, and in a panic he moved to the other side of the room and out of earshot.

In a minute Lincoln came back. "Look here, Charlie, I think we'd better call off dinner for tonight. Marion's in bad shape."

"Is she angry with me?"

"Sort of," he said, almost roughly. "She's not strong and—"

"You mean she's changed her mind about Honoria?"

"She's pretty bitter right now. I don't know. You phone me at the bank tomorrow."

"I wish you'd explain to her I never dreamed these people would come here. I'm just as sore as you are."

"I couldn't explain anything to her now."

Charlie got up. He took his coat and hat and started down the corridor. Then he opened the door of the dining room and said in a strange voice, "Good night, children."

Honoria rose and ran around the table to hug him.

"Good night, sweetheart," he said vaguely, and then trying to make his voice more tender, trying to conciliate something, "Good night, dear children."

V

Charlie went directly to the Ritz bar with the furious idea of finding Lorraine and Duncan, but they were not there, and he realized that in any case there was nothing he could do. He had not touched his drink at the Peters, and now he ordered a whisky-and-soda. Paul came over to say hello.

"It's a great change," he said sadly. "We do about half the business we did. So many fellows I hear about back in the States lost everything, maybe not in the first crash, but then in the second. Your friend George Hardt lost every cent, I hear. Are you back in the States?"

"No, I'm in business in Prague."

"I heard that you lost a lot in the crash."

"I did," and he added grimly, "but I lost everything I wanted in the boom."

"Selling short."

"Something like that."

Again the memory of those days swept over him like a nightmare—the people they had met travelling; then people who couldn't add a row of figures or speak a coherent sentence. The little man Helen had consented to dance with at the ship's party, who had insulted her ten feet from the table; the women and girls carried screaming with drink or drugs out of public places——

—The men who locked their wives out in the snow, because the snow of twenty-nine wasn't real snow. If you didn't want it to be snow, you just paid some money.

He went to the phone and called the Peters' apartment; Lincoln answered.

"I called up because this thing is on my mind. Has Marion said anything definite?"

"Marion's sick," Lincoln answered shortly. "I know this thing isn't altogether your fault, but I can't have her go to pieces about it. I'm afraid we'll have to let it slide for six months; I can't take the chance of working her up to this state again."

"I see."

"I'm sorry, Charlie."

He went back to his table. His whiskey glass was empty, but he shook his head when Alix looked at it questioningly. There wasn't much he could do now except send Honoria some things; he would send her a lot of things tomorrow. He thought rather angrily that this was just money—he had given so many people money. . . .

"No, no more," he said to another waiter. "What do I owe you?"

He would come back some day; they couldn't make him pay forever. But he wanted his child, and nothing was much good now, beside that fact. He wasn't young any more, with a lot of nice thoughts and dreams to have by himself. He was absolutely sure Helen wouldn't have wanted him to be so alone.

QUESTIONS

1. What are the limitations placed on the narration of this story?

2. In the first two extended paragraphs of the story (beginning "He was not really disappointed . . .") what signs suggest an internal narrative perspective? Examine other paragraphs of description or observation. How frequently do they appear to present essentially the same internal narrative perspective (Charlie's)?

3. The last paragraph begins "He would come back some day; they couldn't make him pay forever." Are we to understand these words as statements of fact, told us by the omniscient narrator speaking from an external perspective, or should we understand them as paraphrases of Charlie's thoughts, narrated from an internal perspective? Defend your answer.

4. How does the focus on Charlie Wales affect our sympathy, or lack of it?

5. What is our attitude toward Marion and Lincoln? Is it the same as Charlie's?

6. Fitzgerald could have told the story in the first person, with Charlie Wales as narrator. Would Charlie have been a reliable narrator?

7. In the Ritz bar, in the last scene, Charlie says: "I lost everything I wanted in the boom." What does he mean?

8. Why is the story called "Babylon Revisited"?

In "A Sorrowful Woman," Gail Godwin uses an omniscient narrator to focus attention on an unnamed wife.

A SORROWFUL WOMAN

Gail Godwin   (1937–)

One winter evening she looked at them: the husband durable, receptive, gentle; the child a tender golden three. The sight of them made her so sad and sick she did not want to see them ever again.

She told the husband these thoughts. He was attuned to her; he understood such things. He said he understood. What would she like him to do? "If you could put the boy to bed and read him the story about the monkey who ate too many bananas, I would be grateful." "Of course," he said. "Why, that's a pleasure." And he sent her off to bed.

The next night it happened again. Putting the warm dishes away in the cupboard, she turned and saw the child's gray eyes approving her movements. In the next room was the man, his chin sunk in the open collar of his favorite wool shirt. He was dozing after her good supper. The shirt was the gray of the child's trusting gaze. She began yelping without tears, retching in between. The man woke in alarm and carried her in his arms to bed. The boy followed them up the stairs, saying, "It's all right, Mommy," but this made her scream. "Mommy is sick," the father said, "go and wait for me in your room."

The husband undressed her, abandoning her only long enough to root beneath the eiderdown for her flannel gown. She stood naked except for her bra, which hung by one strap down the side of her body; she had not the impetus to shrug it off. "If only there were instant sleep," she said, hiccuping, and the husband bundled her into the gown and went out and came back with a sleeping draught guaranteed swift. She was to drink a little glass of cognac followed by a big glass of dark liquid and afterward there was just time to say, "Thank you and could you get him a clean pair of pajamas out of the laundry, it came back today."

The next day was Sunday and the husband brought her breakfast in bed and let her sleep until it grew dark again. He took the child for a walk, and when they returned, red-cheeked and boisterous, the father made supper. She heard them laughing in the kitchen. He brought her up a tray of buttered toast, celery sticks, and black bean soup. "I am the luckiest woman," she said, crying real tears. "Nonsense," he said. "You need a rest from us," and went to prepare the sleeping draught, find the child's pajamas, select the story for the night.

She got up on Monday and moved about the house till noon. The boy, delighted to have her back, pretended he was a vicious tiger and followed her from room to room, growling and scratching. Whenever she came close, he would growl and scratch at her. One of his sharp little claws ripped her flesh, just above the wrist, and together they paused to watch a thin red line materialize on the inside of her pale arm and spill over in little beads. "Go away," she said. She got herself upstairs and locked the door. She called the husband's office and said, "I've locked myself away from him. I'm afraid." The husband told her in his richest voice to lie down, take it easy, and he was already on the phone to call one of the baby-sitters they often employed. Shortly after, she heard the girl let herself in, heard the girl coaxing the frightened child to come and play.

After supper several nights later, she hit the child. She had known she was going to do it when the father would see. "I'm sorry," she said, collapsing on the floor. The weeping child had run to hide. "What has happened to me? I'm not myself anymore." The man picked her tenderly from the floor and looked at her with much concern. "Would it help if we got, you know, a girl in? We could fix the room downstairs. I want you to feel freer," he said, understanding these things. "We have the money for a girl. I want you to think about it."

And now the sleeping draught was a nightly thing; she did not have to ask. He went down to the kitchen to mix it; he set it nightly beside her bed. The little glass and the big one, amber and deep rich brown, the flannel gown and the eiderdown.

The man put out the word and found the perfect girl. She was young, dynamic, and not pretty. "Don't bother with the room, I'll fix it up myself." Laughing, she employed her thousand energies. She painted the room white, fed the child lunch, read edifying books, raced the boy to the mailbox, hung her own watercolors on the fresh-painted walls, made spinach soufflé, cleaned a spot from the mother's coat, made them all laugh, danced in stocking feet to music in the white room after reading the child to sleep. She knitted dresses for herself and played chess with the husband. She washed and set the mother's soft ash-blond hair and gave her neck rubs, offered to.

The woman now spent her winter afternoons in the big bedroom. She made a fire in the hearth and put on slacks and an old sweater she had loved at school, and sat in the big chair and stared out the window at snow-ridden branches, or went away into long novels about other people moving through other winters.

The girl brought the child in twice a day, once in the late afternoon when he would tell of his day, all of it tumbling out quickly because there was not much time, and before he went to bed. Often now, the man took his wife to dinner. He made a courtship ceremony of it, inviting her beforehand so she could get used to the idea. They dressed and were beautiful together again and went out into the frosty night. Over candlelight he would say, "I think you are better, you know."

"Perhaps I am," she would murmur. "You look . . . like a cloistered queen," he said once, his voice breaking curiously.

One afternoon the girl brought the child into the bedroom. "We've been out playing in the park. He found something he wants to give you, a surprise." The little boy approached her, smiling mysteriously. He placed his cupped hands in hers and left a live dry thing that spat brown juice in her palm and leapt away. She screamed and wrung her hands to be rid of the brown juice. "Oh, it was only a grasshopper," said the girl. Nimbly she crept to the edge of a curtain, did a quick knee bend, and reclaimed the creature, led the boy competently from the room.

"The girl upsets me," said the woman to her husband. He sat frowning on the side of the bed he had not entered for so long. "I'm sorry, but there it is." The husband stroked his creased brow and said he was sorry, too. He really did not know what they would do without that treasure of a girl. "Why don't you stay here with me in bed," the woman said.

Next morning she fired the girl, who cried and said, "I loved the little boy, what will become of him now?" But the mother turned away her face and the girl took down the watercolors from the walls, sheathed the records she had danced to, and went away.

"I don't know what we'll do. It's all my fault, I know. I'm such a burden, I know that."

"Let me think. I'll think of something." (Still understanding these things.)

"I know you will. You always do," she said.

With great care he rearranged his life. He got up hours early, did the shopping, cooked the breakfast, took the boy to nursery school. "We will manage," he said, "until you're better, however long that is." He did his work, collected the boy from the school, came home and made the supper, washed the dishes, got the child to bed. He managed everything. One evening, just as she was on the verge of swallowing her draught, there was a timid knock on her door. The little boy came in wearing his pajamas. "Daddy has fallen asleep on my bed and I can't get in. There's not room."

Very sedately she left her bed and went to the child's room. Things were much changed. Books were rearranged, toys. He'd done some new drawings. She came as a visitor to her son's room, wakened the father, and helped him to bed. "Ah, he shouldn't have bothered you," said the man, leaning on his wife. "I've told him not to." He dropped into his own bed and fell asleep with a moan. Meticulously she undressed him. She folded and hung his clothes. She covered his body with the bedclothes. She flicked off the light that shone in his face.

The next day she moved her things into the girl's white room. She put her hairbrush on the dresser; she put a note pad and pen beside the bed. She stocked the little room with cigarettes, books, bread, and cheese. She didn't need much.

At first the husband was dismayed. But he was receptive to her needs. He understood these things. "Perhaps the best thing is for you to follow it through," he said. "I want to be big enough to contain whatever you must do."

All day long she stayed in the white room. She was a young queen, a virgin in a tower; she was the previous inhabitant, the girl with all the energies. She tried these personalities on like costumes, then discarded them. The room had a new view of streets she'd never seen that way before. The sun hit the room in late afternoon, and she took to brushing her hair in the sun. One day she decided to write a poem. "Perhaps a sonnet." She took up her pen and pad and began working from words that had lately lain in her mind. She had choices for the sonnet, ABAB or ABBA for a start. She pondered these possibilities until she tottered into a larger choice: she did not have to write a sonnet. Her poem could be six, eight, ten, thirteen lines, it could be any number of lines, and it did not even have to rhyme.

She put down the pen on top of the pad.

In the evenings, very briefly, she saw the two of them. They knocked on her door, a big knock and a little, and she would call "Come in," and the husband would smile though he looked a bit tired, yet somehow this tiredness suited him. He would put her sleeping draught on the bedside table and say, "The boy and I have done all right today," and the child would kiss her. One night she tasted for the first time the power of his baby spit.

"I don't think I can see him anymore," she whispered sadly to the man. And the husband turned away, but recovered admirably and said, "Of course, I see."

So the husband came alone. "I have explained to the boy," he said. "And we are doing fine. We are managing." He squeezed his wife's pale arm and put the two glasses on her table. After he had gone, she sat looking at the arm.

"I'm afraid it's come to that," she said next time. "Just push the notes under the door; I'll read them. And don't forget to leave the draught outside."

The man sat for a long time with his head in his hands. Then he rose and went away from her. She heard him in the kitchen where he mixed the draught in batches now to last a week at a time, storing it in a corner of the cupboard. She heard him come back, leave the big glass and the little one outside on the floor.

Outside her window, the snow was melting from the branches, there were more people on the streets. She brushed her hair a lot and seldom read anymore. She sat in her window and brushed her hair for hours, and saw a boy fall off his new bicycle again and again, a dog chasing a squirrel, an old woman peek slyly over her shoulder and then extract a parcel from a garbage can.

In the evening she read the notes they slipped under her door. The child could not write, so he drew and sometimes painted his. The notes were painstaking at first, the man and boy offering the final strength of their day to her. But sometimes, when they seemed to have had a bad day, there were only hurried scrawls.

One night, when the husband's note had been extremely short, loving but short, and there had been nothing from the boy, she stole out of her room as she often did to get more supplies, but crept upstairs instead and stood outside their doors, listening to the regular breathing of the man and boy asleep. She hurried back to her room and drank the draught.

She woke earlier now. It was spring, there were birds. She listened for sounds of the man and the boy eating breakfast; she listened for the roar of the motor when they drove away. One beautiful noon, she went out to look at her kitchen in the daylight. Things were changed. He had bought some new dishtowels. Had the old ones worn out? The canisters seemed closer to the sink. She inspected the cupboard and saw new things among the old. She got out flour, yeast, salt, milk (he bought a different brand of butter), and baked a loaf of bread and left it cooling on the table.

The force of the two joyful notes slipped under her door that evening pressed her into the corner of the little room; she had hardly space to breathe. As soon as possible, she drank the draught.

Now the days were too short. She was always busy. She woke with the first bird. Worked till the sun set. No time for hair-brushing. Her fingers raced the hours.

Finally, in the nick of time, it was finished one late afternoon. Her veins pumped and her forehead sparkled. She went to the kitchen cupboard, took what was hers, closed herself into the little white room, and brushed her hair for a while.

The man and boy came home and found: five loaves of warm bread, a roast stuffed turkey, a glazed ham, three pies of different fillings, eight molds of the boy's favorite custard, two weeks' supply of fresh-laundered sheets and shirts and towels, two hand-knitted sweaters (both of the same gray color), a sheath of marvelous watercolor beasts accompanied by mad and fanciful stories nobody could ever make up again, and a tablet full of love sonnets addressed to the man. The house was redolent of renewal and spring. The man ran to the little room, could not contain himself to knock, flung back the door.

"Look, Mommy is sleeping," said the boy. "She's tired from doing all our things again." He dawdled in a stream of the last sun for that day and watched his father tenderly roll back her eyelids, lay his ear softly to her breast, test the delicate bones of her wrist. The father put down his face into her fresh-washed hair.

"Can we eat the turkey for supper?" the boy asked.

QUESTIONS

1. An omniscient narrator knows things no first-person participant or observer can know, as, for example, the thoughts, emotions, and motivations of different characters. What are some of the examples of omniscience in this story?

2. All omniscient narrators withhold information, telling only what they think matters in the order that will make the best story. This one does not tell the name of the woman or her husband and tells nothing of their past. Why? Similarly, the narrator tells us the husband "did the shopping . . . took the boy to nursery school . . . did his work," but gives no details of his life outside the house. Why?

3. Give several examples of external narrative perspective from the story. Give several examples of internal narrative perspective. Is it always clear which is which?

4. Is the internal narrative perspective always that of the wife? Mostly so? Does it matter?
5. In what ways are thoughts presented within the story? Can you find good examples of direct interior presentation of thoughts? Indirect?
6. Can you find a passage of thought long enough to be called an interior monologue? If so, is it direct or indirect?
7. In what ways may this story be compared and contrasted to Charlotte Perkins Gilman's "The Yellow Wall-Paper"? Consider both the story and the manner of its telling.

In writing his "Mother and Daughter," D. H. Lawrence used a narrative voice much more far reaching than the ones used by Godwin and Fitzgerald for their stories.

MOTHER AND DAUGHTER

D. H. Lawrence   (1885–1930)

Virginia Bodoin had a good job: she was head of a department in a certain government office, held a responsible position, and earned, to imitate Balzac[1] and be precise about it, seven hundred and fifty pounds a year. That is already something. Rachel Bodoin, her mother, had an income of about six hundred a year, on which she had lived in the capitals of Europe since the effacement of a never very important husband.

Now, after some years of virtual separation and 'freedom', mother and daughter once more thought of settling down. They had become, in course of time, more like a married couple than mother and daughter. They knew one another very well indeed, and each was a little 'nervous' of the other. They had lived together and parted several times. Virginia was now thirty, and she didn't look like marrying. For four years she had been as good as married to Henry Lubbock, a rather spoilt young man who was musical. Then Henry let her down: for two reasons. He couldn't stand her mother. Her mother couldn't stand him. And anybody whom Mrs. Bodoin could not stand she managed to sit on, disastrously. So Henry had writhed horribly, feeling his mother-in-law sitting on him tight, and Virginia after all, in a helpless sort of family loyalty, sitting alongside her mother. Virginia didn't really want to sit on Henry. But when her mother egged her on, she couldn't help it. For ultimately her mother had power over her; a strange *female* power, nothing to do with parental authority. Virginia had long thrown parental authority to the winds. But her mother had another, much subtler form of domination, female and thrilling, so that when Rachel said: "Let's squash him!" Virginia had to rush wickedly and gleefully to the sport. And Henry knew quite well when he was being squashed. So that was one of his reasons for going back on Vinny. He called her Vinny, to the superlative disgust of Mrs. Bodoin, who always corrected him: "My daughter *Virginia*—"

[1]Honoré de Balzac (1799–1850), a French novelist noted for generous and precise detail.

The second reason was, again to be Balzacian, that Virginia hadn't a sou of her own. Henry had a sorry two hundred and fifty. Virginia, at the age of twenty-four, was already earning four hundred and fifty. But she was earning them. Whereas Henry managed to earn about twelve pounds per annum, by his precious music. He had realised that he would find it hard to earn more. So that marrying, except with a wife who could keep him, was rather out of the question. Vinny would inherit her mother's money. But then Mrs. Bodoin had the health and muscular equipment of the Sphinx. She would live for ever, seeking whom she might devour, and devouring him. Henry lived with Vinny for two years, in the married sense of the words: and Vinny felt they were married, minus a mere ceremony. But Vinny had her mother always in the background; often as far back as Paris or Biarritz, but still, within letter reach. And she never realised the funny little grin that came on her own elvish face when her mother, even in a letter, spread her skirts and calmly sat on Henry. She never realised that in spirit she promptly and mischievously sat on him too: she could no more have helped it than the tide can help turning to the moon. And she did not dream that he felt it, and was utterly mortified in his masculine vanity. Women, very often, hypnotise one another, and then, hypnotised, they proceed gently to wring the neck of the man they think they are loving with all their hearts. Then they call it utter perversity on his part, that he doesn't like having his neck wrung. They think he is repudiating a heart-felt love. For they are hypnotised. Women hypnotise one another, without knowing it.

In the end, Henry backed out. He saw himself being simply reduced to nothingness by two women, an old witch with muscles like the Sphinx, and a young, spell-bound witch, lavish, elvish and weak, who utterly spoilt him but who ate his marrow.

Rachel would write from Paris: "My Dear Virginia, as I had a windfall in the way of an investment, I am sharing it with you. You will find enclosed my cheque for twenty pounds. No doubt you will be needing it to buy Henry a suit of clothes, since the spring is apparently come, and the sunlight may be tempted to show him up for what he is worth. I don't want my daughter going around with what is presumably a street-corner musician, but please pay the tailor's bill yourself, or you may have to do it over again later." Henry got a suit of clothes, but it was as good as a shirt of Nessus,[2] eating him away with subtle poison.

So he backed out. He didn't jump out, or bolt, or carve his way out at the sword's point. He sort of faded out, distributing his departure over a year or more. He was fond of Vinny, and he could hardly do without her, and he was sorry for her. But at length he couldn't see her apart from her mother. She was a young, weak, spendthrift witch, accomplice of her tough-clawed witch of a mother.

Henry made other alliances, got a good hold on elsewhere, and gradually extricated himself. He saved his life, but he had lost, he felt, a good deal of his

---

[2]Heracles died as a result of contact with the poisoned blood of Nessus on a shirt given to him by his wife.

youth and marrow. He tended now to go fat, a little puffy, somewhat insignificant. And he had been handsome and striking-looking.

The two witches howled when he was lost to them. Poor Virginia was really half-crazy, she didn't know what to do with herself. She had a violent recoil from her mother. Mrs. Bodoin was filled with furious contempt for her daughter: that she should let such a hooked fish slip out of her hands! That she should allow such a person to turn her down! "I don't quite see my daughter seduced and thrown over by a sponging individual such as Henry Lubbock," she wrote. "But if it has happened, I suppose it is somebody's fault—"

There was a mutual recoil, which lasted nearly five years. But the spell was not broken. Mrs. Bodoin's mind never left her daughter, and Virginia was ceaselessly aware of her mother, somewhere in the universe. They wrote, and met at intervals, but they kept apart in recoil.

The spell, however, was between them, and gradually it worked. They felt more friendly. Mrs. Bodoin came to London. She stayed in the same quiet hotel with her daughter: Virginia had had two rooms in an hotel for the past three years. And, at last, they thought of taking an apartment together.

Virginia was now over thirty. She was still thin and odd and elvish, with a very slight and piquant cast in one of her brown eyes, and she still had her odd, twisted smile, and her slow, rather deep-toned voice, that caressed a man like the stroking of subtle fingertips. Her hair was still a natural tangle of curls, a bit dishevelled. She still dressed with a natural elegance which tended to go wrong and a tiny bit sluttish. She still might have a hole in her expensive and perfectly new stockings, and still she might have to take off her shoes in the drawing-room, if she came to tea, and sit there in her stockinged-feet. True, she had elegant feet: she was altogether elegantly shaped. But it wasn't that. It was neither coquetry nor vanity. It was simply that, after having gone to a good shoemaker and paid five guineas for a pair of perfectly simple and natural shoes, made to her feet, the said shoes would hurt her excruciatingly, when she had walked half a mile in them, and she would simply have to take them off, even if she sat on the kerb to do it. It was a fatality. There was a touch of the *gamin* in her very feet, a certain sluttishness that wouldn't let them stay properly in nice proper shoes. She practically always wore her mother's old shoes. "Of course, I go through life in mother's old shoes. If she died and left me without a supply, I suppose I should have to go in a bath-chair," she would say, with her odd twisted little grin. She was so elegant, and yet a slut. It was her charm, really.

Just the opposite of her mother. They would wear each other's shoes and each other's clothes, which seemed remarkable, for Mrs. Bodoin seemed so much the bigger of the two. But Virginia's shoulders were broad; if she was thin, she had a strong frame, even when she looked a frail rag.

Mrs. Bodoin was one of those women of sixty or so, with a terrible inward energy and a violent sort of vitality. But she managed to hide it. She sat with perfect repose, and folded hands. One thought: What a calm woman! Just as one may look at the snowy summit of a quiescent volcano, in the evening light, and think: What peace!

It was strange *muscular* energy which possessed Mrs. Bodoin, as it possesses, curiously enough, many women over fifty, and is usually distasteful in its manifestations. Perhaps it accounts for the lassitude of the young.

But Mrs. Bodoin recognised the bad taste in her energetic coevals, so she cultivated repose. Her very way of pronouncing the word, in two syllables: re-pòse, making the second syllable run on into the twilight, showed how much suppressed energy she had. Faced with the problem of iron-grey hair and black eyebrows, she was too clever to try dyeing herself back into youth. She studied her face, her whole figure, and decided that it was *positive.* There was no denying it. There was no wispiness, no hollowness, no limp frail blossom-on-a-bending-stalk about her. Her figure, though not stout, was full, strange, and *cambré.* [3] Her face had an aristocratic arched nose, aristocratic, who-the-devil-are-you grey eyes, and cheeks rather long but also rather full. Nothing appealing or youthfully skittish here.

Like an independent woman, she used her wits, and decided most emphatically not to be youthful or skittish or appealing. She would keep her dignity, for she was fond of it. She was positive. She liked to be positive. She was used to her positivity. So she would just *be* positive.

She turned to the positive period; to the eighteenth century, to Voltaire, to Ninon de l'Enclos and the Pompadour, to Madame la Duchesse and Monsieur le Marquis. She decided that she was not much in the line of la Pompadour or la Duchesse, but almost exactly in the line of Monsieur le Marquis. And she was right. With hair silvering to white, brushed back clean from her positive brow and temples, cut short, but sticking out a little behind, with her rather full, pink face and thin black eyebrows plucked to two fine, superficial crescents, her arching nose and her rather full insolent eyes she was perfectly eighteenth century, the early half. That she was Monsieur le Marquis rather than Madame la Marquise made her really modern.

Her appearance was perfect. She wore delicate combinations of grey and pink, maybe with a darkening iron-grey touch, and her jewels were of soft old coloured paste. Her bearing was a sort of alert repose, very calm, but very assured. There was, to use a vulgarism, no getting past her.

She had a couple of thousand pounds she could lay hands on. Virginia, of course, was always in debt. But, after all, Virginia was not to be sniffed at. She made seven hundred and fifty a year.

Virginia was oddly clever, and not clever. She didn't *really* know anything, because anything and everything was interesting to her for the moment, and she picked it up at once. She picked up languages with extraordinary ease, she was fluent in a fortnight. This helped her enormously with her job. She could prattle away with heads of industry, let them come from where they liked. But she didn't *know* any language, not even her own. She picked things up in her sleep, so to speak, without knowing anything about them.

And this made her popular with men. With all her curious facility, they didn't

[3] Well set.

feel small in front of her, because she was like an instrument. She had to be prompted. Some man had to set her in motion, and then she worked, really cleverly. She could collect the most valuable information. She was very useful. She worked with men, spent most of her time with men, her friends were practically all men. She didn't feel easy with women.

Yet she had no lover, nobody seemed eager to marry her, nobody seemed eager to come close to her at all. Mrs. Bodoin said: "I'm afraid Virginia is a one-man woman. I am a one-man woman. So was my mother, and so was my grandmother. Virginia's father was the only man in my life, the only one. And I'm afraid Virginia is the same, tenacious. Unfortunately, the man was what he was, and her life is just left there."

Henry had said, in the past, that Mrs. Bodoin wasn't a one-man woman, she was a no-man woman, and that if she could have had her way, everything male would have been wiped off the face of the earth, and only the female element left.

However, Mrs. Bodoin thought that it was now time to make a move. So she and Virginia took a quite handsome apartment in one of the old Bloomsbury squares, fitted it up and furnished it with extreme care, and with some quite lovely things, got in a very good man, an Austrian, to cook, and they set up married life together, mother and daughter.

At first it was rather thrilling. The two reception-rooms, looking down on the dirty old trees of the Square gardens, were of splendid proportions, and each with three great windows coming down low, almost to the level of the knees. The chimney-piece was late eighteenth century. Mrs. Bodoin furnished the rooms with a gentle suggestion of Louis-Seize merged with Empire, without keeping to any particular style. But she had, saved from her own home, a really remarkable Aubusson carpet. It looked almost new, as if it had been woven two years ago, and was startling, yet somehow rather splendid, as it spread its rose-red borders and wonderful florid array of silver-grey and gold-grey roses, lilies and gorgeous swans and trumpeting volutes away over the floor. Very aesthetic people found it rather loud, they preferred the worn, dim yellowish Aubusson in the big bedroom. But Mrs. Bodoin loved her drawing-room carpet. It was positive, but it was not vulgar. It had a certain grand air in its floridity. She felt it gave her a proper footing. And it behaved very well with her painted cabinets and grey-and-gold brocade chairs and big Chinese vases, which she liked to fill with big flowers: single Chinese peonies, big roses, great tulips, orange lilies. The dim room of London, with all its atmospheric colour, would stand the big, free, fisticuffing flowers.

Virginia, for the first time in her life, had the pleasure of making a home. She was again entirely under her mother's spell, and swept away, thrilled to her marrow. She had had no idea that her mother had got such treasures as the carpets and painted cabinets and brocade chairs up her sleeve: many of them the débris of the Fitzpatrick home in Ireland, Mrs. Bodoin being a Fitzpatrick. Almost like a child, like a bride, Virginia threw herself into the business of fixing up the rooms. "Of course, Virginia, I consider this is your apartment," said Mrs.

Bodoin. "I am nothing but your *dame de compagnie,*[4] and shall carry out your wishes entirely, if you will only express them."

Of course Virginia expressed a few, but not many. She introduced some wild pictures bought from impecunious artists whom she patronised. Mrs. Bodoin thought the pictures positive about the wrong things, but as far as possible, she let them stay: looking on them as the necessary element of modern ugliness. But by that element of modern ugliness, wilfully so, it was easy to see the things that Virginia had introduced into the apartment.

Perhaps nothing goes to the head like setting up house. You can get drunk on it. You feel you are creating something. Nowadays it is no longer the 'home', the domestic nest. It is 'my rooms', or 'my house', the great garment which reveals and clothes 'my personality'. Mrs. Bodoin, deliberately scheming for Virginia, kept moderately cool over it, but even she was thrilled to the marrow, and of an intensity and ferocity with the decorators and furnishers, astonishing. But Virginia was just all the time tipsy with it, as if she had touched some magic button on the grey wall of life, and with an Open Sesame![5] her lovely and coloured rooms had begun to assemble out of fairyland. It was far more vivid and wonderful to her than if she had inherited a duchy.

The mother and daughter, the mother in a sort of faded russet crimson and the daughter in silver, began to entertain. They had, of course, mostly men. It filled Mrs. Bodoin with a sort of savage impatience to entertain women. Besides, most of Virginia's acquaintances were men. So there were dinners and well-arranged evenings.

It went well, but something was missing. Mrs. Bodoin wanted to be gracious, so she held herself rather back. She stayed a little distant, was calm, reposed, eighteenth-century, and determined to be a foil to the clever and slightly-elvish Virginia. It was a pose, and alas, it stopped something. She was very nice with the men, no matter what her contempt of them. But the men were uneasy with her: afraid.

What they all felt, all the men guests, was that *for them,* nothing really happened. Everything that happened was between mother and daughter. All the flow was between mother and daughter. A subtle, hypnotic spell encompassed the two women, and, try as they might, the men were shut out. More than one young man, a little dazzled, *began* to fall in love with Virginia. But it was impossible. Not only was he shut out, he was, in some way, annihilated. The spontaneity was killed in his bosom. While the two women sat, brilliant and rather wonderful, in magnetic connection at opposite ends of the table, like two witches, a double Circe[6] turning the men not into swine—the men would have liked that well enough—but into lumps.

It was tragic. Because Mrs. Bodoin wanted Virginia to fall in love and marry. She really wanted it, and she attributed Virginia's lack of forthcoming to the delinquent Henry. She never realised the hypnotic spell, which of course encom-

[4]Female companion.　[5]The magic words that opened the cave of jewels in "Ali Baba and the Forty Thieves."　[6]The enchantress who turns men to swine in Homer's *Odyssey,* Book X.

passed her as well as Virginia, and made men just an impossibility to both women, mother and daughter alike.

At this time, Mrs. Bodoin hid her humour. She had a really marvellous faculty of humorous imitation. She could imitate the Irish servants from her old home, or the American woman who called on her, or the modern ladylike young men, the asphodels, as she called them: "Of course, you know the asphodel is a kind of onion! Oh yes, just an over-bred onion": who wanted, with their murmuring voices and peeping under their brows, to make her feel very small and very bourgeois. She could imitate them all with a humour that was really touched with genius. But it was devastating. It demolished the objects of her humour so absolutely, smashed them to bits with a ruthless hammer, pounded them to nothing so terribly, that it frightened people, particularly men. It frightened men off.

So she hid it. She hid it. But there it was, up her sleeve, her merciless, hammer-like humour, which just smashed its object on the head and left him brained. She tried to disown it. She tried to pretend, even to Virginia, that she had the gift no more. But in vain the hammer hidden up her sleeve hovered over the head of every guest, and every guest felt his scalp creep, and Virginia felt her inside creep with a little, mischievous, slightly idiotic grin, as still another fool male was mystically knocked on the head. It was a sort of uncanny sport.

No, the plan was not going to work: the plan of having Virginia fall in love and marry. Of course, the men *were* such lumps, such *oeufs farcies.* [7] There was one, at least, that Mrs. Bodoin had real hopes of. He was a healthy and normal and very good-looking boy of good family, with no money, alas, but clerking to the House of Lords and very hopeful, and not very clever, but simply in love with Virginia's cleverness. He was just the one Mrs. Bodoin would have married for herself. True, he was only twenty-six, to Virginia's thirty-one. But he had rowed in the Oxford eight, and adored horses, talked horses adorably, and was simply infatuated by Virginia's cleverness. To him Virginia had the finest mind on earth. She was as wonderful as Plato, but infintely more attractive because she was a woman, and winsome with it. Imagine a winsome Plato with untidy curls and the tiniest little brown-eyed squint and just a hint of woman's pathetic need for a protector, and you may imagine Adrian's feeling for Virginia. He adored her on his knees, but he felt he could protect her.

"Of course, he's just a very nice *boy!*" said Mrs. Bodoin. "He's a boy, and that's all you can say. And he always will be a boy. But that's the very nicest kind of man, the only kind you can live with: the eternal boy. Virginia, aren't you attracted to him?"

"Yes, mother! I think he's an awfully nice *boy,* as you say," replied Virginia, in her rather low, musical, whimsical voice. But the mocking little curl in the intonation put the lid on Adrian. Virginia was not marrying a nice *boy!* She could be malicious too, against her mother's taste. And Mrs. Bodoin let escape her a faint gesture of impatience.

[7]Stuffed eggs.

For she had been planning her own retreat, planning to give Virginia the apartment outright, and half of her own income, if she would marry Adrian. Yes, the mother was already scheming how best she could live with dignity on three hundred a year, once Virginia was happily married to that most attractive if slightly brainless *boy.*

A year later, when Virginia was thirty-two, Adrian, who had married a wealthy American girl and been transferred to a job in the legation at Washington in the meantime, faithfully came to see Virginia as soon as he was in London, faithfully kneeled at her feet, faithfully thought her the most wonderful spiritual being, and faithfully felt that she, Virginia, could have done wonders with him, which wonders would now never be done, for he had married in the meantime.

Virginia was looking haggard and worn. The scheme of a *ménage à deux*[8] with her mother had not succeeded. And now, work was telling on the younger woman. It is true, she was amazingly facile. But facility wouldn't get her all the way. She had to earn her money, and earn it hard. She had to slog, and she had to concentrate. While she could work by quick intuition and without much responsibility, work thrilled her. But as soon as she had to get down to it, as they say, grip and slog and concentrate, in a really responsible position, it wore her out terribly. She had to do it all off her nerves. She hadn't the same sort of fighting power as a man. Where a man can summon his old Adam in him to fight through his work, a woman has to draw on her nerves, and on her nerves alone. For the old Eve in her will have nothing to do with such work. So that mental responsibility, mental concentration, mental slogging wear out a woman terribly, especially if she is head of a department, and not working *for* somebody.

So poor Virginia was worn out. She was thin as a rail. Her nerves were frayed to bits. And she could never forget her beastly work. She would come home at tea-time speechless and done for. Her mother, tortured by the sight of her, longed to say: "Has anything gone wrong, Virginia? Have you had anything particularly trying at the office to-day?" But she learned to hold her tongue, and say nothing. The question would be the last straw to Virginia's poor overwrought nerves, and there would be a little scene which, despite Mrs. Bodoin's calm and forbearance, offended the elder woman to the quick. She had learned, by bitter experience, to leave her child alone, as one would leave a frail tube of vitriol alone. But, of course, she could not keep her *mind* off Virginia. That was impossible. And poor Virginia, under the strain of work and the strain of her mother's awful ceaseless mind, was at the very end of her strength and resources.

Mrs. Bodoin had always disliked the fact of Virginia's doing a job. But now she hated it. She hated the whole government office with violent and virulent hate. Not only was it undignified for Virginia to be tied up there, but it was turning her, Mrs. Bodoin's daughter, into a thin, nagging, fearsome old maid. Could anything be more utterly English and humiliating to a well-born Irishwoman?

After a long day attending to the apartment, skilfully darning one of the brocade chairs, polishing the Venetian mirrors to her satisfaction, selecting

[8]Housekeeping for two.

flowers, doing certain shopping and housekeeping, attending perfectly to every-thing, then receiving callers in the afternoon, with never-ending energy, Mrs. Bodoin would go up from the drawing-room after tea and write a few letters, take her bath, dress with great care—she enjoyed attending to her person—and come down to dinner as fresh as a daisy, but far more energetic than that quiet flower. She was ready now for a full evening.

She was conscious, with gnawing anxiety, of Virginia's presence in the house, but she did not see her daughter till dinner was announced. Virginia slipped in, and away to her room unseen, never going into the drawing-room to tea. If Mrs. Bodoin heard her daughter's key in the latch, she quickly retired into one of the rooms till Virginia was safely through. It was too much for poor Virginia's nerves even to catch sight of anybody in the house, when she came in from the office. Bad enough to hear the murmur of visitors' voices behind the drawing-room door.

And Mrs. Bodoin would wonder: How is she? How is she to-night? I wonder what sort of a day she's had? And this thought would roam prowling through the house, to where Virginia was lying on her back in her room. But the mother would have to consume her anxiety till dinner-time. And then Virginia would appear, with black lines under her eyes, thin, tense, a young woman out of an office, the stigma upon her: badly dressed, a little acid in humour, with an impaired digestion, not interested in anything, blighted by her work. And Mrs. Bodoin, humiliated at the very sight of her, would control herself perfectly, say nothing but the mere smooth nothings of casual speech, and sit in perfect form presiding at a carefully-cooked dinner thought out entirely to please Virginia. Then Virginia hardly noticed what she ate.

Mrs. Bodoin was pining for an evening with life in it. But Virginia would lie on the couch and put on the loud-speaker. Or she would put a humorous record on the gramophone, and be amused, and hear it again, and be amused, and hear it again, six times, and six times be amused by a mildly funny record that Mrs. Bodoin now knew off by heart. "Why, Virginia, I could repeat that record over to you, if you wished it, without your troubling to wind up that gramophone." And Virginia, after a pause in which she seemed not to have heard what her mother said, would reply: "I'm sure you could, mother." And that simple speech would convey such volumes of contempt for all that Rachel Bodoin was or ever could be or ever had been, contempt for her energy, her vitality, her mind, her body, her very existence, that the elder woman would curl. It seemed as if the ghost of Robert Bodoin spoke out of the mouth of the daughter, in deadly venom. Then Virginia would put on the record for the seventh time.

During the second ghastly year, Mrs. Bodoin realised that the game was up. She was a beaten woman, a woman without object or meaning any more. The hammer of her awful female humour, which had knocked so many people on the head, all the people, in fact, that she had come into contact with, had at last flown backwards and hit herself on the head. For her daughter was her other self, her *alter ego*. The secret and the meaning and the power of Mrs. Bodoin's whole life lay in the hammer, that hammer of her living humour which knocked everything on the head. That had been her lust and her passion, knocking everybody and everything humorously on the head. She had felt inspired in it: it was a sort of mission. And she had hoped to hand on the hammer to Virginia, her clever, unsolid but still actual daughter, Virginia. Virginia was the continuation of Rachel's own self. Virginia was Rachel's *alter ego*, her other self.

But, alas, it was a half-truth. Virginia had had a father. The fact, which had been utterly ignored by the mother, was gradually brought home to her by the curious recoil of the hammer. Virginia was her father's daughter. Could anything be more unseemly, horrid, more perverse in the natural scheme of things? For Robert Bodoin had been fully and deservedly knocked on the head by Rachel's hammer. Could anything, then, be more disgusting than that he should resurrect again in the person of Mrs. Bodoin's own daughter, her own *alter ego* Virginia, and start hitting back with a little spiteful hammer that was David's pebble against Goliath's battle-axe!

But the little pebble was mortal. Mrs. Bodoin felt it sink into her brow, her temple, and she was finished. The hammer fell nerveless from her hand.

The two women were now mostly alone. Virginia was too tired to have company in the evening. So there was the gramophone or loud-speaker, or else silence. Both women had come to loathe the apartment. Virginia felt it was the last grand act of bullying on her mother's part, she felt bullied by the assertive Aubusson carpet, by the beastly Venetian mirrors, by the big over-cultured flowers. She even felt bullied by the excellent food, and longed again for a Soho restaurant and her two poky, shabby rooms in the hotel. She loathed the apartment: she loathed everything. But she had not the energy to move. She had not the energy to do anything. She crawled to her work, and for the rest, she lay flat, gone.

It was Virginia's worn-out inertia that really finished Mrs. Bodoin. That was the pebble that broke the bone of her temple: "To have to attend my daughter's funeral, and accept the sympathy of all her fellow-clerks in her office, no, that is a final humiliation which I must spare myself. No! If Virginia must be a lady-clerk, she must be it henceforth on her own responsibility. I will retire from her existence."

Mrs. Bodoin had tried hard to persuade Virginia to give up her work and come and live with her. She had offered her half her income. In vain. Virginia stuck to her office.

Very well! So be it! The apartment was a fiasco, Mrs. Bodoin was longing, longing to tear it to pieces again. One last and final blow of the hammer! "Virginia, don't you think we'd better get rid of this apartment, and live around as we used to do? Don't you think we'll do that?"—"But all the money you've put into it? and the lease for ten years!" cried Virginia, in a kind of inertia.—"Never mind! We had the pleasure of making it. And we've had as much pleasure out of living in it as we shall ever have. Now we'd better get rid of it—quickly—don't you think?"

Mrs. Bodoin's arms were twitching to snatch the pictures off the walls, roll up the Aubusson carpet, take the china out of the ivory-inlaid cabinet there and then, at that very moment.

"Let us wait till Sunday before we decide," said Virginia.

"Till Sunday! Four days! As long as that? Haven't we already decided in our own minds?" said Mrs. Bodoin.

"We'll wait till Sunday, anyhow," said Virginia.

The next evening, the Armenian came to dinner. Virginia called him Arnold, with the French pronunciation, Arnault. Mrs. Bodoin, who barely tolerated him, and could never get his name, which seemed to have a lot of bouyoums in it, called him either the Armenian or the Rahat Lakoum, after the name of the sweetmeat, or simply the Turkish Delight.

"Arnault is coming to dinner to-night, mother."

"Really! The Turkish Delight is coming here to dinner? Shall I provide anything special?" Her voice sounded as if she would suggest snails in aspic.

"I don't think so."

Virginia had seen a good deal of the Armenian at the office when she had to negotiate with him on behalf of the Board of Trade. He was a man of about sixty, a merchant, had been a millionaire, was ruined during the war, but was now coming on again, and represented trade in Bulgaria. He wanted to negotiate with the British Government, and the British Government sensibly negotiated with him: at first through the medium of Virginia. Now things were going satisfactorily between Monsieur Arnault, as Virginia called him, and the Board of Trade, so that a sort of friendship had followed the official relations.

The Turkish Delight was sixty, grey-haired and fat. He had numerous grandchildren growing up in Bulgaria, but he was a widower. He had a grey moustache cut like a brush, and glazed brown eyes over which hung heavy lids with white lashes. His manner was humble, but in his bearing there was a certain dogged conceit. One notices the combination sometimes in Jews. He had been very wealthy and kow-towed to, he had been ruined and humiliated, terribly humiliated, and now, doggedly, he was rising up again, his sons backing him, away in Bulgaria. One felt he was not alone. He had his sons, his family, his tribe behind him, away in the Near East.

He spoke bad English, but fairly fluent guttural French. He did not speak much, but he sat. He sat, with his short, fat thighs, as if for eternity, *there*. There was a strange potency in his fat immobile sitting, as if his posterior were connected with the very centre of the earth. And his brain, spinning away at the one point in question, business, was very agile. Business absorbed him. But not in a nervous, personal way. Somehow the family, the tribe was always felt behind him. It was business for the family, the tribe.

With the English he was humble, for the English like such aliens to be humble, and he had had a long schooling from the Turks. And he was always an outsider. Nobody would ever take any notice of him in society. He would just be an outsider, *sitting*.

"I hope, Virginia, you won't ask that Turkish-carpet gentleman when we have other people. I can bear it," said Mrs. Bodoin. "Some people might mind."

"Isn't it hard when you can't choose your own company in your own house," mocked Virginia.

"No! I don't care. I can meet anything and I'm sure, in the way of selling

Turkish carpets, your acquaintance is very good. But I don't suppose you look on him as a personal friend—?"

"I do. I like him quite a lot."

"Well—! As you will. But consider your *other* friends."

Mrs. Bodoin was really mortified this time. She looked on the Armenian as one looks on the fat Levantine in a fez who tries to sell one hideous tapestries at Port Said, or on the seafront at Nice, as being outside the class of human beings, and in the class of insects. That he had been a millionaire, and might be a millionaire again, only added venom to her feeling of disgust at being forced into contact with such scum. She could not even squash him, or annihilate him. In scum there is nothing to squash, for scum is only the unpleasant residue of that which was never anything but squashed.

However, she was not quite just. True, he was fat, and he sat, with short thighs, like a toad, as if seated for a toad's eternity. His colour was of a dirty sort of paste, his brown eyes were glazed under heavy lids. And he never spoke until spoken to, waiting in his toad's silence, like a slave.

But his thick, fine white hair, which stood up on his head like a soft brush, was curiously virile. And his curious small hands, of the same soft dull paste, had a peculiar, fat, soft masculine breeding of their own. And his dull brown eye could glint with the subtlety of serpents, under the white brush of eyelash. He was tired, but he was not defeated. He had fought, and won, and lost, and was fighting again, always at a disadvantage. He belonged to a defeated race which accepts defeat, but which gets its own back by cunning. He was the father of sons, the head of a family, one of the heads of a defeated but indestructible tribe. He was not alone, and so you could not lay your finger on him. His whole consciousness was patriarchal and tribal. And somehow, he was humble, but he was indestructible.

At dinner he sat half-effaced, humble, yet with the conceit of the humble. His manners were perfectly good, rather French. Virginia chattered to him in French, and he replied with that peculiar nonchalance of the boulevards, which was the only manner he could command when speaking French. Mrs. Bodoin understood, but she was what one would call a heavy-footed linguist, so when she said anything, it was intensely in English. And the Turkish Delight replied in his clumsy English, hastily. It was not his fault that French was being spoken. It was Virginia's.

He was very humble, conciliatory, with Mrs. Bodoin. But he cast at her sometimes that rapid glint of a reptilian glance as if to say: "Yes! I see you! You are a handsome figure. As an *objet de vertu*[9] you are almost perfect." Thus his connoisseur's, antique-dealer's eye would appraise her. But then his thick white eyebrows would seem to add: "But what, under holy Heaven, are you as a woman? You are neither wife nor mother nor mistress, you have no perfume of sex, you are more dreadful than a Turkish soldier or an English official. No man on earth could embrace you. You are a ghoul, you are a strange genie from the underworld!" And he would secretly invoke the holy names to shield him.

[9]Object of quality.

Yet he was in love with Virginia. He saw, first and foremost, the child in her, as if she were a lost child in the gutter, a waif with a faint, fascinating cast in her brown eyes, waiting till someone would pick her up. A fatherless waif! And he was tribal father, father through all the ages.

Then, on the other hand, he knew her peculiar disinterested cleverness in affairs. That, too, fascinated him: that odd, almost second-sight cleverness about business, and entirely impersonal, entirely in the air. It seemed to him very strange. But it would be an immense help to him in his schemes. He did not really understand the English. He was at sea with them. But with her, he would have a clue to everything. For she was, finally, quite a somebody among these English, these English officials.

He was about sixty. His family was established in the East, his grandsons were growing up. It was necessary for him to live in London for some years. This girl would be useful. She had no money, save what she would inherit from her mother. But he would risk that: she would be an investment in his business. And then the apartment. He liked the apartment extremely. He recognised the *cachet,* [10] and the lilies and swans of the Aubusson carpet really did something to him. Virginia said to him: "Mother gave me the apartment." So he looked on that as safe. And finally, Virginia was almost a virgin, probably quite a virgin, and, as far as the paternal Oriental male like himself was concerned, entirely virgin. He had a very small idea of the silly puppy-sexuality of the English, so different from the prolonged male voluptuousness of his own pleasures. And last of all, he was physically lonely, getting old and tired.

Virginia, of course, did not know why she liked being with Arnault. Her cleverness was amazingly stupid when it came to life, to living. She said he was 'quaint'. She said his nonchalant French of the boulevards was 'amusing'. She found his business cunning 'intriguing', and the glint in his dark glazed eyes, under the white, thick lashes, 'shieky'. She saw him quite often, had tea with him in his hotel, and motored with him one day down to the sea.

When he took her hand in his own soft still hands, there was something so caressing, so possessive in his touch, so strange and positive in his leaning towards her, that though she trembled with fear, she was helpless.—"But you are so thin, dear little thin thing, you need repose, repose, for the blossom to open, poor little blossom, to become a little fat!" he said in his French.

She quivered, and was helpless. It certainly was quaint! He was so strange and positive, he seemed to have all the power. The moment he realised that she would succumb into his power, he took full charge of the situation, he lost all his hesitation and his humility. He did not want just to make love to her: he wanted to marry her, for all his multifarious reasons. And he must make himself master of her.

He put her hand to his lips, and seemed to draw her life to his in kissing her thin hand. "The poor child is tired, she needs repose, she needs to be caressed and cared for," he said in his French. And he drew nearer to her.

[10]Style.

She looked up in dread at his glinting, tired dark eyes under the white lashes. But he used all his will, looking back at her heavily and calculating that she must submit. And he brought his body quite near to her, and put his hand softly on her face, and made her lay her face against his breast, as he soothingly stroked her arm with his other hand. "Dear little thing! Dear little thing! Arnault loves her so dearly! Arnault loves her! Perhaps she will marry her Arnault. Dear little girl, Arnault will put flowers in her life, and make her life perfumed with sweetness and content."

She leaned against his breast and let him caress her. She gave a fleeting, half poignant, half vindictive thought to her mother. Then she felt in the air the sense of destiny, destiny. Oh, so nice, not to have to struggle. To give way to destiny.

"Will she marry her old Arnault? Eh? Will she marry him?" he asked in a soothing, caressing voice, at the same time compulsive.

She lifted her head and looked at him: the thick white brows, the glinting, tired dark eyes. How queer and comic! How comic to be in his power! And he was looking a little baffled.

"Shall I?" she said, with her mischievous twist of a grin.

"Mais oui!" he said, with all the sang-froid of his old eyes. *"Mais oui! Je te contenterai, tu le verras."*[11]

"Tu me contenteras!"[12] she said, with a flickering smile of real amusement at his assurance. "Will you really content me?"

"But surely! I assure you it. And you will marry me?"

"You must tell mother," she said, and hid wickedly against his waistcoat again, while the male pride triumphed in him.

Mrs. Bodoin had no idea that Virginia was intimate with the Turkish Delight: she did not inquire into her daughter's movements. During the famous dinner, she was calm and a little aloof, but entirely self-possessed. When, after coffee, Virginia left her alone with the Turkish Delight, she made no effort at conversation, only glanced at the rather short, stout man in correct dinner-jacket, and thought how his sort of fatness called for a fez and the full muslin breeches of a bazaar merchant in *The Thief of Baghdad*.

"Do you really prefer to smoke a hookah?" she asked him, with a slow drawl.

"What is a hookah, please?"

"One of those water-pipes. Don't you all smoke them in the East?"

He only looked mystified and humble, and silence resumed. She little knew what was simmering inside his stillness.

"Madame," he said, "I want to ask you something."

"You do? Then why not ask it?" came her slightly melancholy drawl.

"Yes! It is this. I wish I may have the honour to marry your daughter. She is willing."

There was a moment's blank pause. Then Mrs. Bodoin leaned towards him from her distance with curious portentousness.

"What was that you said?" she asked. "Repeat it!"

[11]"Yes, indeed! I will content you, you will see."   [12]"You will content me?"

"I wish I may have the honour to marry your daughter. She is willing to take me."

His dark, glazed eyes looked at her, then glanced away again. Still leaning forward, she gazed fixedly on him, as if spellbound, turned to stone. She was wearing pink topaz ornaments, but he judged they were paste, moderately good.

"Did I hear you say she is willing to take you?" came the slow, melancholy, remote voice.

"Madame, I think so," he said, with a bow.

"I think we'll wait till she comes," she said, leaning back.

There was silence. She stared at the ceiling. He looked closely round the room, at the furniture, at the china in the ivory-inlaid cabinet.

"I can settle five thousand pounds on Mademoiselle Virginia, madame," came his voice. "Am I correct to assume that she will bring this apartment and its appointments into the marriage settlement?"

Absolute silence. He might as well have been on the moon. But he was a good sitter. He just sat until Virginia came in.

Mrs. Bodoin was still staring at the ceiling. The iron had entered her soul finally and fully. Virginia glanced at her, but said:

"Have a whisky-and-soda, Arnault?"

He rose and came towards the decanters, and stood beside her: a rather squat, stout man with white head, silent with misgiving. There was the fizz of the syphon: then they came to their chairs.

"Arnault has spoken to you, mother?" said Virginia.

Mrs. Bodoin sat up straight and gazed at Virginia with big, owlish eyes, haggard. Virginia was terrified, yet a little thrilled. Her mother was beaten.

"Is it true, Virginia, that you are *willing* to marry this—Oriental gentlemen?" asked Mrs. Bodoin slowly.

"Yes, mother, quite true," said Virginia, in her teasing soft voice.

Mrs. Bodoin looked owlish and dazed.

"May I be excused from having any part in it, or from having anything to do with your future *husband*—I mean having any business to transact with him?" she asked dazedly, in her slow, distinct voice.

"Why, of course!" said Virginia, frightened, smiling oddly.

There was a pause. Then Mrs. Bodoin, feeling old and haggard, pulled herself together again.

"Am I to understand that your future husband would like to possess this apartment?" came her voice.

Virginia smiled quickly and crookedly. Arnault just sat, planted on his posterior, and heard. She reposed on him.

"Well—perhaps!" said Virginia. "Perhaps he would like to know that I possessed it." She looked at him.

Arnault nodded gravely.

"And do you *wish* to possess it?" came Mrs. Bodoin's slow voice. "Is it your intention to *inhabit* it, with your *husband*?" She put eternities into her long, stressed words.

"Yes, I think it is," said Virginia. "You know you *said* the apartment was mine, mother."

"Very well! It shall be so. I shall send my lawyer to this—Oriental gentleman, if you will leave written instructions on my writing-table. May I ask when you think of getting—*married?*"

"When do you think, Arnault?" said Virginia.

"Shall it be in two weeks?" he said, sitting erect, with his fists on his knees.

"In about a fortnight, mother," said Virginia.

"I have heard? In two weeks! Very well! In two weeks everything shall be at your disposal. And now, please excuse me." She rose, made a slight general bow, and moved calmly and dimly from the room. It was killing her, that she could not shriek aloud and beat that Levantine out of the house. But she couldn't. She had imposed the restraint on herself.

Arnault stood and looked with glistening eyes round the room. It would be his. When his sons came to England, here he would receive them.

He looked at Virginia. She, too, was white and haggard now. And she flung away from him, as if in resentment. She resented the defeat of her mother. She was still capable of dismissing him for ever, and going back to her mother.

"Your mother is a wonderful lady," he said, going to Virginia and taking her hand. "But she has no husband to shelter her, she is unfortunate. I am sorry she will be alone. I should be happy if she would like to stay here with us."

The sly old fox knew what he was about.

"I'm afraid there's no hope of that," said Virginia, with a return of her old irony.

She sat on the couch, and he caressed her softly and paternally, and the very incongruity of it, there in her mother's drawing-room, amused her. And because he saw that the things in the drawing-room were handsome and valuable, and now they were his, his blood flushed and he caressed the thin girl at his side with passion, because she represented these valuable surroundings, and brought them to his possession. And he said: "And with me you will be very comfortable, very content, oh, I shall make you content, not like madame your mother. And you will get fatter, and bloom like the rose. I shall make you bloom like the rose. And shall we say next week, hein? Shall it be next week, next Wednesday, that we marry? Wednesday is a good day. Shall it be then?"

"Very well!" said Virginia, caressed again into a luxurious sense of destiny, reposing on fate, having to make no effort, no more effort, all her life.

Mrs. Bodoin moved into an hotel next day, and came into the apartment to pack up and extricate herself and her immediate personal belongings only when Virginia was necessarily absent. She and her daughter communicated by letter, as far as was necessary.

And in five days' time Mrs. Bodoin was clear. All business that could be settled was settled, all her trunks were removed. She had five trunks, and that was all. Denuded and outcast, she would depart to Paris, to live out the rest of her days.

The last day she waited in the drawing-room till Virginia should come home. She sat there in her hat and street things, like a stranger.

"I just waited to say good-bye" she said. "I leave in the morning for Paris. This is my address. I think everything is settled; if not, let me know and I'll attend to it. Well, good-bye!—and I hope you'll be *very happy!*"

She dragged out the last words sinisterly; which restored Virginia, who was beginning to lose her head.

"Why, I think I may be," said Virginia, with the twist of a smile.

"I shouldn't wonder," said Mrs. Bodoin pointedly and grimly. "I think the Armenian grandpapa knows very well what he's about. You're just the harem type, after all." The words came slowly, dropping, each with a plop! of deep contempt.

"I suppose I am! Rather fun!" said Virginia. "But I wonder where I got it? Not from you, mother—" she drawled mischievously.

"I should say *not.*"

"Perhaps daughters go by contraries, like dreams," mused Virginia wickedly. "All the harem was left out of you, so perhaps it all had to be put back into me."

Mrs. Bodoin flashed a look at her.

"You have *all* my *pity!*" she said.

"Thank you, dear. You have just a bit of mine."

QUESTIONS

1. In what ways is the ominiscience in this story less limited than the omniscience in "A Sorrowful Woman" or "Babylon Revisited"? Is Lawrence's omniscience limited at all in significant ways? For instance, does the narrator focus on any character more than on others?

2. What are the differences between Virginia's first suitor and her last? Why is the last more successful?

3. Summarize the relationship between mother and daughter. Does it remain the same throughout the story? Does the narrator approve of one more than the other? Should we?

4. Is it true that "Women hypnotise one another, without knowing it"? Are other observations of the narrator true, or matters of opinion?

5. Can we use the narrator's many opinions and attitudes to draw a character study of him?

6. Explain the meaning of the last two lines of the story.

"The Storm" is a very short story, but observe the cumulative effect of the storyteller's all-encompassing knowledge.

THE STORM

Kate Chopin   *(1851–1904)*

I

The leaves were so still that even Bibi thought it was going to rain. Bobinôt, who was accustomed to converse on terms of perfect equality with his little son, called the child's attention to certain sombre clouds that were rolling with sinister intention from the west, accompanied by a sullen, threatening roar. They were at Friedheimer's store and decided to remain there till the storm had passed. They sat within the door on two empty kegs. Bibi was four years old and looked very wise.

"Mama'll be 'fraid, yes," he suggested with blinking eyes.

"She'll shut the house. Maybe she got Sylvie helpin' her this evenin'," Bobinôt responded reassuringly.

"No; she ent got Sylvie. Sylvie was helpin' her yistiday," piped Bibi.

Bobinôt arose and going across to the counter purchased a can of shrimps, of which Calixta was very fond. Then he returned to his perch on the keg and sat stolidly holding the can of shrimps while the storm burst. It shook the wooden store and seemed to be ripping great furrows in the distant field. Bibi laid his little hand on his father's knee and was not afraid.

II

Calixta, at home, felt no uneasiness for their safety. She sat at a side window sewing furiously on a sewing machine. She was greatly occupied and did not notice the approaching storm. But she felt very warm and often stopped to mop her face on which the perspiration gathered in beads. She unfastened her white sacque at the throat. It began to grow dark, and suddenly realizing the situation she got up hurriedly and went about closing windows and doors.

Out on the small front gallery she had hung Bobinôt's Sunday clothes to air and she hastened out to gather them before the rain fell. As she stepped outside, Alcée Laballière rode in at the gate. She had not seen him very often since her marriage, and never alone. She stood there with Bobinôt's coat in her hands, and the big rain drops began to fall. Alcée rode his horse under the shelter of a side projection where the chickens had huddled and there were plows and a harrow piled up in the corner.

"May I come and wait on your gallery till the storm is over, Calixta?" he asked.

"Come 'long in, M'sieur Alcée."

His voice and her own startled her as if from a trance, and she seized Bobinôt's vest. Alcée, mounting to the porch, grabbed the trousers and snatched Bibi's braided jacket that was about to be carried away by a sudden gust of wind. He expressed an intention to remain outside, but it was soon apparent that he might as well have been out in the open: the water beat in upon the boards in driving sheets, and he went inside, closing the door after him. It was even necessary to put something beneath the door to keep the water out.

"My! what a rain! It's good two years sence it rain' like that," exclaimed Calixta as she rolled up a piece of bagging and Alcée helped her to thrust it beneath the crack.

She was a little fuller of figure than five years before when she married; but she had lost nothing of her vivacity. Her blue eyes still retained their melting quality; and her yellow hair, dishevelled by the wind and rain, kinked more stubbornly than ever about her ears and temples.

The rain beat upon the low, shingled roof with a force and clatter that threatened to break an entrance and deluge them there. They were in the dining room —the sitting room—the general utility room. Adjoining was her bed room, with Bibi's couch along side her own. The door stood open, and the room with its white, monumental bed, its closed shutters, looked dim and mysterious.

Alcée flung himself into a rocker and Calixta nervously began to gather up from the floor the lengths of a cotton sheet which she had been sewing.

"If this keeps up, *Dieu sait*[1] if the levees goin' to stan' it!" she exclaimed.

"What have you got to do with the levees?"

"I got enough to do! An' there's Bobinôt with Bibi out in that storm—if he only didn't left Friedheimer's!"

"Let us hope, Calixta, that Bobinôt's got sense enough to come in out of a cyclone."

She went and stood at the window with a greatly disturbed look on her face. She wiped the frame that was clouded with moisture. It was stiflingly hot. Alcée got up and joined her at the window, looking over her shoulder. The rain was coming down in sheets obscuring the view of far-off cabins and enveloping the distant wood in a gray mist. The playing of the lightning was incessant. A bolt struck a tall chinaberry tree at the edge of the field. It filled all visible space with a blinding glare and the crash seemed to invade the very boards they stood upon.

Calixta put her hands to her eyes, and with a cry, staggered backward. Alcée's arm encircled her, and for an instant he drew her close and spasmodically to him.

"*Bonté!*"[2] she cried, releasing herself from his encircling arm and retreating from the window, "the house'll go next! If I only knew w'ere Bibi was!" She would not compose herself; she would not be seated. Alcée clasped her shoulders and looked into her face. The contact of her warm, palpitating body when he had unthinkingly drawn her into his arms, had aroused all the old-time infatuation and desire for her flesh.

"Calixta," he said, "don't be frightened. Nothing can happen. The house is too low to be struck, with so many tall trees standing about. There! aren't you going to be quiet? say, aren't you?" He pushed her hair back from her face that was warm and steaming. Her lips were as red and moist as pomegranate seed. Her white neck and a glimpse of her full, firm bosom disturbed him powerfully. As she glanced up at him the fear in her liquid blue eyes had given place to a drowsy gleam that unconsciously betrayed a sensuous desire. He looked down into her eyes and there was nothing for him to do but to gather her lips in a kiss. It reminded him of Assumption.

"Do you remember—in Assumption, Calixta?" he asked in a low voice broken by passion. Oh! she remembered; for in Assumption he had kissed her and kissed and kissed her; until his senses would well nigh fail, and to save her he would resort to a desperate flight. If she was not an immaculate dove in those days, she was still inviolate; a passionate creature whose very defenselessness had made her defense, against which his honor forbade him to prevail. Now—well, now—her lips seemed in a manner free to be tasted, as well as her round, white throat and her whiter breasts.

They did not heed the crashing torrents, and the roar of the elements made her laugh as she lay in his arms. She was a revelation in that dim, mysterious chamber; as white as the couch she lay upon. Her firm, elastic flesh that was knowing for the first time its birthright, was like a creamy lily that the sun invites to contribute its breath and perfume to the undying life of the world.

The generous abundance of her passion, without guile or trickery, was like a white flame which penetrated and found response in depths of his own sensuous nature that had never yet been reached.

When he touched her breasts they gave themselves up in quivering ecstasy, inviting his lips. Her mouth was a fountain of delight. And when he possessed her, they seemed to swoon together at the very borderland of life's mystery.

He stayed cushioned upon her, breathless, dazed, enervated, with his heart beating like a hammer upon her. With one hand she clasped his head, her lips lightly touching his forehead. The other hand stroked with a soothing rhythm his muscular shoulders.

The growl of the thunder was distant and passing away. The rain beat softly upon the shingles, inviting them to drowsiness and sleep. But they dared not yield.

The rain was over; and the sun was turning the glistening green world into a palace of gems. Calixta, on the gallery, watched Alcée ride away. He turned and smiled at her with a beaming face; and she lifted her pretty chin in the air and laughed aloud.

III

Bobinôt and Bibi, trudging home, stopped without at the cistern to make themselves presentable.

"My! Bibi, w'at will yo' mama say! You ought to be ashame'. You oughtn' put on those good pants. Look at 'em! An' that mud on yo' collar! How you got that mud on yo' collar, Bibi? I never saw such a boy!" Bibi was the picture of pathetic resignation. Bobinôt was the embodiment of serious solicitude as he strove to remove from his own person and his son's the signs of their tramp over heavy roads and through wet fields. He scraped the mud off Bibi's bare legs and feet with a stick and carefully removed all traces from his heavy brogans. Then, prepared for the worst—the meeting with an over-scrupulous housewife, they entered cautiously at the back door.

Calixta was preparing supper. She had set the table and was dripping coffee at the hearth. She sprang up as they came in.

"Oh, Bobinôt! You back! My! but I was uneasy. W'ere you been during the rain? An' Bibi? he ain't wet? he ain't hurt?" She had clasped Bibi and was kissing him effusively. Bobinôt's explanations and apologies which he had been composing all along the way, died on his lips as Calixta felt him to see if he were dry, and seemed to express nothing but satisfaction at their safe return.

"I brought you some shrimps, Calixta," offered Bobinôt, hauling the can from his ample side pocket and laying it on the table.

"Shrimps! Oh, Bobinôt! you too good fo' anything!" and she gave him a smacking kiss on the cheek that resounded. "*J'vous réponds,*[3] we'll have a feas' to night! umph-umph!"

Bobinôt and Bibi began to relax and enjoy themselves, and when the three seated themselves at table they laughed much and so loud that anyone might have heard them as far away as Laballière's.

IV

Alcée Laballière wrote to his wife, Clarisse, that night. It was a loving letter, full of tender solicitude. He told her not to hurry back, but if she and the babies liked it at Biloxi, to stay a month longer. He was getting on nicely; and though he missed them, he was willing to bear the separation a while longer—realizing that their health and pleasure were the first things to be considered.

V

As for Clarisse, she was charmed upon receiving her husband's letter. She and the babies were doing well. The society was agreeable; many of her old friends and acquaintances were at the bay. And the first free breath since her marriage seemed to restore the pleasant liberty of her maiden days. Devoted as she was to her husband, their intimate conjugal life was something which she was more than willing to forego for a while.

So the storm passed and every one was happy.

QUESTIONS

1. What limitations, if any, are placed on the narrator's omniscience?
2. Why are some of the five scenes treated in greater detail than others?
3. How much of the past history of these people do we know? Why does the author give us so little detail from the past?
4. "So the storm passed and every one was happy": Who says so? Is this the comment of a reliable narrator, or an unreliable one? Is there any sense in which it might be ironic?

In reading Hemingway's "Hills Like White Elephants," we find ourselves placed in the position of silent and invisible observers of a small drama. Why do we get so little help from the narrator as we seek to interpret it?

HILLS LIKE WHITE ELEPHANTS

Ernest Hemingway   *(1899–1961)*

The hills across the valley of the Ebro were long and white. On this side there was no shade and no trees and the station was between two lines of rails in the sun. Close against the side of the station there was the warm shadow of the building and a curtain, made of strings of bamboo beads, hung across the open

[3]"I tell you."

door into the bar, to keep out flies. The American and the girl with him sat at a table in the shade, outside the building. It was very hot and the express from Barcelona would come in forty minutes. It stopped at this junction for two minutes and went on to Madrid.

"What should we drink?" the girl asked. She had taken off her hat and put it on the table.

"It's pretty hot," the man said.

"Let's drink beer."

"Dos cervezas," the man said into the curtain.

"Big ones?" a woman asked from the doorway.

"Yes. Two big ones."

The woman brought two glasses of beer and two felt pads. She put the felt pads and the beer glasses on the table and looked at the man and the girl. The girl was looking off at the line of hills. They were white in the sun and the country was brown and dry.

"They look like white elephants," she said.

"I've never seen one," the man drank his beer.

"No, you wouldn't have."

"I might have," the man said. "Just because you say I wouldn't have doesn't prove anything."

The girl looked at the bead curtain. "They've painted something on it," she said. "What does it say?"

"Anis del Toro. It's a drink."

"Could we try it?"

The man called "Listen" through the curtain. The woman came out from the bar.

"Four reales."

"We want two Anis del Toro."

"With water?"

"Do you want it with water?"

"I don't know," the girl said. "Is it good with water?"

"It's all right."

"You want them with water?" asked the woman.

"Yes, with water."

"It tastes like licorice," the girl said and put the glass down.

"That's the way with everything."

"Yes," said the girl. "Everything tastes of licorice. Especially all the things you've waited so long for, like absinthe."

"Oh, cut it out."

"You started it," the girl said. "I was being amused. I was having a fine time."

"Well, let's try and have a fine time."

"All right. I was trying. I said the mountains looked like white elephants. Wasn't that bright?"

"That was bright."

"I wanted to try this new drink. That's all we do, isn't it—look at things and try new drinks?"

"I guess so."

The girl looked across at the hills.

"They're lovely hills," she said. "They don't really look like white elephants. I just meant the coloring of their skin through the trees."

"Should we have another drink?"

"All right."

The warm wind blew the bead curtain against the table.

"The beer's nice and cool," the man said.

"It's lovely," the girl said.

"It's really an awfully simple operation, Jig," the man said. "It's not really an operation at all."

The girl looked at the ground the table legs rested on.

"I know you wouldn't mind it, Jig. It's really not anything. It's just to let the air in."

The girl did not say anything.

"I'll go with you and I'll stay with you all the time. They just let the air in and then it's all perfectly natural."

"Then what will we do afterward?"

"We'll be fine afterward. Just like we were before."

"What makes you think so?"

"That's the only thing that bothers us. It's the only thing that's made us unhappy."

The girl looked at the bead curtain, put her hand out and took hold of two of the strings of beads.

"And you think then we'll be all right and be happy."

"I know we will. You don't have to be afraid. I've known lots of people that have done it."

"So have I," said the girl. "And afterward they were all so happy."

"Well," the man said, "if you don't want to you don't have to. I wouldn't have you do it if you didn't want to. But I know it's perfectly simple."

"And you really want to?"

"I think it's the best thing to do. But I don't want you to do it if you don't really want to."

"And if I do it you'll be happy and things will be like they were and you'll love me?"

"I love you now. You know I love you."

"I know. But if I do it, then it will be nice again if I say things are like white elephants, and you'll like it?"

"I'll love it. I love it now but I just can't think about it. You know how I get when I worry."

"If I do it you won't ever worry?"

"I won't worry about that because it's perfectly simple."

"Then I'll do it. Because I don't care about me."

"What do you mean?"

"I don't care about me."

"Well, I care about you."

"Oh, yes. But I don't care about me. And I'll do it and then everything will be fine."

"I don't want you to do it if you feel that way."

The girl stood up and walked to the end of the station. Across, on the other side, were fields of grain and trees along the banks of the Ebro. Far away, beyond the river, were mountains. The shadow of a cloud moved across the field of grain and she saw the river through the trees.

"And we could have all this," she said. "And we could have everything and every day we make it more impossible."

"What did you say?"

"I said we could have everything."

"We can have everything."

"No, we can't."

"We can have the whole world."

"No, we can't."

"We can go everywhere."

"No, we can't. It isn't ours any more."

"It's ours."

"No, it isn't. And once they take it away, you never get it back."

"But they haven't taken it away."

"We'll wait and see."

"Come on back in the shade," he said. "You mustn't feel that way."

"I don't feel any way," the girl said. "I just know things."

"I don't want you to do anything that you don't want to do——"

"Nor that isn't good for me," she said. "I know. Could we have another beer?"

"All right. But you've got to realize——"

"I realize," the girl said. "Can't we maybe stop talking?"

They sat down at the table and the girl looked across at the hills on the dry side of the valley and the man looked at her and at the table.

"You've got to realize," he said, "that I don't want you to do it if you don't want to. I'm perfectly willing to go through with it if it means anything to you."

"Doesn't it mean anything to you? We could get along."

"Of course it does. But I don't want anybody but you. I don't want any one else. And I know it's perfectly simple."

"Yes, you know it's perfectly simple."

"It's all right for you to say that, but I do know it."

"Would you do something for me now?"

"I'd do anything for you."

"Would you please please please please please please please stop talking?"

He did not say anything but looked at the bags against the wall of the station. There were labels on them from all the hotels where they had spent nights.

"But I don't want you to," he said, "I don't care anything about it."

"I'll scream," the girl said.

The woman came out through the curtains with two glasses of beer and put them down on the damp felt pads. "The train comes in five minutes," she said.

"What did she say?" asked the girl.

"That the train is coming in five minutes."

The girl smiled brightly at the woman, to thank her.

"I'd better take the bags over to the other side of the station," the man said. She smiled at him.

"All right. Then come back and we'll finish the beer."

He picked up the two heavy bags and carried them around the station to the other tracks. He looked up the tracks but could not see the train. Coming back, he walked through the barroom, where people waiting for the train were drinking. He drank an Anis at the bar and looked at the people. They were all waiting reasonably for the train. He went out through the bead curtain. She was sitting at the table and smiled at him.

"Do you feel better?" he asked.

"I feel fine," she said. "There's nothing wrong with me. I feel fine."

QUESTIONS

1. Considering this story as an example, what are some of the major effects of dramatic method narration?
2. Are there any places in the story where the dramatic method seems less than strictly applied?
3. What "simple operation" are the man and girl talking about? How do we know?
4. Does the girl "feel fine" at the end? How do we know?
5. Does this seem a satisfactory story, or should there be more? Explain your answer.

CHAPTER 5

CHARACTER

In some fictions, the *characters*—the people in the story—are of small interest, as the tale turns on the events. To get the point of a joke we need to know very little about the traveling salesman or the farmer's daughter. Our interest in the people in fairy tales is similarly limited as we attend to the magic of glass slippers or straw turned into gold. Even for some more elaborate forms of fiction, such as satires and allegories, complications of character are frequently unnecessary or inappropriate. In modern short stories, however, character is sometimes crucial. What happens is less important than what it reveals about the people involved.

The people we meet in fiction may be better known to us than those we meet in life, for in life many of the people we claim to "know" we define superficially by their jobs, appearance, or relationship to others. We often know the inmost thoughts of fictional people without their having expressed them out loud. We understand how their lives are shaped by forces they cannot perceive. Because of its length, a short story usually presents no more than one or two characters with any completeness (and, of course, what we know of the characters is mostly limited to the time and events of the story). Novels present a larger number of fully developed characters, explored over a longer time and in relation to more incidents.

For different kinds of characters we need different descriptive terms. An *individualized character* is one developed with emphasis on a personality different from others who share similar backgrounds. Individualized characters are sometimes called *round* or *three-dimensional,* terms suggesting a depth of portrayal that makes them similar to real people. A *type character* is one where the emphasis falls on qualities that suggest a person who is representative of a class. Type characters are sometimes called *flat* or *two-dimensional;* such characters are often defined by one or two dominant traits, the hero on his white horse, the villain twirling his mustache. Both kinds have their place in fiction. Individualized or round characters are the major actors in realistic stories. Type or flat characters play major roles in formula fiction, fables, satire, and allegories, and minor roles in realistic stories. Some authors intentionally mix the two, challenging the reader to understand that an initial impression of character, built on generalizations from a few characteristics, is not necessarily a valid one. The "Good Country People" of Flannery O'Connor's story may not be so good, or so countrified, as we first imagine.

Writers differ in their methods of creating characters. In *summary characterization* a narrator tells us in brief what we need to understand of a character, delineating key personality traits in a few words or sentences: "Alan Austen, as nervous as a kitten . . . ." Sometimes *naming* is a form of summary characterization. We expect a Squire Allworthy or a Mrs. Hopewell to demonstrate the named qualities in their actions, although as students of fiction we soon learn that because writers are fond of irony a woman named Mrs. Hopewell may continually see her hopes undermined; her daughter Joy may not be joyful. The most important forms of characterization in fiction, however, are *action* and *speech:* we understand the people in a story most completely by what they say and do.

THE USE OF FORCE
William Carlos Williams   *(1883–1963)*

They were new patients to me, all I had was the name, Olson. Please come down as soon as you can, my daughter is very sick.

When I arrived I was met by the mother, a big startled looking woman, very clean and apologetic who merely said, Is this the doctor? and let me in. In the back, she added. You must excuse us, doctor, we have her in the kitchen where it is warm. It is very damp here sometimes.

The child was fully dressed and sitting on her father's lap near the kitchen table. He tried to get up, but I motioned for him not to bother, took off my overcoat and started to look things over. I could see that they were all very nervous, eyeing me up and down distrustfully. As often, in such cases, they weren't telling me more than they had to, it was up to me to tell them; that's why they were spending three dollars on me.

The child was fairly eating me up with her cold, steady eyes, and no expression to her face whatever. She did not move and seemed, inwardly, quiet; an unusually attractive little thing, and as strong as a heifer in appearance. But her face was flushed, she was breathing rapidly, and I realized that she had a high fever. She had magnificent blonde hair, in profusion. One of those picture children often reproduced in advertising leaflets and the photogravure sections of the Sunday papers.

She's had a fever for three days, began the father and we don't know what it comes from. My wife has given her things, you know, like people do, but it don't do no good. And there's been a lot of sickness around. So we tho't you'd better look her over and tell us what is the matter.

As doctors often do I took a trial shot at it as a point of departure. Has she had a sore throat?

Both parents answered me together, No . . . No, she says her throat don't hurt her.

Does your throat hurt you? added the mother to the child. But the little girl's expression didn't change nor did she move her eyes from my face.

Have you looked?

I tried to, said the mother, but I couldn't see.

As it happens we had been having a number of cases of diphtheria[1] in the school to which this child went during that month and we were all, quite apparently, thinking of that, though no one had as yet spoken of the thing.

Well, I said, suppose we take a look at the throat first. I smiled in my best professional manner and asking for the child's first name I said, come on, Mathilda, open your mouth and let's take a look at your throat.

Nothing doing.

Aw, come on, I coaxed, just open your mouth wide and let me take a look. Look, I said opening both hands wide, I haven't anything in my hands. Just open up and let me see.

Such a nice man, put in the mother. Look how kind he is to you. Come on, do what he tells you to. He won't hurt you.

At that I ground my teeth in disgust. If only they wouldn't use the word "hurt" I might be able to get somewhere. But I did not allow myself to be hurried or disturbed but speaking quietly and slowly I approached the child again.

As I moved my chair a little nearer suddenly with one catlike movement both her hands clawed instinctively for my eyes and she almost reached them too. In fact she knocked my glasses flying and they fell, though unbroken, several feet away from me on the kitchen floor.

Both the mother and father almost turned themselves inside out in embarrassment and apology. You bad girl, said the mother, taking her and shaking her by one arm. Look what you've done. The nice man . . .

For heaven's sake, I broke in. Don't call me a nice man to her. I'm here to look at her throat on the chance that she might have diphtheria and possibly die of it. But that's nothing to her. Look here, I said to the child, we're going to look at your throat. You're old enough to understand what I'm saying. Will you open it now by yourself or shall we have to open it for you?

Not a move. Even her expression hadn't changed. Her breaths however were coming faster and faster. Then the battle began. I had to do it. I had to have a

---

[1]A disease once common in young children. Death could occur from suffocation caused by the tough, gray membrane that grew to cover the throat or from damage to the heart or kidneys. The disease is now rare because infants are given a series of injections (usually combined with whooping cough and tetanus immunizations).

throat culture for her own protection. But first I told the parents that it was entirely up to them. I explained the danger but said that I would not insist on a throat examination so long as they would take the responsibility.

If you don't do what the doctor says you'll have to go to the hospital, the mother admonished her severely.

Oh yeah? I had to smile to myself. After all, I had already fallen in love with the savage brat, the parents were contemptible to me. In the ensuing struggle they grew more and more abject, crushed, exhausted while she surely rose to magnificent heights of insane fury of effort bred of her terror of me.

The father tried his best, and he was a big man but the fact that she was his daughter, his shame at her behavior and his dread of hurting her made him release her just at the critical moment several times when I had almost achieved success, till I wanted to kill him. But his dread also that she might have diphtheria made him tell me to go on, go on though he himself was almost fainting, while the mother moved back and forth behind us raising and lowering her hands in an agony of apprehension.

Put her in front of you on your lap, I ordered, and hold both her wrists.

But as soon as he did the child let out a scream. Don't you're hurting me. Let go of my hands. Let them go I tell you. Then she shrieked terrifyingly, hysterically. Stop it! Stop it! You're killing me!

Do you think she can stand it, doctor! said the mother.

You get out, said the husband to his wife. Do you want her to die of diphtheria? Come on now, hold her, I said.

Then I grasped the child's head with my left hand and tried to get the wooden tongue depressor between her teeth. She fought, with clenched teeth, desperately! But now I also had grown furious—at a child. I tried to hold myself down but I couldn't. I know how to expose a throat for inspection. And I did my best. When finally I got the wooden spatula behind the last teeth and just the point of it into the mouth cavity, she opened up for an instant but before I could see anything she came down again and gripping the wooden blade between her molars she reduced it to splinters before I could get it out again.

Aren't you ashamed, the mother yelled at her. Aren't you ashamed to act like that in front of the doctor?

Get me a smooth-handled spoon of some sort, I told the mother. We're going through with this. The child's mouth was already bleeding. Her tongue was cut and she was screaming in wild hysterical shrieks. Perhaps I should have desisted and come back in an hour or more. No doubt it would have been better. But I have seen at least two children lying dead in bed of neglect in such cases, and feeling that I must get a diagnosis now or never I went at it again. But the worst of it was that I too had got beyond reason. I could have torn the child apart in my own fury and enjoyed it. It was a pleasure to attack her. My face was burning with it.

The damned little brat must be protected against her own idiocy, one says to one's self at such times. Others must be protected against her. It is social necessity. And all these things are true. But a blind fury, a feeling of adult shame, bred of a longing for muscular release are the operatives. One goes on to the end.

In a final unreasoning assault I overpowered the child's neck and jaws. I forced the heavy silver spoon back of her teeth and down her throat till she gagged. And there it was—both tonsils covered with membrane. She had fought valiantly to keep me from knowing her secret. She had been hiding that sore throat for three days at least and lying to her parents in order to escape just such an outcome as this.

Now truly she *was* furious. She had been on the defensive before but now she attacked. Tried to get off her father's lap and fly at me while tears of defeat blinded her eyes.

QUESTIONS

1. What actions tell us most about the character of the doctor?
2. What does the doctor say to the parents or the child that best illustrates his character? In his role as narrator of his own story, what does he say to the reader that is especially helpful in defining his character?
3. The author, a doctor, must have experienced scenes similar to the one reported here. Is his report convincing?
4. Which elements of the story are most clearly the result of narrating from the perspective of the doctor?
5. How would the story be changed if one of the parents narrated? The girl herself?
6. If you were to tell the story from an omniscient perspective, what limitations would you consider placing on the omniscience?
7. Why has Williams concentrated on such a small incident?

FEET LIVE THEIR OWN LIFE

Langston Hughes   (1902–1967)

"If you want to know about my life," said Simple as he blew the foam from the top of the newly filled glass the bartender put before him, "don't look at my face, don't look at my hands. Look at my feet and see if you can tell how long I been standing on them."

"I cannot see your feet through your shoes," I said.

"You do not need to see through my shoes," said Simple. "Can't you tell by the shoes I wear—not pointed, not rocking-chair, not French-toed, not nothing but big, long, broad, and flat—that I been standing on these feet a long time and carrying some heavy burdens? They ain't flat from standing at no bar, neither, because I always sets at a bar. Can't you tell that? You know I do not hang out in a bar unless it has stools, don't you?"

"That I have observed," I said, "but I did not connect it with your past life."

"Everything I do is connected up with my past life," said Simple. "From

Virginia to Joyce, from my wife to Zarita, from my mother's milk to this glass of beer, everything is connected up."

"I trust you will connect up with that dollar I just loaned you when you get paid," I said. "And who is Virginia? You never told me about her."

"Virginia is where I was borned," said Simple. "I would be borned in a state named after a woman. From that day on, women never give me no peace."

"You, I fear, are boasting. If the women were running after you as much as you run after them, you would not be able to sit here on this bar stool in peace. I don't see any women coming to call you out to go home, as some of these fellows' wives do around here."

"Joyce better not come in no bar looking for me," said Simple. "That is why me and my wife busted up—one reason. I do not like to be called out of no bar by a female. It's a man's prerogative to just set and drink sometimes."

"How do you connect that prerogative with your past?" I asked.

"When I was a wee small child," said Simple, "I had no place to set and think in, being as how I was raised up with three brothers, two sisters, seven cousins, one married aunt, a common-law uncle, and the minister's grandchild—and the house only had four rooms. I never had a place just to set and think. Neither to set and drink—not even much my milk before some hongry child snatched it out of my hand. I were not the youngest, neither a girl, nor the cutest. I don't know why, but I don't think nobody liked me much. Which is why I was afraid to like anybody for a long time myself. When I did like somebody, I was full-grown and then I picked out the wrong woman because I had no practice in liking anybody before that. We did not get along."

"Is that when you took to drink?"

"Drink took to me," said Simple. "Whiskey just naturally likes me but beer likes me better. By the time I got married I had got to the point where a cold bottle was almost as good as a warm bed, especially when the bottle could not talk and the bed-warmer could. I do not like a woman to talk to me too much —I mean about me. Which is why I like Joyce. Joyce most in generally talks about herself."

"I am still looking at your feet," I said, "and I swear they do not reveal your life to me. Your feet are no open book."

"You have eyes but you see not," said Simple. "These feet have stood on every rock from the Rock of Ages to 135th and Lenox. These feet have supported everything from a cotton bale to a hongry woman. These feet have walked ten thousand miles working for white folks and another ten thousand keeping up with colored. These feet have stood at altars, crap tables, free lunches, bars, graves, kitchen doors, betting windows, hospital clinics, WPA[1] desks, social security railings, and in all kinds of lines from soup lines to the draft. If I just had four feet, I could have stood in more places longer. As it is, I done wore out seven hundred pairs of shoes, eighty-nine tennis shoes, twelve summer sandals, also six

[1] Works Projects Administration (1935–1943), a program instituted by Franklin Delano Roosevelt to counter widespread unemployment.

loafers. The socks that these feet have bought could build a knitting mill. The corns I've cut away would dull a German razor. The bunions I forgot would make you ache from now till Judgment Day. If anybody was to write the history of my life, they should start with my feet."

"Your feet are not all that extraordinary," I said. "Besides, everything you are saying is general. Tell me specifically some one thing your feet have done that makes them different from any other feet in the world, just one."

"Do you see that window in that white man's store across the street?" asked Simple. "Well, this right foot of mine broke out that window in the Harlem riots right smack in the middle. Didn't no other foot in the world break that window but mine. And this left foot carried me off running as soon as my right foot came down. Nobody else's feet saved me from the cops that night but these *two* feet right here. Don't tell me these feet ain't had a life of their own."

"For shame," I said, "going around kicking out windows. Why?"

"Why?" said Simple. "You have to ask my great-great-grandpa why. He must of been simple—else why did he let them capture him in Africa and sell him for a slave to breed my great-grandpa in slavery to breed my grandpa in slavery to breed my pa to breed me to look at that window and say, 'It ain't mine! Bam-mmm-mm-m!' and kick it out?"

"This bar glass is not yours either," I said. "Why don't you smash it?"

"It's got my beer in it," said Simple.

Just then Zarita came in wearing her Thursday-night rabbitskin coat. She didn't stop at the bar, being dressed up, but went straight back to a booth. Simple's hand went up, his beer went down, and the glass back to its wet spot on the bar.

"Excuse me a minute," he said, sliding off the stool.

Just to give him pause, the dozens, that old verbal game of maligning a friend's female relatives, came to mind. "Wait," I said. "You have told me about what to ask your great-great-grandpa. But I want to know what to ask your great-great-grand*ma.*"

"I don't play the dozens that far back," said Simple, following Zarita into the smoky juke-box blue of the back room.

QUESTIONS

1. As Simple tells about his feet, what does he also tell about his character?
2. Although Simple does most of the talking, an "I" narrates. How much do we know of the character of the narrator? On what evidence?
3. In other Hughes stories about Simple a reader learns that his real name is Jesse B. Semple. Does his nickname "Simple" characterize him fully, or do we need to make an allowance for irony in his naming?
4. Is there any seriousness in Simple's fooling? Where?

GOOD COUNTRY PEOPLE

Flannery O'Connor   (1925–1964)

Besides the neutral expression that she wore when she was alone, Mrs. Freeman had two others, forward and reverse, that she used for all her human dealings. Her forward expression was steady and driving like the advance of a heavy truck. Her eyes never swerved to left or right but turned as the story turned as if they followed a yellow line down the center of it. She seldom used the other expression because it was not often necessary for her to retract a statement, but when she did, her face came to a complete stop, there was an almost imperceptible movement of her black eyes, during which they seemed to be receding, and then the observer would see that Mrs. Freeman, though she might stand there as real as several grain sacks thrown on top of each other, was no longer there in spirit. As for getting anything across to her when this was the case, Mrs. Hopewell had given it up. She might talk her head off. Mrs. Freeman could never be brought to admit herself wrong on any point. She would stand there and if she could be brought to say anything, it was something like, "Well, I wouldn't of said it was and I wouldn't of said it wasn't," or letting her gaze range over the top kitchen shelf where there was an assortment of dusty bottles, she might remark, "I see you ain't ate many of them figs you put up last summer."

They carried on their most important business in the kitchen at breakfast. Every morning Mrs. Hopewell got up at seven o'clock and lit her gas heater and Joy's. Joy was her daughter, a large blonde girl who had an artificial leg. Mrs. Hopewell thought of her as a child though she was thirty-two years old and highly educated. Joy would get up while her mother was eating and lumber into the bathroom and slam the door, and before long, Mrs. Freeman would arrive at the back door. Joy would hear her mother call, "Come on in," and then they would talk for a while in low voices that were indistinguishable in the bathroom. By the time Joy came in, they had usually finished the weather report and were on one or the other of Mrs. Freeman's daughters, Glynese or Carramae. Joy called them Glycerin and Caramel. Glynese, a redhead, was eighteen and had many admirers; Carramae, a blond, was only fifteen but already married and pregnant. She could not keep anything on her stomach. Every morning Mrs. Freeman told Mrs. Hopewell how many times she had vomited since the last report.

Mrs. Hopewell liked to tell people that Glynese and Carramae were two of the finest girls she knew and that Mrs. Freeman was a *lady* and that she was never ashamed to take her anywhere or introduce her to anybody they might meet. Then she would tell how she had happened to hire the Freemans in the first place and how they were a godsend to her and how she had had them four years. The reason for her keeping them so long was that they were not trash. They were good country people. She had telephoned the man whose name they had given as a reference and he had told her that Mr. Freeman was a good farmer but that his wife was the nosiest woman ever to walk the earth. "She's got to be into everything," the man said. "If she don't get there before the dust settles, you can bet she's dead, that's all. She'll want to know all your business. I can stand him real good," he had said, "but me nor my wife neither could have stood that woman one more minute on this place." That had put Mrs. Hopewell off for a few days.

She had hired them in the end because there were no other applicants but she had made up her mind beforehand exactly how she would handle the woman. Since she was the type who had to be into everything, then, Mrs. Hopewell had decided, she would not only let her be into everything, she would *see to it* that she was into everything—she would give her the responsibility of everything, she would put her in charge. Mrs. Hopewell had no bad qualities of her own but she was able to use other people's in such a constructive way that she never felt the lack. She had hired the Freemans and she had kept them four years.

Nothing is perfect. This was one of Mrs. Hopewell's favorite sayings. Another was: that is life! And still another, the most important, was: well, other people have their opinions too. She would make these statements, usually at the table, in a tone of gentle insistence as if no one held them but her, and the large hulking Joy, whose constant outrage had obliterated every expression from her face, would stare just a little to the side of her, her eyes icy blue, with the look of someone who has achieved blindness by an act of will and means to keep it.

When Mrs. Hopewell said to Mrs. Freeman that life was like that, Mrs. Freeman would say, "I always said so myself." Nothing had been arrived at by anyone that had not first been arrived at by her. She was quicker than Mr. Freeman. When Mrs. Hopewell said to her after they had been on the place a while, "You know, you're the wheel behind the wheel," and winked, Mrs. Freeman had said, "I know it. I've always been quick. It's some that are quicker than others."

"Everybody is different," Mrs. Hopewell said.

"Yes, most people is," Mrs. Freeman said.

"It takes all kinds to make the world."

"I always said it did myself."

The girl was used to this kind of dialogue for breakfast and more of it for dinner; sometimes they had it for supper too. When they had no guest they ate in the kitchen because that was easier. Mrs. Freeman always managed to arrive at some point during the meal and to watch them finish it. She would stand in the doorway if it were summer but in the winter she would stand with one elbow on top of the refrigerator and look down on them, or she would stand by the gas heater, lifting the back of her skirt slightly. Occasionally she would stand against the wall and roll her head from side to side. At no time was she in any hurry to leave. All this was very trying on Mrs. Hopewell but she was a woman of great patience. She realized that nothing is perfect and that in the Freemans she had good country people and that if, in this day and age, you get good country people, you had better hang onto them.

She had had plenty of experience with trash. Before the Freemans she had averaged one tenant family a year. The wives of these farmers were not the kind you would want to be around you for very long. Mrs. Hopewell, who had divorced her husband long ago, needed someone to walk over the fields with her;

and when Joy had to be impressed for these services, her remarks were usually so ugly and her face so glum that Mrs. Hopewell would say, "If you can't come pleasantly, I don't want you at all," to which the girl, standing square and rigid-shouldered with her neck thrust slightly forward, would reply, "If you want me, here I am—LIKE I AM."

Mrs. Hopewell excused this attitude because of the leg (which had been shot off in a hunting accident when Joy was ten). It was hard for Mrs. Hopewell to realize that her child was thirty-two now and that for more than twenty years she had had only one leg. She thought of her still as a child because it tore her heart to think instead of the poor stout girl in her thirties who had never danced a step or had any *normal* good times. Her name was really Joy but as soon as she was twenty-one and away from home, she had had it legally changed. Mrs. Hopewell was certain that she had thought and thought until she had hit upon the ugliest name in any language. Then she had gone and had the beautiful name, Joy, changed without telling her mother until after she had done it. Her legal name was Hulga.

When Mrs. Hopewell thought the name, Hulga, she thought of the broad blank hull of a battleship. She would not use it. She continued to call her Joy to which the girl responded but in a purely mechanical way.

Hulga had learned to tolerate Mrs. Freeman who saved her from taking walks with her mother. Even Glynese and Carramae were useful when they occupied attention that might otherwise have been directed at her. At first she had thought she could not stand Mrs. Freeman for she had found that it was not possible to be rude to her. Mrs. Freeman would take on strange resentments and for days together she would be sullen but the source of her displeasure was always obscure; a direct attack, a positive leer, blatant ugliness to her face—these never touched her. And without warning one day, she began calling her Hulga.

She did not call her that in front of Mrs. Hopewell who would have been incensed but when she and the girl happened to be out of the house together, she would say something and add the name Hulga to the end of it, and the big spectacled Joy-Hulga would scowl and redden as if her privacy had been intruded upon. She considered the name her personal affair. She had arrived at it first purely on the basis of its ugly sound and then the full genius of its fitness had struck her. She had a vision of the name working like the ugly sweating Vulcan[1] who stayed in the furnace and to whom, presumably, the goddess had to come when called. She saw it as the name of her highest creative act. One of her major triumphs was that her mother had not been able to turn her dust into Joy, but the greater one was that she had been able to turn it herself into Hulga. However, Mrs. Freeman's relish for using the name only irritated her. It was as if Mrs. Freeman's beady steel-pointed eyes had penetrated far enough behind her face to reach some secret fact. Something about her seemed to fascinate Mrs. Freeman and then one day Hulga realized that it was the artificial leg. Mrs. Freeman had a special fondness for the details of secret infections, hidden deformities, assaults

---

[1]Roman god of fire, lame blacksmith to the gods and husband of Venus, goddess of love.

upon children. Of diseases, she preferred the lingering or incurable. Hulga had heard Mrs. Hopewell give her the details of the hunting accident, how the leg had been literally blasted off, how she had never lost consciousness. Mrs. Freeman could listen to it any time as if it had happened an hour ago.

When Hulga stumped into the kitchen in the morning (she could walk without making the awful noise but she made it—Mrs. Hopewell was certain—because it was ugly-sounding), she glanced at them and did not speak. Mrs. Hopewell would be in her red kimono with her hair tied around her head in rags. She would be sitting at the table, finishing her breakfast and Mrs. Freeman would be hanging by her elbow outward from the refrigerator, looking down at the table. Hulga always put her eggs on the stove to boil and then stood over them with her arms folded, and Mrs. Hopewell would look at her—a kind of indirect gaze divided between her and Mrs. Freeman—and would think that if she would only keep herself up a little, she wouldn't be so bad looking. There was nothing wrong with her face that a pleasant expression wouldn't help. Mrs. Hopewell said that people who looked on the bright side of things would be beautiful even if they were not.

Whenever she looked at Joy this way, she could not help but feel that it would have been better if the child had not taken the Ph.D. It had certainly not brought her out any and now that she had it, there was no more excuse for her to go to school again. Mrs. Hopewell thought it was nice for girls to go to school to have a good time but Joy had "gone through." Anyhow, she would not have been strong enough to go again. The doctors had told Mrs. Hopewell that with the best of care, Joy might see forty-five. She had a weak heart. Joy made it plain that if it had not been for this condition, she would be far from these red hills and good country people. She would be in a university lecturing to people who knew what she was talking about. And Mrs. Hopewell could very well picture her there, looking like a scarecrow and lecturing to more of the same. Here she went about all day in a six-year-old skirt and a yellow sweat shirt with a faded cowboy on a horse embossed on it. She thought this was funny; Mrs. Hopewell thought it was idiotic and showed simply that she was still a child. She was brilliant but she didn't have a grain of sense. It seemed to Mrs. Hopewell that every year she grew less like other people and more like herself—bloated, rude, and squint-eyed. And she said such strange things! To her own mother she had said—without warning, without excuse, standing up in the middle of a meal with her face purple and her mouth half full—"Woman! do you ever look inside? Do you ever look inside and see what you are *not*? God!" she had cried sinking down again and staring at her plate, "Malebranche[2] was right: we are not our own light. We are not our own light!" Mrs. Hopewell had no idea to this day what brought that on. She had only made the remark, hoping Joy would take it in, that a smile never hurt anyone.

The girl had taken the Ph.D. in philosophy and this left Mrs. Hopewell at a

---

[2]Nicolas Malebranche (1638–1715), French philosopher who attempted to bridge the gap between science and religion by suggesting that scientific knowledge is possible only through the soul's unity with the divine intellect.

complete loss. You could say, "My daughter is a nurse," or "My daughter is a school teacher," or even, "My daughter is a chemical engineer." You could not say, "My daughter is a philosopher." That was something that had ended with the Greeks and Romans. All day Joy sat on her neck in a deep chair, reading. Sometimes she went for walks but she didn't like dogs or cats or birds or flowers or nature or nice young men. She looked at nice young men as if she could smell their stupidity.

One day Mrs. Hopewell had picked up one of the books the girl had just put down and opening it at random, she read, "Science, on the other hand, has to assert its soberness and seriousness afresh and declare that it is concerned solely with what-is. Nothing—how can it be for science anything but a horror and a phantasm? If science is right, then one thing stands firm: science wishes to know nothing of nothing. Such is after all the strictly scientific approach to Nothing. We know it by wishing to know nothing of Nothing." These words had been underlined with a blue pencil and they worked on Mrs. Hopewell like some evil incantation in gibberish. She shut the book quickly and went out of the room as if she were having a chill.

This morning when the girl came, Mrs. Freeman was on Carramae. "She thrown up four times after supper," she said, "and was up twict in the night after three o'clock. Yesterday she didn't do nothing but ramble in the bureau drawer. All she did. Stand up there and see what she could run up on."

"She's got to eat," Mrs. Hopewell muttered, sipping her coffee, while she watched Joy's back at the stove. She was wondering what the child had said to the Bible salesman. She could not imagine what kind of a conversation she could possibly have had with him.

He was a tall gaunt hatless youth who had called yesterday to sell them a Bible. He had appeared at the door, carrying a large black suitcase that weighted him so heavily on one side that he had to brace himself against the door facing. He seemed on the point of collapse but he said in a cheerful voice, "Good morning, Mrs. Cedars!" and set the suitcase down on the mat. He was not a bad-looking young man though he had on a bright blue suit and yellow socks that were not pulled up far enough. He had prominent face bones and a streak of sticky-looking brown hair falling across his forehead.

"I'm Mrs. Hopewell," she said.

"Oh!" he said, pretending to look puzzled but with his eyes sparkling, "I saw it said 'The Cedars,' on the mailbox so I thought you was Mrs. Cedars!" and he burst out in a pleasant laugh. He picked up the satchel and under cover of a pant, he fell forward into her hall. It was rather as if the suitcase had moved first, jerking him after it. "Mrs. Hopewell!" he said and grabbed her hand. "I hope you are well!" and he laughed again and then all at once his face sobered completely. He paused and gave her a straight earnest look and said, "Lady, I've come to speak of serious things."

"Well, come in," she muttered, none too pleased because her dinner was almost ready. He came into the parlor and sat down on the edge of a straight chair and put the suitcase between his feet and glanced around the room as if he were sizing her up by it. Her silver gleamed on the two sideboards; she decided he had never been in a room as elegant as this.

"Mrs. Hopewell," he began, using her name in a way that sounded almost intimate, "I know you believe in Chrustian service."

"Well yes," she murmured.

"I know," he said and paused, looking very wise with his head cocked on one side, "that you're a good woman. Friends have told me."

Mrs. Hopewell never liked to be taken for a fool. "What are you selling?" she asked.

"Bibles," the young man said and his eye raced around the room before he added, "I see you have no family Bible in your parlor, I see that is the one lack you got!"

Mrs. Hopewell could not say, "My daughter is an atheist and won't let me keep the Bible in the parlor." She said, stiffening slightly, "I keep my Bible by my bedside." This was not the truth. It was in the attic somewhere.

"Lady," he said, "the word of God ought to be in the parlor."

"Well, I think that's a matter of taste," she began. "I think . . ."

"Lady," he said, "for a Chrustian, the word of God ought to be in every room in the house besides in his heart. I know you're a Chrustian because I can see it in every line of your face."

She stood up and said, "Well, young man, I don't want to buy a Bible and I smell my dinner burning."

He didn't get up. He began to twist his hands and looking down at them, he said softly, "Well lady, I'll tell you the truth—not many people want to buy one nowadays and besides, I know I'm real simple. I don't know how to say a thing but to say it. I'm just a country boy." He glanced up into her unfriendly face. "People like you don't like to fool with country people like me!"

"Why!" she cried, "good country people are the salt of the earth! Besides, we all have different ways of doing, it takes all kinds to make the world go 'round. That's life!"

"You said a mouthful," he said.

"Why, I think there aren't enough good country people in the world!" she said, stirred. "I think that's what's wrong with it!"

His face had brightened. "I didn't inraduce myself," he said. "I'm Manley Pointer from out in the country around Willohobie, not even from a place, just from near a place."

"You wait a minute," she said. "I have to see about my dinner." She went out to the kitchen and found Joy standing near the door where she had been listening.

"Get rid of the salt of the earth," she said, "and let's eat."

Mrs. Hopewell gave her a pained look and turned the heat down under the vegetables. "*I* can't be rude to anybody," she murmured and went back into the parlor.

He had opened the suitcase and was sitting with a Bible on each knee.

"You might as well put those up," she told him. "I don't want one."

"I appreciate your honesty," he said. "You don't see any more real honest people unless you go way out in the country."

"I know," she said, "real genuine folks!" Through the crack in the door she heard a groan.

"I guess a lot of boys come telling you they're working their way through college," he said, "but I'm not going to tell you that. Somehow," he said, "I don't want to go to college. I want to devote my life to Chrustian service. See," he said, lowering his voice, "I got this heart condition. I may not live long. When you know it's something wrong with you and you may not live long, well then, lady . . ." He paused, with his mouth open, and stared at her.

He and Joy had the same condition! She knew that her eyes were filling with tears but she collected herself quickly and murmured, "Won't you stay for dinner? We'd love to have you!" and was sorry the instant she heard herself say it.

"Yes mam," he said in an abashed voice, "I would sher love to do that!"

Joy had given him one look on being introduced to him and then throughout the meal had not glanced at him again. He had addressed several remarks to her, which she had pretended not to hear. Mrs. Hopewell could not understand deliberate rudeness, although she lived with it, and she felt she had always to overflow with hospitality to make up for Joy's lack of courtesy. She urged him to talk about himself and he did. He said he was the seventh child of twelve and that his father had been crushed under a tree when he himself was eight year old. He had been crushed very badly, in fact, almost cut in two and was practically not recognizable. His mother had got along the best she could by hard working and she had always seen that her children went to Sunday School and that they read the Bible every evening. He was now nineteen year old and he had been selling Bibles for four months. In that time he had sold seventy-seven Bibles and had the promise of two more sales. He wanted to become a missionary because he thought that was the way you could do most for people. "He who losest his life shall find it," he said simply and he was so sincere, so genuine and earnest that Mrs. Hopewell would not for the world have smiled. He prevented his peas from sliding onto the table by blocking them with a piece of bread which he later cleaned his plate with. She could see Joy observing sidewise how he handled his knife and fork and she saw too that every few minutes, the boy would dart a keen appraising glance at the girl as if he were trying to attract her attention.

After dinner Joy cleared the dishes off the table and disappeared and Mrs. Hopewell was left to talk with him. He told her again about his childhood and his father's accident and about various things that had happened to him. Every five minutes or so she would stifle a yawn. He sat for two hours until finally she told him she must go because she had an appointment in town. He packed his Bibles and thanked her and prepared to leave, but in the doorway he stopped and wrung her hand and said that not on any of his trips had he met a lady as nice as her and he asked if he could come again. She had said she would always be happy to see him.

Joy had been standing in the road, apparently looking at something in the distance, when he came down the steps toward her, bent to the side with his heavy valise. He stopped where she was standing and confronted her directly. Mrs. Hopewell could not hear what he said but she trembled to think what Joy would say to him. She could see that after a minute Joy said something and that then the boy began to speak again, making an excited gesture with his free hand. After a minute Joy said something else at which the boy began to speak once more. Then to her amazement, Mrs. Hopewell saw the two of them walk off together, toward the gate. Joy had walked all the way to the gate with him and Mrs. Hopewell could not imagine what they had said to each other, and she had not yet dared to ask.

Mrs. Freeman was insisting upon her attention. She had moved from the refrigerator to the heater so that Mrs. Hopewell had to turn and face her in order to seem to be listening. "Glynese gone out with Harvey Hill again last night," she said. "She had this sty."

"Hill," Mrs. Hopewell said absently, "is that the one who works in the garage?"

"Nome, he's the one that goes to chiropracter school," Mrs. Freeman said. "She had this sty. Been had it two days. So she says when he brought her in the other night he says, 'Lemme get rid of that sty for you,' and she says, 'How?' and he says, 'You just lay yourself down acrost the seat of that car and I'll show you.' So she done it and he popped her neck. Kept on a-popping it several times until she made him quit. This morning," Mrs. Freeman said, "she ain't got no sty. She ain't got no traces of a sty."

"I never heard of that before," Mrs. Hopewell said.

"He ast her to marry him before the Ordinary," Mrs. Freeman went on, "and she told him she wasn't going to be married in no *office.*"

"Well, Glynese is a fine girl," Mrs. Hopewell said. "Glynese and Carramae are both fine girls."

"Carramae said when her and Lyman was married Lyman said it sure felt sacred to him. She said he said he wouldn't take five hundred dollars for being married by a preacher."

"How much would he take?" the girl asked from the stove.

"He said he wouldn't take five hundred dollars," Mrs. Freeman repeated.

"Well we all have work to do," Mrs. Hopewell said.

"Lyman said it just felt more sacred to him," Mrs. Freeman said. "The doctor wants Carramae to eat prunes. Says instead of medicine. Says them cramps is coming from pressure. You know where I think it is?"

"She'll be better in a few weeks," Mrs. Hopewell said.

"In the tube," Mrs. Freeman said. "Else she wouldn't be as sick as she is."

Hulga had cracked her two eggs into a saucer and was bringing them to the table along with a cup of coffee that she had filled too full. She sat down carefully and began to eat, meaning to keep Mrs. Freeman there by questions if for any reason she showed an inclination to leave. She could perceive her mother's eye on her. The first round-about question would be about the Bible salesman and she did not wish to bring it on. "How did he pop her neck?" she asked.

Mrs. Freeman went into a description of how he had popped her neck. She said he owned a '55 Mercury but that Glynese said she would rather marry a man with only a '36 Plymouth who would be married by a preacher. The girl asked what if he had a '32 Plymouth and Mrs. Freeman said what Glynese had said was a '36 Plymouth.

Mrs. Hopewell said there were not many girls with Glynese's common sense. She said what she admired in those girls was their common sense. She said that reminded her that they had a nice visitor yesterday, a young man selling Bibles. "Lord," she said, "he bored me to death but he was so sincere and genuine I couldn't be rude to him. He was just good country people, you know," she said, "—just the salt of the earth."

"I seen him walk up," Mrs. Freeman said, "and then later—I seen him walk off," and Hulga could feel the slight shift in her voice, the slight insinuation, that he had not walked off alone, had he? Her face remained expressionless but the color rose into her neck and she seemed to swallow it down with the next spoonful of egg. Mrs. Freeman was looking at her as if they had a secret together.

"Well, it takes all kinds of people to make the world go 'round," Mrs. Hopewell said. "It's very good we aren't all alike."

"Some people are more alike than others," Mrs. Freeman said.

Hulga got up and stumped, with about twice the noise that was necessary, into her room and locked the door. She was to meet the Bible salesman at ten o'clock at the gate. She had thought about it half the night. She had started thinking of it as a great joke and then she had begun to see profound implications in it. She had lain in bed imagining dialogues for them that were insane on the surface but that reached below to depths that no Bible salesman would be aware of. Their conversation yesterday had been of this kind.

He had stopped in front of her and had simply stood there. His face was bony and sweaty and bright, with a little pointed nose in the center of it, and his look was different from what it had been at the dinner table. He was gazing at her with open curiosity, with fascination, like a child watching a new fantastic animal at the zoo, and he was breathing as if he had run a great distance to reach her. His gaze seemed somehow familiar but she could not think where she had been regarded with it before. For almost a minute he didn't say anything. Then on what seemed an insuck of breath, he whispered, "You ever ate a chicken that was two days old?"

The girl looked at him stonily. He might have just put this question up for consideration at the meeting of a philosophical association. "Yes," she presently replied as if she had considered it from all angles.

"It must have been mighty small!" he said triumphantly and shook all over with little nervous giggles, getting very red in the face, and subsiding finally into his gaze of complete admiration, while the girl's expression remained exactly the same.

"How old are you?" he asked softly.

She waited some time before she answered. Then in a flat voice she said, "Seventeen."

His smiles came in succession like waves breaking on the surface of a little lake. "I see you got a wooden leg," he said. "I think you're real brave. I think you're real sweet."

The girl stood blank and solid and silent.

"Walk to the gate with me," he said. "You're a brave sweet little thing and I liked you the minute I seen you walk in the door."

Hulga began to move forward.

"What's your name?" he asked, smiling down on the top of her head.

"Hulga," she said.

"Hulga," he murmured, "Hulga. Hulga. I never heard of anybody named Hulga before. You're shy, aren't you, Hulga?" he asked.

She nodded, watching his large red hand on the handle of the giant valise.

"I like girls that wear glasses," he said, "I think a lot. I'm not like these people that a serious thought don't ever enter their heads. It's because I may die."

"I may die too," she said suddenly and looked up at him. His eyes were very small and brown, glittering feverishly.

"Listen," he said, "don't you think some people was meant to meet on account of what all they got in common and all? Like they both think serious thoughts and all?" He shifted the valise to his other hand so that the hand nearest her was free. He caught hold of her elbow and shook it a little. "I don't work on Saturday," he said. "I like to walk in the woods and see what Mother Nature is wearing. O'er the hills and far away. Pic-nics and things. Couldn't we go on a pic-nic tomorrow? Say yes, Hulga," he said and gave her a dying look as if he felt his insides about to drop out of him. He had even seemed to sway slightly toward her.

During the night she had imagined that she seduced him. She imagined that the two of them walked on the place until they came to the storage barn beyond the two back fields and there, she imagined, that things came to such a pass that she very easily seduced him and that then, of course, she had to reckon with his remorse. True genius can get an idea across even to an inferior mind. She imagined that she took his remorse in hand and changed it into a deeper understanding of life. She took all his shame away and turned it into something useful.

She set off for the gate at exactly ten o'clock, escaping without drawing Mrs. Hopewell's attention. She didn't take anything to eat, forgetting that food is usually taken on a picnic. She wore a pair of slacks and a dirty white shirt, and as an afterthought, she had put some Vapex on the collar of it since she did not own any perfume. When she reached the gate no one was there.

She looked up and down the empty highway and had the furious feeling that she had been tricked, that he had only meant to make her walk to the gate after the idea of him. Then suddenly he stood up, very tall, from behind a bush on the opposite embankment. Smiling, he lifted his hat which was new and wide-brimmed. He had not worn it yesterday and she wondered if he had bought it for the occasion. It was toast-colored with a red and white band around it and was slightly too large for him. He stepped from behind the bush still carrying the black valise. He had on the same suit and the same yellow socks sucked down in his shoes from walking. He crossed the highway and said, "I knew you'd come!"

The girl wondered acidly how he had known this. She pointed to the valise and asked, "Why did you bring your Bibles?"

He took her elbow, smiling down on her as if he could not stop. "You can never tell when you'll need the word of God, Hulga," he said. She had a moment in which she doubted that this was actually happening and then they began to climb the embankment. They went down into the pasture toward the woods. The boy walked lightly by her side, bouncing on his toes. The valise did not seem to be heavy today; he even swung it. They crossed half the pasture without saying anything and then, putting his hand easily on the small of her back, he asked softly, "Where does your wooden leg join on?"

She turned an ugly red and glared at him and for an instant the boy looked abashed. "I didn't mean you no harm," he said. "I only meant you're so brave and all. I guess God takes care of you."

"No," she said, looking forward and walking fast, "I don't even believe in God."

At this he stopped and whistled. "No!" he exclaimed as if he were too astonished to say anything else.

She walked on and in a second he was bouncing at her side, fanning with his hat. "That's very unusual for a girl," he remarked, watching her out of the corner of his eye. When they reached the edge of the wood, he put his hand on her back again and drew her against him without a word and kissed her heavily.

The kiss, which had more pressure than feeling behind it, produced that extra surge of adrenalin in the girl that enables one to carry a packed trunk out of a burning house, but in her, the power went at once to the brain. Even before he released her, her mind, clear and detached and ironic anyway, was regarding him from a great distance, with amusement but with pity. She had never been kissed before and she was pleased to discover that it was an unexceptional experience and all a matter of the mind's control. Some people might enjoy drain water if they were told it was vodka. When the boy, looking expectant but uncertain, pushed her gently away, she turned and walked on, saying nothing as if such business, for her, were common enough.

He came along panting at her side, trying to help her when he saw a root that she might trip over. He caught and held back the long swaying blades of thorn vine until she had passed beyond them. She led the way and he came breathing heavily behind her. Then they came out on a sunlit hillside, sloping softly into another one a little smaller. Beyond, they could see the rusted top of the old barn where the extra hay was stored.

The hill was sprinkled with small pink weeds. "Then you ain't saved?" he asked suddenly, stopping.

The girl smiled. It was the first time she had smiled at him at all. "In my economy," she said, "I'm saved and you are damned but I told you I didn't believe in God."

Nothing seemed to destroy the boy's look of admiration. He gazed at her now as if the fantastic animal at the zoo had put its paw through the bars and given him a loving poke. She thought he looked as if he wanted to kiss her again and she walked on before he had the chance.

"Ain't there somewheres we can sit down sometime?" he murmured, his voice softening toward the end of the sentence.

"In that barn," she said.

They made for it rapidly as if it might slide away like a train. It was a large two-story barn, cool and dark inside. The boy pointed up the ladder that led into the loft and said, "It's too bad we can't go up there."

"Why can't we?" she asked.

"Yer leg," he said reverently.

The girl gave him a contemptuous look and putting both hands on the ladder, she climbed it while he stood below, apparently awestruck. She pulled herself expertly through the opening and then looked down at him and said, "Well, come on if you're coming," and he began to climb the ladder, awkwardly bringing the suitcase with him.

"We won't need the Bible," she observed.

"You never can tell," he said, panting. After he had got into the loft, he was a few seconds catching his breath. She had sat down in a pile of straw. A wide sheath of sunlight, filled with dust particles, slanted over her. She lay back against a bale, her face turned away, looking out the front opening of the barn where hay was thrown from a wagon into the loft. The two pink-speckled hill-sides lay back against a dark ridge of woods. The sky was cloudless and cold blue. The boy dropped down by her side and put one arm under her and the other over her and began methodically kissing her face, making little noises like a fish. He did not remove his hat but it was pushed far enough back not to interfere. When her glasses got in his way, he took them off of her and slipped them into his pocket.

The girl at first did not return any of the kisses but presently she began to and after she had put several on his cheek, she reached his lips and remained there, kissing him again and again as if she were trying to draw all the breath out of him. His breath was clear and sweet like a child's and the kisses were sticky like a child's. He mumbled about loving her and about knowing when he first seen her that he loved her, but the mumbling was like the sleepy fretting of a child being put to sleep by his mother. Her mind, throughout this, never stopped or lost itself for a second to her feelings. "You ain't said you loved me none," he whispered finally, pulling back from her. "You got to say that."

She looked away from him off into the hollow sky and then down at a black ridge and then down farther into what appeared to be two green swelling lakes. She didn't realize he had taken her glasses but this landscape could not seem exceptional to her for she seldom paid any close attention to her surroundings.

"You got to say it," he repeated. "You got to say you love me."

She was always careful how she committed herself. "In a sense," she began, "if you use the word loosely, you might say that. But it's not a word I use. I don't have illusions. I'm one of those people who see *through* to nothing."

The boy was frowning. "You got to say it. I said it and you got to say it," he said.

The girl looked at him almost tenderly. "You poor baby," she murmured. "It's just as well you don't understand," and she pulled him by the neck, face-down, against her. "We are all damned," she said, "but some of us have taken off our blindfolds and see that there's nothing to see. It's a kind of salvation."

The boy's astonished eyes looked blankly through the ends of her hair. "Okay," he almost whined, "but do you love me or don'tcher?"

"Yes," she said and added, "in a sense. But I must tell you something. There mustn't be anything dishonest between us." She lifted his head and looked him in the eye. "I am thirty years old," she said. "I have a number of degrees."

The boy's look was irritated but dogged. "I don't care," he said. "I don't care a thing about what all you done. I just want to know if you love me or don'tcher?" and he caught her to him and wildly planted her face with kisses until she said, "Yes, yes."

"Okay then," he said, letting her go. "Prove it."

She smiled, looking dreamily out on the shifty landscape. She had seduced him without even making up her mind to try. "How?" she asked, feeling that he should be delayed a little.

He leaned over and put his lips to her ear. "Show me where your wooden leg joins on," he whispered.

The girl uttered a sharp little cry and her face instantly drained of color. The obscenity of the suggestion was not what shocked her. As a child she had sometimes been subject to feelings of shame but education had removed the last traces of that as a good surgeon scrapes for cancer; she would no more have felt it over what he was asking than she would have believed in his Bible. But she was as sensitive about the artificial leg as a peacock about his tail. No one ever touched it but her. She took care of it as someone else would his soul, in private and almost with her own eyes turned away. "No," she said.

"I known it," he muttered, sitting up. "You're just playing me for a sucker."

"Oh no no!" she cried. "It joins on at the knee. Only at the knee. Why do you want to see it?"

The boy gave her a long penetrating look. "Because," he said, "it's what makes you different. You ain't like anybody else."

She sat staring at him. There was nothing about her face or her round freezing-blue eyes to indicate that this had moved her; but she felt as if her heart had stopped and left her mind to pump her blood. She decided that for the first time in her life she was face to face with real innocence. This boy, with an instinct that came from beyond wisdom, had touched the truth about her. When after a minute, she said in a hoarse high voice, "All right," it was like surrendering to him completely. It was like losing her own life and finding it again, miraculously, in his.

Very gently he began to roll the slack leg up. The artificial limb, in a white sock and brown flat shoe, was bound in a heavy material like canvas and ended in an ugly jointure where it was attached to the stump. The boy's face and his voice were entirely reverent as he uncovered it and said, "Now show me how to take it off and on."

She took it off for him and put it back on again and then he took it off himself, handling it as tenderly as if it were a real one. "See!" he said with a delighted child's face. "Now I can do it myself!"

"Put it back on," she said. She was thinking that she would run away with him and that every night he would take the leg off and every morning put it back on again. "Put it back on," she said.

"Not yet," he murmured, setting it on its foot out of her reach. "Leave it off for a while. You got me instead."

She gave a little cry of alarm but he pushed her down and began to kiss her again. Without the leg she felt entirely dependent on him. Her brain seemed to have stopped thinking altogether and to be about some other function that it was not very good at. Different expressions raced back and forth over her face. Every now and then the boy, his eyes like two steel spikes, would glance behind him where the leg stood. Finally she pushed him off and said, "Put it back on me now."

"Wait," he said. He leaned the other way and pulled the valise toward him and opened it. It had a pale blue spotted lining and there were only two Bibles in it. He took one of these out and opened the cover of it. It was hollow and contained a pocket flask of whiskey, a pack of cards, and a small blue box with printing on it. He laid these out in front of her one at a time in an evenly-spaced row, like one presenting offerings at the shrine of a goddess. He put the blue box in her hand. THIS PRODUCT TO BE USED ONLY FOR THE PREVENTION OF DISEASE, she read, and dropped it. The boy was unscrewing the top of the flask. He stopped and pointed, with a smile, to the deck of cards. It was not an ordinary deck but one with an obscene picture on the back of each card. "Take a swig," he said, offering her the bottle first. He held it in front of her, but like one mesmerized, she did not move.

Her voice when she spoke had an almost pleading sound. "Aren't you," she murmured, "aren't you just good country people?"

The boy cocked his head. He looked as if he were just beginning to understand that she might be trying to insult him. "Yeah," he said, curling his lip slightly, "but it ain't held me back none. I'm as good as you any day in the week."

"Give me my leg," she said.

He pushed it farther away with his foot. "Come on now, let's begin to have us a good time," he said coaxingly. "We ain't got to know one another good yet."

"Give me my leg!" she screamed and tried to lunge for it but he pushed her down easily.

"What's the matter with you all of a sudden?" he asked, frowning as he screwed the top on the flask and put it quickly back inside the Bible. "You just a while ago said you didn't believe in nothing. I thought you was some girl!"

Her face was almost purple. "You're a Christian!" she hissed. "You're a fine Christian! You're just like them all—say one thing and do another. You're a perfect Christian, you're . . ."

The boy's mouth was set angrily. "I hope you don't think," he said in a lofty indignant tone, "that I believe in that crap! I may sell Bibles but I know which end is up and I wasn't born yesterday and I know where I'm going!"

"Give me my leg!" she screeched. He jumped up so quickly that she barely saw him sweep the cards and the blue box back into the Bible and throw the Bible into the valise. She saw him grab the leg and then she saw it for an instant slanted forlornly across the inside of the suitcase with a Bible at either side of its opposite ends. He slammed the lid shut and snatched up the valise and swung it down the hole and then stepped through himself.

When all of him had passed but his head, he turned and regarded her with a look that no longer had any admiration in it. "I've gotten a lot of interesting things," he said. "One time I got a woman's glass eye this way. And you needn't to think you'll catch me because Pointer ain't really my name. I use a different name at every house I call at and don't stay nowhere long. And I'll tell you another thing, Hulga," he said, using the name as if he didn't think much of it, "you ain't so smart. I been believing in nothing ever since I was born!" and then the toast-colored hat disappeared down the hole and the girl was left, sitting on the straw in the dusty sunlight. When she turned her churning face toward the opening, she saw his blue figure struggling successfully over the green speckled lake.

Mrs. Hopewell and Mrs. Freeman, who were in the back pasture, digging up onions, saw him emerge a little later from the woods and head across the meadow toward the highway. "Why, that looks like that nice dull young man that tried to sell me a Bible yesterday," Mrs. Hopewell said, squinting. "He must have been selling them to the Negroes back in there. He was so simple," she said, "but I guess the world would be better off if we were all that simple."

Mrs. Freeman's gaze drove forward and just touched him before he disappeared under the hill. Then she returned her attention to the evil-smelling onion shoot she was lifting from the ground. "Some can't be that simple," she said. "I know I never could."

QUESTIONS

1. Characters are more fully developed in this story than in the shorter stories that immediately precede it. How much of the relationship between Hulga and her mother can be seen as common or typical of a mother and daughter relationship? What elements of character serve to individualize Hulga and her mother, setting them apart from a typical mother and daughter?

2. What characteristics do you think Mrs. Hopewell expects to find in "good country people"? How fully does Hulga share her mother's expectations concerning such people?

3. In what ways are Mrs. Freeman and the Bible salesman typical of Mrs. Hopewell's idea of "good country people"?

4. How does the summary characterization of Mrs. Freeman in the first

four sentences of the story prove accurate when measured against
her later actions and speeches?

5. How do the names "Mrs. Hopewell," "Joy," and "Hulga" serve to
characterize?

6. How are the names "Mrs. Freeman" and "Manley Pointer" significant?

7. Apart from the names, what are some of the most memorable uses
of irony in the story?

8. Explain the significance of the Bible salesman's comment to Hulga,
"you ain't so smart. I been believing in nothing ever since I was
born!"

9. If Hulga told her own story, how would it be changed?

10. How and where does the omniscient perspective shift from external
to internal?

THE SHAWL

Cynthia Ozick   (1928–   )

Stella, cold, cold, the coldness of hell. How they walked on the roads together,
Rosa with Magda curled up between sore breasts, Magda wound up in the shawl.
Sometimes Stella carried Magda. But she was jealous of Magda. A thin girl of
fourteen, too small, with thin breasts of her own, Stella wanted to be wrapped
in a shawl, hidden away, asleep, rocked by the march, a baby, a round infant in
arms. Magda took Rosa's nipple, and Rosa never stopped walking, a walking
cradle. There was not enough milk; sometimes Magda sucked air; then she
screamed. Stella was ravenous. Her knees were tumors on sticks, her elbows
chicken bones.

Rosa did not feel hunger; she felt light, not like someone walking but like
someone in a faint, in trance, arrested in a fit, someone who is already a floating
angel, alert and seeing everything, but in the air, not there, not touching the road.
As if teetering on the tips of her fingernails. She looked into Magda's face through
a gap in the shawl: a squirrel in a nest, safe, no one could reach her inside the
little house of the shawl's windings. The face, very round, a pocket mirror of a
face: but it was not Rosa's bleak complexion, dark like cholera, it was another
kind of face altogether, eyes blue as air, smooth feathers of hair nearly as yellow
as the Star[1] sewn into Rosa's coat. You could think she was one of *their* babies.

Rosa, floating, dreamed of giving Magda away in one of the villages. She could
leave the line for a minute and push Magda into the hands of any woman on the
side of the road. But if she moved out of line they might shoot. And even if she
fled the line for half a second and pushed the shawl-bundle at a stranger, would
the woman take it? She might be surprised, or afraid; she might drop the shawl,
and Magda would fall out and strike her head and die. The little round head. Such

[1]Star of David, six-pointed, a symbol of Judaism.

a good child, she gave up screaming, and sucked now only for the taste of the drying nipple itself. The neat grip of the tiny gums. One mite of a tooth tip sticking up in the bottom gum, how shining, an elfin tombstone of white marble, gleaming there. Without complaining, Magda relinquished Rosa's teats, first the left, then the right; both were cracked, not a sniff of milk. The duct crevice extinct, a dead volcano, blind eye, chill hole, so Magda took the corner of the shawl and milked it instead. She sucked and sucked, flooding the threads with wetness. The shawl's good flavor, milk of linen.

It was a magic shawl, it could nourish an infant for three days and three nights. Magda did not die, she stayed alive, although very quiet. A peculiar smell, of cinnamon and almonds, lifted out of her mouth. She held her eyes open every moment, forgetting how to blink or nap, and Rosa and sometimes Stella studied their blueness. On the road they raised one burden of a leg after another and studied Magda's face. "Aryan,"[2] Stella said, in a voice grown as thin as a string; and Rosa thought how Stella gazed at Magda like a young cannibal. And the time that Stella said "Aryan," it sounded to Rosa as if Stella had really said "Let us devour her."

But Magda lived to walk. She lived that long, but she did not walk very well, partly because she was only fifteen months old, and partly because the spindles of her legs could not hold up her fat belly. It was fat with air, full and round. Rosa gave almost all her food to Magda, Stella gave nothing; Stella was ravenous, a growing child herself, but not growing much. Stella did not menstruate. Rosa did not menstruate. Rosa was ravenous, but also not; she learned from Magda how to drink the taste of a finger in one's mouth. They were in a place without pity, all pity was annihilated in Rosa, she looked at Stella's bones without pity. She was sure that Stella was waiting for Magda to die so she could put her teeth into the little thighs.

Rosa knew Magda was going to die very soon; she should have been dead already, but she had been buried away deep inside the magic shawl, mistaken there for the shivering mound of Rosa's breasts; Rosa clung to the shawl as if it covered only herself. No one took it away from her. Magda was mute. She never cried. Rosa hid her in the barracks, under the shawl, but she knew that one day someone would inform; or one day someone, not even Stella, would steal Magda to eat her. When Magda began to walk Rosa knew that Magda was going to die very soon, something would happen. She was afraid to fall asleep; she slept with the weight of her thigh on Magda's body; she was afraid she would smother Magda under her thigh. The weight of Rosa was becoming less and less; Rosa and Stella were slowly turning into air.

Magda was quiet, but her eyes were horribly alive, like blue tigers. She watched. Sometimes she laughed—it seemed a laugh, but how could it be? Magda had never seen anyone laugh. Still, Magda laughed at her shawl when the wind blew its corners, the bad wind with pieces of black in it, that made Stella's and Rosa's eyes tear. Magda's eyes were always clear and tearless. She watched like

---

[2] A term used in Nazi Germany to designate non-Jewish Caucasians.

a tiger. She guarded her shawl. No one could touch it; only Rosa could touch it. Stella was not allowed. The shawl was Magda's own baby, her pet, her little sister. She tangled herself up in it and sucked on one of the corners when she wanted to be very still.

Then Stella took the shawl away and made Magda die.

Afterward Stella said: "I was cold."

And afterward she was always cold, always. The cold went into her heart: Rosa saw that Stella's heart was cold. Magda flopped onward with her little pencil legs scribbling this way and that, in search of the shawl; the pencils faltered at the barracks opening, where the light began. Rosa saw and pursued. But already Magda was in the square outside the barracks, in the jolly light. It was the roll-call arena. Every morning Rosa had to conceal Magda under the shawl against a wall of the barracks and go out and stand in the arena with Stella and hundreds of others, sometimes for hours, and Magda, deserted, was quiet under the shawl, sucking on her corner. Every day Magda was silent, and so she did not die. Rosa saw that today Magda was going to die, and at the same time a fearful joy ran in Rosa's two palms, her fingers were on fire, she was astonished, febrile: Magda, in the sunlight, swaying on her pencil legs, was howling. Ever since the drying up of Rosa's nipples, ever since Magda's last scream on the road, Magda had been devoid of any syllable; Magda was a mute. Rosa believed that something had gone wrong with her vocal cords, with her windpipe, with the cave of her larynx; Magda was defective, without a voice; perhaps she was deaf; there might be something amiss with her intelligence; Magda was dumb. Even the laugh that came when the ash-stippled wind made a clown out of Magda's shawl was only the air-blown showing of her teeth. Even when the lice, head lice and body lice, crazed her so that she became as wild as one of the big rats that plundered the barracks at daybreak looking for carrion, she rubbed and scratched and kicked and bit and rolled without a whimper. But now Magda's mouth was spilling a long viscous rope of clamor.

"Maaaa—"

It was the first noise Magda had ever sent out from her throat since the drying up of Rosa's nipples.

"Maaaa . . . aaa!"

Again! Magda was wavering in the perilous sunlight of the arena, scribbling on such pitiful little bent shins. Rosa saw. She saw that Magda was grieving for the loss of her shawl, she saw that Magda was going to die. A tide of commands hammered in Rosa's nipples: Fetch, get, bring! But she did not know which to go after first, Magda or the shawl. If she jumped out into the arena to snatch Magda up, the howling would not stop, because Magda would still not have the shawl; but if she ran back into the barracks to find the shawl, and if she found it, and if she came after Magda holding it and shaking it, then she would get Magda back, Magda would put the shawl in her mouth and turn dumb again.

Rosa entered the dark. It was easy to discover the shawl. Stella was heaped under it, asleep in her thin bones. Rosa tore the shawl free and flew—she could fly, she was only air—into the arena. The sunheat murmured of another life, of butterflies in summer. The light was placid, mellow. On the other side of the steel fence, far away, there were green meadows speckled with dandelions and deep-colored violets; beyond them, even farther, innocent tiger lilies, tall, lifting their orange bonnets. In the barracks they spoke of "flowers," of "rain": excrement, thick turd-braids, and the slow stinking maroon waterfall that slunk down from the upper bunks, the stink mixed with a bitter fatty floating smoke that greased Rosa's skin. She stood for an instant at the margin of the arena. Sometimes the electricity inside the fence would seem to hum; even Stella said it was only an imagining, but Rosa heard real sounds in the wire: grainy sad voices. The farther she was from the fence, the more clearly the voices crowded at her. The lamenting voices strummed so convincingly, so passionately, it was impossible to suspect them of being phantoms. The voices told her to hold up the shawl, high; the voices told her to shake it, to whip with it, to unfurl it like a flag. Rosa lifted, shook, whipped, unfurled. Far off, very far, Magda leaned across her air-fed belly, reaching out with the rods of her arms. She was high up, elevated, riding someone's shoulder. But the shoulder that carried Magda was not coming toward Rosa and the shawl, it was drifting away, the speck of Magda was moving more and more into the smoky distance. Above the shoulder a helmet glinted. The light tapped the helmet and sparkled it into a goblet. Below the helmet a black body like a domino and a pair of black boots hurled themselves in the direction of the electrified fence. The electric voices began to chatter wildly. "Maamaa, maaa-maaa," they all hummed together. How far Magda was from Rosa now, across the whole square, past a dozen barracks, all the way on the other side! She was no bigger than a moth.

All at once Magda was swimming through the air. The whole of Magda traveled through loftiness. She looked like a butterfly touching a silver vine. And the moment Magda's feathered round head and her pencil legs and balloonish belly and zigzag arms splashed against the fence, the steel voices went mad in their growling, urging Rosa to run and run to the spot where Magda had fallen from her flight against the electrified fence; but of course Rosa did not obey them. She only stood, because if she ran they would shoot, and if she tried to pick up the sticks of Magda's body they would shoot, and if she let the wolf's screech ascending now through the ladder of her skeleton break out, they would shoot; so she took Magda's shawl and filled her own mouth with it, stuffed it in and stuffed it in, until she was swallowing up the wolf's screech and tasting the cinnamon and almond depth of Magda's saliva; and Rosa drank Magda's shawl until it dried.

QUESTIONS

1. How do you know where and when this story occurs?
2. "The Shawl" might have been included in Chapter 4 as an example of internal narrative perspective. Because of the method of narration, we know nothing of Rosa's life before or after the events narrated and we have no judgment of her character as given by an

outside observer. How would you summarize her character? On what evidence?

3. Why does Rosa remain silent and inactive when her child is killed?

4. More than some other stories, this one stresses the link between character and circumstances. It is possible to imagine Rosa's character before the concentration camp? After? To test your imagination against an author's, you might look up Ozick's story "Rosa," set many years later.

5. What is the significance of the shawl?

THE HUNTER

E. L. Doctorow   (1931–   )

The town is terraced in the hill, along the river, a factory town of clapboard houses and public buildings faced in red stone. There is a one-room library called the Lyceum. There are several taverns made from porched homes, Miller and Bud signs hanging in neon in the front windows. Down at water's edge sits the old brassworks, a long two-story brick building with a tower at one end and it is behind locked fences and many of its windows are broken. The river is frozen. The town is dusted in new snow. Along the sides of the streets the winter's accumulated snow is banked high as a man's shoulder. Smoke drifts from the chimneys of the houses and is quickly sucked into the sky. The wind comes up off the river and sweeps up the hill through the houses.

A school bus makes its way through the narrow hill streets. The mothers and fathers stand on the porches above to watch the bus accept their children. It's the only thing moving in the town. The fathers fill their arms with firewood stacked by the front doors and go back inside. Trees are black in the woods behind the homes; they are black against the snow. Sparrow and finch dart from branch to branch and puff their feathers to keep warm. They flutter to the ground and hop on the snow-crust under the trees.

The children enter the school through the big oak doors with the push bars. It is not a large school but its proportions, square and high, create hollow rooms and echoing stairwells. The children sit in their rows with their hands folded and watch their teacher. She is cheery and kind. She has been here just long enough for her immodest wish to transform these children to have turned to awe at what they are. Their small faces have been rubbed raw by the cold; the weakness of their fair skin is brought out in blotches on their cheeks and in the blue pallor of their eyelids. Their eyelids are translucent membranes, so thin and so delicate that she wonders how they sleep, how they keep from seeing through their closed eyes.

She tells them she is happy to see them here in such cold weather, with a hard wind blowing up the valley and another storm coming. She begins the day's work with their exercise, making them squat and bend and jump and swing their arms and somersault so that they can see what the world looks like upside down. How does it look? she cries, trying it herself, somersaulting on the gym mat until she's dizzy.

They are not animated but the exercise alerts them to the mood she's in. They watch her with interest to see what is next. She leads them out of the small, dimly lit gymnasium through the empty halls, up and down the stairs, telling them they are a lost patrol in the caves of a planet somewhere far out in space. They are looking for signs of life. They wander through the unused schoolrooms, where crayon drawings hang from one thumbtack and corkboards have curled away from their frames. Look, she calls, holding up a child's red rubber boot, fished from the depths of a classroom closet. You never can tell!

When they descend to the basement, the janitor dozing in his cubicle is startled awake by a group of children staring at him. He is a large bearish man and wears fatigue pants and a red plaid woolen shirt. The teacher has never seen him wear anything different. His face has a gray stubble. We're a lost patrol, she says to him, have you seen any living creatures hereabouts? The janitor frowns. What? he says. What?

It is warm in the basement. The furnace emits its basso roar. She has him open the furnace door so the children can see the source of heat, the fire in its pit. They are each invited to cast a handful of coal through the door. They do this as a sacrament.

Then she insists that the janitor open the storage rooms and the old lunchroom kitchen, and here she notes unused cases of dried soup mix and canned goods, and then large pots and thick aluminum cauldrons and a stack of metal trays with food compartments. Here, you can't take those, the janitor says. And why not, she answers, this is their school, isn't it? She gives each child a tray or pot, and they march upstairs, banging them with their fists to scare away the creatures of wet flesh and rotating eyes and pulpy horns who may be lying in wait round the corners.

In the afternoon it is already dark, and the school bus receives the children in the parking lot behind the building. The new street lamps installed by the county radiate an amber light. The yellow school bus in the amber light is the color of a dark egg yolk. As it leaves, the children, their faces indistinct behind the windows, turn to stare out at the young teacher. She waves, her fingers opening and closing like a fluttering wing. The bus windows slide past, breaking her image and re-forming it, and giving her the illusion of the stone building behind her sliding along its foundations in the opposite direction.

The bus has turned into the road. It goes slowly past the school. The children's heads lurch in unison as the driver shifts gears. The bus plunges out of sight in the dip of the hill. At this moment the teacher realizes that she did not recognize the driver. He was not the small, burly man with eyeglasses without rims. He was a young man with long light hair and white eyebrows, and he looked at her in the instant he hunched over the steering wheel, with his arms about to make the effort of putting the bus into a turn.

That evening at home the young woman heats water for a bath and pours it in the tub. She bathes and urinates in the bathwater. She brings her hands out of the water and lets it pour through her fingers. She hums a made-up tune. The bathroom is large, with wainscoting of wood strips painted gray. The tub rests on four cast-iron claws. A small window high on the wall is open just a crack and through it the night air sifts into the room. She lies back and the cold air comes along the water line and draws its finger across her neck.

In the morning she dresses and combs her hair back and ties it behind her head and wears small opal teardrop earrings given to her for her graduation from college. She walks to work, opens up the school, turns up the radiator, cleans the blackboard, and goes to the front door to await the children on the yellow bus.

They do not come.

She goes to her teaching room, rearranges the day's lesson on the desk, distributes a sheet of stiff paper to each child's desk. She goes back to the front door and awaits the children.

They are nowhere in sight.

She looks for the school janitor in the basement. The furnace makes a kind of moaning sound, there is rhythmic intensification of its running pitch, and he's staring at it with a perplexed look on his face. He tells her the time, and it is the time on her watch. She goes back upstairs and stands at the front door with her coat on.

The yellow bus comes into the school driveway and pulls up before the front door. She puts her hand on the shoulder of each child descending the steps from the bus. The young man with the blond hair and eyebrows smiles at her.

There have been sacred rites and legendary events in this town. In a semi-pro football game a player was killed. A presidential candidate once came and spoke. A mass funeral was held here for the victims of a shoe-factory fire. She understands the new bus driver has no knowledge of any of this.

On Saturday morning the teacher goes to the old people's home and reads aloud. They sit there and listen to the story. They are the children's faces in another time. She thinks she can even recognize some of the grandmothers and grandfathers by family. When the reading is over those who can walk come up to her and pluck at her sleeves and her collar, interrupting each other to tell her who they are and what they used to be. They shout at each other. They mock each other's words. They waggle their hands in her face to get her to look at them.

She cannot get out of there fast enough. In the street she breaks into a run. She runs until the old people's home is out of sight.

It is very cold, but the sun shines. She decides to walk up to the mansion at the top of the highest hill in town. The hill streets turn abruptly back on themselves like a series of chutes. She wears lace-up boots and jeans. She climbs through snowdrifts in which she sinks up to the thighs.

The old mansion sits in the sun above the tree line. It is said that one of the factory owners built it for his bride, and that shortly after taking possession he killed her with a shotgun. The Greek columns have great chunks missing and she sees chicken wire exposed under the plaster. The portico is hung with icicles, and snow is backed against the house. There is no front door. She goes in. The light of the sun and a fall of snow fill the entrance hall and its grand stairway. She can see the sky through the collapsed ceiling and a crater in the roof. She moves carefully and goes to the door of what must have been the dining room. She opens it. It smells of rot. There is a rustle and a hissing sound and she sees several pairs of eyes constellated in the dark. She opens the door wider. Many cats are backed into a corner of the room. They growl at her and twitch their tails.

She goes out and walks around to the back, an open field white in the sun. There is a pitted aluminum straight ladder leaning against a windowsill in the second floor. She climbs the ladder. The window is punched out and she climbs through the frame and stands in a light and airy bedroom. A hemisphere of ice hangs from the ceiling. It looks like the bottom of the moon. She stands at the window and sees at the edge of the field a man in an orange jacket and red hat. She wonders if he can see her from this distance. He raises a rifle to his shoulder and a moment later she hears an odd smack as if someone has hit the siding of the house with an open palm. She does not move. The hunter lowers his rifle and steps back into the woods at the edge of the field.

That evening the young teacher calls the town physician to ask for something to take. What seems to be the trouble? the doctor says. She conceives of a self-deprecating answer, sounding confident and assertive, even managing a small laugh. He says he will call the druggist and prescribe Valiums, two-milligram so that she won't be made drowsy by them. She walks down to Main Street, where the druggist opens his door and without turning on the store light leads her to the prescription counter in the rear. The druggist puts his hand into a large jar and comes up with a handful of tablets, and feeds the Valium one by one, from his thumb and forefinger, into a vial.

She goes to the movie theater on Main Street and pays her admission. The theater bears the same name as the town. She sits in the dark and swallows a handful of tabs. She cannot discern the picture. The screen is white. Then what she sees forming on the white screen is the town in its blanket of snow, the clapboard houses on the hill, the frozen river, the wind blowing snow along the streets. She sees the children coming out of their doors with their schoolbooks and walking down their steps to the street. She sees her life exactly as it is outside the movie theater.

Later she walks through the downtown. The only thing open is the State News. Several men stand thumbing the magazines. She turns down Mechanic Street and walks past the tool-and-die company and crosses the railroad tracks to the bridge. She begins to run. In the middle of the bridge the wind is a force and she feels it wants to press her through the railing into the river. She runs bent over, feeling as if she is pushing through something, as if it is only giving way to her by tearing.

Across the bridge the road turns sharply left and at the curve, at the foot of a hill of pine trees, is a brown house with a neon sign in the window: The Rapids. She climbs up the porch steps into the Rapids, and looking neither left nor right, walks to the back, where she finds the ladies' room. When she comes out she sits in one of the varnished plywood booths and stares at the table. After a while a man in an apron comes over and she orders a beer. Only then does she look up. The light is dim. A couple of elderly men are at the bar. But alone down at the end, established with his glass and a pack of cigarettes, is the new bus driver with the long blond hair, and he is smiling at her.

He has joined her. For a while nothing is said. He raises his arm and turns in his seat to look toward the bar. He turns his head to look back at her. You want another, he says. She shakes her head no but doesn't say thank you. She digs in her coat pocket and puts a wrinkled dollar beside her bottle. He holds up one finger.

You from around here? he says.

From the eastern part of the state, she says.

I'm from Valdese, he says. Down on Sixteen.

Oh yes.

I know you're their teacher, he says. I'm their driver.

He wears a wool shirt and a denim jacket and jeans. It is what he wears in his bus. He would not own a coat. There is something on a chain around his neck but it is hidden under the shirt. Blond beard stubble lies sparsely on his chin and along the line of his jaw. His cheeks are smooth. He is smiling. One of his front teeth is chipped.

What do you do to get to be a teacher?

You go to college. She sighs: What do you do to be a driver?

It's a county job, he says. You need a chauffeur's license and a clean record.

What is a dirty record?

Why, if you been arrested, you know? If you have any kind of record. Or if you got a bad service discharge.

She waits.

I had a teacher once in the third grade, he says. I believe she was the most beautiful woman I have ever seen. I believe now she was no more'n a girl. Like you. But she was very proud and she had a way of tossing her head and walking that made me wish to be a better student.

She laughs.

He picks up her beer bottle and feigns reproach and holds up his arm to the bartender and signals for two.

It is very easy, she says, to make them fall in love with you. Boys or girls, it's very easy.

And to herself she admits that she tries to do it, to make them love her, she takes on a grace she doesn't really have at any other time. She moves like a dancer, she touches them and brushes against them. She is outgoing and shows no terror, and the mystery of her is created in their regard.

Do you have sisters? she says.

Two. How'd you know that?

They're older than you?

One older, one younger.

What do they do?

Work in the office of the lumber mill down there.

She says: I would trust a man who had sisters.

He tilts his head back and takes a long pull at his beer bottle, and she watches his Adam's apple rise and fall, and the sparse blond stubble on his throat move like reeds lying on the water.

Later they come out of the Rapids and he leads her to his pickup. He is rather short. She climbs in and notices his workboots when he comes up into the cab from the other side. They're clean good boots, new yellow leather. He has trouble starting the engine.

What are you doing here at night if you live in Valdese? she says.

Waiting for you. He laughs and the engine turns over.

They drive slowly across the bridge, and across the tracks. Following her instructions, he goes to the end of the main street and turns up into the hills and brings her to her house. He pulls up in the yard by the side door.

It is a small house and it looks dark and cold. He switches off the engine and the headlights and leans across her lap and presses the button of the glove compartment. He says: Happens I got me some party wine right here. He removes a flat bottle in a brown bag and slams the door, and as he moves back, his arm brushes her thigh.

She stares through the windshield. She says: Stupid goddamn mill hand. Making his play with the teacher. Look at that, with his party wine in a sack. I can't believe it.

She jumps down from the cab, runs around the truck, and up the back steps into her kitchen. She slams the door. There is silence. She waits in the kitchen, not moving, in the dark, standing behind the table, facing the door.

She hears nothing but her own breathing.

All at once the back door is flooded with light, the white curtain on the door glass becomes a white screen, and then the light fades, and she hears the pickup backing out to the street. She is panting and now her rage breaks, and she is crying.

She stands alone in her dark kitchen crying, a bitter scent coming off her body, a smell of burning, which offends her. She heats water on the stove and takes it up to her bath.

On Monday morning the teacher waits for her children at the front door of the school. When the bus turns into the drive, she steps back and stands inside the door. She can see the open door of the bus but she cannot see if he is trying to see her.

She is very animated this morning. This is a special day, children, she announces, and she astonishes them by singing them a song while she accompanies herself on the Autoharp. She lets them strum the Autoharp while she presses the chords. Look, she says to each one, you are making music.

At eleven the photographer arrives. He is a man with a potbelly and a black string tie. I don't get these school calls till spring, he says.

This is a special occasion, the teacher says. We want a picture of ourselves now. Don't we, children?

They watch intently as he sets up his tripod and camera. He has a black valise with brass latches that snap as he opens them. Inside are cables and floodlamps.

Used to be classes of kids, he says. Now look at what's left of you. Heat this whole building for one room.

By the time he is ready, the young teacher has pushed the benches to the blackboard and grouped the children in two rows, the taller ones sitting on the benches, the shorter ones sitting in front of them on the floor, cross-legged. She herself stands at one side. There are fifteen children staring at the camera and their smiling teacher holding her hands in front of her, like an opera singer.

The photographer looks at the scene and frowns. Why, these children ain't fixed up for their picture.

What do you mean?

Why, they ain't got on their ties and their new shoes. You got girls here wearing trousers.

Just take it, she says.

They don't look right. Their hair ain't combed, these boys here.

Take us as we are, the teacher says. She steps suddenly out of line and with a furious motion removes the barrette fastening her hair and shakes her head until her hair falls to her shoulders. The children are startled. She kneels down on the floor in front of them, facing the camera, and pulls two of them into her arms. She brings all of them around her with an urgent opening and closing of her hands, and they gather about her. One girl begins to cry.

She pulls them in around her, feeling their bodies, the thin bones of their arms, their small shoulders, their legs, their behinds.

Take it, she says in a fierce whisper. Take it as we are. We are looking at you. Take it.

QUESTIONS

1. Is the brief characterization of the teacher as "cheery and kind" in the third paragraph an accurate summary of her character as you see it revealed by her actions? What other adjectives would you use to characterize her more fully or more accurately? On what evidence?
2. List some of the things another writer might tell about the teacher that are omitted from this story. Are these things important?
3. Describe Doctorow's narrative perspective in this story.
4. Why is the story called "The Hunter"? Is the reference only to the hunter who appears at the end of the third section or to some other hunter as well? What is being hunted?
5. What elements of setting are most important to the story? To what extent does the setting help us understand the characters?

CHAPTER 6

SETTING

The time and place of a story is its *setting.* The term *ethos* describes not only the physical place the characters inhabit and the time of the plot but also the social, historical, or psychological conditions in which the story unfolds.

Stories dealing with conflicts between human beings or psychological tensions within individuals may use almost any locale or era; descriptions of the surroundings may work simply as backdrops to action, adding little to meaning. However, in stories illustrating the human struggle with physical surroundings, weather conditions, social structure, tradition, or stereotypes, setting or ethos may be more central to our understanding.

When setting is important, the author must define very clearly the limitations or obstacles imposed on the characters from without, so that we as readers understand the terms of the conflict. A writer may present the setting very realistically, as Jack London does in "To Build a Fire," or may combine realism with symbolism to communicate the struggle as Ellison and Cheever do. In either case, the writer must show the reader how a character's surroundings influence what he or she does. In stories where the environment may be totally different from anything the reader has experienced, the writer must place the essential features concretely before the reader's imagination. Even science fiction or fantasy, however removed from the world we inhabit, establishes its authority through details of setting that may be crucial to the plot and characterization.

The first few paragraphs of a story are often important in setting the scene or establishing the ethos. What can extreme cold do? How does racial stereotyping inhibit perception? What effect does social class have on individual emotions? How does the ethos of another time and place shape the behavior of people who live there? In reading the following stories pay particular attention to the physical, social, and historical backgrounds that influence each character.

197

TO BUILD A FIRE

Jack London   (1876–1916)

Day had broken cold and gray, exceedingly cold and gray, when the man turned aside from the main Yukon trail and climbed the high earth-bank, where a dim and little-travelled trail led eastward through the fat spruce timberland. It was a steep bank, and he paused for breath at the top, excusing the act to himself by looking at his watch. It was nine o'clock. There was no sun nor hint of sun, though there was not a cloud in the sky. It was a clear day, and yet there seemed an intangible pall over the face of things, a subtle gloom that made the day dark, and that was due to the absence of sun. This fact did not worry the man. He was used to the lack of sun. It had been days since he had seen the sun, and he knew that a few more days must pass before that cheerful orb, due south, should just peep above the sky line and dip immediately from view.

The man flung a look back along the way he had come. The Yukon lay a mile wide and hidden under three feet of ice. On top of this ice were as many feet of snow. It was all pure white, rolling in gentle undulations where the ice jams of the freeze-up had formed. North and south, as far as his eye could see, it was unbroken white, save for a dark hairline that curved and twisted from around the spruce-covered island to the south, and that curved and twisted away into the north, where it disappeared behind another spruce-covered island. This dark hairline was the trail—the main trail—that led south five hundred miles to the Chilcoot Pass, Dyea, and salt water; and that led north seventy miles to Dawson, and still on to the north a thousand miles to Nulato, and finally to St. Michael, on Bering Sea, a thousand miles and half a thousand more.

But all this—the mysterious, far-reaching hairline trail, the absence of sun from the sky, the tremendous cold, and the strangeness and weirdness of it all —made no impression on the man. It was not because he was long used to it. He was a newcomer in the land, a *chechaquo,* and this was his first winter. The trouble with him was that he was without imagination. He was quick and alert in the things of life, but only in the things, and not in the significances. Fifty degrees below zero meant eighty-odd degrees of frost. Such fact impressed him as being cold and uncomfortable, and that was all. It did not lead him to meditate upon his frailty as a creature of temperature, and upon man's frailty in general, able only to live within certain narrow limits of heat and cold; and from there on it did not lead him to the conjectural field of immortality and man's place in the universe. Fifty degrees below zero stood for a bite of frost that hurt and that must be guarded against by the use of mittens, ear flaps, warm moccasins, and thick socks. Fifty degrees below zero was to him just precisely fifty degrees below zero. That there should be anything more to it than that was a thought that never entered his head.

As he turned to go on, he spat speculatively. There was a sharp, explosive crackle that startled him. He spat again. And again, in the air, before it could fall to the snow, the spittle crackled. He knew that at fifty below spittle crackled on the snow, but this spittle had crackled in the air. Undoubtedly it was colder than fifty below—how much colder he did not know. But the temperature did not matter. He was bound for the old claim on the left fork of Henderson Creek, where the boys were already. They had come over across the divide from the Indian Creek country, while he had come the roundabout way to take a look at the possibilities of getting out logs in the spring from the islands in the Yukon. He would be in to camp by six o'clock; a bit after dark, it was true, but the boys would be there, a fire would be going, and a hot supper would be ready. As for lunch, he pressed his hand against the protruding bundle under his jacket. It was also under his shirt, wrapped up in a handkerchief and lying against the naked skin. It was the only way to keep the biscuits from freezing. He smiled agreeably to himself as he thought of those biscuits, each cut open and sopped in bacon grease, and each enclosing a generous slice of fried bacon.

He plunged in among the big spruce trees. The trail was faint. A foot of snow had fallen since the last sled had passed over, and he was glad he was without a sled, traveling light. In fact, he carried nothing but the lunch wrapped in the handkerchief. He was surprised, however, at the cold. It certainly was cold, he concluded, as he rubbed his numb nose and cheekbones with his mittened hand. He was a warm-whiskered man, but the hair on his face did not protect the high cheekbones and the eager nose that thrust itself aggressively into the frosty air.

At the man's heels trotted a dog, a big native husky, the proper wolf dog, gray-coated and without any visible or temperamental difference from its brother, the wild wolf. The animal was depressed by the tremendous cold. It knew that it was no time for traveling. Its instinct told it a truer tale than was told to the man by the man's judgment. In reality, it was not merely colder than fifty below zero; it was colder than sixty below, than seventy below. It was seventy-five below zero. Since the freezing point is thirty-two above zero, it meant that one hundred and seven degrees of frost obtained. The dog did not know anything about thermometers. Possibly in its brain there was no sharp consciousness of a condition of very cold such as was in the man's brain. But the brute had its instinct. It experienced a vague but menacing apprehension that subdued it and made it slink along at the man's heels, and that made it question eagerly every unwonted movement of the man as if expecting him to go into camp or to seek shelter somewhere and build a fire. The dog had learned fire, and it wanted fire, or else to burrow under the snow and cuddle its warmth away from the air.

The frozen moisture of its breathing had settled on its fur in a fine powder of frost, and especially were its jowls, muzzle, and eyelashes whitened by its crystalled breath. The man's red beard and mustache were likewise frosted, but more solidly, the deposit taking the form of ice and increasing with every warm, moist breath he exhaled. Also, the man was chewing tobacco, and the muzzle of ice held his lips so rigidly that he was unable to clear his chin when he expelled the juice. The result was that a crystal beard of the color and solidity of amber was increasing its length on his chin. If he fell down it would shatter itself, like glass, into brittle fragments. But he did not mind the appendage. It was the penalty all tobacco chewers paid in that country, and he had been out before in two cold snaps. They had not been so cold as this, he knew, but by the spirit thermometer at Sixty Mile he knew they had been registered at fifty below and at fifty-five.

He held on through the level stretch of woods for several miles, crossed a wide flat of nigger heads, and dropped down a bank to the frozen bed of a small stream. This was Henderson Creek, and he knew he was ten miles from the forks. He looked at his watch. It was ten o'clock. He was making four miles an hour, and he calculated that he would arrive at the forks at half-past twelve. He decided to celebrate that event by eating his lunch there.

The dog dropped in again at his heels, with a tail drooping discouragement, as the man swung along the creek bed. The furrow of the old sled trail was plainly visible, but a dozen inches of snow covered the marks of the last runners. In a month no man had come up or down that silent creek. The man held steadily on. He was not much given to thinking, and just then particularly he had nothing to think about save that he would eat lunch at the forks and that at six o'clock he would be in camp with the boys. There was nobody to talk to; and, had there been, speech would have been impossible because of the ice muzzle on his mouth. So he continued monotonously to chew tobacco and to increase the length of his amber beard.

Once in a while the thought reiterated itself that it was very cold and that he had never experienced such cold. As he walked along he rubbed his cheekbones and nose with the back of his mittened hand. He did this automatically, now and again changing hands. But, rub as he would, the instant he stopped his cheekbones went numb, and the following instant the end of his nose went numb. He was sure to frost his cheeks; he knew that, and experienced a pang of regret that he had not devised a nose strap of the sort Bud wore in cold snaps. Such a strap passed across the cheeks, as well, and saved them. But it didn't matter much, after all. What were frosted cheeks? A bit painful, that was all; they were never serious.

Empty as the man's mind was of thoughts, he was keenly observant, and he noticed the changes in the creek, the curves and bends and timber jams, and always he sharply noted where he placed his feet. Once, coming around a bend, he shied abruptly, like a startled horse, curved away from the place where he had been walking, and retreated several paces back along the trail. The creek he knew was frozen clear to the bottom—no creek could contain water in that arctic winter —but he knew also that there were springs that bubbled out from the hillsides and ran along under the snow and on top the ice of the creek. He knew that the coldest snaps never froze these springs, and he knew likewise their danger. They were traps. They hid pools of water under the snow that might be three inches deep, or three feet. Sometimes a skin of ice half an inch thick covered them, and in turn was covered by the snow. Sometimes there were alternate layers of water and ice skin, so that when one broke through he kept on breaking through for a while, sometimes wetting himself to the waist.

That was why he had shied in such panic. He had felt the give under his feet and heard the crackle of a snow-hidden ice skin. And to get his feet wet in such a temperature meant trouble and danger. At the very least it meant delay, for he would be forced to stop and build a fire, and under its protection to bare his feet while he dried his socks and moccasins. He stood and studied the creek bed and its banks, and decided that the flow of water came from the right. He reflected awhile, rubbing his nose and cheeks, then skirted to the left, stepping gingerly and testing the footing for each step. Once clear of the danger, he took a fresh chew of tobacco and swung along at his four-mile gait.

In the course of the next two hours he came upon several similar traps. Usually the snow above the hidden pools had a sunken, candied appearance that advertised the danger. Once again, however, he had a close call; and once, suspecting danger, he compelled the dog to go on in front. The dog did not want to go. It hung back until the man shoved it forward, and then it went quickly across the white, unbroken surface. Suddenly it broke through, floundered to one side, and got away to firmer footing. It had wet its forefeet and legs, and almost immediately the water that clung to it turned to ice. It made quick efforts to lick the ice off its legs, then dropped down in the snow and began to bite out the ice that had formed between the toes. This was a matter of instinct. To permit the ice to remain would mean sore feet. It did not know this. It merely obeyed the mysterious prompting that arose from the deep crypts of its being. But the man knew, having achieved a judgment on the subject, and he removed the mitten from his right hand and helped tear out the ice particles. He did not expose his fingers more than a minute, and was astonished at the swift numbness that smote them. It certainly was cold. He pulled on the mitten hastily, and beat the hand savagely across his chest.

At twelve o'clock the day was at its brightest. Yet the sun was too far south on its winter journey to clear the horizon. The bulge of the earth intervened between it and Henderson Creek, where the man walked under a clear sky at noon and cast no shadow. At half-past twelve, to the minute, he arrived at the forks of the creek. He was pleased at the speed he had made. If he kept it up, he would certainly be with the boys by six. He unbuttoned his jacket and shirt and drew forth his lunch. The action consumed no more than a quarter of a minute, yet in that brief moment the numbness laid hold of the exposed fingers. He did not put the mitten on, but, instead, struck the fingers a dozen sharp smashes against his leg. Then he sat down on a snow-covered log to eat. The sting that followed upon the striking of his fingers against his leg ceased so quickly that he was startled. He had had no chance to take a bite of biscuit. He struck the fingers repeatedly and returned them to the mitten, baring the other hand for the purpose of eating. He tried to take a mouthful, but the ice muzzle prevented. He had forgotten to build a fire and thaw out. He chuckled at his foolishness, and as he chuckled he noted the numbness creeping into the exposed fingers. Also, he noted that the stinging which had first come to his toes when he sat down was already passing away. He wondered whether the toes were warm or numb. He moved them inside the moccasins and decided that they were numb.

He pulled the mitten on hurriedly and stood up. He was a bit frightened. He stamped up and down until the stinging returned into the feet. It certainly was cold, was his thought. That man from Sulphur Creek had spoken the truth when telling how cold it sometimes got in the country. And he had laughed at him at the time! That showed one must not be too sure of things. There was no mistake about it, it *was* cold. He strode up and down, stamping his feet and threshing his arms, until reassured by the returning warmth. Then he got out matches and proceeded to make a fire. From the undergrowth, where high water of the previous spring had lodged a supply of seasoned twigs, he got his firewood. Working carefully from a small beginning, he soon had a roaring fire, over which he thawed the ice from his face and in the protection of which he ate his biscuits. For the moment the cold of space was outwitted. The dog took satisfaction in the fire, stretching out close enough for warmth and far enough away to escape being singed.

When the man had finished, he filled his pipe and took his comfortable time over a smoke. Then he pulled on his mittens, settled the ear flaps of his cap firmly about his ears, and took the creek trail up the left fork. The dog was disappointed and yearned back toward the fire. This man did not know cold. Possibly all the generations of his ancestry had been ignorant of cold, of real cold, of cold one hundred and seven degrees below freezing point. But the dog knew; all its ancestry knew, and it had inherited the knowledge. And it knew that it was not good to walk abroad in such fearful cold. It was the time to lie snug in a hole in the snow and wait for a curtain of cloud to be drawn across the face of outer space whence this cold came. On the other hand, there was no keen intimacy between the dog and the man. The one was the toil slave of the other, and the only caresses it had ever received were the caresses of the whip lash and of harsh and menacing throat sounds that threatened the whip lash. So the dog made no effort to communicate its apprehension to the man. It was not concerned in the welfare of the man; it was for its own sake that it yearned back toward the fire. But the man whistled, and spoke to it with the sound of whip lashes, and the dog swung in at the man's heels and followed after.

The man took a chew of tobacco and proceeded to start a new amber beard. Also, his moist breath quickly powdered with white his mustache, eyebrows, and lashes. There did not seem to be so many springs on the left fork of the Henderson, and for half an hour the man saw no signs of any. And then it happened. At a place where there were no signs, where the soft, unbroken snow seemed to advertise solidity beneath, the man broke through. It was not deep. He wet himself halfway to the knees before he floundered out to the firm crust.

He was angry, and cursed his luck aloud. He had hoped to get into camp with the boys at six o'clock, and this would delay him an hour, for he would have to build a fire and dry out his footgear. This was imperative at that low temperature—he knew that much; and he turned aside to the bank, which he climbed. On top, tangled in the underbrush about the trunks of several small spruce trees, was a highwater deposit of dry firewood—sticks and twigs, principally, but also larger portions of seasoned branches and fine dry last year's grasses. He threw down several large pieces on top of the snow. This served for a foundation and prevented the young flame from drowning itself in the snow it otherwise would melt. The flame he got by touching a match to a small shred of birch bark that he took from his pocket. This burned even more readily than paper. Placing it on the foundation, he fed the young flame with wisps of dry grass and with the tiniest dry twigs.

He worked slowly and carefully, keenly aware of his danger. Gradually, as the flame grew stronger, he increased the size of the twigs with which he fed it. He squatted in the snow, pulling the twigs out from their entanglement in the brush and feeding directly to the flame. He knew there must be no failure. When it is seventy-five below zero, a man must not fail in his first attempt to build a fire—that is, if his feet are wet. If his feet are dry, and he fails, he can run along the trail for half a mile and restore his circulation. But the circulation of wet and freezing feet cannot be restored by running when it is seventy-five below. No matter how fast he runs, the wet feet will freeze the harder.

All this the man knew. The old-timer on Sulphur Creek had told him about it the previous fall, and now he was appreciating the advice. Already all sensation had gone out of his feet. To build the fire he had been forced to remove his mittens, and the fingers had quickly gone numb. His pace of four miles an hour had kept his heart pumping blood to the surface of his body and to all the extremities. But the instant he stopped, the action of the pump eased down. The cold of space smote the unprotected tip of the planet, and he, being on that unprotected tip, received the full force of the blow. The blood of his body recoiled before it. The blood was alive, like the dog, and like the dog it wanted to hide away and cover itself up from the fearful cold. So long as he walked four miles an hour, he pumped that blood, willy-nilly, to the surface; but now it ebbed away and sank down into the recesses of his body. The extremities were the first to feel its absence. His wet feet froze the faster, and his exposed fingers numbed the faster, though they had not yet begun to freeze. Nose and cheeks were already freezing, while the skin of all his body chilled as it lost its blood.

But he was safe. Toes and nose and cheeks would be only touched by the frost, for the fire was beginning to burn with strength. He was feeding it with twigs the size of his finger. In another minute he would be able to feed it with branches the size of his wrist, and then he could remove his wet footgear, and, while it dried, he could keep his naked feet warm by the fire, rubbing them at first, of course, with snow. The fire was a success. He was safe. He remembered the advice of the old-timer on Sulphur Creek, and smiled. The old-timer had been very serious in laying down the law that no man must travel alone in the Klondike after fifty below. Well, here he was; he had had the accident; he was alone; and he had saved himself. Those old-timers were rather womanish, some of them, he thought. All a man had to do was to keep his head, and he was all right. Any man who was a man could travel alone. But it was surprising, the rapidity with which his cheeks and nose were freezing. And he had not thought his fingers could go lifeless in so short a time. Lifeless they were, for he could scarcely make them move together to grip a twig, and they seemed remote from his body and from him. When he touched a twig, he had to look and see whether or not he had hold of it. The wires were pretty well down between him and his finger ends.

All of which counted for little. There was the fire, snapping and crackling and promising life with every dancing flame. He started to untie his moccasins. They

were coated with ice; the thick German socks were like sheaths of iron halfway
to the knees; and the moccasin strings were like rods of steel all twisted and
knotted as by some conflagration. For a moment he tugged with his numb fingers,
then, realizing the folly of it, he drew his sheath knife.

But before he could cut the strings, it happened. It was his own fault or, rather,
his mistake. He should not have built the fire under the spruce tree. He should
have built it in the open. But it had been easier to pull the twigs from the brush
and drop them directly on the fire. Now the tree under which he had done this
carried a weight of snow on its boughs. No wind had blown for weeks, and each
bough was fully freighted. Each time he had pulled a twig he had communicated
a slight agitation to the tree—an imperceptible agitation, so far as he was concerned, but an agitation sufficient to bring about the disaster. High up in the tree
one bough capsized its load of snow. This fell on the boughs beneath, capsizing
them. This process continued, spreading out and involving the whole tree. It grew
like an avalanche, and it descended without warning upon the man and the fire,
and the fire was blotted out! Where it had burned was a mantle of fresh and
disordered snow.

The man was shocked. It was as though he had just heard his own sentence
of death. For a moment he sat and stared at the spot where the fire had been.
Then he grew very calm. Perhaps the old-timer on Sulphur Creek was right. If
he had only had a trail mate he would have been in no danger now. The trail mate
could have built the fire. Well, it was up to him to build the fire over again, and
this second time there must be no failure. Even if he succeeded, he would most
likely lose some toes. His feet must be badly frozen by now, and there would be
some time before the second fire was ready.

Such were his thoughts, but he did not sit and think them. He was busy all
the time they were passing through his mind. He made a new foundation for a
fire, this time in the open, where no treacherous tree could blot it out. Next he
gathered dry grasses and tiny twigs from the high-water flotsam. He could not
bring his fingers together to pull them out, but he was able to gather them by the
handful. In this way he got many rotten twigs and bits of green moss that were
undesirable, but it was the best he could do. He worked methodically, even
collecting an armful of the larger branches to be used later when the fire gathered
strength. And all the while the dog sat and watched him, a certain yearning
wistfulness in its eyes, for it looked upon him as the fire provider, and the fire
was slow in coming.

When all was ready, the man reached in his pocket for a second piece of birch
bark. He knew the bark was there, and, though he could not feel it with his fingers,
he could hear its crisp rustling as he fumbled for it. Try as he would, he could
not clutch hold of it. And all the time, in his consciousness, was the knowledge
that each instant his feet were freezing. This thought tended to put him in a panic,
but he fought against it and kept calm. He pulled on his mittens with his teeth,
and threshed his arms back and forth, beating his hands with all his might against
his sides. He did this sitting down, and he stood up to do it; and all the while
the dog sat in the snow, its wolf brush of a tail curled around warmly over its

forefeet, its sharp wolf ears pricked forward intently as it watched the man. And the man, as he beat and threshed with his arms and hands, felt a great surge of envy as he regarded the creature that was warm and secure in its natural covering.

After a time he was aware of the first faraway signals of sensation in his beaten fingers. The faint tingling grew stronger till it evolved into a stinging ache that was excruciating, but which the man hailed with satisfaction. He stripped the mitten from his right hand and fetched forth the birch bark. The exposed fingers were quickly going numb again. Next he brought out his bunch of sulphur matches. But the tremendous cold had already driven the life out of his fingers. In his effort to separate one match from the others, the whole bunch fell in the snow. He tried to pick it out of the snow, but failed. The dead fingers could neither touch nor clutch. He was very careful. He drove the thought of his freezing feet, and nose, and cheeks, out of his mind, devoting his whole soul to the matches. He watched, using the sense of vision in place of that of touch, and when he saw his fingers on each side the bunch, he closed them—that is he willed to close them, for the wires were down, and the fingers did not obey. He pulled the mitten on the right hand, and beat it fiercely against his knee. Then, with both mittened hands, he scooped the bunch of matches, along with much snow, into his lap. Yet he was no better off.

After some manipulation he managed to get the bunch between the heels of his mittened hands. In this fashion he carried it to his mouth. The ice crackled and snapped when by a violent effort he opened his mouth. He drew the lower jaw in, curled the upper lip out of the way, scraped the bunch with his upper teeth in order to separate a match. He succeeded in getting one, which he dropped on his lap. He was no better off. He could not pick it up. Then he devised a way. He picked it up in his teeth and scratched it on his leg. Twenty times he scratched before he succeeded in lighting it. As it flamed he held it with his teeth to the birch bark. But the burning brimstone went up his nostrils and into his lungs, causing him to cough spasmodically. The match fell into the snow and went out.

The old-timer on Sulphur Creek was right, he thought in the moment of controlled despair that ensued: after fifty below, a man should travel with a partner. He beat his hands, but failed in exciting any sensation. Suddenly he bared both hands, removing the mittens with his teeth. He caught the whole bunch between the heels of his hands. His arm muscles not being frozen enabled him to press the hand heels tightly against the matches. Then he scratched the bunch along his leg. It flared into flame, seventy sulphur matches at once! There was no wind to blow them out. He kept his head to one side to escape the strangling fumes, and held the blazing bunch to the birch bark. As he so held it, he became aware of sensation in his hand. His flesh was burning. He could smell it. Deep down below the surface he could feel it. The sensation developed into pain that grew acute. And still he endured it, holding the flame of the matches clumsily to the bark that would not light readily because his own burning hands were in the way, absorbing most of the flame.

At last, when he could endure no more, he jerked his hands apart. The blazing matches fell sizzling into the snow, but the birch bark was alight. He began laying dry grasses and the tiniest twigs on the flame. He could not pick and choose, for he had to lift the fuel between the heels of his hands. Small pieces of rotten wood and green moss clung to the twigs, and he bit them off as well as he could with his teeth. He cherished the flame carefully and awkwardly. It meant life, and it must not perish. The withdrawal of blood from the surface of his body now made him begin to shiver, and he grew more awkward. A large piece of green moss fell squarely on the little fire. He tired to poke it out with his fingers, but his shivering frame made him poke too far, and he disrupted the nucleus of the little fire, the burning grasses and tiny twigs separating and scattering. He tried to poke them together again, but in spite of the tenseness of the effort, his shivering got away with him, and the twigs were hopelessly scattered. Each twig gushed a puff of smoke and went out. The fire provider had failed. As he looked apathetically about him, his eyes chanced on the dog, sitting across the ruins of the fire from him, in the snow, making restless, hunching movements, slightly lifting one forefoot and then the other, shifting its weight back and forth on them with wistful eagerness.

The sight of the dog put a wild idea into his head. He remembered the tale of the man, caught in a blizzard, who killed a steer and crawled inside the carcass, and so was saved. He would kill the dog and bury his hands in the warm body until the numbness went out of them. Then he could build another fire. He spoke to the dog, calling it to him; but in his voice was a strange note of fear that frightened the animal, who had never known the man to speak in such a way before. Something was the matter, and its suspicious nature sensed danger—it knew not what danger, but somewhere, somehow, in its brain arose an apprehension of the man. It flattened its ears down at the sound of the man's voice, and its restless, hunching movements and the liftings and shiftings of its forefeet became more pronounced; but it would not come to the man. He got on his hands and knees and crawled toward the dog. This unusual posture again excited suspicion, and the animal sidled mincingly away.

The man sat up in the snow for a moment and struggled for calmness. Then he pulled on his mittens, by means of his teeth, and got upon his feet. He glanced down at first in order to assure himself that he was really standing up, for the absence of sensation in his feet left him unrelated to the earth. His erect position in itself started to drive the webs of suspicion from the dog's mind; and when he spoke peremptorily, with the sound of whip lashes in his voice, the dog rendered its customary allegiance and came to him. As it came within reaching distance the man lost his control. His arms flashed out to the dog, and he experienced genuine surprise when he discovered that his hands could not clutch, that there was neither bend nor feeling in the fingers. He had forgotten for the moment that they were frozen and that they were freezing more and more. All this happened quickly, and before the animal could get away, he encircled its body with his arms. He sat down in the snow, and in this fashion held the dog, while it snarled and whined and struggled.

But it was all he could do, hold its body encircled in his arms and sit there. He realized that he could not kill the dog. There was no way to do it. With his helpless hands he could neither draw nor hold his sheath knife nor throttle the animal. He released it, and it plunged wildly away, with tail between its legs, and still snarling. It halted forty feet away and surveyed him curiously, with ears sharply pricked forward.

The man looked down at his hands in order to locate them, and found them hanging on the ends of his arms. It struck him as curious that one should have to use his eyes in order to find out where his hands were. He began threshing his arms back and forth, beating the mittened hands against his sides. He did this for five minutes, violently, and his heart pumped enough blood up to the surface to put a stop to his shivering. But no sensation was aroused in the hands. He had an impression that they hung like weights on the ends of his arms, but when he tried to run the impression down, he could not find it.

A certain fear of death, dull and oppressive, came to him. This fear quickly became poignant as he realized that it was no longer a mere matter of freezing his fingers and toes, or of losing his hands and feet, but that it was a matter of life and death with the chances against him. This threw him into a panic, and he turned and ran up the creek bed along the old, dim trail. The dog joined in behind and kept up with him. He ran blindly, without intention, in fear such as he had never known in his life. Slowly, as he plowed and floundered through the snow, he began to see things again—the banks of the creek, the old timber jams, the leafless aspens, and the sky. The running made him feel better. He did not shiver. Maybe, if he ran on, his feet would thaw out; and, anyway, if he ran far enough, he would reach camp and the boys. Without doubt he would lose some fingers and toes and some of his face; but the boys would take care of him, and save the rest of him when he got there. And at the same time there was another thought in his mind that said he would never get to the camp and the boys; that it was too many miles away, that the freezing had too great a start on him, and that he would soon be stiff and dead. This thought he kept in the background and refused to consider. Sometimes it pushed itself forward and demanded to be heard, but he thrust it back and strove to think of other things.

It struck him as curious that he could run at all on feet so frozen that he could not feel them when they struck the earth and took the weight of his body. He seemed to himself to skim along above the surface, and to have no connection with the earth. Somewhere he had once seen a winged Mercury, and he wondered if Mercury felt as he felt when skimming over the earth.

His theory of running until he reached camp and the boys had one flaw in it: he lacked the endurance. Several times he stumbled, and finally he tottered, crumpled up, and fell. When he tried to rise, he failed. He must sit and rest, he decided, and next time he would merely walk and keep on going. As he sat and regained his breath, he noted that he was feeling quite warm and comfortable. He was not shivering, and it even seemed that a warm glow had come to his chest and trunk. And yet, when he touched his nose or cheeks, there was no sensation. Running would not thaw them out. Nor would it thaw out his hands and feet. Then the thought came to him that the frozen portions of his body must be extending. He tried to keep this thought down, to forget it, to think of something else; he was aware of the panicky feeling that it caused, and he was afraid of the panic. But the thought asserted itself, and persisted, until it produced a vision of his body totally frozen. This was too much, and he made another wild run along the trail. Once he slowed down to a walk, but the thought of the freezing extending itself made him run again.

And all the time the dog ran with him, at his heels. When he fell down a second time, it curled its tail over its forefeet and sat in front of him, facing him, curiously eager and intent. The warmth and security of the animal angered him, and he cursed it till it flattened down its ears appeasingly. This time the shivering came more quickly upon the man. He was losing in his battle with the frost. It was creeping into his body from all sides. The thought of it drove him on, but he ran no more than a hundred feet, when he staggered and pitched headlong. It was his last panic. When he had recovered his breath and control, he sat up and entertained in his mind the conception of meeting death with dignity. However, the conception did not come to him in such terms. His idea of it was that he had been making a fool of himself, running around like a chicken with its head cut off—such was the simile that occurred to him. Well, he was bound to freeze anyway, and he might as well take it decently. With this new-found peace of mind came the first glimmerings of drowsiness. A good idea, he thought, to sleep off to death. It was like taking an anesthetic. Freezing was not so bad as people thought. There were lots worse ways to die.

He pictured the boys finding his body next day. Suddenly he found himself with them, coming along the trail and looking for himself. And, still with them, he came around a turn in the trail and found himself lying in the snow. He did not belong with himself any more, for even then he was out of himself, standing with the boys and looking at himself in the snow. It certainly was cold, was his thought. When he got back to the States he could tell the folks what real cold was. He drifted on from this to a vision of the old-timer on Sulphur Creek. He could see him quite clearly, warm and comfortable, and smoking a pipe.

"You were right, old hoss; you were right," the man mumbled to the old-timer of Sulphur Creek.

Then the man drowsed off into what seemed to him the most comfortable and satisfying sleep he had ever known. The dog sat facing him and waiting. The brief day drew to a close in a long, slow twilight. There were no signs of a fire to be made, and, besides, never in the dog's experience had it known a man to sit like that in the snow and make no fire. As the twilight drew on, its eager yearning for the fire mastered it, and with a great lifting and shifting of forefeet, it whined softly, then flattened its ear down in anticipation of being chidden by the man. But the man remained silent. Later the dog whined loudly. And still later it crept close to the man and caught the scent of death. This made the animal bristle and back away. A little longer it delayed, howling under the stars that leaped and danced and shone brightly in the cold sky. Then it turned and trotted up the trail in the direction of the camp it knew, where were the other food providers and fire providers.

QUESTIONS

1. What words and phrases in the first two paragraphs describe the setting in a way that suggests it will be unusually important to this story?
2. How is the theme of man's frailty against the rigors of nature, introduced in paragraph three, dealt with in the rest of the story?
3. What are the physical details of the man's location: the temperature, his resources, his task?
4. What is the relationship between the man and the dog?
5. What incidents prepare the reader for the climax?

THE OLD CHIEF MSHLANGA

Doris Lessing   (1919–   )

They were good, the years of ranging the bush over her father's farm which, like every white farm, was largely unused, broken only occasionally by small patches of cultivation. In between, nothing but trees, the long sparse grass, thorn and cactus and gully, grass and outcrop and thorn. And a jutting piece of rock which had been thrust up from the warm soil of Africa unimaginable eras of time ago, washed into hollows and whorls by sun and wind that had travelled so many thousands of miles of space and bush, would hold the weight of a small girl whose eyes were sightless for anything but a pale willowed river, a pale gleaming castle —a small girl singing: "Out flew the web and floated wide, the mirror cracked from side to side . . ."[1]

Pushing her way through the green aisles of the mealie stalks, the leaves arching like cathedrals veined with sunlight far overhead, with the packed red earth underfoot, a fine lace of red starred witchweed would summon up a black bent figure croaking premonitions: the Northern witch, bred of cold Northern forests, would stand before her among the mealie fields, and it was the mealie fields that faded and fled, leaving her among the gnarled roots of an oak, snow falling thick and soft and white, the woodcutter's fire glowing red welcome through crowding tree trunks.

A white child, opening its eyes curiously on a sun-suffused landscape, a gaunt and violent landscape, might be supposed to accept it as her own, to take the msasa trees and the thorn trees as familiars, to feel her blood running free and responsive to the swing of the seasons.

This child could not see a msasa tree, or the thorn, for what they were. Her books held tales of alien fairies, her rivers ran slow and peaceful, and she knew the shape of the leaves of an ash or an oak, the names of the little creatures that lived in English streams, when the words "the veld"[2] meant strangeness, though she could remember nothing else.

[1]Alfred, Lord Tennyson, "The Lady of Shalott."   [2]Open pasture land in South Africa (from Dutch).

Because of this, for many years, it was the veld that seemed unreal; the sun was a foreign sun, and the wind spoke a strange language.

The black people on the farm were as remote as the trees and the rocks. They were an amorphous black mass, mingling and thinning and massing like tadpoles, faceless, who existed merely to serve, to say "Yes, Baas," take their money and go. They changed season by season, moving from one farm to the next, according to their outlandish needs, which one did not have to understand, coming from perhaps hundreds of miles North or East, passing on after a few months—where? Perhaps even as far away as the fabled gold mines of Johannesburg, where the pay was so much better than the few shillings a month and the double handful of mealie meal twice a day which they earned in that part of Africa.

The child was taught to take them for granted: the servants in the house would come running a hundred yards to pick up a book if she dropped it. She was called "Nkosikaas"—Chieftainess, even by the black children her own age.

Later, when the farm grew too small to hold her curiosity, she carried a gun in the crook of her arm and wandered miles a day, from vlei[3] to vlei, from kopje[4] to kopje, accompanied by two dogs: the dogs and the gun were an armour against fear. Because of them she never felt fear.

If a native came into sight along the kaffir[5] paths half a mile away, the dogs would flush him up a tree as if he were a bird. If he expostulated (in his uncouth language which was by itself ridiculous) that was cheek. If one was in a good mood, it could be a matter for laughter. Otherwise one passed on, hardly glancing at the angry man in the tree.

On the rare occasions when white children met together they could amuse themselves by hailing a passing native in order to make a buffoon of him; they could set the dogs on him and watch him run; they could tease a small black child as if he were a puppy—save that they would not throw stones and sticks at a dog without a sense of guilt.

Later still, certain questions presented themselves in the child's mind; and because the answers were not easy to accept, they were silenced by an even greater arrogance of manner.

It was even impossible to think of the black people who worked about the house as friends, for if she talked to one of them, her mother would come running anxiously: "Come away; you mustn't talk to natives."

It was this instilled consciousness of danger, of something unpleasant, that made it easy to laugh out loud, crudely, if a servant made a mistake in his English or if he failed to understand an order—there is a certain kind of laughter that is fear, afraid of itself.

One evening, when I was about fourteen, I was walking down the side of a mealie field that had been newly ploughed, so that the great red clods showed fresh and tumbling to the vlei beyond, like a choppy red sea; it was that hushed and listening hour, when the birds send long sad calls from tree to tree, and all

---

[3]Small valley. [4]Small hill. [5]The white South African term for Zulus and related blacks, borrowed from the Arabic slavers' word meaning "nonbeliever."

the colours of earth and sky and leaf are deep and golden. I had my rifle in the curve of my arm, and the dogs were at my heels.

In front of me, perhaps a couple of hundred yards away, a group of three Africans came into sight around the side of a big antheap. I whistled the dogs close in to my skirts and let the gun swing in my hand, and advanced, waiting for them to move aside, off the path, in respect for my passing. But they came on steadily, and the dogs looked up at me for the command to chase. I was angry. It was "cheek" for a native not to stand off a path, the moment he caught sight of you.

In front walked an old man, stooping his weight on to a stick, his hair grizzled white, a dark red blanket slung over his shoulders like a cloak. Behind him came two young men, carrying bundles of pots, assegais,[6] hatchets.

The group was not a usual one. They were not natives seeking work. These had an air of dignity, of quietly following their own purpose. It was the dignity that checked my tongue. I walked quietly on, talking softly to the growling dogs, till I was ten paces away. Then the old man stopped, drawing his blanket close.

"Morning, Nkosikaas," he said, using the customary greeting for any time of the day.

"Good morning," I said, "Where are you going?" My voice was a little truculent.

The old man spoke in his own language, then one of the young men stepped forward politely and said in careful English: "My Chief travels to see his brothers beyond the river."

A Chief! I thought, understanding the pride that made the old man stand before me like an equal—more than an equal, for he showed courtesy, and I showed none.

The old man spoke again, wearing dignity like an inherited garment, still standing ten paces off, flanked by his entourage, not looking at me (that would have been rude) but directing his eyes somewhere over my head at the trees.

"You are the little Nkosikaas from the farm of Baas Jordan?"

"That's right," I said.

"Perhaps your father does not remember," said the interpreter for the old man, "but there was an affair with some goats. I remember seeing you when you were . . ." The young man held his hand at knee level and smiled.

We all smiled.

"What is your name?" I asked.

"This is Chief Mshlanga," said the young man.

"I will tell my father that I met you," I said.

The old man said: "My greetings to your father, little Nkosikaas."

"Good morning," I said politely, finding the politeness difficult, from lack of use.

"Morning, little Nkosikaas," said the old man, and stood aside to let me pass.

[6]Spears.

I went by, my gun hanging awkwardly, the dogs sniffing and growling, cheated of their favourite game of chasing natives like animals.

Not long afterwards I read in an old explorer's book the phrase: "Chief Mshlanga's country." It went like this: "Our destination was Chief Mshlanga's country, to the north of the river; and it was our desire to ask his permission to prospect for gold in his territory."

The phrase "ask his permission" was so extraordinary to a white child, brought up to consider all natives as things to use, that it revived those questions, which could not be suppressed: they fermented slowly in my mind.

On another occasion one of those old prospectors who still move over Africa looking for neglected reefs, with their hammers and tents, and pans for sifting gold from crushed rock, came to the farm and, in talking of the old days, used that phrase again: "This was the Old Chief's country," he said. "It stretched from those mountains over there way back to the river, hundreds of miles of country." That was his name for our district: "The Old Chief's Country"; he did not use our name for it—a new phrase which held no implication of usurped ownership.

As I read more books about the time when this part of Africa was opened up, not much more than fifty years before, I found Old Chief Mshlanga had been a famous man, known to all the explorers and prospectors. But then he had been young; or maybe it was his father or uncle they spoke of—I never found out.

During that year I met him several times in the part of the farm that was traversed by natives moving over the country. I learned that the path up the side of the big red field where the birds sang was the recognized highway for migrants. Perhaps I even haunted it in the hope of meeting him: being greeted by him, the exchange of courtesies, seemed to answer the questions that troubled me.

Soon I carried a gun in a different spirit; I used it for shooting food and not to give me confidence. And now the dogs learned better manners. When I saw a native approaching, we offered and took greetings; and slowly that other landscape in my mind faded, and my feet struck directly on the African soil, and I saw the shapes of tree and hill clearly, and the black people moved back, as it were, out of my life: it was as if I stood aside to watch a slow intimate dance of landscape and men, a very old dance, whose steps I could not learn.

But I thought: this is my heritage, too; I was bred here; it is my country as well as the black man's country; and there is plenty of room for all of us, without elbowing each other off the pavements and roads.

It seemed it was only necessary to let free that respect I felt when I was talking with old Chief Mshlanga, to let both black and white people meet gently, with tolerance for each other's differences: it seemed quite easy.

Then, one day, something new happened. Working in our house as servants were always three natives: cook, houseboy, garden boy. They used to change as the farm natives changed: staying for a few months, then moving on to a new job, or back home to their kraals.[7] They were thought of as "good" or "bad" natives;

---

[7]Native villages.

which meant: how did they behave as servants? Were they lazy, efficient, obedient, or disrespectful? If the family felt good-humoured, the phrase was: "What can you expect from raw black savages?" If we were angry, we said: "These damned niggers, we would be much better off without them."

One day, a white policeman was on his rounds of the district, and he said laughingly: "Did you know you have an important man in your kitchen?"

"What!" exclaimed my mother sharply. "What do you mean?"

"A Chief's son." The policeman seemed amused. "He'll boss the tribe when the old man dies."

"He'd better not put on a Chief's son act with me," said my mother.

When the policeman left, we looked with different eyes at our cook: he was a good worker, but he drank too much at week-ends—that was how we knew him.

He was a tall youth, with very black skin, like black polished metal, his tightly-growing black hair parted white man's fashion at one side, with a metal comb from the store stuck into it; very polite, very distant, very quick to obey an order. Now that it had been pointed out, we said: "Of course, you can see. Blood always tells."

My mother became strict with him now she knew about his birth and prospects. Sometimes, when she lost her temper, she would say: "You aren't the Chief yet, you know." And he would answer her very quietly, his eyes on the ground: "Yes, Nkosikaas."

One afternoon he asked for a whole day off, instead of the customary half-day, to go home next Sunday.

"How can you go home in one day?"

"It will take me half an hour on my bicycle," he explained.

I watched the direction he took; and the next day I went off to look for this kraal; I understood he must be Chief Mshlanga's successor: there was no other kraal near enough our farm.

Beyond our boundaries on that side the country was new to me. I followed unfamiliar paths past *kopjes* that till now had been part of the jagged horizon, hazed with distance. This was Government land, which had never been cultivated by white men; at first I could not understand why it was that it appeared, in merely crossing the boundary, I had entered a completely fresh type of landscape. It was a wide green valley, where a small river sparkled, and vivid waterbirds darted over the rushes. The grass was thick and soft to my calves, the trees stood tall and shapely.

I was used to our farm, whose hundreds of acres of harsh eroded soil bore trees that had been cut for the mine furnaces and had grown thin and twisted, where the cattle had dragged the grass flat, leaving innumerable criss-crossing trails that deepened each season into gullies, under the force of the rains.

This country had been left untouched, save for prospectors whose picks had struck a few sparks from the surface of the rocks as they wandered by; and for migrant natives whose passing had left, perhaps, a charred patch on the trunk of a tree where their evening fire had nestled.

It was very silent; a hot morning with pigeons cooing throatily, the midday

shadows lying dense and thick with clear yellow spaces of sunlight between and
in all that wide green park-like valley, not a human soul but myself.

I was listening to the quick regular tapping of a woodpecker when slowly a
chill feeling seemed to grow up from the small of my back to my shoulders, in
a constricting spasm like a shudder, and at the roots of my hair a tingling
sensation began and ran down over the surface of my flesh, leaving me goose-
fleshed and cold, though I was damp with sweat. Fever? I thought; then uneasily,
turned to look over my shoulder; and realized suddenly that this was fear. It was
extraordinary, even humiliating. It was a new fear. For all the years I had walked
by myself over this country I had never known a moment's uneasiness; in the
beginning because I had been supported by a gun and the dogs, then because I
had learnt an easy friendliness for the Africans I might encounter.

I had read of this feeling, how the bigness and silence of Africa, under the
ancient sun, grows dense and takes shape in the mind, till even the birds seem
to call menacingly, and a deadly spirit comes out of the trees and the rocks. You
move warily, as if your very passing disturbs something old and evil, something
dark and big and angry that might suddenly rear and strike from behind. You
look at groves of entwined trees, and picture the animals that might be lurking
there; you look at the river running slowly, dropping from level to level through
the vlei, spreading into pools where at night the bucks come to drink, and the
crocodiles rise and drag them by their soft noses into underwater caves. Fear
possessed me. I found I was turning round and round, because of that shapeless
menace behind me that might reach out and take me; I kept glancing at the files
of *kopjes* which, seen from a different angle, seemed to change with every step
so that even known landmarks, like a big mountain that had sentinelled my world
since I first became conscious of it, showed an unfamiliar sunlit valley among its
foothills. I did not know where I was. I was lost. Panic seized me. I found I was
spinning round and round, staring anxiously at this tree and that, peering up at
the sun which appeared to have moved into an eastern slant, shedding the sad
yellow light of sunset. Hours must have passed! I looked at my watch and found
that this state of meaningless terror had lasted perhaps ten minutes.

The point was that it was meaningless. I was not ten miles from home: I had
only to take my way back along the valley to find myself at the fence; away among
the foothills of the *kopjes* gleamed the roof of a neighbour's house, and a couple
of hours' walking would reach it. This was the sort of fear that contracts the flesh
of a dog at night and sets him howling at the full moon. It had nothing to do with
what I thought or felt; and I was more disturbed by the fact that I could become
its victim than of the physical sensation itself: I walked steadily on, quietened,
in a divided mind, watching my own pricking nerves and apprehensive glances
from side to side with a disgusted amusement. Deliberately I set myself to think
of this village I was seeking, and what I should do when I entered it—if I could
find it, which was doubtful, since I was walking aimlessly and it might be anywhere in the hundreds of thousands of acres of bush that stretched about me.
With my mind on that village, I realized that a new sensation was added to the
fear: loneliness. Now such a terror of isolation invaded me that I could hardly

walk; and if it were not that I came over the crest of a small rise and saw a village below me, I should have turned and gone home. It was a cluster of thatched huts in a clearing among trees. There were neat patches of mealies and pumpkins and millet, and cattle grazed under some trees at a distance. Fowls scratched among the huts, dogs lay sleeping on the grass, and goats friezed a *kopje* that jutted up beyond a tributary of the river lying like an enclosing arm round the village.

As I came close I saw the huts were lovingly decorated with patterns of yellow and red and ochre mud on the walls; and the thatch was tied in place with plaits of straw.

This was not at all like our farm compound, a dirty and neglected place, a temporary home for migrants who had no roots in it.

And now I did not know what to do next. I called a small black boy, who was sitting on a lot playing a stringed gourd, quite naked except for the strings of blue beads round his neck, and said: "Tell the Chief I am here." The child stuck his thumb in his mouth and stared shyly back at me.

For minutes I shifted my feet on the edge of what seemed a deserted village, till at last the child scuttled off, and then some women came. They were draped in bright cloths, with brass glinting in their ears and on their arms. They also stared, silently; then turned to chatter among themselves.

I said again: "Can I see Chief Mshlanga?" I saw they caught the name; they did not understand what I wanted. I did not understand myself.

At last I walked through them and came past the huts and saw a clearing under a big shady tree, where a dozen old men sat crosslegged on the ground, talking. Chief Mshlanga was leaning back against the tree, holding a gourd in his hand, from which he had been drinking. When he saw me, not a muscle of his face moved, and I could see he was not pleased: perhaps he was afflicted with my own shyness, due to being unable to find the right forms of courtesy for the occasion. To meet me, on our own farm, was one thing; but I should not have come here. What had I expected? I could not join them socially; the thing was unheard of. Bad enough that I, a white girl, should be walking the veld alone as a white man might: and in this part of the bush where only Government officials had the right to move.

Again I stood, smiling foolishly, while behind me stood the groups of brightly-clad, chattering women, their faces alert with curiosity and interest, and in front of me sat the old men, with old lined faces, their eyes guarded, aloof. It was a village of ancients and children and women. Even the two young men who kneeled beside the Chief were not those I had seen with him previously: the young men were all away working on the white men's farms and mines, and the Chief must depend on relatives who were temporarily on holiday for his attendants.

"The small white Nkosikaas is far from home," remarked the old man at last.

"Yes," I agreed, "it is far." I wanted to say: "I have come to pay you a friendly visit, Chief Mshlanga." I could not say it. I might now be feeling an urgent helpless desire to get to know these men and women as people, to be accepted by them as a friend, but the truth was I had set out in a spirit of curiosity: I had wanted to see the village that one day our cook, the reserved and obedient young man who got drunk on Sundays, would one day rule over.

"The child of Nkosi Jordan is welcome," said Chief Mshlanga.

"Thank you," I said, and could think of nothing more to say. There was a silence, while the flies rose and began to buzz around my head; and the wind shook a little in the thick green tree that spread its branches over the old men.

"Good morning," I said at last. "I have to return now to my home."

"Morning, little Nkosikaas," said Chief Mshlanga.

I walked away from the indifferent village, over the rise past the staring amber-eyed goats, down through the tall stately trees into the great rich green valley where the river meandered and the pigeons cooed tales of plenty and the woodpecker tapped softly.

The fear had gone; the loneliness had set into stiff-necked stoicism; there was now a queer hostility in the landscape, a cold, hard, sullen indomitability that walked with me, as strong as a wall, as intangible as smoke; it seemed to say to me: you walk here as a destroyer. I went slowly homewards, with an empty heart: I had learned that if one cannot call a country to heel like a dog, neither can one dismiss the past with a smile in an easy gush of feeling, saying: I could not help it, I am also a victim.

I only saw Chief Mshlanga once again.

One night my father's big red land was trampled down by small sharp hooves, and it was discovered that the culprits were goats from Chief Mshlanga's kraal. This had happened once before, years ago.

My father confiscated all the goats. Then he sent a message to the old Chief that if he wanted them he would have to pay for the damage.

He arrived at our house at the time of sunset one evening, looking very old and bent now, walking stiffly under his regally-draped blanket, leaning on a big stick. My father sat himself down in his big chair below the steps of the house; the old man squatted carefully on the ground before him, flanked by his two young men.

The palaver was long and painful, because of the bad English of the young man who interpreted, and because my father could not speak dialect, but only kitchen kaffir.

From my father's point of view, at least two hundred pounds' worth of damage had been done to the crop. He knew he could not get the money from the old man. He felt he was entitled to keep the goats. As for the old Chief, he kept repeating angrily: "Twenty goats! My people cannot lose twenty goats! We are not rich, like the Nkosi Jordan, to lose twenty goats at once."

My father did not think of himself as rich, but rather as very poor. He spoke quickly and angrily in return, saying that the damage done meant a great deal to him, and that he was entitled to the goats.

At last it grew so heated that the cook, the Chief's son, was called from the kitchen to be interpreter, and now my father spoke fluently in English, and our cook translated rapidly so that the old man could understand how very angry my father was. The young man spoke without emotion, in a mechanical way, his eyes lowered, but showing how he felt his position by a hostile uncomfortable set of the shoulders.

It was now in the late sunset, the sky a welter of colours, the birds singing their last songs, and the cattle, lowing peacefully, moving past us towards their sheds for the night. It was the hour when Africa is most beautiful; and here was this pathetic, ugly scene, doing no one any good.

At last my father stated finally: "I'm not going to argue about it. I am keeping the goats."

The old Chief flashed back in his own language: "That means that my people will go hungry when the dry season comes."

"Go to the police, then," said my father, and looked triumphant.

There was, of course, no more to be said.

The old man sat silent, his head bent, his hands dangling helplessly over his withered knees. Then he rose, the young men helping him, and he stood facing my father. He spoke once again, very stiffly; and turned away and went home to his village.

"What did he say?" asked my father of the young man, who laughed uncomfortably and would not meet his eyes.

"What did he say?" insisted my father.

Our cook stood straight and silent, his brows knotted together. Then he spoke. "My father says: All this land, this land you call yours, is his land, and belongs to our people."

Having made this statement, he walked off into the bush after his father, and we did not see him again.

Our next cook was a migrant from Nyasaland, with no expectations of greatness.

Next time the policeman came on his rounds he was told this story. He remarked: "That kraal has no right to be there; it should have been moved long ago. I don't know why no one has done anything about it. I'll have a chat with the Native Commissioner next week. I'm going over for tennis on Sunday, anyway."

Some time later we heard that Chief Mshlanga and his people had been moved two hundred miles east, to a proper Native Reserve; the Government land was going to be opened up for white settlement soon.

I went to see the village again, about a year afterwards. There was nothing there. Mounds of red mud, where the huts had been, had long swathes of rotting thatch over them, veined with the red galleries of the white ants. The pumpkin vines rioted everywhere, over the bushes, up the lower branches of trees so that the great golden balls rolled underfoot and dangled overhead: it was a festival of pumpkins. The bushes were crowding up, the new grass sprang vivid green.

The settler lucky enough to be allotted the lush warm valley (if he chose to cultivate this particular section) would find, suddenly, in the middle of a mealie field, the plants were growing fifteen feet tall, the weight of the cobs dragging at the stalks, and wonder what unsuspected vein of richness he had struck.

QUESTIONS

1. At what point does the narrative perspective switch from the omniscient storyteller to the first-person narration of the girl? What do we learn about the girl and the circumstances of her life in the opening section?
2. What specific descriptions of the land affect or mirror the girl's emotions?
3. In what ways does the ethos of the place where she lives influence what the child does?
4. Read again the last two paragraphs. What point is made through reporting this last visit to the village? Is there any irony in the "vein of richness" of the last sentence?
5. How would you summarize the narrator's attitude toward the old chief?
6. How do the observations of a girl of fourteen provide an edge to the story that would be missing in the observations of an adult?
7. At the time she writes, the narrator has become an adult. How does that affect the story?
8. What does the narrator mean when she writes, "I had learned that if one cannot call a country to heel like a dog, neither can one dismiss the past with a smile in an easy gush of feeling, saying: I could not help it, I am also a victim"?

FLYING HOME

Ralph Ellison   (1914–   )

When Todd came to, he saw two faces suspended above him in a sun so hot and blinding that he could not tell if they were black or white. He stirred, feeling pain that burned as though his whole body had been laid open to the sun which glared into his eyes. For a moment an old fear of being touched by white hands seized him. Then the very sharpness of the pain began slowly to clear his head. Sounds came to him dimly. He done come to. Who are they? he thought. Naw he aint, I coulda sworn he was white. Then he heard clearly:

"You hurt bad?"

Something within him uncoiled. It was a Negro sound.

"He's still out," he heard.

"Give 'im time. . . . Say, son, you hurt bad?"

Was he? There was that awful pain. He lay rigid, hearing their breathing and trying to weave a meaning between them and his being stretched painfully upon the ground. He watched them warily, his mind traveling back over a painful distance. Jagged scenes, swiftly unfolding as in a movie trailer, reeled through his mind, and he saw himself piloting a tailspinning plane and landing and landing and falling from the cockpit and trying to stand. Then, as in a great silence, he remembered the sound of crunching bone, and now, looking up into the anxious faces of an old Negro man and a boy from where he lay in the same field, the memory sickened him and he wanted to remember no more.

"How you feel, son?"

Todd hesitated, as though to answer would be to admit an inacceptable weakness. Then, "It's my ankle," he said.

"Which one?"

"The left."

With a sense of remoteness he watched the old man bend and remove his boot, feeling the pressure ease.

"That any better?"

"A lot. Thank you."

He had the sensation of discussing someone else, that his concern was with some far more important thing, which for some reason escaped him.

"You done broke it bad," the old man said. "We have to get you to a doctor."

He felt that he had been thrown into a tailspin. He looked at his watch; how long had he been here? He knew there was but one important thing in the world, to get the plane back to the field before his officers were displeased.

"Help me up," he said. "Into the ship."

"But it's broke too bad. . . ."

"Give me you arm!"

"But, son . . ."

Clutching the old man's arm he pulled himself up, keeping his left leg clear, thinking, "I'd never make him understand," as the leather-smooth face came parallel with his own.

"Now, let's see."

He pushed the old man back, hearing a bird's insistent shrill. He swayed giddily. Blackness washed over him, like infinity.

"You best sit down."

"No, I'm O.K."

"But, son, You jus' gonna make it worse. . . ."

It was a fact that everything in him cried out to deny, even against the flaming pain in his ankle. He would have to try again.

"You mess with that ankle they have to cut your foot off," he heard.

Holding his breath, he started up again. It pained so badly that he had to bite his lips to keep from crying out and he allowed them to help him down with a pang of despair.

"It's best you take it easy. We gon' git you a doctor."

Of all the luck, he thought. Of all the rotten luck, now I have done it. The fumes of high-octane gasoline clung in the heat taunting him.

"We kin ride him into town on old Ned," the boy said.

Ned? He turned, seeing the boy point toward an ox team browsing where the buried blade of a plow marked the end of a furrow. Thoughts of himself riding an ox through the town, past streets full of white faces, down the concrete runways of the airfield made swift images of humiliation in his mind. With a pang he remembered his girl's last letter. "Todd," she had written, "I don't need the papers to tell me you had the intelligence to fly. And I have always known you to be as brave as anyone else. The papers annoy me. Don't you be contented to prove over and over again that you're brave or skillful just because you're black, Todd. I think they keep beating that dead horse because they don't want to say why you boys are not yet fighting. I'm really disappointed, Todd. Anyone with brains can learn to fly, but then what? What about using it, and who will you use it for? I wish, dear, you'd write about this. I sometimes think they're playing a trick on us. It's very humiliating. . . ." He wiped cold sweat from his face, thinking, What does she know of humiliation? She's never been down South. Now the humiliation would come. When you must have them judge you, knowing that they never accept your mistakes as your own, but hold it against your whole race —that was humiliation. Yes and humiliation was when you could never be simply yourself, when you were always a part of this old black ignorant man. Sure, he's all right. Nice and kind and helpful. But he's not you. Well, there's one humiliation I can spare myself.

"No," he said, "I have orders not to leave the ship. . . ."

"Aw," the old man said. Then turning to the boy, "Teddy, then you better hustle down to Mister Graves and get him to come. . . ."

"No, wait!" he protested before he was fully aware. Graves might be white. "Just have him get word to the field, please. They'll take care of the rest."

He saw the boy leave, running.

"How far does he have to go?"

"Might' nigh a mile."

He rested back, looking at the dusty face of his watch. But now they know something has happened, he thought. In the ship there was a perfectly good radio, but it was useless. The old fellow would never operate it. That buzzard knocked me back a hundred years, he thought. Irony danced within him like the gnats circling the old man's head. With all I've learned I'm dependent upon this "peasant's" sense of time and space. His leg throbbed. In the plane, instead of time being measured by the rhythms of pain and a kid's legs, the instruments would have told him at a glance. Twisting upon his elbows he saw where dust had powdered the plane's fuselage, feeling the lump form in his throat that was always there when he thought of flight. It's crouched there, he thought, like the abandoned shell of a locust. I'm naked without it. Not a machine, a suit of clothes you wear. And with a sudden embarrassment and wonder he whispered, "It's the only dignity I have. . . ."

He saw the old man watching, his torn overalls clinging limply to him in the heat. He felt a sharp need to tell the old man what he felt. But that would be meaningless. If I tried to explain why I need to fly back, he'd think I was simply afraid of white officers. But it's more than fear . . . a sense of anguish clung to him like the veil of sweat that hugged his face. He watched the old man, hearing him humming snatches of a tune as he admired the plane. He felt a furtive sense of resentment. Such old men often came to the field to watch the pilots with childish eyes. At first it had made him proud; they had been a meaningful part of a new experience. But soon he realized they did not understand his accomplishments and they came to shame and embarrass him, like the distasteful praise of an idiot. A part of the meaning of flying had gone then, and he had not been able to regain it. If I were a prizefighter I would be more human, he thought. Not a monkey doing tricks, but a man. They were pleased simply that he was a Negro who could fly, and that was not enough. He felt cut off from them by age, by understanding, by sensibility, by technology and by his need to measure himself against the mirror of other men's appreciation. Somehow he felt betrayed, as he had when as a child he grew to discover that his father was dead. Now for him any real appreciation lay with his white officers; and with them he could never be sure. Between ignorant black men and condescending whites, his course of flight seemed mapped by the nature of things away from all needed and natural landmarks. under some sealed orders, couched in ever more technical and mysterious terms, his path curved swiftly away from both the shame the old man symbolized and the cloudy terrain of white men's regard. Flying blind, he knew but one point of landing and there he would receive his wings. After that the enemy would appreciate his skill and he would assume his deepest meaning, he thought sadly, neither from those who condescended nor from those who praised without understanding, but from the enemy who would recognize his manhood and skill in terms of hate. . . .

He sighed, seeing the oxen making queer, prehistoric shadows against the dry brown earth.

"You just take it easy, some," the old man soothes. "That boy won't take long. Crazy as he is about airplanes."

"I can wait," he said.

"What kinda airplane you call this here'n?"

"An Advanced Trainer," he said, seeing the old man smile. His fingers were like gnarled dark wood against the metal as he touched the low-slung wing.

"'Bout how fast can she fly?"

"Over two hundred an hour."

"Lawd! That's so fast I bet it don't seem like you moving!"

Holding himself rigid, Todd opened his flying suit. The shade had gone and he lay in a ball of fire.

"You mind if I take a look inside? I was always curious to see . . . ."

"Help yourself. Just don't touch anything."

He heard him climb upon the metal wing, grunting. Now the questions would start. Well, so you don't have to think to answer . . . .

He saw the old man looking over into the cockpit, his eyes bright as a child's.

"You must have to know a lot to work all these here things."

He was silent, seeing him step down and kneel beside him.

"Son, how come you want to fly way up there in the air?"

Because it's the most meaningful act in the world . . . because it makes me less like you, he thought.

But he said: "Because I like it, I guess. It's as good a way to fight and die as I know."

"Yeah? I guess you right," the old man said. "But how long you think before they gonna let you all fight?"

He tensed. This was the question all Negroes asked, put with the same timid hopefulness and longing that always opened a greater void within him than that he had felt beneath the plane the first time he had flown. He felt light-headed. It came to him suddenly that there was something sinister about the conversation, that he was flying unwillingly into unsafe and uncharted regions. If he could only be insulting and tell this old man who was trying to help him to shut up!

"I bet you one thing . . ."

"Yes?"

"That you was plenty scared coming down."

He did not answer. Like a dog on a trail the old man seemed to smell out his fears and he felt anger bubble within him.

"You sho' scared me. When I seen you coming down in that thing with it a-rollin' and a-jumpin' like a pitchin' hoss, I thought sho' you was a goner. I almost had me a stroke!"

He saw the old man grinning, "Ever'thin's been happening round here this morning, come to think of it."

"Like what?" he asked.

"Well, first thing I know, here come two white fellers looking for Mister Rudolph, that's Mister Graves's cousin. That got me worked up right away . . . ."

"Why?"

"Why? 'Cause he done broke outta the crazy house, that's why. He liable to kill somebody," he said. "They oughta have him by now though. Then here you come. First I think it's one of them white boys. Then doggone if you don't fall outta there. Lawd, I'd done heard about you boys but I haven't never seen one o' you-all. Cain't tell you how it felt to see somebody what look like me in a airplane!"

The old man talked on, the sound steaming around Todd's thoughts like air flowing over the fuselage of a flying plane. You were a fool, he thought, remembering how before the spin the sun had blazed bright against the billboard signs beyond the town, and how a boy's blue kite had bloomed beneath him, tugging gently in the wind like a strange, odd-shaped flower. He had once flown such kites himself and tried to find the boy at the end of the invisible cord. But he had been flying too high and too fast. He had climbed steeply away in exultation. Too steeply, he thought. And one of the first rules you learn is that if the angle of thrust is too steep the plane goes into a spin. And then, instead of pulling out of it and going into a dive you let a buzzard panic you. A lousy buzzard!

"Son, what made all that blood on the glass?"

"A buzzard," he said, remembering how the blood and feathers had sprayed back against the hatch. It had been as though he had flown into a storm of blood and blackness.

"Well, I declare! They's lots of 'em around here. They after dead things. Don't eat nothing what's alive."

"A little bit more and he would have made a meal out of me," Todd said grimly.

"They bad luck all right. Teddy's got a name for 'em, calls 'em jimcrows," the old man laughed.

"It's a damned good name."

"They the damnedest birds. Once I seen a hoss all stretched out like he was sick, you know. So I hollers, 'Gid up from there, suh!' Just to make sho! An' doggone, son, if I don't see two ole jimcrows come flying right up outa that hoss's insides! Yessuh! The sun was shinin' on 'em and they couldn't a been no greasier if they'd been eating barbecue."

Todd thought he would vomit, his stomach quivered.

"You made that up," he said.

"Nawsuh! Saw him just like I see you."

"Well, I'm glad it was you."

"You see lots a funny things down here, son."

"No, I'll let you see them," he said.

"By the way, the white folks round here don't like to see you boys up there in the sky. They ever bother you?"

"No."

"Well, they'd like to."

"Someone always wants to bother someone else," Todd said. "How do you know?"

"I just know."

"Well," he said defensively, "no one has bothered us."

Blood pounded in his ears as he looked away into space. He turned, seeing a black spot in the sky, and strained to confirm what he could not clearly see.

"What does that look like to you?" he asked excitedly.

"Just another bad luck, son."

Then he saw the movement of wings with disappointment. It was gliding smoothly down, wings outspread, tail feathers gripping the air, down swiftly— gone behind the green screen of trees. It was like a bird he had imagined there, only the sloping branches of the pines remained, sharp against the pale stretch of sky. He lay barely breathing and stared at the point where it had disappeared, caught in a spell of loathing and admiration. Why did they make them so disgusting and yet teach them to fly so well? It's like when I was up in heaven, he heard, starting.

The old man was chuckling, rubbing his stubbled chin.

"What did you say?"

"Sho', I died and went to heaven . . . maybe by time I tell you about it they be done come after you."

"I hope so," he said wearily.

"You boys ever sit around and swap lies?"

"Not often. Is this going to be one?"

"Well, I ain't so sho', on account of it took place when I was dead."

The old man paused, "That wasn't no lie 'bout the buzzards, though."

"All right," he said.

"Sho' you want to hear 'bout heaven?"

"Please," he answered, resting his head upon his arm.

"Well, I went to heaven and right away started to sproutin' me some wings. Six good ones, they was. Just like them the white angels had. I couldn't hardly believe it. I was so glad that I went off on some clouds by myself and tried 'em out. You know, 'cause I didn't want to make a fool outta myself the first thing. . . ."

It's an old tale, Todd thought. Told me years ago. Had forgotten. But at least it will keep him from talking about buzzards.

He closed his eyes, listening.

". . . First thing I done was to git up on a low cloud and jump off. And doggone, boy, if them wings didn't work! First I tried the right; then I tried the left; then I tried 'em both together. Then Lawd, I started to move on out among the folks. I let 'em see me. . . ."

He saw the old man gesturing flight with his arms, his face full of mock pride as he indicated an imaginary crowd, thinking, It'll be in the newspapers, as he heard, ". . . so I went and found me some colored angels—somehow I didn't believe I was an angel till I seen a real black one, ha, yes! Then I was sho'—but they tole me I better come down 'cause us colored folks had to wear a special kin' a harness when we flew. That was how come they wasn't flyin'. Oh yes, an' you had to be extra strong for a black man even, to fly with one of them harnesses. . . ."

This is a new turn, Todd thought, what's he driving at?

"So I said to myself, I ain't gonna be bothered with no harness! Oh naw! 'Cause if God let you sprout wings you oughta have sense enough not to let nobody make you wear something what gits in the way of flyin'. So I starts to flyin'. Heck, son," he chuckled, his eyes twinkling, "you know I had to let ev'ybody know that old Jefferson could fly good as anybody else. And I could too, fly smooth as a bird! I could even loop-the-loop—only I had to make sho' to keep my long white robe down roun' my ankles. . . ."

Todd felt uneasy. He wanted to laugh at the joke, but his body refused, as of an independent will. He felt as he had as a child when after he had chewed a sugar-coated pill which his mother had given him, she had laughed at his efforts to remove the terrible taste.

". . . Well," he heard, "I was doing all right 'til I got to speeding. Found out I could fan up a right strong breeze, I could fly so fast. I could do all kin'sa stunts too. I started flying up to the stars and divin' down and zooming roun' the moon. Man, I like to scare the devil outa some ole white angels. I was raisin' hell. Not that I meant any harm, son. But I was just feeling good. It was so good to know I was free at last. I accidently knocked the tops offa some stars and they tell me I caused a storm and a coupla lynchings down here in Macon County—though I swear I believe them boys what said that was making up lies on me. . . ."

He's mocking me, Todd thought angrily. He thinks it's a joke. Grinning down at me . . . His throat was dry. He looked at his watch; why the hell didn't they come? Since they had to, why? One day I was flying down one of them heavenly streets. You got yourself into it, Todd thought. Like Jonah in the whale.

"Justa throwin' feathers in everybody's face. An' ole Saint Peter called me in. Said, 'Jefferson, tell me two things, what you doin' flyin' without a harness; an' how come you flyin' so fast?' So I tole him I was flyin' without a harness 'cause it got in my way, but I couldn'ta been flyin' so fast, 'cause I wasn't usin' but one wing. Saint Peter said, 'You wasn't flyin' with but one wing?' 'Yessuh,' I says, scared-like. So he says, 'Well, since you got sucha extra fine pair of wings you can leave off yo' harness awhile. But from now on none of that there one-wing flyin', 'cause you gittin' up too damn much speed!' "

And with one mouth full of bad teeth you're making too damned much talk, thought Todd. Why don't I send him after the boy? His body ached from the hard ground and seeking to shift his position he twisted his ankle and hated himself for crying out.

"It gittin' worse?"

"I . . . I twisted it," he groaned.

"Try not to think about it, son. That's what I do."

He bit his lip, fighting pain with counter-pain as the voice resumed its rhythmical droning. Jefferson seemed caught in his own creation.

". . . After all that trouble I just floated roun' heaven in slow motion. But I forgot, like colored folks will do, and got to flyin' with one wing again. This time I was restin' my old broken arm and got to flyin' fast enough to shame the devil. I was comin' so fast, Lawd, I got myself called befo' ole Saint Peter again. He said, 'Jeff, didn't I warn you 'bout that speedin'?' 'Yessuh,' I says, 'but it was an accident.' He looked at me sad-like and shook his head and I knowed I was gone. He said, 'Jeff, you and that speedin' is a danger to the heavenly community. If I was to let you keep on flyin', heaven wouldn't be nothin' but uproar. Jeff, you got to go!' Son, I argued and pleaded with that old white man, but it didn't do a bit of good. They rushed me straight to them pearly gates and gimme a parachute and a map of the state of Alabama . . ."

Todd heard him laughing so that he could hardly speak, making a screen between them upon which his humiliation glowed like fire.

"Maybe you'd better stop awhile," he said, his voice unreal.

"Ain't much more," Jefferson laughed. "When they gimme the parachute ole Saint Peter ask me if I wanted to say a few words before I went. I felt so bad I couldn't hardly look at him, specially with all them white angels standin' around. Then somebody laughed and made me mad. So I tole him, 'Well, you done took my wings. And you puttin' me out. You got charge of things so's I can't do nothing' about it. But you got to admit just this: While I was up here I was the flyinest sonofabitch what ever hit heaven!' "

At the burst of laughter Todd felt such an intense humiliation that only great violence would wash it away. The laughter which shook the old man like a boiling purge set up vibrations of guilt within him which not even the intricate machinery of the plane would have been adequate to transform and he heard himself screaming, "Why do you laugh at me this way?"

He hated himself at that moment, but he had lost control. He saw Jefferson's mouth fall open, "What—?"

"Answer me!"

His blood pounded as though it would surely burst his temples and he tried to reach the old man and fell, screaming, "Can I help it because they won't let us actually fly? Maybe we are a bunch of buzzards feeding on a dead horse, but we can hope to be eagles, can't we? Can't we?"

He fell back, exhausted, his ankle pounding. The saliva was like straw in his mouth. If he had the strength he would strangle this old man. This grinning, gray-headed clown who made him feel as he felt when watched by the white officers at the field. And yet this old man had neither power, prestige, rank nor technique. Nothing that could rid him of this terrible feeling. He watched him, seeing his face struggle to express a turmoil of feeling.

"What you mean, son? What you talking 'bout . . . ?"

"Go away. Go tell your tales to the white folks."

"But I didn't mean nothing like that. . . . I . . . I wasn't tryin' to hurt your feelings. . . ."

"Please. Get the hell away from me!"

"But I didn't, son. I didn't mean all them things a-tall."

Todd shook as with a chill, searching Jefferson's face for a trace of the mockery he had seen there. But now the face was somber and tired and old. He was confused. He could not be sure that there had ever been laughter there, that Jefferson had ever really laughed in his whole life. He saw Jefferson reach out to touch him and shrank away, wondering if anything except the pain, now causing his vision to waver, was real. Perhaps he had imagined it all.

"Don't let it get you down, son," the voice said pensively.

He heard Jefferson sigh wearily, as though he felt more than he could say. His anger ebbed, leaving only the pain.

"I'm sorry," he mumbled.

"You just wore out with pain, was all . . . ."

He saw him through a blur, smiling. And for a second he felt the embarrassed silence of understanding flutter between them.

"What you was doin' flyin' over this section, son? Wasn't you scared they might shoot you for a crow?"

Todd tensed. Was he being laughed at again. But before he could decide, the pain shook him and a part of him was lying calmly behind the screen of pain that had fallen between them, recalling the first time he had ever seen a plane. It was as though an endless series of hangars had been shaken ajar in the air base of his memory and from each, like a young wasp emerging from its cell, arose the memory of a plane.

The first time I ever saw a plane I was very small and planes were new in the world. I was four-and-a-half and the only plane that I had ever seen was a model suspended from the ceiling of the automobile exhibit at the State Fair. But I did not know that it was only a model. I did not know how large a real plane was, nor how expensive. To me it was a fascinating toy, complete in itself, which my mother said could only be owned by rich little white boys. I stood rigid with admiration, my head straining backwards as I watched the gray little plane describing arcs above the gleaming tops of the automobiles. And I vowed that, rich or poor, someday I would own such a toy. My mother had to drag me out of the exhibit and not even the merry-go-round, the Ferris wheel, or the racing horses could hold my attention for the rest of the Fair. I was too busy imitating the tiny drone of the plane with my lips, and imitating with my hands the motion, swift and circling, that it made in flight.

After that I no longer used the pieces of lumber that lay about our back yard to construct wagons and autos . . . now it was used for airplanes. I built biplanes, using pieces of board for wings, a small box for the fuselage, another piece of wood for the rudder. The trip to the Fair had brought something new into my small world. I asked my mother repeatedly when the Fair would come back again. I'd lie in the grass and watch the sky, and each fighting bird became a soaring plane. I would have been good a year just to have seen a plane again. I became a nuisance to everyone with my questions about airplanes. But planes were new to the old folks, too, and there was little that they could tell me. Only my uncle knew some of the answers. And better still, he could carve propellers from pieces of wood that would whirl rapidly in the wind, wobbling noisily upon oiled nails.

I wanted a plane more than I'd wanted anything, more than I wanted the red wagon with rubber tires, more than the train that ran on a track with its train of cars. I asked my mother over and over again:

"Mamma?"

"What do you want, boy?" she'd say.

"Mamma, will you get mad if I ask you?" I'd say.

"What do you want now? I ain't got time to be answering a lot of fool questions. What do you want?"

"Mamma, when you gonna get me one . . . ?" I'd ask.

"Get you one what?" she'd say.

"You know, Mamma; what I been asking you . . . ."

"Boy," she'd say, "if you don't want a spanking you better come on an' tell me what you talking about so I can get on with my work."

"Aw, Mamma, you know . . . ."

"What I just tell you?" she'd say.

"I mean when you gonna buy me a airplane."

"AIRPLANE! Boy, is you crazy? How many times I have to tell you to stop that foolishness. I done told you them things cost too much. I bet I'm gon' wham the living daylight out of you if you don't quit worrying me 'bout them things!"

But this did not stop me, and a few days later I'd try all over again.

Then one day a strange thing happened. It was spring and for some reason I had been hot and irritable all morning. It was a beautiful spring. I could feel it as I played barefoot in the backyard. Blossoms hung from the thorny black locust trees like clusters of fragrant white grapes. Butterflies flickered in the sunlight above the short new dew-wet grass. I had gone in the house for bread and butter and coming out I heard a steady unfamiliar drone. It was unlike anything I had ever heard before. I tried to place the sound. It was no use. It was a sensation like that I had when searching for my father's watch, heard ticking unseen in a room. It made me feel as though I had forgotten to perform some task that my mother had ordered . . . then I located it, overhead. In the sky, flying quite low and about a hundred yards off was a plane! It came so slowly that it seemed barely to move. My mouth hung wide; my bread and butter fell into the dirt. I wanted to jump up and down and cheer. And when the idea struck I trembled with excitement: "Some little white boy's plane's done flew away and all I got to do is stretch out my hands and it'll be mine!" It was a little plane like that at the Fair, flying no higher than the eaves of our roof. Seeing it come steadily forward I felt the world grow warm with promise. I opened the screen and climbed over it and clung there, waiting. I would catch the plane as it came over and swing down fast and run into the house before anyone could see me. Then no one could come to claim the plane. It droned nearer. Then when it hung like a silver cross in the blue directly above me I stretched out my hand and grabbed. It was like sticking my finger through a soap bubble. The plane flew on, as though I had simply blown my breath after it. I grabbed again, frantically, trying to catch the tail. My fingers clutched the air and disappointment surged tight and hard in my throat. Giving one last desperate grasp, I strained forward. My fingers ripped from the screen, I was falling. The ground burst hard against me. I drummed the earth with my heels and when my breath returned, I lay there bawling.

My mother rushed through the door.

"What's the matter, chile! What on earth is wrong with you?"

"It's gone! It's gone!"

"What gone?"

"The airplane . . ."

"Airplane?"

"Yessum, jus' like the one at the Fair. . . . I . . . I tried to stop it an' it kep' right on going . . ."

"When, boy?"

"Just now," I cried, through my tears.

"Where it go, boy, what way?"

"Yonder, there . . ."

She scanned the sky, her arms akimbo and her checkered apron flapping in the wind as I pointed to the fading plane. Finally she looked down at me, slowly shaking her head.

"It's gone! It's gone!" I cried.

"Boy, is you a fool?" she said. "Don't you see that there's a real airplane 'stead of one of them toy ones?"

"Real . . . ?" I forgot to cry. "Real?"

"Yass, real. Don't you know that thing you reaching for is bigger'n a auto? You here trying to reach for it and I bet it's flying 'bout two hundred miles higher'n this roof." She was disgusted with me. "You come on in this house before somebody else sees what a fool you done turned out to be. You must think these here lil ole arms of you'n is mighty long. . . ."

I was carried into the house and undressed for bed and the doctor was called. I cried bitterly, as much from the disappointment of finding the plane so far beyond my reach as from the pain.

When the doctor came I heard my mother telling him about the plane and asking if anything was wrong with my mind. He explained that I had had a fever for several hours. But I was kept in bed for a week and I constantly saw the plane in my sleep, lying just beyond my fingertips, sailing so slowly that it seemed barely to move. And each time I'd reach out to grab it I'd miss and through each dream I'd hear my grandma warning:

Young man, young man,
Yo' arms too short
To box with God. . . .

"Hey, son!"

At first he did not know where he was and looked at the old man pointing, with blurred eyes.

"Ain't that one of you-all's airplanes coming after you?"

As his vision cleared he saw a small black shape above a distant field, soaring through waves of heat. But he could not be sure and with the pain he feared that somehow a horrible recurring fantasy of being split in twain by the whirling blades of a propeller had come true.

"You think he sees us?" he heard.

"See? I hope so."

"He's coming like a bat outa hell!"

Straining, he heard the faint sound of a motor and hoped it would soon be over.

"How you feeling?"

"Like a nightmare," he said.

"Hey, he's done curved back the other way!"

"Maybe he saw us," he said. "Maybe he's gone to send out the ambulance and ground crew." And, he thought with despair, maybe he didn't even see us.

"Where did you send the boy?"

"Down to Mister Graves," Jefferson said. "Man what owns this land."

"Do you think he phoned?"

Jefferson looked at him quickly.

"Aw sho'. Dabney Graves is got a bad name on accounta them killings but he'll call though. . . ."

"What killings?"

"Them five fellers . . . ain't you heard?" he asked with surprise.

"No."

"Everybody knows 'bout Dabney Graves, especially the colored. He done killed enough of us."

Todd had the sensation of being caught in a white neighborhood after dark.

"What did they do?" he asked.

"Thought they was men," Jefferson said. "An' some he owed money, like he do me. . . ."

"But why do you stay here?"

"You black, son."

"I know, but . . ."

"You have to come by the white folks, too."

He turned away from Jefferson's eyes, at once consoled and accused. And I'll have to come by them soon, he thought with despair. Closing his eyes, he heard Jefferson's voice as the sun burned blood-red upon his lips.

"I got nowhere to go," Jefferson said, "an' they'd come after me if I did. But Dabney Graves is a funny fellow. He's all the time making jokes. He can be mean as hell, then he's liable to turn right around and back the colored against the white folks. I seen him do it. But me, I hates him for that more'n anything else. 'Cause just as soon as he gits tired helping a man he don't care what happens to him. He just leaves him stone cold. And then the other white folks is double hard on anybody he done helped. For him it's just a joke. He don't give a hilla beans for nobody—but hisself. . . ."

Todd listened to the thread of detachment in the old man's voice. It was as though he held his words arm's length before him to avoid their destructive meaning.

"He'd just as soon do you a favor and then turn right around and have you strung up. Me, I stays outa his way 'cause down here that's what you gotta do."

If my ankle would only ease for a while, he thought. The closer I spin toward the earth the blacker I become, flashed through his mind. Sweat ran into his eyes and he was sure that he would never see the plane if his head continued whirling. He tried to see Jefferson, what it was that Jefferson held in his hand? It was a little black man, another Jefferson! A little black Jefferson that shook with fits of belly-laughter while the other Jefferson looked on with detachment. Then Jefferson looked up from the thing in his hand and turned to speak, but Todd was far away, searching the sky for a plane in a hot dry land on a day and age he had long forgotten. He was going mysteriously with his mother through empty streets where black faces peered from behind drawn shades and someone was rapping at a window and he was looking back to see a hand and a frightened face frantically beckoning from a cracked door and his mother was looking down the empty perspective of the street and shaking her head and hurrying him along and at first it was only a flash he saw and a motor was droning as through the sun-glare he saw it gleaming silver as it circled and he was seeing a burst like a puff of white smoke and hearing his mother yell, Come along, boy, I got no time for them fool airplanes, I got no time, and he saw it a second time, the plane flying high, and the burst appeared suddenly and fell slowly, billowing out sparkling like fireworks and he was watching and being hurried along as the air filled with a flurry of white pinwheeling cards that caught in the wind and scattered over the rooftops and into the gutters and a woman was running and snatching a card and reading it and screaming and he darted into the shower, grabbing as in winter he grabbed for snowflakes and bounding away at his mother's, Come in here, boy! Come on, I say! and he was watching as she took the card away, seeing her face grow puzzled and turning taut as her voice quavered, "Niggers Stay From The Polls," and died to a moan of terror as he saw the eyeless sockets of a white hood staring at him from the card and above he saw the plane spiraling gracefully, agleam in the sun like a fiery sword. And seeing it soar he was caught, transfixed between a terrible horror and a horrible fascination.

The sun was not so high now, and Jefferson was calling and gradually he saw three figures moving across the curving roll of the field.

"Look like some doctors, all dressed in white," said Jefferson.

They're coming at last, Todd thought. And he felt such a release of tension within him that he thought he would faint. But no sooner did he close his eyes than he was seized and he was struggling with three white men who were forcing his arms into some kind of coat. It was too much for him, his arms were pinned to his sides as the pain blazed in his eyes, he realized that it was a straitjacket. What filthy joke was this?

"That oughta hold him, Mister Graves," he heard.

His total energies seemed focused in his eyes as he searched their faces. That was Graves; the other two wore hospital uniforms. He was poised between two poles of fear and hate as he heard the one called Graves saying, "He looks kinda purty in that there suit, boys. I'm glad you dropped by."

"This boy ain't crazy, Mister Graves," one of the others said. "He needs a doctor, not us. Don't see how you led us way out here anyway. It might be a joke to you, but your cousin Rudolph liable to kill somebody. White folks or niggers, don't make no difference. . . ."

Todd saw the man turn red with anger. Graves looked down upon him, chuckling.

"This nigguh belongs in a straitjacket, too, boys. I knowed that the minit Jeff's kid said something 'bout a nigguh flyer. You all know you cain't let the nigguh git up that high without his going crazy. The nigguh brain ain't built right for high altitudes. . . ."

Todd watched the drawling red face, feeling that all the unnamed horror and obscenities that he had ever imagined stood materialized before him.

"Let's git outta here," one of the attendants said.

Todd saw the other reach toward him, realizing for the first time that he lay upon a stretcher as he yelled.

"Don't put your hands on me!"

They drew back, surprised.

"What's that you say, nigguh?" asked Graves.

He did not answer and thought that Graves's foot was aimed at his head. It landed on his chest and he could hardly breathe. He coughed helplessly, seeing Graves's lips stretch taut over his yellow teeth, and tried to shift his head. It was as though a half-dead fly was dragging slowly across his face and a bomb seemed to burst within him. Blasts of hot, hysterical laughter tore from his chest, causing his eyes to pop and he felt that the veins in his neck would surely burst. And then a part of him stood behind it all, watching the surprise in Graves's red face and his own hysteria. He thought he would never stop, he would laugh himself to death. It rang in his ears like Jefferson's laughter and he looked for him, centering his eyes desperately upon his face, as though somehow he had become his sole salvation in an insane world of outrage and humiliation. It brought a certain relief. He was suddenly aware that although his body was still contorted it was an echo that no longer rang in his ears. He heard Jefferson's voice with gratitude.

"Mister Graves, the Army done tole him not to leave his airplane."

"Nigguh, Army or no, you gittin' off my land! That airplane can stay 'cause it was paid for by taxpayers' money. But you gittin' off. An' dead or alive, it don't make no difference to me."

Todd was beyond it now, lost in a world of anguish.

"Jeff," Graves said, "you and Teddy come and grab holt. I want you to take this here black eagle over to that nigguh airfield and leave him."

Jefferson and the boy approached him silently. He looked away, realizing and doubting at once that only they could release him from his overpowering sense of isolation.

They bent for the stretcher. One of the attendants moved toward Teddy.

"Think you can manage it, boy?"

"I think I can, suh," Teddy said.

"Well, you better go behind then, and let yo' pa go ahead so's to keep that leg elevated."

He saw the white men walking ahead as Jefferson and the boy carried him along in silence. Then they were pausing and he felt a hand wiping his face; then he was moving again. And it was as though he had been lifted out of his isolation, back into the world of men. A new current of communication flowed between the man and boy and himself. They moved him gently. Far away he heard a mockingbird liquidly calling. He raised his eyes, seeing a buzzard poised unmoving in space. For a moment the whole afternoon seemed suspended and he waited for the horror to seize him again. Then like a song within his head he heard the boy's soft humming and saw the dark bird glide into the sun and glow like a bird of flaming gold.

QUESTIONS

1. What can you deduce about the historical period and geographical location of this story? How does the ethos of the time and place help explain Todd's fears and motivations?
2. In what ways is Todd "flying home"?
3. How can you tell the difference in this narration between present action, memory, and dream and delirium? Can you always tell? What are the signs?
4. After the child reaches for and misses the real airplane, he dreams that his grandmother warns "Yo' arms too short / To box with God." What connection does this incident have with the larger story?
5. Why does Todd become angry at the story the old man tells about flying to heaven?
6. Describe the narrative perspective. Is it effective?

THE SWIMMER

John Cheever   (1912–1982)

It was one of those midsummer Sundays when everyone sits around saying, "I *drank* too much last night." You might have heard it whispered by the parishioners leaving church, heard it from the lips of the priest himself, struggling with his cassock in the *vestiarium,* heard it from the golf links and the tennis courts, heard it from the wildlife preserve where the leader of the Audubon group was suffering from a terrible hangover. "I *drank* too much," said Donald Westerhazy. "We all *drank* too much," said Lucinda Merrill. "It must have been the wine," said Helen Westerhazy. "I *drank* too much of that claret."

This was at the edge of the Westerhazys' pool. The pool, fed by an artesian well with a high iron content, was a pale shade of green. It was a fine day. In the west there was a massive stand of cumulus cloud so like a city seen from a distance —from the bow of an approaching ship—that it might have had a name. Lisbon. Hackensack. The sun was hot. Neddy Merrill sat by the green water, one hand in it, one around a glass of gin. He was a slender man—he seemed to have the especial slenderness of youth—and while he was far from young he had slid down his banister that morning and given the bronze backside of Aphrodite on the hall table a smack, as he jogged toward the smell of coffee in his dining room. He might have been compared to a summer's day, particularly the last hours of one, and while he lacked a tennis racket or a sail bag the impression was definitely one of youth, sport, and clement weather. He had been swimming and now he was breathing deeply, stertorously as if he could gulp into his lungs the components of that moment, the heat of the sun, the intenseness of his pleasure. It all seemed to flow into his chest. His own house stood in Bullet Park, eight miles to the south, where his four beautiful daughters would have had their lunch and might be playing tennis. Then it occurred to him that by taking a dogleg to the southwest he could reach his home by water.

His life was not confining and the delight he took in this observation could not be explained by its suggestion of escape. He seemed to see, with a cartographer's eye, that string of swimming pools, that quasi-subterranean stream that curved across the county. He had made a discovery, a contribution to modern geography; he would name the stream Lucinda after his wife. He was not a practical joker nor was he a fool but he was determinedly original and had a vague and modest idea of himself as a legendary figure. The day was beautiful and it seemed to him that a long swim might enlarge and celebrate its beauty.

He took off a sweater that was hung over his shoulders and dove in. He had an inexplicable contempt for men who did not hurl themselves into pools. He swam a choppy crawl, breathing either with every stroke or every fourth stroke and counting somewhere well in the back of his mind the one-two one-two of a flutter kick. It was not a serviceable stroke for long distances but the domestication of swimming had saddled the sport with some customs and in his part of the world a crawl was customary. To be embraced and sustained by the light green water was less a pleasure, it seemed, than the resumption of a natural condition, and he would have liked to swim without trunks, but this was not possible, considering his project. He hoisted himself up on the far curb—he never used the ladder—and started across the lawn. When Lucinda asked where he was going he said he was going to swim home.

The only maps and charts he had to go by were remembered or imaginary but these were clear enough. First there were the Grahams, the Hammers, the Lears, the Howlands, and the Crosscups. He would cross Ditmar Street to the Bunkers and come, after a short portage, to the Levys, the Welchers, and the public pool in Lancaster. Then there were the Hallorans, the Sachses, the Biswangers, Shirley Adams, the Gilmartins, and the Clydes. The day was lovely, and that he lived in a world so generously supplied with water seemed like a clemency, a beneficence. His heart was high and he ran across the grass. Making his way home by an uncommon route gave him the feeling that he was a pilgrim, an explorer, a man with a destiny, and he knew that he would find friends all along the way; friends would line the banks of the Lucinda River.

He went through a hedge that separated the Westerhazys' land from the Grahams', walked under some flowering apple trees, passed the shed that housed their pump and filter, and came out at the Grahams' pool. "Why, Neddy," Mrs. Graham said, "what a marvelous surprise. I've been trying to get you on the phone all morning. Here, let me get you a drink." He saw then, like any explorer, that the hospitable customs and traditions of the natives would have to be handled with diplomacy if he was ever going to reach his destination. He did not want to mystify or seem rude to the Grahams nor did he have the time to linger there. He swam the length of their pool and joined them in the sun and was rescued, a few minutes later, by the arrival of two carloads of friends from Connecticut. During the uproarious reunions he was able to slip away. He went down by the front of the Grahams' house, stepped over a thorny hedge, and crossed a vacant lot to the Hammers'. Mrs. Hammer, looking up from her roses, saw him swim by although she wasn't quite sure who it was. The Lears heard him splashing past the open windows of their living room. The Howlands and the Crosscups were away. After leaving the Howlands' he crossed Ditmar Street and started for the Bunkers', where he could hear, even at that distance, the noise of a party.

The water refracted the sound of voices and laughter and seemed to suspend it in midair. The Bunkers' pool was on a rise and he climbed some stairs to a terrace where twenty-five or thirty men and women were drinking. The only person in the water was Rusty Towers, who floated there on a rubber raft. Oh, how bonny and lush were the banks of the Lucinda River! Prosperous men and women gathered by the sapphire-colored waters while caterer's men in white coats passed them cold gin. Overhead a red de Haviland trainer was circling around and around and around in the sky with something like the glee of a child in a swing. Ned felt a passing affection for the scene, a tenderness for the gathering, as if it was something he might touch. In the distance he heard thunder. As soon as Enid Bunker saw him she began to scream: "Oh, look who's here! What a marvelous surprise! When Lucinda said that you couldn't come I thought I'd *die.* " She made her way to him through the crowd, and when they had finished kissing she led him to the bar, a progress that was slowed by the fact that he stopped to kiss eight or ten other women and shake the hands of as many men. A smiling bartender he had seen at a hundred parties gave him a gin and tonic and he stood by the bar for a moment, anxious not to get stuck in any conversation that would delay his voyage. When he seemed about to be surrounded he dove in and swam close to the side to avoid colliding with Rusty's raft. At the far end of the pool he bypassed the Tomlinsons with a broad smile and jogged up the garden path. The gravel cut his feet but this was the only unpleasantness. The party was confined to the pool, and as he went toward the house he heard the brilliant, watery sound of voices fade, heard the noise of a radio from the Bunkers' kitchen, where someone was listening to a ball game. Sunday afternoon. He made his way through the parked cars and down the grassy border of their driveway to Alewives Lane. He did not want to be seen on the road in his bathing trunks but there was no traffic and he made the short distance to the Levys' driveway, marked with a PRIVATE PROPERTY sign and a green tube for *The New York Times.* All the doors and windows of the big house were open but there were no signs of life; not even a dog barked. He went around the side of the house to the pool and saw that the Levys had only recently left. Glasses and bottles and dishes of nuts were on a table at the deep end, where there was a bathhouse or gazebo, hung with Japanese lanterns. After swimming the pool he got himself a glass and poured a drink. It was his fourth or fifth drink and he had swum nearly half the length of the Lucinda River. He felt tired, clean, and pleased at that moment to be alone; pleased with everything.

It would storm. The stand of cumulus cloud—that city—had risen and darkened, and while he sat there he heard the percussiveness of thunder again. The de Haviland trainer was still circling overhead and it seemed to Ned that he could almost hear the pilot laugh with pleasure in the afternoon; but when there was another peal of thunder he took off for home. A train whistle blew and he wondered what time it had gotten to be. Four? Five? He thought of the provincial station at that hour, where a waiter, his tuxedo concealed by a raincoat, a dwarf with some flowers wrapped in newspaper, and a woman who had been crying would be waiting for the local. It was suddenly growing dark; it was that moment when the pin-headed birds seem to organize their song into some acute and knowledgeable recognition of the storm's approach. Then there was a fine noise of rushing water from the crown of an oak at his back, as if a spigot there had been turned. Then the noise of fountains came from the crowns of all the tall trees. Why did he love storms, what was the meaning of his excitement when the door sprang open and the rain wind fled rudely up the stairs, why had the simple task of shutting the windows of an old house seemed fitting and urgent, why did the first watery notes of a storm wind have for him the unmistakable sound of good news, cheer, glad tidings? Then there was an explosion, a smell of cordite, and rain lashed the Japanese lanterns that Mrs. Levy had bought in Kyoto the year before last, or was it the year before that?

He stayed in the Levys' gazebo until the storm had passed. The rain had cooled the air and he shivered. The force of the wind had stripped a maple of its red and yellow leaves and scattered them over the grass and the water. Since it was midsummer the tree must be blighted, and yet he felt a peculiar sadness at this sign of autumn. He braced his shoulders, emptied his glass, and started for the Welchers' pool. This meant crossing the Lindleys' riding ring and he was surprised to find it overgrown with grass and all the jumps dismantled. He wondered if the Lindleys had sold their horses or gone away for the summer and put them out to board. He seemed to remember having heard something about the Lindleys and their horses but the memory was unclear. On he went, barefoot through the wet grass, to the Welchers', where he found their pool was dry.

This breach in his chain of water disappointed him absurdly, and he felt like some explorer who seeks a torrential headwater and finds a dead stream. He was disappointed and mystified. It was common enough to go away for the summer but no one ever drained his pool. The Welchers had definitely gone away. The pool furniture was folded, stacked, and covered with a tarpaulin. The bathhouse was locked. All the windows of the house were shut, and when he went around to the driveway in front he saw a FOR SALE sign nailed to a tree. When had he last heard from the Welchers—when, that is, had he and Lucinda last regretted an invitation to dine with them? It seemed only a week or so ago. Was his memory failing or had he so disciplined it in the repression of unpleasant facts that he had damaged his sense of the truth? Then in the distance he heard the sound of a tennis game. This cheered him, cleared away all his apprehensions and let him regard the overcast sky and the cold air with indifference. This was the day that Neddy Merrill swam across the county. That was the day! He started off then for his most difficult portage.

Had you gone for a Sunday afternoon ride that day you might have seen him, close to naked, standing on the shoulders of Route 424, waiting for a chance to cross. You might have wondered if he was the victim of foul play, had his car broken down, or was he merely a fool. Standing barefoot in the deposits of the highway—beer cans, rags, and blowout patches—exposed to all kinds of ridicule, he seemed pitiful. He had known when he started that this was a part of his journey—it had been on his maps—but confronted with the lines of traffic, worming through the summery light, he found himself unprepared. He was laughed at, jeered at, a beer can was thrown at him, and he had no dignity or humor to bring to the situation. He could have gone back, back to the Westerhazys', where Lucinda would still be sitting in the sun. He had signed nothing, vowed nothing, pledged nothing, not even to himself. Why, believing as he did, that all human obduracy was susceptible to common sense, was he unable to turn back? Why was he determined to complete his journey even if it meant putting his life in danger? At what point had this prank, this joke, this piece of horseplay become serious? He could not go back, he could not even recall with any clearness the green water at the Westerhazys', the sense of inhaling the day's components, the friendly and relaxed voices saying that they had *drunk* too much. In the space of an hour, more or less, he had covered a distance that made his return impossible.

An old man, tooling down the highway at fifteen miles an hour, let him get to the middle of the road, where there was a grass divider. Here he was exposed to the ridicule of the northbound traffic, but after ten or fifteen minutes he was able to cross. From here he had only a short walk to the Recreation Center at the edge of the village of Lancaster, where there were some handball courts and a public pool.

The effect of the water on voices, the illusion of brilliance and suspense, was the same here as it had been at the Bunkers' but the sounds here were louder, harsher, and more shrill, and as soon as he entered the crowded enclosure he was confronted with regimentation. "ALL SWIMMERS MUST TAKE A SHOWER BEFORE USING THE POOL. ALL SWIMMERS MUST USE THE FOOTBATH. ALL SWIMMERS MUST WEAR THEIR IDENTIFICATION DISKS." He took a shower, washed his feet in a cloudy and bitter solution, and made his way to the edge of the water. It stank of chlorine and looked to him like a sink. A pair of lifeguards in a pair of towers blew police whistles at what seemed to be regular intervals and abused the swimmers through a public address system. Neddy remembered the sapphire water at the Bunkers' with longing and thought that he might contaminate himself—damage his own prosperousness and charm—by swimming in this murk, but he reminded himself that he was an explorer, a pilgrim, and that this was merely a stagnant bend in the Lucinda River. He dove, scowling with distaste, into the chlorine and had to swim with his head above water to avoid collisions, but even so he was bumped into, splashed, and jostled. When he got to the shallow end both lifeguards were shouting at him: "Hey, you, you without the identification disk, get outa the water." He did, but they had no way of pursuing him and he went through the reek of suntan oil and chlorine out through the hurricane fence and passed the handball courts. By crossing the road he entered the wooded part of the Halloran estate. The woods were not cleared and the footing was treacherous and difficult until he reached the lawn and the clipped beech hedge that encircled their pool.

The Hallorans were friends, an elderly couple of enormous wealth who seemed to bask in the suspicion that they might be Communists. They were zealous reformers but they were not Communists, and yet when they were accused, as they sometimes were, of subversion, it seemed to gratify and excite them. Their beech hedge was yellow and he guessed this had been blighted like the Levys' maple. He called hullo, hullo, to warn the Hallorans of his approach, to palliate his invasion of their privacy. The Hallorans, for reasons that had never been explained to him, did not wear bathing suits. No explanations were in order, really. Their nakedness was a detail in their uncompromising zeal for reform and he stepped politely out of his trunks before he went through the opening in the hedge.

Mrs. Halloran, a stout woman with white hair and a serene face, was reading the *Times*. Mr. Halloran was taking beech leaves out of the water with a scoop. They seemed not surprised or displeased to see him. Their pool was perhaps the oldest in the county, a fieldstone rectangle, fed by a brook. It had no filter or pump and its waters were the opaque gold of the stream.

"I'm swimming across the county," Ned said.

"Why, I didn't know one could," exclaimed Mrs. Halloran.

"Well, I've made it from the Westerhazys'," Ned said. "That must be about four miles."

He left his trunks at the deep end, walked to the shallow end, and swam this stretch. As he was pulling himself out of the water he heard Mrs. Halloran say, "We've been *terribly* sorry to hear about all your misfortunes, Neddy."

"My misfortunes?" Ned asked. "I don't know what you mean."

"Why, we heard that you'd sold the house and that your poor children . . ."

"I don't recall having sold the house," Ned said, "and the girls are at home."

"Yes," Mrs. Halloran sighed. "Yes . . ." Her voice filled the air with an unseasonable melancholy and Ned spoke briskly. "Thank you for the swim."

"Well, have a nice trip," said Mrs. Halloran.

Beyond the hedge he pulled on his trunks and fastened them. They were loose and he wondered if, during the space of an afternoon, he could have lost some weight. He was cold and he was tired and the naked Hallorans and their dark water had depressed him. The swim was too much for his strength but how could he have guessed this, sliding down the banister that morning and sitting in the Westerhazys' sun? His arms were lame. His legs felt rubbery and ached at the joints. The worst of it was the cold in his bones and the feeling that he might never be warm again. Leaves were falling down around him and he smelled wood smoke on the wind. Who would be burning wood at this time of year?

He needed a drink. Whiskey would warm him, pick him up, carry him through the last of his journey, refresh his feeling that it was original and valorous to swim across the county. Channel swimmers took brandy. He needed a stimulant. He crossed the lawn in front of the Hallorans' house and went down a little path to where they had built a house for their only daughter, Helen, and her husband, Eric Sachs. The Sachses' pool was small and he found Helen and her husband there.

"Oh, *Neddy,*" Helen said. "Did you lunch at Mother's?"

"Not *really,*" Ned said. "I *did* stop to see your parents." This seemed to be explanation enough. "I'm terribly sorry to break in on you like this but I've taken a chill and I wonder if you'd give me a drink."

"Why, I'd *love* to," Helen said, "but there hasn't been anything in this house to drink since Eric's operation. That was three years ago."

Was he losing his memory, had his gift for concealing painful facts let him forget that he had sold his house, that his children were in trouble, and that his friend had been ill? His eyes slipped from Eric's face to his abdomen, where he saw three pale, sutured scars, two of them at least a foot long. Gone was his navel, and what, Neddy thought, would the roving hand, bed-checking one's gifts at 3 A.M., make of a belly with no navel, no link to birth, this breach in the succession?

"I'm sure you can get a drink at the Biswangers'," Helen said. "They're having an enormous do. You can hear it from here. Listen!"

She raised her head and from across the road, the lawns, the gardens, the woods, the fields, he heard again the brilliant noise of voices over water. "Well, I'll get wet," he said, still feeling that he had no freedom of choice about his means of travel. He dove into the Sachses' cold water and, gasping, close to drowning, made his way from one end of the pool to the other. "Lucinda and I want *terribly* to see you," he said over his shoulder, his face set toward the Biswangers'. "We're sorry it's been so long and we'll call you *very* soon."

He crossed some fields to the Biswangers' and the sounds of revelry there. They would be honored to give him a drink, they would be happy to give him a drink. The Biswangers invited him and Lucinda for dinner four times a year, six weeks in advance. They were always rebuffed and yet they continued to send out their invitations, unwilling to comprehend the rigid and undemocratic realities of their society. They were the sort of people who discussed the price of things at cocktails, exchanged market tips during dinner, and after dinner told dirty stories to mixed company. They did not belong to Neddy's set—they were not even on Lucinda's Christmas-card list. He went toward their pool with feelings of indifference, charity, and some unease, since it seemed to be getting dark and these were the longest days of the year. The party when he joined it was noisy and large. Grace Biswanger was the kind of hostess who asked the optometrist, the veterinarian, the real-estate dealer, and the dentist. No one was swimming and the twilight, reflected on the water of the pool, had a wintry gleam. There was a bar and he started for this. When Grace Biswanger saw him she came toward him, not affectionately as he had every right to expect, but bellicosely.

"Why, this party has everything," she said loudly, "including a gate crasher."

She could not deal him a social blow—there was no question about this and he did not flinch. "As a gate crasher," he asked politely, "do I rate a drink?"

"Suit yourself," she said. "You don't seem to pay much attention to invitations."

She turned her back on him and joined some guests, and he went to the bar and ordered a whiskey. The bartender served him but he served him rudely. His was a world in which the caterer's men kept the social score, and to be rebuffed by a part-time bartender meant that he had suffered some loss of social esteem. Or perhaps the man was new and uninformed. Then he heard Grace at his back say: "They went for broke overnight—nothing but income—and he showed up drunk one Sunday and asked us to loan him five thousand dollars. . . ." She was always talking about money. It was worse than eating your peas off a knife. He dove into the pool, swam its length and went away.

The next pool on his list, the last but two, belonged to his old mistress, Shirley Adams. If he had suffered any injuries at the Biswangers' they would be cured here. Love—sexual roughhouse in fact—was the supreme elixir, the pain killer, the brightly colored pill that would put the spring back into his step, the joy of life in his heart. They had had an affair last week, last month, last year. He couldn't remember. It was he who had broken it off, his was the upper hand, and he stepped through the gate of the wall that surrounded her pool with nothing so considered as self-confidence. It seemed in a way to be his pool, as the lover, particularly the illicit lover, enjoys the possessions of his mistress with an authority unknown to holy matrimony. She was there, her hair the color of brass, but her figure, at the edge of the lighted, cerulean water, excited in him no profound memories. It had been, he thought, a lighthearted affair, although she had wept when he broke it off. She seemed confused to see him and he wondered if she was still wounded. Would she, God forbid, weep again?

"What do you want?" she asked.

"I'm swimming across the county."

"Good Christ. Will you ever grow up?"

"What's the matter?"

"If you've come here for money," she said, "I won't give you another cent."

"You could give me a drink."

"I could but I won't. I'm not alone."

"Well, I'm on my way."

He dove in and swam the pool, but when he tried to haul himself up onto the curb he found that the strength in his arms and shoulders had gone, and he paddled to the ladder and climbed out. Looking over his shoulder he saw, in the lighted bathhouse, a young man. Going out onto the dark lawn he smelled chrysanthemums or marigolds—some stubborn autumnal fragrance—on the night air, strong as gas. Looking overhead he saw that the stars had come out, but why should he seem to see Andromeda, Cepheus, and Cassiopeia? What had become of the constellations of midsummer? He began to cry.

It was probably the first time in his adult life that he had ever cried, certainly the first time in his life that he had ever felt so miserable, cold, tired, and bewildered. He could not understand the rudeness of the caterer's barkeep or the rudeness of a mistress who had come to him on her knees and showered his trousers with tears. He had swum too long, he had been immersed too long, and his nose and his throat were sore from the water. What he needed then was a drink, some company, and some clean, dry clothes, and while he could have cut directly across the road to his home he went on to the Gilmartins' pool. Here, for the first time in his life, he did not dive but went down the steps into the icy water and swam a hobbled sidestroke that he might have learned as a youth. He staggered with fatigue on his way to the Clydes' and paddled the length of their pool, stopping again and again with his hand on the curb to rest. He climbed up the ladder and wondered if he had the strength to get home. He had done what he wanted, he had swum the county, but he was so stupefied with exhaustion that his triumph seemed vague. Stooped, holding on to the gateposts for support, he turned up the driveway of his own house.

The place was dark. Was it so late that they had all gone to bed? Had Lucinda stayed at the Westerhazys' for supper? Had the girls joined her there or gone someplace else? Hadn't they agreed, as they usually did on Sunday, to regret all their invitations and stay at home? He tried the garage doors to see what cars were in but the doors were locked and rust came off the handles onto his hands. Going toward the house, he saw that the force of the thunderstorm had knocked one of the rain gutters loose. It hung down over the front door like an umbrella rib, but it could be fixed in the morning. The house was locked, and he thought that the stupid cook or the stupid maid must have locked the place up until he remembered that it had been some time since they had employed a maid or a cook. He shouted, pounded on the door, tried to force it with his shoulder, and then, looking in at the windows, saw that the place was empty.

QUESTIONS

1. In the beginning paragraphs of the story, what do we learn about the society Neddy Merrill inhabits?
2. What does Ned's decision to swim home tell us about him?
3. Is there any irony in his calling his route the "Lucinda River"?
4. What are some of the important changes in setting that tell us something is wrong in Ned's world?
5. In this voyage of exploration, what does Ned discover about his world and about himself?
6. What is the author's attitude toward Ned?
7. How is the ethos of Ned's community significantly different from the ethos of the community you inhabit?

CHAPTER 7

METAPHOR, SYMBOL, ALLEGORY

A *metaphor* clarifies meaning by treating something as if it were something else. Money becomes a *nest egg;* a person who fails, a *washout;* a sandwich, a *submarine.* (A *simile* makes the metaphoric comparison explicit: "This looks *like a submarine.*") A *symbol* is an object or act especially significant—a dove, an eagle, a rocking horse. An *allegory* is a story suggesting, metaphorically or symbolically, another story. All of these reflect the way we respond to the world and express our feelings. We see an oak and think of sturdiness, so when we want to describe a friend we say, "He's as sturdy as an oak." We send flowers to loved ones to symbolize things we can't find words for. Our stories, even anecdotes of what happened when we lost our wallet or our purse, tend toward allegory as they reflect other stories that made the same point. When we use allegories or metaphors in conversation, we clarify our point by the comparison: "Just like Eve and the apple!"—"He waddles like a duck." Writers may be more skillful than we are, but their clarification through comparisons or through things that symbolize is natural to all of us. In the following stories, metaphors and symbols abound, and allegories beckon.

"Evangelist" illustrates nicely the difference between actuality and our metaphoric perceptions of it. At the outset, a sour John Pratt sees houses as "old kept women on the look out for some city lecher"; at the end, an elated John Pratt sees them as "veteran soldiers in line, meeting with stoic pride the injuries of time." As with all of us, Pratt's mood affects his vision.

EVANGELIST

Joyce Cary   (1888–1957)

John Pratt, fifty-five, on holiday at the sea, gets up one sunny morning, looks from the window, says, 'It won't last,' and picks from his seven suits the only dark one. He dresses himself with care, and eats for breakfast one piece of dry toast.

'A touch of liver,' he says to himself, takes his umbrella and a bowler,[1] and goes for his morning walk along the Parade.[2]

'Why the bowler?' he asks himself. 'I'm not going back to town.' And suddenly it strikes him that he is bored. 'Impossible,' he says; 'I've only been here a week and my regular time is always a fortnight.'

He looks about him to discover some usual source of pleasure in this charming old place; and immediately he is seized, possessed, overwhelmed with boredom, with the most malignant and hopeless of all boredoms, holiday boredom. It rises from his stomach, it falls from the lukewarm air. Everything in sight is instantly perceived as squalid, mercenary, debased by mean use and vulgar motives. The Regency façades[3] whose delicate taste he has so much admired, which bring him year after year to a place neither smart nor quiet, seem to leer at him with the sly, false primness of old kept women on the look out for some city lecher, willing to set off cracked plaster against lewd dexterity.

He looks at the sea for freshness. But it appears thick, greasy: he murmurs with horror, 'The cesspool of the whole earth.' He sees the drains discharging from a million towns, the rubbish unbucketed from ten thousand years of ships, wrecks full of corpses; the splash of glitter beyond the pier is like the explosion of some hidden corruption. The ozone comes to his nose like a stench.

He sees from the distance a friend, the Colonel in his light-grey suit, stepping briskly. He is whirling his stick—it is plain that he is in his usual high spirits.

Pratt crosses the road to avoid him. A taxi hoots in an angry and distracted manner, but he does not hurry, he would rather be killed than betray the dignity of his despair. The taxi's brakes squawk like Donald Duck—it comes to a stop at his elbow—a furious young man with upstanding black hair and red-rimmed eyes thrusts out his neck and bawls insults. Bystanders laugh and stare. Pratt does not turn his head or quicken his walk. He accepts these humiliations as appropriate to such a morning in such a world.

The shopping housewives with their predatory eyes and anxious wrinkled foreheads fill him with a lofty and scornful pity, as for insects generated by a conspiracy of gases and instinct to toil in blind necessity for the production of more insects.

Yes, he thinks, humanity is like the maggots on a perishing carcass. Its history is the history of maggots; the fly, the buzz, the coupling of flies, the dropping of their poison on every clean thing, the hunt for some ordure, some corpse, the

[1]Hat.   [2]Public promenade, in this instance at a seaside resort.   [3]Early nineteenth-century house fronts.

laying of eggs, and another generation of maggots. Foulness upon foulness. Tides of disgust and scorn rise in his soul; he stalks more grandly; he has become a giant for whom all history is meaner than the dust on his boot soles.

Suddenly he is accosted by a red-faced man, an hotel acquaintance, who starts out of a shop and seizes him by the hand—impossible to avoid this person. The red-faced man is in a fluster. Has Mr. Pratt seen the news? Is there going to be a war, is this it? Should he sell out his investments and pay his debts; should he fetch back his family from abroad?

Pratt draws himself up and out of mere wrath at this intrusion, utters in severe tones such banalities as amaze his own ears. If war comes, he says, it will come, and if not, then not. There are good arguments on both sides of the question. If we believe our freedom is worth defending, then we should be ready to defend it at all costs. For faith is not faith, not what we truly believe, unless we are prepared to die for it. And in a conflict of faith those alone who are prepared to die for what they believe deserve to win. As for bombs, one can die but once. One will die anyhow and possibly much worse than by a bomb.

And all these panic-mongers, are they not more than foolish? Panic is not only useless, it is a treachery—a defeat—an invitation to the enemy within as well as without.

The red-faced man is taken aback by this rigmarole of eloquence. He listens with surprised attention in his green eyes—then with respect. Pratt's unmoved solemnity, his severe tone born of scornful indifference, impress him. He ejaculates murmurs of approval. He says that this is just what he himself has always thought. And this is probably true. He could scarcely have escaped such reflections.

At last he is greatly moved. He turns even redder, his gooseberry eyes shine. He grasps Pratt's hand with fervour and a glance that means, 'This is an important, a solemn occasion. You are a bigger man than I took you for. Men of sense and courage, like ourselves, should be better acquainted.' He departs exalted.

Pratt walks on alone, his step is still majestic but full of spring. He is exhilarated; he looks at the sea and it appears to him noble in its vastness, transcendent in its unconcern, venerable in its intimation of glorious deeds. The houses are like veteran soldiers in line, meeting with stoic pride the injuries of time. The housewives, striving, saving for their families, wear the brows of angels; the battered angels roughly carved on some primitive church. He salutes with heroic elation a world made for heroes. He perceives with joy that it is going to be a fine day, that he is hungry. He whirls his umbrella.

QUESTIONS

1. What do Pratt's suits suggest? The umbrella?
2. How does "my regular time is always a fortnight" establish his character?
3. Where do the metaphors begin? List some of the most telling ones.
4. What is the metaphorical effect of *cracked plaster* (fourth paragraph)?

5.   What is the effect of the allusion to Donald Duck?
6.   What accounts for Pratt's change of mood?
7.   How do the red-faced man's eyes develop a telling metaphor? Do they reflect Pratt's or the narrator's attitude?
8.   What in the story suggests Pratt's concluding metaphors?
9.   What does the final sentence do for the story?
10. In what sense is Pratt an "evangelist"?
11. What aspects of the story are allegorical?

Hawthorne carefully sets the following story in colonial New England to invite an allegorical reading of plausible events, making Robin's crossing of what must be the actual Charles River into the actual Boston seem like a crossing of the Styx into Hell itself. Remember the Boston Tea Party? The story's power lies in its invited, and specious, allegory, until Robin comes to himself, and his share in human meanness. The story is also rich in metaphor and symbol. How does the opening paragraph "serve as a preface to the following adventures"?

MY KINSMAN, MAJOR MOLINEUX

Nathaniel Hawthorne   *(1804–1864)*

After the kings of Great Britain had assumed the right of appointing the colonial governors, the measures of the latter seldom met with the ready and generous approbation which had been paid to those of their predecessors, under the original charters. The people looked with most jealous scrutiny to the exercise of power which did not emanate from themselves, and they usually rewarded their rulers with slender gratitude for the compliances by which, in softening their instructions from beyond the sea, they had incurred the reprehension of those who gave them. The annals of Massachusetts Bay will inform us, that of six governors in the space of about forty years from the surrender of the old charter, under James II, two were imprisoned by a popular insurrection; a third, as Hutchinson[1] inclines to believe, was driven from the province by the whizzing of a musket-ball; a fourth, in the opinion of the same historian, was hastened to his grave by continual bickerings with the House of Representatives; and the remaining two, as well as their successors, till the revolution, were favored with few and brief intervals of peaceful sway. The inferior members of the court party, in times of high political excitement, led scarcely a more desirable life. These remarks may serve as a preface to the following adventures, which chanced upon a summer night, not far from a hundred years ago. The reader, in order to avoid a long and dry detail of colonial affairs, is requested to dispense with an account of the train of circumstances that had caused much temporary inflammation of the popular mind.

It was near nine o'clock of a moonlight evening, when a boat crossed the ferry with a single passenger, who had obtained his conveyance at that unusual hour

[1]Thomas Hutchinson (1711–1780), governor of Massachusetts and Colonial historian.

by the promise of an extra fare. While he stood on the landing-place, searching in either pocket for the means of fulfilling his agreement, the ferryman lifted a lantern, by the aid of which, and the newly risen moon, he took a very accurate survey of the stranger's figure. He was a youth of barely eighteen years, evidently country-bred, and now, as it should seem, upon his first visit to town. He was clad in a coarse gray coat, well worn, but in excellent repair; his under garments were durably constructed of leather, and fitted tight to a pair of serviceable and well-shaped limbs; his stockings of blue yarn were the incontrovertible work of a mother or a sister; and on his head was a three-cornered hat, which in its better days had perhaps sheltered the graver brow of the lad's father. Under his left arm was a heavy cudgel formed of an oak sapling, and retaining a part of the hardened root; and his equipment was completed by a wallet, not so abundantly stocked as to incommode the vigorous shoulders on which it hung. Brown, curly hair, well-shaped features, and bright, cheerful eyes were nature's gifts, and worth all that art could have done for his adornment.

The youth, one of whose names was Robin, finally drew from his pocket the half of a little province bill of five shillings, which, in the depreciation in that sort of currency, did but satisfy the ferryman's demand, with the surplus of a sexangular piece of parchment, valued at three pence. He then walked forward into the town, with as light a step as if his day's journey had not already exceeded thirty miles, and with as eager an eye as if he were entering London city, instead of the little metropolis of a New England colony. Before Robin had proceeded far, however, it occurred to him that he knew not whither to direct his steps; so he paused, and looked up and down the narrow street, scrutinizing the small and mean wooden buildings that were scattered on either side.

"This low hovel cannot be my kinsman's dwelling," thought he, "nor yonder old house, where the moonlight enters at the broken casement; and truly I see none hereabouts that might be worthy of him. It would have been wise to inquire my way of the ferryman, and doubtless he would have gone with me, and earned a shilling from the Major for his pains. But the next man I meet will do as well."

He resumed his walk, and was glad to perceive that the street now became wider, and the houses more respectable in their appearance. He soon discerned a figure moving on moderately in advance, and hastened his steps to overtake it. As Robin drew nigh, he saw that the passenger was a man in years, with a full periwig of gray hair, a wide-skirted coat of dark cloth, and silk stockings rolled above his knees. He carried a long and polished cane, which he struck down perpendicularly before him at every step; and at regular intervals he uttered two successive hems, of a peculiarly solemn and sepulchral intonation. Having made these observations, Robin laid hold of the skirt of the old man's coat, just when the light from the open door and windows of a barber's shop fell upon both their figures.

"Good evening to you, honored sir," said he, making a low bow and still retaining his hold of the skirt. "I pray you tell me whereabouts is the dwelling of my kinsman, Major Molineux."

The youth's question was uttered very loudly; and one of the barbers, whose razor was descending on a well-soaped chin, and another who was dressing a Ramillies wig,[2] left their occupations, and came to the door. The citizen, in the mean time, turned a long-favored countenance upon Robin, and answered him in a tone of excessive anger and annoyance. His two sepulchral hems, however, broke into the very centre of his rebuke, with most singular effect, like a thought of the cold grave obtruding among wrathful passions.

"Let go my garment, fellow! I tell you, I know not the man you speak of. What! I have authority, I have—hem, hem—authority; and if this be the respect you show for your betters, your feet shall be brought acquainted with the stocks by daylight, tomorrow morning!"

Robin released the old man's skirt, and hastened away, pursued by an ill-mannered roar of laughter from the barber's shop. He was at first considerably surprised by the result of his question, but, being a shrewd youth, soon thought himself able to account for the mystery.

"This is some country representative," was his conclusion, "who has never seen the inside of my kinsman's door, and lacks the breeding to answer a stranger civilly. The man is old, or verily—I might be tempted to turn back and smite him on the nose. Ah, *Robin, Robin!* even the barber's boys laugh at you for choosing such a guide! You will be wiser in time, friend Robin."

He now became entangled in a succession of crooked and narrow streets, which crossed each other, and meandered at no great distance from the waterside. The smell of tar was obvious to his nostrils, the masts of vessels pierced the moonlight above the tops of the buildings, and the numerous signs, which Robin paused to read, informed him that he was near the centre of business. But the streets were empty, the shops were closed, and lights were visible only in the second stories of a few dwelling-houses. At length, on the corner of a narrow lane, through which he was passing, he beheld the broad countenance of a British hero swinging before the door of an inn, whence proceeded the voices of many guests. The casement of one of the lower windows was thrown back, and a very thin curtain permitted Robin to distinguish a party at supper, round a well-furnished table. The fragrance of the good cheer steamed forth into the outer air, and the youth could not fail to recollect that the last remnant of his travelling stock of provision had yielded to his morning appetite, and that noon had found and left him dinnerless.

"Oh, that a parchment three-penny might give me a right to sit down at yonder table!" said Robin, with a sigh. "But the Major will make me welcome to the best of his victuals; so I will even step boldly in, and inquire my way to his dwelling."

He entered the tavern, and was guided by the murmur of voices and the fumes of tobacco to the public-room. It was a long and low apartment, with oaken walls, grown dark in the continual smoke, and a floor which was thickly sanded, but of no immaculate purity. A number of persons—the larger part of whom appeared to be mariners, or in some way connected with the sea—occupied the

---

[2]A wig with a long plaited tail and a bow at top and bottom, fashionable after Marlborough's victory at Ramillies, Belgium, in 1706.

wooden benches, or leather-bottomed chairs, conversing on various matters, and occasionally lending their attention to some topic of general interest. Three or four little groups were draining as many bowls of punch, which the West India trade had long since made a familiar drink in the colony. Others, who had the appearance of men who lived by regular and laborious handicraft, preferred the insulated bliss of an unshared potation, and became more taciturn under its influence. Nearly all, in short, evinced a predilection for the Good Creature in some of its various shapes, for this is a vice to which, as Fast Day sermons of a hundred years ago will testify, we have a long hereditary claim. The only guests to whom Robin's sympathies inclined him were two or three sheepish country-men, who were using the inn somewhat after the fashion of a Turkish caravan-sary; they had gotten themselves into the darkest corner of the room, and heedless of the Nicotian[3] atmosphere, were supping on the bread of their own ovens, and the bacon cured in their own chimney-smoke. But though Robin felt a sort of brotherhood with these strangers, his eyes were attracted from them to a person who stood near the door, holding whispered conversation with a group of ill-dressed associates. His features were separately striking almost to grotesqueness, and the whole face left a deep impression on the memory. The forehead bulged out into a double prominence, with a vale between; the nose came boldly forth in an irregular curve, and its bridge was of more than a finger's breadth; the eyebrows were deep and shaggy, and the eyes glowed beneath them like fire in a cave.

While Robin deliberated of whom to inquire respecting his kinsman's dwelling, he was accosted by the innkeeper, a little man in a stained white apron, who had come to pay his professional welcome to the stranger. Being in a second genera-tion from a French Protestant, he seemed to have inherited the courtesy of his parent nation; but no variety of circumstances was ever known to change his voice from the one shrill note in which he now addressed Robin.

"From the country, I presume, sir?" said he, with a profound bow. "Beg leave to congratulate you on your arrival, and trust you intend a long stay with us. Fine town here, sir, beautiful buildings, and much that may interest a stranger. May I hope for the honor of your commands in respect to supper?"

"The man sees a family likeness! The rogue has guessed that I am related to the Major!" thought Robin, who had hitherto experienced little superfluous civility.

All eyes were now turned on the country lad, standing at the door, in his worn three-cornered hat, gray coat, leather breeches, and blue yarn stockings, leaning on an oaken cudgel, and bearing a wallet on his back.

Robin replied to the courteous innkeeper, with such an assumption of confi-dence as befitted the Major's relative. "My honest friend," he said, "I shall make it a point to patronize your house on some occasion, when"—here he could not help lowering his voice—"when I may have more than a parchment three-pence in my pocket. My present business," continued he, speaking with

---

[3]From nicotine.

lofty confidence, "is merely to inquire my way to the dwelling of my kinsman, Major Molineux."

There was a sudden and general movement in the room, which Robin interpreted as expressing the eagerness of each individual to become his guide. But the innkeeper turned his eyes to a written paper on the wall, which he read, or seemed to read, with occasional recurrences to the young man's figure.

"What have we here?" said he, breaking his speech into little dry fragments. " 'Left the house of the subscriber, bounden servant, Hezekiah Mudge,—had on, when he went away, gray coat, leather breeches, master's third-best hat. One pound currency reward to whosoever shall lodge him in any jail in the province.' Better trudge, boy; better trudge!"

Robin had begun to draw his hand towards the lighter end of the oak cudgel, but a strange hostility in every countenance induced him to relinquish his purpose of breaking the courteous innkeeper's head. As he turned to leave the room, he encountered a sneering glance from the bold-featured personage whom he had before noticed; and no sooner was he beyond the door, than he heard a general laugh, in which the innkeeper's voice might be distinguished, like the dropping of small stones into a kettle.

"Now, is it not strange," thought Robin, with his usual shrewdness,—"is it not strange that the confession of an empty pocket should outweigh the name of my kinsman, Major Molineux? Oh, if I had one of those grinning rascals in the woods, where I and my oak sapling grew up together, I would teach him that my arm is heavy though my purse be light!"

On turning the corner of the narrow lane, Robin found himself in a spacious street, with an unbroken line of lofty houses on each side, and a steepled building at the upper end, whence the ringing of a bell announced the hour of nine. The light of the moon, and the lamps from the numerous shop-windows, discovered people promenading on the pavement, and amongst them Robin had hoped to recognize his hitherto inscrutable relative. The result of his former inquiries made him unwilling to hazard another, in a scene of such publicity, and he determined to walk slowly and silently up the street, thrusting his face close to that of every elderly gentleman, in search of the Major's lineaments. In his progress, Robin encountered many gay and gallant figures. Embroidered garments of showy colors, enormous periwigs, gold-laced hats, and silver-hilted swords glided past him and dazzled his optics. Travelled youths, imitators of the European fine gentlemen of the period, trod jauntily along, half dancing to the fashionable tunes which they hummed, and making poor Robin ashamed of his quiet and natural gait. At length, after many pauses to examine the gorgeous display of goods in the shop-windows, and after suffering some rebukes for the impertinence of his scrutiny into people's faces, the Major's kinsman found himself near the steepled building, still unsuccessful in his search. As yet, however, he had seen only one side of the thronged street; so Robin crossed, and continued the same sort of inquisition down the opposite pavement, with stronger hopes than the philosopher seeking an honest man, but with no better fortune. He had arrived about midway towards the lower end, from which his course began, when he overheard the approach of some one who struck down a cane on the flagstones at every step, uttering at regular intervals, two sepulchral hems.

"Mercy on us!" quoth Robin, recognizing the sound.

Turning a corner, which chanced to be close at his right hand, he hastened to pursue his researches in some other part of the town. His patience now was wearing low, and he seemed to feel more fatigue from his rambles since he crossed the ferry, than from his journey of several days on the other side. Hunger also pleaded loudly with him, and Robin began to balance the propriety of demanding, violently, and with lifted cudgel, the necessary guidance from the first solitary passenger whom he should meet. While a resolution to this effect was gaining strength, he entered a street of mean appearance, on either side of which a row of ill-built houses was straggling towards the harbor. The moonlight fell upon no passenger along the whole extent, but in the third domicile which Robin passed there was a half-opened door, and his keen glance detected a woman's garment within.

"My luck may be better here," said he to himself.

Accordingly, he approached the door, and beheld it shut closer as he did so; yet an open space remained, sufficing for the fair occupant to observe the stranger, without a corresponding display on her part. All that Robin could discern was a strip of scarlet petticoat, and the occasional sparkle of an eye, as if the moonbeams were trembling on some bright thing.

"Pretty mistress," for I may call her so with a good conscience, thought the shrewd youth, since I know nothing to the contrary,—"my sweet pretty mistress, will you be kind enough to tell me whereabouts I must seek the dwelling of my kinsman, Major Molineux?"

Robin's voice was plaintive and winning, and the female, seeing nothing to be shunned in the handsome country youth, thrust open the door, and came forth into the moonlight. She was a dainty little figure, with a white neck, round arms, and a slender waist, at the extremity of which her scarlet petticoat jutted out over a hoop, as if she were standing in a balloon. Moreover, her face was oval and pretty, her hair dark beneath the little cap, and her bright eyes possessed a sly freedom, which triumphed over those of Robin.

"Major Molineux dwells here," said this fair woman.

Now, her voice was the sweetest Robin had heard that night, yet he could not help doubting whether that sweet voice spoke Gospel truth. He looked up and down the mean street, and then surveyed the house before which they stood. It was a small, dark edifice of two stories, the second of which projected over the lower floor, and the front apartment had the aspect of a shop for petty commodities.

"Now, truly, I am in luck," replied Robin, cunningly, "and so indeed is my kinsman, the Major, in having so pretty a housekeeper. But I prithee trouble him to step to the door; I will deliver him a message from his friends in the country, and then go back to my lodgings at the inn."

"Nay, the Major has been abed this hour or more," said the lady of the scarlet petticoat; "and it would be to little purpose to disturb him to-night, seeing his evening draught was of the strongest. But he is a kind-hearted man, and it would be as much as my life's worth to let a kinsman of his turn away from the door. You are the good old gentleman's very picture, and I could swear that was his rainy-weather hat. Also he has garments very much resembling those leather small-clothes. But come in, I pray, for I bid you hearty welcome in his name."

So saying, the fair and hospitable dame took our hero by the hand; and the touch was light, and the force was gentleness, and though Robin read in her eyes what he did not hear in her words, yet the slender-waisted woman in the scarlet petticoat proved stronger than the athletic country youth. She had drawn his half-willing footsteps nearly to the threshold, when the opening of a door in the neighborhood startled the Major's housekeeper, and, leaving the Major's kinsman, she vanished speedily into her own domicile. A heavy yawn preceded the appearance of a man, who, like the Moonshine of Pyramus and Thisbe,[4] carried a lantern, needlessly aiding his sister luminary in the heavens. As he walked sleepily up the street, he turned his broad, dull face on Robin, and displayed a long staff, spiked at the end.

"Home, vagabond, home!" said the watchman, in accents that seemed to fall asleep as soon as they were uttered. "Home, or we'll set you in the stocks by peep of day!"

"This is the second hint of this kind," thought Robin. "I wish they would end my difficulties, by setting me there to-night."

Nevertheless, the youth felt an instinctive antipathy towards the guardian of midnight order, which at first prevented him from asking his usual question. But just when the man was about to vanish behind the corner, Robin resolved not to lose the opportunity, and shouted lustily after him,—

"I say, friend! will you guide me to the house of my kinsman, Major Molineux?"

The watchman made no reply, but turned the corner and was gone; yet Robin seemed to hear the sound of drowsy laughter stealing along the solitary street. At that moment, also, a pleasant titter saluted him from the open window above his head; he looked up, and caught the sparkle of a saucy eye; a round arm beckoned to him, and next he heard light footsteps descending the staircase within. But Robin, being of the household of a New England clergyman, was a good youth, as well as a shrewd one; so he resisted temptation, and fled away.

He now roamed desperately, and at random, through the town, almost ready to believe that a spell was on him, like that by which a wizard of his country had once kept three pursuers wandering, a whole winter night, within twenty paces of the cottage which they sought. The streets lay before him, strange and desolate, and the lights were extinguished in almost every house. Twice, however, little parties of men, among whom Robin distinguished individuals in outlandish attire, came hurrying along; but, though on both occasions, they paused to address him, such intercourse did not at all enlighten his perplexity. They did but utter a few words in some language of which Robin knew nothing, and perceiving his inabil-

---

[4]In Shakespeare's *A Midsummer Night's Dream*.

ity to answer, bestowed a curse upon him in plain English and hastened away. Finally, the lad determined to knock at the door of every mansion that might appear worthy to be occupied by his kinsman, trusting that perseverance would overcome the fatality that had hitherto thwarted him. Firm in this resolve, he was passing beneath the walls of a church, which formed the corner of two streets, when, as he turned into a shade of its steeple, he encountered a bulky stranger, muffled in a cloak. The man was proceeding with the speed of earnest business, but Robin planted himself full before him, holding the oak cudgel with both hands across his body as a bar to further passage.

"Halt, honest man, and answer me a question," said he, very resolutely. "Tell me, this instant, whereabouts is the dwelling of my kinsman, Major Molineux!"

"Keep your tongue between your teeth, fool, and let me pass!" said a deep, gruff voice, which Robin partly remembered. "Let me pass, or I'll strike you to the earth!"

"No, no, neighbor!" cried Robin, flourishing his cudgel, and then thrusting its larger end close to the man's muffled face. "No, no, I'm not the fool you take me for, nor do you pass till I have an answer to my question. Whereabouts is the dwelling of my kinsman, Major Molineux?"

The stranger, instead of attempting to force his passage, stepped back into the moonlight, unmuffled his face, and stared full into that of Robin.

"Watch here an hour, and Major Molineux will pass by," said he.

Robin gazed with dismay and astonishment on the unprecedented physiognomy of the speaker. The forehead with its double prominence, the broad hooked nose, the shaggy eyebrows, and fiery eyes were those which he had noticed at the inn, but the man's complexion had undergone a singular, or, more properly, a twofold change. One side of the face blazed an intense red, while the other was black as midnight, the division line being in the broad bridge of the nose; and a mouth which seemed to extend from ear to ear was black or red, in contrast to the color of the cheek. The effect was as if two individual devils, a fiend of fire and a fiend of darkness, had united themselves to form this infernal visage. The stranger grinned in Robin's face, muffled his party-colored features, and was out of sight in a moment.

"Strange things we travellers see!" ejaculated Robin.

He seated himself, however, upon the steps of the church-door, resolving to wait the appointed time for his kinsman. A few moments were consumed in philosophical speculations upon the species of man who had just left him; but having settled this point shrewdly, rationally, and satisfactorily, he was compelled to look elsewhere for his amusement. And first he threw his eyes along the street. It was of more respectable appearance than most of those into which he had wandered; and the moon, creating, like the imaginative power, a beautiful strangeness in familiar objects, gave something of romance to a scene that might not have possessed it in the light of day. The irregular and often quaint architecture of the houses, some of whose roofs were broken into numerous little peaks, while others ascended, steep and narrow, into a single point, and others again were square; the pure snow-white of some of their complexions, the aged darkness of others, and the thousand sparklings, reflected from bright substances in the walls of many; these matters engaged Robin's attention for a while, and then began to grow wearisome. Next he endeavored to define the forms of distant objects, starting away, with almost ghostly indistinctness, just as his eye appeared to grasp them; and finally he took a minute survey of an edifice which stood on the opposite side of the street, directly in front of the church-door, where he was stationed. It was a large, square mansion, distinguished from its neighbors by a balcony, which rested on tall pillars, and by an elaborate Gothic window, communicating therewith.

"Perhaps this is the very house I have been seeking," thought Robin.

Then he strove to speed away the time, by listening to a murmur which swept continually along the street, yet was scarcely audible, except to an unaccustomed ear like his; it was a low, dull, dreamy sound, compounded of many noises, each of which was at too great a distance to be separately heard. Robin marvelled at this snore of a sleeping town, and marvelled more whenever its continuity was broken by now and then a distant shout, apparently loud where it originated. But altogether it was a sleep-inspiring sound, and, to shake off its drowsy influence, Robin arose, and climbed a window-frame, that he might view the interior of the church. There the moonbeams came trembling in, and fell down upon the deserted pews, and extended along the quiet aisles. A fainter yet more awful radiance was hovering around the pulpit, and one solitary ray had dared to rest upon the open page of the great Bible. Had nature, in that deep hour, become a worshipper in the house which man had builded? Or was that heavenly light the visible sanctity of the place,—visible because no earthly and impure feet were within the walls? The scene made Robin's heart shiver with a sensation of loneliness stronger than he had ever felt in the remotest depths of his native woods; so he turned away and sat down again before the door. There were graves around the church, and now an uneasy thought obtruded into Robin's breast. What if the object of his search, which had been so often and so strangely thwarted, were all the time mouldering in his shroud? What if his kinsman should glide through yonder gate, and nod and smile to him in dimly passing by?

"Oh that any breathing thing were here with me!" said Robin.

Recalling his thoughts from the uncomfortable track, he sent them over forest, hill, and stream, and attempted to imagine how that evening of ambiguity and weariness had been spent by his father's household. He pictured them assembled at the door, beneath the tree, the great old tree, which had been spared for its huge twisted trunk and venerable shade, when a thousand leafy brethren fell. There, at the going down of the summer sun, it was his father's custom to perform domestic worship, that the neighbors might come and join with him like brothers of the family, and that the wayfaring man might pause to drink at the fountain, and keep his heart pure by freshening the memory of home. Robin distinguished the seat of every individual of the little audience; he saw the good man in the midst, holding the Scriptures in the golden light that fell from the western clouds; he beheld him close the book and all rise up to pray. He heard the old thanksgiving for daily mercies, the old supplications for their continuance, to which he had so often listened in weariness, but which were now among his dear remembrances. He perceived the slight inequality of his father's voice when he came to speak of the absent one; he noted how his mother turned her face to the broad and knotted trunk; how his elder brother scorned, because the beard was rough upon his upper lip, to permit his features to be moved; how the younger sister drew down a low hanging branch before her eyes; and how the little one of all, whose sports had hitherto broken the decorum of the scene, understood the prayer for her playmate, and burst into clamorous grief. Then he saw them go in at the door; and when Robin would have entered also, the latch tinkled into its place, and he was excluded from his home.

"Am I here, or there?" cried Robin, starting; for all at once, when his thoughts had become visible and audible in a dream, the long, wide, solitary street shone out before him.

He aroused himself, and endeavored to fix his attention steadily upon the large edifice which he had surveyed before. But still his mind kept vibrating between fancy and reality; by turns, the pillars of the balcony lengthened into the tall, bare stems of pines, dwindled down to human figures, settled again into their true shape and size, and then commenced a new succession of changes. For a single moment, when he deemed himself awake, he could have sworn that a visage— one which he seemed to remember, yet could not absolutely name as his kinsman's—was looking towards him from the Gothic window. A deeper sleep wrestled with and nearly overcame him, but fled at the sound of footsteps along the opposite pavement. Robin rubbed his eyes, discerned a man passing at the foot of the balcony, and addressed him in a loud, peevish, and lamentable cry.

"Hallo, friend! must I wait here all night for my kinsman, Major Molineux?"

The sleeping echoes awoke, and answered the voice; and the passenger, barely able to discern a figure sitting in the oblique shade of the steeple, traversed the street to obtain a nearer view. He was himself a gentleman in the prime, of open, intelligent, cheerful, and altogether prepossessing countenance. Perceiving a country youth, apparently homeless and without friends, he accosted him in a tone of real kindness, which had become strange to Robin's ears.

"Well, my good lad, why are you sitting here?" inquired he. "Can I be of service to you in any way?"

"I am afraid not, sir," replied Robin, despondingly; "yet I shall take it kindly, if you'll answer me a single question. I've been searching, half the night, for one Major Molineux; now, sir, is there really such a person in these parts, or am I dreaming?"

"Major Molineux! The name is not altogether strange to me," said the gentleman, smiling. "Have you any objection to telling me the nature of your business with him?"

Then Robin briefly related that his father was a clergyman, settled on a small salary, at a long distance back in the country, and that he and Major Molineux were brothers' children. The Major, having inherited riches, and acquired civil and military rank, had visited his cousin, in great pomp, a year or two before; had manifested much interest in Robin and an elder brother, and, being childless himself, had thrown out hints respecting the future establishment of one of them in life. The elder brother was destined to succeed to the farm which his father cultivated in the interval of sacred duties; it was therefore determined that Robin should profit by his kinsman's generous intentions, especially as he seemed to be rather the favorite, and was thought to possess other necessary endowments.

"For I have the name of being a shrewd youth," observed Robin, in this part of his story.

"I doubt not you deserve it," replied his new friend, good-naturedly; "but pray proceed."

"Well, sir, being nearly eighteen years old, and well grown, as you see," continued Robin, drawing himself up to his full height, "I thought it high time to begin in the world. So my mother and sister put me in handsome trim, and my father gave me half the remnant of his last year's salary, and five days ago I started for this place, to pay the Major a visit. But, would you believe it, sir! I crossed the ferry a little after dark, and have yet found nobody that would show me the way to his dwelling; only, an hour or two since, I was told to wait here, and Major Molineux would pass by."

"Can you describe the man who told you this?" inquired the gentleman.

"Oh, he was a very ill-favored fellow, sir," replied Robin, "with two great bumps on his forehead, a hook nose, fiery eyes; and, what struck me as the strangest, his face was of two different colors. Do you happen to know such a man, sir?"

"Not intimately," answered the stranger, "but I chanced to meet him a little time previous to your stopping me. I believe you may trust his word, and that the Major will very shortly pass through this street. In the mean time, as I have a singular curiosity to witness your meeting, I will sit down here upon the steps and bear you company."

He seated himself accordingly, and soon engaged his companion in animated discourse. It was but of brief continuance, however, for a noise of shouting, which had long been remotely audible, drew so much nearer that Robin inquired its cause.

"What may be the meaning of this uproar?" asked he. "Truly, if your town be always as noisy, I shall find little sleep while I am an inhabitant."

"Why, indeed, friend Robin, there do appear to be three or four riotous fellows abroad to-night," replied the gentleman. "You must not expect all the stillness of your native woods here in our street. But the watch will shortly be at the heels of these lads and"—

"Ay, and set them in the stocks by peep of day," interrupted Robin, recollecting his own encounter with the drowsy lantern-bearer, "But, dear sir, if I may trust my ears, an army of watchmen would never make head against such a multitude of rioters. There were at least a thousand voices went up to make that one shout."

"May not a man have several voices, Robin, as well as two complexions?" said his friend.

"Perhaps a man may; but Heaven forbid that a woman should!" responded the shrewd youth, thinking of the seductive tones of the Major's housekeeper.

The sounds of a trumpet in some neighboring street now became so evident and continual, that Robin's curiosity was strongly excited. In addition to the shouts, he heard frequent bursts from many instruments of discord, and a wild and confused laughter filled up the intervals. Robin rose from the steps, and looked wistfully towards a point whither people seemed to be hastening.

"Surely, some prodigious merry-making is going on," exclaimed he. "I have laughed very little since I left home, sir, and should be sorry to lose an opportunity. Shall we step round the corner by that darkish house, and take our share of the fun?"

"Sit down again, sit down, good Robin," replied the gentleman, laying his hand on the skirt of the gray coat. "You forget that we must wait here for your kinsman; and there is reason to believe that he will pass by, in the course of a very few moments."

The near approach of the uproar had now disturbed the neighborhood; windows flew open on all sides; and many heads, in the attire of the pillow, and confused by sleep suddenly broken, were protruded to the gaze of whoever had leisure to observe them. Eager voices hailed each other from house to house, all demanding the explanation, which not a soul could give. Half-dressed men hurried towards the unknown commotion, stumbling as they went over the stone steps that thrust themselves into the narrow footwalk. The shouts, the laughter, and the tuneless bray, the antipodes of music, came onwards with increasing din, till scattered individuals, and then denser bodies, began to appear round a corner at the distance of a hundred yards.

"Will you recognize your kinsman, if he passes in this crowd?" inquired the gentleman.

"Indeed, I can't warrant it, sir; but I'll take my stand here, and keep a bright lookout," answered Robin, descending to the outer edge of the pavement.

A mighty stream of people now emptied into the street, and came rolling slowly towards the church. A single horseman wheeled the corner in the midst of them, and close behind him came a band of fearful wind-instruments, sending forth a fresher discord now that no intervening buildings kept it from the ear. Then a redder light disturbed the moonbeams, and a dense multitude of torches shone along the street, concealing, by their glare, whatever object they illuminated. The single horseman, clad in a military dress, and bearing a drawn sword, rode onward as the leader, and, by his fierce and variegated countenance, appeared like war personified; the red of one cheek was an emblem of fire and sword; the blackness of the other betokened the mourning that attends them. In his train were wild figures in the Indian dress, and many fantastic shapes without a model, giving the whole march a visionary air, as if a dream had broken forth from some feverish brain, and were sweeping visibly through the midnight streets. A mass of people, inactive, except as applauding spectators, hemmed the procession in; and several women ran along the sidewalk, piercing the confusion of heavier sounds with their shrill voices of mirth or terror.

"The double-faced fellow has his eye upon me," muttered Robin, with an indefinite but an uncomfortable idea that he was himself to bear a part in the pageantry.

The leader turned himself in the saddle, and fixed his glance full upon the country youth, as the steed went slowly by. When Robin had freed his eyes from those fiery ones, the musicians were passing before him, and the torches were close at hand but the unsteady brightness of the latter formed a veil which he could not penetrate. The rattling of wheels over the stones sometimes found its way to his ear, and confused traces of a human form appeared at intervals, and then melted into the vivid light. A moment more, and the leader thundered a command to halt: the trumpets vomited a horrid breath, and then held their peace; the shouts and laughter of the people died away, and there remained only a universal hum, allied to silence. Right before Robin's eyes was an uncovered cart. There the torches blazed the brightest, there the moon shouted out like day, and there, in tar-and-feathery dignity, sat his kinsman, Major Molineux!

He was an elderly man, of large and majestic person, and strong, square features, betokening a steady soul; but steady as it was his enemies had found means to shake it. His face was pale as death, and far more ghastly; the broad forehead was contracted in his agony, so that his eyebrows formed one grizzled line; his eyes were red and wild, and the foam hung white upon his quivering lip. His whole frame was agitated by a quick and continual tremor, which his pride strove to quell, even in those circumstances of overwhelming humiliation. But perhaps the bitterest pang of all was when his eyes met those of Robin; for he evidently knew him on the instant, as the youth stood witnessing the foul disgrace of a head grown gray in honor. They stared at each other in silence, and Robin's knees shook, and his hair bristled, with a mixture of pity and terror. Soon, however, a bewildering excitement began to seize upon his mind; the preceding adventures of the night, the unexpected appearance of the crowd, the torches, the confused din and the hush that followed, the spectre of his kinsman reviled by that great multitude,—all this, and, more than all, a perception of tremendous ridicule in the whole scene, affected him with a sort of mental inebriety. At that moment a voice of sluggish merriment saluted Robin's ears, he turned instinctively, and just behind the corner of the church stood the lantern-bearer, rubbing his eyes, and drowsily enjoying the lad's amazement. Then he heard a peal of laughter like the ringing of silvery bells; a woman twitched his arm, a saucy eye met his, and he saw the lady of the scarlet petticoat. A sharp, dry cachinnation appealed to his memory, and standing on tiptoe in the crowd, with his white apron over his head, he beheld the courteous little innkeeper. And lastly, there sailed over the heads of the multitude a great, broad laugh, broken in the midst by two sepulchral hems, thus, "Haw, haw, haw,—hem, hem,—haw, haw, haw, haw!"

The sound proceeded from the balcony of the opposite edifice, and thither Robin turned his eyes. In front of the Gothic window stood the old citizen, wrapped in a wide gown, his gray periwig exchanged for a nightcap, which was thrust back from his forehead, and his silk stockings hanging about his legs. He supported himself on his polished cane in a fit of convulsive merriment, which manifested itself on his solemn old features like a funny inscription on a tombstone. Then Robin seemed to hear the voices of the barbers, of the guests of the inn, and of all who had made sport of him that night. The contagion was spreading among the multitude, when all at once, it seized upon Robin, and he sent forth a shout of laughter that echoed through the street,—every man shook his sides, every man emptied his lungs, but Robin's shout was the loudest there. The cloud-spirits peeped from their silvery islands, as the congregated mirth went roaring up the sky! The Man in the Moon heard the far bellow. "Oho," quoth he, "the old earth is frolicsome to-night!"

When there was a momentary calm in that tempestuous sea of sound, the leader gave the sign, the procession resumed its march. On they went, like fiends that throng in mockery around some dead potentate, mighty no more, but majestic still in his agony. On they went, in counterfeited pomp, in senseless uproar, in frenzied merriment, trampling all on an old man's heart. On swept the tumult, and left a silent street behind.

"Well, Robin, are you dreaming?" inquired the gentleman, laying his hand on the youth's shoulder.

Robin started, and withdrew his arm from the stone post to which he had instinctively clung, as the living stream rolled by him. His cheek was somewhat pale, and his eye not quite as lively as in the earlier part of the evening.

"Will you be kind enough to show me the way to the ferry?" said he, after a moment's pause.

"You have, then, adopted a new subject of inquiry?" observed his companion, with a smile.

"Why, yes, sir," replied Robin, rather dryly. "Thanks to you, and to my other friends, I have at last met my kinsman, and he will scarce desire to see my face again. I begin to grow weary of a town life, sir. Will you show me the way to the ferry?"

"No, my good friend Robin—not to-night, at least," said the gentleman. "Some few days hence, if you wish it, I will speed you on your journey. Or, if you prefer to remain with us, perhaps, as you are a shrewd youth, you may rise in the world without the help of your kinsman, Major Molineux."

QUESTIONS

1. How does the story's actual beginning in the second paragraph contrast with Hawthorne's preface in the first?

2. What details of Robin's clothing are significant? What do they suggest about the story to come?

3. What position does the "hem-hem" gentleman seem to have in the community? Why is his reaction to Robin different from that of the barbers and their customers?

4. How does the term *shrewd* operate in the story?

5. What are the significant details in the features of the man with the

bumpy forehead? What is his role in the events? What allegorical role does he fill?

6. Who is "the lady of the scarlet petticoat"? What is her allegorical role?
7. Who are the people "in outlandish attire" who address Robin in a strange language?
8. What is the significance of the ray of moonlight on the Bible and Robin's subsequent thoughts?
9. What is the irony in the kindly gentleman's "The name is not altogether strange to me"?
10. How does the reader know whether or not Robin is dreaming?
11. Where do the narrator's sympathies lie, with the American colonists or with the British governor?
12. Why does Robin laugh?
13. Will he stay in Boston or return to the country?

In "Bliss" the omniscient narrator focuses our attention upon the perceptions of Bertha Young, so that we see the world metaphorically and symbolically, as she does. "Why be given a body," Bertha asks, "if you have to keep it shut up in a case like a rare, rare fiddle?" Only at the end do we perceive the dramatic irony that undercuts her vision. What accounts for Bertha's youthful bliss?

BLISS

Katherine Mansfield   (1888–1923)

Although Bertha Young was thirty she still had moments like this when she wanted to run instead of walk, to take dancing steps on and off the pavement, to bowl a hoop, to throw something up in the air and catch it again, or to stand still and laugh at—nothing—at nothing, simply.

What can you do if you are thirty and, turning the corner of your own street, you are overcome, suddenly, by a feeling of bliss—absolute bliss!—as though you'd suddenly swallowed a bright piece of that late afternoon sun and it burned in your bosom, sending out a little shower of sparks into every particle, into every finger and toe? . . .

Oh, is there no way you can express it without being "drunk and disorderly"? How idiotic civilization is! Why be given a body if you have to keep it shut up in a case like a rare, rare fiddle?

"No, that about the fiddle is not quite what I mean," she thought, running up the steps and feeling in her bag for the key—she'd forgotten it, as usual—and rattling the letter-box. "It's not what I mean, because—Thank you, Mary"—she went into the hall. "Is nurse back?"

"Yes, M'm."

"And has the fruit come?"

"Yes, M'm. Everything's come."

"Bring the fruit up to the dining-room, will you? I'll arrange it before I go upstairs."

It was dusky in the dining-room and quite chilly. But all the same Bertha threw off her coat; she could not bear the tight clasp of it another moment, and the cold air fell on her arms.

But in her bosom there was still that bright glowing place—that shower of little sparks coming from it. It was almost unbearable. She hardly dared to breathe for fear of fanning it higher, and yet she breathed deeply, deeply. She hardly dared to look into the cold mirror—but she did look, and it gave her back a woman, radiant, with smiling, trembling lips, with big, dark eyes and an air of listening, waiting for something . . . divine to happen . . . that she knew must happen. . . infallibly.

Mary brought in the fruit on a tray and with it a glass bowl, and a blue dish, very lovely, with a strange sheen on it as though it had been dipped in milk.

"Shall I turn on the light, M'm?"

"No, thank you. I can see quite well."

There were tangerines and apples stained with strawberry pink. Some yellow pears, smooth as silk, some white grapes covered with a silver bloom and a big cluster of purple ones. These last she had bought to tone in with the new dining-room carpet. Yes, that did sound rather far-fetched and absurd, but it was really why she had bought them. She had thought in the shop: "I must have some purples ones to bring the carpet up to the table." And it had seemed quite sense at the time.

When she had finished with them and had made two pyramids of these bright round shapes, she stood away from the table to get the effect—and it really was most curious. For the dark table seemed to melt into the dusky light and the glass dish and the blue bowl to float in the air. This, of course in her present mood, was so incredibly beautiful. . . . She began to laugh.

"No, no. I'm getting hysterical." And she seized her bag and coat and ran upstairs to the nursery.

Nurse sat at a low table giving Little B her supper after her bath. The baby had on a white flannel gown and a blue woollen jacket, and her dark, fine hair was brushed up into a funny little peak. She looked up when she saw her mother and began to jump.

"Now, my lovey, eat it up like a good girl," said Nurse, setting her lips in a way that Bertha knew, and that meant she had come into the nursery at another wrong moment.

"Has she been good, Nanny?"

"She's been a little sweet all the afternoon," whispered Nanny. "We went to the park and I sat down on a chair and took her out of the pram and a big dog came along and put its head on my knee and she clutched its ear, tugged it. Oh, you should have seen her."

Bertha wanted to ask if it wasn't rather dangerous to let her clutch at a strange dog's ear. But she did not dare to. She stood watching them, her hands by her side, like the poor little girl in front of the rich little girl with the doll.

The baby looked up at her again, stared, and then smiled so charmingly that Bertha couldn't help crying:

"Oh, Nanny, do let me finish giving her her supper while you put the bath things away."

"Well, M'm, she oughtn't to be changed hands while she's eating," said Nanny, still whispering. "It unsettles her; it's very likely to upset her."

How absurd it was. Why have a baby if it has to be kept—not in a case like a rare, rare fiddle—but in another woman's arms?

"Oh, I must!" said she.

Very offended, Nanny handed her over.

"Now, don't excite her after her supper. You know you do, M'm. And I have such a time with her after!"

Thank heaven! Nanny went out of the room with the bath towels.

"Now I've got you to myself, my little precious," said Bertha, as the baby leaned against her.

She ate delightfully, holding up her lips for the spoon and then waving her hands. Sometimes she wouldn't let the spoon go; and sometimes, just as Bertha had filled it, she waved it away to the four winds.

When the soup was finished Bertha turned round to the fire.

"You're nice—you're very nice!" said she, kissing her warm baby. "I'm fond of you. I like you."

And, indeed, she loved Little B so much—her neck as she bent forward, her exquisite toes as they shone transparent in the firelight—that all her feeling of bliss came back again, and again she didn't know how to express it—what to do with it.

"You're wanted on the telephone," said Nanny, coming back in triumph and seizing *her* little B.

Down she flew. It was Harry.

"Oh, is that you, Ber? Look here. I'll be late. I'll take a taxi and come along as quickly as I can, but get dinner put back ten minutes—will you? All right?"

"Yes, perfectly. Oh, Harry!"

"Yes?"

What had she to say? She'd nothing to say. She only wanted to get in touch with him for a moment. She couldn't absurdly cry: "Hasn't it been a divine day!"

"What is it?" rapped out the little voice.

"Nothing. *Entendu,*"[1] said Bertha, and hung up the receiver, thinking how more than idiotic civilization was.

They had people coming to dinner. The Norman Knights—a very sound couple—he was about to start a theatre, and she was awfully keen on interior decoration, a young man, Eddie Warren, who had just published a little book of

---

[1]Understood (French).

poems and whom everybody was asking to dine, and a "find" of Bertha's called
Pearl Fulton. What Miss Fulton did, Bertha didn't know. They had met at the
club and Bertha had fallen in love with her, as she always did fall in love with
beautiful women who had something strange about them.

The provoking thing was that, though they had been about together and met
a number of times and really talked, Bertha couldn't yet make her out. Up to a
certain point Miss Fulton was rarely, wonderfully frank, but the certain point was
there, and beyond that she would not go.

Was there anything beyond it? Harry said "No." Voted her dullish, and "cold
like all blond women, with a touch, perhaps, of anaemia of the brain." But Bertha
wouldn't agree with him; not yet, at any rate.

"No, the way she has of sitting with her head a little on one side, and smiling,
has something behind it, Harry, and I must find out what that something is."

"Most likely it's a good stomach," answered Harry.

He made a point of catching Bertha's heels with replies of that kind . . . "liver
frozen, my dear girl," or "pure flatulence," or "kidney disease," . . . and so on.
For some strange reason Bertha liked this, and almost admired it in him very
much.

She went into the drawing-room and lighted the fire; then, picking up the
cushions, one by one, that Mary had disposed so carefully, she threw them back
on to the chairs and the couches. That made all the difference; the room came
alive at once. As she was about to throw the last one she surprised herself by
suddenly hugging it to her, passionately, passionately. But it did not put out the
fire in her bosom. Oh, on the contrary!

The windows of the drawing-room opened on to a balcony overlooking the
garden. At the far end, against the wall, there was a tall, slender pear tree in
fullest, richest bloom; it stood perfect, as though becalmed against the jade-green
sky. Bertha couldn't help feeling, even from this distance, that it had not a single
bud or a faded petal. Down below, in the garden beds, the red and yellow tulips,
heavy with flowers, seemed to lean upon the dusk. A grey cat, dragging its belly,
crept across the lawn, and a black one, its shadow, trailed after. The sight of them,
so intent and so quick, gave Bertha a curious shiver.

"What creepy things cats are!" she stammered, and she turned away from the
window and began walking up and down. . . .

How strong the jonquils smelled in the warm room. Too strong? Oh, no. And
yet, as though overcome, she flung down on a couch and pressed her hands to
her eyes.

"I'm too happy—too happy!" she murmured.

And she seemed to see on her eyelids the lovely pear tree with its wide open
blossoms as a symbol of her own life.

Really—really—she had everything. She was young. Harry and she were as
much in love as ever, and they got on together splendidly and were really good
pals. She had an adorable baby. They didn't have to worry about money. They
had this absolutely satisfactory house and garden. And friends—modern, thrilling
friends, writers and painters and poets or people keen on social questions—just

the kind of friends they wanted. And then there were books, and there was music, and she had found a wonderful little dressmaker, and they were going abroad in the summer, and their new cook made the most superb omelettes . . . .

"I'm absurd. Absurd!" She sat up; but she felt quite dizzy, quite drunk. It must have been the spring.

Yes, it was the spring. Now she was so tired she could not drag herself upstairs to dress.

A white dress, a string of jade beads, green shoes and stockings. It wasn't intentional. She had thought of this scheme hours before she stood at the drawing-room window.

Her petals rustled softly into the hall, and she kissed Mrs. Norman Knight, who was taking off the most amusing orange coat with a procession of black monkeys round the hem and up the fronts.

". . . Why! Why! Why is the middle-class so stodgy—so utterly without a sense of humour! My dear, it's only by a fluke that I am here at all—Norman being the protective fluke. For my darling monkeys so upset the train that it rose to a man and simply ate me with its eyes. Didn't laugh—wasn't amused —that I should have loved. No, just stared—and bored me through and through."

"But the cream of it was," said Norman, pressing a large tortoiseshell-rimmed monocle into his eye, "you don't mind me telling this, Face, do you?" (In their home and among their friends they called each other Face and Mug.) "The cream of it was when she, being full fed, turned to the woman beside her and said: 'Haven't you ever seen a monkey before?' "

"Oh, yes!" Mrs. Norman Knight joined in the laughter. "Wasn't that too absolutely creamy?"

And a funnier thing still was that now her coat was off she did look like a very intelligent monkey—who had even made that yellow silk dress out of scraped banana skins. And her amber ear-rings; they were like little dangling nuts.

"This is a sad, sad fall!" said Mug, pausing in front of Little B's perambulator. "When the perambulator comes into the hall—" and he waved the rest of the quotation away.

The bell rang. It was lean, pale Eddie Warren (as usual) in a state of acute distress.

"It *is* the right house, *isn't* it?" he pleaded.

"Oh, I think so—I hope so," said Bertha brightly.

"I have had such a *dreadful* experience with a taxi-man; he was *most* sinister. I couldn't get him to *stop*. The *more* I knocked and called the *faster* he went. And *in* the moonlight this *bizarre* figure with the *flattened* head *crouching* over the *lit-tle* wheel. . . ."

He shuddered, taking off an immense white silk scarf. Bertha noticed that his socks were white, too—most charming.

"But how dreadful!" she cried.

"Yes, it really was," said Eddie, following her into the drawingroom. "I saw myself *driving* through Eternity in a *timeless* taxi."

He knew the Norman Knights. In fact, he was going to write a play for N. K. when the theatre scheme came off.

"Well, Warren, how's the play?" said Norman Knight, dropping his monocle and giving his eye a moment in which to rise to the surface before it was screwed down again.

And Mrs. Norman Knight: "Oh, Mr. Warren, what happy socks!"

"I *am* so glad you like them," said he, staring at his feet. "They seem to have got so *much* whiter since the moon rose." And he turned his lean sorrowful young face to Bertha. "There *is* a moon, you know."

She wanted to cry: "I am sure there is—often—often!"

He really was a most attractive person. But so was Face, crouched before the fire in her banana skins, and so was Mug, smoking a cigarette and saying as he flicked the ash: "Why doth the bridegroom tarry?"

"There he is, now."

Bang went the front door open and shut. Harry shouted: "Hullo, you people. Down in five minutes." And they heard him swarm up the stairs. Bertha couldn't help smiling; she knew how he loved doing things at high pressure. What, after all, did an extra five minutes matter? But he would pretend to himself that they mattered beyond measure. And then he would make a great point of coming into the drawing-room, extravagantly cool and collected.

Harry had such a zest for life. Oh, how she appreciated it in him. And his passion for fighting—for seeking in everything that came up against him another test of his power and of his courage—that, too, she understood. Even when it made him just occasionally, to other people, who didn't know him well, a little ridiculous perhaps. . . . For there were moments when he rushed into battle where no battle was. . . . She talked and laughed and positively forgot until he had come in (just as she had imagined) that Pearl Fulton had not turned up.

"I wonder if Miss Fulton has forgotten?"

"I expect so," said Harry. "Is she on the 'phone?"

"Ah! There's a taxi, now," And Bertha smiled with that little air of proprietorship that she always assumed while her women finds were new and mysterious. "She lives in taxis."

"She'll run to fat if she does," said Harry coolly, ringing the bell for dinner. "Frightful danger for blond women."

"Harry—don't," warned Bertha, laughing up at him.

Came another tiny moment, while they waited, laughing and talking, just a trifle too much at their ease, a trifle too unaware. And then Miss Fulton, all in silver, with a silver fillet binding her pale blond hair, came in smiling, her head a little on one side.

"Am I late?"

"No, not at all," said Bertha. "Come along." And she took her arm and they moved into the dining-room.

What was there in the touch of that cool arm that could fan—fan—start blazing—blazing—the fire of bliss that Bertha did not know what to do with?

Miss Fulton did not look at her; but then she seldom did look at people directly. Her heavy eyelids lay upon her eyes and the strange half smile came and went upon her lips as though she lived by listening rather than seeing. But Bertha knew, suddenly, as if the longest, most intimate look had passed between them —as if they had said to each other: "You too?"—that Pearl Fulton, stirring the beautiful red soup in the grey plate, was feeling just what she was feeling.

And the others? Face and Mug, Eddie and Harry, their spoons rising and falling—dabbing their lips with their napkins, crumbling bread, fiddling with the forks and glasses and talking.

"I met her at the Alpha show—the weirdest little person. She'd not only cut off her hair, but she seemed to have taken a dreadfully good snip off her legs and arms and her neck and her poor little nose as well."

"Isn't she very *liée*[2] with Michael Oat?"

"The man who wrote *Love in False Teeth?*"

"He wants to write a play for me. One act. One man. Decides to commit suicide. Gives all the reasons why he should and why he shouldn't. And just as he has made up his mind either to do it or not to do it—curtain. Not half a bad idea."

"What's he going to call it—'Stomach Trouble'?"

"I *think* I've come across the *same* idea in a lit-tle French review, *quite* unknown in England."

No, they didn't share it. They were dears—dears—and she loved having them there, at her table, and giving them delicious food and wine. In fact, she longed to tell them how delightful they were, and what a decorative group they made, how they seemed to set one another off and how they reminded her of a play by Tchekof![3]

Harry was enjoying his dinner. It was part of his—well, not his nature, exactly, and certainly not his pose—his—something or other—to talk about food and to glory in his "shameless passion for the white flesh of the lobster" and "the green of pistachio ices—green and cold like the eyelids of Egyptian dancers."

When he looked up at her and said: "Bertha, this is a very admirable *soufflée!*" she almost could have wept with child-like pleasure.

Oh, why did she feel so tender towards the whole world tonight? Everything was good—was right. All that happened seemed to fill again her brimming cup of bliss.

And still, in the back of her mind, there was the pear tree. It would be silver now, in the light of poor dear Eddie's moon, silver as Miss Fulton, who sat there turning a tangerine in her slender fingers that were so pale a light seemed to come from them.

What she simply couldn't make out—what was miraculous—was how she should have guessed Miss Fulton's mood so exactly and so instantly. For she never doubted for a moment that she was right, and yet what had she to go on? Less than nothing.

"I believe this does happen very, very rarely between women. Never between

---

[2]Intimate (French).   [3]Anton Chekhov (1860–1904), Russian dramatist.

men," thought Bertha. "But while I am making the coffee in the drawing-room perhaps she will 'give a sign.' "

What she meant by that she did not know, and what would happen after that she could not imagine.

While she thought like this she saw herself talking and laughing. She had to talk because of her desire to laugh.

"I must laugh or die."

But when she noticed Face's funny little habit of tucking something down the front of her bodice—as if she kept a tiny, secret hoard of nuts there, too—Bertha had to dig her nails into her hands—so as not to laugh too much.

It was over at last. And: "Come and see my new coffee machine," said Bertha.

"We only have a new coffee machine once a fortnight," said Harry. Face took her arm this time; Miss Fulton bent her head and followed after.

The fire had died down in the drawing-room to a red, flickering "nest of baby phoenixes," said Face.

"Don't turn up the light for a moment. It is so lovely." And down she crouched by the fire again. She was always cold . . . "without her little red flannel jacket, of course," thought Bertha.

At that moment Miss Fulton "gave the sign."

"Have you a garden?" said the cool, sleepy voice.

This was so exquisite on her part that all Bertha could do was to obey. She crossed the room, pulled the curtains apart, and opened those long windows.

"There!" she breathed.

And the two women stood side by side looking at the slender, flowering tree. Although it was so still it seemed, like the flame of a candle, to stretch up, to point, to quiver in the bright air, to grow taller and taller as they gazed—almost to touch the rim of the round, silver moon.

How long did they stand there? Both, as it were, caught in that circle of unearthly light, understanding each other perfectly, creatures of another world, and wondering what they were to do in this one with all this blissful treasure that burned in their bosoms and dropped, in silver flowers, from their hair and hands?

For ever—for a moment? And did Miss Fulton murmur: "Yes. Just *that.*" Or did Bertha dream it?

Then the light was snapped on and Face made the coffee and Harry said: "My dear Mrs. Knight, don't ask me about my baby. I never see her. I shan't feel the slightest interest in her until she has a lover," and Mug took his eye out of the conservatory for a moment and then put it under glass again and Eddie Warren drank his coffee and set down the cup with a face of anguish as though he had drunk and seen the spider.

"What I want to do is to give the young men a show. I believe London is simply teeming with first-chop, unwritten plays. What I want to say to 'em is: 'Here's the theatre. Fire ahead.' "

"You know, my dear, I am going to decorate a room for the Jacob Nathans. Oh, I am so tempted to do a fried-fish scheme, with the backs of the chairs shaped like frying pans and lovely chip potatoes embroidered all over the curtains."

"The trouble with our young writing men is that they are still too romantic. You can't put out to sea without being seasick and wanting a basin. Well, why won't they have the courage of those basins?"

"A *dreadful* poem about a *girl* who was *violated* by a beggar *without* a nose in a lit-tle wood. . . ."

Miss Fulton sank into the lowest, deepest chair and Harry handed round the cigarettes.

From the way he stood in front of her shaking the silver box and saying abruptly: "Egyptian? Turkish? Virginian? They're all mixed up," Bertha realized that she not only bored him; he really disliked her. And she decided from the way Miss Fulton said: "No, thank you, I won't smoke," that she felt it, too, and was hurt.

"Oh, Harry, don't dislike her. You are quite wrong about her. She's wonderful, wonderful. And, besides, how can you feel so differently about someone who means so much to me. I shall try to tell you when we are in bed to-night what has been happening. What she and I have shared."

At those last words something strange and almost terrifying darted into Bertha's mind. And this something blind and smiling whispered to her: "Soon these people will go. The house will be quiet—quiet. The lights will be out. And you and he will be alone together in the dark room—the warm bed. . . ."

She jumped up from her chair and ran over to the piano.

"What a pity someone does not play!" she cried. "What a pity somebody does not play."

For the first time in her life Bertha Young desired her husband.

Oh, she'd loved him—she'd been in love with him, of course, in every other way, but just not in that way. And, equally, of course, she'd understood that he was different. They'd discussed it so often. It had worried her dreadfully at first to find that she was so cold, but after a time it had not seemed to matter. They were so frank with each other—such good pals. That was the best of being modern.

But now—ardently! ardently! The word ached in her ardent body! Was this what that feeling of bliss had been leading up to? But then then—

"My dear," said Mrs. Norman Knight, "you know our shame. We are the victims of time and train. We live in Hampstead. It's been so nice."

"I'll come with you into the hall," said Bertha. "I loved having you. But you must not miss the last train. That's so awful, isn't it?"

"Have a whisky, Knight, before you go?" called Harry.

"No, thanks, old chap."

Bertha squeezed his hand for that as she shook it.

"Good night, good-bye," she cried from the top step, feeling that this self of hers was taking leave of them for ever.

When she got back into the drawing-room the others were on the move.

". . . Then you can come part of the way in my taxi."

"I shall be *so* thankful *not* to have to face *another* drive *alone* after my *dreadful* experience."

"You can get a taxi at the rank just at the end of the street. You won't have to walk more than a few yards."

"That's a comfort. I'll go and put on my coat."

Miss Fulton moved towards the hall and Bertha was following when Harry almost pushed past.

"Let me help you."

Bertha knew that he was repenting his rudeness—she let him go. What a boy he was in some ways—so impulsive—so—simple.

And Eddie and she were left by the fire.

"I *wonder* if you have seen Bilks' *new* poem called *Table d'Hôte,*" said Eddie softly. "It's *so* wonderful. In the last Anthology. Have you got a copy? I'd *so* like to *show* it to you. It begins with an *incredibly* beautiful line: 'Why Must it Always be Tomato Soup?'"

"Yes," said Bertha. And she moved noiselessly to a table opposite the drawing-room door and Eddie glided noiselessly after her. She picked up the little book and gave it to him; they had not made a sound.

While he looked it up she turned her head towards the hall. And she saw . . . Harry with Miss Fulton's coat in his arms and Miss Fulton with her back turned to him and her head bent. He tossed the coat away, put his hands on her shoulders and turned her violently to him. His lips said: "I adore you," and Miss Fulton laid her moonbeam fingers on his cheeks and smiled her sleepy smile. Harry's nostrils quivered; his lips curled back in a hideous grin while he whispered: "To-morrow," and with her eyelids Miss Fulton said: "Yes."

"Here it is," said Eddie. "'Why Must it Always be Tomato Soup?' It's so *deeply* true, don't you feel? Tomato soup is so *dreadfully* eternal."

"If you prefer," said Harry's voice, very loud, from the hall, "I can phone you a cab to come to the door."

"Oh, no. It's not necessary," said Miss Fulton, and she came up to Bertha and gave her the slender fingers to hold.

"Good-bye. Thank you so much."

"Good-bye," said Bertha.

Miss Fulton held her hand a moment longer.

"Your lovely pear tree!" she murmured.

And then she was gone, with Eddie following, like the black cat following the grey cat.

"I'll shut up shop," said Harry, extravagantly cool and collected.

"Your lovely pear tree—pear tree—pear tree!"

Bertha simply ran over to the long windows.

"Oh, what is going to happen now?" she cried.

But the pear tree was as lovely as ever and as full of flower and as still.

QUESTIONS

1. What elements do Bertha's metaphors of the afternoon sun and the fiddle share? Where do they recur?

2. Why does she call civilization idiotic? Why does she retract her fiddle metaphor as "not quite what I mean"?

3. What is significant about the two cats Bertha sees as she looks at the pear tree? Are they symbols? Where do they recur?

4. To what extent is the pear tree, as Bertha "seemed to see it on her eyelid," actually "a symbol of her own life"? Why is it like Miss Fulton? How does the pear tree connect with the title and with the closing sentence?

5. What is the irony in Bertha's remark to herself (indirect interior monologue) that "Harry had such a zest for life"? What details in the story illustrate this zest?

6. Why does the touch of Miss Fulton's arm make Bertha's bliss "start blazing."

7. As Bertha and Miss Fulton look at the pear tree, are they "understanding each other perfectly"? Who is asserting that they are?

8. What is the irony in the two paragraphs concerning Harry's passing cigarettes to Miss Fulton? When do we perceive the irony? What does this moment tell us about the three people concerned?

9. How are we to understand the quotation marks around the "Oh, Harry . . ." paragraph?

10. Who is saying "Your lovely pear tree—pear tree—pear tree!"? What does this sentence imply?

In the next story, indirect interior monologue again generates a perpetual dramatic irony: "It was something to have a friend like that."

In Joyce's suave prose, we can examine the question of the author's voice. Who *is* saying "Eight years before . . ."? Who, "It was something to have a friend . . ."? Actually, the narrator says it all. He reports what he wants us to see and hear. His voice may be bitter or amused or wet with tears. He may quote from an ironic margin, as he does here, his character's thoughts about having such a friend. He mimics his character's voice in speech or in mind and then goes on to tell us things in his own voice. To recognize the narrator's voice and his mimicries is to deepen our pleasure in hearing its actualities and ironies and in enjoying his narrative skill. His metaphors and symbols may be his own or those of his character's widened or diminished vision. The narrator of "A Little Cloud" begins in spare, nonmetaphorical assertion and description. To what effect does metaphor enter the story?

A LITTLE CLOUD

James Joyce   (1882–1941)

Eight years before he had seen his friend off at the North Wall and wished him godspeed. Gallaher had got on. You could tell that at once by his travelled air, his well-cut tweed suit, and fearless accent. Few fellows had talents like his and fewer still could remain unspoiled by such success. Gallaher's heart was in the right place and he had deserved to win. It was something to have a friend like that.

Little Chandler's thoughts ever since lunch-time had been of his meeting with Gallaher, of Gallaher's invitation and of the great city London where Gallaher lived. He was called Little Chandler because, though he was but slightly under the average stature, he gave one the idea of being a little man. His hands were white and small, his frame was fragile, his voice was quiet and his manners were refined. He took the greatest care of his fair silken hair and moustache and used perfume discreetly on his handkerchief. The half-moons of his nails were perfect and when he smiled you caught a glimpse of a row of childish white teeth.

As he sat at his desk in the King's Inns he thought what changes those eight years had brought. The friend whom he had known under a shabby and necessitous guise had become a brilliant figure on the London Press. He turned often from his tiresome writing to gaze out of the office window. The glow of a late autumn sunset covered the grass plots and walks. It cast a shower of kindly golden dust on the untidy nurses and decrepit old men who drowsed on the benches; it flickered upon all the moving figures—on the children who ran screaming along the gravel paths and on everyone who passed through the gardens. He watched the scene and thought of life; and (as always happened when he thought of life) he became sad. A gentle melancholy took possession of him. He felt how useless it was to struggle against fortune, this being the burden of wisdom which the ages had bequeathed to him.

He remembered the books of poetry upon his shelves at home. He had bought them in his bachelor days and many an evening, as he sat in the little room off the hall, he had been tempted to take one down from the bookshelf and read out something to his wife. But shyness had always held him back; and so the books had remained on their shelves. At times he repeated lines to himself and this consoled him.

When his hour had struck he stood up and took leave of his desk and of his fellow-clerks punctiliously. He emerged from under the feudal arch of the King's Inns, a neat modest figure, and walked swiftly down Henrietta Street. The golden sunset was waning and the air had grown sharp. A horde of grimy children populated the street. They stood or ran in the roadway or crawled up the steps before the gaping doors or squatted like mice upon the thresholds. Little Chandler gave them no thought. He picked his way deftly through all that minute vermin-like life and under the shadow of the gaunt spectral mansions in which the old nobility of Dublin had roistered. No memory of the past touched him, for his mind was full of a present joy.

He had never been in Corless's but he knew the value of the name. He knew that people went there after the theatre to eat oysters and drink liqueurs; and he had heard that the waiters there spoke French and German. Walking swiftly by at night he had seen cabs drawn up before the door and richly dressed ladies, escorted by cavaliers, alight and enter quickly. They wore noisy dresses and many wraps. Their faces were powdered and they caught up their dresses, when they touched earth, like alarmed Atalantas.[1] He had always passed without turning his head to look. It was his habit to walk swiftly in the street even by day and whenever he found himself in the city late at night he hurried on his way apprehensively and excitedly. Sometimes, however, he courted the causes of his fear. He chose the darkest and narrowest streets and, as he walked boldly forward, the silence that was spread about his footsteps troubled him, the wandering silent figures troubled him; and at times a sound of low fugitive laughter made him tremble like a leaf.

He turned to the right towards Capel Street. Ignatius Gallaher on the London Press! Who would have thought it possible eight years before? Still, now that he reviewed the past, Little Chandler could remember many signs of future greatness in his friend. People used to say that Ignatius Gallaher was wild. Of course, he did mix with a rakish set of fellows at that time, drank freely and borrowed money on all sides. In the end he had got mixed up in some shady affair, some money transaction: at least, that was one version of his flight. But nobody denied him talent. There was always a certain . . . something in Ignatius Gallaher that impressed you in spite of yourself. Even when he was out at elbows and at his wits' end for money he kept up a bold face. Little Chandler remembered (and the remembrance brought a slight flush of pride to his cheek) one of Ignatius Gallaher's sayings when he was in a tight corner:

—Half time, now, boys, he used to say light-heartedly. Where's my considering cap?

That was Ignatius Gallaher all out; and, damn it, you couldn't but admire him for it.

Little Chandler quickened his pace. For the first time in his life he felt himself superior to the people he passed. For the first time his soul revolted against the dull inelegance of Capel Street. There was no doubt about it: if you wanted to succeed you had to go away. You could do nothing in Dublin. As he crossed Grattan Bridge he looked down the river towards the lower quays and pitied the poor stunted houses. They seemed to him a band of tramps, huddled together along the river-banks, their old coats covered with dust and soot, stupefied by the panorama of sunset and waiting for the first chill of night to bid them arise, shake themselves and be gone. He wondered whether he could write a poem to express his idea. Perhaps Gallaher might be able to get it into some London paper for him. Could he write something original? He was not sure what idea he wished to express but the thought that a poetic moment had touched him took life within him like an infant hope. He stepped onward bravely.

Every step brought him nearer to London, farther from his own sober inartistic life. A light began to tremble on the horizon of his mind. He was not so old— thirty-two. His temperament might be said to be just at the point of maturity. There were so many different moods and impressions that he wished to express in verse. He felt them within him. He tried to weigh his soul to see if it was a

---

[1]Atalanta, swift-footed maiden of Greek myth, offered to marry any man who could run fast enough to defeat her in a race.

poet's soul. Melancholy was the dominant note of his temperament, he thought, but it was a melancholy tempered by recurrences of faith and resignation and simple joy. If he could give expression to it in a book of poems perhaps men would listen. He would never be popular: he saw that. He could not sway the crowd but he might appeal to a little circle of kindred minds. The English critics, perhaps, would recognize him as one of the Celtic school by reason of the melancholy tone of his poems; besides that, he would put in allusions. He began to invent sentences and phrases from the notices which his book would get. *Mr. Chandler has the gift of easy and graceful verse. . . . A wistful sadness pervades these poems. . . . The Celtic note.* It was a pity his name was not more Irish-looking. Perhaps it would be better to insert his mother's name before the surname: Thomas Malone Chandler, or better still: T. Malone Chandler. He would speak to Gallaher about it.

He pursued his revery so ardently that he passed his street and had to turn back. As he came near Corless's his former agitation began to overmaster him and he halted before the door in indecision. Finally he opened the door and entered.

The light and noise of the bar held him at the doorway for a few moments. He looked about him, but his sight was confused by the shining of many red and green wine-glasses. The bar seemed to him to be full of people and he felt that the people were observing him curiously. He glanced quickly to right and left (frowning slightly to make his errand appear serious), but when his sight cleared a little he saw that nobody had turned to look at him: and there, sure enough, was Ignatius Gallaher leaning with his back against the counter and his feet planted far apart.

—Hallo, Tommy, old hero, here you are! What is it to be? What will you have? I'm taking whisky: better stuff than we get across the water. Soda? Lithia?[2] No mineral? I'm the same. Spoils the flavour. . . . Here, *garçon,* bring us two halves of malt whisky, like a good fellow. . . . Well, and how have you been pulling along since I saw you last? Dear God, how old we're getting! Do you see any signs of aging in me—eh, what! A little grey and thin on the top—what?

Ignatius Gallaher took off his hat and displayed a large closely cropped head. His face was heavy, pale and clean-shaven. His eyes, which were of bluish slate-colour, relieved his unhealthy pallor and shone out plainly above the vivid orange tie he wore. Between these rival features the lips appeared very long and shapeless and colourless. He bent his head and felt with two sympathetic fingers the thin hair at the crown. Little Chandler shook his head as a denial. Ignatius Gallaher put on his hat again.

—It pulls you down, he said, Press life. Always hurry and scurry, looking for copy and sometimes not finding it: and then, always to have something new in your stuff. Damn proofs and printers, I say, for a few days. I'm deuced glad, I can tell you, to get back to the old country. Does a fellow good, a bit of a holiday. I feel a ton better since I landed again in dear dirty Dublin. . . . Here you are, Tommy. Water? Say when.

---

[2]A medicinal mineral water.

Little Chandler allowed his whisky to be very much diluted.

—You don't know what's good for you, my boy, said Ignatius Gallaher. I drink mine neat.

—I drink very little as a rule, said Little Chandler modestly. An odd half-one or so when I meet any of the old crowd: that's all.

—Ah, well, said Ignatius Gallaher, cheerfully, here's to us and to old times and old acquaintance.

They clinked glasses and drank the toast.

—I met some of the old gang to-day, said Ignatius Gallaher. O'Hara seems to be in a bad way. What's he doing?

—Nothing, said Little Chandler. He's gone to the dogs.

—But Hogan has a good sit, hasn't he?

—Yes; he's in the Land Commission.

—I met him one night in London and he seemed to be very flush. . . . Poor O'Hara! Boose, I suppose?

—Other things, too, said Little Chandler shortly.

Ignatius Gallaher laughed.

—Tommy, he said, I see you haven't changed an atom. You're the very same serious person that used to lecture me on Sunday mornings when I had a sore head and a fur on my tongue. You'd want to knock about a bit in the world. Have you never been anywhere, even for a trip?

—I've been to the Isle of Man, said Little Chandler.

Ignatius Gallaher laughed.

—The Isle of Man! he said. Go to London or Paris: Paris, for choice. That'd do you good.

—Have you seen Paris?

—I should think I have! I've knocked about there a little.

—And is it really so beautiful as they say? asked Little Chandler.

He sipped a little of his drink while Ignatius Gallaher finished his boldly.

—Beautiful? said Ignatius Gallaher, pausing on the word and on the flavour of his drink. It's not so beautiful, you know. Of course, it is beautiful. . . . But it's the life of Paris; that's the thing. Ah, there's no city like Paris for gaiety, movement, excitement. . . .

Little Chandler finished his whisky and, after some trouble, succeeded in catching the barman's eye. He ordered the same again.

—I've been to the Moulin Rouge,[3] Ignatius Gallaher continued when the barman had removed their glasses, and I've been to all the Bohemian cafés. Hot stuff! Not for a pious chap like you, Tommy.

Little Chandler said nothing until the barman returned with the two glasses: then he touched his friend's glass lightly and reciprocated the former toast. He was beginning to feel somewhat disillusioned. Gallaher's accent and way of expressing himself did not please him. There was something vulgar in his friend which he had not observed before. But perhaps it was only the result of living

[3]Paris nightclub.

in London amid the bustle and competition of the Press. The old personal charm was still there under this new gaudy manner. And, after all, Gallaher had lived, he had seen the world. Little Chandler looked at his friend enviously.

—Everything in Paris is gay, said Ignatius Gallaher. They believe in enjoying life—and don't you think they're right? If you want to enjoy yourself properly you must go to Paris. And, mind you, they've a great feeling for the Irish there. When they heard I was from Ireland they were ready to eat me, man.

Little Chandler took four or five sips from his glass.

—Tell me, he said, is it true that Paris is so . . . immoral as they say?

Ignatius Gallaher made a catholic gesture with his right arm.

—Every place is immoral, he said. Of course you do find spicy bits in Paris. Go to one of the students' balls, for instance. That's lively, if you like, when the *cocottes*[4] begin to let themselves loose. You know what they are, I suppose?

—I've heard of them, said Little Chandler.

Ignatius Gallaher drank off his whisky and shook his head.

—Ah, he said, you may say what you like. There's no woman like the Parisienne—for style, for go.

—Then it is an immoral city, said Little Chandler, with timid insistence—I mean, compared with London or Dublin?

—London! said Ignatius Gallaher. It's six of one and half-a-dozen of the other. You ask Hogan, my boy. I showed him a bit about London when he was over there. He'd open your eye. . . . I say, Tommy, don't make punch of that whisky: liquor up.

—No, really. . . .

—O, come on, another one won't do you any harm. What is it? The same again, I suppose?

—Well . . . all right.

—*François,* the same again. . . . Will you smoke, Tommy?

Ignatius Gallaher produced his cigar-case. The two friends lit their cigars and puffed at them in silence until their drinks were served.

—I'll tell you my opinion, said Ignatius Gallaher, emerging after some time from the clouds of smoke in which he had taken refuge, it's a rum world. Talk of immorality! I've heard of cases—what am I saying?—I've known them: cases of . . . immorality. . . .

Ignatius Gallaher puffed thoughtfully at his cigar and then, in a calm historian's tone, he proceeded to sketch for his friend some pictures of the corruption which was rife abroad. He summarized the vices of many capitals and seemed inclined to award the palm to Berlin. Some things he could not vouch for (his friends had told him), but of others he had had personal experience. He spared neither rank nor caste. He revealed many of the secrets of religious houses on the Continent and described some of the practices which were fashionable in high society and ended by telling, with details, a story about an English duchess—a story which he knew to be true. Little Chandler was astonished.

[4]"Loose women."

—Ah, well, said Ignatius Gallaher, here we are in old jog-along Dublin where nothing is known of such things.

—How dull you must find it, said Little Chandler, after all the other places you've seen!

—Well, said Ignatius Gallaher, it's a relaxation to come over here, you know. And, after all, it's the old country, as they say, isn't it? You can't help having a certain feeling for it. That's human nature. . . . But tell me something about yourself. Hogan told me you had . . . tasted the joys of connubial bliss. Two years ago, wasn't it?

Little Chandler blushed and smiled.

—Yes, he said. I was married last May twelve months.

—I hope it's not too late in the day to offer my best wishes, said Ignatius Gallaher. I didn't know your address or I'd have done so at the time.

He extended his hand, which Little Chandler took.

—Well, Tommy, he said, I wish you and yours every joy in life, old chap, and tons of money, and may you never die till I shoot you. And that's the wish of a sincere friend, an old friend. You know that?

—I know that, said Little Chandler.

—Any youngsters? said Ignatius Gallaher.

Little Chandler blushed again.

—We have one child, he said.

—Son or daughter?

—A little boy.

Ignatius Gallaher slapped his friend sonorously on the back.

—Bravo, he said, I wouldn't doubt you, Tommy.

Little Chandler smiled, looked confusedly at his glass and bit his lower lip with three childishly white front teeth.

—I hope you'll spend an evening with us, he said, before you go back. My wife will be delighted to meet you. We can have a little music and—

—Thanks awfully, old chap, said Ignatius Gallaher, I'm sorry we didn't meet earlier. But I must leave tomorrow night.

—To-night, perhaps. . .?

—I'm awfully sorry, old man. You see I'm over here with another fellow, clever young chap he is too, and we arranged to go to a little card-party. Only for that . . .

—O, in that case. . . .

—But who knows? said Ignatius Gallaher considerately. Next year I may take a little skip over here now that I've broken the ice. It's only a pleasure deferred.

—Very well, said Little Chandler, the next time you come we must have an evening together. That's agreed now, isn't it?

—Yes, that's agreed, said Ignatius Gallaher. Next year if I come, *parole d'honneur.*[5]

---

[5]"Word of honor."

—And to clinch the bargain, said Little Chandler, we'll just have one more now.

Ignatius Gallaher took out a large gold watch and looked at it.

—Is it to be the last? he said. Because you know, I have an a.p.

—O, yes, positively, said Little Chandler.

—Very well, then, said Ignatius Gallaher, let us have another one as a *deoc an doruis*—that's good vernacular[6] for a small whisky, I believe.

Little Chandler ordered the drinks. The blush which had risen to his face a few moments before was establishing itself. A trifle made him blush at any time: and now he felt warm and excited. Three small whiskies had gone to his head and Gallaher's strong cigar had confused his mind, for he was a delicate and abstinent person. The adventure of meeting Gallaher after eight years, of finding himself with Gallaher in Corless's surrounded by lights and noise, of listening to Gallaher's stories and of sharing for a brief space Gallaher's vagrant and triumphant life, upset the equipoise of his sensitive nature. He felt acutely the contrast between his own life and his friend's, and it seemed to him unjust. Gallaher was his inferior in birth and education. He was sure that he could do something better than his friend had ever done, or could ever do, something higher than mere tawdry journalism if he only got the chance. What was it that stood in his way? His unfortunate timidity! He wished to vindicate himself in some way, to assert his manhood. He saw behind Gallaher's refusal of his invitation. Gallaher was only patronizing him by his friendliness just as he was patronizing Ireland by his visit.

The barman brought their drinks. Little Chandler pushed one glass towards his friend and took up the other boldly.

—Who knows? he said, as they lifted their glasses. When you come next year I may have the pleasure of wishing long life and happiness to Mr and Mrs Ignatius Gallaher.

Ignatius Gallaher in the act of drinking closed one eye expressively over the rim of his glass. When he had drunk he smacked his lips decisively, set down his glass and said:

—No blooming fear of that, my boy. I'm going to have my fling first and see a bit of life and the world before I put my head in the sack—if I ever do.

—Some day you will, said Little Chandler calmly.

Ignatius Gallaher turned his orange tie and slate-blue eyes full upon his friend.

—You think so? he said

—You'll put your head in the sack, repeated Little Chandler stoutly, like everyone else if you can find the girl.

He had slightly emphasised his tone and he was aware that he had betrayed himself; but, though the colour had heightened in his cheek, he did not flinch from his friend's gaze. Ignatius Gallaher watched him for a few moments and then said:

—If ever it occurs, you may bet your bottom dollar there'll be no mooning and

[6]I.e., Irish Gaelic.

spooning about it. I mean to marry money. She'll have a good fat account at the bank or she won't do for me.

Little Chandler shook his head.

—Why, man alive, said Ignatius Gallaher, vehemently, do you know what it is? I've only to say the word and to-morrow I can have the woman and the cash. You don't believe it? Well, I know it. There are hundreds—what am I saying? —thousands of rich Germans and Jews, rotten with money, that'd only be too glad. . . . You wait a while, my boy. See if I don't play my cards properly. When I go about a thing I mean business, I tell you. You just wait.

He tossed his glass to his mouth, finished his drink and laughed loudly. Then he looked thoughtfully before him and said in a calmer tone:

—But I'm in no hurry. They can wait. I don't fancy tying myself up to one woman, you know.

He imitated with his mouth the act of tasting and made a wry face.

—Must get a bit stale, I should think, he said.

• • •

Little Chandler sat in the room off the hall, holding a child in his arms. To save money they kept no servant but Annie's young sister Monica came for an hour or so in the morning and an hour or so in the evening to help. But Monica had gone home long ago. It was a quarter to nine. Little Chandler had come home late for tea and, moreover, he had forgotten to bring Annie home the parcel of coffee from Bewley's. Of course she was in a bad humour and gave him short answers. She said she would do without any tea but when it came near the time at which the shop at the corner closed she decided to go out herself for a quarter of a pound of tea and two pounds of sugar. She put the sleeping child deftly in his arms and said:

—Here. Don't waken him.

A little lamp with a white china shade stood upon the table and its light fell over a photograph which was enclosed in a frame of crumpled horn. It was Annie's photograph. Little Chandler looked at it, pausing at the thin tight lips. She wore the pale blue summer blouse which he had brought her home as a present one Saturday. It had cost him ten and elevenpence; but what an agony of nervousness it had cost him! How he had suffered that day, waiting at the shop door until the shop was empty, standing at the counter and trying to appear at his ease while the girl piled ladies' blouses before him, paying at the desk and forgetting to take up the odd penny of his change, being called back by the cashier, and, finally, striving to hide his blushes as he left the shop by examining the parcel to see if it was securely tied. When he brought the blouse home Annie kissed him and said it was very pretty and stylish; but when she heard the price she threw the blouse on the table and said it was a regular swindle to charge ten and elevenpence for that. At first she wanted to take it back but when she tried it on she was delighted with it, especially with the make of the sleeves, and kissed him and said he was very good to think of her.

Hm! . . .

He looked coldly into the eyes of the photograph and they answered coldly. Certainly they were pretty and the face itself was pretty. But he found something mean in it. Why was it so unconscious and lady-like? The composure of the eyes irritated him. They repelled him and defied him: there was no passion in them, no rapture. He thought of what Gallaher had said about rich Jewesses. Those dark Oriental eyes, he thought, how full they are of passion, of voluptuous longing! . . . Why had he married the eyes in the photograph?

He caught himself up at the question and glanced nervously around the room. He found something mean in the pretty furniture which he had bought for his house on the hire system. Annie had chosen it herself and it reminded him of her. It too was prim and pretty. A dull resentment against his life awoke within him. Could he not escape from his little house? Was it too late for him to try to live bravely like Gallaher? Could he go to London? There was the furniture still to be paid for. If he could only write a book and get it published, that might open the way for him.

A volume of Byron's poems lay before him on the table. He opened it cautiously with his left hand lest he should waken the child and began to read the first poem in the book:[7]

> Hushed are the winds and still the evening gloom,
>   Not e'en a Zephyr wanders through the grove,
> Whilst I return to view my Margaret's tomb
> And scatter flowers on the dust I love.

He paused. He felt the rhythm of the verse about him in the room. How melancholy it was! Could he, too, write like that, express the melancholy of his soul in verse? There were so many things he wanted to describe: his sensation of a few hours before on Grattan Bridge, for example. If he could get back again into that mood. . . .

The child awoke and began to cry. He turned from the page and tried to hush it: but it would not be hushed. He began to rock it to and fro in his arms but its wailing cry grew keener. He rocked it faster while his eyes began to read the second stanza:

> Within this narrow cell reclines her clay,
>   That clay where once . . .

It was useless. He couldn't read. He couldn't do anything. The wailing of the child pierced the drum of his ear. It was useless, useless! He was a prisoner for life. His arms trembled with anger and suddenly bending to the child's face he shouted:

—Stop!

The child stopped for an instant, had a spasm of fright and began to scream. He jumped up from his chair and walked hastily up and down the room with the child in his arms. It began to sob piteously, losing its breath for four or five

[7]The opening lines of Byron's "On The Death of a Young Lady."

seconds, and then bursting out anew. The thin walls of the room echoed the sound. He tried to soothe it but it sobbed more convulsively. He looked at the contracted and quivering face of the child and began to be alarmed. He counted seven sobs without a break between them and caught the child to his breast in fright. If it died! . . .

The door was burst open and a young woman ran in, panting.

—What is it? What is it? she cried.

The child, hearing its mother's voice, broke out into a paroxysm of sobbing.

—It's nothing, Annie . . . it's nothing. . . . He began to cry . . .

She flung her parcels on the floor and snatched the child from him.

—What have you done to him? she cried, glaring into his face.

Little Chandler sustained for one moment the gaze of her eyes and his heart closed together as he met the hatred in them. He began to stammer:

—It's nothing. . . . He . . . he began to cry. . . . I couldn't . . . I didn't do anything. . . . What?

Giving no heed to him she began to walk up and down the room, clasping the child tightly in her arms and murmuring:

—My little man! My little mannie! Was 'ou frightened, love? . . . There now, love! There now! . . . Lambabaun! Mamma's little lamb of the world! . . . There now!

Little Chandler felt his cheeks suffused with shame and he stood back out of the lamplight. He listened while the paroxysm of the child's sobbing grew less and less; and tears of remorse started to his eyes.

QUESTIONS

1. Where does metaphor enter the story? What distinguishes the narrator's metaphors from Chandler's?
2. What are the "many signs of future greatness" in Gallaher?
3. What is the dramatic irony in Chandler's "poetic moment" and his subsequent thoughts about writing poetry?
4. What is the irony in the sentence concluding the third paragraph?— "He felt how useless it was to struggle against fortune, this being the burden of wisdom which the ages had bequeathed him"? Whose voice do we hear?
5. What are the implications in Chandler's trip to the Isle of Man and Gallaher's amusement at it?
6. Characterize Gallaher. How far do our views and Chandler's views of Gallaher agree? Why does Gallaher envy him?
7. What are the differences in perception between Chandler's view of Gallaher and Chandler's view of his wife?
8. What is the significance of Mrs. Chandler's "My little man!"?
9. In what sense is Chandler "a prisoner for life"?
10. Why does Joyce end with "tears of remorse"?
11. What is the significance of Joyce's title?

In Barth's "Lost in the Funhouse" we can trace allegories on three levels: the funhouse of adolescence, the funhouse of life, and the funhouse of art—especially in creating the funhouse of fiction. The actual funhouse at Ocean City becomes the supreme symbol for all our excursions after pleasure, as Fat May laughs and everyone laughs with her. Barth spoofs the creative act, including that of sex, especially in those persistent fables we create for ourselves, awake and asleep: "each saw himself as the hero of the story," as Barth's young hero says. Barth also spoofs literary criticism and the very act of critical reading we are this instant doing as we seek to understand and enjoy what he seems this instant to be writing. Yet as Barth breaks off his sentences and breaks through the illusion of reality he is creating, he also exhibits the fabulous power of fiction to engage us in belief. What contributes to the illusion that Ambrose and the other characters are real people?

LOST IN THE FUNHOUSE
John Barth   (1930–   )

For whom is the funhouse fun? Perhaps for lovers. For Ambrose it is *a place of fear and confusion.* He has come to the seashore with his family for the holiday, *the occasion of their visit is Independence Day, the most important secular holiday of the United States of America.* A single straight underline is the manuscript mark for italic type, *which in turn* is the printed equivalent to oral emphasis of words and phrases as well as the customary type for titles of complete works, not to mention. Italics are also employed, in fiction stories especially, for "outside," intrusive, or artificial voices, such as radio announcements, the texts of telegrams and newspaper articles, et cetera. They should be used *sparingly.* If passages originally in roman type are italicized by someone repeating them, it's customary to acknowledge the fact. *Italics mine.*

Ambrose was "at that awkward age." His voice came out high-pitched as a child's if he let himself get carried away; to be on the safe side, therefore, he moved and spoke with *deliberate calm* and *adult gravity.* Talking soberly of unimportant or irrelevant matters and listening consciously to the sound of your own voice are useful habits for maintaining control in this difficult interval. *En route* to Ocean City he sat in the back seat of the family car with his brother Peter, age fifteen, and Magda G———, age fourteen, a pretty girl an exquisite young lady, who lived not far from them on B——— Street in the town of D———, Maryland. Initials, blanks, or both were often substituted for proper names in nineteenth-century fiction to enhance the illusion of reality. It is as if the author felt it necessary to delete the names for reasons of tact or legal liability. Interestingly, as with other aspects of realism, it is an *illusion* that is being enhanced, by purely artificial means. Is it likely, does it violate the principle of verisimilitude, that a thirteen-year-old boy could make such a sophisticated observation? A girl of fourteen is *the psychological coeval* of a boy of fifteen or sixteen; a thirteen-year-old boy, therefore, even one precocious in some other respects, might be three years *her emotional junior.*

Thrice a year—on Memorial, Independence, and Labor Days—the family visits Ocean City for the afternoon and evening. When Ambrose and Peter's father was their age, the excursion was made by train, as mentioned in the novel *The 42nd Parallel* by John Dos Passos. Many families from the same neighborhood used to travel together, with dependent relatives and often with Negro servants; schoolfuls of children swarmed through the railway cars; everyone shared everyone else's Maryland fried chicken, Virginia ham, deviled eggs, potato salad, beaten biscuits, iced tea. Nowadays (that is, in 19———, the year of our story) the journey is made by automobile—more comfortably and quickly though without the extra fun though without the *camaraderie* of a general excursion. It's all part of the deterioration of American life, their father declares; Uncle Karl supposes that when the boys take *their* families to Ocean City for the holidays they'll fly in Autogiros. Their mother, sitting in the middle of the front seat like Magda in the second, only with her arms on the seat-back behind the men's shoulders, wouldn't want the good old days back again, the steaming trains and stuffy long dresses; on the other hand she can do without Autogiros, too, if she has to become a grandmother to fly in them.

Description of physical appearance and mannerisms is one of several standard methods of characterization used by writers of fiction. It is also important to "keep the senses operating"; when a detail from one of the five senses, say visual, is "crossed" with a detail from another, say auditory, the reader's imagination is oriented to the scene, perhaps unconsciously. This procedure may be compared to the way surveyors and navigators determine their positions by two or more compass bearings, a process known as triangulation. The brown hair on Ambrose's mother's forearms gleamed in the sun like. Though right-handed, she took her left arm from the seat-back to press the dashboard cigar lighter for Uncle Karl. When the glass bead in its handle glowed red, the lighter was ready for use. The smell of Uncle Karl's cigar smoke reminded one of. The fragrance of the ocean came strong to the picnic ground where they always stopped for lunch, two miles inland from Ocean City. Having to pause for a full hour almost within sound of the breakers was difficult for Peter and Ambrose when they were younger; even at their present age it was not easy to keep their anticipation, *stimulated by the briny spume,* from turning into short temper. The Irish author James Joyce, in his unusual novel entitled *Ulysses,* now available in this country, uses the adjectives *snot-green* and *scrotum-tightening* to describe the sea. Visual, auditory, tactile, olfactory, gustatory. Peter and Ambrose's father, while steering their black 1936 LaSalle sedan with one hand, could with the other remove the first cigarette from a white pack of Lucky Strikes and, more remarkably, light it with a match forefingered from its book and thumbed against the flint paper without being detached. The matchbook cover merely advertised U. S. War Bonds and Stamps. A fine metaphor, simile, or other figure of speech, in addition to its obvious "first-order" relevance to the thing it describes, will be seen upon reflection to have a second order of significance: it may be drawn from the *milieu* of the action, for example, or be particularly appropriate to the sensibility of the narrator, even hinting to the reader things of which the narrator is unaware; or it may cast further and subtler lights upon the thing it describes, sometimes ironically qualifying the more evident sense of the comparison.

To say that Ambrose's and Peter's mother was *pretty* is to accomplish nothing; the reader may acknowledge the proposition, but his imagination is not engaged. Besides, Magda was also pretty, yet in an altogether different way. Although she lived on B——— Street she had very good manners and did better than average in school. Her figure was very well developed for her age. Her right hand lay casually on the plush upholstery of the seat, very near Ambrose's left leg, on which his own hand rested. The space between their legs, between her right and his left leg, was out of the line of sight of anyone sitting on the other side of Magda, as well as anyone glancing into the rear-view mirror. Uncle Karl's face resembled Peter's—rather, vice versa. Both had dark hair and eyes, short husky statures, deep voices. Magda's left hand was probably in a similar position on her left side. The boy's father is difficult to describe; no particular feature of his appearance or manner stood out. He wore glasses and was principal of a T——— County grade school. Uncle Karl was a masonry contractor.

Although Peter must have known as well as Ambrose that the latter, because of his position in the car, would be the first to see the electrical towers of the power plant at V———, the halfway point of their trip, he leaned forward and slightly toward the center of the car and pretended to be looking for them through the flat pinewoods and tuckahoe creeks along the highway. For as long as the boys could remember, "looking for the Towers" had been a feature of the first half of their excursions to Ocean City, "looking for the standpipe" of the second. Though the game was childish, their mother preserved the tradition of rewarding the first to see the Towers with a candy-bar or piece of fruit. She insisted now that Magda play the game; the prize, she said, was "something hard to get nowadays." Ambrose decided not to join in; he sat far back in his seat. Magda, like Peter, leaned forward. Two sets of straps were discernible through the shoulders of her sun dress; the inside right one, a brassiere-strap, was fastened or shortened with a small safety pin. The right armpit of her dress, presumably the left as well, was damp with perspiration. The simple strategy for being first to espy the Towers, which Ambrose had understood by the age of four, was to sit on the right-hand side of the car. Whoever sat there, however, had also to put up with the worst of the sun, and so Ambrose, without mentioning the matter, chose sometimes the one and sometimes the other. Not impossibly Peter had never caught on to the trick, or thought that his brother hadn't simply because Ambrose on occasion preferred shade to a Baby Ruth or tangerine.

The shade-sun situation didn't apply to the front seat, owing to the windshield; if anything the driver got more sun, since the person on the passenger side not only was shaded below by the door and dashboard but might swing down his sunvisor all the way too.

"Is that them?" Magda asked. Ambrose's mother teased the boys for letting Magda win, insinuating that "somebody [had] a girlfriend." Peter and Ambrose's father reached a long thin arm across their mother to butt his cigarette in the dashboard ashtray, under the lighter. The prize this time for seeing the Towers first was a banana. Their mother bestowed it after chiding their father for wasting a half-smoked cigarette when everything was so scarce. Magda, to take the prize, moved her hand from so near Ambrose's that he could have touched it as though accidentally. She offered to share the prize, things like that were so hard to find; but everyone insisted it was hers alone. Ambrose's mother sang an iambic trimeter couplet from a popular song, femininely rhymed:

> "What's good is in the Army;
>   What's left will never harm me."

Uncle Karl tapped his cigar ash out the ventilator window; some particles were sucked by the slipstream back into the car through the rear window on the passenger side. Magda demonstrated her ability to hold a banana in one hand and peel it with her teeth. She still sat forward; Ambrose pushed his glasses back onto the bridge of his nose with his left hand, which he then negligently let fall to the seat cushion immediately behind her. He even permitted the single hair, gold, on the second joint of his thumb to brush the fabric of her skirt. Should she have sat back at that instant, his hand would have been caught under her.

Plush upholstery prickles uncomfortably through gabardine slacks in the July sun. The function of the *beginning* of a story is to introduce the principal characters, establish their initial relationships, set the scene for the main action, expose the background of the situation if necessary, plant motifs and foreshadowings where appropriate, and initiate the first complication or whatever of the "rising action." Actually, if one imagines a story called "The Funhouse," or "Lost in the Funhouse," the details of the drive to Ocean City don't seem especially relevant. The *beginning* should recount the events between Ambrose's first sight of the funhouse early in the afternoon and his entering it with Magda and Peter in the evening. The *middle* would narrate all relevant events from the time he goes in to the time he loses his way; middles have the double and contradictory function of delaying the climax while at the same time preparing the reader for it and fetching him to it. Then the *ending* would tell what Ambrose does while he's lost, how he finally finds his way out, and what everybody makes of the experience. So far there's been no real dialogue, very little sensory detail, and nothing in the way of a *theme.* And a long time has gone by already without anything happening; it makes a person wonder. We haven't even reached Ocean City yet: we will never get out of the funhouse.

The more closely an author identifies with the narrator, literally or metaphorically, the less advisable it is, as a rule, to use the first-person narrative viewpoint. Once three years previously the young people *aforementioned* played Niggers and Masters in the backyard; when it was Ambrose's turn to be Master and theirs to be Niggers Peter had to go serve his evening papers; Ambrose was afraid to punish Magda alone, but she led him to the whitewashed Torture Chamber between the woodshed and the privy in the Slaves Quarters; there she knelt sweating among bamboo rakes and dusty Mason jars, pleadingly embraced his knees, and while bees droned in the lattice as if on an ordinary summer afternoon, purchased clemency at a surprising price set by herself.

Doubtless she remembered nothing of this event; Ambrose on the other hand seemed unable to forget the least detail of his life. He even recalled how, standing beside himself with awed impersonality in the reeky heat, he'd stared the while at an empty cigar box in which Uncle Karl kept stone-cutting chisels: beneath the words *El Producto,* a laureled, loose-toga'd lady regarded the sea from a marble bench; beside her, forgotten or not yet turned to, was a five-stringed lyre. Her chin reposed on the back of her right hand; her left depended negligently from the bench-arm. The lower half of scene and lady was peeled away; the words EXAMINED BY——— were inked there into the wood. Nowadays cigar boxes are made of pasteboard. Ambrose wondered what Magda would have done, Ambrose wondered what Magda would do when she sat back on his hand as he resolved she should. Be angry. Make a teasing joke of it. Give no sign at all. For a long time she leaned forward, playing cow-poker with Peter against Uncle Karl and Mother and watching for the first sign of Ocean City. At nearly the same instant, picnic ground and Ocean City stand-pipe hove into view; an Amoco filling station on their side of the road cost Mother and Uncle Karl fifty cows and the game; Magda bounced back, clapping her right hand on Mother's right arm; Ambrose moved clear "in the nick of time."

At this rate our hero, at this rate our protagonist will remain in the funhouse forever. Narrative ordinarily consists of alternating dramatization and summarization. One symptom of nervous tension, paradoxically, is repeated and violent yawning; neither Peter nor Magda nor Uncle Karl nor Mother reacted in this manner. Although they were no longer small children, Peter and Ambrose were each given a dollar to spend on boardwalk amusements in addition to what money of their own they'd brought along. Magda too, though she protested she had ample spending money. The boys' mother made a little scene out of distributing the bills; she pretended that her sons and Magda were small children and cautioned them not to spend the sum too quickly or in one place. Magda promised with a merry laugh and, having both hands free, took the bill with her left. Peter laughed also and pledged in a falsetto to be a good boy. His imitation of a child was not clever. The boys' father was tall and thin, balding, fair-complexioned. Assertions of that sort are not effective; the reader may acknowledge the proposition, but. We should be much farther along than we are; something has gone wrong; not much of this preliminary rambling seems relevant. Yet everyone begins in the same place; how is it that most go along without difficulty but a few lose their way?

"Stay out from under the boardwalk," Uncle Karl growled from the side of his mouth. The boys' mother pushed his shoulder *in mock annoyance.* They were all standing before Fat May the Laughing Lady who advertised the funhouse. Larger than life, Fat May mechanically shook, rocked on her heels, slapped her thighs while recorded laughter—uproarious, female—came amplified from a hidden loudspeaker. It chuckled, wheezed, wept; tried in vain to catch its breath; tittered, groaned, exploded raucous and anew. You couldn't hear it without laughing yourself, no matter how you felt. Father came back from talking to a Coast-Guardsman on duty and reported that the surf was spoiled with crude oil from tankers recently torpedoed offshore. Lumps of it, difficult to remove, made tarry tidelines on the beach and stuck on swimmers. Many bathed in the surf nevertheless and came out speckled; others paid to use a municipal pool and only sunbathed on the beach. We would do the latter. We would do the latter. We would do the latter.

Under the boardwalk, matchbook covers, grainy other things. What is the story's theme? Ambrose is ill. He perspires in the dark passages; candied apples-on-a-stick, delicious-looking, disappointing to eat. Funhouses need men's and ladies' room at intervals. Others perhaps have also vomited in corners and corridors; may even have had bowel movements liable to be stepped in in the dark. The word *fuck* suggests suction and/or and/or flatulence. Mother and Father; grandmothers and grandfathers on both sides; great-grandmothers and great-grandfathers on four sides, et cetera. Count a generation as thirty years: in approximately the year when Lord Baltimore was granted charter to the province of Maryland by Charles I, five hundred twelve women—English, Welsh, Bavarian, Swiss—of every class and character, received into themselves the penises the intromittent organs of five hundred twelve men, ditto, in every circumstance and posture, to conceive the five hundred twelve ancestors of the two hundred fifty-six ancestors of the et cetera et cetera et cetera et cetera et cetera et cetera et cetera et cetera of the author, of the narrator, of this story, *Lost in the Funhouse.* In alleyways, ditches, canopy beds, pinewoods, bridal suites, ship's cabins, coach-and-fours, coaches-and-four, sultry toolsheds; on the cold sand under boardwalks, littered with *El Producto* cigar butts, treasured with Lucky Strike cigarette stubs, Coca-Cola caps, gritty turds, cardboard lollipop sticks, matchbook covers warning that A Slip of the Lip Can Sink a Ship. The shluppish whisper, continuous as seawash round the globe, tidelike falls and rises with the circuit of dawn and dusk.

Magda's teeth. She *was* left-handed. Perspiration. They've gone all the way, through, Magda and Peter, they've been waiting for hours with Mother and Uncle Karl while Father searches for his lost son; they draw french-fried potatoes from a paper cup and shake their heads. They've named the children they'll one day have and bring to Ocean City on holidays. Can spermatozoa properly be thought of as male animalcules when there are no female spermatozoa? They grope through hot, dark windings, past Love's Tunnel's fearsome obstacles. Some perhaps lose their way.

Peter suggested then and there that they do the funhouse; he had been through it before, so had Magda, Ambrose hadn't and suggested, his voice cracking on account of Fat May's laughter, that they swim first. All were chuckling, couldn't help it; Ambrose's father, Ambrose's and Peter's father came up grinning like a lunatic with two boxes of syrup-coated popcorn, one for Mother, one for Magda; the men were to help themselves. Ambrose walked on Magda's right; being by nature left-handed, she carried the box in her left hand. Up front the situation was reversed.

"What are you limping for?" Magda inquired of Ambrose. He supposed in a husky tone that his foot had gone to sleep in the car. Her teeth flashed. "Pins and needles?" It was the honeysuckle on the lattice of the former privy that drew the bees. Imagine being stung there. How long is this going to take?

The adults decided to forgo the pool; but Uncle Karl insisted they change into swimsuits and do the beach. "He wants to watch the pretty girls," Peter teased, and ducked behind Magda from Uncle Karl's pretended wrath. "You've got all the pretty girls you need right here," Magda declared, and Mother said: "Now that's the gospel truth." Magda scolded Peter, who reached over her shoulder to sneak some popcorn. "Your brother and father aren't getting any." Uncle Karl wondered if they were going to have fireworks that night, what with the shortages. It wasn't the shortages, Mr. M———— replied; Ocean City had fireworks from pre-war. But it was too risky on account of the enemy submarines, some people thought.

"Don't seem like Fourth of July without fireworks," said Uncle Karl. The inverted tag in dialogue writing is still considered permissible with proper names or epithets, but sounds old-fashioned with personal pronouns. "We'll have 'em again soon enough," predicted the boys' father. Their mother declared she could do without fireworks: they reminded her too much of the real thing. Their father said all the more reason to shoot off a few now and again. Uncle Karl asked *rhetorically* who needed reminding, just look at people's hair and skin.

"The oil, yes," said Mrs. M————.

Ambrose had a pain in his stomach and so didn't swim but enjoyed watching the others. He and his father burned red easily. Magda's figure was exceedingly well developed for her age. She too declined to swim, and got mad, and became angry when Peter attempted to drag her into the pool. She always swam, he insisted; what did she mean not swim? Why did a person come to Ocean City?

"Maybe I want to lay here with Ambrose," Magda teased.

Nobody likes a pedant.

"Aha," said Mother. Peter grabbed Magda by one ankle and ordered Ambrose to grab the other. She squealed and rolled over on the beach blanket. Ambrose pretended to help hold her back. Her tan was darker than even Mother's and Peter's. "Help out, Uncle Karl!" Peter cried. Uncle Karl went to seize the other ankle. Inside the top of her swimsuit, however, you could see the line where the sunburn ended and, when she hunched her shoulders and squealed again, one nipple's auburn edge. Mother made them behave themselves. "*You* should certainly know," she said to Uncle Karl. Archly. "That when a lady says she doesn't feel like swimming, a gentleman doesn't ask questions." Uncle Karl said excuse *him;* Mother winked at Magda; Ambrose blushed; stupid Peter kept saying "Phooey on *feel like!*" and tugging at Magda's ankle; then even he got the point, and cannonballed with a holler into the pool.

"I swear," Magda said, in mock *in feigned* exasperation.

The diving would make a suitable literary symbol. To go off the high board you had to wait in a line along the poolside and up the ladder. Fellows tickled girls and goosed one another and shouted to the ones at the top to hurry up, or razzed them for bellyfloppers. Once on the springboard some took a great while posing or clowning or deciding on a dive or getting up their nerve; others ran right off. Especially among the younger fellows the idea was to strike the funniest pose or do the craziest stunt as you fell, a thing that got harder to do as you kept on and kept on. But whether you hollered *Geronimo!* or *Sieg heil!,* held your nose or "rode a bicycle," pretended to be shot or did a perfect jacknife or changed your mind halfway down and ended up with nothing, it was over in two seconds, after all that wait. Spring, pose, splash. Spring, neat-o, splash. Spring, aw fooey, splash.

The grown-ups had gone on; Ambrose wanted to converse with Magda; she was remarkably well developed for her age; it was said that that came from rubbing with a turkish towel, and there were other theories. Ambrose could think of nothing to say except how good a diver Peter was, who was showing off for her benefit. You could pretty well tell by looking at their bathing suits and arm muscles how far along the different fellows were. Ambrose was glad he hadn't gone in swimming, the cold water shrank you up so. Magda pretended to be uninterested in the diving; she probably weighed as much as he did. If you knew your way around in the funhouse like your own bedroom, you could wait until a girl came along and then slip away without ever getting caught, even if her boyfriend was right with her. She'd think *he* did it! It would be better to be the boyfriend, and act outraged, and tear the funhouse apart.

Not act; *be.*

"He's a master diver," Ambrose said. In feigned admiration. "You really have to slave away at it to get that good." What would it matter anyhow if he asked her right out whether she remembered, even teased her with it as Peter would have?

There's no point in going farther; this isn't getting anybody anywhere; they haven't even come to the funhouse yet. Ambrose is off the track, in some new or old part of the place that's not supposed to be used; he strayed into it by some one-in-a-million chance, like the time the roller-coaster car left the tracks in the nineteen-teens against all the laws of physics and sailed over the boardwalk in the dark. And they can't locate him because they don't know where to look. Even the designer and operator have forgotten this other part, that winds around on itself like a whelk shell. That winds around the right part like the snakes on Mercury's caduceus. Some people, perhaps, don't "hit their stride" until their twenties, when the growing-up business is over and women appreciate other things besides wisecracks and teasing and strutting. Peter didn't have one-tenth the imagination *he* had, not one-tenth. Peter did this naming-their-children thing as a joke, making up names like Aloysius and Murgatroyd, but Ambrose knew *exactly* how it would feel to be married and have children of your own, and be a loving husband and father, and go comfortably to work in the mornings and to bed with your wife at night, and wake up with her there. With a breeze coming through the sash and birds and mockingbirds singing in the Chinese-cigar trees. His eyes watered, there aren't enough ways to say that. He would be quite famous in his line of work. Whether Magda was his wife or not, one evening when he was wise-lined and gray at the temples he'd smile gravely, at a fashionable dinner party, and remind her of his youthful passion. The time they went with his family to Ocean City; the *erotic fantasies* he used to have about her. How long ago it seemed, and childish! Yet tender, too, *n'est-ce pas?*[1] Would she have imagined that the world-famous whatever remembered how many strings were on the lyre on the bench beside the girl on the label of the cigar box he'd stared at in the toolshed at age ten while she, age eleven. Even then he had felt *wise beyond his years;* he'd stroked her hair and said in his deepest voice and correct English, as to a dear child: "I shall never forget this moment."

But though he had breathed heavily, groaned as if ecstatic, what he'd really felt throughout was an odd detachment, as though someone else were Master. Strive as he might to be transported, he heard his mind take notes upon the scene: *This is what they call* passion. *I am experiencing it.* Many of the digger machines were out of order in the penny arcades and could not be repaired or replaced for the duration. Moreover the prizes, made now in USA, were less interesting than formerly, pasteboard items for the most part, and some of the machines wouldn't work on white pennies. The gypsy fortune-teller machine might have provided a foreshadowing of the climax of this story if Ambrose had operated it. It was even dilapidateder than most: the silver coating was worn off the brown metal handles, the glass windows around the dummy were cracked and taped, her kerchiefs and silks long-faded. If a man lived by himself, he could take a department-store mannequin with flexible joints and modify her in certain ways. *However:* by the time he was that old he'd have a real woman. There was a machine that stamped your name around a white-metal coin with a star in the middle: A————. His son would be the second, and when the lad reached thirteen or so he would put a strong arm around his shoulder and tell him calmly: "It is perfectly normal. We have all been through it. It will not last forever." Nobody knew how to be what they were right. He'd smoke a pipe, teach his son how to fish and softcrab, assure him he needn't worry about himself. Magda would certainly give, Magda would certainly yield a great deal of milk, although guilty of occasional solecisms. It don't taste so bad. Suppose the lights came on now!

The day wore on. You think you're yourself, but there are other persons in you. Ambrose gets hard when Ambrose doesn't want to, *and obversely.* Ambrose watches them disagree; Ambrose watches him watch. In the funhouse mirror-room you can't see yourself go on forever, because no matter how you stand, your head gets in the way. Even if you had a glass periscope, the image of your eye would cover up the thing you really wanted to see. The police will come; there'll be a story in the papers. That must be where it happened. Unless he can find a surprise exit, an unofficial backdoor or escape hatch opening on an alley, say, and then stroll up to the family in front of the funhouse and ask where everybody's been; *he's* been out of the place for ages. That's just where it happened, in that last lighted room: Peter and Magda found the right exit; he found one that you weren't supposed to find and strayed off into the works somewhere. In a perfect funhouse you'd be able to go only one way, like the divers off the highboard; getting lost would be impossible; the doors and halls would work like minnow traps or the valves in veins.

[1] Is it not? (French).

On account of German U-boats, Ocean City was "browned out": streetlights were shaded on the seaward side; shop-windows and boardwalk amusement places were kept dim, not to silhouette tankers and Liberty-ships for torpedoing. In a short story about Ocean City, Maryland, during World War II, the author could make use of the image of sailors on leave in the penny arcades and shooting galleries, sighting through the crosshairs of toy machine guns at swastika'd subs, while out in the black Atlantic a U-boat skipper squints through his periscope at real ships outlined by the glow of penny arcades. After dinner the family strolled back to the amusement end of the boardwalk. The boys' father had burnt red as always and was masked with Noxzema, a minstrel in reverse. The grown-ups stood at the end of the boardwalk where the Hurricane of '33 had cut an inlet from the ocean to Assawoman Bay.

"Pronounced with a long *o,*" Uncle Karl reminded Magda with a wink. His shirt sleeves were rolled up; Mother punched his brown biceps with the arrowed heart on it and said his mind was naughty. Fat May's laugh came suddenly from the funhouse, as if she'd just got the joke; the family laughed too at the coincidence. Ambrose went under the boardwalk to search for out-of-town matchbook covers with the aid of his pocket flashlight; he looked out from the edge of the North American continent and wondered how far their laughter carried over the water. Spies in rubber rafts; survivors in lifeboats. If the joke had been beyond his understanding, he could have said: "*The laughter was over his head.*" And let the reader see the serious wordplay on second reading.

He turned the flashlight on and then off at once even before the woman whooped. He sprang away, heart athud, dropping the light. What had the man grunted? Perspiration drenched and chilled him by the time he scrambled up to the family. "See anything?" his father asked. His voice wouldn't come; he shrugged and violently brushed sand from his pants legs.

"Let's ride the old flying horses!" Magda cried. I'll never be an author. It's been forever already, everybody's gone home, Ocean City's deserted, the ghost crabs are tickling across the beach and down the littered cold streets. And the empty halls of clapboard hotels and abandoned funhouses. A tidal wave; an enemy air raid; a monster-crab swelling like an island from the sea. *The inhabitants fled in terror.* Magda clung to his trouser leg; he alone knew the maze's secret. "He gave his life that we might live," said Uncle Karl with a scowl of pain, as he. The fellow's hands had been tattooed; the woman's legs, the woman's fat white legs had. *An astonishing coincidence.* He yearned to tell Peter. He wanted to throw up for excitement. They hadn't even chased him. He wished he were dead.

One possible ending would be to have Ambrose come across another lost person in the dark. They'd match their wits together against the funhouse, struggle like Ulysses past obstacle after obstacle, help and encourage each other. Or a girl. By the time they found the exit they'd be closest friends, sweethearts if it were a girl; they'd know each other's inmost souls, be bound together *by the cement of shared adventure;* then they'd emerge into the light and it would turn out that his friend was a Negro. A blind girl. President Roosevelt's son. Ambrose's former archenemy.

Shortly after the mirror room he'd groped along a musty corridor, his heart already misgiving him at the absence of phosphorescent arrows and other signs. He'd found a crack of light—not a door, it turned out, but a seam between the plyboard wall panels—and squinting up to it, he spied a small old man, *in appearance not unlike* the photographs at home of Ambrose's late grandfather, nodding upon a stool beneath a bare, speckled bulb. A crude panel of toggle- and knife-switches hung beside the open fuse box near his head; elsewhere in the little room were wooden levers and ropes belayed to boat cleats. At the time, Ambrose wasn't lost enough to rap or call; later he couldn't find that crack. Now it seemed to him that he'd possibly dozed off for a few minutes somewhere along the way; certainly he was exhausted from the afternoon's sunshine and the evening's problems; he couldn't be sure he hadn't dreamed part or all of the sight. Had an old black wall fan droned like bees and shimmied two flypaper streamers? Had the funhouse operator—gentle, somewhat sad and tired-appearing, in expression not unlike the photographs at home of Ambrose's late Uncle Konrad—murmured in his sleep? Is there really such a person as Ambrose, or is he a figment of the author's imagination? Was it Assawoman Bay or Sinepuxent? Are there other errors of fact in this fiction? Was there another sound besides the little slap slap of thigh on ham, like water sucking at the chine-boards of a skiff?

When you're lost, the smartest thing to do is stay put till you're found, hollering if necessary. But to holler guarantees humiliation as well as rescue; keeping silent permits some saving of face—you can act surprised at the fuss when your rescuers find you and swear you weren't lost, if they do. What's more you might find your own way yet, *however belatedly.*

"Don't tell me your foot's still asleep!" Magda exclaimed as the three young people walked from the inlet to the area set aside for ferris wheels, carrousels, and other carnival rides, they having decided in favor of the vast and ancient merry-go-round instead of the funhouse. What a sentence, everything was wrong from the outset. People don't know what to make of him, he doesn't know what to make of himself, he's only thirteen, *athletically and socially inept,* not astonishingly bright, but there are antennae; he has . . . some sort of receivers in his head; things speak to him, he understands more than he should, the world winks at him through its objects, grabs grinning at his coat. Everybody else is in on some secret he doesn't know; they've forgotten to tell him. Through simple *procrastination* his mother put off his baptism until this year. Everyone else had it done as a baby; he'd assumed the same of himself, as had his mother, so she claimed, until it was time for him to join Grace Methodist-Protestant and the oversight came out. He was mortified, but pitched sleepless through his private catechizing, intimidated by the ancient mysteries, a thirteen year old would never say that, resolved to experience conversion like St. Augustine. When the water touched his brow and Adam's sin left him, he contrived by a strain like defecation to bring tears into his eyes—but felt nothing. There was some simple, radical difference about him; he hoped it was genius, feared it was madness, devoted himself to amiability and inconspicuousness. Alone on the seawall near his house he was seized by the terrifying transports he'd thought to find in toolshed, in Communion-cup. The grass was alive! The town, the river, himself, were not imaginary; time roared in his ears like wind; the world was *going on!* This part ought to be dramatized. The Irish author James Joyce once wrote. Ambrose M——— is going to scream.

There is no *texture of rendered sensory detail,* for one thing. The faded distorting mirrors beside Fat May; the impossibility of choosing a mount when one had but a single ride on the great carrousel; the *vertigo attendant on his recognition* that Ocean City was worn out, the place of fathers and grandfathers, straw-boatered men and parasoled ladies survived by their amusements. Money spent, the three paused at Peter's insistence beside Fat May to watch the girls get their skirts blown up. The object was to tease Magda, who said: "I swear, Peter M———, you've got a one-track mind! Amby and me aren't *interested* in such things." In the tumbling-barrel, too, just inside the Devil's-mouth entrance to the funhouse, the girls were upended and their boyfriends and others could see up their dresses if they cared to. Which was the whole point, Ambrose realized. Of the entire funhouse! If you looked around, you noticed that almost all the people on the boardwalk were paired off into couples except the small children; in a way, that was the whole point of Ocean City! If you had X-ray eyes and could see everything going on at that instant under the boardwalk and in all the hotel rooms and cars and alleyways, you'd realize that all that normally *showed,* like restaurants and dance halls and clothing and test-your-strength machines, was merely preparation and intermission. Fat May screamed.

Because he watched the goings-on from the corner of his eye, it was Ambrose who spied the half-dollar on the boardwalk near the tumbling-barrel. Losers weepers. The first time he'd heard some people moving through a corridor not far away, just after he'd lost sight of the crack of light, he'd decided not to call to them, for fear they'd guess he was scared and poke fun; it sounded like roughnecks; he'd hoped they'd come by and he could follow in the dark without their knowing. Another time he'd heard just one person, unless he imagined it, bumping along as if on the other side of the plywood; perhaps Peter coming back for him, or Father, or Magda lost too. Or the owner and operator of the funhouse. He'd called out once, as though merrily: "Anybody know where the heck we are?" But the query was too stiff, his voice cracked, when the sounds stopped he was terrified: maybe it was a queer who waited for fellows to get lost, or a long-haired filthy monster that lived in some cranny of the farmhouse. He stood rigid for hours it seemed like, scarcely respiring. His future was shockingly clear, in outline. He tried holding his breath to the point of unconsciousness. There ought to be a button you could push to end your life absolutely without pain; disappear in a flick, like turning out a light. He would push it instantly! He despised Uncle Karl. But he despised his father too, for not being what he was supposed to be. Perhaps his father hated *his* father, and so on, and his son would hate him, and so on. Instantly!

Naturally he didn't have nerve enough to ask Magda to go through the funhouse with him. With incredible nerve and to everyone's surprise he invited Magda, quietly and politely, to go through the funhouse with him. "I warn you, I've never been through it before," he added, *laughing easily;* "but I reckon we can manage somehow. The important thing to remember, after all, is that it's meant to be a *fun* house; that is, a place of amusement. If people really got lost or injured or too badly frightened in it, the owner'd go out of business. There'd even be lawsuits. No character in a work of fiction can make a speech this long without interruption or acknowledgment from the other characters."

Mother teased Uncle Karl: "Three's a crowd, I always heard." But actually Ambrose was relieved that Peter now had a quarter too. Nothing was what it looked like. Every instant, under the surface of the Atlantic Ocean, millions of living animals devoured one another. Pilots were falling in flames over Europe; women were being forcibly raped in the South Pacific. His father should have taken him aside and said: "There is a simple secret to getting through the funhouse, as simple as being first to see the Towers. Here it is. Peter does not know it; neither does your Uncle Karl. You and I are different. Not surprisingly, you've often wished you weren't. Don't think I haven't noticed how unhappy your childhood has been! But you'll understand, when I tell you, why it had to be kept secret until now. And you won't regret not being like your brother and your uncle. *On the contrary!*" If you knew all the stories behind all the people on the boardwalk, you'd see that *nothing* was what it looked like. Husbands and wives often hated each other; parents didn't necessarily love their children; et cetera. A child took things for granted because he had nothing to compare his life to and everybody acted as if things were as they should be. Therefore each saw himself as the hero of the story, when the truth might turn out to be that he's the villain, or the coward. And there wasn't one thing you could do about it!

Hunchbacks, fat ladies, fools—that no one chose what he was was unbearable. In the movies he'd meet a beautiful young girl in the funhouse; they'd have hairs-breadth escapes from real dangers; he'd do and say the right things; she also; in the end they'd be lovers; their dialogue lines would match up; he'd be perfectly at ease; she'd not only like him well enough, she'd think he was *marvelous.* she'd lie awake thinking about *him,* instead of vice versa—the way *his* face looked in different lights and how he stood and exactly what he'd said—and yet that would be only one small episode in his wonderful life, among many many others. Not a *turning point* at all. What had happened in the toolshed was nothing. He hated, he loathed his parents! One reason for not writing a lost-in-the-funhouse story is that either everybody's felt what Ambrose feels, in which case it goes without saying, or else no normal person feels such things, in which case Ambrose is a freak. "Is anything more tiresome, in fiction, than the problems of sensitive adolescents?" And it's all too long and rambling, as if the author. For all a person knows the first time through, the end could be just around any corner; perhaps, *not impossibly* it's been within reach any number of times. On the other hand he may be scarcely past the start, with everything yet to get through, an intolerable idea.

Fill in: His father's raised eyebrows when he announced his decision to do the funhouse with Magda. Ambrose understands now, but didn't then, that his father was wondering whether he knew what the funhouse was *for*—especially since he didn't object, as he should have, when Peter decided to come along too. The ticket-woman, witchlike, mortifying him when inadvertently he gave her his name-coin instead of the half-dollar, then unkindly calling Magda's attention to the birthmark on his temple: "Watch out for him, girlie, he's a marked man!" She wasn't even cruel, he understood, only vulgar and insensitive. Somewhere in the world there was a young woman with such splendid understanding that she'd see him entire, like a poem or story, and find his words so valuable after all that when he confessed his apprehensions she would explain why they were in fact the very things that made him precious to her . . . and to Western Civilization! There was no such girl, the simple truth being. Violent yawns as they approached the mouth. Whispered advice from an old-timer on a bench near the barrel: "Go crabwise and ye'll get an eyeful without upsetting!" Composure vanished at the first pitch: Peter hollered joyously, Magda tumbled, shrieked, clutched her skirt; Ambrose scrambled crabwise, tight-lipped with terror, was soon out, watched his dropped name-coin slide among the couples. Shame-faced he saw that to get through expeditiously was not the point; Peter feigned assistance in order to trip Magda up, shouted "I see Christmas!" when her legs went flying. The old man, his latest betrayer, cackled approval. A dim hall then of black-thread cobwebs and re-corded gibber: he took Magda's elbow to steady her against revolving discs set in the slanted floor to throw your feet out from under, and explained to her in a calm, deep voice his theory that each phase of the funhouse was triggered either automatically, by a series of photoelectric devices, or else manually by operators stationed at peepholes. But he lost his voice thrice as the discs unbalanced him; Magda was anyhow squealing; but at one point she clutched him about the waist to keep from falling, and her right cheek pressed for a moment against his belt-buckle. Heroically he drew her up, it was his chance to clutch her close as if for support and say: "I love you." He even put an arm lightly about the small of her back before a sailor-and-girl pitched into them from behind, sorely treading his left big toe and knocking Magda asprawl with them. The sailor's girl was a string-haired hussy with a loud laugh and light blue drawers; Ambrose realized that he wouldn't have said "I love you" anyhow, and was smitten with self-contempt. How much better it would be to be that common sailor! A wiry little Seaman 3rd, the fellow squeezed a girl to each side and stumbled hilarious into the mirror room, closer to Magda in thirty seconds than Ambrose had got in thirteen years. She giggled at something the fellow said to Peter; she drew her hair from her eyes with a movement so womanly it struck Ambrose's heart; Peter's smacking her backside then seemed particularly coarse. But Magda made a pleased indignant face and cried, "All right for *you,* mister!" and pursued Peter into the maze without a backward glance. The sailor followed after, leisurely, drawing his girl against his hip; Ambrose understood not only that they were all so relieved to be rid of his burdensome company that they didn't even notice his absence, but that he himself shared their relief. Stepping from the treacherous passage at last into the mirror-maze, he saw once again, more clearly than ever, how readily he deceived himself into supposing he was a person. He even foresaw, wincing at his dreadful self-knowledge, that he would repeat the deception, at ever-rarer intervals, all his wretched life, so fearful were the alternatives. Fame, madness, suicide; perhaps all three. It's not believable that so young a boy could articulate that reflection, and in fiction the merely true must always yield to the plausible. Moreover, the symbolism is in places heavy-footed. Yet Ambrose M——— understood, as few adults do, that the famous loneliness of the great was no popular myth but a general truth—furthermore, that it was as much cause as effect.

All the preceding except the last few sentences is exposition that should've been done earlier or interspersed with the present action instead of lumped together. No reader would put up with so much with such *prolixity.* It's interesting that Ambrose's father, though presumably an intelligent man (as indicated by his role as grade-school principal), neither encouraged nor discouraged his sons at all in any way—as if he either didn't care about them or cared all right but didn't know how to act. If this fact should contribute to one of them's becoming a celebrated but wretchedly unhappy scientist, was it a good thing or not? He too might someday face the question; it would be useful to know whether it had tortured his father for years, for example, or never once crossed his mind.

In the maze two important things happened. First, our hero found a name-coin someone else had lost or discarded: *AMBROSE,* suggestive of the famous lightship and of his late grandfather's favorite dessert, which his mother used to prepare on special occasions out of coconut, oranges, grapes, and what else. Second, as he wondered at the endless replication of his image in the mirrors, second, as he *lost himself in the reflection* that the necessity for an observer makes perfect observation impossible, better make him eighteen at least, yet that would render other things unlikely, he heard Peter and Magda chuckling somewhere together in the maze. "Here!" "No here!" they shouted to each other; Peter said, "Where's Amby?" Magda murmured. "Amb?" Peter called. In a pleased, friendly voice. He didn't reply. The truth was, his brother was a *happy-go-lucky youngster* who'd've been better off with a regular brother of his own, but who seldom complained of his lot and was generally cordial. Ambrose's throat ached; there aren't enough different ways to say that. He stood quietly while the two young people giggled and thumped through the glittering maze, hurrah'd their discovery of its exit, cried out in joyful alarm at what next beset them. Then he set his mouth and followed after, as he supposed, took a wrong turn, strayed into the pass *wherein he lingers yet.*

The action of conventional dramatic narrative may be represented by a diagram called Freitag's Triangle:[2]

or more accurately by a variant of that diagram:

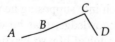

in which *AB* represents the exposition, *B* the introduction of conflict, *BC* the "rising action," complication, or development of the conflict, *C* the climax, or

[2]See Gustave Freytag, *Technique of the Drama,* translated by Elias J. MacEwan, 1895.

turn of the action, *CD* the dénouement, or resolution of the conflict. While there is no reason to regard this pattern as an absolute necessity, like many other conventions it became conventional because great numbers of people over many years learned by trial and error that it was effective; one ought not to forsake it, therefore, unless one wishes to forsake as well the effect of drama or has clear cause to feel that deliberate violation of the "normal" pattern can better can better effect that effect. This can't go on much longer; it can go on forever. He died telling stories to himself in the dark; years later, when that vast unsuspected area of the funhouse came to light, the first expedition found his skeleton in one of its labyrinthine corridors and mistook it for part of the entertainment. He died of starvation telling himself stories in the dark; but unbeknownst unbeknownst to him, an assistant operator of the funhouse, happening to overhear him, crouched just behind the plyboard partition and wrote down his every word. The operator's daughter, an exquisite young woman with a figure unusually well developed for her age, crouched just behind the partition and transcribed his every word. Though she had never laid eyes on him, she recognized that here was one of Western Culture's truly great imaginations, the eloquence of whose suffering would be an inspiration to unnumbered. And her heart was torn between her love for the misfortunate young man (yes, she loved him, though she had never laid though she knew him only—but how well!—through his words, and the deep, calm voice in which he spoke them) between her love et cetera and her womanly intuition that only in suffering and isolation could he give voice et cetera. Lone dark dying. Quietly she kissed the rough plyboard, and a tear fell upon the page. Where she had written in shorthand *Where she had written in shorthand* Where she had written in shorthand *Where she* et cetera. A long time ago we should have passed the apex of Freitag's Triangle and made brief work of the *dénouement;* the plot doesn't rise by meaningful steps but winds upon itself, digresses, retreats, hesitates, sighs, collapses, expires. The climax of the story must be its protagonist's discovery of a way to get through the funhouse. But he has found none, may have ceased to search.

What relevance does the war have to the story? Should there be fireworks outside or not?

Ambrose wandered, languished, dozed. Now and then he fell into his habit of rehearsing to himself the unadventurous story of his life, narrated from the third-person point of view, from his earliest memory parenthesis of maple leaves stirring in the summer breath of tidewater Maryland end of parenthesis to the present moment. Its principal events, on this telling, would appear to have been *A, B, C,* and *D.*

He imagined himself years hence, successful, married, at ease in the world, the trials of his adolescence far behind him. He has come to the seashore with his family for the holiday: how Ocean City has changed! But at one seldom at one ill-frequented end of the boardwalk a few derelict amusements survive from times gone by: the great carrousel from the turn of the century, with its monstrous griffins and mechanical concert band; the roller coaster rumored since 1916 to have been condemned; the mechanical shooting gallery in which only the image of our enemies changed. His own son laughs with Fat May and wants to know what a funhouse is; Ambrose hugs the sturdy lad close and smiles around his pipestem at his wife.

The family's going home. Mother sits between Father and Uncle Karl, who teases him good-naturedly who chuckles over the fact that the comrade with whom he'd fought his way shoulder to shoulder through the funhouse had turned out to be a blind Negro girl—to their mutual discomfort, as they'd opened their souls. But such are the walls of custom, which even. Whose arm is where? How must it feel. He dreams of a funhouse vaster by far than any yet constructed; but by then they may be out of fashion, like steamboats and excursion trains. Already quaint and seedy: the draperied ladies on the frieze of the carrousel are his father's father's mooncheeked dreams; if he thinks of it more he will vomit his apple-on-a-stick.

He wonders: will he become a regular person? Something has gone wrong; his vaccination didn't take; at the Boy-Scout initiation campfire he only pretended to be deeply moved, as he pretends to this hour that it is not so bad after all in the funhouse, and that he has a little limp. How long will it last? He envisions a truly astonishing funhouse, incredibly complex yet utterly controlled from a great central switchboard like the console of a pipe organ. Nobody had enough imagination. He could design such a place himself, wiring and all, and he's only thirteen years old. He would be its operator: panel lights would show what was up in every cranny of its cunning of its multifarious vastness; a switch-flick would ease this fellow's way, complicate that's, to balance things out; if anyone seemed lost or frightened, all the operator had to do was.

He wishes he had never entered the funhouse. But he has. Then he wishes he were dead. But he's not. Therefore he will construct funhouses for others and be their secret operator—though he would rather be among the lovers for whom funhouses are designed.

QUESTIONS

1. For all its apparent formlessness, what parts of the story could be diagrammed on Freytag's triangle? What does the last sentence contribute to the story's form?
2. What details render the funhouse symbolic?
3. In what general way does the narrator limit his omniscience?
4. What happens to the narrator's omniscience in the fourth paragraph with the two adjacent but broken sentences: "The brown hair on Ambrose's mother's forearms gleamed in the sun like," and "The smell of Uncle Karl's cigar smoke reminded one of"? to what do these two sentences relate later in the narration?
5. What is Barth doing with his punctuation in "Peter and Ambrose's father" and "Ambrose's and Peter's mother"?
6. Who says, "Nobody likes a pedant" after Magda says, "Maybe I want to lay here with Ambrose"? Why?
7. What kind of background does Barth sketch for Magda, particularly through her language?

   8.   What is the dramatic irony in the paragraph (fourth from the end)
          where Ambrose "imagined himself years hence"?
   9.   In "The Monkey's Paw," Mrs. White says, "Sounds like the *Arabian
          Nights.*" What is the similarity between what Jacobs does with that
          remark and what Barth is doing?
   10. "So far," says the narrator, "there's been nothing in the way of a
          theme" (p. 283). What is the story's theme?
   11. What does the story, with all its spoofing, ultimately imply about the
          fictive illusion of reality?
   12. Does Ambrose get out of the funhouse?

   The bowl in Ann Beattie's "Janus" is a symbol. Andrea thinks it perfect, and
others seem to agree. It is "both subtle and noticeable." How does Beattie
develop her symbol and what, ultimately, does it symbolize?

JANUS

Ann Beattie   (1947–)

The bowl was perfect. Perhaps it was not what you'd select if you faced a shelf
of bowls, and not the sort of thing that would inevitably attract a lot of attention
at a crafts fair, yet it had real presence. It was as predictably admired as a mutt
who has no reason to suspect he might be funny. Just such a dog, in fact, was
often brought out (and in) along with the bowl.

   Andrea was a real-estate agent, and when she thought that some prospective
buyers might be dog-lovers, she would drop off her dog at the same time she
placed the bowl in the house that was up for sale. She would put a dish of water
in the kitchen for Mondo, take his squeaking plastic frog out of her purse and
drop it on the floor. He would pounce delightedly, just as he did every day at
home, batting around his favorite toy. The bowl usually sat on a coffee table,
though recently she had displayed it on top of a pine blanket chest and on a
lacquered table. It was once placed on a cherry table beneath a Bonnard still-life,
where it held its own.

   Everyone who has purchased a house or who has wanted to sell a house must
be familiar with some of the tricks used to convince a buyer that the house is quite
special: a fire in the fireplace in early evening; jonquils in a pitcher on the kitchen
counter, where no one ordinarily has space to put flowers; perhaps the slight
aroma of spring, made by a single drop of scent vaporizing from a lamp bulb.

   The wonderful thing about the bowl, Andrea thought, was that it was both
subtle and noticeable—a paradox of a bowl. Its glaze was the color of cream and
seemed to glow no matter what light it was placed in. There were a few bits of
color in it—tiny geometric flashes—and some of these were tinged with flecks of
silver. They were as mysterious as cells seen under a microscope; it was difficult
not to study them, because they shimmered, flashing for a split second, and then
resumed their shape. Something about the colors and their random placement

suggested motion. People who liked country furniture always commented on the bowl, but then it turned out that people who felt comfortable with Biedermeier loved it just as much. But the bowl was not at all ostentatious, or even so noticeable that anyone would suspect that it had been put in place deliberately. They might notice the height of the ceiling on first entering a room, and only when their eye moved down from that, or away from the refraction of sunlight on a pale wall, would they see the bowl. Then they would go immediately to it and comment. Yet they always faltered when they tried to say something. Perhaps it was because they were in the house for a serious reason, not to notice some object.

Once, Andrea got a call from a woman who had not put in an offer on a house she had shown her. That bowl, she said—would it be possible to find out where the owners had bought that beautiful bowl? Andrea pretended that she did not know what the woman was referring to. A bowl, somewhere in the house? Oh, on a table under the window. Yes, she would ask, of course. She let a couple of days pass, then called back to say that the bowl had been a present and the people did not know where it had been purchased.

When the bowl was not being taken from house to house, it sat on Andrea's coffee table at home. She didn't keep it carefully wrapped (although she transported it that way, in a box); she kept it on the table, because she liked to see it. It was large enough so that it didn't seem fragile, or particularly vulnerable if anyone sideswiped the table or Mondo blundered into it at play. She had asked her husband to please not drop his house key in it. It was meant to be empty.

When her husband first noticed the bowl, he had peered into it and smiled briefly. He always urged her to buy things she liked. In recent years, both of them had acquired many things to make up for all the lean years when they were graduate students, but now that they had been comfortable for quite a while, the pleasure of new possessions dwindled. Her husband had pronounced the bowl "pretty," and he had turned away without picking it up to examine it. He had no more interest in the bowl than she had in his new Leica.

She was sure that the bowl brought her luck. Bids were often put in on houses where she had displayed the bowl. Sometimes the owners, who were always asked to be away or to step outside when the house was being shown, didn't even know that the bowl had been in their house. Once—she could not imagine how—she left it behind, and then she was so afraid that something might have happened to it that she rushed back to the house and sighed with relief when the woman owner opened the door. The bowl, Andrea explained—she had purchased a bowl and set it on the chest for safekeeping while she toured the house with the prospective buyers, and she . . . She felt like rushing past the frowning woman and seizing her bowl. The owner stepped aside, and it was only when Andrea ran to the chest that the lady glanced at her a little strangely. In the few seconds before Andrea picked up the bowl, she realized that the owner must have just seen that it had been perfectly placed, that the sunlight struck the bluer part of it. Her pitcher had been moved to the far side of the chest, and the bowl predominated. All the way home, Andrea wondered how she could have left the bowl behind. It was like leaving a friend at an outing—just walking off. Sometimes there were stories in the paper about families forgetting a child somewhere and driving to the next city. Andrea had only gone a mile down the road before she remembered.

In time, she dreamed of the bowl. Twice, in a waking dream—early in the morning, between sleep and a last nap before rising—she had a clear vision of it. It came into sharp focus and startled her for a moment—the same bowl she looked at every day.

She had a very profitable year selling real estate. Word spread, and she had more clients than she felt comfortable with. She had the foolish thought that if only the bowl were an animate object she could thank it. There were times when she wanted to talk to her husband about the bowl. He was a stockbroker, and sometimes told people that he was fortunate to be married to a woman who had such a fine aesthetic sense and yet could also function in the real world. They were a lot alike, really—they had agreed on that. They were both quiet people— reflective, slow to make value judgments, but almost intractable once they had come to a conclusion. They both liked details, but while ironies attracted her, he was more impatient and dismissive when matters became many-sided or unclear. But they both knew this; it was the kind of thing they could talk about when they were alone in the car together, coming home from a party or after a weekend with friends. But she never talked to him about the bowl. When they were at dinner, exchanging their news of the day, or while they lay in bed at night listening to the stereo and murmuring sleepy disconnections, she was often tempted to come right out and say that she thought that the bowl in the living room, the cream-colored bowl, was responsible for her success. But she didn't say it. She couldn't begin to explain it. Sometimes in the morning, she would look at him and feel guilty that she had such a constant secret.

Could it be that she had some deeper connection with the bowl—a relationship of some kind? She corrected her thinking: how could she imagine such a thing, when she was a human being and it was a bowl? It was ridiculous. Just think of how people lived together and loved each other . . . But was that always so clear, always a relationship? She was confused by these thoughts, but they remained in her mind. There was something within her now, something real, that she never talked about.

The bowl was a mystery, even to her. It was frustrating, because her in-volvement with the bowl contained a steady sense of unrequited good fortune; it would have been easier to respond if some sort of demand were made in return. But that only happened in fairy tales. The bowl was just a bowl. She did not believe that for one second. What she believed was that it was some-thing she loved.

In the past, she had sometimes talked to her husband about a new property she was about to buy or sell—confiding some clever strategy she had devised to persuade owners who seemed ready to sell. Now she stopped doing that, for all her strategies involved the bowl. She became more deliberate with the bowl, and more possessive. She put it in houses only when no one was there, and removed it when she left the house. Instead of just moving a pitcher or a dish, she would remove all the other objects from a table. She had to force herself to handle them carefully, because she didn't really care about them. She just wanted them out of sight.

She wondered how the situation would end. As with a lover, there was no exact scenario of how matters would come to a close. Anxiety became the operative force. It would be irrelevant if the lover rushed into someone else's arms, or wrote her a note and departed to another city. The horror was the possibility of the disappearance. That was what mattered.

She would get up at night and look at the bowl. It never occurred to her that she might break it. She washed and dried it without anxiety, and she moved it often, from coffee table to mahogany corner table or wherever, without fearing an accident. It was clear that she would not be the one who would do anything to the bowl. The bowl was only handled by her, set safely on one surface or another; it was not very likely that anyone would break it. A bowl was a poor conductor of electricity: it would not be hit by lightning. Yet the idea of damage persisted. She did not think beyond that—to what her life would be without the bowl. She only continued to fear that some accident would happen. Why not, in a world where people set plants where they did not belong, so that visitors touring a house would be fooled into thinking that dark corners got sunlight—a world full of tricks?

She had first seen the bowl several years earlier, at a crafts fair she had visited half in secret, with her lover. He had urged her to buy the bowl. She didn't *need* any more things, she told him. But she had been drawn to the bowl, and they had lingered near it. Then she went on to the next booth, and he came up behind her, tapping the rim against her shoulder as she ran her fingers over a wood carving. "You're still insisting that I buy that?" she said. "No," he said. "I bought it for you." He had bought her other things before this—things she liked more, at first—the child's ebony-and-turquoise ring that fitted her little finger; the wooden box, long and thin, beautifully dovetailed, that she used to hold paper clips; the soft gray sweater with a pouch pocket. It was his idea that when he could not be there to hold her hand she could hold her own—clasp her hands inside the lone pocket that stretched across the front. But in time she became more attached to the bowl than to any of his other presents. She tried to talk herself out of it. She owned other things that were more striking or valuable. It wasn't an object whose beauty jumped out at you; a lot of people must have passed it by before the two of them saw it that day.

Her lover had said that she was always too slow to know what she really loved. Why continue with her life the way it was? Why be two-faced, he asked her. He had made the first move toward her. When she would not decide in his favor, would not change her life and come to him, he asked her what made her think she could have it both ways. And then he made the last move and left. It was a decision meant to break her will, to shatter her intransigent ideas about honoring previous commitments.

Time passed. Alone in the living room at night, she often looked at the bowl sitting on the table, still and safe, unilluminated. In its way, it was perfect: the world cut in half, deep and smoothly empty. Near the rim, even in dim light, the eye moved toward one small flash of blue, a vanishing point on the horizon.

QUESTIONS

1. What is the implication of Beattie's title?
2. What irony do you find accumulating behind the opening sentence as the story proceeds?
3. What are the various "tricks" in the story?
4. How does the bowl accord differently with Bonnard and Biedermeier?
5. Why do people falter when they try to say something about the bowl? Whose answer to that question is the "Perhaps it was because . . ."?
6. What does the bowl's "steady sense of unrequited good fortune" contribute to the story's suspense?
7. What is the effect of the remark "But that only happened in fairy tales"?
8. What is the effect of the delayed introduction of the husband? Of the lover?
9. What statements point up the bowl's symbolic meaning?

CHAPTER 8

THEME

Telling stories to make a point is as old as the hills and as current as gossip. When Aesop's fox says of the grapes he cannot reach, "I thought those grapes were ripe, but now I see they are quite sour," the lesson (through the dramatic irony) is clear. Jesus tells the story of the Prodigal Son (Luke 15.11–32) to make a point. Meaning is more important than plot or characterization. Modern stories are rarely so pointedly didactic, but as we have seen, they too aim to illustrate something as they offer a complex interpretation of life and art. Even a pointless story about a shaggy dog makes a point about fictive engagement and human gullibility. It has a *theme*. Broadly, a story's theme is its subject (love, marriage, death, deception), or, more properly, its idea about the subject (love ennobles or debases, marriage fulfills or depletes). The theme may dominate a story, or it may lie more subtly under the surface.

In Margaret Atwood's "When It Happens," the theme that civilization will collapse into savagery, which lurks uneasily with the atomic warheads at the edges of modern consciousness, begins with green tomato pickles. What does Mrs. Burridge's careful preparation have to do with the story as it unfolds?

WHEN IT HAPPENS

Margaret Atwood   (1939–   )

Mrs. Burridge is putting up green tomato pickles. There are twelve quarts in each lot with a bit left over, and that is the end of the jars. At the store they tell her there's a strike on at the factory where they get made. She doesn't know anything about that but you can't buy them anywhere, and even before this they were double what they were last year; she considers herself lucky she had those in the cellar. She has a lot of green tomatoes because she heard on the weather last night there was going to be a killer frost, so she put on her parka and her work gloves and took the lantern out to the garden in the pitch-dark and picked off all the ones she could see, over three bushels. She can lift the full baskets herself but she asked Frank to carry them in for her; he grumbles, but he likes it when she asks. In the morning the news said the growers had been hit and that would shoot the price up—not that the growers would get any of it themselves; everyone knows it's the stores that make the money.

She feels richer than she did yesterday, but on the other hand there isn't that much you can do with green tomatoes. The pickles hardly made a dint in them, and Frank has said, as he does every year, that they will never eat twenty-four quarts of green tomato pickle with just the two of them, and the children gone. Except when they come to visit and eat me out of house and home, Mrs. Burridge adds silently. The truth is, she has always made two batches and the children never liked it anyway; it was Frank ate them all and she knows perfectly well he'll do it again, without even noticing. He likes it on bread and cheese when he's watching the hockey games; during every commercial he goes out to the kitchen and makes himself another slice, even if he's just had a big meal, leaving a trail of crumbs and bits of pickle from the counter across the floor and over the front-room rug to his big chair. It used to annoy Mrs. Burridge, especially the crumbs, but now she watches him with a kind of sadness; she once thought their life together would go on forever but she has come to realize this is not the case.

She doesn't even feel like teasing him about his spare tire anymore, though she does it all the same because he would miss it if she stopped. "There you go," she says, in the angular, prodding, metallic voice she cannot change because everyone expects it from her; if she spoke any other way, they would think she was ill. "You keep on munching away like that and it'll be easy for me to get you out of bed in the mornings. I'll just give you a push and you'll roll all the way down the stairs like a barrel." And he answers in his methodical voice, pretending to be lazy even though he isn't, "You need a little fun in life," as though his pickles and cheese were slightly disreputable, almost like an orgy. Every year he tells her she's made too much, but there would be a fuss, all right, if he went down to the cellar one day and there wasn't any left.

Mrs. Burridge has made her own pickles since 1952, which was the first year she had the garden. She remembers it especially because her daughter Sarah was on the way and she had trouble bending down to do the weeding. When she herself was growing up everyone did their own pickles, and their own canning and preserving too. But after the war most women gave it up; there was more money then and it was easier to buy things at the store. Mrs. Burridge never gave it up, though most of her friends thought she was wasting her time, and now she is glad she didn't—it kept her in practice while the others were having to learn all over again. Though with the sugar going up the way it is, she can't understand how long anyone is going to be able to afford even the homemade things.

On paper Frank is making more money than he ever did; yet they seem to have less to spend. They could always sell the farm, she supposes, to people from the city who would use it as a weekend place; they could get what seems like a very high price—several of the farms south of them have gone that way. But Mrs. Burridge does not have much faith in money; also it is a waste of the land and this is her home, she has it arranged the way she wants it.

When the second batch is on and simmering, she goes to the back door, opens it and stands with her arms folded across her stomach, looking out. She catches herself doing this four or five times a day now and she doesn't quite know why. There isn't much to see, just the barn and the back field with the row of dead elms Frank keeps saying he's going to cut down, and the top of Clarke's place sticking over the hill. She isn't sure what she is looking for but she has the odd idea she may see something burning, smoke coming up from the horizon, a column of it or perhaps more than one column off to the south. This is such a peculiar thought for her to have that she hasn't told it to anyone else. Yesterday Frank saw her standing at the back door and asked her about it at dinner; anything he wants to talk to her about he saves up till dinner, even if he thinks about it in the morning. He wondered why she was at the back door, doing nothing at all, for over ten minutes, and Mrs. Burridge told him a lie, which made her very uneasy. She said she heard a strange dog barking, which wasn't a good story because their own dogs were right there and they didn't notice a thing. But Frank let it pass; perhaps he thinks she is getting funny in her old age and doesn't want to call attention to it, which would be like him. He'll track mud all over her nice shiny kitchen floor but he'd hate to hurt anyone's feelings. Mrs. Burridge decides, a little wistfully, that despite his pigheadedness he is a kind and likable man, and for her this is like renouncing a cherished and unquestionable belief, such as the flatness of the earth. He has made her angry so many times.

When the pickles are cool she labels them as she always does with the name and the date and carries them down the cellar stairs. The cellar is the old kind, with stone walls and a dirt floor. Mrs. Burridge likes to have everything neat— she still irons her sheets—so she had Frank build her some shelves right after they were married. The pickles go on one side, jams and jellies on the other, and the quarts of preserves along the bottom. It used to make her feel safe to have all that food in the cellar; she would think to herself, Well, if there's a snowstorm or anything and we're cut off, it won't be so bad. It doesn't make her feel safe anymore. Instead she thinks that if she has to leave suddenly, she won't be able to take any of the jars with her—they'd be too heavy to carry.

She comes back up the stairs after the last trip. It's not as easy as it used to be; her knee still bothers her as it has ever since she fell six years ago, when she tripped on the second-last step. She's asked Frank a million times to fix the stairs but he hasn't done it—that's what she means by pigheaded. If she asks him more than twice to do something, he calls it nagging, and maybe it is, but who's going to do it if he won't? The cold, vacant hole at the back of this question is too much for her.

She has to stop herself from going to the back door again. Instead she goes to the back window and looks out; she can see almost the same things anyway.

Frank is going toward the barn, carrying something that looks like a wrench. The way he walks, slower than he used to, bent forward a little—from the back he's like an old man; how many years has he been walking that way?—makes her think, *He can't protect me.* She doesn't think this on purpose; it simply occurs to her. And it isn't only him, it's all of them, they've lost the power—you can tell by the way they walk. They are all waiting, just as Mrs. Burridge is, for whatever it is to happen. Whether they realize it or not. Lately when she's gone to the Dominion Store in town she has seen a look on the faces of the women there—she knows most of them, she wouldn't be mistaken—an anxious, closed look, as if they are frightened of something but won't talk about it. They're wondering what they will do; perhaps they think there's nothing they can do. This air of helplessness exasperates Mrs. Burridge, who has always been practical.

For weeks she has wanted to go to Frank and ask him to teach her how to use the gun. In fact, he has two guns, a shotgun and a .22 rifle; he used to like going after a few ducks in the fall, and of course there are the groundhogs—they have to be shot because of the holes they make in the fields Frank drives over on the tractor five or six times a year. A lot of men get injured by overturning tractors. But she can't ask him because she can't explain to him why she needs to know, and if she doesn't explain, he will only tease. "Anyone can shoot a gun," he'll say. "All you have to do is pull the trigger. . . . Oh, you mean you want to hit something, well now, that's different—who you planning to kill?" Perhaps he won't say that; perhaps this is only the way he talked twenty years ago, before she stopped taking an interest in things outside the house. But Mrs. Burridge will never know because she will never ask. She doesn't have the heart to say to him, *Maybe you'll be dead. Maybe you'll go off somewhere when it happens, maybe there will be a war.* She can remember the last war.

Nothing has changed outside the window, so she turns away and sits down at the kitchen table to make out her shopping list. Tomorrow is their day for going into town. She tries to plan the day so she can sit down at intervals; otherwise her feet start swelling up. That began with Sarah and got worse with the other two children and it's never really gone away. All her life, ever since she got married, she has made lists of things that have to be bought, sewed, planted, cooked, stored; she already has her list made for next Christmas, all the names and the gift she will buy for each, and the list of what she needs for Christmas dinner. But she can't seem to get interested in it; it's too far away. She can't believe in a distant future that is orderly like the past, she no longer seems to have the energy; it's as if she is saving it up for when she will have to use it.

She is even having trouble with the shopping list. Instead of concentrating on the paper—she writes on the backs of the used-up days off the page-a-day calendar Frank gives her every New Year's—she is gazing around the kitchen, looking at all the things she will have to leave behind when she goes. That will be the hardest part. Her mother's china, her silver, even though it is an old-fashioned pattern and the silver is wearing off, the egg timer in the shape of a chicken Sarah gave her when she was twelve, the ceramic salt and pepper shakers, green horses with perforated heads that one of the other children brought from the fair. She thinks of walking up the stairs, the sheets folded in the chest, the towels stacked neatly on the shelves, the beds made, the quilt that was her grandmother's—it makes her want to cry. On her bureau, the wedding picture, herself in a shiny satin gown (the satin was a mistake; it emphasized her hips), Frank in the suit he has not worn since except to funerals, his hair cut too short on the sides and a surprising tuft at the top, like a woodpecker's. The children when they were babies. She thinks of her girls now and hopes they will not have babies; it is no longer the right time for it.

Mrs. Burridge wishes someone would be more precise so she could make better plans. Everyone knows something is going to happen, you can tell by reading the newspapers and watching the television, but nobody is sure what it will be, nobody can be exact. She has her own ideas about it, though. At first it will simply become quieter. She will have an odd feeling that something is wrong but it will be a few days before she is able to pin it down. Then she will notice that the planes are no longer flying over on their way to the Malton Airport, and that the noise from the highway two miles away, which is quite distinct when the leaves are off the trees, has almost disappeared. The television will be noncommittal about it; in fact, the television, which right now is filled with bad news, of strikes, shortages, famines, layoffs and price increases, will become sweet-tempered and placating, and long intervals of classical music will appear on the radio. About this time Mrs. Burridge will realize that the news is being censored as it was during the war.

Mrs. Burridge is not positive about what will happen next; that is, she knows what will happen but she is not positive about the order. She expects it will be the gas and oil: the oil deliveryman will simply not turn up at his usual time and one morning the corner filling station will be closed. Just that, no explanations, because of course they—she does not know who "they" are, but she has always believed in their existence—they do not want people to panic. They are trying to keep things looking normal; possibly they have already started on this program and that is in fact why things still do look normal. Luckily she and Frank have the diesel fuel tank in the shed, it is three-quarters full; and they don't use the filling station anyway, they have their own gas pump. She has Frank bring in the old wood stove, the one they stored under the barn when they had the furnace and the electricity put in, and for once, she blesses Frank's habit of putting things off. She was after him for years to take that stove to the dump. He cuts down the dead elms, finally, and they burn them in the stove.

The telephone wires are blown down in a storm and no one comes to fix them; or this is what Mrs. Burridge deduces. At any rate, the phone goes dead. Mrs. Burridge doesn't particularly mind, she never liked using the phone much anyway, but it does make her feel cut off.

About now men begin to appear on the back road, the gravel road that goes past the gate, walking usually by themselves, sometimes in pairs. They seem to be heading north. Most of them are young, in their twenties, Mrs. Burridge would guess. They are not dressed like the men around here. It's been so long since she has seen anyone *walking* along this road that she becomes alarmed. She begins leaving the dogs off their chains—she has kept them chained at night ever since one of them bit a Jehovah's Witness early one Sunday morning. Mrs. Burridge doesn't hold with the Witnesses—she is United Church of Christ—but she respects their perseverence; at least they have the courage of their convictions which is more than you can say for some members of her own church, and she always buys a *Watchtower*. Maybe they have been right all along.

It is about this time too that she takes one of the guns, she thinks it will be the shotgun, as she will have a better chance of hitting something, and hides it, along with the shells, under a piece of roofing behind the barn. She does not tell Frank; he will have the .22. She has already picked out the spot.

They do not want to waste the little gasoline they still have left in the pump so they do not make unnecessary trips. They begin to eat the chickens, which Mrs. Burridge does not look forward to. She hates cleaning and plucking them, and the angriest she ever got at Frank was the time he and Henry Clarke decided to go into turkey farming. They did it, too, despite all she had to say against it, and she had to cope with the turkeys' escaping and scratching in the garden and impossible to catch—in her opinion they were the stupidest birds in God's creation—and she had to clean and pluck a turkey a week until luckily the blackhead[1] wiped out a third of the flock, which was enough to discourage them and they sold off the rest at a loss. It was the only time she was actually glad to see Frank lose money on one of his ventures.

Mrs. Burridge will feel things are getting serious on the day the electricity goes off and does not come back on. She knows, with a kind of fatalism, that this will happen in November, when the freezer is full of the vegetables but before it is cold enough to keep the packages frozen outside. She stands and looks at the plastic bags of beans and corn and spinach and carrots, melting and sodden, and thinks, *Why couldn't they have waited till spring?* It is the waste, of food and also of her hard work, that aggravates her the most. She salvages what she can. During the Depression, she remembers, they used to say those on farms were better off than those in the city, because at least they had food; if you could keep the farm, that is; but she is no longer sure this is true. She feels beleaguered, isolated, like someone shut up inside a fortress, though no one has bothered them, in fact no one has passed their way for days, not even the solitary walking men.

With the electricity off they can no longer get the television. The radio stations, when they broadcast at all, give out nothing but soothing music, which Mrs. Burridge does not find soothing in the least.

One morning she goes to the back door and looks out and there are the columns of smoke, right where she's been expecting to see them, off to the south. She calls Frank and they stand watching. The smoke is thick and black, oily, as if something has exploded. She does not know what Frank is thinking; she herself

[1] An infectious disease of turkeys and chickens.

is wondering about the children. She has had no news of them in weeks, but how could she? They stopped delivering mail some time ago now.

Fifteen minutes later, Henry Clarke drives into the yard in his half-ton truck. This is very unusual, as no one has been driving anywhere lately. There is another man with him, and Mrs. Burridge identifies him as the man three farms up who moved in four or five years ago. Frank goes out and talks with them, and they drive over to the gas pump and start pumping the rest of the precious gas into the truck. Frank comes back to the house. He tells her there's a little trouble down the road, they are going along to see about it and she isn't to worry. He goes into the back room, comes out with the .22, asks her where the shotgun is. She says she doesn't know. He searches for it, fruitlessly—she can hear him swearing, he does not swear in her presence—until he gives up. He comes out, kisses her good-bye, which is unusual too, and says he'll be back in a couple of hours. She watches the three of them drive off in Henry Clarke's truck, toward the smoke, she knows he will not come back. She supposes she ought to feel more emotional about it, but she is well prepared; she has been saying good-bye to him silently for years.

She re-enters the house and closes the door. She is fifty-one, her feet hurt and she does not know where she can go, but she realizes she cannot stay here. There will now be a lot of hungry people, those that can make it this far out of the cities will be young and tough, her house is a beacon, signaling warmth and food. It will be fought over, but not by her.

She goes upstairs, searches in the cupboard and puts on her heavy slacks and her two thickest sweaters. Downstairs, she gathers up all the food that will be light enough for her to carry: raisins, cooking chocolate, dried prunes and apricots, half a loaf of bread, some milk powder that she puts into a quart freezer bag, a piece of cheese. Then she unearths the shotgun from behind the barn. She thinks briefly of killing the livestock, the chickens, the heifers and the pig so no one will do it who does not know the right way; but she herself does not know the right way, she has never killed anything in her life, Frank always did it, so she contents herself with opening the henhouse door and the gate into the back field. She hopes the animals will run away but she knows they probably will not.

She takes one last look around the house. As an afterthought she adds her toothbrush to the bundle: she does not like the feel of unbrushed teeth. She does not go down into the cellar but she has an image of her carefully sealed bottles and jars, red and yellow and purple, shattered on the floor in a sticky puddle that looks like blood. Those who come will be wasteful, what they cannot eat themselves they will destroy. She thinks about setting fire to the house herself, before anyone else can do it.

Mrs. Burridge sits at her kitchen table. On the back of her calendar page—it's for a Monday—she has written *Oatmeal* in her evenly spaced public-school handwriting that always got a star and has not changed very much since then. The dogs are a problem. After some thought she unchains them, but she does not let them past the gate: at a crucial moment they might give her away. She walks north in her heavy boots, carrying her parka because it is not yet cold enough to put it on, and her package of food and the shotgun, which she has taken care to load. She passes the cemetery where her father and mother and her grandmother and grandfather are buried; the church used to be there but it burned down sixteen years ago and was rebuilt closer to the highway. Frank's people are in the other cemetery, his go back to the great-grandfather but they are Anglican, not that he kept it up. There is no one else on the road; she feels a little foolish. What if she is wrong and Frank comes back after all; what if nothing, really, is the matter? *Shortening,* she writes. She intends to make a lemon meringue pie for Sunday, when two of the children are coming up from the city for dinner.

It is almost evening and Mrs. Burridge is tired. She is in a part of the country she cannot remember, though she has stayed on the same road and it is a road she knows well; she has driven along it many times with Frank. But walking is not the same as driving. On one side there is a field, no buildings, and on the other a woodlot; a stream flows through a culvert under the road. Mrs. Burridge kneels down to drink: the water is ice-cold and tastes of iron. Later there will be a frost; she can feel it. She puts on her parka and her gloves and turns into the forest, where she will not be seen. There she will eat some raisins and cheese and try to rest, waiting for the moon to rise so she can continue walking. It is now quite dark. She smells earth, wood, rotting leaves.

Suddenly her eye is caught by a flicker of red, and before she can turn back —how can this happen so quickly?—it takes shape, it is a small fire, off to the right, and two men are crouching near it. They have seen her too: one of them rises and comes toward her. His teeth bared, he is smiling; he thinks she will be easy, an old woman. He says something but she cannot imagine what it is, she does not know how people dressed like that would talk.

They have spotted her gun, their eyes have fastened on it, they want it. Mrs. Burridge knows what she must do. She must wait until they are close enough and then she must raise the gun and shoot them, using one barrel for each, aiming at the faces. Otherwise they will kill her, she has no doubt about that. She will have to be fast, which is too bad because her hands feel thick and wooden; she is afraid, she does not want the loud noise or the burst of red that will follow, she has never killed anything in her life. She has no pictures beyond this point. You never know how you will act in a thing like that until it actually happens.

Mrs. Burridge looks at the kitchen clock. On her list she writes *Cheese;* they are eating more cheese now than they used to because of the price of meat. She gets up and goes to the kitchen door.

QUESTIONS

1. How does Mrs. Burridge's "peculiar thought" about a column of smoke (sixth paragraph) operate in the plot to set the story's theme? What earlier hints are there?
2. How does Frank's personality contrast with Mrs. Burridge's? Why does she wistfully decide that he is "a kind and likable man"?

3. What is the significance in her realizing that once the jars and quarts of preserves made her feel safe?
4. In the story's plotting, where and how do you discover the title's phrase, *when it happens?*
5. Contrary to usual narration, the story proceeds in the present tense: "Mrs. Burridge *is putting;* she *says;* Frank *answers."* How does this present-tense mode convey the story's actualities and its theme? How does the author, grammatically, convey the past?
6. As Mrs. Burridge sits making her shopping list, the tense shifts to the present: "He cuts down the dead elms, finally, and they burn them in the stove." Where does this place the events that follow? What is the actuality?
7. How does *cheese* in the final paragraph emphasize the theme?
8. What is the theme?

In Ursula Le Guin's "The Ones Who Walk Away from Omelas," theme dominates. The story is an unusual science-fiction meditation in which the narrator imagines, rejects, and revises the details of her fictive country, even asking the reader to "imagine it as your fancy bids," as if the details really do not change the theme. Her theme in broadest terms is the question of happiness. How does she answer that question?

THE ONES WHO WALK AWAY FROM OMELAS

Ursula K. Le Guin   (1929–   )

With a clamor of bells that set the swallows soaring, the Festival of Summer came to the city Omelas, bright-towered by the sea. The rigging of the boats in harbor sparkled with flags. In the streets between houses with red roofs and painted walls, between old moss-grown gardens and under avenues of trees, past great parks and public buildings, processions moved. Some were decorous: old people in long stiff robes of mauve and grey, grave master workmen, quiet, merry women carrying their babies and chatting as they walked. In other streets the music beat faster, a shimmering of gong and tambourine, and the people went dancing, the procession was a dance. Children dodged in and out, their high calls rising like the swallows' crossing flights over the music and the singing. All the processions wound towards the north side of the city, where on the great water-meadow called the Green Fields boys and girls, naked in the bright air, with mud-stained feet and ankles and long, lithe arms, exercised their restive horses before the race. The horses wore no gear at all but a halter without bit. Their manes were braided with streamers of silver, gold, and green. They flared their nostrils and pranced and boasted to one another; they were vastly excited, the horse being the only animal who has adopted our ceremonies as his own. Far off to the north and west the mountains stood up half encircling Omelas on her bay. The air of morning was so clear that the snow still crowning the Eighteen Peaks burned with white-gold fire across the miles of sunlit air, under the dark blue of the sky. There was just enough wind to make the banners that marked the racecourse snap and flutter now and then. In the silence of the broad green meadows one could hear the music winding through the city streets, farther and nearer and ever approaching, a cheerful faint sweetness of the air that from time to time trembled and gathered together and broke out into the great joyous clanging of the bells.

Joyous! How is one to tell about joy? How describe the citizens of Omelas?

They were not simple folk, you see, though they were happy. But we do not say the words of cheer much any more. All smiles have become archaic. Given a description such as this one tends to make certain assumptions. Given a description such as this one tends to look next for the King, mounted on a splendid stallion and surrounded by his noble knights, or perhaps in a golden litter borne by great-muscled slaves. But there was no king. They did not use swords, or keep slaves. They were not barbarians. I do not know the rules and laws of their society, but I suspect that they were singularly few. As they did without monarchy and slavery, so they also got on without the stock exchange, the advertisement, the secret police, and the bomb. Yet I repeat that these were not simple folk, not dulcet shepherds, noble savages, bland utopians. They were not less complex than us. The trouble is that we have a bad habit, encouraged by pedants and sophisticates, of considering happiness as something rather stupid. Only pain is intellectual, only evil interesting. This is the treason of the artist: a refusal to admit the banality of evil and the terrible boredom of pain. If you can't lick 'em, join 'em. If it hurts, repeat it. But to praise despair is to condemn delight, to embrace violence is to lose hold of everything else. We have almost lost hold; we can no longer describe a happy man, nor make any celebration of joy. How can I tell you about the people of Omelas? They were not naïve and happy children —though their children were, in fact, happy. They were mature, intelligent, passionate adults whose lives were not wretched. O miracle! but I wish I could describe it better. I wish I could convince you. Omelas sounds in my words like a city in a fairy tale, long ago and far away, once upon a time. Perhaps it would be best if you imagined it as your own fancy bids, assuming it will rise to the occasion, for certainly I cannot suit you all. For instance, how about technology? I think that there would be no cars or helicopters in and above the streets; this follows from the fact that the people of Omelas are happy people. Happiness is based on a just discrimination of what is necessary, what is neither necessary nor destructive, and what is destructive. In the middle category, however—that of the unnecessary but undestructive, that of comfort, luxury, exuberance, etc.—they could perfectly well have central heating, subway trains, washing machines, and all kinds of marvelous devices not yet invented here, floating light-sources, fuel-less power, a cure for the common cold. Or they could have none of that: it doesn't matter. As you like it. I incline to think that people from towns up and down the coast have been coming in to Omelas during the last days before the Festival on very fast little trains and double-decked trams, and that the train station of Omelas is actually the handsomest building in town, though plainer than the magnificent Farmers' Market. But even granted trains, I fear that Omelas so far strikes some of you as goody-goody. Smiles, bells, parades, horses, bleh. If so, please add an orgy. If an orgy would help, don't hesitate. Let us not, however, have temples from which issue beautiful nude priests and priestesses already half in ecstasy and ready to copulate with any man or woman, lover or stranger, who desires union with the deep godhead of the blood, although that was my first idea. But really it would be better not to have any temples in Omelas—at least, not manned temples. Religion yes, clergy no. Surely the beautiful nudes can just wander about, offering themselves like divine soufflés to the hunger of the needy and the rapture of the flesh. Let them join the processions. Let tambourines be struck above the copulations, and the glory of desire be proclaimed upon the gongs, and (a not unimportant point) let the offspring of these delightful rituals be beloved and looked after by all. One thing I know there is none of in Omelas is guilt. But what else should there be? I thought at first there were no drugs, but that is puritanical. For those who like it, the faint insistent sweetness of *drooz* may perfume the ways of the city, *drooz* which first brings a great lightness and brilliance to the mind and limbs, and then after some hours a dreamy languor, and wonderful visions at last of the very arcana and inmost secrets of the Universe, as well as exciting the pleasure of sex beyond all belief; and it is not habit-forming. For more modest tastes I think there ought to be beer. What else, what else belongs in the joyous city? The sense of victory, surely, the celebration of courage. But as we did without clergy, let us do without soldiers. The joy built upon successful slaughter is not the right kind of joy; it will not do; it is fearful and it is trivial. A boundless and generous contentment, a magnanimous triumph felt not against some outer enemy but in communion with the finest and fairest in the souls of all men everywhere and the splendor of the world's summer: this is what swells the hearts of the people of Omelas, and the victory they celebrate is that of life. I really don't think many of them need to take *drooz*.

Most of the processions have reached the Green Fields by now. A marvelous smell of cooking goes forth from the red and blue tents of the provisioners. The faces of small children are amiably sticky; in the benign grey beard of a man a couple of crumbs of rich pastry are entangled. The youths and girls have mounted their horses and are beginning to group around the starting line of the course. An old woman, small, fat, and laughing, is passing out flowers from a basket, and tall young men wear her flowers in their shining hair. A child of nine or ten sits at the edge of the crowd, alone, playing on a wooden flute. People pause to listen, and they smile, but they do not speak to him, for he never ceases playing and never sees them, his dark eyes wholly rapt in the sweet, thin magic of the tune.

He finishes, and slowly lowers his hands holding the wooden flute.

As if that little private silence were the signal, all at once a trumpet sounds from the pavilion near the starting line: imperious, melancholy, piercing. The horses rear on their slender legs, and some of them neigh in answer. Sober-faced, the young riders stroke the horses' necks and soothe them, whispering, "Quiet, quiet, there my beauty, my hope. . . ." They begin to form in rank along the starting line. The crowds along the racecourse are like a field of grass and flowers in the wind. The Festival of Summer has begun.

Do you believe? Do you accept the festival, the city, the joy? No? Then let me describe one more thing.

In a basement under one of the beautiful public buildings of Omelas, or perhaps in the cellar of one of its spacious private homes, there is a room. It has one locked door, and no window. A little light seeps in dustily between cracks in the boards, secondhand from a cobwebbed window somewhere across the cellar. In one corner of the little room a couple of mops, with stiff, clotted, foul-smelling heads, stand near a rusty bucket. The floor is dirt, a little damp to the touch, as cellar dirt usually is. The room is about three paces long and two wide: a mere broom closet or disused tool room. In the room a child is sitting. It could be a boy or a girl. It looks about six, but actually is nearly ten. It is feeble-minded. Perhaps it was born defective, or perhaps it has become imbecile through fear, malnutrition, and neglect. It picks its nose and occasionally fumbles vaguely with its toes or genitals, as it sits hunched in the corner farthest from the bucket and the two mops. It is afraid of the mops. It finds them horrible. It shuts its eyes, but it knows the mops are still standing there; and the door is locked; and nobody will come. The door is always locked; and nobody ever comes, except that sometimes—the child has no understanding of time or interval—sometimes the door rattles terribly and opens, and a person, or several people, are there. One of them may come in and kick the child to make it stand up. The others never come close, but peer in at it with frightened, disgusted eyes. The food bowl and the water jug are hastily filled, the door is locked, the eyes disappear. The people at the door never say anything, but the child, who has not always lived in the tool room, and can remember sunlight and its mother's voice, sometimes speaks. "I will be good," it says. "Please let me out. I will be good!" They never answer. The child used to scream for help at night, and cry a good deal, but now it only makes a kind of whining, "eh-haa, eh-haa," and it speaks less and less often. It is so thin there are no calves to its legs; its belly protrudes; it lives on a half-bowl of corn meal and grease a day. It is naked. Its buttocks and thighs are a mass of festered sores, as it sits in its own excrement continually.

They all know it is there, all the people of Omelas. Some of them have come to see it, others are content merely to know it is there. They all know that it has to be there. Some of them understand why, and some do not, but they all understand that their happiness, the beauty of their city, the tenderness of their friendships, the health of their children, the wisdom of their scholars, the skill of their makers, even the abundance of their harvest and the kindly weathers of their skies, depend wholly on this child's abominable misery.

This is usually explained to children when they are between eight and twelve, whenever they seem capable of understanding; and most of those who come to see the child are young people, though often enough an adult comes, or comes back, to see the child. No matter how well the matter has been explained to them, these young spectators are always shocked and sickened at the sight. They feel disgust, which they had thought themselves superior to. They feel anger, outrage, impotence, despite all the explanations. They would like to do something for the child. But there is nothing they can do. If the child were brought up into the sunlight out of that vile place, if it were cleaned and fed and comforted, that would be a good thing, indeed; but if it were done, in that day and hour all the prosperity and beauty and delight of Omelas would wither and be destroyed. Those are the terms. To exchange all the goodness and grace of every life in Omelas for that single, small improvement: to throw away the happiness of thousands for the chance of the happiness of one: that would be to let guilt within the walls indeed.

The terms are strict and absolute; there may not even be a kind word spoken to the child.

Often the young people go home in tears, or in a tearless rage, when they have seen the child and faced this terrible paradox. They may brood over it for weeks or years. But as time goes on they begin to realize that even if the child could be released, it would not get much good of its freedom: a little vague pleasure of warmth and food, no doubt, but little more. It is too degraded and imbecile to know any real joy. It has been afraid too long ever to be free of fear. Its habits are too uncouth for it to respond to humane treatment. Indeed, after so long it would probably be wretched without walls about it to protect it, and darkness for its eyes, and its own excrement to sit in. Their tears at the bitter injustice dry when they begin to perceive the terrible justice of reality, and to accept it. Yet it is their tears and anger, the trying of their generosity and the acceptance of their helplessness, which are perhaps the true source of the splendor of their lives. Theirs is no vapid, irresponsible happiness. They know that they, like the child, are not free. They know compassion. It is the existence of the child, and their knowledge of its existence, that makes possible the nobility of their architecture, the poignancy of their music, the profundity of their science. It is because of the child that they are so gentle with children. They know that if the wretched one were not there snivelling in the dark, the other one, the flute-player, could make no joyful music as the young riders line up in their beauty for the race in the sunlight of the first morning of summer.

Now do you believe in them? Are they not more credible? But there is one more thing to tell, and this is quite incredible.

At times one of the adolescent girls or boys who go to see the child does not go home to weep or rage, does not, in fact, go home at all. Sometimes also a man or woman much older falls silent for a day or two, and then leaves home. These people go out into the street, and walk down the street alone. They keep walking, and walk straight out of the city of Omelas, through the beautiful gates. They keep walking across the farmlands of Omelas. Each one goes alone, youth or girl, man or woman. Night falls; the traveler must pass down village streets, between the houses with yellow-lit windows, and on out into the darkness of the fields. Each alone, they go west or north, towards the mountains. They go on. They leave Omelas, they walk ahead into the darkness, and they do not come back. The place they go towards is a place even less imaginable to most of us than the city of happiness. I cannot describe it at all. It is possible that it does not exist. But they seem to know where they are going, the ones who walk away from Omelas.

QUESTIONS

1. What actual cultures do the details of Le Guin's description suggest for this imaginary city?
2. Who is the narrator Le Guin projects with "our ceremonies" in the first paragraph and with the "they" in the third?
3. What does she suggest with "all smiles have become archaic"?
4. How does the narrative perspective change with "Given a description such as this . . ."? What does "They were not less complex than us" suggest about the perspective?
5. What does Le Guin suggest by "we can no longer describe a happy man, nor make any celebrations of joy"?
6. What is the effect of "Omelas sounds in my words like a city in a fairy tale"? What other stories in this book have invoked something similar?
7. What does Le Guin imply about the narrator with ". . . washing machines, and all kinds of devices not yet invented here"? And, eight sentences later, with "that was my first idea"?
8. What do these shifts say about defining happiness?
9. What is the significance of the child playing the wooden flute?
10. What do the ones who walk away imply about happiness?

Futuristic utopias with anti-utopian themes are perhaps the twentieth century's major contribution to the eternal tutelage of fiction. But science-fiction writers, as with Le Guin and with Lem's "The Seventh Sally"—note the chivalric diction—characteristically imagine, out there in infinite space, primitive, ancient, or medieval societies. The visitors to outer space encounter horses without gear, banners, wooden flutes, kings, castles, mythologies emerging. Why does the twentieth-century imagination turn for meaning to these curious time warps?

THE SEVENTH SALLY*

Or How Trurl's Own Perfection Led to No Good

Stanislaw Lem   (1921–)

The Universe is infinite but bounded, and therefore a beam of light, in whatever direction it may travel, will after billions of centuries return—if powerful enough —to the point of its departure; and it is no different with rumor, that flies about from star to star and makes the rounds of every planet. One day Trurl heard distant reports of two mighty constructor-benefactors, so wise and so accomplished that they had no equal; with this news he ran to Klapaucius, who explained to him that these were not mysterious rivals, but only themselves, for their fame had circumnavigated space. Fame, however, has this fault, that it says nothing of one's failures, even when those very failures are the product of a great

*Translated by Michael Kandel.

perfection. And he who would doubt this, let him recall the last of the seven sallies[1] of Trurl, which was undertaken without Klapaucius, whom certain urgent duties kept at home at the time.

In those days Trurl was exceedingly vain, receiving all marks of veneration and honor paid to him as his due and a perfectly normal thing. He was heading north in his ship, as he was the least familiar with that region, and had flown through the void for quite some time, passing spheres full of the clamor of war as well as spheres that had finally obtained the perfect peace of desolation, when suddenly a little planet came into view, really more of a stray fragment of matter than a planet.

On the surface of this chunk of rock someone was running back and forth, jumping and waving his arms in the strangest way. Astonished by a scene of such total loneliness and concerned by those wild gestures of despair, and perhaps of anger as well, Trurl quickly landed.

He was approached by a personage of tremendous hauteur, iridium and vanadium all over and with a great deal of clanging and clanking, who introduced himself as Excelsius the Tartarian, ruler of Pancreon and Cyspenderora; the inhabitants of both these kingdoms had, in a fit of regicidal madness, driven His Highness from the throne and exiled him to this barren asteroid, eternally adrift among the dark swells and currents of gravitation.

Learning in turn the identity of his visitor, the deposed monarch began to insist that Trurl—who after all was something of a professional when it came to good deeds—immediately restore him to his former position. The thought of such a turn of events brought the flame of vengeance to the monarch's eyes, and his iron fingers clutched the air, as if already closing around the throats of his beloved subjects.

Now Trurl had no intention of complying with this request of Excelsius, as doing so would bring about untold evil and suffering, yet at the same time he wished somehow to comfort and console the humiliated king. Thinking a moment or two, he came to the conclusion that, even in this case, not all was lost, for it would be possible to satisfy the king completely—without putting his former subjects in jeopardy. And so, rolling up his sleeves and summoning up all his mastery, Trurl built the king an entirely new kingdom. There were plenty of towns, rivers, mountains, forests and brooks, a sky with clouds, armies full of derring-do, citadels, castles and ladies' chambers; and there were marketplaces, gaudy and gleaming in the sun, days of back-breaking labor, nights full of dancing and song until dawn, and the gay clatter of swordplay. Trurl also carefully set into this kingdom a fabulous capital, all in marble and alabaster, and assembled a council of hoary sages, and winter palaces and summer villas, plots, conspirators, false witnesses, nurses, informers, teams of magnificent steeds, and plumes waving crimson in the wind; and then he crisscrossed that atmosphere with silver fanfares and twenty-one gun salutes, also threw in the necessary handful of traitors, another of heroes, added a pinch of prophets and seers, and one messiah and one great poet each, after which he bent over and set the works in motion,

---

[1]The first six sallies are recounted in *The Cyberiad,* the source of the present story.

deftly making last-minute adjustments with his microscopic tools as it ran, and he gave the women of that kingdom beauty, the men—sullen silence and surliness when drunk, the officials—arrogance and servility, the astronomers—an enthusiasm for stars, and the children—a great capacity for noise. And all of this, connected, mounted and ground to precision, fit into a box, and not a very large box, but just the size that could be carried about with ease. This Trurl presented to Excelsius, to rule and have dominion over forever; but first he showed him where the input and output of his brand-new kingdom were, and how to program wars, quell rebellions, exact tribute, collect taxes, and also instructed him in the critical points and transition states of that microminiaturized society—in other words the maxima and minima of palace coups and revolutions—and explained everything so well, that the king, an old hand in the running of tyrannies, instantly grasped the directions and, without hesitation, while the constructor watched, issued a few trial proclamations, correctly manipulating the control knobs, which were carved with imperial eagles and regal lions. These proclamations declared a state of emergency, martial law, a curfew and a special levy. After a year had passed in the kingdom, which amounted to hardly a minute for Trurl and the king, by an act of the greatest magnanimity—that is, by a flick of the finger at the controls—the king abolished one death penalty, lightened the levy and deigned to annul the state of emergency, whereupon a tumultuous cry of gratitude, like the squeaking of tiny mice lifted by their tails, rose up from the box, and through its curved glass cover one could see, on the dusty highways and along the banks of lazy rivers that reflected the fluffy clouds, the people rejoicing and praising the great and unsurpassed benevolence of their sovereign lord.

And so, though at first he had felt insulted by Trurl's gift, in that the kingdom was too small and very like a child's toy, the monarch saw that the thick glass lid made everything inside seem large; perhaps too he dully understood that size was not what mattered here, for government is not measured in meters and kilograms, and emotions are somehow the same, whether experienced by giants or dwarfs—and so he thanked the constructor, if somewhat stiffly. Who knows, he might even have liked to order him thrown in chains and tortured to death, just to be safe—that would have been a sure way of nipping in the bud any gossip about how some common vagabond tinkerer presented a mighty monarch with a kingdom.

Excelsius was sensible enough, however, to see that this was out of the question, owing to a very fundamental disproportion, for fleas could sooner take their host into captivity than the king's army seize Trurl. So with another cold nod, he stuck his orb and scepter under his arm, lifted the box kingdom with a grunt, and took it to his humble hut of exile. And as blazing day alternated with murky night outside, according to the rhythm of the asteroid's rotation, the king, who was acknowledged by his subjects as the greatest in the world, diligently reigned, bidding this, forbidding that, beheading, rewarding—in all these ways incessantly spurring his little ones on to perfect fealty and worship of the throne.

As for Trurl, he returned home and related to his friend Klapaucius, not without pride, how he had employed his constructor's genius to indulge the autocratic aspirations of Excelsius and, at the same time, safeguard the democratic aspirations of his former subjects. But Klapaucius, surprisingly enough, had no words of praise for Trurl; in fact, there seemed to be rebuke in his expression.

"Have I understood you correctly?" he said at last. "You gave that brutal despot, that born slave master, that slavering sadist of a painmonger, you gave him a whole civilization to rule and have dominion over forever? And you tell me, moreover, of the cries of joy brought on by the repeal of a fraction of his cruel decrees! Trurl, how could you have done such a thing?!"

"You must be joking!" Trurl exclaimed. "Really, the whole kingdom fits into a box three feet by two by two and a half . . . it's only a model . . ."

"A model of what?"

"What do you mean, of what? Of a civilization, obviously, except that it's a hundred million times smaller."

"And how do you know there aren't civilizations a hundred million times larger than our own? And if there were, would ours then be a model? And what importance do dimensions have anyway? In that box kingdom, doesn't a journey from the capital to one of the corners take months—for those inhabitants? And don't they suffer, don't they know the burden of labor, don't they die?"

"Now just a minute, you know yourself that all these processes take place only because I programmed them, and so they aren't genuine. . . ."

"Aren't genuine? You mean to say the box is empty, and the parades, tortures and beheadings are merely an illusion?"

"Not an illusion, no, since they have reality, though purely as certain microscopic phenomena, which I produced by manipulating atoms," said Trurl. "The point is, these births, loves, acts of heroism and denunciations are nothing but the minuscule capering of electrons in space, precisely arranged by the skill of my nonlinear craft, which—"

"Enough of your boasting, not another word!" Klapaucius snapped. "Are these processes self-organizing or not?"

"Of course they are!"

"And they occur among infinitesimal clouds of electrical charge?"

"You know they do."

"And the phenomenological events of dawns, sunsets and bloody battles are generated by the concatenation of real variables?"

"Certainly."

"And are not we as well, if you examine us physically, mechanistically, statistically and meticulously, nothing but the minuscule capering of electron clouds? Positive and negative charges arranged in space? And is our existence not the result of subatomic collisions and the interplay of particles, though we ourselves perceive those molecular cartwheels as fear, longing, or meditation? And when you day-dream, what transpires within your brain but the binary algebra of connecting and disconnecting circuits, the continual meandering of electrons?"

"What, Klapaucius, would you equate our existence with that of an imitation kingdom locked up in some glass box?!" cried Trurl. "No, really, that's going too far! My purpose was simply to fashion a simulator of statehood, a model cybernetically perfect, nothing more!"

"Trurl! Our perfection is our curse, for it draws down upon our every endeavor no end of unforeseeable consequences!" Klapaucius said in a stentorian voice. "If an imperfect imitator, wishing to inflict pain, were to build himself a crude idol of wood or wax, and further give it some makeshift semblance of a sentient being, his torture of the thing would be a paltry mockery indeed! But consider a succession of improvements on this practice! Consider the next sculptor, who builds a doll with a recording in its belly, that it may groan beneath his blows; consider a doll which, when beaten, begs for mercy, no longer a crude idol, but a homeostat; consider a doll that sheds tears, a doll that bleeds, a doll that fears death, though it also longs for the peace that only death can bring! Don't you see, when the imitator is perfect, so must be the imitation, and the semblance becomes the truth, the pretense a reality! Trurl, you took an untold number of creatures capable of suffering and abandoned them forever to the rule of a wicked tyrant. . . . Trurl, you have committed a terrible crime!"

"Sheer sophistry!" shouted Trurl, all the louder because he felt the force of his friends's argument. "Electrons meander not only in our brains, but in phonograph records as well, which proves nothing, and certainly gives no grounds for such hypostatical analogies! The subjects of that monster Excelsius do in fact die when decapitated, sob, fight, and fall in love, since that is how I set up the parameters, but it's impossible to say, Klapaucius, that they feel anything in the process—the electrons jumping around in their heads will tell you nothing of that!"

"And if I were to look inside your head, I would also see nothing but electrons," replied Klapaucius. "Come now, don't pretend not to understand what I'm saying, I know you're not that stupid! A phonograph record won't run errands for you, won't beg for mercy or fall on its knees! You say there's no way of knowing whether Excelsius' subjects groan, when beaten, purely because of the electrons hopping about inside—like wheels grinding out the mimicry of a voice—or whether they really groan, that is, because they honestly experience the pain? A pretty distinction, this! No, Trurl, a sufferer is not one who hands you his suffering, that you may touch it, weigh it, bite it like a coin; a sufferer is one who behaves like a sufferer! Prove to me here and now, once and for all, that they do not feel, that they do not think, that they do not in any way exist as beings conscious of their enclosure between the two abysses of oblivion—the abyss before birth and the abyss that follows death—prove this to me, Trurl, and I'll leave you be! Prove that you only *imitated* suffering, and did not *create* it!"

"You know perfectly well that's impossible," answered Trurl quietly. "Even before I took my instruments in hand, when the box was still empty, I had to anticipate the possibility of precisely such a proof—in order to rule it out. For otherwise the monarch of that kingdom sooner or later would have gotten the impression that his subjects were not real subjects at all, but puppets, marionettes. Try to understand, there was no other way to do it! Anything that would have destroyed in the littlest way the illusion of complete reality, would have also destroyed the importance, the dignity of governing, and turned it into nothing but a mechanical game. . . ."

"I understand, I understand all too well!" cried Klapaucius. "Your intentions were the noblest—you only sought to construct a kingdom as lifelike as possible, so similar to a real kingdom, that no one, absolutely no one, could ever tell the difference, and in this, I am afraid, you were successful! Only hours have passed since your return, but for them, the ones imprisoned in that box, whole centuries have gone by—how many beings, how many lives wasted, and all to gratify and feed the vanity of King Excelsius!"

Without another word Trurl rushed back to his ship, but saw that his friend was coming with him. When he had blasted off into space, pointed the bow between two great clusters of eternal flame and opened the throttle all the way, Klapaucius said:

"Trurl, you're hopeless. You always act first, think later. And now what do you intend to do when we get there?"

"I'll take the kingdom away from him!"

"And what will you do with it?"

"Destroy it!" Trurl was about to shout, but choked on the first syllable when he realized what he was saying. Finally he mumbled:

"I'll hold an election. Let them choose just rulers from among themselves."

"You programmed them all to be feudal lords or shiftless vassals. What good would an election do? First you'd have to undo the entire structure of the kingdom, then assemble from scratch. . . ."

"And where," exclaimed Trurl, "does the changing of structures end and the tampering with minds begin?!" Klapaucius had no answer for this, and they flew on in gloomy silence, till the planet of Excelsius came into view. As they circled it, preparing to land, they beheld a most amazing sight.

The entire planet was covered with countless signs of intelligent life. Microscopic bridges, like tiny lines, spanned every rill and rivulet, while the puddles, reflecting the stars, were full of microscopic boats like floating chips. . . . The night side of the sphere was dotted with glimmering cities, and on the day side one could make out flourishing metropolises, though the inhabitants themselves were much too little to observe, even through the strongest lens. Of the king there was not a trace, as if the earth had swallowed him up.

"He isn't here," said Trurl in an awed whisper. "What have they done with him? Somehow they managed to break through the walls of their box and occupy the asteroid. . . ."

"Look!" said Klapaucius, pointing to a little cloud no larger than a thimble and shaped like a mushroom; it slowly rose into the atmosphere. "They've discovered atomic energy. . . . And over there—you see that bit of glass? It's the remains of the box, they've made it into some sort of temple. . . ."

"I don't understand. It was only a model, after all. A process with a large number of parameters, a simulation, a mock-up for a monarch to practice on, with the necessary feedback, variables, multistats . . ." muttered Trurl, dumbfounded.

"Yes. But you made the unforgivable mistake of over-perfecting your replica. Not wanting to build a mere clocklike mechanism, you inadvertently—in your punctilious way—created that which was possible, logical and inevitable, that which became the very antithesis of a mechanism. . . ."

"Please no more!" cried Trurl. And they looked out upon the asteroid in silence, when suddenly something bumped their ship, or rather grazed it slightly. They saw this object, for it was illumined by the thin ribbon of flame that issued from its tail. A ship, probably, or perhaps an artificial satellite, though remarkably similar to one of those steel boots the tyrant Excelsius used to wear. And when the constructors raised their eyes, they beheld a heavenly body shining high above the tiny planet—it hadn't been there previously—and they recognized, in that cold pale orb, the stern features of Excelsius himself, who had in this way become the Moon of the Microminians.

QUESTIONS

1. How does the bounded universe, with its returning beam of light, bear on the way the story ends?
2. What is Trurl's mistake in this expedition, of which he is "exceedingly vain"?
3. What is the satire in Lem's fifth paragraph—and elsewhere?
4. For what does Klapaucius, the superior "constructor-benefactor," reprimand Trurl? How are they both proved wrong?
5. What is "the very antithesis of mechanism" that Trurl has created?
6. What are the implications of the tiny atomic explosion Trurl and Klapaucius see? How does this relate to spheres clamoring with war and spheres "that had finally attained the perfect peace of desolation" that Trurl passes as he sets out (second paragraph)?
7. What elements of Greek mythology appear in the Microminians' culture?
8. What are the political and social themes in this story?

Jorge Luis Borges once remarked after a lecture on the reality of fiction: "All life is a parable, though we do not know what it means." Here he makes an allegory on the biblical account of Christ, with realistic details from Argentina precisely placed in March, 1928. What is he saying about religion in this parable of modern life?

THE GOSPEL ACCORDING TO MARK*

Jorge Luis Borges   (1899–1986)

These events took place at La Colorada ranch, in the southern part of the township of Junín,[1] during the last days of March, 1928. The protagonist was a medical student named Baltasar Espinosa. We may describe him, for now, as one of the common run of young men from Buenos Aires, with nothing more note-

---

*Translated by Norman Thomas di Giovanni in collaboration with the author.

[1]In Argentina, west of Buenos Aires.

worthy about him than an almost unlimited kindness and a capacity for public speaking that had earned him several prizes at the English school in Ramos Mejía. He did not like arguing, and preferred having his listener rather than himself in the right. Although he was fascinated by the probabilities of chance in any game he played, he was a bad player because it gave him no pleasure to win. His wide intelligence was undirected; at the age of thirty-three, he still lacked credit for graduation, by one course—the course to which he was most drawn. His father, who was a freethinker (like all the gentlemen of his day), had introduced him to the lessons of Herbert Spencer,[2] but his mother, before leaving on a trip for Montevideo, once asked him to say the Lord's Prayer and make the sign of the cross every night. Through the years, he had never gone back on that promise.

Espinosa was not lacking in spirit; one day, with more indifference than anger, he had exchanged two or three punches with a group of fellow-students who were trying to force him to take part in a university demonstration. Owing to an acquiescent nature, he was full of opinions, or habits of mind, that were questionable: Argentina mattered less to him than a fear that in other parts of the world people might think of us as Indians; he worshiped France but despised the French; he thought little of Americans but approved the fact that there were tall buildings, like theirs, in Buenos Aires; he believed the gauchos of the plains to be better riders than those of hill or mountain country. When his cousin Daniel invited him to spend the summer months out at La Colorada, he said yes at once —not because he was really fond of the country, but more out of his natural complacency and also because it was easier to say yes than to dream up reasons for saying no.

The ranch's main house was big and slightly run-down; the quarters of the foreman, whose name was Gutre, were close by. The Gutres were three: the father, an unusually uncouth son, and a daughter of uncertain paternity. They were tall, strong, and bony, and had hair that was on the reddish side and faces that showed traces of Indian blood. They were barely articulate. The foreman's wife had died years before.

There in the country, Espinosa began learning things he never knew, or even suspected—for example, that you do not gallop a horse when approaching settlements, and that you never go out riding except for some special purpose. In time, he was to come to tell the birds apart by their calls.

After a few days, Daniel had to leave for Buenos Aires to close a deal on some cattle. At most, this bit of business might take him a week. Espinosa, who was already somewhat weary of hearing about his cousin's incessant luck with women and his tireless interest in the minute details of men's fashion, preferred staying on at the ranch with his textbooks. But the heat was unbearable, and even the night brought no relief. One morning at daybreak, thunder woke him. Outside, the wind was rocking the Australian pines. Listening to the first heavy drops of rain, Espinosa thanked God. All at once, cold air rolled in. That afternoon, the Salado overflowed its banks.

[2]Spencer (1820–1903) was an English philosopher and a proponent of scientific determinism.

The next day, looking out over the flooded fields from the gallery of the main house, Baltasar Espinosa thought that the stock metaphor comparing the pampa[3] to the sea was not altogether false—at least, not that morning—though W. H. Hudson[4] had remarked that the sea seems wider because we view it from a ship's deck and not from a horse or from eye level.

The rain did not let up. The Gutres, helped or hindered by Espinosa, the town dweller, rescued a good part of the livestock, but many animals were drowned. There were four roads leading to La Colorada; all of them were under water. On the third day, when a leak threatened the foreman's house, Espinosa gave the Gutres a room near the tool shed, at the back of the main house. This drew them all closer, they ate together in the big dining room. Conversation turned out to be difficult. The Gutres, who knew so much about country things, were hard put to it to explain them. One night, Espinosa asked them if people still remembered the Indian raids from back when the frontier command was located there in Junín. They told him yes, but they would have given the same answer to a question about the beheading of Charles I.[5] Espinosa recalled his father's saying that almost every case of longevity that was cited in the country was really a case of bad memory or of a dim notion of dates. Gauchos are apt to be ignorant of the year of their birth or of the name of the man who begot them.

In the whole house, there was apparently no other reading matter than a set of the *Farm Journal,* a handbook of veterinary medicine, a deluxe edition of the Uruguayan epic *Tabaré, a History of Shorthorn Cattle in Argentina,* a number of erotic or detective stories, and a recent novel called *Don Segundo Sombra.* Espinosa, trying in some way to bridge the inevitable after-dinner gap, read a couple of chapters of this novel to the Gutres, none of whom could read or write. Unfortunately, the foreman had been a cattle drover, and the doings of the hero, another cattle drover, failed to whet his interest. He said that the work was light, that drovers always traveled with a packhorse that carried everything they needed, and that, had he not been a drover, he would never have seen such far-flung places as the Laguna de Gómez, the town of Bragado, and the spread of the Núñez family in Chacabuco. There was a guitar in the kitchen; the ranch hands, before the time of the events I am describing, used to sit around in a circle. Someone would tune the instrument without ever getting around to playing it. This was known as a guitarfest.

Espinosa, who had grown a beard, began dallying in front of the mirror to study his new face, and he smiled to think how, back in Buenos Aires he would bore his friends by telling them the story of the Salado flood. Strangely enough, he missed places he never frequented and never would: a corner of Cabrera Street on which there was a mailbox; one of the cement lions of a gateway on Jujuy Street, a few blocks from the Plaza del Once; an old barroom with a tiled floor, whose exact whereabouts he was unsure of. As for his brothers and his father,

---

[3]Treeless plains.   [4]An English writer (1841–1922), born in Argentina.   [5]An English king, beheaded in 1649.

they would already have learned from Daniel that he was isolated—etymologically, the word was perfect—by the floodwaters.

Exploring the house, still hemmed in by the watery waste, Espinosa came across an English Bible. Among the blank pages at the end, the Guthries—such was their original name—had left a handwritten record of their lineage. They were natives of Inverness;[6] had reached the New World, no doubt as common laborers, in the early part of the nineteenth century; and had intermarried with Indians. The chronicle broke off sometime during the eighteen-seventies, when they no longer knew how to write. After a few generations, they had forgotten English; their Spanish, at the time Espinosa knew them, gave them trouble. They lacked any religious faith, but there survived in their blood, like faint tracks, the rigid fanaticism of the Calvinist and the superstitions of the pampa Indian. Espinosa later told them of his find, but they barely took notice.

Leafing through the volume, his fingers opened it at the beginning of the Gospel according to St. Mark. As an exercise in translation, and maybe to find out whether the Gutres understood any of it, Espinosa decided to begin reading them that text after their evening meal. It surprised him that they listened attentively, absorbed. Maybe the gold letters on the cover lent the book authority. It's still there in their blood, Espinosa thought. It also occurred to him that the generations of men, throughout recorded time, have always told and retold two stories—that of a lost ship which searches the Mediterranean sea for a dearly loved island, and that of a god who is crucified on Golgotha.[7] Remembering his lessons in elocution from his schooldays in Ramos Mejía, Espinosa got to his feet when he came to the parables.

The Gutres took to bolting their barbecued meat and their sardines so as not to delay the Gospel. A pet lamb that the girl adorned with a small blue ribbon had injured itself on a strand of barbed wire. To stop the bleeding, the three had wanted to apply a cobweb to the wound, but Espinosa treated the animal with some pills. The gratitude that this treatment awakened in them took him aback. (Not trusting the Gutres at first, he'd hidden away in one of his books the two hundred and forty pesos he had brought with him.) Now, the owner of the place away, Espinosa took over and gave timid orders, which were immediately obeyed. The Gutres, as if lost without him, liked following him from room to room and along the gallery that ran around the house. While he read to them, he noticed that they were secretly stealing the crumbs he had dropped on the table. One evening, he caught them unawares, talking about him respectfully, in very few words.

Having finished the Gospel according to St. Mark, he wanted to read another of the three Gospels that remained, but the father asked him to repeat the one he had just read, so that they could understand it better. Espinosa felt that they were like children, to whom repetition is more pleasing than variations or novelty. That night—this is not to be wondered at—he dreamed of the Flood;[8] the hammer

---

[6]In Scotland.   [7]Where Christ was crucified. See Mark 15.22.   [8]The story of the flood is told in Genesis, chapters 6–8.

blows of the building of the Ark woke him up, and he thought that perhaps they were thunder. In fact, the rain, which had let up, started again. The cold was bitter. The Gutres had told him that the storm had damaged the roof of the tool shed, and that they would show it to him when the beams were fixed. No longer a stranger now, he was treated by them with special attention, almost to the point of spoiling him. None of them liked coffee, but for him there was always a small cup into which they heaped sugar.

The new storm had broken out on a Tuesday. Thursday night, Espinosa was awakened by a soft knock at his door, which—just in case—he always kept locked. He got out of bed and opened it; there was the girl. In the dark he could hardly make her out, but by her footsteps he could tell she was barefoot, and moments later, in bed, that she must have come all the way from the other end of the house naked. She did not embrace him or speak a single word; she lay beside him, trembling. It was the first time she had known a man. When she left, she did not kiss him; Espinosa realized that he didn't even know her name. For some reason that he did not want to pry into, he made up his mind that upon returning to Buenos Aires he would tell no one about what had taken place.

The next day began like the previous ones, except that the father spoke to Espinosa and asked him if Christ had let Himself be killed so as to save all other men on earth. Espinosa, who was a freethinker but who felt committed to what he had read to the Gutres, answered, "Yes, to save everyone from Hell."

Gutre then asked, "What's Hell?"

"A place under the ground where souls burn and burn."

"And the Roman soldiers who hammered in the nails—were they saved too?"

"Yes," said Espinosa, whose theology was rather dim.

All along, he was afraid that the foreman might ask him about what had gone on the night before with his daughter. After lunch, they asked him to read the last chapters over again.

Espinosa slept a long nap that afternoon. It was a light sleep, disturbed by persistent hammering and by vague premonitions. Toward evening, he got up and went out onto the gallery. He said, as if thinking aloud, "The waters have dropped. It won't be long now."

"It won't be long now," Gutre repeated, like an echo.

The three had been following him. Bowing their knees to the stone pavement, they asked his blessing. Then they mocked at him, spat on him, and shoved him toward the back part of the house. The girl wept. Espinosa understood what awaited him on the other side of the door. When they opened it, he saw a patch of sky. A bird sang out. A goldfinch, he thought. The shed was without a roof; they had pulled down the beams to make the cross.

QUESTIONS

1. What are the implications in the hero's name? (Balthasar was one of the Magi; Belshazzar was the King of Babylon who saw the handwriting on the wall; *espina* means "thorn" in Spanish.)

2. Why does Borges say *for now* in the third sentence?
3. What relevance has Espinosa's "almost unlimited kindness" and his "capacity for public speaking"?
4. What is the significance of Espinosa's age?
5. What is the significance of his parents' teachings?
6. What kind of personality does Borges present in his first two paragraphs?
7. What are the implications of "Espinosa thanked God," when the rain begins?
8. What does the Guthrie Bible suggest about the Gutres and the present situation?
9. What are the ironies concerning the pet lamb?
10. What significance do you see in the Gutres "stealing crumbs he had dropped on the table"?
11. Is the Gospel according to Mark significantly different from those of Matthew, Luke, and John? (Write a paper on this if time permits.)
12. Why does Borges bring in the flood?
13. What significance has the girl's visit on Thursday night?
14. What is the irony in "they had pulled down the beams to make the cross"? What other ironies does Borges generate from the biblical account?
15. What is significant about the Gutres retaining in their blood faint traces of Calvinist fanaticism and Indian superstition?
16. What is Borges saying about religion?

Our next hero is the opposite of Espinosa. He is a city dweller. He is hypersensitive about his relation to society. He confides to us in the first person. But he, like Espinosa, is alienated. What twentieth-century theme do both reflect?

THE THROWER-AWAY*

Heinrich Böll   *(1917–1985)*

For the last few weeks I have been trying to avoid people who might ask me what I do for a living. If I really had to put a name to my occupation, I would be forced to utter a word which would alarm people. So I prefer the abstract method of putting down my confession on paper.

Until recently I would have been prepared at any time to make an oral confession. I almost insisted. I called myself an inventor, a scholar, even a student, and, in the melodramatic mood of incipient intoxication, an unrecognized genius. I basked in the cheerful fame which a frayed collar can radiate; arrogantly, as if it were mine by right, I exacted reluctant credit from suspicious shopkeepers who watched margarine, ersatz coffee and cheap tobacco disappear into my pockets; I reveled in my unkempt appearance, and at break-

*Der Wegwerfer (1957), translated by Leila Vennewitz.

fast, lunch and dinner I drank the nectar of Bohemian life: the bliss of knowing one is not conforming.

But for the past few weeks I have been boarding the streetcar every morning
just before 7:30 at the corner of the Roonstrasse;[1] like everyone else I meekly hold
out my season ticket to the conductor. I have on a gray double-breasted suit, a
striped shirt, a dark-green tie, I carry my sandwiches in a flat aluminum box and
hold the morning paper, lightly rolled, in my hand. I look like a citizen who has
managed to avoid introspection. After the third stop I get up to offer my seat to
one of the elderly working women who have got on at the housing settlement.
Having sacrificed my seat on the altar of social compassion, I continue to read
the newspaper standing up, now and again letting myself be heard in the capacity
of arbitrator when morning irritation is inclined to make people unjust. I correct
the worst political and historical errors (by explaining, for instance, that there is
a certain difference between SA and USA);[2] as soon as anyone puts a cigarette
to his lips I discreetly hold my lighter in front of his nose and, with the aid of
the tiny but dependable flame, light his morning cigarette for him. Thus I complete the picture of a well-groomed fellow-citizen who is still young enough for
people to say he "has nice manners."

I seem to have been successful in donning the mask which makes it impossible
to ask me about my occupation. I am evidently taken for an educated businessman dealing in attractively packaged and agreeably smelling articles such as
coffee, tea or spices, or in valuable small objects which are pleasing to the eye such
as jewelry or watches; a man who practices his profession in a nice old-fashioned
office with dark oil paintings of merchant forebears hanging on the walls, who
phones his wife about ten, who knows how to imbue his apparently impassive
voice with that hint of tenderness which betrays affection and concern. Since I
also participate in the usual jokes and do not refrain from laughing when every
morning at the Lohengrinstrasse the clerk from City Hall shouts out "When does
the next swan leave?", since I do not withhold my comments concerning either
the events of the day or the results of the football pools, I am obviously regarded
as someone who, although prosperous (as can be seen from his suit material), has
an attitude toward life which is deeply rooted in the principles of democracy. An
air of integrity encases me the way the glass coffin encased Snow White.

When a passing truck provides the streetcar window with a background for
a moment, I check up on the expression on my face: isn't it perhaps rather too
pensive, almost verging on the sorrowful? I assiduously erase the remnants of
brooding and do my best to give my face the expression I want it to wear: neither
reserved nor familiar, neither superficial nor profound.

My camouflage seems to be successful, for when I get out at the Marienplatz
and dive into the maze of streets in the Old Town, where there is no lack of nice

[1]Roon Street, a street in Böll's native Cologne. Marienplatz and the Old Town are also actual,
but the streetcar did not, and still does not, stop at either Roonstrasse or Marienplatz. The
translator substitutes a fictive Lohengrinstrasse and its joke for Böll's original fictive street and
its political joke that would mystify non-Germans. The UBIA company is also fictive. [2]SA stands
for *Sturmabteilung*, Hitler's "Storm Troopers."

old-fashioned offices, where notaries and lawyers abound, no one suspects that I pass through a rear entrance into the UBIA building—a firm that can boast of supporting 350 people and of insuring the lives of 400,000. The commissionaire greets me with a smile at the delivery entrance, I walk past him, go down to the basement, and start in on my work, which has to be completed by the time the employees come pouring into the office at 8:30. The activity that I pursue every morning between 8 and 8:30 in the basement of this respected establishment is devoted entirely to destruction. I throw away.

It took me years to invent my profession, to endow it with mathematical plausibility. I wrote treatises; graphs and charts covered—and still cover—the walls of my apartment. For years I climbed along abscissas and up ordinates, wallowed in theories, and savored the glacial ecstasy of solving formulas. Yet since practicing my profession and seeing my theories come to life, I am filled with a sense of sadness such as may come over a general who finds himself obliged to descend from the heights of strategy to the plains of tactics.

I enter my workroom, exchange my jacket for a gray smock, and immediately set to work. I open the mailbags which the commissionaire has already picked up earlier from the main post office, and I empty them into the two wooden bins which, constructed according to my design, hang to the right and left on the wall over my worktable. This way I only need to stretch out my hands, somewhat like a swimmer, and begin swiftly to sort the mail.

First I separate the circulars from the letters, a purely routine job, since a glance at the postage suffices. At this stage a knowledge of the postal tariff renders hesitation unnecessary. After years of practice I am able to complete this phase within half an hour, and by this time it is half past eight and I can hear the footsteps of the employees pouring into the offices overhead. I ring for the commissionaire, who takes the sorted letters to the various departments. It never fails to sadden me, the sight of the commissionaire carrying off in a metal tray the size of a briefcase the remains of what had once filled three mailbags. I might feel triumphant, for this, the vindication of my theory of throwing away, has for years been the objective of my private research; but, strangely enough, I do not feel triumphant. To have been right is by no means always a reason for rejoicing.

After the departure of the commissionaire there remains the task of examining the huge pile of printed matter to make sure it contains no letter masquerading behind the wrong postage, no bill mailed as a circular. This work is almost always superfluous, for the probity of the mailing public is nothing short of astounding. I must admit that here my calculations were incorrect: I had overestimated the number of postal defrauders.

Rarely has a post card, a letter or a bill sent as printed matter escaped my notice; about half past nine I ring for the commissionaire, who takes the remaining objects of my careful scrutiny to the departments.

The time has now come when I require some refreshment. The commissionaire's wife brings me my coffee, I take my sandwich out of the flat aluminum box, sit down for my break, and chat with the commissionaire's wife about her children. Is Alfred doing somewhat better in arithmetic? Has Gertrude been able to catch up in spelling? Alfred is not doing any better in arithmetic, whereas Gertrude has been able to catch up in spelling. Have the tomatoes ripened properly, are the rabbits plump, and was the experiment with the melons successful? The tomatoes have not ripened properly, but the rabbits are plump, while the experiment with the melons is still undecided. Serious problems, such as whether one should stock up on potatoes or not, matters of education, such as whether one should enlighten one's children or be enlightened by them, are the subjects of our intense consideration.

Just before eleven the commissionaire's wife leaves, and usually she asks me to let her have some travel folders. She is collecting them, and I smile at her enthusiasm, for I have retained tender memories of travel folders. As a child I also collected travel folders, I used to fish them out of my father's waste-paper basket. Even as a boy it bothered me that my father would take mail from the mailman and throw it into the waste-paper basket without looking at it. This action wounded my innate propensity for economy: there was something that had been designed, set up, printed, put in an envelope, and stamped, that had passed through the mysterious channels by which the postal service actually causes our mail to arrive at our addresses; it was weighted with the sweat of the draftsman, the writer, the printer, the office boy who had stuck on the stamps; on various levels and in various tariffs it had cost money: all this only to end—without being deemed worthy of so much as a glance—in a waste-paper basket?

At the age of eleven I had already adopted the habit of taking out of the waste-paper basket, as soon as my father had left for the office, whatever had been thrown away. I would study it, sort it, and put it away in a chest which I used to keep toys in. Thus by the time I was twelve I already possessed an imposing collection of wine-merchants' catalogues, as well as prospectuses on naturopathy and natural history. My collection of travel folders assumed the dimensions of a geographical encyclopedia; Dalmatia was as familiar to me as the Norwegian fjords, Scotland as close as Zakopane, the forests of Bohemia soothed me while the waves of the Atlantic disquieted me; hinges were offered me, houses and buttons, political parties asked for my vote, charities for my money; lotteries promised me riches, religious sects poverty. I leave it to the reader's imagination to picture what my collection was like when at the age of seventeen, suddenly bored with it all, I offered my collection to a junk dealer who paid me 7 marks and 60 pfennigs for it.

Having finished school, I embarked in my father's footsteps and set my foot on the first rung of the civil service ladder. With the 7 marks and 60 pfennigs I bought a package of squared paper and three colored crayons, and my attempt to gain a foothold in the civil service turned into a laborious detour, for a happy thrower-away was slumbering in me while I filled the role of an unhappy junior clerk. All my free time was devoted to intricate calculations.

Stop-watch, pencil, slide-rule, squared paper, these were the props of my obsession; I calculated how long it took to open a circular of small, medium or large size, with or without pictures, give it a quick glance, satisfy oneself of its uselessness, and then throw it in the wastepaper basket, a process requiring a minimum of five seconds and a maximum of twenty-five; if the circular is at all attractive, either the text or the pictures, several minutes, often a quarter of an hour, must be allowed for this. By conducting bogus negotiations with printing firms, I also worked out the minimum production costs for circulars. Indefatigably I checked the results of my studies and adjusted them (it did not occur to me until two years later that the time of the cleaning-women who have to empty the waste-paper baskets had to be included in my calculations); I applied the results of my research to firms with ten, twenty, a hundred or more employees; and I arrived at results which an expert on economics would not have hesitated to describe as alarming.

Obeying my sense of loyalty, I began by offering my results to my superiors; although I had reckoned with the possibility of ingratitude, I was nevertheless shocked at the extent of that ingratitude. I was accused of neglecting my duties, suspected of nihilism, pronounced "a mental case," and discharged. To the great sorrow of my kind parents, I abandoned my promising career, began new ones, broke these off too, forsook the warmth of the parental hearth, and, as I have already said, eked out my existence as an unrecognized genius. I took pleasure in the humiliation of vainly peddling my invention, and spent years in a blissful state of being antisocial, so consistently that my punch-card in the central files which had long ago been punched with the symbol for "mental case" was now stamped with the confidential symbol for "antisocial."

In view of these circumstances, it can readily be imagined what a shock it was when the obviousness of my results at last became obvious to someone else—the manager of UBIA, how deeply humiliated I was to have to wear a dark-green tie, yet I must continue to go around in disguise as I am terrified of being found out. I try anxiously to give my face the proper expression when I laugh at the Lohengrin joke, since there is no greater vanity than that of the wags who populate the streetcar every morning. Sometimes, too, I am afraid the streetcar may be full of people who the previous day have done work which I am about to destroy that very morning: printers, typesetters, draftsmen, writers who compose the wording of advertisements, commercial artists, envelope stuffers, packers, apprentices of all kinds. From 8 to 8:30 every morning I ruthlessly destroy the products of respected paper mills, worthy printing establishments, brilliant commercial artists, the texts of talented writers; coated paper, glossy paper, copperplate, I take it all, just as it comes from the mailbag, and without the faintest sentimentality tie it up into handy bundles for the waste-paper dealer. In the space of one hour I destroy the output of 200 work-hours and save UBIA a further 100 hours, so that altogether (here I must lapse into my own jargon) I achieve a concentrate of 1:300.

When the commissionaire's wife leaves with the empty coffeepot and the travel folders, I knock off. I wash my hands, exchange my smock for my jacket, pick up the morning paper, and leave the UBIA building by the rear entrance. I stroll through the town and wonder how I can escape from tactics and get back into strategy. That which intoxicated me as a formula, I find disappointing, since it can be performed so easily. Strategy translated into action can be carried out by hacks. I shall probably establish schools for throwers-away. I may possibly also attempt to have throwers-away placed in post offices, perhaps even in printing establishments; an enormous amount of energy, valuable commodities, and intelligence could be utilized as well as postage saved; it might even be feasible to conceive, compose, and set brochures up in type but not print them. These are all problems still requiring a lot of study.

However, the mere throwing away of mail as such has almost ceased to interest me; any improvements on that level can be worked out by means of the basic formula. For a long time now I have been devoting my attention to calculations concerning wrapping paper and the process of wrapping: this is virgin territory where nothing has been done, here one can strive to spare humanity those unprofitable efforts under the burden of which it is groaning. Every day billions of throwing-away movements are made, energies are dissipated which, could they but be utilized, would suffice to change the face of the earth. It would be a great advantage if one were permitted to undertake experiments in department stores; should one dispense with the wrapping process altogether, or should one post an expert thrower-away right next to the wrapping table who unwraps what has just been wrapped and immediately ties the wrapping paper into bundles for the waste-paper dealer? These are problems meriting some thought. In any case it has struck me that in many shops the customers implore the clerk not to wrap the purchased article, but that they have to submit to having it wrapped. Clinics for nervous diseases are rapidly filling with patients who complain of an attack of nerves whenever they unwrap a bottle of perfume or a box of chocolates, or open a packet of cigarettes, and at the moment I am making an intensive study of a young man from my neighborhood who earned his living as a book reviewer but at times was unable to practice his profession because he found it impossible to undo the twisted wire tied around the parcel, and even when he did find himself equal to this physical exertion, he was incapable of penetrating the massive layer of gummed paper with which the corrugated paper is stuck together. The man appears deeply disturbed and has now gone over to reviewing the books unread and placing the parcels on his bookshelves without unwrapping them. I leave it to the reader's imagination to depict for himself the effect of such a case on our intellectual life.

While walking through the town between eleven and one I observe all sorts of details: I spend some time unobtrusively in the department stores, hovering around the wrapping tables; I stand in front of tobacco shops and pharmacies and note down minor statistics; now and again I even purchase something, so as to allow the senseless procedure to be performed on myself and to discover how much effort is required actually to take possession of the article one wishes to own.

So between eleven and one in my impeccable suit I complete the picture of a man who is sufficiently prosperous to afford a bit of leisure—who at about one o'clock enters a sophisticated little restaurant, casually chooses the most expensive meal, and scribbles some hieroglyphics on his beer coaster which could equally well be stock quotations or flights of poetry; who knows how to praise or decry the quality of the meat with arguments which betray the connoisseur

to even the most blasé waiter; who, when it comes to choosing dessert, hesitates
with a knowing air between cake, ice cream and cheese; and who finishes off his
scribblings with a flourish which proves that they were stock quotations after all.

Shocked at the results of my calculations I leave the little restaurant. My
expression becomes more and more thoughtful while I search for a small café
where I can pass the time till three o'clock and read the evening paper. At three
I re-enter the UBIA building by the rear door to take care of the afternoon mail,
which consists almost exclusively of circulars. It is a matter of scarcely fifteen
minutes to pick out the ten or twelve letters; I don't even have to wash my hands
after it, I just brush them off, take the letters to the commissionaire, leave the
building, and at the Marienplatz board the streetcar, glad that on the way home
I do not need to laugh at the Lohengrin joke. When the dark tarpaulin of a passing
truck makes a background for the streetcar window, I can see my face: it is
relaxed, that is to say pensive, almost brooding, and I relish the fact that I do
not have to put on any other face, for at this hour none of my morning fellow-
travellers has finished work. I get out at the Roonstrasse, buy some fresh rolls,
a piece of cheese or sausage, some ground coffee, and walk up to my little
apartment, the walls of which are hung with graphs and charts, with hectic
curves: between the abscissas and ordinates I capture the lines of a fever going
up and up; not a single one of my curves goes down, not a single one of my
formulas has the power to soothe me. I groan under the burden of my vision of
economics, and while the water is boiling for the coffee I place my slide-rule, my
notes, pencil and paper in readiness.

My apartment is sparsely furnished, it looks more like a laboratory. I drink
my coffee standing up and hastily swallow a sandwich, the epicure I was at noon
is now a thing of the past. Wash hands, light a cigarette, then I set my stop-watch
and unwrap the nerve tonic I bought that morning on my stroll through the town:
outer wrapping paper, cellophane covering, carton, inside wrapping paper, directions for use secured by a rubber band: thirty-seven seconds. The nervous energy
consumed in unwrapping exceeds the nervous energy which the tonic promises
to impart to me, but there may be subjective reasons for this which I shall
disregard in my calculations. One thing is certain: the wrapping is worth more
than the contents, and the cost of the twenty-five yellow tablets is out of all
proportion to their value. But these are considerations verging on the moral
aspect, and I would prefer to keep away from morality altogether. My field of
speculation is one of pure economics.

Numerous articles are waiting to be unwrapped by me, many slips of paper
are waiting to be evaluated; green, red, blue ink, everything is ready. It is usually
late by the time I get to bed, and as I fall asleep I am haunted by my formulas,
whole worlds of useless paper roll over me; some formulas explode like dynamite,
the noise of the explosion sounds like a burst of laughter: it is my own, my
laughter at the Lohengrin joke originating in my fear of the clerk from City Hall.
Perhaps he has access to the punch-card file, has picked out my card, discovered
that it contains not only the symbol for "mental case" but the second, more
dangerous one for "antisocial." There is nothing more difficult to fill than a tiny

hole like that in a punch-card; perhaps my laughter at the Lohengrin joke is the price I have to pay for my anonymity. I would not like to admit face to face what I find easier to do in writing: that I am a thrower-away.

QUESTIONS

1. Why is the narrator embarrassed about his occupation?
2. How does the bliss of nonconformity relate to his present life and attitude? Why is wearing a dark-green tie humiliating?
3. What is the point of the joke about Lohengrinstrasse?
4. How is checking his expression as a truck passes the streetcar, twice mentioned, significant?
5. How would the narrator know about the entries "mental case" and "antisocial" on his punch card in the central files? What is an author's central problem with first-person narration?
6. What are the ultimate conclusions of the narrator's plans for throwing away and for eliminating wrapping? Why does he, on reaching his apartment, groan at his vision of economics?
7. What is the effect of timing the unwrapping of the nerve medicine?
8. What is the effect of the laughter in the final paragraph?
9. What is Böll satirizing? What is his theme?

Another modern city symbolizes a twentieth-century theme, a kind of mulligan stew of chaos reflected realistically in the Washington, D.C., of February 1957. "Entropy," as Pynchon illustrates, concerns the random loss of energy in thermodynamics, as heat transfers into mechanical work. What is he also saying about the loss in the effort of human communication?

ENTROPY

Thomas Pynchon   *(1937–)*

> *Boris has just given me a summary of his views. He is a weather prophet. The weather will continue bad, he says. There will be more calamities, more death, more despair. Not the slightest indication of a change anywhere. . . . We must get into step, a lockstep toward the prison of death. There is no escape. The weather will not change.*
>
>   *—Tropic of Cancer*[1]

Downstairs, Meatball Mulligan's lease-breaking party was moving into its 40th hour. On the kitchen floor, amid a litter of empty champagne fifths, were Sandor Rojas and three friends, playing spit in the ocean and staying awake on Heidseck and benzedrine pills. In the living room Duke, Vincent, Krinkles and Paco sat crouched over a 15-inch speaker which had been bolted into the top of a wastepa-

---

[1]A novel by Henry Miller (1891–1980).

per basket, listening to 27 watts' worth of *The Heroes' Gate at Kiev*. They all wore
hornrimmed sunglasses and rapt expressions, and smoked funny-looking cigarettes which contained not, as you might expect, tobacco, but an adulterated form
of *cannabis sativa*. This group was the Duke di Angelis quartet. They recorded
for a local label called Tambú and had to their credit one 10″ LP entitled *Songs
of Outer Space*.[2] From time to time one of them would flick the ashes from his
cigarette into the speaker cone to watch them dance around. Meatball himself was
sleeping over by the window, holding an empty magnum to his chest as if it were
a teddy bear. Several government girls, who worked for people like the State
Department and NSA, had passed out on couches, chairs and in one case the
bathroom sink.

This was in early February of '57 and back then there were a lot of American
expatriates around Washington, D.C., who would talk, every time they met you,
about how someday they were going to go over to Europe for real but right now
it seemed they were working for the government. Everyone saw a fine irony in
this. They would stage, for instance, polyglot parties where the newcomer was
sort of ignored if he couldn't carry on simultaneous conversations in three or four
languages. They would haunt Armenian delicatessens for weeks at a stretch and
invite you over for bulghour and lamb in tiny kitchens whose walls were covered
with bullfight posters. They would have affairs with sultry girls from Andalucía
or the Midi who studied economics at Georgetown. Their Dôme was a collegiate
Rathskeller out on Wisconsin Avenue called the Old Heidelberg and they had to
settle for cherry blossoms instead of lime trees when spring came, but in its
lethargic way their life provided, as they said, kicks.

At the moment, Meatball's party seemed to be gathering its second wind.
Outside there was rain. Rain splatted against the tar paper on the roof and was
fractured into a fine spray off the noses, eyebrows and lips of wooden gargoyles
under the eaves, and ran like drool down the windowpanes. The day before, it
had snowed and the day before that there had been winds of gale force and before
that the sun had made the city glitter bright as April, though the calendar read
early February. It is a curious season in Washington, this false spring. Somewhere
in it are Lincoln's Birthday and the Chinese New Year, and a forlornness in the
streets because cherry blossoms are weeks away still and, as Sarah Vaughan has
put it, spring will be a little late this year. Generally crowds like the one which
would gather in the Old Heidelberg on weekday afternoons to drink Würtzburger
and to sing Lili Marlene (not to mention The Sweetheart of Sigma Chi) are
inevitably and incorrigibly Romantic. And as every good Romantic knows, the
soul *(spiritus, ruach, pneuma)* is nothing, substantially, but air; it is only natural
that warpings in the atmosphere should be recapitulated in those who breathe it.
So that over and above the public components—holidays, tourist attractions—
there are private meanderings, linked to the climate as if this spell were a *stretto*
passage in the year's fugue: haphazard weather, aimless loves, unpredicted com-

---

[2]Since outer space lacks air to carry sound waves, these songs would be silent, a concept the
group continues to work on.

mitments: months one can easily spend *in* fugue, because oddly enough, later on, winds, rains, passions of February and March are never remembered in that city, it is as if they had never been.

The last bass notes of *The Heroes' Gate* boomed up through the floor and woke Callisto from an uneasy sleep. The first thing he became aware of was a small bird he had been holding gently between his hands, against his body. He turned his head sidewise on the pillow to smile down at it, at its blue hunched-down head and sick, lidded eyes, wondering how many more nights he would have to give it warmth before it was well again. He had been holding the bird like that for three days: it was the only way he knew to restore its health. Next to him the girl stirred and whimpered, her arm thrown across her face. Mingled with the sounds of the rain came the first tentative, querulous morning voices of the other birds, hidden in philodendrons and small fan palms: patches of scarlet, yellow and blue laced through this Rousseau-like fantasy, this hothouse jungle it had taken him seven years to weave together. Hermetically sealed, it was a tiny enclave of regularity in the city's chaos, alien to the vagaries of the weather, of national politics, of any civil disorder. Through trial-and-error Callisto had perfected its ecological balance, with the help of the girl its artistic harmony, so that the swayings of its plant life, the stirrings of its birds and human inhabitants were all as integral as the rhythms of a perfectly-executed mobile. He and the girl could no longer, of course, be omitted from that sanctuary; they had become necessary to its unity. What they needed from outside was delivered. They did not go out.

"Is he all right," she whispered. She lay like a tawny question mark facing him, her eyes suddenly huge and dark and blinking slowly. Callisto ran a finger beneath the feathers at the base of the bird's neck; caressed it gently. "He's going to be well, I think. See: he hears his friends beginning to wake up." The girl had heard the rain and the birds even before she was fully awake. Her name was Aubade: she was part French and part Annamese, and she lived on her own curious and lonely planet, where the clouds and the odor of poincianas, the bitterness of wine and the accidental fingers at the small of her back or feathery against her breasts came to her reduced inevitably to the terms of sound: of music which emerged at intervals from a howling darkness of discordancy. "Aubade," he said, "go see." Obedient, she arose; padded to the window, pulled aside the drapes and after a moment said: "It is 37. Still 37." Callisto frowned. "Since Tuesday, then," he said. "No change." Henry Adams,[3] three generations before his own, had stared aghast at Power; Callisto found himself now in much the same state over Thermodynamics, the inner life of that power, realizing like his predecessor that the Virgin and the dynamo stand as much for love as for power; that the two are indeed identical; and that love therefore not only makes the world go round but also makes the boccie ball spin, the nebula precess. It was this latter or sidereal element which disturbed him. The cosmologists had predicted an eventual heat-death for the universe (something like Limbo: form and motion abolished, heat-energy identi-

---

[3]In *The Education of Henry Adams* (1907), Adams defines the universal forces as the Virgin (spiritual) versus the Dynamo (physical energy).

cal at every point in it); the meteorologists, day-to-day, staved it off by contradicting with a reassuring array of varied temperatures.

But for three days now, despite the changeful weather, the mercury had stayed at 37 degrees Fahrenheit. Leery at omens of apocalypse, Callisto shifted beneath the covers. His fingers pressed the bird more firmly, as if needing some pulsing or suffering assurance of an early break in the temperature.

It was that last cymbal crash that did it. Meatball was hurled wincing into consciousness as the synchronized wagging of heads over the wastebasket stopped. The final hiss remained for an instant in the room, then melted into the whisper of rain outside. "Aarrgghh," announced Meatball in the silence, looking at the empty magnum. Krinkles, in slow motion, turned, smiled and held out a cigarette. "Tea time, man," he said. "No, no," said Meatball. "How many times I got to tell you guys. Not at my place. You ought to know, Washington is lousy with Feds." Krinkles looked wistful. "Jeez, Meatball," he said, "you don't want to do nothing no more." "Hair of dog," said Meatball. "Only hope. Any juice left?" He began to crawl toward the kitchen. "No champagne, I don't think," Duke said. "Case of tequila behind the icebox." They put on an Earl Bostic side. Meatball paused at the kitchen door, glowering at Sandor Rojas. "Lemons," he said after some thought. He crawled to the refrigerator and got out three lemons and some cubes, found the tequila and set about restoring order to his nervous system. He drew blood once cutting the lemons and had to use two hands squeezing them and his foot to crack the ice tray but after about ten minutes he found himself, through some miracle, beaming down into a monster tequila sour. "That looks yummy," Sandor Rojas said. "How about you make me one." Meatball blinked at him. *"Kitchi lofass a shegitbe,"*[4] he replied automatically, and wandered away into the bathroom. "I say," he called out a moment later to no one in particular. "I say, there seems to be a girl or something sleeping in the sink." He took her by the shoulders and shook. "Wha," she said. "You don't look too comfortable," Meatball said. "Well," she agreed. She stumbled to the shower, turned on the cold water and sat down crosslegged in the spray. "That's better," she smiled.

"Meatball," Sandor Rojas yelled from the kitchen. "Somebody is trying to come in the window. A burglar, I think. A second-story man." "What are you worrying about," Meatball said. "We're on the third floor." He loped back into the kitchen. A shaggy woebegone figure stood out on the fire escape, raking his fingernails down the windowpane. Meatball opened the window. "Saul," he said.

"Sort of wet out," Saul said. He climbed in, dripping. "You heard, I guess."

"Miriam left you," Meatball said, "or something, is all I heard."

There was a sudden flurry of knocking at the front door. "Do come in," Sandor Rojas called. The door opened and there were three coeds from George Washington, all of whom were majoring in philosophy. They were each holding a gallon of Chianti. Sandor leaped up and dashed into the living room. "We heard there was a party," one blonde said. "Young blood," Sandor shouted. He was an

[4]Hungarian for shove it.

ex-Hungarian freedom fighter who had easily the worst chronic case of what certain critics of the middle class have called Don Giovannism in the District of Columbia. *Purche porti la gonnella, voi sapete quel che fa.*[5] Like Pavlov's dog: a contralto voice or a whiff of Arpège and Sandor would begin to salivate. Meatball regarded the trio blearily as they filed into the kitchen; he shrugged. "Put the wine in the icebox," he said "and good morning."

Aubade's neck made a golden bow as she bent over the sheets of foolscap, scribbling away in the green murk of the room. "As a young man at Princeton," Callisto was dictating, nestling the bird against the gray hairs of his chest, "Callisto had learned a mnemonic device for remembering the Laws of Thermodynamics: you can't win, things are going to get worse before they get better, who says they're going to get better. At the age of 54, confronted with Gibbs'[6] notion of the universe, he suddenly realized that undergraduate cant had been oracle, after all. That spindly maze of equations became, for him, a vision of ultimate, cosmic heat-death. He had known all along, of course, that nothing but a theoretical engine or system ever runs at 100% efficiency; and about the theorem of Clausius,[7] which states that the entropy of an isolated system always continually increases. It was not, however, until Gibbs and Boltzmann[8] brought to this principle the methods of statistical mechanics that the horrible significance of it all dawned on him: only then did he realize that the isolated system—galaxy, engine, human being, culture, whatever—must evolve spontaneously toward the Condition of the More Probable. He was forced, therefore, in the sad dying fall of middle age, to a radical reëvaluation of everything he had learned up to then; all the cities and seasons and casual passions of his days had now to be looked at in a new and elusive light. He did not know if he was equal to the task. He was aware of the dangers of the reductive fallacy and, he hoped, strong enough not to drift into the graceful decadence of an enervated fatalism. His had always been a vigorous, Italian sort of pessimism: like Machiavelli, he allowed the forces of *virtù* and *fortuna*[9] to be about 50/50; but the equations now introduced a random factor which pushed the odds to some unutterable and indeterminate ratio which he found himself afraid to calculate." Around him loomed vague hothouse shapes; the pitifully small heart fluttered against his own. Counterpointed against his words the girl heard the chatter of birds and fitful car honkings scattered along the wet morning and Earl Bostic's alto rising in occasional wild peaks through the floor. The architectonic purity of her world was constantly threatened by such hints of anarchy: gaps and excrescences and skew lines, and a shifting or tilting of planes to which she had continually to readjust lest the whole structure shiver into a disarray of discrete and meaningless signals. Callisto had described the process once as a kind of "feedback": she crawled into dreams each night with a sense of exhaustion, and a desperate resolve never to relax that

---

[5]"As long as she wears a skirt, you know what will happen." Leporello's Catalogue Aria in Mozart's *Don Giovanni*.   [6]Josiah Willard Gibbs (1839–1903), thermodynamic mathematician. [7]Rudolf Julius Emanuel Clausius (1822–88) conceived and named entropy.   [8]Ludwig Boltzmann (1804–1906) named a constant amid entropy's variables.   [9]Ability and luck.

vigilance. Even in the brief periods when Callisto made love to her, soaring above the bowing of taut nerves in haphazard double-stops would be the one singing string of her determination.

"Nevertheless," continued Callisto, "he found in entropy or the measure of disorganization for a closed system an adequate metaphor to apply to certain phenomena in his own world. He saw, for example, the younger generation responding to Madison Avenue with the same spleen his own had once reserved for Wall Street: and in American 'consumerism' discovered a similar tendency from the least to the most probable, from differentiation to sameness, from ordered individuality to a kind of chaos. He found himself, in short, restating Gibbs' prediction in social terms, and envisioned a heat-death for his culture in which ideas, like heat-energy, would no longer be transferred, since each point in it would ultimately have the same quantity of energy; and intellectual motion would, accordingly, cease." He glanced up suddenly. "Check it now," he said. Again she rose and peered out at the thermometer. "37," she said. "The rain has stopped." He bent his head quickly and held his lips against a quivering wing. "Then it will change soon," he said, trying to keep his voice firm.

Sitting on the stove Saul was like any big rag doll that a kid has been taking out some incomprehensible rage on. "What happened," Meatball said. "If you feel like talking, I mean."

"Of course I feel like talking," Saul said. "One thing I did, I slugged her."

"Discipline must be maintained."

"Ha, ha. I wish you'd been there. Oh Meatball, it was a lovely fight. She ended up throwing a *Handbook of Chemistry and Physics* at me, only it missed and went through the window, and when the glass broke I reckon something in her broke too. She stormed out of the house crying, out in the rain. No raincoat or anything."

"She'll be back."

"No."

"Well." Soon Meatball said: "It was something earthshattering, no doubt. Like who is better, Sal Mineo or Ricky Nelson."

"What it was about," Saul said, "was communication theory. Which of course makes it very hilarious."

"I don't know anything about communication theory."

"Neither does my wife. Come right down to it, who does? That's the joke."

When Meatball saw the kind of smile Saul had on his face he said: "Maybe you would like tequila or something."

"No. I mean, I'm sorry. It's a field you can go off the deep end in, is all. You get where you're watching all the time for security cops: behind bushes, around corners. MUFFET is top secret."

"Wha."

"Multi-unit factorial field electronic tabulator."

"You were fighting about that."

"Miriam has been reading science fiction again. That and *Scientific American.* It seems she is, as we say, bugged at this idea of computers acting like people.

I made the mistake of saying you can just as well turn that around, and talk about human behavior like a program fed into an IBM machine."

"Why not," Meatball said.

"Indeed, why not. In fact it is sort of crucial to communication, not to mention information theory. Only when I said that she hit the roof. Up went the balloon. And I can't figure out *why*. If anybody should know why, I should. I refuse to believe the government is wasting taxpayers' money on me, when it has so many bigger and better things to waste it on."

Meatball made a moue. "Maybe she thought you were acting like a cold, dehumanized amoral scientist type."

"My god," Saul flung up an arm. "Dehumanized. How much more human can I get? I worry, Meatball, I do. There are Europeans wandering around North Africa these days with their tongues torn out of their heads because those tongues have spoken the wrong words. Only the Europeans thought they were the right words."

"Language barrier," Meatball suggested.

Saul jumped down off the stove. "That," he said, angry, "is a good candidate for sick joke of the year. No, ace, it is *not* a barrier. If it is anything it's a kind of leakage. Tell a girl: 'I love you.' No trouble with two-thirds of that, it's a closed circuit. Just you and she. But that nasty four-letter word in the middle, *that's* the one you have to look out for. Ambiguity. Redundance. Irrelevance, even. Leakage. All this is noise. Noise screws up your signal, makes for disorganization in the circuit."

Meatball shuffled around. "Well, now, Saul," he muttered, "you're sort of, I don't know, expecting a lot from people. I mean, you know. What it is is, most of the things we say, I guess, are mostly noise."

"Ha! Half of what you just said, for example."

"Well, you do it too."

"I know." Saul smiled grimly. "It's a bitch, ain't it."

"I bet that's what keeps divorce lawyers in business. Whoops."

"Oh I'm not sensitive. Besides," frowning, "you're right. You find I think that most 'successful' marriages—Miriam and me, up to last night—are sort of founded on compromises. You never run at top efficiency, usually all you have is a minimum basis for a workable thing. I believe the phrase is Togetherness."

"Aarrgghh."

"Exactly. You find that one a bit noisy, don't you. But the noise content is different for each of us because you're a bachelor and I'm not. Or wasn't. The hell with it."

"Well sure," Meatball said, trying to be helpful, "you were using different words. By 'human being' you meant something that you can look at like it was a computer. It helps you think better on the job or something. But Miriam meant something entirely—"

"The hell with it."

Meatball fell silent. "I'll take that drink," Saul said after a while.

The card game had been abandoned and Sandor's friends were slowly getting wasted on tequila. On the living room couch, one of the coeds and Krinkles were engaged in amorous conversation. "No," Krinkles was saying, "no, I can't put Dave *down*. In fact I give Dave a lot of credit, man. Especially considering his accident and all." The girl's smile faded. "How terrible," she said. "What accident?" "Hadn't you heard?" Krinkles said. "When Dave was in the army, just a private E-2, they sent him down to Oak Ridge on special duty. Something to do with the Manhattan Project. He was handling hot stuff one day and got an overdose of radiation. So now he's got to wear lead gloves all the time." She shook her head sympathetically. "What an awful break for a piano-player."

Meatball had abandoned Saul to a bottle of tequila and was about to go to sleep in a closet when the front door flew open and the place was invaded by five enlisted personnel of the U.S. Navy, all in varying stages of abomination. "This is the place," shouted a fat, pimply seaman apprentice who had lost his white hat. "This here is the hoorhouse that chief was telling us about." A stringy-looking 3rd class boatswain's mate pushed him aside and cased the living room. "You're right, Slab," he said. "But it don't look like much, even for Stateside. I seen better tail in Naples, Italy." "How much, hey," boomed a large seaman with adenoids, who was holding a Mason jar full of white lightning. "Oh, my god," said Meatball.

Outside the temperature remained constant at 37 degrees Fahrenheit. In the hothouse Aubade stood absently caressing the branches of a young mimosa, hearing a motif of sap-rising, the rough and unresolved anticipatory theme of those fragile pink blossoms which, it is said, insure fertility. That music rose in a tangled tracery: arabesques of order competing fugally with the improvised discords of the party downstairs, which peaked sometimes in cusps and ogees of noise. That precious signal-to-noise ratio, whose delicate balance required every calorie of her strength, seesawed inside the small tenuous skull as she watched Callisto, sheltering the bird. Callisto was trying to confront any idea of the heat-death now, as he nuzzled the feathery lump in his hands. He sought correspondences. Sade, of course. And Temple Drake, gaunt and hopeless in her little park in Paris, at the end of *Sanctuary*. Final equilibrium. *Nightwood*. And the tango. Any tango, but more than any perhaps the sad sick dance in Stravinsky's *L'Histoire du Soldat*. He thought back: what had tango music been for them after the war, what meanings had he missed in all the stately coupled automatons in the *cafés-dansants,* or in the metronomes which had ticked behind the eyes of his own partners? Not even the clean constant winds of Switzerland could cure the *grippe espagnole:*[10] Stravinsky had had it, they all had had it. And how many musicians were left after Passchendaele, after the Marne? It came down in this case to seven: violin, double-bass. Clarinet, bassoon. Cornet, trombone. Tympani. Almost as if any tiny troupe of saltimbanques had set about conveying the same information as a full pit-orchestra. There was hardly a full complement left in Europe. Yet with violin and tympani Stravinsky had managed to communicate in that tango the same exhaustion, the same airlessness one saw in the slicked-

---

[10]The epidemic of Spanish flu in Europe and America, 1918.

down youths who were trying to imitate Vernon Castle,[11] and in their mistresses, who simply did not care. *Ma maîtresse.* Celeste. Returning to Nice after the second war he had found that café replaced by a perfume shop which catered to American tourists. And no secret vestige of her in the cobblestones or in the old pension next door; no perfume to match her breath heavy with the sweet Spanish wine she always drank. And so instead he had purchased a Henry Miller novel and left for Paris, and read the book on the train so that when he arrived he had been given at least a little forewarning. And saw that Celeste and the others and even Temple Drake were not all that had changed. "Aubade," he said, "my head aches." The sound of his voice generated in the girl an answering scrap of melody. Her movement toward the kitchen, the towel, the cold water, and his eyes following her formed a weird and intricate canon; as she placed the compress on his forehead his sigh of gratitude seemed to signal a new subject, another series of modulations.

"No," Meatball was still saying, "no, I'm afraid not. This is not a house of ill repute. I'm sorry, really I am." Slab was adamant. "But the chief said," he kept repeating. The seaman offered to swap the moonshine for a good piece. Meatball looked around frantically, as if seeking assistance. In the middle of the room, the Duke di Angelis quartet were engaged in a historic moment. Vincent was seated and the others standing: they were going through the motions of a group having a session, only without instruments. "I say," Meatball said. Duke moved his head a few times, smiled faintly, lit a cigarette, and eventually caught sight of Meatball. "Quiet, man," he whispered. Vincent began to fling his arms around, his fists clenched; then, abruptly, was still, then repeated the performance. This went on for a few minutes while Meatball sipped his drink moodily. The navy had withdrawn to the kitchen. Finally at some invisible signal the group stopped tapping their feet and Duke grinned and said, "At least we ended together."

Meatball glared at him. "I say," he said. "I have this new conception, man," Duke said. "You remember your namesake. You remember Gerry."[12]

"No," said Meatball. "I'll remember April, if that's any help."

"As a matter of fact," Duke said, "it was Love for Sale. Which shows how much you know. The point is, it was Mulligan, Chet Baker and that crew, way back then, out yonder. You dig?"

"Baritone sax," Meatball said. "Something about a baritone sax."

"But no piano, man. No guitar. Or accordion. You know what that means."

"Not exactly," Meatball said.

"Well first let me just say, that I am no Mingus, no John Lewis. Theory was never my strong point. I mean things like reading were always difficult for me and all—"

"I know," Meatball said drily. "You got your card taken away because you changed key on Happy Birthday at a Kiwanis Club picnic."

[11] A professional ballroom dancer (1887–1918) who, with his wife, Irene, captivated New York and Paris before World War I. [12] Gerry Mulligan, jazz musician, as are Chet Baker, Charlie Mingus, and John Lewis.

"Rotarian. But it occurred to me, in one of these flashes of insight, that if that first quartet of Mulligan's had no piano, it could only mean one thing."

"No chords," said Paco, the baby-faced bass.

"What he is trying to say," Duke said, "is no root chords. Nothing to listen to while you blow a horizontal line. What one does in such a case is, one *thinks* the roots."

A horrified awareness was dawning on Meatball. "And the next logical extension," he said.

"Is to think everything," Duke announced with simple dignity. "Roots, line, everything."

Meatball looked at Duke, awed. "But," he said.

"Well," Duke said modestly, "there are a few bugs to work out."

"But," Meatball said.

"Just listen," Duke said. "You'll catch on." And off they went again into orbit, presumably somewhere around the asteroid belt. After a while Krinkles made an embouchure and started moving his fingers and Duke clapped his hand to his forehead. "Oaf!" he roared. "The new head we're using, you remember, I wrote last night?" "Sure," Krinkles said, "the new head. I come in on the bridge. All your heads I come in then." "Right," Duke said. "So why—" "Wha," said Krinkles, "16 bars, I wait, I come in—" "16?" Duke said. "No. No, Krinkles. Eight you waited. You want me to sing it? A cigarette that bears a lipstick's traces, an airline ticket to romantic places." Krinkles scratched his head. "These Foolish Things, you mean." "Yes," Duke said, "yes, Krinkles. Bravo." "Not I'll Remember April," Krinkles said. *"Minghe morte,"*[13] said Duke. "I *figured* we were playing it a little slow," Krinkles said. Meatball chuckled. "Back to the old drawing board," he said. "No, man," Duke said, "back to the airless void." And they took off again, only it seemed Paco was playing in G sharp while the rest were in E flat, so they had to start all over.

In the kitchen two of the girls from George Washington and the sailors were singing Let's All Go Down and Piss on the Forrestal. There was a two-handed, bilingual *morra*[14] game on over by the icebox. Saul had filled several paper bags with water and was sitting on the fire escape, dropping them on passersby in the street. A fat government girl in a Bennington sweatshirt, recently engaged to an ensign attached to the Forrestal, came charging into the kitchen, head lowered, and butted Slab in the stomach. Figuring this was as good an excuse for a fight as any, Slab's buddies piled in. The *morra* players were nose-to-nose, screaming *trois, sette* at the tops of their lungs. From the shower the girl Meatball had taken out of the sink announced that she was drowning. She had apparently sat on the drain and the water was now up to her neck. The noise in Meatball's apartment had reached a sustained, ungodly crescendo.

Meatball stood and watched, scratching his stomach lazily. The way he figured, there were only about two ways he could cope: (a) lock himself in the

---

[13]Screw it to death (Italian).   [14]An Italian game in which a player tries to match the number of fingers extended simultaneously by his opponent.

closet and maybe eventually they would all go away, or (b) try to calm everybody down, one by one. (a) was certainly the more attractive alternative. But then he started thinking about that closet. It was dark and stuffy and he would be alone. He did not feature being alone. And then this crew off the good ship Lollipop or whatever it was might take it upon themselves to kick down the closet door, for a lark. And if that happened he would be, at the very least, embarrassed. The other way was more a pain in the neck, but probably better in the long run.

So he decided to try and keep his lease-breaking party from deteriorating into total chaos: he gave wine to the sailors and separated the *morra* players; he introduced the fat government girl to Sandor Rojas, who would keep her out of trouble; he helped the girl in the shower to dry off and get into bed; he had another talk with Saul; he called a repairman for the refrigerator, which someone had discovered was on the blink. This is what he did until nightfall, when most of the revellers had passed out and the party trembled on the threshold of its third day.

Upstairs Callisto, helpless in the past, did not feel the faint rhythm inside the bird begin to slacken and fail. Aubade was by the window, wandering the ashes of her own lovely world; the temperature held steady, the sky had become a uniform darkening gray. Then something from downstairs—a girl's scream, an overturned chair, a glass dropped on the floor, he would never know what exactly —pierced that private time-warp and he became aware of the faltering, the constriction of muscles, the tiny tossings of the bird's head; and his own pulse began to pound more fiercely, as if trying to compensate. "Aubade," he called weakly, "he's dying." The girl, flowing and rapt, crossed the hothouse to gaze down at Callisto's hands. The two remained like that, poised, for one minute, and two, while the heartbeat ticked a graceful diminuendo down at last into stillness. Callisto raised his head slowly. "I held him," he protested, impotent with the wonder of it, "to give him the warmth of my body. Almost as if I were communicating life to him, or a sense of life. What has happened? Has the transfer of heat ceased to work? Is there no more . . ." He did not finish.

"I was just at the window," she said. He sank back, terrified. She stood a moment more, irresolute; she had sensed his obsession long ago, realized somehow that that constant 37 was now decisive. Suddenly then, as if seeing the single and unavoidable conclusion to all this she moved swiftly to the window before Callisto could speak; tore away the drapes and smashed out the glass with two exquisite hands which came away bleeding and glistening with splinters; and turned to face the man on the bed and wait with him until the moment of equilibrium was reached, when 37 degrees Fahrenheit should prevail both outside and inside, and forever, and the hovering, curious dominant of their separate lives should resolve into a tonic of darkness and the final absence of all motion.

QUESTIONS

1. In *Slow Learner,* Pynchon says of "Entropy": "The story is a fine example of a procedural error beginning writers are always being cautioned against. It is simply wrong to begin with a theme . . . and

then try to force characters and events to conform to it." Do you agree?

2.   What is Pynchon's point about "American expatriates around Washington, D.C."?

3.   What relevance for the story has Pynchon's allusion to this rainy spring as "a *stretto* passage in the year's fugue"?

4.   How does Aubade's perceiving physical sensations as music, by strength of will, support Pynchon's theme?

5.   Since entropy concerns transferring heat to other energy, how does Callisto's treatment of the bird carry out Pynchon's theme?

6.   What does Meatball do to restore order on the chaos he himself has invited?

7.   What does Krinkles mean by "Tea time, man"? How about, later: "Sandor's friends were slowly getting *wasted* on tequila"? How has slang changed since 1958? Can you find other evidence for either change or stability in slang between then and now?

8.   What closed systems do Callisto and Aubade create? Where is the entropy in them?

9.   What can you fill in of Callisto's history from his age, remarks, and reminiscences?

10. Callisto buys "a Henry Miller novel and left for Paris." What connection do you see with Pynchon's heading his story with a quotation from Miller's *Tropic of Cancer* (1934), an autobiographical novel about an American expatriate's life in Paris?

11. What is the relationship between Callisto's recollection of Stravinsky's *L'Histoire du Soldat* and what the Duke di Angelis quartet is up to? What is the connection between their name and their *Songs for Outer Space*? How does this relate to Pynchon's theme?

12. What contrasts does Pynchon make between the Callisto-Aubade ending and the Meatball ending? What do they suggest?

13. What is Pynchon's theme?

CHAPTER 9

LONGER FICTION

Here, to try your skills, are two extended stories, the first really a short novel, or *novelette*. Tolstoy, the Russian aristocrat turned visionary peasant, projected the modern dilemma, public and private, in his *War and Peace* (1865–1872) and *Anna Karenina* (1875–1876). His *The Death of Ivan Ilych* (1884) is a masterpiece of dramatic and circumstantial irony. Perhaps no other work moves so closely to the process of dying. What picture does Tolstoy give of nineteenth-century medical practice? Does the modern reader have any difference of perspective? What does Tolstoy imply about the medical and legal professions?

Conrad, a Polish boy fleeing Russian pogroms, became a sailor of the world and a preeminent author in English, his third language (after French), which he found to be the true language of his imagination. His "Secret Sharer" is an imaginative fictionalization of his feelings on taking his first command of a ship. In what way does this exotic tale "tell of you"?

THE DEATH OF IVAN ILYCH*

LEO TOLSTOY   *(1828–1910)*

I

During an interval in the Melvinski trial in the large building of the Law Courts, the members and public prosecuter met in Ivam Egorovich Shebek's private room, where the conversation turned on the celebrated Krasovski case. Fëdor Vasilievich warmly maintained that it was not subject to their jurisdiction, Ivan Egorovich maintained the contrary, while Peter Ivanovich, not having entered

*Translated by Louise and Aylmer Maude.

into the discussion at the start, took no part in it but looked through the *Gazette* which had just been handed in.

"Gentlemen," he said, "Ivan Ilych has died!"

"You don't say so!"

"Here, read it yourself," replied Peter Ivanovich, handing Fëdor Vasilievich the paper still damp from the press. Surrounded by a black border were the words: "Praskovya Fëdorovna Goloviná, with profound sorrow, informs relatives and friends of the demise of her beloved husband Ivan Ilych Golovin, Member of the Court of Justice, which occurred on February the 4th of this year 1882. The funeral will take place on Friday at one o'clock in the afternoon."

Ivan Ilych had been a colleague of the gentlemen present and was liked by them all. He had been ill for some weeks with an illness said to be incurable. His post had been kept open for him, but there had been conjectures that in case of his death Alexeev might receive his appointment, and that either Vinnikov or Shtabel would succeed Alexeev. So on receiving the news of Ivan Ilych's death the first thought of each of the gentlemen in that private room was of the changes and promotions it might occasion among themselves or their acquaintances.

"I shall be sure to get Shtabel's place or Vinnikov's," thought Fëdor Vasilievich. "I was promised that long ago, and the promotion means an extra eight hundred rubles a year for me besides the allowance."

"Now I must apply for my brother-in-law's transfer from Kaluga," thought Peter Ivanovich. "My wife will be very glad and then she won't be able to say that I never do anything for her relations."

"I thought he would never leave his bed again," said Peter Ivanovich aloud. "It's very sad."

"But what really was the matter with him?"

"The doctors couldn't say—at least they could, but each of them said something different. When last I saw him I thought he was getting better."

"And I haven't been to see him since the holidays. I always meant to go."

"Had he any property?"

"I think his wife had a little—but something quite trifling."

"We shall have to go to see her, but they live so terribly far away."

"Far away from you, you mean. Everything's far away from your place."

"You see, he never can forgive my living on the other side of the river," said Peter Ivanovich, smiling at Shebek. Then, still talking of the distances between different parts of the city, they returned to the Court.

Besides considerations as to the possible transfers and promotions likely to result from Ivan Ilych's death, the mere fact of the death of a near acquaintance aroused, as usual, in all who heard of it the complacent feeling that "it is he who is dead and not I."

Each one thought or felt, "Well, he's dead but I'm alive!" But the more intimate of Ivan Ilych's acquaintances, his so-called friends, could not help thinking also that they would now have to fulfil the very tiresome demands of propriety by attending the funeral service and paying a visit of condolence to the widow.

Fëdor Vasilievich and Peter Ivanovich had been his nearest acquaintances.

Peter Ivanovich had studied law with Ivan Ilych and had considered himself to be under obligations to him.

Having told his wife at dinner-time of Ivan Ilych's death and of his conjecture that it might be possible to get her brother transferred to their circuit, Peter Ivanovich sacrificed his usual nap, put on his evening clothes, and drove to Ivan Ilych's house.

At the entrance stood a carriage and two cabs. Leaning against the wall in the hall downstairs near the cloak-stand was a coffin-lid covered with cloth of gold, ornamented with gold cord and tassels, that had been polished up with metal powder. Two ladies in black were taking off their fur cloaks. Peter Ivanovich recognized one of them as Ivan Ilych's sister, but the other was a stranger to him. His colleague Schwartz was just coming downstairs, but on seeing Peter Ivanovich enter he stopped and winked at him, as if to say: "Ivan Ilych has made a mess of things—not like you and me."

Schwartz's face with his Piccadilly whiskers and his slim figure in evening dress had as usual an air of elegant solemnity which contrasted with the playfulness of his character and had a special piquancy here, or so it seemed to Peter Ivanovich.

Peter Ivanovich allowed the ladies to precede him and slowly followed them upstairs. Schwartz did not come down but remained where he was, and Peter Ivanovich understood that he wanted to arrange where they should play bridge that evening. The ladies went upstairs to the widow's room, and Schwartz with seriously compressed lips but a playful look in his eyes, indicated by a twist of his eyebrows the room to the right where the body lay.

Peter Ivanovich, like everyone else on such occasions, entered feeling uncertain what he would have to do. All he knew was that at such times it is always safe to cross oneself. But he was not quite sure whether one should make obeisances while doing so. He therefore adopted a middle course. On entering the room he began crossing himself and made a slight movement resembling a bow. At the same time, as far as the motion of his head and arm allowed, he surveyed the room. Two young men—apparently nephews, one of whom was a high-school pupil—were leaving the room, crossing themselves as they did so. An old woman was standing motionless, and a lady with strangely arched eyebrows was saying something to her in a whisper. A vigorous, resolute Church Reader, in a frock-coat, was reading something in a loud voice with an expression that precluded any contradiction. The butler's assistant, Gerasim, stepping lightly in front of Peter Ivanovich, was strewing something on the floor. Noticing this, Peter Ivanovich was immediately aware of a faint odor of a decomposing body.

The last time he had called on Ivan Ilych, Peter Ivanovich had seen Gerasim in the study. Ivan Ilych had been particularly fond of him and he was performing the duty of a sick nurse.

Peter Ivanovich continued to make the sign of the cross, slightly inclining his head in an intermediate direction between the coffin, the Reader, and the icons on the table in a corner of the room. Afterwards, when it seemed to him that this movement of his arm in crossing himself had gone on too long, he stopped and began to look at the corpse.

The dead man lay, as dead men always lie, in a specially heavy way, his rigid limbs sunk in the soft cushions of the coffin, with the head forever bowed on the pillow. His yellow waxen brow with bald patches over his sunken temples was thrust up in the way peculiar to the dead, the protruding nose seeming to press on the upper lip. He was much changed and had grown even thinner since Peter Ivanovich had last seen him, but, as is always the case with the dead, his face was handsomer and above all more dignified than when he was alive. The expression on the face said that what was necessary had been accomplished, and accomplished rightly. Besides this there was in that expression a reproach and a warning to the living. This warning seemed to Peter Ivanovich out of place, or at least not applicable to him. He felt a certain discomfort and so he hurriedly crossed himself once more and turned and went out of the door—too hurriedly and too regardless of propriety, as he himself was aware.

Schwartz was waiting for him in the adjoining room with legs spread wide apart and both hands toying with his top-hat behind his back. The mere sight of that playful, well-groomed, and elegant figure refreshed Peter Ivanovich. He felt that Schwartz was above all these happenings and would not surrender to any depressing influences. His very look said that this incident of a church service for Ivan Ilych could not be a sufficient reason for infringing the order of the session—in other words, that it would certainly not prevent his unwrapping a new pack of cards and shuffling them that evening while a footman placed four fresh candles on the table: in fact, that there was no reason for supposing that this incident would hinder their spending the evening agreeably. Indeed he said this in a whisper as Peter Ivanovich passed him, proposing that they should meet for a game at Fëdor Vasilievich's. But apparently Peter Ivanovich was not destined to play bridge that evening. Praskovya Fëdorovna (a short, fat woman who despite all efforts to the contrary had continued to broaden steadily from her shoulders downwards and who had the same extraordinarily arched eyebrows as the lady who had been standing by the coffin), dressed all in black, her head covered with lace, came out of her own room with some other ladies, conducted them to the room where the dead body lay, and said: "The service will begin immediately. Please go in."

Schwartz, making an indefinite bow, stood still, evidently neither accepting nor declining this invitation. Praskovya Fëdorovna, recognizing Peter Ivanovich, sighed, went close up to him, took his hand, and said: "I know you were a true friend of Ivan Ilych . . ." and looked at him awaiting some suitable response. And Peter Ivanovich knew that, just as it had been the right thing to cross himself in that room, so what he had to do here was to press her hand, sigh, and say, "Believe me. . . ." So he did all this and as he did it felt that the desired result had been achieved: that both he and she were touched.

"Come with me. I want to speak to you before it begins," said the widow. "Give me your arm."

Peter Ivanovich gave her his arm and they went to the inner rooms, passing Schwartz, who winked at Peter Ivanovich compassionately.

"That does for our bridge! Don't object if we find another player. Perhaps you can cut in when you do escape," said his playful look.

Peter Ivanovich sighed still more deeply and despondently, and Praskovya Fëdorovna pressed his arm gratefully. When they reached the drawing-room, upholstered in pink cretonne and lighted by a dim lamp, they sat down at the table —she on a sofa and Peter Ivanovich on a low pouffe, the springs of which yielded spasmodically under his weight. Praskovya Fëdorovna had been on the point of warning him to take another seat, but felt that such a warning was out of keeping with her present condition and so changed her mind. As he sat down on the pouffe Peter Ivanovich recalled how Ivan Ilych had arranged this room and had consulted him regarding this pink cretonne with green leaves. The whole room was full of furniture and knick-knacks, and on her way to the sofa the lace of the widow's black shawl caught on the carved edge of the table. Peter Ivanovich rose to detach it, and the springs of the pouffe, relieved of his weight, rose also and gave him a push. The widow began detaching her shawl herself, and Peter Ivanovich again sat down, suppressing the rebellious springs of the pouffe under him. But the widow had not quite freed herself and Peter Ivanovich got up again, and again the pouffe rebelled and even creaked. When this was all over she took out a clean cambric handkerchief and began to weep. The episode with the shawl and the struggle with the pouffe had cooled Peter Ivanovich's emotions and he sat there with a sullen look on his face. This awkward situation was interrupted by Sokolov, Ivan Ilych's butler, who came to report that the plot in the cemetery that Praskovya Fëdorovna had chosen would cost two hundred rubles. She stopped weeping and, looking at Peter Ivanovich with the air of a victim, remarked in French that it was very hard for her. Peter Ivanovich made a silent gesture signifying his full conviction that it must indeed be so.

"Please smoke," she said in a magnanimous yet crushed voice, and turned to discuss with Sokolov the price of the plot for the grave.

Peter Ivanovich while lighting his cigarette heard her inquiring very circumstantially into the prices of different plots in the cemetery and finally decide which she would take. When that was done she gave instructions about engaging the choir. Sokolov then left the room.

"I look after everything myself," she told Peter Ivanovich, shifting the albums that lay on the table; and noticing that the table was endangered by his cigarette-ash, she immediately passed him an ashtray, saying as she did so: "I consider it an affectation to say that my grief prevents my attending to practical affairs. On the contrary, if anything can—I won't say console me, but—distract me, it is seeing to everything concerning him." She again took out her handkerchief as if preparing to cry, but suddenly, as if mastering her feeling, she shook herself and began to speak calmly. "But there is something I want to talk to you about."

Peter Ivanovich bowed, keeping control of the springs of the pouffe, which immediately began quivering under him.

"He suffered terribly the last few days."

"Did he?" said Peter Ivanovich.

"Oh, terribly! He screamed unceasingly, not for minutes but for hours. For the last three days he screamed incessantly. It was unendurable. I cannot understand how I bore it; you could hear him three rooms off. Oh, what I have suffered!"

"Is it possible that he was conscious all that time?" asked Peter Ivanovich.

"Yes," she whispered. "To the last moment. He took leave of us a quarter of an hour before he died, and asked us to take Volodya away."

The thought of the sufferings of this man he had known so intimately, first as a merry little boy, then as a school-mate, and later as a grown-up colleague, suddenly struck Peter Ivanovich with horror, despite an unpleasant consciousness of his own and this woman's dissimulation. He again saw that brow, and that nose pressing down on the lip, and felt afraid for himself.

"Three days of frightful suffering and then death! Why, that might suddenly, at any time, happen to me," he thought, and for a moment felt terrified. But— he did not himself know how—the customary reflection at once occurred to him that this had happened to Ivan Ilych and not to him, and that it should not and could not happen to him, and that to think that it could would be yielding to depression which he ought not to do, as Schwartz's expression plainly showed. After which reflection Peter Ivanovich felt reassured, and began to ask with interest about the details of Ivan Ilych's death, as though death was an accident natural to Ivan Ilych but certainly not to himself.

After many details of the really dreadful physical sufferings Ivan Ilych had endured (which details he learnt only from the effect those sufferings had produced on Praskovya Fëdorovna's nerves) the widow apparently found it necessary to get to business.

"Oh, Peter Ivanovich, how hard it is! How terribly, terribly hard!" and she again began to weep.

Peter Ivanovich sighed and waited for her to finish blowing her nose. When she had done so he said, "Believe me . . ." and she again began talking and brought out what was evidently her chief concern with him—namely, to question him as to how she could obtain a grant of money from the government on the occasion of her husband's death. She made it appear that she was asking Peter Ivanovich's advice about her pension, but he soon saw that she already knew about that to the minutest detail, more even than he did himself. She knew how much could be got out of the government in consequence of her husband's death, but wanted to find out whether she could not possibly extract something more. Peter Ivanovich tried to think of some means of doing so, but after reflecting for a while and, out of propriety, condemning the government for its niggardliness, he said he thought that nothing more could be got. Then she sighed and evidently began to devise means of getting rid of her visitor. Noticing this, he put out his cigarette, rose, pressed her hand, and went out into the anteroom.

In the dining-room where the clock stood that Ivan Ilych had liked so much and had bought at an antique shop, Peter Ivanovich met a priest and a few acquaintances who had come to attend the service, and he recognized Ivan Ilych's daughter, a handsome young woman. She was in black and her slim figure appeared slimmer than ever. She had a gloomy, determined, almost angry expression, and bowed to Peter Ivanovich as though he were in some way to blame. Behind her, with the same offended look, stood a wealthy young man, an examining magistrate, whom Peter Ivanovich also knew and who was her fiancé, as he had heard. He bowed mournfully to them and was about to pass into the death-chamber, when from under the stairs appeared the figure of Ivan Ilych's school boy son, who was extremely like his father. He seemed a little Ivan Ilych, such as Peter Ivanovich remembered when they studied law together. His tear-stained eyes had in them the look that is seen in the eyes of boys of thirteen or fourteen who are not pure-minded. When he saw Peter Ivanovich he scowled morosely and shamefacedly. Peter Ivanovich nodded to him and entered the death-chamber. The service began: candles, groans, incense, tears, and sobs. Peter Ivanovich stood looking gloomily down at his feet. He did not look once at the dead man, did not yield to any depressing influence, and was one of the first to leave the room. There was no one in the anteroom, but Gerasim darted out of the dead man's room, rummaged with his strong hands among the fur coats to find Peter Ivanovich's, and helped him on with it.

"Well, friend Gerasim," said Peter Ivanovich, so as to say something. "It's a sad affair, isn't it?"

"It's God's will. We shall all come to it some day," said Gerasim, displaying his teeth—the even, white teeth of a healthy peasant—and, like a man in the thick of urgent work, he briskly opened the front door, called the coachman, helped Peter Ivanovich into the sledge, and sprang back to the porch as if in readiness for what he had to do next.

Peter Ivanovich found the fresh air particularly pleasant after the smell of incense, the dead body, and carbolic acid.

"Where to, sir?" asked the coachman.

"It's not too late even now. . . . I'll call round on Fëdor Vasilievich."

He accordingly drove there and found them just finishing the first rubber, so that it was quite convenient for him to cut in.

II

Ivan Ilych's life had been most simple and most ordinary and therefore most terrible.

He had been a member of the Court of Justice, and died at the age of forty-five. His father had been an official who after serving in various ministries and departments in Petersburg had made the sort of career which brings men to positions from which by reason of their long service they cannot be dismissed, though they are obviously unfit to hold any responsible position, and for whom therefore posts are specially created, which though fictitious carry salaries of from six to ten thousand rubles that are not fictitious, and in receipt of which they live on to a great age.

Such was the Privy Councillor and superfluous member of various superfluous institutions, Ilya Epimovich Golovin.

He had three sons, of whom Ivan Ilych was the second. The eldest son was following in his father's footsteps only in another department, and was already approaching that stage in the service at which a similar sinecure would be reached. The third son was a failure. He had ruined his prospects in a number of positions and was now serving in the railway department. His father and brothers, and still more their wives, not merely disliked meeting him, but avoided remembering his existence unless compelled to do so. His sister had married Baron Greff, a Petersburg official of her father's type. Ivan Ilych was *le phénix de la famille*[1] as people said. He was neither as cold and formal as his elder brother nor as wild as the younger, but was a happy mean between them—an intelligent, polished, lively, and agreeable man. He had studied with his younger brother at the School of Law, but the latter had failed to complete the course and was expelled when he was in the fifth class. Ivan Ilych finished the course well. Even when he was at the School of Law he was just what he remained for the rest of his life: a capable, cheerful, good-natured, and sociable man, though strict in the fulfilment of what he considered to be his duty: and he considered his duty to be what was so considered by those in authority. Neither as a boy nor as a man was he a toady, but from early youth was by nature attracted to people of high station as a fly is drawn to the light, assimilating their ways and views of life and establishing friendly relations with them. All the enthusiasms of childhood and youth passed without leaving much trace on him; he succumbed to sensuality, to vanity, and latterly among the highest classes to liberalism, but always within limits which his instinct unfailingly indicated to him as correct.

At school he had done things which had formerly seemed to him very horrid and made him feel disgusted with himself when he did them; but when later on he saw that such actions were done by people of good position and that they did not regard them as wrong, he was able not exactly to regard them as right, but to forget about them entirely or not be at all troubled at remembering them.

Having graduated from the School of Law and qualified for the tenth rank of the civil service, and having received money from his father for his equipment, Ivan Ilych ordered himself clothes at Scharmer's, the fashionable tailor, hung a medallion inscribed *respice finem*[2] on his watch-chain, took leave of his professor and the prince who was patron of the school, had a farewell dinner with his comrades at Donon's first-class restaurant, and with his new and fashionable portmanteau, linen, clothes, shaving and other toilet appliances, and a travelling rug all purchased at the best shops, he set off for one of the provinces where, through his father's influence, he had been attached to the Governor as an official for special service.

In the province Ivan Ilych soon arranged as easy and agreeable a position for himself as he had had at the School of Law. He performed his official tasks, made his career, and at the same time amused himself pleasantly and decorously. Occasionally he paid official visits to country districts, where he behaved with dignity both to his superiors and inferiors, and performed the duties entrusted to

---

[1]The phoenix [paragon] of the family.   [2]Reflect on the end.

him, which related chiefly to the sectarians,[3] with an exactness and incorruptible honesty of which he could not but feel proud.

In official matters, despite his youth and taste for frivolous gaiety, he was exceedingly reserved, punctilious, and even severe; but in society he was often amusing and witty, and always good-natured, correct in his manner, and *bon enfant*,[4] as the Governor and his wife—with whom he was like one of the family —used to say of him.

In the province he had an affair with a lady who made advances to the elegant young lawyer, and there was also a milliner; and there were carousals with aides-de-camp who visited the district, and after-supper visits to a certain outlying street of doubtful reputation; and there was too some obsequiousness to his chief and even to his chief's wife, but all this was done with such a tone of good breeding that no hard names could be applied to it. It all came under the heading of the French saying: "*Il faut que jeunesse se passe.*"[5] It was all done with clean hands, in clean linen, with French phrases, and above all among people of the best society and consequently with the approval of people of rank.

So Ivan Ilych served for five years and then came a change in his official life. The new and reformed judicial institutions were introduced, and new men were needed. Ivan Ilych became such a new man. He was offered the post of examining magistrate, and he accepted it though the post was in another province and obliged him to give up the connections he had formed and to make new ones. His friends met to give him a send-off; they had a group-photograph taken and presented him with a silver cigarette-case, and he set off to his new post.

As examining magistrate Ivan Ilych was just as *comme il faut*[6] and decorous a man, inspiring general respect and capable of separating his official duties from his private life, as he had been when acting as an official on special service. His duties now as examining magistrate were far more interesting and attractive than before. In his former position it had been pleasant to wear an undress uniform made by Scharmer, and to pass through the crowd of petitioners and officials who were timorously awaiting an audience with the Governor, and who envied him as with free and easy gait he went straight into his chief's private room to have a cup of tea and a cigarette with him. But not many people had been directly dependent on him—only police officials and the sectarians when he went on special missions—and he liked to treat them politely, almost as comrades, as if he were letting them feel that he who had the power to crush them was treating them in this simple, friendly way. There were then but few such people. But now, as an examining magistrate, Ivan Ilych felt that everyone without exception, even the most important and self-satisfied, was in his power, and that he need only write a few words on a sheet of paper with a certain heading, and this or that important, self-satisfied person would be brought before him in the role of an accused person or a witness, and if he did not choose to allow him to sit down, would have to stand before him and answer his questions. Ivan Ilych never abused his power; he tried on the contrary to soften its expression, but the consciousness

---

[3]Religious dissenters. [4]Good fellow. [5]Youth will be served. [6]Correct.

of it and of the possibility of softening its effect, supplied the chief interest and attraction of his office. In his work itself, especially in his examinations, he very soon acquired a method of eliminating all considerations irrelevant to the legal aspect of the case, and reducing even the most complicated case to a form in which it would be presented on paper only in its externals, completely excluding his personal opinion of the matter, while above all observing every prescribed formality. The work was new and Ivan Ilych was one of the first men to apply the new Code of 1864.[7]

On taking up the post of examining magistrate in a new town, he made new acquaintances and connections, placed himself on a new footing, and assumed a somewhat different tone. He took up an attitude of rather dignified aloofness towards the provincial authorities, but picked out the best circle of legal gentlemen and wealthy gentry living in the town and assumed a tone of slight dissatisfaction with the government, of moderate liberalism, and of enlightened citizenship. At the same time, without at all altering the elegance of his toilet, he ceased shaving his chin and allowed his beard to grow as it pleased.

Ivan Ilych settled down very pleasantly in this new town. The society there, which inclined towards opposition to the Governor, was friendly, his salary was larger, and he began to play *vint*,[8] which he found added not a little to the pleasure of life; for he had a capacity for cards, played good-humoredly, and calculated rapidly and astutely, so that he usually won.

After living there for two years he met his future wife, Praskovya Fëdorovna Mikhel, who was the most attractive, clever, and brilliant girl of the set in which he moved, and among other amusements and relaxations from his labors as examining magistrate, Ivan Ilych established light and playful relations with her.

While he had been an official on special service he had been accustomed to dance, but now as an examining magistrate it was exceptional for him to do so. If he danced now, he did it as if to show that though he served under the reformed order of things, and had reached the fifth official rank, yet when it came to dancing he could do it better than most people. So at the end of an evening he sometimes danced with Praskovya Fëdorovna, and it was chiefly during these dances that he captivated her. She fell in love with him. Ivan Ilych had at first no definite intention of marrying, but when the girl fell in love with him he said to himself: "Really, why shouldn't I marry?"

Praskovya Fëdorovna came of a good family, was not bad-looking, and had some little property. Ivan Ilych might have aspired to a more brilliant match, but even this was good. He had his salary, and she, he hoped, would have an equal income. She was well connected, and was a sweet, pretty, and thoroughly correct young woman. To say that Ivan Ilych married because he fell in love with Praskovya Fëdorovna and found that she sympathized with his views of life would be as incorrect as to say that he married because his social circle approved

[7]The emancipation of the serfs in 1861 was followed by a thorough all-round reform of judicial proceedings. [L. and A. Maude]   [8]A form of bridge. [L. and A. Maude]

of the match. He was swayed by both these considerations: the marriage gave him personal satisfaction, and at the same time it was considered the right thing by the most highly placed of his associates.

So Ivan Ilych got married.

The preparations for marriage and the beginning of married life, with its conjugal caresses, the new furniture, new crockery, and new linen, were very pleasant until his wife became pregnant—so that Ivan Ilych had begun to think that marriage would not impair the easy, agreeable, gay, and always decorous character of his life, approved of by society and regarded by himself as natural, but would even improve it. But from the first months of his wife's pregnancy, something new, unpleasant, depressing, and unseemly, and from which there was no way of escape, unexpectedly showed itself.

His wife, without any reason—*de gaieté de coeur*[9] as Ivan Ilych expressed it to himself—began to disturb the pleasure and propriety of their life. She began to be jealous without any cause, expected him to devote his whole attention to her, found fault with everything, and made coarse and ill-mannered scenes.

At first Ivan Ilych hoped to escape from the unpleasantness of this state of affairs by the same easy and decorous relation to life that had served him heretofore: he tried to ignore his wife's disagreeable moods, continued to live in his usual easy and pleasant way, invited friends to his house for a game of cards, and also tried going out to his club or spending his evenings with friends. But one day his wife began upbraiding him so vigorously, using such coarse words, and continued to abuse him every time he did not fulfil her demands, so resolutely and with such evident determination not to give way till he submitted—that is, till he stayed at home and was bored just as she was—that he became alarmed. He now realized that matrimony—at any rate with Praskovya Fëdorovna—was not always conducive to the pleasures and amenities of life, but on the contrary often infringed both comfort and propriety, and that he must therefore entrench himself against such infringement. And Ivan Ilych began to seek for means of doing so. His official duties were the one thing that imposed upon Praskovya Fëdorovna, and by means of his official work and the duties attached to it he began struggling with his wife to secure his own independence.

With the birth of their child, the attempts to feed it and the various failures in doing so, and with the real and imaginary illnesses of mother and child, in which Ivan Ilych's sympathy was demanded but about which he understood nothing, the need of securing for himself an existence outside his family life became still more imperative.

As his wife grew more irritable and exacting and Ivan Ilych transferred the center of gravity of his life more and more to his official work, so did he grow to like his work better and become more ambitious than before.

Very soon, within a year of his wedding, Ivan Ilych had realized that marriage, though it may add some comforts to life, is in fact a very intricate and difficult affair towards which in order to perform one's duty, that is, to lead a decorous

---

[9]Out of sheer wantonness.

life approved of by society, one must adopt a definite attitude just as towards one's official duties.

And Ivan Ilych evolved such an attitude towards married life. He only required of it those conveniences—dinner at home, housewife, and bed—which it could give him, and above all that propriety of external forms required by public opinion. For the rest he looked for light-hearted pleasure and propriety, and was very thankful when he found them, but if he met with antagonism and querulousness he at once retired into his separate fenced-off world of official duties, where he found satisfaction.

Ivan Ilych was esteemed a good official, and after three years was made Assistant Public Prosecutor. His new duties, their importance, the possibility of indicting and imprisoning anyone he chose, the publicity his speeches received, and the success he had in all these things, made his work still more attractive.

More children came. His wife became more and more querulous and ill-tempered, but the attitude Ivan Ilych had adopted towards his home life rendered him almost impervious to her grumbling.

After seven years' service in that town he was transferred to another province as Public Prosecutor. They moved, but were short of money and his wife did not like the place they moved to. Though the salary was higher the cost of living was greater, besides which two of their children died and family life became still more unpleasant for him.

Praskovya Fëdorovna blamed her husband for every inconvenience they encountered in their new home. Most of the conversations between husband and wife, especially as to the children's education, led to topics which recalled former disputes, and those disputes were apt to flare up again at any moment. There remained only those rare periods of amorousness which still came to them at times but did not last long. These were islets at which they anchored for a while and then again set out upon that ocean of veiled hostility which showed itself in their aloofness from one another. This aloofness might have grieved Ivan Ilych had he considered that it ought not to exist, but he now regarded the position as normal, and even made it the goal at which he aimed in family life. His aim was to free himself more and more from those unpleasantnesses and to give them a semblance of harmlessness and propriety. He attained this by spending less and less time with his family, and when obliged to be at home he tried to safeguard his position by the presence of outsiders. The chief thing however was that he had his official duties. The whole interest of his life now centered in the official world and that interest absorbed him. The consciousness of his power, being able to ruin anybody he wished to ruin, the importance, even the external dignity of his entry into court, or meetings with his subordinates, his success with superiors and inferiors, and above all his masterly handling of cases, of which he was conscious —all this gave him pleasure and filled his life, together with chats with his colleagues, dinners, and bridge. So that on the whole Ivan Ilych's life continued to flow as he considered it should do—pleasantly and properly.

So things continued for another seven years. His eldest daughter was already sixteen, another child had died, and only one son was left, a schoolboy and a subject of dissension. Ivan Ilych wanted to put him in the School of Law, but to spite him Praskovya Fëdorovna entered him at the High School. The daughter had been educated at home and had turned out well: the boy did not learn badly either.

III

So Ivan Ilych lived for seventeen years after his marriage. He was already a Public Prosecutor of long standing, and had declined several proposed transfers while awaiting a more desirable post, when an unanticipated and unpleasant occurrence quite upset the peaceful course of his life. He was expecting to be offered the post of presiding judge in a University town, but Happe somehow came to the front and obtained the appointment instead. Ivan Ilych became irritable, reproached Happe, and quarrelled both with him and with his immediate superiors—who became colder to him and again passed him over when other appointments were made.

This was in 1880, the hardest year of Ivan Ilych's life. It was then that it became evident on the one hand that his salary was insufficient for them to live on, and on the other that he had been forgotten, and not only this, but that what was for him the greatest and most cruel injustice appeared to others a quite ordinary occurrence. Even his father did not consider it his duty to help him. Ivan Ilych felt himself abandoned by everyone, and that they regarded his position with a salary of 3,500 rubles as quite normal and even fortunate. He alone knew that with the consciousness of the injustices done him, with his wife's incessant nagging, and with the debts he had contracted by living beyond his means, his position was far from normal.

In order to save money that summer he obtained leave of absence and went with his wife to live in the country at her brother's place.

In the country, without his work, he experienced *ennui* for the first time in his life, and not only *ennui* but intolerable depression, and he decided that it was impossible to go on living like that, and that it was necessary to take energetic measures.

Having passed a sleepless night pacing up and down the veranda, he decided to go to Petersburg and bestir himself, in order to punish those who had failed to appreciate him and to get transferred to another ministry.

Next day, despite many protests from his wife and her brother, he started for Petersburg with the sole object of obtaining a post with a salary of five thousand rubles a year. He was no longer bent on any particular department, or tendency, or kind of activity. All he now wanted was an appointment to another post with a salary of five thousand rubles, either in the administration, in the banks, with the railways, in one of the Empress Marya's Institutions, or even in the customs —but it had to carry with it a salary of five thousand rubles and be in a ministry other than that in which they had failed to appreciate him.

And this quest of Ivan Ilych's was crowned with remarkable and unexpected success. At Kursk an acquaintance of his, F. I. Ilyin, got into the first-class carriage, sat down beside Ivan Ilych, and told him of a telegram just received by the Governor of Kursk announcing that a change was about to take place in the ministry: Peter Ivanovich was to be superseded by Ivan Semënovich.

The proposed change, apart from its significance for Russia, had a special significance for Ivan Ilych, because by bringing forward a new man, Peter Petrovich, and consequently his friend Zachar Ivanovich, it was highly favorable for Ivan Ilych, since Zachar Ivanovich was a friend and colleague of his.

In Moscow this news was confirmed, and on reaching Petersburg Ivan Ilych found Zachar Ivanovich and received a definite promise of an appointment in his former department of Justice.

A week later he telegraphed to his wife: "Zachar in Miller's place. I shall receive appointment on presentation of report."

Thanks to this change of personnel, Ivan Ilych had unexpectedly obtained an appointment in his former ministry which placed him two stages above his former colleagues besides giving him five thousand rubles salary and three thousand five hundred rubles for expenses connected with his removal. All his ill humor towards his former enemies and the whole department vanished, and Ivan Ilych was completely happy.

He returned to the country more cheerful and contented than he had been for a long time. Praskovya Fëdorovna also cheered up and a truce was arranged between them. Ivan Ilych told of how he had been fêted by everybody in Petersburg, how all those who had been his enemies were put to shame and now fawned on him, how envious they were of his appointment, and how much everybody in Petersburg had liked him.

Praskovya Fëdorovna listened to all this and appeared to believe it. She did not contradict anything, but only made plans for their life in the town to which they were going. Ivan Ilych saw with delight that these plans were his plans, that he and his wife agreed, and that, after a stumble, his life was regaining its due and natural character of pleasant lightheartedness and decorum.

Ivan Ilych had come back for a short time only, for he had to take up his new duties on the 10th of September. Moreover, he needed time to settle into the new place, to move all his belongings from the province, and to buy and order many additional things: in a word, to make such arrangements as he had resolved on, which were almost exactly what Praskovya Fëdorovna too had decided on.

Now that everything had happened so fortunately, and that he and his wife were at one in their aims and moreover saw so little of one another, they got on together better than they had done since the first years of marriage. Ivan Ilych had thought of taking his family away with him at once, but the insistence of his wife's brother and her sister-in-law, who had suddenly become particularly amiable and friendly to him and his family, induced him to depart alone.

So he departed, and the cheerful state of mind induced by his success and by the harmony between his wife and himself, the one intensifying the other, did not leave him. He found a delightful house, just the thing both he and his wife had dreamt of. Spacious, lofty reception rooms in the old style, a convenient and dignified study, rooms for his wife and daughter, a study for his son—it might have been specially built for them. Ivan Ilych himself superintended the arrangements, chose the wallpapers, supplemented the furniture (preferably with antiques which he considered particularly *comme il faut*), and supervised the upholstering. Everything progressed and progressed and approached the ideal he had set himself: even when things were only half completed they exceeded his expectations. He saw what a refined and elegant character, free from vulgarity, it would all have when it was ready. On falling asleep he pictured to himself how the reception-room would look. Looking at the yet unfinished drawing-room he could see the fireplace, the screen, the what-not, the little chairs dotted here and there, the dishes and plates on the walls, and the bronzes, as they would be when everything was in place. He was pleased by the thought of how his wife and daughter, who shared his taste in this matter, would be impressed by it. They were certainly not expecting as much. He had been particularly successful in finding, and buying cheaply, antiques which gave a particularly aristocratic character to the whole place. But in his letter he intentionally understated everything in order to be able to surprise them. All this so absorbed him that his new duties—though he liked his official work—interested him less than he had expected. Sometimes he even had moments of absentmindedness during the Court Sessions, and would consider whether he should have straight or curved cornices for his curtains. He was so interested in it all that he often did things himself, rearranging the furniture, or rehanging the curtains. Once when mounting a stepladder to show the upholsterer, who did not understand, how he wanted the hangings draped, he made a false step and slipped, but being a strong and agile man he clung on and only knocked his side against the knob of the window frame. The bruised place was painful but the pain soon passed, and he felt particularly bright and well just then. He wrote: "I feel fifteen years younger." He thought he would have everything ready by September, but it dragged on till mid-October. But the result was charming not only in his eyes but to everyone who saw it.

In reality it was just what is usually seen in the houses of people of moderate means who want to appear rich, and therefore succeed only in resembling others like themselves: there were damasks, dark wood, plants, rugs, and dull and polished bronzes—all the things people of a certain class have in order to resemble other people of that class. His house was so like the others that it would never have been noticed, but to him it all seemed to be quite exceptional. He was very happy when he met his family at the station and brought them to the newly furnished house all lit up, where a footman in a white tie opened the door into the hall decorated with plants, and when they went on into the drawing-room and the study uttering exclamations of delight. He conducted them everywhere, drank in their praises eagerly, and beamed with pleasure. At tea that evening, when Praskovya Fëdorovna among other things asked him about his fall, he laughed and showed them how he had gone flying and had frightened the upholsterer.

"It's a good thing I'm a bit of an athlete. Another man might have been killed, but I merely knocked myself, just here; it hurts when it's touched, but it's passing off already—it's only a bruise."

So they began living in their new home—in which, as always happens, when they got thoroughly settled in they found they were just one room short—and with the increased income, which as always was just a little (some five hundred rubles) too little, but it was all very nice.

Things went particularly well at first, before everything was finally arranged and while something had still to be done: this thing bought, that thing ordered, another thing moved, and something else adjusted. Though there were some disputes between husband and wife, they were both so well satisfied and had so much to do that it all passed off without any serious quarrels. When nothing was left to arrange it became rather dull and something seemed to be lacking, but they were then making acquaintances, forming habits, and life was growing fuller.

Ivan Ilych spent his mornings at the law courts and came home to dinner, and at first he was generally in a good humor, though he occasionally became irritable just on account of his house. (Every spot on the tablecloth or the upholstery, and every broken window-blind string, irritated him. He had devoted so much trouble to arranging it all that every disturbance of it distressed him.) But on the whole his life ran its course as he believed life should do: easily, pleasantly, and decorously.

He got up at nine, drank his coffee, read the paper, and then put on his undress uniform and went to the law courts. There the harness in which he worked had already been stretched to fit him and he donned it without a hitch: petitioners, inquiries at the chancery, the chancery itself, and the sittings public and administrative. In all this the thing was to exclude everything fresh and vital, which always disturbs the regular course of official business, and to admit only official relations with people, and then only on official grounds. A man would come, for instance, wanting some information. Ivan Ilych, as one in whose sphere the matter did not lie, would have nothing to do with him: but if the man had some business with him in his official capacity, something that could be expressed on officially stamped paper, he would do everything, positively everything he could within the limits of such relations, and in doing so would maintain the semblance of friendly human relations, that is, would observe the courtesies of life. As soon as the official relations ended, so did everything else. Ivan Ilych possessed this capacity to separate his real life from the official side of affairs and not mix the two, in the highest degree, and by long practice and natural aptitude had brought it to such a pitch that sometimes, in the manner of a virtuoso, he would even allow himself to let the human and official relations mingle. He let himself do this just because he felt that he could at any time he chose resume the strictly official attitude again and drop the human relation. And he did it all easily, pleasantly, correctly, and even artistically. In the intervals between the sessions he smoked, drank tea, chatted a little about politics, a little about general topics, a little about cards, but most of all about official appointments. Tired, but with the feelings of a virtuoso—one of the first violins who has played his part in an orchestra with precision—he would return home to find that his wife and daughter had been out paying calls, or had a visitor, and that his son had been to school, had done his homework with his tutor, and was duly learning what is taught at High Schools.

Everything was as it should be. After dinner, if they had no visitors, Ivan Ilych sometimes read a book that was being much discussed at the time, and in the evening settled down to work, that is, read official papers, compared the depositions of witnesses, and noted paragraphs of the Code applying to them. This was neither dull nor amusing. It was dull when he might have been playing bridge, but if no bridge was available it was at any rate better than doing nothing or sitting with his wife. Ivan Ilych's chief pleasure was giving little dinners to which he invited men and women of good social position, and just as his drawing-room resembled all other drawing-rooms so did his enjoyable little parties resemble all other such parties.

Once they even gave a dance. Ivan Ilych enjoyed it and everything went off well, except that it led to a violent quarrel with his wife about the cakes and sweets. Praskovya Fëdorovna had made her own plans, but Ivan Ilych insisted on getting everything from an expensive confectioner and ordered too many cakes, and the quarrel occurred because some of those cakes were left over and the confectioner's bill came to forty-five rubles. It was a great and disagreeable quarrel. Praskovya Fëdorovna called him "a fool and an imbecile," and he clutched at his head and made angry allusions to divorce.

But the dance itself had been enjoyable. The best people were there, and Ivan Ilych had danced with Princess Trufonova, a sister of the distinguished founder of the Society "Bear my Burden."

The pleasures connected with his work were pleasures of ambition; his social pleasures were those of vanity; but Ivan Ilych's greatest pleasure was playing bridge. He acknowledged that whatever disagreeable incident happened in his life, the pleasure that beamed like a ray of light above everything else was to sit down to bridge with good players, not noisy partners, and of course to four-handed bridge (with five players it was annoying to have to stand out, though one pretended not to mind), to play a clever and serious game (when the cards allowed it), and then to have supper and drink a glass of wine. After a game of bridge, especially if he had won a little (to win a large sum was unpleasant), Ivan Ilych went to bed in specially good humor.

So they lived. They formed a circle of acquaintances among the best people and were visited by people of importance and by young folk. In their views as to their acquaintances, husband, wife, and daughter were entirely agreed, and tacitly and unanimously kept at arm's length and shook off the various shabby friends and relations who, with much show of affection, gushed into the drawing-room with its Japanese plates on the walls. Soon these shabby friends ceased to obtrude themselves and only the best people remained in the Golovins' set.

Young men made up to Lisa, and Petrishchev, an examining magistrate and Dmitri Ivanovich Petrishchev's son and sole heir, began to be so attentive to her that Ivan Ilych had already spoken to Praskovya Fëdorovna about it, and considered whether they should not arrange a party for them, or get up some private theatricals.

So they lived, and all went well, without change, and life flowed pleasantly.

IV

They were all in good health. It could not be called ill health if Ivan Ilych sometimes said that he had a queer taste in his mouth and felt some discomfort in his left side.

But this discomfort increased and, though not exactly painful, grew into a sense of pressure in his side accompanied by ill humor. And his irritability became worse and worse and began to mar the agreeable, easy, and correct life that had established itself in the Golovin family. Quarrels between husband and wife became more and more frequent, and soon the ease and amenity disappeared and even the decorum was barely maintained. Scenes again became frequent, and very few of those islets remained on which husband and wife could meet without an explosion. Praskovya Fëdorovna now had good reason to say that her husband's temper was trying. With characteristic exaggeration she said he had always had a dreadful temper, and that it had needed all her good nature to put up with it for twenty years. It was true that now the quarrels were started by him. His bursts of temper always came just before dinner, often just as he began to eat his soup. Sometimes he noticed that a plate or dish was chipped, or the food was not right, or his son put his elbow on the table, or his daughter's hair was not done as he liked it, and for all this he blamed Praskovya Fëdorovna. At first she retorted and said disagreeable things to him, but once or twice he fell into such a rage at the beginning of dinner that she realized it was due to some physical derangement brought on by taking food, and so she restrained herself and did not answer, but only hurried to get the dinner over. She regarded this self-restraint as highly praiseworthy. Having come to the conclusion that her husband had a dreadful temper and made her life miserable, she began to feel sorry for herself, and the more she pitied herself the more she hated her husband. She began to wish he would die; yet she did not want him to die because then his salary would cease. And this irritated her against him still more. She considered herself dreadfully unhappy just because not even his death could save her, and though she concealed her exasperation, that hidden exasperation of hers increased his irritation also.

After one scene in which Ivan Ilych had been particularly unfair and after which he had said in explanation that he certainly was irritable but that it was due to his not being well, she said that if he was ill it should be attended to, and insisted on his going to see a celebrated doctor.

He went. Everything took place as he had expected and as it always does. There was the usual waiting and the important air assumed by the doctor, with which he was so familiar (resembling that which he himself assumed in court), and the sounding and listening, and the questions which called for answers that were foregone conclusions and were evidently unnecessary, and the look of importance which implied that "if only you put yourself in our hands we will arrange everything—we know indubitably how it has to be done, always in the same way for everybody alike." It was all just as it was in the law courts. The doctor put on just the same air towards him as he himself put on towards an accused person.

The doctor said that so-and-so indicated that there was so-and-so inside the patient, but if the investigation of so-and-so did not confirm this, then he must assume that and that. If he assumed that and that, then . . . and so on. To Ivan Ilych only one question was important: was his case serious or not? But the doctor ignored that inappropriate question. From his point of view it was not the one under consideration, the real question was to decide between a floating kidney, chronic catarrh, or appendicitis. It was not a question of Ivan Ilych's life or death, but one between a floating kidney and appendicitis. And that question the doctor solved brilliantly, as it seemed to Ivan Ilych, in favor of the appendix, with the reservation that should an examination of the urine give fresh indications the matter would be reconsidered. All this was just what Ivan Ilych had himself brilliantly accomplished a thousand times in dealing with men on trial. The doctor summed up just as brilliantly, looking over his spectacles triumphantly and even gaily at the accused. From the doctor's summing up Ivan Ilych concluded that things were bad, but that for the doctor, and perhaps for everybody else, it was a matter of indifference, though for him it was bad. And this conclusion struck him painfully, arousing in him a great feeling of pity for himself and of bitterness towards the doctor's indifference to a matter of such importance.

He said nothing of this, but rose, placed the doctor's fee on the table, and remarked with a sigh: "We sick people probably often put inappropriate questions. But tell me, in general, is this complaint dangerous, or not? . . ."

The doctor looked at him sternly over his spectacles with one eye, as if to say: "Prisoner, if you will not keep to the questions put to you, I shall be obliged to have you removed from the court."

"I have already told you what I consider necessary and proper. The analysis may show something more." And the doctor bowed.

Ivan Ilych went out slowly, seated himself disconsolately in his sledge, and drove home. All the way home he was going over what the doctor had said, trying to translate those complicated, obscure, scientific phrases into plain language and find in them an answer to the question: "Is my condition bad? Is it very bad? Or is there as yet nothing much wrong?" And it seemed to him that the meaning of what the doctor had said was that it was very bad. Everything in the streets seemed depressing. The cabmen, the houses, the passers-by, and the shops, were dismal. His ache, this dull gnawing ache that never ceased for a moment, seemed to have acquired a new and more serious significance from the doctor's dubious remarks. Ivan Ilych now watched it with a new and oppressive feeling.

He reached home and began to tell his wife about it. She listened, but in the middle of his account his daughter came in with her hat on, ready to go out with her mother. She sat down reluctantly to listen to this tedious story, but could not stand it long, and her mother too did not hear him to the end.

"Well, I am very glad," she said. "Mind now to take your medicine regularly. Give me the prescription and I'll send Gerasim to the chemist's." And she went to get ready to go out.

While she was in the room Ivan Ilych had hardly taken time to breathe, but he sighed deeply when she left it.

"Well," he thought, "perhaps it isn't so bad after all."

He began taking his medicine and following the doctor's directions, which had been altered after the examination of the urine. But then it happened that there was a contradiction between the indications drawn from the examination of the urine and the symptoms that showed themselves. It turned out that what was happening differed from what the doctor had told him, and that he had either forgotten, or blundered, or hidden something from him. He could not, however, be blamed for that, and Ivan Ilych still obeyed his orders implicitly and at first derived some comfort from doing so.

From the time of his visit to the doctor, Ivan Ilych's chief occupation was the exact fulfilment of the doctor's instructions regarding hygiene and the taking of medicine, and the observation of his pain and his excretions. His chief interests came to be people's ailments and people's health. When sickness, deaths, or recoveries were mentioned in his presence, especially when the illness resembled his own, he listened with agitation which he tried to hide, asked questions, and applied what he heard to his own case.

The pain did not grow less, but Ivan Ilych made efforts to force himself to think that he was better. And he could do this so long as nothing agitated him. But as soon as he had any unpleasantness with his wife, any lack of success in his official work, or held bad cards at bridge, he was at once acutely sensible of his disease. He had formerly borne such mischances, hoping soon to adjust what was wrong, to master it and attain success, or make a grand slam. But now every mischance upset him and plunged him into despair. He would say to himself: "There now, just as I was beginning to get better and the medicine had begun to take effect, comes this accursed misfortune, or unpleasantness. . . ." And he was furious with the mishap, or with the people who were causing the unpleasantness and killing him, for he felt that this fury was killing him but could not restrain it. One would have thought that it should have been clear to him that this exasperation with circumstances and people aggravated his illness, and that he ought therefore to ignore unpleasant occurrences. But he drew the very opposite conclusion: he said that he needed peace, and he watched for everything that might disturb it and became irritable at the slightest infringement of it. His condition was rendered worse by the fact that he read medical books and consulted doctors. The progress of his disease was so gradual that he could deceive himself when comparing one day with another—the difference was so slight. But when he consulted the doctors it seemed to him that he was getting worse, and even very rapidly. Yet despite this he was continually consulting them.

That month he went to see another celebrity, who told him almost the same as the first had done but put his questions rather differently, and the interview with this celebrity only increased Ivan Ilych's doubts and fears. A friend of a friend of his, a very good doctor, diagnosed his illness again quite differently from the others, and though he predicted recovery, his questions and suppositions bewildered Ivan Ilych still more and increased his doubts. A homoeopathist diagnosed the disease in yet another way, and prescribed medicine which Ivan Ilych took secretly for a week. But after a week, not feeling any improvement and having lost confidence both in the former doctor's treatment and in this one's, he became still more despondent. One day a lady acquaintance mentioned a cure effected by a wonder-working icon. Ivan Ilych caught himself listening attentively and beginning to believe that it had occurred. This incident alarmed him. "Has my mind really weakened to such an extent?" he asked himself. "Nonsense! It's all rubbish. I mustn't give way to nervous fears but having chosen a doctor must keep strictly to his treatment. That is what I will do. Now it's all settled. I won't think about it, but will follow the treatment seriously till summer, and then we shall see. From now there must be no more of this wavering!" This was easy to say but impossible to carry out. The pain in his side oppressed him and seemed to grow worse and more incessant, while the taste in his mouth grew stranger and stranger. It seemed to him that his breath had a disgusting smell, and he was conscious of a loss of appetite and strength. There was no deceiving himself: something terrible, new, and more important than anything before in his life, was taking place within him of which he alone was aware. Those about him did not understand or would not understand it, but thought everything in the world was going on as usual. That tormented Ivan Ilych more than anything. He saw that his household, especially his wife and daughter who were in a perfect whirl of visiting, did not understand anything of it and were annoyed that he was so depressed and so exacting, as if he were to blame for it. Though they tried to disguise it he saw that he was an obstacle in their path, and that his wife had adopted a definite line in regard to his illness and kept to it regardless of anything he said or did. Her attitude was this: "You know," she would say to her friends, "Ivan Ilych can't do as other people do, and keep to the treatment prescribed for him. One day he'll take his drops and keep strictly to his diet and go to bed in good time, but the next day unless I watch him he'll suddenly forget his medicine, eat sturgeon—which is forbidden—and sit up playing cards till one o'clock in the morning."

"Oh, come, when was that?" Ivan Ilych would ask in vexation. "Only once at Peter Ivanovich's."

"And yesterday with Shebek."

"Well, even if I hadn't stayed up, this pain would have kept me awake."

"Be that as it may you'll never get well like that, but will always make us wretched."

Praskovya Fëdorovna's attitude to Ivan Ilych's illness, as she expressed it both to others and to him, was that it was his own fault and was another of the annoyances he caused her. Ivan Ilych felt that this opinion escaped her involuntarily—but that did not make it easier for him.

At the law courts too, Ivan Ilych noticed, or thought he noticed, a strange attitude towards himself. It sometimes seemed to him that people were watching him inquisitively as a man whose place might soon be vacant. Then again, his friends would suddenly begin to chaff him in a friendly way about his low spirits, as if the awful, horrible, and unheard-of thing that was going on within him, incessantly gnawing at him and irresistibly drawing him away, was a very agreeable subject for jests. Schwartz in particular irritated him by his jocularity, vivacity, and *savoir-faire,* which reminded him of what he himself had been ten years ago.

Friends came to make up a set and they sat down to cards. They dealt, bending the new cards to soften them, and he sorted the diamonds in his hand and found he had seven. His partner said "No trumps" and supported him with two diamonds. What more could be wished for? It ought to be jolly and lively. They would make a grand slam. But suddenly Ivan Ilych was conscious of that gnawing pain, that taste in his mouth, and it seemed ridiculous that in such circumstances he should be pleased to make a grand slam.

He looked at his partner Mikhail Mikhaylovich, who rapped the table with his strong hand and instead of snatching up the tricks pushed the cards courteously and indulgently towards Ivan Ilych that he might have the pleasure of gathering them up without the trouble of stretching out his hand for them. "Does he think I am too weak to stretch out my arm?" thought Ivan Ilych, and forgetting what he was doing he over-trumped his partner, missing the grand slam by three tricks. And what was most awful of all was that he saw how upset Mikhail Mikhaylovich was about it but did not himself care. And it was dreadful to realize why he did not care.

They all saw that he was suffering, and said: "We can stop if you are tired. Take a rest." Lie down? No, he was not at all tired, and he finished the rubber. All were gloomy and silent. Ivan Ilych felt that he had diffused this gloom over them and could not dispel it. They had supper and went away, and Ivan Ilych was left alone with the consciousness that his life was poisoned and was poisoning the lives of others, and that this poison did not weaken but penetrated more and more deeply into his whole being.

With this consciousness, and with physical pain besides the terror, he must go to bed, often to lie awake the greater part of the night. Next morning he had to get up again, dress, go to the law courts, speak, and write; or if he did not go out, spend at home those twenty-four hours a day each of which was a torture. And he had to live thus all alone on the brink of an abyss, with no one who understood or pitied him.

V

So one month passed and then another. Just before the New Year his brother-in-law came to town and stayed at their house. Ivan Ilych was at the law courts and Praskovya Fëdorovna had gone shopping. When Ivan Ilych came home and entered his study he found his brother-in-law there—a healthy, florid man— unpacking his portmanteau himself. He raised his head on hearing Ivan Ilych's footsteps and looked up at him for a moment without a word. That stare told Ivan Ilych everything. His brother-in-law opened his mouth to utter an exclamation of surprise but checked himself, and that action confirmed it all.

"I have changed, eh?"

"Yes, there is a change."

And after that, try as he would to get his brother-in-law to return to the subject of his looks, the latter would say nothing about it. Praskovya Fëdorovna came home and her brother went out to her. Ivan Ilych locked the door and began to examine himself in the glass, first full face, then in profile. He took up a portrait of himself taken with his wife, and compared it with what he saw in the glass. The change in him was immense. Then he bared his arms to the elbow, looked at them, drew the sleeves down again, sat down on an ottoman, and grew blacker than night.

"No, no, this won't do!" he said to himself, and jumped up, went to the table, took up some law papers, and began to read them, but could not continue. He unlocked the door and went into the reception room. The door leading to the drawing-room was shut. He approached it on tiptoe and listened.

"No, you are exaggerating!" Praskovya Fëdorovna was saying.

"Exaggerating! Don't you see it? Why, he's a dead man! Look at his eyes—there's no light in them. But what is it that is wrong with him?"

"No one knows. Nikolaevich said something, but I don't know what. And Leshchetitsky[10] said quite the contrary. . . ."

Ivan Ilych walked away, went to his own room, lay down, and began musing: "The kidney, a floating kidney." He recalled all the doctors had told him of how it detached itself and swayed about. And by an effort of imagination he tried to catch that kidney and arrest it and support it. So little was needed for this, it seemed to him. "No, I'll go to see Peter Ivanovich[11] again." He rang, ordered the carriage, and got ready to go.

"Where are you going, Jean?" asked his wife, with a specially sad and exceptionally kind look.

This exceptionally kind look irritated him. He looked morosely at her.

"I must go to see Peter Ivanovich."

He went to see Peter Ivanovich, and together they went to see his friend, the doctor. He was in, and Ivan Ilych had a long talk with him.

Reviewing the anatomical and physiological details of what in the doctor's opinion was going on inside him, he understood it all.

There was something, a small thing, in the vermiform appendix. It might all come right. Only stimulate the energy of one organ and check the activity of another, then absorption would take place and everything would come right. He got home rather late for dinner, ate his dinner, and conversed cheerfully, but could not for a long time bring himself to go back to work in his room. At last however, he went to his study and did what was necessary, but the consciousness that he had put something aside—an important, intimate matter which he would revert to when his work was done—never left him. When he had finished his work he remembered that this intimate matter was the thought of his vermiform appendix. But he did not give himself up to it, and went to the drawing-room for tea. There were callers there, including the examining magistrate who was a desirable match for his daughter, and they were conversing, playing the piano,

---

[10]*Nikolaevich, Leshchetitsky:* two doctors, the latter a celebrated specialist. [L. and A. Maude]

[11]*Peter Ivanovich:* That was the friend whose friend was a doctor. [L. and A. Maude]

and singing. Ivan Ilych, as Praskovya Fëdorovna remarked, spent that evening more cheerfully than usual, but he never for a moment forgot that he had postponed the important matter of the appendix. At eleven o'clock he said good-night and went to his bedroom. Since his illness he had slept alone in a small room next to his study. He undressed and took up a novel by Zola, but instead of reading it he fell into thought, and in his imagination that desired improvement in the vermiform appendix occurred. There was the absorption and evacuation and the re-establishment of normal activity. "Yes, that's it!" he said to himself. "One need only assist nature, that's all." He remembered his medicine, rose, took it, and lay down on his back watching for the beneficent action of the medicine and for it to lessen the pain. "I need only take it regularly and avoid all injurious influences. I am already feeling better, much better." He began touching his side: it was not painful to the touch. "There, I really don't feel it. It's much better already." He put out the light and turned on his side. . . . "The appendix is getting better, absorption is occurring." Suddenly he felt the old, familiar, dull, gnawing pain, stubborn and serious. There was the same familiar loathsome taste in his mouth. His heart sank and he felt dazed. "My God! My God!" he muttered. "Again, again! and it will never cease." And suddenly the matter presented itself in a quite different aspect. "Vermiform appendix! Kidney!" he said to himself. "It's not a question of appendix or kidney, but of life and . . . death. Yes, life was there and now it is going, going and I cannot stop it. Yes. Why deceive myself? Isn't it obvious to everyone but me that I'm dying, and that it's only a question of weeks, days . . . it may happen this moment. There was light and now there is darkness. I was here and now I'm going there! Where?" A chill came over him, his breathing ceased, and he felt only the throbbing of his heart.

"When I am not, what will there be? There will be nothing. Then where shall I be when I am no more? Can this be dying? No, I don't want to!" He jumped up and tried to light the candle, felt for it with trembling hands, dropped candle and candlestick on the floor, and fell back on his pillow.

"What's the use? It makes no difference," he said to himself, staring with wide-open eyes into the darkness. "Death. Yes, death. And none of them know or wish to know it, and they have no pity for me. Now they are playing." (He heard through the door the distant sound of a song and its accompaniment.) "It's all the same to them, but they will die too! Fools! I first, and they later, but it will be the same for them. And now they are merry . . . the beasts!"

Anger choked him and he was agonizingly, unbearably miserable. "It is impossible that all men have been doomed to suffer this awful horror!" He raised himself.

"Something must be wrong. I must calm myself—must think it all over from the beginning." And he again began thinking. "Yes, the beginning of my illness: I knocked my side, but I was still quite well that day and the next. It hurt a little, then rather more. I saw the doctors, then followed despondency and anguish, more doctors, and I drew nearer to the abyss. My strength grew less and I kept coming nearer and nearer, and now I have wasted away and there is no light in my eyes. I think of the appendix—but this is death! I think of mending the appendix, and all the while here is death! Can it really be death?" Again terror seized him and he gasped for breath. He leant down and began feeling for the matches, pressing with his elbow on the stand beside the bed. It was in his way and hurt him, he grew furious with it, pressed on it still harder, and upset it. Breathless and in despair he fell on his back, expecting death to come immediately.

Meanwhile the visitors were leaving. Praskovya Fëdorovna was seeing them off. She heard something fall and came in.

"What has happened?"

"Nothing. I knocked it over accidentally."

She went out and returned with a candle. He lay there panting heavily, like a man who has run a thousand yards, and stared upwards at her with a fixed look.

"What is it, Jean?"

"No . . . o . . . thing. I upset it." ("Why speak of it? She won't understand," he thought.)

And in truth she did not understand. She picked up the stand, lit his candle, and hurried away to see another visitor off. When she came back he still lay on his back, looking upwards.

"What is it? Do you feel worse?"

"Yes."

She shook her head and sat down.

"Do you know, Jean, I think we must ask Leshchetitsky to come and see you here."

This meant calling in the famous specialist, regardless of expense. He smiled malignantly and said "No." She remained a little longer and then went up to him and kissed his forehead.

While she was kissing him he hated her from the bottom of his soul and with difficulty refrained from pushing her away.

"Good-night. Please God you'll sleep."

"Yes."

VI

Ivan Ilych saw that he was dying, and he was in continual despair.

In the depth of his heart he knew he was dying, but not only was he not accustomed to the thought, he simply did not and could not grasp it.

The syllogism he had learnt from Kiezewetter's Logic:[12] "Caius is a man, men are mortal, therefore Caius is mortal," had always seemed to him correct as applied to Caius, but certainly not as applied to himself. That Caius—man in the abstract—was mortal, was perfectly correct, but he was not Caius, not an abstract man, but a creature quite, quite separate from all others. He had been little Vanya, with a mamma and a papa, with Mitya and Volodya, with the toys, a coachman and a nurse, afterwards with Katenka and with all the joys, griefs, and delights

---

[12]Karl Kiezewetter, *Outline of Logic According to Kantian Principles.*

of childhood, boyhood, and youth. What did Caius know of the smell of that striped leather ball Vanya had been so fond of? Had Caius kissed his mother's hand like that, and did the silk of her dress rustle so for Caius? Had he rioted like that at school when the pastry was bad? Had Caius been in love like that? Could Caius preside at a session as he did? "Caius really was mortal, and it was right for him to die; but for me, little Vanya, Ivan Ilych, with all my thoughts and emotions, it's altogether a different matter. It cannot be that I ought to die. That would be too terrible."

Such was his feeling.

"If I had to die like Caius I should have known it was so. An inner voice would have told me so, but there was nothing of the sort in me and I and all my friends felt that our case was quite different from that of Caius. And now here it is!" he said to himself. "It can't be. It's impossible! But here it is. How is this? How is one to understand it?"

He could not understand it, and tried to drive this false, incorrect, morbid thought away and to replace it by other proper and healthy thoughts. But that thought, and not the thought only but the reality itself, seemed to come and confront him.

And to replace that thought he called up a succession of others, hoping to find in them some support. He tried to get back into the former current of thoughts that had once screened the thought of death from him. But strange to say, all that had formerly shut off, hidden, and destroyed his consciousness of death, no longer had that effect. Ivan Ilych now spent most of his time in attempting to re-establish that old current. He would say to himself: "I will take up my duties again—after all I used to live by them." And banishing all doubts he would go to the law courts, enter into conversation with his colleagues, and sit carelessly as was his wont, scanning the crowd with a thoughtful look and leaning both his emaciated arms on the arms of his oak chair; bending over as usual to a colleague and drawing his papers nearer he would interchange whispers with him, and then suddenly raising his eyes and sitting erect would pronounce certain words and open the proceedings. But suddenly in the midst of those proceedings the pain in his side, regardless of the stage the proceedings had reached, would begin its own gnawing work. Ivan Ilych would turn his attention to it and try to drive the thought of it away, but without success. *It* would come and stand before him and look at him, and he would be petrified and the light would die out of his eyes, and he would again begin asking himself whether *It* alone was true. And his colleagues and subordinates would see with surprise and distress that he, the brilliant and subtle judge, was becoming confused and making mistakes. He would shake himself, try to pull himself together, manage somehow to bring the sitting to a close, and return home with the sorrowful consciousness that his judicial labors could not as formerly hide from him what he wanted them to hide, and could not deliver him from *It.* And what was worst of all was that *It* drew his attention to itself not in order to make him take some action but only that he should look at *It,* look it straight in the face: look at it and, without doing anything, suffer inexpressibly.

And to save himself from this condition Ivan Ilych looked for consolations— new screens—and new screens were found and for a while seemed to save him, but then they immediately fell to pieces or rather became transparent, as if *It* penetrated them and nothing could veil *It.*

In these latter days he would go into the drawing-room he had arranged—that drawing-room where he had fallen and for the sake of which (how bitterly ridiculous it seemed) he had sacrificed his life—for he knew that his illness originated with that knock. He would enter and see that something had scratched the polished table. He would look for the cause of this and find that it was the bronze ornamentation of an album, that had got bent. He would take up the expensive album which he had lovingly arranged, and feel vexed with his daughter and her friends for their untidiness—for the album was torn here and there and some of the photographs turned upside down. He would put it carefully in order and bend the ornamentation back into position. Then it would occur to him to place all those things in another corner of the room, near the plants. He could call the footman, but his daughter or wife would come to help him. They would not agree, and his wife would contradict him, and he would dispute and grow angry. But that was all right, for then he did not think about *It. It* was invisible.

But then, when he was moving something himself, his wife would say: "Let the servants do it. You will hurt yourself again." And suddenly *It* would flash through the screen and he would see it. It was just a flash, and he hoped it would disappear, but he would involuntarily pay attention to his side. "It sits there as before, gnawing just the same!" And he could no longer forget *It,* but could distinctly see it looking at him from behind the flowers. "What is it all for?"

"It really is so! I lost my life over that curtain as I might have done when storming a fort. Is that possible? How terrible and how stupid. It can't be true! It can't, but it is."

He would go to his study, lie down, and again be alone with *It:* face to face with *It.* And nothing could be done with *It* except to look at it and shudder.

VII

How it happened it is impossible to say because it came about step by step, unnoticed, but in the third month of Ivan Ilych's illness, his wife, his daughter, his son, his acquaintances, the doctors, the servants, and above all he himself, were aware that the whole interest he had for other people was whether he would soon vacate his place, and at last release the living from the discomfort caused by his presence and be himself released from his sufferings.

He slept less and less. He was given opium and hypodermic injections of morphine, but this did not relieve him. The dull depression he experienced in a somnolent condition at first gave him a little relief, but only as something new, afterwards it became as distressing as the pain itself or even more so.

Special foods were prepared for him by the doctors' orders, but all those foods became increasingly distasteful and disgusting to him.

For his excretions also special arrangements had to be made, and this was a torment to him every time—a torment from the uncleanliness, the unseemliness, and the smell, and from knowing that another person had to take part in it.

But just through this most unpleasant matter, Ivan Ilych obtained comfort. Gerasim, the butler's young assistant, always came in to carry the things out. Gerasim was a clean, fresh peasant lad, grown stout on town food and always cheerful and bright. At first the sight of him, in his clean Russian peasant costume, engaged on that disgusting task embarrassed Ivan Ilych.

Once when he got up from the commode too weak to draw up his trousers, he dropped into a soft armchair and looked with horror at his bare, enfeebled thighs with the muscles so sharply marked on them.

Gerasim with a firm light tread, his heavy boots emitting a pleasant smell of tar and fresh winter air, came in wearing a clean Hessian apron, the sleeves of his print shirt tucked up over his strong, bare young arms; and refraining from looking at his sick master out of consideration for his feelings, and restraining the joy of life that beamed from his face, he went up to the commode.

"Gerasim!" said Ivan Ilych in a weak voice.

Gerasim started, evidently afraid he might have committed some blunder, and with a rapid movement turned his fresh, kind, simple young face which just showed the first downy signs of a beard.

"Yes, sir?"

"That must be very unpleasant for you. You must forgive me. I am helpless."

"Oh, why, sir," and Gerasim's eyes beamed and he showed his glistening white teeth, "what's a little trouble? It's a case of illness with you, sir."

And his deft strong hands did their accustomed task, and he went out of the room stepping lightly. Five minutes later he as lightly returned.

Ivan Ilych was still sitting in the same position in the armchair.

"Gerasim," he said when the latter had replaced the freshly-washed utensil. "Please come here and help me." Gerasim went up to him. "Lift me up. It is hard for me to get up, and I have sent Dmitri away."

Gerasim went up to him, grasped his master with his strong arms deftly but gently, in the same way that he stepped—lifted him, supported him with one hand, and with the other drew up his trousers and would have set him down again, but Ivan Ilych asked to be led to the sofa. Gerasim, without an effort and without apparent pressure, led him, almost lifting him, to the sofa and placed him on it.

"Thank you. How easily and well you do it all!"

Gerasim smiled again and turned to leave the room. But Ivan Ilych felt his presence such a comfort that he did not want to let him go.

"One thing more, please move up that chair. No, the other one—under my feet. It is easier for me when my feet are raised."

Gerasim brought the chair, set it down gently in place, and raised Ivan Ilych's legs on to it. It seemed to Ivan Ilych that he felt better while Gerasim was holding up his legs.

"It's better when my legs are higher," he said. "Place that cushion under them."

Gerasim did so. He again lifted the legs and placed them, and again Ivan Ilych felt better while Gerasim held his legs. When he set them down Ivan Ilych fancied he felt worse.

"Gerasim," he said. "Are you busy now?"

"Not at all, sir," said Gerasim, who had learnt from the townsfolk how to speak to gentlefolk.

"What have you still to do?"

"What have I to do? I've done everything except chopping the logs for tomorrow."

"Then hold my legs up a bit higher, can you?"

"Of course I can. Why not?" And Gerasim raised his master's legs higher and Ivan Ilych thought that in that position he did not feel any pain at all.

"And how about the logs?"

"Don't trouble about that, sir. There's plenty of time."

Ivan Ilych told Gerasim to sit down and hold his legs, and began to talk to him. And strange to say it seemed to him that he felt better while Gerasim held his legs up.

After that Ivan Ilych would sometimes call Gerasim and get him to hold his legs on his shoulders, and he liked talking to him. Gerasim did it all easily, willingly, simply, and with a good nature that touched Ivan Ilych. Health, strength, and vitality in other people were offensive to him, but Gerasim's strength and vitality did not mortify but soothed him.

What tormented Ivan Ilych most was the deception, the lie, which for some reason they all accepted, that he was not dying but was simply ill, and that he only need keep quiet and undergo a treatment and then something very good would result. He however knew that do what they would nothing would come of it, only still more agonizing suffering and death. This deception tortured him —their not wishing to admit what they all knew and what he knew, but wanting to lie to him concerning his terrible condition, and wishing and forcing him to participate in that lie. Those lies—lies enacted over him on the eve of his death and destined to degrade this awful, solemn act to the level of their visitings, their curtains, their sturgeon for dinner—were a terrible agony for Ivan Ilych. And strangely enough, many times when they were going through their antics over him he had been within a hairbreadth of calling out to them: "Stop lying! You know and I know that I am dying. Then at least stop lying about it!" But he had never had the spirit to do it. The awful, terrible act of his dying was, he could see, reduced by those about him to the level of a casual, unpleasant, and almost indecorous incident (as if someone entered a drawing-room diffusing an unpleasant odor) and this was done by that very decorum which he had served all his life long. He saw that no one felt for him, because no one even wished to grasp his position. Only Gerasim recognized it and pitied him. And so Ivan Ilych felt at ease only with him. He felt comforted when Gerasim supported his legs (sometimes all night long) and refused to go to bed, saying: "Don't you worry, Ivan Ilych. I'll get sleep enough later on," or when he suddenly became familiar and exclaimed: "If you weren't sick it would be another matter, but as it is, why should I grudge a little trouble?'' Gerasim alone did not lie; everything showed that he alone understood the facts of the case and did not consider it necessary to disguise them, but simply felt sorry for his emaciated and enfeebled master. Once when Ivan Ilych was sending him away he even said straight out: "We shall all of us die, so why should I grudge a little trouble?"—expressing the fact that he did not think his work burdensome, because he was doing it for a dying man and hoped someone would do the same for him when his time came.

Apart from this lying, or because of it, what most tormented Ivan Ilych was that no one pitied him as he wished to be pitied. At certain moments after prolonged suffering he wished most of all (though he would have been ashamed to confess it) for someone to pity him as a sick child is pitied. He longed to be petted and comforted. He knew he was an important functionary, that he had a beard turning grey, and that therefore what he longed for was impossible, but still he longed for it. And in Gerasim's attitude towards him there was something akin to what he wished for, and so that attitude comforted him. Ivan Ilych wanted to weep, wanted to be petted and cried over, and then his colleague Shebek would come, and instead of weeping and being petted, Ivan Ilych would assume a serious, severe, and profound air, and by force of habit would express his opinion on a decision of the Court of Cassation and would stubbornly insist on that view. This falsity around him and within him did more than anything else to poison his last days.

VIII

It was morning. He knew it was morning because Gerasim had gone, and Peter the footman had come and put out the candles, drawn back one of the curtains, and begun quietly to tidy up. Whether it was morning or evening, Friday or Sunday, made no difference, it was all just the same: the gnawing, unmitigated, agonizing pain, never ceasing for an instant, the consciousness of life inexorably waning but not yet extinguished, the approach of that ever dreaded and hateful Death which was the only reality, and always the same falsity. What were days, weeks, hours, in such a case?

"Will you have some tea, sir?"

"He wants things to be regular, and wishes the gentlefolk to drink tea in the morning," thought Ivan Ilych, and only said "No."

"Wouldn't you like to move onto the sofa, sir?"

"He wants to tidy up the room, and I'm in the way. I am uncleanliness and disorder," he thought, and said only:

"No, leave me alone."

The man went on bustling about. Ivan Ilych stretched out his hand. Peter came up, ready to help.

"What is it, sir?"

"My watch."

Peter took the watch which was close at hand and gave it to his master.

"Half-past eight. Are they up?"

"No, sir, except Vladimir Ivanovich" (the son) "who has gone to school. Praskovya Fёdorovna ordered me to wake her if you asked for her. Shall I do so?"

"No, there's no need to." "Perhaps I'd better have some tea," he thought, and added aloud: "Yes, bring me some tea."

Peter went to the door, but Ivan Ilych dreaded being left alone. "How can I keep him here? Oh yes, my medicine." "Peter, give me my medicine." "Why not? Perhaps it may still do me some good." He took a spoonful and swallowed it. "No, it won't help. It's all tomfoolerly, all deception," he decided as soon as he became aware of the familiar, sickly, hopeless taste. "No, I can't believe in it any longer. But the pain, why this pain? If it would only cease just for a moment!" And he moaned. Peter turned towards him. "It's all right. Go and fetch me some tea."

Peter went out. Left alone Ivan Ilych groaned not so much with pain, terrible though that was, as from mental anguish. Always and forever the same, always these endless days and nights. If only it would come quicker! If only *what* would come quicker? Death, darkness? . . . No, no! Anything rather than death!

When Peter returned with the tea on a tray, Ivan Ilych stared at him for a time in perplexity, not realizing who and what he was. Peter was disconcerted by that look and his embarrassment brought Ivan Ilych to himself.

"Oh, tea! All right, put it down. Only help me to wash and put on a clean shirt."

And Ivan Ilych began to wash. With pauses for rest, he washed his hands and then his face, cleaned his teeth, brushed his hair, and looked in the glass. He was terrified by what he saw, especially by the limp way in which his hair clung to his pallid forehead.

While his shirt was being changed he knew that he would be still more frightened at the sight of his body, so he avoided looking at it. Finally he was ready. He drew on a dressing-gown, wrapped himself in a plaid, and sat down in the armchair to take his tea. For a moment he felt refreshed, but soon as he began to drink the tea he was again aware of the same taste, and the pain also returned. He finished it with an effort, and then lay down stretching out his legs, and dismissed Peter.

Always the same. Now a spark of hope flashes up, then a sea of despair rages, and always pain; always pain, always despair, and always the same. When alone he had a dreadful and distressing desire to call someone, but he knew beforehand that with others present it would be still worse. "Another dose of morphine— to lose consciousness. I will tell him, the doctor, that he must think of something else. It's impossible, impossible, to go on like this."

An hour and another pass like that. But now there is a ring at the door bell. Perhaps it's the doctor? It is. He comes in fresh, hearty, plump, and cheerful, with that look on his face that seems to say: "There now, you're in a panic about something, but we'll arrange it all for you directly!" The doctor knows this expression is out of place here, but he has put it on once for all and can't take it off—like a man who has put on a frock-coat in the morning to pay a round of calls.

The doctor rubs his hands vigorously and reassuringly.

"Brr! How cold it is! There's such a sharp frost; just let me warm myself!" he says, as if it were only a matter of waiting till he was warm, and then he would put everything right.

"Well now, how are you?"

Ivan Ilych feels that the doctor would like to say: "Well, how are our affairs?" but that even he feels that this would not do, and says instead: "What sort of a night have you had?"

Ivan Ilych looks at him as much as to say: "Are you really never ashamed of lying?" But the doctor does not wish to understand this question, and Ivan Ilych says: "Just as terrible as ever. The pain never leaves me and never subsides. If only something. . . ."

"Yes, you sick people are always like that. . . . There, now I think I am warm enough. Even Praskovya Fëdorovna, who is so particular, could find no fault with my temperature. Well, now I can say good-morning," and the doctor presses his patient's hand.

Then, dropping his former playfulness, he begins with a most serious face to examine the patient, feeling his pulse and taking his temperature, and then begins the sounding and auscultation.

Ivan Ilych knows quite well and definitely that all this is nonsense and pure deception, but when the doctor, getting down on his knee, leans over him, putting his ear first higher then lower, and performs various gymnastic movements over him with a significant expression on his face, Ivan Ilych submits to it all as he used to submit to the speeches of the lawyers, though he knew very well that they were all lying and why they were lying.

The doctor, kneeling on the sofa, is still sounding him when Praskovya Fëdorovna's silk dress rustles at the door and she is heard scolding Peter for not having let her know of the doctor's arrival.

She comes in, kisses her husband, and at once proceeds to prove that she has been up a long time already, and only owing to a misunderstanding failed to be there when the doctor arrived.

Ivan Ilych looks at her, scans her all over, sets against her the whiteness and plumpness and cleanness of her hands and neck, the gloss of her hair, and the sparkle of her vivacious eyes. He hates her with his whole soul. And the thrill of hatred he feels for her makes him suffer from her touch.

Her attitude towards him and his disease is still the same. Just as the doctor had adopted a certain relation to his patient which he could not abandon, so had she formed one towards him—that he was not doing something he ought to do and was himself to blame, and that she reproached him lovingly for this—and she could not now change that attitude.

"You see he doesn't listen to me and doesn't take his medicine at the proper time. And above all he lies in a position that is no doubt bad for him—with his legs up."

She described how he made Gerasim hold his legs up.

The doctor smiled with a contemptuous affability that said: "What's to be done? These sick people do have foolish fancies of that kind, but we must forgive them."

When the examination was over the doctor looked at his watch, and then Praskovya Fëdorovna announced to Ivan Ilych that it was of course as he pleased, but she had sent today for a celebrated specialist who would examine him and have a consultation with Michael Danilovich (their regular doctor).

"Please don't raise any objections. I am doing this for my own sake," she said ironically, letting it be felt that she was doing it all for his sake and only said this to leave him no right to refuse. He remained silent, knitting his brows. He felt that he was so surrounded and involved in a mesh of falsity that it was hard to unravel anything.

Everything she did for him was entirely for her own sake, and she told him she was doing for herself what she actually was doing for herself, as if that was so incredible that he must understand the opposite.

At half-past eleven the celebrated specialist arrived. Again the sounding began and the significant conversations in his presence and in another room, about the kidneys and the appendix, and the questions and answers, with such an air of importance that again, instead of the real question of life and death which now alone confronted him, the question arose of the kidney and appendix which were not behaving as they ought to and would now be attacked by Michael Danilovich and the specialist and forced to amend their ways.

The celebrated specialist took leave of him with a serious though not hopeless look, and in reply to the timid question Ivan Ilych, with eyes glistening with fear and hope, put to him as to whether there was a chance of recovery, said that he could not vouch for it but there was a possibility. The look of hope with which Ivan Ilych watched the doctor out was so pathetic that Praskovya Fëdorovna, seeing it, even wept as she left the room to hand the doctor his fee.

The gleam of hope kindled by the doctor's encouragement did not last long. The same room, the same pictures, curtains, wallpaper, medicine bottles, were all there, and the same aching suffering body, and Ivan Ilych began to moan. They gave him a subcutaneous injection and he sank into oblivion.

It was twilight when he came to. They brought him his dinner and he swallowed some beef tea with difficulty, and then everything was the same again and night was coming on.

After dinner, at seven o'clock, Praskovya Fëdorovna came into the room in evening dress, her full bosom pushed up by her corset, and with traces of powder on her face. She had reminded him in the morning that they were going to the theatre. Sarah Bernhardt was visiting the town and they had a box, which he had insisted on their taking. Now he had forgotten about it and her toilet offended him, but he concealed his vexation when he remembered that he had himself insisted on their securing a box and going because it would be an instructive and aesthetic pleasure for the children.

Praskovya Fëdorovna came in, self-satisfied but yet with a rather guilty air. She sat down and asked how he was, but, as he saw, only for the sake of asking and not in order to learn about it, knowing that there was nothing to learn—and then went on to what she really wanted to say: that she would not on any account have gone but that the box had been taken and Helen and their daughter were going, as well as Petrischev (the examining magistrate, their daughter's fiancé), and that it was out of the question to let them go alone; but that she would have much preferred to sit with him for a while; and he must be sure to follow the doctor's orders while she was away.

"Oh, and Fëdor Petrovich" (the fiancé) "would like to come in. May he? And Lisa?"

"All right."

Their daughter came in in full evening dress, her fresh young flesh exposed (making a show of that very flesh which in his own case caused so much suffering), strong, healthy, evidently in love, and impatient with illness, suffering, and death, because they interfered with her happiness.

Fëdor Petrovich came in too, in evening dress, his hair curled *à la Capoul*,[13] a tight stiff collar round his long sinewy neck, an enormous white shirt-front, and narrow black trousers tightly stretched over his strong thighs. He had one white glove tightly drawn on, and was holding his opera hat in his hand.

Following him the schoolboy crept in unnoticed, in a uniform, poor little fellow, and wearing gloves. Terribly dark shadows showed under his eyes, the meaning of which Ivan Ilych knew well.

His son had always seemed pathetic to him, and now it was dreadful to see the boy's frightened look of pity. It seemed to Ivan Ilych that Vasya was the only one besides Gerasim who understood and pitied him.

They all sat down and again asked how he was. A silence followed. Lisa asked her mother about the opera-glasses, and there was an altercation between mother and daughter as to who had taken them and where they had been put. This occasioned some unpleasantness.

Fëdor Petrovich inquired of Ivan Ilych whether he had ever seen Sarah Bernhardt. Ivan Ilych did not at first catch the question, but then replied: "No, have you seen her before?"

"Yes, in *Adrienne Lecouvreur*."[14]

Praskovya Fëdorovna mentioned some rôles in which Sarah Bernhardt was particularly good. Her daughter disagreed. Conversation sprang up as to the elegance and realism of of her acting—the sort of conversation that is always repeated and is always the same.

In the midst of the conversation Fëdor Petrovich glanced at Ivan Ilych and became silent. The others also looked at him and grew silent. Ivan Ilych was staring with glittering eyes straight before him, evidently indignant with them. This had to be rectified, but it was impossible to do so. The silence had to be broken, but for a time no one dared to break it and they all became afraid that the conventional deception would suddenly become obvious and the truth be-

---

[13]A hair style named after Victor Capoul (1839–1924), a French singer.   [14]A play by Eugène Scribe (1791–1861) and Ernest Legouvé (1807–1903), French playwrights.

come plain to all. Lisa was the first to pluck up courage and break that silence, but by trying to hide what everybody was feeling, she betrayed it.

"Well, if we are going it's time to start," she said, looking at her watch, a present from her father, and with a faint and significant smile at Fëdor Petrovich relating to something known only to them. She got up with a rustle of her dress.

They all rose, said good-night, and went away.

When they had gone it seemed to Ivan Ilych that he felt better; the falsity had gone with them. But the pain remained—that same pain and that same fear that made everything monotonously alike, nothing harder and nothing easier. Everything was worse.

Again minute followed minute and hour followed hour. Everything remained the same and there was no cessation. And the inevitable end of it all became more and more terrible.

"Yes, send Gerasim here," he replied to a question Peter asked.

IX

His wife returned late at night. She came in on tiptoe, but he heard her, opened his eyes, and made haste to close them again. She wished to send Gerasim away and to sit with him herself, but he opened his eyes and said: "No, go away."

"Are you in great pain?"

"Always the same."

"Take some opium."

He agreed and took some. She went away.

Till about three in the morning he was in a state of stupefied misery. It seemed to him that he and his pain were being thrust into a narrow, deep black sack, but though they were pushed further and further in they could not be pushed to the bottom. And this, terrible enough in itself, was accompanied by suffering. He was frightened yet wanted to fall through the sack, he struggled but yet cooperated. And suddenly he broke through, fell, and regained consciousness. Gerasim was sitting at the foot of the bed dozing quietly and patiently, while he himself lay with his emaciated stockinged legs resting on Gerasim's shoulders; the same shaded candle was there and the same unceasing pain.

"Go away, Gerasim," he whispered.

"It's all right, sir. I'll stay a while."

"No. Go away."

He removed his legs from Gerasim's shoulders, turned sideways onto his arm, and felt sorry for himself. He only waited till Gerasim had gone into the next room and then restrained himself no longer but wept like a child. He wept on account of his helplessness, his terrible loneliness, the cruelty of man, the cruelty of God, and the absence of God.

"Why hast Thou done all this? Why hast Thou brought me here? Why, why dost Thou torment me so terribly?"

He did not expect an answer and yet wept because there was no answer and could be none. The pain again grew more acute, but he did not stir and did not call. He said to himself: "Go on! Strike me! But what is it for? What have I done to Thee? What is it for?"

Then he grew quiet and not only ceased weeping but even held his breath and became all attention. It was as though he were listening not to an audible voice but to the voice of his soul, to the current of thoughts arising within him.

"What is it you want? was the first clear conception capable of expression in words that he heard.

"What do you want? What do you want?" he repeated to himself.

"What do I want? To live and not to suffer," he answered.

And again he listened with such concentrated attention that even his pain did not distract him.

"To live? How?" asked his inner voice.

"Why, to live as I used to—well and pleasantly." the voice repeated.

"As you lived before, well and pleasantly?"

And in imagination he began to recall the best moments of his pleasant life. But strange to say none of those best moments of his pleasant life now seemed at all what they had then seemed—none of them except the first recollections of childhood. There, in childhood, there had been something really pleasant with which it would be possible to live if it could return. But the child who had experienced that happiness existed no longer, it was like a reminiscence of somebody else.

As soon as the period began which had produced the present Ivan Ilych, all that had then seemed joys now melted before his sight and turned into something trivial and often nasty.

And the further he departed from childhood and the nearer he came to the present the more worthless and doubtful were the joys. This began with the School of Law. A little that was really good was still found there—there was lightheartedness, friendship, and hope. But in the upper classes there had already been fewer of such good moments. Then during the first years of his official career, when he was in the service of the Governor, some pleasant moments again occurred; they were the memories of love for a woman. Then all became confused and there was still less of what was good; later on again there was still less that was good, and the further he went the less there was. His marriage, a mere accident, then the disenchantment that followed it, his wife's bad breath and the sensuality and hypocrisy: then that deadly official life and those preoccupations about money, a year of it, and two, and ten, and twenty, and always the same thing. And the longer it lasted the more deadly it became. "It is as if I had been going downhill while I imagined I was going up. And that is really what it was. I was going up in public opinion, but to the same extent life was ebbing away from me. And now it is all done and there is only death."

"Then what does it mean? Why? It can't be that life is so senseless and horrible. But if it really has been so horrible and senseless, why must I die and die in agony? There is something wrong!"

"Maybe I did not live as I ought to have done," it suddenly occurred to him. "But how could that be, when I did everything properly?" he replied, and immediately dismissed from his mind this, the sole solution of all the riddles of life and death, as something quite impossible.

"Then what do you want now? To live? Live how? Live as you lived in the law courts when the usher proclaimed 'The judge is coming!' The judge is coming, the judge!" he repeated to himself. "Here he is, the judge. But I am not guilty!" he exclaimed angrily. "What is it for?" And he ceased crying, but turning his face to the wall continued to ponder on the same question: Why, and for what purpose, is there all this horror? But however much he pondered he found no answer. And whenever the thought occurred to him, as it often did, that it all resulted from his not having lived as he ought to have done, he at once recalled the correctness of his whole life and dismissed so strange an idea.

X

Another fortnight passed. Ivan Ilych now no longer left his sofa. He would not lie in bed but lay on the sofa, facing the wall nearly all the time. He suffered ever the same unceasing agonies and in his loneliness pondered always on the same insoluble question: "What is this? Can it be that it is Death?" And the inner voice answered: "Yes, it is Death."

"Why these sufferings?" And the voice answered, "For no reason—they just are so." Beyond and besides this there was nothing.

From the very beginning of his illness, ever since he had first been to see the doctor, Ivan Ilych's life had been divided between two contrary and alternating moods: now it was despair and the expectation of this uncomprehended and terrible death, and now hope and an intently interested observation of the functioning of his organs. Now before his eyes there was only a kidney or an intestine that temporarily evaded its duty, and now only that incomprehensible and dreadful death from which it was impossible to escape.

These two states of mind had alternated from the very beginning of his illness, but the further it progressed the more doubtful and fantastic became the conception of the kidney, and the more real the sense of impending death.

He had but to call to mind what he had been three months before and what he was now, to call to mind with what regularity he had been going downhill, for every possibility of hope to be shattered.

Latterly during that loneliness in which he found himself as he lay facing the back of the sofa, a loneliness in the midst of a populous town and surrounded by numerous acquaintances and relations but that yet could not have been more complete anywhere—either at the bottom of the sea or under the earth—during that terrible loneliness Ivan Ilych had lived only in memories of the past. Pictures of his past rose before him one after another. They always began with what was nearest in time and then went back to what was most remote—to his childhood—and rested there. If he thought of the stewed prunes that had been offered him that day, his mind went back to the raw shrivelled French plums of his childhood, their peculiar flavor and the flow of saliva when he sucked their stones, and along with the memory of that taste came a whole series of memories of those days: his nurse, his brother, and their toys. "No, I mustn't think of that. . . . It is too painful," Ivan Ilych said to himself, and brought himself back to the present—to the button on the back of the sofa and the creases in its morocco. "Morocco is expensive, but it does not wear well: there had been a quarrel about it. It was a different kind of quarrel and a different kind of morocco that time when we tore father's portfolio and were punished, and mamma brought us some tarts. . . ." And again his thoughts dwelt on his childhood, and again it was painful and he tried to banish them and fix his mind on something else.

Then again together with that chain of memories another series passed through his mind—of how his illness had progressed and grown worse. There also the further back he looked the more life there had been. There had been more of what was good in life and more of life itself. The two merged together. "Just as the pain went on getting worse and worse, so my life grew worse and worse," he thought. "There is one bright spot there at the back, at the beginning of life, and afterwards all becomes blacker and blacker and proceeds more and more rapidly—in inverse ratio to the square of the distance from death," thought Ivan Ilych. And the example of a stone falling downwards with increasing velocity entered his mind. Life, a series of increasing sufferings, flies further and further towards its end—the most terrible suffering. "I am flying. . . ." He shuddered, shifted himself, and tried to resist, but was already aware that resistance was impossible, and again, with eyes weary of gazing but unable to cease seeing what was before them, he stared at the back of the sofa and waited—awaiting that dreadful fall and shock and destruction.

"Resistance is impossible!" he said to himself. "If I could only understand what it is all for! But that too is impossible. An explanation would be possible if it could be said that I have not lived as I ought to. But it is impossible to say that," and he remembered all the legality, correctitude, and propriety of his life. "That at any rate can certainly not be admitted," he thought, and his lips smiled ironically as if someone could see that smile and be taken in by it. "There is no explanation! Agony, death. . . . What for?"

XI

Another two weeks went by in this way and during that fortnight an event occurred that Ivan Ilych and his wife had desired. Petrischev formally proposed. It happened in the evening. The next day Praskovya Fëdorovna came into her husband's room considering how best to inform him of it, but that very night there had been a fresh change for the worse in his condition. She found him still lying on the sofa but in a different position. He lay on his back, groaning and staring fixedly straight in front of him.

She began to remind him of his medicines, but he turned his eyes towards her with such a look that she did not finish what she was saying; so great an animosity, to her in particular, did that look express.

"For Christ's sake let me die in peace!" he said.

She would have gone away, but just then their daughter came in and went up to say good morning. He looked at her as he had done at his wife, and in reply to her inquiry about his health said dryly that he would soon free them all of himself. They were both silent and after sitting with him for a while went away.

"Is it our fault?" Lisa said to her mother. "It's as if we were to blame! I am sorry for papa, but why should we be tortured?"

The doctor came at his usual time. Ivan Ilych answered "Yes" and "No," never taking his angry eyes from him, and at last said: "You know you can do nothing for me, so leave me alone."

"We can ease your sufferings."

"You can't even do that. Let me be."

The doctor went into the drawing-room and told Praskovya Fëdorovna that the case was very serious and that the only resource left was opium to allay her husband's sufferings, which must be terrible.

It was true, as the doctor said, that Ivan Ilych's physical sufferings were terrible, but worse than the physical sufferings were his mental sufferings, which were his chief torture.

His mental sufferings were due to the fact that that night, as he looked at Gerasim's sleepy, good-natured face with its prominent cheekbones, the question suddenly occurred to him: "What if my whole life has really been wrong?"

It occurred to him that what had appeared perfectly impossible before, namely that he had not spent his life as he should have done, might after all be true. It occurred to him that his scarcely perceptible attempts to struggle against what was considered good by the most highly placed people, those scarcely noticeable impulses which he had immediately suppressed, might have been the real thing, and all the rest false. And his professional duties and the whole arrangement of his life and of his family, and all his social and official interests, might all have been false. He tried to defend all those things to himself and suddenly felt the weakness of what he was defending. There was nothing to defend.

"But if that is so," he said to himself, "and I am leaving this life with the consciousness that I have lost all that was given me and it is impossible to rectify it—what then?"

He lay on his back and began to pass his life in review in quite a new way. In the morning when he saw first his footman, then his wife, then his daughter, and then the doctor, their every word and movement confirmed to him the awful truth that had been revealed to him during the night. In them he saw himself—all that for which he had lived—and saw clearly that it was not real at all, but a terrible and huge deception which had hidden both life and death. This consciousness intensified his physical suffering tenfold. He groaned and tossed about, and pulled at his clothing which choked and stifled him. And he hated them on that account.

He was given a large dose of opium and became unconscious, but at noon his sufferings began again. He drove everybody away and tossed from side to side.

His wife came to him and said:

"Jean, my dear, do this for me. It can't do any harm and often helps. Healthy people often do it."

He opened his eyes wide.

"What? Take communion? Why? It's unnecessary! However. . . ."

She began to cry.

"Yes, do, my dear. I'll send for our priest. He is such a nice man."

"All right. Very well," he muttered.

When the priest came and heard his confession, Ivan Ilych was softened and seemed to feel a relief from his doubts and consequently from his sufferings, and for a moment there came a ray of hope. He again began to think of the vermiform appendix and the possibility of correcting it. He received the sacrament with tears in his eyes.

When they laid him down again afterwards he felt a moment's ease, and the hope that he might live awoke in him again. He began to think of the operation that had been suggested to him. "To live! I want to live!" he said to himself.

His wife came in to congratulate him after his communion, and when uttering the usual conventional words she added:

"You feel better, don't you?"

Without looking at her he said "Yes."

Her dress, her figure, the expression of her face, the tone of her voice, all revealed the same thing. "This is wrong, it is not as it should be. All you have lived for and still live for is falsehood and deception, hiding life and death from you." And as soon as he admitted that thought, his hatred and his agonizing physical suffering again sprang up, and with that suffering a consciousness of the unavoidable, approaching end. And to this was added a new sensation of grinding shooting pain and a feeling of suffocation.

The expression of his face when he uttered that "yes" was dreadful. Having uttered it, he looked her straight in the eyes, turned on his face with a rapidity extraordinary in his weak state and shouted:

"Go away! Go away and leave me alone!"

XII

From that moment the screaming began that continued for three days, and was so terrible that one could not hear it through the two closed doors without horror. At the moment he answered his wife he realized that he was lost, that there was no return, that the end had come, the very end, and his doubts were still unsolved and remained doubts.

"Oh! Oh! Oh!" he cried in various intonations. He had begun by screaming "I won't!" and continued screaming on the letter O.

For three whole days, during which time did not exist for him, he struggled in that black sack into which he was being thrust by an invisible, resistless force. He struggled as a man condemned to death struggles in the hands of the executioner, knowing that he cannot save himself. And every moment he felt that despite all his efforts he was drawing nearer and nearer to what terrified him. He felt that his agony was due to his being thrust into that black hole and still more to his not being able to get right into it. He was hindered from getting into it by his conviction that his life had been a good one. That very justification of his life held him fast and prevented his moving forward, and it caused him most torment of all.

Suddenly some force struck him in the chest and side, making it still harder to breathe, and he fell through the hole and there at the bottom was a light. What had happened to him was like the sensation one sometimes experiences in a railway carriage when one thinks one is going backwards while one is really going forwards and suddenly becomes aware of the real direction.

"Yes, it was all not the right thing," he said to himself, "but that's no matter. It can be done. But what *is* the right thing?" he asked himself, and suddenly grew quiet.

This occurred at the end of the third day, two hours before his death. Just then his schoolboy son had crept softly in and gone up to the bedside. The dying man was still screaming desperately and waving his arms. His hand fell on the boy's head, and the boy caught it, pressed it to his lips, and began to cry.

At that very moment Ivan Ilych fell through and caught sight of the light, and it was revealed to him that though his life had not been what it should have been, this could still be rectified. He asked himself, "What *is* the right thing?" and grew still, listening. Then he felt that someone was kissing his hand. He opened his eyes, looked at his son, and felt sorry for him. His wife came up to him and he glanced at her. She was gazing at him open-mouthed, with undried tears on her nose and cheek and a despairing look on her face. He felt sorry for her too.

"Yes, I am making them wretched," he thought. "They are sorry, but it will be better for them when I die." He wished to say this but had not the strength to utter it. "Besides, why speak? I must act," he thought. With a look at his wife he indicated his son and said: "Take him away . . . sorry for him . . . sorry for you too. . . ." He tried to add, "Forgive me," but said "forgo" and waved his hand, knowing that He whose understanding mattered would understand.

And suddenly it grew clear to him that what had been oppressing him and would not leave him was all dropping away at once from two sides, from ten sides, and from all sides. He was sorry for them, he must act so as not to hurt them: release them and free himself from these sufferings. "How good and how simple!" he thought. "And the pain?" he asked himself. "What has become of it? Where are you, pain?"

He turned his attention to it.

"Yes, here it is. Well, what of it? Let the pain be."

"And death . . . where is it?"

He sought his former accustomed fear of death and did not find it. "Where is it? What death?" There was no fear because there was no death.

In place of death there was light.

"So that's what it is!" he suddenly exclaimed aloud. "What joy!"

To him all this happened in a single instant, and the meaning of that instant did not change. For those present his agony continued for another two hours. Something rattled in his throat, his emaciated body twitched, then the gasping and rattle became less and less frequent.

"It is finished!" said someone near him.

He heard these words and repeated them in his soul.

"Death is finished," he said to himself. "It is no more!"

He drew in a breath, stopped in the midst of a sigh, stretched out, and died.

QUESTIONS

1. How does the beginning relate to the end?
2. What is Tolstoy's irony as the lawyers discuss Ivan's death, and a few "so-called friends" decide that they must "fulfill the very tiresome demands of propriety"? What force do the words *proper, decorum,* and *pleasant* gather as the story goes on?
3. What does the widow's remark "Oh, what I have suffered!" confirm about the story as a whole?
4. What is the significance of Gerasim, whom we do not meet until the end of section I?
5. Tolstoy tells us that Ivan's youthful philanderings were all done "with clean hands, in clean linen, with French phrases." What is the effect of his own French phrases? *"Il faut que jeunesse se passe,"* they said. What does this passage say about the life depicted?
6. What does Ivan's attitude about marriage tell us about him?
7. Soon after Ivan's marriage (section II), a brief paragraph begins: "His wife, without any reason. . . ." Whose viewpoint is this? What irony is the author achieving, and how?
8. In the third paragraph from the end of section II, we find a sentence beginning "Though the salary was higher. . . ." What is the effect of the clause that starts with "besides which"?
9. In a long paragraph toward the end of section III beginning "He got up at nine," the translators write: "There the harness in which he worked had already been stretched to fit him and he donned it without a hitch." Do you think they render Tolstoy's metaphor accurately?
10. In the long paragraph toward the end of section IV (p. 365), what are the ironies in "those about him did not understand or would not understand" his trouble, "but thought everything in the world was going on as usual"?
11. What does "the sounding and auscultation" (section VIII, p. 376) mean?
12. As the story moves on, how are we involved in the indifference to death and also in its progress?
13. When his family comes in to see him on their way to the opera (section VIII), what is significant in the phrase "the schoolboy crept in unnoticed . . . poor little fellow . . ."? Why *the schoolboy* rather than "his son" or "Vasya"? What is significant in "now it was dread-

ful" in the next paragraph? What role does the boy play in the story's meaning?

14. What is "the sole solution of all the riddles of life and death" (section IX, next-to-last paragraph)?

15. What ultimately is the significance of Ilych's death?

In Conrad's *The Secret Sharer,* the captain's "double," as he soon calls him, swims up from the mysterious sea to disturb his assumed command of it. Conrad engages the pre-Freudian psychology of the doppelgänger, the dark alter ego, in a story about coming of age in facing the challenges of freedom and responsibility. Like "My Kinsman, Major Molineux," it makes actuality seem supernatural, but from a different point of view. What is this difference? Note the touches with which Conrad builds his eerie impression and its hints of insanity.

THE SECRET SHARER
Joseph Conrad   *(1857–1924)*

I

On my right hand there were lines of fishing-stakes resembling a mysterious system of half-submerged bamboo fences, incomprehensible in its division of the domain of tropical fishes, and crazy of aspect as if abandoned for ever by some nomad tribe of fishermen now gone to the other end of the ocean; for there was no sign of human habitation as far as the eye could reach. To the left a group of barren islets, suggesting ruins of stone walls, towers, and blockhouses, had its foundations set in a blue sea that itself looked solid, so still and stable did it lie below my feet; even the track of light from the westering sun shone smoothly, without that animated glitter which tells of an imperceptible ripple. And when I turned my head to take a parting glance at the tug which had just left us anchored outside the bar, I saw the straight line of the flat shore joined to the stable sea, edge to edge, with a perfect and unmarked closeness, in one levelled floor half brown, half blue under the enormous dome of the sky. Corresponding in their insignificance to the islets of the sea, two small clumps of trees, one on each side of the only fault in the impeccable joint, marked the mouth of the river Meinam[1] we had just left on the first preparatory stage of our homeward journey; and, far back on the inland level, a larger and loftier mass, the grove surrounding the great Paknam pagoda, was the only thing on which the eye could rest from the vain task of exploring the monotonous sweep of the horizon. Here and there gleams as of a few scattered pieces of silver marked the windings of the great river; and on the nearest of them, just within the bar, the tug steaming right into the land became lost to my sight, hull and funnel and masts, as though the impassive earth had swallowed her up without an effort, without a tremor. My eye followed

---

[1]The Chao Phraya River, running through the heart of Bangkok, past the Paknam pagoda, and into the Gulf of Siam.

the light cloud of her smoke, now here, now there, above the plain, according to the devious curves of the stream, but always fainter and farther away, till I lost it at last behind the mitre-shaped hill of the great pagoda. And then I was left alone with my ship, anchored at the head of the Gulf of Siam.

She floated at the starting-point of a long journey, very still in an immense stillness, the shadows of her spars flung far to the eastward by the setting sun. At that moment I was alone on her decks. There was not a sound in her—and around us nothing moved, nothing lived, not a canoe on the water, not a bird in the air, not a cloud in the sky. In this breathless pause at the threshold of a long passage we seemed to be measuring our fitness for a long and arduous enterprise, the appointed task of both our existences to be carried out, far from all human eyes, with only sky and sea for spectators and for judges.

There must have been some glare in the air to interfere with one's sight, because it was only just before the sun left us that my roaming eyes made out beyond the highest ridge of the principal islet of the group something which did away with the solemnity of perfect solitude. The tide of darkness flowed on swiftly; and with tropical suddenness a swarm of stars came out above the shadowy earth, while I lingered yet, my hand resting lightly on my ship's rail as if on the shoulder of a trusted friend. But, with all that multitude of celestial bodies staring down at one, the comfort of quiet communion with her was gone for good. And there were also disturbing sounds by this time—voices, footsteps forward; the steward flitted along the maindeck, a busily ministering spirit; a hand-bell tinkled urgently under the poop-deck. . . .

I found my two officers waiting for me near the supper table, in the lighted cuddy. We sat down at once, and as I helped the chief mate, I said:

"Are you aware that there is a ship anchored inside the islands? I saw her mastheads above the ridge as the sun went down."

He raised sharply his simple face, overcharged by a terrible growth of whisker, and emitted his usual ejaculations: "Bless my soul, sir! You don't say so!"

My second mate was a round-cheeked, silent young man, grave beyond his years, I thought; but as our eyes happened to meet I detected a slight quiver on his lips. I looked down at once. It was not my part to encourage sneering on board my ship. It must be said, too, that I knew very little of my officers. In consequence of certain events of no particular significance, except to myself, I had been appointed to the command only a fortnight before. Neither did I know much of the hands forward. All these people had been together for eighteen months or so, and my position was that of the only stranger on board. I mention this because it has some bearing on what is to follow. But what I felt most was my being a stranger to the ship; and if all the truth must be told, I was somewhat of a stranger to myself. The youngest man on board (barring the second mate), and untried as yet by a position of the fullest responsibility, I was willing to take the adequacy of the others for granted. They had simply to be equal to their tasks; but I wondered how far I should turn out faithful to that ideal conception of one's own personality every man sets up for himself secretly.

Meanwhile the chief mate, with an almost visible effect of collaboration on the part of his round eyes and frightful whiskers, was trying to evolve a theory of the anchored ship. His dominant trait was to take all things into earnest consideration. He was of a painstaking turn of mind. As he used to say, he "liked to account to himself" for practically everything that came in his way, down to a miserable scorpion he had found in his cabin a week before. The why and the wherefore of that scorpion—how it got on board and came to select his room rather than the pantry (which was a dark place and more what a scorpion would be partial to), and how on earth it managed to drown itself in the inkwell of his writing-desk —had exercised him infinitely. The ship within the islands was much more easily accounted for; and just as we were about to rise from table he made his pronouncement. She was, he doubted not, a ship from home lately arrived. Probably she drew too much water to cross the bar except at the top of spring tides. Therefore she went into that natural harbour to wait for a few days in preference to remaining in an open roadstead.

"That's so," confirmed the second mate, suddenly, in his slightly hoarse voice. "She draws over twenty feet. She's the Liverpool ship *Sephora* with a cargo of coal. Hundred and twenty-three days from Cardiff." We looked at him in surprise.

"The tugboat skipper told me when he came on board for your letters, sir," explained the young man. "He expects to take her up the river the day after tomorrow."

After thus overwhelming us with the extent of his information he slipped out of the cabin. The mate observed regretfully that he "could not account for that young fellow's whims." What prevented him telling us all about it at once, he wanted to know.

I detained him as he was making a move. For the last two days the crew had had plenty of hard work, and the night before they had very little sleep. I felt painfully that I—a stranger—was doing something unusual when I directed him to let all hands turn in without setting an anchor-watch. I proposed to keep on deck myself till one o'clock or thereabouts. I would get the second mate to relieve me at that hour.

"He will turn out the cook and the steward at four," I concluded, "and then give you a call. Of course at the slightest sign of any sort of wind we'll have the hands up and make a start at once."

He concealed his astonishment. "Very well, sir." Outside the cuddy he put his head in the second mate's door to inform him of my unheard-of caprice to take a five hours' anchor-watch on myself. I heard the other raise his voice incredulously—"What? The Captain himself?" Then a few more murmurs, a door closed, then another. A few moments later I went on deck.

My strangeness, which had made me sleepless, had prompted that unconventional arrangement, as if I had expected in those solitary hours of the night to get on terms with the ship of which I knew nothing, manned by men of whom I knew very little more. Fast alongside a wharf, littered like any ship in port with a tangle of unrelated things, invaded by unrelated shore people, I had hardly seen her yet properly. Now, as she lay cleared for sea, the stretch of her main-deck seemed to me very fine under the stars. Very fine, very roomy for her size, and very inviting. I descended the poop and paced the waist, my mind picturing to myself the coming passage through the Malay Archipelago, down the Indian Ocean, and up the Atlantic. All its phases were familiar enough to me, every characteristic, all the alternatives which were likely to face me on the high seas —everything! . . . except the novel responsibility of command. But I took heart from the reasonable thought that the ship was like other ships, the men like other men, and that the sea was not likely to keep any special surprises expressly for my discomfiture.

Arrived at that comforting conclusion, I bethought myself of a cigar and went below to get it. All was still down there. Everybody at the after end of the ship was sleeping profoundly. I came out again on the quarter-deck, agreeably at ease in my sleeping-suit on that warm breathless night, barefooted, a glowing cigar in my teeth, and, going forward, I was met by the profound silence of the fore end of the ship. Only as I passed the door of the forecastle I heard a deep, quiet, trustful sigh of some sleeper inside. And suddenly I rejoiced in the great security of the sea as compared with the unrest of the land, in my choice of that untempted life presenting no disquieting problems, invested with an elementary moral beauty by the absolute straightforwardness of its appeal and by the singleness of its purpose.

The riding-light in the fore-rigging burned with a clear, untroubled, as if symbolic, flame, confident and bright in the mysterious shades of the night. Passing on my way aft along the other side of the ship, I observed that the rope side-ladder, put over, no doubt, for the master of the tug when he came to fetch away our letters, had not been hauled in as it should have been. I became annoyed at this, for exactitude in small matters is the very soul of discipline. Then I reflected that I had myself peremptorily dismissed my officers from duty, and by my own act had prevented the anchor-watch being formally set and things properly attended to. I asked myself whether it was wise ever to interfere with the established routine of duties even from the kindest of motives. My action might have made me appear eccentric. Goodness only knew how that absurdly whiskered mate would "account" for my conduct, and what the whole ship thought of that informality of their new captain. I was vexed with myself.

Not from compunction certainly, but, as it were mechanically, I proceeded to get the ladder in myself. Now a side-ladder of that sort is a light affair and comes in easily, yet my vigorous tug, which should have brought it flying on board, merely recoiled upon my body in a totally unexpected jerk. What the devil! . . . I was so astounded by the immovableness of that ladder that I remained stock-still, trying to account for it to myself like that imbecile mate of mine. In the end, of course, I put my head over the rail.

The side of the ship made an opaque belt of shadow on the darkling glassy shimmer of the sea. But I saw at once something elongated and pale floating very close to the ladder. Before I could form a guess a faint flash of phosphorescent light, which seemed to issue suddenly from the naked body of a man, flickered in the sleeping water with the elusive, silent play of summer lightning in a night sky. With a gasp I saw revealed to my stare a pair of feet, the long legs, a broad livid back immersed right up to the neck in a greenish cadaverous glow. One hand, awash, clutched the bottom rung of the ladder. He was complete but for the head. A headless corpse! The cigar dropped out of my gaping mouth with a tiny plop and a short hiss quite audible in the absolute stillness of all things under heaven. At that I suppose he raised up his face, a dimly pale oval in the shadow of the ship's side. But even then I could only barely make out down there the shape of his black-haired head. However, it was enough for the horrid, frost-bound sensation which had gripped me about the chest to pass off. The moment of vain exclamations was past, too. I only climbed on the spare spar and leaned over the rail as far as I could, to bring my eyes nearer to that mystery floating alongside.

As he hung by the ladder, like a resting swimmer, the sea-lightning played about his limbs at every stir; and he appeared in it ghastly, silvery, fish-like. He remained as mute as a fish, too. He made no motion to get out of the water, either. It was inconceivable that he should not attempt to come on board, and strangely troubling to suspect that perhaps he did not want to. And my first words were prompted by just that troubled incertitude.

"What's the matter?" I asked in my ordinary tone, speaking down to the face upturned exactly under mine.

"Cramp," it answered, no louder. Then slightly anxious, "I say, no need to call any one."

"I was not going to," I said.

"Are you alone on deck?"

"Yes."

I had somehow the impression that he was on the point of letting go the ladder to swim away beyond my ken—mysterious as he came. But, for the moment, this being appearing as if he had risen from the bottom of the sea (it was certainly the nearest land to the ship) wanted only to know the time. I told him. And he, down there, tentatively:

"I suppose your captain's turned in?"

"I am sure he isn't," I said.

He seemed to struggle with himself, for I heard something like the low, bitter murmur of doubt. "What's the good?" His next words came out with a hesitating effort.

"Look here, my man. Could you call him out quietly?"

I thought the time had come to declare myself.

"*I* am the captain."

I heard a "By Jove!" whispered at the level of the water. The phosphorescence flashed in the swirl of the water all about his limbs, his other hand seized the ladder.

"My name's Leggatt."

The voice was calm and resolute. A good voice. The self-possession of that man had somehow induced a corresponding state in myself. It was very quietly that I remarked:

"You must be a good swimmer."

"Yes. I've been in the water practically since nine o'clock. The question for me now is whether I am to let go this ladder and go on swimming till I sink from exhaustion, or—to come on board here."

I felt this was no mere formula of desperate speech, but a real alternative in the view of a strong soul. I should have gathered from this that he was young; indeed, it is only the young who are ever confronted by such clear issues. But at this time it was pure intuition on my part. A mysterious communication was established already between us two—in the face of that silent, darkened tropical sea. I was young, too; young enough to make no comment. The man in the water began suddenly to climb up the ladder, and I hastened away from the rail to fetch some clothes.

Before entering the cabin I stood still, listening in the lobby at the foot of the stairs. A faint snore came through the closed door of the chief mate's room. The second mate's door was on the hook, but the darkness in there was absolutely soundless. He, too, was young and could sleep like a stone. Remained the steward, but he was not likely to wake up before he was called. I got a sleeping-suit out of my room and, coming back on deck, saw the naked man from the sea sitting on the main-hatch, glimmering white in the darkness, his elbows on his knees and his head in his hands. In a moment he had concealed his damp body in a sleeping-suit of the same grey-stripe pattern as the one I was wearing and followed me like my double on the poop. Together we moved right aft, barefooted, silent.

"What is it?" I asked in a deadened voice, taking the lighted lamp out of the binnacle, and raising it to his face.

"An ugly business."

He had rather regular features; a good mouth; light eyes under somewhat heavy, dark eyebrows; a smooth, square forehead; no growth on his cheeks; a small, brown moustache, and a well-shaped, round chin. His expression was concentrated, meditative, under the inspecting light of the lamp I held up to his face; such as a man thinking hard in solitude might wear. My sleeping-suit was just right for his size. A well-knit young fellow of twenty-five at most. He caught his lower lip with the edge of the white, even teeth.

"Yes," I said, replacing the lamp in the binnacle. The warm, heavy tropical night closed upon his head again.

"There's a ship over there," he murmured.

"Yes, I know. The *Sephora*. Did you know of us?"

"Hadn't the slightest idea. I am the mate of her—" He paused and corrected himself. "I should say I *was*."

"Aha! Something wrong?"

"Yes. Very wrong indeed. I've killed a man."

"What do you mean? Just now?"

"No, on the passage. Weeks ago. Thirty-nine south. When I say a man—"

"Fit of temper," I suggested, confidently.

The shadowy, dark head, like mine, seemed to nod imperceptibly above the ghostly grey of my sleeping-suit. It was, in the night, as though I had been faced by my own reflection in the depths of a sombre and immense mirror.

"A pretty thing to have to own up to for a Conway[2] boy," murmured my double, distinctly.

"You're a Conway boy?"

"I am," he said, as if startled. Then, slowly . . . "Perhaps you too—"

It was so; but being a couple of years older I had left before he joined. After a quick interchange of dates a silence fell; and I thought suddenly of my absurb mate with his terrific whiskers and the "Bless my soul—you don't say so" type of intellect. My double gave me an inkling of his thoughts by saying: "My father's a parson in Norfolk. Do you see me before a judge and jury on that charge? For myself I can't see the necessity. There are fellows that an angel from heaven— And I am not that. He was one of those creatures that are just simmering all the time with a silly sort of wickedness. Miserable devils that have no business to live at all. He wouldn't do his duty and wouldn't let anybody else do theirs. But what's the good of talking! You know well enough the sort of ill-conditioned snarling cur—"

He appealed to me as if our experiences had been as identical as our clothes. And I knew well enough the pestiferous danger of such a character where there are no means of legal repression. And I knew well enough also that my double there was no homicidal ruffian. I did not think of asking him for details, and he told me the story roughly in brusque, disconnected sentences. I needed no more. I saw it all going on as though I were myself inside that other sleeping-suit.

"It happened while we were setting a reefed foresail, at dusk. Reefed foresail! You understand the sort of weather. The only sail we had left to keep the ship running; so you may guess what it had been like for days. Anxious sort of job, that. He gave me some of his cursed insolence at the sheet. I tell you I was overdone with this terrific weather that seemed to have no end to it. Terrific, I tell you—and a deep ship. I believed the fellow himself was half crazed with funk. It was no time for gentlemanly reproof, so I turned round and felled him like an ox. He up and at me. We closed just as an awful sea made for the ship. All hands saw it coming and took to the rigging, but I had him by the throat, and went on shaking him like a rat, the men above us yelling, 'Look out! look out!' Then a crash as if the sky had fallen on my head. They say that for over ten minutes hardly anything was to be seen of the ship—just the three masts and a bit of the forecastle head and of the poop all awash driving along in a smother of foam. It was a miracle that they found us, jammed together behind the forebits. It's clear that I meant business, because I was holding him by the throat still when they picked us up. He was black in the face. It was too much for them. It seems they rushed us aft together, gripped as we were, screaming 'Murder!' like a lot of lunatics, and broke into the cuddy. And the ship running for her life, touch and go all the time, any minute her last in a sea fit to turn your hair grey only a-looking at it. I understand that the skipper, too, started raving like the rest of them. The

[2] A British training ship.

man had been deprived of sleep for more than a week, and to have this sprung on him at the height of a furious gale nearly drove him out of his mind. I wonder they didn't fling me overboard after getting the carcass of their precious shipmate out of my fingers. They had rather a job to separate us, I've been told. A sufficiently fierce story to make an old judge and a respectable jury sit up a bit. The first thing I heard when I came to myself was the maddening howling of that endless gale, and on that the voice of the old man. He was hanging on to my bunk, staring into my face out of his sou'wester.

" 'Mr. Leggatt, you have killed a man. You can act no longer as chief mate of this ship.' "

His care to subdue his voice made it sound monotonous. He rested a hand on the end of the skylight to steady himself with, and all that time did not stir a limb, so far as I could see. "Nice little tale for a quiet tea-party," he concluded in the same tone.

One of my hands, too, rested on the end of the skylight; neither did I stir a limb, so far as I knew. We stood less than a foot from each other. It occurred to me that if old "Bless my soul—you don't say so" were to put his head up the companion and catch sight of us, he would think he was seeing double, or imagine himself come upon a scene of weird witchcraft; the strange captain having a quiet confabulation by the wheel with his own grey ghost. I became very much concerned to prevent anything of the sort. I heard the other's soothing undertone.

"My father's a parson in Norfolk," it said. Evidently he had forgotten he had told me this important fact before. Truly a nice little tale.

"You had better slip down into my stateroom now," I said, moving off stealthily. My double followed my movements; our bare feet made no sound; I let him in, closed the door with care, and, after giving a call to the second mate, returned on deck for my relief.

"Not much sign of any wind yet," I remarked when he approached.

"No, sir. Not much," he assented, sleepily, in his hoarse voice, with just enough deference, no more, and barely suppressing a yawn.

"Well, that's all you have to look out for. You have got your orders."

"Yes, sir."

I paced a turn or two on the poop and saw him take up his position face forward with his elbow in the ratlines of the mizzen-rigging before I went below. The mate's faint snoring was still going on peacefully. The cuddy lamp was burning over the table on which stood a vase with flowers, a polite attention from the ship's provision merchant—the last flowers we should see for the next three months at the very least. Two bunches of bananas hung from the beam symmetrically, one on each side of the rudder-casing. Everything was as before in the ship —except that two of her captain's sleeping-suits were simultaneously in use, one motionless in the cuddy, the other keeping very still in the captain's stateroom.

It must be explained here that my cabin had the form of the capital letter L the door being within the angle and opening into the short part of the letter. A couch was to the left, the bed-place to the right; my writing-desk and the chronometers' table faced the door. But any one opening it, unless he stepped right inside, had no view of what I call the long (or vertical) part of the letter. It contained some lockers surmounted by a bookcase; and a few clothes, a thick jacket or two, caps, oilskin coat, and such like, hung on hooks. There was at the bottom of that part a door opening into my bath-room, which could be entered also directly from the saloon. But that way was never used.

The mysterious arrival had discovered the advantage of this particular shape. Entering my room, lighted strongly by a big bulkhead lamp swung on gimbals above my writing-desk, I did not see him anywhere till he stepped out quietly from behind the coats hung in the recessed part.

"I heard somebody moving about, and went in there at once," he whispered.

I, too, spoke under my breath.

"Nobody is likely to come in here without knocking and getting permission."

He nodded. His face was thin and the sunburn faded, as though he had been ill. And no wonder. He had been, I heard presently, kept under arrest in his cabin for nearly seven weeks. But there was nothing sickly in his eyes or in his expression. He was not a bit like me, really; yet, as we stood leaning over my bed-place, whispering side by side, with our dark heads together and our backs to the door, anybody bold enough to open it stealthily would have been treated to the uncanny sight of a double captain busy talking in whispers with his other self.

"But all this doesn't tell me how you came to hang on to our side-ladder," I inquired, in the hardly audible murmurs we used, after he had told me something more of the proceedings on board the *Sephora* once the bad weather was over.

"When we sighted Java Head I had had time to think all those matters out several times over. I had six weeks of doing nothing else, and with only an hour or so every evening for a tramp on the quarter-deck."

He whispered, his arms folded on the side of my bed-place, staring through the open port. And I could imagine perfectly the manner of this thinking out— a stubborn if not a steadfast operation; something of which I should have been perfectly incapable.

"I reckoned it would be dark before we closed with the land," he continued, so low that I had to strain my hearing, near as we were to each other, shoulder touching shoulder almost. "So I asked to speak to the old man. He always seemed very sick when he came to see me—as if he could not look me in the face. You know, that foresail saved the ship. She was too deep to have run long under bare poles. And it was I that managed to set it for him. Anyway, he came. When I had him in my cabin—he stood by the door looking at me as if I had the halter round my neck already—I asked him right away to leave my cabin door unlocked at night while the ship was going through Sunda Straits. There would be the Java coast within two or three miles, off Angier Point. I wanted nothing more. I've had a prize for swimming my second year in the Conway."

"I can believe it," I breathed out.

"God only knows why they locked me in every night. To see some of their faces you'd have thought they were afraid I'd go about at night strangling people. Am I a murdering brute? Do I look it? By Jove! If I had been he wouldn't have trusted himself like that into my room. You'll say I might have chucked him aside and bolted out, there and then—it was dark already. Well, no. And for the same reason I wouldn't think of trying to smash the door. There would have been a rush to stop me at the noise, and I did not mean to get into a confounded scrimmage. Somebody else might have got killed—for I would not have broken out only to get chucked back, and I did not want any more of that work. He refused, looking more sick than ever. He was afraid of the men, and also of that old second mate of his who had been sailing with him for years—a grey-headed old humbug; and his steward, too, had been with him devil knows how long— seventeen years or more—a dogmatic sort of loafer who hated me like poison, just because I was the chief mate. No chief mate ever made more than one voyage in the *Sephora,* you know. Those two old chaps ran the ship. Devil only knows what the skipper wasn't afraid of (all his nerve went to pieces altogether in that hellish spell of bad weather we had)—of what the law would do to him—of his wife, perhaps. Oh, yes! she's on board. Though I don't think she would have meddled. She would have been only too glad to have me out of the ship in any way. The 'brand of Cain'[3] business, don't you see. That's all right. I was ready enough to go off wandering on the face of the earth—and that was price enough to pay for an Abel of that sort. Anyhow, he wouldn't listen to me. 'This thing must take its course. I represent the law here.' He was shaking like a leaf. 'So you won't?' 'No!' 'Then I hope you will be able to sleep on that,' I said, and turned my back on him. 'I wonder that *you* can,' cries he, and locks the door.

"Well, after that, I couldn't. Not very well. That was three weeks ago. We have had a slow passage through the Java Sea; drifted about Carimata[4] for ten days. When we anchored here they thought, I suppose, it was all right. The nearest land (and that's five miles) is the ship's destination; the consul would soon set about catching me; and there would have been no object in bolting to these islets there. I don't suppose there's a drop of water on them. I don't know how it was, but to-night that steward, after bringing me my supper, went out to let me eat it, and left the door unlocked. And I ate it—all there was, too. After I had finished I strolled out on the quarter-deck. I don't know that I meant to do anything. A breath of fresh air was all I wanted, I believe. Then a sudden temptation came over me. I kicked off my slippers and was in the water before I had made up my mind fairly. Somebody heard the splash and they raised an awful hullabaloo. 'He's gone! Lower the boats! He's committed suicide! No, he's swimming.' Certainly I was swimming. It's not so easy for a swimmer like me to commit suicide by drowning. I landed on the nearest islet before the boat left the ship's side. I heard them pulling about in the dark, hailing, and so on, but after a bit they gave up. Everything quieted down and the anchorage became as still as death. I sat down on a stone and began to think. I felt certain they would start searching for me at daylight. There was no place to hide on those stony things—and if there had been, what would have been the good? But now I was clear of that ship, I

---

[3]After Cain killed his brother Abel, the Lord made him "a fugitive and a vagabond" and then "the Lord set a mark upon Cain, lest any finding him should kill him" (Genesis 4.14–15). [4]The Karimata islands, near Borneo.

was not going back. So after a while I took off all my clothes, tied them up in a bundle with a stone inside, and dropped them in the deep water on the outer side of that islet. That was suicide enough for me. Let them think what they liked, but I didn't mean to drown myself. I meant to swim till I sank—but that's not the same thing. I struck out for another of these little islands, and it was from that one that I first saw your riding-light. Something to swim for. I went on easily, and on the way I came upon a flat rock a foot or two above water. In the daytime, I dare say, you might make it out with a glass from your poop. I scrambled up on it and rested myself for a bit. Then I made another start. That last spell must have been over a mile."

His whisper was getting fainter and fainter, and all the time he stared straight out through the port-hole, in which there was not even a star to be seen. I had not interrupted him. There was something that made comment impossible in his narrative, or perhaps in himself; a sort of feeling, a quality, which I can't find a name for. And when he ceased, all I found was a futile whisper: "So you swam for our light?"

"Yes—straight for it. It was something to swim for. I couldn't see any stars low down because the coast was in the way, and I couldn't see the land, either. The water was like glass. One might have been swimming in a confounded thousand-feet deep cistern with no place for scrambling out anywhere; but what I didn't like was the notion of swimming round and round like a crazed bullock before I gave out; and as I didn't mean to go back . . . No. Do you see me being hauled back, stark naked, off one of these little islands by the scruff of the neck and fighting like a wild beast? Somebody would have got killed for certain, and I did not want any of that. So I went on. Then your ladder—"

"Why didn't you hail the ship?" I asked, a little louder.

He touched my shoulder lightly. Lazy footsteps came right over our heads and stopped. The second mate had crossed from the other side of the poop and might have been hanging over the rail, for all we knew.

"He couldn't hear us talking—could he?" My double breathed into my very ear, anxiously.

His anxiety was an answer, a sufficient answer, to the question I had put to him. An answer containing all the difficulty of that situation. I closed the porthole quietly, to make sure. A louder word might have been overheard.

"Who's that?" he whispered then.

"My second mate. But I don't know much more of the fellow than you do."

And I told him a little about myself. I had been appointed to take charge while I least expected anything of the sort, not quite a fortnight ago. I didn't know either the ship or the people. Hadn't had the time in port to look about me or size anybody up. And as to the crew, all they knew was that I was appointed to take the ship home. For the rest, I was almost as much of a stranger on board as himself, I said. And at the moment I felt it most acutely. I felt that it would take very little to make me a suspect person in the eyes of the ship's company.

He had turned about meantime; and we, the two strangers in the ship, faced each other in identical attitudes.

"Your ladder—" he murmured, after a silence. "Who'd have thought of finding a ladder hanging over at night in a ship anchored out here! I felt just then a very unpleasant faintness. After the life I've been leading for nine weeks, anybody would have got out of condition. I wasn't capable of swimming round as far as your rudder-chains. And, lo and behold! there was a ladder to get hold of. After I gripped it I said to myself, 'What's the good?' When I saw a man's head looking over I thought I would swim away presently and leave him shouting —in whatever language it was. I didn't mind being looked at. I—I liked it. And then you speaking to me so quietly—as if you had expected me—made me hold on a little longer. It had been a confounded lonely time—I don't mean while swimming. I was glad to talk a little to somebody that didn't belong to the *Sephora*. As to asking for the captain, that was a mere impulse. It could have been no use, with all the ship knowing about me and the other people pretty certain to be round here in the morning. I don't know—I wanted to be seen, to talk with somebody, before I went on. I don't know what I would have said. . . . 'Fine night, isn't it?' or something of the sort."

"Do you think they will be round here presently?" I asked with some incredulity.

"Quite likely," he said, faintly.

He looked extremely haggard all of a sudden. His head rolled on his shoulders.

"H'm. We shall see then. Meantime get into that bed," I whispered. "Want help? There."

It was a rather high bed-place with a set of drawers underneath. This amazing swimmer really needed the lift I gave him by seizing his leg. He tumbled in, rolled over on his back, and flung one arm across his eyes. And then, with his face nearly hidden, he must have looked exactly as I used to look in that bed. I gazed upon my other self for a while before drawing across carefully the two green serge curtains which ran on a brass rod. I thought for a moment of pinning them together for greater safety, but I sat down on the couch, and once there I felt unwilling to rise and hunt for a pin. I would do it in a moment. I was extremely tired, in a peculiarly intimate way, by the strain of stealthiness, by the effort of whispering and the general secrecy of this excitement. It was three o'clock by now and I had been on my feet since nine, but I was not sleepy; I could not have gone to sleep. I sat there, fagged out, looking at the curtains, trying to clear my mind of the confused sensation of being in two places at once, and greatly bothered by an exasperating knocking in my head. It was a relief to discover suddenly that it was not in my head at all, but on the outside of the door. Before I could collect myself the words "Come in" were out of my mouth, and the steward entered with a tray, bringing in my morning coffee. I had slept, after all, and I was so frightened that I shouted, "This way! I am here, steward," as though he had been miles away. He put down the tray on the table next the couch and only then said, very quietly, "I can see you are here, sir." I felt him give me a keen look, but I dared not meet his eyes just then. He must have wondered why I had drawn the curtains of my bed before going to sleep on the couch. He went out, hooking the door open as usual.

I heard the crew washing decks above me. I knew I would have been told at once if there had been any wind. Calm, I thought, and I was doubly vexed. Indeed, I felt dual more than ever. The steward reappeared suddenly in the doorway. I jumped up from the couch so quickly that he gave a start.

"What do you want here?"

"Close your port, sir—they are washing decks."

"It is closed," I said, reddening.

"Very well, sir." But he did not move from the doorway and returned my stare in an extraordinary, equivocal manner for a time. Then his eyes wavered, all his expression changed, and in a voice unusually gentle, almost coaxingly:

"May I come in to take the empty cup away, sir?"

"Of course!" I turned my back on him while he popped in and out. Then I unhooked and closed the door and even pushed the bolt. This sort of thing could not go on very long. The cabin was as hot as an oven, too. I took a peep at my double, and discovered that he had not moved, his arm was still over his eyes; but his chest heaved; his hair was wet; his chin glistened with perspiration. I reached over him and opened the port.

"I must show myself on deck," I reflected.

Of course, theoretically, I could do what I liked, with no one to say nay to me within the whole circle of the horizon; but to lock my cabin door and take the key away I did not dare. Directly I put my head out of the companion I saw the group of my two officers, the second mate barefooted, the chief mate in long india-rubber boots, near the break of the poop, and the steward half-way down the poop-ladder talking to them eagerly. He happened to catch sight of me and dived, the second ran down on the main-deck shouting some order or other, and the chief mate came to meet me, touching his cap.

There was a sort of curiosity in his eye that I did not like. I don't know whether the steward had told them that I was "queer" only, or downright drunk, but I know the man meant to have a good look at me. I watched him coming with a smile which, as he got into point-blank range, took effect and froze his very whiskers. I did not give him time to open his lips.

"Square the yards by lifts and braces before the hands go to breakfast."

It was the first particular order I had given on board that ship; and I stayed on deck to see it executed, too. I had felt the need of asserting myself without loss of time. That sneering young cub got taken down a peg or two on that occasion, and I also seized the opportunity of having a good look at the face of every foremast man as they filed past me to go to the after braces. At breakfast time, eating nothing myself, I presided with such frigid dignity that the two mates were only too glad to escape from the cabin as soon as decency permitted; and all the time the dual working of my mind distracted me almost to the point of insanity. I was constantly watching myself, my secret self, as dependent on my actions as my own personality, sleeping in that bed, behind that door which faced me as I sat at the head of the table. It was very much like being mad, only it was worse because one was aware of it.

I had to shake him for a solid minute, but when at last he opened his eyes it was in the full possession of his senses, with an inquiring look.

"All's well so far," I whispered. "Now you must vanish into the bath-room."

He did so, as noiseless as a ghost, and then I rang for the steward, and facing him boldly, directed him to tidy up my stateroom while I was having my bath —"and be quick about it." As my tone admitted of no excuses, he said, "Yes, sir," and ran off to fetch his dust-pan and brushes. I took a bath and did most of my dressing, splashing, and whistling softly for the steward's edification, while the secret sharer of my life stood drawn up bolt upright in that little space, his face looking very sunken in daylight, his eyelids lowered under the stern, dark line of his eyebrows drawn together by a slight frown.

When I left him there to go back to my room the steward was finishing dusting. I sent for the mate and engaged him in some insignificant conversation. It was, as it were, trifling with the terrific character of his whiskers; but my object was to give him an opportunity for a good look at my cabin. And then I could at last shut, with a clear conscience, the door of my stateroom and get my double back into the recessed part. There was nothing else for it. He had to sit still on a small folding stool, half smothered by the heavy coats hanging there. We listened to the steward going into the bath-room out of the saloon, filling the water-bottles there, scrubbing the bath, setting things to rights, whisk, bang, clatter—out again into the saloon—turn the key—click. Such was my scheme for keeping my second self invisible. Nothing better could be contrived under the circumstances. And there we sat; I at my writing-desk ready to appear busy with some papers, he behind me out of sight of the door. It would not have been prudent to talk in daytime; and I could not have stood the excitement of that queer sense of whispering to myself. Now and then, glancing over my shoulder, I saw him far back there, sitting rigidly on the low stool, his bare feet close together, his arms folded, his head hanging on his breast—and perfectly still. Anybody would have taken him for me.

I was fascinated by it myself. Every moment I had to glance over my shoulder. I was looking at him when a voice outside the door said:

"Beg pardon, sir."

"Well!" . . . I kept my eyes on him, and so when the voice outside the door announced, "There's a ship's boat coming our way, sir," I saw him give a start —the first movement he had made for hours. But he did not raise his bowed head.

"All right. Get the ladder over."

I hesitated. Should I whisper something to him? But what? His immobility seemed to have been never disturbed. What could I tell him he did not know already? . . . Finally I went on deck.

II

The skipper of the *Sephora* had a thin red whisker all round his face, and the sort of complexion that goes with hair of that colour; also the particular, rather smeary shade of blue in the eyes. He was not exactly a showy figure; his shoulders were high, his stature but middling—one leg slightly more bandy than the other. He shook hands, looking vaguely around. A spiritless tenacity was his main characteristic, I judged. I behaved with a politeness which seemed to disconcert him. Perhaps he was shy. He mumbled to me as if he were ashamed of what he was saying; gave his name (it was something like Archbold—but at this distance of years I hardly am sure), his ship's name, and a few other particulars of that sort, in the manner of a criminal making a reluctant and doleful confession. He had had terrible weather on the passage out—terrible—terrible—wife aboard, too.

By this time we were seated in the cabin and the steward brought in a tray with a bottle and glasses. "Thanks! No." Never took liquor. Would have some water, though. He drank two tumblerfuls. Terrible thirsty work. Ever since daylight had been exploring the islands round his ship.

"What was that for—fun?" I asked, with an appearance of polite interest.

"No!" He sighed. "Painful duty."

As he persisted in his mumbling and I wanted my double to hear every word, I hit upon the notion of informing him that I regretted to say I was hard of hearing.

"Such a young man, too!" he nodded, keeping his smeary blue, unintelligent eyes fastened upon me. "What was the cause of it—some disease?" he inquired, without the least sympathy and as if he thought that, if so, I'd got no more than I deserved.

"Yes; disease," I admitted in a cheerful tone which seemed to shock him. But my point was gained, because he had to raise his voice to give me his tale. It is not worth while to record that version. It was just over two months since all this had happened, and he had thought so much about it that he seemed completely muddled as to its bearings, but still immensely impressed.

"What would you think of such a thing happening on board your own ship? I've had the *Sephora* for these fifteen years. I am a well-known shipmaster."

He was densely distressed—and perhaps I should have sympathised with him if I had been able to detach my mental vision from the unsuspected sharer of my cabin as though he were my second self. There he was on the other side of the bulkhead, four or five feet from us, no more, as we sat in the saloon. I looked politely at Captain Archbold (if that was his name), but it was the other I saw, in a grey sleeping-suit, seated on a low stool, his bare feet close together, his arms folded, and every word said between us falling into the ears of his dark head bowed on his chest.

"I have been at sea now, man and boy, for seven-and-thirty years, and I've never heard of such a thing happening in an English ship. And that it should be my ship. Wife on board, too."

I was hardly listening to him.

"Don't you think," I said, "that the heavy sea which, you told me, came aboard just then might have killed the man? I have seen the sheer weight of a sea kill a man very neatly, by simply breaking his neck."

"Good God!" he uttered, impressively, fixing his smeary blue eyes on me. "The sea! No man killed by the sea ever looked like that." He seemed positively scandalised at my suggestion. And as I gazed at him, certainly not prepared for anything original on his part, he advanced his head close to mine and thrust his tongue out at me so suddenly that I couldn't help starting back.

After scoring over my calmness in this graphic way he nodded wisely. If I had seen the sight, he assured me, I would never forget it as long as I lived. The weather was too bad to give the corpse a proper sea burial. So next day at dawn they took it up on the poop, covering its face with a bit of bunting; he read a short prayer, and then, just as it was, in its oilskins and long boots, they launched it amongst those mountainous seas that seemed ready every moment to swallow up the ship herself and the terrified lives on board of her.

"That reefed foresail saved you," I threw in.

"Under God—it did," he exclaimed fervently. "It was by a special mercy, I firmly believe, that it stood some of those hurricane squalls."

"It was the setting of that sail which—" I began.

"God's own hand in it," he interrupted me. "Nothing less could have done it. I don't mind telling you that I hardly dared give the order. It seemed impossible that we could touch anything without losing it, and then our last hope would have been gone."

The terror of that gale was on him yet. I let him go on for a bit, then said, casually—as if returning to a minor subject:

"You were very anxious to give up your mate to the shore people, I believe?"

He was. To the law. His obscure tenacity on that point had in it something incomprehensible and a little awful; something, as it were, mystical, quite apart from his anxiety that he should not be suspected of "countenancing any doings of that sort." Seven-and-thirty virtuous years at sea, of which over twenty of immaculate command, and the last fifteen in the *Sephora,* seemed to have laid him under some pitiless obligation.

"And you know," he went on, groping shamefacedly amongst his feelings, "I did not engage that young fellow. His people had some interest with my owners. I was in a way forced to take him on. He looked very smart, very gentlemanly, and all that. But do you know—I never liked him, somehow. I am a plain man. You see, he wasn't exactly the sort for the chief mate of a ship like the *Sephora.*"

I had become so connected in thoughts and impressions with the secret sharer of my cabin that I felt as if I, personally, were being given to understand that I, too, was not the sort that would have done for the chief mate of a ship like the *Sephora.* I had no doubt of it in my mind.

"Not at all the style of man. You understand," he insisted, superfluously, looking hard at me.

I smiled urbanely. He seemed at a loss for a while.

"I suppose I must report a suicide."

"Beg pardon?"

"Sui-cide! That's what I'll have to write to my owners directly I get in."

"Unless you manage to recover him before to-morrow," I assented, dispassionately. . . . "I mean, alive."

He mumbled something which I really did not catch, and I turned my ear to him in a puzzled manner. He fairly bawled:

"The land—I say, the mainland is at least seven miles off my anchorage."

"About that."

My lack of excitement, of curiosity, of surprise, of any sort of pronounced interest, began to arouse his distrust. But except for the felicitous pretence of deafness I had not tried to pretend anything. I had felt utterly incapable of playing the part of ignorance properly, and therefore was afraid to try. It is also certain that he had brought some ready-made suspicions with him, and that he viewed my politeness as a strange and unnatural phenomenon. And yet how else could I have received him? Not heartily! That was impossible for psychological reasons, which I need not state here. My only object was to keep off his inquiries. Surlily? Yes, but surliness might have provoked a point-blank question. From its novelty to him and from its nature, punctilious courtesy was the manner best calculated to restrain the man. But there was the danger of his breaking through my defence bluntly. I could not, I think, have met him by a direct lie, also for psychological (not moral) reasons. If he had only known how afraid I was of his putting my feeling of identity with the other to the test! But, strangely enough—(I thought of it only afterwards)—I believe that he was not a little disconcerted by the reverse side of that weird situation, by something in me that reminded him of the man he was seeking—suggested a mysterious similitude to the young fellow he had distrusted and disliked from the first.

However that might have been, the silence was not very prolonged. He took another oblique step.

"I reckon I had no more than a two-mile pull to your ship. Not a bit more."

"And quite enough, too, in this awful heat," I said.

Another pause full of mistrust followed. Necessity, they say, is mother of invention, but fear, too, is not barren of ingenious suggestions. And I was afraid he would ask me point-blank for news of my other self.

"Nice little saloon, isn't it?" I remarked, as if noticing for the first time the way his eyes roamed from one closed door to the other. "And very well fitted out, too. Here, for instance," I continued, reaching over the back of my seat negligently and flinging the door open, "is my bath-room."

He made an eager movement, but hardly gave it a glance. I got up, shut the door of the bath-room, and invited him to have a look round, as if I were very proud of my accommodation. He had to rise and be shown round, but he went through the business without any raptures whatever.

"And now we'll have a look at my stateroom," I declared, in a voice as loud as I dared to make it, crossing the cabin to the starboard side with purposely heavy steps.

He followed me in and gazed around. My intelligent double had vanished. I played my part.

"Very convenient—isn't it?"

"Very nice. Very comf . . ." He didn't finish and went out brusquely as if to escape from some unrighteous wiles of mine. But it was not to be. I had been too frightened not to feel vengeful; I felt I had him on the run, and I meant to keep him on the run. My polite insistence must have had something menacing in it, because he gave in suddenly. And I did not let him off a single item; mate's room, pantry, storerooms, the very sail-locker which was also under the poop—he had to look into them all. When at last I showed him out on the quarter-deck he drew a long, spiritless sigh, and mumbled dismally that he must really be going back to his ship now. I desired my mate, who had joined us, to see to the captain's boat.

The man of whiskers gave a blast on the whistle which he used to wear hanging round his neck, and yelled, "*Sephora's* away!" My double down there in my cabin must have heard, and certainly could not feel more relieved than I. Four fellows came running out from somewhere forward and went over the side, while my own men, appearing on deck too, lined the rail. I escorted my visitor to the gangway ceremoniously, and nearly overdid it. He was a tenacious beast. On the very ladder he lingered, and in that unique, guiltily conscientious manner of sticking to the point:

"I say . . . you . . . you don't think that—"

I covered his voice loudly:

"Certainly not. . . . I am delighted. Goodbye."

I had an idea of what he meant to say, and just saved myself by the privilege of defective hearing. He was too shaken generally to insist, but my mate, close witness of that parting, looked mystified and his face took on a thoughtful cast. As I did not want to appear as if I wished to avoid all communication with my officers, he had the opportunity to address me.

"Seems a very nice man. His boat's crew told our chaps a very extraordinary story, if what I am told by the steward is true. I suppose you had it from the captain, sir?"

"Yes. I had a story from the captain."

"A very horrible affair—isn't it, sir?"

"It is."

"Beats all these tales we hear about murders in Yankee ships."

"I don't think it beats them. I don't think it resembles them in the least."

"Bless my soul—you don't say so! But of course I've no acquaintance whatever with American ships, not I, so I couldn't go against your knowledge. It's horrible enough for me. . . . But the queerest part is that those fellows seemed to have some idea the man was hidden aboard here. They had really. Did you ever hear of such a thing?"

"Preposterous—isn't it?"

We were walking to and fro athwart the quarter-deck. No one of the crew forward could be seen (the day was Sunday), and the mate pursued:

"There was some little dispute about it. Our chaps took offence. 'As if we would harbour a thing like that,' they said. 'Wouldn't you like to look for him in our coal-hole?' Quite a tiff. But they made it up in the end. I suppose he did drown himself. Don't you, sir?"

"I don't suppose anything."

"You have no doubt in the matter, sir?"

"None whatever."

I left him suddenly. I felt I was producing a bad impression, but with my double down there it was most trying to be on deck. And it was almost as trying to be below. Altogether a nerve-trying situation. But on the whole I felt less torn in two when I was with him. There was no one in the whole ship whom I dared take into my confidence. Since the hands had got to know his story, it would have been impossible to pass him off for any one else, and an accidental discovery was to be dreaded now more than ever. . . .

The steward being engaged in laying the table for dinner, we could talk only with our eyes when I first went down. Later in the afternoon we had a cautious try at whispering. The Sunday quietness of the ship was against us; the stillness of air and water around her was against us; the elements, the men were against us—everything was against us in our secret partnership; time itself—for this could not go on forever. The very trust in Providence was, I suppose, denied to his guilt. Shall I confess that this thought cast me down very much? And as to the chapter of accidents which counts for so much in the book of success, I could only hope that it was closed. For what favourable accident could be expected?

"Did you hear everything?" were my first words as soon as we took up our position side by side, leaning over my bed-place.

He had. And the proof of it was his earnest whisper, "The man told you he hardly dared to give the order."

I understood the reference to be to that saving foresail.

"Yes. He was afraid of it being lost in the setting."

"I assure you he never gave the order. He may think he did, but he never gave it. He stood there with me on the break of the poop after the maintopsail blew away, and whimpered about our last hope—positively whimpered about it and nothing else—and the night coming on! To hear one's skipper go on like that in such weather was enough to drive any fellow out of his mind. It worked me up into a sort of desperation. I just took it into my own hands and went away from him, boiling, and—But what's the use telling you? *You* know! . . . Do you think that if I had not been pretty fierce with them I should have got the men to do anything? Not it! The bo's'n perhaps? Perhaps! It wasn't a heavy sea—it was a sea gone mad! I suppose the end of the world will be something like that; and a man may have the heart to see it coming once and be done with it—but to have to face it day after day—I don't blame anybody. I was precious little better than the rest. Only—I was an officer of that old coal-wagon, anyhow—"

"I quite understand," I conveyed that sincere assurance into his ear. He was out of breath with whispering; I could hear him pant slightly. It was all very simple. The same strung-up force which had given twenty-four men a chance, at least, for their lives, had, in a sort of recoil, crushed an unworthy mutinous existence.

But I had no leisure to weigh the merits of the matter—footsteps in the saloon, a heavy knock. "There's enough wind to get under way with, sir." Here was the call of a new claim upon my thoughts and even upon my feelings.

"Turn the hands up," I cried through the door. "I'll be on deck directly."

I was going out to make the acquaintance of my ship. Before I left the cabin our eyes met—the eyes of the only two strangers on board. I pointed to the recessed part where the little camp-stool awaited him and laid my finger on my lips. He made a gesture—somewhat vague—a little mysterious, accompanied by a faint smile, as if of regret.

This is not the place to enlarge upon the sensations of a man who feels for the first time a ship move under his feet to his own independent word. In my case they were not unalloyed. I was not wholly alone with my command; for there was that stranger in my cabin. Or rather, I was not completely and wholly with her. Part of me was absent. That mental feeling of being in two places at once affected me physically as if the mood of secrecy had penetrated my very soul. Before an hour had elapsed since the ship had begun to move, having occasion to ask the mate (he stood by my side) to take a compass bearing of the Pagoda, I caught myself reaching up to his ear in whispers. I say I caught myself, but enough had escaped to startle the man. I can't describe it otherwise than by saying that he shied. A grave, preoccupied manner, as though he were in possession of some perplexing intelligence, did not leave him henceforth. A little later I moved away from the rail to look at the compass with such a stealthy gait that the helmsman noticed it—and I could not help noticing the unusual roundness of his eyes. These are trifling instances, though it's to no commander's advantage to be suspected of ludicrous eccentricities. But I was also more seriously affected. There are to a seaman certain words, gestures, that should in given conditions come as naturally, as instinctively as the winking of a menaced eye. A certain order should spring on to his lips without thinking; a certain sign should get itself made, so to speak, without reflection. But all unconscious alertness had abandoned me. I had to make an effort of will to recall myself back (from the cabin) to the conditions of the moment. I felt that I was appearing an irresolute commander to those people who were watching me more or less critically.

And, besides, there were the scares. On the second day out, for instance, coming off the deck in the afternoon (I had straw slippers on my bare feet) I stopped at the open pantry door and spoke to the steward. He was doing something there with his back to me. At the sound of my voice he nearly jumped out of his skin, as the saying is, and incidentally broke a cup.

"What on earth's the matter with you?" I asked, astonished.

He was extremely confused. "Beg your pardon, sir. I made sure you were in your cabin."

"You see I wasn't."

"No, sir. I could have sworn I had heard you moving in there not a moment ago. It's most extraordinary . . . very sorry, sir."

I passed on with an inward shudder. I was so identified with my secret double that I did not even mention the fact in those scanty, fearful whispers we exchanged. I suppose he had made some slight noise of some kind or other. It would have been miraculous if he hadn't at one time or another. And yet, haggard as he appeared, he looked always perfectly self-controlled, more than calm—almost invulnerable. On my suggestion he remained almost entirely in the bathroom, which, upon the whole, was the safest place. There could be really no shadow of an excuse for any one ever wanting to go in there, once the steward had done with it. It was a very tiny place. Sometimes he reclined on the floor, his legs bent, his head sustained on one elbow. At others I would find him on the camp-stool, sitting in his grey sleeping-suit and with his cropped dark hair like a patient, unmoved convict. At night I would smuggle him into my bed-place, and we would whisper together, with the regular footfalls of the officer of the watch passing and repassing over our heads. It was an infinitely miserable time. It was lucky that some tins of fine preserves were stowed in a locker in my stateroom; hard bread I could always get hold of; and so he lived on stewed chicken, pate de foie gras, asparagus, cooked oysters, sardines—on all sorts of abominable sham delicacies out of tins. My early morning coffee he always drank; and it was all I dared do for him in that respect.

Every day there was the horrible maneuvering to go through so that my room and then the bath-room should be done in the usual way. I came to hate the sight of the steward, to abhor the voice of that harmless man. I felt that it was he who would bring on the disaster of discovery. It hung like a sword over our heads.

The fourth day out, I think (we were then working down the east side of the Gulf of Siam, tack for tack, in light winds and smooth water)—the fourth day, I say, of this miserable juggling with the unavoidable, as we sat at our evening meal, that man, whose slightest movement I dreaded, after putting down the dishes ran up on deck busily. This could not be dangerous. Presently he came down again; and then it appeared that he had remembered a coat of mine which I had thrown over a rail to dry after having been wetted in a shower which had passed over the ship in the afternoon. Sitting stolidly at the head of the table I became terrified at the sight of the garment on his arm. Of course he made for my door. There was no time to lose.

"Steward," I thundered. My nerves were so shaken that I could not govern my voice and conceal my agitation. This was the sort of thing that made my terrifically whiskered mate tap his forehead with his forefinger. I had detected him using that gesture while talking on deck with a confidential air to the carpenter. It was too far to hear a word, but I had no doubt that this pantomime could only refer to the strange new captain.

"Yes, sir," the pale-faced steward turned resignedly to me. It was this maddening course of being shouted at, checked without rhyme or reason, arbitrarily chased out of my cabin, suddenly called into it, sent flying out of his pantry on incomprehensible errands, that accounted for the growing wretchedness of his expression.

"Where are you going with that coat?"

"To your room, sir."

"Is there another shower coming?"

"I'm sure I don't know, sir. Shall I go up again and see, sir?"

"No! never mind."

My object was attained, as of course my other self in there would have heard everything that passed. During this interlude my two officers never raised their eyes off their respective plates; but the lip of that confounded cub, the second mate, quivered visibly.

I expected the steward to hook my coat on and come out at once. He was very slow about it; but I dominated my nervousness sufficiently not to shout after him. Suddenly I became aware (it could be heard plainly enough) that the fellow for some reason or other was opening the door of the bath-room. It was the end. The place was literally not big enough to swing a cat in. My voice died in my throat and I went stony all over. I expected to hear a yell of surprise and terror, and made a movement, but had not the strength to get on my legs. Everything remained still. Had my second self taken the poor wretch by the throat? I don't know what I could have done next moment if I had not seen the steward come out of my room, close the door, and then stand quietly by the sideboard.

"Saved," I thought. "But, no! Lost! Gone! He was gone!"

I laid my knife and fork down and leaned back in my chair. My head swam. After a while, when sufficiently recovered to speak in a steady voice, I instructed my mate to put the ship round at eight o'clock himself.

"I won't come on deck," I went on. "I think I'll turn in, and unless the wind shifts I don't want to be disturbed before midnight. I feel a bit seedy."

"You did look middling bad a little while ago," the chief mate remarked without showing any great concern.

They both went out, and I stared at the steward clearing the table. There was nothing to be read on that wretched man's face. But why did he avoid my eyes I asked myself. Then I thought I should like to hear the sound of his voice.

"Steward!"

"Sir!" Startled as usual.

"Where did you hang up that coat?"

"In the bath-room, sir." The usual anxious tone. "It's not quite dry yet, sir."

For some time longer I sat in the cuddy. Had my double vanished as he had come? But of his coming there was an explanation, whereas his disappearance would be inexplicable. . . . I went slowly into my dark room, shut the door, lighted the lamp, and for a time dared not turn round. When at last I did I saw him standing bolt-upright in the narrow recessed part. It would not be true to say I had a shock, but an irresistible doubt of his bodily existence flitted through my mind. Can it be, I asked myself, that he is not visible to other eyes than mine? It was like being haunted. Motionless, with a grave face, he raised his hands slightly at me in a gesture which meant clearly, "Heavens! what a narrow escape!" Narrow indeed. I think I had come creeping quietly as near insanity as any man who has not actually gone over the border. That gesture restrained me, so to speak.

The mate with the terrific whiskers was now putting the ship on the other tack. In the moment of profound silence which follows upon the hands going to their stations I heard on the poop his raised voice: "Hard alee!" and the distant shout of the order repeated on the maindeck. The sails, in that light breeze, made but a faint fluttering noise. It ceased. The ship was coming round slowly; I held my breath in the renewed stillness of expectation; one wouldn't have thought that there was a single living soul on her decks. A sudden brisk shout, "Mainsail haul!" broke the spell, and in the noisy cries and rush overhead of the men running away with the main-brace we two, down in my cabin, came together in our usual position by the bed-place.

He did not wait for my question. "I heard him fumbling here and just managed to squat myself down in the bath," he whispered to me. "The fellow only opened the door and put his arm in to hang the coat up. All the same—"

"I never thought of that," I whispered back, even more appalled than before at the closeness of the shave, and marvelling at that something unyielding in his character which was carrying him through so finely. There was no agitation in his whisper. Whoever was being driven distracted, it was not he. He was sane. And the proof of his sanity was continued when he took up the whispering again.

"It would never do for me to come to life again."

It was something that a ghost might have said. But what he was alluding to was his old captain's reluctant admission of the theory of suicide. It would obviously serve his turn—if I had understood at all the view which seemed to govern the unalterable purpose of his action.

"You must maroon me as soon as ever you can get amongst these islands off the Cambodge[5] shore," he went on.

"Maroon you! We are not living in a boy's adventure tale," I protested. His scornful whispering took me up.

"We aren't indeed! There's nothing of a boy's tale in this. But there's nothing else for it. I want no more. You don't suppose I am afraid of what can be done to me? Prison or gallows or whatever they may please. But you don't see me coming back to explain such things to an old fellow in a wig and twelve respectable tradesmen, do you? What can they know whether I am guilty or not—or of *what* I am guilty, either? That's my affair. What does the Bible say?[6] 'Driven off the face of the earth.' Very well. I am off the face of the earth now. As I came at night so I shall go."

"Impossible!" I murmured. "You can't."

"Can't? . . . Not naked like a soul on the Day of Judgment. I shall freeze on to this sleeping-suit. The Last Day is not yet—and . . . you have understood thoroughly. Didn't you?"

I felt suddenly ashamed of myself. I may say truly that I understood—and my hesitation in letting that man swim away from my ship's side had been a mere sham sentiment, a sort of cowardice.

"It can't be done now till next night," I breathed out. "The ship is on the off-shore tack and the wind may fail us."

"As long as I know that you understand," he whispered. "But of course you do. It's a great satisfaction to have got somebody to understand. You seem to have been there on purpose." And in the same whisper, as if we two whenever we talked had to say things to each other which were not fit for the world to hear, he added, "It's very wonderful."

---

[5]Cambodian.   [6]Of Cain (Genesis 4.14).

We remained side by side talking in our secret way—but sometimes silent or just exchanging a whispered word or two at long intervals. And as usual he stared through the port. A breath of wind came now and again into our faces. The ship might have been moored in dock, so gently and on an even keel she slipped through the water, that did not murmur even at our passage, shadowy and silent like a phantom sea.

At midnight I went on deck, and to my mate's great surprise put the ship round on the other tack. His terrible whiskers flitted round me in silent criticism. I certainly should not have done it if it had been only a question of getting out of that sleepy gulf as quickly as possible. I believe he told the second mate, who relieved him, that it was a great want of judgment. The other only yawned. That intolerable cub shuffled about so sleepily and lolled against the rails in such a slack, improper fashion that I came down on him sharply.

"Aren't you properly awake yet?"

"Yes, sir! I am awake."

"Well, then, be good enough to hold yourself as if you were. And keep a lookout. If there's any current we'll be closing with some islands before daylight."

The east side of the gulf is fringed with islands, some solitary, others in groups. On the blue background of the high coast they seem to float on silvery patches of calm water, arid and grey, or dark green and rounded like clumps of evergreen bushes, with the larger ones, a mile or two long, showing the outlines of ridges, ribs of grey rock under the dank mantle of matted leafage. Unknown to trade, to travel, almost to geography, the manner of life they harbour is an unsolved secret. There must be villages—settlements of fishermen at least—on the largest of them, and some communication with the world is probably kept up by native craft. But all that forenoon, as we headed for them, fanned along by the faintest of breezes, I saw no sign of man or canoe in the field of the telescope I kept on pointing at the scattered group.

At noon I gave no orders for a change of course, and the mate's whiskers became much concerned and seemed to be offering themselves unduly to my notice. At last I said:

"I am going to stand right in. Quite in—as far as I can take her."

The stare of extreme surprise imparted an air of ferocity also to his eyes, and he looked truly terrific for a moment.

"We're not doing well in the middle of the gulf," I continued, casually. "I am going to look for the land breezes to-night."

"Bless my soul! Do you mean, sir, in the dark amongst the lot of all them islands and reefs and shoals?"

"Well—if there are any regular land breezes at all on this coast one must get close inshore to find them, mustn't one?"

"Bless my soul!" he exclaimed again under his breath. All that afternoon he wore a dreamy, contemplative appearance which in him was a mark of perplexity. After dinner I went into my stateroom as if I meant to take some rest. There we two bent our dark heads over a half-unrolled chart lying on my bed.

"There," I said. "It's got to be Koh-ring. I've been looking at it ever since sunrise. It has got two hills and a low point. It must be inhabited. And on the coast opposite there is what looks like the mouth of a biggish river—with some town, no doubt, not far up. It's the best chance for you that I can see."

"Anything. Koh-ring let it be."

He looked thoughtfully at the chart as if surveying chances and distances from a lofty height—and following with his eyes his own figure wandering on the blank land of Cochin-China,[7] and then passing off that piece of paper clean out of sight into uncharted regions. And it was as if the ship had two captains to plan her course for her. I had been so worried and restless running up and down that I had not had the patience to dress that day. I had remained in my sleeping-suit, with straw slippers and a soft floppy hat. The closeness of the heat in the gulf had been most oppressive, and the crew were used to see me wandering in that airy attire.

"She will clear the south point as she heads now," I whispered into his ear. "Goodness only knows when, though, but certainly after dark. I'll edge her in to half a mile, as far as I may be able to judge in the dark—"

"Be careful," he murmured, warningly—and I realised suddenly that all my future, the only future for which I was fit, would perhaps go irretrievably to pieces in any mishap to my first command.

I could not stop a moment longer in the room. I motioned him to get out of sight and made my way on the poop. That unplayful cub had the watch. I walked up and down for a while thinking things out, then beckoned him over.

"Send a couple of hands to open the two quarter-deck ports," I said, mildly.

He actually had the impudence, or else so forgot himself in his wonder at such an incomprehensible order, as to repeat:

"Open the quarter-deck ports! What for, sir?"

"The only reason you need concern yourself about is because I tell you to do so. Have them opened wide and fastened properly."

He reddened and went off, but I believe made some jeering remark to the carpenter as to the sensible practice of ventilating a ship's quarter-deck. I know he popped into the mate's cabin to impart the fact to him because the whiskers came on deck, as it were by chance, and stole glances at me from below—for signs of lunacy or drunkenness, I suppose.

A little before supper, feeling more restless than ever, I rejoined, for a moment, my second self. And to find him sitting so quietly was surprising, like something against nature, inhuman.

I developed my plan in a hurried whisper.

"I shall stand in as close as I dare and then put her round. I will presently find means to smuggle you out of here into the sail-locker, which communicates with the lobby. But there is an opening, a sort of square for hauling the sails out, which gives straight on the quarter-deck and which is never closed in fine weather, so as to give air to the sails. When the ship's way is deadened in stays and all the hands are aft at the main-braces you will have a clear road to

[7]South Vietnam.

slip out and get overboard through the open quarter-deck port. I've had them both fastened up. Use a rope's end to lower yourself into the water so as to avoid a splash—you know. It could be heard and cause some beastly complication."

He kept silent for a while, then whispered, "I understand."

"I won't be there to see you go," I began with an effort. "The rest . . . I only hope I have understood, too."

"You have. From first to last"—and for the first time there seemed to be a faltering, something strained in his whisper. He caught hold of my arm, but the ringing of the supper bell made me start. He didn't though; he only released his grip.

After supper I didn't come below again till well past eight o'clock. The faint, steady breeze was loaded with dew; and the wet, darkened sails held all there was of propelling power in it. The night, clear and starry, sparkled darkly, and the opaque, lightless patches shifting slowly against the low stars were the drifting islets. On the port bow there was a big one more distant and shadowily imposing by the great space of sky it eclipsed.

On opening the door I had a back view of my very own self looking at a chart. He had come out of the recess and was standing near the table.

"Quite dark enough," I whispered.

He stepped back and leaned against my bed with a level, quiet glance. I sat on the couch. We had nothing to say to each other. Over our heads the officer of the watch moved here and there. Then I heard him move quickly. I knew what that meant. He was making for the companion; and presently his voice was outside my door.

"We are drawing in pretty fast, sir. Land looks rather close."

"Very well," I answered. "I am coming on deck directly."

I waited till he was gone out of the cuddy, then rose. My double moved too. The time had come to exchange our last whispers, for neither of us was ever to hear each other's natural voice.

"Look here!" I opened a drawer and took out three sovereigns. "Take this anyhow. I've got six and I'd give you the lot, only I must keep a little money to buy some fruit and vegetables for the crew from native boats as we go through Sunda Straits."

He shook his head.

"Take it," I urged him, whispering desperately. "No one can tell what—"

He smiled and slapped meaningly the only pocket of the sleeping-jacket. It was not safe, certainly. But I produced a large old silk handkerchief of mine, and tying the three pieces of gold in a corner, pressed it on him. He was touched, I suppose, because he took it at last and tied it quickly round his waist under the jacket, on his bare skin.

Our eyes met; several seconds elapsed, till, our glances still mingled, I extended my hand and turned the lamp out. Then I passed through the cuddy, leaving the door of my room wide open. . . . "Steward!"

He was still lingering in the pantry in the greatness of his zeal, giving a rub-up to a plated cruet stand the last thing before going to bed. Being careful not to wake up the mate, whose room was opposite, I spoke in an undertone.

He looked round anxiously. "Sir!"

"Can you get me a little hot water from the galley?"

"I am afraid, sir, the galley fire's been out for some time now."

"Go and see."

He flew up the stairs.

"Now," I whispered, loudly, into the saloon—too loudly, perhaps, but I was afraid I couldn't make a sound. He was by my side in an instant—the double captain slipped past the stairs—through a tiny dark passage . . . a sliding door. We were in the sail-locker, scrambling on our knees over the sails. A sudden thought struck me. I saw myself wandering barefooted, bareheaded, the sun beating on my dark poll. I snatched off my floppy hat and tried hurriedly in the dark to ram it on my other self. He dodged and fended off silently. I wonder what he thought had come to me before he understood and suddenly desisted. Our hands met gropingly, lingered united in a steady, motionless clasp for a second. . . . No word was breathed by either of us when they separated. I was standing quietly by the pantry door when the steward returned.

"Sorry, sir. Kettle barely warm. Shall I light the spirit-lamp?"

"Never mind."

I came out on deck slowly. It was now a matter of conscience to shave the land as close as possible—for now he must go overboard whenever the ship was put in stays. Must! There could be no going back for him. After a moment I walked over to leeward and my heart flew into my mouth at the nearness of the land on the bow. Under any other circumstances I would not have held on a minute longer. The second mate had followed me anxiously.

I looked on till I felt I could command my voice.

"She will weather," I said then in a quiet tone.

"Are you going to try that, sir?" he stammered out incredulously.

I took no notice of him and raised my tone just enough to be heard by the helmsman.

"Keep her good full."

"Good full, sir."

The wind fanned my cheek, the sails slept, the world was silent. The strain of watching the dark loom of the land grow bigger and denser was too much for me. I had shut my eyes—because the ship must go closer. She must! The stillness was intolerable. Were we standing still?

When I opened my eyes the second view started my heart with a thump. The black southern hill of Koh-ring seemed to hang right over the ship like a towering fragment of the everlasting night. On that enormous mass of blackness there was not a gleam to be seen, not a sound to be heard. It was gliding irresistibly towards us and yet seemed already within reach of the hand. I saw the vague figures of the watch grouped in the waist, gazing in awed silence.

"Are you going on, sir?" inquired an unsteady voice at my elbow.

I ignored it. I had to go on.

"Keep her full. Don't check her way. That won't do now," I said, warningly.

"I can't see the sails very well," the helmsman answered me, in strange, quavering tones.

Was she close enough? Already she was, I won't say in the shadow of the land, but in the very blackness of it, already swallowed up as it were, gone too close to be recalled, gone from me altogether.

"Give the mate a call," I said to the young man who stood at my elbow as still as death. "And turn all hands up."

My tone had a borrowed loudness reverberated from the height of the land. Several voices cried out together: "We are all on deck, sir."

Then stillness again, with the great shadow gliding closer, towering higher, without a light, without a sound. Such a hush had fallen on the ship that she might have been a bark of the dead floating in slowly under the very gate of Erebus.

"My God! Where are we?"

It was the mate moaning at my elbow. He was thunderstruck, and as it were deprived of the moral support of his whiskers. He clapped his hands and absolutely cried out, "Lost!"

"Be quiet," I said, sternly.

He lowered his tone, but I saw the shadowy gesture of his despair. "What are we doing here?"

"Looking for the land wind."

He made as if to tear his hair, and addressed me recklessly.

"She will never get out. You have done it, sir. I knew it'd end in something like this. She will never weather, and you are too close now to stay. She'll drift ashore before she's round. O my God!"

I caught his arm as he was raising it to batter his poor devoted head, and shook it violently.

"She's ashore already," he wailed, trying to tear himself away.

"Is she? . . . Keep good full there!"

"Good full, sir," cried the helmsman in a frightened, thin, child-like voice.

I hadn't let go the mate's arm and went on shaking it. "Ready about, do you hear? You go forward"—shake—"and stop there"—shake—"and hold your noise"—shake—"and see these head-sheets properly overhauled"—shake, shake —shake.

And all the time I dared not look towards the land lest my heart should fail me. I released my grip at last and he ran forward as if fleeing for dear life.

I wondered what my double there in the sail-locker thought of this commotion. He was able to hear everything—and perhaps he was able to understand why, on my conscience, it had to be thus close—no less. My first order "Hard alee!" re-echoed ominously under the towering shadow of Koh-ring as if I had shouted in a mountain gorge. And then I watched the land intently. In that smooth water and light wind it was impossible to feel the ship coming-to. No! I could not feel her. And my second self was making now ready to slip out and lower himself overboard. Perhaps he was gone already . . . .

The great black mass brooding over our very mast-heads began to pivot away from the ship's side silently. And now I forgot the secret stranger ready to depart, and remembered only that I was a total stranger to the ship. I did not know her. Would she do it? How was she to be handled?

I swung the mainyard and waited helplessly. She was perhaps stopped, and her very fate hung in the balance, with the black mass of Koh-ring like the gate of the everlasting night towering over her taffrail. What would she do now? Had she way on her yet? I stepped to the side swiftly, and on the shadowy water I could see nothing except a faint phosphorescent flash revealing the glassy smoothness of the sleeping surface. It was impossible to tell—and I had not learned yet the feel of my ship. Was she moving? What I needed was something easily seen, a piece of paper, which I could throw overboard and watch. I had nothing on me. To run down for it I didn't dare. There was no time. All at once my strained, yearning stare distinguished a white object floating within a yard of the ship's side. White on the black water. A phosphorescent flash passed under it. What was that thing? . . . I recognized my own floppy hat. It must have fallen off his head . . . and he didn't bother. Now I had what I wanted—the saving mark for my eyes. But I hardly thought of my other self, now gone from the ship, to be hidden for ever from all friendly faces, to be a fugitive and a vagabond on the earth, with no brand of the curse on his sane forehead to stay a slaying hand . . . too proud to explain.

And I watched the hat—the expression of my sudden pity for his mere flesh. It had been meant to save his homeless head from the dangers of the sun. And now—behold—it was saving the ship, by serving me for a mark to help out the ignorance of my strangeness. Ha! It was drifting forward, warning me just in time that the ship had gathered sternway.

"Shift the helm," I said in a low voice to the seaman standing still like a statue.

The man's eyes glistened wildly in the binnacle light as he jumped round to the other side and spun round the wheel.

I walked to the break of the poop. On the over-shadowed deck all hands stood by the forebraces waiting for my order. The stars ahead seemed to be gliding from right to left. And all was so still in the world that I heard the quiet remark, "She's round," passed in a tone of intense relief between two seamen.

"Let go and haul."

The foreyards ran round with a great noise, amidst cheery cries. And now the frightful whiskers made themselves heard giving various orders. Already the ship was drawing ahead. And I was alone with her. Nothing! no one in the world should stand now between us, throwing a shadow on the way of silent knowledge and mute affection, the perfect communion of a seaman with his first command.

Walking to the taffrail, I was in time to make out, on the very edge of a darkness thrown by a towering black mass like the very gateway of Erebus—yes, I was in time to catch an evanescent glimpse of my white hat left behind to mark the spot where the secret sharer of my cabin and of my thoughts, as though he were my second self, had lowered himself into the water to take his punishment: a free man, a proud swimmer striking out for a new destiny.

QUESTIONS

1. Does Conrad intend his title to mean "the hidden sharer" or "the sharer of secrets"? How do you know?
2. How does Conrad's first sentence set his theme about human boundaries and the mystery beyond?
3. What is the effect of "alone" in concluding the first paragraph? of "long journey" in beginning the second?
4. Conrad's young captain says that he was "the only stranger on board" and a stranger to his ship and himself. What does this suggest as to how the story will develop?
5. How is the chief mate's habit of accounting for everything significant?
6. The new captain, with a cigar in his teeth, comments to himself on the sea's "absolute straightforwardness . . . and singleness of purpose." In what way is this true? In what way ironic?
7. How does the swimmer's appearance affect the story?
8. What does Leggatt's name suggest?
9. How soon does the captain find a bond between him and Leggatt?
10. Why does Conrad put his captain and Leggatt in gray-striped "sleeping suits"?
11. What leads the captain to call Leggatt "my double" almost as soon as their conversation begins?
12. Check the diagram below against Conrad's description of the captain's cabin. Where in the story do we learn that the short part of the "L" is on the ship's starboard side?
13. What is significant in the way Leggatt, the parson's son, takes the "brand of Cain"? The doppelgänger psychology assumed a good rational consciousness and an evil irrational subconsciousness. How much of this theory is Conrad using?
14. Why does the *Sephora*'s captain say that only God could have set the foresail?
15. Is the captain's pretense of deafness necessary? What is the result?

Plan of Captain's Quarters

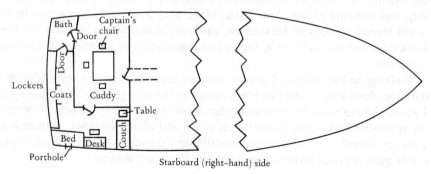

Starboard (right-hand) side

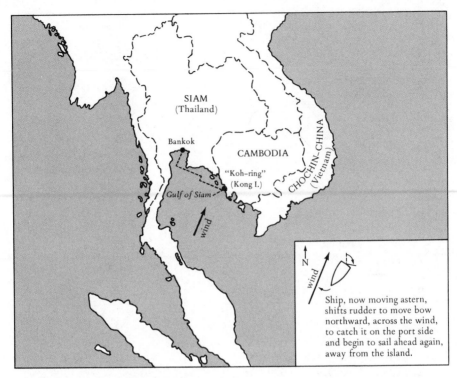

SIAM
(Thailand)

Bankok

CAMBODIA

CHOCHIN-CHINA
(Vietnam)

"Koh–ring"
(Kong I.)

Gulf of Siam

wind

N

wind

Ship, now moving astern,
shifts rudder to move bow
northward, across the wind,
to catch it on the port side
and begin to sail ahead again,
away from the island.

16. What attitude does the *Sephora*'s captain have toward Leggatt? Why? What is his attitude toward the protagonist-captain and its results?

17. Why does the protagonist feel unable "for psychological (not moral) reasons" to lie directly about Leggatt, if asked?

18. Why does the captain feel "less torn in two" when with Leggatt?

19. Why does the captain feel that the "very trust in Providence" was denied Leggatt and him? How about Leggatt's "You seem to have been there on purpose" four pages later?

20. What effect does the secret sharer have on the captain's ability to sail his ship?

21. What is the significance of the captain's giving Leggatt his floppy hat? How does it function to save the ship and the captain's career? The diagram at the top of the page shows how well Conrad, the experienced sailor, has worked out the physical details.

22. What is the significance of "a bark of the dead floating in slowly under the very gate of Erebus," "My God! Where are we?" and "Lost!"?

23. Why do the stars seem to be gliding from right to left?

24. What is the psychological significance of Leggatt's separating from the captain? How do their personalities differ?

25. What does the ship symbolize?

POETRY

ON POETRY

SOUND

A poet has to accept the language given at birth, so we have first to ask what the peculiar strengths and difficulties of the English language are as a medium of poetry. First, it is a heavily accented language (French critics speak of "the British thump"); second, it has a high proportion of consonants to vowels; third, most of the words in common use, including most of the words of native English origin, are monosyllables or near monosyllables; and fourth, it has very few inflections. There are other characteristics that will emerge in the more specific commentaries, but these will do to go on with. All four, of course, are closely interconnected.

Every monosyllable has a separate accent, however slight, and because the English language is so heavily accented, and so full of consonants as well, the effect is like that of riding a bucking and plunging horse that is capable of great speed and power if brought under control or of merely running away with its rider if not. Partly because of the lack of inflections, English is very full of such phrases as "the house," "by him," "when I," "of love," "to be," and the like. These phrases are iambic (short-long) in rhythm, and help to make iambic the normal meter for English poetry:

> When I consider how my light is spent (Milton: "On His Blindness").
> And I with thee will choose to live (Milton: "Il Penseroso").

The first line quoted is iambic pentameter, or five iambic feet; the second iambic tetrameter, or four feet. The iambic pentameter has been the backbone of English poetry from Chaucer to our own day, but tetrameters or octosyllabics are used a good deal too, especially when high speed is wanted. Longer lines than the pentameter are seldom used for long poems, because in English the rhythm is apt to get clattery and turn into doggerel when there are too many beats in a line, especially if rhyme is added. In fact, anything unusual that a poet does to rhythm or rhyme in English is likely to sound obtrusive, to call more attention to itself than would normally be wanted. So such unusual features, when we find them in competent poets, are being used for special effects.

At the beginning of *Paradise Lost,* Milton describes the expelling of Satan from heaven thus:

Hurled headlong flaming from the ethereal sky.

The rhythm of "headlong flaming" is trochaic (long-short), because the trochaic is a "falling" rhythm and is also a more energetic rhythm in English than the more usual iambic. We notice too that the use of a long word ("ethereal") makes the rhythm lighter because, with the heavy accent in English, a long word brings in a ripple of unaccented syllables. This principle, that the longer words in English (mostly borrowed from Greek or Latin) lighten the rhythm because of their lightly stressed syllables, meets us everywhere: in Cummings' "O sweet spontaneous earth," in Wordsworth's "From low to high doth dissolution climb," in Whitman's "A reminiscence sing," and so on.

Special effect poems in unusual rhythms include Tennyson's "Charge of the Light Brigade," where the prevailing rhythm is dactylic (long-short-short), because the theme is a cavalry charge. In this passage from Swinburne's "Atalanta in Calydon" an anapestic rhythm (short-short-long) mingles with the iambic one, and goes with the sense of bursting energy that the poem celebrates:

When the hounds of spring are on winter's traces,
  The mother of months in meadow or plain
Fills the shadows and windy places
  With lisp of leaves and ripple of rain.

In the second and fourth lines there is also a heavy alliteration (beginning with the same letter) in the texture; this again is there to mark the driving power of emerging life in the spring.

The same principles apply to rhyme. Most rhymes are very resonant in English, and even the simplest double rhymes, like the "traces-places" rhyme above, are generally used rather sparingly. Triple rhymes usually belong to light verse, as in Byron's

But O! ye lords of ladies intellectual,
Inform us truly: have they not henpecked you all?

where the poet is writing deliberate or intentional doggerel. In Hopkins' sonnet, "That Nature is a Heraclitean Fire," we find such rhymes as "resurrection-dejection-deck shone." Here again what would be in other contexts doggerel rhymes are being used for a special reason: they go with the complex and syncopated rhythm of the poem.

Poetry is language used with the greatest possible intensity, and one obvious way in which it can express intensity is in its movement and sound. Poetry is never very far from dancing and singing or from other energetic actions like marching and horseback riding, and, as already suggested, English is an excellent vehicle for high speeds. Thus Edith Sitwell:

> Nobody comes to give him his rum but the
> Rim of the sky hippopotamus-glum
> Enhances the chances to bless with a benison
> Alfred Lord Tennyson crossing the bar laid . . .

Here the movement is so fast that it drags the meaning along after it: there is a meaning, and the words will eventually make some sense, but the meaning can wait. Here we are in the world of the nursery rhyme, where the bouncing rhythm is what carries the poem. We may notice two things in particular. First, a very emphatic rhyme scheme cuts across the arrangement of the lines, which gives a syncopated rhythm suggesting the jazz rhythms popular in the 1920s, which the poem is in part imitating. Second, while there is a rolling dactylic meter, there are also four main beats or accents to the line.

This four-beat line is the most primitive measure in English; it is the rhythm of Old English poetry, where as a rule the first three beats alliterate to increase the emphasis, as in the adaptation of the Old English poem "The Seafarer" by Ezra Pound:

> Chill its chains are; chafing sighs
> Hew my heart round and hunger begot
> Mere-weary mood. Lest man know not . . .

It is also the rhythm of most nursery rhymes and most ballads. The ballad is often in a four-lined stanza with four and three accents alternating (or, counting by syllables, eight-six-eight-six, the "common meter" of hymnbooks). This is really a continuous four-beat line with a rest at the end of every other line. Thus in "Sir Patrick Spens":

> The kíng síts in Dumferling tówn,
> Drínking the bloód-red wíne: (rest)
> "O whére will Í get goód sailór
> To sáil this shíp of miné?" (rest).

Originally the ballad (from the Latin *ballare,* to dance; cf. "ball") had a background of dancing as well as singing, and for dancing one needs a continuous rhythm.

After English poetry adopted meters in the Middle Ages, the old four-beat rhythm could still be heard as a secondary rhythm syncopating against it. If we look at Hamlet's famous "to be or not to be" soliloquy on the page, we see iambic pentameter lines; but if we listen to an actor speaking the lines on a stage, we also hear something like this:

> To BE or NOT to be, THAT is the QUEStion:
> WHEther 'tis NOBler in the MIND to SUFfer
> The SLINGS and ARrows of outRAGEous FORtune,
> Or to TAKE ARMS against a SEA of TROUBles . . .

The conflict of the two rhythms against each other, in Shakespeare as elsewhere, is largely what provides the subtlety and complexity of what we hear. In a high-speed poem like Browning's "How They Brought the Good News from Ghent to Aix," the speed comes from both the anapestic meter and the heavy accent of the four main beats:

> I sprang to the stirrup, and Joris, and he;
> I galloped, Dirck galloped, we galloped all three;
> "Good speed!" cried the watch, as the gatebolts undrew;
> "Speed!" echoed the wall to us galloping through . . .

But of course poetry has to have its andante and adagio movements as well. In the stopped couplets of Dryden or Pope, the iambic pentameter takes charge, and the four beats we heard in Hamlet's soliloquy fade into the background:

> Tim'rous by nature, of the Rich in awe,
> I come to Counsel learned in the Law:
> You'll give me, like a friend both sage and free,
> Advice; and (as you use) without a Fee.

We can still hear the four main stresses, but a strict meter and rhyme scheme controls them. If such verse as this (from Pope's "Imitation of the First Satire of the Second Book of Horace") is read aloud to us, we have a sense of constantly fulfilled expectation. If we hear the line "You'll give me, like a friend both sage and free," we don't know what the next line will be, but we do know that it will be an impeccable iambic pentameter, with the last word a perfect rhyme to "free." Such strict meter and rhyme give the effect of *wit,* of high intelligence in full control of its material. Similarly with E. A. Robinson's "Richard Cory":

> So on we worked, and waited for the light,
>   And went without the meat, and cursed the bread;
> And Richard Cory, one calm summer night,
>   Went home and put a bullet through his head.

The punch line is surprising, but, once we have had the surprise, inevitable. Such a combination of relaxed easy movement and deadly accuracy would be impossible without the firmly established meter and rhyme.

The capacity of English for high speed also has something to do with the fact that, because it has so few inflections, it depends on a fixed word order. If we hear someone say at a station, "When does go this train?" there is no disturbance of logical order, but we know that the speaker's native language is not English. The skeleton of word order is the sequence subject-predicate-object, as in "John loves Mary," where *John* is the subject, *loves* the predicate, and *Mary* the object. "Mary loves John" is clearly a different statement, and "John Mary loves" means nothing because it could mean both. In Latin we would normally say "Johannes Mariam amat," but we could rearrange the words in any order, because the *m* on the word *Mariam* shows that that is the object whatever the order. Latin verse often seems to the student who is accustomed to the unvarying linear drive of English from subject through predicate to object like a very tangled ball of yarn. In Gray's "Elegy Written in a Country Churchyard" we read:

> The boast of heraldry, the pomp of power,
>   And all that beauty, all that wealth e'er gave,
> Awaits alike th' inevitable hour . . .

Here the *s* on "awaits" shows that "hour" is the subject and the first two lines the object. It is very unusual to alter the word order in this way, but in such a slow and meditative movement it is perhaps appropriate sometimes to pause and rearrange our impressions of the words.

In still slower movements we become more aware of such features of English as its clusters of consonants. In the passage given in this book from Pope's "Essay on Criticism," Pope gives examples of how to vary the speed and rhythm to fit the subject being talked about, and says:

> When Ajax strives some rock's vast weight to throw,
> The line too labours, and the words move slow.

What makes the first line laborious is the number of consonants we have to stop and spit out before we can go on to the next word. If we are to read poetry with an ear as sharp as Pope's, we have to be conscious of every sound. If we try to introduce "ghost story," "wasp's nest," or "priest's stole" into ordinary conversation, we soon realize how much eliding, or cutting out of consonants, we do; but we cannot read poetry in this way. Thus in Ben Jonson's little song beginning:

> Slow, slow, fresh fount, keep time with my salt tears

there are two *t*'s in "salt tears," not one, and getting them both out will bring us down to the speed Jonson wants.

The same song goes on:

> Droop, herbs and flowers,
> Fall, grief, in showers;

Here we come back to something noted earlier: that monosyllables have separate accents and thus slow down the rhythm. In a passage just before the one quoted from Pope's "Essay on Criticism," Pope gives horrible examples of bad ways to write and cautions against an overuse of monosyllables with this one:

> And ten low words oft creep in one dull line.

The trouble with this line is not the ten monosyllables but the ten heavy stressed accents: such a line has no rhythm at all. So when Milton is describing the scenery of hell, he says:

> Rocks, caves, lakes, fens, bogs, dens, and shades of death
>
> *(Paradise Lost,* Book 2, 621)

Both the rhythm and the harsh discordant inner rhyme "fens-dens" tell our ears that the scenery of hell is not attractive.

Monosyllables, however, are very useful to a skillful poet. Even in an unobtrusive line like Shakespeare's "When icicles hang by the wall," we should notice how the lively anapestic meter can still "hang" the icicle for a suspended instant. Or, again, placing two heavy accents, usually monosyllables, together in the middle of a line (called a spondee), can often give the effect of something ominous or foreboding, as in a wonderful little poem written by Sir Thomas Wyatt at the beginning of the sixteenth century:

> Perchaunce thee lie withered and old
> These winter nights that are so cold,
> Plaining in vain unto the moon:
> Thy wishes then dare not be told.

On the other hand, the absence of inflectional endings means that English can seldom manage the gentle caressing rhythm that we find so often in, say, German lyrics. In the Middle English that Chaucer used there were still a large number of such endings, and modern English can seldom match the lightness of such lines in Chaucer as

> And trewèly to tellen attè lastè.

or

> And whan we weren esèd attè bestè.

Writing lyrics in English is like carving in oak: it can be done all right, but we need to allow for the toughness of the medium. In Housman's *A Shropshire Lad* we have:

With rue my heart is laden
  For golden friends I had,
For many a rose-lipt maiden
  And many a lightfoot lad.

The delicate charm needed is skillfully brought out, but the curiously old-fashioned words used show that the poet is not finding it easy.

So far we have dealt with poetry that is also verse, that is, has certain features like a regularly recurring rhythm that can be identified. But we can have verse that is not acceptable as poetry, or what we usually call doggerel, and we can have poetry in "free verse," with none of these specific features. If we look at, say, Whitman's "Dalliance of the Eagles," we can see that the furious gyrating and twisting movement is just as effective without a metrical framework. In other free verse, such as we have in William Carlos Williams, we can see what makes it "poetry" if we look at what the arrangement of lines on the page does to our reading of it. There is no continuous linear movement through the syntax of one sentence after another, as in prose; the rhythm keeps returning on itself, driving towards its own center, forcing us to grasp the total meaning of the words.

MEANING

We said a moment ago that poetry is language used with the greatest possible intensity, and this means, first of all, that in reading poetry we have to step up the intensity of our reading, beginning with the movements and sounds. In prose, or more specifically nonliterary prose, there is a low-keyed intensity, because the words are being used to describe something else. In poetry the words exist for their own sake, and the primary relation of each word, including nouns and verbs, is to the other words, not to the things or actions they describe. In this world, surrounded as we are with such masses of verbiage, mostly passing for prose, we get feelings of panic about the amount of material we have to "cover." We have to start reading poetry by dismissing this panic. Reading poetry is a technique of meditation; we must keep reading and rereading the same poem for quite a while before its real intensity will emerge.

When it does, we can begin to see that poetry is *figured* speech, made up of patterns of words that bring things together in ways that would be quite impossible if the writer were trying to describe something in experience. The most frequent figures are metaphor (this is that), simile (this is like that), and metonymy (this is put for that). We have metaphor in Shakespeare's:

Thou that art now the world's fresh ornament,
  And only herald of the gaudy spring.

We have simile in T. S. Eliot's:

> When the evening is spread out against the sky
> Like a patient etherized upon a table.

We have metonymy in Dylan Thomas's:

> The force that through the green fuse drives the flower.

These figures are not decorative or ornamental; they are modes of thinking. A great poet is a great thinker too, but rather than thinking conceptually or in ideas like a philosopher, the poet thinks in images, and sets these images beside one another or on top of each other, leaving it to us to make the connections. We said that the metaphor usually takes the form "this is that," but Ezra Pound says that real metaphor just puts things together, as in his little two-line poem "In a Station of the Metro":

> The apparition of these faces in the crowd,
> Petals on a wet, black bough.

We may feel that this is not good grammar, and that we need some predicate in between, such as "is," "is like," "reminds me of," "suggests to me," "is linked in my mind with," or whatever; but it is clear that as soon as we have put one down we have ruined the poem. Similarly:

> O Western wind, when wilt thou blow,
> The small rain down can rain?
> Christ, if my love were in my arms,
> And I in my bed again!

Here the juxtaposing of uncomfortable weather and comfortable bed is easier to follow; it is not a logical connection, but an emotional connection of a kind we have all had in some form or other. The important thing is that the poem simply presents the two images: it does not talk about them, still less about the relation between them.

Thinking in metaphor, simile, and metonymy is in some ways a primitive way of thinking; it has no relation to telling the "truth" as we usually understand truth, where we put a body of words up against something it's supposed to describe and say it's "true" if it's an adequate counterpart of that something. It's because of the primitive nature of poetic thinking that all literatures, in all human societies, begin with poetry; prose develops only much later. But while it's primitive it's also extremely concentrated. Suppose I were writing an essay about eighteenth-century England and were trying to explain how the common-sense philosophy of John Locke helped to establish the cultural climate out of which the Industrial Revolution emerged. This revolution brought in new inventions, like the spinning jenny, but also other things like mass migrations, exploitation, and imperialism, which had very little to do with common sense. As I keep writing, it may occur to me that there is a grotesque analogy here with the Biblical story of the fall of man, with Adam so well adjusted to this world until, with the creation of Eve from his body, another person, and consequently a human community, a wholly unexpected complication, emerged in which he lost that world. But the more I labor at this analogy, the more strained and unconvincing it would get; my readers couldn't follow it, and I would finally have to cut it; one can't do this kind of thing in prose. Yeats, in poetry, can say it all in twenty syllables or so:

> Locke sank into a swoon,
> The garden died:
> God took the spinning-jenny
> Out of his side.

Or, again, Hopkins writes of the instability of all things, and of how, for him, the resurrection of Christ establishes something permanent and solid in the middle of it. He ends:

> This Jack, joke, poor potsherd, patch, matchwood, immortal diamond . . .

Heraclitus said that everything was in a state of flux, a constant flowing or burning, so that one very central image of his pessimistic philosophy (he was called the weeping philosopher) would be a burnt match. If we held the opposite view, that there was something in reality that did not disintegrate, about the best image we could use would be a diamond, the hardest known substance and as precious as the match is the opposite. Yet both match and diamond are made of the same substance, namely carbon, just as the physical body of man ("potsherd" because it's compared in the Bible to a potter's vessel) is of the same substance as the spiritual body that enters the resurrection. Hopkins wrote the poem out of a profound belief in the resurrection. We don't have to share the belief to respond to the poem, but we do have to see that the belief is imaginatively possible.

The greater intensity of poetry as compared with prose, we said, is partly a greater intensity of sound: that is why rhyme, alliteration, pun, and assonance (similarity of sound) belong to it. Such resemblances of sound are accidents in a language until a poet uses them; then they become elements of design. Here we have "jack-joke," "patch-match," diamond as gem and diamond as suit in a pack of cards. The "jack" in cards, also called knave or valet (servant), suggests man in his ordinary state, of no use except as a servant of God and usually unreliable as that. When Pope describes a card game in his long mock-epic "The Rape of the Lock," he says

> The Knave of Diamonds tries his wily arts,

indicating that this particular card has a shifty reputation in card lore. The sound link between jack and joke turns up another card, the joker or fool (the fool was often called "patch" in Shakespeare's day). In the background, not in the poem, but within its range of allusions, is the contrast between ordinary humanity, weak and suggestible, and Christ the invincible: Paul calls them the first and second Adam. The Greek word *adamas,* unconquerable, is the origin of our word diamond.

Poetry, we see, can be endlessly allusive. If you try to write poetry, you will soon find that the kind of poetry you produce will depend entirely on what kind of poetry you have read and will be full of echoes of it. You may be expressing your ideas or emotions, but you can never express them directly; they must go inside some poetic structure, or what is called a convention. Young poets usually gather in groups and write like each other, but as they get older they strike their individual roots into literature and learn more and more from the poets of the past. But the notion that they can write outside the framework of the literary tradition itself is pure illusion, and all great poets gave it up long before they became great poets. When Yeats tells, for the thousandth time in poetry, the classical myth of Leda and the swan and says

> A shudder in the loins engenders there
> The broken wall, the burning roof and tower
> And Agamemnon dead

he is indirectly telling us that, because Homer wrote about the Trojan War at the beginning of our literary tradition, that is the most important war for readers of poetry to know about, and the word "Agamemnon" can fall on our ears with a resonant crash that no less familiar name can match. True, Whitman urged his Muse to "migrate from Greece and Ionia" on the ground that we had heard enough about the Trojan War, and come to "a better, fresher, busier sphere" in the United States. But fortunately, Whitman's real Muse made him write like a poet and ignored his advertising copy. The *content* of poetry constantly changes, but its inner structure does not, just as a new baby is always a different individual but never constitutes a different species.

The allusiveness of poetry is a by-product of the fact that the study of literature is as coherent and systematic as the study of any other subject. Just as every genuine discovery in science is true because it is consistent with other genuine discoveries, so every great work of the imagination is imaginatively consistent with other works in the same medium. Even so, this allusiveness in poetry may put some of us off. Why, we may say, should we have to look up so many references? OK, they may be part of our cultural heritage, and it may be very interesting to see how classical and biblical stories and echoes from earlier poets are used in poetry, but, with so complicated a world facing us in this century, is it really worth so much time and effort to learn a special elitist language?

Some poets are explicitly allusive, like Milton, or like Eliot or Yeats in our day. They make us look things up and consult footnotes, and we find ourselves rapidly getting an education in comparative mythology, religion, and literature. Others, like Wordsworth or Robert Frost, keep their language as free of special reference as they can, and they are the ones who may give us a clue to the question we're looking at. We notice that some poems—we might call them emblematic poems—set up a single central image and stare hard at it, as, to take random examples, Blake does with his tiger and worm-eaten rose, W. C. Williams with his red wheelbarrow, or Whitman with his live-oaks in Louisiana. Sometimes the poet tells us that the image is the distilled essence of an intense experience, as Rossetti does in "The Woodspurge." The poet doesn't use these images as a pretext for talking about something else, as is done in certain kinds of allegory, where the "real" meaning is something different. If we look at Robert Frost's poem, "Stopping by Woods on a Snowy Evening," long enough and hard enough, we begin to see that it is collecting a great variety of experiences into that single, solemn, hushed moment. But we can't say, for instance, "the poem is really about death," because it is, just as really, about stopping by woods on a snowy evening. It's as though the central image of the poem had been placed in a reverberating sound chamber and were expressing some kind of infinite resonance in its very concrete and specific theme.

Explicitly allusive poems, then, like Milton's "Lycidas" or Eliot's "Prufrock," create a resonance by their allusions against everything else we've read in literature, as well as an infinite amount that we haven't. (This goes for poets too, who haven't read the poems written after their death that echo them, and that they echo by anticipation.) Such poems tell us that the whole world of literature is one gigantic imaginative body and that studying literature is entering into that body of human imaginative experience, not just reading one thing after another. But implicit allusion, like that of Frost's poem, raises an even bigger question.

Wallace Stevens has a poem called "Description Without Place," a long and very difficult poem, which says that we do not live directly in the world of nature, like animals and plants—we live within our own constructs of the world. These constructs, in their totality, are what we call cultures or civilizations. They are what, as Stevens says, make everything that we see in Spain look Spanish. A great deal of these constructs consists of words, and at the center of it all is the body of words we call poetry. Because the metaphors and images and analogies of poetry are what tell us most clearly that we cannot see or understand or act or feel except from within the human construct that we entered at birth. Nature knows nothing of up or down, of inside or outside, of beginning or ending, of before and not yet. All these are notions we impose on nature. It is the poets who keep reducing our experience to these simple and essential things, and they who lead us to the engine room of creation, the energy and intensity of the constructing process itself.

CHAPTER 1

TYPES OF POEMS

LYRIC

Think of a lyre. It is a stringed instrument, a small harp. The poet knows how to play a bit, and is trying to find the sounds to suit an emotional state. He or she hums an accompaniment, seeking a rhythm and melody, and begins to find words that can express feelings even better than musical notes. As the words become more interesting, the music becomes secondary to the discovery of a poem. Perhaps the lyre is laid aside in favor of the rhythm of the language and the subtly musical variations of the words.

The poet is a lyrist, or lyricist. The poem is a lyric, probably the most ancient form of poetic composition. Its creator may have lived in ancient Greece, or Anglo-Saxon England, or the Australian Bush of the early twentieth century—or may live today in an apartment in Toronto, a condominium in Ann Arbor, a tract house in Phoenix, or a farmhouse outside of Fargo. The poetic impulse knows no limits in time or space. The maker of lyrics attempts to express deep-seated personal feelings, trying the words and rhythms one way, then another, and so again and again. The process may be easy, or it may take weeks or years. Between times the poet goes about other business. Somewhere along the way the maker recites the poem to a friend or prints it on a sheet or in a book. If it is good enough—if enough people like it—it becomes a part of the shared artistic heritage of humanity and finds renewed expression down the years in the throats and minds of countless people who never knew the maker. Consider the following lyric:

Western wind, when wilt thou blow,
The small rain down can rain?

432

Christ, if my love were in my arms,
And I in my bed again! 4

The poem comes from England in the fifteenth century. As with many fine lyrics, nobody knows now who wrote it, but it has delighted numerous readers and listeners. Read it several times, trying to recapture the feeling of the person who made it. What is there in these few words that so many since have admired? Start simply with the pleasure in the reading. Find some delight in the way the words move in your throat or sound in your mind. Try to imagine yourself the maker. The poem is your poem. What are you trying to say? What do you like best about the way you have said it?

Perhaps this particular poem holds no delight for you. Perhaps you can make no sense of it at all. If so, your case is not unusual, and not without remedy. Not all poems are for all people, any more than all paintings are, or all music or all movies or all automobiles. Leave this poem and go on to another. You may want to return to this one later. Perhaps you will see it differently after you have read some others that you find more immediately appealing. Perhaps others who have admired this poem are in some way wrong about it, but if your mind is inquisitive you will want to return to it from time to time to discover whether you can yet see it as they do.

Meanwhile, try this one:

Waly, Waly, Love Be Bonny

O waly,[1] waly, up the bank,
  And waly, waly, down the brae,[2]
And waly, waly, yon burn[3] side,
  Where I and my love were wont to gae.[4] 4

I leant my back upon an oak,
  I thought it was a trusty tree;
But first it bent, and then it broke,
  Just as my love proved false to me. 8

O waly, waly, love is bonny,
  A little while when it is new;
But when it's old, it waxes cold,
  And fades away like morning dew. 12

O wherefore should I busk[5] my head?
  O wherefore should I comb my hair?
For my true love has me forsook,
  And says he'll never love me more. 16

Now Arthur's Seat[6] shall be my bed,
  The sheets shall ne'er be filled by me:

[1]Woefully. [2]Steep bank. [3]Brook. [4]Go. [5]Dress. [6]A hill outside Edinburgh.

Saint Anthony's well[7] shall be my drink,
  Since my true love has forsaken me.   **20**

Martinmas[8] wind, when wilt thou blow,
  And shake the green leaves off the tree?
O gentle death, when wilt thou come?
  For of my life I am weary.   **24**

'Tis not the frost, that freezes fell,[9]
  Nor blowing snow's inclemency;
'Tis not such cold that makes me cry,
  But my love's heart grown cold to me.   **28**

When we came in by Glasgow town,
  We were a comely sight to see,
My love was clad in black velvet,
  And I myself in cramasie.[10]   **32**

But had I wist,[11] before I kissed,
  That love had been so ill to win,
I'd locked my heart in a case of gold,
  And pinned it with a silver pin.   **36**

And oh! if my young babe were born,
  And set upon the nurse's knee,
And I my self were dead and gone:
  For a maid again I'll never be.   **40**

---

[7]Near Arthur's Seat.   [8]Feast of St. Martin, November 11.   [9]Cruelly.   [10]Crimson.   [11]Known.

"Waly, Waly" is another old poem, longer than "Western Wind," and, depending upon a number of matters peculiar to you as an individual, perhaps more immediately attractive or more puzzling still. Like "Western Wind" it is anonymous, its author no longer known. We can assume that it was already old in the eighteenth century when it was first printed. It has experienced a large part of its popularity as a folk song, being passed down orally in singing families and communities until well into the twentieth century. In the form in which we have printed it (we have modernized some of the lines), it is obviously Scottish, but in other versions it loses its evidence of that particular locality and becomes localized elsewhere, or nowhere. In other versions, it loses some stanzas or picks up others.

You have probably already noticed that the sixth stanza contains some haunting echoes of "Western Wind." Did this poet know the other poem? Perhaps, but, if not, the poet at least seems familiar with the same ways of thinking, aware of the same poetic conventions, attuned to the same rhythms. Here is an interesting point: Poems reflect upon one another. The more we read, the more easily we understand and enjoy them, having accumulated the means to compare each new poem intelligently with a large number of others.

Does the sixth stanza here reflect any light upon the single stanza of "Western Wind"? What is the poet trying to convey? It seems clear that the speaker, weary of life, is asking for death. But what has that to do with "Martinmas wind" and with shaking the leaves off the tree? A dictionary will tell us that Martinmas comes each year on November 11. A wind on that day would blow the leaves off the trees that are soon going to lose them anyway, because winter is coming. The speaker seems to be asking for winter to come more quickly and seems to be associating winter with death. This is not a difficult or unusual association. We can easily imagine moods that might find expression in these words. We write the words, try them different ways, set them to music, and find we are pleased. We have written a lyric.

Let us return briefly to "Western Wind." The similarities in the lines suggest similar things happening in the poem. If the Martinmas wind that shakes the leaves from the trees is a harbinger of winter, is the western wind that brings small rain also suggesting a season? What season? We might put ourselves in the poet's place and try to understand the emotion he or she desires to convey. The poet didn't say "north wind" or "east wind," for those winds would presumably not express the proper feeling. Not "south wind" either. Each of those winds would bring a different kind of weather. If you live in the country almost anywhere in North America and are observant of natural phenomena, or if you are a meteorologist, you have noticed yourself what this English poet had observed centuries ago in the similar weather patterns of England. The west wind brings the light rains ("the small rain") of spring. "April showers bring May flowers." The poet wants the spring because spring will bring a reunion with a loved one. Have they been separated in some way that will end in the spring, or is the poet merely playing upon the natural association of spring and love? The poem doesn't say.

The poem "Waly, Waly" covers more ground. In this poem the speaker wants not love, but death. The poem asks not for spring, but winter. Why? The other stanzas help to fill in the story. Although not all of its details are clear, we know enough to summarize the outline.

By the end of the fourth stanza, we have discovered that the speaker is a woman and by the end of the final stanza we know why she wants to die. We also know why she looks forward to a later rather than immediate death. She respects the life of her unborn child. She wants to see it safely cared for. And then she asks for relief from her shame and sorrow. We have called this a lyric rather than a narrative poem, yet it is also a narrative, a story in small, dramatic scope. Every lyric, indeed, is a brief dramatic statement from some larger life's story at which we can only guess from the emotions expressed and the details given.

If we consider "Waly, Waly" from another perspective, we will notice that some stanzas contribute nothing to the story but express the speaker's emotion in different ways, as if she were trying one way of making poetry out of her

feelings and then another. With this hint and that, obliquely she circles round
the situation, each time adding to, or qualifying, our understanding of her emotions. Obviously if we want greater compression or want to stick more closely
to the story, we can leave out some of the stanzas. This is exactly what some
versions of "Waly, Waly" do. Just as obviously, if we wish to dwell upon the
emotion or clarify the story we can add another stanza or two. Such changes
are part of the folk process. In some songs related to this one, for example, the
stanza about the oak is coupled with one about a rose:

> I put my finger to the bush
>   To pluck a rose of fairest kind;
> The thorn it pricked me at a touch,
>   And O, I left that rose behind.

This stanza does not appear in the version of "Waly, Waly" we have used. If
you were a poet, would you put it in or leave it out? What would you gain or
lose? We must balance fullness of statement against the power of compression.
Our opinions may differ. The extreme compression of "Western Wind," for
instance, may be either an advantage or a disadvantage. Some people believe
it a fragment of a lost folk song.

Here is another anonymous Scottish song.

The Bonny Earl of Murray*

> Ye highlands and ye lowlands,
>   Oh! where have ye been?
> They have slain the Earl of Murray,
>   And have laid him on the green.   4
>
> Now woe be to thee, Huntley!
>   And wherefore did ye so?
> I bade you bring him with you,
>   But forbade you him to slay.   8
>
> He was a braw¹ gallant,
>   And he rode at the ring;
> And the bonny Earl of Murray,
>   Oh! he might have been a king.   12
>
> He was a braw gallant,
>   And he played at the ball;
> And the bonny Earl of Murray
>   Was the flower among them all.   16

*Francis J. Child, *English and Scottish Popular Ballads,* 181A. We have normalized the spelling.

¹Brave.

He was a braw gallant,
  And he played at the glove;
And the bonny Earl of Murray,
  Oh! he was the Queen's love.   20

Oh! long will his lady
  Look o'er the Castle Downe,[2]
Ere she see the Earl of Murray
  Come sounding through the town.   24

[2]Doune Castle, belonging to the Earl of Murray (or Moray).

Like "Waly, Waly" the poem has obviously a story lying behind it, but the poet seems less concerned with telling the story than with communicating his feelings about it. We can, if we wish, look up the details, for the story is based in historical fact. The "Bonny Earl of Murray" died mysteriously at Donibristle on February 7, 1592. But myriads of people have found this folk song attractive without knowing the history. We can do the same. We can see that a man named Huntley has killed the Earl of Murray. We can see that the Earl was admired for his athletic prowess and that he was loved by the queen (was Huntley jealous?). We can see that the Earl might, in time, have been a king. This is all we learn, but probably all we need to know.

But who is the anonymous speaker and exactly what emotion is he or she trying to express? In "Western Wind" and "Waly, Waly," the speaker was the center of events as far as we could see into them: the person in love, the girl betrayed. Is this speaker someone close to the Earl of Murray, perhaps a friend or relation? Not according to anything we can be sure of in the poem. The poet appears to have been a person in command, though the orders not to slay the Earl were disobeyed. From a position of authority, the poet speaks to all Scots ("Ye highlands and ye lowlands") and implies that all are involved in the guilt ("Oh! where have ye been?") and now share the sense of loss. The poet seems, in short, to address the poem to a country mourning a national hero. He or she wants to remind people of a promise now lost for the whole nation ("he might have been a king"). The poet wants also to remind them of the personal dimensions of a national tragedy:

Oh! long will his lady
  Look o'er the Castle Downe,
Ere she see the Earl of Murray
  Come sounding through the town.

We do not need to live in Scotland in the sixteenth century to appreciate these emotions.

Let us change the mood. Lyrics, as we are beginning to see, appear often to be one form or another of lamentation. The poet, in solitude, desires something he or she does not have or wishes to undo something now past correction. Human emotions in solitude often take just that turn. But other emotions are possible. Lyrics can celebrate the poet's entire satisfaction with the current state of affairs, or they can suggest, as the next one does, that even if something has been lost, not everything has. There are more fish than one in the sea. Or, in the language of "The Brazos River," there are more rivers than one in Texas.

The Brazos River*

We crossed the broad Pecos, we forded the Nueces,
We swum the Guadalupe, we followed the Brazos,
Red River runs rusty, the Wichita clear,
But down by the Brazos I courted my dear.   4

    Then la, la, la, lee, lee, lee, give me your hand,
    La, la, la, lee, lee, lee, give me your hand,
    La, la, la, lee, lee, lee, give me your hand,
    There's a-many a river that waters the land.   8

The fair Angelina runs glossy and gliding,
The crooked Colorado runs weaving and winding,
And the slow San Antonio, it courses the plain,
But I never will walk by the Brazos again.   12

    Then la, la, la, lee, lee, lee, pole the boat on,
    La, la, la, lee, lee, lee, pole the boat on,
    La, la, la, lee, lee, lee, pole the boat on,
    My Brazos River sweetheart has left me and gone.   16

She kissed me, she hugged me, she called me her dandy,
The Trinity's muddy, the Brazos quicksandy,
She hugged me, she kissed me, she called me her own,
But down by the Brazos she left me alone.   20

    Then la, la, la, lee, lee, lee, give me your hand,
    La, la, la, lee, lee, lee, give me your hand,
    La, la, la, lee, lee, lee, give me your hand,
    The Trinity's muddy, but the Brazos quicksand.   24

The girls of Little River, they're plump and they're pretty,
The Sabine and the Sulphur have many a beauty,
On the banks of the Natchez there's girls by the score,
And down by the Brazos I'll wander no more.   28

*"The Brazos River" was recorded by Vance Randolph in 1942 from the singing of Mrs. Irene Carlisle of Fayetteville, Arkansas. Our source is that recording, number AFS 5397A2, from the Archive of Folk Song, Library of Congress.

Then la, la, la, lee, lee, lee, give me your hand,
La, la, la, lee, lee, lee, give me your hand,
La, la, la, lee, lee, lee, give me your hand,
There's a-many a river that waters the land.   32

To this point we have been illustrating our concepts with anonymous poems. For lyrics this is easy to do, because the lyric is in its essence a simple outpouring of emotion. All people have emotions and many have sat or wandered by themselves, trying to shape their feelings into poems. Many people not otherwise known as poets have created works that passed into the anonymous stream of oral tradition because other people liked them and kept them alive. But a number of the best lyrics in English have been created by people who established reputations as poets and whose names are therefore available to us. Let us examine a few.

Loveliest of Trees, the Cherry Now

A. E. Housman   (1859–1936)

Loveliest of trees, the cherry now
Is hung with bloom along the bough,
And stands about the woodland ride
Wearing white for Eastertide.   4

Now, of my threescore years and ten,
Twenty will not come again,
And take from seventy springs a score,
It only leaves me fifty more.   8

And since to look at things in bloom
Fifty springs are little room,
About the woodlands I will go
To see the cherry hung with snow.   12

Like the poems that we have already examined, Housman's is mostly concerned with the speaker's emotional response to his situation. In some respects, both the situation and the emotion seem quite simple. It is spring. The speaker tells us the cherry trees are in bloom. The speaker is twenty years old, and he expects to live fifty more years, until he has reached the normal human expectancy of "threescore years and ten." Through the simple subtraction that he performs for us, we see that he thinks of fifty years as a short time ("It *only* leaves me fifty more"); we begin to see, in other words, that the source of his emotion is his sense of how short life is, of how little time he has left. He feels a sense of loss, but it is followed by a sense of recovery. In the last stanza, he seems to be saying that since time is short, he will use it well by doing the things he most enjoys. This is a poem of mixed emotions, like "The Brazos River": something has been lost, but much remains. Yet the emotions here seem much more subtly mixed than they are in "The Brazos River."

The cherry is not for this speaker just any tree. It is the "Loveliest of trees." We may not agree with him, but we know what he means. We can share his emotional response to cherry trees in bloom in the spring. Just so, we did not know the Earl of Murray, but we have observed the death of other men whom we admired and that the nation looked up to. The poem moves us because it touches our emotions in ways similar to the way that the original experience touched the poet. All poetry acts upon us this way (or it does not act upon us at all). We have felt similar emotions in comparable experiences. We read the poem, and it becomes our poem because it says something to us that we would have liked to have said ourselves, if not about cherry trees, then about other things cherished. The poem is a concrete expression of abstract truths we have all responded to. We are surrounded by things that we love. Life is short. We can make the most of our time by spending it at those activities that bring life's beauty home to us.

The last word, "snow," is a puzzle to some readers, but need not be. The two most obvious possibilities of meaning do not contradict but support one another. As a first possibility, the word may carry its ordinary, literal meaning. The poet says that since fifty springs provide such a limited time to enjoy the cherries, he will visit them in the winter as well, when they are covered not with blossoms, but with snow. In other words, he will take full advantage of all his human opportunities to enjoy their beauty. As a second possibility, the poet may not mean real snow, but may intend the word in a figurative or metaphoric sense. The blossoms, as the first stanza makes clear, are white. In the last line he may be telling us that they make the trees look as though they were "hung with snow." The message is essentially the same. Given his awareness of the shortness of life, he will expend his present moments enjoying the beauty of the trees and the wonder and mystery of life they represent.

But why does the poet end a poem about spring with an ambiguous reference to snow? The poem, we may say, is not about spring. It is about the brevity of life. Blossoms remind us of spring and youth (when we are twenty —or were, or soon will be). Snow reminds us of winter and death (when we shall have run out our threescore years and ten). In one brilliant word at the end of the poem the poet reminds us of both our hopes and our human limitations. For this effect it does not matter whether the snow is literal or figurative, since the fundamental image is the same and in either case it is played off against the blossoms.

Faced with a knowledge of the shortness of our lives, most of us will not spend our time wandering in cherry orchards, either in spring or in winter, but we can respond to the desire to grasp at fleeting beauty and vitality. The poet's experience of looking at blossoms and being reminded of snow becomes for us a fitting response to life's brevity. We, too, are moved by the thought that lies behind the bittersweet double image.

Although the word "snow" may be read both with a literal and a metaphoric sense, both readings are consistent with the poetic effect of the other lines. Both affirm the poet's desire to extract all the enjoyment he can from the fleeting moments of his existence. The poem is memorable because its clear and effective communication is not hurt but assisted by the ambiguity of the last word. An accomplished reader of poetry learns to welcome the enrichment of such extended meanings without using their existence as an excuse to believe that a poem can mean anything he or she wants it to.

When a poem is well made, momentary delight turns sometimes into a lifelong possession. Not all our emotions are serious. Not all moments that we treasure are of earth-shaking importance. The grass at our feet and the clouds overhead, if seen clearly, can supply the emotion for a lyric.

Cut Grass

Philip Larkin   (1922–1985)

Cut grass lies frail:
Brief is the breath
Mown stalks exhale.
Long, long the death   4

It dies in the white hours
Of young-leafed June
With chestnut flowers,
With hedges snowlike strewn,   8

White lilac bowed,
Lost lanes of Queen Anne's lace,
And that high-builded cloud
Moving at summer's pace.   12

Which words in "Cut Grass" remind us of death? In what ways? What do the grass and clouds here have in common? Is there any point, besides the music of the sounds, to the rhyming of "breath" and "death" and "frail" and "exhale"? Compare the "hedges snowlike strewn" here with Housman's "cherry hung with snow." Is the point similar? How would you summarize the emotion of this poem?

Emotion is fundamental to the lyric, but the emotion is heightened by the form. If we look back over the lyrics already presented, we see that all were rigidly controlled by meter and rhyme. Like the lyre player, the poet must discover the pitch and rhythm, the words and arrangements that will present an idea most memorably. At times he or she may discover that a form as exacting as the sonnet will serve admirably:

Composed Upon Westminster Bridge, September 3, 1802

William Wordsworth   *(1770–1850)*

Earth has not anything to show more fair:
Dull would he be of soul who could pass by
A sight so touching in its majesty:
This City now doth, like a garment, wear   4
The beauty of the morning; silent, bare,
Ships, towers, domes, theatres, and temples lie
Open unto the fields, and to the sky;
All bright and glittering in the smokeless air.   8
Never did sun more beautifully steep
In his first splendour, valley, rock, or hill;
Ne'er saw I, never felt, a calm so deep!
The river glideth at his own sweet will: 12
Dear God! the very houses seem asleep;
And all that mighty heart is lying still!

A lesser poet could not achieve this effect in a form so difficult. Wordsworth, despite the sonnet's complicated demands of rhyme and meter, has managed to keep his emotion pure and create a poem that sings with a stately music. At its best, indeed, the sonnet turns out to be a remarkably useful lyric form.

Although written by a highly sophisticated modern poet, the following lyric is in a style much like that of the anonymous lyrics with which we began.

Down by the Salley Gardens

W. B. Yeats   *(1865–1939)*

Down by the salley[1] gardens my love and I did meet;
She passed the salley gardens with little snow-white feet.
She bid me take love easy, as the leaves grow on the tree;
But I, being young and foolish, with her would not agree.   4
In a field by the river my love and I did stand,
And on my leaning shoulder she laid her snow-white hand.
She bid me take life easy, as the grass grows on the weirs,[2]
But I was young and foolish, and now am full of tears.   8

[1]Willow.   [2]Milldams.

What are we to make of this? Like the folk poets, Yeats leaves much of his story untold. He wants less to tell a story than to express a state of mind, to find the words that will convey his emotion. Has he succeeded? Does the music in his lines bring his feelings home to us? Does omitting the details heighten the force of the tears? What is the effect of the repetition, with changes, of lines 3 and 4 as lines 7 and 8? Why compare love and life to leaves and grass? What do you suppose was the essence of the young man's foolishness?

NARRATIVE

A *narrative poem* is a story in verse. The impulse to tell stories this way is as old as human memory. Like the lyric impulse, the narrative impulse is fundamental to human nature. The tellers were originally also singers. They wish to give their story a form, and their meters help other singers to remember it and pass it along, just as they enchant their listeners. As the centuries wear on, the words may outlast the music. And, as with the lyrics, poets may engage in the sounds and rhythms of the words alone.

The first three of the following poems are, again, anonymous folksongs. The last three were written by poets whose names we know. All have a story to tell and tell it in different ways.

Edward*

"Why does your brand[1] so drop with blood,
                Edward, Edward?
Why does your brand so drop with blood,
  And why so sad gang[2] ye, O?"   **4**
"O I have killed my hawk so good,
                Mother, Mother.
O I have killed my hawk so good,
  And I had no more but he, O."   **8**

"Your hawk's blood was never so red,
                Edward, Edward.
Your hawk's blood was never so red,
  My dear son I tell thee, O."   **12**
"O I have killed my red-roan steed,
                Mother, Mother.
O I have killed my red-roan steed,
  That erst[3] was so fair and free, O."   **16**

"Your steed was old, and ye have got more,
                Edward, Edward.
Your steed was old, and ye have got more,
  Some other dule[4] ye drie,[5] O."   **20**
"O I have killed my father dear,
                Mother, Mother.

*Francis J. Child, *English and Scottish Popular Ballads*, 13B. We have normalized the spelling.
[1]Sword. [2]Go. [3]Once. [4]Sorrow. [5]Suffer.

O I have killed my father dear,
    Alas, and woe is me, O!"   24

"And what penance will ye drie for that,
                Edward, Edward?
And what penance will ye drie for that?
    My dear son, now tell me, O."   28
"I'll set my feet in yonder boat,
                Mother, Mother.
I'll set my feet in yonder boat,
    And I'll fare over the sea, O."   32

"And what will ye do with your towers and your hall,
                Edward, Edward?
And what will ye do with your towers and your hall,
    That were so fair to see, O?"   36
"I'll let them stand till they down fall,
                Mother, Mother.
I'll let them stand till they down fall,
    For here never more may I be, O."   40

"And what will ye leave to your bairns[6] and your wife,
                Edward, Edward?
And what will ye leave to your bairns and your wife,
    When ye gang over the sea, O?"   44
"The world's room, let them beg through life,
                Mother, Mother.
The world's room, let them beg through life,
    For them never more will I see, O."   48

"And what will ye leave to your own mother dear,
                Edward, Edward?
And what will ye leave to your own mother dear?
    My dear son, now tell me, O."   52
"The curse of hell from me shall ye bear,
                Mother, Mother.
The curse of hell from me shall ye bear,
    Such counsels ye gave to me, O."   56

---

[6]Children.

The story of Edward is much older than even the Scottish version printed here, existing in a number of languages other than English. Its roots are in the Middle Ages, but it lives on with twentieth-century folksingers, both British and American.

Where is its staying power? Certainly, the story itself is engaging. Edward has killed his father, but we don't know that at the outset. The manner of telling is part of the attraction; it is a succession of suspenses. The listener wonders until the end of the third stanza why Edward's sword is dripping with blood. He also may wonder why the mother seems unperturbed on learning that her son has killed her husband. She merely asks him what penance he will do. Only in the last line does the poet tell us (if we are alert) why she was not upset, or even surprised. The elements of a mystery are heightened first by the horror of patricide, then by the further horror of the mother's instigation. There is no punishment for such wickedness—or is there? The son says "I'll set my feet in yonder boat, / and I'll fare over the sea, O." Among some ancient seafaring peoples the normal punishment for murder was to be set upon the open sea in an oarless boat. The son accepts his punishment. But the mother? How calmly she asks about the blood on the sword. How willingly she lets the son go to his judgment. How eagerly she asks what he will leave behind. The poem is an intense study of character.

We could say more. Notice the abruptness of the beginning. Notice the repetition. Notice the rhythm of the lines. The poem is entirely dialogue, wholly the mother's questions and the son's answers. Are any of these elements important? They are if they help us to feel the effect of the poem, if they help to locate it among our memorable literary experiences.

Another ancient poem tells a story of the jealousy of two sisters.

The Two Sisters

There was an old man in the North Countrie,
    Bow down, bow down.
There was an old man in the North Countrie,
And he had daughters, one, two, three.   4
    Love will be true, true to my love,
    Love will be true to you.

There was a young man came courting there,
And he did choose the youngest fair.   8

He gave to the youngest a gay gold ring,
And to the oldest not a single thing.

He gave to the youngest a beaver hat,
And the oldest she thought hard of that.   12

"Sister, O sister, let's walk the sea shore,
To see the ships come sailing o'er."

They were walking along on yonder sea-brim
When the oldest shoved the youngest in.   16

"O sister, O sister, hand me your hand,
    And you may have my house and land."

"O sister, O sister, hand me your glove,
    And you may have my own true love."   20

"I'll neither hand you hand nor glove,
    For all I want is your true love."

So down she sank and away she swam
    Until she reached the old mill dam.   24

The miller threw out his old grab-hook
    And pulled the fair maiden out of the brook.

"O miller, O miller, here's three gold rings,
    If you'll take me to my father's again."   28

He up with her fingers and off with her rings
    And threw her back in the brook again.

The miller was hung at his mill gate
    For drowning of my sister Kate.   32

Although this song, too, exists in some fine Scottish versions, this is a version from North America. What is the story? Are any elements unclear? Does it bear any resemblances to "Edward"? Both are family tragedies, for instance. Does this have any bearing on their enduring popularity? Are other elements particularly worthy of comment?

Sir Patrick Spens*

The king sits in Dumferling town,
    Drinking the blood-red wine:
"O where will I get good sailor,
    To sail this ship of mine?"   4

Up and spoke an elderly knight,
    Sat at the king's right knee:
"Sir Patrick Spens is the best sailor
    That sails upon the sea."   8

The king has written a braid[1] letter,
    And signed it with his hand,
And sent it to Sir Patrick Spens,
    Was walking on the sand.   12

*Child 58A. We have normalized the spelling.
[1]Informal.

The first line that Sir Patrick read,
    A loud laugh laughed he;
The next line that Sir Patrick read,
    The tear blinded his eye.   16

"O who is this has done this deed,
    This ill deed done to me,
To send me out this time o' the year,
    To sail upon the sea!   20

"Make haste, make haste, my merry men all,
    Our good ship sails the morn."
"O say not so, my master dear,
    For I fear a deadly storm.   24

"Late late yestreen I saw the new moon,
    With the old moon in her arm,
And I fear, I fear, my dear master,
    That we will come to harm."   28

O our Scots nobles were right loath
    To wet their cork-heeled shoon,[2]
But long o'er all the play were played,
    Their hats they swam aboon.[3]   32

O long, long may their ladies sit,
    With their fans into their hand,
Or e'er they see Sir Patrick Spens
    Come sailing to the land.   36

O long, long may the ladies stand,
    With their gold combs in their hair,
Waiting for their own dear lords,
    For they'll see them no more.   40

Half o'er, half o'er to Aberdour,
    It's fifty fathoms deep,
And there lies good Sir Patrick Spens,
    With the Scots lords at his feet.   44

[2]Shoes. [3]Above.

What is the story? Sir Patrick Spens put to sea at his king's command, despite his misgivings and the warning of one of his followers, and went down with his ship and his men. Why should we care? We can't care, in fact—not unless it is a good story, well told, with some relationship to our own lives. Does it have these qualities? We have no king we must obey, but can imagine ourselves doing something against our better judgment out of loyalty to another. We can imagine a tragedy ensuing. In this sense, we can participate in the story of Sir Patrick Spens, can understand his bravery, and can sympathize with his fate. If we judge it a good story, and well told, we will return to it again and again, as others have before us. Thousands of ships have gone down in various seas. Few are remembered so vividly.

Part of the poem's power is its grim sense of irony. The best sailor in the kingdom drowns. His men are loath to wet even the heels of their shoes in such a bad season, but their hats swim fifty fathoms overhead before they are through. Their ladies will wait long, the poet says in grim understatement, meaning they will wait forever. Stanzas 9 and 10 enhance the tragedy memorably by turning to the ladies ashore. We may remember, however, that an almost identical stanza ends "The Bonny Earl of Murray." We don't need to ask which came first; the question is probably beyond answering in any case. A more interesting question is whether "Sir Patrick Spens" needs to work this traditional formula twice, or whether once, as in "The Bonny Earl of Murray," would have been enough.

There is not much to the story of Richard Cory. You can easily retell it. But can you retell so memorably?

Richard Cory

Edwin Arlington Robinson   (1869–1935)

Whenever Richard Cory went down town,
We people on the pavement looked at him:
He was a gentleman from sole to crown,
Clean favored, and imperially slim.   4

And he was always quietly arrayed,
And he was always human when he talked;
But still he fluttered pulses when he said,
"Good-morning," and he glittered when he walked.   8

And he was rich—yes, richer than a king—
And admirably schooled in every grace:
In fine, we thought that he was everything
To make us wish that we were in his place.   12

So on we worked, and waited for the light,
And went without the meat, and cursed the bread.
And Richard Cory, one calm summer night,
Went home and put a bullet through his head.   16

Who are "we people on the pavement"? What is the "light" of line 13? Why would anybody curse bread? What does line 14 mean? How many ironies can you find? Is "one calm summer night" one of them?

Another story with few details was written as a song by John Lennon and Paul McCartney.

Eleanor Rigby

John Lennon   (1940–1980)
and Paul McCartney   (1942–)

Ah, look at all the lonely people!
Ah, look at all the lonely people!

Eleanor Rigby
Picks up the rice in the church where a wedding has been,
Lives in a dream,   5
Waits at the window
Wearing the face that she keeps in a jar by the door.
Who is it for?

All the lonely people,
Where do they all come from?   10
All the lonely people,
Where do they all belong?

Father McKenzie,
Writing the words of a sermon that no one will hear—
No one comes near.   15
Look at him working,
Darning his socks in the night when there's nobody there.
What does he care?

All the lonely people,
Where do they all come from?   20
All the lonely people,
Where do they all belong?

Eleanor Rigby
Died in the church and was buried along with her name.
Nobody came.   25
Father McKenzie,
Wiping the dirt from his hands as he walks from the grave—
No one was saved.

All the lonely people,
Where do they all come from?   30
All the lonely people,
Where do they all belong?

Ah, look at all the lonely people!
Ah, look at all the lonely people!

Tell what you know of the stories of Eleanor Rigby and Father McKenzie. What details illustrate their lives most effectively? In what ways do their two lives connect? How do you explain "wearing the face that she keeps in the jar by the door"? How many ironies can you find? In what way does the refrain "all the lonely people" help explain the popularity of this song that names only two?

Here is a very different kind of narrative verse:

Hurt Hawks

Robinson Jeffers   (1887–1962)

I

The broken pillar of the wing jags from the clotted shoulder,
The wing trails like a banner in defeat,
No more to use the sky forever but live with famine
And pain a few days: cat nor coyote
Will shorten the week of waiting for death, there is game without
    talons.   5
He stands under the oak-bush and waits
The lame feet of salvation; at night he remembers freedom
And flies in a dream, the dawns ruin it.
He is strong and pain is worse to the strong, incapacity is worse.
The curs of the day come and torment him   10
At distance, no one but death the redeemer will humble that head,
The intrepid readiness, the terrible eyes.
The wild God of the world is sometimes merciful to those
That ask mercy, not often to the arrogant.
You do not know him, you communal people, or you have forgotten
    him;   15
Intemperate and savage, the hawk remembers him;
Beautiful and wild, the hawks, and men that are dying, remember
    him.

II

I'd sooner, except the penalties, kill a man than a hawk; but the
    great redtail
Had nothing left but unable misery
From the bone too shattered for mending, the wing that trailed
    under his talons when he moved.   20
We had fed him six weeks, I gave him freedom,
He wandered over the foreland hill and returned in the evening,
    asking for death,
Not like a beggar, still eyed with the old

Implacable arrogance. I gave him the lead gift in the twilight. What
    fell was relaxed,
Owl-downy, soft feminine feathers; but what   25
Soared: the fierce rush: the night-herons by the flooded river cried
    fear at its rising
Before it was quite unsheathed from reality.

What is the story here? The poem lacks the insistent rhythm and rhyme of the usual narrative poem. Does it lose or gain? What does the subject have to do with the form? The poet, of course, wants to do more than merely tell a story in verse. The story means something to him. He has an emotion, an attitude, or a thought he wishes to convey. His poem is not simply narrative, any more than lyric poems are simply lyric. Here the narrator says "I'd sooner, except the penalties, kill a man than a hawk." Can this be true? If true, what does it tell of him? In your own words, how would you describe "the wild God of the world" of this poem?

The narrative or the lyric element dominates some poems and serves lesser roles in others. Similarly, some poems are more descriptive, others more discursive or thoughtful, more interested in ideas. Something of "Hurt Hawks" is descriptive, something discursive. Other poems emphasize one or the other of these elements, but nothing seems quite as fundamental to poetry as the lyric or the narrative impulse.

CHAPTER 2

THE POEM AS DRAMA

SITUATION

Many poems revolve around an inherently dramatic situation. Sometimes poets have experienced or observed an event that they wish to record in verse. Sometimes they have imagined an event. The poem may take the form of a complete narrative or an incident presented in isolation, or it may amount to no more than the expression of an emotion for which the reader may infer an active cause. As readers we may classify the poem as narrative, lyric, descriptive, discursive, or by such other designations as we find helpful, yet if the poem was worth writing the poet was probably driven to it by an inner need, something like the need to dramatize.

The poem comes to us as a verbal communication, but as we first approach it we cannot be certain either that the voice is the poet's or that it is addressed to us as readers. Perhaps the poet has invented a voice other than his or her own. Perhaps the poet has written a love poem or a letter to a patron. In any event, we may suppose that something has happened to prompt this communication at this time. We can define the dramatic situation if we can answer three questions: Who speaks the words of the poem? To whom is the poem addressed? Under what circumstances is the poem spoken? Careful and complete answers to these questions will frequently take us a long way into understanding.

The Walk

Thomas Hardy   *(1840–1928)*

You did not walk with me
Of late to the hill-top tree
    By the gated ways,
    As in earlier days;   4
    You were weak and lame,
    So you never came,
And I went alone, and I did not mind,
Not thinking of you as left behind.   8

I walked up there to-day
Just in the former way;
    Surveyed around
    The familiar ground   12
    By myself again:
    What difference, then?
Only that underlying sense
Of the look of a room on returning thence.   16

Who speaks the poem? Perhaps the poet, at least someone long in the habit of walking to a tree at the top of a hill. To whom is the poem addressed? Clearly not directly to the reader, but to a "you" who used to walk up the hill also, a "you" who later became too "weak and lame" for the habitual walk. In what circumstances is the poem spoken? Something has happened to make a difference in the lives of the two people, although the speaker still takes his habitual walk, just as he had been doing "of late," without the "you." "What difference, then?" he asks and then answers himself: "Only that underlying sense / Of the look of a room on returning thence." One question prompts another in the mind of the reader. Why should the room look different? Most obviously, if the person is no longer there. The poem radiates a sense of loss, and probably refers to the final loss of death. The speaker communicates his anguish over the loss of a loved one, someone no longer able to greet him on his return. He speaks in the form of an *apostrophe,* an address either to an inanimate object or an individual not present to receive the communication.

If we want completely to answer the question: "To whom is the poem addressed?" we will probably now add that, although it is an apostrophe addressed directly to the "you," it is also addressed indirectly to the sympathetic ear of the reader, asking him or her to share in the emotion. On the evidence of the poem, we cannot say much more than this. We cannot identify for certain the sex of either the speaker or the "you." We cannot even be sure of a death, although we may feel it strongly, since the person addressed may simply have gone away—as the result of a quarrel, say, or to enter a hospital. The poem obtains its power from what it says and also from what it does not say. By attempting to provide careful and complete answers to the three questions that define its dramatic situation, we are forced a long way into the complexities of a poem that looks quite simple on the surface.

If we remain unsatisfied with answers we derive from the poem itself, we may examine its connection with the life of the poet, Thomas Hardy. So doing, we discover "The Walk" to be one of a number of frankly autobiographical poems Hardy wrote in his seventies, not long after the death of Emma Hardy, to whom he had been married for almost 40 years. Such knowledge defines the situation more precisely than is apparent in the poem alone. Does our added understanding make the poem in any way a different or a better work of art?

In the next poem, little question of an autobiographical basis arises. The poet has imagined a verbal exchange between a redwood tree and a person.

Kind

A. R. Ammons   (1926-   )

> I can't understand it
>   said the giant redwood
>   I have attained height and distant view,
>   am easy with time,
>
>   and yet you search the   5
>   wood's edge
> for weeds
> that find half-dark room in margins
>   of stone
>   and are   10
> as everybody knows
>   here and gone in a season
>
>   O redwood I said in this matter
> I may not be able to argue from reason
> but preference sends me stooping   15
> seeking
>   the least,
>   as finished as you
>   and with a flower

Who speaks? A redwood tree and a person, with the person reporting the conversation. To whom do they speak? To each other (and the reader as auditor). Under what circumstances do they speak? The person has displayed his fascination with weeds rather than trees and has been asked to explain himself.

By means of his fable, Ammons suggests something about one individual's preference for small and transient perfections over loftier things.

Not Waving But Drowning

Stevie Smith   (1902–1971)

Nobody heard him, the dead man,
But still he lay moaning:
I was much further out than you thought
And not waving but drowning.   4

Poor chap, he always loved larking
And now he's dead
It must have been too cold for him his heart gave way,
They said.   8

Oh, no no no, it was too cold always
(Still the dead one lay moaning)
I was much too far out all my life
And not waving but drowning.   12

Here are the words of three speakers: a narrator, a dead man, and a collective "they." The narrator speaks to the reader, and the "they" speak to each other. The most important speaker, however, is the dead man, who speaks to the "they" but is heard only by the narrator and the reader. The point of the poem is the failure of communication. The dead man was misunderstood as he was drowning, just as he had been misunderstood (and therefore "drowning") all his life.

Robert Frost's "Home Burial" extends a dramatic situation to a length in which it possesses the complications of a miniature stage play.

Home Burial

Robert Frost   (1874–1963)

He saw her from the bottom of the stairs
Before she saw him. She was starting down,
Looking back over her shoulder at some fear.
She took a doubtful step and then undid it
To raise herself and look again. He spoke   5
Advancing toward her: "What is it you see
From up there always?—for I want to know."
She turned and sank upon her skirts at that,
And her face changed from terrified to dull.
He said to gain time: "What is it you see?"   10

Mounting until she cowered under him.
"I will find out now—you must tell me, dear."
She, in her place, refused him any help,
With the least stiffening of her neck and silence.
She let him look, sure that he wouldn't see,   15
Blind creature; and awhile he didn't see.
But at last he murmured, "Oh," and again, "Oh."

"What is it—what?" she said.
                                        "Just that I see."

"You don't," she challenged. "Tell me what it is."
"The wonder is I didn't see at once.   20
I never noticed it from here before.
I must be wonted to it—that's the reason.
The little graveyard where my people are!
So small the window frames the whole of it.
Not so much larger than a bedroom, is it?   25
There are three stones of slate and one of marble,
Broad-shouldered little slabs there in the sunlight
On the sidehill. We haven't to mind *those*.
But I understand: it is not the stones,
But the child's mound—"
                        "Don't, don't, don't, don't," she cried. 30

She withdrew, shrinking from beneath his arm
That rested on the banister, and slid downstairs;
And turned on him with such a daunting look,
He said twice over before he knew himself:
"Can't a man speak of his own child he's lost?"   35

"Not you!—Oh, where's my hat? Oh, I don't need it!
I must get out of here. I must get air.—
I don't know rightly whether any man can."

"Amy! Don't go to someone else this time.
Listen to me. I won't come down the stairs."   40
He sat and fixed his chin between his fists.
"There's something I should like to ask you, dear."

"You don't know how to ask it."
                                "Help me, then."

Her fingers moved the latch for all reply.

"My words are nearly always an offense.   45
I don't know how to speak of anything
So as to please you. But I might be taught,
I should suppose. I can't say I see how.
A man must partly give up being a man

With womenfolk. We could have some arrangement   50
By which I'd bind myself to keep hands off
Anything special you're a-mind to name.
Though I don't like such things 'twixt those that love.
Two that don't love can't live together without them.
But two that do can't live together with them."   55
She moved the latch a little. "Don't—don't go.
Don't carry it to someone else this time.
Tell me about it if it's something human.
Let me into your grief. I'm not so much
Unlike other folks as your standing there   60
Apart would make me out. Give me my chance.
I do think, though, you overdo it a little.
What was it brought you up to think it the thing
To take your mother-loss of a first child
So inconsolably—in the face of love.   65
You'd think his memory might be satisfied—"

"There you go sneering now!"
                                        "I'm not, I'm not!
You make me angry. I'll come down to you.
God, what a woman! And it's come to this,
A man can't speak of his own child that's dead."   70

"You can't because you don't know how to speak.
If you had any feelings, you that dug
With your own hand—how could you?—his little grave;
I saw you from that very window there,
Making the gravel leap and leap in air,   75
Leap up, like that, like that, and land so lightly
And roll back down the mound beside the hole.
I thought, Who is that man? I didn't know you.
And I crept down the stairs and up the stairs
To look again, and still your spade kept lifting.   80
Then you came in. I heard your rumbling voice
Out in the kitchen, and I don't know why,
But I went near to see with my own eyes.
You could sit there with the stains on your shoes
Of the fresh earth from your own baby's grave   85
And talk about your everyday concerns.
You had stood the spade up against the wall
Outside there in the entry, for I saw it."

"I shall laugh the worst laugh I ever laughed.
I'm cursed. God, if I don't believe I'm cursed."   90

"I can repeat the very words you were saying:
'Three foggy mornings and one rainy day

Will rot the best birch fence a man can build.'
Think of it, talk like that at such a time!
What had how long it takes a birch to rot   95
To do with what was in the darkened parlor?
You *couldn't* care! The nearest friends can go
With anyone to death, comes so far short
They might as well not try to go at all.
No, from the time when one is sick to death,   100
One is alone, and he dies more alone.
Friends make pretense of following to the grave,
But before one is in it, their minds are turned
And making the best of their way back to life
And living people, and things they understand. 105
But the world's evil. I won't have grief so
If I can change it. Oh, I won't, I won't!"

"There, you have said it all and you feel better.
You won't go now. You're crying. Close the door.
The heart's gone out of it: why keep it up?   110
Amy! There's someone coming down the road!"

"*You*—oh, you think the talk is all. I must go—
Somewhere out of this house. How can I make you—"

"If—you—do!" She was opening the door wider.
"Where do you mean to go? First tell me that.   115
I'll follow and bring you back by force. I *will!*—"

Observe that there are three speakers in "Home Burial." Who are they? To whom does each speak? What are the circumstances that have prompted the exchange between husband and wife? How would you describe the husband? Refer to specific phrases and lines to illustrate his character. What qualities does the wife have? Mention specific words and sentences that reveal her character. What overheard sentence does the woman find most offensive? Why? Can you find a meaning in the sentence that the wife appears not to understand?

Consider the visual images (the pictures) of the poem: In how many places are the husband and wife shown as separated? What future do you predict for this couple? Why?

The dramatic situation in the next poem is largely a dream, but not entirely.

Dream Barker

Jean Valentine   (1934–   )

We met for supper in your flat-bottomed boat.
I got there first: in a white dress: I remember
Wondering if you'd come. Then you shot over the bank,

A Virgilian[1] Nigger Jim,[2] and poled us off
To a little sea-food barker's cave you knew. 5

What'll you have? you said. Eels hung down,
Bamboozled claws hung up from the crackling weeds.
The light was all behind us. To one side
In a dish of ice was a shell shaped like a sand-dollar
But worked with Byzantine blue and gold. *What's that?* 10

Well, I've never seen it before, you said,
And I don't know how it tastes.
Oh well, said I, *if it's bad,*
I'm not too hungry, are you? We'd have the shell . . .
I know just how you feel, you said 15

And asked for it; we held out our hands.
Six Dollars! barked the barker, *For This Beauty!*
We fell down laughing in your flat-bottomed boat,

And then I woke up: in a white dress:
Dry as a bone on dry land, Jim, 20
Bone dry, old, in a dry land, Jim, my Jim.

---

[1]Of the Roman poet Virgil (70–19 B.C.).   [2]From Twain's *Huckleberry Finn.*

Probably "Dream Barker" is an apostrophe. What does that mean? How does
it affect your understanding of the poem? What words and phrases define the
dream experience? What is the usual association with a white dress? How does
the tradition fit into this poem? How do you interpret ". . . if it's bad . . . We'd
have the shell . . . ?" What does the adjective "dry" in the last stanza communicate? How is the last stanza a contrast to the rest of the poem? Characterize the
speaker.

In the following poem an old man speaks to any listener, or to the reader.
How do we know he is old? What experience has prompted the poem?

The Brothers

Edwin Muir   (1887–1959)

Last night I watched my brothers play,
The gentle and the reckless one,
In a field two yards away.
For half a century they were gone
Beyond the other side of care 5
To be among the peaceful dead.
Even in a dream how could I dare
Interrogate that happiness
So wildly spent yet never less?

For still they raced about the green   10
And were like two revolving suns;
A brightness poured from head to head,
So strong I could not see their eyes
Or look into their paradise.
What were they doing, the happy ones?   15
Yet where I was they once had been.

I thought, How could I be so dull,
Twenty thousand days ago,
Not to see they were beautiful?
I asked them, Were you really so   20
As you are now, that other day?
And the dream was soon away.

For then we played for victory
And not to make each other glad.
A darkness covered every head,   25
Frowns twisted the original face,
And through that mask we could not see
The beauty and the buried grace.

I have observed in foolish awe
The dateless mid-days of the law   30
And seen indifferent justice done
By everyone on everyone.
And in a vision I have seen
My brothers playing on the green.

What specific memories does the speaker have of his brothers? Why are the brothers' heads in "brightness" in line 12 and "darkness" in line 25? What "green" do the brothers play on? Support your answer.

In the next poem, from an Omaha Indian ritual, a priest apostrophizes the sun, moon, and stars. The ceremony is called "Introduction of the Child to the Cosmos."

Ho! Ye Sun, Moon, Stars

Ho! Ye Sun, Moon, Stars, all ye that move in the heavens,
   I bid you hear me!
Into your midst has come a new life.
   Consent ye, I implore!
Make its path smooth, that it may reach the brow of the first hill!   5

Ho! Ye Winds, Clouds, Rain, Mist, all ye that move in the air,
   I bid you hear me!

Into your midst has come a new life.
    Consent ye, I implore!
Make its path smooth, that it may reach the brow of the second hill!   10

Ho! Ye Hills, Valleys, Rivers, Lakes, Trees, Grasses, all ye of the earth,
    I bid you hear me!
Into your midst has come a new life.
    Consent ye, I implore!
Make its path smooth, that it may reach the brow of the third hill!   15

Ho! Ye Birds, great and small, that fly in the air,
Ho! Ye Animals, great and small, that dwell in the forest,
Ho! Ye Insects that creep among the grasses and burrow in the
    ground—
    I bid you hear me!
Into your midst has come a new life.   20
    Consent ye, I implore!
Make its path smooth, that it may reach the brow of the fourth hill!

Ho! All ye of the heavens, all ye of the air, all ye of the earth:
    I bid you hear me!
Into your midst has come a new life.   25
    Consent ye, consent ye all, I implore!
Make its path smooth—then shall it travel beyond the four hills!

What is the logic behind the order in which the priest apostrophizes things?
What does the poem suggest about Native American religion?

As a final example of how understanding the dramatic situation can assist one
to an understanding of the whole poem, consider the following lines by Thom
Gunn.

Moly

Thom Gunn   *(1929–)*

Nightmare of beasthood, snorting, how to wake.
I woke. What beasthood skin she made me take?

Leathery toad that ruts for days on end,
Or cringing dribbling dog, man's servile friend,   4

Or cat that prettily pounces on its meat,
Tortures it hours, then does not care to eat:

Parrot, moth, shark, wolf, crocodile, ass, flea.
What germs, what jostling mobs there were in me.   8

    These seem like bristles, and the hide is tough.
No claw or web here: each foot ends in hoof.

Into what bulk has method disappeared?
Like ham, streaked. I am gross—grey, gross, flap-eared.   12

The pale-lashed eyes my only human feature.
My teeth tear, tear. I am the snouted creature

That bites through anything, root, wire, or can.
If I was not afraid I'd eat a man.   16

Oh a man's flesh already is in mine.
Hand and foot poised for risk. Buried in swine. \

   I root and root, you think that it is greed,
It is, but I seek out a plant I need.   20

Direct me, gods, whose changes are all holy,
To where it flickers deep in grass, the moly:

Cool flesh of magic in each leaf and shoot,
From milky flower to the black forked root.   24

From this fat dungeon I could rise to skin
And human title, putting pig within.

I push my big grey wet snout through the green,
Dreaming the flower I have never seen.   28

First we need to recall the Circe episode in book 10 of Homer's *Odyssey*, since Gunn assumes a common knowledge of this famous incident. The beautiful Circe turned Odysseus's men to swine, though they retained their human minds; Odysseus was protected from her enchantment by the magic herb moly, which was given to him by the messenger of the gods, Hermes. In "Moly," Gunn imagines the story from a perspective different from Homer's. Who speaks? In what circumstances? At what point does the speaker first fully understand his new shape? What is the "fat dungeon" of line 25? Explain "putting pig within" (line 26). What does it suggest of the speaker's attitude toward his permanent nature?

CHARACTER

Any poem rooted in an inherently dramatic situation projects the character of the speaker, but poets heighten the characterization when they present speakers markedly different from themselves. For these poems, poets deliberately dramatize, evoking a sense of character as important to poetic effect. Frequently a poet emphasizes one character, a speaker who reveals personality through language and point of view. In such a poem, the poet speaks through the mask, or *persona*, of another person's experiences, projecting, like a dramatist, a different personality.

A male writer may adopt the character (or persona) of a woman, or a woman of a man. A young man may adopt the character of an old one, or a brave man of a coward, or an honest man of a thief. A twentieth-century English writer may adopt the character of an ancient Greek warrior changed by enchantment into a pig, as Thom Gunn does in "Moly." The possibilities are as limitless as the human imagination. This section presents a series of these dramatizations, as the speakers reveal themselves through their various voices.

Ulysses

Alfred, Lord Tennyson   *(1809–1892)*

It little profits that an idle king,
By this still hearth, among these barren crags,
Matched with an agèd wife, I mete and dole
Unequal laws unto a savage race,
That hoard, and sleep, and feed, and know not me.   5
I cannot rest from travel: I will drink
Life to the lees:[1] all times I have enjoyed
Greatly, have suffered greatly, both with those
That loved me, and alone; on shore, and when
Through scudding drifts the rainy Hyades[2]   10
Vext the dim sea: I am become a name
For always roaming with a hungry heart;
Much have I seen and known; cities of men
And manners, climates, councils, governments,
Myself not least, but honoured of them all;   15
And drunk delight of battle with my peers,
Far on the ringing plains of windy Troy.
I am a part of all that I have met;
Yet all experience is an arch wherethrough
Gleams that untravelled world, whose margin fades   20
For ever and for ever when I move.
How dull it is to pause, to make an end,
To rust unburnished, not to shine in use!
As though to breathe were life. Life piled on life
Were all too little, and of one to me   25
Little remains: but every hour is saved
From that eternal silence, something more,
A bringer of new things; and vile it were
For some three suns to store and hoard myself,
And this gray spirit yearning in desire   30

---

[1]Sediment at the bottom of a wine glass or bottle.   [2]A constellation associated, in rising, with rain.

To follow knowledge like a sinking star,
Beyond the utmost bound of human thought.

    This is my son, mine own Telemachus,
To whom I leave the sceptre and the isle—
Well-loved of me, discerning to fulfil   35
This labour, by slow prudence to make mild
A rugged people, and through soft degrees
Subdue them to the useful and the good.
Most blameless is he, centred in the sphere
Of common duties, decent not to fail   40
In offices of tenderness, and pay
Meet adoration to my household gods,
When I am gone. He works his work, I mine.

    There lies the port; the vessel puffs her sail:
There gloom the dark broad seas. My mariners,   45
Souls that have toiled, and wrought, and thought with me—
That ever with a frolic welcome took
The thunder and the sunshine, and opposed
Free hearts, free foreheads—you and I are old;
Old age hath yet his honour and his toil;   50
Death closes all: but something ere the end,
Some work of noble note, may yet be done,
Not unbecoming men that strove with Gods.
The lights begin to twinkle from the rocks.
The long day wanes: the slow moon climbs: the deep   55
Moans round with many voices. Come, my friends,
'Tis not too late to seek a newer world.
Push off, and sitting well in order smite
The sounding furrows; for my purpose holds
To sail beyond the sunset, and the baths   60
Of all the western stars, until I die.
It may be that the gulfs will wash us down:
It may be we shall touch the Happy Isles,
And see the great Achilles, whom we knew.
Though much is taken, much abides; and though   65
We are not now that strength which in old days
Moved earth and heaven; that which we are, we are;
One equal temper of heroic hearts,
Made weak by time and fate, but strong in will
To strive, to seek, to find, and not to yield.   70

    The speaker is Ulysses himself, and we can define him further by considering the time and place from which he speaks. An old man, he has long since completed his wandering journey home, won back his wife, and regained his throne. Tennyson takes up where Homer's *Odyssey* left off. He imagines himself Ulysses. Given Ulysses's history and temperament, how would he respond to his aging in Ithaca? The poem presents Tennyson's answer. In what lines does Ulysses most clearly indicate his attitude toward his past, his present, and his future? What lines most clearly suggest his attitude toward his son? His wife? His country? His mariners? Explain lines 19 to 21. Explain the comparisons involving wine (lines 6–7) and rust (lines 22–23). Do they have anything in common? We may wish to consider Tennyson's "Ulysses" not simply as the portrait of one man, but of a type. What type?

My Last Duchess[1]

Ferrara

Robert Browning   *(1812–1889)*

That's my last Duchess painted on the wall,
Looking as if she were alive. I call
That piece a wonder, now: Frà Pandolf's hands
Worked busily a day, and there she stands.
Will 't please you sit and look at her? I said   5
'Frà Pandolf' by design, for never read
Strangers like you that pictured countenance,
The depth and passion of its earnest glance,
But to myself they turned (since none puts by
The curtain I have drawn for you, but I)   10
And seemed as they would ask me, if they durst,
How such a glance came there; so, not the first
Are you to turn and ask thus. Sir, 't was not
Her husband's presence only, called that spot
Of joy into the Duchess' cheek: perhaps   15
Frà Pandolf chanced to say 'Her mantle laps
'Over my lady's wrist too much,' or 'Paint
'Must never hope to reproduce the faint
'Half-flush that dies along her throat:' such stuff
Was courtesy, she thought, and cause enough   20
For calling up that spot of joy. She had
A heart—how shall I say?—too soon made glad,
Too easily impressed; she liked whate'er
She looked on, and her looks went everywhere.

[1]Alfonso II, a sixteenth-century Duke of Ferrara, in Italy, negotiated a second marriage after the death of his first young wife. Browning imagined the details and also, apparently, the painter, Frà Pandolf, and the sculptor, Claus of Innsbruck.

Sir, 't was all one! My favour at her breast,   25
The dropping of the daylight in the West,
The bough of cherries some officious fool
Broke in the orchard for her, the white mule
She rode with round the terrace—all and each
Would draw from her alike the approving speech,   30
Or blush, at least. She thanked men,—good! but thanked
Somehow—I know not how—as if she ranked
My gift of a nine-hundred-years-old name
With anybody's gift. Who'd stoop to blame
This sort of trifling? Even had you skill   35
In speech—(which I have not)—to make your will
Quite clear to such an one, and say, 'Just this
'Or that in you disgusts me; here you miss,
'Or there exceed the mark'—and if she let
Herself be lessoned so, nor plainly set   40
Her wits to yours, forsooth, and made excuse,
—E'en then would be some stooping; and I choose
Never to stoop. Oh sir, she smiled, no doubt,
Whene'er I passed her; but who passed without
Much the same smile? This grew; I gave commands;   45
Then all smiles stopped together. There she stands
As if alive. Will 't please you rise? We'll meet
The company below, then. I repeat,
The Count your master's known munificence
Is ample warrant that no just pretence   50
Of mine for dowry will be disallowed;
Though his fair daughter's self, as I avowed
At starting, is my object. Nay, we'll go
Together down, sir. Notice Neptune, though,
Taming a sea-horse, thought a rarity,   55
Which Claus of Innsbruck cast in bronze for me!

"My Last Duchess" is one of Browning's several distinctive *dramatic mono-logues.* Browning has imagined not only a character and a situation, but a listener other than the reader. In Tennyson's "Ulysses" the character speaks in *soliloquy,* addressing himself only, or, as in a play by Shakespeare, speaking his thoughts aloud to clarify his motives or explain himself to the playgoing audi-ence. In "My Last Duchess," however, the Duke of Ferrara addresses his re-marks not to himself or to us, but to another imagined figure who silently shares the stage with him.

"My Last Duchess" is a fine illustration of an obvious truth; a speaker is not always aware of the effect of his words. The Duke obviously has a high opinion of himself, but his words reveal a man neither poet nor reader can admire. What is repellent about him? What details reveal his attitudes? Where do our attitudes differ? Here is what we call *dramatic irony;* a character's words or acts have implications opposite to what he or she assumes or intends. Dramatic irony is the frequent effect of first-person narration, as here, when the Duke asserts himself in his "I" and "my." What can we infer about his imagined listener? Are we to assume that he says nothing at all?

The River-Merchant's Wife: A Letter

Ezra Pound   *(1885–1972)*

While my hair was still cut straight across my forehead
I played about the front gate, pulling flowers.
You came by on bamboo stilts, playing horse,
You walked about my seat, playing with blue plums.
And we went on living in the village of Chōkan: 5
Two small people, without dislike or suspicion.

At fourteen I married My Lord you.
I never laughed, being bashful.
Lowering my head, I looked at the wall.
Called to, a thousand times, I never looked back.   10

At fifteen I stopped scowling,
I desired my dust to be mingled with yours
Forever and forever and forever.
Why should I climb the look out?

At sixteen you departed,   15
You went into far Ku-tō-en, by the river of swirling eddies,
And you have been gone five months.
The monkeys make sorrowful noise overhead.

You dragged your feet when you went out.
By the gate now, the moss is grown, the different mosses,   20
Too deep to clear them away!
The leaves fall early this autumn, in wind.
The paired butterflies are already yellow with August
Over the grass in the West garden;
They hurt me. I grow older.   25
If you are coming down through the narrows of the river Kiang,
Please let me know beforehand,
And I will come out to meet you
          As far as Chō-fū-Sa.

          By Rihaku (Li T'ai Po)

In this translation, Ezra Pound adopts a female persona, an eighth-century Chinese teenager. How convincing is the result? What lines most effectively suggest her age and gender? What details most effectively suggest a Chinese setting? What changes are recorded between the beginning and end of the poem? What has caused them? Are there any similarities between the lives of these young people and those of young people in twentieth-century America?

Our last example is the longest and in some respects the most difficult. The speaker is J. Alfred Prufrock; readers will understand much in the poem when they begin to see Prufrock as a personality with a past, a present, and a future. Prufrock speaks to a "you" who may be difficult to define, but Eliot evidently parallels Prufrock's speech with the speech in Italian he quotes as his epigraph (both Guido and Prufrock may be seen as describing their private hells to listeners they believe condemned to similar fates). Finally, the conditions that prompt Prufrock to speak become more clear when we consider that Eliot has given the poem a pointedly ironic title; this "love song" contains little that most people would call "love."

The Love Song of J. Alfred Prufrock

T. S. Eliot   (1888–1965)

S'io credessi che mia risposta fosse
a persona che mai tornasse al mondo,
questa fiamma staria senza più scosse.
Ma per ciò che giammai di questo fondo
non tornò vivo alcun, s'i'odo il vero,
senza tema d'infamia ti rispondo.[1]

Let us go then, you and I,
When the evening is spread out against the sky
Like a patient etherised upon a table;
Let us go, through certain half-deserted streets,
The muttering retreats   5
Of restless nights in one-night cheap hotels
And sawdust restaurants with oyster-shells:
Streets that follow like a tedious argument
Of insidious intent
To lead you to an overwhelming question . . .   10

---

[1]In Dante's *Inferno* the poet, a visitor to Hell, has asked Guido da Montefeltro, whose soul burns in eternal flame, who he is and how he came there. The Italian lines given here begin Guido's reply: "If I believed my answer were to one who might return to the world, this flame would shake [because I would speak] no more. But since, if I hear true, none ever came alive from this abyss, I answer you without fear of infamy" (xxvii, 61–66).

Oh, do not ask, 'What is it?'
Let us go and make our visit.

In the room the women come and go
Talking of Michelangelo.[2]

The yellow fog that rubs its back upon the window-panes,   **15**
The yellow smoke that rubs its muzzle on the window-panes,
Licked its tongue into the corners of the evening,
Lingered upon the pools that stand in drains,
Let fall upon its back the soot that falls from chimneys,
Slipped by the terrace, made a sudden leap,   **20**
And seeing that it was a soft October night,
Curled once about the house and fell asleep.

And indeed there will be time
For the yellow smoke that slides along the street
Rubbing its back upon the window-panes;   **25**
There will be time, there will be time
To prepare a face to meet the faces that you meet;
There will be time to murder and create,
And time for all the works and days[3] of hands
That lift and drop a question on your plate;   **30**
Time for you and time for me,
And time yet for a hundred indecisions,
And for a hundred visions and revisions,
Before the taking of a toast and tea.

In the room the women come and go   **35**
Talking of Michelangelo.

And indeed there will be time
To wonder, 'Do I dare?' and, 'Do I dare?'
Time to turn back and descend the stair,
With a bald spot in the middle of my hair—   **40**
(They will say: 'How his hair is growing thin!')
My morning coat, my collar mounting firmly to the chin,
My necktie rich and modest, but asserted by a simple pin—
(They will say: 'But how his arms and legs are thin!')
Do I dare   **45**
Disturb the universe?
In a minute there is time
For decisions and revisions which a minute will reverse.

[2]Michelangelo created; these people talk.   [3]*Works and Days,* by Hesiod (eighth century B.C.), an account of agricultural labor.

For I have known them all already, known them all—
Have known the evenings, mornings, afternoons,   50
I have measured out my life with coffee spoons;
I know the voices dying with a dying fall[4]
Beneath the music from a farther room.
    So how should I presume?

And I have known the eyes already, known them all—   55
The eyes that fix you in a formulated phrase,
And when I am formulated, sprawling on a pin,
When I am pinned and wriggling on the wall,
Then how should I begin
To spit out all the butt-ends of my days and ways?   60
    And how should I presume?

And I have known the arms already, known them all—
Arms that are braceleted and white and bare
(But in the lamplight, downed with light brown hair!)
Is it perfume from a dress   65
That makes me so digress?
Arms that lie along a table, or wrap about a shawl.
    And should I then presume?
    And how should I begin?

                        •   •   •

Shall I say, I have gone at dusk through narrow streets   70
And watched the smoke that rises from the pipes
Of lonely men in shirt-sleeves, leaning out of windows? . . .

I should have been a pair of ragged claws
Scuttling across the floors of silent seas.

                        •   •   •

And the afternoon, the evening, sleeps so peacefully!   75
Smoothed by long fingers,
Asleep . . . tired . . . or it malingers,
Stretched on the floor, here beside you and me.
Should I, after tea and cakes and ices,
Have the strength to force the moment to its crisis?   80
But though I have wept and fasted, wept and prayed,
Though I have seen my head (grown slightly bald) brought in upon a
        platter,[5]

---

[4]Cf. Shakespeare, *Twelfth Night,* Act I, Scene 1, lines 1–4: "If music be the food of love, play on. / Give me excess of it, that, surfeiting, / The appetite may sicken, and so die. / That strain again! It had a dying fall." Music, love, and romance are distant from Prufrock, in "a farther room."   [5]Like John the Baptist. See Mark 6. 17–28; Matthew 14. 3–11.

I am no prophet—and here's no great matter;
I have seen the moment of my greatness flicker,
And I have seen the eternal Footman hold my coat, and snicker,   85
And in short, I was afraid.

And would it have been worth it, after all,
After the cups, the marmalade, the tea,
Among the porcelain, among some talk of you and me,
Would it have been worth while,   90
To have bitten off the matter with a smile,
To have squeezed the universe into a ball[6]
To roll it towards some overwhelming question,
To say: 'I am Lazarus, come from the dead,[7]
Come back to tell you all, I shall tell you all'—   95
If one, settling a pillow by her head,
      Should say: 'That is not what I meant at all.
      That is not it, at all.'

And would it have been worth it, after all,
Would it have been worth while,   100
After the sunsets and the dooryards and the sprinkled streets,
After the novels, after the teacups, after the skirts that trail along the
      floor—
And this, and so much more?—
It is impossible to say just what I mean!
But as if a magic lantern threw the nerves in patterns on a screen: 105
Would it have been worth while
If one, settling a pillow or throwing off a shawl,
And turning toward the window, should say:
      'That is not it at all,
      That is not what I meant, at all.'   110

· · ·

No! I am not Prince Hamlet,[8] nor was meant to be;
Am an attendant lord, one that will do
To swell a progress, start a scene or two,
Advise the prince; no doubt, an easy tool,
Deferential, glad to be of use,   115
Politic, cautious, and meticulous;

[6]Cf. Andrew Marvell's "To His Coy Mistress": 'Let us roll all our strength and all / Our sweetness up into one ball, / And tear our pleasures with rough strife / Through the iron gates of life."
[7]John 11. 1–44 tells of Christ's raising Lazarus from the dead. Another Lazarus appears in Luke 16. 19–31, where the passage ends: "If they hear not Moses and the prophets, neither will they be persuaded, though one rose from the dead."   [8]Prufrock considers himself like Shakespeare's Hamlet in procrastination but not in action. In the play of life he is not a tragic hero but a Polonius, Rosencrantz, or Guildenstern—perhaps even the stock comic character, the Fool.

Full of high sentence,[9] but a bit obtuse;
At times, indeed, almost ridiculous—
Almost, at times, the Fool.

I grow old . . . I grow old . . .   120
I shall wear the bottoms of my trousers rolled.

Shall I part my hair behind? Do I dare to eat a peach?
I shall wear white flannel trousers, and walk upon the beach.
I have heard the mermaids singing, each to each.

I do not think that they will sing to me.   125

I have seen them riding seaward on the waves
Combing the white hair of the waves blown back
When the wind blows the water white and black.

We have lingered in the chambers of the sea
By sea-girls wreathed with seaweed red and brown   130
Till human voices wake us, and we drown.

[9]Sententiousness, pomposity.

How old is Prufrock? How do you know? What else do you know about him?
Summarize his character. How does the name "J. Alfred Prufrock" help to
characterize him? In what ways would Prufrock like his life to be different? How
do you know? In what ways would Prufrock's life be different if he were "a pair
of ragged claws" (line 73)? What would he gain? What would he lose? Would
what "have been worth it, after all" (lines 87, 99)? Will Prufrock change? What
is the "overwhelming question" (line 10)?

CHAPTER 3

LANGUAGE

DENOTATION AND CONNOTATION

The *denotation* of a word is its direct reference, its dictionary definition. It is the thing the word stands for, a concept without emotional coloring. The *connotation* is the feeling or emotion aroused in the mind of speaker or listener. Certain words possess powerful connotations for most people, though the precise feelings aroused may vary: *God, Hiroshima, love, Communist.* Others are more simply denotative *(chair, street),* though even these may be connotative for some people; *dog* and *cat* may be emotional words for people afraid of animals. Careful control of connotations is vital to poetry. As readers, we must be alert to the meanings of words, but we must also observe the associations the poet evokes.

Through images of estate and garden the following poem contrasts the emotional satisfactions of possession with the pain of irretrievable loss.

Those Hours When Happy Hours Were My Estate

Edna St. Vincent Millay   (1892–1950)

Those hours when happy hours were my estate,—
Entailed, as proper, for the next in line,
Yet mine the harvest, and the title mine—
Those acres, fertile, and the furrow straight,
From which the lark would rise—all of my late
Enchantments, still, in brilliant colours, shine,
But striped with black, the tulip, lawn and vine,

4

473

Like gardens looked at through an iron gate.   8
Yet not as one who never sojourned there
I view the lovely segments of a past
I lived with all my senses, well aware
That this was perfect, and it would not last: 12
I smell the flower, though vacuum-still the air;
I feel its texture, though the gate is fast.

The speaker has, in fact, not lost a garden. What has she lost? What words
and phrases serve most powerfully to convey her feelings through their connotations? Describe the connotations of *estate, fertile, lark, black, gardens, vacuum-
still.* What is the denotation and the connotation of *furrow straight?* Of *iron gate*
(why not a *wooden gate*)?

In the next poem we start with associations suggested by the name "Iona."
An island, scarcely three miles long, off the west coast of Scotland, it remained
a powerful center of Celtic culture for three centuries after St. Columba established a mission there in 563. Vast numbers of kings, chieftains, and holy men
were buried in its rocky soil.

Iona: The Graves of the Kings

Robinson Jeffers   (1887–1962)

I wish not to lie here.
There's hardly a plot of earth not blessed for burial, but here
One might dream badly.   3

In beautiful seas a beautiful
And sainted island, but the dark earth so shallow on the rock
Gorged with bad meat.   6

Kings buried in the lee of the saint,
Kings of fierce Norway, blood-boltered[1] Scotland, bitterly dreaming
Treacherous Ireland.   9

Imagine what delusions of grandeur,
What suspicion-agonized eyes, what jellies of arrogance and terror
This earth has absorbed.   12

---

[1]Blood-spattered. A "bolter" is a sieve, or a cloth used for sifting. Cf. "blood-boltered Banquo,"
Shakespeare's *Macbeth,* iv, i, 123.

What are the denotations and connotations in *graves* (why not *tombs*)?
Consider *gorged, meat, lee,* especially *jellies.* Do you think Jeffers remembers
King Lear, in which Cornwall shouts as he stamps out Gloucester's remaining
eye "Out, vile jelly! Where is thy lustre now?" What kind of people are these
kings?

Shakespeare was a master both of precise meanings and of vital associations. In the following poem the speaker denies to his mistress the beauty usually associated with roses and perfumes, but does he mean that she is not beautiful?

My Mistress' Eyes Are Nothing Like the Sun

William Shakespeare   (1564–1616)

My mistress' eyes are nothing like the sun;
Coral is far more red than her lips' red:
If snow be white, why then her breasts are dun;
If hairs be wires, black wires grow on her head.   4
I have seen roses damask'd, red and white,
But no such roses see I in her cheeks;
And in some perfumes is there more delight
Than in the breath that from my mistress reeks.   8
I love to hear her speak, yet well I know
That music hath a far more pleasing sound:
I grant I never saw a goddess go,—
My mistress, when she walks, treads on the ground: 12
   And yet, by heaven, I think my love as rare
   As any she belied with false compare.

William Carlos Williams, too, could play that game. The woman described by his speaker is more like a weed than an anemone, but does the comparison make her less beautiful?

Queen-Ann's-Lace

William Carlos Williams   (1883–1963)

Her body is not so white as
anemone petals nor so smooth—nor
so remote a thing. It is a field
of the wild carrot taking
the field by force; the grass   5
does not raise above it.
Here is no question of whiteness,
white as can be, with a purple mole
at the center of each flower.
Each flower is a hand's span   10
of her whiteness. Wherever
his hand has lain there is
a tiny purple blemish. Each part
is a blossom under his touch
to which the fibres of her being   15

stem one by one, each to its end,
until the whole field is a
white desire, empty, a single stem,
a cluster, flower by flower,
a pious wish to whiteness gone over—   20
or nothing.

How is Williams's poem like Shakespeare's? Look up *Queen Anne's lace* in your
dictionary, preferably one with a picture to help you judge Williams's denotative
accuracy. What do you make of *purple mole?* Of *fibres of her being?* Why does
he conclude "or nothing"?
    In still another description of a lovely woman, the following speaker plays
with some mildly off-color double meanings ("Love likes a gander, and adores
a goose"), but that is only part of the fun.

I Knew a Woman

Theodore Roethke   (1908–1963)

I knew a woman, lovely in her bones,
When small birds sighed, she would sigh back at them;
Ah, when she moved, she moved more ways than one:
The shapes a bright container can contain!
Of her choice virtues only gods should speak,   5
Or English poets who grew up on Greek
(I'd have them sing in chorus, cheek to cheek).

How well her wishes went! She stroked my chin,
She taught me Turn, and Counter-turn, and Stand;
She taught me Touch, that undulant white skin;   10
I nibbled meekly from her proffered hand;
She was the sickle; I, poor I, the rake,
Coming behind her for her pretty sake
(But what prodigious mowing we did make).

Love likes a gander, and adores a goose: 15
Her full lips pursed, the errant note to seize;
She played it quick, she played it light and loose;
My eyes, they dazzled at her flowing knees;
Her several parts could keep a pure repose,
Or one hip quiver with a mobile nose   20
(She moved in circles, and those circles moved).

Let seed be grass, and grass turn into hay:
I'm martyr to a motion not my own;
What's freedom for? To know eternity.
I swear she cast a shadow white as stone.   25

But who would count eternity in days?
These old bones live to learn her wanton ways:
(I measure time by how a body sways).

What is the usual denotation of "container"? Does the word ordinarily have any significant connotation? What meanings and associations does it have here? What other words and phrases lend important effects to the poem through their associations?

The last poem in this section deals with death, almost invariably an emotional subject. Observe which words work most powerfully by association.

Sylvia Plath committed suicide at thirty-one by turning on a gas oven, evidently her fourth attempt, which, like the others, may have contained a buried expectation of rescue. Her father was of German descent, hence her allusions to death camps and Herr Doktor. Lazarus, four days dead, had been buried in a cave closed by a stone. Jesus ordered the stone removed and called Lazarus. "And he that was dead came forth, bound hand and foot with grave-clothes; and his face was bound about with a napkin. Jesus saith unto them, Loose him, and let him go" (John 11.44).

Lady Lazarus

Sylvia Plath   (1932–1963)

I have done it again.
One year in every ten
I manage it—   3

A sort of walking miracle, my skin
Bright as a Nazi lampshade,[1]
My right foot   6

A paperweight,
My face a featureless, fine
Jew linen.   9

Peel off the napkin
O my enemy.
Do I terrify?—   12

The nose, the eye pits, the full set of teeth?
The sour breath
Will vanish in a day.   15

Soon, soon the flesh
The grave cave ate will be
At home on me   18

[1]Made of skin from a death camp victim.

And I a smiling woman.
I am only thirty.
And like the cat I have nine times to die.   21

This is Number Three.
What a trash
To annihilate each decade.   24

What a million filaments.
The peanut-crunching crowd
Shoves in to see   27

Them unwrap me hand and foot—
The big strip tease.
Gentlemen, ladies,   30

These are my hands,
My knees.
I may be skin and bone,   33

Nevertheless, I am the same, identical woman.
The first time it happened I was ten.
It was an accident.   36

The second time I meant
To last it out and not come back at all.
I rocked shut   39

As a seashell.
They had to call and call
And pick the worms off me like sticky pearls.   42

Dying
Is an art, like everything else.
I do it exceptionally well.   45

I do it so it feels like hell.
I do it so it feels real.
I guess you could say I've a call.   48

It's easy enough to do it in a cell.
It's easy enough to do it and stay put.
It's the theatrical   51

Comeback in broad day
To the same place, the same face, the same brute
Amused shout: 54

"A miracle!"
That knocks me out.
There is a charge   57

For the eyeing of my scars, there is a charge
For the hearing of my heart—
It really goes. 60

And there is a charge, a very large charge,
For a word or a touch
Or a bit of blood 63

Or a piece of my hair or my clothes.
So, so, Herr Doktor.
So, Herr Enemy. 66

I am your opus,
I am your valuable,
The pure gold baby 69

That melts to a shriek.
I turn and burn.
Do not think I underestimate your great concern. 72

Ash, ash—
You poke and stir.
Flesh, bone, there is nothing there— 75

A cake of soap,
A wedding ring,
A gold filling. 78

Herr God, Herr Lucifer,
Beware
Beware. 81

Out of the ash
I rise with my red hair
And I eat men like air. 84

What are the connotations of *a Nazi lampshade,* of *a cake of soap,* of *miracle, opus,* and *great concern?* What is Plath picturing with the ashes, and with rising from them?

ALLUSION

Sylvia Plath has alluded to Lazarus, to the phoenix, to German death camps, to her father, and to her own attempts at suicide: "I have done it again." An *allusion* is any meaningful reference, direct or indirect. "A Socrates" suggests a wise teacher; "a Judas," a treacherous friend. Yeats writes "Another Troy must rise and set," calling up the whole tragic Trojan war, along with the course of the sun. Shakespeare's Falstaff alludes to the biblical "Dives who lived in purple" to describe amusingly the color of Bardolf's face. T. S. Eliot in *The Waste Land,* with a cryptic "To Carthage then I came / Burning," calls up the young St. Augustine's wayward life. Most allusions refer to the heritage of Western culture: Greek and Roman myths, the Bible, Shakespeare, memorable historical events. Some are less evident, like Eliot's to Augustine, or like Plath's personal ones, which require some biographical assistance. Some are very hard indeed to puzzle out and remain ambiguous. But all are meaningful, challenging the reader's attention and expanding the poem's significance.

Terence, This Is Stupid Stuff

A. E. Housman   (1859–1936)

"Terence, this is stupid stuff:
You eat your victuals fast enough;
There can't be much amiss, 'tis clear,
To see the rate you drink your beer.
But oh, good Lord, the verse you make,   5
It gives a chap the belly-ache.
The cow, the old cow, she is dead;
It sleeps well, the horned head:
We poor lads, 'tis our turn now
To hear such tunes as killed the cow.   10
Pretty friendship 'tis to rhyme
Your friends to death before their time
Moping melancholy mad:
Come, pipe a tune to dance to, lad."
     Why, if 'tis dancing you would be,   15
There's brisker pipes than poetry.
Say, for what were hop-yards meant,
Or why was Burton built on Trent?
Oh many a peer[1] of England brews
Livelier liquor than the Muse,   20
And malt does more than Milton can
To justify God's ways to man.
Ale, man, ale's the stuff to drink
For fellows whom it hurts to think:
Look into the pewter pot   25
To see the world as the world's not.
And faith, 'tis pleasant till 'tis past:

[1]Nobleman. Wealth from breweries sometimes led to peerages.

The mischief is that 'twill not last.
Oh I have been to Ludlow[2] fair
And left my necktie God knows where,   30
And carried half-way home, or near,
Pints and quarts of Ludlow beer:
Then the world seemed none so bad,
And I myself a sterling lad;
And down in lovely muck I've lain,   35
Happy till I woke again.
Then I saw the morning sky:
Heigho, the tale was all a lie;
The world, it was the old world yet,
I was I, my things were wet,   40
And nothing now remained to do
But begin the game anew.
    Therefore, since the world has still
Much good, but much less good than ill,
And while the sun and moon endure   45
Luck's a chance, but trouble's sure,
I'd face it as a wise man would,
And train for ill and not for good.
'Tis true, the stuff I bring for sale
Is not so brisk a brew as ale: 50
Out of a stem that scored[3] the hand
I wrung it in a weary land.
But take it: if the smack is sour,
The better for the embittered hour;
It should do good to heart and head   55
When your soul is in my soul's stead;
And I will friend you, if I may,
In the dark and cloudy day.

    There was a king reigned in the East:
There, when kings will sit to feast,   60
They get their fill before they think
With poisoned meat and poisoned drink.
He gathered all that springs to birth
From the many-venomed earth;
First a little, thence to more,   65
He sampled all her killing store;
And easy, smiling, seasoned sound,
Sate the king when healths went round.
They put arsenic in his meat

---

[2] A Shropshire market town.　　[3] Scratched, cut.

And stared aghast to watch him eat;   70
They poured strychnine in his cup
And shook to see him drink it up:
They shook, they stared as white's their shirt:
Them it was their poison hurt.
—I tell the tale that I heard told.   75
Mithridates, he died old.

In this poem the most important allusion is to Mithridates, a king whose story is told in Pliny's *Natural History*. Perhaps because he fears Mithridates will not be familiar to his readers, Housman recapitulates the story in the last section of the poem, making the allusion largely self-explanatory. He leaves it to the reader, however, to perceive the relationship between Mithridates and the rest of the poem. Other allusions help to clarify the attitude toward life upon which the relationship rests. Burton upon Trent is an English town famous for its breweries. The allusion to Milton ("And malt does more than Milton can / To justify God's ways to man") reminds us that in the opening lines of *Paradise Lost* Milton says he wrote the poem to "justify the ways of God to men." The line "Terence, this is stupid stuff" also involves an allusion: Terence was a Latin comic dramatist (ca. 190–159 B.C.), and Housman was Professor of Latin at Cambridge. Terence's reputation for a polished Latin style may have prompted Housman's choice of this pseudonym for himself. The poem gains force when read in its original position near the end of a volume of poems that are not comic, but "moping melancholy mad," Housman's *A Shropshire Lad*. A good dictionary or encyclopedia will usually clarify such allusions as "Mithridates" and "Terence," but the opening lines of "Terence, This is Stupid Stuff" are more immediately clear to those who have already savored Housman in the poems preceding it. How does Housman characterize his poems? What does he mean by carrying pints and quarts of Ludlow beer "half-way home, or near"? Explain "When your soul is in my soul's stead." What point does Housman make with Mithridates?

The following poem is enriched by knowledge of Homer's *Odyssey*.

Ulysses

Robert Graves   (1895–1985)

To the much-tossed Ulysses, never done
    With woman whether gowned as wife or whore,
Penelope and Circe seemed as one:
She like a whore made his lewd fancies run,
    And wifely she a hero to him bore.   5

Their counter-changings terrified his way:
    They were the clashing rocks, Symplegades,
Scylla and Charybdis too were they;
Now they were storms frosting the sea with spray
    And now the lotus island's drunken ease.   10

They multiplied into the Sirens' throng,
  Forewarned by fear of whom he stood bound fast
Hand and foot helpless to the vessel's mast,
Yet would not stop his ears: daring their song
  He groaned and sweated till that shore was past.   15

One, two and many: flesh had made him blind,
  Flesh had one pleasure only in the act,
Flesh set one purpose only in the mind—
Triumph of flesh and afterwards to find
  Still those same terrors wherewith flesh was racked.   20

His wiles were witty and his fame far known,
Every king's daughter sought him for her own,
  Yet he was nothing to be won or lost.
  All lands to him were Ithaca: love-tossed
He loathed the fraud, yet would not bed alone.   25

Penelope was the wife of Ulysses; Circe, an enchantress whose attractions kept him for a year from continuing his journey homeward. In the mind of Ulysses, as Graves portrays him, they stand for two extremes of woman, "wife or whore," but seem also "as one." By identifying with woman the difficulties that Ulysses met in his wanderings (Symplegades, Scylla, Charybdis, storms, the lotus island, and the Sirens), Graves makes the *Odyssey* into a metaphoric voyage by a man "love-tossed," who "loathed the fraud, yet would not bed alone."

The title of the next poem fixes the scene in a museum of fine arts. The first few lines present a generalization about the "Old Masters" that is specifically illustrated in two paintings by Pieter Breughel.

Musée des Beaux Arts

W. H. Auden   *(1907–1973)*

About suffering they were never wrong,
The Old Masters: how well they understood
Its human position; how it takes place
While someone else is eating or opening a window or just walking
    dully along;   5
How, when the aged are reverently, passionately waiting
For the miraculous birth, there always must be
Children who did not specially want it to happen, skating
On a pond at the edge of the wood:
They never forgot   10
That even the dreadful martyrdom must run its course
Anyhow in a corner, some untidy spot
Where the dogs go on with their doggy life and the torturer's horse
Scratches its innocent behind on a tree.

In Breughel's *Icarus,* for instance: how everything turns away   15
Quite leisurely from the disaster; the ploughman may
Have heard the splash, the forsaken cry,
But for him it was not an important failure; the sun shone
As it had to on the white legs disappearing into the green
Water; and the expensive delicate ship that must have seen   20
Something amazing, a boy falling out of the sky,
Had somewhere to get to and sailed calmly on.

Auden alludes to Breughel's "The Massacre of the Innocents" and "The Fall of Icarus," but he evokes the paintings in sufficient detail for our understanding. We do need, however, to know something of the Icarus of ancient Greek myth: a boy who flew too near the sun on wings of feathers and wax, which the sun melted, plunging him into the sea. What point is Auden making? What are his most effective details?

The Second Coming

W. B. Yeats   (1865–1939)

Turning and turning in the widening gyre
The falcon cannot hear the falconer;
Things fall apart; the centre cannot hold;
Mere anarchy is loosed upon the world,
The blood-dimmed tide is loosed, and everywhere   5
The ceremony of innocence is drowned;
The best lack all conviction, while the worst
Are full of passionate intensity.

Surely some revelation is at hand;
Surely the Second Coming is at hand.   10
The Second Coming! Hardly are those words out
When a vast image out of *Spiritus Mundi*
Troubles my sight: somewhere in sands of the desert
A shape with lion body and the head of a man,
A gaze blank and pitiless as the sun,   15
Is moving its slow thighs, while all about it
Reel shadows of the indignant desert birds.
The darkness drops again; but now I know
That twenty centuries of stony sleep
Were vexed to nightmare by a rocking cradle,   20
And what rough beast, its hour come round at last,
Slouches towards Bethlehem to be born?

The most important allusion here is to the widespread belief that Christ will appear on earth once more, in a "Second Coming." The speaker of this poem suggests that the Second Coming will present mankind not with a savior, like the first coming, but with a ravening beast. In the "gyre" Yeats describes a widening cone similar to the path of an upward-flying falcon, but similar also to his own image for the periodic movement of history, from one gyre into another opposing one. In the term *"Spiritus Mundi"* he suggests that his vision derives from a "Spirit of the World," an ever-present, animating principle.

Frequently, as here, the reader needs not only to identify the allusion, but to understand it in the poet's particular focus. Yeats is writing about political tension and violence in Ireland, taking it as typical of the modern world. How does his beast surrounded by indignant birds contrast with the biblical Bethlehem?

Yeats makes another powerful biblical allusion in the following poem.

Fragments

W. B. Yeats   (1865–1939)

I

Locke sank into a swoon;
The Garden died;
God took the spinning-jenny
Out of his side.   4

II

Where got I that truth?
Out of a medium's mouth,
Out of nothing it came,
Out of the forest loam,   8
Out of dark night where lay
The crowns of Nineveh.

The first stanza alludes to the Garden of Eden and the story in Genesis of how God created Eve from the rib of the sleeping Adam. It alludes also to the British philosopher John Locke (1632–1704) and to the invention of the spinning jenny. Why does the speaker consider Locke to be like Adam, why is the creation of the spinning jenny analogous to the creation of Eve, and why does the Garden die? Locke asserted that all knowledge came through the senses rather than from intuition or divine revelation. Yeats also assigns to Locke the theory George Berkeley developed from him that the mind's perception constitutes the perceived reality. The spinning jenny, invented by James Hargreaves in about 1764, could spin sixteen or more threads simultaneously. It is in a sense the mother of the industrial age, which ended the divinity of Eden and the garden of an agricultural economy. Nineveh was the site of a civilization that died centuries before the birth of Locke. What is Yeats saying about sensory knowledge, technology, and the modern world? What does his allusion to Nineveh imply?

Here are two sonnets likewise commenting on the ruins of time. Both allude to Ozymandias, better known as Rameses II (1324–1258 B.C.), of whom one Memnon carved a seated colossus, ninety feet high, from solid stone. Diodorus, the Sicilian Greek historian describes it in the first century B.C. as "the greatest in all Egypt," without "the least flaw, or any other blemish," and inscribed: "I am Osymandyas, king of kings; if any would know how great I am, and where I lie, let him excel me in any of my works." This translation from Diodorus first appeared in 1700 and was quoted several times afterwards—once in *The Encyclopaedia Britannica* of 1812, six years before Shelley wrote his sonnet. He and his friend Smith had been looking through Richard Pococke's two-volume *A Description of the East* (1742), with engraved illustrations, which describes but does not picture the colossus as "broke off about the middle of the trunk," and gives measurements of the foot and the head and shoulders lying in the sand, but mentions no inscription. Shelley and Smith evidently remembered their standing legs from pictures of several other ruined statues. Leigh Hunt published Shelley's poem in his *Examiner* on January 11, 1818, and Smith's companion piece in the next issue, February 1.

Ozymandias

Percy Bysshe Shelley   (1792–1822)

I met a traveller from an antique land
Who said: Two vast and trunkless legs of stone
Stand in the desert . . . Near them, on the sand,
Half sunk, a shattered visage lies, whose frown,
And wrinkled lip, and sneer of cold command,   5
Tell that its sculptor well those passions read
Which yet survive, stamped on these lifeless things,
The hand that mocked them, and the heart that fed:
And on the pedestal these words appear:
"My name is Ozymandias, king of kings: 10
Look on my works, ye Mighty, and despair!"
Nothing beside remains. Round the decay
Of that colossal wreck, boundless and bare
The lone and level sands stretch far away.

On a Stupendous Leg of Granite, Discovered Standing by Itself in the Deserts of Egypt, with the Inscription Inserted Below

Horatio H. Smith   (1779–1849)[1]

In Egypt's sandy silence, all alone,
    Stands a gigantic leg, which far off throws
    The only shadow that the desert knows.

---

[1]Smith, a tremendously popular figure in London society, had made a fortune as a stockbroker and a literary reputation by parodying, with his brother, the styles of eminent poets beginning with Wordsworth (not including young Shelley). He went on to write some twenty historical novels and a number of witty poems and essays.

"I am great Ozymandias," saith the stone, 4
  "The king of kings: this mighty city shows
The wonders of my hand." The city's gone!
  Nought but the leg remaining to disclose
The site of that forgotten Babylon. 8

We wonder, and some hunter may express
Wonder like ours, when thro' the wilderness,
  Where London *stood,* holding the wolf in chace,
He meets some fragment huge, and stops to guess 12
  What powerful, but unrecorded, race,
  Once dwelt in that annihilated place.

What is the effect of Shelley's traveler? Are the hand and heart the king's or the sculptor's (taking *mocked* as "mimicked" or "imitated," as some have done)? See what you can do with a paraphrase beginning with *whose frown.* What is the force of Shelley's *colossal?* Of Smith's *shadow, Babylon,* and *annihilated?* In what ways are the poems similar, in what ways different? You might try a paper comparing them, perhaps making a case for one as the better of the two.

  Like Smith, John Ashbery contemplates a bleak future against a sense of loss. But his allusion is literary, biographical, and immediately contemporary—a typically twentieth-century focus. His title and ninth line allude to a sonnet of Gérard Nerval (1808–1855), considered the father of modern French poetry, a writer and poem much esteemed by twentieth-century poets: "El Desdichado" (1854), Spanish for "The Unfortunate" or "The Outcast." Its opening lines are:

Je suis le Ténébreux,—le Veuf,—l'Inconsolé,
Le Prince d'Aquitaine à la Tour abolie

(I am the Shadowed,—the Widower,—the Unconsoled,
The Prince of Aquitaine of the abolished Tower)

T. S. Eliot climaxes *The Waste Land* by quoting the second line. Ashbery left graduate studies in English to write art criticism in France for the European edition of the *New York Herald Tribune.* He has taught English at Brooklyn College. Since 1980, he has been art critic and editor at *Newsweek.*

The Desperado

John Ashbery   (1927–)

What kind of life is this that we are leading
That so much strong vagary can slip by unnoticed?
Is there a future? It seems that all we'd planned
To find in it is rolling around now, spending itself. 4

You step aside, and the rock invasion from the fifties
Dissipates in afternoon smoke. And disco
Retreats a little, wiping large brown eyes.
They come along here. Now, all will be gone.   8

I am the shadowed, widower, the unconsoled.
But if it weren't for me I should also be the schoolmaster
Coaching, pruning young spring thoughts
Surprised to be here, in this air.   12

But their barely restrained look suits the gray
Importance of what we expect to be confronted with
Any day. Send the odious one a rebuke. Can one deny
Any longer that it is, and going to be?   16

Explain *rock invasion* and *disco*. What does the allusion to Nerval do for the
poem? Explain *if it weren't for me*. What do we expect to be confronted with?
    Here is another poem loaded with personal and contemporary allusion. The
title alludes to Billie Holiday (1915–1959), also known as Lady Day, the great
black singer of jazz and blues. O'Hara was a curator at New York's Museum
of Modern Art, influential in recognizing and writing about the Abstract Impres-
sionism of such artists and friends, as Willem de Kooning and Jackson Pollock,
that flourished in the 1950s.

The Day Lady Died

Frank O'Hara   (1926–1966)

It is 12:20 in New York a Friday
three days after Bastille day,[1] yes
it is 1959 and I go get a shoeshine
because I will get off the 4:19 in Easthampton[2]
at 7:15 and then go straight to dinner   5
and I don't know the people who will feed me

I walk up the muggy street beginning to sun
and have a hamburger and a malted and buy
an ugly NEW WORLD WRITING to see what the poets
in Ghana are doing these days
                                    I go on to the bank   10
and Miss Stillwagon (first name Linda I once heard)
doesn't even look up my balance for once in her life
and in the GOLDEN GRIFFIN[3] I get a little Verlaine

[1]July 14, the French national holiday celebrating the fall of the Bastille prison in 1789 at the outset
of the French Revolution.   [2]Easthampton village on the southeastern shore of Long Island, a
popular summer resort favored by the artists O'Hara knew.   [3]A bookstore near the Museum of
Modern Art.

for Patsy[4] with drawings by Bonnard although I do
think of Hesiod, trans. Richmond Lattimore or 15
Brendan Behan's new play or *Le Balcon* or *Les Nègres*
of Genet, but I don't, I stick with Verlaine
after practically going to sleep with quandariness

and for Mike I just stroll into the PARK LANE
Liquor Store and ask for a bottle of Strega and 20
then I go back where I came from to 6th Avenue
and the tobacconist in the Ziegfeld Theatre and
casually ask for a carton of Gauloises and a carton
of Picayunes, and a NEW YORK POST with her face on it

and I am sweating a lot by now and thinking of 25
leaning on the john door in the 5 SPOT
while she whispered a song along the keyboard
to Mal Waldron[5] and everyone and I stopped breathing

[4]Patsy Southgate, an artist. He buys an edition of the French poet Paul Verlaine (1844–1896) illustrated by the eminent French artist Pierre Bonnard (1867–1947) and considers Richmond Lattimore's new translation of Hesiod and plays by Behan and Genêt recently produced on Broadway. [5]Billie Holiday's accompanist (b. 1925).

What is the effect of O'Hara's precise details? Comment on his title. Why doesn't he say something like "In Memoriam, Billie Holiday"? Why is he buying gifts for Patsy and Mike? How do you picture "the 5 SPOT"? What is the effect of O'Hara's omissions of punctuation? Comment on *I stopped breathing*.

Like Ashbery's and O'Hara's (and Sylvia Plath's), James Merrill's allusions are largely personal, with a gathering of modern history and literature. His father was Charles Edward Merrill, a founder of the tremendously prosperous investment company now known as Merrill Lynch Pierce Fenner & Smith. He married, as Merrill says, "each thirteenth year." How does that number reflect on the poem and the childhood Merrill describes?

The Broken Home

James Merrill   (1926–)

Crossing the street,
I saw the parents and the child
At their window, gleaming like fruit
With evening's mild gold leaf. 4

In a room on the floor below,
Sunless, cooler—a brimming
Saucer of wax, marbly and dim—
I have lit what's left of my life. 8

I have thrown out yesterday's milk
And opened a book of maxims.
The flame quickens. The word stirs.

Tell me, tongue of fire,   **12**
That you and I are as real
At least as the people upstairs.

My father, who had flown in World War I,
Might have continued to invest his life   **16**
In cloud banks well above Wall Street and wife.
But the race was run below, and the point was to win.

Too late now, I make out in his blue gaze
(Through the smoked glass of being thirty-six)   **20**
The soul eclipsed by twin black pupils, sex
And business; time was money in those days.

Each thirteenth year he married. When he died
There were already several chilled wives   **24**
In sable orbit—rings, cars, permanent waves.
We'd felt him warming up for a green bride.

He could afford it. He was "in his prime"
At three score ten. But money was not time.   **28**

When my parents were younger this was a popular act:
A veiled woman would leap from an electric, wine-dark car
To the steps of no matter what—the Senate or the Ritz Bar—
And bodily, at newsreel speed, attack   **32**

No matter whom—Al Smith or José Maria Sert
Or Clemenceau[1]—veins standing out on her throat
As she yelled *War mongerer! Pig! Give us the vote!*,
And would have to be hauled away in her hobble skirt.   **36**

What had the man done? Oh, made history.
Her business (he had implied) was giving birth,
Tending the house, mending the socks.

Always that same old story—   **40**
Father Time and Mother Earth,
A marriage on the rocks.

One afternoon, red, satyr-thighed
Michael, the Irish setter, head   **44**

[1]Alfred E. Smith (1873–1944), governor of New York and candidate for president in 1928; José Maria Sert (1876–1945), Spanish mural painter who decorated the lobby of the Waldorf-Astoria Hotel in 1930; Georges Clemenceau (1841–1929), French premier who opposed Woodrow Wilson at the Paris Peace Conference.

Passionately lowered, led
The child I was to a shut door. Inside,

Blinds beat sun from the bed.
The green-gold room throbbed like a bruise.   48
Under a sheet, clad in taboos
Lay whom we sought, her hair undone, outspread,

And of a blackness found, if ever now, in old
Engravings where the acid bit.   52
I must have needed to touch it
Or the whiteness—was she dead?
Her eyes flew open, startled strange and cold.
The dog slumped to the floor. She reached for me. I fled.   56

Tonight they have stepped out onto the gravel.
The party is over. It's the fall
Of 1931. They love each other still.

She: Charlie, I can't stand the pace.   60
He: Come on, honey—why, you'll bury us all!

A lead soldier guards my windowsill:
Khaki rifle, uniform, and face.
Something in me grows heavy, silvery, pliable.   64

How intensely people used to feel!
Like metal poured at the close of a proletarian novel,
Refined and glowing from the crucible,
I see those two hearts, I'm afraid,   68
Still. Cool here in the graveyard of good and evil,
They are even so to be honored and obeyed.

. . . Obeyed, at least, inversely. Thus
I rarely buy a newspaper, or vote.   72
To do so, I have learned, is to invite
The tread of a stone guest[2] within my house.

Shooting this rusted bolt, though, against him,
I trust I am no less time's child than some   76
Who on the heath impersonate Poor Tom[3]
Or on the barricades risk life and limb.

Nor do I try to keep a garden, only
An avocado in a glass of water—   80
Roots pallid, gemmed with air. And later,

[2]A stone statue wreaks revenge on Don Juan in Molière's play and Mozart's opera.   [3]Edgar, in Shakespeare's *King Lear,* calls himself "Poor Tom" and pretends madness when disowned by his father.

When the small gilt leaves have grown
Fleshy and green, I let them die, yes, yes,
And start another. I am earth's no less.   84

A child, a red dog roam the corridors,
Still, of the broken home. No sound. The brilliant
Rag runners halt before wide-open doors.
My old room! Its wallpaper—cream, medallioned   88
With pink and brown—brings back the first nightmares,
Long summer colds, and Emma, sepia-faced,
Perspiring over broth carried upstairs
Aswim with golden fats I could not taste.   92

The real house became a boarding school.
Under the ballroom ceiling's allegory
Someone at last may actually be allowed
To learn something; or, from my window, cool   96
With the unstiflement of the entire story,
Watch a red setter stretch and sink in cloud.

What relevance does the first stanza have for the poem? What is the weight of
invest in the fifth stanza? Of *sable* in the seventh? Explain *But money was not
time.* What relevance does the veiled woman have? Why is the red setter
satyr-thighed? Explain the incident of the woman "clad in taboos . . . whom
we sought" What is Merrill's attitude toward his parents? Toward his childhood?
Who is Emma? Explain the implications of the last line. You might try a paper
on the significance of personal allusion in poetry, with evidence from Ashbery,
O'Hara, and Merrill.

IRONY

All irony entails a reversal either of meaning or of expectation. Someone says
or does something opposite to what he or she would normally be expected to
do or say. Although literature can compound ironies for some of its most
complicated and subtle effects, they generally fall into one of three categories:
verbal ironies, dramatic ironies, and situational ironies.

1. *Verbal irony*—saying something contrary to what it means. Someone comes
in dripping rainwater and says "What lovely weather!" Verbal ironies depend
on their context. The rainstorm makes the "lovely" ironic. And so the poet will
control the *context* in his or her language, the surroundings that will turn a
"lovely" into a "dreadful."
2. *Dramatic irony*—saying or doing something while unaware of its ironic
contrast with the whole truth. Someone says, "This is the happiest day of my

life" and dances a jig, while the audience, and perhaps some of the people on stage, know that his mortgage has been foreclosed and his family wiped out at the intersection. When Oedipus, the great riddle solver, says he will find the unknown sinner, a thrill of ironic horror runs through the audience, who knows that he himself is the culprit. When Jack Benny smiles blissfully as he fiddles, the audience dies with laughter at the musical atrocity. Poetic monologues like Browning's "My Last Duchess" frequently generate dramatic irony.

3. *Situational irony*—events turning out the opposite of what is expected or what should be (also called *circumstantial irony* and the *irony of fate*), as when it rains on the Weather Bureau's picnic. A swimmer attempting a rescue is drowned, but the drowning nonswimmer is pulled to shore and survives. The ironic situation—the *ought* upended by the *is*—is integral to dramatic irony. The very quality of innocent joy in Browning's duchess drives the jealous duke to have her murdered. And the ironic situation turns the speaker's unknowing words ironic. Situational irony is the very essence of both comedy and tragedy. The young lovers run into the worst possible luck, until everything clears up happily. The most noble spirits go to their death, while the featherheads survive.

Ironies vary from bitter to hilarious, from tragic to comic, and in all the subtleties of human attitudes between. They are also frequently complex. A speaker may feign the ignorance of dramatic irony, frequently for a laugh, as Shakespeare's Falstaff does. Or a speaker may intend a verbal irony that becomes a dramatic irony in his or her ignorance of all the facts: calling a stormy day "lovely" in deliberate verbal irony, without realizing that someone's possessions have perished in the flood. In discussing irony, we must distinguish the differing perspectives and contexts of knowledge that produce the oppositions; we must know from what point of view the irony appears.

Here is a neatly ironic commentary on the situation of our competitive struggles within our ideal Garden of Eden.

The Trees in the Garden Rained Flowers

Stephen Crane   *(1871–1900)*

The trees in the garden rained flowers.
Children ran there joyously.
They gathered the flowers
Each to himself.
Now there were some   5
Who gathered great heaps—
Having opportunity and skill—
Until, behold, only chance blossoms
Remained for the feeble.

Then a little spindling tutor 10
Ran importantly to the father, crying:
"Pray, come hither!
See this unjust thing in your garden!"
But when the father had surveyed,
He admonished the tutor: 15
"Not so, small sage!
This thing is just.
For, look you,
Are not they who possess the flowers
Stronger, bolder, shrewder 20
Than they who have none?
Why should the strong—
The beautiful strong—
Why should they not have the flowers?"

Upon reflection, the tutor bowed to the ground. 25
"My Lord," he said,
"The stars are displaced
By this towering wisdom."

The words at the end are clearly ironic from the perspective of the author and the reader, but are they ironic to the tutor as well? Is this verbal or dramatic irony? Are the stars displaced? Is the wisdom towering? Whom does the author imply is the wiser, the father or the spindling tutor, the small sage?

The British White Star liner *Titanic,* on her maiden voyage, collided with an iceberg and sank on the night of April 14, 1912. What ironies does the poem associate with her sinking?

The Convergence of the Twain

(Lines on the Loss of the "Titanic")

Thomas Hardy   (1840–1928)

I

In a solitude of the sea
Deep from human vanity,
And the Pride of Life that planned her, stilly couches she. 3

II

Steel chambers, late the pyres
Of her salamandrine[1] fires,
Cold currents thrid,[2] and turn to rhythmic tidal lyres. 6

---

[1]Hardy associates aquatic salamanders with the mythical salamanders that could live in fire.
[2]Thread.

III

Over the mirrors meant
To glass the opulent
The sea-worm crawls—grotesque, slimed, dumb, indifferent.   9

IV

Jewels in joy designed
To ravish the sensuous mind
Lie lightless, all their sparkles bleared and black and blind.   12

V

Dim moon-eyed fishes near
Gaze at the gilded gear
And query: "What does this vaingloriousness down here?" . . .   15

VI

Well: while was fashioning
This creature of cleaving wing,
The Immanent Will that stirs and urges everything   18

VII

Prepared a sinister mate
For her—so gaily great—
A Shape of Ice, for the time far and dissociate.   21

VIII

And as the smart ship grew
In stature, grace, and hue,
In shadowy silent distance grew the Iceberg too.   24

IX

Alien they seemed to be:
No mortal eye could see
The intimate welding of their later history.   27

X

Or sign that they were bent
By paths coincident
On being anon twin halves of one august event.   30

XI

Till the Spinner of the Years
Said "Now!" And each one hears,
And consummation comes, and jars two hemispheres.   33

What is ironic about the ship's name? What does Hardy imply about the Immanent Will and man's aspirations?

In 1887, Great Britain celebrated Queen Victoria's fiftieth year on the throne. This is Housman's commentary:

1887

A. E. Housman   (1859–1936)

From Clee to heaven the beacon burns,
    The shires have seen it plain,
From north and south the sign returns
    And beacons burn again.   4

Look left, look right, the hills are bright,
    The dales are light between,
Because 'tis fifty years to-night
    That God has saved the Queen.   8

Now, when the flames they watch not towers
    About the soil they trod,
Lads, we'll remember friends of ours
    Who shared the work with God.   12

To skies that knit their heartstrings right,
    To fields that bred them brave,
The saviors come not home to-night:
    Themselves they could not save.   16

It dawns in Asia, tombstones show
    And Shropshire names are read;
And the Nile spills his overflow
    Beside the Severn's dead.   20

We pledge in peace by farm and town
    The Queen they served in war,
And fire the beacons up and down
    The land they perished for.   24

'God save the Queen' we living sing,
   From height to height 'tis heard;
And with the rest your voices ring,
   Lads of the Fifty-third.   28

Oh, God will save her, fear you not:
   Be you the men you've been,
Get you the sons your fathers got,
   And God will save the Queen.   32

Who does save the queen? Who are "Lads of the Fifty-third"?
Here is a similar comment from World War I.

Dulce et Decorum Est

Wilfred Owen   *(1893–1918)*

Bent double, like old beggars under sacks,
Knock-kneed, coughing like hags, we cursed through sludge,
Till on the haunting flares we turned our backs,
And towards our distant rest began to trudge.
Men marched asleep. Many had lost their boots,   5
But limped on, blood-shod. All went lame, all blind;
Drunk with fatigue; deaf even to the hoots
Of gas-shells dropping softly behind.

Gas! GAS! Quick, boys!—An ecstasy of fumbling,
Fitting the clumsy helmets just in time,   10
But someone still was yelling out and stumbling
And floundering like a man in fire or lime.—
Dim through the misty panes and thick green light,
As under a green sea, I saw him drowning.

In all my dreams before my helpless sight   15
He plunges at me, guttering, choking, drowning.

If in some smothering dreams, you too could pace
Behind the wagon that we flung him in,
And watch the white eyes writhing in his face,
His hanging face, like a devil's sick of sin;   20
If you could hear, at every jolt, the blood
Come gargling from the froth-corrupted lungs,
Bitter as the cud
Of vile, incurable sores on innocent tongues,—
My friend, you would not tell with such high zest   25
To children ardent for some desperate glory,
The old Lie: Dulce et decorum est
Pro patria mori.

Owen's title and concluding line come from Horace's reverent evocation of the Roman belief "Sweet and fitting it is to die for one's country" (*Odes* III.ii). Why is the Latin especially ironic for the young British officer?

Here is an ironic view of World War II, when the first recruits were trained without full equipment.

Naming of Parts

Henry Reed   (1914–)

To-day we have naming of parts. Yesterday,
We had daily cleaning. And to-morrow morning,
We shall have what to do after firing. But to-day,
To-day we have naming of parts. Japonica
Glistens like coral in all of the neighbouring gardens,
      And to-day we have naming of parts.   6

This is the lower sling swivel. And this
Is the upper sling swivel, whose use you will see,
When you are given your slings. And this is the piling swivel,
Which in your case you have not got. The branches
Hold in the gardens their silent, eloquent gestures,
      Which in our case we have not got.   12

This is the safety-catch, which is always released
With an easy flick of the thumb. And please do not let me
See anyone using his finger. You can do it quite easy
If you have any strength in your thumb. The blossoms
Are fragile and motionless, never letting anyone see
      Any of them using their finger.   18

And this you can see is the bolt. The purpose of this
Is to open the breech, as you see. We can slide it
Rapidly backwards and forwards: we call this
Easing the spring. And rapidly backwards and forwards
The early bees are assaulting and fumbling the flowers:
      They call it easing the Spring.   24

They call it easing the Spring: it is perfectly easy
If you have any strength in your thumb: like the bolt,
And the breech, and the cocking-piece, and the point of balance,
Which in our case we have not got; and the almond-blossom
Silent in all of the gardens and the bees going backwards and
      forwards,
      For to-day we have naming of parts.   30

You hear two voices in this poem. Whose are they? Identify the lines each speaks (or thinks). Are the ironies apparent to both speakers? What is the situational irony? Is there any dramatic irony?

We have contemplated dramatic irony in Browning's "My Last Duchess." Here is another famous example.

The Bishop Orders His Tomb at Saint Praxed's Church

Rome, 15—

Robert Browning　　　*(1812–1889)*

Vanity, saith the preacher, vanity![1]
Draw round my bed: is Anselm keeping back?
Nephews—sons mine . . . ah, God, I know not! Well—
She, men would have to be your mother once,
Old Gandolf[2] envied me, so fair she was!　　　　　　　　5
What's done is done, and she is dead beside,
Dead long ago, and I am Bishop since,
And as she died so must we die ourselves,
And thence ye may perceive the world's a dream.
Life, how and what is it? As here I lie　　　　　　　　10
In this state-chamber, dying by degrees,
Hours and long hours in the dead night, I ask
'Do I live, am I dead?' Peace, peace seems all.
Saint Praxed's ever was the church for peace;
And so, about this tomb of mine. I fought　　　　　　　15
With tooth and nail to save my niche, ye know:
—Old Gandolf cozened[3] me, despite my care;
Shrewd was that snatch from out the corner South
He graced his carrion with, God curse the same!
Yet still my niche is not so cramped but thence　　　　20
One sees the pulpit o' the epistle-side,
And somewhat of the choir, those silent seats,
And up into the aery dome where live
The angels, and a sunbeam's sure to lurk:
And I shall fill my slab of basalt there,　　　　　　　25
And 'neath my tabernacle take my rest,
With those nine columns round me, two and two,
The odd one at my feet where Anselm stands:
Peach-blossom marble all, the rare, the ripe
As fresh-poured red wine of a mighty pulse.　　　　　30
—Old Gandolf with his paltry onion-stone,
Put me where I may look at him! True peach,

[1]Cf. Eccles. 1. 2.　[2]An imagined person, like the speaker.　[3]Cheated.

Rosy and flawless: how I earned the prize!
Draw close: that conflagration of my church
—What then? So much was saved if aught were missed!   35
My sons, ye would not be my death? Go dig
The white-grape vineyard where the oil-press stood,
Drop water gently till the surface sink,
And if ye fine . . . Ah God, I know not, I! . . .
Bedded in store of rooten fig-leaves soft,   40
And corded up in a tight olive-frail,[4]
Some lump, ah God, of *lapis lazuli*,[5]
Big as a Jew's head cut off at the nape,
Blue as a vein o'er the Madonna's breast . . .
Sons, all have I bequeathed you, villas, all,   45
That brave Frascati[6] villa with its bath,
So, let the blue lump poise between my knees,
Like God the Father's globe on both his hands
Ye worship in the Jesu Church so gay,
For Gandolf shall not choose but see and burst!   50
Swift as a weaver's shuttle fleet our years:
Man goeth to the grave, and where is he?
Did I say basalt for my slab, sons? Black—
'T was ever antique-black I meant! How else
Shall ye contrast my frieze to come beneath?   55
The bas-relief in bronze ye promised me,
Those Pans and Nymphs ye wot of, and perchance
Some tripod, thyrsus,[7] with a vase or so,
The Saviour at his sermon on the mount,
Saint Praxed in a glory,[8] and one Pan   60
Ready to twitch the Nymph's last garment off,
And Moses with the tables[9] . . . but I know
Ye mark me not! What do they whisper thee,
Child of my bowels, Anselm? Ah, ye hope
To revel down my villas while I gasp   65
Bricked o'er with beggar's mouldy travertine[10]
Which Gandolf from his tomb-top chuckles at!
Nay, boys, ye love me—all of jasper, then!
'T is jasper ye stand pledged to, lest I grieve
My bath must needs be left behind, alas!   70
One block, pure green as a pistachio-nut,
There's plenty jasper somewhere in the world—
And have I not Saint Praxed's ear to pray
Horses for ye, and brown Greek manuscripts,

[4]Olive basket.   [5]A valuable blue stone.   [6]A wealthy Roman suburb.   [7]Staff.   [8]Gold rays, signifying sanctity.   [9]Tablets with the Ten Commandments.   [10]Inexpensive limestone.

And mistresses with great smooth marbly limbs? 75
—That's if ye carve my epitaph aright,
Choice Latin, picked phrase, Tully's[11] every word,
No gaudy ware like Gandolf's second line—
Tully, my masters? Ulpian[12] serves his need!
And then how I shall lie through centuries, 80
And hear the blessed mutter of the mass,
And see God made and eaten all day long,[13]
And feel the steady candle-flame, and taste
Good strong thick stupefying incense-smoke!
For as I lie here, hours of the dead night, 85
Dying in state and by such slow degrees,
I fold my arms as if they clasped a crook,[14]
And stretch my feet forth straight as stone can point,
And let the bedclothes, for a mortcloth,[15] drop
Into great laps and folds of sculptor's-work: 90
And as yon tapers dwindle, and strange thoughts
Grow, with a certain humming in my ears,
About the life before I lived this life,
And this life too, popes, cardinals and priests,
Saint Praxed at his sermon on the mount, 95
Your tall pale mother with her talking eyes,
And new-found agate urns as fresh as day,
And marble's language, Latin pure, discreet,
—Aha, ELUCESCEBAT[16] quoth our friend?
No Tully, said I, Ulpian at the best! 100
Evil and brief hath been my pilgrimage.
All *lapis,* all, sons! Else I give the Pope
My villas! Will ye ever eat my heart?
Ever your eyes were as a lizard's quick
They glitter like your mother's for my soul, 105
Or ye would heighten my impoverished frieze,
Piece out its starved design, and fill my vase
With grapes, and add a vizor and a Term,[17]
And to the tripod ye would tie a lynx
That in his struggle throws the thyrsus down, 110
To comfort me on my entablature[18]
Whereon I am to lie till I must ask
'Do I live, am I dead?' There, leave me, there!
For ye have stabbed me with ingratitude

[11]Marcus Tullius Cicero, an esteemed stylist.   [12]A later Latin writer.   [13]Through transubstantiation; in the Eucharist.   [14]Bishop's crozier.   [15]Cloth used as covering for a body or coffin.
[16]"He was illustrious"; but the bishop thinks the verb form not up to Tully's standard.   [17]Pillar.
[18]Raised platform.

To death—ye wish it—God, ye wish it! Stone—   115
Gritstone, a-crumble! Clammy squares which sweat
As if the corpse they keep were oozing through—
And no more *lapis* to delight the world!
Well go! I bless ye. Fewer tapers there,
But in a row: and, going, turn your backs   120
—Ay, like departing altar-ministrants,
And leave me in my church, the church for peace,
That I may watch at leisure if he leers—
Old Gandolf, at me, from his onion-stone,
As still he envied me, so far she was!   125

What is the bishop's dominant characteristic? Why is his monologue dramatically ironic? Point to some of the details that characterize his views, especially
those concerning the mass. St. Praxed was a woman. Explain line 95. Who was
the woman who was so fair? Whom does the bishop address? What might
Gandolf's position have been? Explain the dramatic irony in the opening line.
Will the bishop get his tomb?

CHAPTER 4

IMAGE, METAPHOR, SYMBOL

IMAGES: THE PRIMARY VISION

An *image* is an imitation. The word derives from the Latin *imago,* meaning a copy or a likeness. A painting is an image and so is a statue. A poem, too, is an image. It is an imitation of life, with the poet's perceptions made accessible to the perceptions of others by means of the sensual responses shared by all humans.

Because it is an imitation, an *image* is also an appeal to the senses. Painters construct their imitation almost entirely in terms of the sense of sight. They create a *visual image* that makes their conception permanently accessible to the perceptions of others. Sculptors appeal to the senses of sight and touch, creating both visual and *tactile images.* Musicians appeal primarily to the sense of hearing, creating *auditory images.* Because poets use language as their medium, they may extend their use of imagery further than painters, sculptors, or musicians. In addition to visual, tactile, and auditory imagery, they may also use imagery that appeals to our senses of smell and taste. Whenever we discover such an appeal in a poem we may speak of the imagery involved. As a rule, however, the two most common images found in poems are those of sound and sight. *Auditory imagery* is important in poetry because sound is a necessary part of the spoken word. *Visual imagery* is still more important because it is through the eyes that we as humans take in the largest portion of our knowledge of the world.

Occasionally a poet will create the effect of a poem almost exclusively with visual imagery.

The Red Wheelbarrow

William Carlos Williams   *(1883–1963)*

so much depends
upon

a red wheel
barrow

glazed with rain
water

beside the white
chickens.

This poem is almost, but not quite, a painting in words. Putting aside for the moment the provocative beginning, "so much depends upon . . ." we are struck by the almost exclusively visual nature of the images that follow. Williams has carefully excluded a number of sensory experiences that might have given the images qualities less like those of a painting and more like those of most poems. He uses no words that evoke the sounds of the chickens as they go clucking about their business (perhaps they are making no sounds) or the sound of the rain as it drums upon the wheelbarrow and drips from its edges (perhaps it has stopped raining). He evokes no smell of the barnyard or of the ozone that accompanies the rain. The limitations of the imagery suggest an impressionistic painting; the emphasis is on bright color and the arrangement of forms. Yet the poem is clearly something different from a painting. Although Williams has told us there are chickens present, he has not told us how many, as the painter must do, or what kind they are (except that they are white) or even whether they are hens or roosters. He has told us that the wheelbarrow is red, but beyond that he has not specified its size or shape or whether it is wooden or metal.

Images in poetry are almost always more suggestive than explicit, springing to life when the words expand in the mind of the reader. The ability to read poetry well involves the ability to respond actively to the signals verbalized by the poet. We have seen chickens, wheelbarrows, and rain. The poet gives us the signals that require us to put these elements together in a composition. But why? What does it mean? Williams has introduced the images with the statement that so much depends upon them, but what exactly does that statement mean? Does the poem suggest that as humans we are in some way dependent upon our ability to visualize the world about us? To transmit that vision to others? Whatever the poem means, it makes us aware, as all good art does, that our responses to the world are changed when we view it through the eyes of another. We see things then that we hadn't seen before. The world becomes for us not simply what we make of it in our own direct contact with it; it becomes also a world shaped for us in the images, or the "imitations," of others.

What poets see is not necessarily what we would see if we were standing in their place. We might look long and intently at a barnyard without seeing it the way that Williams asks us to see it in his poem. The life that poets imitate is partly the life external to their mental processes, but it is also partly the life that goes on within their heads. An image may spring from a direct sensory experience (Williams may have seen the chickens, the wheelbarrow, and the rain), or it may be uncovered from the storehouse of the poet's mind (Williams may have only been thinking about those things). The word *imagination* is related to the word *image* in this important fundamental sense. The poet's imagination is his or her ability to imitate life both externally, as it appears to others, and internally, as he or she conceives of it within the recesses of the mind. As readers who reconstitute the images from the words of the poem, we share in the imaginative processes of the poet. Our minds are opened and enlightened as the poet's has been. Our imaginations are enlivened and our lives enriched through contact with a mental process different from our own, and perhaps deeper and richer.

Within the longer poem that follows the imagery is still heavily visual.

A Flock of Guinea Hens Seen from a Car

Eudora Welty   *(1909–)*

The lute and the pear are your half sisters,
The mackerel moon a full first cousin,
And you were born to appear seemly, even when running on guinea
    legs,
As maiden-formed, as single-minded as raindrops,
Ellipses, small homebodies of great orbits (little knots at the back
    like apron strings),   5
Perfected, sealed off, engraved like a dozen perfect consciences,
As egglike as the eggs you know best, triumphantly speckled . . .
But fast!
Side-eyed with emancipation, no more lost than a string of pearls are
    lost from one another,
You cross the road in the teeth of Pontiacs   10
As over a threshold, into waving, gregarious grasses,
Welcome wherever you go—the Guinea Sisters.

Bobbins with the threads of innumerable visits behind you,
As light on your feet
As the daughters[1] of Mr. Barrett of Wimpole Street,   15
Do you ever wonder where Africa has fled?

Is the strangeness of your origins packed tight in those
       little nutmeg heads, so ceremonious, partly naked?
Is there time to ask each other what became of the family wings?

[1]The poet Elizabeth Barrett Browning and her sisters.

Do you dream?
Princess of Dapple,   20
Princess of Moonlight,
Princess of Conch,
Princess of Guinealand,
Though you roost in the care of S. Thomas Truly, Rt. 1
(There went his mailbox flying by),   25
The whole world knows you've never yet given up the secret of
     where you've hidden your nests.

Which images come closest to describing the scene as it might appear to any objective viewer? Which images seem most to belong to the subjective reaction of the poet herself? Consider the first two lines:

The lute and the pear are your half sisters,
The mackerel moon a full first cousin, . . .

Although there are no lutes or pears literally present in the scene the poet describes, as seen from her car, the mental images of lutes and pears share a likeness of shape that makes them "half sisters" to the guinea hens; although we as readers may have no clear idea of the shape of guinea hens before we read this line, we begin to see a picture as we complete it. With the introduction of the mackerel moon in the second line we begin to understand something of the coloration of the hens (they are barred like a "mackerel moon"). The images are both external and internal at the same time. The poet has seen what we would see but has forced us to perceive it also in the way that it appears in her mind. Do other images in the poem also operate in this way, requiring us to respond to what the poet has seen and also to what she has been reminded of?

Since in fact we rarely stand in the place where the poet has stood, we are often in our reading confronted with instances wherein we cannot be certain which elements of a poem possessed an objective existence and which were manufactured by the poet. Yet by a curious paradox the distinction between objective reality and subjective reality that existed before the creation of the poem ceases to be of serious importance once the poem has come into being. Once an image has been fixed in a poem by the imagination of the poet it possesses the same artistic reality as any other image in the poem. The lute and the pear and the guinea hens share forever the relationship created by the poet. If she has used her imagination well, these images will become a part of our experience (perhaps even a larger part than real lutes, real pears, or real guinea hens).

The effect of imagery is to fix a perceptual moment, taking it outside of time and giving it the lasting quality of art. All experiences available to our senses are subject to change—except the images of art.

In the following poem the poet takes an experience common in the country and gives it an existence more memorable to many people than the similar experiences they themselves have had. Long after one has forgotten what it felt like—or might have felt like—to pick apples, reading this poem can make the experience come to life again.

After Apple-Picking

Robert Frost   (1874–1963)

My long two-pointed ladder's sticking through a tree
Toward heaven still,
And there's a barrel that I didn't fill
Beside it, and there may be two or three
Apples I didn't pick upon some bough.   5
But I am done with apple-picking now.
Essence of winter sleep is on the night,
The scent of apples: I am drowsing off.
I cannot rub the strangeness from my sight
I got from looking through a pane of glass   10
I skimmed this morning from the drinking trough
And held against the world of hoary grass.
It melted, and I let it fall and break.
But I was well
Upon my way to sleep before it fell,   15
And I could tell
What form my dreaming was about to take.
Magnified apples appear and disappear,
Stem end and blossom end,
And every fleck of russet showing clear.   20
My instep arch not only keeps the ache;
It keeps the pressure of a ladder-round.
I feel the ladder sway as the boughs bend.
And I keep hearing from the cellar bin
The rumbling sound   25
Of load on load of apples coming in.
For I have had too much
Of apple-picking: I am overtired
Of the great harvest I myself desired.
There were ten thousand thousand fruit to touch,   30
Cherish in hand, lift down, and not let fall.
For all
That struck the earth,
No matter if not bruised or spiked with stubble,
Went surely to the cider-apple heap   35

As of no worth.
One can see what will trouble
This sleep of mine, whatever sleep it is.
Were he not gone,
The woodchuck could say whether it's like his   40
Long sleep, as I describe its coming on,
Or just some human sleep.

Again, the greater part of the imagery is visual. Here, however, there are also some effective tactile images, or appeals to the sense of touch. Where are they? Note also how we are invited to hear "from the cellar bin / The rumbling sound / Of load on load of apples coming in."

Frost derives his imagery almost exclusively from the immediate experience, straying only so far as a dream about apples and a question whether the woodchuck's hibernating sleep is like the sleep the narrator feels "coming on." He begins specifically, with his ladder sticking through the tree, generating imagery as he goes. Keats, in the following sonnet, begins with the overwhelming images generated from seeing the specific Grecian sculptures that do not enter the poem until it is almost over.

On Seeing the Elgin Marbles

John Keats   (1795–1821)

My spirit is too weak—mortality
    Weighs heavily on me like unwilling sleep,
    And each imagined pinnacle and steep
Of godlike hardship tells me I must die   4
Like a sick eagle looking at the sky.
    Yet 'tis a gentle luxury to weep
    That I have not the cloudy winds to keep
Fresh for the opening of the morning's eye.   8
Such dim-conceivèd glories of the brain
    Bring round the heart an undescribable feud;
So do these wonders a most dizzy pain,
    That mingles Grecian grandeur with the rude   12
Wasting of old Time, with a billowy main,
    A sun, a shadow of a magnitude.

The Elgin Marbles are a collection of statuary and friezes from the Parthenon at Athens, brought to England by Lord Elgin at the beginning of the nineteenth century and put on public display in the British Museum. It might seem odd at first sight that Keats chose to write a poem about them without ever giving any clear idea what they look like. But is it odd? Is the subject the marbles themselves or the poet's emotions on seeing them, or his thoughts about something else?

When does he actually begin talking about the marbles? Identify the images. Is the eagle important as an eagle or as the representation of an idea? Does "mortality / Weighs heavily on me" convey an image? If it does, what is its effect? What are we to make of the collection of images at the end: "a billowy main, / A sun, a shadow of a magnitude"?

Much visual imagery is essentially *static;* the pictures stand suspended in time, frozen in inactivity like paintings or photographs. In *kinetic imagery* a sense of motion is important, as it is in the movies, first called "motion pictures," or cinema (*cinema* and *kinetic* come from the same Greek root). Strong kinetic imagery of approaching darkness is essential to the success of the following poem.

You, Andrew Marvell

Archibald MacLeish   (1892–1982)

And here face down beneath the sun
And here upon earth's noonward height
To feel the always coming on
The always rising of the night: 4

To feel creep up the curving east
The earthy chill of dusk and slow
Upon those under lands the vast
And ever climbing shadow grow   8

And strange at Ecbatan[1] the trees
Take leaf by leaf the evening strange
The flooding dark about their knees
The mountains over Persia change   12

And now at Kermanshah the gate
Dark empty and the withered grass
And through the twilight now the late
Few travelers in the westward pass   16

And Baghdad darken and the bridge
Across the silent river gone
And through Arabia the edge
Of evening widen and steal on   20

And deepen on Palmyra's street
The wheel rut in the ruined stone
And Lebanon fade out and Crete
High through the clouds and overblown   24

[1]From Ecbatan, a city in ancient Persia, to Spain and Africa, the poet's mind moves westward with the sun, passing over sites of ancient civilizations.

And over Sicily the air
Still flashing with the landward gulls
And loom and slowly disappear
The sails above the shadowy hulls   28

And Spain go under and the shore
Of Africa the gilded sand
And evening vanish and no more
The low pale light across that land   32

Nor now the long light on the sea:

And here face downward in the sun
To feel how swift how secretly
The shadow of the night comes on . . .   36

Although kinetic imagery is not as insistent in the following poem as it is in
"You, Andrew Marvell," in a number of places it is important.

Mr. Flood's Party

Edwin Arlington Robinson   *(1869–1935)*

Old Eben Flood, climbing alone one night
Over the hill between the town below
And the forsaken upland hermitage
That held as much as he should ever know   4
On earth again of home, paused warily.
The road was his with not a native near;
And Eben, having leisure, said aloud,
For no man else in Tilbury Town to hear: 8

"Well, Mr. Flood, we have the harvest moon
Again, and we may not have many more;
The bird is on the wing, the poet[1] says,
And you and I have said it here before.   12
Drink to the bird." He raised up to the light
The jug that he had gone so far to fill,
And answered huskily: "Well, Mr. Flood,
Since you propose it, I believe I will."   16

Alone, as if enduring to the end
A valiant armor of scarred hopes outworn,
He stood there in the middle of the road

[1]Edward Fitzgerald, in *The Rubáiyát of Omar Khayyám:* "Come, fill the Cup, and in the Fire of
Spring / Your Winter-garment of Repentence fling: / The Bird of Time has but a little way / To
flutter—and the Bird is on the wing."

Like Roland's[2] ghost winding[3] a silent horn.   20
Below him, in the town among the trees,
Where friends of other days had honored him,
A phantom salutation of the dead
Rang thinly till old Eben's eyes were dim.   24

Then, as a mother lays her sleeping child
Down tenderly, fearing it may awake,
He set the jug down slowly at his feet
With trembling care, knowing that most things break;   28
And only when assured that on firm earth
It stood, as the uncertain lives of men
Assuredly did not, he paced away,
And with his hand extended paused again: 32

"Well, Mr. Flood, we have not met like this
In a long time; and many a change has come
To both of us, I fear, since last it was
We had a drop together. Welcome home!"   36
Convivially returning with himself,
Again he raised the jug up to the light;
And with an acquiescent quaver said:
"Well, Mr. Flood, if you insist, I might.   40

"Only a very little, Mr. Flood—
For auld lang syne. No more, sir; that will do."
So, for the time, apparently it did,
And Eben evidently thought so too;   44
For soon amid the silver loneliness
Of night he lifted up his voice and sang,
Secure, with only two moons listening,
Until the whole harmonious landscape rang—   48

"For auld lang syne." The weary throat gave out,
The last word wavered, and the song was done.
He raised again the jug regretfully
And shook his head, and was again alone.   52
There was not much that was ahead of him,
And there was nothing in the town below—
Where strangers would have shut the many doors
That many friends had opened long ago.   56

---

[2]A romantic hero killed at Roncesvalles in 778.   [3]Winding: blowing.

List some of the most important kinetic images. How much do they contribute to the total success of the poem? Explain the specific picture and the emotional

connotation in "Roland's ghost winding a silent horn." What are the two moons
in the next-to-last stanza? How does the dialogue and its accompanying activities, which the poet pictures for us, emphasize the theme?

   Mr. Flood's song awakens auditory as well as visual imagery. Notice how
Vaughan, in "The Waterfall," heightens his auditory imagery to enhance his
visual imagery, especially of the fall itself, which becomes a symbol of God's
spiritual continuity. List some of the most important kinetic images. How do they
contribute to the total success of the poem?

The Waterfall

Henry Vaughan   (1622–1695)

With what deep murmurs through time's silent stealth
Doth thy transparent, cool and watery wealth
        Here flowing fall,
        And chide, and call,
As if his liquid, loose retinue stayed   5
Lingering, and were of this steep place afraid,
        The common pass
        Where, clear as glass,
        All must descend
        Not to an end: 10
But quickened by this deep and rocky grave,
Rise to a longer course more bright and brave,
Dear stream! dear bank, where often I
Have sat, and pleased my pensive eye,
Why, since each drop of thy quick[1] store   15
Runs thither, whence it flowed before,
Should poor souls fear a shade or night,
Who came sure from a sea of light?
Or since those drops are all sent back
So sure to thee, that none doth lack,   20
Why should frail flesh doubt any more
That what God takes, He'll not restore?
O useful element and clear!
My sacred wash and cleanser[2] here,
My first consigner unto those   25
Fountains of life, where the lamb goes?
What sublime truths, and wholesome themes,
Lodge in thy mystical, deep streams!
Such as dull man can never find
Unless that Spirit lead his mind,   30
Which first upon thy face did move,

[1]Living.   [2]By baptism.

And hatched all with his quickening love.
As this loud brook's incessant fall
In streaming rings restagnates all,
Which reach by course the bank, and then   35
Are no more seen, just so pass men.
O my invisible estate,
My glorious liberty, still late!
Thou art the channel my soul seeks,
Not this with cataracts and creeks.   40

Vaughan's *restagnates* puzzles modern readers, until they discover its archaic meaning of "overflows." What does Vaughan seem to say at first? What is his final image of the way men pass? Explain Vaughan's argument about poor souls fearing.

George Herbert's "Easter Wings" develops the kind of visual imagery Vaughan traces at the outset of "The Waterfall," creating the *shaped poem,* or *picture poem,* whose shape on the page pictures its subject.

Easter Wings[1]

George Herbert   (1593–1633)

Lord, who createdst man in wealth and store,[2]
    Though foolishly he lost the same,
        Decaying more and more
            Till he became
                Most poor: 5
                With thee
                O let me rise
        As larks, harmoniously,
    And sing this day thy victories:
Then shall the fall further the flight in me.   10

My tender age in sorrow did begin:
    And still with sicknesses and shame
        Thou didst so punish sin,
            That I became
                Most thin.   15
                With thee
            Let me combine,
        And feel this day thy victory;
    For, if I imp[3] my wing on thine,
Affliction shall advance the flight in me.   20

[1]Early printings turned the poem on its side, with the lines running vertically, enhancing the image of wings in upward flight.   [2]Abundance.   [3]Graft.

How does this poem picture "Easter wings"? How does the shape of the poem
enhance its message?

Consider the uses and effects of the various kinds of imagery in the following
poems.

Morning Song

Sylvia Plath   (1932–1963)

Love set you going like a fat gold watch.
The midwife slapped your footsoles, and your bald cry
Took its place among the elements.

Our voices echo, magnifying your arrival. New statue.
In a drafty museum, your nakedness   5
Shadows our safety. We stand round blankly as walls.

I'm no more your mother
Than the cloud that distils a mirror to reflect its own slow
Effacement at the wind's hand.

All night your moth-breath   10
Flickers among the flat pink roses. I wake to listen:
A far sea moves in my ear.

One cry, and I stumble from bed, cow-heavy and floral
In my Victorian nightgown.
Your mouth opens clean as a cat's. The window square   15

Whitens and swallows its dull stars. And now you try
Your handful of notes;
The clear vowels rise like balloons.

What does Plath's image of the cloud picture? How does it convey her feeling
about motherhood? What about the far sea and the balloons?

The Bear on the Delhi Road

Earle Birney   (1904–)

Unreal   tall as a myth
by the road the Himalayan bear
is beating the brilliant air
with his crooked arms
About him two men   bare   5
spindly as locusts   leap

One pulls on a ring
in the great soft nose   His mate
flicks   flicks with a stick
up at the rolling eyes   10

They have not led him here
down from the fabulous hills
to this bald alien plain
and the clamorous world   to kill
but simply to teach him to dance   15

They are peaceful both   these spare
men of Kashmir   and the bear
alive is their living   too
If   far on the Delhi way
around him galvanic they dance   20
it is merely to wear   wear
from his shaggy body the tranced
wish forever to stay
only an ambling bear
four-footed in berries   25

It is no more joyous for them
in this hot dust to prance
out of reach of the praying claws
sharpened to paw for ants
in the shadows of deodars   30
It is not easy to free
myth from reality
or rear this fellow up
to lurch   lurch with them
in the tranced dancing of men   35

What do the spatial breaks in the lines of "The Bear on the Delhi Road" convey?

Carentan O Carentan[1]

Louis Simpson   *(1923–   )*

Trees in the old days used to stand
And shape a shady lane
Where lovers wandered hand in hand
Who came from Carentan.   4

[1] A French port town, the site of a severe battle on June 8–12, 1944, a few days after D-Day.

This was the shining green canal
Where we came two by two
Walking at combat-interval.
Such trees we never knew.   8

The day was early June, the ground
Was soft and bright with dew.
Far away the guns did sound,
But here the sky was blue.   12

The sky was blue, but there a smoke
Hung still above the sea
Where the ships together spoke
To towns we could not see.   16

Could you have seen us through a glass
You would have said a walk
Of farmers out to turn the grass,
Each with his own hay-fork.   20

The watchers in their leopard suits[2]
Waited till it was time,
And aimed between the belt and boot
And let the barrel climb.   24

I must lie down at once, there is
A hammer at my knee.
And call it death or cowardice,
Don't count again on me.   28

Everything's all right, Mother,
Everyone gets the same
At one time or another.
It's all in the game.   32

I never strolled, nor ever shall,
Down such a leafy lane.
I never drank in a canal,
Nor ever shall again.   36

There is a whistling in the leaves
And it is not the wind,
The twigs are falling from the knives
That cut men to the ground.   40

[2]Camouflage uniforms.

Tell me, Master-Sergeant,
The way to turn and shoot.
But the Sergeant's silent
That taught me how to do it.   44

O Captain, show us quickly
Our place upon the map.
But the Captain's sickly
And taking a long nap.   48

Lieutenant, what's my duty,
My place in the platoon?
He too's a sleeping beauty,
Charmed by that strange tune.   52

Carentan O Carentan
Before we met with you
We never yet had lost a man
Or known what death could do.   56

What does the image of the lane do for "Carentan O Carentan"? What other images support it? What effect do the balladlike structure and language have?

Heat

H. D. [Hilda Doolittle]   *(1886–1961)*

O wind, rend open the heat,
cut apart the heat,
rend it to tatters.

Fruit cannot drop
through this thick air—   5
fruit cannot fall into heat
that presses up and blunts
the points of pears
and rounds the grapes.

Cut the heat—   10
plough through it,
turning it on either side
of your path.

How does the imagery of the wind in "Heat" change from first to last stanzas? How about "thick air"? Are these images supportive or inconsistent?

The Cool Web

Robert Graves   (1895–1985)

Children are dumb to say how hot the day is,
How hot the scent is of the summer rose,
How dreadful the black wastes of evening sky,
How dreadful the tall soldiers drumming by.   4

But we have speech, to chill the angry day,
And speech, to dull the rose's cruel scent.
We spell away the overhanging night,
We spell away the soldiers and the fright.   8

There's a cool web of language winds us in,
Retreat from too much joy or too much fear:
We grow sea-green at last and coldly die
In brininess and volubility.   12

But if we let our tongues lose self-possession,
Throwing off language and its watery clasp
Before our death, instead of when death comes,
Facing the wide glare of the children's day,   16
Facing the rose, the dark sky and the drums
We shall go mad no doubt and die that way.

Explain in detail how Graves suggests the world's imagery affects children and adults differently. What is the function of the "cool web of language"?

METAPHOR: THE DOUBLE VISION

A *metaphor* is an implied comparison between objects that are in important respects dissimilar. It is a form of imagery and is therefore, like an image, rooted in a sensual perception that is usually visual.

In its simple form an image carries no metaphor. The poet implies no comparison, forces no double response. Complex images, however, tend toward metaphor. Suggesting a likeness between two essentially unlike objects, or between a physical object and an abstraction, the poet creates a double vision that serves as one of the chief ingredients of most successful poems.

There Is a Garden in Her Face

Thomas Campion   (1567–1620)

There is a garden in her face,
Where roses and white lillies grow;
A heavenly paradise is that place,   3

Wherein all pleasant fruits do flow.
   There cherries grow, which none may buy
   Till "Cherry ripe" themselves do cry.[1]   6

   Those cherries fairly do enclose
Of orient pearl a double row,
   Which when her lovely laughter shows,   9
They look like rosebuds filled with snow.
   Yet them nor peer nor prince can buy,
   Till "Cherry ripe" themselves do cry.   12

   Her eyes like angels watch them still;
Her brows like bended bows do stand,
   Threatening with piercing frowns to kill   15
All that attempt with eye or hand
   Those sacred cherries to come nigh,
   Till "Cherry ripe" themselves do cry.   18

[1]Until they cry out like street vendors, announcing goods for sale.

The controlling metaphor in this poem implies a comparison between a girl's face and a garden. *Similes* spell out this metaphorical comparison with *like, as,* or *as if,* as in Christina Rossetti's "Goblin Market":

Laura stretched her gleaming neck
Like a rush-imbedded swan,
Like a lily from the beck

The *plain metaphor* makes the analogy in one leap: "She *is* a swan, a lily." The *implied metaphor* gives her swanlike or lilylike qualities without naming *swan* or *lily.* "O so white! O so soft! . . . is she!" writes Jonson, after mentioning the lily and swansdown. The implied metaphor seems often like a pun, because ordinary words suddenly project their pictorial potential, as when Shakespeare says: "And summer's *lease* hath all too short a *date,*" and we get the sudden picture of summer as a person renting a house with a short lease. Implied metaphors can be wonderfully compounded, as when, in another poem, Shakespeare shifts his picture in a kind of montage; an old man with shaking limbs is like a barren tree in autumn with its boughs shaking in the cold wind, and the tree's bare limbs, deserted by birds, are like a ruined choir loft in one of the monastic chapels ruined by Henry VIII, where the choirboys used to sing like birds:

That time of year thou mayst in me behold
When yellow leaves, or none, or few, do hang
Upon those boughs which shake against the cold,
Bare ruin'd choirs, where late the sweet birds sang.

Metaphors may also be compounded with symbols, as in that most amazing of poems, Gerard Manley Hopkins's "The Windhover," where the windhover, a type of falcon, wings stretched against the sky, symbolizes Christ on the cross as well as Christ as Prince of Morning, Heir to the Kingdom of Heaven, and as a chivalric knight gloriously riding and managing his horse:

> I caught this morning morning's minion, kingdom of daylight's dauphin, dapple-dawn-
>   drawn Falcon, in his riding
>   Of the rolling level underneath him steady air, and striding
> High there, how he rung upon the rein of a wimpling wing
> In his ecstasy! . . .

And even another metaphor has burst into the picture, since the curved wing of the falcon is like the curving fabric of a nun's or monk's wimple, or hood, fluttering on either side of the face.

The poet's fancy can even invert the metaphor, so that the real becomes the fancied and the fancied the real, as in this stanza by Ebenezer Jones where the fancied flame of autumn becomes the actuality, and the actual crocus becomes the *as if*. The figurative flame is like the crocus, rather than the crocus being like a flame, and the concentration on the beautiful flower itself is startingly intense.

> And the woodland haunter
> Shall not cease to saunter
>   When, far down some glade,
> Of the great world's burning,
> One soft flame upturning,
> Seems, to his discerning,
>   Crocus in the shade.

Metaphors frequently fade with use, becoming *dead metaphors,* like the *jacket* of a book, or the *hood* of a car, or the *limb* of a tree for a human arm or leg. "A very limb lopped off!" cries Shakespeare's Hotspur when he learns that his father's army can't join the battle. Thus writers frequently inject a burst of life by reviving the dead, bringing the metaphorical double vision back to our delighted attention. Shakespeare does it even more subtly with "those boughs that shake against the cold," giving us metaphorically the tree's wintry branches and the aged human arms and legs without saying *limbs* at all.

Even before their death, some metaphors become *conventional* and carry no great surprise; others are *unconventional,* and remain surprising in their originality.

About an Excavation

Charles Reznikoff   *(1894–1976)*

About an excavation
a flock of bright red lanterns
has settled.   3

This poem illustrates admirably the essential double vision of metaphor. We see a group of red lanterns, but we also see a flock of birds. The poem is a record of that isolated double perception. If the perception had been single, the poet might have written:

About an excavation
a flock of birds
has settled.

Or, alternatively:

About an excavation
a number of bright red lanterns
have been placed.

Each of these revisions presents an image. Reznikoff's poem implies a comparison by presenting two images simultaneously. The metaphor in this poem is less conventional than the metaphors in the Campion poem. Do you find the metaphors in both poems successful?

Because poets share with other humans the ability to perceive externally and internally at the same time, images in poetry have a way of turning into metaphors. Poets compare what they see to what they have seen, what exists to what they imagine could exist, what is real to what they believe to be ideal. A straight descriptive image frequently expands into the metaphorical double vision. Laura with her gleaming neck becomes first a swan then a ship. In the following poem, Ferril's commonplace "adrift" releases the matter-of-fact into the metaphorical.

Always Begin Where You Are

Thomas Hornsby Ferril   *(1896–   )*

Always begin right here where you are
And work out from here:
If adrift, feel the feel of the oar in the oarlock first,
If saddling a horse let your right knee slug   4

The belly of the horse like an uppercut,
Then cinch his suck,
Then mount and ride away
To any dream deserving the sensible world.   8

None of the images of rowing or riding, taken by themselves, goes far toward implying a comparison. Taken side by side, they imply a comparison with each other (rowing is like riding), but the poet wants us to see more than that. "Always begin right here where you are," he says, "And work out from here." The images, in other words, are metaphoric examples for any endeavor. By the time we finish the poem, we know that the horse we "mount and ride away / To any dream deserving the sensible world" is no physical horse we can find in any pasture.

A metaphor always has two terms. Something is being compared to something else. Yet sometimes the second term has been left vague, as when Ferril requires the reader to imagine other activities to compare to rowing and riding. Sometimes both terms are clear, but the likeness is obscure, as perhaps in the baby's "moth-breath" of Plath's "Morning Song."

A *riddle* is a form of metaphor in which one term is expressed and the other left for guessing.

Consider the following children's riddle:

Twenty white horses on a red hill:
Now they prance,
Now they dance,
Now they stand still.

A reader adept at riddles will sense a clue in the unlikely "red hill." What may be compared to white horses on a red hill? What moves and stands still "Now"? The answer is teeth and gums. The child's twenty teeth (the twenty "milk teeth" before the molars arrive) move as he or she speaks the riddle and stand still when he or she ceases speaking. The metaphor, then, is a solved riddle, and to some extent all poems attract us with the riddle's invitation, "What do I mean?" Some poems are indeed riddles, like Emily Dickinson's "I Like to See It Lap the Miles" (p. 559) or this poem by Poe.

The Haunted Palace

Edgar Allan Poe   (1809–1849)

In the greenest of our valleys
    By good angels tenanted,
Once a fair and stately palace—
    Radiant palace—reared its head.   4

In the monarch Thought's dominion—
  It stood there!
Never seraph spread a pinion
  Over fabric half so fair!   8

Banners yellow, glorious, golden,
  On its roof did float and flow,
(This—all this—was in the olden
  Time long ago,)   12
And every gentle air that dallied,
  In that sweet day,
Along the ramparts plumed and pallid,
  A wingéd odor went away.   16

Wanderers in that happy valley,
  Through two luminous windows, saw
Spirits moving musically,
  To a lute's well-tuned law,   20
Round about a throne where, sitting,
  Porphyrogene,[1]
In state his glory well befitting,
  The ruler of the realm was seen.   24

And all with pearl and ruby glowing
  Was the fair palace door,
Through which came flowing, flowing, flowing,
  And sparkling evermore,   28
A troop of Echoes, whose sweet duty
  Was but to sing,
In voices of surpassing beauty,
  The wit and wisdom of their king.   32

But evil things, in robes of sorrow,
  Assailed the monarch's high estate.
(Ah, let us mourn!—for never morrow
  Shall dawn upon him desolate!)   36
And round about his home the glory
  That blushed and bloomed,
Is but a dim-remembered story
  Of the old time entombed.   40

And travellers, now, within that valley,
  Through the red-litten windows see
Vast forms, that move fantastically
  To a discordant melody,   44

---

[1] A Greek-derived name, "born to the purple," or to royalty.

While, like a ghastly rapid river,
  Through the pale door
A hideous throng rush out forever
And laugh—but smile no more.   **48**

Poe inserted this poem into his story "The Fall of the House of Usher" as a
way of underlining one of the main themes. Readers sometimes miss the point,
for although they respond well enough to the main imagery they fail to see the
intended metaphoric comparison. For such readers the poem remains an unperceived and unsolved riddle. The palace is, of course, a human head. The banners
are hair, the windows eyes, the door the mouth, and so on. The most important
description is not of a palace but of insanity.

A *personification* is a metaphor that gives human qualities to something not
human. Personification thus turns an abstraction into a visual image, as when
we say Justice is blind or Fate is cruel. Even the unpoetic sometimes see the sun
as smiling or clouds as frowning. In the following poem, Drayton personifies a
deathbed scene from the dead metaphor "love is dying."

Since There's No Help, Come Let Us Kiss and Part

Michael Drayton   (1563–1631)

Since there's no help, come let us kiss and part;
Nay, I have done, you get no more of me,
And I am glad, yea, glad with all my heart
That thus so cleanly I myself can free;   **4**
Shake hands for ever, cancel all our vows,
And when we meet any time again,
Be it not seen in either of our brows
That we one jot of former love retain.   **8**
Now at the last gasp of Love's latest breath,
When, his pulse failing, Passion speechless lies,
When Faith is kneeling by his bed of death,
And Innocence is closing up his eyes,   **12**
  Now if thou wouldst, when all have given him over,
  From death to life thou mightst him yet recover.   **14**

What roles in an actual dying would the four personifications fill? How would
each abstraction be appropriate to the role of an actual person? The personifications in the scene are helpless. What does this do for the closing couplet?

An *extended metaphor* stretches through several lines or a whole poem. In
the following poem, Reid extends the metaphor of the sea as hills of home
through his first long stanza, then suggests a set of parallels in the rest of the
poem.

Calenture[1]

Alastair Reid   (1926–   )

He never lives to tell,
but other men bring back the tale
of how, after days of gazing at the sea
unfolding itself incessantly and greenly—
hillsides of water crested with clouds of foam—   5
heavy with a fading dream of home,
he climbs aloft one morning and, looking down,
cries out at seeing a different green,
farms, woods, grasslands, an extending plain,
hazy meadows, a long tree-fledged horizon,   10
swallows flashing in the halcyon sun,
his ship riding in deep rippling grain,
the road well-known to him, the house, the garden,
figures at the gate, till, dazed by his passion,
he suddenly climbs down and begins to run.   15
Stunned by his joy, the others watch him drown.

Such calenture, they say,
is not unknown in lovers long at sea,

yet such a like fever did she make in me,
this green-leaved summer morning, that I,   20
seeing her confirm a wish made lovingly,
felt gate, trees, grass, birds, garden glimmer over,
a ripple cross her face, the sky quiver,
the cropped lawn sway in waves, the house founder,
the light break into flecks, the path shimmer,   25
till, seeing her eyes clear and true at the center,
I walked toward her on the flowering water.

[1]A delirium in which sailors in tropic seas are said to desire to jump into the sea, which they imagine to be green fields.

A *mixed metaphor* is usually a mistake, with several physical impossibilities clashing their images together. If we were to write, "The web of fate rolled blindly in its iron groove," we would probably communicate little beyond an insensitivity to language. Yet mixed metaphors are not unknown to good poetry. An important element of the metaphoric vision is a sense of how each metaphor relates to the communication of the rest of the poem; a poet possessing that sense may use fundamentally different images to support and not undermine one another.

Question

May Swenson   (1919–)

Body my house
my horse my hound
what will I do
when you are fallen

Where will I sleep   5
How will I ride
What will I hunt
Where can I go
without my mount
all eager and quick   10
How will I know
in thicket ahead
is danger or treasure
when Body my good
bright dog is dead   15

How will it be
to lie in the sky
without roof or door
and wind for an eye

With cloud for shift   20
how will I hide?

Within the first seven words the poet tells us that the body is like a house,
a horse, and a hound. Is this a mixed metaphor? If so, point out its inconsistencies. If not, tell what unifies these disparate items.

In the following poem, Jeffers gives us metaphors of a volcano, flowers, fruit,
mother, meteors, mountains, something shining, a monster, servants and masters, and a trap.

Shine, Perishing Republic

Robinson Jeffers   (1887–1962)

While this America settles in the mould of its vulgarity, heavily
        thickening to empire,
And protest, only a bubble in the molten mass, pops and sighs out,
        and the mass hardens,   4

I sadly smiling remember that the flower fades to make fruit, the fruit
    rots to make earth.
Out of the mother; and through the spring exultances, ripeness and
    decadence; and home to the mother.   8

You making haste haste on decay: not blameworthy; life is good, be it
    stubbornly long or suddenly
A mortal splendor: meteors are not needed less than mountains:
    shine, perishing republic.   12

But for my children, I would have them keep their distance from the
    thickening center; corruption
Never has been compulsory, when the cities lie at the monster's feet
    there are left the mountains.   16

And boys, be in nothing so moderate as in love of man, a clever servant,
    insufferable master.
There is the trap that catches noblest spirits, that caught—they say—
    God, when he walked on earth.   20

Jeffers's title, repeated in line 12, is an *apostrophe:* an address to an imaginary
or absent person or a personification—another version of metaphor. How do
these various metaphors consort and support one another, or are they in fact
unfortunately mixed?

The double vision of metaphor is allied to the duality fundamental to all
figurative language: language that communicates a meaning other than that
conveyed by the literal sense of the words. Although we speak of roses in a girl's
cheeks, we do not mean that she literally has plants growing out of the side of
her face. Similarly, other forms of figurative language require the reader or
listener to maintain a double understanding, balancing what we have said against
what we have not said. *Overstatement,* or *hyperbole* ("hie-PER-bo-lee"), communicates by exaggeration, as when we say, "I've told you a thousand times,"
but mean we have said it three or four. In *understatement,* we say much less
than we hope will be understood, as when we say, "It will be to your advantage
to listen well," meaning some disaster will occur if you don't. When we use
litotes ("lie-TOTE-ees"), we affirm one meaning by negating a contrary one, as
when we say we have attended "not a few" movies in our time. Poets may
support the primary vision of the image and the double vision of the metaphor
by hyperbole, understatement, or litotes, attaching them to the sensory experience of the poem. These figures, however, are generally less important to the
total effect than either image or metaphor.

In *metonymy,* one thing stands for another associated with it; we speak of
the wishes of "the oval office," but mean the wishes of the president. Metonymy
is often ranked in importance with metaphor and simile as one of three primary

figures. A subordinate figure, *synecdoche,* makes a part stand for a whole: we speak of "wheels," but mean "automobile." Both are kinds of metaphor, of course, and they are sometimes difficult to keep distinct. Consider, for example, Shakespeare's phrase "rosy lips and cheeks" in the following sonnet:

Let Me Not to the Marriage of True Minds

William Shakespeare   (1564–1616)

Let me not to the marriage of true minds
Admit impediments. Love is not love
Which alters when it alteration finds,
Or bends with the remover to remove: 4
O, no! it is an ever-fixed mark,
That looks on tempests and is never shaken;
It is the star to every wandering bark,
Whose worth's unknown, although his height be taken.   8
Love's not Time's fool, though rosy lips and cheeks
Within his bending sickle's compass come;
Love alters not with his brief hours and weeks,
But bears it out even to the edge of doom.   12
    If this be error, and upon me proved,
    I never writ, nor no man ever loved.

The "rosy lips and cheeks" are a part of the body that Time, personified, cuts down with "his bending sickle"; considered in this way, the phrase is an excellent example of synecdoche. But because Time is a metaphor and the action of his sickle metaphoric, we may also suggest that "rosy lips and cheeks" stand for or are associated with youth and health; considered in this way the phrase looks like metonymy. The label is finally not important provided that we understand the metaphoric double vision that operates throughout the poem to underscore its meaning. Explain the metaphor of love as a star, including the point about worth and height.

    Look for and enjoy the various kinds of metaphor in the following poems.

An Ode: To Himself

Ben Jonson   (1573–1637)

Where dost thou careless lie,
    Buried in ease and sloth?
Knowledge that sleeps doth die;   3
And this security,
    It is the common moth
That eats on wits and arts, and oft destroys them both.   6

Are all the Aonian springs
    Dried up? Lies Thespia[1] waste?
Doth Clarius'[2] harp want strings,   9
That not a nymph now sings?
    Or droop they, as disgraced
To see their seats and bowers by chattering pies[3] defaced?   12

If hence thy silence be,
    As 'tis too just a cause,
Let this thought quicken thee: 15
Minds that are great and free,
    Should not on fortune pause;
'Tis crown enough to virtue still, her own applause.   18

What though the greedy fry[4]
    Be taken with false baits
Of worded balladry,   21
And think it poesie?
    They die with their conceits,
And only piteous scorn upon their folly waits.   24

Then take in hand thy lyre,
    Strike in thy proper strain;
With Japhet's[5] line, aspire   27
Sol's[6] chariot for new fire
    To give the world again;
Who aided him, will thee, the issue of Jove's brain.   30

And since our dainty age
    Cannot endure reproof,
Make not thyself a page   33
To that strumpet, the stage;
    But sing high and aloof,
Safe from the wolf's black jaw, and the dull ass's hoof.   36

---

[1]The Aonian springs and the town of Thespia were both sacred to the muses. [2]Apollo's (from his place of worship in Claros). [3]Magpies. [4]Young fishes. [5]Iapetus, father of Prometheus, who stole fire from the gods. [6]The sun's.

Where in the first line means "wherefore, why." Explain the aptness of *security* as a moth. What kind of a metaphor is *virtue* (line 18) Who are the *greedy fry?* Explain *conceits.* How is the myth of Prometheus appropriate? Who is "the issue of Jove's brain"? What is Jonson telling himself to do in the last stanza? What might the wolf and the ass represent in actuality?

A Red, Red Rose

Robert Burns   (1759–1796)

O my Luve's like a red, red rose,
  That's newly sprung in June;
O my Luve's like the melodie
  That's sweetly play'd in tune.—   4

As fair art thou, my bonie lass,
  So deep in luve am I;
And I will luve thee still, my Dear,
  Till a'[1] the seas gang[2] dry.—   8

Till a' the seas gang dry, my Dear,
  And the rocks melt wi' the sun:
I will luve thee still, my Dear,
  While the sands o' life shall run.—   12

And fare thee weel, my only Luve!
  And fare thee weel, a while!
And I will come again, my Luve,
  Tho' it were ten thousand mile!—   16

[1]All. [2]Go.

Do the similes of Burns's first stanza clash with or support one another? What other forms of figurative language can you find in the poem? Where?

She Walks in Beauty

George Gordon, Lord Byron   (1788–1824)

I

She walks in Beauty, like the night
  Of cloudless climes and starry skies;
And all that's best of dark and bright
  Meet in her aspect and her eyes:
Thus mellowed to that tender light
  Which Heaven to gaudy day denies.   6

II

One shade the more, one ray the less,
  Had half impaired the nameless grace
Which waves in every raven tress,
  Or softly lightens o'er her face;

Where thoughts serenely sweet express,
  How pure, how dear their dwelling-place.   **12**

III

And on that cheek, and o'er that brow,
  So soft, so calm, yet eloquent,
The smiles that win, the tints that glow,
  But tell of days in goodness spent,
A mind at peace with all below,
  A heart whose love is innocent!   **18**

What is the governing metaphor of "She Walks in Beauty"? Comment on *gaudy day, raven, dwelling-place, at peace with all below*.

When Daffodils Begin to Peer

William Shakespeare   (1564–1616)

When daffodils begin to peer,
  With heigh, the doxy[1] over the dale!
Why, then comes in the sweet o' the year,
  For the red blood reigns in the winter's pale.[2]   **4**

The white sheet bleaching on the hedge,
  With hey, the sweet birds, O how they sing!
Doth set my pugging[3] tooth on edge,
  For a quart of ale is a dish for a king.   **8**

The lark, that tirra-lyra chants,
  With heigh, with heigh, the thrush and the jay!
Are summer songs for me and my aunts,[4]
  While we lie tumbling in the hay.   **12**

[1]Wench. [2]Paleness; also, area of authority. [3]Thieving. [4]Prostitutes.

Explain the metaphor about the daffodils. Can you find the three metaphors punned into being by *reigns* and *pale?* How does the white sheet connect with the other stanzas? What are the particularly springish things in this song?

After Great Pain, a Formal Feeling Comes

Emily Dickinson   (1830–1886)

After great pain, a formal feeling comes—
The Nerves sit ceremonious, like Tombs—
The stiff Heart questions was it He, that bore,
And Yesterday, or Centuries before?   **4**

The Feet, mechanical, go round—
Of Ground, or Air, or Ought[1]—
A Wooden way
Regardless grown,   8
A Quartz contentment, like a stone—

This is the Hour of Lead—
Remembered, if outlived,
As Freezing persons, recollect the Snow—   12
First—Chill—then Stupor—then the letting go—

[1]Nothing; or, perhaps, obligation.

Is the great pain physical or emotional? What does Dickinson mean by a *formal feeling?* What is the reference to *He?* What are the various metaphors? How does the poet draw force and unity from them?

The Force That Through the Green Fuse Drives the Flower

Dylan Thomas   (1914–1953)

The force that through the green fuse drives the flower
Drives my green age; that blasts the roots of trees
Is my destroyer.
And I am dumb to tell the crooked rose
My youth is bent by the same wintry fever.   5

The force that drives the water through the rocks
Drives my red blood; that dries the mouthing streams
Turns mine to wax.
And I am dumb to mouth unto my veins
How at the mountain spring the same mouth sucks.   10

The hand that whirls the water in the pool
Stirs the quicksand; that ropes the blowing wind
Hauls my shroud sail.
And I am dumb to tell the hanging man
How of my clay is made the hangman's lime.   15

The lips of time leech to the fountain head;
Love drips and gathers, but the fallen blood
Shall calm her sores.
And I am dumb to tell a weather's wind
How time has ticked a heaven round the stars.   20

And I am dumb to tell the lover's tomb
How at my sheet goes the same crooked worm.

What is "the force"? What pictorial metaphor do you get with *fuse* in the first line? How does it connect with the second? In the second stanza, comment on the way similar-sounding words culminate in the metaphorical *mouth.* Comment on *shroud sail.* Can you explain *Love drips and gathers?* What is the visual metaphor in time's ticking? Comment on *sheet.*

A Valediction:[1] Forbidding Mourning

John Donne   (1572–1631)

As virtuous men pass mildly away,
   And whisper to their souls to go,
Whilst some of their sad friends do say
   The breath goes now, and some say, No;   **4**

So let us melt, and make no noise,
   No tear-floods, nor sigh-tempests move:
'Twere profanation of our joys
   To tell the laity our love.   **8**

Moving of th' earth[2] brings harms and fears,
   Men reckon what it did and meant;
But trepidation of the spheres,[3]
   Though greater far, is innocent.[4]   **12**

Dull sublunary[5] lovers' love
   (Whose soul is sense[6]) cannot admit
Absence, because it doth remove
   Those things which elemented[7] it.   **16**

But we by a love so much refined
   That our selves know not what it is,
Inter-assuréd of the mind,
   Care less, eyes, lips, and hands to miss.   **20**

Our two souls therefore, which are one,
   Though I must go, endure not yet
A breach,[8] but an expansion,
   Like gold to airy thinness beat.   **24**

If they be two, they are two so
   As stiff twin compasses[9] are two;
Thy soul, the fixed foot, makes no show
   To move, but doth, if th' other do.   **28**

[1]Farewell. [2]An earthquake. [3]In Ptolemaic astronomy, the spheres supported the stars, planets, sun, and moon. [4]Not sinister. [5]Beneath the moon, earthly. Contrasted with the lovers of the poem, whose love is higher and greater. [6]The love of ordinary lovers has its essence in the senses. [7]Composed. [8]Break. [9]Instrument for drawing circles.

And though it in the center sit,
    Yet when the other far doth roam,
It leans and hearkens after it,
    And grows erect, as that comes home.   32

Such wilt thou be to me, who must
    Like th' other foot, obliquely run;
Thy firmness makes my circle just,
    And makes me end where I begun.   36

What is the meaning of Donne's opening deathbed simile? In the third stanza, "trepidation" describes a movement, or trembling, that Ptolemaic astronomers assumed existed in the spheres supporting heavenly bodies. How does Donne's comparison of movement of the earth and of the spheres in this stanza illuminate his point about the parting of the lovers? Explain his metaphor of the gold. Explain how his compass metaphor works.

SYMBOL AND ALLEGORY

The double vision of metaphor originates in our desire to connect the disparate elements of earthly phenomena. Symbols spontaneously connect these elements, and allegory extends the connection throughout a story. Any item catches our attention only because it symbolizes something. The crab's dead claw in the sand arrests us because it symbolizes—though we don't realize it—life's clutching against the eternal tide. Many things have acquired conventional symbolic meanings, as one or another of their natural qualities has caught the human imagination. A garden, for instance, is naturally pleasant, peaceful, hopeful, as grass and buds declare again and again life's renewal. The ancient Golden Age and the Biblical Eden both pictured a garden of perpetual spring. Any garden in literature will have this natural suggestiveness, and the author will very likely, and indeed naturally, add some touch to remind us that all gardens reflect something of the Garden of Eden. A snake, for instance, will inevitably symbolize the dangers in beautiful gardens and will bring to mind the most famous of snakes in the grass, Satan himself, who, disguised as a serpent, destroyed the Garden's innocent bliss.

The dove is another natural symbol, long made traditional in literature. Doves —white, soft, and cooing—flocked around the temples of Venus, the Greek goddess of love, as her own sacred birds. Thus the dove naturally seems to symbolize Love. When Noah sends out a dove from the Ark, and the dove returns with an olive leaf to show that trees are emerging, both the dove and the olive come to symbolize the peace that follows God's wrathful flood. Love naturally has transposed into peace. Next, in the New Testament, when John baptizes Jesus in the Jordan River: "Lo, the heavens were opened unto him, and he saw the Spirit of God descending like a dove, and lighting upon him: and lo a voice from heaven, saying, This is my beloved Son, in whom I am well pleased" (Matt. 3.16–17). Pagan Love has become the Spirit of God—which is Love for his beloved Son. Finally, in the minds of Christian symbolizers, the dove becomes associated with the tongues of fire that descended on the apostles at the Pentecost—50 days after Easter and Christ's resurrection—filling them with the Holy Ghost (God's Spirit) and affirming the resurrection to the skeptical bystanders. In thousands of paintings and stained-glass windows, and through centuries of Bible reading, the dove and the fire become fixed as symbols for the Holy Spirit, for Love, and the peace that passeth understanding, emphasized in literature and thought in one aspect or another—a symbol so universal indeed that it is now also the dominant symbol in Communist countries for peace and community. Christianity, indeed, has so thoroughly imbued Western culture through the centuries, that even the obviously non-Christian writers of the twentieth century cannot resist returning again and again to characters symbolically analogous to Christ, to crosses, and other traditional symbols.

One Christian symbol in particular shows how a natural suggestiveness deepens into a symbol the more men think about it: the fish. Again, ancient societies chose the fish as a token of fertility, perhaps from some more primitive intuition that life, and the salty fecundity of woman, had emerged from the sea. Venus, goddess of love, we will remember, rose from the sea. Again, Christian history and thought projected an ancient symbol into higher significance, and again by natural association. Christ's apostles were fishermen. Christ is soon helping them bring in a tremendous catch, soon punning that he will be a fisher of men, soon feeding a multitude with a few loaves and fishes. Soon the fish becomes a symbol for Christ's spiritual fertility, and becomes an acronym, a secret sign, for the early Christian underground. The *ichthus*, a fish drawn in Roman catacombs and on tombstones (from the Greek word for fish, *ichthys*) was taken as the initial sounds of the Latinized Greek phrase for "Jesus Christ, Son of God, Savior": I*ēsous* CH*ristos*, TH*eou* HY*ios*, *Soter*—ICHTHYS. So the fish symbolizes Christ and his spiritual power. And any fish, like any garden, in a story or poem, may well carry these symbolic implications. Our job as readers of—and writers about—literature is to decide whether the writer intended them, or whether a fish is simply a fish and nothing more.

In the following passage, Keats makes the abstract "thing of beauty" a symbol for all aspiration, and then picks up the particular symbols—a bower, flowers, sun, moon.

[From] Endymion: Book I

John Keats   (1795–1821)

A thing of beauty is a joy for ever:
Its loveliness increases; it will never
Pass into nothingness; but still will keep
A bower[1] quiet for us, and a sleep

---

[1]Rustic cottage, retreat.

Full of sweet dreams, and health, and quiet breathing.   5
Therefore, on every morrow, are we wreathing
A flowery band to bind us to the earth,
Spite of despondence, of the inhuman dearth
Of noble natures, of the gloomy days,
Of all the unhealthy and o'er-darkened ways   10
Made for our searching—yes, in spite of all,
Some shape of beauty moves away the pall[2]
From our dark spirits. Such the sun, the moon,
Trees, old and young, sprouting a shady boon
For simple sheep; and such are daffodils   15
With the green world they live in; and clear rills[3]
That for themselves a cooling covert[4] make
'Gainst the hot season; the mid-forest brake,[5]
Rich with a sprinkling of fair musk-rose[6] blooms;
And such too is the grandeur of the dooms[7]   20
We have imagined for the mighty dead,
All lovely tales that we have heard or read—
An endless fountain of immortal drink,
Pouring unto us from the heaven's brink.

Nor do we merely feel these essences   25
For one short hour; no, even as the trees
That whisper round a temple become soon
Dear as the temple's self, so does the moon,
The passion poesy, glories infinite,
Haunt us till they become a cheering light   30
Unto our souls, and bound to us so fast
That, whether there be shine or gloom o'ercast,
They always must be with us, or we die.

[2]Funeral covering.   [3]Small brooks.   [4]Hidden nook.   [5]Thicket.   [6]A Mediterranean rose, usually white.   [7]Destinies.

Within these lines Keats asserts the value of natural beauty:

> . . . daffodils
> With the green world they live in; and clear rills
> That for themselves a cooling covert make
> 'Gainst the hot season. . . .

He reminds us also of our heritage of literature:

> . . . the grandeur of the dooms
> We have imagined for the mighty dead;

All lovely tales that we have heard or read—
An endless fountain of immortal drink,
Pouring unto us from the heaven's brink.

Fundamental to the argument is the idea that both the natural objects of the world and the created objects of art possess meanings deeper and more complex than their surface appearance. Why will a thing of beauty be a joy forever? Why will its loveliness increase? How does the mind counteract gloom and daily discouragement? What are Keats's specific natural symbols of hope? What are his literary ones?

The poet's daffodil may symbolize a larger meaning. The poet's story suggests an *allegory* when his explicit narrative implies a loftier set of events. The great medieval play *Everyman* signifies in its homely details the lives of all men. Dante's *Inferno* journeys to a Hell fraught with meanings for us all. Bryant's "Waterfowl" first symbolizes the great bird—probably some kind of crane—then allegorizes its flight.

To a Waterfowl

William Cullen Bryant   (1794–1878)

Whither, midst falling dew,
While glow the heavens with the last steps of day:
Far, through their rosy depths, dost thou pursue
    Thy solitary way?   4

Vainly the fowler's eye
Might mark thy distant flight to do thee wrong,
As, darkly seen against the crimson sky,
    Thy figure floats along.   8

Seek'st thou the plashy brink
Of weedy lake, or marge of river wide,
Or where the rocking billows rise and sink
    On the chafed ocean-side?   12

There is a Power whose care
Teaches thy way along that pathless coast—
The desert and illimitable air—
    Lone wandering, but not lost.   16

All day thy wings have fanned,
At that far height, the cold, thin atmosphere,
Yet stoop not, weary, to the welcome land,
    Though the dark night is near.   20

And soon that toil shall end;
Soon shalt thou find a summer home, and rest,
And scream among thy fellows; reeds shall bend,
    Soon, o'er thy sheltered nest.   24

    Thou'rt gone, the abyss of heaven
Hath swallowed up thy form; yet, on my heart
Deeply has sunk the lesson thou hast given,
    And shall not soon depart.   28

    He who, from zone to zone,
Guides through the boundless sky thy certain flight,
In the long way that I must tread alone,
    Will lead my steps aright.   32

What does the waterfowl symbolize? How is its flight allegorical? What is the
effect of "scream among thy fellows" (line 23)? In what way does each element
of the bird's situation parallel the situation of the narrator, the "I" who emerges
in the last stanza?

Not all writers announce their allegorical intent.

Whoso List to Hunt

Thomas Wyatt   *(1503–1542)*

Whoso list[1] to hunt, I know where is an hind,
    But as for me, alas, I may no more;
    The vain travail hath wearied me so sore,
I am of them that farthest come behind.   4
Yet may I by no means my wearied mind
    Draw from the deer, but as she fleeth afore
    Fainting I follow; I leave off therefore,
Since in a net I seek to hold the wind.   8
Who list her hunt, I put him out of doubt,
    As well as I, may spend his time in vain.
And graven with diamonds in letters plain,
There is written her fair neck round about,   12
    "*Noli me tangere,*[2] for Caesar's I am,
    And wild for to hold, though I seem tame."

[1]Wishes.   [2]Touch me not.

Wyatt's allegorical hunt may describe his pursuit of Anne Boleyn, who became
Henry VIII's queen. What details would support this interpretation?

In the following poem, what does Frost's little evening journey allegorize?

Stopping by Woods on a Snowy Evening

Robert Frost   *(1874–1963)*

Whose woods these are I think I know.
His house is in the village, though;
He will not see me stopping here
To watch his woods fill up with snow.   4

My little horse must think it queer
To stop without a farmhouse near
Between the woods and frozen lake
The darkest evening of the year.   8

He gives his harness bells a shake
To ask if there is some mistake.
The only other sound's the sweep
Of easy wind and downy flake.   12

The woods are lovely, dark, and deep,
But I have promises to keep,
And miles to go before I sleep,
And miles to go before I sleep.   16

What effect does the ownership of the woods have on the poem? What do the woods filling with snow symbolize? How is the poet traveling? Comment on *easy wind and downy flake.* What is the effect of *But?* What is the effect of repeating the last two lines?

What does the rose symbolize in the following poem?

The Sick Rose

William Blake   *(1757–1827)*

O rose, thou art sick:
The invisible worm
That flies in the night,
In the howling storm,   4
Has found out thy bed
Of crimson joy;
And his dark secret love
Does thy life destroy.   8

Is the rose actually sick? What is the invisible worm? Could this be a simple statement of fact and yet symbolize something? Comment on the force of *bed.*

Two years before the Civil War, abolitionist John Brown led an attack on the U.S. government arsenal at Harper's Ferry, Virginia (now West Virginia), on

October 16, 1859. After a trial in Charles Town, in the Shenandoah Valley, he
was hanged on December 2, 1859.

The Portent

Herman Melville   *(1819–1891)*

Hanging from the beam,
  Slowly swaying (such the law),
Gaunt the shadow on your green,
  Shenandoah!
The cut is on the crown
(Lo, John Brown),
And the stabs shall heal no more.

Hidden in the cap   8
  Is the anguish none can draw;
So your future veils its face,
  Shenandoah!
But the streaming beard is shown   12
(Weird John Brown),
The meteor of the war.

Explain Melville's title. How would you characterize his apostrophe to Shenandoah? What does John Brown's shadow symbolize? Describe Brown's appearance as he hangs there. Look up *weird* and explain its force. Why is *meteor*
apt?

    What is the actuality in the following poem, and what becomes symbolic?

In Just-

E. E. Cummings   *(1894–1962)*

in Just-
spring when the world is mud-
luscious the little
lame balloonman

whistles far and wee   5

and eddieandbill come
running from marbles and
piracies and it's   10
spring

when the world is puddle-wonderful

the queer
old balloonman whistles
far   and   wee
and bettyandisbel come dancing   15
from hop-scotch and jump-rope and

it's
spring
and
        the   20

    goat-footed

balloonMan   whistles
far
and
wee   25

Explain the effect of Cummings's spacing, beginning with his odd hyphen after
Just-. Who might eddieandbill and bettyandisbel be? Does leaving them uncapi-
talized and running them together have anything to do with symbolism? Comment on *puddle-wonderful*. Follow the evolution of the descriptions of the
balloon man. What is the actuality? What does he symbolize? Is the evolution
of the whistle significant?

Symbols and allegories tend to shade into one another, since both share the
metaphorical process—something represented by something else. Consider the
elements of metaphor, symbol, and allegory in the following two poems.

Hymn to Cynthia[1]

Ben Jonson   *(1573–1637)*

Queen and huntress, chaste and fair,
Now the sun is laid to sleep,
Seated in thy silver chair,
State in wonted manner keep:
    Hesperus[2] entreats thy light,
    Goddess excellently bright.   6

Earth, let not thy envious shade
Dare itself to interpose;
Cynthia's shining orb was made
Heaven to clear, when day did close:
    Bless us then with wished sight,
    Goddess excellently bright.   12

[1]Diana, goddess of the moon; also traditionally a name for Queen Elizabeth I.   [2]The evening star.

Lay thy bow of pearl apart,
And thy crystal-shining quiver;
Give unto the flying hart[3]
Space to breathe, how short soever:
    Thou that mak'st a day of night,
    Goddess excellently bright.   **18**

[3]Male deer.

What does the moon symbolize in "Hymn to Cynthia"? What is allegorical about it? What are the personifications? How might the earth interpose an envious shade? Why envious? Explain the allusion to the bow and quiver.

The Chambered Nautilus[1]

Oliver Wendell Holmes   (1809–1894)

This is the ship of pearl, which, poets feign,
    Sails the unshadowed main,—
    The venturous bark that flings
On the sweet summer wind its purpled wings
In gulfs enchanted, where the Siren[2] sings,   **5**
    And coral reefs lie bare,
Where the cold sea-maids rise to sun their streaming hair.

Its webs of living gauze no more unfurl;
    Wrecked is the ship of pearl!
    And every chambered cell,   **10**
Where its dim dreaming life was wont to dwell,
As the frail tenant shaped his growing shell,
    Before thee lies revealed,—
Its irised[3] ceiling rent, its sunless crypt unsealed!

Year after year beheld the silent toil   **15**
    That spread his lustrous coil;
    Still, as the spiral grew,
He left the past year's dwelling for the new,
Stole with soft step its shining archway through,
    Built up its idle door,   **20**
Stretched in his last-found home, and knew the old no more.

[1]The pearly nautilus of the South Pacific builds a spiral shell, adding a chamber each year. The ancients believed it could erect a membrane as a sail.   [2]One of the winged sea nymphs who, by their singing, lured sailors to destruction on the rocks.   [3]Rainbowed.

Thanks for the heavenly message brought by thee,
    Child of the wandering sea,
    Cast from her lap, forlorn!
From thy dead lips a clearer note is born   25
Than ever Triton[4] blew from wreathèd horn!
    While on mine ear it rings,
Through the deep caves of thought I hear a voice that sings:—

Build thee more stately mansions, O my soul,
    As the swift seasons roll!   30
    Leave thy low-vaulted past!
Let each new temple, nobler than the last,
Shut thee from heaven with a dome more vast,
    Till thou at length art free,
Leaving thine outgrown shell by life's unresting sea!   35

---

[4]Sea god. Cf. Wordsworth's sonnet "The World Is Too Much With Us," last line: "Or hear old
Triton blow his wreathèd horn."

How does the mythical nautilus of the first stanza contrast with the actuality of
the second? What is the allegory? How does the poet interpret it? What has
suggested his metaphor of the deep caves of thought? What is the effect of each
year's "dome more vast"? Explain the symbol and its effectiveness in the last
line.

CHAPTER 5

SOUNDS

SOUND PATTERNS

Hickory dickory dock
Fee fie foe fum

Sounds strike us first. We enjoy them in themselves, even when they mean nothing. Poetry, as in these nursery rhymes, calls forth for our enjoyment the sounds of language, those chiming variations, especially when they also imitate the rhythms we know as we breathe, or walk, or clap our hands in time. So let us say that the sounds of poetry consist in rhyme and meter: (1) sounds matched to each other, and (2) the rhythms of language matched to measured time.

Rhyme

We may segregate the rhyming sounds of poetry into *alliteration, assonance, consonance, full rhyme,* and *reiteration.* All are repetitions, in which we enjoy the similarities among the differences in language.

1. *Alliteration.* First sounds of words (or of accented syllables) the same: "a *L*ittle *L*ost al*L*iteration."

   *W*estern *w*ind, when *w*ilt thou blow

(The *hw* sound of *wh*en comes close, and indeed is identical, a full alliteration, in some pronunciations.)

2. *Assonance.* Middle vowel sounds the same: smoky loam; glad rag; hot rod.

> Ere she *see* the *Ea*rl of Murray
> Come sounding through the town

(She see the makes a triple assonance, if we say "thee" for *the;* *Ea*rl / Murray shows how similar sounds, not spelling, make the assonance.)

3. *Consonance.* End-consonant sounds the same in words or syllables but vowels different (called "slant rhyme" when rhymed at line-ends): *bored / third, supple / apple, cried / bleed, love / over.*

> When*as* in *sil*ks my *Jul*ia *goes*

4. *Reiteration.* The same word repeated, often with different force:

> *Tiger, Tiger,* burning bright
> *Then, then* (me thinks) how sweetly flowes
> Of hammered *gold* and *gold* enamelling

Whole lines are often repeated, as in Frost's "Stopping by Woods" or in the refrains of ballads. Repetition of words, phrases, or lines may bring us back to the familiar, may emphasize a point, or, frequently, may give new emphasis or meaning to the repeated words.

5. *Rhyme.* Words ending in the same sound: *bird / third,* usually at line-ends ("Does it rhyme?"). Slant rhyme *(bird / soared)* also counts as "rhyme" at line-ends, and may even include approximations like *cob / rap* or *cot / mad.* Contrasting with *exact rhymes,* the *slant rhymes* are also called *off rhymes* and *approximate rhymes.* Words that look alike but sound slanted, like *love / move,* are also called *eye rhymes.* Most rhymes are *masculine,* matching the accented final syllable: *hate / fate, report / contort.* Words adding an unstressed syllable make *feminine rhymes (double rhymes): candy / dandy.* Three syllables make a *triple rhyme: ratified / stratified.* Rhyme, like all patterns of sound, depends on repetition with variation. A couplet rhyming *sore* with *soar* leaves us unfulfilled, unless the poet wants to amuse us with a clinker.

A poet frequently orchestrates all or most of these rhyming sounds together, sometimes stressing one sound in different combinations to augment meaning, as Robert Herrick does the *s* sounds in the poem below, which seem to suggest the sound of water and the liquid sound of silks rubbing together:

Whenas in silks my *Julia* goes,
Then, then (me thinks) how sweetly flowes
That liquefaction of her clothes.

Next, when I cast mine eyes and see
That brave Vibration each way free;
O how that glittering taketh me!

The reiterated *then* and the end-rhymes are obvious. But note the alliterated *th*'s *(Then, then, thinks)*, the *l*'s *(-ly, flowes, liquefaction)*, and the *br*'s in *brave* and *-brations* that also combine in assonance with *way*. Other assonances are *in-silks, me-sweetly, That-faction, -tion-of, Next-when, cast-and, I-mine-eyes, each-free*. Consonance appears in *Whenas-goes, sil-Jul, then-thin, when-mine*, and merges with alliteration in *brave-vibration* and *glittering-taketh*. The way Herrick's sounds flow and echo probably eludes precise demonstration, as when the *a* in *that* deepens to *brave* and then squeezes up into the *ee*'s of *each* and *free* or as *o* flows into *-ow*, as if one were hearing the different vowels recited. With the swishing *s*'s underlining the silken image, we can only point in admiration to Herrick's orchestrated sounds as we attempt to explain to our readers the total effect of this little poem.

Meter

Meter is the drummer in the poetic band: *rattity-tat-ta-tat-ta-tat*. Or perhaps we should say that meter is the bass drum's steady beat, with the snare drum's *rattity-tat* marking its varieties, as in the opening line of Andrew Marvell's "To His Coy Mistress": *"Had we but world enough and time"*—*rattity-tat-ta-tat-ta-tat*. This is *iambic* meter, which has predominated in English for over four hundred years. Three other meters—*anapestic, trochaic, dactylic*—lend iambic an occasional foot, for variety, and produce a few poems.

Modern verse is predominantly "free," with no regular pattern. And some modern poets have tried other systems in place of the four traditional meters, writing "syllabic verse" in which all lines have a predetermined number of syllables but no regular beat, or "rhythmic verse," with, say, three beats to each line of loosely varying numbers of syllables. Others have tried *shaped poems*, grouping their words on the page to look like keys or locomotives, or scattering them around to suggest swooping pigeons or sheer dramatic pause and emphasis. When analyzing a poem we need to discover if it has a metrical pattern or no pattern, and what that pattern is.

Dipodic Verse

Sometimes looking like free verse, dipodic ("two-footed") verse survives from Old English poetry in a light-hearted rocking meter, with two half lines, each with two stresses falling among scattered light syllables. Nursery rhymes picked up the pattern:

ᵁ — | ᵁ ᵁ — ᵁ **|** ᵁ — | ᵁ ᵁ — |
There was an old woman who lived in a shoe.

ᵁ — | ᵁ ᵁ ᵁ — ᵁ **|** ᵁ — | ᵁ ᵁ ᵁ ᵁ ᵁ — |
She had so many children she didn't know what to do.

From this emerged a more patterned light verse, which will scan in alternating heavy and light iambic feet (ᵁ —): ta-DA, ta-da, ta-DA, ta-da:

ᵁ — | ᵁ ᵁ — | ᵁ—|ᵁ — **|** ᵁ—|ᵁ — | ᵁ—|ᵁ — |
Go down to Kew in lilac-time, in lilac-time, in lilac-time

But it really rollicks better when read more quickly in the old dipodic way, with the lighter heavies falling in with the lights (tap your foot to the accented syllables):

ᵁ — | ᵁ ᵁ ᵁ —ᵁ ᵁ **|** ᵁ—ᵁ ᵁ | ᵁ—ᵁ ᵁ |
Go down to Kew in lilac-time, in lilac-time, in lilac-time

ᵁ — | ᵁ ᵁ ᵁ—ᵁ ᵁ **|** ᵁ —|ᵁ ᵁ ᵁ — ᵁ |
Go down to Kew in lilac-time (it isn't far from London!)

ᵁ —| ᵁ ᵁ ᵁ — ᵁ ᵁ **|** ᵁ —|ᵁ ᵁ ᵁ — ᵁ ᵁ|
And you shall wander hand in hand with love in summer's wonderland

ᵁ — | ᵁ ᵁ ᵁ—ᵁ ᵁ **|** ᵁ—|ᵁ ᵁ ᵁ — ᵁ |
Go down to Kew in lilac-time (it isn't far from London)!

Alfred Noyes, "The Barrel-Organ"

Noyes's refrain illustrates another trait of dipodics: to slow down the two-footed run at the end, with a three-stressed, and more conventional, pattern. We can keep on running, as in the scansion above, but we will probably slow down to conventional iambics:

ᵁ —|ᵁ — | ᵁ — ᵁ|
it isn't far from London

Regular Meters

Most metrical poems will be in iambics, with feet from the other three meters occasionally substituted for variety. Here are the four regular meters:

RISING METERS

Iambic: ᵁ —
Anapestic: ᵁ ᵁ —

FALLING METERS

Trochaic: — ᵁ
Dactylic: — ᵁ ᵁ

The number of these metrical units, or feet, in a line also gives the verse a name:

1 foot: monometer
2 feet: dimeter
3 feet: trimeter

4 feet: tetrameter
5 feet: pentameter
6 feet: hexameter
7 feet: heptameter

Thus we have *iambic tetrameter,* lines of four iambic feet, or *dactylic hexameter,* lines of six dactylic feet. All meters will show some variations, substituting other kinds of feet, but the dominant foot is usually easily recognizable—indeed, *must* be recognizable for us to say, "This is an iambic pentameter poem," or "This is an anapestic poem in stanzas of two tetrameter lines and a dimeter." *Scansion*—marking off the feet—will help your analysis:

IAMBIC TETRAMETER

Had we but world enough and time

ANAPESTIC TETRAMETER

The pop-lars are felled; farewell to the shade

And the whis-pering sound of the cool colonade!

William Cowper, "The Poplar Field"

TROCHAIC TETRAMETER

Tell me not in mournful numbers

Longfellow, "A Psalm of Life"

DACTYLIC HEXAMETER

This is the forest prim-eval. The murmuring pines and the hemlocks

Bearded with moss....

Longfellow, "Evangeline"

Scansion

Scanning the lines of a poem—marking off the beat and its variations in metrical feet—helps you to perceive the metrical sound effects and to describe their striking features. The regular iambic pentameter line—ten syllables, five stresses—scans like this:

What oft was thought, but ne'er so well expressed

The iambic also regularly admits an extra light syllable at the line-end, a "feminine ending" (the regular one is "masculine"), giving the five-stress line an occasional eleventh syllable:

Like to the lark at break of day arising.

Scanning will tune your ear to the way in which meter underlines certain of the slurred syllables of speech, lifting them into metrical regularity, as the poet imposes his or her will on language and stretches out its latent accents in metrical pleasure. Each of the following lines, in ordinary speech, would have only four stresses:

True Wít is Náture to advántage drést

And leáves the wofld to dárkness and to mé

Deép in the shády sádness of a vále

But each of the poets (Pope, Gray, Keats), in the context of his other lines and regular beat, stretches them into iambic meter:

True Wit is Nature to advantage drest

And leaves the world to darkness and to me

Deep in the sha- dy sad- ness of a vale

In reading them metrically, we lift into meter, just slightly, the otherwise unaccented syllables *to, and, of.* Keats and Yeats (and others) can even extrude iambic pentameter from ordinarily three-stressed lines, showing how this kind of mastery is most pleasing when exerted on big polysyllabic words. Each of the following lines would show only three stresses in ordinary speech *(sun, shad-, mag,* and *Mon-, own, -nif-).* But the meaning seems to emerge with the beat as the poets stretch them out along the metrical frame:

A sun—a shad- ow of a mag- nitude.

Monuments of his own magnif- icence

Thus scansion identifies the metrical pattern for you, and leads you to discern the poet's mastery in bending language to the pleasures of meter.

By scanning, you will discover that iambic has three regular variations:

Inverted foot: | — ∪ | (a trochee)
Spondee: | — — |
Ionic double-foot: | ∪ ∪ | — — |

We have already seen how frequently the inverted foot begins an iambic line: *Had we but world; Like to the lark; Monuments of.* The spondee is rarer, but see how it energizes Dylan Thomas's iambic line:

∪ — | ∪ — | ∪ — | — — | ∪ — |
The force that through the green fuse drives the flower

Some lines from Housman's "To an Athlete Dying Young" will show nicely how the inverted foot and the double ionic can vary the iambic march without missing a beat:

∪ — | ∪ — | ∪ — | ∪ — |
So set, before its echoes fade,

∪ — | — — ∪ | ∪ — | ∪ — |
The fleet foot on the sill of shade,

∪ — | ∪ ∪ | — — | ∪ — |
And hold to the low lintel up

∪ — | ∪ — | ∪ — | ∪ — |
The still-defended challenge-cup.

Some writers like an extra ("hypermetric") light syllable. Others hold their iambics close, allowing only the three regular variations. The punctuation also varies the meter, of course, either in midline caesuras or at endline, as when a conductor momentarily suspends the baton in midair and the orchestra pauses before resuming the beat. Scanning will tell you what kind of a metrist you have, so you can describe his or her metrical bent, and the way the sound effects flow and twirl over the march of the meter.

The poet has two more strings to his or her sounding bow. Since rhyme augments the natural pause at the line's end, poets may underline that pause in either rhymed or unrhymed lines by an *end-stop*—any punctuation to mark the pause:

O long, long may the ladies stand,
  With their gold combs in their hair,

Or they may use *enjambment,* a *run-on line,* in which the sense rushes on into the next line:

That is no country for old men. The young
In one another's arms. . . .

Finally, poets use *caesuras:* any punctuation that pauses within a line. A *masculine caesura* pauses at the end of a metrical foot:

The salmon falls, the mackerel-crowded seas

A *feminine caesura* pauses midfoot, like the commas after *Fish* and *begotten* in Yeats's lines:

> Fish, flesh, or fowl, commend all summer long
> Whatever is begotten, born, and dies.

There you have a nice illustration of a *run-on line,* two *feminine caesuras,* and three *masculine caesuras.*

Rhyme Scheme

Ultimately, through rhyme, the pleasures of sound fall into larger patterns. As with meter, we can enjoy variations only as we perceive and enjoy a regular rhyming pattern, skipping away and touching base. To see the regularity and enjoy the release, we must first detect the pattern. Conversely, we must assure ourselves that another poem, apparently unrhymed or in altogether free verse, derives its pleasures elsewhere. So we discover rhyme scheme by assigning letters to the sounds at line-ends:

> O long, long may the ladies stand,   *a*
>   With their gold combs in their hair,   *b*
> Waiting for their own dear lords,   *c*
>   For they'll see them no more.   *b*

This is a typical *ballad stanza,* from "Sir Patrick Spens," a quatrain of alternate iambic tetrameters and trimeters rhymed *abcb.*

Marking the scheme in longer stanzas, especially freely rhyming stanzas, can reveal a pattern otherwise not noticed, as the apparently casual flow of language chimes into patterns metrical and stanzaic:

> Laura stretched her gleaming neck   *a*
> Like a rush-embedded swan,   *b*
> Like a lily from the beck,   *a*
> Like a moonlit poplar branch,   *c*
> Like a vessel at the launch   *c*
> When its last restraint is gone.   *b*
>
>   *Christina Rossetti, "Goblin Market"*

You will notice that *branch / launch* looks like a consonance, a "slant rhyme," though it may have rhymed exactly in the poet's pronunciation. Marking the rhyme scheme will thus bring out unnoticed slant rhymes and even more remote approximations.

> That is no country for old men. The young   *a*
> In one another's arms, birds in the trees,   *b*
> —Those dying generations—at their song,   *a*

The salmon-falls, the mackerel-crowded seas,	*b*
Fish, flesh, or fowl, commend all summer long	*a*
Whatever is begotten, born, and dies.	*b*
Caught in that sensual music all neglect	*c*
Monuments of unageing intellect.	*c*

Yeats, *"Sailing to Byzantium"*

In marking the rhymes, we are surprised to discover how simple and straightforward Yeats's stanzaic scheme is, and as we move through the poem (see pp. 677–678), we can admire how confidently (and characteristically) he can force a rhyme to keep his sense and his pattern both, even rhyming *magnificence* with *dress,* for instance:

. . . and louder sing	*a*
For every tatter in its mortal dress,	*b*
Nor is there singing school but studying	*a*
Monuments of its own magnificence	*b*

Or, more conventionally, *wall / soul / animal:*

O sages standing in God's holy fire	*a*
As in the gold mosaic of a wall,	*b*
Come from the holy fire, perne in a gyre,	*a*
And be the singing-masters of my soul.	*b*
Consume my heart away; sick with desire	*a*
And fastened to a dying animal	*b*
It knows not what it is. . . .	

EXPLORING SOUND PATTERNS

Let us examine a sonnet rich in the patterned sounds of poetry to explore some of the variations in rhyme and meter and especially the effect of reiteration. Note how the three repetitions of *state* accumulate meaning.

When in Disgrace with Fortune and Men's Eyes

William Shakespeare　　(1564–1616)

When in disgrace with fortune and men's eyes
I all alone beweep my outcast state,
And trouble deaf heaven with my bootless[1] cries,
And look upon myself, and curse my fate,
Wishing me like to one more rich in hope,

4

[1]Useless, unrewarding.

Featured like him, like him with friends possessed,
Desiring this man's art, and that man's scope,
With what I most enjoy contented least;   8
Yet in these thoughts myself almost despising,
Haply I think on thee,—and then my state,
Like to the lark at break of day arising
From sullen earth, sings hymns at heaven's gate;   12
    For thy sweet love remembered such wealth brings
    That then I scorn to change my state with kings.

Scan the first line. What is the meter? What is the variation? Scan the third line. What does the poet accomplish metrically with *trouble deaf heaven?* What is the effect of *like him, like him?* Give in your own words the meaning of the first and the second *state;* then explain the effect of that final punning *state.* Where are the caesuras? Are there any feminine ones? How about the rhymes? What is the effect of the run-on lines as against the end-stopped ones? How does the idea of riches (fortune) operate in this poem?

The following poem is a treasure house of alliteration, consonance, and assonance.

God's Grandeur

Gerard Manley Hopkins   *(1844–1889)*

The world is charged with the grandeur of God.
  It will flame out, like shining from shook foil;
  It gathers to a greatness, like the ooze of oil
Crushed. Why do men then now not reck[1] his rod?   4
Generations have trod, have trod, have trod;
  And all is seared with trade; bleared, smeared with toil;
  And wears man's smudge and shares man's smell: the soil
Is bare now, nor can foot feel, being shod.   8

And for all this, nature is never spent;
  There lives the dearest freshness deep down things;
And though the last lights off the black West went
  Oh, morning, at the brown brink eastward, springs—   12
Because the Holy Ghost over the bent
  World broods with warm breast and with ah! bright wings.

[1]Take heed of.

See what you can do in illustrating how alliteration, consonance, assonance, caesura, reiteration, and run-ons augment this remarkable sonnet. What is the rhyme scheme? Comment on the metaphor of the *bent world.*

The following selection is famous for the way its sounds support its meaning.

Zephyr blows, the stream flows, the torrent roars, Ajax strives, and Camilla scours—all in lines suited in sound to their varied activities. Notice how the lines linked by rhyme are also linked by thought, and how the rhymes underscore meaning in these skillful *rhymed couplets.* Note also how alliteration, like rhyme, can link concepts and underscore meaning—"soft . . . strain," "smooth stream," "loud . . . lash"—and how the consonance "strain when" blends with the assonance on *e* in "when Zephyr gently."

[From] Essay on Criticism

Alexander Pope   (1668–1744)

True ease in writing comes from art, not chance,
As those move easiest who have learned to dance.
'Tis not enough no harshness gives offence,
The sound must seem an Echo to the sense: 4
Soft is the strain when Zephyr gently blows,
And the smooth stream in smoother numbers flows;
But when loud surges lash the sounding shore,
The hoarse, rough verse should like the torrent roar: 8
When Ajax strives some rock's vast weight to throw,
The line too labours, and the words move slow;
Not so, when swift Camilla scours the plain,
Flies o'er th' unbending corn, and skims along the main.   12

What is the effect of the assonance in "loud . . . sounding"? Of the repeated *m*'s in "smooth stream in smoother numbers"? Of the varied *o* sounds from *aw* to *oh* to *oo* in "soft . . . blows . . . smooth"? Does Pope use any run-ons? Why or why not? Identify the caesuras and describe their effect.

This selection illustrates two more poetic effects. Its pleasing combinations of sound are called *euphony.* The opposite—harsh, discordant sounds—is *cacophony.* Pope's lines on Ajax approach cacophony, as the line illustrates his labors; certainly they are less euphonious than the lines on Zephyr.

Identify the sounds that contribute to the euphony of the following poem. Note the internal rhymes.

The Splendor Falls

Alfred, Lord Tennyson   (1809–1892)

The splendor falls on castle walls
    And snowy summits old in story:
The long light shakes across the lakes,   3
    And the wild cataract leaps in glory.
Blow, bugle, blow, set the wild echoes flying,
Blow, bugle; answer, echoes, dying, dying, dying.   6

O hark, O hear! how thin and clear,
 And thinner, clearer, farther going!
O sweet and far from cliff and scar   9
 The horns of Elfland faintly blowing!
Blow, let us hear the purple glens replying:
Blow, bugle; answer, echoes, dying, dying, dying. 12

 O love, they die in yon rich sky,
  They faint on hill or field or river:
 Our echoes roll from soul to soul,   15
  And grow for ever and for ever.
Blow, bugle, blow, set the wild echoes flying,
And answer, echoes, answer, dying, dying, dying. 18

Onomatopoeia is a word sounding its meaning: the "buzz" of a bee, the "clop, clop" of horses' hooves, the "sizzling" of bacon in a skillet. Show how Tennyson reflects the sound of a bugle in his language. What is the effect of his inner rhyme? Of reiteration? This is a romantic picture—castles, mountains, elfland. How does *O love* point the poet's meaning?

The following poems are also memorable for their varied sound effects.

Dover Beach

Matthew Arnold *(1822–1888)*

The sea is calm to-night.
The tide is full, the moon lies fair
Upon the straits;—on the French coast the light
Gleams and is gone; the cliffs of England stand,
Glimmering and vast, out in the tranquil bay.   5
Come to the window, sweet is the night-air!

Only, from the long line of spray
Where the sea meets the moon-blanched land,
Listen! you hear the grating roar
Of pebbles which the waves draw back, and fling, 10
At their return, up the high strand,
Begin, and cease, and then again begin,
With tremulous cadence slow, and bring
The eternal note of sadness in.

Sophocles long ago   15
Heard it on the Ægæan, and it brought
Into his mind the turbid ebb and flow
Of human misery;[1] we

[1] Cf. *Antigone*, II, 583–591.

Find also in the sound a thought,
Hearing it by this distant northern sea. 20

The Sea of Faith
Was once, too, at the full, and round earth's shore
Lay like the folds of a bright girdle furled.
But now I only hear
Its melancholy, long, withdrawing roar, 25
Retreating, to the breath
Of the night-wind, down the vast edges drear
And naked shingles[2] of the world.

Ah, love, let us be true
To one another! for the world, which seems 30
To lie before us like a land of dreams,
So various, so beautiful, so new,
Hath really neither joy, nor love, nor light,

Nor certitude, nor peace, nor help for pain;
And we are here as on a darkling[3] plain 35
Swept with confused alarms of struggle and flight,
Where ignorant armies clash by night.

[2]Pebbly beaches. [3]Becoming dark.

Where are the effects of *onomatopoeia* in "Dover Beach"? How is the picture in the first stanza reflected in the fifth? How does the sound of the surf at the foot of the cliffs of England (second stanza) translate in the closing stanza?

Felix Randal

Gerard Manley Hopkins *(1844–1889)*

Felix Randal the farrier,[1] O is he dead then? my duty all ended,
Who have watched his mould of man, big-boned and
     hardy-handsome
Pining, pining, till time when reason rambled in it and some
Fatal four disorders, fleshed there, all contended? 4

Sickness broke him. Impatient, he cursed at first, but mended
Being anointed and all; though a heavenlier heart began some
Months earlier, since I had our sweet reprieve and ransom
Tendered to him.[2] Ah well, God rest him all road ever he offended! 8

[1]Blacksmith. [2]Had confessed him and given him absolution (Hopkins was a priest).

This seeing the sick endears them to us, us too it endears.
My tongue had taught thee comfort, touch had quenched thy tears,
Thy tears that touched my heart, child, Felix, poor Felix Randal;

How far from then forethought of, all thy more boisterous years,   12
When thou at the random grim forge, powerful amidst peers,
Didst fettle[3] for the great grey drayhorse his bright and battering
    sandal!

[3]Prepare.

Comment on the sound effects of "Felix Randal," especially *boisterous* and the
last line. Why is the final rhyme both surprising and apt? What is the rhyme
scheme? What about the meter?

Like "Felix Randal," the following poem is a sonnet, but with conventional
meter. Nevertheless, Donne charges it with struggle by his many caesuras.
Scanning it will help you appreciate both its energy and Donne's metrical skill.

Batter My Heart, Three-Personed God

John Donne   *(1572–1631)*

Batter my heart, three-personed God; for You
As yet but knock, breathe, shine, and seek to mend;
That I may rise and stand, o'erthrow me, and bend
Your force to break, blow, burn, and make me new.   4
I, like an usurped town, to another due,[1]
Labor to admit You, but oh, to no end;
Reason, Your viceroy in me, me should defend,
But is captived, and proves weak or untrue.   8
Yet dearly I love You, and would be loved fain,[2]
But am betrothed unto Your enemy.
Divorce me, untie or break that knot again;
Take me to You, imprison me, for I,   12
Except You enthrall me, never shall be free,
Nor ever chaste, except You ravish me.

[1]Owed.   [2]Joyfully.

How does Donne metaphorically cast himself in this little allegorical drama?
Does his metaphor change? What actual struggle does the military-sexual imagery convey?

Slow, Slow, Fresh Fount

Ben Jonson   (1573–1637)

Slow, slow, fresh fount, keep time with my salt tears;
Yet slower yet, O faintly gentle springs;
List to the heavy part the music bears:
    Woe weeps out her division when she sings.
        Droop, herbs and flowers,   5
        Fall, grief, in showers;
        Our beauties are not ours:
           Oh, could I still
(Like melting snow upon some craggy hill)
        Drop, drop, drop, drop   10
Since nature's pride is now a withered daffodil.

Jonson uses *division* in a seventeenth-century sense: a rapid melodic passage, thought of as dividing long notes into a number of short ones. Point out some of the onomatopoetic effects. Where are the personifications? Is *Woe* a different kind from the others? What is the effect of the final rhyme?

Read the following aloud to savor the crowd of language and images roaring out fun at Alfred Lord Tennyson.

Sir Beelzebub

Edith Sitwell   (1887–1964)

When
Sir
Beelzebub[1] called for his syllabub[2] in the hotel in Hell
        Where Proserpine[3] first fell,
Blue as the gendarmerie[4] were the waves of the sea   5

      (Rocking and shocking the bar-maid).

Nobody comes to give him his rum but the
Rim of the sky hippopotamus-glum
Enhances the chances to bless with a benison[5]
Alfred Lord Tennyson[6] crossing the bar laid   10
With cold vegetation from pale deputations

[1]A devil; Satan.   [2]A drink or dessert made of milk or cream, curdled with wine, cider, or, in this instance, rum.   [3]Persephone, who was carried to the underworld by Hades.   [4]Police.   [5]Blessing.
[6]Poet laureate. His "Crossing the Bar" is a poem on death, "In Memoriam" an elegy for a friend.

Of temperance workers (all signed In Memoriam)
Hoping with glory to trip up the Laureate's feet

    (Moving in classical metres) . . .

Like Balaclava,[7] the lava came down from the   15
Roof, and the sea's blue wooden gendarmerie
Took them in charge while Beelzebub roared for his rum.

    . . . None of them come!

[7]In the Crimea, scene of the battle that occasioned Tennyson's "The Charge of the Light Brigade."

What happened to Proserpine in the hotel? What is Sitwell's pun on feet? What is Sitwell imagining to be happening to Tennyson?

    The following poem is a riddle. What is the *it?*

I Like to See It Lap the Miles

Emily Dickinson   *(1830–1886)*

I like to see it lap the Miles—
And lick the Valleys up—
And stop to feed itself at Tanks—
And then—prodigious step

Around a Pile of Mountains—   5
And supercilious peer
In Shanties—by the sides of Roads—
And then a Quarry pare

To fit its Ribs
And crawl between   10
Complaining all the while
In horrid—hooting stanza—
Then chase itself down Hill—

And neigh like Boanerges[1]—
Then—punctual as a Star   15
Stop—docile and omnipotent
At its own stable door—

[1]A surname meaning "sons of thunder," given by Christ to James and John (Mark 3.17); any loud preacher.

See what you can do with Dickinson's metaphors. Consider *lap* and *lick*. Do they suggest the same metaphorical picture? How about *crawl* and *hooting stanza?* What are the rhymes? How does the meter fit the sense?

Next is an unusual achievement of meter and onomatopoetics. No one before or after Tennyson has managed a three-stress line with only three words.

Break, Break, Break

Alfred, Lord Tennyson   *(1809–1892)*

Break, break, break,
   On thy cold gray stones, O Sea!
And I would that my tongue could utter
   The thoughts that arise in me.   4

O well for the fisherman's boy,
   That he shouts with his sister at play!
O well for the sailor lad,
   That he sings in his boat on the bay!   8

And the stately ships go on
   To their haven under the hill;
But O for the touch of a vanished hand,
   And the sound of a voice that is still!   12

Break, break, break,
   At the foot of thy crags, O Sea!
But the tender grace of a day that is dead
   Will never come back to me.   16

What is the predominant metrical foot? What is the dominant number of beats per line? Which lines change the pattern? What is the onomatopoetic effect of the first two lines? Scan them to show how the meter underlines the sense.

Iambic pentameter—the ten-syllable line of five iambic feet ($\cup$ —)—has been the dominant English meter for centuries, as poets since Chaucer have adopted it for their own time and idiom. It captures English sound and syntax easily and naturally. Shakespeare's dramatic passages in this meter resound as verse, but they resound also as speech. Frost's New England farmers speak in ten-syllable verse remarkably close to the colloquial conversation of their nonversified neighbors. *Blank verse,* or unrhymed iambic pentameter, imitates speech particularly well. Much of Frost is blank verse. Shakespeare's plays, too, are blank verse, except for occasional passages of prose or song or when a rhymed couplet brings the audience up sharp to close a scene: ". . . . The play's the thing / Wherein I'll catch the conscience of the King." Blank verse works well, also, for meditative poems such as the following.

Lines

Composed a Few Miles above Tintern Abbey,[1] *on Revisiting the Banks of the Wye During a Tour. July 13, 1798*

William Wordsworth   *(1770–1850)*

Five years have past; five summers, with the length
Of five long winters! and again I hear
These waters, rolling from their mountain-springs
With a soft inland murmur.—Once again
Do I behold these steep and lofty cliffs,   5
That on a wild secluded scene impress
Thoughts of more deep seclusion; and connect
The landscape with the quiet of the sky.
The day is come when I again repose
Here, under this dark sycamore, and view   10
These plots of cottage-ground, these orchard-tufts,
Which at this season, with their unripe fruits,
Are clad in one green hue, and lose themselves
'Mid groves and copses.[2] Once again I see
These hedge-rows, hardly hedge-rows, little lines   15
Of sportive wood run wild: these pastoral farms,
Green to the very door; and wreaths of smoke
Sent up, in silence, from among the trees!
With some uncertain notice, as might seem
Of vagrant dwellers in the houseless woods,   20
Or of some Hermit's cave, where by his fire
The Hermit sits alone.

                These beauteous forms,
Through a long absence, have not been to me
As is a landscape to a blind man's eye: 25
But oft, in lonely rooms, and 'mid the din
Of towns and cities, I have owed to them
In hours of weariness, sensations sweet,
Felt in the blood, and felt along the heart;
And passing even into my purer mind,   30
With tranquil restoration:—feelings too
Of unremembered pleasure: such, perhaps,
As have no slight or trivial influence
On that best portion of a good man's life,
His little, nameless, unremembered, acts   35
Of kindness and of love. Nor less, I trust,
To them I may have owed another gift,

[1]Ruined medieval abbey in Monmouthshire in the valley of the river Wye.   [2]Thickets.

Of aspect more sublime; that blessed mood
In which the burthen of the mystery,
In which the heavy and the weary weight   40
Of all this unintelligible world,
Is lightened:—that serene and blessed mood,
In which the affections gently lead us on,—
Until, the breath of this corporeal frame
And even the motion of our human blood   45
Almost suspended, we are laid asleep
In body, and become a living soul:
While with an eye made quiet by the power
Of harmony, and the deep power of joy,
We see into the life of things.   50
          If this
Be but a vain belief, yet, oh! how oft—
In darkness and amid the many shapes
Of joyless daylight; when the fretful stir
Unprofitable, and the fever of the world,   55
Have hung upon the beatings of my heart—
How oft, in spirit, have I turned to thee,
O sylvan Wye! thou wanderer thro' the woods,
How often has my spirit turned to thee!

   And now, with gleams of half-extinguished thought,   60
With many recognitions dim and faint,
And somewhat of a sad perplexity,
The picture of the mind revives again:
While here I stand, not only with the sense
Of present pleasure, but with pleasing thoughts   65
That in this moment there is life and food
For future years. And so I dare to hope,
Though changed, no doubt, from what I was when first
I came among these hills; when like a roe
I bounded o'er the mountains, by the sides   70
Of the deep rivers, and the lonely streams,
Wherever nature led: more like a man
Flying from something that he dreads than one
Who sought the thing he loved. For nature then
(The coarser pleasures of my boyish days,   75
And their glad animal movements all gone by)
To me was all in all.—I cannot paint
What then I was. The sounding cataract
Haunted me like a passion: the tall rock,
The mountain, and the deep and gloomy wood,   80
Their colours and their forms, were then to me

An appetite; a feeling and a love,
That had no need of a remoter charm,
By thought supplied, nor any interest
Unborrowed from the eye.—That time is past,   85
And all its aching joys are now no more,
And all its dizzy raptures. Not for this
Faint I, nor mourn nor murmur; other gifts
Have followed; for such loss, I would believe,
Abundant recompense. For I have learned   90
To look on nature, not as in the hour
Of thoughtless youth; but hearing oftentimes
The still, sad music of humanity,
Nor harsh nor grating, though of ample power
To chasten and subdue. And I have felt   95
A presence that disturbs me with the joy
Of elevated thoughts; a sense sublime
Of something far more deeply interfused,
Whose dwelling is the light of setting suns,
And the round ocean and the living air,   100
And the blue sky, and in the mind of man:
A motion and a spirit, that impels
All thinking things, all objects of all thought,
And rolls through all things. Therefore am I still
A lover of the meadows and the woods,   105
And mountains; and of all that we behold
From this green earth; of all the mighty world
Of eye, and ear,—both what they half create,
And what perceive; well pleased to recognise
In nature and the language of the sense   110
The anchor of my purest thoughts, the nurse,
The guide, the guardian of my heart, and soul
Of all my moral being.
              Nor perchance,
If I were not thus taught, should I the more   115
Suffer my genial spirits to decay:
For thou art with me here upon the banks
Of this fair river; thou my dearest Friend,[3]
My dear, dear Friend; and in thy voice I catch
The language of my former heart, and read   120
My former pleasures in the shooting lights
Of thy wild eyes. Oh! yet a little while
May I behold in thee what I was once,
My dear, dear Sister! and this prayer I make,

[3]Wordsworth's sister Dorothy.

Knowing that Nature never did betray   125
The heart that loved her; 'tis her privilege,
Through all the years of this our life, to lead
From joy to joy: for she can so inform
The mind that is within us, so impress
With quietness and beauty, and so feed   130
With lofty thoughts, that neither evil tongues,
Rash judgments, nor the sneers of selfish men,
Nor greetings where no kindness is, nor all
The dreary intercourse of daily life,
Shall e'er prevail against us, or disturb   135
Our cheerful faith, that all which we behold
Is full of blessings. Therefore let the moon
Shine on thee in thy solitary walk;
And let the misty mountain-winds be free
To blow against thee: and, in after years,   140
When these wild ecstasies shall be matured
Into a sober pleasure; when thy mind
Shall be a mansion for all lovely forms,
Thy memory be as a dwelling-place
For all sweet sounds and harmonies; oh! then,   145
If solitude, or fear, or pain, or grief,
Should be thy portion, with what healing thoughts
Of tender joy wilt thou remember me,
And these my exhortations! Nor, perchance—
If I should be where I no more can hear   150
Thy voice, nor catch from thy wild eyes these gleams
Of past existence—wilt thou then forget
That on the banks of this delightful stream
We stood together; and that I, so long
A worshipper of Nature, hither came   155
Unwearied in that service: rather say
With warmer love—oh! with far deeper zeal
Of holier love. Nor wilt thou then forget,
That after many wanderings, many years
Of absence, these steep woods and lofty cliffs,   160
And this green pastoral landscape, were to me
More dear, both for themselves and for thy sake!

As Wordsworth revisits these rural hills, he contemplates his daily city life. What is that life like? What other pessimistic traces does the poem include? What happens in the city when Wordsworth remembers the Wye? What are the unremembered acts? What is his "sad perplexity" (line 62)? What does he hope for the future? How does he remember his past? What has he lost? What gained? Explain the world of eye and ear "both what they half create, / And what perceive" (lines 108–109). How does his sister's presence enhance this visit? What power does he attribute to Nature? Scan the fourth line. What metrical details do you discover?

Adding rhyme to iambic pentameter heightens the pleasures and forces of perceived structure. Pope favored the *heroic couplet:* a rhymed couplet of iambic pentameter, frequently closing the thought on the rhyme of the second line. The following lines introduce his long poem "An Essay on Man," in which Pope invites his philosopher-friend to survey life as if it were a vast English estate, with a maze, formal gardens, vistas, and wild copses, and they were two gentlemen out for a morning's shoot.

[The Wild Garden]¹

Alexander Pope   (1688–1744)

Awake, my St. John! leave all meaner things
To low ambition, and the pride of Kings.
Let us (since Life can little more supply
Than just to look about us and to die)   4
Expatiate free o'er all this scene of Man;
A mighty maze! but not without a plan;
A Wild, where weeds and flowers promiscuous shoot,
Or Garden, tempting with forbidden fruit.   8
Together let us beat this ample field,
Try what the open, what the covert yield;
The latent tracts, the giddy heights explore
Of all who blindly creep, or sightless soar;   12
Eye Nature's walks, shoot Folly as it flies,
And catch the Manners living as they rise;
Laugh where we must, be candid where we can;
But vindicate the ways of God to Man.   16

¹*An Essay on Man,* I, 1–16. Henry St. John, Viscount Bolingbroke, Secretary of State under Queen Anne, had been deposed and attainted for treason by George I.

Why is the world like a maze? What is the reference to the garden? What kind of people might Pope's metaphor of creatures that creep and soar refer to? Explain the metaphor in "shoot Folly as it flies." In reference to "Manners," Pope makes a metaphor of the eighteenth-century practice of catching small birds by beating the shrubbery and driving them into nets. What is Pope saying about God's world and man's view of it in the next-to-last line? What is the force of *But?*

The sonnet, too, uses iambic pentameter, adding to the demands of meter the demands of a complicated rhyme scheme:

When I Have Fears That I May Cease to Be

John Keats   (1795–1821)

When I have fears that I may cease to be
  Before my pen has gleaned my teeming brain,
Before high-pilèd books, in charactery,[1]
  Hold like rich garners the full ripened grain;   4
When I behold, upon the night's starred face,
  Huge cloudy symbols of a high romance,
And think that I may never live to trace
  Their shadows with the magic hand of chance;   8
And when I feel, fair creature of an hour,
  That I shall never look upon thee more,
Never have relish in the fairy power
  Of unreflecting love; then on the shore   12
Of the wide world I stand alone and think
Till love and fame to nothingness do sink.

[1]The characters, or letters, on the pages.

Why does Keats fear death? What is the force of the "I" standing in the middle of the next-to-last line? What is Keats's conclusion?

Another selection from Pope concludes our survey of iambic pentameter. The colloquial flexibility Pope can control in the couplet is nowhere more brilliant than in the opening of his epistle to his close friend and doctor, John Arbuthnot. Pope, now rich and famous from his labors, has leased a villa on the Thames at Twickenham *("Twit'nam"),* with a grotto, which he used for contemplation and study, tunneling under the road in back to his garden on the hillside beyond. Pope is complaining in amused hyperbole of how every amateur and struggling poet in London is after him for help. The John of the first line is not Arbuthnot but Pope's servant, John Serle.

An Epistle to Dr. Arbuthnot

Alexander Pope   (1688–1744)

Shut, shut the door, good *John!* fatigu'd I said,
Tye up the knocker, say I'm sick, I'm dead,
The Dog-star rages! nay 'tis past a doubt,
All *Bedlam,* or *Parnassus,* is let out:
Fire in each eye, and Papers in each hand,   5
They rave, recite, and madden round the land.
    What Walls can guard me, or what Shades can hide?
They pierce my Thickets, thro' my Grot they glide,
By land, by water, they renew the charge,
They stop the Chariot, and they board the Barge.   10

No place is sacred, not the Church is free,
Ev'n *Sunday* shines no *Sabbath-day* to me:
Then from the *Mint* walks forth the Man of Ryme,[1]
Happy! to catch me, just at Dinner-time.
  Is there a Parson, much be-mus'd in Beer,[2]   15
A maudlin Poetess, a ryming Peer,
A Clerk, foredoom'd his Father's soul to cross,
Who pens a Stanza when he should *engross?*
Is there, who lock'd from Ink and Paper, scrawls
With desp'rate Charcoal round his darken'd walls?   20
All fly to *Twit'nam,* and in humble strain
Apply to me, to keep them mad or vain.
Arthur, whose giddy Son neglects the Laws,[3]
Imputes to me and my damn'd works the cause.
Poor *Cornus*[4] sees his frantic Wife elope,   25
And curses Wit, and Poetry, and *Pope.*

[1]The area around the Mint, near the Tower, was one of London's several sanctuaries where debtors were free from arrest, as they were on Sundays. [2]Pope is punning on the name of the Rev. Mr. Laurence Eusden, poet laureate from 1718 until his death in 1730 (Pope published *Arbuthnot* in January 1735), who was something of a tippler. [3]Arthur Moore and his son, James Moore Smythe, a poet and playwright with whom Pope had had a literary quarrel. [4]Pope invents a name for any cuckold, from the Latin *cornu,* "horn," on the ancient notion that horns grew from the forehead of a faithless wife's husband.

To enjoy the remarkable ease with which Pope contains his language precisely within the couplet's metrical bounds, scan the first six lines. How many caesuras, masculine and feminine, do you find? What are the noniambic feet? What accounts for the variety within the highly regular iambic beat? Explain the references to the dog star, Bedlam, and Parnassus. Point out some instances of hyperbole, especially that of the man deprived of ink and paper.

    One foot shorter than iambic pentameter, iambic tetrameter became the leading measure of the seventeenth century, nowhere more superbly turned than in Marvell's couplets.

The Garden

Andrew Marvell   *(1621–1678)*

  How vainly men themselves amaze
To win the palm, the oak, or bays,[1]
And their incessant labors see
Crowned from some single herb, or tree,
Whose short and narrow-vergéd shade   5
Does prudently their toils upbraid;

[1]Crowns: palm for athletics, oak for public service, bays for poetry.

While all flowers and all trees do close[2]
To weave the garlands of repose!

    Fair Quiet, have I found thee here,
And Innocence, thy sister dear?   10
Mistaken long, I sought you then
In busy companies of men.
Your sacred plants, if here below,
Only among the plants will grow;
Society is all but rude   15
To this delicious solitude.

    No white nor red was ever seen
So amorous as this lovely green.
Fond lovers, cruel as their flame,
Cut in these trees their mistress' name: 20
Little, alas, they know or heed
How far these beauties hers exceed!
Fair trees, wheresoe'er your barks I wound,
No name shall but your own be found.

    When we have run our passion's heat,   25
Love hither makes his best retreat.
The gods, that mortal beauty chase,
Still in a tree did end their race:
Apollo hunted Daphne so,
Only that she might laurel grow;   30
And Pan did after Syrinx speed,
Not as a nymph, but for a reed.

    What wondrous life is this I lead!
Ripe apples drop about my head;
The luscious clusters of the vine   35
Upon my mouth do crush their wine;
The nectarine and curious peach
Into my hands themselves do reach;
Stumbling on melons, as I pass,
Insnared with flowers, I fall on grass.   40

    Meanwhile the mind, from pleasure less,
Withdraws into its happiness;
The mind, that ocean where each kind
Does straight its own resemblance find;
Yet it creates, transcending these,   45
Far other worlds and other seas,
Annihilating all that's made
To a green thought in a green shade.

[2]Unite.

Here at the fountain's sliding foot,
Or at some fruit tree's mossy root,   50
Casting the body's vest[3] aside,
My soul into the boughs does glide:
There, like a bird, it sits and sings,
Then whets[4] and combs its silver wings,
And, till prepared for longer flight,   55
Waves in its plumes the various light.

    Such was that happy garden-state,
While man there walked without a mate:
After a place so pure and sweet,
What other help could yet be meet![5]   60
But 'twas beyond a mortal's share
To wander solitary there:
Two paradises 'twere in one
To live in paradise alone.

    How well the skillful gardener drew   65
Of flowers and herbs this dial new,
Where, from above, the milder sun
Does through a fragrant zodiac run;
And as it works, th' industrious bee
Computes its time as well as we!   70
How could such sweet and wholesome hours
Be reckoned but with herbs and flowers?

[3]Garment. [4]Preens. [5]Fitting.

What is the pun on *upbraid* in the first stanza? How does Marvell contrast his love of the garden with love of women? Explain the allusions to Apollo and Pan. Explain the psychology in the sixth stanza. Explain the simile of the soul as a bird. Explain "Two paradises 'twere in one / To live in paradise alone." The last stanza refers to an actual formal knot garden laid out like a sun dial. What is the pun on *time?*

    The tetrameter line and the trimeter remain favorites, quicker than pentameter and frequently underscored by rhyme.

April Inventory

W. D. Snodgrass   *(1926–)*

The green catalpa tree has turned
All white; the cherry blooms once more.
In one whole year I haven't learned
A blessed thing they pay you for.
The blossoms snow down in my hair;
The trees and I will soon be bare.

6

The trees have more than I to spare.
The sleek, expensive girls I teach,
Younger and pinker every year,
Bloom gradually out of reach.
The pear tree lets its petals drop
Like dandruff on a tabletop.   12

The girls have grown so young by now
I have to nudge myself to stare.
This year they smile and mind me how
My teeth are falling with my hair.
In thirty years I may not get
Younger, shrewder, or out of debt.   18

The tenth time, just a year ago,
I made myself a little list
Of all the things I'd ought to know,
Then told my parents, analyst,
And everyone who's trusted me
I'd be substantial, presently.   24

I haven't read one book about
A book or memorized one plot.
Or found a mind I did not doubt.
I learned one date. And then forgot.
And one by one the solid scholars
Get the degrees, the jobs, the dollars.   30

And smile above their starchy collars.
I taught my classes Whitehead's notions;
One lovely girl, a song of Mahler's.
Lacking a source-book or promotions,
I showed one child the colors of
A luna moth and how to love.   36

I taught myself to name my name,
To bark back, loosen love and crying;
To ease my woman so she came,
To ease an old man who was dying.
I have not learned how often I
Can win, can love, but choose to die.   42

I have not learned there is a lie
Love shall be blonder, slimmer, younger;
That my equivocating eye
Loves only by my body's hunger;
That I have forces, true to feel,
Or that the lovely world is real.   48

While scholars speak authority
And wear their ulcers on their sleeves,
My eyes in spectacles shall see
These trees procure and spend their leaves.
There is a value underneath
The gold and silver in my teeth.   **54**

Though trees turn bare and girls turn wives,
We shall afford our costly seasons;
There is a gentleness survives
That will outspeak and has its reasons.
There is a loveliness exists,
Preserves us, not for specialists.   **60**

How would you characterize Snodgrass's attitude and tone of voice? What does he conclude? What is his rhyme scheme? What does he gain when he rhymes from one stanza to the next?

My Papa's Waltz

Theodore Roethke   *(1908–1963)*

The whiskey on your breath
Could make a small boy dizzy;
But I hung on like death:
Such waltzing was not easy.   **4**

We romped until the pans
Slid from the kitchen shelf;
My mother's countenance
Could not unfrown itself.   **8**

The hand that held my wrist
Was battered on one knuckle;
At every step you missed
My right ear scraped a buckle.   **12**

You beat time on my head
With a palm caked hard by dirt,
Then waltzed me off to bed
Still clinging to your shirt.   **16**

What is Roethke's attitude toward his father? What is his mother's present attitude? How do his meter and feminine rhymes (especially the slanted *dizzy/easy*) convey the drunken effect? Note the variation as *Slid* takes a *rhetorical stress,* an emphasis from meaning rather than meter, once more emphasizing the tipsiness.

Often, as with Tennyson's "Break, Break," a poet varies his effect with lines markedly different from the prevailing meter.

La Belle Dame Sans Merci

John Keats   (1795–1821)

I

Oh, what can ail thee, knight-at-arms,
   Alone and palely loitering?
The sedge has withered from the lake,
   And no birds sing!   4

II

Oh, what can ail thee, knight-at-arms,
   So haggard and so woe-begone?
The squirrel's granary is full,
   And the harvest's done.   8

III

I see a lily on thy brow,
   With anguish moist and fever-dew,
And on thy cheek a fading rose
   Fast withereth too.   12

IV

I met a lady in the meads
   Full beautiful, a fairy's child,
Her hair was long, her foot was light,
   And her eyes were wild.   16

V

I made a garland for her head,
   And bracelets too, and fragrant zone;
She looked at me as she did love,
   And made sweet moan.   20

VI

I set her on my pacing steed,
   And nothing else saw all day long;
For sidelong would she bend, and sing
   A fairy's song.   24

VII

She found me roots of relish sweet,
  And honey wild, and manna dew;
And sure in language strange she said,
  'I love thee true'.   28

VIII

She took me to her elfin grot,
  And there she wept, and sighed full sore,
And there I shut her wild wild eyes
  With kisses four.   32

IX

And there she lullèd me asleep,
  And there I dreamed—Ah! woe betide!—
The latest dream I ever dreamed
  On the cold hill side.   36

X

I saw pale kings, and princes too,
  Pale warriors, death-pale were they all;
They cried—'La belle Dame sans merci
  Hath thee in thrall!'   40

XI

I saw their starved lips in the gloom
  With horrid warning gapèd wide,
And I awoke, and found me here
  On the cold hill side.   44

XII

And this is why I sojourn here,
  Alone and palely loitering,
Though the sedge is withered from the lake,
  And no birds sing.   48

What does this allegory say about seeking perpetual spring and perpetual beauty? What is the effect of the opening questioner? What kind of person is he? Why does the lady weep and sigh full sore? What is the effect of the dimeter line with which Keats closes his stanza? How does it vary from the regular iambic pattern, especially with "And no birds sing"?
  Within the general context of iambics, poets have achieved a number of

effectively varied metrical patterns. Ben Jonson, in celebrating the beauty of his "Charis" (pronounced KARis), a lady of the court otherwise unknown, creates an unusual and beautiful stanza.

Her Triumph

Ben Jonson   (1573–1637)

See the chariot at hand here of Love
    Wherein my lady rideth:
Each that drawes is a swan, or a dove,
    And well the carre Love guideth.
As she goes, all hearts doe duty   5
      Unto her beauty;
And enamour'd, doe wish, so they might
      But enjoy such a sight,
    That they still were to run by her side,
Through swords, through seas, whether she would ride.   10

Doe but looke on her eyes; they doe light
    All that Loves world compriseth:
Doe but looke on her haire; it is bright
    As Loves starre when it riseth:
Doe but marke, her forhead's smoother   15
      Then words that sooth her:
And from her arched browes, such a grace
      Sheds itselfe through the face,
    As alone there triumphs to the life
All the gaine, all the good, of the elements strife.   20

Have you seen but a bright lillie grow,
Before rude hands have touch'd it?
    Ha' you mark'd but the fall o'the snow
Before the soyle hath smutch'd it?
Ha' you felt the wooll of bever?   25
      Or swans downe ever?
Or have smelt o'the bud o'the brier?
      Or the nard in the fire?
Or have tasted the bag of the bee?
O so white! O so soft! O so sweet is she!   30

Jonson alternates anapestic and iambic trimeters for four lines, with feminine endings on the iambics. The fifth line merges the two meters by beginning with an anapest. For the short sixth line Jonson adopts from Latin the concluding measure of a Sapphic stanza, the same beat that concludes Latin and Greek hexameters: $- \cup\cup | - \cup$, which British schoolboys call the "strawberry jampot" to match the meter. If you scan the whole poem, you will see how very nearly Jonson matches the pattern he works out in his first stanza in his next two, almost syllable for syllable. How does the last line draw together the details of the last stanza?

Michael Drayton, Jonson's contemporary, develops a swinging stanza from the Latin dactyllic meter: — ∪ ∪. He rhymes three dactyllic dimeters, caps them with a jampot, repeats the pattern, and then rhymes the jampot. He is celebrating Henry V's famous victory over a very much larger French army at Agincourt on October 25, 1415, St. Crispin's Day. Drayton wants to emulate the warlike ballads of the Welsh harpers (Cambro-Britons).

To the Cambro-Britons and Their Harp:

His Ballad of Agincourt

Michael Drayton   *(1563–1631)*

Fair stood the wind for France,
When we our sails advance,
Nor now to prove our chance,
   Longer will tarry;   4
But putting to the main
At Kaux, the mouth of Seine,
With all his martial train,
   Landed King Harry.   8

And taking many a fort,
Furnished in warlike sort,
Marcheth towards Agincourt,
   In happy hour;   12
Skirmishing day by day
With those that stopped his way,
Where the French gen'ral lay
   With all his power.   16

Which in his height of pride,
King Henry to deride,
His ransom to provide
   To the King sending;   20
Which he neglects the while
As from a nation vile,
Yet with an angry smile
   Their fall portending.   24

And turning to his men,
Quoth our brave Henry then:

Though they to one be ten,
  Be not amazed.   28
Yet have we well begun,
Battles so bravely won
Have ever to the sun
  By fame been raised.   32

And for myself, quoth he,
This my full rest shall be,
England ne'er mourn for me,
  Nor more esteem me;   36
Victor I will remain,
Or on this earth lie slain,
Never shall she sustain
  Loss to redeem me.   40

Poitiers and Crecy[1] tell,
When most their pride did swell,
Under our swords they fell;
  No less our skill is   44
Than when our grandsire great,
Claiming the regal seat
By many a warlike feat,
  Lopped the French lilies.   48

The Duke of York so dread
The eager vaward[2] led;
With the main Henry sped
  Amongst his henchmen.   52
Excester[3] had the rear,
A braver man not there,
Oh Lord, how hot they were
  On the false Frenchmen!   56

They now to fight are gone,
Armor on armor shone,
Drum now to drum did groan,
  To hear was wonder,   60
That with cries they make
The very earth did shake,
Trumpet to trumpet spake,
  Thunder to thunder.   64

Well it thine age became,
Oh noble Erpingham,

[1]Sites of earlier English victories in the Hundred Years' War. [2]Vanguard. [3]Exeter.

Which didst the signal aim
　　To our hid forces;
When from a meadow by,
Like a storm suddenly,
The English archery
　　Struck the French horses.　　　　　　　　72

With Spanish yew so strong,
Arrows a cloth-yard long,
That like to serpents stung,
　　Piercing the weather;　　　　　　　　　76
None from his fellow starts,
But playing manly parts,
And like true English hearts,
　　Stuck close together.　　　　　　　　　80

When down their bows they threw,
And forth their bilboes⁴ drew,
And on the French they flew,
　　Not one was tardy;　　　　　　　　　　84
Arms were from shoulders sent,
Scalps to the teeth were rent,
Down the French peasants went;
　　Our men were hardy.　　　　　　　　　88

This while our noble King,
His broad sword brandishing,
Down the French host did ding,
　　As to o'erwhelm it;　　　　　　　　　　92
And many a deep wound lent,
His arms with blood besprent,
And many a cruel dent
　　Bruiséd his helmet.　　　　　　　　　　96

Gloster, that Duke so good,
Next of the royal blood,
For famous England stood
　　With his brave brother;　　　　　　　　100
Clarence, in steel so bright,
Though but a maiden knight,
Yet in that furious fight,
　　Scarce such another.　　　　　　　　　104

Warwick in blood did wade,
Oxford the foe invade,

⁴Swords.

And cruel slaughter made,
    Still as they ran up;   108
Suffolk his ax did ply,
Beaumont and Willoughby
Bare them right doughtily,
    Ferrers and Fanhope.   112

Upon Saint Crispin's day
Fought was this noble fray,
Which fame did not delay
    To England to carry;   116
Oh, when shall English men
With such acts fill a pen,
Or England breed again
    Such a King Harry?   120

How does the meter aid the account of the battle, which Drayton gives accurately, including the triumph of English archery? What is the effect of naming names?

   L. E. Sissman recalls the glory of Agincourt by playfully celebrating a modern victory in Drayton's meter and stanza.

Henley, July 4: 1914–1964

L. E. Sissman   (1928–1976)

Fifty years after Capt. Leverett Saltonstall's Harvard junior varsity became the first American eight to win the Grand Challenge Cup at Henley in England, Saltonstall . . . will lead his crew back to the scene of its triumph. Every man who pulled an oar in the victorious 1914 Harvard crew, as well as the coxswain, is not only alive but is preparing to return to Henley on July 1. They will take to a shell again on the picturesque Thames course during the forthcoming regatta.

                                                    —The New York Times

Fair stands the wind again
For nine brave Harvard men
Sung by both tongue and pen,
    Sailing for Henley   4
Fifty years after they
Won the great rowing fray
On Independence Day,
    Boyish and manly.   8

On Independence Day
Fifty light years away
They took the victor's bay
    From mighty Britain.   12

They were a City joke
Till they put up the stroke
And their strong foemen broke,
   As it is written.   16

Leverett Saltonstall
Is the first name of all
That noble roll we call,
   That band of brothers.   20
Curtis, Talcott, and Meyer,
Morgan and Lund set fire
To England's funeral pyre,
   They and three others.   24

That young and puissant crew
Quickened their beat and flew
Past all opponents, who
   Watched them in wonder.   28
Fifty years later, we
See them across the sea
Echo that memory
   Like summer thunder.   32

Fair stands the wind again;
Thames, bear them softly, then.
Far came these rowing men
   In every weather.   36
What though their stroke has slowed?
(How long they all have rowed!)
Oarsmen, accept our ode,
   Blades of a feather.   40

The "City" in Sissman's second stanza refers to London's business district.
Comment on his rhyming and naming names and on the last line.

In the following poem, William Carlos Williams also gets some interesting
effects from dactyls.

The Dance

William Carlos Williams   *(1883–1963)*

In Breughel's[1] great picture, The Kermess,[2]
the dancers go round, they go round and
around, the squeal and the blare and the
tweedle of bagpipes, a bugle and fiddles   4

---

[1]Pieter Breughel (1520?–1569), a Flemish painter.   [2]Fair.

tipping their bellies (round as the thick-
sided glasses whose wash they impound)
their hips and their bellies off balance
to turn them. Kicking and rolling about   8
the Fair Grounds, swinging their butts, those
shanks must be sound to bear up under such
rollicking measures, prance as they dance
In Breughel's great picture, The Kermess.   12

Williams's lines vary from three to four stresses and from eight to eleven syllables. How does the generally dactylic movement organize the poem metrically,
like a dance?

Poets in the twentieth century have often tried new metrical schemes. As
early as 1875, Gerard Manley Hopkins was experimenting with what he called
sprung rhythm, in which the stress count is regular, but the unstressed syllables
vary in number. Similarly, William Carlos Williams's *variable foot* is a verse unit
with one stress, but an indeterminate number of unstressed syllables. Marianne
Moore writes *syllabic verse,* ignoring stress and counting only syllables. Her "No
Swan So Fine," for example, sets up a pattern of syllable counts in the first stanza
(7/8/6/8/8/5/9/) that she repeats almost precisely in the second stanza.

No Swan So Fine

Marianne Moore   (1887–1972)

"No water so still as the
     dead fountains of Versailles."[1] No swan,
with swart blind look askance
and gondoliering legs, so fine
     as the chintz china one with fawn-   5
brown eyes and toothed gold
collar on to show whose bird it was.

Lodged in the Louis Fifteenth
     candelabrum-tree of cockscomb-
tinted buttons, dahlias,   10
sea urchins, and everlastings,
     it perches on the branching foam
of polished sculptured
flowers—at ease and tall. The king is dead.

---

[1]A quotation taken by Moore from a magazine article. The palace at Versailles, built by Louis
XIV, has many fountains.

Do you find syllabic metrics effective? Why does Moore allow herself an extra syllable in the last line, the only line with two caesuras? What is Moore actually describing? What is the effect of "The king is dead"?

Like Moore, Dylan Thomas at times used a rigid syllable count to shape his stanzas. In the following poem, he also allowed himself minor variations from the pattern.

Poem in October

Dylan Thomas   (1914–1953)

It was my thirtieth year to heaven
Woke to my hearing from harbour and neighbour wood
   And the mussel pooled and the heron
      Priested shore
      The morning beckon   5
With water praying and call of seagull and rook
And the knock of sailing boats on the net webbed wall
   Myself to set foot
      That second
   In the still sleeping town and set forth.   10

My birthday began with the water-
Birds and the birds of the winged trees flying my name
   Above the farms and the white horses
      And I rose
      In rainy autumn   15
And walked abroad in a shower of all my days.
High tide and the heron dived when I took the road
   Over the border
      And the gates
   Of the town closed as the town awoke.   20

A springful of larks in a rolling
Cloud and the roadside bushes brimming with whistling
   Blackbirds and the sun of October
      Summery
      On the hill's shoulder.   25
Here were fond climates and sweet singers suddenly
Come in the morning where I wandered and listened
   To the rain wringing
      Wind blow cold
   In the wood faraway under me.   30

Pale rain over the dwindling harbour
And over the sea wet church the size of a snail
  With its horns through mist and the castle
    Brown as owls
    But all the gardens   35
Of spring and summer were blooming in the tall tales
Beyond the border and under the lark full cloud.
  There could I marvel
    My birthday
Away but the weather turned around.   40

  It turned away from the blithe country
And down the other air and the blue altered sky
  Streamed again a wonder of summer
    With apples
    Pears and red currants   45
And I saw in the turning so clearly a child's
Forgotten mornings when he walked with his mother
  Through the parables
    Of sun light
And the legends of the green chapels   50

  And the twice told fields of infancy
That his tears burned my cheeks and his heart moved in mine.
  These were the woods the river and sea
    Where a boy
    In the listening   55
Summertime of the dead whispered the truth of his joy
To the trees and the stones and the fish in the tide.
  And the mystery
    Sang alive
Still in the water and singingbirds.   60

  And there could I marvel my birthday
Away but the weather turned around. And the true
  Joy of the long dead child sang burning
    In the sun.
    It was my thirtieth   65
Year to heaven stood there then in the summer noon
Though the town below lay leaved with October blood.
  O may my heart's truth
    Still be sung
On this high hill in a year's turning.   70

Count the syllables in each line of the first stanza so that you can see the pattern.
Notice how two short lines bracket two longer lines in the middle of each stanza.

Find the place where Thomas incorporates the first phrase into another line; how is the second use different from the first? Is the syllabic pattern apparent when you read lines from this poem aloud? What is the image in "the heron / Priested shore"? *Dylan* means "water" in Welsh: how are the birds "flying my name"? How does the weather turn around? Explain the image of the church like a snail. What are the parables and the legends (lines 48–50)? Compare Thomas's account with Wordsworth's in "Tintern Abbey."

In *free verse,* which we will discuss in Chapter 7, the poet discards all restrictions of stress and syllable count. Lines are organized by a "feel" for rhythm or by some largely subjective standard, as when Allen Ginsberg wrote of his "Howl" that each line is "a single breath unit." Generally, free verse poets have subscribed to T. S. Eliot's dictum, "No verse is free for the man who wants to do a good job," even though they have not always been able to explain their methods.

CHAPTER 6

TRADITIONAL FORMS

STRUCTURAL ELEMENTS

A number of patterns have become conventional in poetry, as poets have repeated favorite combinations of sound. To discover these patterns, we examine such structural elements as meter, rhyme scheme, and stanza.

Couplets and Quatrains
Of the many metered and rhyming patterns possible in English, a few simple arrangements of *couplets* (two lines) and *quatrains* (four lines) have proved basic.

Tetrameter couplet (iambic tetrameter)
A common couplet pairs two iambic tetrameter lines:

The grave's a fine and private place,
But none, I think, do there embrace.

    Marvell, "To His Coy Mistress"

Closed couplet (iambic pentameter)
Also called the *heroic couplet, balanced couplet,* and *pentameter couplet,* this classic unit is at its best when thoughts are balanced against each other in lines and half-lines, as they are in Sir John Denham's famous address to the River Thames:

O could I flow like thee, and make thy stream
My great example, as it is my theme.
Tho' deep, yet clear; tho' gentle, yet not dull;
Strong, without rage; without o'erflowing, full.

       Sir John Denham, "Cooper's Hill"

Common meter

Common meter, also called the *ballad stanza,* alternates iambic tetrameter
and trimeter lines in a 4/3/4/3 pattern, rhyming them *abcb* or *abab:*

She lived unknown, and few could know
    When Lucy ceased to be;
But she is in her grave, and, oh,
    The difference to me!

      *William Wordsworth, "She Dwelt
        Among the Untrodden Ways"*

Long meter

Long meter lengthens the second and fourth lines of common meter to make
four tetrameter lines (4/4/4/4):

As virtuous men pass mildly away,
    And whisper to their souls to go,
Whilst some of their sad friends do say
    The breath goes now, and some say, No. . . .

      *John Donne, "A Valediction: Forbidding
             Mourning"*

Short meter

Short meter shortens the first line of common meter to trimeter, creating a
3/3/4/3 stanza:

The Heart asks Pleasure—first—
And then—Excuse from Pain—
And then—those little Anodynes
That deaden suffering—

      *Emily Dickinson, "The Heart
        Asks Pleasure—First"*

Envelope quatrain

Some quatrains enclose a couplet with rhymes on the first and fourth lines,
abba. When the lines are tetrameter, this is often called the *"In Memoriam"*
stanza, after the Tennyson poem that begins:

Strong Son of God, immortal Love,
   Whom we, that have not seen thy face,
   By faith, and faith alone, embrace,
Believing where we cannot prove. . . .

Pentameter quatrain

Some quatrains extend the line to pentameter, rhyming usually in one of the patterns common in the shorter lines of tetrameter:

The troubles of our proud and angry dust
   Are from eternity, and shall not fail.
Bear them we can, and if we can we must.
   Shoulder the sky, my lad, and drink your ale.

>   *A. E. Housman, "The Chestnut Casts His*
>   *Flambeaux"*

Stanzas

A *stanza* is a kind of verse paragraph, repeating as a unit a fixed number of lines with a particular meter and rhyme scheme and ordinarily set off from other stanzas by an extra space. Couplets, usually printed one after another, are usually not considered stanzas. Quatrains are commonly considered stanzas, and printed with spaces between them to emphasize their structural cohesion. Stanzas longer than four lines are often created by combining shorter units, as, for example, a quatrain and a couplet:

The green catalpa tree has turned   *a*
All white; the cherry blooms once more.   *b*
In one whole year I haven't learned   *a*
A blessed thing they pay you for.   *b*
The blossoms snow down in my hair;   *c*
The trees and I will soon be bare.   *c*

>   *W. D. Snodgrass, "April Inventory"*

If we examine the rest of "April Inventory," we will see this pattern repeated ten times; Snodgrass's poem has ten stanzas, each with six iambic tetrameter lines, rhyming *ababcc*. Once we have the habit of observing stanzaic form, we begin to notice forms repeated by various poets. We can find this one also, for example, in Thomas Campion's "There is a Garden in Her Face" and Matthew Arnold's "To Marguerite."

Traditional Forms

When an entire poem is considered as a unit, its form is the shape dictated by its structural elements: meter, rhyme scheme, stanza, and number of lines. Of the many traditional forms, the ballad and sonnet have been most popular.

The villanelle and sestina, which we will also consider below, are less common.

BALLAD

A *ballad* is a song that tells a story. A *folk ballad* (or *traditional ballad*) has been shaped by oral transmission; the words of the original composer have been modified as the song has passed from one singer to another so that the song is finally a collaboration of numerous forgotten singers.* A *broadside ballad* is one commemorating some local atrocity, printed on one side of a sheet of paper and hawked in the streets like newspapers. Broadside ballads are usually cruder than folk ballads, which have been worn smooth by oral transmission. A *literary ballad* is written by a sophisticated poet in imitation of folk or broadside ballads.

"The Wife of Usher's Well" illustrates the traditional *ballad stanza:* a 4/3/4/3 iambic stanza, identical to common meter, usually rhyming *abcb* in folk songs.

The Wife of Usher's Well

There lived a wife at Usher's Well,
    And a wealthy wife was she;
She had three stout and stalwart sons,
    And sent them oer the sea.   4

They hadna been a week from her,
    A week but barely ane,
When word came to the carline[1] wife
    That her three sons were gane.   8

They hadna been a week from her,
    A week but barely three,
When word came to the carline wife
    That her sons she'd never see.   12

'I wish the wind may never cease,
    Nor fashes[2] in the flood,
Till my three sons come hame to me,
    In earthly flesh and blood'   16

It fell about the Martinmass,[3]
    When nights are lang and mirk,[4]

*For English folk ballads, the basic source is Francis J. Child, *The English and Scottish Popular Ballads.* For American folk ballads see such collections as Alan Lomax, *The Folksongs of North America;* Vance Randolph, *Ozark Folksongs;* Newman Ivey White, *The Frank C. Brown Collection of North Carolina Folklore.*

[1]Old woman, witch. [2]Troubles. [3]Feast of St. Martin, November 11. [4]Dark.

The carline wife's three sons came hame,
　　And their hats were o the birk.[5]   **20**

It neither grew in syke[6] nor ditch,
　　Nor yet in ony sheugh;[7]
But at the gates of Paradise,
　　That birk grew fair eneugh.   **24**

'Blow up the fire, my maidens,
　　Bring water from the well;
For a' my house shall feast this night,
　　Since my three sons are well.'   **28**

And she has made to them a bed,
　　She's made it large and wide,
And she's taen[8] her mantle her about,
　　Sat down at the bed-side.   **32**

Up then the crew the red, red cock,
　　And up and crew the gray;
The eldest to the youngest said,
　　'T is time we were away.   **36**

The cock he hadna crawd but once,
　　And clapped his wings at a',
When the youngest to the eldest said,
　　Brother, we must awa.   **40**

'The cock doth craw, the day-doth daw,
　　The channerin[9] worm doth chide;
Gin[10] we be mist[11] out o our place,
　　A sair[12] pain we maun[13] bide.   **44**

'Fare ye weel, my mother dear!
　　Fareweel to barn and byre![14]
And fare ye weel, the bonny lass
　　That kindles my mother's fire!   **48**

---

[5]Birch. [6]Grove. [7]Dell. [8]Taken. [9]Plaintive. [10]If. [11]Missed. [12]Sore. [13]Must. [14]Cow shed.

Repetitions of meter and rhyme are standard to ballads. Most also repeat phrases or lines. Which repetitions of lines or parts of lines seem most important in "The Wife of Usher's Well"? Why? Alliteration is another repeated sound pattern in this poem. Where? What is the effect? Where have the sons been and where are they going at the end? How do you know? Explain the irony of the alliterative "stout and stalwart" (line 3).

With its feminine rhymes, "Barbara Allan" illustrates the flexibility of the traditional ballad stanza. In a few stanzas, it also adds rhymes to the first and third lines, creating an *abab* pattern.

Barbry Ellen[1]

All in the merry month of May,
    When the green buds they were swelling,
Young William Green on his death-bed lay,
    For the love of Barbry Ellen.   **4**

He sent his servant to the town,
    To the place where she was dwelling,
Saying, my master bids you come,
    If your name is Barbry Ellen.   **8**

Then slowly, slowly she got up,
    And slowly came she nigh him,
And when she pulled the curtains back,
    Young man, I think you're dying.   **12**

O yes, I'm sick, I'm very very sick,
    And I never will be any better,
Until I have the love of one,
    The love of Barbry Ellen.   **16**

O don't you remember in yonder town,
    In the place where you were dwelling,
You drank the health of the ladies all around,
    But you slighted Barbry Ellen.   **20**

O yes, I remember in yonder town,
    In the place where I was dwelling,
I drank the health of the ladies all around,
    But my love was to Barbry Ellen.   **24**

He turned his pale face to the wall,
    And death was in him dwelling.
Adieu, adieu, my kind friends all,
    Be kind to Barbry Ellen.   **28**

As she was going through the field,
    She heard the death bells knelling,
And every stroke they seemed to say,
    Hard-hearted Barbry Ellen.   **32**

[1]This version of "Barbara Allan" (Child 84) was collected in Pine Mountain, Kentucky in 1916.

She looked east, she looked west,
   And saw the pale corpse coming.
Go bring him here and lay him down,
   And let me look upon him.   **36**

The more she looked, the more she grieved,
   Until she burst out crying.
Go take him away, go take him away,
   For I am now a-dying.   **40**

O Mother, O Mother, come make my bed,
   Come make it soft and narrow;
Sweet William died for me today,
   I'll die for him tomorrow.   **44**

O Father, O Father, come dig my grave,
   O dig it deep and narrow;
Sweet William died for love of me,
   And I will die for sorrow.   **48**

They buried her in the old churchyard,
   And William's grave was nigh her,
And out of his grave there grew a red rose,
   And out of hers a briar.   **52**

They grew and grew to the old church tower,
   And they could not grow any higher,
They grew and grew till they tied love knots,
   And the rose wrapped round the briar.   **56**

In your own words, what is the story of "Barbry Ellen"? Has she been "hard-hearted"? Defend your answer. What is the symbolism of the rose and briar? Why is it the rose that wraps around the briar, rather than the briar around the rose?

Although scanning in iambs 4/3/4/3, the essential beat of a traditional ballad is really 4/4/4/4, with the three-beat line sometimes filled out with an "Oh" or a "Ho." Thus here the last syllable of each trimeter line, unstressed in reading, picks up an extra beat from the music:

$$\smile \;\underline{} \mid \smile \;\;\underline{} \mid \smile \underline{} \mid \smile \;\underline{} \mid$$
I'll die for him tomorrow .

The background music also lets the lines with ten or eleven syllables, rather than the eight of a standard iambic tetrameter line, slip easily into the same four-beat pattern.

As I Walked Out One Evening

W. H. Auden   *(1907–1973)*

As I walked out one evening,
   Walking down Bristol Street,
The crowds upon the pavement
   Were fields of harvest wheat.   4

And down by the brimming river
   I heard a lover sing
Under an arch of the railway:
   'Love has no ending.   8

'I'll love you, dear, I'll love you
   Till China and Africa meet,
And the river jumps over the mountain
   And the salmon sing in the street,   12

'I'll love you till the ocean
   Is folded and hung up to dry
And the seven stars go squawking
   Like geese about the sky.   16

The years shall run like rabbits,
   For in my arms I hold
The Flower of the Ages,
   And the first love of the world.'   20

But all the clocks in the city
   Began to whirr and chime:
'O let not Time deceive you,
   You cannot conquer Time.   24

'In the burrows of the Nightmare
   Where Justice naked is,
Time watches from the shadow
   And coughs when you would kiss.   28

'In headaches and in worry
   Vaguely life leaks away,
And Time will have his fancy
   To-morrow or to-day.   32

'Into many a green valley
   Drifts the appalling snow;
Time breaks the threaded dances
   And the diver's brilliant bow.   36

'O plunge your hands in water,
   Plunge them in up to the wrist;
Stare, stare in the basin
   And wonder what you've missed.   **40**

'The glacier knocks in the cupboard,
   The desert sighs in the bed,
And the crack in the tea-cup opens
   A lane to the land of the dead.   **44**

'Where the beggars raffle the banknotes
   And the Giant is enchanting to Jack,
And the Lily-white Boy is a Roarer,
   And Jill goes down on her back.   **48**

'O look, look in the mirror,
   O look in your distress;
Life remains a blessing
   Although you cannot bless.   **52**

'O stand, stand at the window
   As the tears scald and start;
You shall love your crooked neighbour
   With your crooked heart.'   **56**

It was late, late in the evening,
   The lovers they were gone;
The clocks had ceased their chiming,
   And the deep river ran on.   **60**

In this literary ballad a highly sophisticated poet has adapted the techniques of the folk poet to his own use. In normal scansion the first and third lines of each stanza would be considered iambic trimeter, with feminine endings:

$$\cup \perp \quad \cup \quad \_ \mid \cup \quad \_ \quad \cup \mid$$
As I walked out one evening;

$$\cup \quad \_ \quad \mid \cup \_ \mid \cup \quad \_ \quad \cup \mid$$
The crowds upon the pavement.

Yet so common is the traditional folk stanza and so careful is Auden's adaptation that the lines can easily be seen as iambic tetrameter, with the missing stress dictated by a silent melody:

$$\cup \perp \quad \cup \quad \_ \mid \cup \_ \mid \cup \quad \_ \mid$$
As I walked out one evening [oh];

$$\cup \quad \_ \mid \cup \_ \mid \cup \quad \_ \mid \cup \quad \_ \mid$$
The crowds upon the pavement [ho].

Many traditional ballads fill out the full 4/4/4/4 beat, as does E. E. Cummings in the following poem.

Anyone Lived in a Pretty How Town

E. E. Cummings   *(1894–1962)*

anyone lived in a pretty how town
(with up so floating many bells down)
spring summer autumn winter
he sang his didn't he danced his did.   4

Women and men(both little and small)
cared for anyone not at all
they sowed their isn't they reaped their same
sun moon stars rain   8

children guessed(but only a few
and down they forgot as up they grew
autumn winter spring summer)
that noone loved him more by more   12

when by now and tree by leaf
she laughed his joy she cried his grief
bird by snow and stir by still
anyone's any was all to her   16

someones married their everyones
laughed their cryings and did their dance
(sleep wake hope and then)they
said their nevers they slept their dream   20

stars rain sun moon
(and only the snow can begin to explain
how children are apt to forget to remember
with up so floating many bells down)   24

one day anyone died i guess
(and noone stooped to kiss his face)
busy folk buried them side by side
little by little and was by was   28

all by all and deep by deep
and more by more they dream their sleep
noone and anyone earth by april
wish by spirit and if by yes.   32

Women and men(both dong and ding)
summer autumn winter spring
reaped their sowing and went their came
sun moon stars rain   36

Like Auden and the folk poets, Cummings uses his insistent rhythms to fill out some lines otherwise short:

$$\cup \; \_ | \cup \;\; \_ | \cup \;\; \_ | \cup \;\; \_ |$$
$$\text{sun} \quad \text{moon} \quad \text{stars} \quad \text{rain.}$$

Other irregularities vary slightly without greatly changing the fundamental four-beat rhythm.

One of the most accomplished twentieth-century ballad makers, Woody Guthrie in the next song extended the basic four-stress pattern to accommodate a melodic line with a ONE-two-three beat:

$$\cup | \; \_ \;\; \cup \;\; \cup | \_ \; \cup \;\; \cup | \_ \; \cup \;\; \cup | \_ \; \cup \;\; \cup |$$
$$\text{The crops are all in and the peaches are rotting} \quad .$$

Considered by itself, the verbal structure has the effect of an irregular dactylic tetrameter.

Plane Wreck at Los Gatos[1]

Woody Guthrie   (1912–1967)

The crops are all in and the peaches are rotting,
The oranges are piled in their creosote dumps;
You're flying them back to the Mexican border
To pay all their money to wade back again.   4

   Refrain:

          Goodbye to my Juan, Goodbye Rosalita;
          Adiós mes amigos, Jesús and Marie,
          You won't have a name when you ride the big airplane:
          And all they will call you will be deportee.   8

My father's own father he waded that river;
They took all the money he made in his life;
My brothers and sisters come working the fruit trees
And they rode the truck till they took down and died.   12

Some of us are illegal and some are not wanted,
Our work contract's out and we have to move on;
Six hundred miles to that Mexico border,
They chase us like outlaws, like rustlers, like thieves.   16

We died in your hills, we died in your deserts,
We died in your valleys and died on your plains;
We died 'neath your trees and we died in your bushes,
Both sides of this river we died just the same.   20

[1]On January 28, 1948, a plane crash in California killed twenty-eight migrant workers being deported to Mexico.

The sky plane took fire over Los Gatos Canyon,
A fireball of lightning and shook all our hills.
Who are all these friends all scattered like dry leaves?
The radio says they are just deportees.   24

Is this the best way we can grow our big orchards?
Is this the best way we grow our good fruit?
To fall like dry leaves to rot on my topsoil
And be called by no name except deportees?   28

The last two poems in this section show the influence of the traditional ballad stanza, though they also show considerable variation from it.

A Runnable Stag

John Davidson   *(1857–1909)*

When the pods went pop on the broom, green broom,[1]
    And apples began to be golden-skinned,
We harboured[2] a stag in the Priory[3] coomb,[4]
    And we feathered[5] his trail up-wind, up-wind,
    We feathered his trail up-wind—   5
        A stag of warrant, a stag, a stag,
        A runnable stag, a kingly crop,
        Brow, bay and tray[6] and three on top,
        A stag, a runnable stag.

Then the huntsman's horn rang yap, yap, yap,   10
    And 'Forwards' we heard the harbourer[7] shout;
But 'twas only a brocket[8] that broke a gap
    In the beechen underwood, driven out,
    From the underwood antlered out
        By warrant and might of the stag, the stag,   15
        The runnable stag, whose lordly mind
        Was bent on sleep, though beamed[9] and tined
        He stood, a runnable stag.

So we tufted the covert[10] till afternoon
    With Tinkerman's Pup and Bell-of-the-North;[11]   20
And hunters were sulky and hounds out of tune
    Before we tufted the right stag forth,
    Before we tufted him forth,
        The stag of warrant, the wily stag,

[1]A shrub of the pea family.   [2]Traced.   [3]Monastery or nunnery.   [4]Small valley.   [5]Set the hounds on.   [6]Brow, bay and tray: first, second, and third branches of a stag's horns.   [7]The person charged with tracing the stag.   [8]A two-year-old stag.   [9]Having fourth-year horns, or tines.   [10]Beat the undergrowth.   [11]Names of the hounds.

The runnable stag with his kingly crop,   25
Brow, bay and tray and three on top,
The royal and runnable stag.

It was Bell-of-the-North and Tinkerman's Pup
That stuck to the scent till the copse was drawn.[12]
'Tally ho! tally ho!' and the hunt was up,   30
The tufters whipped and the pack laid on,
The resolute pack laid on,
 And the stag of warrant away at last,
 The runnable stag, the same, the same,
 His hoofs on fire, his horns like flame,   35
 A stag, a runnable stag.

'Let your gelding be: if you check or chide
He stumbles at once and you're out of the hunt;
For three hundred gentlemen, able to ride,
 On hunters accustomed to bear the brunt,   40
 Accustomed to bear the brunt,
  Are after the runnable stag, the stag,
  The runnable stag with his kingly crop,
  Brow, bay and tray and three on top,
  The right, the runnable stag.'   45

By perilous paths in coomb and dell,
 The heather, the rocks, and the river-bed,
The pace grew hot, for the scent lay well,
 And a runnable stag goes right ahead,
 The quarry went right ahead—   50
  Ahead, ahead, and fast and far;
  His antlered crest, his cloven hoof,
  Brow, bay and tray and three aloof,
  The stag, the runnable stag.

For a matter of twenty miles and more,   55
 By the densest hedge and the highest wall,
Through herds of bullocks he baffled the lore
 Of harbourer, huntsman, hounds and all,
 Of harbourer, hounds and all—
  The stag of warrant, the wily stag,   60
  For twenty miles, and five and five,
  He ran, and he never was caught alive,
  This stag, this runnable stag.

When he turned at bay in the leafy gloom,
 In the emerald gloom where the brook ran deep,   65
He heard in the distance the rollers[13] boom,

[12]The wood was searched.   [13]Waves, billows.

And he saw in a vision of peaceful sleep,
  In a wonderful vision of sleep,
    A stag of warrant, a stag, a stag,
    A runnable stag in a jewelled bed,   70
    Under the sheltering ocean dead,
      A stag, a runnable stag.

So a fateful hope lit up his eye,
  And he opened his nostrils wide again,
And he tossed his branching antlers high   75
  As he headed the hunt down the Charlock glen,
  As he raced down the echoing glen,
    For five miles more, the stag, the stag,
    For twenty miles, and five and five,
    Not to be caught now, dead or alive,   80
      The stag, the runnable stag.

Three hundred gentlemen, able to ride,
  Three hundred horses as gallant and free,
Behind him escape on the evening tide,
  Far out till he sank in the Severn Sea,[14]   85
  Till he sank in the depths of the sea—
    The stag, the buoyant stag, the stag
    That slept at last in a jewelled bed
    Under the sheltering ocean spread,
      The stag, the runnable stag.   90

[14]At the mouth of the Severn River, between Gloucestershire and Monmouthshire, England.

Each stanza in "A Runnable Stag" begins with four lines that present a common variation of the ballad stanza: a 4/4/4/4 stress pattern, rhyming *abab*. What is the form of the fifth line of each stanza? Consider the last four lines of each stanza as a unit, an envelope quatrain. In what ways is the form of this unit similar to and different from the "In Memoriam" stanza described on page 585? Where are the three-beat lines in each stanza? What is the effect?

Recruiting Drive

Charles Causley   *(1917–)*

Under the willow the willow
  I heard the butcher-bird sing,
Come out you fine young fellow
  From under your mother's wing.   4
I'll show you the magic garden
  That hangs in the beamy air,

The way of the lynx and the angry Sphinx
　　And the fun of the freezing fair.　　　　　　　　　　**8**

Lie down lie down with my daughter
　　Beneath the Arabian tree,
Gaze on your face in the water
　　Forget the scribbling sea.　　　　　　　　　　　　　**12**
Your pillow the nine bright shiners
　　Your bed the spilling sand,
But the terrible toy of my lily-white boy
　　Is the gun in his innocent hand.　　　　　　　　　　**16**

You must take off your clothes for the doctor
　　And stand as straight as a pin,
His hand of stone on your white breast-bone
　　Where the bullets all go in.　　　　　　　　　　　　**20**
They'll dress you in lawn and linen
　　And fill you with Plymouth gin,
O the devil may wear a rose in his hair
　　I'll wear my fine doe-skin.　　　　　　　　　　　　　**24**

My mother weeps as I leave her
　　But I tell her it won't be long,
The murderers wail in Wandsworth Gaol[1]
　　But I shoot a more popular song.　　　　　　　　　　**28**
Down in the enemy country
　　Under the enemy tree
There lies a lad whose heart has gone bad
　　Waiting for me, for me.　　　　　　　　　　　　　　**32**

He says I have no culture
　　And that when I've stormed the pass
I shall fall on the farm with a smoking arm
　　And ravish his bonny lass.　　　　　　　　　　　　**36**
Under the willow the willow
　　Death spreads her dripping wings
And caught in the snare of the bleeding air
　　The butcher-bird sings, sings, sings.　　　　　　　　**40**

---

[1]A London prison.

Consider each stanza in "Recruiting Drive" as a combination of two quatrains. In what ways do the quatrains resemble traditional ballad stanzas? How are they different? Where is interior rhyme found in this poem? What is a butcher-bird? Look up its habits if you don't know them. Why did Causley choose that bird to sing the song in this poem?

SONNET

The sonnet, a more tightly controlled form than the ballad, was introduced into English about 1530 in translations of Petrarch's Italian sonnets (written two centuries earlier). The *Petrarchan* pattern divides its fourteen iambic pentameter lines into an *octave* of eight lines, posing a problem, and a *sestet* of six, reaching a solution. The octave, two envelope quatrains, rhymes *abbaabba.* The sestet is two triads rhymed *cdecde,* with variations allowed, such as *cdedce,* or even *cddcee,* which, with its final couplet, moves toward Shakespeare. But however the poet arranges the three rhymes in the sestet, the overall limit is five rhymes only. Here is Milton's famous sonnet on his blindness, in which he "paragraphs" his quatrains and triads to emphasize his Petrarchan pattern:

On His Blindness

John Milton   (1608–1674)

When I consider how my light is spent,	*a*
Ere half my days, in this dark world and wide,	*b*
And that one Talent which is death to hide,	*b*
Lodg'd with me useless, though my Soul more bent	*a*
To serve therewith my Maker, and present	*a*
My true account, lest he returning chide;	*b*
Doth God exact day-labour, light denied,	*b*
I fondly ask; But patience to prevent	*a*
That murmur, soon replies, God doth not need	*c*
Either man's work or his own gifts; who best	*d*
Bear his mild yoke, they serve him best, his state	*e*
Is Kingly. Thousands at his bidding speed	*c*
And post o'er Land and Ocean without rest:	*d*
They also serve who only stand and wait.	*e*

Shakespeare loosened up the Petrarchan pattern into three quatrains and a summary couplet, affording himself seven rhymes instead of five, since rhymes are harder to find in English than in Italian: *abab cdcd efef gg.* Within his new rhyming structure, however, he sometimes kept the two-part thought pattern of the Italian sonnet.

Shall I Compare Thee to a Summer's Day?

William Shakespeare   (1564–1616)

Shall I compare thee to a summer's day?	*a*
Thou art more lovely and more temperate:	*b*
Rough winds do shake the darling buds of May,	*a*
And summer's lease hath all too short a date:	*b*

Sometime too hot the eye of heaven shines,	*c*
And often is his gold complexion dimmed;	*d*
And every fair from fair sometime declines,	*c*
By chance, or nature's changing course untrimmed;	*d*
But thy eternal summer shall not fade,	*e*
Nor lose possession of that fair thou ow'st,[1]	*f*
Nor shall death brag thou wander'st in his shade,	*e*
When in eternal lines to time thou grow'st;	*f*
So long as men can breathe, or eyes can see,	*g*
So long lives this, and this gives life to thee.	*g*

[1]Ownest.

How is the thought of the first two quatrains unified? What turn in thought is signaled by the "But" beginning line 9? What is the "this" of the last line?

Shakespeare's sonnets frequently do not turn so sharply after line 8, however. Often the quatrains serve as natural containers for three stages of thought leading to the strong conclusion of the couplet.

When to the Sessions of Sweet Silent Thought

William Shakespeare   (1564–1616)

When to the sessions of sweet silent thought	*a*
I summon up remembrance of things past,	*b*
I sigh the lack of many a thing I sought,	*a*
And with old woes new wail my dear time's waste.	*b*
Then can I drown an eye, unus'd to flow,	*c*
For precious friends hid in death's dateless night,	*d*
And weep afresh love's long since cancell'd woe,	*c*
And moan the expense of many a vanish'd sight.	*d*
Then can I grieve at grievances foregone,	*e*
And heavily from woe to woe tell o'er	*f*
The sad account of fore-bemoaned moan	*e*
Which I new pay as if not paid before.	*f*
But if the while I think on thee, dear friend,	*g*
All losses are restor'd and sorrows end.	*g*

Summarize the thought of the first quatrain. Of the second quatrain. Of the third. How does the couplet resolve the problem expressed in the first twelve lines?

Some poets have created mixed sonnets, blending the characteristics of Italian and Shakespearean types.

Leda and the Swan[1]

W. B. Yeats   (1865–1939)

A sudden blow: the great wings beating still
Above the staggering girl, her thighs caressed
By the dark webs, her nape caught in his bill,
He holds her helpless breast upon his breast.   4

How can those terrified vague fingers push
The feathered glory from her loosening thighs?
And how can body, laid in that white rush,
But feel the strange heart beating where it lies?   8

A shudder in the loins engenders there
The broken wall, the burning roof and tower[2]
And Agamemnon dead.[3]
                    Being so caught up,
So mastered by the brute blood of the air,   12
Did she put on his knowledge with his power
Before the indifferent beak could let her drop?

[1]Leda, raped by Zeus in the form of a swan, later gave birth to Helen of Troy and Clytemnestra.
[2]The destruction of Troy, in a war fought over Helen.   [3]Killed by his wife Clytemnestra.

What is the rhyme scheme of "Leda and the Swan"? How does it blend Italian and Shakespearean form? Yeats's rhyming patterns here create three main divisions for his sonnet. The break in line 11 creates a fourth. Does the thought also fall into four divisions? Explain.

Design

Robert Frost   (1874–1963)

I found a dimpled spider, fat and white,
On a white heal-all,[1] holding up a moth
Like a white piece of rigid satin cloth—
Assorted characters of death and blight   4
Mixed ready to begin the morning right,
Like the ingredients of a witches' broth—
A snow-drop spider, a flower like a froth,
And dead wings carried like a paper kite.   8

[1]A flower that is usually blue.

What had that flower to do with being white,
The wayside blue and innocent heal-all?
What brought the kindred spider to that height,
Then steered the white moth thither in the night?   12
What but design of darkness to appall?—
If design govern in a thing so small.

"Design" begins on the Italian pattern. Show where and how it changes. Frost's poem has only three rhyme sounds. What does he gain by creating this extra difficulty for himself?

To Sleep

John Keats   (1795–1821)

O soft embalmer of the still midnight,
   Shutting with careful fingers and benign
Our gloom-pleased eyes, embowered from the light,
   Enshaded in forgetfulness divine: 4
O soothest Sleep! If so it please thee, close,
   In midst of this thine hymn, my willing eyes,
Or wait the 'Amen', ere thy poppy[1] throws
   Around my bed its lulling charities.   8
Then save me, or the passèd day will shine
Upon my pillow, breeding many woes;
   Save me from curious conscience, that still hoards
Its strength for darkness, burrowing like a mole;   12
   Turn the key deftly in the oilèd wards,[2]
And seal the hushèd casket of my soul.

[1]The opium poppy.   [2]The ridges of a lock that allow a particular key to pass, but not others.

"To Sleep" begins on the Shakespearean pattern. Show where and how it changes. The last six lines resemble an Italian sestet. How are they different?
   Here are some more sonnets to illustrate the possibilities of the form.

What Lips My Lips Have Kissed

Edna St. Vincent Millay   (1892–1950)

What lips my lips have kissed, and where, and why,
I have forgotten, and what arms have lain
Under my head till morning; but the rain
Is full of ghosts tonight, that tap and sigh   4

Upon the glass and listen for reply,
And in my heart there stirs a quiet pain
For unremembered lads that not again
Will turn to me at midnight with a cry.   8
Thus in the winter stands the lonely tree,
Nor knows what birds have vanished one by one,
Yet knows its boughs more silent than before:
I cannot say what loves have come and gone,   12
I only know that summer sang in me
A little while, that in me sings no more.

The World Is Too Much with Us

William Wordsworth   *(1770–1850)*

The world is too much with us; late and soon,
Getting and spending, we lay waste our powers:
Little we see in Nature that is ours;
We have given our hearts away, a sordid boon![1]   4
This Sea that bares her bosom to the moon;
The winds that will be howling at all hours,
And are up-gathered now like sleeping flowers;
For this, for everything, we are out of tune;   8
It moves us not.—Great God! I'd rather be
A Pagan suckled in a creed outworn;
So might I, standing on this pleasant lea,[2]
Have glimpses that would make me less forlorn;   12
Have sight of Proteus[3] rising from the sea;
Or hear old Triton blow his wreathèd horn.

[1]Gift. [2]Meadow. [3]Proteus and Triton: sea gods.

When Serpents Bargain for the Right to Squirm

E. E. Cummings   *(1894–1962)*

when serpents bargain for the right to squirm
and the sun strikes to gain a living wage—
when thorns regard their roses with alarm
and rainbows are insured against old age   4

when every thrush may sing no new moon in
if all screech-owls have not okayed his voice
—and any wave signs on the dotted line
or else an ocean is compelled to close   8

when the oak begs permission of the birch
to make an acorn—valleys accuse their
mountains of having altitude—and march
denounces april as a saboteur   12

then we'll believe in that incredible
unanimal mankind(and not until)

Praise in Summer

Richard Wilbur   (1921–)

Obscurely yet most surely called to praise,
As sometimes summer calls us all, I said
The hills are heavens full of branching ways
Where star-nosed moles fly overhead the dead;   4
I said the trees are mines in air, I said
See how the sparrow burrows in the sky!
And then I wondered why this mad *instead*
Perverts our praise to uncreation, why   8
Such savor's in this wrenching things awry.
Does sense so stale that it must needs derange
The world to know it? To a praiseful eye
Should it not be enough of fresh and strange   12
That trees grow green, and moles can course in clay,
And sparrows sweep the ceiling of our day?

Bright Star! Would I Were Steadfast as Thou Art

John Keats   (1795–1821)

Bright star! Would I were steadfast as thou art—
   Not in lone splendour hung aloft the night
And watching, with eternal lids apart,
   Like nature's patient, sleepless eremite,[1]   4
The moving waters at their priestlike task
   Of pure ablution[2] round earth's human shores,
Or gazing on the new soft-fallen mask
   Of snow upon the mountains and the moors;   8
No—yet still steadfast, still unchangeable,
   Pillowed upon my fair love's ripening breast,

[1]Hermit. [2]Washing, especially as a religious ceremony.

To feel for ever its soft fall and swell,
   Awake for ever in a sweet unrest,   **12**
Still, still to hear her tender-taken breath,
And so live ever—or else swoon to death.

The Windhover[1]

To Christ Our Lord

Gerard Manley Hopkins   *(1844–1889)*

I caught this morning morning's minion,[2] king-
   dom of daylight's dauphin,[3] dapple-dawn-drawn Falcon, in his riding
Of the rolling level underneath him steady air, and striding
High there, how he rung upon the rein[4] of a wimpling[5] wing   **4**
In his ecstasy! then off, off forth on swing,
   As a skate's heel sweeps smooth on a bow-bend: the hurl and gliding
Rebuffed the big wind. My heart in hiding
Stirred for a bird,—the achieve of, the mastery of the thing!   **8**

Brute beauty and valour and act, oh, air, pride, plume, here
   Buckle! AND the fire that breaks from thee then, a billion
Times told lovelier, more dangerous, O my chevalier![6]

   No wonder of it: shéer plód makes plough down sillion[7]   **12**
Shine, and blue-bleak embers, ah my dear,
   Fall, gall themselves, and gash gold-vermilion.

[1]The kestrel, a bird that can hover against the wind.   [2]Favorite.   [3]Heir to the throne of France.
[4]Like a horse running in rings at the end of a rein.   [5]Rippling.   [6]Christ.   [7]Furrow.

Mortal Limit

Robert Penn Warren   *(1905–)*

I saw the hawk ride updraft in the sunset over Wyoming.
It rose from coniferous darkness, past gray jags
Of mercilessness, past whiteness, into the gloaming
Of dream-spectral light above the last purity of snow-snags.   **4**
There—west—were the Tetons. Snow-peaks would soon be
In dark profile to break constellations. Beyond what height
Hangs now the black speck? Beyond what range will gold eyes see
New ranges rise to mark a last scrawl of light?   **8**
Or, having tasted that atmosphere's thinness, does it

Hang motionless in dying vision before
It knows it will accept the mortal limit,
And swing into the great circular downwardness that will restore   12
The breath of earth? Of rock? Of rot? Of other such
Items, and the darkness of whatever dream we clutch?

VILLANELLE

A *villanelle* has five *tercets* (three-line stanzas) and a quatrain, all on two rhymes repeated in an *aba* pattern, with the last stanza *abaa*. The whole first and third lines are repeated alternately, as the final lines of stanzas two, three, four, and five, and together to conclude the quatrain. Of the following examples, the first is in iambic trimeter, the others in iambic pentameter.

The House on the Hill

Edwin Arlington Robinson   *(1869–1935)*

They are all gone away,
  The House is shut and still,
There is nothing more to say.

Through broken walls and gray
  The winds blow bleak and shrill.
They are all gone away.   6

Nor is there one to-day
  To speak them good or ill:
There is nothing more to say.   9

Why is it then we stray
  Around the sunken sill?
They are all gone away,   12

And our poor fancy-play
  For them is wasted skill:
There is nothing more to say.   15

There is ruin and decay
  In the House on the Hill:
They are all gone away,
There is nothing more to say.   18

A successful villanelle repeats lines worth repeating. Does the repetition in "The House on the Hill" seem worthwhile? Who "are all gone away"? Can you answer the question asked in lines 10 and 11?

Do Not Go Gentle into That Good Night

Dylan Thomas   (1914–1953)

Do not go gentle into that good night,
Old age should burn and rave at close of day;
Rage, rage against the dying of the light.   3

Though wise men at their end know dark is right,
Because their words had forked no lightning they
Do not go gentle into that good night.   6

Good men, the last wave by, crying how bright
Their frail deeds might have danced in a green bay,
Rage, rage against the dying of the light.   9

Wild men who caught and sang the sun in flight,
And learn, too late, they grieved it on its way,
Do not go gentle into that good night.   12

Grave men, near death, who see with blinding sight
Blind eyes could blaze like meteors and be gay,
Rage, rage against the dying of the light.   15

And you, my father, there on the sad height,
Curse, bless, me now with your fierce tears, I pray.
Do not go gentle into that good night.   18
Rage, rage against the dying of the light.

To whom is the poem addressed? In what circumstances is it spoken? Observe that the two repeated lines end on "night" and "light." What do these words symbolize? Where else in the poem do you find dark and bright images to place beside the ideas of night and light? Do these other images support the same general symbolism? Explain the differences between men who are "wise," "good," "wild," and "grave."

The Waking

Theodore Roethke   (1908–1963)

I wake to sleep, and take my waking slow.
I feel my fate in what I cannot fear.
I learn by going where I have to go.   3

We think by feeling. What is there to know?
I hear my being dance from ear to ear.
I wake to sleep, and take my waking slow.   6

Of those so close beside me, which are you?
God bless the Ground! I shall walk softly there,
And learn by going where I have to go.   9

Light takes the Tree; but who can tell us how?
The lowly worm climbs up the winding stair;
I wake to sleep, and take my waking slow.   12

Great Nature has another thing to do
To you and me; so take the lively air,
And, lovely, learn by going where to go.   15

This shaking keeps me steady. I should know.
What falls away is always. And is near.
I wake to sleep, and take my waking slow.   18
I learn by going where I have to go.

What is the effect of the small changes in the repeated lines of "The Waking"?
Beginning with lines two and four, show how feeling is important to this poem.

SESTINA

The *sestina* has 6 six-line stanzas and a three-line *envoy,* or conclusion. Instead
of rhyme, it ends the lines of each stanza with the same six words. Within the
three lines of the envoy the six key words are repeated again, three within the
lines and three at the ends.

In its strict form, the sestina interweaves the repeated words systematically.
After the first stanza establishes the key words, each succeeding stanza rearranges the end words of the one preceding, beginning with the last, then following with the first, then the fifth, second, fourth, and third. In Kipling's "Sestina
of the Tramp-Royal," therefore, the order of the end words for the first three
stanzas is: *all, world, good, long, done, die / die, all, done, world, along,
good / good, die, long, all, world, done.* Save for the minor substitution in two
places of "along" for "long," the sestina follows through in strict form until the
end. In the envoy, Kipling follows a pattern that repeats the first three words of
the sixth stanza in order in the middle of the lines *(world, long, die)* and the last
three in order at the ends *(done, good, all).*

Sestina of the Tramp-Royal

Rudyard Kipling   *(1865–1936)*

Speakin' in general, I 'ave tried 'em all—
The 'appy roads that take you o'er the world.
Speakin' in general, I 'ave found them good   3
For such as cannot use one bed too long,

But must get 'ence, the same as I 'ave done,
An' go observin' matters till they die.   6

What do it matter where or 'ow we die,
So long as we've our 'ealth to watch it all—
The different ways that different things are done,   9
An' men an' women lovin' in this world;
Takin' our chances as they come along,
An' when they ain't, pretendin' they are good?   12

In cash or credit—no, it aren't no good;
You 'ave to 'ave the 'abit or you'd die,
Unless you lived your life but one day long,   15
Nor didn't prophesy nor fret at all,
But drew your tucker[1] some'ow from the world,
An' never bothered what you might ha' done.   18

But, Gawd, what things are they I 'aven't done?
I've turned my 'and to most, an' turned it good,
In various situations round the world—   21
For 'im that doth not work must surely die;
But that's no reason man should labour all
'Is life on one same shift—life's none so long.   24

Therefore, from job to job I've moved along.
Pay couldn't 'old me when my time was done,
For something in my 'ead upset it all,   27
Till I 'ad dropped whatever 'twas for good,
An', out at sea, be'eld the dock-lights die,
An' met my mate—the wind that tramps the world!   30

It's like a book, I think, this bloomin' world,
Which you can read and care for just so long,
But presently you feel that you will die   33
Unless you get the page you're readin' done,
An' turn another—likely not so good;
But what you're after is to turn 'em all.   36

Gawd bless this world! Whatever she 'ath done—
Excep' when awful long—I've found it good.
So write, before I die, "'E liked it all!"   39

[1]Daily rations.

In the next sestina, the writer has abandoned the strict order of repetition, but kept the general form.

Rink Keeper's Sestina

Hockey, hockey

George Draper   (1942–   )

Call me Zamboni.[1] Nights my job is hockey.
I make the ice and watch the kids take slapshots
At each other. They act like Esposito,[2]   **3**
As tough in the slot as Phil, as wild with fury
In fights. Their coaches tell me this is pleasure.
But it isn't pleasure. What it is, is Hockey.   **6**

Now let me tell you what I mean by Hockey.
I mean the fights. I mean young kids in fury,
And all these coaches yelling for more slapshots.   **9**
I tell you, blood is spilled here. This is pleasure?
It seems to me the coaches should teach hockey,
Not how to act like Schultz or Esposito.   **12**

Look, I have nothing against Phil Esposito.
He's one of the greats, no question, it's a pleasure
To watch him play. My point is, why teach fury?   **15**
If I know life (at least if I know hockey),
Then fury's here to stay. We don't need Hockey
To tell us that, we don't need fights and slapshots.   **18**

Like yesterday. I heard a coach yell, "Slapshots!
Take slapshots, son! You think Phil Esposito
Hangs back? And hit! And hit again! That's hockey!"   **21**
But he was wrong. The kid was ten. That's Hockey.
You could tell the boy admired his coach's fury.
It won't be long before he hits with pleasure.   **24**

Sure, I'm no saint. I know. I've gotten pleasure
From fury, too, like any man. And hockey
At times gets changed around in me to Hockey.   **27**
I've yelled for blood at Boston Garden. Slapshots?
They've thrilled me. I've seen men clobber Esposito
And loved it when he hit them back with fury.   **30**

But you know what? Before these days of fury,
When indoor rinks were just a gleam in Hockey
Fanatics' eyes, there was no greater pleasure   **33**
Than winter mornings. Black ice. (Esposito

---

[1]Inventor of a machine that renews or "makes" the ice in ice-skating rinks.   [2]Like Schultz
(below), a National Hockey League player.

Knew days like this as a boy.) Some friends. No slapshots,
But a clear, cold sky. Choose teams. Drop the puck. Play hockey.   36

Yes, before big Hockey (sorry, Esposito),
Before the fury and all the blazing slapshots,
We had great pleasure outdoors playing hockey.   39

What differences does Draper suggest between "hockey" and "Hockey"? Summarize the attitudes expressed toward "fury" and "pleasure."

Sestina

Elizabeth Bishop   *(1911–1979)*

September rain falls on the house.
In the failing light, the old grandmother
sits in the kitchen with the child   3
beside the Little Marvel Stove,
reading the jokes from the almanac,
laughing and talking to hide her tears.   6

She thinks that her equinoctial tears
and the rain that beats on the roof of the house
were both foretold by the almanac,   9
but only known to a grandmother.
The iron kettle sings on the stove.
She cuts some bread and says to the child,   12

It's time for tea now; but the child
is watching the teakettle's small hard tears
dance like mad on the hot black stove,   15
the way the rain must dance on the house.
Tidying up, the old grandmother
hangs up the clever almanac   18

on its string. Birdlike, the almanac
hovers half open above the child,
hovers above the old grandmother   21
and her teacup full of dark brown tears.
She shivers and says she thinks the house
feels chilly, and puts more wood in the stove.   24

It was to be, says the Marvel Stove.
I know what I know, says the almanac.
With crayons the child draws a rigid house   27
and a winding pathway. Then the child
puts in a man with buttons like tears
and shows it proudly to the grandmother.   30

But secretly, while the grandmother
busies herself about the stove,
the little moons fall down like tears   33
from between the pages of the almanac
into the flower bed the child
has carefully placed in the front of the house.   36

Time to plant tears, says the almanac.
The grandmother sings to the marvellous stove
and the child draws another inscrutable house.   39

In how many places does Bishop's "Sestina" seem to be a poem about time?
How many kinds of tears appear in the poem? What is the relationship between
time and tears? Why are the only two people mentioned a child and a grandmother? Explain why "house," "stove," and "almanac" deserve the repetition
this sestina gives them.

CHAPTER 7

FREE VERSE

Poems in *free verse* abandon traditional structures. Lines of varied length follow no strict meters. Rhyme is often missing; when it appears, the sounds fall into random rather than repeated patterns. Lines may be grouped into verse paragraphs, but within a poem these units generally do not repeat a given structure.

Freedom from traditional structure does not mean that the poem has no structure at all, but rather that the structure is organic to that one piece, as the poet has tried to make form follow content. Successful free verse establishes on its own terms the repetitions of sound and rhythm that distinguish poetry from prose. As William Carlos Williams expressed it, "No verse can be free, it must be governed by some measure, but not by the old measure."

Poets organize the looser rhythms of free verse in several ways, determining the length of the line, for instance, by content, visual effect, or sound. Walt Whitman typically writes an end-stopped line, with each unit containing a single part of an ongoing description. We might envision this as a movie camera establishing a scene, cutting from background to foreground, moving from this view to that—each line describing what is seen in a single shot. Lawrence Ferlinghetti's "Constantly Risking Absurdity" balances lines across the page in imitation of the acrobat it describes. Stephen Crane follows speech patterns in his "A Man Said to the Universe," and other poets determine the length of line by how many words can be spoken with one breath. Whatever standard the poet uses, the effect is to make each line a unit of attention. We read prose continuously, but poetry line by line.

In reading the following Whitman poem, note how each line focuses on a different perspective of the scene.

Cavalry Crossing a Ford

Walt Whitman   (1819–1892)

A line in long array where they wind betwixt green islands,
They take a serpentine course, their arms flash in the sun—hark to
    the musical clank,
Behold the silvery river, in it the splashing horses loitering stop to
    drink,   3
Behold the brown-faced men, each group, each person a picture, the
    negligent rest on the saddles,
Some emerge on the opposite bank, others are just entering the ford
    —while,
Scarlet and blue and snowy white,   6
The guidon[1] flags flutter gayly in the wind.

---

[1]A flag identifying a military unit.

Observe that Whitman does not end his line each time he comes to a natural pause. Consider lines 2, 3, and 4, for example: what unifies the elements of each line, distinguishing each from the next? Lines 6 and 7 depict flags. What has Whitman gained by separating his description into two lines? Is anything gained by ending the poem with lines that are shorter than the long ones of the middle of the poem?

A Man Said to the Universe

Stephen Crane   (1871–1900)

A man said to the universe:
"Sir, I exist!"
"However," replied the universe,
"The fact has not created in me
A sense of obligation."   5

How are the two speeches in "A Man Said to the Universe" different? How does the difference help communicate the idea of the poem? In contrast to Whitman's practice, this poem contains a run-on line. Where is it? What is the effect?

In free verse, as in traditional verse, repetition of words, phrases, or parallel grammatical structures ties lines or stanzas together. The placement of rhymes or of other sound repetitions may call attention to ideas the poet wants us to connect. Images may be repeated with subtle variations to underscore meaning through comparison or contrast, and by establishing thematic, metaphoric, or symbolic emphasis.

The Purse-Seine

Robinson Jeffers   (1887–1962)

Our sardine fishermen work at night in the dark of the moon;
    daylight or moonlight
They could not tell where to spread the net, unable to see the
    phosphorescence of the shoals of fish.
They work northward from Monterey, coasting Santa Cruz; off New
    Year's Point or off Pigeon Point
The look-out man will see some lakes of milk-color light on the sea's
    night-purple; he points, and the helmsman
Turns the dark prow, the motorboat circles the gleaming shoal and
    drifts out her seine-net. They close the circle   5
And purse the bottom of the net, then with great labor haul it in.

                             I cannot tell you
How beautiful the scene is, and a little terrible, then, when the
    crowded fish
Know they are caught, and wildly beat from one wall to the other of
    their closing destiny the phosphorescent
Water to a pool of flame, each beautiful slender body sheeted with
    flame, like a live rocket
A comet's tail wake of clear yellow flame; while outside the
    narrowing   10
Floats and cordage of the net great sea-lions come up to watch,
    sighing in the dark; the vast walls of night
Stand erect to the stars.

                  Lately I was looking from a night mountain-top
On a wide city, the colored splendor, galaxies of light: how could I
    help but recall the seine-net
Gathering the luminous fish? I cannot tell you how beautiful the city
    appeared, and a little terrible.
I thought, We have geared the machines and locked all together into
    interdependence; we have built the great cities; now   15
There is no escape. We have gathered vast populations incapable of
    free survival, insulated
From the strong earth, each person in himself helpless, on all
    dependent. The circle is closed, and the net
Is being hauled in. They hardly feel the cords drawing, yet they
    shine already. The inevitable mass-disasters
Will not come in our time nor in our children's, but we and our
    children
Must watch the net draw narrower, government take all powers—or
    revolution, and the new government   20

Take more than all, add to kept bodies kept souls—or anarchy, the
   mass-disasters.

                    These things are Progress;
Do you marvel our verse is troubled or frowning, while it keeps its
   reason? Or it lets go, lets the mood flow
In the manner of the recent young men into mere hysteria, splintered
   gleams, crackled laughter. But they are quite wrong.
There is no reason for amazement: surely one always knew that
   cultures decay, and life's end is death.

Examine "The Purse-Seine," identifying significant repetition of words and
phrases. What does the repeating accomplish? List the likenesses in the two
major images. What ideas are suggested by these similarities?

Robert Bly has said that the term *free verse* "implies not a technique, but a
longing." For many poets this longing encompasses the intellectual content of
the poem as well as the structure. Ideas may be presented in a disjointed,
fragmented way similar to psychoanalytic free association or to the methods of
stream-of-consciousness fiction. To understand such poetry, the reader must
enter into the poet's mind and try to see why images evoke specific ideas or
concepts.

A Supermarket in California

Allen Ginsberg   (1926–   )

What thoughts I have of you tonight, Walt Whitman,[1] for I walked
down the sidestreets under the trees with a headache self-conscious
looking at the full moon.

In my hungry fatigue, and shopping for images, I went into the neon
fruit supermarket, dreaming of your enumerations!

What peaches and what penumbras! Whole families shopping at night!
Aisles full of husbands! Wives in the avocados, babies in the tomatoes!
—and you, Garcia Lorca,[2] what were you doing down by the water-
melons?

I saw you, Walt Whitman, childless, lonely old grubber, poking among
the meats in the refrigerator and eyeing the grocery boys.

I heard you asking questions of each: Who killed the pork chops?
What price bananas? Are you my Angel?   5

I wandered in and out of the brilliant stacks of cans following you, and
followed in my imagination by the store detective.

We strode down the open corridors together in our solitary fancy
tasting artichokes, possessing every frozen delicacy, and never passing
the cashier.

[1]An American poet (1819–1892). [2]A Spanish poet (1899–1936).

Where are we going, Walt Whitman? The doors close in an hour.
Which way does your beard point tonight?
(I touch your book and dream of our odyssey in the supermarket and
feel absurd.)
Will we walk all night through solitary streets? The trees add shade
to shade, lights out in the houses, we'll both be lonely.   10
Will we stroll dreaming of the lost America of love past blue automobiles in driveways, home to our silent cottage?
Ah, dear father, graybeard, lonely old courage-teacher, what America
did you have when Charon³ quit poling his ferry and you got out on a
smoking bank and stood watching the boat disappear on the black waters
of Lethe?⁴

---

³Charon transported dead souls over the river Styx.   ⁴River of forgetfulness.

In "A Supermarket in California," what qualities does Allen Ginsberg associate with Walt Whitman? In what ways does he consider Whitman a "courage-
teacher?" Are there any similarities between the Whitman poems in this book
and Ginsberg's poem? Be specific. How does the line structure in this poem
compare to the line structure of Jeffers's "The Purse-Seine?" Is the subject matter
of this poem traditionally poetic? What about the language?

The Far Field

Theodore Roethke   *(1908–1963)*

1

I dream of journeys repeatedly:
Of flying like a bat deep into a narrowing tunnel,
Of driving alone, without luggage, out a long peninsula,
The road lined with snow-laden second growth,
A fine dry snow ticking the windshield,   5
Alternate snow and sleet, no on-coming traffic,
And no lights behind, in the blurred side-mirror,
The road changing from glazed tarface to a rubble of stone,
Ending at last in a hopeless sand-rut,
Where the car stalls,   10
Churning in a snowdrift
Until the headlights darken.

2

At the field's end, in the corner missed by the mower,
Where the turf drops off into a grass-hidden culvert,

Haunt of the cat-bird, nesting-place of the field-mouse,   15
Not too far away from the ever-changing flower-dump,
Among the tin cans, tires, rusted pipes, broken machinery,—
One learned of the eternal;
And in the shrunken face of a dead rat, eaten by rain and
    ground-beetles
(I found it lying among the rubble of an old coal bin)   20
And the tom-cat, caught near the pheasant-run,
Its entrails strewn over the half-grown flowers,
Blasted to death by the night watchman.

I suffered for birds, for young rabbits caught in the mower,
My grief was not excessive.   25
For to come upon warblers in early May
Was to forget time and death:
How they filled the oriole's elm, a twittering restless cloud, all one
    morning,
And I watched and watched till my eyes blurred from the bird
    shapes,—
Cape May, Blackburnian, Cerulean,—   30
Moving, elusive as fish, fearless,
Hanging, bunched like young fruit, bending the end branches,
Still for a moment,
Then pitching away in half-flight,
Lighter than finches,   35
While the wrens bickered and sang in the half-green hedgerows,
And the flicker drummed from his dead tree in the chicken-yard.

—Or to lie naked in sand,
In the silted shallows of a slow river,
Fingering a shell,   40
Thinking:
Once I was something like this, mindless,
Or perhaps with another mind, less peculiar;
Or to sink down to the hips in a mossy quagmire;
Or, with skinny knees, to sit astride a wet log,   45
Believing:
I'll return again,
As a snake or a raucous bird,
Or, with luck, as a lion.

I learned not to fear infinity,   50
The far field, the windy cliffs of forever,
The dying of time in the white light of tomorrow,
The wheel turning away from itself,
The sprawl of the wave,
The on-coming water.   55

3

The river turns on itself,
The tree retreats into its own shadow.
I feel a weightless change, a moving forward
As of water quickening before a narrowing channel
When banks converge, and the wide river whitens;   60
Or when two rivers combine, the blue glacial torrent
And the yellowish-green from the mountainy upland,—
At first a swift rippling between rocks,
Then a long running over flat stones
Before descending to the alluvial plain,   65
To the clay banks, and the wild grapes hanging from the elmtrees.
The slightly trembling water
Dropping a fine yellow silt where the sun stays;
And the crabs bask near the edge,
The weedy edge, alive with small snakes and bloodsuckers,—   70
I have come to a still, but not a deep center,
A point outside the glittering current;
My eyes stare at the bottom of a river,
At the irregular stones, iridescent sandgrains,
My mind moves in more than one place,   75
In a country half-land, half-water.

I am renewed by death, thought of my death,
The dry scent of a dying garden in September,
The wind fanning the ash of a low fire.
What I love is near at hand,   80
Always, in earth and air.

4

The lost self changes,
Turning toward the sea,
A sea-shape turning around,—
An old man with his feet before the fire,   85
In robes of green, in garments of adieu.

A man faced with his own immensity
Wakes all the waves, all their loose wandering fire.
The murmur of the absolute, the why
Of being born fails on his naked ears.   90
His spirit moves like monumental wind
That gentles on a sunny blue plateau.
He is the end of things, the final man.

All finite things reveal infinitude:
The mountain with its singular bright shade   95
Like the blue shine on freshly frozen snow,
The after-light upon ice-burdened pines;
Odor of basswood on a mountain-slope,
A scent beloved of bees;
Silence of water above a sunken tree: 100
The pure serene of memory in one man,—
A ripple widening from a single stone
Winding around the waters of the world.

In the first line of "The Far Field" the speaker says, "I dream of journeys repeatedly." He then describes a dream journey in the following line and another in the next ten. What do they have in common? What other journeys are described or implied in the following sections? Analyze the way the poem is broken into groups of lines. Why do the four major divisions come where they do? Can you see reasons for the subdivisions? Some elements of this poem seem to arise from free association. Which ones? What connects them?

Consider lines 50 through 55. What is being said here? In what ways are these lines related to the rest of the poem?

Show where alliteration, assonance, and consonance contribute to the effect of the last four lines. Show how sound patterns are also important in selected lines or passages elsewhere in the poem.

Three more poems in free verse follow. In reading each, pay particular attention to the nontraditional elements of structure and content.

[handwritten: Circus – all rehearsed, theatrical – like poetry. An allegory between poet + acrobat]

Constantly Risking Absurdity   *[handwritten: irregular. No punctuation. No metre. simple language]*

Lawrence Ferlinghetti   (1920–)

[handwritten left margin: About poems – working on imagery but gives us an acrobat]

Constantly risking absurdity   *[handwritten: criticism]*
                and death   *[handwritten: loss of sales]*
    whenever he performs   *[handwritten: act → an illusion. You mustn't accept what the poet says is the truth.]*
        [handwritten: an elitist thing]   above the heads
                    of his audience
    the poet like an acrobat   *[handwritten: assonance]*
        climbs on rime
            to a high wire of his own making
and balancing on eyebeams   *[handwritten: everyone looking at them / a spotlight on him; eyes reading the poem]*
            above a sea of faces
    paces his way
        to the other side of day   *[handwritten: imagination / unconsciousness]*   12[?]
performing entrechats   *[handwritten: acrobat prefers he's going to fall off]*
        [handwritten: pun]
    and sleight-of-foot tricks   *[handwritten: doesn't come naturally]*
        [handwritten: metre]

[handwritten bottom: Nothing truthful about the poem. It's v. theatrical / artificial. Sentences follow like an acrobat walking precariously.]

and other high theatrics
                    and all without mistaking
            any thing
                    for what it may not be *metaphors*   18

    For he's the super realist *— people thinks he's telling them some*
                                    inner emotions (Not True)
        (write's taut) who must perforce perceive
            taut truth   *alliteration*
                    before the taking of each stance or step
        in his supposed advance
    personification toward that still higher perch   24
where Beauty stands and waits   *our*
                    with gravity *— seriousness*
                    to start her death-defying leap *earth*

                        showing his irrelivence —
    And he   *Always putting on a act. Pathetic victim*
            a little charleychaplin man
                    who may or may not catch   30
            her fair eternal form
                    spreadeagled in the empty air
        of existence   *Not resolved at end.*
                                  Ambiguous

At First I Was Given Centuries

Margaret Atwood   (1939–)

At first I was given centuries
to wait in caves, in leather
tents, knowing you would never come back

Then it speeded up: only
several years between   5
the day you jangled off
into the mountains, and the day (it was
spring again) I rose from the embroidery
frame at the messenger's entrance.

That happened twice, or was it   10
more; and there was once, not so
long ago, you failed,
and came back in a wheelchair
with a moustache and a sunburn
and were insufferable.   15

Time before last though, I remember
I had a good eight months between
running alongside the train, skirts hitched, handing

you violets in at the window
and opening the letter; I watched   20
your snapshot fade for twenty years.

And last time (I drove to the airport
still dressed in my factory
overalls, the wrench
I had forgotten sticking out of the back   25
pocket; there you were,
zippered and helmeted, it was zero
hour, you said Be
Brave) it was at least three weeks before
I got the telegram and could start regretting.   30

But recently, the bad evenings
there are only seconds
between the warning on the radio and the
explosion; my hands
don't reach you   35

and on quieter nights
you jump up from
your chair without even touching your dinner
and I can scarcely kiss you goodbye
before you run out into the street and they shoot   40

Corsons Inlet

A. R. Ammons   (1926–)

I went for a walk over the dunes again this morning
to the sea,
then turned right along
        the surf   4
                    rounded a naked headland
                    and returned

        along the inlet shore:

it was muggy sunny, the wind from the sea steady and high,   8
crisp in the running sand,
        some breakthroughs of sun
        but after a bit

continuous overcast: 12

the walk liberating, I was released from forms,
from the perpendiculars,
        straight lines, blocks, boxes, binds

of thought 16
into the hues, shadings, rises, flowing bends and blends
    of sight:

      I allow myself eddies of meaning:
yield to a direction of significance 20
running
like a stream through the geography of my work:
  you can find
in my sayings 24
      swerves of action
        like the inlet's cutting edge:
      there are dunes of motion,
organizations of grass, white sandy paths of remembrance 28
in the overall wandering of mirroring mind:
but Overall is beyond me: is the sum of these events
I cannot draw, the ledger I cannot keep, the accounting
beyond the account: 32

in nature there are few sharp lines: there are areas of
primrose
    more or less dispersed;
disorderly orders of bayberry; between the rows 36
of dunes,
irregular swamps of reeds,
though not reeds alone, but grass, bayberry, yarrow, all . . .
predominantly reeds: 40

I have reached no conclusions, have erected no boundaries,
shutting out and shutting in, separating inside
    from outside: I have
    drawn no lines: 44
    as

manifold events of sand
change the dune's shape that will not be the same shape
tomorrow, 48

so I am willing to go along, to accept
the becoming
thought, to stake off no beginnings or ends, establish
    no walls: 52

by transitions the land falls from grassy dunes to creek
to undercreek: but there are no lines, though
    change in that transition is clear
    as any sharpness: but "sharpness" spread out, 56

allowed to occur over a wider range
than mental lines can keep:

the moon was full last night: today, low tide was low:
black shoals of mussels exposed to the risk   60
of air
and, earlier, of sun,
waved in and out with the waterline, waterline inexact,
caught always in the event of change: 64
    a young mottled gull stood free on the shoals
    and ate
to vomiting: another gull, squawking possession, cracked a crab,
picked out the entrails, swallowed the soft-shelled legs, a ruddy   68
turnstone running in to snatch leftover bits:

risk is full: every living thing in
siege: the demand is life, to keep life: the small
white blacklegged egret, how beautiful, quietly stalks and spears   72
    the shallows, darts to shore
      to stab—what? I couldn't
  see against the black mudflats—a frightened
fiddler crab?   76

    the news to my left over the dunes and
reeds and bayberry clumps was
    fall: thousands of tree swallows
    gathering for flight: 80
    an order held
    in constant change: a congregation
rich with entropy: nevertheless, separable, noticeable
  as one event,   84
      not chaos: preparations for
flight from winter,
cheet, cheet, cheet, cheet, wings rifling the green clumps,
beaks   88
at the bayberries
  a perception full of wind, flight, curve,
  sound:
  the possibility of rule as the sum of rulelessness: 92
the "field" of action
with moving, incalculable center:

in the smaller view, order tight with shape:
blue tiny flowers on a leafless weed: carapace of crab: 96
snail shell:
    pulsations of order
        in the bellies of minnows: orders swallowed,

broken down, transferred through membranes 100
to strengthen larger orders: but in the large view, no
lines or changeless shapes: the working in and out, together
      and against, of millions of events: this,
         so that I make 104
         no form of
         formlessness:

orders as summaries, as outcomes of actions override
or in some way result, not predictably (seeing me gain 108
the top of a dune,
the swallows
could take flight—some other fields of bayberry
         could enter fall 112
         berryless) and there is serenity:

         no arranged terror: no forcing of image, plan,
or thought:
no propaganda, no humbling of reality to precept: 116

terror pervades but is not arranged, all possibilities
of escape open: no route shut, except in
    the sudden loss of all routes:

         I see narrow orders, limited tightness, but will 120
not run to that easy victory:
         still around the looser, wider forces work:
         I will try
         to fasten into order enlarging grasps of disorder, widening 124
scope, but enjoying the freedom that
Scope eludes my grasp, that there is no finality of vision,
that I have perceived nothing completely,
         that tomorrow a new walk is a new walk. 128

CHAPTER 8

TIME AND PLACE

Many poems stand forth comparatively free of specific indications of birth. Others are closely tied to a particular event, a way of life, a manner of thought peculiar to the poet or the time that brought them forth. Although we are often tempted to read poems in isolation, relating them as best we can to our own vision of the world, we sometimes gain much by an effort to enter into another time, another place, another human circumstance.

In "Crossing Brooklyn Ferry," Whitman loads us with images different in many details from those we associate with the New York City of our day. In places he speaks directly to us, reminding us that his is a voice of a century ago. But as he tells us that his time and place is not ours, he also demonstrates that it is.

Crossing Brooklyn Ferry[1]

Walt Whitman   *(1819–1892)*

1

Flood-tide below me! I see you face to face!
Clouds of the west—sun there half an hour high—I see you also face
    to face.

Crowds of men and women attired in the usual costumes, how curious
    you are to me!

---

[1]"Crossing Brooklyn Ferry" was called "Sun-Down Poem" when first published in 1856, in the second edition of *Leaves of Grass.* Whitman gave it its present title later. We present Whitman's improved 1881 version.

On the ferry-boats the hundreds and hundreds that cross, returning
    home, are more curious to me than you suppose,
And you that shall cross from shore to shore years hence are more
    to me, and more in my meditations, than you might suppose.   5

2

The impalpable sustenance of me from all things at all hours of the day,
The simple, compact, well-join'd scheme, myself disintegrated, every
    one disintegrated yet part of the scheme,
The similitudes of the past and those of the future,
The glories strung like beads on my smallest sights and hearings, on
    the walk in the street and the passage over the river,
The current rushing so swiftly and swimming with me far away,   10
The others that are to follow me, the ties between me and them,
The certainty of others, the life, love, sight, hearing of others.

Others will enter the gates of the ferry and cross from shore to shore,
Others will watch the run of the flood-tide,
Others will see the shipping of Manhattan north and west, and the
    heights of Brooklyn to the south and east,   15
Others will see the islands large and small;
Fifty years hence, others will see them as they cross, the sun half an
    hour high,
A hundred years hence, or ever so many hundred years hence, others
    will see them,
Will enjoy the sunset, the pouring-in of the flood-tide, the
    falling-back to the sea of the ebb-tide.

3

It avails not, time nor place—distance avails not,   20
I am with you, you men and women of a generation, or ever so
    many generations hence,
Just as you feel when you look on the river and sky, so I felt,
Just as any of you is one of a living crowd, I was one of a crowd,
Just as you are refresh'd by the gladness of the river and the bright
    flow, I was refresh'd,
Just as you stand and lean on the rail, yet hurry with the swift
    current, I stood yet was hurried,   25
Just as you look on the numberless masts of ships and the
    thick-stemm'd pipes of steamboats, I look'd.

I too many and many a time cross'd the river of old,
Watched the Twelfth-month[2] sea-gulls, saw them high in the air
    floating with motionless wings, oscillating their bodies,

[2]The Quaker name for December.

Saw how the glistening yellow lit up parts of their bodies and left the
    rest in strong shadow,
Saw the slow-wheeling circles and the gradual edging toward the
    south,   30
Saw the reflection of the summer sky in the water,
Had my eyes dazzled by the shimmering track of beams,
Look'd at the fine centrifugal spokes of light round the shape of my
    head in the sunlit water,
Look'd on the haze on the hills southward and south-westward,
Look'd on the vapor as it flew in fleeces tinged with violet,   35
Look'd toward the lower bay to notice the vessels arriving,
Saw their approach, saw aboard those that were near me,
Saw the white sails of schooners and sloops, saw the ships at anchor,
The sailors at work in the rigging or out astride the spars,
The round masts, the swinging motion of the hulls, the slender
    serpentine pennants,   40
The large and small steamers in motion, the pilots in their
    pilothouses,
The white wake left by the passage, the quick tremulous whirl of the
    wheels,
The flags of all nations, the falling of them at sunset,
The scallop-edged waves in the twilight, the ladled cups, the
    frolicsome crests and glistening,
The stretch afar growing dimmer and dimmer, the gray walls of the
    granite storehouses by the docks,   45
On the river the shadowy group, the big steam-tug closely flank'd on
    each side by the barges, the hay-boat, the belated lighter,
On the neighboring shore the fires from the foundry chimneys
    burning high and glaringly into the night,
Casting their flicker of black contrasted with wild red and yellow
    light over the tops of houses, and down into the clefts of streets.

4

These and all else were to me the same as they are to you,
I loved well those cities, loved well the stately and rapid river,   50
The men and women I saw were all near to me,
Others the same—others who look back on me because I look'd
    forward to them,
(The time will come, though I stop here to-day and to-night.)

5

What is it then between us?
What is the count of the scores or hundreds of years between us?   55

Whatever it is, it avails not—distance avails not, and place avails not,
I too lived, Brooklyn of ample hills was mine,
I too walk'd the streets of Manhattan island, and bathed in the
    waters around it,
I too felt the curious abrupt questionings stir within me,
In the day among crowds of people sometimes they came upon me,   60
In my walks home late at night or as I lay in my bed they came
    upon me,
I too had been struck from the float forever held in solution,
I too had receiv'd identity by my body,
That I was I knew was of my body, and what I should be I knew I
    should be of my body.

6

It is not upon you alone the dark patches fall,   65
The dark threw its patches down upon me also,
The best I had done seem'd to me blank and suspicious,
My great thoughts as I supposed them, were they not in reality
    meagre?
Nor is it you alone who know what it is to be evil,
I am he who knew what it was to be evil,   70
I too knitted the old knot of contrariety,
Blabb'd, blush'd, resented, lied, stole, grudg'd,
Had guile, anger, lust, hot wishes I dared not speak,
Was wayward, vain, greedy, shallow, sly, cowardly, malignant,
The wolf, the snake, the hog, not wanting in me,   75
The cheating look, the frivolous word, the adulterous wish, not
    wanting,
Refusals, hates, postponements, meanness, laziness, none of these
    wanting,
Was one with the rest, the days and haps of the rest,
Was call'd by my nighest name by clear loud voices of young men as
    they saw me approaching or passing,
Felt their arms on my neck as I stood, or the negligent leaning of
    their flesh against me as I sat,   80
Saw many I loved in the street or ferry-boat or public assembly, yet
    never told them a word,
Lived the same life with the rest, the same old laughing, gnawing,
    sleeping,
Play'd the part that still looks back on the actor or actress,
The same old role, the role that is what we make it, as great as we
    like,
Or as small as we like, or both great and small.   85

7

Closer yet I approach you,
What thought you have of me now, I had as much of you—I laid in
    my stores in advance,
I consider'd long and seriously of you before you were born.

Who was to know what should come home to me?
Who knows but I am enjoying this?   90
Who knows, for all the distance, but I am as good as looking at you
    now, for all you cannot see me?

8

Ah, what can ever be more stately and admirable to me than
    mast-hemm'd Manhattan?
River and sunset and scallop-edg'd waves of flood-tide?
The sea-gulls oscillating their bodies, the hay-boat in the twilight,
    and the belated lighter?
What gods can exceed these that clasp me by the hand, and with
    voices I love call me promptly and loudly by my nighest name
    as I approach?   95
What is more subtle than this which ties me to the woman or man
    that looks in my face?
Which fuses me into you now, and pours my meaning into you?

We understand then do we not?
What I promis'd without mentioning it, have you not accepted?
What the study could not teach—what the preaching could not
    accomplish is accomplish'd, is it not?   100

9

Flow on, river! flow with the flood-tide, and ebb with the ebb-tide!
Frolic on, crested and scallop-edg'd waves!
Gorgeous clouds of the sunset! drench with your splendor me, or the
    men and women generations after me!
Cross from shore to shore, countless crowds of passengers!
Stand up, tall masts of Mannahatta! stand up, beautiful hills of
    Brooklyn!   105
Throb, baffled and curious brain! throw out questions and answers!
Suspend here and everywhere, eternal float of solution!
Gaze, loving and thirsting eyes, in the house or street or public
    assembly!
Sound out, voices of young men! loudly and musically call me by my
    nighest name!
Live, old life! play the part that looks back on the actor or actress!   110
Play the old role, the role that is great or small according as one
    makes it!

Consider, you who peruse me, whether I may not in unknown ways
    be looking upon you;
Be firm, rail over the river, to support those who lean idly, yet haste
    with the hasting current;
Fly on, sea-birds! fly sideways, or wheel in large circles high in the
    air;
Receive the summer sky, you water, and faithfully hold it till all
    downcast eyes have time to take it from you!   115
Diverge, fine spokes of light, from the shape of my head, or any
    one's head, in the sunlit water!
Come on, ships from the lower bay! pass up or down, white-sail'd
    schooners, sloops, lighters!
Flaunt away, flags of all nations! be duly lower'd at sunset!
Burn high your fires, foundry chimneys! cast black shadows at
    nightfall! cast red and yellow light over the tops of the houses!
Appearances, now or henceforth, indicate what you are,   120
You necessary film, continue to envelop the soul,
About my body for me, and your body for you, be hung our divinest
    aromas,
Thrive, cities—bring your freight, bring your shows, ample and
    sufficient rivers,
Expand, being than which none else is perhaps more spiritual,
Keep your places, objects than which none else is more lasting.   125

You have waited, you always wait, you dumb, beautiful ministers,
We receive you with free sense at last, and are insatiate
    hence-forward,
Not you any more shall be able to foil us, or withhold yourselves
    from us,
We use you, and do not cast you aside—we plant you permanently
    within us,
We fathom you not—we love you—there is perfection in you also,   130
You furnish your parts toward eternity,
Great or small, you furnish your parts toward the soul.

In what important ways is the scene described by Whitman different from what we would see today in the same place? What did Whitman see that would still be visible to us? What did he see that would have been visible hundreds or thousands of years before his time? What did he see that was new to the middle of the nineteenth century, omens of things to come? What was his attitude toward these things? Is our attitude the same? Why or why not?

You may want to compare this poem to Wordsworth's "Composed Upon Westminster Bridge, September 3, 1802," another poem very much of its time and place. What are the similarities? What are the differences? With the proper thesis, this would make a good essay.

In his *Walt Whitman: A Life,* Justin Kaplan said of this poem that "The ferry plying between Brooklyn and Manhattan also plied between now and forever, the one and the many." What did he mean? What passages in the poem most clearly support Kaplan's idea about "now and forever"? About "the one and the many"? Whitman ends with a grand philosophical statement, Emersonian and transcendental, voicing ideas widespread in his time. Kaplan's observation is one way of expressing it briefly. Explain it more fully in your own words, paraphrasing from line 120 onward, "Appearances, now or henceforth, indicate what you are."

The next poem, by a poet otherwise not much read, has been widely quoted and owes much of its fame to the fact that it is inscribed on a tablet at the base of the Statue of Liberty.

The New Colossus

Emma Lazarus   (1849–1887)

Not like the brazen giant of Greek fame,
With conquering limbs astride from land to land;
Here at our sea-washed, sunset gates shall stand
A mighty woman with a torch, whose flame   4
Is the imprisoned lightning, and her name
Mother of Exiles. From her beacon-hand
Glows world-wide welcome; her mild eyes command
The air-bridged harbor that twin cities frame.   8
"Keep, ancient lands, your storied pomp!" cries she
With silent lips. "Give me your tired, your poor,
Your huddled masses yearning to breathe free,
The wretched refuse of your teeming shore.   12
Send these, the homeless, tempest-tost to me,
I lift my lamp beside the golden door!"

"The New Colossus" was written in anticipation of the erection of the Statue of Liberty, dedicated in 1886. The harbor the statue looks upon is no longer merely "air-bridged" (a ship entering it from the Atlantic Ocean has already passed under the Verrazano Narrows Bridge). Aside from this perhaps minor reminder of the passage of time, does the poem describe a scene that has changed? Today most immigrants arriving in New York come by plane. As they approach the landing field, they see the Statue of Liberty either not at all or only as a small figure in a large panorama. In what ways does this poem seem more appropriate to immigrants arriving by ship?

During its first century, the United States had no federal laws restricting immigration. The first law, passed by Congress in 1882, placed a head tax on immigrants and excluded convicts, idiots, and paupers. Later laws extended the regulations, barring immigration from certain countries and, by 1921, setting up strict quotas for others. In what ways might this poem be seen as a rebuke to the idea of restriction? What in the history of the past century has caused some Americans to have second thoughts about the open invitation of this poem's last five lines?

With the next two poems we move to the time of World War II. Auden's "September 1, 1939" records the thoughts of an English poet who had earlier that year moved to the United States.

September 1, 1939[1]

W. H. Auden   (1907–1973)

I sit in one of the dives
Of Fifty-Second Street[2]
Uncertain and afraid
As the clever hopes expire
Of a low dishonest decade:[3]   5
Waves of anger and fear
Circulate over the bright
And darkened lands of the earth,
Obsessing our private lives;
The unmentionable odour of death   10
Offends the September night.

Accurate scholarship can
Unearth the whole offence
From Luther[4] until now
That has driven a culture mad,   15
Find what occurred at Linz,[5]
What huge imago made
A psychopathic god:
I and the public know
What all schoolchildren learn,   20
Those to whom evil is done[6]
Do evil in return.

[1]The date on which Hitler's panzer tanks rolled into Poland and launched World War II. [2]New York City. [3]The decade of the 1930s was "low" because of the worldwide Great Depression and also "low" and "dishonest" in rationalizing Hitler's national and international crimes with such "clever hopes" as those with which Britain's Neville Chamberlain and France's Edouard Daladier agreed at Munich (September 30, 1938) to give Hitler his way with Czechoslovakia in exchange for what they thought was "peace in our time," as Chamberlain phrased it from the *Book of Common Prayer*, "Evening Prayer." [4]Martin Luther (c. 1483–1546), founder of the Lutheran Church and, as Auden sees it, initiator of German nationalism in his Protestant break with Rome. [5]The capital of Upper Austria, in the vicinity of which Hitler grew up and where he made his first major speech. [6]Contrary to Auden's assumption, Hitler had a somewhat pampered though lonely youth.

Exiled Thucydides[7] knew
All that a speech can say
About Democracy,   25
And what dictators do,
The elderly rubbish they talk
To an apathetic grave;
Analysed all in his book,
The enlightenment driven away,   30
The habit-forming pain,
Mismanagement and grief:
We must suffer them all again.

Into his neutral air
Where blind skyscrapers use   35
Their full height to proclaim
The strength of Collective Man,
Each language pours its vain
Competitive excuse:
But who can live for long   40
In an euphoric dream;
Out of the mirror they stare,
Imperialism's face
And the international wrong.

Faces along the bar   45
Cling to their average day:
The lights must never go out,
The music must always play,
All the conventions conspire
To make this fort assume   50
The furniture of home;
Lest we should see where we are,
Lost in a haunted wood,
Children afraid of the night
Who have never been happy or good.   55

The windiest militant trash
Important Persons shout
Is not so crude as our wish:
What mad Nijinsky wrote
About Diaghilev[8]   60

---

[7]A Greek historian (c. 460–403 B.C.), author of the unfinished *History of the Peloponnesian War*, exiled for twenty years when his Athenian fleet failed to thwart the capture of a city. He analyzes Athens' claims to empire and the democracy that continued uninhibited in all the Greek states. The speeches he constructs for the leaders of both sides are notable.   [8]Vaslav Nijinsky (1890–1950), a Russian ballet dancer, wrote to Sergei Diaghilev (1872–1929), his producer, that he, Nijinsky, loved the whole world whereas Diaghilev loved only himself.

Is true of the normal heart;
For the error bred in the bone
Of each woman and each man
Craves what it cannot have,
Not universal love   65
But to be loved alone.

From the conservative dark
Into the ethical life
The dense commuters come,
Repeating their morning vow,   70
'I *will* be true to the wife,
I'll concentrate more on my work',
And helpless governors wake
To resume their compulsory game:
Who can release them now,   75
Who can reach the deaf,
Who can speak for the dumb?

All I have is a voice
To undo the folded lie,
The romantic lie in the brain   80
Of the sensual man-in-the-street
And the lie of Authority
Whose buildings grope the sky:
There is no such thing as the State
And no one exists alone;   85
Hunger allows no choice
To the citizen or the police;
We must love one another or die.

Defenceless under the night
Our world in stupor lies;   90
Yet, dotted everywhere,
Ironic points of light
Flash out wherever the Just
Exchange their messages:
May I, composed like them   95
Of Eros and of dust,
Beleaguered by the same
Negation[9] and despair,
Show an affirming flame.

[9]Auden puns on the League of Nations, the congress of countries established in 1920 to affirm the Peace of Versailles concluding World War I, which, as World War II sadly demonstrated, had failed of its hopes to legitimatize worldwide peace.

The footnotes accompanying Auden's poem help show how rooted it is in his time and place as well as how Auden enriches his analysis of the twentieth century with allusions to Luther and Thucydides. Examining Auden's life in the years immediately preceding 1939, we discover that he observed war at first hand in China and Spain. How might this knowledge enrich our understanding of lines 38–44? What does Auden mean by "There is no such thing as the State / And no one exists alone"? Explain the importance of love in the developing thought of the last four stanzas. What relationships does Auden suggest between troubles in the rest of the world and people in New York?

In the next poem, an American poet, who had long lived in England and become an English citizen, responds to the bombing of London in the early years of the same war. For this major effort by a twentieth-century master, we offer full footnotes and an analysis designed to show how an attempt to understand a poem in terms of the poet's time and place drives us toward an exploration not only of public events, but of the poet's life, his work, and his reading.

Little Gidding

T. S. Eliot   *(1888–1965)*

I

Midwinter spring is its own season
Sempiternal though sodden towards sundown,
Suspended in time, between pole and tropic.
When the short day is brightest, with frost and fire,
The brief sun flames the ice, on pond and ditches,   5
In windless cold that is the heart's heat,
Reflecting in a watery mirror
A glare that is blindness in the early afternoon.
And glow more intense than blaze of branch, or brazier,
Stirs the dumb spirit: no wind, but pentecostal fire[1]   10
In the dark time of the year. Between melting and freezing
The soul's sap quivers. There is no earth smell
Or smell of living thing. This is the spring time
But not in time's covenant. Now the hedgerow
Is blanched for an hour with transitory blossom   15
Of snow, a bloom more sudden
Than that of summer, neither budding nor fading,
Not in the scheme of generation.
Where is the summer, the unimaginable
Zero summer?

[1]On the feast of the Pentecost, Christ's apostles were confronted with "a sound from heaven as of a rushing mighty wind. . . . And there appeared unto them cloven tongues like as of fire. . . . And they were all filled with the Holy Ghost, and began to speak with other tongues, as the Spirit gave them utterance" (Acts 2.2–4). Pentecost (or Whitsunday) is celebrated in May or June, seven Sundays after Easter.

                    If you came this way,   20
Taking the route you would be likely to take
From the place you would be likely to come from,
If you came this way in may time, you would find the hedges
White again, in May, with voluptuary sweetness.
It would be the same at the end of the journey,   25
If you came at night like a broken king,[2]
If you came by day not knowing what you came for,
It would be the same, when you leave the rough road
And turn behind the pig-sty to the dull façade
And the tombstone. And what you thought you came for   30
Is only a shell, a husk of meaning
From which the purpose breaks only when it is fulfilled
If at all. Either you had no purpose
Or the purpose is beyond the end you figured
And is altered in fulfilment. There are other places[3]   35
Which also are the world's end, some at the sea jaws,
Or over a dark lake, in a desert or a city—
But this is the nearest, in place and time,
Now and in England.

                    If you came this way,
Taking any route, starting from anywhere,   40
At any time or at any season,
It would always be the same: you would have to put off
Sense and notion. You are not here to verify,
Instruct yourself, or inform curiosity
Or carry report. You are here to kneel   45
Where prayer has been valid. And prayer is more
Than an order of words, the conscious occupation
Of the praying mind, or the sound of the voice praying.
And what the dead had no speech for, when living,
They can tell you, being dead: the communication   50
Of the dead is tongued with fire beyond the language of the living.
Here, the intersection of the timeless moment
Is England and nowhere. Never and always.

II

Ash on an old man's sleeve
Is all the ash the burnt roses leave.   55
Dust in the air suspended
Marks the place where a story ended.

---

[2]Charles I is supposed to have visited Little Gidding after his final defeat.   [3]Eliot had in mind several specific places of religious refuge: the holy islands of Iona and Lindisfarne (off the coasts of Scotland and England), the lake at Glendalough (Ireland), the desert associated with St. Anthony of Egypt, the city of Padua in Italy.

Dust inbreathed was a house—
The wall, the wainscot and the mouse.
The death of hope and despair,
   This is the death of air.   60

There are flood and drouth
Over the eyes and in the mouth,
Dead water and dead sand
Contending for the upper hand.   65
The parched eviscerate soil
Gapes at the vanity of toil,
Laughs without mirth.
   This is the death of earth.

Water and fire succeed   70
The town, the pasture and the weed.
Water and fire deride
The sacrifice that we denied.
Water and fire shall rot
The marred foundations we forgot,   75
Of sanctuary and choir.
   This is the death of water and fire.

In the uncertain hour before the morning[4]
   Near the ending of interminable night
   At the recurrent end of the unending   80
After the dark dove with the flickering tongue
   Had passed below the horizon of his homing
   While the dead leaves still rattled on like tin
Over the asphalt where no other sound was
   Between three districts whence the smoke arose   85
   I met one walking, loitering and hurried
As if blown towards me like the metal leaves
   Before the urban dawn wind unresisting.
   And as I fixed upon the down-turned face
That pointed scrutiny with which we challenge   90
   The first-met stranger in the waning dusk
   I caught the sudden look of some dead master
Whom I had known, forgotten, half recalled
   Both one and many; in the brown baked features
   The eyes of a familiar compound ghost   95
Both intimate and unidentifiable.
   So I assumed a double part, and cried
   And heard another's voice cry: 'What! are *you* here?'[5]

[4]Eliot wrote "This section of a poem . . . cost me far more time and trouble and vexation than any passage of the same length that I have ever written." His intention was to create "the nearest equivalent to a canto of the *Inferno* or the *Purgatorio,* in style as well as content, that I could achieve."

Although we were not. I was still the same,
   Knowing myself yet being someone other—   100
   And he a face still forming; yet the words sufficed
To compel the recognition they preceded.
   And so, compliant to the common wind,
   Too strange to each other for misunderstanding,
In concord at this intersection time   105
   Of meeting nowhere, no before and after,
   We trod the pavement in a dead patrol.
I said: 'The wonder that I feel is easy,
   Yet ease is cause of wonder. Therefore speak:
   I may not comprehend, may not remember.'   110
And he: 'I am not eager to rehearse
   My thoughts and theory which you have forgotten.
   These things have served their purpose: let them be.
So with your own, and pray they be forgiven
   By others, as I pray you to forgive   115
   Both bad and good. Last season's fruit is eaten
And the fullfed beast shall kick the empty pail.
   For last year's words belong to last year's language
   And next year's words await another voice.
But, as the passage now presents no hindrance   120
   To the spirit unappeased and peregrine
   Between two worlds become much like each other,
So I find words I never thought to speak
   In streets I never thought I should revisit
   When I left my body on a distant shore.   125
Since our concern was speech, and speech impelled us
   To purify the dialect of the tribe[6]
   And urge the mind to aftersight and foresight,
Let me disclose the gifts reserved for age
   To set a crown upon your lifetime's effort.   130
   First, the cold friction of expiring sense
Without enchantment, offering no promise
   But bitter tastelessness of shadow fruit
   As body and soul begin to fall asunder.
Second, the conscious impotence of rage   135
   At human folly, and the laceration
   Of laughter at what ceases to amuse.
And last, the rending pain of re-enactment

---

[5]The line recalls Dante's meeting in Hell with Brunetto Latini, his former teacher (*Inferno*, XV).
Latini's prediction of Dante's future ill treatment at the hands of his countrymen parallels Eliot's
fears concerning the lasting value and acceptance of his own work.   [6]Translating "Donner un sens
plus pur aux mots de la tribu" from Stéphane Mallarmé's "Le Tombeau d'Edgar Poe," the line
defines an ambition shared by many poets, including Dante and Yeats.

Of all that you have done, and been; the shame
Of motives late revealed, and the awareness   140
Of things ill done and done to others' harm
    Which once you took for exercise of virtue.
Then fools' approval stings, and honour stains.
From wrong to wrong the exasperated spirit
    Proceeds, unless restored by that refining fire   145
    Where you must move in measure, like a dancer."[7]
The day was breaking. In the disfigured street
    He left me, with a kind of valediction,
And faded on the blowing of the horn.[8]

III

There are three conditions which often look alike[9]   150
Yet differ completely, flourish in the same hedgerow:
Attachment to self and to things and to persons, detachment
From self and from things and from persons; and, growing between
    them, indifference
    Which resembles the others as death resembles life,
Being between two lives—unflowering, between   155
The live and the dead nettle. This is the use of memory:
For liberation—not less of love but expanding
Of love beyond desire, and so liberation
From the future as well as the past. Thus, love of a country
Begins as attachment to our own field of action   160
And comes to find that action of little importance
Though never indifferent. History may be servitude,
History may be freedom. See, now they vanish,
The faces and places, with the self which, as it could, loved them,
    To become renewed, transfigured, in another pattern.   165

Sin is Behovely, but
All shall be well, and
All manner of thing shall be well.[10]
If I think, again, of this place,
And of people, not wholly commendable,   170
Of no immediate kin or kindness,
But some of peculiar genius,

---

[7]The spirit moving "in measure" in a "refining fire" recalls especially "Sailing to Byzantium" and "Byzantium," by Yeats, the poet who in Eliot's time wrote most memorably of the problems of aging. Cf. also "Vacillation." Yeats had died in 1939.   [8]The all-clear signal. The ghost of Hamlet's father disappears in similar fashion: "It faded on the crowing of the cock" (*Hamlet*, I, i, 157).
[9]The thought here owes much to the *Bhagavad-Gita*, which Eliot considered "the next greatest philosophical poem" to *The Divine Comedy*. See especially, in the translation by Swami Prabhavananda and Christopher Isherwood, parts V, VI, XIV, XVIII.   [10]Three lines from *Revelations of Divine Love*, by Dame Julian of Norwich, a fourteenth-century English mystic. Her vision shows the pain resulting from sin as a necessary step toward self-knowledge.

All touched by a common genius,
United in the strife which divided them;
If I think of a king at nightfall,[11]   175
Of three men, and more, on the scaffold
And a few who died forgotten
In other places, here and abroad,
And of one who died blind and quiet,[12]
Why should we celebrate   180
These dead men more than the dying?
It is not to ring the bell backward
Nor is it an incantation
To summon the spectre of a Rose.[13]
We cannot revive old factions   185
We cannot restore old policies
Or follow an antique drum.
These men, and those who opposed them
And those whom they opposed
Accept the constitution of silence   190
And are folded in a single party.
Whatever we inherit from the fortunate
We have taken from the defeated
What they had to leave us—a symbol:
A symbol perfected in death.   195
And all shall be well and
All manner of thing shall be well
By the purification of the motive
In the ground of our beseeching.[14]

IV

The dove descending breaks the air   200
With flame of incandescent terror
Of which the tongues declare
The one discharge from sin and error.
The only hope, or else despair
   Lies in the choice of pyre or pyre—   205
   To be redeemed from fire by fire.

Who then devised the torment? Love.
Love is the unfamiliar Name
Behind the hands that wove
The intolerable shirt of flame   210
Which human power cannot remove.[15]

[11]Charles I.   [12]John Milton.   [13]Specifically, the rose, in various forms, long associated with the English royalty dethroned with the beheading of Charles I (1649). The reference recalls, however, the rose's traditional symbolic value as an emblem of earthly beauty (cf. 1. 55) and its use, in Dante and at the end of this poem, as a symbol of eternity.   [14]Dame Julian, after fifteen years of searching, discovered that "the ground of our beseeching" is "Love," Cf. 1. 207.

We only live, only suspire
Consumed by either fire or fire.

V

What we call the beginning is often the end[16]
And to make an end is to make a beginning.   215
The end is where we start from. And every phrase
And sentence that is right (where every word is at home,
Taking its place to support the others,
The word neither diffident nor ostentatious,
An easy commerce of the old and the new,   220
The common word exact without vulgarity,
The formal word precise but not pedantic,
The complete consort dancing together)
Every phrase and every sentence is an end and a beginning,
Every poem an epitaph. And any action   225
Is a step to the block, to the fire, down the sea's throat
Or to an illegible stone: and that is where we start.
We die with the dying:
See, they depart, and we go with them.
We are born with the dead: 230
See, they return, and bring us with them.
The moment of the rose and the moment of the yew-tree[17]
Are of equal duration. A people without history
Is not redeemed from time, for history is a pattern
Of timeless moments. So, while the light fails   235
On a winter's afternoon, in a secluded chapel
History is now and England.

With the drawing of this Love and the voice of this Calling[18]

We shall not cease from exploration
And the end of all our exploring   240
Will be to arrive where we started
And know the place for the first time.
Through the unknown, remembered gate
When the last of earth left to discover
Is that which was the beginning;   245

[15]Deianira hoped to regain the love of her husband, Hercules, by giving him a shirt stained with the blood of Nessus. The shirt burst into flames, adhering to the skin as Hercules tore at it. Badly burned, he had himself immolated on a funeral pyre.   [16]Cf. "In my beginning is my end" and "In my end is my beginning," the first and last words of Eliot's *East Coker.*   [17]Simply, the rose is a symbol of transient life, the yew-tree a symbol of death.   [18]A line from an anonymous fourteenth-century religious work, *The Cloud of Unknowing.* The book takes its title from the "cloud" that surrounds human effort, save as God's light breaks through. Cf. the darkness and pentecostal fire of this poem.

At the source of the longest river
The voice of the hidden waterfall
And the children in the apple-tree
Not known, because not looked for
But heard, half-heard, in the stillness   250
Between two waves of the sea.
Quick now, here, now, always—[19]
A condition of complete simplicity
(Costing not less than everything)
And all shall be well and   255
All manner of thing shall be well
When the tongues of flame are in-folded
Into the crowned knot of fire
And the fire and the rose are one.[20]

---

[19]By repeating here the third-from-the-last line of the first *Quartet, Burnt Norton,* Eliot stresses an idea that is important to all four poems and to his work as a whole. All times meet in the present moment, which is the moment of intersection with eternity.   [20]Cf. Dante's *Paradiso,* XXXIII, in which all the disparate elements of the universe are gathered by the force of love into "un semplice lume," one simple flame. Dante's lines, wrote Eliot, attain "the highest point that poetry has ever reached or ever can reach."

The fourth of T. S. Eliot's *Four Quartets, Little Gidding* is the last major poem of one of the twentieth-century's most accomplished poets. Eliot was fifty-four in 1942, when *Little Gidding* was first published. Undergirding the poem is a carefully nurtured poetic skill first apparent twenty-five years earlier in *Prufrock and Other Observations.* Supporting it also is a philosophic and religious stance thoughtfully developed in a number of prose essays and shaped in poetic form especially vivid in *The Waste Land, Ash-Wednesday* and the three earlier *Quartets. Little Gidding* is in addition constructed solidly upon the conditions of the immediate time and place in which it was written. In 1942 Eliot lived and worked in wartime in a London that had learned to accept the explosions and fires of German bombs as a recurring part of ordinary existence. Out of the materials of incoherence and despair Eliot built a shapely monument of affirmation.

Although the atmosphere of World War II surrounds the poem, the confusion and destruction enter its lines directly only in the second section of part II, where an air raid warden on a dawn patrol "After the dark dove with the flickering tongue / Had passed below the horizon of his homing" meets and converses with a "dead master" in the calm preceding the blowing of the all-clear signal. The rest of the poem builds toward and falls away from this structural midpoint. The poem's beginning takes us miles into the English countryside and centuries into the past; the end takes us out of time and place entirely, enfolding all that has happened and will happen into "the fire and the rose" of eternity.

Part I

In Part I the poet meditates upon a midwinter visit to Little Gidding, the site of an Anglican religious community founded in 1625 and destroyed by Puritans not long after. In the nineteenth century a chapel was erected there. Into this now peaceful setting, seventy-five miles from London, the narrator has come seeking in a place "where prayer has been valid" a respite from the turmoil of his everyday existence. In passages structurally kin (as the entire poem is) to the repetitions and thematic variations of a formal musical composition, the narrator considers the visit from three different perspectives.

The first twenty lines spring from the observation that the sun sometimes shines at its brightest even in the darkest days of winter, flaming in reflection from the ice. The snow mimics spring, forming blossoms on the hedges. In this spring which is not spring, ("not in time's convenant"), the narrator perceives the religious symbolism of "pentecostal fire / In the dark time of the year." These lines anticipate, thematically, the dark time in the second section of Part II: the dive bombers attacking London. The question "Where is the summer, the unimaginable / Zero summer?" applies to the destruction of Little Gidding, the bombing of London, and to the dark, midwinter time of an aging poet.

In the next group of lines the narrator adopts a "you" perspective, inviting the reader's participation in the meditation. "If you came this way" he says to himself, and also to the reader made sympathetic by the universal appeal of the problem with which the poem begins, "you would find the hedges / White again, in May." Then, paradoxically, you would find the same "If you came at night." The brightness that flames in midwinter, we begin to understand, is symbolic of a brightness not easily enclosed in any particular "husk of meaning." We travel to places like Little Gidding for reasons that we do not fully understand, seeking to fulfill purposes that are "altered in fulfilment." In other times we might have sought answers in places other than this particular "world's end," but this one is convenient and will serve.

The next section is more general in its description of need and more specific in its suggestion of remedy. It does not matter where you come from or when you come. All the world's problems drive toward one solution: the validity of the kind of prayer that breaks through the boundaries of sense to arrive at "the intersection of the timeless moment" that is "never and always." Through prayerful communion with the dead, we learn that

> . . . what the dead had no speech for, when living,
> They can tell you, being dead: the communication
> Of the dead is tongued with fire beyond the language of the living.

Reminding us of the inadequacy of language to deal effectively with our most deeply felt needs, the narrator prepares us for his predawn meeting with the dead master.

Part II

Part II begins with a lyric on the death of the four elements that the ancients saw as the structural building blocks of the universe: air, earth, water, and fire. In three carefully metered and rhyming stanzas, the poet describes the end of those attributes of existence that humans care most for, both those that possess physical being (roses, houses, eyes and mouths, towns and pastures) and those that exist as abstract ambitions or fears (hope, despair, toil, sacrifice). The key word is the "vanity" of the second stanza, carrying with it centuries of biblical and literary associations. "Vanity of vanities, saith the Preacher, vanity of vanities; all is vanity" (Eccles. 1.2). The reader steeped in Eliot will see in the symbols of the passage a number of insistent echoes from earlier poems: the "lonely men in shirtsleeves" of *The Love Song of J. Alfred Prufrock,* the dust and watery death of *The Waste Land,* the Rose, the Garden, and the sand of *Ash-Wednesday,* the rose garden and dust of *Burnt Norton,* the house, wainscot, and mouse of *East Coker,* the "ground swell" of the sea and the "significant soil" of *The Dry Salvages.* Eliot here mourns and at the same celebrates the termination of all things earthly, including his own poetic endeavor in his lifetime.

The air raid section follows. Walking before dawn through streets deserted in the wake of the latest bombing, the narrator meets and converses with "some dead master," a composite figure modeled upon Dante, Yeats, and other individuals important to Eliot. The section moves in three-line units of careful iambic pentameter, with alternate feminine and masculine endings: not precisely the *terza rima* of Dante's *Divine Comedy,* but a meticulous adaptation to suit the requirements of twentieth-century English. The darkness before dawn, the surrounding smoke, the timeless meeting with an individual recognized and yet not recognized evoke especially the atmosphere of the *Inferno,* in which Dante converses with individuals long dead. After the death of the world contemplated in the preceding lyric, these lines compel the narrator to consider the death of his poetic voice (for "next year's words await another voice") and turn his attention to the disappointments of age. Faced with "expiring sense," "the conscious impotence of rage," and "the rending pain of re-enactment / Of all that you have done, and been," the aging poet can be restored to vitality only by the "refining fire" of eternity, celebrated in both Eastern and Western religions, that envelops and transcends the fires of this temporal world.

Part III

In the first section of Part III Eliot summarizes some of the most important teachings of the *Bhagavad-Gita,* the Hindu religious text that served him also as a major source for the discussion that dominates the last half of *The Dry Salvages,* setting the stage in that work for the intellectual and religious stance of *Little Gidding.* In the lines of this poem there is no direct reference to the plight of Arjuna or the response of Krishna, but instead a transformation of Eastern teachings to suit a Western setting. The "three conditions which often look alike" characterize reactions theoretically possible to the poet contemplating the memory of the destroyed Anglican religious community, the present reality of the bombing of London, and his own inevitable aging and death. Between the sensual "attachment to self and to things and to persons" characteristic of much earthly life and the spiritual detachment necessary as a preparation for eternal salvation, there lies the emptiness of indifference, "which resembles the others as death resembles life." Only by retaining a delicate tension between love for "faces and places" and acceptance of the knowledge that ultimately "they vanish" can we learn to accept "our own field of action" as necessary to an eternal order "renewed, transfigured, in another pattern."

All things come to the same end and that end is good. That, in essence, is the message of the second section of Part III, but it includes also the important corollary that all things tending toward that end are also good because they are part of a timeless order inscrutable to humans encapsulated in the particulars of their times and places. "Sin is Behovely": so wrote the fourteenth-century English mystic Julian of Norwich, meaning by that phrase that sin, too, has a necessary place in the Divine Plan. In the lines that follow, the poet applies that thought to the war that long ago destroyed Little Gidding, preparing himself and the reader for the application of it, in Part IV, to the bombing of London in his own time. Charles I is the king we are asked to remember. He was beheaded, just as Little Gidding was destroyed, in the civil and religious strife that tore England apart in the seventeenth century. Others died as he did, publicly, "on the scaffold," while still others "died forgotten." Milton, a poet much embroiled in politics, "died blind and quiet." Yet Eliot asks us to consider that however much we regret the past we cannot change it: "We cannot revive old factions / We cannot restore old policies." More important, the men who followed their different opinions to destructive ends in the seventeenth century now "Accept the constitution of silence/And are folded in a single party." The rose, symbolic in life of English factionalism, stands in death as a symbol of the perfection of eternity. In the last two lines of this section the poet adds an important qualification to the idea that "All shall be well"; the motives of our human actions must be purified through prayers arising from love.

Part IV

In the first of these two lyric stanzas Eliot returns to the London of 1942. Applying the lesson of the preceding section, he merges the image of the bombers with the image of the Pentecostal Holy Ghost, with its "tongues like as of fire" (Acts 2.3). We may be redeemed from earthly fire only by the fire of God's love. The second stanza enforces the point. Hercules' "intolerable shirt of flame," although intended as a gift of human love, caused him a pain relieved only when he placed himself upon his own funeral pyre. The public fires of London and the private fires of Hercules are as one in the all-consuming, all-redeeming fire of eternity. Humanity's only hope, as opposed to our otherwise inevitable despair, resides in our ability to make an active choice of the eternal fire that offers "The one discharge from sin and error."

Part V

Defining his choices through his words, the poet seeks always that identification with the timeless that came to the apostles when, inspired with the Holy Ghost, they began to "speak with other tongues" (Acts 2.4). Caught in the here and now, he strives toward the wisdom half-grasped in the speech of the dead master, that "communication" of Part I that "is tongued with fire beyond the language of the living." Struggling toward truth, he discovers that "Every phrase and every sentence is an end and a beginning, / Every poem an epitaph." Paradoxically, humanity can reach through to eternity only by living each moment now, for it is only within time that we come to know the timeless. "We die with the dying. . . . We are born with the dead." At the end of the first section of Part V, the light that bursts forth in midwinter in Little Gidding at the beginning of the poem now "fails" on that same "winter's afternoon," but only to remind the poet that there is no escaping from the present. "History is now and England."

Nor is there any escaping from the work of the present. The "Love" and "Calling" in a line borrowed from a fourteenth-century religious work foreshadow the active commitment required of us in the poem's summation. Just as all time is one time, so all movement forward takes us but to the place where we began. Eliot here echoes earlier movements in the *Four Quartets:* the gate into the rose garden remembered from *Burnt Norton,* the concern with beginnings and ends that runs through *East Coker,* the sea waves of *The Dry Salvages.* More generally, the lines remind us of all beginnings: the children we once were, the voices of waterfalls heard but not yet seen, the sources of rivers—indeed, we should probably be reminded of the garden of Eden that was the world's first garden. In "the stillness / Between two waves," we are reminded of the silence and stability of eternity. Finally, "all shall be well" not in our earthly time, but in that time to come when all beginnings and endings and all manners of expression and activity "are in-folded / Into the crowned knot of fire / And the fire and the rose are one."

CHAPTER 9

TRADITIONAL THEMES

A *theme* is a recurring element of subject matter, a connective thread that sews together a number of other elements. A *theme* is also an insistent idea, a thought about the subject matter and not simply the matter itself. In some poems, subject matter and thought about subject matter are essentially the same. In discussing others, however, precise distinctions between *thematic material* and *thematic idea* are helpful. In a poem about death, for instance, the thematic material might be recurring references to dead leaves or withered flowers or the scent of chrysanthemums, and the thematic idea might be that death is a release or a termination of all existence.

Because subjects and ideas are limited, poets have returned frequently to a limited number of traditional thematic materials and ideas. The poet's experience may be new, of course. The writing may convey the excitement of discovery and the joys of emotional enlargement and intellectual enlightenment. A poem, said Robert Frost, "begins in delight and ends in wisdom." Yet, in a broad sense, innumerable writers have produced the delight and wisdom before. The new particulars illustrate the old truths anew and lead us to realize them anew. Great poetry celebrates both the new and the old at the same time. We can see a poem both in its own time and place and in the wider context of all times and places. The greater the poem, the more surely it joins the timeless company of the great ones on similar themes, and any thematic grouping will enhance our pleasure and understanding.

The following poems illustrate common poetic themes. As you read them, you will observe how different poems can be generated from similar materials. For study purposes, the questions to ask take us back to the earlier chapters of this book. What differences occur when one poet develops a theme through a lyric, another through a narrative? Which poems of a group exploit a dramatic situation most effectively or depend most on description of a character or creation of a persona? How does the language of one poem—its denotations and connotations, its allusions and ironies—distinguish it from others? Which poems explore similar themes through similar images, metaphors, or symbols? Which ones treat an old subject in strikingly original ways? Which are private and personal, which more public or historical in their references? Which invite allegorical interpretations? What are the differences between poems in their patterns of rhyme and meter? Which poets develop their thoughts through traditional structures—through couplets and quatrains or sonnets or other strict forms—and which attempt unfamiliar combinations or free verse? For which poems is a reader most helped by an enlarged understanding of the time and place in which they were written?

WHERE ARE THE SNOWS OF YESTERYEAR?

Ubi sunt qui ante nos fuerunt? wrote the medieval poets, again and again—"Where are those who were before us?" And *ubi sunt* has come to designate the whole group of poems lamenting the irrecoverable past. Each of the following poems asks the same question, by implication if not explicitly. The answers vary, of course, but the lamenting question remains, perhaps ultimately unanswerable.

The Ruin[1]

Wondrous this masonry   wasted by Fate!
Giant-built battlements   shattered and broken!
The roofs are in ruin,   the towers are wrecked,
The frost-covered bastions   battered and fallen.
Rime[2] whitens mortar;   the cracking walls 5
Have sagged and toppled,   weakened by Time.
The clasp of earth   and the clutch of the grave
Grip the proud builders,   long perished and gone,
While a hundred generations   have run.
Hoary with lichen   and ruddy of hue 10
This wall has outlasted,   unshaken by storm,
Reign after reign;   now ravaged and wrecked
The lofty arch   is leveled in ruin. . . .
   Firmly the builder   laid the foundations,
Cunningly bound them   with iron bands; 15
Stately the palaces,   splendid the baths,
Towers and pinnacles   pointing on high;

[1]This anonymous Old English poem presumably describes the Roman ruins at Bath.   [2]Frost.

Many a mead-hall   rang with their revelry,
Many a court   with the clangor of arms,
Till Fate the all-leveling   laid them low.   20
A pestilence rose   and corpses were rife,
And death laid hold   on the warrior-host.
    Then their bulwarks were broken,   their fortresses fell,
The hands to restore them   were helpless and still.
Desolate now are the courts,   and the dome,   25
With arches discolored,   is stripped of its tiles.
Where of old once the warrior   walked in his pride,
Gleaming with gold   and wanton with wine,
Splendidly shining   in glittering mail,
The structure lies fallen   and scattered in ruin.   30
Around him he saw   a treasure of silver,
Riches of pearl   and precious stones,
In a shining city   of far-flung sway.
There stood courts of stone,   with a gushing spring
Of boiling water   in welling floods,   35
And a wall embosomed   in gleaming embrace
The spot where the hot baths   burst into air.

Translated by Charles W. Kennedy

Ubi Sunt Qui Ante Nos Fuerunt?

Were beth they biforen us weren,	Where are those that were before us,
Houndes ladden and hauekes beren	Hounds led and hawks bore,
And hadden feld and wode?	And had field and wood?
The riche levedies in hoere bour,	The rich ladies in their bowers,
That wereden gold in hoere tressour,	That wore gold in their coiffures,
With hoere brightte rode,	With their bright faces, 6
Eten and drounken and maden hem glad;	Ate and drank and made themselves glad;
Hoere lif was al with gamen i-lad;	Their lives were all with pleasure led;
Men keneleden hem beforen;	Men knelt before them;
They beren hem wel swithe heye—	They bore themselves right haughtily—
And in a twincling of an eye	And in the twinkling of an eye
Hoere soules weren forloren.	Their souls were lost. 12
Were is that lawing and that song,	Where is that laughter and that song,
That trayling and that proude yong,	Those trailing garments and that proud gait,
Tho hauekes and tho houndes?	Those hawks and those hounds?
Al that joye is went away;	All that joy has gone away;
That wele is comen to welaway,	That wealth has come to wellaway,
To manie harde stoundes.	To many hard times. 18
Hoere paradis hy nomen here,	Their paradise they took here,
And nou they lien in helle i-fere—	And now they lie in hell together—
The fuir hit brennes hevere.	The fire it burns ever.
Long is ay and long is ho,	Long is aye and long is always,

Long is wy and long is wo—
  Thennes ne cometh they nevere.

Dreghy here, man, thenne if thou wilt,
A luitel pine, that me the bit.
  Withdrau thine eyes ofte.
They thi pine be ounrede,
And thou thenke on thi mede,
  Hit sal the thinken softe.

If that fend, that foule thing,
Thorou wikke roun, thorou fals egging,
  Nethere the haveth i-cast,
Oup, and be god chaunpioun!
Stond, ne fal namore adoun
  For a luytel blast.

Thou tak the rode to thi staf
And thenk on him that thereonne yaf
  His lif that wes so lef.
He hit yaf for the; thou yelde hit him
Ayein his fo. That staf thou nim
  And wrek him of that thef.

Of rightte bileve thou nim that sheld
The wiles that thou best in that feld.
  Thin hond to strenkthen fonde
And kep thy fo with staves ord
And do that traytre seien that word.
  Biget that murie londe

Thereinne is day withouten night,
Withouten ende strenkthe and might,
  And wreche of everich fo,
Mid god himselwen eche lif
And pes and rest withoute strif,
  Wele withouten wo.

Mayden moder, hevene quene,
Thou might and const and owest to bene
  Oure sheld ayein the fende,
Help ous sunne for to flen
That we moten thi sone i-seen
  In joye withouten hende.

Long is alas and long is woe—
  Thence they shall come never.   24

Endure here, man, then if thou wilt,
The little pain that thou art bid.
  Put away thy comforts often.
Though thy pain be hard,
If thou consider thy reward,
  Thou shalt think it soft.   30

If that fiend, that foul thing,
Through wicked counsel, through false tempting,
  Downward hast thee cast,
Up, and be a good champion!
Stand, and fall no more adown
  For a little blast.   36

Take thou the cross for thy staff,
And think on Him that thereon gave
  His life that was so lief.
He gave it for thee; repay it to Him
Against His foe. Take thou that staff
  And avenge Him on that thief.   42

Of right belief take thou the shield,
While thou art in the field;
  Seek to strengthen thy hand,
And keep thy foe at staff's end,
And make that traitor say surrender.
  Attain that pleasant land.   48

Therein is day without night,
Strength without end, and might,
  And vengeance on every foe;
With God himself eternal life,
And peace and rest without strife,
  Well-being without woe.   54

Maiden mother, heaven's queen,
Thou might and can and ought to be
  Our shield against the fiend.
Help us sin to flee,
That we may thy son see
  In joy without end.   60

Translated by George Perkins

The Ballad of Dead Ladies

François Villon   *(1431–?)*

Tell me now in what hidden way is
  Lady Flora[1] the lovely Roman?
Where's Hipparchia,[2] and where is Thais,[3]

[1]A courtesan mentioned by Juvenal. [2]Identity uncertain. [3]A courtesan who followed Alexander the Great.

Neither of them the fairer woman?   4
  Where is Echo,[4] beheld of no man,
Only heard on river and mere,—
  She whose beauty was more than human? . . .
But where are the snows of yester-year?   8

Where's Héloise,[5] the learned nun,
  For whose sake Abeillard, I ween,
Lost manhood and put priesthood on?
  (From Love he won such dule and teen!)[6]   12
  And where, I pray you, is the Queen
Who willed that Buridan should steer
  Sewed in a sack's mouth down the Seine?[7] . . .
But where are the snows of yester-year?   16

White Queen Blanche,[8] like a queen of lilies,
  With a voice like any mermaiden—
Bertha Broadfoot, Beatrice, Alice,[9]
  And Ermengarde the lady of Maine,[10]—   20
  And that good Joan[11] whom Englishmen
At Rouen doomed and burned her there,—
  Mother of God, where are they then? . . .
But where are the snows of yester-year?   24

Nay, never ask this week, fair lord,
  Where they are gone, nor yet this year,
Except with this for an overword,—
  But where are the snows of yester-year?   28

Translated by D. G. Rossetti

---

[4]Nymph of Greek myth, who pined away for unrequited love, leaving only a voice.   [5]Héloise and Abélard: famous twelfth-century lovers.   [6]Servitude and grief.   [7]According to legend, Buridan (a fourteenth-century professor at the University of Paris) paid in this manner for his love of Jeanne de Navarre.   [8]Blanche de Castille.   [9]Three heroines of *Hervi de Metz,* a medieval *chanson de geste.*   [10]Twelfth-century heiress of the French province.   [11]Of Arc.

With Rue My Heart Is Laden

A. E. Housman   (1859–1936)

With rue my heart is laden
  For golden friends I had,
For many a rose-lipt maiden
  And many a lightfoot lad.   4

By brooks too broad for leaping
  The lightfoot boys are laid;
The rose-lipt girls are sleeping
  In fields where roses fade.   **8**

Calmly We Walk Through This April's Day

Delmore Schwartz   *(1913–1966)*

Calmly we walk through this April's day,
Metropolitan poetry here and there,
In the park sit pauper and *rentier,*[1]
The screaming children, the motor-car
Fugitive about us, running away,   **5**
Between the worker and the millionaire
Number provides all distances,
It is Nineteen Thirty-Seven now,
Many great dears are taken away,
What will become of you and me   **10**
(This is the school in which we learn . . .)
Besides the photo and the memory?
(. . . that time is the fire in which we burn.)

(This is the school in which we learn . . .)
What is the self amid this blaze?   **15**
What am I now that I was then
Which I shall suffer and act again,
The theodicy[2] I wrote in my high school days
Restored all life from infancy,
The children shouting are bright as they run   **20**
(This is the school in which they learn . . .)
Ravished entirely in their passing play!
(. . . that time is the fire in which they burn.)

Avid its rush, that reeling blaze!
Where is my father and Eleanor?   **25**
Not where are they now, dead seven years,
But what they were then?
                  No more? No more?
From Nineteen-Fourteen to the present day,
Bert Spira and Rhoda consume, consume
Not where they are now (where are they now?)   **30**
But what they were then, both beautiful;

[1]A stockholder. [2]A vindication of God's permitting evil to exist.

Each minute bursts in the burning room,
The great globe reels in the solar fire,
Spinning the trivial and unique away.
(How all things flash! How all things flare!)   35
What am I now that I was then?
May memory restore again and again
The smallest color of the smallest day:
Time is the school in which we learn,
Time is the fire in which we burn.   40

THE VANITY OF HUMAN WISHES

We never cease wishing, though we wish in vain, and what we gain we may
lose or not like after all. We can be certain of nothing except the passing of time
and of life. These ideas have been common in poetry from earliest times: "Vanity
of vanities, saith the Preacher, vanity of vanities; all is vanity" (Eccles. 1.2).

What If a Day, or a Month, or a Year

Thomas Campion   *(1567–1620)*

What if a day, or a month, or a year
Crown thy delights with a thousand sweet contentings?
Cannot a chance of a night or an hour
Cross thy desires with as many sad tormentings?   4
   Fortune, honor, beauty, youth
   Are but blossoms dying;
   Wanton pleasure, doting love,
   Are but shadows flying.   8
   All our joys are but toys,
   Idle thoughts deceiving;
   None have power of an hour
   In their lives' bereaving.   12

Earth's but a point to the world, and a man
Is but a point to the world's compared ceinture[1]
Shall then a point of a point be so vain
As to triumph in a seely[2] points adventure?   16
   All is hazard that we have,
   There is nothing biding;
   Days of pleasure are like streams
   Through fair meadows gliding.   20
   Weal and woe, time doth go,

---

[1]Belt, girdle.   [2]Wretched.

Time is never turning:
Secret fates guide our states,
Both in mirth and mourning.   24

A Litany in Time of Plague

Thomas Nashe   *(1567–1601)*

Adieu, farewell, earth's bliss;
This world uncertain is;
Fond[1] are life's lustful joys;
Death proves them all but toys;
None from his darts can fly;   5
I am sick, I must die.
   Lord, have mercy on us!

Rich men, trust not in wealth,
Gold cannot buy you health;
Physic himself must fade.   10
All things to end are made,
The plague full swift goes by;
I am sick, I must die
   Lord, have mercy on us!

Beauty is but a flower   15
Which wrinkles will devour;
Brightness falls from the air;
Queens have died young and fair;
Dust hath closed Helen's[2] eye.
I am sick, I must die.   20
   Lord, have mercy on us!

Strength stoops unto the grave,
Worms feed on Hector[3] brave;
Swords may not fight with fate,
Earth still holds ope her gate.   25
"Come, come!" the bells do cry.
I am sick, I must die.
   Lord, have mercy on us.

Wit with his wantonness
Tasteth death's bitterness;   30
Hell's executioner
Hath no ears for to hear
What vain art can reply.

[1]Foolish. [2]Helen of Troy. [3]A Trojan hero.

I am sick, I must die.
   Lord, have mercy on us.   35

Haste, therefore, each degree,
To welcome destiny;
Heaven is our heritage,
Earth but a player's stage;
Mount we unto the sky.   40
I am sick, I must die.
   Lord, have mercy on us.

A Palinode[1]

Edmund Bolton   (c. 1575–c. 1633)

As withereth the primrose by the river,
As fadeth summer's sun from gliding fountains,
As vanisheth the light-blown bubble ever,
As melteth snow upon the mossy mountains: 4
So melts, so vanisheth, so fades, so withers
The rose, the shine, the bubble, and the snow,
Of praise, pomp, glory, joy, which short life gathers,
Fair praise, vain pomp, sweet glory, brittle joy.   8
The withered primrose by the mourning river,
The faded summer's sun from weeping fountains,
The light-blown bubble, vanishéd for ever,
The molten snow upon the naked mountains,   12
   Are emblems that the treasures we uplay
   Soon wither, vanish, fade, and melt away.

For as the snow, whose lawn did overspread
Th' ambitious hills which giant-like did threat   16
To pierce the heaven with their aspiring head,
Naked and bare doth leave their craggy seat;
Whenas the bubble, which did empty fly
The dalliance of the undiscernéd wind   20
On whose calm rolling waves it did rely,
Hath shipwreck made where it did dalliance find;
And when the sunshine which dissolved the snow,
Colored the bubble with a pleasant vary,[2]   24
And made the rathe[3] and timely primrose grow,
Swarth[4] clouds withdrawn, which longer time do tarry:

[1]A song of retraction or recantation.   [2]Variation.   [3]Eager.   [4]Dark, swarthy.

Oh, what is praise, pomp, glory, joy, but so
As shine by fountains, bubbles, flowers, or snow?   28

Elegy Written in a Country Churchyard

Thomas Gray   *(1716–1771)*

The curfew tolls the knell of parting day,
   The lowing herd wind slowly o'er the lea,[1]
The plowman homeward plods his weary way,
   And leaves the world to darkness and to me.   4

Now fades the glimmering landscape on the sight,
   And all the air a solemn stillness holds,
Save where the beetle wheels his droning flight,
   And drowsy tinklings lull the distant folds;   8

Save that from yonder ivy-mantled tower
   The moping owl does to the moon complain
Of such, as wandering near her secret bower,
   Molest her ancient solitary reign.   12

Beneath those rugged elms, that yew tree's shade,
   Where heaves the turf in many a moldering heap,
Each in his narrow cell forever laid,
   The rude forefathers of the hamlet sleep.   16

The breezy call of incense-breathing Morn,
   The swallow twittering from the straw-built shed,
The cock's shrill clarion, or the echoing horn,[2]
   No more shall rouse them from their lowly bed.   20

For them no more the blazing hearth shall burn,
Or busy housewife ply her evening care;
No children run to lisp their sire's return,
   Or climb his knees the envied kiss to share.   24

Oft did the harvest to their sickle yield,
   Their furrow oft the stubborn glebe[3] has broke;
How jocund did they drive their team afield!
   How bowed the woods beneath their sturdy stroke!   28

Let not Ambition mock their useful toil,
   Their homely joys, and destiny obscure;
Nor Grandeur hear with a disdainful smile
   The short and simple annals of the poor.   32

[1]Pasture. [2]Hunter's horn. [3]Soil.

The boast of heraldry, the pomp of power,
   And all that beauty, all that wealth e'er gave,
Awaits alike the inevitable hour.
   The paths of glory lead but to the grave.   **36**

Nor you, ye proud, impute to these the fault,
   If Memory o'er their tomb no trophies[4] raise,
Where through the long-drawn aisle and fretted[5] vault
   The pealing anthem swells the note of praise.   **40**

Can storied urn or animated bust[6]
   Back to its mansion call the fleeting breath?
Can Honor's voice provoke[7] the silent dust,
   Or Flattery soothe the dull cold ear of Death?   **44**

Perhaps in this neglected spot is laid
   Some heart once pregnant with celestial fire;
Hands that the rod of empire might have swayed,
   Or waked to ecstasy the living lyre.   **48**

But Knowledge to their eyes her ample page
   Rich with the spoils of time did ne'er unroll;
Chill Penury repressed their noble rage,
   And froze the genial current of the soul.   **52**

Full many a gem of purest ray serene,
   The dark unfathomed caves of ocean bear:
Full many a flower is born to blush unseen,
   And waste its sweetness on the desert air.   **56**

Some village Hampden,[8] that with dauntless breast
   The little tyrant of his fields withstood;
Some mute inglorious Milton[9] here may rest,
   Some Cromwell[10] guiltless of his country's blood.   **60**

The applause of listening senates to command,
   The threats of pain and ruin to despise,
To scatter plenty o'er a smiling land,
   And read their history in a nation's eyes,   **64**

Their lot forbade: nor circumscribed alone
   Their growing virtues, but their crimes confined;
Forbade to wade through slaughter to a throne,
   And shut the gates of mercy on mankind,   **68**

---

[4]For example, memorials celebrating the triumphs of military heroes.   [5]Ornamented with intersecting bars.   [6]An urn with a narrative epitaph or a lifelike bust.   [7]Call forth.   [8]John Hampden (1597–1643), a hero of the English Civil War.   [9]John Milton (1608–1674), an English poet. [10]Oliver Cromwell (1599–1658), a soldier and statesman.

The struggling pangs of conscious truth to hide,
    To quench the blushes of ingenuous shame,
Or heap the shrine of Luxury and Pride
    With incense kindled at the Muse's flame.   72

Far from the madding crowd's ignoble strife,
    Their sober wishes never learned to stray;
Along the cool sequestered vale of life
    They kept the noiseless tenor of their way.   76

Yet even these bones from insult to protect
    Some frail memorial still erected nigh,
With uncouth rhymes and shapeless sculpture decked,
    Implores the passing tribute of a sigh.   80

Their name, their years, spelt by the unlettered Muse,
    The place of fame and elegy supply:
And many a holy text around she strews,
    That teach the rustic moralist to die.   84

For who to dumb Forgetfulness a prey,
    This pleasing anxious being e'er resigned,
Left the warm precincts of the cheerful day,
    Nor cast one longing lingering look behind?   88

On some fond breast the parting soul relies,
    Some pious drops the closing eye requires;
Even from the tomb the voice of Nature cries,
    Even in our ashes live their wonted fires.   92

For thee, who mindful of the unhonored dead
    Dost in these lines their artless tale relate;
If chance, by lonely contemplation led,
    Some kindred spirit shall inquire thy fate,   96

Haply some hoary-headed swain may say,
    "Oft have we seen him at the peep of dawn
Brushing with hasty steps the dews away
    To meet the sun upon the upland lawn.   100

"There at the foot of yonder nodding beech
    That wreathes its old fantastic roots so high,
His listless length at noontide would he stretch,
    And pore upon the brook that babbles by.   104

"Hard by yon wood, now smiling as in scorn,
    Muttering his wayward fancies he would rove,
Now drooping, woeful wan, like one forlorn,
    Or crazed with care, or crossed in hopeless love.   108

"One morn I missed him on the customed hill,
   Along the heath and near his favorite tree;
Another came; nor yet beside the rill,
   Nor up the lawn, nor at the wood was he;   112

"The next with dirges due in sad array
   Slow through the churchway path we saw him borne.
Approach and read (for thou canst read) the lay,
   Graved on the stone beneath yon aged thorn."   116

The Epitaph

Here rests his head upon the lap of Earth
   A youth to Fortune and to Fame unknown.
Fair Science[11] *frowned not on his humble birth,*
   And Melancholy marked him for her own.   120

Large was his bounty, and his soul sincere,
   Heaven did a recompense as largely send:
He gave to Misery all he had, a tear,
   He gained from Heaven ('twas all he wished) a friend.   124

No farther seek his merits to disclose,
   Or draw his frailties from their dread abode
(There they alike in trembling hope repose),
   The bosom of his Father and his God.   128

[11]Learning.

Hamatreya[1]

Ralph Waldo Emerson   *(1803–1882)*

Bulkeley, Hunt, Willard, Hosmer, Meriam, Flint,[2]
Possessed the land which rendered to their toil
Hay, corn, roots, hemp, flax, apples, wool and wood.
Each of these landlords walked amidst his farm,
Saying, "Tis mine, my children's and my name's.   5
How sweet the west wind sounds in my own trees!
How graceful climb those shadows on my hill!
I fancy these pure waters and the flags
Know me, as does my dog: we sympathize;
And, I affirm, my actions smack of the soil.'   10
Where are these men? Asleep beneath their grounds:

[1]The poem is based on a passage in the *Vishnu Purana,* a Hindu religious work, in which Maitreya (Hamatreya) is taught an "Earth Song" similar to Emerson's.   [2]Early settlers of Concord, Mass.

And strangers, fond as they, their furrows plough.
Earth laughs in flowers, to see her boastful boys
Earth-proud, proud of the earth which is not theirs;
Who steer the plough, but cannot steer their feet   15
Clear of the grave.
They added ridge to valley, brook to pond,
And sighed for all that bounded their domain;
'This suits me for a pasture; that's my park;
We must have clay, lime, gravel, granite-ledge,   20
And misty lowland, where to go for peat.
The land is well,—lies fairly to the south.
'T is good, when you have crossed the sea and back,
To find the sitfast acres where you left them.'
Ah! the hot owner sees not Death, who adds   25
Him to his land, a lump of mould the more.
Hear what the Earth says:—

Earth-Song

'Mine and yours;
Mine, not yours.
Earth endures;   30
Stars abide—
Shine down in the old sea;
Old are the shores;
But where are old men?
I who have seen much,   35
Such have I never seen.

'The lawyer's deed
Ran sure,
In tail,
To them, and to their heirs   40
Who shall succeed,
Without fail,
Forevermore.

'Here is the land,
Shaggy with wood,   45
With its old valley,
Mound and flood.
But the heritors?—

Fled like the flood's foam.
The lawyer, and the laws,   50
And the kingdom,
Clean swept herefrom.

'They called me theirs,
Who so controlled me;
Yet every one   55
Wished to stay, and is gone,
How am I theirs,
If they cannot hold me,
But I hold them?'

When I heard the Earth-song   60
I was no longer brave;
My avarice cooled
Like lust in the chill of the grave.

SEIZE THE DAY

Carpe diem, quam minimum credula postero—"seize today, and trust tomorrow little"—wrote Horace (*Odes* I, xi, 8), giving a name and an attitude to a
whole class of poems: *carpe diem*. Since life is short, we must grasp what
pleasures we have. This is the poetry of youth, especially of the youth persuading
his girl to join him.

Lesbia

(Catullus No. 5)

Catullus   (84?–54? B.C.)

Let's live, my Lesbia, and love.
For sour old murmurs we won't give
One cent. Suns set and still can rise,
But once our little daylight dies   4
We sleep one never-ending night.
Give me a thousand kisses straight,
Then a hundred, then another
Thousand with a hundred smother.
Thousands, a hundred—thousands more   8
We'll make, mix, and forget before
Some evil eye gets envious,
Knowing how many times we kiss.[1]   12

Translated by Sheridan Baker

---

[1]Knowing the exact number of anything enabled a person to *invidere:* to envy and to cast an evil
eye, bringing bad luck. So Catullus not only rushes his thousands and hundreds, but also wants

the lovers themselves to lose count, to be doubly safe (and doubly happy). In prose, line for line, this famous poem translates: "Let us live, my Lesbia, and let us love./And let us estimate the murmurs of the severe old people at one [very small coin]./Suns can set (die) and come back:/ For us, when once the brief light sets (dies),/One perpetual night must be slept./Gimme a thousand kisses,* then a hundred,/Then another thousand, then a second hundred,/Then all the way to another thousand, then a hundred,/Then, when we will have made many thousands,/We will stir them all to confusion, so we will not know,/Or so someone bad cannot look with the evil eye,/When he will know how many there are of kisses."

---

*Catullus's *Da mi basia mille* is apparently intimate slang, with *basia,* for *kisses,* appearing for the first time in recorded Latin.

My Sweetest Lesbia*

Thomas Campion   (1567–1620)

My sweetest Lesbia, let us live and love,
And, though the sager sort our deeds reprove,
Let us not weigh them: heaven's great lamps do dive
Into their west, and straight again revive,
But, soon as once set is our little light,
Then must we sleep one ever-during night.   6

If all would lead their lives in love like me,
Then bloody swords and armor should not be;
No drum nor trumpet peaceful sleeps should move,
Unless alarm came from the camp of love:
But fools do live, and waste their little light,
And seek with pain their ever-during night.   12

When timely death my life and fortune ends,
Let not my hearse be vexed with mourning friends,
But let all lovers, rich in triumph, come,
And with sweet pastimes grace my happy tomb;
And, Lesbia, close up thou my little light,
And crown with love my ever-during night.   18

*Based upon and partly translated from Catullus No. 5, with some influence from Propertius.

Fragment

On the Back of the ms. of Canto I.

George Gordon, Lord Byron   (1788–1824)

I would to Heaven that I were so much clay,
    As I am blood, bone, marrow, passion, feeling—
Because at least the past were passed away,
    And for the future—(but I write this reeling,

Having got drunk exceedingly to-day,
  So that I seem to stand upon the ceiling)
I say—the future is a serious matter—
And so—for God's sake—hock[1] and soda-water!   8

[1]White Rhine wine.

To the Virgins, to Make Much of Time

Robert Herrick   (1591–1624)

Gather ye rosebuds while ye may,
  Old time is still a-flying:
And this same flower that smiles today,
  Tomorrow will be dying.   4

The glorious lamp of heaven, the sun,
  The higher he's a-getting;
The sooner will his race be run,
  And nearer he's to setting.   8

That age is best which is the first,
  When youth and blood are warmer;
But being spent, the worse, and worst
  Times, still succeed the former.   12

Then be not coy, but use your time;
  And while ye may, go marry:
For having lost but once your prime,
  You may forever tarry.   16

Corinna's Going A-Maying

Robert Herrick   (1591–1624)

Get up! get up for shame! the blooming morn
Upon her wings presents the god unshorn.[1]
  See how Aurora[2] throws her fair
  Fresh-quilted colors through the air:
  Get up, sweet slug-a-bed, and see   5
  The dew bespangling herb and tree.
Each flower has wept and bowed toward the east
Above an hour since, yet you not dressed;
  Nay, not so much as out of bed?
  When all the birds have matins[3] said,   10

[1]Apollo, god of the sun, with his streaming rays. [2]Goddess of the dawn. [3]Morning prayers.

And sung their thankful hymns, 'tis sin,
Nay, profanation to keep in,
Whenas a thousand virgins on this day
Spring, sooner than the lark, to fetch in May.[4]

Rise, and put on your foliage, and be seen   15
To come forth, like the springtime, fresh and green,
And sweet as Flora.[5] Take no care
For jewels for your gown or hair;
Fear not; the leaves will strew
Gems in abundance upon you;   20
Besides, the childhood of the day has kept,
Against you come, some orient pearls[6] unwept;
Come and receive them while the light
Hangs on the dew-locks of the night,
And Titan[7] on the eastern hill   25
Retires himself, or else stands still
Till you come forth. Wash, dress, be brief in praying:
Few beads[8] are best when once we go a-Maying.

Come, my Corinna, come; and, coming, mark
How each field turns a street, each street a park   30
Made green and trimmed with trees; see how
Devotion gives each house a bough
Or branch: each porch, each door ere this,
An ark, a tabernacle is,[9]
Made up of whitethorn neatly interwove,   35
As if here were those cooler shades of love.
Can such delights be in the street
And open fields, and we not see 't?
Come, we'll abroad; and let's obey
The proclamation made for May,   40
And sin no more, as we have done, by staying;
But, my Corinna, come, let's go a-Maying.

There's not a budding boy or girl this day
But is got up and gone to bring in May;
A deal of youth, ere this, is come   45
Back, and with whitethorn laden home.
Some have dispatched their cakes and cream
Before that we have left to dream;
And some have wept and wooed, and plighted troth,

---

[4]Boughs of hawthorn ("whitethorn," 1. 35) were traditionally gathered as May Day decorations for streets and houses. [5]Goddess of flowers. [6]Pearls from the East. [7]The sun. [8]Prayers. [9]Each decorated porch or door is like a place of religious shelter or worship.

And chose their priest, ere we can cast off sloth.   50
   Many a green-gown has been given,
   Many a kiss, both odd and even;
   Many a glance, too, has been sent
   From out the eye, love's firmament;
Many a jest told of the keys betraying   55
This night, and locks picked; yet we're not a-Maying.

Come, let us go while we are in our prime,
And take the harmless folly of the time.
   We shall grow old apace, and die
   Before we know our liberty.   60
   Our life is short, and our days run
   As fast away as does the sun;
And, as a vapor or a drop of rain
Once lost, can ne'er be found again;
   So when or you or I are made   65
   A fable, song, or fleeting shade,
   All love, all liking, all delight
   Lies drowned with us in endless night.
Then while time serves, and we are but decaying,
Come, my Corinna, come, let's go a-Maying.   70

To His Coy Mistress

Andrew Marvell   (1621–1678)

Had we but world enough, and time,
This coyness, lady, were no crime.
We would sit down, and think which way
To walk, and pass our long love's day.
Thou by the Indian Ganges' side   5
Should'st rubies find: I by the tide
Of Humber would complain. I would
Love you ten years before the flood:
And you should, if you please, refuse
Till the conversion of the Jews.   10
My vegetable love should grow
Vaster then empires, and more slow.
An hundred years should go to praise
Thine eyes, and on thy forehead gaze.
Two hundred to adore each breast: 15
But thirty thousand to the rest.

An age at least to every part,
And the last age should show your heart.
For, lady, you deserve this state;
Nor would I love at lower rate.   20
    But at my back I always hear
Time's winged chariot hurrying near:
And yonder all before us lie
Deserts of vast eternity.
Thy beauty shall no more be found;   25
Nor, in thy marble vault, shall sound
My echoing song: then worms shall try
That long preserved virginity:
And your quaint honor turn to dust;
And into ashes all my lust.   30
The grave's a fine and private place,
But none I think do there embrace.
    Now therefore, while the youthful hue
Sits on thy skin like morning dew,
And while thy willing soul transpires   35
At every pore with instant fires,
Now let us sport us while we may;
And now, like amorous birds of prey,
Rather at once our time devour,
Than languish in his slow-chapped power.   40
Let us roll all our strength, and all
Our sweetness, up into one ball:
And tear our pleasures with rough strife,
Thorough the iron gates of life.
Thus, though we cannot make our sun   45
Stand still, yet we will make him run.

The Ecstasy

John Donne   (1572–1631)

Where, like a pillow on a bed,
    A pregnant bank swelled up to rest
The violet's reclining head,
    Sat we two, one another's best.
Our hands were firmly cemented   5
    With a fast balm, which thence did spring.
Our eye-beams twisted, and did thread
    Our eyes upon one double string;
So to intergraft our hands, as yet
    Was all our means to make us one;   10

And pictures in our eyes to get
  Was all our propagation.
As 'twixt two equal armies, Fate
  Suspends uncertain victory,
Our souls (which to advance their state,   **15**
  Were gone out) hung 'twixt her and me.
And whilst our souls negotiate there,
  We like sepulchral statues lay;
All day the same our postures were,
  And we said nothing all the day.   **20**
If any, so by love refined
  That he soul's language understood,
And by good love were grown all mind,
  Within convenient distance stood,
He (though he know not which soul spake,   **25**
  Because both meant, both spake the same)
Might thence a new concoction take,
  And part far purer than he came.
This ecstasy doth unperplex,
  We said, and tell us what we love;   **30**
We see by this it was not sex;
  We see we saw not what did move;[1]
But as all several[2] souls contain
  Mixture of things, they know not what,
Love these mixed souls doth mix again,   **35**
  And makes both one, each this and that.
A single violet transplant.
  The strength, the color, and the size
(All which before was poor, and scant)
  Redoubles still, and multiplies.   **40**
When love, with one another so
  Interinanimates two souls,
That abler soul, which thence doth flow,
  Defects of loneliness controls.
We then, who are this new soul, know,   **45**
  Of what we are composed, and made,
For, th' atomies[3] of which we grow,
  Are souls, whom no change can invade.
But O alas, so long, so far
  Our bodies why do we forbear?   **50**
They are ours, though they are not we; we are
  The intelligences, they the sphere.[4]

---

[1]We did not understand what motivated us.   [2]Separate.   [3]Atoms.   [4]As the spheres of Ptolemaic astronomy were believed to be governed by "intelligences," so we govern our bodies.

We owe them thanks because they thus,
    Did us to us at first convey,
Yielded their forces, sense, to us,   55
    Nor are dross to us, but allay.[5]
On man heaven's influence works not so
    But that it first imprints the air,
So soul into the soul may flow,
    Though it to body first repair.   60
As our blood labors to beget
    Spirits as like souls as it can,
Because such fingers need to knit
    That subtle knot which makes us man:
So must pure lovers' souls descend   65
    T' affections, and to faculties
Which sense may reach and apprehend;
    Else a great Prince in prison lies.
To our bodies turn we then, that so
    Weak men on love revealed may look;   70
Love's mysteries in souls do grow,
    But yet the body is his book.
And if some lover, such as we,
    Have heard this dialogue of one,
Let him still mark us; he shall see   75
    Small change when we are to bodies gone.

[5]A "dross" is an impurity in a mixture; an "allay" (alloy) strengthens it.

LOVE

"All you need is love," sang the Beatles, giving new impetus to a sentiment ages old. But what is love, and how do we distinguish true from false?

As You Came from the Holy Land*

As you came from the holy land
    Of Walsingham,[1]
Met you not with my true love,
    By the way as you came?   4

"How should I know your true love
    That have met many a one

*Sometimes attributed to Sir Walter Raleigh (c. 1552–1618).
[1]The shrine of Our Lady of Walsingham.

As I came from the holy land,
    That have come, that have gone?"   **8**

She is neither white nor brown,
    But as the heavens fair;
There is none hath her form so divine,
    On the earth, in the air.   **12**

"Such a one did I meet, good sir,
    With angel-like face,
Who like a nymph, like a queen, did appear
    In her gait, in her grace."   **16**

She hath left me here alone,
    All alone unknown,
Who sometime loved me as her life,
    And called me her own.   **20**

"What is the cause she hath left thee alone,
    And a new way doth take,
That sometime did thee love as herself,
    And her joy did thee make?"   **24**

I have loved her all my youth,
    But now am old as you see;
Love liketh not the falling fruit,
    Nor the withered tree.   **28**

For love is a careless child,
    And forgets promise past;
He is blind, he is deaf, when he list,[2]
    And in faith never fast.   **32**

His desire is fickle found,
    And a trustless joy;
He is won with a world of despair,
    And is lost with a toy.   **36**

"Such is the love of womenkind,
    Or the word 'love' abused,
Under which many childish desires
    And conceits are excused.   **40**

"But love, it is a durable fire
    In the mind ever burning,
Never sick, never dead, never cold,
    From itself never turning."   **44**

[2]Wants, desires.

Over the Hills and Far Away[1]

John Gay   (1685–1732)

Macheath: Were I laid on Greenland's coast,
And in my arms embraced my lass,
Warm amidst eternal frost,
Too soon the half year's night would pass.   4

Polly: Were I sold on Indian soil,
Soon as the burning day was closed,
I could mock the sultry toil,
When on my charmer's breast reposed.   8

Macheath: And I would love you all the day,
Polly: Every night would kiss and play,
Macheath: If with me you'd fondly stray
Polly: Over the hills and far away.   12

---

[1]In this song from *The Beggar's Opera* (1728), Macheath, the outlaw, and Polly, his beloved, sing of the love they might share if things were different.

When Faces Called Flowers

E. E. Cummings   (1894–1962)

when faces called flowers float out of the ground
and breathing is wishing and wishing is having—
but keeping is downward and doubting and never
—it's april(yes,april;my darling)it's spring!
yes the pretty birds frolic as spry as can fly   5
yes the little fish gambol as glad as can be
(yes the mountains are dancing together)

when every leaf opens without any sound
and wishing is having and having is giving—
but keeping is doting and nothing and nonsense   10
—alive;we're alive,dear:it's(kiss me now)spring!
now the pretty birds hover so she and so he
now the little fish quiver so you and so i
(now the mountains are dancing,the mountains)

when more than was lost has been found has been found   15
and having is giving and giving is living—
but keeping is darkness and winter and cringing
—it's spring(all our night becomes day)o,it's spring!
all the pretty birds dive to the heart of the sky

all the little fish climb through the mind of the sea   20
(all the mountains are dancing;are dancing)

Song

Sir John Suckling   (1609–1642)

Why so pale and wan fond lover?
        Prithee why so pale?
Will, when looking well can't move her,
        Looking ill prevail?
        Prithee why so pale?   5

Why so dull and mute young sinner?
        Prithee why so mute?
Will, when speaking well can't win her,
        Saying nothing do't?
        Prithee why so mute?   10

Quit, quit, for shame, this will not move,
        This cannot take her;

If of her self she will not love,
        Nothing can make her:
        The Devil take her!   15

Song: To Celia

Ben Jonson   (1573–1637)

Drink to me only with thine eyes,
And I will pledge with mine;
Or leave a kiss but in the cup,
And I'll not look for wine.
The thirst that from the soul doth rise,
Doth ask a drink divine:
But might I of Jove's nectar sup,
I would not change for thine.   8

I sent thee late a rosy wreath,
Not so much honoring thee,
As giving it a hope, that there
It could not withered be.   12
But thou thereon did'st only breathe,
And sent'st it back to me;

Since when it grows and smells, I swear,
Not of itself, but thee.   16

To My Dear and Loving Husband

Anne Bradstreet   (c. 1612–1672)

If ever two were one, then surely we.
If ever man were loved by wife, then thee;
If ever wife was happy in a man,
Compare with me, ye women, if you can.   4
I prize thy love more than whole mines of gold
Or all the riches that the East doth hold.
My love is such that rivers cannot quench,
Nor ought but love from thee, give recompense.   8
Thy love is such I can no way repay,
The heavens reward thee manifold, I pray.
Then while we live, in love let's so persevere
That when we live no more, we may live ever.   12

John Anderson My Jo

Robert Burns   (1759–1796)

John Anderson my jo,[1] John,
    When we were first acquent,[2]
Your locks were like the raven,
    Your bonny brow was brent,[3]   4
But now your brow is beld,[4] John,
    Your locks are like the snow,
But blessings on your frosty pow,[5]
    John Anderson, my jo.   8

John Anderson my jo, John,
    We clamb[6] the hill thegither,[7]
And mony a canty[8] day, John,
    We've had wi' ane anither;   12
Now we maun[9] totter down, John,
    And hand in hand we'll go,
And sleep thegither at the foot,
    John Anderson, my jo.   16

---

[1]Sweetheart. [2]Acquainted. [3]Smooth, unwrinkled. [4]Bald. [5]Head. [6]Climbed. [7]Together.
[8]Jolly. [9]Must.

They Flee from Me

Thomas Wyatt   *(1503–1542)*

They flee from me, that sometime did me seek,
With naked foot stalking in my chamber.
I have seen them, gentle, tame, and meek,
That now are wild, and do not remember
That sometime they put themselves in danger   5
To take bread at my hand; and now they range,
Busily seeking with a continual change.

Thanked be Fortune it hath been otherwise,
Twenty times better; but once in special,
In thin array, after a pleasant guise,   10
When her loose gown from her shoulders did fall,
And she me caught in her arms long and small,
And therewith all sweetly did me kiss
And softly said, "Dear heart, how like you this?"

It was no dream, I lay broad waking.   15
But all is turned, thorough my gentleness,
Into a strange fashion of forsaking;
And I have leave to go, of her goodness,
And she also to use newfangleness.
But since that I so kindely[1] am served,   20
I fain would know what she hath deserved.

[1]"Naturally," an older meaning, but with an ironic pun on the modern meaning of "kindly."

Love Among the Ruins

Robert Browning   *(1812–1889)*

I

Where the quiet-colored end of evening smiles,
    Miles and miles
On the solitary pastures where our sheep
    Half-asleep
Tinkle homeward thro' the twilight, stray or stop   4
    As they crop—
Was the site once of a city great and gay,
    (So they say)
Of our country's very capital, its prince   8
    Ages since

Held his court in, gathered councils, wielding far
    Peace or war.   12

II

Now,—the country does not even boast a tree,
    As you see,
To distinguish slopes of verdure, certain rills
    From the hills   16
Intersect and give a name to, (else they run
    Into one)
Where the domed and daring palace shot its spires
    Up like fires   20
O'er the hundred-gated circuit of a wall
    Bounding all,
Made of marble, men might march on nor be pressed,
    Twelve abreast.   24

III

And such plenty and perfection, see, of grass
    Never was!
Such a carpet as, this summer time, o'erspreads
    And embeds   28
Every vestige of the city, guessed alone,
    Stock or stone—
Where a multitude of men breathed joy and woe
    Long ago;   32
Lust of glory pricked their hearts up, dread of shame
    Struck them tame;
And that glory and that shame alike, the gold
    Bought and sold.   36

IV

Now,—the single little turret that remains
    On the plains,
By the caper[1] overrooted, by the gourd
    Overscored,   40
While the patching houseleek's[2] head of blossom winks
    Through the chinks—
Marks the basement whence a tower in ancient time
    Sprang sublime,   44
And a burning ring, all round, the chariots traced
    As they raced,

---

[1] A Mediterranean bush. Its green flower buds are pickled for salads and sauces.   [2] A plant related to the onion.

And the monarch and his minions and his dames
  Viewed the games.

48

V

And I know, while thus the quiet-colored eve
  Smiles to leave
To their folding, all our many-tinkling fleece
  In such peace,

52

And the slopes and rills in undistinguished grey
  Melt away—
That a girl with eager eyes and yellow hair
  Waits me there

56

In the turret whence the charioteers caught soul
  For the goal,
When the king looked, where she looks now, breathless, dumb
  Till I come.

60

VI

But he looked upon the city, every side,
  Far and wide,
All the mountains topped with temples, all the glades'
  Colonnades,

64

All the causeys,[3] bridges, aqueducts,—and then,
  All the men!
When I do come, she will speak not, she will stand,
  Either hand

68

On my shoulder, give her eyes the first embrace
  Of my face,
Ere we rush, ere we extinguish sight and speech
  Each on each.

72

VII

In one year they sent a million fighters forth
  South and North,
And they built their gods a brazen pillar high
  As the sky,

76

Yet reserved a thousand chariots in full force—
  Gold, of course.
Oh heart! oh blood that freezes, blood that burns!
  Earth's returns

80

For whole centuries of folly, noise and sin!
  Shut them in,
With their triumphs and their glories and the rest!
  Love is best!

84

[3]Causeways.

Love Is Not All

Edna St. Vincent Millay   (1892–1950)

Love is not all: it is not meat nor drink
Nor slumber nor a roof against the rain;
Nor yet a floating spar to men that sink
And rise and sink and rise and sink again;   4
Love can not fill the thickened lung with breath,
Nor clean the blood, nor set the fractured bone;
Yet many a man is making friends with death
Even as I speak, for lack of love alone.   8
It well may be that in a difficult hour,
Pinned down by pain and moaning for release,
Or nagged by want past resolution's power,
I might be driven to sell your love for peace,   12
Or trade the memory of this night for food.
It well may be. I do not think I would.

AGE

Youth passes away, and age brings other problems. Although the subject matter
in the following poems is in a broad sense the same, the ideas it generates are
by no means identical.

Sailing to Byzantium[1]

W. B. Yeats   (1865–1939)

I

That[2] is no country for old men. The young
In one another's arms, birds in the trees
—Those dying generations—at their song,
The salmon-falls, the mackerel-crowded seas,   4
Fish, flesh, or fowl, commend all summer long
Whatever is begotten, born, and dies.
Caught in that sensual music all neglect
Monuments of unageing intellect.   8

II

An aged man is but a paltry thing,
A tattered coat upon a stick, unless

---

[1]The ancient name for the modern Istanbul. Byzantium here symbolizes a time and place devoted
to the permanence of art and artifice as opposed to the transience of "Whatever is begotten, born,
and dies."   [2]The country, presumably Ireland, that the speaker leaves behind.

Soul clap its hands and sing, and louder sing
For every tatter in its mortal dress,   12
Nor is there singing school but studying
Monuments of its own magnificence;
And therefore I have sailed the seas and come
To the holy city of Byzantium.   16

III

O sages standing in God's holy fire
As in the gold mosaic of a wall,
Come from the holy fire, perne in a gyre,[3]
And be the singing-masters of my soul.   20
Consume my heart away; sick with desire
And fastened to a dying animal
It knows not what it is; and gather me
Into the artifice of eternity.   24

IV

Once out of nature I shall never take
My bodily form from any natural thing,
But such a form as Grecian goldsmiths make
Of hammered gold and gold enamelling   28
To keep a drowsy Emperor awake;
Or set upon a golden bough to sing[4]
To lords and ladies of Byzantium
Of what is past, or passing, or to come.   32

---

[3]To move in a gyrating motion like a perne (sometimes "pirn"), or weaver's bobbin. [4]Yeats had read "that in the Emperor's palace at Byzantium was a tree made of gold and silver, and artificial birds that sang."

That Time of Year Thou Mayst in Me Behold

William Shakespeare   (1565–1616)

That time of year thou mayst in me behold
When yellow leaves, or none, or few, do hang
Upon those boughs which shake against the cold,
Bare ruined choirs, where late the sweet birds sang.   4
In me thou see'st the twilight of such day
As after sunset fadeth in the west;
Which by and by black night doth take away,
Death's second self, that seals up all in rest.   8
In me thou see'st the glowing of such fire,

That on the ashes of his youth doth lie,
As the deathbed whereon it must expire
Consumed with that which it was nourished by.   12
    This thou perceiv'st, which makes thy love more strong,
    To love that well which thou must leave ere long.

Survivor

Archibald MacLeish   *(1892–1982)*

On an oak in autumn
there'll always be
one leaf left at the top of the tree
that won't let go with the rest and rot—
won't cast loose and skitter and sail   5
and end in a puddle of rain in a swale
and fatten the earth and be fruitful . . .
                        No,

it won't and it won't and it won't let go.
It rattles a kind of a jig tattoo,   10
a telegrapher's tattle that *will* get through
like an SOS from a struggling ship
over and over, a dash and a skip.

You cover your head with your quilt and still
that telegrapher's key on Conway hill   15
calls to Polaris.[1]

        I can spell:
I know what it says . . . I know too well.
I pull my pillow over my ear
but I hear.   20

[1]The North Star.

The Ivy Crown[1]

William Carlos Williams   *(1883–1963)*

The whole process is a lie,
        unless

                crowned by excess,

[1]From *Journey to Love,* published in 1955, when Williams was 72, and addressed to his wife of many years, Florence (Flossie).

it break forcefully,
   one way or another,   **5**
     from its confinement—

or find a deeper well.
   Antony and Cleopatra[2]
     were right;

they have shown   **10**
   the way. I love you
     or I do not live

at all.

Daffodil time
   is past. This is   **15**
     summer, summer!

the heart says,
   and not even the full of it.
     No doubts

are permitted—   **20**
   though they will come
     and may

before our time
   overwhelm us.
     We are only mortal **25**

but being mortal
   can defy our fate.
     We may

by an outside chance
   even win! We do not   **30**
     look to see

jonquils and violets
   come again
     but there are,

still,   **35**
   the roses!

Romance has no part in it.
   The business of love is
     cruelty *which,*

[2]Famous as older lovers.

by our wills,   40
       we transform
             to live together.

It has its seasons,
       for and against,
             whatever the heart   45

fumbles in the dark
       to assert
             toward the end of May.

Just as the nature of briars
       is to tear flesh,   50
             I have proceeded

through them.
       Keep
             the briars out,

they say.   55
       You cannot live
             and keep free of

briars.

Children pick flowers.
       Let them.   60
             Though having them

in hand
       they have no further use for them
             but leave them crumpled

at the curb's edge.   65
At our age the imagination
       across the sorry facts
             lifts us

to make roses
       stand before thorns.   70
             Sure

love is cruel
       and selfish
             and totally obtuse—
at least, blinded by the light,   75
       young love is.
             But we are older,

I to love
　　　and you to be loved,
　　　　　we have,   80
no matter how,
　　　by our wills survived
　　　　　to keep

the jeweled prize
　　　always   85
　　　　　at our finger tips.

We will it so
　　　and so it is
　　　　　past all accident.

MUTABILITY

All things flow. You can never put your foot in the same river twice. These observations, paraphrased from the Greek philosopher Heraclitus, are essential to the concept of *mutability* (a word that derives from the Latin word for *change*). You can never put your foot in the same river twice because the river will change, will become a different river, even as you take your foot from the water and put it back. The same law applies, as poets have frequently observed, to all things accessible to the five senses. What should be our response to a world in which change may be our only constant? Can we somehow escape the law of mutability? Are there planes of existence, beyond the reach of our senses, not subject to earthly change? Poems on mutability provide a variety of responses.

Mutability

William Wordsworth   (1770–1850)

From low to high doth dissolution climb,
And sink from high to low, along a scale
Of awful notes, whose concord shall not fail;
A musical but melancholy chime,   4
Which they can hear who meddle not with crime,
Nor avarice, nor over-anxious care.
Truth fails not; but her outward forms that bear
The longest date do melt like frosty rime,   8
That in the morning whitened hill and plain
And is no more; drop like the tower sublime
Of yesterday, which royally did wear
His crown of weeds, but could not even sustain   12
Some casual shout that broke the silent air,
Or the unimaginable touch of Time.

Death, Be Not Proud

John Donne   (1572–1631)

Death, be not proud, though some have called thee
Mighty and dreadful, for thou art not so;
For those whom thou think'st thou dost overthrow
Die not, poor Death, nor yet canst thou kill me.   4
From rest and sleep, which but thy pictures be,
Much pleasure; then from thee much more must flow,
And soonest our best men with thee do go,
Rest of their bones, and soul's delivery.   8
Thou art slave to fate, chance, kings, and desperate men,
And dost with poison, war, and sickness dwell,
And poppy[1] or charms can make us sleep as well
And better than thy stroke; why swell'st thou then?   12
One short sleep last, we wake eternally
And death shall be no more; Death, thou shalt die.

[1]The opium poppy.

To the Stone-Cutters

Robinson Jeffers   (1887–1962)

Stone-cutters fighting time with marble, you foredefeated
Challengers of oblivion
Eat cynical earnings, knowing rock splits, records fall down,
The square-limbed Roman letters
Scale in the thaws, wear in the rain. The poet as well   5
Builds his monument mockingly;
For man will be blotted out, the blithe earth die, the brave sun
Die blind and blacken to the heart:
Yet stones have stood for a thousand years, and pained thoughts
    found
The honey of peace in old poems.   10

As I Ebb'd with the Ocean of Life

Walt Whitman   (1819–1892)

1

As I ebb'd with the ocean of life,
As I wended the shores I know,
As I walk'd where the ripples continually wash you Paumanok,[1]

[1]Indian name for Long Island, where Whitman was born.

Where they rustle up hoarse and sibilant,
Where the fierce old mother[2] endlessly cries for her castaways,   5
I musing late in the autumn day, gazing off southward,
Held by this electric self out of the pride of which I utter poems,
Was seiz'd by the spirit that trails in the lines underfoot,
The rim, the sediment that stands for all the water and all the land
    of the globe.

Fascinated, my eyes reverting from the south, dropt, to follow those
    slender windrows,   10
Chaff, straw, splinters of wood, weeds, and the sea-gluten,
Scum, scales from shining rocks, leaves of salt-lettuce, left by the
    tide,
Miles walking, the sound of breaking waves the other side of me,
Paumanok there and then as I thought the old thought of likenesses,[3]
These you presented to me you fish-shaped island,   15
As I wended the shores I know,
As I walk'd with that electric self seeking types.

2

As I wend to the shores I know not,
As I list to the dirge, the voice of men and women wreck'd,
As I inhale the impalpable breezes that set in upon me,   20
As the ocean so mysterious rolls toward me closer and closer,
I too but signify at the utmost a little wash'd-up drift,
A few sands and dead leaves to gather,
Gather, and merge myself as part of the sands and drift.

O baffled, balk'd, bent to the very earth,   25
Oppress'd with myself that I have dared to open my mouth,
Aware now that amid all that blab whose echoes recoil upon me I
    have not once had the least idea who or what I am,
But that before all my arrogant poems the real Me stands yet
    untouch'd, untold, altogether unreach'd,
Withdrawn far, mocking me with mock-congratulatory signs and
    bows,
With peals of distant ironical laughter at every word I have written,   30
Pointing in silence to these songs, and then to the sand beneath.

I perceive I have not really understood anything, not a single object, and
    that no man ever can,
Nature here in sight of the sea taking advantage of me to dart upon
    me and sting me,
Because I have dared to open my mouth to sing at all.

[2]The sea. [3]Correspondences between man and nature, the "types" of line 17.

3

You oceans both, I close with you,   35
We murmur alike reproachfully rolling sands and drift, knowing not
    why,
These little shreds indeed standing for you and me and all.

You friable⁴ shore with trails of debris,
You fish-shaped island, I take what is underfoot,
What is yours is mine my father.⁵   40

I too Paumanok,
I too have bubbled up, floated the measureless float, and been wash'd
    on your shores,
I too am but a trail of drift and debris,
I too leave little wrecks upon you, you fish-shaped island.

I throw myself upon your breast my father,   45
I cling to you so that you cannot unloose me,
I hold you so firm till you answer me something.

Kiss me my father,
Touch me with your lips as I touch those I love,
Breathe to me while I hold you close the secret of the murmuring I
    envy.   50

4

Ebb, ocean of life, (the flow will return,)
Cease not your moaning you fierce old mother,
Endlessly cry for your castaways, but fear not, deny not me,
Rustle not up so hoarse and angry against my feet as I touch you or
    gather from you.

I mean tenderly by you and all,   55
I gather for myself and for this phantom looking down where we
    lead, and following me and mine.

Me and mine, loose windrows, little corpses,
Froth, snowy white, and bubbles,
(See, from my dead lips the ooze exuding at last,
See, the prismatic colors glistening and rolling,)   60
Tufts of straw, sands, fragments,
Buoy'd hither from many moods, one contradicting another,
From the storm, the long calm, the darkness, the swell,
Musing, pondering, a breath, a briny tear, a dab of liquid or soil,
Up just as much out of fathomless workings fermented and thrown,   65

⁴Easily crumbled.   ⁵Paumanok (Long Island).

A limp blossom or two, torn, just as much over waves floating,
    drifted at random,
Just as much for us that sobbing dirge of Nature,
Just as much whence we come that blare of the cloud-trumpets,
We, capricious, brought hither we know not whence, spread out
    before you,
You up there walking or sitting,   70
Whoever you are, we too lie in drifts at your feet.

Directive

Robert Frost   *(1874–1963)*

Back out of all this now too much for us,
Back in a time made simple by the loss
Of detail, burned, dissolved, and broken off
Like graveyard marble sculpture in the weather,
There is a house that is no more a house   5
Upon a farm that is no more a farm
And in a town that is no more a town.
The road there, if you'll let a guide direct you
Who only has at heart your getting lost,
May seem as if it should have been a quarry—   10
Great monolithic knees the former town
Long since gave up pretense of keeping covered.
And there's a story in a book about it:
Besides the wear of iron wagon wheels
The ledges show lines ruled southeast-northwest,   15
The chisel work of an enormous Glacier
That braced his feet against the Arctic Pole.
You must not mind a certain coolness from him
Still said to haunt this side of Panther Mountain.
Nor need you mind the serial ordeal   20
Of being watched from forty cellar holes
As if by eye pairs out of forty firkins.[1]
As for the woods' excitement over you
That sends light rustle rushes to their leaves,
Charge that to upstart inexperience.   25
Where were they all not twenty years ago?
They think too much of having shaded out
A few old pecker-fretted apple trees.
Make yourself up a cheering song of how
Someone's road home from work this once was,   30

[1] Small wooden tubs.

Who may be just ahead of you on foot
Or creaking with a buggy load of grain.
The height of the adventure is the height
Of country where two village cultures faded
Into each other. Both of them are lost.   35
And if you're lost enough to find yourself
By now, pull in your ladder road behind you
And put a sign up CLOSED to all but me.
Then make yourself at home. The only field
Now left's no bigger than a harness gall.   40
First there's the children's house of make-believe,
Some shattered dishes underneath a pine,
The playthings in the playhouse of the children.
Weep for what little things could make them glad.
Then for the house that is no more a house,   45
But only a belilaced cellar hole,
Now slowly closing like a dent in dough.
This was no playhouse but a house in earnest.
Your destination and your destiny's
A brook that was the water of the house,   50
Cold as a spring as yet so near its source,
Too lofty and original to rage.
(We know the valley streams that when aroused
Will leave their tatters hung on barb and thorn.)
I have kept hidden in the instep arch   55
Of an old cedar at the waterside
A broken drinking goblet like the Grail[2]
Under a spell so the wrong ones can't find it,
So can't get saved, as Saint Mark says they mustn't.[3]
(I stole the goblet from the children's playhouse.)   60
Here are your waters and your watering place.
Drink and be whole again beyond confusion.

[2]The cup Christ drank from at the Last Supper.   [3]See Mark 16.16.

DEATH

Death is the final constant. It serves as the ultimate common denominator, eventually reducing all living things to the same condition. How should we as humans confront the death of others? In what way should we contemplate the fact of our own end?

Lycidas

John Milton

(1608–1674)

In this Monody[1] the Author bewails a learned Friend, unfortunately drowned in his passage from Chester on the Irish Seas, 1637; and by occasion, foretells the ruin of our corrupted Clergy, then in their height.

Yet once more, O ye laurels,[2] and once more,
Yet myrtles brown, with ivy never sere,[3]
I come to pluck your berries harsh and crude,
And with forced fingers rude
Shatter your leaves before the mellowing year.   5
Bitter constraint and sad occasion dear
Compels me to disturb your season due;
For Lycidas is dead, dead ere his prime,
Young Lycidas, and hath not left his peer.
Who would not sing for Lycidas? he knew   10
Himself to sing, and build the lofty rhyme.
He must not float upon his watery bier
Unwept, and welter to the parching wind,
Without the meed[4] of some melodious tear.
    Begin, then, Sisters[5] of the sacred well   15
That from beneath the seat of Jove doth spring;
Begin, and somewhat loudly sweep the string.
Hence with denial vain and coy excuse:
So may some gentle Muse
With lucky words favour my destined urn,   20
And as he passes turn,
And bid fair peace be to my sable shroud!
    For we were nursed upon the self-same hill,
Fed the same flock, by fountain, shade, and rill;
Together both, ere the high lawns appeared   25
Under the opening eyelids of the Morn,
We drove a-field, and both together heard
What time the grey-fly winds her sultry horn,
Battening[6] our flocks with the fresh dews of night,
Oft till the star that rose at evening bright   30

[1]A lament or dirge sung by a single voice. Milton writes in the form of a *pastoral elegy*, drawing his imagery from an idyllic vision of a shepherd's life, in a tradition dating from classical antiquity. The friend was Edward King, who had been a fellow student with Milton at Cambridge. [2]Laurel, myrtle, and ivy, all evergreen, were traditional materials for poetic garlands, symbolic of inspiration. [3]Withered. [4]Reward. [5]The Muses, who were associated with the sacred well of Aganippe, at the foot of Mt. Helicon. [6]Fattening.

Toward heaven's descent had sloped his westering wheel.
Meanwhile the rural ditties were not mute;
Tempered to th' oaten flute,
Rough Satyrs danced, and Fauns with cloven heel
From the glad sound would not be absent long;   35
And old Damaetas[7] loved to hear our song.
        But, oh! the heavy change, now thou art gone,
Now thou art gone and never must return!
Thee, Shepherd, thee the woods and desert caves,
With wild thyme and the gadding[8] vine o'ergrown,   40
And all their echoes, mourn.
The willows, and the hazel copses green,
Shall now no more be seen
Fanning their joyous leaves to thy soft lays.
As killing as the canker to the rose,   45
Or taint-worm to the weanling herds that graze,
Or frost to flowers, that their gay wardrobe wear,
When first the white-thorn blows;[9]
Such, Lycidas, thy loss to shepherd's ear.
        Where were ye, Nymphs, when the remorseless deep   50
Closed o'er the head of your loved Lycidas?
For neither were ye playing on the steep
Where your old bards, the famous Druids,[10] lie,
Nor on the shaggy top of Mona high,
Nor yet where Deva spreads her wizard stream.   55
Ay me! I fondly[11] dream
"Had ye been there," . . . for what could that have done?
What could the Muse herself that Orpheus[12] bore,
The Muse herself, for her enchanting son,
Whom universal nature did lament,   60
When, by the rout that made the hideous roar,
His gory visage down the stream was sent,
Down the swift Hebrus to the Lesbian shore?
        Alas! what boots[13] it with uncessant care
To tend the homely, slighted, shepherd's trade,   65
And strictly meditate the thankless Muse?
Were it not better done, as others use,
To sport with Amaryllis in the shade,

---

[7]A conventional pastoral name, though Milton may have had in mind a particular Cambridge tutor.   [8]Wandering.   [9]Blossoms.   [10]The Druids, Celtic priests, were buried on the "steep" of Kerig-y-Druidion in Wales. Mona is the Isle of Anglesey and Deva the River Dee (considered "wizard" or magic by the local inhabitants). All are near the site of King's drowning.   [11]Foolishly.   [12]Calliope, Muse of epic poetry, was the mother of Orpheus, whose music was fabled for its power over nature. Orpheus was torn apart by screaming Maenads, who threw his head into the River Hebrus, whence it floated to Lesbos.   [13]Profits.

Or with the tangles of Neaera's hair?[14]
Fame is the spur that the clear spirit doth raise   70
(That last infirmity of noble mind)
To scorn delights and live laborious days;
But the fair guerdon[15] when we hope to find,
And think to burst out into sudden blaze,
Comes the blind Fury with th' abhorrèd shears,   75
And slits the thin-spun life.[16] "But not the praise,"
Phoebus[17] replied, and touched my trembling ears:
"Fame is no plant that grows on mortal soil,
Nor in the glistering foil[18]
Set off to the world, nor in broad rumour lies,   80
But lives and spreads aloft by those pure eyes
And perfect witness of all-judging Jove;
As he pronounces lastly on each deed,
Of so much fame in Heaven expect thy meed."
     O fountain Arethuse, and thou honoured flood,   85
Smooth-sliding Mincius,[19] crowned with vocal reeds,
That strain I heard was of a higher mood.
But now my oat[20] proceeds,
And listens to the Herald of the Sea,[21]
That came in Neptune's plea.   90
He asked the waves, and asked the felon winds,
What hard mishap hath doomed this gentle swain?
And questioned every gust of rugged wings
That blows from off each beakèd promontory.
They knew not of his story;   95
And sage Hippotades[22] their answer brings,
That not a blast was from his dungeon strayed:
The air was calm, and on the level brine
Sleek Panopè[23] with all her sisters played.
It was that fatal and perfidious bark,   100
Built in th' eclipse, and rigged with curses dark,
That sunk so low that sacred head of thine.
     Next, Camus,[24] reverend sire, went footing slow,
His mantle hairy, and his bonnet sedge,[25]
Inwrought with figures dim, and on the edge   105
Like to that sanguine flower[26] inscribed with woe.

[14]Amaryllis and Neaera: conventional pastoral names.   [15]Reward.   [16]Atropos, one of the three
Fates, cut the thread of a person's life after her sisters had spun and measured it.   [17]Phoebus
Apollo, god of poetic inspiration.   [18]Setting, often for an inferior gem.   [19]Arethuse: fountain in
Sicily associated with the poet Theocritus; Mincius: river in Italy associated with the poet Virgil.
[20]Oaten pipe; song.   [21]Triton, who pleads Neptune's innocence in the death of King.   [22]Aeolus,
god of the winds.   [23]A sea nymph.   [24]God of the river Cam; hence, a representative of Cambridge
University.   [25]Marsh grass.   [26]The hyacinth, with bloody marks AI AI ("Alas, alas") commemorating the accidental death of the youthful Hyancinthus at the hands of Apollo.

"Ah! who hath reft," quoth he, "my dearest pledge?"
Last came, and last did go,
The Pilot of the Galilean Lake;[27]
Two massy keys he bore of metals twain 	110
(The golden opes, the iron shuts amain).
He shook his mitred locks,[28] and stern bespake:—
"How well could I have spared for thee, young swain,
Enow of such as, for their bellies' sake,
Creep, and intrude, and climb into the fold! 	115
Of other care they little reckoning make
Than how to scramble at the shearers' feast,
And shove away the worthy bidden guest.
Blind mouths! that scarce themselves know how to hold
A sheep-hook, or have learnt aught else the least 	120
That to the faithful herdman's art belongs!
What recks it them? What need they? They are sped,
And, when they list,[29] their lean and flashy songs
Grate on their scrannel[30] pipes of wretched straw;
The hungry sheep look up, and are not fed, 	125
But, swoln with wind and the rank mist they draw,
Rot inwardly, and foul contagion spread;
Besides what the grim wolfe with privy[31] paw
Daily devours apace, and nothing said.
But that two-handed engine at the door[32] 	130
Stands ready to smite once, and smite no more,"
    Return, Alpheus,[33] the dread voice is past
That shrunk thy streams; return, Sicilian-Muse,
And call the vales, and bid them hither cast
Their bells and flowerets of a thousand hues. 	135
Ye valleys low, where the mild whispers use
Of shades, and wanton winds, and gushing brooks,
On whose fresh lap the swart star[34] sparely looks,
Throw hither all your quaint enamelled eyes,
That on the green turf suck the honeyed showers, 	140
And purple all the ground with vernal flowers.
Bring the rathe[35] primrose that forsaken dies,
The tufted crow-toe, and pale jessamine,
The white pink, and the pansy freaked with jet,
The glowing violet, 	145
The musk rose, and the well-attired woodbine,
With cowslips wan that hang the pensive head,

---

[27]St. Peter, who holds the keys to Heaven. 	[28]He wears a bishop's miter. 	[29]Choose. 	[30]Meager.
[31]Secret, with an allusion to Roman Catholicism. 	[32]An instrument of death, though the specific
meaning is obscure. 	[33]A river god who loved Arethusa. 	[34]Sirius, the Dog Star, thought to have
a "swart," or dark, malignant influence in late summer. 	[35]Early.

And every flower that sad embroidery wears;
Bid amaranthus[36] all his beauty shed,
And daffadillies fill their cups with tears,   150
To strew the laureate hearse where Lycid lies.
For so, to interpose a little ease,
Let our frail thoughts dally with false surmise.
Ay me! whilst thee the shores and sounding seas
Wash far away, where'er thy bones are hurled;   155
Whether beyond the stormy Hebrides,[37]
Where thou perhaps under the whelming tide
Visit'st the bottom of the monstrous world;
Or whether thou, to our moist vows denied,
Sleep'st by the fable of Bellerus[38] old,   160
Where the great Vision of the guarded mount[39]
Looks toward Namancos and Bayona's hold.
Look homeward, Angel, now, and melt with ruth:[40]
And, O ye dolphins, waft the hapless youth.

  Weep no more, woeful shepherds, weep no more,   165
For Lycidas, your sorrow, is not dead,
Sunk though he be beneath the watery floor.
So sinks the day-star in the ocean bed,
And yet anon repairs his drooping head,
And tricks his beams, and with new-spangled ore   170
Flames in the forehead of the morning sky:
So Lycidas sunk low, but mounted high,
Through the dear might of him that walked the waves,[41]
Where, other groves and other streams along,
With nectar pure his oozy locks he laves,[42]   175
And hears the unexpressive nuptial song,
In the blest kingdoms meek of joy and love.
There entertain him all the Saints above,
In solemn troops, and sweet societies,
That sing, and singing in their glory move,   180
And wipe the tears for ever from his eyes.
Now, Lycidas, the shepherds weep no more;
Henceforth thou art the Genius of the shore,
In thy large recompense, and shalt be good
To all that wander in that perilous flood.   185

  Thus sang the uncouth[43] swain to th' oaks and rills,
While the still morn went out with sandals grey:

---

[36]A legendary flower supposed never to fade.   [37]Off the coast of Scotland, at the northern end of
the Irish Sea.   [38]A legendary giant supposed to be buried at Land's End, Cornwall.
[39]From St. Michael's Mount at the tip of Cornwall, the archangel gazes toward Namancos and Bayona, strongholds of Catholicism in northern Spain.   [40]Pity.   [41]Christ.
[42]Bathes.   [43]Unlettered.

He touched the tender stops of various quills,
With eager thought warbling his Doric[44] lay;
And now the sun had stretched out all the hills,   **190**
And now was dropped into the western bay;
At last he rose, and twitched his mantle blue:
To-morrow to fresh woods, and pastures new.

[44]Simple, pastoral.

Burial

Alice Walker   (1944–   )

I

They have fenced in the dirt road
that once led to Wards Chapel
A.M.E.[1] church,
and cows graze
among the stones that   **5**
mark my family's graves.
The massive oak is gone
from out the church yard,
but the giant space is left
unfilled;   **10**
despite the two-lane blacktop
that slides across
the old, unalterable
roots.

II

Today I bring my own child here;   **15**
to this place where my father's
grandmother rests undisturbed
beneath the Georgia sun,
above her the neatstepping hooves
of cattle.   **20**
Here the graves soon grow back into the land.
Have been known to sink. To drop open without
warning. To cover themselves with wild ivy,
blackberries. Bittersweet and sage.
No one knows why. No one asks.   **25**
When Burning Off Day comes, as it does
some years,

[1]African Methodist Episcopalian.

the graves are haphazardly cleared and snakes
hacked to death and burned sizzling
in the brush. . . . The odor of smoke, oak   30
leaves, honeysuckle.
Forgetful of geographic resolutions as birds,
the farflung young fly South to bury
the old dead.

III

The old women move quietly up   35
and touch Sis Rachel's face.
"Tell Jesus I'm coming," they say.
"Tell Him I ain't goin' to *be*
long."
My grandfather turns his creaking head   40
away from the lavender box.
He does not cry. But looks afraid.
For years he called her "Woman";
shortened over the decades to
" 'Oman."   45
On the cut stone for " 'Oman's" grave
he did not notice
they had misspelled her name.

(The stone reads *Racher Walker*—not "Rachel"—
Loving Wife, Devoted Mother.)   50

IV

As a young woman, who had known her? Tripping
eagerly, "loving wife," to my grandfather's
bed. Not pretty, but serviceable. A hard
worker, with rough, moist hands. Her own two
babies dead before she came.   55
Came to seven children.
To aprons and sweat.
Came to quiltmaking.
Came to canning and vegetable gardens
big as fields.   60
Came to fields to plow.
Cotton to chop.
Potatoes to dig.
Came to multiple measles, chickenpox,
and croup.   65
Came to water from springs.

Came to leaning houses one story high.
Came to rivalries. Saturday night battles.
Came to straightened hair, Noxzema, and
feet washing at the Hardshell Baptist church.   70
Came to zinnias around the woodpile.
Came to grandchildren not of her blood
whom she taught to dip snuff without
sneezing.

Came to death blank, forgetful of it all.   75

When he called her " 'Oman" she no longer
listened. Or heard, or knew, or felt.

V

It is not until I see my first grade teacher
review her body that I cry.
Not for the dead, but for the gray in my   80
first grade teacher's hair. For memories
of before I was born, when teacher and
grandmother loved each other; and later
above the ducks made of soap and the orange-
legged chicks Miss Reynolds drew over   85
my own small hand
on paper with wide blue lines.

VI

Not for the dead, but for memories. None of
them sad. But seen from the angle of her
death.

In Memory of W. B. Yeats

(D. Jan. 1939)

W. H. Auden   (1907–1973)

I

He disappeared in the dead of winter:
The brooks were frozen, the airports almost deserted,
And snow disfigured the public statues;
The mercury sank in the mouth of the dying day.
What instruments we have agree   5
The day of his death was a dark cold day.

Far from his illness
The wolves ran on through the evergreen forests,
The peasant river was untempted by the fashionable quays;[1]
By mourning tongues   10
The death of the poet was kept from his poems.

But for him it was his last afternoon as himself,
An afternoon of nurses and rumours;
The provinces of his body revolted,
The squares of his mind were empty,   15
Silence invaded the suburbs,
The current of his feeling failed; he became his admirers.

Now he is scattered among a hundred cities
And wholly given over to unfamiliar affections,
To find his happiness in another kind of wood   20
And be punished under a foreign code of conscience.
The words of a dead man
Are modified in the guts of the living.
But in the importance of noise of to-morrow
When the brokers are roaring like beasts on the floor of the Bourse,[2] 25
And the poor have the sufferings to which they are fairly
    accustomed,
And each in the cell of himself is almost convinced of his freedom,
A few thousand will think of this day
As one thinks of a day when one did something slightly unusual.
What instruments we have agree   30
The day of his death was a dark cold day.

II

You were silly like us; your gift survived it all:
The parish of rich women, physical decay,
Yourself. Mad Ireland hurt you into poetry.
Now Ireland has her madness and her weather still,   35
For poetry makes nothing happen: it survives
In the valley of its making where executives
Would never want to tamper, flows on south
From ranches of isolation and the busy griefs,
Raw towns that we believe and die in; it survives,   40
A way of happening, a mouth.

III

Earth, receive an honoured guest:
William Yeats is laid to rest.

[1] Paved landing places for loading ships.   [2] Stock exchange.

Let the Irish vessel lie
Emptied of its poetry.   45

In the nightmare of the dark
All the dogs of Europe bark,
And the living nations wait,
Each sequestered in its hate;

Intellectual disgrace   50
Stares from every human face,
And the seas of pity lie
Locked and frozen in each eye.

Follow, poet, follow right
To the bottom of the night,   55
With your unconstraining voice
Still persuade us to rejoice;

With the farming of a verse
Make a vineyard of the curse,
Sing of human unsuccess   60
In a rapture of distress;

In the deserts of the heart
Let the healing fountain start,
In the prison of his days
Teach the free man how to praise.   65

Out of the Cradle Endlessly Rocking

Walt Whitman   (1819–1892)

Out of the cradle endlessly rocking,
Out of the mocking-bird's throat, the musical shuttle,
Out of the Ninth-month[1] midnight,
Over the sterile sands and the fields beyond, where the child leaving
    his bed wander'd alone, bareheaded, barefoot,
Down from the shower'd halo,   5
Up from the mystic play of shadows twining and twisting as if they
    were alive,
Out from the patches of briers and blackberries,
From the memories of the bird that chanted to me,
From your memories sad brother,[2] from the fitful risings and fallings
    I heard,
From under that yellow half-moon late-risen and swollen as if with
    tears,   10

[1]The Quaker name for September.   [2]The bird.

romantic

From those beginning notes of yearning and love there in the mist,
From the thousand responses of my heart never to cease,
From the myriad thence-arous'd words,
From the word stronger and more delicious than any,
From such as now they start the scene revisiting,   15
As a flock, twittering, rising, or overhead passing,
Borne hither, ere all eludes me, hurriedly,
A man, yet by these tears a little boy again,
Throwing myself on the sand, confronting the waves,
I, chanter of pains and joys, uniter of here and hereafter,   20
Taking all hints to use them, but swiftly leaping beyond them,
A reminiscence sing

Once Paumanok,[3]
When the lilac-scent was in the air and Fifth-month grass was
    growing,
Up this seashore in some briers,   25
Two feather'd guests from Alabama, two together,
And their nest, and four light-green eggs spotted with brown,
And every day the he-bird to and fro near at hand,
And every day the she-bird crouch'd on her nest; silent, with bright
    eyes,
And every day I, a curious boy, never too close, never disturbing
    them,   30
Cautiously peering, absorbing, translating.

Shine! shine! shine![4]
Pour down your warmth, great sun!
While we bask, we two together.

Two together!   35
Winds blow south, or winds blow north,
Day come white, or night come black,
Home, or rivers and mountains from home,
Singing all time, minding no time,
While we two keep together.   40

Till of a sudden,
May-be kill'd, unknown to her mate,
One forenoon the she-bird crouch'd not on the nest,
Nor return'd that afternoon, nor the next,
Nor ever appear'd again.   45

And thenceforward all summer in the sound of the sea,
And at night under the full of the moon in calmer weather,

---

[3]The Indian name for Long Island, where Whitman was born.   [4]Here and later, the songs of the
bird, as translated by the poet, appear in italics.

Over the hoarse surging of the sea,
Or flitting from brier to brier by day,
I saw, I heard at intervals the remaining one, the he-bird,   50
The solitary guest from Alabama.

Blow! blow! blow!
Blow up sea-winds along Paumanok's shore;
I wait and I wait till you blow my mate to me.

Yes, when the stars glisten'd,   55
All night long on the prong of a moss-scallop'd stake,
Down almost amid the slapping waves,
Sat the lone singer wonderful causing tears.

He call'd on his mate,
He pour'd forth the meanings which I of all men know.   60

Yes my brother I know,
The rest might not, but I have treasur'd every note,
For more than once dimly down to the beach gliding,
Silent, avoiding the moonbeams, blending myself with the shadows,
Recalling now the obscure shapes, the echoes, the sounds and sights
    after their sorts,   65
The white arms out in the breakers tirelessly tossing,
I, with bare feet, a child, the wind wafting my hair,
Listen'd long and long.

Listen'd to keep, to sing, now translating the notes,
Following you my brother.   70

Soothe! soothe! soothe!
Close on its wave soothes the wave behind,
And again another behind embracing and lapping, every one close,
But my love soothes not me, not me.

Low hangs the moon, it rose late,   75
It is lagging—O I think it is heavy with love, with love.

O madly the sea pushes upon the land,
With love, with love.

O night! do I not see my love fluttering out among the breakers?
What is that little black thing I see there in the white?   80

Loud! loud! loud!
Loud I call to you, my love!
High and clear I shoot my voice over the waves,
Surely you must know who is here, is here,
You must know who I am, my love.   85

transfered emotions unrequited love

Low-hanging moon!
What is that dusky spot in your brown yellow?
O it is the shape, the shape of my mate!
O moon do not keep her from me any longer.

Land! Land! O land!   90
Whichever way I turn, O I think you could give me my mate back
    again if you only would,
For I am almost sure I see her dimly whichever way I look.

O rising stars!
Perhaps the one I want so much will rise, will rise with some of you.

O throat! O trembling throat!   95
Sound clearer through the atmosphere!
Pierce the woods, the earth,
Somewhere listening to catch you must be the one I want.

Shake out carols!
Solitary here, the night's carols!   100
Carols of lonesome love! death's carols!
Carols under that lagging, yellow, waning moon!
O under that moon where she droops almost down into the sea!
O reckless despairing carols.

But soft! sink low!   105
Soft! let me just murmur,
And do you wait a moment you husky-nois'd sea,
For somewhere I believe I heard my mate responding to me,
So faint, I must be still, be still to listen,
But not altogether still, for then she might not come immediately to
    me.   110

Hither my love!
Here I am! here!
With this just-sustain'd note I announce myself to you,
This gentle call is for you my love, for you.

Do not be decoy'd elsewhere,   115
That is the whistle of the wind, it is not my voice,
That is the fluttering, the fluttering of the spray,
Those are the shadows of leaves.

O darkness! O in vain!
O I am very sick and sorrowful.   120

O brown halo in the sky near the moon, dropping upon the sea!
O troubled reflection in the sea!

O throat! O throbbing heart!
And I singing uselessly, uselessly all the night.

O past! O happy life! O songs of joy!   125
In the air, in the woods, over fields,
Loved! loved! loved! loved! loved!
But my mate no more, no more with me!
We two together no more.

The aria sinking,   130
All else continuing, the stars shining,
The winds blowing, the notes of the bird continuous echoing,
With angry moans the fierce old mother[5] incessantly moaning,
On the sands of Paumanok's shore gray and rustling,
The yellow half-moon enlarged, sagging down, drooping, the face of
    the sea almost touching,   135
The boy ecstatic, with his bare feet the waves, with his hair the
    atmosphere dallying,
The love in the heart long pent, now loose, now at last tumultuously
    bursting,
The aria's meaning, the ears, the soul, swiftly depositing,
The strange tears down the cheeks coursing,
The colloquy[6] there, the trio, each uttering,   140
The undertone, the savage old mother incessantly crying,
To the boy's soul's questions sullenly timing, some drown'd secret
    hissing,
To the outsetting bard.

Demon or bird! (said the boy's soul,)
Is it indeed toward your mate you sing? or is it really to me?   145
For I, that was a child, my tongue's use sleeping, now I have heard
    you,
Now in a moment I know what I am for, I awake,
And already a thousand singers, a thousand songs, clearer, louder
    and more sorrowful than yours,
A thousand warbling echoes have started to life within me, never to
    die.

O you singer solitary, singing by yourself, projecting me,   150
O solitary me listening, never more shall I cease perpetuating you,
Never more shall I escape, never more the reverberations,
Never more the cries of unsatisfied love be absent from me,
Never again leave me to be the peaceful child I was before what
    there in the night,
By the sea under the yellow and sagging moon,   155

[5]The sea.   [6]Discourse.

The messenger there arous'd, the fire, the sweet hell within,
The unknown want, the destiny of me.

O give me the clew! (it lurks in the night here somewhere,)
O if I am to have so much, let me have more!

A word then, (for I will conquer it,)   160
The word final, superior to all,
Subtle, sent up—what is it?—I listen;
Are you whispering it, and have been all the time, you sea-waves?
Is that it from your liquid rims and wet sands?

Whereto answering, the sea,   165
Delaying not, hurrying not,
Whisper'd me through the night, and very plainly before daybreak,
Lisp'd to me the low and delicious word death,
And again death, death, death, death,
Hissing melodious, neither like the bird nor like my arous'd child's
    heart,
                                                                     170
But edging near as privately for me rustling at my feet,
Creeping thence steadily up to my ears and laving me softly all over,
Death, death, death, death, death.

Which I do not forget,
But fuse the song of my dusky demon and brother,   175
That he sang to me in the moonlight on Paumanok's gray beach,
With the thousand responsive songs at random,
My own songs awaked from that hour,
And with them the key, the word up from the waves,
The word of the sweetest song and all songs,   180
That strong and delicious word which, creeping to my feet,
(Or like some old crone rocking the cradle, swathed in sweet
    garments, bending aside,)
The sea whisper'd me.

CHAPTER 10

POEMS
FOR STUDY

When April with His Sweet Showers[1]

Geoffrey Chaucer   *(c. 1343–1400)*

Whan that Aprill with his shoures soote
The droghte of March hath perced to the roote,
And bathed every veyne in swich licour
Of which vertue engendred is the flour;   4
When Zephirus eek with his sweete breeth
Inspired hath in every holt and heeth
The tendre croppes, and the yonge sonne
Hath in the Ram his halve cours yronne,   8
And smale foweles maken melodye,
That slepen al the nyght with open yë
(So priketh hem nature in hir corages),—
Thanne longen folk to goon on pilgrimages,   12
And palmeres for to seken straunge strondes,
To ferne halwes, kowthe in sondry londes;
And specially from every shires ende
Of Engelond to Caunterbury they wende,   16
The hooly blisful martir for to seke,
That hem hath holpen whan that they were seeke.

---

[1]The opening lines of the General Prologue to *The Canterbury Tales:* "When April with his sweet showers / The drought of March has pierced to the root, / And bathed every vein in such liqúor / Of which virtue engendered is the flower; / When Zephyrus, also, with his sweet breath /

Inspired has in every wood and heath / The tender shoots, and the young sun / Has in the Ram his half course run, / And small birds make melody, / That sleep all night with open eye / (So nature pricks them in their hearts),— / Then folk long to go on pilgrimages, / And palmers to seek strange shores, / To far shrines, known in sundry lands; / And specially from every shire's end / Of England to Canterbury they wend, / The holy, blissful martyr for to seek, / Who had helped them when they were sick."

Zephyrus: the west wind. The Ram: sign of the Zodiac; Aries. Palmers: so called because pilgrims wore palm branches as a sign they had been to the Holy Land. Blissful martyr: St. Thomas à Becket, murdered at Canterbury in 1170.

When Daisies Pied

William Shakespeare   (1564–1616)

When daisies pied, and violets blue,
   And lady-smocks all silver-white,
And cuckoo-buds of yellow hue
    Do paint the meadows with delight,   **4**
The cuckoo then on every tree
Mocks married men,[1] for thus sings he,
        "Cuckoo;
Cuckoo, cuckoo"—O word of fear,
Unpleasing to a married ear!   **8**

When shepherds pipe on oaten straws,
   And merry larks are ploughmen's clocks;
When turtles tread,[2] and rooks and daws,
   And maidens bleach their summer smocks,   **12**
The cuckoo then on every tree
Mocks married men; for thus sings he,
        "Cuckoo;
Cuckoo, cuckoo"—O word of fear,
Unpleasing to a married ear!   **16**

[1]Because his song suggests the word *cuckold*.   [2]Turtledoves mate.

When Icicles Hang by the Wall

William Shakespeare   (1564–1616)

When icicles hang by the wall,
   And Dick the shepherd blows his nail,
And Tom bears logs into the hall,
   And milk comes frozen home in pail;
When blood is nipped, and ways be foul,
Then nightly sings the staring owl,
        "Tu-whit, tu-who!"—

A merry note,
While greasy Joan doth keel[1] the pot.

When all aloud the wind doth blow,
    And coughing drowns the parson's saw,[2]
And birds sit brooding in the snow,
    And Marian's nose looks red and raw;
When roasted crabs[3] hiss in the bowl,
Then nightly sings the staring owl,
        "Tu-whit, tu-who!"—

A merry note,
While greasy Joan doth keel the pot.

[1]Stir.   [2]Platitude.   [3]Crab apples.

Hark, Hark, the Lark

William Shakespeare   (1564–1616)

Hark, hark, the lark at heaven's gate sings,
    And Phoebus gins[1] arise,
His steeds to water at those springs
    On chaliced[2] flowers that lies;
And winking Mary-buds[3] begin to ope their golden eyes;   5
With every thing that pretty is, my lady sweet, arise:
            Arise, arise!

[1]The sun begins to.   [2]Cup-shaped.   [3]Marigold buds.

Fear No More the Heat o' the Sun

William Shakespeare   (1564–1616)

Fear no more the heat o' the sun,
Nor the furious winter's rages,
Thou thy worldly task hast done,
Home art gone, and ta'en thy wages.   3
Golden lads and girls all must,
As chimney-sweepers, come to dust.   6
Fear no more the frown o' the great,
Thou art past the tyrant's stroke;
Care no more to clothe and eat,   9
To thee the reed is as the oak.
The sceptre, learning, physic,[1] must
All follow this and come to dust.   12

[1]Medical science.

Fear no more the lightning-flash.
Nor th' all-dreaded thunder-stone.[2]
Fear not slander, censure rash.   15
Thou hast finished joy and moan.
All lovers young, all lovers must
Consign to thee and come to dust.   18
No exorciser harm thee.
Nor no witchcraft charm thee.
Ghost unlaid forbear thee.   21
Nothing ill come near thee.
Quiet consummation have,
And renowned be thy grave.   24

[2]Thunderbolt.

Blow, Blow, Thou Winter Wind

William Shakespeare   (1564–1616)

Blow, blow, thou winter wind,
Thou art not so unkind
    As man's ingratitude;
Thy tooth is not so keen,
Because thou art not seen,   5
    Although thy breath be rude.
Heigh-ho, sing heigh-ho! unto the green holly,
Most friendship is feigning, most loving mere folly.
Then heigh-ho, the holly!
    This life is most jolly.   10

Freeze, freeze, thou bitter sky,
That dost not bite so nigh
    As benefits forgot;
Though thou the waters warp,
Thy sting is not so sharp   15
    As friend remembered not.
Heigh-ho, sing heigh-ho! etc.

Still to Be Neat

Ben Jonson   (1573–1637)

Still to be neat, still to be dressed,
As you were going to a feast;
Still to be powdered, still perfumed: 3
Lady, it is to be presumed,

Though art's hid causes are not found,
All is not sweet, all is not sound. 6

Give me a look, give me a face,
That makes simplicity a grace;
Robes loosely flowing, hair as free: 9
Such sweet neglect more taketh me
Than all the adulteries of art:
They strike mine eyes, but not my heart. 12

Call for the Robin Redbreast and the Wren

John Webster   (1580–1625)

Call for the robin redbreast and the wren,
Since o'er shady groves they hover,
And with leaves and flowers do cover
The friendless bodies of unburied men. 4
Call unto his funeral dole[1]
The ant, the field mouse, and the mole,
To rear him hillocks that shall keep him warm,
And, when gay tombs are robbed, sustain no harm; 8
But keep the wolf far thence, that's foe to men,
For with his nails he'll dig them up again.

[1]Lamentation.

Delight in Disorder

Robert Herrick   (1591–1674)

A sweet disorder in the dress
Kindles in clothes a wantonness.
A lawn[1] about the shoulders thrown
Into a fine distraction; 4
An erring lace, which here and there
Enthralls the crimson stomacher;[2]
A cuff neglectful, and thereby
Ribbons to flow confusedly; 8
A winning wave, deserving note,
In a tempestuous petticoat;
A careless shoestring, in whose tie
I see a wild civility; 12
Do more bewitch me than when art
Is too precise in every part.

[1]Shawl of fine linen.   [2]An ornamental cloth worn over the chest.

The Bad Season Makes the Poet Sad

Robert Herrick   (1591–1674)

Dull to myself, and almost dead to these
My many fresh and fragrant mistresses,
Lost to all music now, since everything
Puts on the semblance here of sorrowing.   4
Sick is the land to th' heart; and doth endure
More dangerous faintings by her desp'rate cure.
But if that golden age would come again,
And Charles[1] here rule, as he before did reign,   8
If smooth and unperplexed the seasons were,
As when the sweet Maria[2] livéd here,
I should delight to have my curls half drowned
In Tyrian dews, and head with roses crowned.   12
And once more yet (ere I am laid out dead)
Knock at a star with my exalted head.

[1]Charles I, beheaded 1649.   [2]Henrietta Maria, Charles's Queen.

The Pulley

George Herbert   (1593–1633)

When God at first made man,
Having a glass of blessings standing by,
"Let us," said he, "pour on him all we can:
Let the world's riches, which dispersed lie,
    Contract into a span."   5

So strength first made a way;
Then beauty flowed, then wisdom, honor, pleasure:
When almost all was out, God made a stay,
Perceiving that, alone of all his treasure,
    Rest in the bottom lay.   10

"For if I should," said he,
"Bestow this jewel also on my creature,
He would adore my gifts instead of me,
And rest in Nature, not the God of Nature:
    So both should losers be.   15

"Yet let him keep the rest,
But keep them with repining restlessness:
Let him be rich and weary, that at least,

If goodness lead him not, yet weariness
   May toss him to my breast."   20

Song

Edmund Waller   (1607–1687)

  Go, lovely rose!
Tell her that wastes her time and me
   That now she knows,
When I resemble[1] her to thee,
How sweet and fair she seems to be.   5

  Tell her that's young,
And shuns to have her graces spied,
   That hadst thou sprung
In deserts, where no men abide,
Thou must have uncommended died.   10

  Small is the worth
Of beauty from the light retired;
   Bid her come forth,
Suffer herself to be desired,
And not blush so to be admired.   15

  Then die! that she
The common fate of all things rare
   May read in thee;
How small a part of time they share
That are so wondrous sweet and fair!   20

[1]Compare.

On His Having Arrived at the Age of Twenty-Three

John Milton   (1608–1674)

How soon hath Time, the subtle thief of youth,
   Stolen on his wing my three-and-twentieth year!
   My hasting days fly on with full career,
   But my late spring no bud or blossom shew'th.[1]   4
Perhaps my semblance might deceive the truth
   That I to manhood am arrived so near;
   And inward ripeness doth much less appear,
   That some more timely-happy spirits endu'th.[2]   8

[1]Showeth. [2]Endow, clothe.

Yet, be it less or more, or soon or slow,
  It shall be still in strictest measure even[3]
  To that same lot, however mean or high,
Toward which Time leads me, and the will of Heaven,   12
  All is, if I have grace to use it so,
  As ever in my great Task-Master's eye.

[3]Equal.

Song

Sir John Suckling   (1609–1672)

No, no, fair heretic, it needs must be
  But an ill love in me,
  And worse for thee.
For were it in my power
To love thee now this hour   5
  More than I did the last,
"Twould then so fall
  I might not love at all.
Love that can flow, and can admit increase,
Admits as well an ebb, and may grow less.   10

True love is still the same; the torrid zones
  And those more frigid ones,
  It must not know;
For love, grown cold or hot,
Is lust or friendship, not   15
  The thing we have;
For that's a flame would die,
  Held down or up too high.
Then think I love more than I can express,
And would love more, could I but love thee less.   20

His Metrical Prayer: Before Execution[1]

James Graham   (1612–1650)

Let them bestow on every airth[2] a limb;
Open all my veins, that I may swim
To thee my Maker, in that crimson lake;
Then place my par-boiled head upon a stake;   4

[1]James Graham, Marquis of Montrose, was hanged, disembowelled, and dismembered. His intestines were burned and his remains distributed throughout Scotland. [2]Compass point.

Scatter my ashes, strew them in the air:
Lord since thou know'st where all these atoms are,
I'm hopeful thou'lt recover once my dust,
And confident thou'lt raise me with the just.   8

Whilst Alexis Lay Pressed

John Dryden   (1631–1700)

Whilst *Alexis* lay pressed
  In her arms he loved best,
With his hands round her neck,
  And his head on her breast,
He found the fierce pleasure too hasty to stay,   5
And his soul in the tempest just flying away.

When *Celia* saw this,
With a sigh, and a kiss,
She cried, Oh my dear, I am robbed of my bliss;
'Tis unkind to your love, and unfaithfully done,   10
To leave me behind you, and die all alone.

The youth, though in haste,
And breathing his last,
In pity died slowly, while she died more fast;
Till at length she cried, Now, my dear, now let us go,   15
Now die, my *Alexis,* and I will die too.

Thus intranced they did lie,
Till *Alexis* did try
To recover new breath, that again he might die:
Then often they did; but the more they did so,   20
The nymph died more quick, and the shepherd more slow.

Harvest Home

John Dryden   (1631–1700)

Your hay it is mowed, and your corn is reaped;
Your barns will be full, and your hovels heaped:
  Come, my boys, come;
  Come, my boys, come;
And merrily roar out Harvest Home.   5

Chorus. Come, my boys, come, &c.

We ha' cheated the parson, we'll cheat him again,
For why should a blockhead ha' one in ten?[1]
  One in ten,
  One in ten,
For why should a blockhead ha' one in Ten?   10

For prating so long like a book-learned sot,
Till pudding and dumpling burn to pot,
  Burn to pot,
  Burn to pot,
Till pudding and dumpling burn to pot.   15

Chorus. Burn to pot, etc.

We'll toss off our ale till we canno' stand,
And hoigh for the honor of old *England:*
  Old *England,*
  Old *England,*
And hoigh for the honor of Old *England.*   20

Chorus. Old *England,* etc.

---

[1]A tithe; one-tenth of a person's annual production given to the clergy.

[Man]*

Alexander Pope   (1688–1744)

Know then thyself, presume not God to scan;
The proper study of mankind is Man.
Placed on this isthmus of a middle state,
A being darkly wise, and rudely great: 4
With too much knowledge for the sceptic side,
With too much weakness for the stoic's pride,
He hangs between; in doubt to act, or rest,
In doubt to deem himself a god, or beast;   8
In doubt his mind or body to prefer,
Born but to die, and reasoning but to err;
Alike in ignorance, his reason such,
Whether he thinks too little, or too much: 12
Chaos of thought and passion, all confused;
Still by himself abused, or disabused;
Created half to rise, and half to fall;
Great lord of all things, yet a prey to all;   16

An Essay on Man, II, 1–18.

Sole judge of truth, in endless error hurled:
The glory, jest, and riddle of the world!

Ode

On a Distant Prospect[1] of
Eton College

Thomas Gray   (1716–1771)

Ye distant spires, ye antique towers,
That crown the watery glade,
Where grateful Science still adores
Her Henry's[2] holy shade;
And ye, that from the stately brow   5
Of Windsor's heights the expanse below
Of grove, of lawn, of mead survey,
Whose turf, whose shade, whose flowers among
Wanders the hoary Thames along
His silver-winding way.   10

   Ah happy hills, ah pleasing shade,
Ah fields beloved in vain,
Where once my careless childhood strayed,
A stranger yet to pain!
I feel the gales, that from ye blow,   15
A momentary bliss bestow,
As waving fresh their gladsome wing,
My weary soul they seem to soothe,
And, redolent of joy and youth,
To breathe a second spring.   20

   Say, Father Thames, for thou hast seen
Full many a sprightly race
Disporting on thy margent green
The paths of pleasure trace,
Who foremost now delight to cleave   25
With pliant arm thy glassy wave?
The captive linnet which enthrall?[3]
What idle progeny succeed[4]
To chase the rolling circle's[5] speed,
Or urge the flying ball?   30

[1]View.   [2]Henry VI, founder of Eton.   [3]Which boys imprison linnets?   [4]Take the place of earlier
schoolboys.   [5]Hoop.

While some on earnest business bent
Their murmuring labors ply
'Gainst graver hours, that bring constraint
To sweeten liberty:
Some bold adventurers disdain   35
The limits of their little reign,
And unknown regions dare descry:[6]
Still as they run they look behind,
They hear a voice in every wind,
And snatch a fearful joy.   40

    Gay hope is theirs by fancy fed,
Less pleasing when possessed;
The tear forgot as soon as shed,
The sunshine of the breast:
Theirs buxom health of rosy hue,   45
Wild wit, invention ever-new,
And lively cheer of vigor born;
The thoughtless day, the easy night,
The spirits pure, the slumbers light,
That fly the approach of morn.   50

    Alas, regardless of their doom,
The little victims play!
No sense have they of ills to come,
Nor care beyond today:
Yet see how all around 'em wait   55
The ministers of human fate,
And black Misfortune's baleful train!
Ah, show them where in ambush stand
To seize their prey the murderous band!
Ah, tell them, they are men!   60

    These shall the fury Passions tear,
The vultures of the mind,
Disdainful Anger, pallid Fear,
And Shame that skulks behind;
Or pining Love shall waste their youth,   65
Or Jealousy with rankling tooth,
That inly gnaws the secret heart,
And Envy wan, and faded Care,
Grim-visaged comfortless Despair,
And Sorrow's piercing dart.   70

    Ambition this[7] shall tempt to rise,
Then whirl the wretch from high,

___
[6]Discover. [7]This one.

To bitter Scorn a sacrifice,
And grinning Infamy.
The stings of Falsehood those[8] shall try,   75
And hard Unkindness' altered eye,
That mocks the tear it forced to flow;
And keen Remorse with blood defiled,
And moody Madness laughing wild
Amid severest woe.   80

   Lo, in the vale of years beneath
A grisly troop are seen,
The painful family of Death,
More hideous than their queen:
This racks the joints, this fires the veins,   85
That every laboring sinew strains,
Those in the deeper vitals rage:
Lo, Poverty, to fill the band,
That numbs the soul with icy hand,
And slow-consuming Age.   90

   To each his sufferings: all are men,
Condemned alike to groan,
The tender for another's pain;
The unfeeling for his own.
Yet ah! why should they know their fate?   95
Since sorrow never comes too late,
And happiness too swiftly flies.
Thought would destroy their paradise.
No more; where ignorance is bliss,
'Tis folly to be wise.   100

[8]Those others.

When Lovely Woman Stoops to Folly

Oliver Goldsmith   (1730–1774)

When lovely woman stoops to folly,
  And finds too late that men betray,
What charm can soothe her melancholy,
  What art can wash her guilt away?   4

The only art her guilt to cover,
  To hide her shame from every eye,
To give repentance to her lover,
  And wring his bosom—is to die.   8

The Clod and the Pebble

William Blake   (1757–1827)

'Love seeketh not itself to please,
Nor for itself hath any care,
But for another gives its ease
And builds a Heaven in Hell's despair.'   4

   So sang a little clod of clay,
   Trodden with the cattle's feet;
   But a pebble of the brook
   Warbled out these meters meet: 8

'Love seeketh only self to please,
To bind another to its delight,
Joys in another's loss of ease,
And builds a Hell in Heaven's despite.'   12

The Tiger

William Blake   (1757–1827)

Tiger, tiger, burning bright
In the forests of the night,
What immortal hand or eye
Could frame thy fearful symmetry?   4

In what distant deeps or skies
Burnt the fire of thine eyes?
On what wings dare he aspire?
What the hand dare seize the fire?   8

And what shoulder and what art
Could twist the sinews of thy heart?
And when thy heart began to beat,
What dread hand? And what dread feet?   12

What the hammer? What the chain?
In what furnace was thy brain?
What the anvil? What dread grasp
Dare its deadly terrors clasp?   16

When the stars threw down their spears
And watered Heaven with their tears,
Did he smile his work to see?
Did he who made the Lamb make thee?   20

Tiger, tiger, burning bright
In the forests of the night,
What immortal hand or eye
Dare frame thy fearful symmetry?   24

And Did Those Feet[1]

William Blake   (1757–1827)

And did those feet in ancient time
Walk upon England's mountains green?
And was the holy Lamb of God
On England's pleasant pastures seen?   4

And did the Countenance Divine
Shine forth upon our clouded hills?
And was Jerusalem builded here,
Among these dark Satanic Mills?[2]   8

Bring me my Bow of burning gold:
Bring me my Arrows of desire:
Bring me my Spear: O clouds unfold!
Bring me my Chariot of fire!   12

I will not cease from Mental Fight,
Nor shall my Sword sleep in my hand,
Till we have built Jerusalem
In England's green & pleasant Land.   16

[1]The feet of Jesus, who was believed by some to have visited England in the company of Joseph of Arimathea. The poem is from the preface to Blake's prophetic poem *Milton.*   [2]Millstones as symbolic of society; the mills of the industrial revolution.

Ah, Sunflower

William Blake   (1757–1827)

Ah, sunflower, weary of time,
Who countest the steps of the sun,
Seeking after that sweet golden clime
Where the traveller's journey is done;   4

Where the youth pined away with desire
And the pale virgin shrouded in snow
Arise their graves and aspire
Where my sunflower wishes to go.   8

London

William Blake   (1757–1827)

I wander through each chartered street
Near where the chartered Thames does flow,
And mark in every face I meet
Marks of weakness, marks of woe.   **4**

In every cry of every man,
In every infant's cry of fear,
In every voice, in every ban,
The mind-forged manacles I hear—   **8**

How the chimney-sweeper's cry
Every blackening church appalls,
And the hapless soldier's sigh
Runs in blood down palace walls;   **12**

But most through midnight streets I hear
How the youthful harlot's curse
Blasts the new-born infant's tear
And blights with plagues the marriage hearse.   **16**

Mock on, Mock on, Voltaire, Rousseau![1]

William Blake   (1757–1827)

Mock on, mock on, Voltaire, Rousseau!
Mock on, mock on—'Tis all in vain!
You throw the sand against the wind,
And the wind blows it back again.   **4**

And every sand becomes a gem
Reflected in the beams divine;
Blown back they blind the mocking eye,
But still in Israel's paths they shine.   **8**

The atoms of Democritus
And Newton's particles of light[2]
Are sands upon the Red Sea shore,
Where Israel's tents do shine so bright.   **12**

---

[1]Symbols, to Blake, of eighteenth-century skepticism.   [2]Democritus held atoms to be the primary materials of the universe. Newton thought light was composed of particles.

To a Louse

On Seeing One on a Lady's Bonnet at Church

Robert Burns   (1759–1796)

Ha! whare ye gaun, Ye crowlan ferlie![1]
Your impudence protects you sairly:[2]
I canna say but ye strunt rarely,   3
   Owre *gawze* and *lace;*
Tho' faith, I fear ye dine but sparely,
   On sic a place.   6

Ye ugly, creepan, blastet wonner,[3]
Detested, shunn'd, by saunt an' sinner,
How daur ye set your fit[4] upon her,   9
   Sae fine a *Lady!*
Gae somewhere else and seek you dinner,
   On some poor body.   12

Swith, in some beggar's haffet squattle;[5]
There ye may creep, and sprawl, and sprattle,
Wi' ither kindred, jumping cattle,   15
   In shoals and nations;
Whare *horn* nor *bane*[6] ne'er daur unsettle,
   Your thick plantations.   18

Now haud[7] you there, ye're out o' sight,
Below the fatt'rels,[8] snug and tight,
Na faith ye yet! ye'll no be right,   21
   Till ye've got on it,
The vera tapmost, towrin height
   O' *Miss's bonnet.*   24

My sooth! right bauld[9] ye set your nose out,
As plump an' gray as onie grozet:[10]
O for some rank, mercurial rozet,[11]   27
   Or fell, red smeddum,[12]
I'd gie you sic a heart does o't,
   Wad dress your droddum![13]   30

I wad na been surpriz'd to spy
You on an auld wife's *flainen toy;*[14]

---

[1]Crawling wonder. [2]Sorely. [3]Wonder. [4]Foot. [5]Off! in some beggar's whisker squat. [6]Horn nor bone [comb]. [7]Hold. [8]Ribbons. [9]Bold. [10]Gooseberry. [11]Resin. [12]Powder. [13]Backside. [14]Flannel cap.

Or aiblins[15] some bit duddie[16] boy,   33
  On 's *wylecoat;*[17]
But Miss's fine *Lunardi,*[18] fye!
  How daur ye do't?   36

O *Jenny* dinna toss your head,
An' set your beauties a' abroad![19]
Ye little ken[20] what cursed speed   39
  The blastie's[21] makin!
Thae[22] *winks* and *finger-ends,* I dread,
  Are notice takin!   42

O wad some Pow'r the giftie gie[23] us
To see oursels as others see us!
It wad frae monie a blunder free us   45
  An' foolish notion:
What airs in dress an' gait wad lea'e us,
  And ev' n Devotion!   48

[15]Perhaps. [16]Small, ragged. [17]Waistcoat. [18]Bonnet. [19]All abroad. [20]Know. [21]Dwarf's.
[22]Those. [23]Gift give.

She Dwelt Among the Untrodden Ways

William Wordsworth   (1770–1850)

She dwelt among the untrodden ways
  Beside the springs of Dove,
A Maid whom there were none to praise
  And very few to love: 4

A violet by a mossy stone
  Half hidden from the eye!
—Fair as a star, when only one
  Is shining in the sky.   8

She lived unknown, and few could know
  When Lucy ceased to be;
But she is in her grave, and, oh,
  The difference to me!   12

A Slumber Did My Spirit Seal

William Wordsworth   (1770–1850)

A slumber did my spirit seal;
  I had no human fears:
She seemed a thing that could not feel
  The touch of earthly years.   4

No motion has she now, no force;
   She neither hears nor sees;
Rolled round in earth's diurnal[1] course,
   With rocks, and stones, and trees.   8

[1]Daily.

Ode

*Intimations of Immortality from Recollections
of Early Childhood*

William Wordsworth   *(1770–1850)*

*The Child is father of the Man;
And I could wish my days to be
Bound each to each by natural piety.*[1]

I

There was a time when meadow, grove, and stream,
The earth, and every common sight,
      To me did seem
      Apparelled in celestial light,
The glory and the freshness of a dream.   5
It is not now as it hath been of yore;—
      Turn wheresoe'er I may,
      By night or day,
The things which I have seen I now can see no more.

II

      The Rainbow comes and goes,   10
      And lovely is the Rose,
      The Moon doth with delight
Look round her when the heavens are bare;
      Waters on a starry night
      Are beautiful and fair;   15
   The sunshine is a glorious birth;
   But yet I know, where'er I go,
That there hath past away a glory from the earth.

III

Now, while the birds thus sing a joyous song,
   And while the young lambs bound   20
    As to the tabor's[2] sound,

[1]The last three lines of Wordsworth's "My Heart Leaps Up."   [2]A small drum.

To me alone there came a thought of grief:
A timely utterance gave that thought relief,
      And I again am strong:
The cataracts blow their trumpets from the steep;
No more shall grief of mine the season wrong;   25
I hear the Echoes through the mountains throng,
The Winds come to me from the fields of sleep,
      And all the earth is gay;
        Land and sea
      Give themselves up to jollity,   30
        And with the heart of May
      Doth every Beast keep holiday;—
        Thou Child of Joy,
Shout round me, let me hear thy shouts, thou happy Shepherd-boy!

IV

Ye blessed Creatures, I have heard the call   35
  Ye to each other make; I see
The heavens laugh with you in your jubilee;
    My heart is at your festival,
        My head hath its coronal,[3]
The fulness of your bliss, I feel—I feel it all.   40
      Oh evil day! if I were sullen
      While Earth herself is adorning,
        This sweet May-morning,
      And the Children are culling
        On every side,   45
      In a thousand valleys far and wide,
      Fresh flowers; while the sun shines warm,
And the Babe leaps up on his Mother's arm:—
      I hear, I hear, with joy I hear!
      —But there's a Tree, of many, one,   50
A single Field which I have looked upon,
Both of them speak of something that is gone:
      The Pansy at my feet
      Doth the same tale repeat:
Whither is fled the visionary gleam?   55
Where is it now, the glory and the dream?

V

Our birth is but a sleep and a forgetting:
The Soul that rises with us, our life's Star,
    Hath had elsewhere its setting,
      And cometh from afar: 60

[3]Crown of flowers.

Not in entire forgetfulness,
And not in utter nakedness,
But trailing clouds of glory do we come
    From God, who is our home:
Heaven lies about us in our infancy!   65
Shades of the prison-house begin to close
    Upon the growing Boy,
        But He
Beholds the light, and whence it flows,
    He sees it in his joy;   70
The Youth, who daily farther from the east
    Must travel, still is Nature's Priest,
    And by the vision splendid
    Is on his way attended;
At length the Man perceives it die away,
And fade into the light of common day.   75

VI

Earth fills her lap with pleasures of her own;
Yearnings she hath in her own natural kind,
And, even with something of a Mother's mind,
    And no unworthy aim,
    The homely[4] Nurse doth all she can   80
To make her Foster-child, her Inmate Man,
    Forget the glories he hath known,
And that imperial palace whence he came.

VII

Behold the Child among his new-born blisses,
A six years' Darling of a pigmy size!   85
See, where 'mid work of his own hand he lies,
Frettied by sallies of his mother's kisses,
With light upon him from his father's eyes!
See, at his feet, some little plan or chart,
Some fragment from his dream of human life,   90
Shaped by himself with newly-learned art;
    A wedding or a festival,
    A mourning or a funeral;
        And this hath now his heart,
    And unto this he frames his song: 95
        Then will he fit his tongue
To dialogues of business, love, or strife;
    But it will not be long

4Simple, unpretentious.

Ere this be thrown aside,
    And with new joy and pride   100
The little Actor cons another part;
Filling from time to time his "humorous stage"[5]
With all the Persons, down to palsied Age,
That Life brings with her in her equipage;
    As if his whole vocation   105
    Were endless imitation.

VIII

Thou, whose exterior semblance doth belie,
    Thy Soul's immensity;
Thou best Philosopher, who yet dost keep
Thy heritage, thou Eye among the blind,   110
That, deaf and silent, read'st the eternal deep,
Haunted for ever by the eternal mind,—
    Mighty Prophet! Seer blest!
    On whom those truths do rest,
Which we are toiling all our lives to find,   115
In darkness lost, the darkness of the grave;
Thou, over whom thy Immortality
Broods like the Day, a Master o'er a Slave,
A Presence which is not to be put by;
Thou little Child, yet glorious in the might   120
Of heaven-born freedom on thy being's height,
Why with such earnest pains dost thou provoke
The years to bring the inevitable yoke,
Thus blindly with thy blessedness at strife?
Full soon thy Soul shall have her earthly freight,   125
And custom lie upon thee with a weight,
Heavy as frost, and deep almost as life!

IX

    O joy! that in our embers
    Is something that doth live,
    That nature yet remembers   130
    What was so fugitive!
The thought of our past years in me doth breed
Perpetual benediction: not indeed
For that which is most worthy to be blest;
Delight and liberty, the simple creed   135
Of Childhood, whether busy or at rest,
With new-fledged hope still fluttering in his breast:—

[5]Displaying the "humors," or characteristic temperaments, of people.

Not for these I raise
   The song of thanks and praise;
  But for those obstinate questionings   140
  Of sense and outward things,
  Fallings from us, vanishings;
   Blank misgivings of a Creature
Moving about in worlds not realised,
High instincts before which our mortal Nature   145
Did tremble like a guilty Thing surprised:
   But for those first affections,
   Those shadowy recollections,
  Which, be they what they may,
Are yet the fountain light of all our day,   150
Are yet a master light of all our seeing;
  Uphold us, cherish, and have power to make
Our noisy years seem moments in the being
Of the eternal Silence: truths that wake,
    To perish never;   155
Which neither listlessness, nor mad endeavour,
    Nor Man nor Boy,
Nor all that is at enmity with joy,
Can utterly abolish or destroy!
    Hence in a season of calm weather   160
    Though inland far we be,
Our Souls have sight of that immortal sea
    Which brought us hither,
    Can in a moment travel thither,
And see the Children sport upon the shore,   165
And hear the mighty waters rolling evermore.

X

Then sing, ye Birds, sing, sing a joyous song!
    And let the young Lambs bound
    As to the tabor's sound!
We in thought will join your throng,
    Ye that pipe and ye that play,   170
    Ye that through your hearts to-day
    Feel the gladness of the May!
What though the radiance which was once so bright
Be now for ever taken from my sight,
    Though nothing can bring back the hour   175
Of splendour in the grass, of glory in the flower;
    We will grieve not, rather find
    Strength in what remains behind;
    In the primal sympathy

Which having been must ever be; 180
In the soothing thoughts that spring
Out of human suffering;
In the faith that looks through death,
In years that bring the philosophic mind.

XI

And O, ye Fountains, Meadows, Hills, and Groves, 185
Forebode not any severing of our loves!
Yet in my heart of hearts I feel your might;
I only have relinquished one delight
To live beneath your more habitual sway.
I love the Brooks which down their channels fret, 190
Even more than when I tripped lightly as they;
The innocent brightness of a new-born Day
        Is lovely yet;
The Clouds that gather round the setting sun
Do take a sober colouring from an eye 195
That hath kept watch o'er man's mortality;
Another race hath been, and other palms are won.
Thanks to the human heart by which we live,
Thanks to its tenderness, its joys, and fears,
To me the meanest flower that blows[6] can give 200
Thoughts that do often lie too deep for tears.

[6]Blooms.

Kubla Khan[1]

Samuel Taylor Coleridge   *(1772–1834)*

In Xanadu did Kubla Khan
A stately pleasure-dome decree:
Where Alph, the sacred river, ran
Through caverns measureless to man
    Down to a sunless sea. 5
So twice five miles of fertile ground
With walls and towers were girdled round:
And there were gardens bright with sinuous rills,[2]
Where blossomed many an incense-bearing tree;
And here were forests ancient as the hills, 10
Enfolding sunny spots of greenery.

[1]Kubla Khan was a thirteenth-century Mongol ruler, but the place names and most of the supporting details are imaginary. Coleridge said he composed the poem in a drug-induced dream.
[2]Small brooks.

But oh! that deep romantic chasm which slanted
Down the green hill athwart a cedarn cover!
A savage place! as holy and enchanted
As e'er beneath a waning moon was haunted   15
By woman wailing for her demon-lover![3]
And from this chasm, with ceaseless turmoil seething,
As if this earth in fast thick pants were breathing,
A mighty fountain momently was forced:
Amid whose swift half-intermitted burst   20
Huge fragments vaulted like rebounding hail,
Or chaffy grain beneath the thresher's flail:
And 'mid these dancing rocks at once and ever
It flung up momently the sacred river.
Five miles meandering with a mazy motion   25
Through wood and dale the sacred river ran,
Then reached the caverns measureless to man,
And sank in tumult to a lifeless ocean:
And 'mid this tumult Kubla heard from far
Ancestral voices prophesying war!   30
    The shadow of the dome of pleasure
    Floated midway on the waves;
    Where was heard the mingled measure
    From the fountain and the caves.
It was a miracle of rare device,   35
A sunny pleasure-dome with caves of ice!

    A damsel with a dulcimer
    In a vision once I saw:
    It was an Abyssinian maid,
    And on her dulcimer she played,   40
    Singing of Mount Abora.
    Could I revive within me
    Her symphony and song,
    To such a deep delight 'twould win me,
That with music loud and long,   45
I would build that dome in air,
That sunny dome! those caves of ice!
And all who heard should see them there,
And all should cry, Beware! Beware!
His flashing eyes, his floating hair!   50
Weave a circle round him thrice,[4]
And close your eyes with holy dread,
For he on honey-dew hath fed,
And drunk the milk of Paradise.

---

[3]The demon lover is common in folklore and folksong.   [4]A charm against intrusion.

Ode to the West Wind

Percy Bysshe Shelley   (1792–1822)

1

O wild West Wind, thou breath of Autumn's being,
Thou, from whose unseen presence the leaves dead
Are driven, like ghosts from an enchanter fleeing,

Yellow, and black, and pale, and hectic red,
Pestilence-stricken multitudes: O thou,   5
Who chariotest to their dark wintry bed

The wingéd seeds, where they lie cold and low,
Each like a corpse within its grave, until
Thine azure sister of the Spring shall blow

Her clarion[1] o'er the dreaming earth, and fill   10
(Driving sweet buds like flocks to feed in air)
With living hues and odors plain and hill:

Wild Spirit, which are moving everywhere;
Destroyer and preserver; hear, oh, hear!

2

Thou on whose stream, mid the steep sky's commotion,   15
Loose clouds like earth's decaying leaves are shed,
Shook from the tangled boughs of Heaven and Ocean,

Angels of rain and lightning: there are spread
On the blue surface of thine aëry surge,
Like the bright hair uplifted from the head   20

Of some fierce Maenad,[2] even from the dim verge
Of the horizon to the zenith's height,
The locks of the approaching storm. Thou dirge

Of the dying year, to which this closing night
Will be the dome of a vast sepulcher,   25
Vaulted with all thy congregated might

Of vapors, from whose solid atmosphere
Black rain, and fire, and hail will burst: oh, hear!

3

Thou who didst waken from his summer dreams
The blue Mediterranean, where he lay,   30
Lulled by the coil of his crystálline streams,

[1]Trumpet. [2]A female worshiper of Bacchus; a frenzied, dancing woman.

Beside a pumice isle in Baiae's bay,[3]
And saw in sleep old palaces and towers
Quivering within the wave's intenser day,

All overgrown with azure moss and flowers   35
So sweet, the sense faints picturing them! Thou
For whose path the Atlantic's level powers

Cleave themselves into chasms, while far below
The sea-blooms and the oozy woods which wear
The sapless foliage of the ocean, know   40

Thy voice, and suddenly grow gray with fear,
And tremble and despoil themselves: oh, hear!

4

If I were a dead leaf thou mightest bear;
If I were a swift cloud to fly with thee;
A wave to pant beneath thy power, and share   45

The impulse of thy strength, only less free
Than thou, O uncontrollable! If even
I were as in my boyhood, and could be

The comrade of thy wanderings over Heaven,
As then, when to outstrip thy skyey speed   50
Scarce seem a vision; I would ne'er have striven

As thus with thee in prayer in my sore need.
Oh, lift me as a wave, a leaf, a cloud!
I fall upon the thorns of life! I bleed!

A heavy weight of hours has chained and bowed   55
One too like thee: tameless, and swift, and proud.

5

Make me thy lyre,[4] even as the forest is:
What if my leaves are falling like its own!
The tumult of thy mighty harmonies

Will take from both a deep, autumnal tone,   60
Sweet though in sadness. Be thou, Spirit fierce,
My spirit! Be thou me, impetuous one!

Drive my dead thoughts over the universe
Like withered leaves to quicken a new birth!
And, by the incantation of this verse,   65

[3]Near Naples.   [4]An aeolian harp (or lyre) plays when the wind blows over its strings.

Scatter, as from an unextinguished hearth
Ashes and sparks, my words among mankind!
Be through my lips to unawakened earth

The trumpet of a prophecy! O Wind,
If Winter comes, can Spring be far behind!   70

Badger

John Clare   (1793–1864)

When midnight comes a host of dogs and men
Go out and track the badger to his den,
And put a sack within the hole, and lie
Till the old grunting badger passes by.   4
He comes and hears—they let the strongest loose.
The old fox hears the noise and drops the goose.
The poacher shoots and hurries from the cry,
And the old hare half wounded buzzes by.   8
They get a forkèd stick to bear him down
And clap the dogs and take him to the town,
And bait him all the day with many dogs,
And laugh and shout and fright the scampering hogs.   12
He runs along and bites at all he meets:
They shout and hollo down the noisy streets.

He turns about to face the loud uproar
And drives the rebels to their very door.   16
The frequent stone is hurled where'er they go;
When badgers fight, then every one's a foe.
The dogs are clapped and urged to join the fray;
The badger turns and drives them all away.   20
Though scarcely half as big, demure and small,
He fights with dogs for hours and beats them all.
The heavy mastiff, savage in the fray,
Lies down and licks his feet and turns away.   24
The bulldog knows his match and waxes cold,
The badger grins and never leaves his hold.
He drives the crowd and follows at their heels
And bites them through—the drunkard swears and reels.   28

The frighted women take the boys away,
The blackguard laughs and hurries on the fray.
He tries to reach the woods; an awkward race,
But sticks and cudgels quickly stop the chase.   32
He turns again and drives the noisy crowd

And beats the many dogs in noises loud.
He drives away and beats them every one,
And then they loose them all and set them on.   34
He falls as dead and kicked by boys and men,
Then starts and grins and drives the crowd again;
Till kicked and torn and beaten out he lies
And leaves his hold and cackles, groans, and dies.   36

Gypsies

John Clare   (1793–1864)

The snow falls deep; the forest lies alone;
The boy goes hasty for his load of brakes,[1]
Then thinks upon the fire and hurries back;
The gypsy knocks his hands and tucks them up,   4
And seeks his squalid camp, half hid in snow,
Beneath the oak which breaks away the wind,
And bushes close in snow like hovel warm;
There tainted mutton wastes upon the coals,   8
And the half-wasted dog squats close and rubs,
Then feels the heat too strong, and goes aloof;
He watches well, but none a bit can spare,
And vainly waits the morsel thrown away.   12
'Tis thus they live—a picture to the place,
A quiet, pilfering, unprotected race.

[1]Brushwood.

On First Looking into Chapman's Homer[1]

John Keats   (1795–1821)

Much have I travelled in the realms of gold,
    And many goodly states and kingdoms seen;
    Round many western islands have I been
Which bards in fealty[2] to Apollo[3] hold.   4
Oft of one wide expanse had I been told
    That deep-browed Homer ruled as his demesne;[4]
    Yet did I never breathe its pure serene
Till I heard Chapman speak out loud and bold.   8
Then felt I like some watcher of the skies
    When a new planet swims into his ken;

[1]The translation of Homer by George Chapman, an Elizabethan poet.   [2]Allegiance.   [3]God of the
sun and also music and poetry.   [4]Domain.

Or like stout Cortez when with eagle eyes
   He stared at the Pacific, and all his men   12
Looked at each other with a wild surmise—
   Silent, upon a peak in Darien.[5]

[5]Keats confused Cortez with Balboa, who first saw the Pacific from a "peak in Darien" (Panama).

Ode to a Nightingale

John Keats   *(1795–1821)*

I

My heart aches, and a drowsy numbness pains
   My sense, as though of hemlock[1] I had drunk,
Or emptied some dull opiate to the drains
   One minute past, and Lethe-wards[2] had sunk.
'Tis not through envy of thy happy lot,   5
   But being too happy in thine happiness—
      That thou, light-wingèd Dryad[3] of the trees,
         In some melodious plot
Of beechen green, and shadows numberless,
   Singest of summer in full-throated ease.   10

II

Oh, for a draught of vintage that hath been
   Cooled a long age in the deep-delvèd earth,
Tasting of Flora and the country green,
   Dance, and Provençal song, and sunburnt mirth!
Oh, for a beaker full of the warm South,   15
   Full of the true, the blushful Hippocrene,[4]
      With beaded bubbles winking at the brim,
         And purple-stainèd mouth,
That I might drink, and leave the world unseen,
   And with thee fade away into the forest dim—   20

III

Fade far away, dissolve, and quite forget
   What thou among the leaves hast never known,
The weariness, the fever, and the fret
   Here, where men sit and hear each other groan;

[1]Poisonous herb. [2]Toward the river of forgetfulness in Hades. [3]Wood nymph. [4]A sacred spring on Mount Helicon.

Where palsy shakes a few, sad, last gray hairs, 25
    Where youth grows pale, and spectre-thin, and dies;
        Where but to think is to be full of sorrow
           And leaden-eyed despairs;
Where Beauty cannot keep her lustrous eyes,
    Or new Love pine at them beyond to-morrow. 30

IV

Away! away! For I will fly to thee,
    Not charioted by Bacchus and his pards,[5]
But on the viewless wings of Poesy,
    Though the dull brain perplexes and retards.
Already with thee! Tender is the night, 35
    And haply the Queen-Moon is on her throne,
        Clustered around by all her starry fays;[6]
           But here there is no light,
Save what from heaven is with the breezes blown
    Through verdurous[7] glooms and winding mossy ways. 40

V

I cannot see what flowers are at my feet,
    Nor what soft incense hangs upon the boughs,
But, in embalmèd darkness, guess each sweet
    Wherewith the seasonable month endows
The grass, the thicket, and the fruit-tree wild— 45
    White hawthorn, and the pastoral eglantine;
        Fast-fading violets covered up in leaves;
           And mid-May's eldest child,
The coming musk-rose, full of dewy wine,
    The murmurous haunt of flies on summer eves. 50

VI

Darkling,[8] I listen; and, for many a time
    I have been half in love with easeful Death,
Called him soft names in many a musèd rhyme,
    To take into the air my quiet breath;
Now more than ever seems it rich to die, 55
    To cease upon the midnight with no pain,
        While thou art pouring forth thy soul abroad
           In such an ecstasy.

[5]Bacchus, god of wine, was sometimes depicted with leopards. [6]Fairies. [7]Green-foliaged.
[8]In the dark.

Still wouldst thou sing, and I have ears in vain—
    To thy high requiem become a sod.   60

VII

Thou wast not born for death, immortal Bird!
  No hungry generations tread thee down;
The voice I hear this passing night was heard
  In ancient days by emperor and clown:
Perhaps the self-same song that found a path   65
  Through the sad heart of Ruth, when, sick for home,
    She stood in tears amid the alien corn;[9]
      The same that oft-times hath
Charmed magic casements, opening on the foam
Of perilous seas in fairy lands forlorn.   70

VIII

Forlorn! The very word is like a bell
  To toll me back from thee to my sole self!
Adieu! The fancy cannot cheat so well
  As she is famed to do, deceiving elf.
Adieu! adieu! Thy plaintive anthem fades   75
  Past the near meadows, over the still stream,
    Up the hill-side; and now 'tis buried deep
      In the next valley-glades:
Was it a vision, or a waking dream?
  Fled is that music . . . Do I wake or sleep?   80

[9]Cf. Ruth 2.3.

Ode on a Grecian Urn

John Keats   *(1795–1821)*

I

Thou still unravished bride of quietness,
  Thou foster-child of silence and slow time,
Sylvan[1] historian, who canst thus express
  A flowery tale more sweetly than our rhyme!

[1]Woodland.

What leaf-fringed legend haunts about thy shape   5
   Of deities or mortals, or of both,
      In Tempe or the dales of Arcady?[2]
   What men or gods are these? What maidens loath?
What mad pursuit? What struggle to escape?
      What pipes and timbrels?[3] What wild ecstasy?   10

II

Heard melodies are sweet, but those unheard
   Are sweeter; therefore, ye soft pipes, play on;
Not to the sensual ear, but, more endeared,
   Pipe to the spirit ditties of no tone.
Fair youth beneath the trees, thou canst not leave   15
Thy song, nor ever can those trees be bare;
      Bold lover, never, never canst thou kiss,
Though winning near the goal—yet do not grieve:
   She cannot fade, though thou hast not thy bliss,
      For ever wilt thou love, and she be fair!   20

III

Ah, happy, happy boughs, that cannot shed
   Your leaves, nor ever bid the spring adieu;
And, happy melodist, unwearièd,
   For ever piping songs for ever new!
More happy love, more happy, happy love!   25
   For ever warm and still to be enjoyed,
      For ever panting, and for ever young—
All breathing human passion far above,
   That leaves a heart high-sorrowful and cloyed,
      A burning forehead, and a parching tongue.   30

IV

Who are these coming to the sacrifice?
   To what green altar, O mysterious priest,
Lead'st thou that heifer lowing at the skies,
   And all her silken flanks with garlands dressed?
What little town by river or sea shore,   35
   Or mountain-built with peaceful citadel,
      Is emptied of this folk, this pious morn?

[2]Tempe: a valley in Greece; Arcady: Arcadia, Greek state associated with a pastoral ideal.
[3]Small drums.

And, little town, thy streets for evermore
  Will silent be; and not a soul to tell
    Why thou art desolate can e'er return.   40

V

O Attic[4] shape! Fair attitude! With brede[5]
  Of marble men and maidens overwrought,
With forest branches and the trodden weed—
  Thou, silent form, dost tease us out of thought
As doth eternity. Cold pastoral!   45
  When old age shall this generation waste,
    Thou shalt remain, in midst of other woe
Than ours, a friend to man, to whom thou say'st,
  'Beauty is truth, truth beauty'—that is all
    Ye know on earth, and all ye need to know.   50

[4]From the region of Athens. [5]Interwoven pattern; braid.

Ode on Melancholy

John Keats   *(1795–1821)*

I

No, no, go not to Lethe,[1] neither twist
  Wolf's-bane,[2] tight-rooted, for its poisonous wine;
Nor suffer thy pale forehead to be kissed
  By nightshade, ruby grape of Proserpine;[3]
Make not your rosary of yew-berries,[4]   5
  Nor let the beetle, nor the death-moth be
    Your mournful Psyche,[5] nor the downy owl
A partner in your sorrow's mysteries;
  For shade to shade will come too drowsily,
    And drown the wakeful anguish of the soul.   10

II

But when the melancholy fit shall fall
  Sudden from heaven like a weeping cloud,
That fosters the droop-headed flowers all,
  And hides the green hill in an April shroud;

[1]The river of forgetfulness. [2]A common poisonous plant, as is nightshade, 1. 4. [3]Persephone, queen of the underworld. [4]Symbolic of death. [5]Psyche: The soul, often pictured as a butterfly, in mourning for her lost lover, Cupid.

Then glut thy sorrow on a morning rose,   15
   Or on the rainbow of the salt sand-wave,
   Or on the wealth of globèd peonies;
Or if thy mistress some rich anger shows,
   Imprison her soft hand, and let her rave,
     And feed deep, deep upon her peerless eyes.   20

III

She dwells with Beauty—Beauty that must die;
   And Joy, whose hand is ever at his lips
Bidding adieu; and aching Pleasure nigh,
   Turning to poison while the bee-mouth sips.
Aye, in the very temple of Delight   25
   Veiled Melancholy has her sovran shrine,
     Though seen of none save him whose strenuous
       tongue
   Can burst Joy's grape against his palate fine;
His soul shall taste the sadness of her might,
     And be among her cloudy trophies hung.   30

To Autumn

John Keats   *(1795–1821)*

I

Season of mists and mellow fruitfulness,
   Close bosom friend of the maturing sun,
Conspiring with him how to load and bless
   With fruit the vines that round the thatch-eaves run:
To bend with apples the mossed cottage-trees,   5
   And fill all fruit with ripeness to the core;
     To swell the gourd, and plump the hazel shells
     With a sweet kernel; to set budding more,
And still more, later flowers for the bees,
Until they think warm days will never cease,   10
     For summer has o'er-brimmed their clammy cells.

II

Who hath not seen thee oft amid thy store?[1]
   Sometimes whoever seeks abroad may find
Thee sitting careless on a granary floor,
   Thy hair soft-lifted by the winnowing wind;   15

---

[1]Abundance.

Or on a half-reaped furrow sound asleep,
Drowsed with the fume of poppies, while thy hook[2]
Spares the next swath and all its twinèd flowers;
And sometimes like a gleaner[3] thou dost keep
Steady thy laden head across a brook;   20
Or by a cider-press, with patient look,
Thou watchest the last oozings hours by hours,

III

Where are the songs of spring? Aye, where are they?
Think not of them, thou hast thy music too—
While barrèd clouds bloom the soft-dying day,   25
And touch the stubble-plains with rosy hue.
Then in a wailful choir the small gnats mourn
Among the river sallows,[4] borne aloft
Or sinking as the light wind lives or dies;
And full-grown lambs loud bleat from hilly bourn;[5]   30
Hedge-crickets sing; and now with treble soft
The red-breast whistles from a garden-croft;[6]
And gathering swallows twitter in the skies.

[2]Sickle.   [3]One who gathers after reapers.   [4]Willows.   [5]Field.   [6]Enclosed field, kitchen garden.

To Helen

Edgar Allan Poe   (1809–1849)

Helen, thy beauty is to me
Like those Nicéan barks of yore,
That gently, o'er a perfumed sea,
The weary, way-worn wanderer bore
To his own native shore.   5

On desperate seas long wont to roam,
Thy hyacinth hair, thy classic face,
Thy Naiad[1] airs have brought me home
To the glory that was Greece,
And the grandeur that was Rome.   10

Lo! in yon brilliant window-niche
How statue-like I see thee stand,
The agate lamp within thy hand!
Ah, Psyche, from the regions which
Are Holy-Land!   15

[1]Water nymph.

The Eagle

Alfred, Lord Tennyson   (1809–1892)

He clasps the crag with crookèd hands;
Close to the sun in lonely lands,
Ringed with the azure world, he stands.   3

The wrinkled sea beneath him crawls;
He watches from his mountain walls,
And like a thunderbolt he falls.   6

[From] The Rubáiyát of Omar Khayyám

Translated by Edward FitzGerald[1]   (1809–1883)

I

Awake! for Morning in the Bowl of Night
Has flung the Stone that puts the Stars to Flight:
   And Lo! the Hunter of the East has caught
The Sultán's Turret in a Noose of Light   (1st)[2]   4

III

  And, as the Cock crew, those who stood before
The Tavern shouted—"Open then the Door!
   "You know how little while we have to stay,
"And, once departed, may return no more."   (1st)   8

VII

Come, fill the Cup, and in the Fire of Spring
Your Winter-garment of Repentence fling:
   The Bird of Time has but a little way
To flutter—and the Bird is on the Wing.   (2nd)   12

[1]FitzGerald (1809–1883), except for five of his childhood years and a year of his youth in Paris, never left England. He had already translated some Persian poets when his friend, Professor E. B. Cowell, an orientalist, discovered in the Bodleian Library, Oxford, a manuscript of Omar Khayyám (d. 1123 or 1132), written in deep purple ink dusted with gold. This "rubáiyát"—which means simply "quatrainiad"—FitzGerald translated into English quatrains that no subsequent translator has equaled. He expanded and revised his first edition of 75 quatrains (1859) into a second of 110 (1868). He trimmed this to a third edition of 101 (1872), polishing further for a fourth (1879).

   Our selections follow the order of the second edition. The roman numerals indicate the stanza in the edition shown in parenthesis. But we have overruled the poet, as popularity has frequently done too, in preferring some of his earlier versions. *Khayyám* means "the tentmaker." [2]Fitz-Gerald's note: "Flinging a stone into the cup was the signal for 'To horse!' in the desert."

XII

Here with a little Bread beneath the Bough,
A Flask of Wine, a Book of Verse—and Thou
   Beside me singing in the Wilderness—
Oh, Wilderness were Paradise enow!   (2nd)[3]   **16**

XIII

Some for the Glories of This World; and some
Sigh for the Prophet's Paradise to come;
   Ah, take the Cash and let the Credit go,
Nor heed the rumble of a distant Drum!   (3rd)   **20**

XXI

Ah, my Beloved, fill the Cup that clears
To-day of past Regrets and future Fears:
   To-morrow! Why, To-morrow I may be
Myself with Yesterday's Sev'n thousand Years.   (2nd)[4]   **24**

XXVII

Myself when young did eagerly frequent
Doctor and Saint, and heard great argument
   About it and about: but evermore
Came out by the same door where in I went.   (3rd)   **28**

XXXII

Into the Universe, and *Why* not knowing
Nor *Whence,* like Water willy-nilly flowing;
   And out of it, as Wind along the Waste,
I know not *Whither,* willy-nilly blowing.   (2nd)   **32**

XL

For I remember stopping by the way
To watch a Potter thumping his wet Clay:
   And with its all-obliterated Tongue
It murmur'd—"Gently, Brother, gently, pray!"   (2nd)   **36**

[3]The popular version of this most famous of Omar's quatrains is that of the third edition, reading:

      A Book of Verses underneath the Bough,
      A Jug of Wine, a Loaf of Bread—and Thou . . .

But the first line loses some metrical verve, and FitzGerald loses Omar's point by swelling his bit of bread to a loaf, and his flask to a jug. Omar says that a modest supply of earth's bounties, with friendship, can make a desert surpass the Sultan's palace. FitzGerald's third edition also drops the "Here," so characteristic of Omar's here and now.   [4]FitzGerald's note: "A thousand years to each Planet."

XLVIII

While the Rose blows along the River Brink,
With old Khayyám the Ruby Vintage drink:
　　And when the Angel with his darker Draught
Draws up to Thee—take that, and do not shrink.　　　　(1st)　　　**40**

XLIII

The Grape that can with Logic absolute
The Two-and-Seventy jarring Sects confute:
　　The subtle Alchemist that in a Trice
Life's leaden Metal into Gold transmute.　　　　　　　(1st)　　　**44**

XLVII

And fear not lest Existence closing *your*
Account, should lose, or know the type no more;
　　The Eternal Sáki from the Bowl has pour'd
Millions of Bubbles like us, and will pour.　　　　　(2nd)　　　**48**

XXXVIII

One Moment in Annihilation's Waste,
One Moment, of the Well of Life to taste—
　　The Stars are setting and the Caravan
Starts for the Dawn of Nothing—Oh, make haste!　　　(1st)[5]　　**52**

LV

You know, my Friends, with what a brave Carouse
I made a Second Marriage in my house;
　　Divorced old barren Reason from my Bed,
And took the Daughter of the Vine to Spouse.　　　　(3rd)　　　**56**

LXIII

Why, be this Juice the growth of God, who dare
Blaspheme the twisted tendril as a Snare?
　　A Blessing, we should use it, should we not?
And if a Curse—why, then, Who set it there?　　　　(2nd)　　　**60**

LXVI

Oh threats of Hell and Hopes of Paradise!
One thing at least is certain—*This* Life flies:
　　One thing is certain and the rest is lies;
The Flower that once is blown for ever dies.　　　　(2nd)　　　**64**

---

[5]FitzGerald's note: "The caravan travelling by night (after their New Year's Day of the vernal equinox) by command of Mohammed, I believe."

LXIX

But helpless Pieces of the Game He plays
Upon this Chequer-board of Nights and Days;
   Hither and thither moves, and checks, and slays,
And one by one back in the Closet lays.   (3rd)   68

LXXVI

The Moving Finger writes; and, having writ,
Moves on: nor all your Piety nor Wit
   Shall lure it back to cancel half a Line,
Nor all your Tears wash out a Word of it.   (2nd)   72

LXXII

And that inverted Bowl they call The Sky,
Whereunder crawling coop'd we live and die,
   Lift not your hands to *It* for help—for It
As impotently moves as you or I.   (4th)   76

LXXXI

Oh, Thou, who Man of baser Earth didst make,
And ev'n with Paradise devise the Snake:
   For all the Sin wherewith the Face of Man
Is blacken'd—Man's forgiveness give—and take!   (3rd)   80

XCVIII

Ah, with the Grape my fading Life provide,
And wash my Body whence the Life has died,
   And lay me, shrouded in the living Leaf,
By some not unfrequented Garden-side.   (2nd)   84

CI

Indeed the Idols I have loved so long
Have done my credit in Men's eye much wrong:
   Have drown'd my Glory in a shallow Cup,
And sold my Reputation for a Song.   (2nd)   88

XCV

And much as Wine has play'd the Infidel,
And robb'd me of my Robe of Honour—Well,
   I wonder often what the Vintners buy
One half so precious as the stuff they sell.   (3rd)   92

LXXII

Alas, that Spring should vanish with the Rose!
That Youth's sweet-scented Manuscript should close!
   The Nightingale that in the Branches sang,
Ah, whence, and whither flown again, who knows!   (1st)   **96**

XCIX

Ah Love! could you and I with Him conspire
To grasp this sorry Scheme of Things entire,
   Would we not shatter it to bits—and then
Re-mould it nearer to the Heart's Desire!   (3rd)   **100**

LXXIV

Ah, Moon of my Delight, who know'st no wane,
The Moon of Heav'n is rising once again:
   How oft hereafter rising shall she look
Through this same Garden after me—in vain!   (1st)   **104**

LXXV

And when Thyself with shining Foot shall pass
Among the Guests Star-scattered on the Grass,
   And in thy joyous Errand reach the Spot
Where I made one—turn down an empty Glass!   (1st)   **108**

                Tamám Shud[6]

[6]It is completed.

The Dalliance of the Eagles

Walt Whitman   *(1819–1892)*

Skirting the river road, (my forenoon walk, my rest,)
Skyward in air a sudden muffled sound, the dalliance of the eagles,
The rushing amorous contact high in space together,
The clinching interlocking claws, a living, fierce, gyrating wheel,
Four beating wings, two beaks, a swirling mass tight grappling,   **5**
In tumbling turning clustering loops, straight downward falling,
Till o'er the river pois'd, the twain yet one, a moment's lull,
A motionless still balance in the air, then parting, talons loosing,
Upward again on slow-firm pinions slanting, their separate diverse
    flight,
She hers, he his, pursuing.   **10**

To Marguerite

Matthew Arnold   *(1822–1888)*

Yes! in the sea of life enisled,
With echoing straits between us thrown,
Dotting the shoreless watery wild,   3
We mortal millions live *alone.*
The islands feel the enclasping flow,
And then their endless bounds they know.   6

But when the moon their hollows lights,
And they are swept by balms of spring,
And in their glens, on starry nights,   9
The nightingales divinely sing;
And lovely notes, from shore to shore,
Across the sounds and channels pour—   12

Oh! then a longing like despair
Is to their farthest caverns sent;
For surely once, they feel, we were   15
Parts of a single continent!
Now round us spreads the watery plain—
Oh might our marges meet again!   18

Who order'd, that their longing's fire
Should be, as soon as kindled, cool'd?
Who renders vain their deep desire?—   21
A God, a God their severance ruled!
And bade betwixt their shores to be
The unplumb'd, salt, estranging sea.   24

The Woodspurge

Dante Gabriel Rossetti   *(1828–1882)*

The wind flapped loose, the wind was still,
Shaken out dead from tree and hill;
I had walked on at the wind's will,—
I sat now, for the wind was still.   4

Between my knees my forehead was,—
My lips, drawn in, said not Alas!
My hair was over in the grass,
My naked ears heard the day pass.   8

My eyes, wide open, had the run
Of some ten weeds to fix upon;
Among those few out of the sun,
The woodspurge flowered, three cups in one.   12

From perfect grief there need not be
Wisdom or even memory;
One thing then learnt remains to me—
The woodspurge has a cup of three.   16

The Heart Asks Pleasure—First

Emily Dickinson   (1830–1886)

The Heart asks Pleasure—first—
And then—Excuse from Pain—
And then—those little Anodynes
That deaden suffering—   4

And then—to go to sleep—
And then—if it should be
The will of its Inquisitor
The privilege to die—   8

When the Hounds of Spring Are on Winter's Traces

Algernon Charles Swinburne   (1834–1909)

When the hounds of spring are on winter's traces,
   The mother of months[1] in meadow or plain
Fills the shadows and windy places
   With lisp of leaves and ripple of rain;   4
And the brown bright nightingale[2] amorous
Is half assuaged for Itylus,
For the Thracian ships and the foreign faces,
   The tongueless vigil, and all the pain.   8

Come with bows bent and with emptying of quivers,
   Maiden most perfect, lady of light,
With a noise of winds and many rivers,
   With a clamour of waters, and with might;   12
Bind on thy sandals, O thou most fleet,
Over the splendour and speed of thy feet;
For the faint east quickens, the wan west shivers,
   Round the feet of the day and the feet of the night.   16

[1]Diana (Artemis), the huntress, goddess of the moon and, hence, "mother of months."
[2]Philomela was raped by Tereus, king of Thrace, who cut out her tongue so that she could not
tell her sister Procne, his wife. Procne, however, found out and in revenge served Tereus a meal
cooked from the flesh of his son Itylus. The gods changed Philomela into the nightingale and
Procne into the sparrow, while Tereus became the hawk, who pursues them. The story is told in
Ovid, *Metamorphoses*, VI.

Where shall we find her, how shall we sing to her,
　Fold our hands round her knees, and cling?
O that man's heart were as fire and could spring to her,
　Fire, or the strength of the streams that spring!　　　20
For the stars and the winds are unto her
As raiment, as songs of the harp-player;
For the risen stars and the fallen cling to her,
　And the southwest-wind and the west-wind sing.　　　24

For winter's rains and ruins are over,
　And all the season of snows and sins;
The days dividing lover and lover,
　The light that loses, the night that wins;　　　28
And time remembered is grief forgotten,
And frosts are slain and flowers begotten,
And in green underwood and cover
　Blossom by blossom the spring begins.　　　32

The full streams feed on flower of rushes,
　Ripe grasses trammel a travelling foot,
The faint fresh flame of the young year flushes
　From leaf to flower and flower to fruit;　　　36
And fruit and leaf are as gold and fire,
And the oat[3] is heard above the lyre,
And the hoofèd heel of a satyr[4] crushes
　The chestnut-husk at the chestnut-root.　　　40

And Pan[5] by noon and Bacchus[6] by night,
　Fleeter of foot than the fleet-foot kid,
Follows with dancing and fills with delight
　The Maenad and the Bassarid;[7]　　　44
And soft as lips that laugh and hide
The laughing leaves of the trees divide,
And screen from seeing and leave in sight
　The god pursuing, the maiden hid.　　　48

The ivy falls with the Bacchanal's hair
　Over her eyebrows hiding her eyes;
The wild vine slipping down leaves bare
　Her bright breast shortening into sighs;　　　52
The wild vine slips with the weight of its leaves,
But the berried ivy catches and cleaves
To the limbs that glitter, the feet that scare
　The wolf that follows, the fawn that flies.　　　56

---

[3]Reed pipe.　[4]A demigod, part man, part horse.　[5]God of shepherds, part goat.　[6]God of wine.
[7]Followers of Pan and Bacchus.

I Look into My Glass

Thomas Hardy   (1840–1928)

I look into my glass,
And view my wasting skin,
And say, "Would God it came to pass
My heart had shrunk as thin!"   4

For then, I, undistrest
By hearts grown cold to me,
Could lonely wait my endless rest
With equanimity.   8

But Time, to make me grieve,
Part steals, lets part abide;
And shakes this fragile frame at eve
With throbbings of noontide.   12

The Self-Unseeing

Thomas Hardy   (1840–1928)

Here is the ancient floor,
Footworn and hollowed and thin,
Here was the former door
Where the dead feet walked in.   4

She sat here in her chair,
Smiling into the fire;
He who played stood there,
Bowing it higher and higher.   8

Childlike, I danced in a dream;
Blessings emblazoned that day;
Everything glowed with a gleam;
Yet we were looking away!   12

In Tenebris[1]

Thomas Hardy   (1840–1928)

"Percussion sum sicut foenum, et aruit cor meum."[2]

—*Psalm 102*

Wintertime nighs;
But my bereavement-pain
It cannot bring again:
Twice no one dies.   4

[1]In darkness.   [2]"My heart is smitten, and withered like grass."

    Flower-petals flee;
But, since it once hath been,
No more that severing scene
    Can harrow me.   **8**

    Birds faint in dread:
I shall not lose old strength
In the lone frost's black length:
    Strength long since fled!   **12**

    Leaves freeze to dun;
But friends can not turn cold
This season as of old
    For him with none.   **16**

    Tempests may scath;[3]
But love can not make smart
Again this year his heart
    Who no heart hath.   **20**

    Black is night's cope;[4]
But death will not appal
One who, past doubtings all,
    Waits in unhope.   **24**

[3]Scathe, injure. [4]Priest's vestment, covering.

Channel Firing

Thomas Hardy   *(1840–1928)*

That night your great guns, unawares,
Shook all our coffins as we lay,
And broke the chancel window-squares,
We thought it was the Judgment-day   **4**

And sat upright. While drearisome
Arose the howl of wakened hounds:
The mouse let fall the altar-crumb,
The worms drew back into the mounds,   **8**

The glebe[1] cow drooled. Till God called, "No;
It's gunnery practice out at sea
Just as before you went below;
The world is as it used to be: **12**

[1]Land belonging to a parish church.

"All nations striving to make
Red war yet redder. Mad as hatters
They do no more for Christés sake
Than you who are helpless in such matters.   16

"That this is not the judgment-hour
For some of them's a blessed thing,
For if it were they'd have to scour
Hell's floor for so much threatening. . . .   20

"Ha, ha. It will be warmer when
I blow the trumpet (if indeed
I ever do; for you are men,
And rest eternal sorely need)."   24

So down we lay again. "I wonder,
Will the world ever saner be,"
Said one, "than when He sent us under
In our indifferent century!"   28

And many a skeleton shook his head.
"Instead of preaching forty year,"
My neighbor Parson Thirdly said,
"I wish I had stuck to pipes and beer."   32

Again the guns disturbed the hour,
Roaring their readiness to avenge,
As far inland as Stourton Tower,
And Camelot, and starlit Stonehenge.[2]   36

---

[2]Stourton Tower: the so-called "Arthur's Tower" on the National Trust estate of Stourhead, near Mere, Wiltshire; Camelot: seat of King Arthur's court, sometimes thought to be in Somerset; Stonehenge: ancient stone circle near Amesbury, Wiltshire.

Pied[1] Beauty

Gerard Manley Hopkins   *(1844–1889)*

Glory be to God for dappled things—
   For skies of couple-colour as a brinded[2] cow;
     For rose-moles all in stipple upon trout that swim;
Fresh-firecoal chestnut-falls; finches' wings;
   Landscape plotted and pieced—fold, fallow,[3] and plough;   5
     And áll trádes, their gear and tackle and trim.

---

[1]Variegated; colored with spots or patches.   [2]Brindled; streaked or spotted.   [3]Fold: an enclosure for animals; fallow: uncultivated land.

All things counter, original, spare, strange;
  Whatever is fickle, freckled (who knows how?)
    With swift, slow; sweet, sour; adazzle, dim;
He fathers-forth whose beauty is past change: 10
                        Praise him.

To an Athlete Dying Young

A. E. Housman   *(1859–1936)*

The time you won your town the race
We chaired you through the market-place;
Man and boy stood cheering by,
And home we brought you shoulder-high.   4

To-day, the road all runners come,
Shoulder-high we bring you home,
And set you at your threshold down,
Townsman of a stiller town.   8

Smart lad, to slip betimes away
From fields where glory does not stay
And early though the laurel[1] grows
It withers quicker than the rose.   12

Eyes the shady night has shut
Cannot see the record cut,
And silence sounds no worse than cheers
After earth has stopped the ears: 16

Now you will not swell the rout[2]
Of lads that wore their honours out,
Runners whom renown outran
And the name died before the man.   20

So set, before its echoes fade,
The fleet foot on the sill of shade,
And hold to the low lintel[3] up
The still-defended challenge-cup.   24

And round that early-laurelled head
Will flock to gaze the strengthless dead,
And find unwithered on its curls
The garland briefer than a girl's.   28

[1]Used to crown winners of athletic events.   [2]Crowd.   [3]Crosspiece over a door.

On Wenlock Edge the Wood's in Trouble

A. E. Housman   *(1859–1936)*

On Wenlock Edge[1] the wood's in trouble;
  His forest fleece the Wrekin[2] heaves;
The gale, it plies the saplings double,
  And thick on Severn[3] snow the leaves.   4

'Twould blow like this through holt and hanger[4]
  When Uricon[5] the city stood:
'Tis the old wind in the old anger,
  But then it threshed another wood.   8

Then, 'twas before my time, the Roman
  At yonder heaving hill would stare:
The blood that warms an English yeoman,
  The thoughts that hurt him, they were there.   12

There, like the wind through woods in riot,
  Through him the gale of life blew high;
The tree of man was never quiet:
  Then 'twas the Roman, now 'tis I.   16

The gale, it plies the saplings double,
  It blows so hard, 'twill soon be gone:
To-day the Roman and his trouble
  Are ashes under Uricon.   20

[1]A ridge in Shropshire. [2]A hill in Shropshire. [3]A Shropshire river. [4]Woods and wooded slopes. [5]A Roman city near where Shrewsbury now stands.

The Chestnut Casts His Flambeaux

A. E. Housman   *(1859–1936)*

The chestnut casts his flambeaux,[1] and the flowers
  Stream from the hawthorn on the wind away,
The doors clap to, the pane is blind with showers.
  Pass me the can, lad; there's an end of May.   4

There's one spoilt spring to scant our mortal lot,
  One season ruined of our little store.
May will be fine next year as like as not:
  Oh ay, but then we shall be twenty-four.   8

We for a certainty are not the first
  Have sat in taverns while the tempest hurled

[1]Torches; here, blossoms.

Their hopeful plans to emptiness, and cursed
  Whatever brute and blackguard made the world.   12

It is in truth iniquity on high
  To cheat our sentenced souls of aught they crave,
And mar the merriment as you and I
  Fare on our long fool's-errand to the grave.   16

Iniquity it is; but pass the can.
  My lad, no pair of kings our mothers bore;
Our only portion is the estate of man:
  We want the moon, but we shall get no more.   20

If here to-day the cloud of thunder lours[2]
  To-morrow it will hie on far behests;
The flesh will grieve on other bones than ours
  Soon, and the soul will mourn in other breasts.   24

The troubles of our proud and angry dust
  Are from eternity, and shall not fail.
Bear them we can, and if we can we must.
  Shoulder the sky, my lad, and drink your ale.   28

[2]Lowers, scowls.

The Night Is Freezing Fast

A. E. Housman   (1859–1936)

The night is freezing fast,
  To-morrow comes December;
    And winterfalls of old   3
Are with me from the past;
  And chiefly I remember
    How Dick would hate the cold.   6

Fall, winter, fall; for he,
  Prompt hand and headpiece clever,
    Has woven a winter robe,   9
And made of earth and sea
  His overcoat for ever,
    And wears the turning globe.   12

The Lake Isle of Innisfree

W. B. Yeats   (1865–1939)

I will arise and go now, and go to Innisfree,[1]
And a small cabin build there, of clay and wattles made:

[1]An island in Lough Gill, near Sligo, Ireland.

Nine bean-rows will I have there, a hive for the honeybee,
And live alone in the bee-loud glade.   4

And I shall have some peace there, for peace comes dropping slow,
Dropping from the veils of the morning to where the cricket sings;
There midnight's all a glimmer, and noon a purple glow,
And evening full of the linnet's wings.   8

I will arise and go now, for always night and day
I hear lake water lapping with low sounds by the shore;
While I stand on the roadway, or on the pavements grey,
I hear it in the deep heart's core.   12

A Prayer for My Daughter[1]

W. B. Yeats   *(1865–1939)*

Once more the storm is howling, and half hid
Under this cradle-hood and coverlid
My child sleeps on. There is no obstacle
But Gregory's wood and one bare hill
Whereby the haystack- and roof-levelling wind,   5
Bred on the Atlantic, can be stayed;
And for an hour I have walked and prayed
Because of the great gloom that is in my mind.

I have walked and prayed for this young child an hour
And heard the sea-wind scream upon the tower,   10
And under the arches of the bridge, and scream
In the elms above the flooded stream;
Imagining in excited reverie
That the future years had come,
Dancing to a frenzied drum,   15
Out of the murderous innocence of the sea.

May she be granted beauty and yet not
Beauty to make a stranger's eye distraught,
Or hers before a looking-glass, for such,
Being made beautiful overmuch,   20
Consider beauty a sufficient end,
Lose natural kindness and maybe
The heart-revealing intimacy
That chooses right, and never find a friend.

Helen[2] being chosen found life flat and dull   25
And later had much trouble from a fool,

[1]Anne Butler Yeats, born February 26, 1919. [2]Helen of Troy, for whom the Trojan War was fought.

While that great Queen,[3] that rose out of the spray,
Being fatherless could have her way
Yet chose a bandy-leggèd smith for man.
It's certain that fine women eat   30
A crazy salad with their meat
Whereby the Horn of Plenty is undone.

In courtesy I'd have her chiefly learned;
Hearts are not had as a gift but hearts are earned
By those that are not entirely beautiful;   35
Yet many, that have played the fool
For beauty's very self, has charm made wise,
And many a poor man that has roved,
Loved and thought himself beloved,
From a glad kindness cannot take his eyes.   40

May she become a flourishing hidden tree
That all her thoughts may like the linnet be,
And have no business but dispensing round
Their magnanimities of sound,
Nor but in merriment begin a chase,   45
Nor but in merriment a quarrel.
O may she live like some green laurel
Rooted in one dear perpetual place.

My mind, because the minds that I have loved,
The sort of beauty that I have approved,   50
Prosper but little, has dried up of late,
Yet knows that to be choked with hate
May well be of all evil chances chief.
If there's no hatred in a mind
Assault and battery of the wind   55
Can never tear the linnet from the leaf.

An intellectual hatred is the worst,
So let her think opinions are accursed.
Have I not seen the loveliest woman born[4]
Out of the mouth of Plenty's horn,   60
Because of her opinionated mind
Barter that horn and every good
By quiet natures understood
For an old bellows full of angry wind?

Considering that, all hatred driven hence,   65
The soul recovers radical innocence

---

[3]Aphrodite sprang out of sea foam. She married Hephaestus, a blacksmith. [4]Maud Gonne, a vocal Irish patriot, long loved by Yeats.

And learns at last that it is self-delighting,
Self-appeasing, self-affrighting,
And that its own sweet will is Heaven's will;
She can, though every face should scowl   70
And every windy quarter howl
Or every bellows burst, be happy still.

And may her bridegroom bring her to a house
Where all's accustomed, ceremonious;
For arrogance and hatred are the wares   75
Peddled in the thoroughfares.
How but in custom and in ceremony
Are innocence and beauty born?
Ceremony's a name for the rich horn,
And custom for the spreading laurel tree.   80

Among School Children

W. B. Yeats   (1865–1939)

I

I walk through the long schoolroom questioning;
A kind old nun in a white hood replies;
The children learn to cipher and to sing,
To study reading-books and history,   4
To cut and sew, be neat in everything
In the best modern way—the children's eyes
In momentary wonder stare upon
A sixty-year-old smiling public man.   8

II

I dream of a Ledaean[1] body, bent
Above a sinking fire, a tale that she
Told of a harsh reproof, or trivial event
That changed some childish day to tragedy—   12
Told, and it seemed that our two natures blent
Into a sphere from youthful sympathy,
Or else, to alter Plato's parable,[2]
Into the yolk and white of the one shell.   16

III

And thinking of that fit of grief or rage
I look upon one child or t'other there

---

[1]As beautiful as Leda, loved by Zeus.   [2]In the *Symposium* it is suggested that human males and females were once one complete unit. Through love they try to reunite.

And wonder if she stood so at that age—
For even daughters of the swan can share   20
Something of every paddler's heritage—
And had that colour upon cheek or hair,
And thereupon my heart is driven wild:
She stands before me as a living child.   24

IV

Her present image floats into the mind—
Did Quattrocento[3] finger fashion it
Hollow of cheek as though it drank the wind
And took a mess of shadows for its meat?   28
And I though never of Ledaean kind
Had pretty plumage once—enough of that,
Better to smile on all that smile, and show
There is a comfortable kind of old scarecrow.   32

V

What youthful mother, a shape upon her lap
Honey of generation had betrayed,
And that must sleep, shriek, struggle to escape
As recollection or the drug decide,   36
Would think her son, did she but see that shape
With sixty or more winters on its head,
A compensation for the pang of his birth,
Or the uncertainty of his setting forth?   40

VI

Plato thought nature but a spume that plays
Upon a ghostly paradigm of things;[4]
Solider Aristotle played the taws
Upon the bottom of a king of kings;[5]   44
World-famous golden-thighed Pythagoras[6]
Fingered upon a fiddle-stick or strings
What a star sang and careless Muses heard:
Old clothes upon old sticks to scare a bird.   48

VII

Both nuns and mothers worship images,
But those the candles light are not as those

---

[3]The fifteenth century in Italy, a time of great artistic activity.   [4]Plato taught that things in nature are but imperfect copies of ideal forms.   [5]Aristotle was tutor to Alexander the Great.   [6]Pythagorus emphasized mathematical relationships in music and in the universe.

That animate a mother's reveries,
But keep a marble or a bronze repose. 52
And yet they too break hearts—O Presences
That passion, piety or affection knows,
And that all heavenly glory symbolise—
O self-born mockers of man's enterprise; 56

VIII

Labour is blossoming or dancing where
The body is not bruised to pleasure soul,
Nor beauty born out of its own despair,
Nor blear-eyed wisdom out of midnight oil. 60
O chestnut-tree, great-rooted blossomer,
Are you the leaf, the blossom or the bole?
O body swayed to music, O brightening glance,
How can we know the dancer from the dance? 64

Two Songs from a Play

W. B. Yeats   *(1865–1939)*

I

I saw a staring virgin stand
Where holy Dionysus[1] died,
And tear the heart out of his side,
And lay the heart upon her hand 4
And bear that beating heart away;
And then did all the Muses sing
Of Magnus Annus[2] at the spring,
As though God's death were but a play. 8

Another Troy[3] must rise and set,
Another lineage feed the crow,
Another Argo's painted prow
Drive to a flashier bauble yet.[4] 12
The Roman Empire stood appalled:
It dropped the reigns of peace and war
When that fierce virgin and her Star[5]
Out of the fabulous darkness called. 16

II

In pity for man's darkening thought
He walked that room and issued thence

[1]Greek god of vegetation and wine. [2]A great or long year. [3]Scene of the Trojan War.
[4]Jason sought the Golden Fleece in a ship called the Argo. [5]Mary and the Star of Bethlehem.

In Galilean turbulence;[6]
The Babylonian starlight brought   20

A fabulous, formless darkness in;
Odour of blood when Christ was slain
Made all Platonic[7] tolerance vain
And vain all Doric[8] discipline.   24

Everything that man esteems
Endures a moment or a day.
Love's pleasure drives his love away,
The painter's brush consumes his dreams;   28
The herald's cry, the soldier's tread
Exhaust his glory and his might:
Whatever flames upon the night
Man's own resinous heart has fed.   32

---

[6]Jesus began his miracles in Galilee during a time of disorder.   [7]Plato, a Greek philosopher
(427–347 B.C.).   [8]A Greek architectural style characterized by simplicity of form.

The Mill

Edwin Arlington Robinson   *(1869–1935)*

The miller's wife had waited long,
    The tea was cold, the fire was dead;
And there might yet be nothing wrong
    In how he went and what he said: 4
"There are no millers any more,"
    Was all that she had heard him say:
And he had lingered at the door
    So long that it seemed yesterday.   8

Sick with a fear that had no form
    She knew that she was there at last;
And in the mill there was a warm
    And mealy fragrance of the past.   12
What else there was would only seem
    To say again what he had meant;
And what was hanging from a beam
    Would not have heeded where she went.   16

And if she thought it followed her,
    She may have reasoned in the dark

That one way of the few there were
  Would hide her and would leave no mark: 20
Black water, smooth above the weir
  Like starry velvet in the night,
Though ruffled once, would soon appear
  The same as ever to the sight.   24

Mending Wall

Robert Frost   (1874–1963)

Something there is that doesn't love a wall,
That sends the frozen-ground-swell under it
And spills the upper boulders in the sun,
And makes gaps even two can pass abreast.
The work of hunters is another thing: 5
I have come after them and made repair
Where they have left not one stone on a stone,
But they would have the rabbit out of hiding,
To please the yelping dogs. The gaps I mean,
No one has seen them made or heard them made,   10
But at spring mending-time we find them there.
I let my neighbor know beyond the hill;
And on a day we meet to walk the line
And set the wall between us once again.
We keep the wall between us as we go.   15
To each the boulders that have fallen to each.
And some are loaves and some so nearly balls
We have to use a spell to make them balance:
"Stay where you are until our backs are turned!"
We wear our fingers rough with handling them.   20
Oh, just another kind of outdoor game,
One on a side. It comes to little more:
There where it is we do not need the wall:
He is all pine and I am apple orchard.
My apple trees will never get across   25
And eat the cones under his pines, I tell him.
He only says, "Good fences make good neighbors."
Spring is the mischief in me, and I wonder
If I could put a notion in his head:
"*Why* do they make good neighbors? Isn't it   30
Where there are cows? But here there are no cows.
Before I built a wall I'd ask to know
What I was walling in or walling out,
And to whom I was like to give offense.

Something there is that doesn't love a wall,   35
That wants it down." I could say "Elves" to him,
But it's not elves exactly, and I'd rather
He said it for himself. I see him there,
Bringing a stone grasped firmly by the top
In each hand, like an old-stone savage armed.   40
He moves in darkness as it seems to me,
Not of woods only and the shade of trees.
He will not go behind his father's saying,
And he likes having thought of it so well
He says again, "Good fences make good neighbors."   45

Dust of Snow

Robert Frost   (1874–1963)

The way a crow
Shook down on me
The dust of snow
From a hemlock tree   4

Has given my heart
A change of mood
And saved some part
Of a day I had rued.   8

Two Tramps in Mud Time

Robert Frost   (1874–1963)

Out of the mud two strangers came
And caught me splitting wood in the yard.
And one of them put me off my aim
By hailing cheerily "Hit them hard!"   4
I knew pretty well why he dropped behind
And let the other go on a way.
I knew pretty well what he had in mind:
He wanted to take my job for pay.   8

Good blocks of oak it was I split,
As large around as the chopping block;
And every piece I squarely hit
Fell splinterless as a cloven rock.   12
The blows that a life of self-control
Spares to strike for the common good,

That day, giving a loose to my soul,
I spent on the unimportant wood.   16

The sun was warm but the wind was chill.
You know how it is with an April day
When the sun is out and the wind is still,
You're one month on in the middle of May.   20
But if you so much as dare to speak,
A cloud comes over the sunlit arch,
A wind comes off a frozen peak,
And you're two months back in the middle of March. 24

A bluebird comes tenderly up to alight
And turns to the wind to unruffle a plume,
His song so pitched as not to excite
A single flower as yet to bloom.   28
It is snowing a flake: and he half knew
Winter was only playing possum.
Except in color he isn't blue,
But he wouldn't advise a thing to blossom.   32

The water for which we may have to look
In summertime with a witching wand,
In every wheelrut's now a brook,
In every print of a hoof a pond.   36
Be glad of water, but don't forget
The lurking frost in the earth beneath
That will steal forth after the sun is set
And show on the water its crystal teeth.   40

The time when most I loved my task
These two must make me love it more
By coming with what they came to ask.
You'd think I never had felt before   44
The weight of an ax-head poised aloft,
The grip on earth of outspread feet,
The life of muscles rocking soft
And smooth and moist in vernal heat.   48

Out of the woods two hulking tramps
(From sleeping God knows where last night,
But not long since in the lumber camps).
They thought all chopping was theirs of right.   52
Men of the woods and lumberjacks,
They judged me by their appropriate tool.
Except as a fellow handled an ax
They had no way of knowing a fool.   56

Nothing on either side was said.
They knew they had but to stay their stay
And all their logic would fill my head:
As that I had no right to play   60
With what was another man's work for gain.
My right might be love but theirs was need.
And where the two exist in twain
Theirs was the better right—agreed.   64

But yield who will to their separation,
My object in living is to unite
My avocation and my vocation
As my two eyes make one in sight.   68
Only where love and need are one,
And the work is play for mortal stakes,
Is the deed ever really done
For Heaven and the future's sakes.   72

Fire and Ice

Robert Frost   (1874–1963)

Some say the world will end in fire,
Some say in ice.
From what I've tasted of desire
I hold with those who favor fire.   4
But if it had to perish twice,
I think I know enough of hate
To say that for destruction ice
Is also great   8
And would suffice.

Once by the Pacific

Robert Frost   (1874–1963)

The shattered water made a misty din.
Great waves looked over others coming in,
And thought of doing something to the shore
That water never did to land before.   4
The clouds were low and hairy in the skies,
Like locks blown forward in the gleam of eyes.
You could not tell, and yet it looked as if
The shore was lucky in being backed by cliff,   8
The cliff in being backed by continent;

It looked as if a night of dark intent
Was coming, and not only a night, an age.
Someone had better be prepared for rage.   12
There would be more than ocean-water broken
Before God's last *Put out the Light* was spoken.

Anecdote of the Jar

Wallace Stevens   (1879–1955)

I placed a jar in Tennessee,
And round it was, upon a hill.
It made the slovenly wilderness
Surround that hill.   4

The wilderness rose up to it,
And sprawled around, no longer wild.
The jar was round upon the ground
And tall and of a port in air.   8

It took dominion everywhere.
The jar was gray and bare.
It did not give of bird or bush,
Like nothing else in Tennessee.   12

The Snow Man

Wallace Stevens   (1879–1955)

One must have a mind of winter
To regard the frost and the boughs
Of the pine-trees crusted with snow;   3

And have been cold a long time
To behold the junipers shagged with ice,
The spruces rough in the distant glitter   6

Of the January sun; and not to think
Of any misery in the sound of the wind,
In the sound of a few leaves,   9

Which is the sound of the land
Full of the same wind
That is blowing in the same bare place   12

For the listener, who listens in the snow,
And, nothing himself, beholds
Nothing that is not there and the nothing that is.   15

The Idea of Order at Key West

Wallace Stevens   (1879–1955)

She sang beyond the genius of the sea.
The water never formed to mind or voice,
Like a body wholly body, fluttering
Its empty sleeves; and yet its mimic motion
Made constant cry, caused constantly a cry,   5
That was not ours although we understood,
Inhuman, of the veritable ocean.

The sea was not a mask. No more was she.
The song and water were not medleyed sound
Even if what she sang was what she heard,   10
Since what she sang was uttered word by word.
It may be that in all her phrases stirred
The grinding water and the gasping wind;
But it was she and not the sea we heard.

For she was the maker of the song she sang.   15
The ever-hooded, tragic-gestured sea
Was merely a place by which she walked to sing.
Whose spirit is this? we said, because we knew
It was the spirit that we sought and knew
That we should ask this often as she sang.   20

If it was only the dark voice of the sea
That rose, or even colored by many waves;
If it was only the outer voice of sky
And cloud, of the sunken coral water-walled,
However clear, it would have been deep air,   25
The heaving speech of air, a summer sound
Repeated in a summer without end
And sound alone. But it was more than that,
More even than her voice, and ours, among
The meaningless plungings of water and the wind,   30
Theatrical distances, bronze shadows heaped
On high horizons, mountainous atmospheres
Of sky and sea.

　　　It was her voice that made
The sky acutest at its vanishing.
She measured to the hour its solitude.   35
She was the single artificer of the world
In which she sang. And when she sang, the sea,
Whatever self it had, became the self
That was her song, for she was the maker. Then we,

As we beheld her striding there alone,   40
Knew that there never was a world for her
Except the one she sang and, singing, made.

Ramon Fernandez,[1] tell me, if you know,
Why, when the singing ended and we turned
Toward the town, tell why the glassy lights,   45
The lights in the fishing boats at anchor there,
As the night descended, tilting in the air,
Mastered the night and portioned out the sea,
Fixing emblazoned zones and fiery poles,
Arranging, deepening, enchanting night.   50

Oh! Blessed rage for order, pale Ramon,
The maker's rage to order words of the sea,
Words of the fragrant portals, dimly-starred,
And of ourselves and of our origins,
In ghostlier demarcations, keener sounds.   55

---

[1]Although there was a French literary critic by this name (1894–1944), Stevens wrote that he
intended it as an invention.

Of Modern Poetry

Wallace Stevens   *(1879–1955)*

The poem of the mind in the act of finding
What will suffice. It has not always had
To find: the scene was set; it repeated what
Was in the script.
                    Then the theatre was changed
To something else. Its past was a souvenir.   5

It has to be living, to learn the speech of the place.
It has to face the men of the time and to meet
The women of the time. It has to think about war
And it has to find what will suffice. It has
To construct a new stage. It has to be on that stage   10
And, like an insatiable actor, slowly and
With meditation, speak words that in the ear,
In the delicatest ear of the mind, repeat,
Exactly, that which it wants to hear, at the sound
Of which, an invisible audience listens,   15
Not to the play, but to itself, expressed
In an emotion as of two people, as of two
Emotions becoming one. The actor is
A metaphysician in the dark, twanging

An instrument, twanging a wiry string that gives   **20**
Sounds passing through sudden rightnesses, wholly
Containing the mind, below which it cannot descend,
Beyond which it has no will to rise.
                              It must
Be the finding of a satisfaction, and may
Be of a man skating, a woman dancing, a woman   **25**
Combing. The poem of the act of the mind.

The Sparrow

(To My Father)

William Carlos Williams   *(1883–1963)*

This sparrow
          who comes to sit at my window
                    is a poetic truth
more than a natural one.
          His voice,   **5**
                    his movements,
his habits—
          how he loves to
                    flutter his wings
in the dust—   **10**
          all attest it;
                    granted, he does it
to rid himself of lice
          but the relief he feels
                    makes him   **15**
cry out lustily—
          which is a trait
                    more related to music
than otherwise.
          Wherever he finds himself   **20**
                    in early spring,
on back streets
          or beside palaces,
                    he carries on
unaffectedly   **25**
          his amours.
                    It begins in the egg,
his sex genders it:
          What is more pretentiously
                    useless   **30**

or about which
              we more pride ourselves?
                            It leads as often as not
to our undoing.
              The cockerel, the crow   35
                            with their challenging voices
cannot surpass
              the insistence
                            of his cheep!
Once   40
              at El Paso
                            toward evening,
I saw—and heard!—
              ten thousand sparrows
                            who had come in from   45
the desert
              to roost. They filled the trees
                            of a small park. Men fled
(with ears ringing!)
              from their droppings,   50
                            leaving the premises
to the alligators
              who inhabit
                            the fountain. His image   55
is familiar
              as that of the aristocratic
                            unicorn, a pity
there are not more oats eaten
              nowadays
                            to make living easier   60
for him.
              At that,
                            his small size,
keen eyes,
              serviceable beak   65
                            and general truculence
assure his survival—
              to say nothing
                            of his innumerable
brood.   70
              Even the Japanese
                            know him
and have painted him
              sympathetically,
                            with profound insight   75

into his minor
    characteristics.
       Nothing even remotely
subtle
    about his lovemaking.   **80**
       He crouches
before the female,
    drags his wings,
       waltzing,
throws back his head   **85**
    and simply—
       yells! The din
is terrific.
    The way he swipes his bill
       across a plank   **90**
to clean it,
    is decisive.
       So with everything
he does. His coppery
    eyebrows   **95**
       give him the air
of being always
    a winner—and yet
       I saw once,
the female of his species   **100**
    clinging determinedly
       to the edge of
a water pipe,
    catch him
       by his crown-feathers **105**
to hold him
    silent,
       subdued,
hanging above the city streets
    until   **110**
       she was through with him.
What was the use
    of that?
       She hung there
herself,   **115**
    puzzled at her success.
       I laughed heartily.
Practical to the end,
    it is the poem
       of his existence   **120**

that triumphed
                finally;
                        a wisp of feathers
flattened to the pavement,
                wings spread symmetrically   125
                        as if in flight,
the head gone,
                the black escutcheon of the breast
                        undecipherable,
an effigy of a sparrow,   130
                a dried wafer only,
                        left to say
and it says it
                without offense,
                        beautifully;   135
This was I,
                a sparrow.
                        I did my best;
farewell.

Prophecy

Elinor Wylie   (1885–1928)

I shall lie hidden in a hut
    In the middle of an alder wood,
With the back door blind and bolted shut,
    And the front door locked for good.   4

I shall lie folded like a saint,
    Lapped in a scented linen sheet,
On a bedstead striped with bright-blue paint,
    Narrow and cold and neat.   8

The midnight will be glassy black
    Behind the panes, with wind about
To set his mouth against a crack
    And blow the candle out.   12

Blue Girls

John Crowe Ransom   (1888–1974)

Twirling your blue skirts, travelling the sward
Under the towers of your seminary,
Go listen to your teachers old and contrary
Without believing a word.   4

Tie the white fillets then about your hair
And think no more of what will come to pass
Than bluebirds that go walking on the grass
And chattering on the air.   8

Practise your beauty, blue girls, before it fail;
And I will cry with my loud lips and publish
Beauty which all our power shall never establish,
It is so frail.   12

For I could tell you a story which is true;
I know a woman with a terrible tongue,
Blear eyes fallen from blue,
All her perfections tarnished—yet it is not long   16
Since she was lovelier than any of you.

Winter Remembered

John Crowe Ransom   (1888–1974)

Two evils, monstrous either one apart,
Possessed me, and were long and loath at going:
A cry of Absence, Absence, in the heart,
And in the wood the furious winter blowing.   4

Think not, when fire was bright upon my bricks,
And past the tight boards hardly a wind could enter,
I glowed like them, the simple burning sticks,
Far from my cause, my proper heat and center.   8

Better to walk forth in the frozen air
And wash my wound in the snows; that would be healing;
Because my heart would throb less painful there,
Being caked with cold, and past the smart of feeling.   12

And where I walked, the murderous winter blast
Would have this body bowed, these eyeballs streaming,
And though I think this heart's blood froze not fast
It ran too small to spare one drop for dreaming.   16

Dear love, these fingers that had known your touch,
And tied our separate forces first together,
Were ten poor idiot fingers not worth much,
Ten frozen parsnips hanging in the weather.   20

This Beast That Rends Me

Edna St. Vincent Millay   (1892–1950)

This beast that rends me in the sight of all,
This love, this longing, this oblivious thing,
That has me under as the last leaves fall,
Will glut, will sicken, will be gone by spring.   4
The wound will heal, the fever will abate,
The knotted hurt will slacken in the breast;
I shall forget before the flickers mate
Your look that is today my east and west.   8
Unscathed, however, from a claw so deep
Though I should love again I shall not go:
Along my body, waking while I sleep,
Sharp to the kiss, cold to the hand as snow,   12
The scar of this encounter like a sword
Will lie between me and my troubled lord.

Since Feeling Is First

E. E. Cummings   (1894–1962)

since feeling is first
who pays any attention
to the syntax of things
will never wholly kiss you;

wholly to be a fool   5
while Spring is in the world
my blood approves,
and kisses are a better fate
than wisdom
lady i swear by all flowers. Don't cry   10
—the best gesture of my brain is less than
your eyelids' flutter which says

we are for each other: then
laugh, leaning back in my arms
for life's not a paragraph   15

And death i think is no parenthesis

O Sweet Spontaneous

E. E. Cummings   (1894–1962)

O sweet spontaneous
earth how often have
the
doting

        fingers of   5
prurient philosophers pinched
and
poked

thee
, has the naughty thumb   10
of science prodded
thy

        beauty . how
often have religions taken
thee upon their scraggy knees   15
squeezing and

buffeting thee that thou mightest conceive
gods
        (but
true   20

to the incomparable
couch of death thy
rhythmic
lover

        thou answerest   25

them only with

        spring)

After I Had Worked All Day

Charles Reznikoff   (1894–1976)

After I had worked all day at what I earn my living,
I was tired. Now my own work has lost another day,
I thought, but began slowly,
and slowly my strength came back to me.
Surely, the tide comes in twice a day.   5

To Be Sung on the Water

Louise Bogan   (1897–1970)

Beautiful, my delight,
Pass, as we pass the wave.
Pass, as the mottled night
Leaves what it cannot save,
Scattering dark and bright.   5

Beautiful, pass and be
Less than the guiltless shade
To which our vows were said;
Less than the sound of the oar
To which our vows were made,—   10
Less than the sound of its blade
Dipping the stream once more.

To Brooklyn Bridge

Hart Crane   (1899–1932)

How many dawns, chill from his rippling rest
The seagull's wings shall dip and pivot him,
Shedding white rings of tumult, building high
Over the chained bay waters Liberty—   4

Then, with inviolate curve, forsake our eyes
As apparitional as sails that cross
Some page of figures to be filed away;
—Till elevators drop us from our day . . .   8

I think of cinemas, panoramic sleights
With multitudes bent toward some flashing scene
Never disclosed, but hastened to again,
Foretold to other eyes on the same screen;   12

And Thee,[1] across the harbor, silver-paced
As though the sun took step of thee, yet left
Some motion ever unspent in thy stride,—
Implicitly thy freedom staying thee!   16

Out of some subway scuttle, cell or loft
A bedlamite[2] speeds to thy parapets,
Tilting there momently, shrill shirt ballooning,
A jest falls from the speechless caravan.   20

[1]The bridge.   [2]Mad person.

Down Wall,[3] from girder into street noon leaks,
A rip-tooth of the sky's acetylene;
All afternoon the cloud-flown derricks turn . . .
Thy cables breathe the North Atlantic still.   24

And obscure as that heaven of the Jews,
Thy guerdon[4] . . . Accolade thou dost bestow
Of anonymity time cannot raise:
Vibrant reprieve and pardon thou dost show.   28

O harp and altar, of the fury fused,
(How could mere toil align thy choiring strings!)
Terrific threshold of the prophet's pledge,
Prayer of pariah,[5] and the lover's cry,—   32

Again the traffic lights that skim thy swift
Unfractioned idiom, immaculate sigh of stars,
Beading thy path—condense eternity:
And we have seen night lifted in thine arms.   36

Under thy shadow by the piers I waited;
Only in darkness is thy shadow clear.
The City's fiery parcels all undone,
Already snow submerges an iron year . . .   40

O Sleepless as the river under thee,
Vaulting the sea, the prairies' dreaming sod,
Unto us lowliest sometime sweep, descend
And of the curveship lend a myth to God.   44

[3]Wall Street, in Manhattan, near the bridge. [4]Reward [5]Outcast.

The Zebras

Roy Campbell   (1901–1957)

From the dark woods that breathe of fallen showers,
Harnessed with level rays in golden reins,
The zebras draw the dawn across the plains
Wading knee-deep among the scarlet flowers.   4
The sunlight, zithering their flanks with fire,
Flashes between the shadows as they pass
Barred with electric tremors through the grass
Like wind along the gold strings of a lyre.   8

Into the flushed air snorting rosy plumes
That smoulder round their feet in drifting fumes,
With dove-like voices call the distant fillies,

While round the herds the stallion wheels his flight,   12
Engine of beauty volted with delight,
To roll his mare among the trampled lilies.

Only the Polished Skeleton

Countee Cullen   (1903–1946)

The heart has need of some deceit
  To make its pistons rise and fall;
For less than this it would not beat,
  Nor flush the sluggish vein at all.   4

With subterfuge and fraud the mind
  Must fend and parry thrust for thrust,
With logic brutal and unkind
  Beat off the onslaughts of the dust.   8

Only the polished skeleton,
  Of flesh relieved and pauperized,
Can rest at ease and think upon
  The worth of all it so despised.   12

The Fury of Aerial Bombardment

Richard Eberhart   (1904–)

You would think the fury of aerial bombardment
Would rouse God to relent; the infinite spaces
Are still silent. He looks on shock-pried faces.
History, even, does not know what is meant.   4

You would feel that after so many centuries
God would give man to repent; yet he can kill
As Cain could, but with multitudinous will,
No farther advanced than in his ancient furies.   8

Was man made stupid to see his own stupidity?
Is God by definition indifferent, beyond us all?
Is the eternal truth man's fighting soul
Wherein the Beast ravens in its own avidity?   12

Of Van Wettering I speak, and Averill,
Names on a list, whose faces I do not recall
But they are gone to early death, who late in school
Distinguished the belt feed lever from the belt holding pawl.[1]   16

---

[1]Machine gun parts.

The Conspirators

Frederic Prokosch   (1908–   )

And if the dead, and the dead
Of spirit now join, and in their horrifying ritual
Proceed till at last with oriental grace
End their concluding dance with the candles guttering,
The cymbals sobbing, the wind harassing the curtains,   5
The chill from the flood embracing the golden stairway.
The scent devoured and the bowls blown clean of incense:

Ah then, farewell, sweet northern music;
No longer the flight of the mind across the continents,
The dazzling flight of our words across the tempestuous   10
Black, or the firelit recital of a distant battle.

No. All that we loved is lost, if the intricate
Languor of recollected centuries
Descends in its terrible sweetness on our limbs.
No shot will echo; no fire; no agonizing   15
Cry will resound in the city's thickets: only,
The ivy falling gently across the bridges,
The larches piercing the roofs, the reclining steeples,
The cellars rich with the agony of the reptiles,
The contemplative worms, the victorious rodents,   20
And at last, the climax entrancingly serene,
The inconclusive note drowned on the ascendant:
Our lovely shapes in marble still shine through the greenery,
Our exquisite silver bones still glide with the glaciers
That split our familiar hills, still fall with the avalanche   25
And weaving their vast wing's thunder over the Indies
The birds, the birds, sob for the time of man.

Airman

Stephen Spender   (1909–   )

He will watch the hawk with an indifferent eye
     Or pitifully;
Nor on those eagles that so feared him, now   3
     Will strain his brow;
Weapons men use, stone, sling and strong-thewed bow
     He will not know.   6

This aristocrat, superb of all instinct,
     With death close linked

Had paced the enormous cloud, almost had won   9
 War on the sun;
Till now, like Icarus[1] mid-ocean-drowned,
 Hands, wings, are found.   12

[1]Flying on wings of wax and feathers too close to the sun, Icarus fell into the sea and drowned, when the sun melted the wax.

Montana Pastoral

J. V. Cunningham   (1911–1985)

I am no shepherd of a child's surmises.
I have seen fear where the coiled serpent rises,

Thirst where the grasses burn in early May
And thistle, mustard, and the wild oat stay.   4

There is dust in this air. I saw in the heat
Grasshoppers busy in the threshing wheat.

So to this hour. Through the warm dusk I drove
To blizzards sifting on the hissing stove,   8

And found no images of pastoral will,
But fear, thirst, hunger, and this huddled chill.

Coffee

J. V. Cunningham   (1911–1985)

When I awoke with cold
And looked for you, my dear,
And the dusk inward rolled,
Not light or dark, but drear.   4

Unabsolute, unshaped,
That no glass can oppose,
I fled not to escape
Myself, but to transpose.   8

I have so often fled
Wherever I could drink
Dark coffee and there read
More than a man would think   12

That I say I waste time
For contemplation's sake:

In an uncumbered clime
Minute inductions wake,   16

Insight flows in my pen.
I know nor fear nor haste.
Time is my own again.
I waste it for the waste.   20

Dream Songs: 4

John Berryman   (1914–1972)

Filling her compact & delicious body
with chicken páprika, she glanced at me
twice.   3
Fainting with interest, I hungered back
and only the fact of her husband & four other people
kept me from springing on her   6

or falling at her little feet and crying
'You are the hottest one for years of night
Henry's dazed eyes   9
have enjoyed, Brilliance.' I advanced upon
(despairing) my spumoni.—Sir Bones: is stuffed,
de world, wif feeding girls.   12

—Black hair, complexion Latin, jewelled eyes
downcast . . . The slob beside her   feasts . . . What wonders is
she sitting on, over there?   15
The restaurant buzzes. She might as well be on Mars.
Where did it all go wrong? There ought to be a law against Henry.
—Mr. Bones: there is.   18

Dream Songs: 14

John Berryman   (1914–1972)

Life, friends, is boring. We must not say so.
After all, the sky flashes, the great sea yearns,
we ourselves flash and yearn,   3
and moreover my mother told me as a boy
(repeatedly) 'Ever to confess you're bored
means you have no   6

Inner Resources.' I conclude now I have no
inner resources, because I am heavy bored.
Peoples bore me,   9
literature bores me, especially great literature,
Henry bores me, with his plights & gripes
as bad as achilles,[1]   12

who loves people and valiant art, which bores me.
And the tranquil hills, & gin, look like a drag
and somehow a dog   15
has taken itself & its tail considerably away
into mountains or sea or sky, leaving
behind: me, wag.   18

[1]Achilles is often sulky in Homer's *Iliad.*

Rescue the Dead

David Ignatow (1914–)

Finally, to forgo love is to kiss a leaf,
is to let rain fall nakedly upon your head,
is to respect fire,
is to study man's eyes and his gestures
as he talks,   5
is to set bread upon the table
and a knife discreetly by,
is to pass through crowds
like a crowd of oneself.
Not to love is to live.   10

To love is to be led away
into a forest where the secret grave
is dug, singing, praising darkness
under the trees.

To live is to sign your name,   15
is to ignore the dead,
is to carry a wallet
and shake hands.

To love is to be a fish.
My boat wallows in the sea.   20
You who are free,
rescue the dead.

The Death of the Ball Turret Gunner

Randall Jarrell   (1914–1965)

From my mother's sleep I fell into the State,
And I hunched in its belly till my wet fur froze.
Six miles from earth, loosed from its dream of life,
I woke to black flak and the nightmare fighters.
When I died they washed me out of the turret with a hose.

Skunk Hour

(For Elizabeth Bishop)[1]

Robert Lowell   (1917–1977)

Nautilus Island's hermit
heiress still lives through winter in her Spartan cottage;
her sheep still graze above the sea.   3
Her son's a bishop. Her farmer
is first selectman in our village;
she's in her dotage.   6

Thirsting for
the hierarchic privacy
of Queen Victoria's century,   9
she buys up all
the eyesores facing her shore,
and lets them fall.   12

The season's ill—
we've lost our summer millionaire,
who seemed to leap from an L. L. Bean[2]   15
catalogue. His nine-knot yawl
was auctioned off to lobstermen.
A red fox stain covers Blue Hill.   18

And now our fairy
decorator brightens his shop for fall;
his fishnet's filled with orange cork,   21
orange, his cobbler's bench and awl;
there is no money in his work,
he'd rather marry.   24

One dark night,
my Tudor Ford climbed the hill's skull;

---

[1]An American poet born in 1911. Lowell wrote that he modeled the poem on her "The Armadillo," which is dedicated to him.   [2]A Maine dealer in sporting goods and clothing.

I watched for love-cars. Lights turned down, 27
they lay together, hull to hull,
where the graveyard shelves on the town. . . .
My mind's not right. 30

A car radio bleats,
"Love, O careless Love. . . ."³ I hear
my ill-spirit sob in each blood cell, 33
as if my hand were at its throat. . . .
I myself am hell;⁴
nobody's here— 36

only skunks, that search
in the moonlight for a bite to eat.
They march on their soles up Main Street: 39
white stripes, moonstruck eyes' red fire
under the chalk-dry and spar spire
of the Trinitarian Church. 42

I stand on top
of our back steps and breathe the rich air—
a mother skunk with her column of kittens swills the garbage pail. 45
She jabs her wedge-head in a cup
of sour cream, drops her ostrich tail,
and will not scare. 48

---

³From the folk song "Careless Love," the lament of a pregnant girl.   ⁴Like Milton's Satan in
Paradise Lost: "Which way I fly is Hell; myself am Hell" (IV,75).

Church Going

Philip Larkin   (1922–1985)

Once I am sure there's nothing going on
I step inside, letting the door thud shut.
Another church: matting, seats, and stone,
And little books; sprawlings of flowers, cut
For Sunday, brownish now; some brass and stuff 5
Up at the holy end; the small neat organ;
And a tense, musty, unignorable silence,
Brewed God knows how long. Hatless, I take off
My cycle-clips in awkward reverence,

Move forward, run my hand around the font. 10
From where I stand, the roof looks almost new—
Cleaned, or restored? Someone would know: I don't.
Mounting the lectern, I peruse a few

Hectoring[1] large-scale verses, and pronounce
'Here endeth' much more loudly than I'd meant.   **15**
The echoes snigger briefly. Back at the door
I sign the book, donate an Irish sixpence,
Reflect the place was not worth stopping for.

Yet stop I did: in fact I often do,
And always end much at a loss like this,   **20**
Wondering what to look for; wondering, too,
When churches fall completely out of use
What we shall turn them into, if we shall keep
A few cathedrals chronically on show,
Their parchment, plate and pyx[2] in locked cases,   **25**
And let the rest rent-free to rain and sheep.
Shall we avoid them as unlucky places?

Or, after dark, will dubious women come
To make their children touch a particular stone;
Pick simples[3] for a cancer; or on some   **30**
Advised night see walking a dead one?
Power of some sort or other will go on
In games, in riddles, seemingly at random;
But superstition, like belief, must die,
And what remains when disbelief has gone?   **35**
Grass, weedy pavement, brambles, buttress, sky,

A shape less recognisable each week,
A purpose more obscure. I wonder who
Will be the last, the very last, to seek
This place for what it was; one of the crew   **40**
That tap and jot and know what rood-lofts[4] were?
Some ruin-bibber, randy for antique,
Or Christmas-addict, counting on a whiff
Of gown-and-bands and organ-pipes and myrrh?
Or will he be my representative,   **45**

Bored, uninformed, knowing the ghostly silt
Dispersed, yet tending to this cross of ground
Through suburb scrub because it held unspilt
So long and equably what since is found
Only in separation—marriage, and birth,   **50**
And death, and thoughts of these—for whom was built

[1]Bullying, threatening. [2]Container for the Eucharist wafer. [3]Medicinal herbs. [4]Church galleries, located over the rood screen.

This special shell? For, though I've no idea
What this accoutred frowsty⁵ barn is worth,
It pleases me to stand in silence here;

A serious house on serious earth it is,   55
In whose blent air all our compulsions meet,
Are recognised, and robed as destinies.
And that much never can be obsolete,
Since someone will forever be surprising
A hunger in himself to be more serious,   60
And gravitating with it to this ground,
Which, he once heard, was proper to grow wise in,
If only that so many dead lie round.

⁵Musty.

Poetry of Departures

Philip Larkin   (1922–1985)

Sometimes you hear, fifth-hand,
As epitaph:
*He chucked up everything
And just cleared off*,
And always the voice will sound
Certain you approve
This audacious, purifying,
Elemental move.   8

And they are right, I think.
We all hate home
And having to be there:
I detest my room,   12
Its specially-chosen junk,
The good books, the good bed,
And my life, in perfect order:
So to hear it said   16

He walked out on the whole crowd
Leaves me flushed and stirred,
Like *Then she undid her dress*
Or *Take that you bastard;*   20
Surely I can, if he did?
And that helps me stay

Sober and industrious.
But I'd go today,   24

Yes, swagger the nut-strewn roads,
Crouch in the fo'c'sle[1]
Stubbly with goodness, if
It weren't so artificial,   28
Such a deliberate step backwards
To create an object:
Books; china; a life
Reprehensibly perfect.   32

[1]The forecastle, location of the sailors' quarters on a merchant ship.

Cherrylog Road

James Dickey   (1923–   )

Off Highway 106
At Cherrylog Road I entered
The '34 Ford without wheels,   3
Smothered in kudzu,[1]
With a seat pulled out to run
Corn whiskey down from the hills,   6

And then from the other side
Crept into an Essex
With a rumble seat of red leather   9
And then out again, aboard
A blue Chevrolet, releasing
The rust from its other color,   12

Reared up on three building blocks.
None had the same body heat;
I changed with them inward, toward   15
The weedy heart of the junkyard,
For I knew that Doris Holbrook
Would escape from her father at noon   18

And would come from the farm
To seek parts owned by the sun
Among the abandoned chassis,   21
Sitting in each in turn
As I did, leaning forward
As in a wild stock-car race   24

[1]A rambling, viny plant.

In the parking lot of the dead.
Time after time, I climbed in
And out the other side, like   27
An envoy or movie star
Met at the station by crickets.
A radiator cap raised its head,   30

Become a real toad or a kingsnake
As I neared the hub of the yard,
Passing through many states,   33
Many lives, to reach
Some grandmother's long Pierce-Arrow
Sending platters of blindness forth   36

From its nickel hubcaps
And spilling its tender upholstery
On sleepy roaches,   39
The glass panel in between
Lady and colored driver
Not all the way broken out,   42

The back-seat phone
Still on its hook.
I got in as though to exclaim,   45
"Let us go to the orphan asylum,
John; I have some old toys
For children who say their prayers."   48

I popped with sweat as I thought
I heard Doris Holbrook scrape
Like a mouse in the southern-state sun   51
That was eating the paint in blisters
From a hundred car tops and hoods.
She was tapping like code,   54

Loosening the screws,
Carrying off headlights,
Sparkplugs, bumpers,   57
Cracked mirrors and gear-knobs,
Getting ready, already,
To go back with something to show   60

Other than her lips' new trembling
I would hold to me soon, soon,
Where I sat in the ripped back seat   63
Talking over the interphone,
Praying for Doris Holbrook
To come from her father's farm   66

And to get back there
With no trace of me on her face
To be seen by her red-haired father   69
Who would change, in the squalling barn,
Her back's pale skin with a strop,
Then lay for me   72

In a bootlegger's roasting car
With a string-triggered 12-gauge shotgun
To blast the breath from the air.   75
Not cut by the jagged windshields,
Through the acres of wrecks she came
With a wrench in her hand,   78

Through dust where the blacksnake dies
Of boredom, and the beetle knows
The compost has no more life.   81
Someone outside would have seen
The oldest car's doors inexplicably
Close from within: 84

I held her and held her and held her,
Convoyed at terrific speed
By the stalled, dreaming traffic around us,   87
So the blacksnake, stiff
With inaction, curved back
Into life, and hunted the mouse   90

With deadly overexcitement,
The beetles reclaimed their field
As we clung, glued together,   93
With the hooks of the seat springs
Working through to catch us red-handed
Amidst the gray breathless batting   96

That burst from the seat at our backs.
We left by separate doors
Into the changed, other bodies   99
Of cars, she down Cherrylog Road
And I to my motorcycle
Parked like the soul of the junkyard   102

Restored, a bicycle fleshed
With power, and tore off
Up Highway 106, continually   105
Drunk on the wind in my mouth,
Wringing the handlebar for speed,
Wild to be wreckage forever.   108

The Skein

Carolyn Kizer   (1925–   )

Moonlight through my gauze curtains
Turns them to nets for snaring wild birds,
Turns them into woven traps, into shrouds.
The old, restless grief keeps me awake.
I wander around, holding a scarf or shawl;   5
In the muffled moonlight I wander around
Folding it carefully, shaking it out again.
Everyone says my old lover is happy.
I wish they said he was coming back to me.
I hesitate here, my scarf like a skein of yarn   10
Binding my two hands loosely
            that would reach for paper and pen.

So I memorize these lines,
Dew on the scarf, dappling my nightdress also.
O love long gone, it is raining in our room!   15
So I memorize these lines,
            without salutation, without close.

Down at the Docks

Kenneth Koch   (1925–   )

Down at the docks
Where everything is sweet and inclines
At night
To the sound of canoes   4
I planted a maple tree
And every night
Beneath it I studied the cosmos
Down at the docks.   8

Sweet ladies, listen to me.
The dock is made of wood
The maple tree's not made of wood
It is wood   12
Wood comes from it
As music comes from me
And from this mandolin I've made
Out of the maple tree.   16

Jealous gentlemen, study how
Wood comes from the maple
Then devise your love

So that it seems   20
To come from where
All is it yet something more
White spring flowers and leafy bough
Jealous gentlemen.   24

Arrogant little waves
Knocking at the dock
It's for you I've made this chanson
For you and that big dark blue.   28

To Christ Our Lord

Galway Kinnell   (1927–)

The legs of the elk punctured the snow's crust
And wolves floated lightfooted on the land
Hunting Christmas elk living and frozen;
Inside snow melted in a basin, and a woman basted
A bird spread over coals by its wings and head.   5

Snow had sealed the windows; candles lit
The Christmas meal. The Christmas grace chilled
The cooked bird, being long-winded and the room cold.
During the words a boy thought, is it fitting
To eat this creature killed on the wing?   10

He had killed it himself, climbing out
Alone on snowshoes in the Christmas dawn,
The fallen snow swirling and the snowfall gone,
Heard its throat scream as the rifle shouted,
Watched it drop, and fished from the snow the dead.   15

He had not wanted to shoot. The sound
Of wings beating into the hushed air
Had stirred his love, and his fingers
Froze in his gloves, and he wondered,
Famishing, could he fire? Then he fired.   20

Now the grace praised his wicked act. At its end
The bird on the plate
Stared at his stricken appetite.
There had been nothing to do but surrender,
To kill and to eat; he ate as he had killed, with wonder. 25

At night on snowshoes on the drifting field
He wondered again, for whom had love stirred?
The stars glittered on the snow and nothing answered.

Then the Swan spread her wings, cross of the cold north,
The pattern and mirror of the acts of earth.   30

Grandmother Watching at Her Window

W. S. Merwin   (1927–)

There was always the river or the train
Right past the door, and someone might be gone
Come morning. When I was a child I mind
Being held up at a gate to wave
Good-bye, good-bye to I didn't know who,   5
Gone to the War, and how I cried after.
When I married I did what was right
But I knew even that first night
That he would go. And so shut my soul tight
Behind my mouth, so he could not steal it   10
When he went. I brought the children up clean
With my needle, taught them that stealing
Is the worst sin; knew if I loved them
They would be taken away, and did my best
But must have loved them anyway   15
For they slipped through my fingers like stitches.
Because God loves us always, whatever
We do. You can sit all your life in churches
And teach your hands to clutch when you pray
And never weaken, but God loves you so dearly   20
Just as you are, that nothing you are can stay,
But all the time you keep going away, away.

Evening

James Wright   (1927–1980)

I called him to come in,
The wide lawn darkened so.
Laughing, he held his chin
And hid beside a bush.
The light gave him a push;   4
Shadowy grass moved slow.
He crept on agile toes
Under a sheltering rose.

His mother, still beyond
The bare porch and the door,

Called faintly, out of sound,
And vanished with her voice.   12
I caught his curious eyes
Measuring me, and more—
The light dancing behind
My shoulder in the wind.   16

Then, struck beyond belief
By the child's voice I heard,
I saw his hair turn leaf,
His dancing toes divide   20
To hoofs on either side,
One hand become a bird.
Startled, I held my tongue
To hear what note he sang.   24

Where was the boy gone now?
I stood on the grass, alone.
Swung from the apple bough,
The bees ignored my cry.   28
A dog roved past, and I
Turned up a sinking stone,
But found beneath no more
Than grasses dead last year.   32

Suddenly, lost and cold,
I knew the yard lay bare.
I longed to touch and hold
My child, my talking child,   36
Laughing or tame or wild,
Solid in light and air,
The supple hands, the face
To fill that barren place.   40

Slowly, the leaves descended,
The birds resolved to hands;
Laugh, and the charm was ended,
The hungry boy stepped forth.   44
He stood on the hard earth,
Like one who understands
Fairy and ghost, but less
Our human loneliness.   48

Then, on the withering lawn
He walked beside my arm.
Trees and the sun were gone,
Everything gone but us.   52

His mother sang in the house,
And kept our supper warm,
And loved us, God knows how,
The wide earth darkened so.   56

For the Record

Adrienne Rich   (1929–)

The clouds and the stars didn't wage this war
the brooks gave no information
if the mountain spewed stones of fire into the river   3
it was not taking sides
the raindrop faintly swaying under the leaf
had no political opinions   6

and if here or there a house
filled with backed-up raw sewage
or poisoned those who lived there   9
with slow fumes, over years
the houses were not at war
nor did the tinned-up buildings   12

intend to refuse shelter
to homeless old women and roaming children
they had no policy to keep them roaming   15
or dying, no, the cities were not the problem
the bridges were non-partisan
the freeways burned, but not with hatred   18

Even the miles of barbed-wire
stretched around crouching temporary huts
designed to keep the unwanted   21
at a safe distance, out of sight
even the boards that had to absorb
year upon year, so many human sounds   24

so many depths of vomit, tears
slow-soaking blood
had not offered themselves for this   27
The trees didn't volunteer to be cut into boards
nor the thorns for tearing flesh
Look around at all of it   30

and ask whose signature
is stamped on the orders, traced
in the corner of the building plans   33

Ask where the illiterate, big-bellied
women were, the drunks and crazies,
the ones you fear most of all: ask where you were.   36

Second Glance at a Jaguar

Ted Hughes   (1930–   )

Skinful of bowls, he bowls them,
The hip going in and out of joint, dropping the spine
With urgency of his hurry
Like a cat going along under thrown stones, under cover,
Glancing sideways, running   5
Under his spine. A terrible, stump-legged waddle
Like a thick Aztec disemboweller,
Club-swinging, trying to grind some square
Socket between his hind legs round,
Carrying his head like a brazier of spilling embers,   10
And the black bit of his mouth, he takes it
Between his back teeth, he has to wear his skin out,
He swipes a lap at the water-trough as he turns,
Swivelling the ball of his heel on the polished spot,
Showing his belly like a butterfly,   15
At every stride he has to turn a corner
In himself and correct it. His head
Is like the worn-down stump of another whole jaguar,
His body is just the engine shoving it forward,
Lifting the air up and shoving on under,   20
The weight of his fangs hanging the mouth open,
Bottom jaw combing the ground. A gorged look,
Gangster, club-tail lumped along behind gracelessly,
He's wearing himself to heavy ovals,
Muttering some mantra,[1] some drum-song of murder   25
To keep his rage brightening, making his skin
Intolerable, spurred by the rosettes, the cain-brands,
Wearing the spots off from the inside,
Rounding some revenge. Going like a prayer-wheel,
The head dragging forward, the body keeping up,   30
The hind legs lagging. He coils, he flourishes
The blackjack tail as if looking for a target,
Hurrying through the underworld, soundless.

[1]Mystic word used in Hindu or Buddhist ritual or meditation.

Daddy

Sylvia Plath   *(1932–1963)*

You do not do, you do not do
Any more, black shoe
In which I have lived like a foot
For thirty years, poor and white,
Barely daring to breathe or Achoo.   5

Daddy, I have had to kill you.
You died before I had time—
Marble-heavy, a bag full of God,
Ghastly statue with one grey toe
Big as a Frisco seal   10

And a head in the freakish Atlantic
Where it pours bean green over blue
In the waters off beautiful Nauset.
I used to pray to recover you.
Ach, du.[1]   15

In the German tongue, in the Polish town
Scraped flat by the roller
Of wars, wars, wars.
But the name of the town is common.
My Polack friend   20

Says there are a dozen or two.
So I never could tell where you
Put your foot, your root,
I never could talk to you.
The tongue stuck in my jaw.   25

It stuck in a barb wire snare.
Ich,[2] ich, ich, ich,
I could hardly speak.
I thought every German was you.
And the language obscene   30

An engine, an engine
Chuffing me off like a Jew.
A Jew to Dachau, Auschwitz, Belsen.[3]
I began to talk like a Jew.
I think I may well be a Jew.   35

[1]Ah, you (German).   [2]I (German).   [3]Death camps in World War II.

The snows of the Tyrol, the clear beer of Vienna
Are not very pure or true.
With my gypsy ancestress and my weird luck
And my Taroc[4] pack and my Taroc pack
I may be a bit of a Jew.   40

I have always been scared of *you*,
With your Luftwaffe,[5] your gobbledygoo.
And your neat moustache
And your Aryan eye, bright blue.
Panzer-man,[6] panzer-man, O You—   45

Not God but a swastika
So black no sky could squeak through.
Every woman adores a Fascist,
The boot in the face, the brute
Brute heart of a brute like you.   50

You stand at the blackboard, daddy,
In the picture I have of you,
A cleft in your chin instead of your foot
But no less a devil for that, no not
Any less the black man who   55

Bit my pretty red heart in two.
I was ten when they buried you.
At twenty I tried to die
And get back, back, back to you.
I thought even the bones would do.   60

But they pulled me out of the sack,
And they stuck me together with glue.
And then I knew what to do.
I made a model of you,
A man in black with a Meinkampf[7] look   65

And a love of the rack and the screw.
And I said I do, I do.
So daddy, I'm finally through.
The black telephone's off at the root,
The voices just can't worm through.   70

If I've killed one man, I've killed two—
The vampire who said he was you
And drank my blood for a year,

[4]Fortune-telling cards; frequently spelled "Tarot."   [5]German Air Force.   [6]Soldier in an armored division.   [7]Adolf Hitler's autobiography was called *Mein Kampf* ("My Struggle").

Seven years, if you want to know.
Daddy, you can lie back now.   75

There's a stake in your fat black heart
And the villagers never liked you.
They are dancing and stamping on you.
They always *knew* it was you.
Daddy, daddy, you bastard, I'm through.   80

The Lost Baby Poem

Lucille Clifton   (1936–)

the time i dropped your almost body down
down to meet the waters under the city
and run one with the sewage to the sea
what did i know about waters rushing back   4
what did i know about drowning
or being drowned

you would have been born into winter
in the year of the disconnected gas   8
and no car   we would have made the thin
walk over Genesee hill into the Canada wind
to watch you slip like ice into strangers' hands
you would have fallen naked as snow into winter   12
if you were here i could tell you these
and some other things

if i am ever less than a mountain
for your definite brothers and sisters   16
let the rivers pour over my head
let the sea take me for a spiller
of seas   let black men call me stranger
always   for your never named sake   20

The Snapper

William Heyen   (1940–)

He is the pond's old father, its brain
and dark, permanent presence.

He is the snapper, and smells
rich and sick as a mat of weeds; and wears   4

a beard of leeches that suck frog, fish,
and snake blood from his neck; and drags

a tail ridged as though hacked out
with an ax. He rises: mud swirls   8

and blooms, lilies bob, water washes
his moss-humped back where, buried

deep in his sweet flesh, the pond ebbs
and flows its sure, slow heart.   12

DRAMA

ON DRAMA

SPECTACLE

The word "theater" is derived from a Greek word meaning *to see,* and this indicates that the basis of what goes on in a theater is spectacle, something to look at. The words in themselves often have a secondary function. Many, if not most, major developments of drama have been closely associated with music, where singing frequently takes over from speaking, and sometimes music and spectacle converge in the dance so that words get squeezed out altogether. In any case it is spectacle that has been the most popular feature of drama in all ages and cultures. If we start to read Shakespeare's plays, for instance, in what scholars regard as their chronological order, we find very early on three plays on the Wars of the Roses in the reign of Henry VI and a tragedy called *Titus Andronicus.* If our only contact with these plays is through reading, we may find the Henry VI plays rather dull and *Titus Andronicus* in particular almost childishly grotesque and horrible. Yet whenever any dramatic company works up enough nerve to give these plays a proper production, we discover that they can be made into superb pieces of spectacular theater. We have to realize, then, that Shakespeare was not educating himself through written texts, as we do for the most part, but through experience with audiences who wanted, and were ready to respond to, spectacle.

Later on, Shakespeare began his *Henry V* with a prologue apologizing for not giving his audience more spectacle, and what may be his last play, *Henry VIII,* again seems rather a dull play to read, because it is really a costume piece, a historical panorama with long processions of noblemen in full parade dress. So while an excellent film can be made of Shakespeare's *Henry V* (and of most of his other plays too), still, if Shakespeare's theater had possessed the resources

799

of the modern cinema, it is clear that we should never have had Shakespeare. The more spectacular the play, the less important the words are, and an audience, unless it is a specially educated audience, will not listen long if there is not enough to see. It's sometimes said that this emphasis on the visual is peculiar to Western culture; it's been suggested that when we say we listen "to" music, the word *to* indicates that we're putting even music into a visual and spatial context. But the emphasis on spectacle is quite as marked in Oriental drama too.

Through most of its history the verbal drama has been squeezed between musical forms on the one hand (opera, ballet, revue) and spectacular ones on the other (pantomime, circus, masque), which, as already noted, often combine to reduce the verbal content still further. One comedy by the best of the Roman dramatists, Terence, was not played through on its first performance, because the audience went out during the intermission to watch a rope-dancing act and failed to return. In later Roman times, when such circus entertainment had expanded into gladiatorial battles and chariot races, serious drama seems to have disappeared from stage almost altogether. If stage drama is not crowded out today by the competition of movies, television, and ball games, that is partly because of the efforts made by books like this one to stress the importance of verbal education and partly out of a need for greater variety. The most popular dramatic forms, because they are mass produced, tend to be highly conventionalized; this is true of sitcoms and similar stereotyped dramatic forms in television, as it was of their predecessors in radio and cinema a generation or so ago, when they were the most popular forms. It is not much wonder if we find a tendency on the part of playwrights to nag and scold their audiences for wanting something more lowbrow; this tendency has run through the history of drama from Aristophanes to Bernard Shaw and beyond. We may assume that a parallel tendency to say "nothing ever happens in these new-fangled plays; they're all just a lot of talk" has recurred in audiences for the same length of time.

DRAMATIC ROLES

But there are some very profound and central human experiences that only verbal drama can express. We might begin by looking at two types of these experiences in particular. In the first place, we act out dramatic roles constantly in our own lives. Someone we know comes into our room, and we instantly adopt a role that is based on our knowledge of the person's character and mannerisms. The person leaves, and we start dramatizing ourselves to ourselves, like Hamlet; if we aren't consciously talking to ourselves, as he did, we are unconsciously throwing our minds into some sort of inner dialogue. Cutting out all the babble and chatter that goes on inside us takes a high degree of concentration and mental discipline, and all this chatter is dramatic in one way or another. Some people speak of a "persona" as the part of ourselves that expresses the social aspect of our life; the word means mask and refers to the fact that in the plays of ancient Greece the actors wore masks. The phrase *dramatis personae,* before the list of characters at the beginning of a play, originally meant "the masks to be used for the performance." But we don't have just one mask; we have any number of them, and it's highly significant that our words *person* and *personality* come from the same dramatic metaphor. They suggest that we can never take a mask off and show the "real self" underneath. There's nothing under a "persona" except another persona; there's no core to that onion. The Greek equivalent of persona is *hypocrites,* from which our word *hypocrite* comes. This sounds bad, and suggests that if we are better people we can remove all deceitful disguises and speak with utter sincerity and truthfulness. Perhaps we can, but when we do we are entering into a dramatic role of sincerity and are wearing *that* mask.

So one of the things drama does is to reflect back to us the dramas we carry on with each other and with ourselves. In some plays, especially modern ones, that reflection results in an exaggeration so marked that if we come to this kind of drama unaccustomed to theatrical conventions we might assume that all the characters are simply insane. But if we listen closely to the interaction of the things we say with the things that are also in our minds that we don't say, along with an occasional echo of things we don't dare say to ourselves or even consciously think, we might hear something not so very different. And we have all gone through conversations that seemed so pointless and meaningless, with so many empty clichés mechanically spoken whether they related to anything else said or not, as to make the most disjointed onstage dialogue seem like the soberest realism.

Our second type of dramatic experience is an extension of the same principle to the characters in a play, who are so often locked inside subdramas of their own, so that the play we are watching often becomes a bundle of subsidiary dramas. Take the conclusion of Miller's *Death of a Salesman,* where we observe the personas that the Loman family have adopted in relation to one another forcefully challenged as fraudulent. Wife and sons must now confront Willy in the light of new knowledge and a new understanding of their own roles—either that or refuse the knowledge and its implications and allow life to go on as it has in the past, with each family member adopting an old mask again. And Willy's final choice when he goes off to die is to continue to play the role he has cast himself in from the beginning, saving the family with an act he persists in viewing as heroic, however hollow others might judge that heroism to be. However we interpret the words at the end of the play, they make it clear that Miller is not simply writing a play and the audience merely listening to it. There's a group of intermediate dramas, some of them within the characters and some of them within our own previous experiences, and it's the interactions of all these that make up the whole drama. Miller's genius as a playwright resulted in part from his ability to create the Loman family both as characters and as the subdramatists of their own lives.

ILLUSION AND IRONY

It's also important that when we assume a dramatic role in relation to someone else we become partly a dramatic construct of that someone else. Anyone who has thrown himself into a set role, like Willy Loman in *Death of a Salesman,* is in danger of suddenly realizing that he's not sure whether he's himself or merely a kind of ventriloquist's dummy, an echo of what other people or other people's values have made out of him. Something similar is the reason for the tensions between the people in Williams's *The Glass Menagerie,* as Tom and Laura try desperately to find their own identities apart from the expectations of their mother. Laura, we discover, succeeds at most in establishing a quite fragile identity, easily shattered, and Tom becomes himself only by satisfying his mother that he is a "selfish dreamer," although that is certainly not his preferred view of himself, nor is it one we are sure an audience should accept. The play abounds with references to the world as an illusion and to our places in it as illusory.

Similarly, in Shakespeare's *The Tempest,* at the beginning of the second act, we find Antonio and Sebastian in a state of giggling hysteria that gradually turns venomous as they plot to murder Alonso when he's asleep. They plot this because they're realists, because this is the kind of thing you do in the real world to get on and get ahead. Earlier, when Gonzalo says that the island is fresh and green, they see it realistically as totally barren. Later the hero, Ferdinand, sees the masque put on by Ariel and the other spirits working for Prospero, which is of course an illusion, like all dramatic performances. By the end of the play we realize that these notions of reality and illusion are exactly the opposite of those being presented by the play itself. The masque symbolizes a far profounder reality than actual existence ever affords; the squalid plot of Antonio and Sebastian shows that they are the ones who are plunged in illusion. And on top of that we have Prospero's speech after the masque, pointing out that the difference between reality and illusion is itself an illusion, what we call reality being simply an illusion that lasts a little longer.

One form of drama that has been popular at various times is the puppet play, where we can see that the movements and sounds of the characters are being produced by somebody else offstage. But of course human actors are to some degree puppets also, considering how much authors and directors have to do with their acting. Audiences, again, are always in a state of greater freedom than the characters on the stage, simply because they are able to walk out of the theater; and in the great majority of plays they know more about what is going on in the whole action of the play than the characters on the stage are supposed to know. All this makes for the situation that we call irony, where the spectator knows more than the participator.

Irony is an obvious source of the comic; in many comedies we find a type of character that Shakespeare's friend and contemporary Ben Jonson called a "humor," a character like a miser or hypochondriac or snob or jealous husband or father or glutton or pedant, who is identified with a single leading characteristic and can't do anything not connected with exhibiting it. Such characters are funny because they have made themselves into puppets, mechanically responding to every stimulus in the same way. The characters in *The Cherry Orchard,* for example, are humors, wandering around in a daze created by their own dreams and snobberies. Lyubov, who compulsively gives too much money to beggars because she resents the fact that she's not wealthy anymore and can't afford to, is the central humor of the play.

But irony is a feature of tragedy also. In *Oedipus Rex,* the audience already knows the outlines of the story and so keeps anticipating all the horrific discoveries that Oedipus makes about himself. In *Hamlet,* the prince, motivated by the desire to set right a monarchy made "rotten" by regicide, fratricide and adultery, brings about the total collapse of Denmark's royal family. Order—when it comes —results from the advent of a new dynasty from another country. In *Death of a Salesman,* again, the audience, while it may not know the end of that particular story, still does know that Willy Loman's version of the American dream is a lot of nonsense and that no good can come of pursuing it.

In general, there's a broad division between tragedy and comedy, which is mainly a difference in endings; a tragedy traditionally ends in the death or disaster of the central character and a comedy with some kind of party, such as a wedding. The pervading mood of tragedy is likely to be sombre and that of comedy festive, but we can have tragedies full of wit and humor, like *Romeo and Juliet* or "black" comedies that seem very gloomy or bitter. The original idea was that tragedy showed us death and comedy showed us a passage through, if not actual death, at least something quite ominous, to renewed life.

In Aristophanes's *Lysistrata,* the women barricade the Acropolis, and the chorus of old men scrambles up with wood to set the place on fire, so as either to roast the women alive or smoke them out. They are too old to be drafted for military service or to be affected by the sexual strike, but the intensity of their hatred for the women who want to intervene in public affairs long enough to stop the war with Sparta is not just good fun. This is "Old" Comedy, and was succeeded on the stage by "New" Comedy, where, usually, a young man wants a young woman, is opposed by his or her father, but finally gets her. He is often helped, in Roman comedies, by a clever slave, who may be threatened with anything from flogging to crucifixion by the father.

Tragedy usually focuses on a heroic figure of greater authority or articulateness than we have. Tragedy is an event; it does not depend on the moral quality of the hero. The hero may be the mature and responsible Oedipus, utterly unconscious of anything he could have done to provoke the wrath of the gods, or he may be loaded down with the foulest crimes, like Macbeth. The one thing he must be is a hero, somebody worth writing a tragedy about. Willy Loman may not be what we ordinarily think of as a hero, but, as his wife says, small men can get just as exhausted as big ones, and however absurd his values may be he has fought hard for them. And, in the sight of watching angels or someone equally removed from the human scene, his values might be much less absurd than Macbeth's ambition.

Is the final meaning of drama, then, simply that everything is illusion and that nothing is real? Not quite. We notice that Oedipus keeps driving himself through the most agonizing self-discoveries because, as he says, he is determined to find out who he is. In *Death of a Salesman,* Biff says of his father: "He never knew who he was," but he's reached a profounder level of insight himself when he says of himself simply "I'm nothing, Pop." In *The Glass Menagerie,* Tom finally leaves home, but in his last speech he tells us how his life has been dominated by the persistent reality of his memories. At the end of *The Tempest,* Gonzalo says that "all of us [found] ourselves when no man was his own." At the end of a play, then, there is often left behind some sense of identity that has been attained by somebody, in however perverse a way, and this sense of identity, a reality that can only be pointed to by illusion, seems to be what is really underneath all the masks and stage paint and lighting. Sometimes a character in the play attains it; sometimes, as in *The Cherry Orchard,* nobody does. In that case the gaining of a sense of identity is a job for the people in the audience, as Prospero indicates when he says, in the Epilogue to *The Tempest,* the play's over; I've done what I can; now it's all yours.

CHAPTER 1

TRAGEDY

THE GREEK THEATER

Imagine yourself an actor and playwright. As the "wright" you will make the play (not write it), just as a wheelwright and wainwright used to make wheels and wagons. Your tools are words, actors, and whatever physical support the budget will allow: costumes, perhaps, and a painted backdrop or two. You have been asked to provide a play to highlight the spring festival your university holds annually in its football stadium. You will use one end of the stadium. You will stand near the goal line and face the 14,000 spectators the stadium can seat from the curve at the end to the line at your right and left. At your back will be a structure of wood and canvas to serve as setting and as a place to change costumes, but you will have no curtains, no electric lights, and no microphones. You will step out in daylight, before thousands, and hold their attention for three or four hours. It won't be easy.

But it can be done. Or at least it once was done regularly in ancient Greece, for what we have described is essentially an ancient Greek theater. Unless your stadium is among the largest in the country you won't be able to seat 14,000 people at one end, but the theater of Dionysus at Athens held approximately that number. Other theaters in the ancient world accommodated perhaps as many as 50,000. All were open to the sky, illuminated naturally by daylight. A *skene* (from which comes our word *scene*), originally a tent or wooden hut, faced the semicircle of seats. In front of the *skene* was the *proskenion* (our *proscenium*) and in front of that a circular *orchestra* for the chorus.

How will you make all those people hear? How will you get their attention and keep them interested? The *skene* will help to enclose your voice in the amphitheater, but your play will do best with speeches suited to public declamation; you won't want to write any intimate, whispery passages. Perhaps you will invent some mechanical magnification. Your players could wear masks cleverly constructed to serve as sounding boards or megaphones. But will the people in the back rows be able to see? Perhaps the masks could enlarge facial features, emphasizing emotional attributes. The actors might be physically heightened by elevated shoes or clogs. The play then will not want much movement, but will depend upon strong, easily projected emotions and large, unmistakable gestures. For subject matter, you may well decide upon some familiar story, with characters everyone knows, a dean or a football hero or a recent president of the United States. If you take a new story, you will want to keep it simple. You will reach your audience more easily that way, but to keep them with you perhaps you had better throw in a chorus and some dancing.

You have reinvented Greek theater. Unfortunately, it is not likely to work well for you, for the theatrical *conventions* of today are far different from those of Sophocles's day. Your audience is accustomed to the psychological isolation of a seat in a darkened theater, looking upon a brightly lit stage or screen. Greek theater was communal, festive, religious. Your audience wants the novelty of a

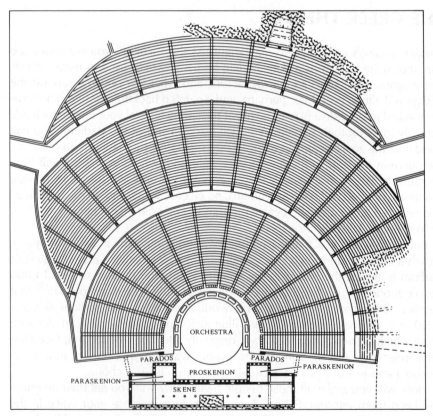

Theater of Dionysus, Fourth Century B.C.
(Adapted from Dörpfeld and Reisch, *Griechische Theater*, 1896)

new story. Greek audiences wanted endless variations on stories known since childhood. Your audience wants close-ups and electronic amplification. Greek audiences wanted the magic of painted masks and the ritual affirmations of choral interludes.

OEDIPUS REX

You can read *Oedipus Rex* as you would any nondramatic work of literature, recreating its images upon the stage of your mind as you do the images of a poem or a story. But you are much more free than you are with a poem or a story to imagine how the actors look and move and how the setting surrounding them appears: all the physical details made concrete in a production. Develop your imagination as you may, you can never experience the play quite the way its first audiences did, but you can sense its ancient greatness if you imagine the Greek stage: the masks, the declamatory voices, the sweeping gestures, the bright blue Mediterranean sky above, the shared responses of thousands. Or you can stage the play in your mind in a darkened twentieth-century theater, either with living actors or with pictures projected upon a screen; done well it retains its power to move deeply. Among literary genres, only the play has quite this protean nature, taking a large part of its identity from its production. To read a play well is to become part stage manager, part actor, and part audience.

OEDIPUS REX*

Sophocles   *(496?–406* B.C.*)*

Persons Represented

OEDIPUS	**MESSENGER**
A PRIEST	**SHEPHERD OF LAÏOS**
CREON	**SECOND MESSENGER**
TEIRESIAS	**CHORUS OF THEBAN ELDERS**
IOCASTÊ	

The Scene: Before the palace of Oedipus, King of Thebes. A central door and two lateral doors open onto a platform which runs the length of the façade. On the platform, right and left, are altars; and three steps lead down into the "orchestra," or chorus-ground. At the beginning of the action these steps are crowded by Suppliants[1] who have brought branches and chaplets of olive leaves and who lie in various attitudes of despair. Oedipus enters.

*English version by Dudley Fitts and Robert Fitzgerald.

[1]Persons entreating favors.

Prologue[2]

OEDIPUS: My children, generations of the living
In the line of Kadmos,[3] nursed at his ancient hearth:
Why have you strewn yourselves before these altars
In supplication, with your boughs and garlands?
The breath of incense rises from the city   5
With a sound of prayer and lamentation.
                                        Children,
I would not have you speak through messengers,
And therefore I have come myself to hear you—
I, Oedipus, who bear the famous name.
(To a Priest.) You, there, since you are eldest in the company,
Speak for them all, tell me what preys upon you,   10
Whether you come in dread, or crave some blessing:
Tell me, and never doubt that I will help you
In every way I can; I should be heartless
Were I not moved to find you suppliant here.
PRIEST: Great Oedipus, O powerful King of Thebes!   15
You see how all the ages of our people
Cling to your altar steps: here are boys
Who can barely stand alone, and here are priests
By weight of age, as I am a priest of God,
And young men chosen from those yet unmarried;   20
As for the others, all that multitude,
They wait with olive chaplets in the squares,
At the two shrines of Pallas,[4] and where Apollo[5]
Speaks in the glowing embers.
                                Your own eyes
Must tell you: Thebes is in her extremity   25
And can not lift her head from the surge of death.
A rust consumes the buds and fruits of the earth;
The herds are sick; children die unborn,
And labor is vain. The god of plague and pyre
Raids like detestable lightning through the city,   30
And all the house of Kadmos is laid waste,
All emptied, and all darkened: Death alone
Battens upon the misery of Thebes.

You are not one of the immortal gods, we know;
Yet we have come to you to make our prayer   35

[2]Introduction, or foreword to the action.   [3]Cadmus, legendary Phoenician founder of the city of
Thebes. Here, as in the names Iocastê (Jocasta) and Laïos (Laius), Fitts and Fitzgerald prefer
spellings more like the Greek than are the usual English forms.   [4]Pallas Athena, goddess of
wisdom.   [5]Phoebus Apollo, the sun god. At his shrine, fortunes were told in a variety of ways,
including from embers.

As to the man of all men best in adversity
And wisest in the ways of God. You saved us
From the Sphinx,[6] that flinty singer, and the tribute
We paid to her so long; yet you were never
Better informed than we, nor could we teach you: 40
It was some god breathed in you to set us free.

Therefore, O mighty King, we turn to you:
Find us our safety, find us a remedy,
Whether by counsel of the gods or men.
A king of wisdom tested in the past   45
Can act in a time of troubles, and act well.
Noblest of men, restore
Life to your city! Think how all men call you
Liberator for your triumph long ago;
Ah, when your years of kingship are remembered,   50
Let them not say *We rose, but later fell*—
Keep the State from going down in the storm!
Once, years ago, with happy augury,
You brought us fortune; be the same again!
No man questions your power to rule the land: 55
But rule over men, not over a dead city!
Ships are only hulls, citadels are nothing,
When no life moves in the empty passageways.
OEDIPUS: Poor children! You may be sure I know
All that you longed for in your coming here.   60
I know that you are deathly sick; and yet,
Sick as you are, not one is as sick as I.
Each of you suffers in himself alone
His anguish, not another's; but my spirit
Groans for the city, for myself, for you.   65

I was not sleeping, you are not waking me.
No, I have been in tears for a long while
And in my restless thought walked many ways.
In all my search, I found one helpful course,
And that I have taken: I have sent Creon,   70
Son of Menoikeus, brother of the Queen,
To Delphi, Apollo's place of revelation,
To learn there, if he can,
What act or pledge of mine may save the city.

[6]A monster with female head and the body of a lion. She had terrorized Thebes, killing all who
could not answer her riddle ("What goes on four legs in the morning, two at noon, three in the
evening?"). Oedipus answered correctly, "Man" (as a baby, an adult, and in age supported by a
cane) and destroyed the monster.

I have counted the days, and now, this very day,   75
I am troubled, for he has overstayed his time.
What is he doing? He has been gone too long.
Yet whenever he comes back, I should do ill
To scant whatever hint the god may give.

PRIEST: It is a timely promise. At this instant   80
They tell me Creon is here.

OEDIPUS: O Lord Apollo!
May his news be fair as his face is radiant!

PRIEST: It could not be otherwise: he is crowned with bay,
The chaplet is thick with berries.

OEDIPUS: We shall soon know;
He is near enough to hear us now.

(Enter Creon)

                                 O Prince: 85
Brother: son of Menoikeus:
What answer do you bring us from the god?

CREON: It is favorable. I can tell you, great afflictions
Will turn out well, if they are taken well.

OEDIPUS: What was the oracle? These vague words   90
Leave me still hanging between hope and fear.

CREON: Is it your pleasure to hear me with all these
Gathered around us? I am prepared to speak,
But should we not go in?

OEDIPUS: Let them all hear it.
It is for them I suffer, more than for myself.   95

CREON: Then I will tell you what I heard at Delphi.
In plain words
The god commands us to expel from the land of Thebes
An old defilement that it seems we shelter.
It is a deathly thing, beyond expiation.   100
We must not let it feed upon us longer.

OEDIPUS: What defilement? How shall we rid ourselves of it?

CREON: By exile or death, blood for blood. It was
Murder that brought the plague-wind on the city.

OEDIPUS: Murder of whom? Surely the god has named him?   105

CREON: My lord: long ago Laïos was our king,
Before you came to govern us.

OEDIPUS: I know;
I learned of him from others; I never saw him.

CREON: He was murdered; and Apollo commands us now
To take revenge upon whoever killed him.   110

OEDIPUS: Upon whom? Where are they? Where shall we find a clue
To solve that crime, after so many years?

CREON: Here in this land, he said.

If we make enquiry,

We may touch things that otherwise escape us.

OEDIPUS: Tell me: Was Laïos murdered in his house,   115

Or in the fields, or in some foreign country?

CREON: He said he planned to make a pilgrimage.

He did not come home again.

OEDIPUS: And was there no one,

No witness, no companion, to tell what happened?

CREON: They were all killed but one, and he got away   120

So frightened that he could remember one thing only.

OEDIPUS: What was that one thing? One may be the key

To everything, if we resolve to use it.

CREON: He said that a band of highwaymen attacked them,

Outnumbered them, and overwhelmed the King.   125

OEDIPUS: Strange, that a highwayman should be so daring—

Unless some faction here bribed him to do it.

CREON: We thought of that. But after Laïos' death

New troubles arose and we had no avenger.

OEDIPUS: What troubles could prevent your hunting down the

killers?   130

CREON: The riddling Sphinx's song

Made us deaf to all mysteries but her own.

OEDIPUS: Then once more I must bring what is dark to light.

It is most fitting that Apollo shows,

As you do, this compunction for the dead.   135

You shall see how I stand by you, as I should,

To avenge the city and the city's god,

And not as though it were for some distant friend,

But for my own sake, to be rid of evil.

Whoever killed King Laïos might—who knows?—   140

Decide at any moment to kill me as well.

By avenging the murdered king I protect myself.

Come, then, my children: leave the altar steps,

Lift up your olive boughs!

One of you go

And summon the people of Kadmos to gather here.   145

I will do all that I can; you may tell them that.

(Exit a Page)

So, with the help of God,

We shall be saved—or else indeed we are lost.

PRIEST: Let us rise, children. It was for this we came,

And now the King has promised it himself.   150

Phoibos has sent us an oracle; may he descend
Himself to save us and drive out the plague.

(Exeunt Oedipus and Creon into the palace by the central door. The Priest and the Suppliants disperse right and left. After a short pause the Chorus enters the orchestra.)

Parodos[7]

Strophe[8] 1

CHORUS: What is God singing in his profound
   Delphi of gold and shadow?
What oracle for Thebes, the sunwhipped city?
   Fear unjoints me, the roots of my heart tremble.
Now I remember, O Healer, your power, and wonder;   5
   Will you send doom like a sudden cloud, or weave it
Like nightfall of the past?
Speak, speak to us, issue of holy sound:
   Dearest to our expectancy: be tender!

Antistrophe 1

Let me pray to Athenê, the immortal daughter of Zeus,   10
   And to Artemis[9] her sister
Who keeps her famous throne in the market ring,
   And to Apollo, bowman at the far butts of heaven—
O gods, descend! Like three streams leap against
   The fires of our grief, the fires of darkness;   15
Be swift to bring us rest!

As in the old time from the brilliant house
Of air you stepped to save us, come again!

Strophe 2

Now our afflictions have no end,
Now all our stricken host lies down   20
And no man fights off death with his mind;

The noble plowland bears no grain,
And groaning mothers can not bear—

See, how our lives like birds take wing,
Like sparks that fly when a fire soars,   25
To the shore of the god of evening.

Antistrophe 2

[7]An entrance song delivered by the chorus.   [8]A song accompanied by a dance right to left. The *antistrophe* accompanies a dance back again.   [9]Goddess of the moon and hunting.

The plague burns on, it is pitiless,
Though pallid children laden with death
Lie unwept in the stony ways,

And old gray women by every path   30
Flock to the strand about the altars

There to strike their breasts and cry
Worship of Phoibos in wailing prayers:
Be kind, God's golden child!

Strophe 3

There are no swords in this attack by fire,   35
No shields, but we are ringed with cries.
Send the besieger plunging from our homes
Into the vast sea-room of the Atlantic
Or into the waves that foam eastward of Thrace—
For the day ravages what the night spares—   40
Destroy our enemy, lord of the thunder!
Let him be riven by lightning from heaven!

Antistrophe 3

Phoibos Apollo, stretch the sun's bowstring,
That golden cord, until it sing for us,
Flashing arrows in heaven!
                    Artemis, Huntress,   45
Race with flaring lights upon our mountains!

O scarlet god, O golden-banded brow,
O Theban Bacchos in a storm of Maenads,[10]

(Enter Oedipus, center)

Whirl upon Death, that all the Undying hate!
Come with blinding cressets, come in joy!   50

Scene I

OEDIPUS: Is this your prayer? It may be answered. Come,
Listen to me, act as the crisis demands,
And you shall have relief from all these evils.

Until now I was a stranger to this tale,
As I had been a stranger to the crime.   5
Could I track down the murderer without a clue?

[10]Bacchus, god of wine and revelry, with female attendants.

But now, friends,
As one who became a citizen after the murder,
I make this proclamation to all Thebans:
If any man knows by whose hand Laïos, son of Labdakos,   10
Met his death, I direct that man to tell me everything,
No matter what he fears for having so long withheld it.
Let it stand as promised that no further trouble
Will come to him, but he may leave the land in safety.

Moreover: If anyone knows the murderer to be foreign,   15
Let him not keep silent: he shall have his reward from me.
However, if he does conceal it; if any man
Fearing for his friend or for himself disobeys this edict,
Hear what I propose to do:

I solemnly forbid the people of this country,   20
Where power and throne are mine, ever to receive that man
Or speak to him, no matter who he is, or let him
Join in sacrifice, lustration, or in prayer.
I decree that he be driven from every house,
Being, as he is, corruption itself to us: the Delphic   25
Voice of Zeus has pronounced this revelation.
Thus I associate myself with the oracle
And take the side of the murdered king.

As for the criminal, I pray to God—
Whether it be a lurking thief, or one of a number—   30
I pray that that man's life be consumed in evil and wretchedness.
And as for me, this curse applies no less
If it should turn out that the culprit is my guest here,
Sharing my hearth.
                    You have heard the penalty.
I lay it on you now to attend to this   35
For my sake, for Apollo's, for the sick
Sterile city that heaven has abandoned.
Suppose the oracle had given you no command:
Should this defilement go uncleansed for ever?
You should have found the murderer: your king,   40
A noble king, had been destroyed!
                              Now I,
Having the power that he held before me,
Having his bed, begetting children there
Upon his wife, as he would have, had he lived—
Their son would have been my children's brother,   45
If Laïos had had luck in fatherhood!

(But surely ill luck rushed upon his reign)—
I say I take the son's part, just as though
I were his son, to press the fight for him
And see it won! I'll find the hand that brought   50
Death to Labdakos' and Polydoros' child,
Heir of Kadmos' and Agenor's line.
And as for those who fail me,
May the gods deny them the fruit of the earth,
Fruit of the womb, and may they rot utterly!   55
Let them be wretched as we are wretched, and worse!

For you, for loyal Thebans, and for all
Who find my actions right, I pray the favor
Of justice, and of all the immortal gods.
CHORAGOS.[11] Since I am under oath, my lord, I swear   60
    I did not do the murder, I can not name
    The murderer. Might not the oracle
    That has ordained the search tell where to find him?
OEDIPUS: An honest question. But no man in the world
    Can make the gods do more than the gods will.   65
CHORAGOS: There is one last expedient—
OEDIPUS: Tell me what it is.
    Though it seem slight, you must not hold it back.
CHORAGOS: A lord clairvoyant to the lord Apollo,
    As we all know, is the skilled Teiresias.
    One might learn much about this from him, Oedipus.   70
OEDIPUS: I am not wasting time:
    Creon spoke of this, and I have sent for him—
    Twice, in fact; it is strange that he is not here.
CHORAGOS: The other matter—that old report—seems useless.
OEDIPUS: Tell me. I am interested in all reports.   75
CHORAGOS: The King was said to have been killed by highwaymen.
OEDIPUS: I know. But we have no witnesses to that.
CHORAGOS: If the killer can feel a particle of dread,
    Your curse will bring him out of hiding!
OEDIPUS: No.
    The man who dared that act will fear no curse.   80

(Enter the blind seer Teiresias, led by a Page)

CHORAGOS: But there is one man who may detect the criminal.
    This is Teiresias, this is the holy prophet
    In whom, alone of all men, truth was born.
OEDIPUS: Teiresias: seer: student of mysteries,

[11]Leader of the chorus.

Of all that's taught and all that no man tells,   85
Secrets of Heaven and secrets of the earth:
Blind though you are, you know the city lies
Sick with plague; and from this plague, my lord,
We find that you alone can guard or save us.

Possibly you did not hear the messengers?   90
Apollo, when we sent to him,
Sent us back word that this great pestilence
Would lift, but only if we established clearly
The identity of those who murdered Laïos.
They must be killed or exiled.
                         Can you use   95
Birdflight or any art of divination
To purify yourself, and Thebes, and me
From this contagion? We are in your hands.
There is no fairer duty
Than that of helping others in distress.   100

TEIRESIAS: How dreadful knowledge of the truth can be
    When there's no help in truth! I knew this well,
    But did not act on it: else I should not have come.

OEDIPUS: What is troubling you? Why are your eyes so cold?

TEIRESIAS: Let me go home. Bear your own fate, and I'll   105
    Bear mine. It is better so: trust what I say.

OEDIPUS: What you say is ungracious and unhelpful
    To your native country. Do not refuse to speak.

TEIRESIAS: When it comes to speech, your own is neither temperate
    Nor opportune. I wish to be more prudent.   110

OEDIPUS: In God's name, we all beg you—

TEIRESIAS: You are all ignorant.
    No; I will never tell you what I know.
    Now it is my misery; then, it would be yours.

OEDIPUS: What! You do know something, and will not tell us?
    You would betray us all and wreck the State?   115

TEIRESIAS: I do not intend to torture myself, or you.
    Why persist in asking? You will not persuade me.

OEDIPUS: What a wicked old man you are! You'd try a stone's
    Patience! Out with it! Have you no feeling at all?

TEIRESIAS: You call me unfeeling. If you could only see   120
    The nature of your own feelings . . .

OEDIPUS: Why,
    Who would not feel as I do? Who could endure
    Your arrogance toward the city?

TEIRESIAS: What does it matter!
    Whether I speak or not, it is bound to come.

OEDIPUS: Then, if "it" is bound to come, you are bound to tell me.   125
TEIRESIAS: No, I will not go on. Rage as you please.
OEDIPUS: Rage? Why not!
                              And I'll tell you what I think:
　You planned it, you had it done, you all but
　Killed him with your own hands: if you had eyes,
　I'd say the crime was yours, and yours alone.   130
TEIRESIAS: So? I charge you, then,
　Abide by the proclamation you have made:
　From this day forth
　Never speak again to these men or to me;
　You yourself are the pollution of this country.   135
OEDIPUS: You dare say that! Can you possibly think you have
　Some way of going free, after such insolence?
TEIRESIAS: I have gone free. It is the truth sustains me.
OEDIPUS: Who taught you shamelessness? It was not your craft.
TEIRESIAS: You did. You made me speak. I did not want to.   140
OEDIPUS: Speak what? Let me hear it again more clearly.
TEIRESIAS: Was it not clear before? Are you tempting me?
OEDIPUS: I did not understand it. Say it again.
TEIRESIAS: I say that you are the murderer whom you seek.
OEDIPUS: Now twice you have spat out infamy. You'll pay for it!   145
TEIRESIAS: Would you care for more? Do you wish to be really angry?
OEDIPUS: Say what you will. Whatever you say is worthless.
TEIRESIAS: I say you live in hideous shame with those
　Most dear to you. You can not see the evil.
OEDIPUS: It seems you can go on mouthing like this for ever.   150
TEIRESIAS: I can, if there is power in truth.
OEDIPUS: There is:
　But not for you, not for you,
　You sightless, witless, senseless, mad old man!
TEIRESIAS: You are the madman. There is no one here
　Who will not curse you soon, as you curse me.   155
OEDIPUS: You child of endless night! You can not hurt me
　Or any other man who sees the sun.
TEIRESIAS: True: it is not from me your fate will come.
　That lies within Apollo's competence,
　As it is his concern.
OEDIPUS: Tell me: 160
　Are you speaking for Creon, or for yourself?
TEIRESIAS: Creon is no threat. You weave your own doom.
OEDIPUS: Wealth, power, craft of statesmanship!
　Kingly position, everywhere admired!
　What savage envy is stored up against these,   165
　If Creon, whom I trusted, Creon my friend,

For this great office which the city once
Put in my hands unsought—if for this power
Creon desires in secret to destroy me!

He has brought this decrepit fortune-teller, this   170
Collector of dirty pennies, this prophet fraud—
Why, he is no more clairvoyant than I am!
                                        Tell us:
Has your mystic mummery ever approached the truth?
When that hellcat the Sphinx was performing here,
What help were you to these people?   175
Her magic was not for the first man who came along:
It demanded a real exorcist. Your birds—
What good were they? or the gods, for the matter of that?
But I came by,
Oedipus, the simple man, who knows nothing—   180
I thought it out for myself, no birds helped me!
And this is the man you think you can destroy,
That you may be close to Creon when he's king!
Well, you and your friend Creon, it seems to me,
Will suffer most. If you were not an old man,   185
You would have paid already for your plot.
CHORAGOS: We can not see that his words or yours
Have been spoken except in anger, Oedipus,
And of anger we have no need. How can God's will
Be accomplished best? That is what most concerns us.   190
TEIRESIAS: You are a king. But where argument's concerned
I am your man, as much a king as you.
I am not your servant, but Apollo's.
I have no need of Creon to speak for me.

Listen to me. You mock my blindness, do you?   195
But I say that you, with both your eyes, are blind:
You can not see the wretchedness of your life,
Nor in whose house you live, no, nor with whom.
Who are your father and mother? Can you tell me?
You do not even know the blind wrongs   200
That you have done them, on earth and in the world below.
But the double lash of your parents' curse will whip you
Out of this land some day, with only night
Upon your precious eyes.
Your cries then—where will they not be heard?   205
What fastness of Kithairon will not echo them?
And that bridal-descant of yours—you'll know it then,
The song they sang when you came here to Thebes

And found your misguided berthing.
All this, and more, that you can not guess at now,   210
Will bring you to yourself among your children.

Be angry, then. Curse Creon. Curse my words.
I tell you, no man that walks upon the earth
Shall be rooted out more horribly than you.
OEDIPUS: Am I to bear this from him?—Damnation   215
  Take you! Out of this place! Out of my sight!
TEIRESIAS: I would not have come at all if you had not asked
  me.
OEDIPUS: Could I have told that you'd talk nonsense, that
  You'd come here to make a fool of yourself, and of me?
TEIRESIAS: A fool? Your parents thought me sane enough.   220
OEDIPUS: My parents again!—Wait: who were my parents?
TEIRESIAS: This day will give you a father, and break your heart.
OEDIPUS: Your infantile riddles! Your damned abracadabra!
TEIRESIAS: You were a great man once at solving riddles.
OEDIPUS: Mock me with that if you like; you will find it true.   225
TEIRESIAS: It was true enough. It brought about your ruin.
OEDIPUS: But if it saved this town?
TEIRESIAS *(to the Page):*   Boy, give me your hand.
OEDIPUS: Yes, boy; lead him away.
                      —While you are here
  We can do nothing. Go; leave us in peace.
TEIRESIAS: I will go when I have said what I have to say.   230
  How can you hurt me? And I tell you again:
  The man you have been looking for all this time,
  The damned man, the murderer of Laïos,
  That man is in Thebes. To your mind he is foreignborn,
  But it will soon be shown that he is a Theban,   235
  A revelation that will fail to please.
                      A blind man,
  Who has his eyes now; a penniless man, who is rich now;
  And he will go tapping the strange earth with his staff;
  To the children with whom he lives now he will be
  Brother and father—the very same; to her   240
  Who bore him, son and husband—the very same
  Who came to his father's bed, wet with his father's blood.

  Enough. Go think that over.
  If later you find error in what I have said,
  You may say that I have no skill in prophecy.   245

(Exit Teiresias, led by his Page. Oedipus goes into the palace.)

Ode[12] I

Strophe 1

CHORUS: The Delphic stone of prophecies
　　Remembers ancient regicide
　　And a still bloody hand.
　　That killer's hour of flight has come.
　　He must be stronger than riderless   5
　　Coursers of untiring wind,
　　For the son of Zeus[13] armed with his father's thunder
　　Leaps in lightning after him;
　　And the Furies[14] follow him, the sad Furies.

Antistrophe 1

　　Holy Parnassos' peak of snow   10
　　Flashes and blinds that secret man,
　　That all shall hunt him down:
　　Though he may roam the forest shade
　　Like a bull gone wild from pasture
　　To rage through glooms of stone.   15
　　Doom comes down on him; flight will not avail him;
　　For the world's heart calls him desolate,
　　And the immortal Furies follow, for ever follow.

Strophe 2

　　But now a wilder thing is heard
　　From the old man skilled at hearing Fate in the wingbeat of a
　　　　bird.   20
　　Bewildered as a blown bird, my soul hovers and can not find
　　Foothold in this debate, or any reason or rest of mind.
　　But no man ever brought—none can bring
　　Proof of strife between Thebes' royal house,
　　Labdakos' line, and the son of Polybos,[15]   25
　　And never until now has any man brought word
　　Of Laïos dark death staining Oedipus the King.

Antistrophe 2

　　Divine Zeus and Apollo hold
　　Perfect intelligence alone of all tales ever told;
　　And well though this diviner works, he works in his own night;   30
　　No man can judge that rough unknown or trust in second sight,
　　For wisdom changes hands among the wise.
　　Shall I believe my great lord criminal
　　At a raging word that a blind old man let fall?
　　I saw him, when the carrion woman faced him of old,   35
　　Prove his heroic mind! These evil words are lies.

---

[12]A choral song.   [13]Apollo was a son of Zeus.   [14]Avenging spirits.   [15]Oedipus is at this point thought to be a son of Polybos, who had adopted him as a baby. His true father, Laïos, was of "Labdakos' line."

Scene II

CREON: Men of Thebes:
  I am told that heavy accusations
  Have been brought against me by King Oedipus.

  I am not the kind of man to bear this tamely.

  If in these present difficulties   5
  He holds me accountable for any harm to him
  Through anything I have said or done—why, then,
  I do not value life in this dishonor.
  It is not as though this rumor touched upon
  Some private indiscretion. The matter is grave.   10
  The fact is that I am being called disloyal
  To the State, to my fellow citizens, to my friends.
CHORAGOS: He may have spoken in anger, not from his mind.
CREON: But did you not hear him say I was the one
  Who seduced the old prophet into lying?   15
CHORAGOS: The thing was said; I do not know how seriously.
CREON: But you were watching him! Were his eyes steady?
  Did he look like a man in his right mind?
CHORAGOS: I do not know.
  I can not judge the behavior of great men.
  But here is the King himself.

(Enter Oedipus)

OEDIPUS: So you dared come back.   20
  Why? How brazen of you to come to my house,
  You murderer!
                Do you think I do not know
  That you plotted to kill me, plotted to steal my throne?
  Tell me, in God's name: am I coward, a fool,
  That you should dream you could accomplish this?   25
  A fool who could not see your slippery game?
  A coward, not to fight back when I saw it?
  You are the fool, Creon, are you not? hoping
  Without support or friends to get a throne?
  Thrones may be won or bought: you could do neither.   30
CREON: Now listen to me. You have talked; let me talk, too.
  You can not judge unless you know the facts.
OEDIPUS: You speak well: there is one fact; but I find it hard
  To learn from the deadliest enemy I have.
CREON: That above all I must dispute with you.   35
OEDIPUS: That above all I will not hear you deny.

CREON: If you think there is anything good in being stubborn
  Against all reason, then I say you are wrong.
OEDIPUS: If you think a man can sin against his own kind
  And not be punished for it, I say you are mad.   **40**
CREON: I agree. But tell me: what have I done to you?
OEDIPUS: You advised me to send for that wizard, did you not?
CREON: I did. I should do it again.
OEDIPUS: Very well. Now tell me:
  How long has it been since Laïos—
CREON: What of Laïos?
OEDIPUS: Since he vanished in that onset by the road?   **45**
CREON: It was long ago, a long time.
OEDIPUS: And this prophet,
  Was he practicing here then?
CREON: He was; and with honor, as now.
OEDIPUS: Did he speak of me at that time?
CREON: He never did;
  At least, not when I was present.
OEDIPUS: But . . . the enquiry?
  I suppose you held one?
CREON: We did, but we learned nothing.   **50**
OEDIPUS: Why did the prophet not speak against me then?
CREON: I do not know; and I am the kind of man
  Who holds his tongue when he has no facts to go on.
OEDIPUS: There's one fact that you know, and you could tell it.
CREON: What fact is that? If I know it, you shall have it.   **55**
OEDIPUS: If he were not involved with you, he could not say
  That it was I who murdered Laïos.
CREON: If he says that, you are the one that knows it!—
  But now it is my turn to question you.
OEDIPUS: Put your questions. I am no murderer.   **60**
CREON: First then: You married my sister?
OEDIPUS: I married your sister.
CREON: And you rule the kingdom equally with her?
OEDIPUS: Everything that she wants she has from me.
CREON: And I am the third, equal to both of you?
OEDIPUS: That is why I call you a bad friend.   **65**
CREON: No. Reason it out, as I have done.
  Think of this first. Would any sane man prefer
  Power, with all a king's anxieties,
  To that same power and the grace of sleep?
  Certainly not I.   **70**
  I have never longed for the king's power—only his rights.
  Would any wise man differ from me in this?
  As matters stand, I have my way in everything

With your consent, and no responsibilities.
If I were king, I should be a slave to policy.   75

How could I desire a scepter more
Than what is now mine—untroubled influence?
No, I have not gone mad; I need no honors,
Except those with the perquisites I have now.
I am welcome everywhere; every man salutes me,   80
And those who want your favor seek my ear,
Since I know how to manage what they ask.
Should I exchange this ease for that anxiety?
Besides, no sober mind is treasonable.
I hate anarchy   85
And never would deal with any man who likes it.

Test what I have said. Go to the priestess
At Delphi, ask if I quoted her correctly.
And as for this other thing: if I am found
Guilty of treason with Teiresias,   90
Then sentence me to death! You have my word
It is a sentence I should cast my vote for—
But not without evidence!
                         You do wrong
When you take good men for bad, bad men for good.
A true friend thrown aside—why, life itself   95
Is not more precious!
                      In time you will know this well:
For time, and time alone, will show the just man,
Though scoundrels are discovered in a day.
CHORAGOS: This is well said, and a prudent man would ponder it.
   Judgments too quickly formed are dangerous.   100
OEDIPUS: But is he not quick in his duplicity?
   And shall I not be quick to parry him?
   Would you have me stand still, hold my peace, and let
   This man win everything, through my inaction?
CREON: And you want—what is it, then? To banish me?   105
OEDIPUS: No, not exile. It is your death I want,
   So that all the world may see what treason means.
CREON: You will persist, then? You will not believe me?
OEDIPUS: How can I believe you?
CREON: Then you are a fool.
OEDIPUS: To save myself?
CREON: In justice, think of me.   110
OEDIPUS: You are evil incarnate.
CREON: But suppose that you are wrong?

OEDIPUS: Still I must rule.
CREON: But not if you rule badly.
OEDIPUS: O city, city!
CREON: It is my city, too!
CHORAGOS: Now, my lords, be still. I see the Queen,
Iocastê, coming from her palace chambers;   115
And it is time she came, for the sake of you both.
This dreadful quarrel can be resolved through her.

(Enter Iocastê)

IOCASTÊ: Poor foolish men, what wicked din is this?
With Thebes sick to death, is it not shameful
That you should rake some private quarrel up?   120
(To Oedipus) Come into the house.
                                 —And you, Creon, go now:
Let us have no more of this tumult over nothing.
CREON: Nothing? No, sister: what your husband plans for me
Is one of two great evils: exile or death.
OEDIPUS: He is right.
                    Why, woman, I have caught him squarely   125
Plotting against my life.
CREON: No! Let me die
Accurst if ever I have wished you harm!
IOCASTÊ: Ah, believe it, Oedipus!
In the name of the gods, respect this oath of his
For my sake, for the sake of these people here!   130

Strophe 1

CHORAGOS: Open your mind to her, my lord. Be ruled by her, I beg you!
OEDIPUS: What would you have me do?
CHORAGOS: Respect Creon's word. He has never spoken like a fool,
And now he has sworn an oath.
OEDIPUS: You know what you ask?
CHORAGOS: I do.
OEDIPUS: Speak on, then.
CHORAGOS: A friend so sworn should not be baited so,   135
In blind malice, and without final proof.
OEDIPUS: You are aware, I hope, that what you say
Means death for me, or exile at the least.

Strophe 2

CHORAGOS: No, I swear by Helios, first in Heaven!
May I die friendless and accurst,   140
The worst of deaths, if ever I meant that!
It is the withering fields
That hurt my sick heart;

Must we bear all these ills,
And now your bad blood as well?   145
OEDIPUS: Then let him go. And let me die, if I must,
Or be driven by him in shame from the land of Thebes.
It is your unhappiness, and not his talk,
That touches me.
              As for him—
Wherever he is, I will hate him as long as I live.   150
CREON: Ugly in yielding, as you were ugly in rage!
Natures like yours chiefly torment themselves.
OEDIPUS: Can you not go? Can you not leave me?
CREON: I can.
You do not know me; but the city knows me,
And in its eyes I am just, if not in yours.   155

(Exit Creon)

                                        Antistrophe 1

CHORAGOS: Lady Iocastê, did you not ask the King to go to his chambers?
IOCASTÊ: First tell me what has happened.
CHORAGOS: There was suspicion without evidence; yet it rankled
As even false charges will.
IOCASTÊ: On both sides?
CHORAGOS: On both.
IOCASTÊ: But what was said?
CHORAGOS: Oh let it rest, let it be done with!   160
Have we not suffered enough?
OEDIPUS: You see to what your decency has brought you:
You have made difficulties where my heart saw none.

                                        Antistrophe 2

CHORAGOS: Oedipus, it is not once only I have told you—
You must know I should count myself unwise   165
To the point of madness, should I now forsake you—
You, under whose hand,
In the storm of another time,
Our dear land sailed out free.
But now stand fast at the helm!   170
IOCASTÊ: In God's name, Oedipus, inform your wife as well:
Why are you so set in this hard anger?
OEDIPUS: I will tell you, for none of these men deserves
My confidence as you do. It is Creon's work,
His treachery, his plotting against me.   175
IOCASTÊ: Go on, if you can make this clear to me.
OEDIPUS: He charges me with the murder of Laïos.

IOCASTÊ: Has he some knowledge? Or does he speak from hearsay?

OEDIPUS: He would not commit himself to such a charge,
But he has brought in that damnable soothsayer   180
To tell his story.

IOCASTÊ: Set your mind at rest.
If it is a question of soothsayers, I tell you
That you will find no man whose craft gives knowledge
Of the unknowable.

                    Here is my proof:

An oracle was reported to Laïos once   185
(I will not say from Phoibos himself, but from
His appointed ministers, at any rate)
That his doom would be death at the hands of his own son—
His son, born of his flesh and of mine!

Now, you remember the story: Laïos was killed   190
By marauding strangers where three highways meet;
But his child had not been three days in this world
Before the King had pierced the baby's ankles
And left him to die on a lonely mountainside.

Thus, Apollo never caused that child   195
To kill his father, and it was not Laïos' fate
To die at the hands of his son, as he had feared.
This is what prophets and prophecies are worth!
Have no dread of them.

                    It is God himself
Who can show us what he wills, in his own way.   200

OEDIPUS: How strange a shadowy memory crossed my mind,
Just now while you were speaking; it chilled my heart.

IOCASTÊ: What do you mean? What memory do you speak of?

OEDIPUS: If I understand you, Laïos was killed
At a place where three roads meet.

IOCASTÊ: So it was said;   205
We have no later story.

OEDIPUS: Where did it happen?

IOCASTÊ: Phokis, it is called: at a place where the Theban Way
Divides into the roads toward Delphi and Daulia.

OEDIPUS: When?

IOCASTÊ: We had the news not long before you came
And proved the right to your succession here.   210

OEDIPUS: Ah, what net has God been weaving for me?

IOCASTÊ: Oedipus! Why does this trouble you?

OEDIPUS: Do not ask me yet.

First, tell me how Laïos looked, and tell me
How old he was.

IOCASTÊ: He was tall, his hair just touched
With white; his form was not unlike your own.   215

OEDIPUS: I think that I myself may be accurst
By my own ignorant edict.

IOCASTÊ: You speak strangely.
It makes me tremble to look at you, my King.

OEDIPUS: I am not sure that the blind man can not see.
But I should know better if you were to tell me—   220

IOCASTÊ: Anything—though I dread to hear you ask it.

OEDIPUS: Was the King lightly escorted, or did he ride
With a large company, as a ruler should?

IOCASTÊ: There were five men with him in all: one was a herald;
And a single chariot, which he was driving.   225

OEDIPUS: Alas, that makes it plain enough!
                                          But who—
Who told you how it happened?

IOCASTÊ: A household servant,
The only one to escape.

OEDIPUS: And is he still
A servant of ours?

IOCASTÊ: No; for when he came back at last
And found you enthroned in the place of the dead king,   230
He came to me, touched my hand with his, and begged
That I would send him away to the frontier district
Where only the shepherds go—
As far away from the city as I could send him.
I granted his prayer; for although the man was a slave,   235
He had earned more than this favor at my hands.

OEDIPUS: Can he be called back quickly?

IOCASTÊ: Easily.
But why?

OEDIPUS: I have taken too much upon myself
Without enquiry; therefore I wish to consult him.

IOCASTÊ: Then he shall come.
                                  But am I not one also   240
To whom you might confide these fears of yours?

OEDIPUS: That is your right; it will not be denied you,
Now least of all; for I have reached a pitch
Of wild foreboding. Is there anyone
To whom I should sooner speak?   245
Polybos of Corinth is my father.
My mother is a Dorian: Meropê.
I grew up chief among the men of Corinth

Until a strange thing happened—
Not worth my passion, it may be, but strange.   250
At a feast, a drunken man maundering in his cups
Cries out that I am not my father's son!

I contained myself that night, though I felt anger
And a sinking heart. The next day I visited
My father and mother, and questioned them. They stormed,   255
Calling it all the slanderous rant of a fool;
And this relieved me. Yet the suspicion
Remained always aching in my mind;
I knew there was talk; I could not rest;
And finally, saying nothing to my parents,   260
I went to the shrine at Delphi.
The god dismissed my question without reply;
He spoke of other things.
                         Some were clear,
Full of wretchedness, dreadful, unbearable:
As, that I should lie with my own mother, breed   265
Children from whom all men would turn their eyes;
And that I should be my father's murderer.

I heard all this, and fled. And from that day
Corinth to me was only in the stars
Descending in that quarter of the sky,   270
As I wandered farther and farther on my way
To a land where I should never see the evil
Sung by the oracle. And I came to this country
Where, so you say, King Laïos was killed.

I will tell you all that happened there, my lady.   275

There were three highways
Coming together at a place I passed;
And there a herald came towards me, and a chariot
Drawn by horses, with a man such as you describe
Seated in it. The groom leading the horses   280
Forced me off the road at his lord's command;
But as this charioteer lurched over towards me
I struck him in my rage. The old man saw me
And brought his double goad down upon my head
As I came abreast.
                         He was paid back, and more!   285
Swinging my club in this right hand I knocked him

Out of his car, and he rolled on the ground.

                        I killed him.

I killed them all.
Now if that stranger and Laïos were—kin,
Where is a man more miserable than I?   290
More hated by the gods? Citizen and alien alike
Must never shelter me or speak to me—
I must be shunned by all.
                   And I myself
Pronounced this malediction upon myself!

Think of it: I have touched you with these hands,   295
These hands that killed your husband. What defilement!

Am I all evil, then? It must be so,
Since I must flee from Thebes, yet never again
See my own countrymen, my own country,
For fear of joining my mother in marriage   300
And killing Polybos, my father.
                      Ah,
If I was created so, born to this fate,
Who could deny the savagery of God?

O holy majesty of heavenly powers!
May I never see that day! Never!   305
Rather let me vanish from the race of men
Than know the abomination destined me!
CHORAGOS: We too, my lord, have felt dismay at this.
    But there is hope: you have yet to hear the shepherd.
OEDIPUS: Indeed, I fear no other hope is left me.   310
IOCASTÊ: What do you hope from him when he comes?
OEDIPUS: This much:
    If his account of the murder tallies with yours,
    Then I am cleared.
IOCASTÊ: What was it that I said
    Of such importance?
OEDIPUS: Why "marauders," you said,
    Killed the King, according to this man's story.   315
    If he maintains that still, if there were several,
    Clearly the guilt is not mine: I was alone.
    But if he says one man, singlehanded, did it,
    Then the evidence all points to me.
IOCASTÊ: You may be sure that he said there were several; 320

And can he call back that story now? He can not.
The whole city heard it as plainly as I.
But suppose he alters some detail of it:
He can not ever show that Laïos' death
Fulfilled the oracle: for Apollo said   325
My child was doomed to kill him; and my child—
Poor baby!—it was my child that died first.

No. From now on, where oracles are concerned,
I would not waste a second thought on any.
OEDIPUS: You may be right.
                                But come: let someone go   330
For the shepherd at once. This matter must be settled.
IOCASTÊ: I will send for him.
I would not wish to cross you in anything,
And surely not in this.—Let us go in.

(Exeunt into the palace)

Ode II

Strophe 1

CHORUS: Let me be reverent in the ways of right,
    Lowly the paths I journey on;
    Let all my words and actions keep
    The laws of the pure universe
    From highest Heaven handed down.   5
    For Heaven is their bright nurse,
    Those generations of the realms of light;
    Ah, never of mortal kind were they begot,
    Nor are they slaves of memory, lost in sleep:
    Their Father is greater than Time, and ages not.   10

Antistrophe 1

    The tyrant is a child of Pride
    Who drinks from his great sickening cup
    Recklessness and vanity,
    Until from his high crest headlong
    He plummets to the dust of hope.   15
    That strong man is not strong.
    But let no fair ambition be denied;
    May God protect the wrestler for the State
    In government, in comely policy,
    Who will fear God, and on His ordinance wait.

Strophe 2

    Haughtiness and the high hand of disdain
    Tempt and outrage God's holy law;

And any mortal who dares hold
No immortal Power in awe
Will be caught up in a net of pain: 25
The price for which his levity is sold.
Let each man take due earnings, then,
And keep his hands from holy things,
And from blasphemy stand apart—
Else the crackling blast of heaven   30
Blows on his head, and on his desperate heart;
Though fools will honor impious men,
In their cities no tragic poet sings.

Antistrophe 2

Shall we lose faith in Delphi's obscurities,
We who have heard the world's core   35
Discredited, and the sacred wood
Of Zeus at Elis praised no more?
The deeds and the strange prophecies
Must make a pattern yet to be understood.
Zeus, if indeed you are lord of all,   40
Throned in light over night and day,
Mirror this in your endless mind:
Our masters call the oracle
Words on the wind, and the Delphic vision blind!
Their hearts no longer know Apollo,   45
And reverence for the gods has died away.

Scene III

(Enter Iocastê)

IOCASTÊ: Princes of Thebes, it has occurred to me
   To visit the altars of the gods, bearing
   These branches as a suppliant, and this incense.
   Our King is not himself: his noble soul
   Is overwrought with fantasies of dread,   5
   Else he would consider
   The new prophecies in the light of the old.
   He will listen to any voice that speaks disaster,
   And my advice goes for nothing.

(She approaches the altar, right)

                              To you, then, Apollo,
   Lycean lord, since you are nearest, I turn in prayer.   10
   Receive these offerings, and grant us deliverance
   From defilement. Our hearts are heavy with fear

When we see our leader distracted, as helpless sailors
Are terrified by the confusion of their helmsman.

(Enter Messenger)

MESSENGER: Friends, no doubt you can direct me: 15
Where shall I find the house of Oedipus,
Or, better still, where is the King himself?

CHORAGOS: It is this very place, stranger; he is inside.
This is his wife and mother of his children.

MESSENGER: I wish her happiness in a happy house,   20
Blest in all the fulfillment of her marriage.

IOCASTÊ: I wish as much for you: your courtesy
Deserves a like good fortune. But now, tell me:
Why have you come? What have you to say to us?

MESSENGER: Good news, my lady, for your house and your
    husband.   25

IOCASTÊ: What news? Who sent you here?

MESSENGER: I am from Corinth.
The news I bring ought to mean joy for you,
Though it may be you will find some grief in it.

IOCASTÊ: What is it? How can it touch us in both ways?

MESSENGER: The people of Corinth, they say,   30
Intend to call Oedipus to be their king.

IOCASTÊ: But old Polybos—is he not reigning still?

MESSENGER: No. Death holds him in his sepulchre.

IOCASTÊ: What are you saying? Polybos is dead?

MESSENGER: If I am not telling the truth, may I die myself.   35

IOCASTÊ *(to a Maidservant)*: Go in, go quickly; tell this to your master.

O riddlers of God's will, where are you now!
This was the man whom Oedipus, long ago,
Feared so, fled so, in dread of destroying him—
But it was another fate by which he died.   40

(Enter Oedipus, center)

OEDIPUS: Dearest Iocastê, why have you sent for me?

IOCASTÊ: Listen to what this man says, and then tell me
What has become of the solemn prophecies.

OEDIPUS: Who is this man? What is his news for me?

IOCASTÊ: He has come from Corinth to announce your father's
    death!   45

OEDIPUS: Is it true, stranger? Tell me in your own words.

MESSENGER: I can not say it more clearly: the King is dead.

OEDIPUS: Was it by treason? Or by an attack of illness?

MESSENGER: A little thing brings old men to their rest.

OEDIPUS: It was sickness, then?

MESSENGER: Yes, and his many years.   50

OEDIPUS: Ah!

Why should a man respect the Pythian hearth,[16] or
Give heed to the birds that jangle above his head?
They prophesied that I should kill Polybos,
Kill my own father; but he is dead and buried,   55
And I am here—I never touched him, never,
Unless he died of grief for my departure,
And thus, in a sense, through me. No. Polybos
Has packed the oracles off with him underground.
They are empty words.

IOCASTÊ: Had I not told you so?   60

OEDIPUS: You had; it was my faint heart that betrayed me.

IOCASTÊ: From now on never think of those things again.

OEDIPUS: And yet—must I not fear my mother's bed?

IOCASTÊ: Why should anyone in this world be afraid,
Since Fate rules us and nothing can be foreseen?   65
A man should live only for the present day.

Have no more fear of sleeping with your mother:
How many men, in dreams, have lain with their mothers!
No reasonable man is troubled by such things.

OEDIPUS: That is true, only—   70
If only my mother were not still alive!
But she is alive. I can not help my dread.

IOCASTÊ: Yet this news of your father's death is wonderful.

OEDIPUS: Wonderful. But I fear the living woman.

MESSENGER: Tell me, who is this woman that you fear?   75

OEDIPUS: It is Meropê, man; the wife of King Polybos.

MESSENGER: Meropê? Why should you be afraid of her?

OEDIPUS: An oracle of the gods, a dreadful saying.

MESSENGER: Can you tell me about it or are you sworn to silence?

OEDIPUS: I can tell you, and I will.   80

Apollo said through his prophet that I was the man
Who should marry his own mother, shed his father's blood
With his own hands. And so, for all these years
I have kept clear of Corinth, and no harm has come—
Though it would have been sweet to see my parents again.   85

MESSENGER: And is this the fear that drove you out of Corinth?

OEDIPUS: Would you have me kill my father?

MESSENGER: As for that
You must be reassured by the news I gave you.

[16]The shrine at Delphi, where a priestess spoke with inspiration from the god Apollo.

OEDIPUS: If you could reassure me, I would reward you.

MESSENGER: I had that in mind, I will confess: I thought   90
    I could count on you when you returned to Corinth.

OEDIPUS: No: I will never go near my parents again.

MESSENGER: Ah, son, you still do not know what you are doing—

OEDIPUS: What do you mean? In the name of God tell me!

MESSENGER: —If these are your reasons for not going home.   95

OEDIPUS: I tell you, I fear the oracle may come true.

MESSENGER: And guilt may come upon you through your parents?

OEDIPUS: That is the dread that is always in my heart.

MESSENGER: Can you not see that all your fears are groundless?

OEDIPUS: How can you say that? They are my parents, surely?   100

MESSENGER: Polybos was not your father.

OEDIPUS: Not my father?

MESSENGER: No more your father than the man speaking to you.

OEDIPUS: But you are nothing to me!

MESSENGER: Neither was he.

OEDIPUS: Then why did he call me son?

MESSENGER: I will tell you:
    Long ago he had you from my hands, as a gift.   105

OEDIPUS: Then how could he love me so, if I was not his?

MESSENGER: He had no children, and his heart turned to you.

OEDIPUS: What of you? Did you buy me? Did you find me by chance?

MESSENGER: I came upon you in the crooked pass of Kithairon.

OEDIPUS: And what were you doing there?

MESSENGER: Tending my flocks.   110

OEDIPUS: A wandering shepherd?

MESSENGER: But your savior, son, that day.

OEDIPUS: From what did you save me?

MESSENGER: Your ankles should tell you that.

OEDIPUS: Ah, stranger, why do you speak of that childhood pain?

MESSENGER: I cut the bonds that tied your ankles together.

OEDIPUS: I have had the mark as long as I can remember.   115

MESSENGER: That was why you were given the name you bear.

OEDIPUS: God! Was it my father or my mother who did it?
    Tell me!

MESSENGER: I do not know. The man who gave you to me
    Can tell you better than I.   120

OEDIPUS: It was not you that found me, but another?

MESSENGER: It was another shepherd gave you to me.

OEDIPUS: Who was he? Can you tell me who he was?

MESSENGER: I think he was said to be one of Laïos' people.

OEDIPUS: You mean the Laïos who was king here years ago?   125

MESSENGER: Yes; King Laïos; and the man was one of his herdsmen.

OEDIPUS: Is he still alive? Can I see him?
MESSENGER: These men here
  Know best about such things.
OEDIPUS: Does anyone here
  Know this shepherd that he is talking about?
  Have you seen him in the fields, or in the town?   130
  If you have, tell me. It is time things were made plain.
CHORAGOS: I think the man he means is that same shepherd
  You have already asked to see. Iocastê perhaps
  Could tell you something.
OEDIPUS: Do you know anything
  About him, Lady? Is he the man we have summoned?   135
  Is that the man this shepherd means?
IOCASTÊ: Why think of him?
  Forget this herdsman. Forget it all.
  This talk is a waste of time.
OEDIPUS: How can you say that,
  When the clues to my true birth are in my hands?
IOCASTÊ: For God's love, let us have no more questioning!   140
  Is your life nothing to you?
  My own is pain enough for me to bear.
OEDIPUS: You need not worry. Suppose my mother a slave,
  And born of slaves: no baseness can touch you.
IOCASTÊ: Listen to me, I beg you: do not do this thing!   145
OEDIPUS: I will not listen; the truth must be made known.
IOCASTÊ: Everything that I say is for your own good!
OEDIPUS: My own good
  Snaps my patience, then; I want none of it.
IOCASTÊ: You are fatally wrong! May you never learn who you
    are!
OEDIPUS: Go, one of you, and bring the shepherd here.   150
  Let us leave this woman to brag of her royal name.
IOCASTÊ: Ah, miserable!
  That is the only word I have for you now.
  That is the only word I can ever have.

(Exit into the palace)

CHORAGOS: Why has she left us, Oedipus? Why has she gone   155
  In such a passion of sorrow? I fear this silence:
  Something dreadful may come of it.
OEDIPUS: Let it come!
  However base my birth, I must know about it.
  The Queen, like a woman, is perhaps ashamed
  To think of my low origin. But I   160

Am a child of Luck; I can not be dishonored.
Luck is my mother; the passing months, my brothers,
Have seen me rich and poor.
                    If this is so,
How could I wish that I were someone else?
How could I not be glad to know my birth?   165

Ode III

Strophe

CHORUS: If ever the coming time were known
    To my heart's pondering,
    Kithairon, now by Heaven I see the torches
    At the festival of the next full moon,
    And see the dance, and hear the choir sing   5
    A grace to your gentle shade:
    Mountain where Oedipus was found,
    O mountain guard of a noble race!
    May the god who heals us lend his aid,
    And let that glory come to pass   10
    For our king's cradling-ground.

Antistrophe

    Of the nymphs that flower beyond the years,
    Who bore you, royal child,
    To Pan of the hills or the timberline Apollo,
    Cold in delight where the upland clears,   15
    Or Hermês for whom Kyllenê's[17] heights are piled?
    Or flushed as evening cloud,
    Great Dionysos, roamer of mountains,
    He—was it he who found you there,
    And caught you up in his own proud   20
    Arms from the sweet god-ravisher
    Who laughed by the Muses' fountains?

Scene IV

OEDIPUS: Sirs: though I do not know the man,
    I think I see him coming, this shepherd we want:
    He is old, like our friend here, and the men
    Bringing him seem to be servants of my house.
    But you can tell, if you have ever seen him.   5

(Enter Shepherd escorted by servants)

[17]The mountain birthplace of Hermês, messenger of the gods.

CHORAGOS: I know him, he was Laïos' man. You can trust him.

OEDIPUS: Tell me first, you from Corinth: is this the shepherd
  We were discussing?

MESSENGER: This is the very man.

OEDIPUS *(to Shepherd):* Come here. No, look at me. You must answer
  Everything I ask.—You belonged to Laïos?   10

SHEPHERD: Yes: born his slave, brought up in his house.

OEDIPUS: Tell me: what kind of work did you do for him?

SHEPHERD: I was a shepherd of his, most of my life.

OEDIPUS: Where mainly did you go for pasturage?

SHEPHERD: Sometimes Kithairon, sometimes the hills near-by.   15

OEDIPUS: Do you remember ever seeing this man out there?

SHEPHERD: What would he be doing there? This man?

OEDIPUS: This man standing here. Have you ever seen him before?

SHEPHERD: No. At least, not to my recollection.

MESSENGER: And that is not strange, my lord. But I'll refresh   20
  His memory: he must remember when we two
  Spent three whole seasons together, March to September,
  On Kithairon or thereabouts. He had two flocks;
  I had one. Each autumn I'd drive mine home
  And he would go back with his to Laïos' sheepfold.—   25
  Is this not true, just as I have described it?

SHEPHERD: True, yes; but it was all so long ago.

MESSENGER: Well, then: do you remember, back in those days
  That you gave me a baby boy to bring up as my own?

SHEPHERD: What if I did? What are you trying to say?   30

MESSENGER: King Oedipus was once that little child.

SHEPHERD: Damn you, hold your tongue!

OEDIPUS: No more of that!
  It is your tongue needs watching, not this man's.

SHEPHERD: My King, my Master, what is it I have done wrong?

OEDIPUS: You have not answered his question about the boy.   35

SHEPHERD: He does not know . . . He is only making trouble . . .

OEDIPUS: Come, speak plainly, or it will go hard with you.

SHEPHERD: In God's name, do not torture an old man!

OEDIPUS: Come here, one of you; bind his arms behind him.

SHEPHERD: Unhappy king! What more do you wish to learn?   40

OEDIPUS: Did you give this man the child he speaks of?

SHEPHERD: I did.
  And I would to God I had died that very day.

OEDIPUS: You will die now unless you speak the truth.

SHEPHERD: Yet if I speak the truth, I am worse than dead.

OEDIPUS: Very well; since you insist upon delaying—   45

SHEPHERD: No! I have told you already that I gave him the boy.

OEDIPUS: Where did you get him? From your house? From somewhere
    else?

SHEPHERD: Not from mine, no. A man gave him to me.

OEDIPUS: Is that man here? Do you know whose slave he was?

SHEPHERD: For God's love, my King, do not ask me any more!   **50**

OEDIPUS: You are a dead man if I have to ask you again.

SHEPHERD: Then . . . Then the child was from the palace of Laïos.

OEDIPUS: A slave child? or a child of his own line?

SHEPHERD: Ah, I am on the brink of dreadful speech!

OEDIPUS: And I of dreadful hearing. Yet I must hear.   **55**

SHEPHERD: If you must be told, then . . .

                            They said it was Laïos' child,

But it is your wife who can tell you about that.

OEDIPUS: My wife!—Did she give it to you?

SHEPHERD: My lord, she did.

OEDIPUS: Do you know why?

SHEPHERD: I was told to get rid of it.

OEDIPUS: An unspeakable mother!

SHEPHERD: There had been prophecies . . .   **60**

OEDIPUS: Tell me.

SHEPHERD: It was said that the boy would kill his own father.

OEDIPUS: Then why did you give him over to this old man?

SHEPHERD: I pitied the baby, my King,

And I thought that this man would take him far away

To his own country.

                    He saved him—but for what a fate!   **65**

For if you are what this man says you are,

No man living is more wretched than Oedipus.

OEDIPUS: Ah God!

    It was true!

             All the prophecies!

                    —Now,

O Light, may I look on you for the last time!   **70**

I, Oedipus,

Oedipus, damned in his birth, in his marriage damned,

Damned in the blood he shed with his own hand!

(He rushes into the palace)

Ode IV

Strophe 1

CHORUS: Alas for the seed of men.

What measure shall I give these generations
That breathe on the void and are void
And exist and do not exist?

Who bears more weight of joy   5
Than mass of sunlight shifting in images,
Or who shall make his thought stay on
That down time drifts away?

Your splendor is all fallen.

O naked brow of wrath and tears,   10
O change of Oedipus!
I who say your days call no man blest—
Your great days like ghósts góne.

That mind was a strong bow.
Deep, how deep you drew it then, hard archer,   15
At a dim fearful range,
And brought dear glory down!

You overcame the stranger—
The virgin with her hooking lion claws—
And though death sang, stood like a tower   20
To make pale Thebes take heart.

Fortress against our sorrow!

Divine king, giver of laws,
Majestic Oedipus!
No prince in Thebes had ever such renown,   25
No prince won such grace of power.

And now of all men ever known
Most pitiful is this man's story:
His fortunes are most changed, his state
Fallen to a low slave's   30
Ground under bitter fate.

O Oedipus, most royal one!
The great door that expelled you to the light
Gave at night—ah, gave night to your glory:
As to the father, to the fathering son.   35
All understood too late.

How could that queen whom Laïos won,
The garden that he harrowed at his height,
Be silent when that act was done?

But all eyes fail before time's eye,   40
All actions come to justice there.
Though never willed, though far down the deep past,
Your bed, your dread sirings,
Are brought to book at last.
Child by Laïos doomed to die,   45
Then doomed to lose that fortunate little death,
Would God you never took breath in this air
That with my wailing lips I take to cry:

For I weep the world's outcast.

I was blind, and now I can tell why: 50
Asleep, for you had given ease of breath
To Thebes, while the false years went by.

Exodos[18]

(Enter, from the palace, Second Messenger)

SECOND MESSENGER: Elders of Thebes, most honored in this land,
What horrors are yours to see and hear, what weight
Of sorrow to be endured, if, true to your birth,
You venerate the line of Labdakos!
I think neither Istros nor Phasis, those great rivers,   5
Could purify this place of the corruption
It shelters now, or soon must bring to light—
Evil not done unconsciously, but willed.

The greatest griefs are those we cause ourselves.
CHORAGOS: Surely, friend, we have grief enough already;   10
What new sorrow do you mean?
SECOND MESSENGER: The Queen is dead.
CHORAGOS: Iocastê? Dead? But at whose hand?
SECOND MESSENGER: Her own.
The full horror of what happened, you can not know,
For you did not see it; but I, who did, will tell you
As clearly as I can how she met her death.   15

When she had left us,
In passionate silence, passing through the court,
She ran to her apartment in the house,
Her hair clutched by the fingers of both hands.
She closed the doors behind her; then, by that bed   20

[18]Final scene.

Where long ago the fatal son was conceived—
That son who should bring about his father's death—
We heard her call upon Laïos, dead so many years,
And heard her wail for the double fruit of her marriage,
A husband by her husband, children by her child.   25

Exactly how she died I do not know:
For Oedipus burst in moaning and would not let us
Keep vigil to the end: it was by him
As he stormed about the room that our eyes were caught.
From one to another of us he went, begging a sword,   30
Cursing the wife who was not his wife, the mother
Whose womb had carried his own children and himself.
I do not know: it was none of us aided him,
But surely one of the gods was in control!
For with a dreadful cry   35
He hurled his weight, as though wrenched out of himself,
At the twin doors: the bolts gave, and he rushed in.
And there we saw her hanging, her body swaying
From the cruel cord she had noosed about her neck.
A great sob broke from him, heartbreaking to hear,   40
As he loosed the rope and lowered her to the ground.

I would blot out from my mind what happened next!
For the King ripped from her gown the golden brooches
That were her ornament, and raised them, and plunged them down
Straight into his own eyeballs, crying, "No more,   45
No more shall you look on the misery about me,
The horrors of my own doing! Too long you have known
The faces of those whom I should never have seen,
Too long been blind to those for whom I was searching!
From this hour, go in darkness!" And as he spoke,   50
He struck at his eyes—not once, but many times;
And the blood spattered his beard,
Bursting from his ruined sockets like red hail.
So from the unhappiness of two this evil has sprung,
A curse on the man and woman alike. The old   55
Happiness of the house of Labdakos
Was happiness enough: where is it today?
It is all wailing and ruin, disgrace, death—all
The misery of mankind that has a name—   60
And it is wholly and for ever theirs.

CHORAGOS: Is he in agony still? Is there no rest for him?
SECOND MESSENGER: He is calling for someone to lead him to the gates
So that all the children of Kadmos may look upon

His father's murderer, his mother's—no,
I can not say it!
      And then he will leave Thebes,   65
Self-exiled, in order that the curse
Which he himself pronounced may depart from the house.
He is weak, and there is none to lead him,
So terrible is his suffering.
       But you will see:
Look, the doors are opening; in a moment   70
You will see a thing that would crush a heart of stone.

(The central door is opened; Oedipus, blinded, is led in)

CHORAGOS: Dreadful indeed for men to see.
 Never have my own eyes
 Looked on a sight so full of fear.

 Oedipus!   75
What madness came upon you, what daemon
Leaped on your life with heavier
Punishment than a mortal man can bear?
No: I can not even
Look at you, poor ruined one.   80
And I would speak, question, ponder,
If I were able. No.
You make me shudder.
OEDIPUS: God. God.
Is there a sorrow greater?   85
Where shall I find harbor in this world?
My voice is hurled far on a dark wind.
What has God done to me?
CHORAGOS: Too terrible to think of, or to see.

              Strophe 1

OEDIPUS: O cloud of night,   90
Never to be turned away: night coming on,
I can not tell how: night like a shroud!

My fair winds brought me here.
       Oh God. Again
The pain of the spikes where I had sight,
The flooding pain   95
Of memory, never to be gouged out.
CHORAGOS: This is not strange.
 You suffer it all twice over, remorse in pain,
 Pain in remorse.

Antistrophe 1

OEDIPUS: Ah dear friend   100
   Are you faithful even yet, you alone?
   Are you still standing near me, will you stay here,
   Patient, to care for the blind?
                              The blind man!
   Yet even blind I know who it is attends me,
   By the voice's tone—   105
   Though my new darkness hide the comforter.
CHORAGOS: Oh fearful act!
   What god was it drove you to rake black
   Night across your eyes?

Strophe 2

OEDIPUS: Apollo. Apollo. Dear   110
   Children, the god was Apollo.
   He brought my sick, sick fate upon me.
   But the blinding hand was my own!
   How could I bear to see
   When all my sight was horror everywhere?   115
CHORAGOS: Everywhere; that is true.
OEDIPUS: And now what is left?
   Images? Love? A greeting even,
   Sweet to the senses? Is there anything?
   Ah, no, friends: lead me away.   120
   Lead me away from Thebes.
                         Lead the great wreck
   And hell of Oedipus, whom the gods hate.
CHORAGOS: Your fate is clear, you are not blind to that.
   Would God you had never found it out!

Antistrophe 2

OEDIPUS: Death take the man who unbound   125
   My feet on that hillside
   And delivered me from death to life! What life?
   If only I had died,
   This weight of monstrous doom
   Could not have dragged me and my darlings down.   130
CHORAGOS: I would have wished the same.
OEDIPUS: Oh never to have come here
   With my father's blood upon me! Never
   To have been the man they call his mother's husband!
   Oh accurst! Oh child of evil,   135
   To have entered that wretched bed—
                              the selfsame one!
   More primal than sin itself, this fell to me.
CHORAGOS: I do not know how I can answer you.
   You were better dead than alive and blind.

OEDIPUS: Do not counsel me any more. This punishment   140
  That I have laid upon myself is just.
  If I had eyes,
  I do not know how I could bear the sight
  Of my father, when I came to the house of Death,
  Or my mother: for I have sinned against them both   145
  So vilely that I could not make my peace
  By strangling my own life.
               Or do you think my children,
  Born as they were born, would be sweet to my eyes?
  Ah never, never! Nor this town with its high walls,
  Nor the holy images of the gods.
                   For I,   150
  Thrice miserable!—Oedipus, noblest of all the line
  Of Kadmos, have condemned myself to enjoy
  These things no more, by my own malediction
  Expelling that man whom the gods declared
  To be a defilement in the house of Laïos.   155
  After exposing the rankness of my own guilt,
  How could I look men frankly in the eyes?
  No, I swear it,
  If I could have stifled my hearing at its source,
  I would have done it and made all this body   160
  A tight cell of misery, blank to light and sound:
  So I should have been safe in a dark agony
  Beyond all recollection.
              Ah Kithairon!
  Why did you shelter me? When I was cast upon you,
  Why did I not die? Then I should never   165
  Have shown the world my execrable birth.

  Ah Polybos! Corinth, city that I believed
  The ancient seat of my ancestors: how fair
  I seemed, your child! And all the while this evil
  Was cancerous within me!
              For I am sick   170
  In my daily life, sick in my origin.

  O three roads, dark ravine, woodland and way
  Where three roads met: you, drinking my father's blood,
  My own blood, spilled by my own hand: can you remember
  The unspeakable things I did there, and the things   175
  I went on from there to do?
            O marriage, marriage!
  The act that engendered me, and again the act

Performed by the son in the same bed—

Ah, the net

Of incest, mingling fathers, brothers, sons,
With brides, wives, mothers: the last evil   180
That can be known by men: no tongue can say
How evil!

No. For the love of God, conceal me

Somewhere far from Thebes; or kill me; or hurl me
Into the sea, away from men's eyes for ever.
Come, lead me. You need not fear to touch me.   185
Of all men, I alone can bear this guilt.

(Enter Creon)

CHORAGOS: We are not the ones to decide; but Creon here
    May fitly judge of what you ask. He only
    Is left to protect the city in your place.
OEDIPUS: Alas, how can I speak to him? What right have I   190
    To beg his courtesy whom I have deeply wronged?
CREON: I have not come to mock you, Oedipus,
    Or to reproach you either.
    (To Attendants)   —You, standing there:
    If you have lost all respect for man's dignity,
    At least respect the flame of Lord Helios: 195
    Do not allow this pollution to show itself
    Openly here, an affront to the earth
    And Heaven's rain and the light of day. No, take him
    Into the house as quickly as you can.
    For it is proper   200
    That only the close kindred see his grief.
OEDIPUS: I pray you in God's name, since your courtesy
    Ignores my dark expectation, visiting
    With mercy this man of all men most execrable:
    Give me what I ask—for your good, not for mine.   205
CREON: And what is it that you would have me do?
OEDIPUS: Drive me out of this country as quickly as may be
    To a place where no human voice can ever greet me.
CREON: I should have done that before now—only,
    God's will had not been wholly revealed to me.   210
OEDIPUS: But his command is plain: the parricide
    Must be destroyed. I am that evil man.
CREON: That is the sense of it, yes; but as things are,
    We had best discover clearly what is to be done.
OEDIPUS: You would learn more about a man like me?   215
CREON: You are ready now to listen to the god.

OEDIPUS: I will listen. But it is to you
That I must turn for help. I beg you, hear me.

The woman in there—
Give her whatever funeral you think proper: 220
She is your sister.
                    —But let me go, Creon!
Let me purge my father's Thebes of the pollution
Of my living here, and go out to the wild hills,
To Kithairon, that has won such fame with me,
The tomb my mother and father appointed for me,   225
And let me die there, as they willed I should.
And yet I know
Death will not ever come to me through sickness
Or in any natural way: I have been preserved
For some unthinkable fate. But let that be.   230
As for my sons, you need not care for them.
They are men, they will find some way to live.
But my poor daughters, who have shared my table,
Who never before have been parted from their father—
Take care of them, Creon; do this for me.   235
And will you let me touch them with my hands
A last time, and let us weep together?
Be kind, my lord,
Great prince, be kind!
                    Could I but touch them,
They would be mine again, as when I had my eyes.   240

(Enter Antigone and Ismene, attended)

Ah, God!
Is it my dearest children I hear weeping?
Has Creon pitied me and sent my daughters?
CREON: Yes, Oedipus: I knew that they were dear to you
In the old days, and know you must love them still.   245
OEDIPUS: May God bless you for this—and be a friendlier
Guardian to you than he has been to me!

Children, where are you?
Come quickly to my hands: they are your brother's—
Hands that have brought your father's once clear eyes   250
To this way of seeing—
                    Ah dearest ones,
I had neither sight nor knowledge then, your father
By the woman who was the source of his own life!
And I weep for you—having no strength to see you—

I weep for you when I think of the bitterness   255
That men will visit upon you all your lives.
What homes, what festivals can you attend
Without being forced to depart again in tears?
And when you come to marriageable age,
Where is the man, my daughters, who would dare   260
Risk the bane that lies on all my children?
Is there any evil wanting? Your father killed
His father; sowed the womb of her who bore him;
Engendered you at the fount of his own existence!
That is what they will say of you.

                         Then, whom   265
Can you ever marry? There are no bridegrooms for you,
And your lives must wither away in sterile dreaming.
O Creon, son of Menoikeus!
You are the only father my daughters have,
Since we, their parents, are both of us gone for ever.   270
They are your own blood: you will not let them
Fall into beggary and loneliness;
You will keep them from the miseries that are mine!
Take pity on them; see, they are only children,
Friendless except for you. Promise me this,   275
Great Prince, and give me your hand in token of it.

(Creon clasps his right hand)

    Children:
    I could say much, if you could understand me,
    But as it is, I have only this prayer for you:
    Live where you can, be as happy as you can—   280
    Happier, please God, than God has made your father!
CREON: Enough. You have wept enough. Now go within.
OEDIPUS: I must; but it is hard.
CREON: Times eases all things.
OEDIPUS: But you must promise . . .
CREON: Say what you desire.
OEDIPUS: Send me from Thebes!
CREON: God grant that I may!   285
OEDIPUS: But since God hates me . . .
CREON: No, he will grant your wish.
OEDIPUS: You promise?
CREON: I can not speak beyond my knowledge.
OEDIPUS: Then lead me in.
CREON: Come now, and leave your children.
OEDIPUS: No! Do not take them from me!
CREON: Think no longer

That you are in command here, but rather think   290
How, when you were, you served your own destruction.

(Exeunt into the house all but the Chorus; the Choragos chants directly to the audience)

CHORAGOS: Men of Thebes: look upon Oedipus.

This is the king who solved the famous riddle
And towered up, most powerful of men.
No mortal eyes but looked on him with envy,   295
Yet in the end ruin swept over him.
Let every man in mankind's frailty
Consider his last day; and let none
Presume on his good fortune until he find
Life, at his death, a memory without pain.   300

GREEK TRAGEDY

Oedipus Rex, one of the first and greatest tragedies, is the play Aristotle had most immediately in mind in his famous definition:

Tragedy, then, is an imitation of an action that is serious, complete, and of a certain magnitude; in language embellished with each kind of artistic ornament, the several kinds being found in separate parts of the play; in the form of action, not of narrative; through pity and fear effecting the proper purgation of these emotions.

(S. H. Butcher translation)

Aristotle's definition, in his *Poetics,* has remained central to the Western world's understanding of tragedy for over two thousand years. However we envision *Oedipus Rex,* as we play it on the stage in our mind, we will want to ask ourselves what in it has transcended the particulars of time and space.

Certainly the action is serious. Oedipus murders his father, marries his mother and begets children, discovers his history, blinds himself, and goes into exile. All this the audience already knew, since Sophocles took the *story* (the chronological set of events upon which the play is based) from the common ground of Greek myth. The story, we may say, was inherently tragic, but it was not a tragedy until Sophocles put his playwright's hand to it. A tragedy, in other words, is an author's shaping of serious events into meaningful art. Our business as students is to examine the constituent elements.

For Aristotle, the most important element was *plot,* which we may define as the author's arrangement of the events of the story. Although the story of Oedipus begins with a prophecy made at his birth, Sophocles confines his plot to the day Oedipus discovers his identity. All springs from Oedipus's promise to discover and punish the murderer of Laïos. The events are compressed into a *unified plot:* a chain in which each single event is the necessary or probable result of an event that has gone before. Only at the end does the chain terminate. This compressed sense of inevitability lies at the heart of Greek tragedy. Once the chain of events has begun, it moves link by iron link to its inescapable conclusion. Another kind of arrangement, not in the Greek view suitable for tragedy, is the *episodic plot:* a series of events not logically linked to one another by necessity or probability.[1]

Two important elements of plot are reversal and recognition. *Reversal* (Greek *Peripeteia*) is a change of fortune, from good to bad in tragedy, from bad to good in comedy. Although Oedipus still lives at the end of the play, his fortunes are horribly reversed. For Aristotle, *reversal of intention* is most important; Oedipus intends to triumph, but ironically ruins himself. Similarly, the messenger intends to be helpful, but only hastens the tragic revelation by telling Oedipus that King Polybos was not his father. And Oedipus's search for the murderer discloses only himself. Twinned naturally with reversal is *discovery* or *recognition* (Greek *anagnorisis*), when a character comes into self-knowledge or learns more about his or her community or place in the world. Oedipus's discovery of who he is profoundly alters his sense of self, his relation to his family and community, and his understanding of his place in the universe.

Character is for Aristotle next in importance to plot. A complex summary of all that an individual is and does, character in literary works tends to be most meaningful when it helps define a significant choice, which turns the plot. As Aristotle expresses it: "Character is that which reveals moral purpose, showing what kinds of things a man chooses or avoids." Many literary works use *stock characters, flat characters,* or *type characters,* people whose choices will be obvious from their simple positions or personalities: the boastful soldier, the gambler with a heart of gold, the hypocritical preacher. Others use *individualized characters* or *round characters,* personalities we must understand in depth before we can understand how they function. Oedipus may at first seem flat, easily defined by his pride, his stubbornness, or his hasty judgment, but the more we consider him, the more we perceive a complexity that defies easy summary. To understand the play, we must ask why Oedipus makes his choices. To say simply that he was fated will not do, since prediction is not necessarily predestination. The oracle foresaw that, being the kind of man he was, he would act in a given way in a particular situation. In Oedipus we can see the vital part character plays in forging the links of probability and necessity in a relentlessly unified plot. The events are probable or necessary because the character is so defined that he can act in no other way.

A tragic character must be *good* in his moral purposes; he or she must intend

---

[1]Writers on tragedy have sometimes emphasized the *three unities* of plot, time, and place, though Aristotle emphasizes only plot. Unity of time and place follow naturally from a unified plot —showing all action at one place during one span of time—a concept arising from the limited staging possibilities of the Greek theater, though it was often an ideal of later writers, particularly in seventeenth-century France, whose theaters were actually more versatile. Unities of time and place (and sometimes even plot) were considerably less important in the fluid Elizabethan theater.

to do right. In Greek tragedy the main character is also noble, so that his or her moral purposes affect all society. The tragic irony occurs when good intentions misfire. Out of this come the tragic emotions of pity and fear: *pity,* the emotion we experience as witnesses to undeserved misfortune, and *fear,* the emotion aroused when the misfortune occurs to a person like ourselves. The person is good, but cannot be spotless. He or she must in some degree be responsible for his or her fate through a *tragic flaw* in character or an *error of judgment* (alternative translations of the Greek *hamartia*). Although we blame Oedipus in part for what happens, we cannot blame him totally or we do not pity him. Although we admire him, we cannot consider him perfect, or we lose the tragic emotion of fear.

In his definition of tragedy, Aristotle stresses the importance for the audience of *catharsis* (or *purgation*) of the emotions of pity and fear. Watching the play, we release pent-up emotions; we leave the theater healthier than we went in. Not all writers have agreed upon the benefits of tragedy, or even that there are any benefits. For the Greeks, however, the experience was clearly communal, rooted in religious ritual and fostered by a shared vision of humanity's place in the eternal scheme of things.

Even in its most Grecian elements, the Greek theater provides a way of seeing and a vocabulary that helps us understand the plays of later cultures. The *chorus,* for example, is hardly ever used again. Yet later playwrights frequently use a *chorus character,* a person who, like the Greek chorus, stands apart from the passions of the play and verbalizes the judgment of an intelligent, compassionate bystander. So, too, the Greeks had a derrick on top of the skene to lower a god out of the heavens, when necessary. The term *deus ex machina* ("god out of the machine") now describes any unlikely solution to a problem, as if the author were intervening from heaven. In its entirety, the Greek vision of tragedy remains a necessary starting point for understanding later tragic visions of the Western world down to our own day.

QUESTIONS

1. In what ways, specifically, is the plot of *Oedipus Rex* different from the story? Why does the play begin where it does, rather than, for example, some years before?

2. How do probability and necessity link the events? Pick two or three successive scenes to show how these concepts apply. Observe the important linkage between character and plot in this play, as one event follows another because of forces within characters that cause them to react as they do.

3. The arrival of the messenger, near the beginning of Scene III, seems coincidental. In what way is this arrival also probable? How does the news brought by the messenger help explain the probability or necessity of the actions in the rest of the play?

4. Where is there a reversal of fortune or expectation in this play? Is there more than one?
5. What lines most clearly show Oedipus's discovery?
6. Oedipus is proud, stubborn, hasty in his judgment. What else is he? Show how his character explains important choices of action.
7. Do we pity Oedipus? Why? Does the play arouse fear in us? How so?
8. Is Oedipus good? Explain. What is his tragic flaw?
9. We often find important clues to understanding a Greek play in the words of the chorus. In this play, which speeches of the chorus (or its leader) help us most?

THE ELIZABETHAN THEATER

To imagine the size of the Globe theater in London, where Shakespeare produced many of his plays, consider first the dimensions of a Greek theater. Within that huge amphiteater, seating tens of thousands, was the *orchestra,* a circular acting area 85 feet in diameter.[1] Shakespeare's Globe was an octagonal building of approximately the size of the Greek orchestra. Elizabethan actors and audiences shared the space Greek spectators viewed from their many ranks of seats. From one side of the English octagon, the stage jutted into the midst of the standees (the *groundlings*), so that the actors played to an audience almost surrounding them. Up the other seven sides of the octagon were three levels of galleries, for those who could pay a bit more for a loftier view of the proceedings. Although perhaps two to three thousand spectators could cram into the Globe, the farthest seat in the house was perhaps only 60 feet from center stage. The galleries and stage were roofed, the rest open to the sky.

With such a stage, the playwright will want no masks, unless for comedies. Every gesture, every grimace will be clearly visible, though the playwright may wish to underline them in dialogue for those off to the side. No clogs will be wanted here; the actors in their natural dimensions will be large enough for this stage. With the actors freed from clogs and masks, and clearly distinguishable by face, the playwright will write for freer movement and more variety of tone, introducing numerous extra characters. A theater of such intimacy will, of course, have its own problems. It may demand some swordplay to stir the audience up from time to time, some *comic relief* to give them a break from the tension of tragedy, an occasional direct address from actor to audience in at least partial acknowledgment that they stand so close.

An important feature of the Globe theater, unlike anything in the Greek (save for the occasional *deus ex machina*), was the three stories of its height. On the first level, behind the stage, a curtained inner stage allowed for bedroom exchanges or death scenes that did not necessitate dragging a corpse offstage. On

---

[1]In the Theater of Dionysus at Athens up to the middle of the fifth century B.C., when it was reduced to 65 feet.

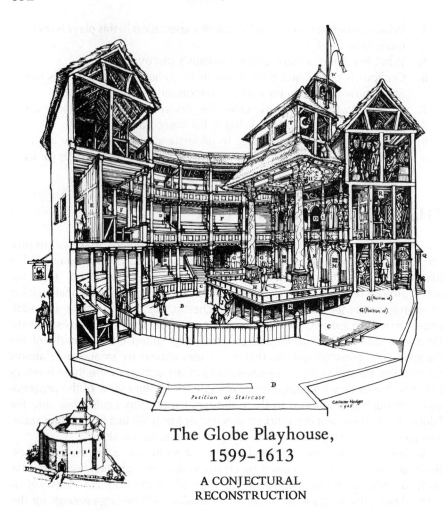

The Globe Playhouse, 1599–1613

A CONJECTURAL RECONSTRUCTION

AA	Main entrance
B	The Yard
CC	Entrances to lowest gallery
D	Entrances to staircase and upper galleries
E	Corridor serving the different sections of the middle gallery
F	Middle gallery ('Twopenny Rooms')
G	'Gentlemen's Rooms' or 'Lords' Rooms'
H	The stage
J	The hanging being put up round the stage
K	The 'Hell' under the stage
L	The stage trap, leading down to the Hell

MM	Stage doors
N	Curtained 'place behind the stage'
O	Gallery above the stage, used as required sometimes by musicians, sometimes by spectators, and often as part of the play
P	Back-stage area (the tiring-house)
Q	Tiring-house door
R	Dressing-rooms
S	Wardrobe and storage
T	The hut housing the machine for lowering enthroned gods, etc., to the stage
U	The 'Heavens'
W	Hoisting the playhouse flag

The Globe Theater, London, 1599–1613
(From *The Globe Restored* by C. Walter Hodges, published by Oxford University Press)

either side of this curtained area were doors for entrances and exits to and from the main stage. A trap door midstage allowed for the appearance of devils and ghosts. On the second level, a gallery provided another acting area and behind that was a second inner stage. On either side of the gallery, windows provided still more acting space. On the third level was a musicians' gallery, perhaps occasionally used for acting.

Not much of this was the invention of the moment. The general plan had evolved over centuries by way of medieval pageant wagons and performances in inn yards and marketplaces, as had the playwright's way of using it and the audience's manner of responding. The net result, by the time of Shakespeare, was a theatrical experience of remarkable fluidity. To change a scene, the actors merely left one acting area as another group appeared on another. Thus quickly the action moves from Scotland to England, say, or from Rome to Alexandria. If necessary, a word or an item of costume will fix a new scene in the imaginations of the audience. Frequently, no precise idea of place is necessary; in the turmoil of battle, for example, the scene may change several times within minutes without the audience knowing or much caring precisely where each incident occurs. In such a theater, the unities of time and place may seem irrelevant. Even unity of plot seems challenged.

Just as we cannot experience the Greek theater, we can never experience the theater of Shakespeare exactly as his first audiences did, although some theaters seek to duplicate the Globe playhouse (we can reproduce the theater, but not the audience). As we read the play, we set the stage in our minds: the Globe theater as we imagine it, the vastly different fluidity of the motion picture, or the twentieth-century stage in any of its variations. Always we seek to provide the fullest scope for the dramatic potential in the playwright's words.

HAMLET

The Globe tooks its name from the round earth. Its sign was Atlas holding up the globe. The world was a stage, and the stage was the world. And on that stage Shakespeare put Hamlet—modern man himself emerging from Renaissance confidence into profound uncertainty. When Shakespeare wrote his play in 1601 or 1602, the world was indeed out of joint. Protestant and Catholic beliefs in authority and in what happened after death clashed violently. Early in 1601, Shakespeare's friend, the handsome, heroic, and melancholy Earl of Essex, perhaps a partial model for Shakespeare's Dane, rebelled against his divinely appointed but aging queen and lost his head. Sixty years before (1543), Copernicus had flung the stable earth from its center in God's universe to wander subordinately around the sun. And soon (1637), Descartes cast all reality inward into one's sole consciousness, into the solipsistic "I": *cogito ergo sum,* "I think therefore I am." Bacon, in his *Advancement of Learning* (1604) and *Novum Organum* (1620), likewise threw out past certainty for a new inductive searching for science.

All this Shakespeare, by some intuitive miracle, embodies in *Hamlet,* based on an old revenge tragedy in which the hero must play mad to save his skin and carry out his purpose. That Shakespeare's hero now conducts an inductive experiment, his play-within-the-play, to establish the facts is only one of the remarkable modernizations. But more significantly still, Shakespeare in *Hamlet* creates something altogether new in tragedy. The Greek audience walked out into the sunlight purged of pity and terror. Shakespeare brought this catharsis into the play itself as his hero, just before death, experiences the illumination and calm of mind formerly reserved for the audience alone.

HAMLET, PRINCE OF DENMARK*

William Shakespeare   *(1564–1616)*

Dramatis Personæ

CLAUDIUS, King of Denmark
HAMLET, son to the late, and nephew to the present King
HORATIO, friend to Hamlet
POLONIUS, Lord Chamberlain
LAERTES, son to Polonius
VOLTIMAND
CORNELIUS
ROSENCRANTZ
GUILDENSTERN } courtiers.
OSRIC
A GENTLEMAN
A PRIEST
MARCELLUS
BERNARDO } officers.
FRANCISCO, a soldier
REYNALDO, servant to Polonius
PLAYERS
Two CLOWNS, gravediggers
FORTINBRAS, prince of Norway
A NORWEGIAN CAPTAIN
ENGLISH AMBASSADORS
GERTRUDE, Queen of Denmark, and mother to Hamlet
OPHELIA, daughter to Polonius
LORDS, LADIES, OFFICERS, SOLDIERS, SAILORS, MESSENGERS, and other ATTENDANTS
GHOST of Hamlet's father

Scene: Denmark.

*Edited, with notes, by Sheridan Baker.

Act I

Scene I

Elsinore. A platform of the castle. Enter Francisco on patrol. Enter to him Bernardo.

BERNARDO: Who's there?

FRANCISCO: Nay, answer me: stand, and unfold yourself.

BERNARDO: Long live the king!

FRANCISCO: Bernardo?

BERNARDO: He.   5

FRANCISCO: You come most carefully upon your hour.

BERNARDO: 'Tis now struck twelve. Get thee to bed, Francisco.

FRANCISCO: For this relief much thanks. 'Tis bitter cold,
    And I am sick at heart.

BERNARDO: Have you had quiet guard?

FRANCISCO: Not a mouse stirring.   10

BERNARDO: Well, good night.
    If you do meet Horatio and Marcellus,
    The rivals of my watch, bid them make haste.

FRANCISCO: I think I hear them. Stand, ho! Who's there?

(Enter Horatio and Marcellus.)

HORATIO: Friends to this ground.

MARCELLUS: And liegemen to the Dane.   15

FRANCISCO: Give you good night.

MARCELLUS: O, farewell, honest soldier.
    Who hath reliev'd you?

FRANCISCO: Bernardo has my place.
    Give you good night.   *(Exit.)*

MARCELLUS: Holla! Bernardo!

BERNARDO: Say,
    What, is Horatio there?

HORATIO: A piece of him.

BERNARDO: Welcome, Horatio. Welcome, good Marcellus.   20

MARCELLUS: What, has this thing appear'd again to-night?

BERNARDO: I have seen nothing.

MARCELLUS: Horatio says 'tis but our fantasy,
    And will not let belief take hold of him
    Touching this dreaded sight, twice seen of us: 25
    Therefore I have entreated him along
    With us to watch the minutes of this night;
    That if again this apparition come,
    He may approve our eyes and speak to it.

13 *rivals,* companions.

HORATIO: Tush, tush, 'twill not appear.

BERNARDO: Sit down awhile;   30
   And let us once again assail your ears,
   That are so fortified against our story
   What we have two nights seen.

HORATIO: Well, sit we down,
   And let us hear Bernardo speak of this.

BERNARDO: Last night of all,   35
   When yond same star that's westward from the pole
   Had made his course to illume that part of heaven
   Where now it burns, Marcellus and myself,
   The bell then beating one—

(Enter Ghost.)

MARCELLUS: Peace! Break thee off! Look, where it comes again!   40
BERNARDO: In the same figure, like the king that's dead.
MARCELLUS: Thou art a scholar; speak to it, Horatio.
BERNARDO: Looks it not like the king? Mark it, Horatio.
HORATIO: Most like: it harrows me with fear and wonder.
BERNARDO: It would be spoke to.
MARCELLUS: Question it, Horatio.   45
HORATIO: What art thou that usurp'st this time of night
   Together with that fair and warlike form
   In which the majesty of buried Denmark
   Did sometimes march? By heaven I charge thee, speak!
MARCELLUS: It is offended.
BERNARDO: See, it stalks away!   50
HORATIO: Stay! speak, speak! I charge thee, speak!   *(Exit Ghost.)*
MARCELLUS: 'Tis gone, and will not answer.
BERNARDO: How now, Horatio! You tremble and look pale.
   Is not this something more than fantasy?
   What think you on 't?   55
HORATIO: Before my God, I might not this believe
   Without the sensible and true avouch
   Of mine own eyes.
MARCELLUS: Is it not like the king?
HORATIO: As thou art to thyself:
   Such was the very armour he had on   60
   When he the ambitious Norway combated;
   So frown'd he once, when, in an angry parle,
   He smote the sledded Polacks on the ice.
   'Tis strange.
MARCELLUS: Thus twice before, and jump at this dead hour,   65
   With martial stalk hath he gone by our watch.

---

42 *scholar,* "You know Latin." Verses for exorcising evil spirits were in Latin.   **65** *jump,* just.

HORATIO: In what particular thought to work I know not;
   But in the gross and scope of my opinion,
   This bodes some strange eruption to our state.
MARCELLUS: Good now, sit down, and tell me, he that knows,   70
   Why this same strict and most observant watch
   So nightly toils the subject of the land,
   And why such daily cast of brazen cannon,
   And foreign mart for implements of war;
   Why such impress of shipwrights, whose sore task   75
   Does not divide the Sunday from the week;
   What might be toward, that this sweaty haste
   Doth make the night joint-labourer with the day:
   Who is 't that can inform me?
HORATIO: That can I;
   At least, the whisper goes so. Our last king,   80
   Whose image even but now appear'd to us,
   Was, as you know, by Fortinbras of Norway,
   Thereto prick'd on by a most emulate pride,
   Dared to the combat; in which our valiant Hamlet—
   For so this side of our known world esteem'd him—   85
   Did slay this Fortinbras; who, by a seal'd compact,
   Well ratified by law and heraldry,
   Did forfeit, with his life, all those his lands
   Which he stood seiz'd of, to the conqueror:
   Against the which, a moiety competent   90
   Was gagèd by our king; which had return'd
   To the inheritance of Fortinbras,
   Had he been vanquisher; as, by the same covenant,
   And carriage of the article design'd,
   His fell to Hamlet. Now, sir, young Fortinbras,   95
   Of unimprovèd mettle hot and full,
   Hath in the skirts of Norway here and there
   Shark'd up a list of lawless resolutes,
   For food and diet, to some enterprise
   That hath a stomach in 't; which is no other—   100
   As it doth well appear unto our state—
   But to recover of us, by strong hand
   And terms compulsatory, those foresaid lands
   So by his father lost: and this, I take it,
   Is the main motive of our preparations,   105
   The source of this our watch and the chief head
   Of this post-haste and romage in the land.

72 *toils the subject of this land,* makes the subjects of this land toil.   **73** *cast,* casting.   **77** *toward,* in preparation.   **82** *Fortinbras of Norway,* former King of Norway, father of young Fortinbras. **84** *Hamlet,* the dead king, young Hamlet's father.   **90** *moiety competent,* an equal half (of land). **91** *gagèd,* pledged.   **96** *unimproved,* untested.

BERNARDO: I think it be no other but e'en so.
    Well may it sort that this portentous figure
    Comes armed through our watch, so like the king   110
    That was and is the question of these wars.
HORATIO: A mote it is to trouble the mind's eye.
    In the most high and palmy state of Rome,
    A little ere the mightiest Julius fell,
    The graves stood tenantless and the sheeted dead   115
    Did squeak and gibber in the Roman streets;
    As stars with trains of fire and dews of blood,
    Disasters in the sun; and the moist star
    Upon whose influence Neptune's empire stands
    Was sick almost to doomsday with eclipse;   120
    And even the like precurse of fierce events,
    As harbingers preceding still the fates
    And prologue to the omen coming on,
    Have heaven and earth together demonstrated
    Unto our climatures and countrymen.—   125
    But soft, behold! lo, where it comes again!

(Enter Ghost again.)

    I'll cross it, though it blast me. Stay, illusion!
    If thou hast any sound, or use of voice,
    Speak to me.
    If there be any good thing to be done,   130
    That may to thee do ease and grace to me,
    Speak to me.
    If thou art privy to thy country's fate,
    Which, happily, foreknowing may avoid,
    O, speak!   135
    Or if thou has uphoarded in thy life
    Extorted treasure in the womb of earth,
    For which, they say, you spirits oft walk in death, *(The cock crows.)*
    Speak of it: stay, and speak! Stop it, Marcellus!
MARCELLUS: Shall I strike at it with my partisan?   140
HORATIO: Do, if it will not stand.
BERNARDO: 'Tis here!
HORATIO: 'Tis here!
MARCELLUS: 'Tis gone!   *(Exit Ghost.)*
    We do it wrong, being so majestical,
    To offer it the show of violence;
    For it is, as the air, invulnerable,   145
    And our vain blows malicious mockery.

---

118 *moist star,* the moon.   **127** *cross,* cross his path, an invitation to his evil influence.
140 *partisan,* spear with hatchet edges.

BERNARDO: It was about to speak, when the cock crew.
HORATIO: And then it started, like a guilty thing
Upon a fearful summons. I have heard,
The cock, that is the trumpet to the morn,   150
Doth with his lofty and shrill-sounding throat
Awake the god of day; and, at his warning,
Whether in sea or fire, in earth or air,
The extravagant and erring spirit hies
To his confine; and of the truth herein   155
This present object made probation.
MARCELLUS: It faded on the crowing of the cock.
Some say that ever 'gainst that season comes
Wherein our Saviour's birth is celebrated,
The bird of dawning singeth all night long;   160
And then, they say, no spirit dare stir abroad;
The nights are wholesome; then no planets strike,
No fairy takes, nor witch hath power to charm,
So hallow'd and so gracious is the time.
HORATIO: So have I heard and do in part believe it.   165
But, look, the morn, in russet mantle clad,
Walks o'er the dew of yon high eastward hill;
Break we our watch up; and by my advice,
Let us impart what we have seen to-night
Unto young Hamlet; for, upon my life,   170
This spirit, dumb to us, will speak to him.
Do you consent we shall acquaint him with it,
As needful in our loves, fitting our duty?
MARCELLUS: Let's do 't, I pray; and I this morning know
Where we shall find him most conveniently.   175

(Exeunt.)

Act I

Scene II

A room of state in the castle. Enter the King, Queen, Hamlet, Polonius, Laertes,
Ophelia, Voltimand, Cornelius, Lords Attendant.

KING: Though yet of Hamlet our dear brother's death
The memory be green, and that it us befitted
To bear our hearts in grief and our whole kingdom
To be contracted in one brow of woe,
Yet so far hath discretion fought with nature   5
That we with wisest sorrow think on him,
Together with remembrance of ourselves.

---

154 *extravagant and erring,* wandering.   **160** *bird of dawning,* the cock.

Therefore our sometime sister, now our queen,
The imperial jointress to this warlike state,
Have we, as 'twere with a defeated joy,— 10
With an auspicious and a dropping eye,
With mirth in funeral and with dirge in marriage,
In equal scale weighing delight and dole,—
Taken to wife: nor have we herein barr'd
Your better wisdoms, which have freely gone 15
With this affair along. For all, our thanks.
Now follows, that you know, young Fortinbras,
Holding a weak supposal of our worth,
Or thinking by our late dear brother's death
Our state to be disjoint and out of frame, 20
Colleagued with the dream of his advantage,
He hath not fail'd to pester us with message,
Importing the surrender of those lands
Lost by his father, with all bonds of law,
To our most valiant brother. So much for him. 25
Now for ourself and for this time of meeting.
Thus much the business is: we have here writ
To Norway, uncle of young Fortinbras,—
Who, impotent and bed-rid, scarcely hears
Of this his nephew's purpose, to suppress 30
His further gait herein; in that the levies,
The lists and full proportions, are all made
Out of his subject; and we here dispatch
You, good Cornelius, and you, Voltimand,
For bearers of this greeting to old Norway, 35
Giving to you no further personal power
To business with the king, more than the scope
Of these delated articles allow.
Farewell, and let your haste commend your duty.

CORNELIUS: } In that and all things will we show our duty.
VOLTIMAND: } 40

KING: We doubt it nothing: heartily farewell.

       (Exeunt Voltimand and Cornelius.)
And now, Laertes, what's the news with you?
You told us of some suit. What is 't, Laertes?
You cannot speak of reason to the Dane,
And lose your voice. What wouldst thou beg, Laertes, 45
That shall not be my offer, not thy asking?
The head is not more native to the heart,
The hand more instrumental to the mouth,

---

14 *barr'd . . . wisdoms,* ignored our wiser counselors.   **33** *subject,* from the King of Norway's subjects.

Than is the throne of Denmark to thy father.
What wouldst thou have, Laertes?

LAERTES: My dread lord,   50
Your leave and favour to return to France;
From whence though willingly I came to Denmark,
To show my duty in your coronation,
Yet now, I must confess, that duty done,
My thoughts and wishes bend again toward France   55
And bow them to your gracious leave and pardon.

KING: Have you your father's leave? What says Polonius?

POLONIUS: He hath, my lord, wrung from me my slow leave
By laboursome petition, and at last
Upon his will I seal'd my hard consent.   60
I do beseech you, give him leave to go.

KING: Take thy fair hour, Laertes; time be thine,
And thy best graces spend it at thy will!
But now, my cousin Hamlet, and my son,—

HAMLET: *(Aside)* A little more than kin, and less than kind.   65

KING: How is it that the clouds still hang on you?

HAMLET: Not so, my lord; I am too much i' the sun.

QUEEN: Good Hamlet, cast thy nighted colour off,
And let thine eye look like a friend on Denmark.
Do not forever with thy vailèd lids   70
Seek for thy noble father in the dust:
Thou know'st 'tis common; all that lives must die,
Passing through nature to eternity.

HAMLET: Ay, madam, it is common.

QUEEN: If it be,
Why seems it so particular with thee?   75

HAMLET: Seems, madam! nay, it is; I know not "seems."
'Tis not alone my inky cloak, good mother,
Nor customary suits of solemn black,
Nor windy suspiration of forc'd breath,
No, nor the fruitful river in the eye,   80
Nor the dejected 'haviour of the visage,
Together with all forms, moods, shapes of grief,
That can denote me truly: these indeed seem,
For they are actions that a man might play:
But I have that within which passeth show;   85
These but the trappings and the suits of woe.

KING: 'Tis sweet and commendable in your nature, Hamlet,
To give these mourning duties to your father:
But, you must know, your father lost a father;

---

64 *cousin,* used for any relative.   **65** *kind,* natural family.   **67** *i' the sun,* "in the public eye," and punning on *son.*   **85** *passeth,* surpasses.

That father lost, lost his, and the survivor bound   90
In filial obligation for some term
To do obsequious sorrow: but to persèver
In obstinate condolement is a course
Of impious stubbornness; 'tis unmanly grief;
It shows a will most incorrect to heaven,   95
A heart unfortified, a mind impatient,
An understanding simple and unschool'd:
For what we know must be and is as common
As any the most vulgar thing to sense,
Why should we in our peevish opposition   100
Take it to heart? Fie! 'tis a fault to heaven,
A fault against the dead, a fault to nature,
To reason most absurd, whose common theme
Is death of fathers, and who still hath cried,
From the first corse till he that died to-day,   105
"This must be so." We pray you, throw to earth
This unprevailing woe, and think of us
As of a father; for let the world take note,
You are the most immediate to our throne;
And with no less nobility of love   110
Than that which dearest father bears his son,
Do I impart toward you. For your intent
In going back to school in Wittenberg,
It is most retrograde to our desire:
And we beseech you, bend you to remain   115
Here, in the cheer and comfort of our eye,
Our chiefest courtier, cousin, and our son.
QUEEN: Let not thy mother lose her prayers, Hamlet:
  I pray thee, stay with us; go not to Wittenberg.
HAMLET: I shall in all my best obey you, madam.   120
KING: Why, 'tis a loving and a fair reply:
  Be as ourself in Denmark. Madam, come;
  This gentle and unforc'd accord of Hamlet
  Sits smiling to my heart: in grace whereof,
  No jocund health that Denmark drinks today,   125
  But the great cannon to the clouds shall tell,
  And the king's rouse the heavens shall bruit again,
  Re-speaking earthly thunder. Come away.

---

105 *first corse,* first corpse, that of Abel, whom his brother Cain killed, bringing death and murder into the world. Claudius unwittingly refers to his own crime. He later remembers Cain explicitly (III.iii.37).   **113** *Wittenberg,* German university; noted for the Protestant reformation. Luther was appointed professor of philosophy in 1508 and nailed his 95 articles to the door of the city's church in 1517. Hamlet and Horatio are thus students of the "new philosophy," questioning accepted religious doctrine and authority.   **127** *rouse,* deep draught; *bruit again,* re-echo.

(Exeunt all but Hamlet.)

HAMLET: O, that this too too solid flesh would melt,
    Thaw and resolve itself into a dew!   130
    Or that the Everlasting had not fix'd
    His canon 'gainst self-slaughter! O God! God!
    How weary, stale, flat and unprofitable,
    Seem to me all the uses of this world!
    Fie on 't! ah fie! 'tis an unweeded garden,   135
    That grows to seed; things rank and gross in nature
    Possess it merely. That it should come to this!
    But two months dead: nay, not so much, not two:
    So excellent a king; that was, to this,
    Hyperion to a satyr; so loving to my mother   140
    That he might not beteem the winds of heaven
    Visit her face too roughly. Heaven and earth!
    Must I remember? why, she would hang on him,
    As if increase of appetite had grown
    By what it fed on: and yet, within a month—   145
    Let me not think on 't—Frailty, thy name is woman!—
    A little month, or ere those shoes were old
    With which she follow'd my poor father's body,
    Like Niobe, all tears:—why she, even she—
    O God! a beast, that wants discourse of reason,   150
    Would have mourn'd longer—married with my uncle,
    My father's brother, but no more like my father
    Than I to Hercules: within a month:
    Ere yet the salt of most unrighteous tears
    Had left the flushing in her gallèd eyes,   155
    She married. O, most wicked speed, to post
    With such dexterity to incestuous sheets!
    It is not nor it cannot come to good:
    But break, my heart; for I must hold my tongue.

(Enter Horatio, Marcellus, and Bernardo.)

HORATIO: Hail to your lordship!
HAMLET: I am glad to see you well: 160
    Horatio,—or I do forget myself.
HORATIO: The same, my lord, and your poor servant ever.

---

129 *solid flesh.* Shakespeare wrote Hamlet's role for Richard Burbage, coowner and leading actor of his company, a chunky fellow, who may also have played Falstaff. See the queen's remark "He's fat" (V.ii.298), and Hamlet's "I have of late . . . foregone all custom of exercises" (II.ii.308).   **132** *canon,* law.   **137** *merely,* completely.   **140** *Hyperion,* Greek sun god, the most beautiful of gods. **149** *Niobe,* The gods, angered at Niobe's bragging about her children, killed them and turned her into a rock, from which her tears continued to stream.

HAMLET: Sir, my good friend; I'll change that name with you:
And what make you from Wittenberg, Horatio?
Marcellus? 165

MARCELLUS: My good lord—

HAMLET: I am very glad to see you —*(To Bernardo:)* Good even, sir.
But what, in faith, make you from Wittenberg?

HORATIO: A truant disposition, good my lord.

HAMLET: I would not hear your enemy say so, 170
Nor shall you do mine ear that violence,
To make it truster of your own report
Against yourself: I know you are no truant.
But what is your affair in Elsinore?
We'll teach you to drink deep ere you depart. 175

HORATIO: My lord, I came to see your father's funeral.

HAMLET: I pray thee, do not mock me, fellow-student;
I think it was to see my mother's wedding.

HORATIO: Indeed, my lord, it follow'd hard upon.

HAMLET: Thrift, thrift, Horatio! the funeral bak'd meats 180
Did coldly furnish forth the marriage tables.
Would I had met my dearest foe in heaven
Or ever I had seen that day, Horatio!
My father!—methinks I see my father.

HORATIO: Where, my lord?

HAMLET: In my mind's eye, Horatio. 185

HORATIO: I saw him once; he was a goodly king.

HAMLET: He was a man, take him for all in all,
I shall not look upon his like again.

HORATIO: My lord, I think I saw him yesternight.

HAMLET: Saw? who? 190

HORATIO: My lord, the king your father.

HAMLET: The king my father!

HORATIO: Season your admiration for a while
With an attent ear, till I may deliver,
Upon the witness of these gentlemen,
This marvel to you.

HAMLET: For God's love, let me hear. 195

HORATIO: Two nights together had these gentlemen,
Marcellus and Bernardo, on their watch,
In the dead vast and middle of the night,
Been thus encounter'd. A figure like your father,
Arm'd at point exactly, cap-a-pe, 200
Appears before them, and with solemn march
Goes slow and stately by them: thrice he walk'd

163 *change,* exchange.   **200** *cap-a-pe,* from head to foot.

By their oppress'd and fear-surprisèd eyes,
Within his truncheon's length; whilst they, distill'd
Almost to jelly with the act of fear,   205
Stand dumb and speak not to him. This to me
In dreadful secrecy impart they did;
And I with them the third night kept the watch:
Where, as they had deliver'd, both in time,
Form of the thing, each word made true and good,   210
The apparition comes: I knew your father;
These hands are not more like.

HAMLET: But where was this?
MARCELLUS: My lord, upon the platform where we watch'd.
HAMLET: Did you not speak to it?
HORATIO: My lord, I did;
But answer made it none: yet once me-thought   215
It lifted up it head and did address
Itself to motion, like as it would speak;
But even then the morning cock crew loud,
And at the sound it shrunk in haste away,
And vanish'd from our sight.
HAMLET: 'Tis very strange.   220
HORATIO: As I do live, my honour'd lord, 'tis true;
And we did think it writ down in our duty
To let you know of it.
HAMLET: Indeed, indeed, sirs, but this troubles me.
Hold you the watch to-night?
MARCELLUS: }   We do, my lord.
BERNARDO: }   225
HAMLET: Arm'd, say you?
MARCELLUS: }   Arm'd, my lord.
BERNARDO: }
HAMLET: From top to toe?
MARCELLUS: }   My lord, from head to foot.
BERNARDO: }
HAMLET: Then saw you not his face?
HORATIO: O, yes, my lord; he wore his beaver up.   230
HAMLET: What, look'd he frowningly?
HORATIO: A countenance more in sorrow than in anger.
HAMLET: Pale or red?
HORATIO: Nay, very pale.
HAMLET: And fix'd his eyes upon you?
HORATIO: Most constantly.
HAMLET: I would I had been there.   235

230 *beaver,* visor of his helmet.

HORATIO: It would have much amaz'd you.

HAMLET: Very like, very like. Stay'd it long?

HORATIO: While one with moderate haste might tell a hundred.

MARCELLUS: } Longer, longer.
BERNARDO: }

HORATIO: Not when I saw 't.

HAMLET: His beard was grizzled,—no?   240

HORATIO: It was, as I have seen it in his life,
A sable silver'd.

HAMLET: I will watch to-night;
Perchance 'twill walk again.

HORATIO: I warrant it will.

HAMLET: If it assume my noble father's person,
I'll speak to it, though hell itself should gape   245
And bid me hold my peace. I pray you all,
If you have hitherto conceal'd this sight,
Let it be tenable in your silence still;
And whatsoever else shall hap to-night,
Give it an understanding, but no tongue: 250
I will requite your loves. So, fare you well.
Upon the platform, 'twixt eleven and twelve,
I'll visit you.

ALL: Our duty to your honour.

HAMLET: Your loves, as mine to you. Farewell.

(Exeunt all but Hamlet.)

My father's spirit in arms! all is not well;   255
I doubt some foul play: would the night were come!
Till then sit still, my soul: foul deeds will rise,
Though all the earth o'erwhelm them, to men's eyes.   *(Exit.)*

Act I

Scene III

Polonius's apartment in the castle. Enter Laertes and Ophelia.

LAERTES: My necessaries are embark'd; farewell:
And, sister, as the winds give benefit
And convoy is assistant, do not sleep,
But let me hear from you.

OPHELIA: Do you doubt that?

LAERTES: For Hamlet and the trifling of his favour,   5
Hold it a fashion and a toy in blood,

---

256 *doubt,* suspect.   **3** *convoy is assistant,* a ship is ready.

A violet in the youth of primy nature,
Forward, not permanent, sweet, not lasting,
The perfume and suppliance of a minute;
No more.

OPHELIA: No more but so?

LAERTES: Think it no more: 10
For nature, crescent, does not grow alone
In thews and bulk, but, as this temple waxes,
The inward service of the mind and soul
Grows wide withal. Perhaps he loves you now,
And now no soil nor cautel doth besmirch 15
The virtue of his will; but you must fear,
His greatness weigh'd, his will is not his own;
For he himself is subject to his birth:
He may not, as unvalu'd persons do,
Carve for himself, for on his choice depends 20
The safety and health of this whole state;
And therefore must his choice be circumscrib'd
Unto the voice and yielding of that body
Whereof he is the head. Then if he says he loves you,
It fits your wisdom so far to believe it 25
As he in his particular act and place
May give his saying deed; which is no further
Than the main voice of Denmark goes withal.
Then weigh what loss your honour may sustain,
If with too credent ear you list his songs, 30
Or lose your heart, or your chaste treasure open
To his unmaster'd importunity.
Fear it, Ophelia, fear it, my dear sister,
And keep you in the rear of your affection,
Out of the shot and danger of desire. 35
The chariest maid is prodigal enough,
If she unmask her beauty to the moon;
Virtue itself 'scapes not calumnious strokes;
The canker galls the infants of the spring,
Too oft before their buttons be disclos'd, 40
And in the morn and liquid dew of youth
Contagious blastments are most imminent.
Be wary then; best safety lies in fear:
Youth to itself rebels, though none else near.

OPHELIA: I shall th' effect of this good lesson keep, 45

---

11 *crescent,* growing. **12** *temple,* the body. **14** *withal,* also. **15** *cautel,* deceit. **17** *His great-ness weigh'd,* when you consider his high rank. **19** *unvalu'd persons,* commoners. **23** *that body,* the state.

As watchman to my heart. But, good my brother,
Do not, as some ungracious pastors do,
Show me the steep and thorny way to heaven,
Whiles, like a puff'd and reckless libertine,
Himself the primrose path of dalliance treads,   50
And recks not his own rede.
LAERTES: O, fear me not.
I stay too long: but here my father comes.

(Enter Polonius.)

A double blessing is a double grace;
Occasion smiles upon a second leave.
POLONIUS: Yet here, Laertes! aboard, aboard, for shame!   55
The wind sits in the shoulder of your sail,
And you are stay'd for. There, my blessing with thee!
And these few precepts in thy memory
See thou character. Give thy thoughts no tongue,
Nor any unproportion'd thought his act.   60
Be thou familiar, but by no means vulgar.
Those friends thou hast, and their adoption tried,
Grapple them to thy soul with hoops of steel;
But do not dull thy palm with entertainment
Of each new-hatch'd, unfledg'd comrade. Beware   65
Of entrance to a quarrel, but being in,
Bear 't that th' opposed may beware of thee.
Give every man thy ear, but few thy voice;
Take each man's censure, but reserve thy judgment.
Costly thy habit as thy purse can buy,   70
But not express'd in fancy; rich, not gaudy;
For the apparel oft proclaims the man,
And they in France of the best rank and station
Are of a most select and generous chief in that.
Neither a borrower nor a lender be;   75
For loan oft loses both itself and friend,
And borrowing dulls the edge of husbandry.
This above all: to thine own self be true,
And it must follow, as the night the day,
Thou canst not then be false to any man.   80
Farewell; my blessing season this in thee!
LAERTES: Most humbly do I take my leave, my lord.

---

47 *ungracious,* lacking God's grace.   **51** *recks,* heeds; *rede,* advice; *fear me not,* don't worry about
me.   **59** *character,* write down.   **64** *dull . . . entertainment,* "numb your hand by welcoming."
70 *habit,* clothes.

POLONIUS: The time invites you; go, your servants tend.

LAERTES: Farewell, Ophelia; and remember well
What I have said to you.

OPHELIA: 'Tis in my memory lock'd,   85
And you yourself shall keep the key of it.

LAERTES: Farewell.   *(Exit.)*

POLONIUS: What is 't, Ophelia, he hath said to you?

OPHELIA: So please you, something touching the Lord Hamlet.

POLONIUS: Marry, well bethought: 90
'Tis told me, he hath very oft of late
Given private time to you; and you yourself
Have of your audience been most free and bounteous.
If it be so, as so 't is put on me,
And that in way of caution, I must tell you,   95
You do not understand yourself so clearly
As it behooves my daughter and your honour.
What is between you? give me up the truth.

OPHELIA: He hath, my lord, of late made many tenders
Of his affection to me.   100

POLONIUS: Affection! pooh! you speak like a green girl,
Unsifted in such perilous circumstance.
Do you believe his tenders, as you call them?

OPHELIA: I do not know, my lord, what I should think.

POLONIUS: Marry, I'll teach you: think yourself a baby;   105
That you have ta'en these tenders for true pay,
Which are not sterling. Tender yourself more dearly;
Or—not to crack the wind of the poor phrase,
Running it thus—you'll tender me a fool.

OPHELIA: My lord, he hath impórtun'd me with love   110
In honourable fashion.

POLONIUS: Ay, fashion you may call it; go to, go to.

OPHELIA: And hath given countenance to his speech, my lord,
With almost all the holy vows of heaven.

POLONIUS: Ay, springes to catch woodcocks. I do know,   115
When the blood burns, how prodigal the soul
Lends the tongue vows: these blazes, daughter,
Giving more light than heat, extinct in both,
Even in their promise, as it is a-making,
You must not take for fire. From this time   120
Be somewhat scanter of your maiden presence;
Set your entreatments at a higher rate

---

90 *Marry,* by the Virgin Mary.   **115** *springes,* snares; *woodcocks,* stupid birds, hence easily trapped
118 *extinct,* extinguished.

Than a command to parley. For Lord Hamlet,
Believe so much in him, that he is young,
And with a larger tether may he walk   125
Than may be given you: in few, Ophelia,
Do not believe his vows, for they are brokers,
Not of that dye which their investments show,
But mere implorators of unholy suits,
Breathing like sanctified and pious bawds,   130
The better to beguile. This is for all:
I would not, in plain terms, from this time forth,
Have you so slander any moment leisure,
As to give words or talk with the Lord Hamlet.
Look to 't, I charge you; come your ways.   135

OPHELIA: I shall obey, my lord.   *(Exeunt.)*

Act I

Scene IV

The Platform. Enter Hamlet, Horatio, and Marcellus.

HAMLET: The air bites shrewdly; it is very cold.
HORATIO: It is a nipping and an eager air.
HAMLET: What hour now?
HORATIO: I think it lacks of twelve.
MARCELLUS: No, it is struck.
HORATIO: Indeed? I heard it not: then it draws near the season   5
    Wherein the spirit held his wont to walk.

(A flourish of trumpets, and two pieces of ordnance shot off.)

    What does this mean, my lord?
HAMLET: The king doth wake to-night and takes his rouse,
    Keeps wassail, and the swaggering up-spring reels;
    And, as he drains his draughts of Rhenish down,   10
    The kettle-drum and trumpet thus bray out
    The triumph of his pledge.
HORATIO: Is it a custom?
HAMLET: Ay, marry, is 't:
    But to my mind, though I am native here
    And to the manner born, it is a custom   15
    More honour'd in the breach than the observance.
    This heavy-headed revel east and west

---

123 *command to parley,* offer to discuss terms of surrender.   **124** *so much,* only so much.
128 *investments,* clothing, with a monetary pun, and on *suits* following.   **2** *eager,* sharp.   **8** *wake,*
stay up; *takes his rouse,* is drinking heavily.   **9** *Keeps wassail,* holds a drinking bout; *up-spring,*
upstart.   **16** *More honour'd in the breach,* that would be more honorable if it were omitted.

Makes us traduc'd and tax'd of other nations:
They clepe us drunkards, and with swinish phrase
Soil our addition; and indeed it takes   20
From our achievements, though perform'd at height,
The pith and marrow of our attribute.
So, oft it chances in particular men,
That for some vicious mole of nature in them,
As, in their birth—wherein they are not guilty,   25
Since nature cannot choose his origin—
By the o'ergrowth of some complexion,
Oft breaking down the pales and forts of reason,
Or by some habit that too much o'er-leavens
The form of plausive manners, that these men,   30
Carrying, I say, the stamp of one defect,
Being nature's livery, or fortune's star,—
Their virtues else—be they as pure as grace,
As infinite as man may undergo—
Shall in the general censure take corruption   35
From that particular fault: the dram of eale
Doth all the noble substance often dout
To his own scandal.

    HORATIO: Look, my lord, it comes!

(Enter Ghost.)

    HAMLET: Angels and ministers of grace defend us!
Be thou a spirit of health or goblin damn'd,   40
Bring with thee airs from heaven or blasts from hell,
Be thy intents wicked or charitable,
Thou comest in such a questionable shape
That I will speak to thee: I'll call thee Hamlet,
King, father, royal Dane; O, answer me!   45
Let me not burst in ignorance, but tell
Why thy canóniz'd bones, hearsèd in death,
Have burst their cerements; why the sepúlchre,
Wherein we saw thee quietly inurn'd,
Hath op'd his ponderous and marble jaws,   50
To cast thee up again. What may this mean,
That thou, dead corse, again in cómplete steel
Revisit'st thus the glimpses of the moon,

---

18 *traduc'd and tax'd,* censured and reproached.   **19** *clepe,* call.   **19–20** *with . . . addition,* asperse our good name by calling us swine.   **21** *perform'd at height,* to the best of our ability.   **22** *attribute,* reputation.   **27** *complexion,* natural quality.   **28** *pales,* defenses.   **29** *o'er-leavens,* puts too much yeast into the dough.   **30** *plausive,* pleasing   **35** *general censure,* popular opinion.   **36** *eale,* probably a pun on *evil* and *oil.*   **37** *dout,* do out, banish.   **40** *spirit of health,* blessed spirit. **48** *cerements,* winding sheet.

Making night hideous; and we fools of nature
So horridly to shake our disposition   55
With thoughts beyond the reaches of our souls?
Say, why is this? wherefore? what should we do?

(Ghost beckons Hamlet.)

HORATIO: It beckons you to go away with it,
As if it some impartment did desire
To you alone.
MARCELLUS: Look, with what courteous action   60
It waves you to a more removèd ground:
But do not go with it.
HORATIO: No, by no means.
HAMLET: It will not speak; then I will follow it.
HORATIO: Do not, my lord.
HAMLET: Why, what should be the fear?
I do not set my life at a pin's fee;   65
And for my soul, what can it do to that,
Being a thing immortal as itself?
It waves me forth again; I'll follow it.
HORATIO: What if it tempt you toward the flood, my lord,
Or to the dreadful summit of the cliff   70
That beetles o'er his base into the sea,
And there assume some other horrible form,
Which might deprive your sovereignty of reason
And draw you into madness? think of it:
The very place puts toys of desperation,   75
Without more motive, into every brain
That looks so many fathoms to the sea
And hears it roar beneath.
HAMLET: It waves me still.
Go on; I'll follow thee.
MARCELLUS: You shall not go, my lord.
HAMLET: Hold off your hands.   80
HORATIO: Be rul'd; you shall not go.
HAMLET: My fate cries out,
And makes each petty artery in this body
As hardy as the Nemean lion's nerve.
Still am I call'd. Unhand me, gentleman.
By heaven, I'll make a ghost of him that lets me!   85
I say, away! Go on, I'll follow thee.

(Exeunt Ghost and Hamlet.)

___

69 *flood,* the sea, at the base of the castle's walls.   **71** *beetles,* overhangs.   **83** *Nemean lion,* a
monster slain by Hercules.   **85** *lets,* stops, like the *let* in tennis.

HORATIO: He waxes desperate with imagination.
MARCELLUS: Let's follow; 'tis not fit thus to obey him.
HORATIO: Have after. To what issue will this come?
MARCELLUS: Something is rotten in the state of Denmark.   90
HORATIO: Heaven will direct it.
MARCELLUS: Nay, let's follow him.

(Exeunt)

Act I

Scene V

Another part of the platform. Enter Ghost and Hamlet.

HAMLET: Where wilt thou lead me? speak! I'll go no further.
GHOST: Mark me.
HAMLET: I will.
GHOST: My hour is almost come,
  When I to sulph'rous and tormenting flames
  Must render up myself.
HAMLET: Alas, poor ghost!
GHOST: Pity me not, but lend thy serious hearing   5
  To what I shall unfold.
HAMLET: Speak. I am bound to hear.
GHOST: So art thou to revenge, when thou shalt hear.
HAMLET: What?
GHOST: I am thy father's spirit,
  Doom'd for a certain term to walk the night,   10
  And for the day confin'd to fast in fires,
  Till the foul crimes done in my days of nature
  Are burnt and purg'd away. But that I am forbid
  To tell the secrets of my prison-house,
  I could a tale unfold whose lightest word   15
  Would harrow up thy soul, freeze thy young blood,
  Make thy two eyes, like stars, start from their spheres,
  Thy knotted and combinèd locks to part
  And each particular hair to stand an end,
  Like quills upon the fretful porpentine: 20
  But this eternal blazon must not be
  To ears of flesh and blood. List, list, O, list!
  If thou didst ever thy dear father love—

91 *Heaven will direct it,* through Horatio, his spokesman, Shakespeare sets his thesis: contrary to what seems to be, God is in control.   **12** *foul crimes,* sins every human commits.   **20** *porpentine,* porcupine.

HAMLET: O God!

GHOST: Revenge his foul and most unnatural murder.   25

HAMLET: Murder!

GHOST: Murder most foul, as in the best it is;
  But this most foul, strange and unnatural.

HAMLET: Haste me to know't, that I, with wings as swift
  As meditation or the thoughts of love,   30
  May sweep to my revenge.

GHOST: I find thee apt;
  And duller shouldst thou be than the fat weed
  That roots itself in ease on Lethe wharf,
  Wouldst thou not stir in this. Now, Hamlet, hear:
  'Tis given out that, sleeping in my orchard,   35
  A serpent stung me; so the whole ear of Denmark
  Is by a forgèd process of my death
  Rankly abus'd: but know, thou noble youth,
  The serpent that did sting thy father's life
  Now wears his crown.

HAMLET: O my prophetic soul!   40
  My uncle!

GHOST: Ay, that incestuous, that adulterate beast,
  With witchcraft of his wit, with traitorous gifts,—
  O wicked wit and gifts, that have the power
  So to seduce!—won to his shameful lust   45
  The will of my most seeming-virtuous queen.
  O Hamlet, what a falling-off was there
  From me, whose love was of that dignity
  That it went hand in hand even with the vow
  I made to her in marriage, and to decline   50
  Upon a wretch whose natural gifts were poor
  To those of mine!
  But virtue, as it never will be mov'd,
  Though lewdness court it in a shape of heaven,
  So lust, though to a radiant angel link'd,   55
  Will sate itself in a celestial bed,
  And prey on garbage.
  But, soft! methinks I scent the morning air;
  Brief let me be. Sleeping within my orchard,
  My custom always of the afternoon,   60
  Upon my secure hour thy uncle stole,
  With juice of cursèd hebenon in a vial,

---

33 *Lethe,* the river, or lake, in Hell, whose drinking gave forgetfulness.   37 *process,* account.
62 *hebenon,* henbane, the yew tree, with berries considered poisonous, traditionally planted in church-yards.

And in the porches of my ears did pour
The leperous distillment; whose effect
Holds such an enmity with blood of man   65
That swift as quicksilver it courses through
The natural gates and alleys of the body,
And with a sudden vigour it doth posset
And curd, like eager droppings into milk,
The thin and wholesome blood: so did it mine;   70
And a most instant tetter bark'd about,
Most lazar-like, with vile and loathsome crust,
All my smooth body.
Thus was I, sleeping, by a brother's hand
Of life, of crown, of queen, at once dispatch'd: 75
Cut off even in the blossoms of my sin,
Unhousel'd, disappointed, unanel'd,
No reckoning made, but sent to my account
With all my imperfections on my head:
O, horrible! O, horrible! most horrible!   80
If thou hast nature in thee, bear it not;
Let not the royal bed of Denmark be
A couch for luxury and damned incest.
But, howsoever thou pursuest this act,
Taint not thy mind, nor let thy soul contrive   85
Against thy mother aught: leave her to heaven
And to those thorns that in her bosom lodge,
To prick and sting her. Fare thee well at once!
The glow-worm shows the matin to be near,
And 'gins to pale his uneffectual fire: 90
Adieu, adieu! Hamlet, remember me.   *(Exit.)*
HAMLET: O all you host of heaven! O earth! What else?
And shall I couple hell? O, fie! Hold, hold, my heart;
And you, my sinews, grow not instant old,
But bear me stiffly up. Remember thee!   95
Ay, thou poor ghost, while memory holds a seat
In this distracted globe. Remember thee!
Yea, from the table of my memory
I'll wipe away all trivial fond records,
All saws of books, all forms, all pressures past,   100
That youth and observation copied there;
And thy commandment all alone shall live

---

71 *instant tetter,* immediate scab.   **72** *lazar-like,* like leprosy.   **77** *Unhousel'd . . . unanel'd,* without having received the sacrament, unprepared (through confession), without anointing with holy oil.   **78** *reckoning,* of his sins through confession.   **89** *matin,* morning.   **97** *globe,* head of mine. **98** *table,* tablet.   **99** *fond,* foolish.   **100** *saws,* wise sayings; *forms,* ideas; *pressures past,* impressions from the past.

Within the book and volume of my brain,
Unmix'd with baser matter: yes, by heaven!
O most pernicious woman!   105
O villain, villain, smiling, damnèd villain!
My tables,—meet it is I set it down,
That one may smile, and smile, and be a villain;
At least I'm sure it may be so in Denmark.

(Writing.)

So, uncle, there you are. Now to my word;   110
It is "Adieu, adieu! remember me."
I have sworn 't.

MARCELLUS: *(Within)* My lord! my lord!
HORATIO:
MARCELLUS: *(Within)* Lord Hamlet!
HORATIO: *(Within)* Heaven secure him!
HAMLET: So be it!
HORATIO: *(Within)* Hillo, ho, ho, my lord!   115
HAMLET: Hillo, ho, ho, boy! come, bird, come.

(Enter Horatio and Marcellus.)

MARCELLUS: How is 't, my noble lord?
HORATIO: What news, my lord?
HAMLET: O, wonderful!
HORATIO: Good my lord, tell it.
HAMLET: No, you will reveal it.
HORATIO: Not I, my lord, by heaven!
MARCELLUS: Nor I, my lord.   120
HAMLET: How say you, then; would heart of man once think it?
But you'll be secret?
HORATIO:
                      Ay, by heaven, my lord.
MARCELLUS:
HAMLET: There's ne'er a villain dwelling in all Denmark
But he's an arrant knave.
HORATIO: There needs no ghost, my lord, come from the grave   125
To tell us this.
HAMLET: Why, right; you are i' the right;
And so, without more circumstance at all,
I hold it fit that we shake hands and part;
You, as your business and desire shall point you;
For every man has business and desire,   130
Such as it is; and for mine own poor part,
Look you, I'll go pray.

---

110 *word,* watchword. **116** *Hillo . . . come,* falconer's call to retrieve his bird. **121** *once think,* ever believe.

HORATIO: These are but wild and whirling words, my lord.

HAMLET: I'm sorry they offend you, heartily;
   Yes, faith, heartily.

HORATIO: There's no offence, my lord.   135

HAMLET: Yes, by Saint Patrick, but there is, Horatio,
   And much offence too. Touching this vision here,
   It is an honest ghost, that let me tell you:
   For your desire to know what is between us,
   O'ermaster 't as you may. And now, good friends,   140
   As you are friends, scholars, and soldiers,
   Give me one poor request.

HORATIO: What is 't, my lord? we will.

HAMLET: Never make known what you have seen to-night.

HORATIO:
MARCELLUS: } My lord, we will not.

HAMLET: Nay, but swear 't.

HORATIO: In faith,   145
   My lord, not I.

MARCELLUS: Nor I, my lord, in faith.

HAMLET: Upon my sword.

MARCELLUS: We have sworn, my lord, already.

HAMLET: Indeed, upon my sword, indeed.

GHOST: *(Beneath)* Swear.

HAMLET: Ah, ha, boy! say'st thou so? art thou there, truepenny?   150
   Come on—you hear this fellow in the cellarage—
   Consent to swear.

HORATIO: Propose the oath, my lord.

HAMLET: Never to speak of this that you have seen,
   Swear by my sword.

GHOST: *(Beneath)* Swear.   155

HAMLET: Hic et ubique? Then we'll shift our ground.
   Come hither, gentlemen,
   And lay your hands again upon my sword:
   Never to speak of this that you have heard,
   Swear by my sword.   160

GHOST: *(Beneath)* Swear.

HAMLET: Well said, old mole! Canst work i' the earth so fast?
   A worthy pioner! Once more remove, good friends.

HORATIO: O day and night, but this is wondrous strange!

HAMLET: And therefore as a stranger give it welcome.   165
   There are more things in heaven and earth, Horatio,

---

136 *Saint Patrick,* the keeper of Purgatory.   **138** *honest,* actual, not a demon in disguise.
147 *Upon my sword,* because the hilt formed a cross.   **150** *truepenny,* trusty fellow.   **156** *Hic et ubique?* Here and everywhere?   **163** *pioner,* military miner who tunnels under fortifications. *remove,* shift your position.

Than are dreamt of in your philosophy.
But come;
Here, as before, never, so help you mercy,
How strange or odd soe'er I bear myself, 170
As I perchance hereafter shall think meet
To put an antic disposition on,
That you, at such times seeing me, never shall,
With arms encumber'd thus, or this headshake,
Or by pronouncing of some doubtful phrase, 175
As "Well, well, we know," or "We could, an if we would,"
Or "If we list to speak," or "There be, an if they might,"
Or such ambiguous giving out, to note
That you know aught of me: this not to do,
So grace and mercy at your most need help you, 180
Swear.

GHOST: *(Beneath)* Swear.

HAMLET: Rest, rest, perturbèd spirit! *(They swear.)* So, gentle-
men,
With all my love I do commend me to you;
And what so poor a man as Hamlet is 185
May do, to express his love and friending to you,
God willing, shall not lack. Let us go in together;
And still your fingers on your lips, I pray.
The time is out of joint; O cursèd spite,
That ever I was born to set it right! 190
Nay, come, let's go together. *(Exeunt.)*

Act II

Scene I

Polonius's apartment in the castle. Enter Polonius and Reynaldo.

POLONIUS: Give him this money and these notes, Reynaldo.
REYNALDO: I will, my lord.
POLONIUS: You shall do marvellous wisely, good Reynaldo,
Before you visit him, to make inquire
Of his behaviour.
REYNALDO: My lord, I did intend it. 5
POLONIUS: Marry, well said; very well said. Look you, sir,
Inquire me first what Danskers are in Paris;
And how, and who, what means, and where they keep,
What company, at what expense; and finding

---

167 *your philosophy,* "than science dreams of," not Horatio's personal philosophy.   **172** *antic
disposition,* mad behavior.   **184** *commend . . . you,* put myself in your hands.   **7** *Danskers,* Danes.
8 *means,* money

By this encompassment and drift of question   10
That they do know my son, come you more nearer
Than your particular demands will touch it:
Take you, as 'twere, some distant knowledge of him;
As thus, "I know his father and his friends,
And in part him;" do you mark this, Reynaldo?   15
REYNALDO: Ay, very well, my lord.
POLONIUS: "And in part him; but" you may say "not well:
But, if 't be he I mean, he's very wild;
Addicted so and so;" and there put on him
What forgeries you please; marry, none so rank   20
As may dishonour him; take heed of that;
But, sir, such wanton, wild and usual slips
As are companions noted and most known
To youth and liberty.
REYNALDO: As gaming, my lord.
POLONIUS: Ay, or drinking, fencing, swearing, quarrelling,   25
Drabbing; you may go so far.
REYNALDO: My lord, that would dishonour him.
POLONIUS: 'Faith, no; as you may season it in the charge.
You must not put another scandal on him,
That he is open to incontinency;   30
That's not my meaning: but breathe his faults so quaintly
That they may seem the taints of liberty,
The flash and outbreak of a fiery mind,
A savageness in unreclaimèd blood,
Of general assault.
REYNALDO: But, my good lord,—   35
POLONIUS: Wherefore should you do this?
REYNALDO: Ay, my lord,
I would know that.
POLONIUS: Marry, sir, here's my drift;
And, I believe, it is a fetch of warrant:
You laying these slight sullies on my son,
As 'twere a thing a little soil'd i' the working,   40
Mark you,
Your party in converse, him you would sound,
Having ever seen in the prenominate crimes
The youth you breathe of guilty, be assured
He closes with you in this consequence;   45
"Good sir," or so, or "friend," or "gentleman,"

---

10 *encompassment,* roundabout approach.   **12** *particular demands,* specific questions.   **13** *Take you,* pretend.   **26** *Drabbing,* whoring.   **28** *season it,* tone it down.   **31** *quaintly,* artfully.   **34** *unreclaimèd,* untamed.   **35** *general assault,* common to all.   **38** *fetch of warrant,* device that is sure to work.   **43** *prenominate,* already mentioned.   **45** *closes . . . in this consequence,* agrees with you as follows.

According to the phrase or the addition
Of man and country.
REYNALDO: Very good, my lord.
POLONIUS: And then, sir, does he this—he does
  —what was I about to say? By the mass, I was about to say something: 50
  Where did I leave?
REYNALDO: At "closes in the consequence," at "friend or so," and
  "gentleman."
POLONIUS: At "closes in the consequence," ay, marry;
  He closes thus: "I know the gentleman;   55
  I saw him yesterday, or t'other day,
  Or then, or then; with such, or such; and, as you say,
  There was a' gaming; there o'ertook in 's rouse;
  There falling out at tennis;" or perchance,
  "I saw him enter such a house of sale,"   60
  Videlicet, a brothel, or so forth.
  See you now;
  Your bait of falsehood takes this carp of truth;
  And thus do we of wisdom and of reach,
  With windlasses and with assays of bias,   65
  By indirections find directions out:
  So by my former lecture and advice,
  Shall you my son. You have me, have you not?
REYNALDO: My lord, I have.
POLONIUS: God be wi' you; fare you well.
REYNALDO: Good my lord!   70
POLONIUS: Observe his inclination in yourself.
REYNALDO: I shall, my lord.
POLONIUS: And let him ply his music.
REYNALDO: Well, my lord.
POLONIUS: Farewell!

(Exit Reynaldo.)

(Enter Ophelia.)

  How now, Ophelia! what's the matter?
OPHELIA: O, my lord, my lord, I have been so affrighted!   75
POLONIUS: With what, i' the name of God?
OPHELIA: My lord, as I was sewing in my closet,
  Lord Hamlet, with his doublet all unbrac'd,
  No hat upon his head; his stockings foul'd,
  Ungarter'd, and down-gyvèd to his ancle;   80
  Pale as his shirt; his knees knocking each other;
  And with a look so piteous in purport

---

58 *o'ertook in 's rouse*, drunk.   **61** *Videlicet*, that is to say.   **65** *bias*, a curve in bowling.
71 *in yourself*, by your own inclinations.   **77** *closet*, private sitting room.   **78** *unbrac'd*, unfastened.   **80** *down-gyvèd*, hanging down like fetters.

As if he had been loosèd out of hell
To speak of horrors—he comes before me.
POLONIUS: Mad for thy love?
OPHELIA: My lord, I do not know;   85
But truly, I do fear it.
POLONIUS: What said he?
OPHELIA: He took me by the wrist and held me hard;
Then goes he to the length of all his arm;
And, with his other hand thus o'er his brow,
He falls to such perusal of my face   90
As he would draw it. Long stay'd he so;
At last, a little shaking of mine arm
And thrice his head thus waving up and down,
He rais'd a sigh so piteous and profound
As it did seem to shatter all his bulk   95
And end his being. That done, he lets me go,
And, with his head over his shoulder turn'd,
He seem'd to find his way without his eyes;
For out o' doors he went without their helps,
And, to the last, bended their light on me.   100
POLONIUS: Come, go with me: I will go seek the king.
This is the very ecstasy of love,
Whose violent property fordoes itself
And leads the will to desperate undertakings
As oft as any passion under heaven   105
That does afflict our natures. I am sorry.
What, have you given him any hard words of late?
OPHELIA: No, my good lord, but, as you did command,
I did repel his letters and denied
His access to me.
POLONIUS: That hath made him mad.   110
I am sorry that with better heed and judgment
I had not quoted him; I fear'd he did but trifle,
And meant to wrack thee; but, beshrew my jealousy!
By heaven, it is as proper to our age
To cast beyond ourselves in our opinions   115
As it is common for the younger sort
To lack discretion. Come, go we to the king:
This must be known; which, being kept close, might move
More grief to hide than hate to utter love.
Come.   (*Exeunt.*)   120

---

85 *for thy love,* for love of you.   **102** *ecstasy,* insanity.   **112** *quoted,* observed.   **113** *wrack,* wreck; *jealousy,* suspicion.   **118** *being kept close,* if it were concealed.   **118–119** *might move . . . utter love,* might cause more grief through its concealment than it would arouse hatred (on the part of Hamlet or his parents) through telling about the love.

Act II

Scene II

A room in the castle. Enter King, Queen, Rosencrantz, Guildenstern, and others.

 KING: Welcome, dear Rosencrantz and Guildenstern!
  Moreover that we much did long to see you,
  The need we have to use you did provoke
  Our hasty sending. Something have you heard
  Of Hamlet's transformation; so call it,   5
  Sith nor the exterior nor the inward man
  Resembles that it was. What it should be,
  More than his father's death, that thus hath put him
  So much from the understanding of himself,
  I cannot dream of: I entreat you both,   10
  That, being of so young days brought up with him,
  And sith so neighbour'd to his youth and haviour,
  That you vouchsafe your rest here in our court
  Some little time; so by your companies
  To draw him on to pleasures, and to gather,   15
  So much as from occasion you may glean,
  Whether aught, to us unknown, afflicts him thus,
  That, open'd, lies within our remedy.
 QUEEN: Good gentlemen, he hath much talk'd of you;
  And sure I am two men there are not living   20
  To whom he more adheres. If it will please you
  To show us so much gentry and good will
  As to expend your time with us awhile,
  For the supply and profit of our hope,
  Your visitation shall receive such thanks   25
  As fits a king's remembrance.
 ROSENCRANTZ: Both your majesties
  Might, by the sovereign power you have of us,
  Put your dread pleasures more into command
  Than to entreaty.
 GUILDENSTERN: But we both obey,
  And here give up ourselves, in the full bent   30
  To lay our service freely at your feet,
  To be commanded.
 KING: Thanks, Rosencrantz and gentle Guildenstern.
 QUEEN: Thanks, Guildenstern and gentle Rosencrantz;
  And I beseech you instantly to visit   35

---

13 *vouchsafe your rest,* agree to stay. **26** *fits,* befits. **30** *in . . . bent,* as much as we can—a metaphor from archery.

My too much chang èd son. Go, some of you,
And bring these gentlemen where Hamlet is.
GUILDENSTERN: Heavens make our presence and our practices
Pleasant and helpful to him!
QUEEN: Ay, amen!

(Exeunt Rosencrantz, Guildenstern, and some Attendants.)

(Enter Polonius.)

POLONIUS: The ambassadors from Norway, my good lord,   40
Are joyfully return'd.
KING: Thou still hast been the father of good news.
POLONIUS: Have I, my lord? I assure my good liege,
I hold my duty, as I hold my soul,
Both to my God and to my gracious king;   45
And I do think, or else this brain of mine
Hunts not the trail of policy so sure
As it hath us'd to do, that I have found
The very cause of Hamlet's lunacy.
KING: O, speak of that; that do I long to hear.   50
POLONIUS: Give first admittance to the ambassadors;
My news shall be the fruit to that great feast.
KING: Thyself do grace to them, and bring them in.   *(Exit Polonius.)*
He tells me, my dear Gertrude, he hath found
The head and source of all your son's distemper.   55
QUEEN: I doubt it is no other but the main:
His father's death, and our o'erhasty marriage.
KING: Well, we shall sift him.

(Enter Polonius, Voltimand, and Cornelius.)

                    Welcome, my good friends!
Say, Voltimand, what from our brother Norway?
VOLTIMAND: Most fair return of greetings and desires.   60
Upon our first, he sent out to suppress
His nephew's levies; which to him appear'd
To be a preparation 'gainst the Polack;
But, better look'd into, he truly found
It was against your highness: whereat griev'd,   65
That so his sickness, age, and impotence
Was falsely borne in hand, sends out arrests
On Fortinbras; which he, in brief, obeys;
Receives rebuke from Norway, and in fine
Makes vow before his uncle never more   70

42 *still,* always.   67 *arrests,* a royal summons.

To give the assay of arms against your majesty.
Whereon old Norway, overcome with joy,
Gives him three thousand crowns in annual fee,
And his commission to employ those soldiers,
So levied as before, against the Polack,   75
With an entreaty, herein further shown,

(Giving a paper.)

That it might please you to give quiet pass
Through your dominions for this enterprise,
On such regards of safety and allowance
As therein are set down.
KING: It likes us well;   80
And at our more consider'd time we'll read,
Answer, and think upon this business.
Meantime we thank you for your well-took labour.
Go to your rest; at night we'll feast together:
Most welcome home!

(Exeunt Voltimand and Cornelius.)

POLONIUS: This business is well ended.   85
My liege, and madam, to expostulate
What majesty should be, what duty is,
Why day is day, night night, and time is time,
Were nothing but to waste night, day, and time.
Therefore, since brevity is the soul of wit,   90
And tediousness the limbs and outward flourishes,
I will be brief. Your noble son is mad.
Mad call I it; for, to define true madness,
What is 't but to be nothing else but mad?
But let that go.
QUEEN: More matter, with less art.   95
POLONIUS: Madam, I swear I use no art at all.
That he is mad, 'tis true: 'tis true 'tis pity;
And pity 'tis 'tis true: a foolish figure;
But farewell it, for I will use no art.
Mad let us grant him, then; and now remains   100
That we find out the cause of this effect,
Or rather say, the cause of this defect,
For this effect defective comes by cause;
Thus it remains, and the remainder thus.
Perpend.   105
I have a daughter—have while she is mine—

90 *wit*, good sense.   **98** *figure*, figure of speech.   **105** *Perpend*, consider.

Who, in her duty and obedience, mark,
Hath given me this. Now gather, and surmise.

(Reads)

> "To the celestial and my soul's idol,
> the most beautified Ophelia,"   110

That's an ill phrase, a vile phrase; "beautified" is a vile phrase; but you
shall hear. Thus:

(Reads)

> "In her excellent white bosom, these, &c."

QUEEN: Came this from Hamlet to her?

POLONIUS: Good madam, stay awhile; I will be faithful.   115

(Reads)

> "Doubt thou the stars are fire;
>   Doubt that the sun doth move;
> Doubt truth to be a liar;
>   But never doubt I love.
> "O dear Ophelia, I am ill at these numbers;   120
> I have not art to reckon my groans; but that
> I love thee best, O most best, believe it.
> Adieu.
>   "Thine evermore, most dear lady,
>   whilst this machine is to him,
>   HAMLET."

This, in obedience, hath my daughter shown me,   125
And more above, hath his solicitings,
As they fell out by time, by means and place,
All given to mine ear.

KING: But how hath she
Receiv'd his love?

POLONIUS: What do you think of me?

KING: As of a man faithful and honourable.   130

POLONIUS: I would fain prove so. But what might you think,
When I had seen this hot love on the wing—
As I perceiv'd it, I must tell you that,
Before my daughter told me—what might you,
Or my dear majesty your queen here, think,   135
If I had play'd the desk or table-book,
Or given my heart a winking, mute and dumb,
Or look'd upon this love with idle sight;
What might you think? No, I went round to work,
And my young mistress thus I did bespeak: 140

---

119 *ill at these numbers,* unskillful at this verse making.   **124** *machine,* body.   **127** *above,* besides.
136 *play'd . . . table-book,* shut the knowledge up as in a desk or notebook.

"Lord Hamlet is a prince, out of thy star;
This must not be;" and then I prescripts gave her,
That she should lock herself from his resort,
Admit no messengers, receive no tokens.
Which done, she took the fruits of my advice;   145
And he, repulsed—a short tale to make—
Fell into a sadness, then into a fast,
Thence to a watch, thence into a weakness,
Thence to a lightness, and, by this declension,
Into the madness wherein now he raves,   150
And all we mourn for.
KING: Do you think 'tis this?
QUEEN: It may be, very likely.
POLONIUS: Hath there been such a time—I'd fain know that—
That I have positively said "'Tis so,"
When it proved otherwise?
KING: Not that I know.   155
POLONIUS: *(Pointing to his head and shoulder)*
Take this from this, if this be otherwise:
If circumstances lead me, I will find
Where truth is hid, though it were hid indeed
Within the centre.
KING: How may we try it further?
POLONIUS: You know, sometimes he walks four hours together   160
Here in the lobby.
QUEEN: So he does indeed.
POLONIUS: At such a time I'll loose my daughter to him:
Be you and I behind an arras then;
Mark the encounter; if he love her not
And be not from his reason fall'n thereon,   165
Let me be no assistant for a state,
But keep a farm and carters.
KING: We will try it.
QUEEN: But, look, where sadly the poor wretch comes reading.
POLONIUS: Away, I do beseech you, both away.
I'll board him presently.

(Exeunt King, Queen, and Attendants.)

(Enter Hamlet, reading.)

O, give me leave,
How does my good Lord Hamlet?
HAMLET: Well, God-a-mercy.

---

141 *star,* in a sphere above yours.   **148** *watch,* insomnia.   **156** *this be otherwise,* if I be wrong.
159 *centre,* center of the earth; *try,* test.   **163** *arras,* tapestry hanging loose against the wall.

POLONIUS: Do you know me, my lord?

HAMLET: Excellent well; you are a fishmonger.

POLONIUS: Not I, my lord.   175

HAMLET: Then I would you were so honest a man.

POLONIUS: Honest, my lord!

HAMLET: Ay, sir; to be honest, as this world goes, is to be one man picked
    out of ten thousand.

POLONIUS: That's very true, my lord.   180

HAMLET: For if the sun breed maggots in a dead dog, being a god kissing
    carrion,—Have you a daughter?

POLONIUS: I have, my lord.

HAMLET: Let her not walk i' the sun: conception is a blessing; but not
    as your daughter may conceive. Friend, look to 't.   185

POLONIUS: *(Aside)* How say you by that? Still harping on my daughter:
    yet he knew me not at first; he said I was a fishmonger: he is far gone,
    far gone: and truly in my youth I suffered much extremity for love;
    very near this. I'll speak to him again. What do you read, my lord?

HAMLET: Words, words, words.   190

POLONIUS: What is the matter, my lord?

HAMLET: Between who?

POLONIUS: I mean, the matter that you read, my lord.

HAMLET: Slanders, sir: for the satirical rogue says here that old men have
    grey beards, that their faces are wrinkled, their eyes purging thick   195
    amber and plum-tree gum and that they have a plentiful lack of wit,
    together with most weak hams: all which, sir, though I most power-
    fully and potently believe, yet I hold it not honesty to have it thus
    set down, for yourself, sir, should be old as I am, if like a crab you
    could go backward.   200

POLONIUS: *(Aside)* Though this be madness, yet there is method in 't.
    Will you walk out of the air, my lord?

HAMLET: Into my grave.

POLONIUS: Indeed, that is out o' the air. *(Aside)* How pregnant some-
    times his replies are! a happiness that often madness hits on, which
    reason and sanity could not so prosperously be delivered of. I will   205
    leave him, and suddenly contrive the means of meeting between him
    and my daughter.—My honourable lord, I will most humbly take
    my leave of you.

HAMLET: You cannot, sir, take from me any thing that I will more
    willingly part withal: except my life, except my life, except my life.

POLONIUS: Fare you well, my lord.   210

HAMLET: These tedious old fools!

(Enter Rosencrantz and Guildenstern.)

---

175 *fishmonger,* a term for "whoremonger" or "bawd."   **183** *conception,* (1) understanding, (2)
pregnancy.   **198** *honesty,* decency.   **204** *happiness,* pointedness.   **206** *suddenly,* immediately.

POLONIUS: You go to seek the Lord Hamlet; there he is.
ROSENCRANTZ: [*To* POLONIUS] God save you, sir!

(Exit Polonius.)

GUILDENSTERN: My honoured lord! 215
ROSENCRANTZ: My most dear lord!
HAMLET: My excellent good friends! How dost thou, Guildenstern? Ah,
    Rosencrantz! Good lads, how do ye both?
ROSENCRANTZ: As the indifferent children of the earth.
GUILDENSTERN: Happy, in that we are not overhappy;
    On Fortune's cap we are not the very button. 220
HAMLET: Nor the soles of her shoe?
ROSENCRANTZ: Neither, my lord.
HAMLET: Then you live about her waist, or in the middle of her favours?
GUILDENSTERN: 'Faith, her privates we.
HAMLET: In the secret parts of Fortune? O, most true; she is a strumpet.
    What's the news? 225
ROSENCRANTZ: None, my lord, but that the world's grown honest.
HAMLET: Then is doomsday near; but your news is not true. Let me
    question more in particular: what have you, my good friends, de-
    served at the hands of Fortune, that she sends you to prison hither?
GUILDENSTERN: Prison, my lord!
HAMLET: Denmark's a prison.
ROSENCRANTZ: Then is the world one. 230
HAMLET: A goodly one; in which there are many confines, wards, and
    dungeons, Denmark being one o' the worst.
ROSENCRANTZ: We think not so, my lord.
HAMLET: Why, then, 'tis none to you; for there is nothing either good
    or bad, but thinking makes it so: to me it is a prison.
ROSENCRANTZ: Why then, your ambition makes it one; 'tis too narrow
    for your mind.
HAMLET: O God, I could be bounded in a nutshell and count myself a
    king of infinite space, were it not that I have bad dreams. 235
GUILDENSTERN: Which dreams indeed are ambition, for the very sub-
    stance of the ambitious is merely the shadow of a dream.
HAMLET: A dream itself is but a shadow.
ROSENCRANTZ: Truly, and I hold ambition of so airy and light a quality
    that it is but a shadow's shadow.
HAMLET: Then are our beggars bodies, and our monarchs and out-
    stretched heroes the beggars' shadows. Shall we to the court? for,
    by my fay, I cannot reason.

218 *indifferent,* ordinary.   239 *beggars bodies . . . beggars' shadows,* "Then beggars, without ambition, are the actual bodies, real people, and monarchs and overreaching heroes are but the elongated
shadows of beggars."

ROSENCRANTZ: ⎫
GUILDENSTERN: ⎭   We'll wait upon you.   240

HAMLET: No such matter; I will not sort you with the rest of my servants, for, to speak to you like an honest man, I am most dreadfully attended. But, in the beaten way of friendship, what make you at Elsinore?

ROSENCRANTZ: To visit you, my lord; no other occasion.   245

HAMLET: Beggar that I am, I am even poor in thanks; but I thank you: and sure, dear friends, my thanks are too dear a halfpenny. Were you not sent for? Is it your own inclining? Is it a free visitation? Come, deal justly with me: come, come; nay, speak.

GUILDENSTERN: What should we say, my lord?   250

HAMLET: Why, any thing, but to the purpose. You were sent for; and there is a kind of confession in your looks which your modesties have not craft enough to colour: I know the good king and queen have sent for you.

ROSENCRANTZ: To what end, my lord?   255

HAMLET: That you must teach me. But let me conjure you, by the rights of our fellowship, by the consonancy of our youth, by the obligation of our ever-preservèd love, and by what more dear a better proposer could charge you withal, be even and direct with me, whether you were sent for, or no?   260

ROSENCRANTZ: *(Aside to Guildenstern.)* What say you?

HAMLET: *(Aside)* Nay, then, I have an eye of you.—If you love me, hold not off.

GUILDENSTERN: My lord, we were sent for.

HAMLET: I will tell you why; so shall my anticipation prevent your discovery, and your secrecy to the king and queen moult no feather.   265 I have of late—but wherefore I know not—lost all my mirth, forgone all custom of exercises; and indeed it goes so heavily with my disposition that this goodly frame, the earth, seems to me a sterile promontory, this most excellent canopy, the air, look you, thisbrave o'erhanging firmament, this majestical roof fretted with golden fire,   270 why, it appears no other thing to me than a foul and pestilent congregation of vapours. What a piece of work is a man! how noble in reason! how infinite in faculty! in form and moving how express and admirable! in action how like an angel! in apprehension how like a god! the beauty of the world! the paragon of animals! And yet, to   275 me, what is this quintessence of dust? Man delights not me; no, nor woman neither, though by your smiling you seem to say so.

---

240 *wait upon,* accompany.   **253** *colour,* disguise.   **256** *conjure,* urge.   **259** *charge you withal,* urge you with; *even,* straightforward.   **262** *an eye of you,* an eye on you.   **265** *prevent your discovery,* anticipate your disclosure.   **269** *brave,* beautiful.   **270** *fretted,* adorned.   **273** *faculty,* capacity.   **276** *quintessence,* the fifth or purest essence of which the heavenly bodies were supposed to be composed, and presumed latent in all things.

ROSENCRANTZ: My lord, there was no such stuff in my thoughts.

HAMLET: Why did you laugh then, when I said "man delights not me"?

ROSENCRANTZ: To think, my lord, if you delight not in man, what lenten
entertainment the players shall receive from you: we coted them on
the way; and hither are they coming, to offer you service.   280

HAMLET: He that plays the king shall be welcome; his majesty shall have
tribute of me; the adventurous knight shall use his foil and target;
the lover shall not sigh gratis; the humorous man shall end his part
in peace; the clown shall make those laugh whose lungs are tickle
o' the sere; and the lady shall say her mind freely, or the blank verse   285
shall halt for 't. What players are they?

ROSENCRANTZ: Even those you were wont to take delight in, the tragedi-
ans of the city.

HAMLET: How chances it they travel? Their residence, both in reputation
and profit, was better both ways.

ROSENCRANTZ: I think their inhibition comes by the means of the late
innovation.

HAMLET: Do they hold the same estimation they did when I was in the
city? are they so followed?   290

ROSENCRANTZ: No, indeed, are they not.

HAMLET: How comes it? do they grow rusty?

ROSENCRANTZ: Nay, their endeavour keeps in the wonted pace: but
there is, sir, an aery of children, little eyases, that cry out on the top
of question, and are most tyrannically clapped for 't: these are now   295
the fashion, and so berattle the common stages—so they call them
—that many wearing rapiers are afraid of goose-quills and dare
scarce come thither.

HAMLET: What, are they children? who maintains 'em? how are they
escoted? Will they pursue the quality no longer than they can sing?   300
will they not say afterwards, if they should grow themselves to
common players—as it is most like, if their means are no better—
their writers do them wrong, to make them exclaim against their
own succession?

280 *lenten entertainment,* meagre reception.   280 *coted,* overtook and passed.   283 *foil and target,*
rapier and shield.   283 *humorous man,* the humor character, the one ruled by a single folly; *in peace,*
without interruption from the audience.   285 *tickle o' the sere,* quick on the trigger.   286 *or
. . . for't,* even though the blank verse has to limp for her to do it.   288 *residence,* in one of the
city theatres.   289 *inhibition,* formal prohibition from acting.   289 *late innovation,* recent novelty,
probably the acting of the Children of the Revels in the Blackfriars' Theatre.   290 *so followed,* as
popular as they were.   294 *aery,* nest.   294 *eyases,* young hawks.   295 *on . . . question,* at a pitch
shriller than ordinary conversation.   295 *tyrannically,* violently.   296 *berattle,* run down.
297 *wearing rapiers,* gentlemen of fashion.   297 *goose-quills,* pens of satirists.   300 *escoted,* supported.   300 *pursue the quality,* continue in their profession.   301 *than . . . sing,* until their voices
change.   302 *common,* regular.   302 *like,* likely.   302 *means are no better,* if no better opportunity offers.   304 *succession,* future profession.

ROSENCRANTZ: 'Faith, there has been much to do on both sides; and the 305
nation holds it no sin to tarre them to controversy: there was, for
a while, no money bid for argument, unless the poet and the player
went to cuffs in the question.

HAMLET: Is 't possible?

GUILDENSTERN: O, there has been much throwing about of brains. 310

HAMLET: Do the boys carry it away?

ROSENCRANTZ: Ay, that they do, my lord; Hercules and his load too.

HAMLET: It is not very strange; for mine uncle is king of Denmark, and
those that would make mows at him while my father lived, give
twenty, forty, fifty, an hundred ducats a-piece for his picture in 315
little. 'Sblood, there is something in this more than natural, if philosophy could find it out.

(Flourish of trumpets within.)

GUILDENSTERN: There are the players.

HAMLET: Gentlemen, you are welcome to Elsinore. Your hands, come
then! The appurtenance of welcome is fashion and ceremony: let me 320
comply with you in this garb, lest my extent to the players, which,
I tell you, must show fairly outward, should more appear like
entertainment than yours. You are welcome; but my uncle-father
and aunt-mother are deceived.

GUILDENSTERN: In what, my dear lord? 325

HAMLET: I am but mad north-north-west: when the wind is southerly I
know a hawk from a handsaw.

(Reenter Polonius.)

POLONIUS: Well be with you, gentlemen!

HAMLET: Hark you, Guildenstern; and you too: at each ear a hearer: that
great baby you see there is not yet out of his swaddling-clouts.

ROSENCRANTZ: Happily he's the second time come to them; for they say
an old man is twice a child. 330

HAMLET: I will prophesy he comes to tell me of the players; mark it. You
say right, sir: o' Monday morning; 'twas so indeed.

POLONIUS: My lord, I have news to tell you.

HAMLET: My lord, I have news to tell you.
When Roscius was an actor in Rome,—

---

305 *to do,* commotion.   **305** *both sides,* i.e., the children and the adult companies.   **306** *tarre,* egg
on.   **307** *argument,* plot for a play.   **308** *went to cuffs,* came to blows; *question,* controversy.
311 *carry it away,* win out.   **312** *Hercules...load,* the Globe Theatre; its sign was Hercules carrying
a globe on his shoulders.   **314** *mows,* faces.   **316** *picture in little,* miniature.   **320** *appurtenance
...ceremony,* the proper accompaniment of welcome is fashionable ceremony.   **321** *extent,* expression of welcome.   **323** *entertainment,* proper hospitality.   **326** *hawk...handsaw,* a proverbial
phrase for "I know what's what."   **330** *Happily,* perhaps.   **334** *Roscius,* famous Roman actor.

POLONIUS: The actors are come hither, my lord.   335

HAMLET: Buzz, buzz!

POLONIUS: Upon mine honour,—

HAMLET: Then came each actor on his ass,—

POLONIUS: The best actors in the world, either for tragedy, comedy,
    history, pastoral, pastoral-comical, historical-pastoral, tragical-his-   340
    torical, tragical-comical-historical-pastoral, scene individable, or
    poem unlimited: Seneca cannot be too heavy, nor Plautus too light.
    For the law of writ and the liberty, these are the only men.

HAMLET: O Jephthah, judge of Israel, what a treasure hadst thou!

POLONIUS: What a treasure had he, my lord?   345

HAMLET: Why,

    "One fair daughter, and no more,
    The which he loved passing well."

POLONIUS: *(Aside)* Still on my daughter.

HAMLET: Am I not i' the right, old Jephthah?   350

POLONIUS: If you call me Jephthah, my lord, I have a daughter that I
    love passing well.

HAMLET: Nay, that follows not.

POLONIUS: What follows, then, my lord?

HAMLET: Why,

    "As by lot, God wot," and then, you know,
    "It came to pass, as most like it was,"—the first row of the pious   355
    chanson will show you more, for look, where my abridgement
    comes.

(Enter four or five Players.)

    You are welcome, masters; welcome, all. I am glad to see thee well.
    Welcome, good friends. O, my old friend! thy face is valanced since
    I saw thee last; comest thou to beard me in Denmark? What, my   360
    young lady and mistress! By'r lady, your ladyship is nearer to
    heaven than when I saw you last, by the altitude of a chopine. Pray
    God, your voice, like a piece of uncurrent gold, be not cracked
    within the ring. Masters, you are all welcome. We'll e'en to 't like
    French falconers, fly at any thing we see: we'll have a speech   365
    straight. Come, give us a taste of your quality; come, a passionate
    speech.

FIRST PLAYER: What speech, my lord?

---

341 *scene individable,* play observing unity of place; *poem unlimited,* a play not limited to one place.
343 *law . . . liberty,* written or extempory plays.   **344** *Jephthah . . . Israel,* title of a popular ballad
about Jephthah, who sacrificed his daughter (Judges, II. 30–40).   **356** *row,* stanza; *pious chanson,*
sacred ballad.   **359** *valanced,* fringed with a beard.   **362** *chopine,* thick-soled shoe.   **364** *cracked
. . . ring,* a crack in a gold coin within a ring enclosing the sovereign's head at the center made it
unfit for legal tender. The voices of boys, who played the female roles, would eventually "crack" as
they matured.   **366** *straight,* at once.

HAMLET: I heard thee speak me a speech once, but it was never acted;
or, if it was, not above once; for the play, I remember, pleased not   370
the million; 'twas caviare to the general; but it was—as I received
it, and others, whose judgements in such matters cried in the top
of mine—an excellent play, well digested in the scenes, set down
with as much modesty as cunning. I remember, one said there were
no sallets in the lines to make the matter savoury, nor no matter in   375
the phrase that might indict the author of affectation; but called it
an honest method, as wholesome as sweet, and by very much more
handsome than fine. One speech in it I chiefly loved: 'twas Æneas'
tale to Dido; and thereabout of it especially, where he speaks of
Priam's slaughter; if it live in your memory, begin at this line: let   380
me see, let me see—
"The rugged Pyrrhus, like the Hyrcanian beast,"—
it is not so:—it begins with Pyrrhus:—
"The rugged Pyrrhus, he whose sable arms,
Black as his purpose, did the night resemble   385
When he lay couched in the ominous horse,
Hath now this dread and black complexion smear'd
With heraldry more dismal; head to foot
Now is he total gules; horridly trick'd
With blood of fathers, mothers, daughters, sons,   390
Baked and impasted with the parching streets,
That lend a tyrannous and damned light
To their lord's murder: roasted in wrath and fire,
And thus o'er-sized with coagulate gore,
With eyes like carbuncles, the hellish Pyrrhus   395
Old grandsire Priam seeks."
So, proceed you.
POLONIUS: 'Fore God, my lord, well spoken, with good accent and good
discretion.
FIRST PLAYER: "Anon he finds him
Striking too short at Greeks; his antique sword,   400
Rebellious to his arm, lies where it falls,
Repugnant to command: unequal match'd,
Pyrrhus at Priam drives; in rage strikes wide;
But with the whiff and wind of his fell sword
The unnerved father falls. Then senseless Ilium,   405
Seeming to feel this blow, with flaming top

---

371 *caviare to the general,* like caviar, not relished by the crowd.   **375** *sallets,* "sallads," spicy jests.
382 *Pyrrhus,* the son of Achilles; *Hyrcanian beast,* the tiger of Hyrcania, a wild district north of the
Caspian Sea.   **384** *sable arms,* with a black design on his shield.   **388** *heraldry,* symbols.
389 *gules,* heraldic term for red; *trick'd,* heraldic term for "decorated."   **391** *impasted,* made into
a paste and baked; *parching,* because of the fire raging in the city.   **394** *o'er-sized,* glued over.
405 *senseless Ilium,* the citadel of Troy, incapable of feeling.

Stoops to his base, and with a hideous crash
Takes prisoner Pyrrhus' ear: for, lo! his sword,
Which was declining on the milky head
Of reverend Priam, seem'd i' the air to stick: 410
So, as a painted tyrant, Pyrrhus stood,
And like a neutral to his will and matter,
Did nothing.
But, as we often see, against some storm,
A silence in the heavens, the rack stand still,   415
The bold winds speechless and the orb below
As hush as death, anon the dreadful thunder
Doth rend the region, so, after Pyrrhus' pause,
Arousèd vengeance sets him new awork;
And never did the Cyclops' hammers fall   420
On Mars's armour, forg'd for proof eterne,
With less remorse than Pyrrhus' bleeding sword
Now falls on Priam.
Out, out, thou strumpet, Fortune! All you gods,
In general synod, take away her power;   425
Break all the spokes and fellies from her wheel,
And bowl the round nave down the hill of heaven,
As low as to the fiends!"
POLONIUS: This is too long.
HAMLET: It shall to the barber's, with your beard. Prithee, say on: he's
    for a jig or a tale of bawdry, or he sleeps: say on: come to Hecuba.

                                                                  430
FIRST PLAYER: "But who, O, who had seen the mobled queen—"
HAMLET: "The mobled queen?"
POLONIUS: That's good; "mobled queen" is good.
FIRST PLAYER: "Run barefoot up and down, threatening the flames
    With bisson rheum; a clout upon that head   435
    Where late the diadem stood, and for a robe,
    About her lank and all o'er-teemèd loins,
    A blanket, in the alarm of fear caught up;
    Who this had seen, with tongue in venom steep'd,
    'Gainst Fortune's state would treason have pronounc'd: 440
    But if the gods themselves did see her then
    When she saw Pyrrhus make malicious sport
    In mincing with his sword her husband's limbs,
    The instant burst of clamour that she made,
    Unless things mortal move them not at all,   445

407 *his,* its.   408 *Takes prisoner,* that is, deafens.   411 *painted tyrant,* a tyrant as depicted
on painted wall cloth.   414 *against,* just before.   421 *for proof eterne,* to last forever.   426 *fellies,*
segments of the rim.   427 *nave,* hub.   431 *mobled,* muffled, with a scarf wrapped.   435 *bisson
rheum,* blinding tears.   437 *o'er-teemed,* worn out from childbearing.

Would have made milch the burning eyes of heaven,
And passion in the gods."
POLONIUS: Look, wh'er he has not turned his colour and has tears in 's
    eyes. Pray you, no more.
HAMLET: 'Tis well; I'll have thee speak out the rest soon. Good my lord,
    will you see the players well bestowed? Do you hear, let them be well   **450**
    used; for they are the abstract and brief chronicles of the time: after
    your death you were better have a bad epitaph than their ill report
    while you live.
POLONIUS: My lord, I will use them according to their desert.
HAMLET: God's bodykins, man, much better; use every man after his
    desert, and who should 'scape whipping? Use them after your own
    honour and dignity: the less they deserve, the more merit is in your
    bounty. Take them in.   **455**
POLONIUS: Come, sirs.
HAMLET: Follow him, friends: we'll hear a play to-morrow. *(Exit
    Polonius with all the Players but the First.)* Dost thou hear me, old
    friend; can you play the Murder of Gonzago?
FIRST PLAYER: Ay, my lord.
HAMLET: We'll ha't to-morrow night. You could, for a need, study a
    speech of some dozen or sixteen lines, which I would set down and
    insert in 't, could you not?
FIRST PLAYER: Ay, my lord.   **460**
HAMLET: Very well. Follow that lord; and look you mock him not. *(Exit
    First Player.)* My good friends, I'll leave you till night: you are
    welcome to Elsinore.
ROSENCRANTZ: Good my lord!
HAMLET: Ay, so, God be wi' ye; *(Exeunt Rosencrantz and Guildenstern.)*
    Now I am alone.
    O, what a rogue and peasant slave am I!
    Is it not monstrous that this player here,   **465**
    But in a fiction, in a dream of passion,
    Could force his soul so to his own conceit
    That from her working all his visage wann'd,
    Tears in his eyes, distraction in 's aspect,
    A broken voice, and his whole function suiting   **470**
    With forms to his conceit? and all for nothing!
    For Hecuba!
    What's Hecuba to him, or he to Hecuba,
    That he should weep for her? What would he do,
    Had he the motive and the cue for passion   **475**
    That I have? He would drown the stage with tears

---

446 *milch,* milky; *eyes of heaven,* the stars.   **448** *wh'er,* whether.   **450** *bestowed,* lodged.
451 *abstract,* summary.   **467** *conceit,* conception.

And cleave the general ear with horrid speech,
Make mad the guilty and appal the free,
Confound the ignorant, and amaze indeed
The very faculties of eyes and ears. 480
Yet I,
A dull and muddy-mettled rascal, peak,
Like John-a-dreams, unpregnant of my cause,
And can say nothing; no, not for a king,
Upon whose property and most dear life 485
A damn'd defeat was made. Am I a coward?
Who calls me villain? breaks my pate across?
Plucks off my beard, and blows it in my face?
Tweaks me by the nose? gives me the lie i' the throat,
As deep as to the lungs? who does me this? 490
Ha!
'Swounds, I should take it: for it cannot be
But I am pigeon-liver'd and lack gall
To make oppression bitter, or ere this
I should have fatted all the region kites 495
With this slave's offal. Bloody, bawdy villain!
Remorseless, treacherous, lecherous, kindless villain!
O, vengeance!
Why, what an ass am I! This is most brave,
That I, the son of a dear father murder'd, 500
Prompted to my revenge by heaven and hell,
Must, like a whore, unpack my heart with words,
And fall a-cursing, like a very drab,
A scullion!
Fie upon 't! foh! About, my brain! I have heard 505
That guilty creatures sitting at a play
Have by the very cunning of the scene
Been struck so to the soul that presently
They have proclaim'd their malefactions;
For murder, though it have no tongue, will speak 510
With most miraculous organ. I'll have these players
Play something like the murder of my father
Before mine uncle. I'll observe his looks;
I'll tent him to the quick: if he but blench,
I know my course. The spirit that I have seen 515
May be the devil: and the devil hath power
To assume a pleasing shape; yea, and perhaps
Out of my weakness and my melancholy,

---

478 *free,* innocent.   **482** *peak,* to become peakèd, sickly.   **493** *pigeon-liver'd,* the pigeon's liver was supposed to secrete no gall, hence their gentleness.   **495** *region,* of the upper air.   **497** *kindless,* unnatural.   **499** *most brave,* very fine.   **514** *tent,* probe; *blench,* flinch.

As he is very potent with such spirits,
Abuses me to damn me. I'll have grounds   520
More relative than this: the play's the thing
Wherein I'll catch the conscience of the king.

(Exit.)

Act III

Scene I

A room in the castle. Enter King, Queen, Polonius, Ophelia, Rosencrantz, Guildenstern, and Lords.

KING: And can you, by no drift of circumstance,
  Get from him why he puts on this confusion,
  Grating so harshly all his days of quiet
  With turbulent and dangerous lunacy?
ROSENCRANTZ: He does confess he feels himself distracted;   5
  But from what cause he will by no means speak.
GUILDENSTERN: Nor do we find him forward to be sounded,
  But, with a crafty madness, keeps aloof,
  When we would bring him on to some confession
  Of his true state.
QUEEN: Did he receive you well?   10
ROSENCRANTZ: Most like a gentleman.
GUILDENSTERN: But with much forcing of his disposition.
ROSENCRANTZ: Niggard of question, but, of our demands,
  Most free in his reply.
QUEEN: Did you assay him
  To any pastime?   15
ROSENCRANTZ: Madam, it so fell out, that certain players
  We o'er-raught on the way: of these we told him;
  And there did seem in him a kind of joy
  To hear of it. They are about the court,
  And, as I think, they have already order   20
  This night to play before him.
POLONIUS: 'Tis most true:
  And he beseech'd me to entreat your majesties
  To hear and see the matter.
KING: With all my heart; and it doth much content me
  To hear him so inclin'd.   25
  Good gentlemen, give him a further edge,
  And drive his purpose on to these delights.
ROSENCRANTZ: We shall, my lord.

---

519 *spirits,* humors, of melancholy.   **521** *this,* the ghost's testimony.   **1** *drift of circumstance,* roundabout method.   **14** *assay him,* try to interest him.

(Exeunt Rosencrantz and Guildenstern.)

KING: Sweet Gertrude, leave us too;
     For we have closely sent for Hamlet hither,
     That he, as 'twere by accident, may here   30
     Affront Ophelia.
     Her father and myself, lawful espials,
     Will so bestow ourselves that, seeing, unseen,
     We may of their encounter frankly judge,
     And gather by him, as he is behav'd,   35
     If 't be the affliction of his love or no
     That thus he suffers for.
QUEEN: I shall obey you.
     And for your part, Ophelia, I do wish
     That your good beauties be the happy cause
     Of Hamlet's wildness. So shall I hope your virtues   40
     Will bring him to his wonted way again,
     To both your honours.
OPHELIA: Madam, I wish it may.

(Exit Queen.)

POLONIUS: Ophelia, walk you here. Gracious, so please you,
     We will bestow ourselves. *(To Ophelia)* Read on this book;
     That show of such an exercise may colour   45
     Your loneliness. We are oft to blame in this,
     'Tis too much prov'd, that with devotion's visage
     And pious action we do sugar o'er
     The devil himself.
KING: *(Aside)* O, 'tis too true!
     How smart a lash that speech doth give my conscience!   50
     The harlot's cheek, beautied with plastering art,
     Is not more ugly to the thing that helps it
     Than is my deed to my most painted word.
     O heavy burthen!
POLONIUS: I hear him coming. Let's withdraw, my lord.
                              (Exeunt King and Polonius.)   55

(Enter Hamlet.)

HAMLET: To be, or not to be: that is the question:
     Whether 'tis nobler in the mind to suffer
     The slings and arrows of outrageous fortune,
     Or to take arms against a sea of troubles,
     And by opposing end them? To die: to sleep;   60

---

29 *closely*, secretly.   **31** *Affront*, meet.   **32** *espials*, spies.   **34** *frankly*, easily.   **43** *Gracious*,
"Gracious Polonius."   **45** *exercise*, religious devotion; *colour*, explain.   **58** *slings*, missiles from
a sling.

No more; and by a sleep to say we end
The heart-ache and the thousand natural shocks
That flesh is heir to, 'tis a consummation
Devoutly to be wish'd. To die, to sleep;
To sleep: perchance to dream: ay, there's the rub;   65
For in that sleep of death what dreams may come
When we have shuffled off this mortal coil,
Must give us pause. There's the respect
That makes calamity of so long life;
For who would bear the whips and scorns of time,   70
The oppressor's wrong, the proud man's contumely,
The pangs of déspis'd love, the law's delay,
The insolence of office and the spurns
That patient merit of the unworthy takes,
When he himself might his quietus make   75
With a bare bodkin? who would fardels bear,
To grunt and sweat under a weary life,
But that the dread of something after death,
The undiscover'd country from whose bourn
No traveller returns, puzzles the will   80
And makes us rather bear those ills we have
Than fly to others that we know not of?
Thus conscience does make cowards of us all;
And thus the native hue of resolution
Is sicklied o'er with the pale cast of thought,   85
And enterprises of great pitch and moment
With this regard their currents turn awry,
And lose the name of action. Soft you now!
The fair Ophelia! Nymph, in thy orisons
Be all my sins remember'd.

OPHELIA: Good my lord,   90
How does your honour for this many a day?

HAMLET: I humbly thank you; well, well, well.

OPHELIA: My lord, I have remembrances of yours,
That I have longed long to re-deliver;
I pray you, now receive them.

HAMLET: No, not I;   95
I never gave you aught.

OPHELIA: My honour'd lord, you know right well you did;

---

67 *shuffled,* cast; *coil,* (1) turmoil, (2) the flesh coiled around the soul.   68 *respect,* consideration.
72 *déspis'd,* rejected.   73 *office,* officials.   75 *quietus,* full discharge of a debt, the debt of life owed
to God.   76 *bare bodkin,* mere dagger (Hamlet, the punster, would also be aware of *bare* as "naked"
and of the *bodkin,* or bone awl, for punching holes in leather and cloth; the *bodkin* or little dagger
as ornamental hairpin comes into fashion some thirty years later); *fardels,* burdens.   79 *undis-*
cover'd, unexplored; *bourn,* boundary.   83 *conscience,* reflection.   86 *pitch,* height, a term in
falconry.   87 *With this regard,* because of this consideration.   89 *orisons,* prayers.

And, with them, words of so sweet breath compos'd
As made the things more rich: their perfume lost,
Take these again; for to the noble mind   100
Rich gifts wax poor when givers prove un-kind.
There, my lord.

HAMLET: Ha, ha! are you honest?

OPHELIA: My lord?

HAMLET: Are you fair?   105

OPHELIA: What means your lordship?

HAMLET: That if you be honest and fair, your honesty should admit no
   discourse to your beauty.

OPHELIA: Could beauty, my lord, have better commerce than with
   honesty?   110

HAMLET: Ay, truly; for the power of beauty will sooner transform
   honesty from what it is to a bawd than the force of honesty can
   translate beauty into his likeness: this was sometime a paradox, but
   now the time gives it proof. I did love you once.

OPHELIA: Indeed, my lord, you made me believe so.   115

HAMLET: You should not have believed me; for virtue cannot so inoculate our old stock but we shall relish of it: I loved you not.

OPHELIA: I was the more deceived.

HAMLET: Get thee to a nunnery: why wouldst thou be a breeder of
   sinners? I am myself indifferent honest; but yet I could accuse me   120
   of such things that it were better my mother had not borne me. I
   am very proud, revengeful, ambitious, with more offences at my
   beck than I have thoughts to put them in, imagination to give them
   shape, or time to act them in. What should such fellows as I
   do crawling between earth and heaven? We are arrant knaves,   125
   all; believe none of us. Go thy ways to a nunnery. Where's your
   father?

OPHELIA: At home, my lord.

HAMLET: Let the doors be shut upon him, that he may play the fool no
   where but in's own house. Farewell.   130

OPHELIA: O, help him, you sweet heavens!

HAMLET: If thou dost marry, I'll give thee this plague for thy dowry: be
   thou as chaste as ice, as pure as snow, thou shalt not escape
   calumny. Get thee to a nunnery, go; farewell. Or, if thou wilt needs
   marry, marry a fool; for wise men know well enough what monsters   135
   you make of them. To a nunnery, go, and quickly too. Farewell.

OPHELIA: O heavenly powers, restore him!

HAMLET: I have heard of your paintings too, well enough; God has given

---

103 *honest,* chaste.   **114** *the time,* present age.   **116–117** *inoculate,* graft.   **117** *relish of,* taste.
120 *indifferent honest,* fairly virtuous.   **123** *beck,* bidding.   **135** *monsters,* cuckolds, supposed to
sprout horns.

you one face, and you make yourselves another. You jig, you amble,
and you lisp, and nick-name God's creatures, and make your wan-   140
tonness your ignorance. Go to, I'll no more on 't; it hath made me
mad. I say, we will have no more marriages: those that are married
already, all but one, shall live; the rest shall keep as they are. To a
nunnery, go.   (*Exit.*)

OPHELIA: O, what a noble mind is here o'er-thrown!   145
The courtier's, soldier's, scholar's, eye, tongue, sword;
The expectancy and rose of the fair state,
The glass of fashion and the mould of form,
The observ'd of all observers, quite, quite down!
And I, of ladies most deject and wretched,   150
That suck'd the honey of his music vows,
Now see that noble and most sovereign reason,
Like sweet bells jangled, out of tune and harsh;
That unmatch'd form and feature of blown youth
Blasted with ecstasy. O, woe is me,   155
To have seen what I have seen, see what I see!

(Enter King and Polonius.)

KING: Love! His affections do not that way tend;
Nor what he spake, though it lack'd form a little,
Was not like madness. There's something in his soul,
O'er which his melancholy sits on brood;   160
And I do doubt the hatch and the disclose
Will be some danger; which for to prevent,
I have in quick determination
Thus set it down: he shall with speed to England,
For the demand of our neglected tribute: 165
Haply the seas and countries different
With variable objects shall expel
This something-settled matter in his heart,
Whereon his brains still beating puts him thus
From fashion of himself. What think you on 't?   170
POLONIUS: It shall do well: but yet do I believe
The origin and commencement of his grief
Sprung from neglected love. How now, Ophelia!
You need not tell us what Lord Hamlet said;

---

139 *jig,* jiggle.   **140** *nick-name God's creatures,* changing the Christian name as you have changed
the God-given face, with a probable reference to the Elizabethan fashion of playful animal names for
certain courtiers.   **141** *make . . . ignorance,* pretend you are too innocent to understand what you
are saying.   **144** *nunnery,* Throughout this scene, Hamlet seems to mean what he says: a convent;
some commentators argue that he uses the Elizabethan ironic euphemism for a brothel, perhaps
punning both ways as he browbeats Ophelia.   **154** *blown,* blossomed.   **155** *ecstasy,* madness.
161 *doubt,* expect.   **168** *something-settled matter,* obsession.   **169** *still beating,* always pondering.

We heard it all. My lord, do as you please;   **175**
But, if you hold it fit, after the play
Let his queen mother all alone entreat him
To show his grief: let her be round with him;
And I'll be plac'd, so please you, in the ear
Of all their conference. If she find him not,   **180**
To England send him, or confine him where
Your wisdom best shall think.

KING: It shall be so:
Madness in great ones must not unwatch'd go.

(Exeunt.)

Act III

Scene II

A hall in the castle. Enter Hamlet and two or three Players.

HAMLET: Speak the speech, I pray you, as I pronounced it to you,
trippingly on the tongue; but if you mouth it, as many of your
players do, I had as lief the town-crier spoke my lines. Nor do not
saw the air too much with your hand, thus, but use all gently; for
in the very torrent, tempest, and, as I may say, the whirlwind of   **5**
passion, you must acquire and beget a temperance that may give it
smoothness. O, it offends me to the soul to hear a robustious peri-
wig-pated fellow tear a passion to tatters, to very rags, to split the
ears of the groundlings, who for the most part are capable of nothing
but inexplicable dumb-shows and noise: I would have such a fellow   **10**
whipped for o'er-doing Termagant; it out-herods Herod: pray you,
avoid it.

FIRST PLAYER: I warrant your honour.

HAMLET: Be not too tame neither, but let your own discretion be your
tutor: suit the action to the word, the word to the action; with this   **15**
special observance, that you o'er-step not the modesty of nature; for
any thing so over-done is from the purpose of playing, whose end,
both at the first and now, was and is, to hold, as 't were, the mirror
up to nature; to show virtue her own feature, scorn her own image,
and the very age and body of the time his form and pressure. Now   **20**
this overdone, or come tardy off, though it make the unskillful
laugh, cannot but make the judicious grieve; the censure of the
which one must in your allowance o'erweigh a whole theatre of

---

180 *find him,* find him out.   **3** *your players,* actors in general.   **9** *groundlings,* those who stood
on the ground in an Elizabethan theatre and so the least intelligent of the audience.   **9** *capable of,*
can appreciate.   **11** *Termagant,* a violent and noisy character in the mystery plays, supposed to be
a god of the Saracens; Herod, acted as a ranting tyrant in the mystery plays.   **20** *pressure,* impression.   **21** *allowance,* estimation.

others. O, there be players that I have seen play, and heard others
praise, and that highly, not to speak it profanely, that, neither   25
having the accent of Christians nor the gait of Christian, pagan, nor
man, have so strutted and bellowed that I have thought some of
nature's journeymen had made men and not made them well, they
imitated humanity so abominably.

FIRST PLAYER: I hope we have reformed that indifferently with us,
sir.   30

HAMLET: O, reform it altogether. And let those that play your clowns
speak no more than is set down for them; for there be of them that
will themselves laugh, to set on some quantity of barren spectators
to laugh too, though, in the mean time, some necessary question of
the play be then to be considered; that's villanous, and shows a most   35
pitiful ambition in the fool that uses it. Go, make you ready.

(Exeunt players.)

(Enter Polonius, Rosencrantz, and Guildenstern.)

How now, my lord! will the king hear this piece of work?

POLONIUS: And the queen too, and that presently.

HAMLET: Bid the players make haste. *(Exit Polonius.)* Will you two help
to hasten them?   40

ROSENCRANTZ:
GUILDENSTERN: We will, my lord.

(Exeunt Rosencrantz and Guildenstern.)

HAMLET: What ho! Horatio!

(Enter Horatio.)

HORATIO: Here, sweet lord, at your service.

HAMLET: Horatio, thou art e'en as just a man
As e'er my conversation cop'd withal.   45

HORATIO: O, my dear lord,—

HAMLET: Nay, do not think I flatter;
For what advancement may I hope from thee
That no revénue hast but thy good spirits,
To feed and clothe thee? Why should the poor be flatter'd?
No, let the candied tongue lick absurd pomp,   50
And crook the pregnant hinges of the knee
Where thrift may follow fawning. Dost thou hear?
Since my dear soul was mistress of her choice
And could of men distinguish, her election

---

28 *journeymen,* not yet masters of their trade.   **30** *indifferently,* fairly well.   **37** *piece of work,*
masterpiece.   **44** *just,* well balanced.   **45** *conversation coped withal,* my experience has dealt with.
51 *pregnant hinges,* full-of-purpose joints.   **52** *thrift,* profit.

Hath seal'd thee for herself; for thou hast been   55
As one, in suffering all, that suffers nothing,
A man that Fortune's buffets and rewards
Hast ta'en with equal thanks: and blest are those
Whose blood and judgement are so well commingled,
That they are not a pipe for Fortune's finger   60
To sound what stop she please. Give me that man
That is not passion's slave, and I will wear him
In my heart's core, ay, in my heart of heart,
As I do thee. Something too much of this!
There is a play to-night before the king;   65
One scene of it comes near the circumstance
Which I have told thee of my father's death.
I prithee, when thou seest that act afoot,
Even with the very comment of thy soul
Observe mine uncle: if his occulted guilt   70
Do not itself unkennel in one speech,
It is a damnèd ghost that we have seen,
And my imaginations are as foul
As Vulcan's stithy. Give him heedful note;
For I mine eyes will rivet to his face,   75
And after we will both our judgements join
In censure of his seeming.
HORATIO: Well, my lord:
If he steal aught the whilst this play is playing,
And 'scape detecting, I will pay the theft.
HAMLET: They are coming to the play; I must be idle.   80
Get you a place.

(*A flourish. Danish march. Enter King, Queen, Polonius, Ophelia, Rosencrantz, Guildenstern, and others, with the Guard carrying torches.*)

KING: How fares our cousin Hamlet?
HAMLET: Excellent, i' faith; of the chameleon's dish: I eat the air, pro-
     mise-crammed; you cannot feed capons so.
KING: I have nothing with this answer, Hamlet; these words are not mine.
HAMLET: No, nor mine now. (*To Polonius*) My lord, you played once
     i' the university, you say?   85
POLONIUS: That did I, my lord, and was accounted a good actor.
HAMLET: What did you enact?
POLONIUS: I did enact Julius Cæsar: I was killed i' the Capitol; Brutus
     killed me.

---

70 *occulted,* concealed.   72 *damnèd ghost,* a devil.   74 *stithy,* smithy.   77 *censure,* judgment.
80 *be idle,* seem crazy.   83 *chameleon's dish,* the air, so the Elizabethans believed.   84 *I . . . with,*
I can make nothing of.   84 *nor mine,* no answer to my question.

HAMLET: It was a brute part of him to kill so capital a calf there. Be the
    players ready?

ROSENCRANTZ: Ay, my lord; they stay upon your patience.   90

QUEEN: Come hither, my dear Hamlet, sit by me.

HAMLET: No, good mother, here's metal more attractive.

POLONIUS: *(To the King)* O, ho! do you mark that?

HAMLET: Lady, shall I lie in your lap?

(Lying down at Ophelia's feet.)

OPHELIA: No, my lord.   95

HAMLET: I mean, my head upon your lap?

OPHELIA: Ay, my lord.

HAMLET: Do you think I meant country matters?

OPHELIA: I think nothing, my lord.

HAMLET: That's a fair thought to lie between maids' legs.   100

OPHELIA: What is, my lord?

HAMLET: Nothing.

OPHELIA: You are merry, my lord.

HAMLET: Who, I?

OPHELIA: Ay, my lord.   105

HAMLET: O God, your only jig-maker. What should a man do but be
    merry? For, look you, how cheerfully my mother looks, and my
    father died within these two hours.

OPHELIA: Nay, 'tis twice two months, my lord.

HAMLET: So long? Nay then, let the devil wear black, for I'll have a suit
    of sables. O heavens! died two months ago, and not forgotten yet?
    Then there's hope a great man's memory may outlive his life half   110
    a year; but by'r lady, he must build churches then, or else shall he
    suffer not thinking on, with the hobby-horse, whose epitaph is "For,
    O, for, O, the hobby-horse is forgot."

(Hautboys play. The dumb-show enters.)

*(Enter a King and a Queen very lovingly, the Queen embracing him, and he her.
She kneels, and makes show of protestation unto him. He takes her up, and declines
his head upon her neck: lays him down upon a bank of flowers: she, seeing him*

89 *part,* act.   **90** *stay . . . patience,* wait until you are ready.   **98** *country matters,* a bawdy remark
based on something like making hay and a pun on the vulgar word for the female pudendum.
102 *Nothing,* a zero, a round 0, to indicate what lies between a maid's legs.   **106** *jig-maker,* writer
of a jig, a song-and-dance afterpiece.   **107** *twice two months,* Hamlet evidently exaggerates in
insisting on only two months at the outset (I.ii.138) and below.   **109** *sables,* black fur for mourning.
112 *not thinking on,* not being remembered.   **113** *hobby-horse is forgot,* A horse figure fastened
around the waist of a morris dancer in May Day festivities. The line is probably from some ballad
satirizing the Puritan opposition to May Days; hobby horse was also a term for prostitute.
114 *dumb-show,* pantomimes frequently introduced early English plays, summarizing the action to
come.

asleep, leaves him. Anon comes in a fellow, takes off his crown, kisses it, and pours poison in the King's ears, and exits. The Queen returns; finds the King dead, and makes passionate action. The Poisoner, with some two or three Mutes, comes in again, seeming to lament with her. The dead body is carried away. The Poisoner wooes the Queen with gifts; she seems loath and unwilling awhile, but in the end accepts his love.) (Exeunt.)

OPHELIA: What means this, my lord?

HAMLET: Marry, this is miching mallecho; it means mischief. 115

OPHELIA: Belike this show imports the argument of the play.

(Enter Prologue.)

HAMLET: We shall know by this fellow: the players cannot keep counsel; they'll tell all.

OPHELIA: Will he tell us what this show meant?

HAMLET: Ay, or any show that you'll show him; be not you ashamed to show, he'll not shame to tell you what it means.

OPHELIA: You are naught, you are naught. I'll mark the play. 120

PROLOGUE: For us, and for our tragedy,
  Here stooping to your clemency,
  We beg your hearing patiently.

(Exit.)

HAMLET: Is this a prologue, or the posy of a ring?

OPHELIA: 'Tis brief, my lord. 125

HAMLET: As woman's love.

(Enter two Players, King and Queen.)

PLAYER KING: Full thirty times hath Phœbus' cart gone round
  Neptune's salt wash and Tellus' orbèd ground,
  And thirty dozen moons with borrow'd sheen
  About the world have times twelve thirties been, 130
  Since love our hearts and Hymen did our hands
  Unite commutual in most sacred bands.

PLAYER QUEEN: So many journeys may the sun and moon
  Make us again count o'er ere love be done!
  But, woe is me, you are so sick of late, 135
  So far from cheer and from your former state,
  That I distrust you. Yet, though I distrust,
  Discomfort you, my lord, it nothing must;
  For women's fear and love holds quantity;

---

115 *miching mallecho,* from the Spanish *malhecho,* which literally means mischief, sneaky mischief. **120** *naught,* naughty, indecent.   **124** *posy of a ring,* a rime engraved on the inside of a ring. **128** *Tellus' . . . ground,* the round earth.   **137** *distrust,* am worried about you.   **139** *quantity,* proportion.

In neither aught, or in extremity.   140
Now, what my love is, proof hath made you know;
And as my love is siz'd, my fear is so:
Where love is great, the littlest doubts are fear;
Where little fears grow great, great love grows there.
PLAYER KING: 'Faith, I must leave thee, love, and shortly too;   145
My operant powers their functions leave to do:
And thou shalt live in this fair world behind,
Honour'd, belov'd; and haply one as kind
For husband shalt thou—
PLAYER QUEEN: O, confound the rest!
Such love must needs be treason in my breast: 150
In second husband let me be accurst!
None wed the second but who kill'd the first.
HAMLET: *(Aside)* Wormwood, wormwood.
PLAYER QUEEN: The instances that second marriage move
Are base respects of thrift, but none of love.   155
A second time I kill my husband dead,
When second husband kisses me in bed.
PLAYER KING: I do believe you think what now you speak;
But what we do determine oft we break.
Purpose is but the slave to memory,   160
Of violent birth, but poor validity;
Which now, like fruit unripe, sticks on the tree,
But fall, unshaken, when they mellow be.
Most necessary 'tis that we forget
To pay ourselves what to ourselves is debt: 165
What to ourselves in passion we propose,
The passion ending, doth the purpose lose.
The violence of either grief or joy
Their own enactures with themselves destroy;
Where joy most revels, grief doth most lament;   170
Grief joys, joy grieves, on slender accident.
This world is not for aye, nor 'tis not strange
That even our loves should with our fortunes change;
For 'tis a question left us yet to prove,
Whether love lead fortune, or else fortune love.   175
The great man down, you mark his favourite flies;
The poor advanc'd makes friends of enemies.
And hitherto doth love on fortune tend;

---

140 *In neither aught, or in extremity,* In neither fear nor love is there no concern at all, but in extremity there is a great deal.   **146** *functions leave to do,* functions stop functioning.   **149** *confound the rest,* strike dumb the rest of what you were going to say.   **154** *instances,* motives.   **155** *respects,* considerations.

For who not needs shall never lack a friend,
And who in want a hollow friend doth try,   180
Directly seasons him his enemy.
But, orderly to end where I begun,
Our wills and fates do so contrary run
That our devices still are overthrown;
Our thoughts are ours, their ends none of our own: 185
So think thou wilt no second husband wed;
But die thy thoughts when thy first lord is dead.
PLAYER QUEEN: Nor earth to me give food, nor heaven light!
Sport and repose lock from me day and night!
To desperation turn my trust and hope!   190
An anchor's cheer in prison be my scope!
Each opposite that blanks the face of joy
Meet what I would have well and it destroy!
Both here and hence pursue me lasting strife,
If, once a widow, ever I be wife!   195
HAMLET: If she should break it now!
PLAYER KING: 'Tis deeply sworn. Sweet, leave me here awhile;
My spirits grow dull, and fain I would beguile
The tedious day with sleep.   *(Sleeps.)*
PLAYER QUEEN: Sleep rock thy brain;
And never come mischance between us twain!   200

(Exit.)

HAMLET: Madam, how like you this play?
QUEEN: The lady doth protest too much, methinks.
HAMLET: O, but she'll keep her word.
KING: Have you heard the argument? Is there no offence in 't?
HAMLET: No, no, they do but jest, poison in jest; no offence i' the
    world.   205
KING: What do you call the play?
HAMLET: The Mouse-trap. Marry, how? Tropically. This play is the
    image of a murder done in Vienna: Gonzago is the duke's name; his
    wife, Baptista. You shall see anon; 't is a knavish piece of work: but
    what o' that? Your majesty and we that have free souls, it touches   210
    us not: let the galled jade wince, our withers are unwrung.

(Enter Lucianus.)

185 *ends,* results.   **191** *anchor's,* anchorite's; *cheer,* fare.   **192** *opposite that blanks,* adverse event
that blots out.   **193** *would have well,* should like.   **202** *protest,* vow.   **204** *argument,* plot.
207 *Tropically,* figuratively.   **209** *anon,* presently.   **210** *free,* free from guilt.   **211** *galled jade,*
old horse galled with harness sores.   **211** *withers,* horse's shoulders; *unwrung,* unchafed.

This is one Lucianus, nephew to the king.

OPHELIA: You are as good as a chorus, my lord.

HAMLET: I could interpret between you and your love, if I could see the
    puppets dallying.   215

OPHELIA: You are keen, my lord, you are keen.

HAMLET: It would cost you a groaning to take off my edge.

OPHELIA: Still better, and worse.

HAMLET: So you must take your husbands. Begin, murderer; pox, leave
    thy damnable faces, and begin. Come: "the croaking raven doth
    bellow for revenge."

LUCIANUS: Thoughts black, hands apt, drugs fit, and time agreeing;   220
    Confederate season, else no creature seeing;
    Thou mixture rank, of midnight weeds collected,
    With Hecate's ban thrice blasted, thrice infected,
    Thy natural magic and dire property,
    On wholesome life usurp immediately.   225

(Pours the poison into the sleeper's ears.)

HAMLET: He poisons him i' the garden for 's estate. His name's Gonzago.
    The story is extant, and writ in choice Italian. You shall see anon
    how the murderer gets the love of Gonzago's wife.

OPHELIA: The king rises.

HAMLET: What, frighted with false fire!

QUEEN: How fares my lord?

POLONIUS: Give o'er the play.   230

KING: Give me some light! Away!

ALL: Lights, lights, lights!

(Exeunt all but Hamlet and Horatio.)

HAMLET: Why, let the stricken deer go weep,
        The hart ungallèd play;
        For some must watch, while some must sleep: 235
        So runs the world away.
  Would not this, sir, and a forest of feathers—if the rest of my fortunes
    turn Turk with me—with two Provincial roses on my razèd shoes,
    get me a fellowship in a cry of players, sir?

---

215 *interpret,* like an actor who explained the action of puppets.   **216** *keen,* bitter, also sexually
aroused.   **221** *Confederate season,* the time cooperating.   **223** *Hecate,* goddess of witchcraft; *ban,*
curse.   **228** *false fire,* discharge of a blank cartridge.   **233** *stricken . . . weep,* a wounded deer was
thought to leave the herd to weep and die alone.   **237** *this,* this play; *feathers,* that decorated an
actor's hat.   **238** *turn Turk,* prove false, like a Christian who turns Moslem.   **238** *Provincial roses,*
a variety of large rose, here the huge rosettes on this imaginary actor's shoes; *razèd,* ornamented by
open work.   **239** *cry,* pack of hounds.

HORATIO: Half a share.   240

HAMLET: A whole one, I.
    For thou dost know, O Damon dear,
      This realm dismantled was
    Of Jove himself; and now reigns here
      A very, very—pajock.   245

HORATIO: You might have rhymed.

HAMLET: O good Horatio, I'll take the ghost's word for a thousand
    pound. Didst perceive?

HORATIO: Very well, my lord.

HAMLET: Upon the talk of the poisoning?   250

HORATIO: I did very well note him.

HAMLET: Ah, ha! Come, some music! come, the recorders!
    For if the king like not the comedy,
    Why then, belike, he likes it not, perdy.
    Come, some music!   255

(Re-enter Rosencrantz and Guildenstern.)

GUILDENSTERN: Good my lord, vouchsafe me a word with you.

HAMLET: Sir, a whole history.

GUILDENSTERN: The king, sir,—

HAMLET: Ay, sir, what of him?

GUILDENSTERN: Is in his retirement marvellous distempered.   260

HAMLET: With drink, sir?

GUILDENSTERN: No, my lord, rather with choler.

HAMLET: Your wisdom should show itself more richer to signify this to
    his doctor; for, for me to put him to his purgation would perhaps
    plunge him into far more choler.   265

GUILDENSTERN: Good my lord, put your discourse into some frame and
    start not so wildly from my affair.

HAMLET: I am tame, sir; pronounce.

GUILDENSTERN: The queen, your mother, in most great affliction of
    spirit, hath sent me to you.   270

HAMLET: You are welcome.

GUILDENSTERN: Nay, good my lord, this courtesy is not of the right
    breed. If it shall please you to make me a wholesome answer, I will
    do your mother's commandment; if not, your pardon and my return
    shall be the end of my business.   275

HAMLET: Sir, I cannot.

GUILDENSTERN: What, my lord?

240 *Half a share,* Shakespeare's company divided the ownership among the actors, the less important receiving only half a share.   **242** *Damon,* the Greeks Damon and Pythias were ideally faithful friends.   **243** *dismantled,* deprived.   **244** *Jove,* Hamlet alludes to his father.   **245** *pajock,* peacock, thought to be cruel and lustful.   **252** *recorders,* a kind of flute.   **254** *perdy,* corruption of *par dieu,* by God.   **262** *choler,* a bilious attack with a play on the meaning anger.   **263** *to signify,* by reporting.   **266** *frame,* logical form.

HAMLET: Make you a wholesome answer; my wit's diseased; but, sir, such answer as I can make, you shall command; or, rather, as you say, my mother: therefore no more, but to the matter: my mother, you say,— 280

ROSENCRANTZ: Then thus she says; your behaviour hath struck her into amazement and admiration.

HAMLET: O wonderful son, that can so astonish a mother! But is there no sequel at the heels of this mother's admiration? Impart. 285

ROSENCRANTZ: She desires to speak with you in her closet, ere you go to bed.

HAMLET: We shall obey, were she ten times our mother. Have you any further trade with us?

ROSENCRANTZ: My lord, you once did love me. 290

HAMLET: So do I still, by these pickers and stealers.

ROSENCRANTZ: Good my lord, what is your cause of distemper? You do, surely, bar the door upon your own liberty, if you deny your griefs to your friend.

HAMLET: Sir, I lack advancement. 295

ROSENCRANTZ: How can that be, when you have the voice of the king himself for your succession in Denmark?

HAMLET: Ay, sir, but "While the grass grows," —the proverb is something musty.

(Enter Players with recorders.)

O, the recorders! let me see one. To withdraw with you:—why do you 300 go about to recover the wind of me, as if you would drive me into a toil?

GUILDENSTERN: O, my lord, if my duty be too bold, my love is too unmannerly.

HAMLET: I do not well understand that. Will you play upon this pipe? 305

GUILDENSTERN: My lord, I cannot.

HAMLET: I pray you.

GUILDENSTERN: Believe me, I cannot.

HAMLET: I do beseech you.

GUILDENSTERN: I know no touch of it, my lord. 310

HAMLET: 'Tis as easy as lying; govern these ventages with your fingers and thumb, give it breath with your mouth, and it will discourse most eloquent music. Look you, these are the stops.

---

291 *pickers and stealers,* hands, referring to the phrase in the English catechism, "To keep my hands from picking and stealing." **293** *deny,* refuse to impart. **298** *"While . . . grows,"* the last part of this proverb is, "the silly horse starves." **300** *withdraw,* speak in private. **301** *recover the wind,* to get downwind in hunting and track your quarry. **302** *toil,* net. **303** *if . . . unmannerly,* if I have been officious in doing my duty by you it is my love for you that is to blame. **311** *ventages,* stops on the recorder.

GUILDENSTERN: But these cannot I command to any utterance of har-
    mony; I have not the skill.   315
HAMLET: Why, look you now, how unworthy a thing you make of me!
    You would play upon me; you would seem to know my stops; you
    would pluck out the heart of my mystery; you would sound me from
    my lowest note to the top of my compass; and there is much music,
    excellent voice, in this little organ; yet cannot you make it speak.   320
    'Sblood, do you think I am easier to be played on than a pipe? Call
    me what instrument you will, though you can fret me, yet you
    cannot play upon me.

(Enter Polonius.)

    God bless you, sir!
POLONIUS: My lord, the queen would speak with you, and presently.   325
HAMLET: Do you see yonder cloud that's almost in shape of a camel?
POLONIUS: By the mass, and 'tis like a camel, indeed.
HAMLET: Methinks it is like a weasel.
POLONIUS: It is backed like a weasel.
HAMLET: Or like a whale?   330
POLONIUS: Very like a whale.
HAMLET: Then I will come to my mother by and by. *(Aside.)* They fool
    me to the top of my bent. *(Aloud.)* I will come by and by.
POLONIUS: I will say so.
HAMLET: By and by is easily said.   335

(Exit Polonius.)

    Leave me, friends.

(Exeunt all but Hamlet.)

    'Tis now the very witching time of night,
    When churchyards yawn and hell itself breathes out
    Contagion to this world: now could I drink hot blood,
    And do such bitter business as the day   340
    Would quake to look on. Soft! now to my mother.
    O heart, lose not thy nature; let not ever
    The soul of Nero enter this firm bosom;
    Let me be cruel, not unnatural:
    I will speak daggers to her, but use none;   345
    My tongue and soul in this be hypocrites;
    How in my words soever she be shent,
    To give them seals never, my soul, consent!

(Exit.)

322 *fret,* pun (1) irritate, (2) finger the frets on a stringed instrument.   332 *fool,* treat me like a fool.
337 *witching time,* midnight.   343 *Nero,* who murdered his mother.   347 *shent,* rebuked.
348 *To . . . seals,* confirm them with official seals.

Act III

Scene III

A room in the castle. Enter King, Rosencrantz, and Guildenstern.

KING: I like him not, nor stands it safe with us
    To let his madness range. Therefore prepare you;
    I your commission will forthwith dispatch,
    And he to England shall along with you.
    The terms of our estate may not endure   5
    Hazard so near us as doth hourly grow
    Out of his lunacies.

GUILDENSTERN: We will ourselves provide.
    Most holy and religious fear it is
    To keep those many many bodies safe
    That live and feed upon your majesty.   10

ROSENCRANTZ: The single and peculiar life is bound,
    With all the strength and armour of the mind,
    To keep itself from noyance; but much more
    That spirit upon whose weal depend and rest
    The lives of many. The cease of majesty   15
    Dies not alone; but, like a gulf, doth draw
    What's near it with it; it is a massy wheel,
    Fix'd on the summit of the highest mount,
    To whose huge spokes ten thousand lesser things
    Are mortis'd and adjoin'd; which, when it falls,   20
    Each small annexment, petty consequence,
    Attends the boisterous ruin. Never alone
    Did the king sigh, but with a general groan.

KING: Arm you, I pray you, to this speedy voyage;
    For we will fetters put upon this fear,   25
    Which now goes too free-footed.

ROSENCRANTZ:
                    We will haste us.
GUILDENSTERN:

(Exeunt Rosencrantz and Guildenstern.)

(Enter Polonius.)

POLONIUS: My lord, he's going to his mother's closet:
    Behind the arras I'll convey myself
    To hear the process; I'll warrant she'll tax him home;
    And, as you said, and wisely was it said,   30
    'Tis meet that some more audience than a mother,

---

7 *provide,* make ready.   **13** *noyance,* harm.   **15** *cease,* death; *majesty,* a king.   **23** *general,* universal.   **29** *tax him home,* censure him severely.

Since nature make them partial, should o'er-hear
The speech, of vantage. Fare you well, my liege.
I'll call upon you ere you go to bed,
And tell you what I know.

KING: Thanks, dear my lord.   35

(Exit Polonius.)

O, my offence is rank, it smells to heaven;
It hath the primal eldest curse upon 't,
A brother's murder. Pray can I not,
Though inclination be as sharp as will:
My stronger guilt defeats my strong intent;   40
And, like a man to double business bound,
I stand in pause where I shall first begin,
And both neglect. What if this cursèd hand
Were thicker than itself with brother's blood,
Is there not rain enough in the sweet heavens   45
To wash it white as snow? Whereto serves mercy
But to confront the visage of offence?
And what's in prayer but this two-fold force,
To be forestallèd ere we come to fall,
Or pardon'd being down? Then I'll look up;   50
My fault is past. But, O, what form of prayer
Can serve my turn? "Forgive me my foul murder"?
That cannot be; since I am still possess'd
Of those effects for which I did the murder,
My crown, mine own ambition, and my queen.   55
May one be pardon'd and retain the offence?
In the corrupted currents of this world
Offence's gilded hand may shove by justice,
And oft 'tis seen the wicked prize itself
Buys out the law; but 'tis not so above;   60
There is no shuffling, there the action lies
In his true nature; and we ourselves compell'd,
Even to the teeth and forehead of our faults,
To give in evidence. What then? what rests?
Try what repentance can: what can it not?   65
Yet what can it when one can not repent?
O wretched state! O bosom black as death!
O limèd soul, that, struggling to be free,
Art more engag'd! Help, angels! Make assay!
Bow, stubborn knees; and, heart with strings of steel,   70

37 *primal eldest curse,* the curse put upon Cain, the first fratricide.   **64** *rests,* remains.   **68** *limèd,* caught as a bird with birdlime.

Be soft as sinews of the new-born babe!
All may be well.   *(Retires and kneels.)*

(Enter Hamlet.)

HAMLET: Now might I do it pat, now he is praying;
    And now I'll do 't. And so he goes to heaven;
    And so am I reveng'd. That would be scann'd: 75
    A villain kills my father; and for that,
    I, his sole son, do this same villain send
    To heaven.
    O, this is hire and salary, not revenge.
    He took my father grossly, full of bread;   80
    With all his crimes broad blown, as flush as May;
    And how his audit stands who knows save heaven?
    But in our circumstance and course of thought,
    'Tis heavy with him; and am I then reveng'd,
    To take him in the purging of his soul,   85
    When he is fit and season'd for his passage?
    No!
    Up, sword; and know thou a more horrid hent.
    When he is drunk asleep, or in his rage,
    Or in the incestuous pleasure of his bed;   90
    At gaming, swearing, or about some act
    That has no relish of salvation in 't;
    Then trip him, that his heels may kick at heaven,
    And that his soul may be as damn'd and black
    As hell, whereto it goes. My mother stays: 95
    This physic but prolongs thy sickly days.

(Exit.)

KING: *(Rising)* My words fly up, my thoughts remain below:
    Words without thoughts never to heaven go.

(Exit.)

Act III

Scene IV

The Queen's closet. Enter Queen and Polonius.

POLONIUS: He will come straight. Look you lay home to him;
    Tell him his pranks have been too broad to bear with,

---

75 *scann'd,* looked into.   **80** *full of bread,* without a repentant fast.   **81** *broad blown,* in full flower.
88 *hent,* intention.   **95** *stays,* waits.   **96** *physic,* purgation through prayer.   **1** *straight,* right
away; *lay home,* speak plain truth.

And that your grace hath screen'd and stood between
Much heat and him. I'll sconce me even here.
Pray you, be round with him.   5

HAMLET: *(Within)* Mother, mother, mother!

QUEEN: I'll warrant you,
Fear me not. Withdraw, I hear him coming.

(Polonius hides behind the arras.)

(Enter Hamlet.)

HAMLET: Now, mother, what's the matter?

QUEEN: Hamlet, thou hast thy father much offended.

HAMLET: Mother, you have my father much offended.   10

QUEEN: Come, come, you answer with an idle tongue.

HAMLET: Go, go, you question with a wicked tongue.

QUEEN: Why, how now, Hamlet!

HAMLET: What's the matter now?

QUEEN: Have you forgot me?

HAMLET: No, by the rood, not so:
You are the queen, your husband's brother's wife;   15
And—would it were not so!—you are my mother.

QUEEN: Nay, then, I'll set those to you that can speak.

HAMLET: Come, come, and sit you down; you shall not budge;
You go not till I set you up a glass
Where you may see the inmost part of you.   20

QUEEN: What wilt thou do? thou wilt not murder me?
Help, help, ho!

POLONIUS: *(Behind)* What, ho! Help! Help! Help!

HAMLET: *(Drawing)* How now! a rat? Dead, for a ducat, dead!

(Makes a thrust through the arras.)

POLONIUS: *(Behind)* O! I am slain!

(Falls and dies.)

QUEEN: O me, what hast thou done?

HAMLET: Nay, I know not.   25
Is it the king?

QUEEN: O, what a rash and bloody deed is this!

HAMLET: A bloody deed! almost as bad, good mother,
As kill a king, and marry with his brother.

QUEEN: As kill a king!

HAMLET: Ay, lady, 'twas my word.   30

---

4 *heat,* anger of the King.   **14** *rood,* holy cross.   **23** *Dead, for a ducat,* I'll wager a ducat that he
is dead.

(Lifts up the arras and discovers Polonius.)

Thou wretched, rash, intruding fool, farewell!
I took thee for thy better. Take thy fortune;
Thou find'st to be too busy is some danger.
Leave wringing of your hands. Peace! sit you down
And let me wring your heart; for so I shall,   35
If it be made of penetrable stuff,
If damnèd custom have not brass'd it so
That it be proof and bulwark against sense.
QUEEN: What have I done, that thou dar'st wag thy tongue
In noise so rude against me?
HAMLET: Such an act   40
That blurs the grace and blush of modesty,
Calls virtue hypocrite, takes off the rose
From the fair forehead of an innocent love
And sets a blister there, makes marriage-vows
As false as dicers' oaths. O, such a deed   45
As from the body of contraction plucks
The very soul, and sweet religion makes
A rhapsody of words, heaven's face doth glow;
Yea, this solidity and compound mass,
With tristful visage, as against the doom,   50
Is thought-sick at the act.
QUEEN: Ay me, what act,
That roars so loud, and thunders in the index?
HAMLET: Look here, upon this picture, and on this.
The counterfeit presentment of two brothers.
See, what a grace was seated on this brow;   55
Hyperion's curls; the front of Jove himself;
An eye like Mars, to threaten and command;
A station like the herald Mercury
New-lighted on a heaven-kissing hill;
A combination and a form indeed,   60
Where every god did seem to set his seal,
To give the world assurance of a man.
This was your husband. Look you now, what follows.
Here is your husband; like a mildew'd ear,
Blasting his wholesome brother. Have you eyes?   65

---

33 *busy,* prying.   **38** *sense,* reason and feeling.   **44** *blister,* women guilty of adultery were branded
on the forehead.   **46** *body of contraction,* the contents of the marriage contract.   **49** *solidity
... mass,* this solid earth compounded of various elements.   **52** *index,* preface.   **54** *counterfeit
presentment,* painted portrait.   **56** *Hyperion,* a Greek sun god; *front,* forehead.   **58** *station,* standing position, posture.   **59** *New-lighted,* just alighted.   **64** *ear,* ear of wheat.   **65** *Blasting,* blight-
ing.

Could you on this fair mountain leave to feed,
And batten on this moor? Ha! have you eyes?
You cannot call it love, for at your age
The hey-day in the blood is tame, it's humble,
And waits upon the judgement; and what judgement   70
Would step from this to this? Sense, sure, you have,
Else could you not have motion; but sure, that sense
Is apoplex'd, for madness would not err,
Nor sense to ecstasy was ne'er so thrall'd
But it reserved some quantity of choice,   75
To serve in such a difference. What devil was 't
That thus hath cozen'd you at hoodman-blind?
Eyes without feeling, feeling without sight,
Ears without hands or eyes, smelling sans all,
Or but a sickly part of one true sense   80
Could not so mope.
O shame! Where is thy blush? Rebellious hell,
If thou canst mutine in a matron's bones,
To flaming youth let virtue be as wax,
And melt in her own fire: proclaim no shame   85
When the compulsive ardour gives the charge,
Since frost itself as actively doth burn
And reason pandars will.

QUEEN: O Hamlet, speak no more!
Thou turn'st mine eyes into my very soul;
And there I see such black and grainèd spots   90
As will not leave their tinct.

HAMLET: Nay, but to live
In the rank sweat of an enseamèd bed,
Stew'd in corruption, honeying and making love
Over the nasty sty,—

QUEEN: O, speak to me no more!
These words like daggers enter in mine ears.   95
No more, sweet Hamlet!

HAMLET: A murderer and a villain!
A slave that is not twentieth part the tithe
Of your precedent lord; a vice of kings;
A cutpurse of the empire and the rule,
That from a shelf the precious diadem stole,   100
And put it in his pocket!

---

66 *leave to feed,* stop feeding. **67** *batten,* stuff yourself. **71** *Sense,* the five senses. **74** *ecstasy,* insanity. **75** *quantity,* ability. **77** *cozen'd,* cheated. **83** *mutine,* rebel. **90** *grainèd,* ingrained. **91** *leave their tinct,* lose their color. **92** *enseamed,* covered with grease. **97** *tithe,* tenth. **98** *vice of,* clown among. The Vice was the clown of the morality plays.

QUEEN: No more!

HAMLET: A king of shreds and patches,—

(Enter Ghost.)

Save me, and hover o'er me with your wings;
You heavenly guards! What would your gracious figure?

QUEEN: Alas, he's mad!   105

HAMLET: Do you not come your tardy son to chide,
That, laps'd in time and passion, lets go by
The important acting of your dread command?
O, say!

GHOST: Do not forget. This visitation   110
Is but to whet thy almost blunted purpose.
But, look, amazement on thy mother sits.
O, step between her and her fighting soul!
Conceit in weakest bodies strongest works.
Speak to her, Hamlet.

HAMLET: How is it with you, lady?   115

QUEEN: Alas, how is 't with you,
That you do bend your eye on vacancy
And with the incorporal air do hold discourse?
Forth at your eyes your spirits wildly peep;
And, as the sleeping soldiers in the alarm,   120
Your bedded hairs, like life in excrements,
Start up, and stand an end. O gentle son,
Upon the heat and flame of thy distemper
Sprinkle cool patience. Whereon do you look?

HAMLET: On him, on him! Look you, how pale he glares!   125
His form and cause conjoin'd, preaching to stones,
Would make them capable. Do not look upon me,
Lest with this piteous action you convert
My stern effects; then what I have to do
Will want true colour; tears perchance for blood.   130

QUEEN: To whom do you speak this?

HAMLET: Do you see nothing there?

QUEEN: Nothing at all; yet all that is I see.

HAMLET: Nor did you nothing hear?

QUEEN: No, nothing but ourselves.

HAMLET: Why, look you there! look, how it steals away!
My father, in his habit as he liv'd!   135
Look, where he goes, even now, out at the portal!   *(Exit Ghost.)*

114 *Conceit,* imagination.   **121** *excrements,* dung.   **127** *capable,* of emotion.   **128–129** *convert*
. . . *effects,* turn me from my stern purpose.   **130** *want true colour,* lose its true purpose.
135 *habit,* clothes.

QUEEN: This is the very coinage of your brain:
This bodiless creation ecstasy
Is very cunning in.
HAMLET: Ecstasy!
My pulse, as yours, doth temperately keep time,   140
And makes as healthful music. It is not madness
That I have utter'd. Bring me to the test,
And I the matter will re-word, which madness
Would gambol from. Mother, for love of grace,
Lay not that flattering unction to your soul,   145
That not your trespass, but my madness speaks.
It will but skin and film the ulcerous place,
Whiles rank corruption, mining all within,
Infects unseen. Confess yourself to heaven;
Repent what's past; avoid what is to come;   150
And do not spread the compost on the weeds
To make them ranker. Forgive me this my virtue;
For in the fatness of these pursy times
Virtue itself of vice must pardon beg,
Yea, curb and woo for leave to do him good.   155
QUEEN: O Hamlet, thou hast cleft my heart in twain.
HAMLET: O, throw away the worser part of it,
And live the purer with the other half.
Good night; but go not to mine uncle's bed;
Assume a virtue, if you have it not.   160
That monster, custom, who all sense doth eat,
Of habits devil, is angel yet in this,
That to the use of actions fair and good
He likewise gives a frock or livery,
That aptly is put on. Refrain to-night,   165
And that shall lend a kind of easiness
To the next abstinence: the next more easy;
For use almost can change the stamp of nature,
And either curb the devil, or throw him out
With wondrous potency. Once more, good night: 170
And when you are desirous to be bless'd,
I'll blessing beg of you. For this same lord,

(Pointing to Polonius.)

I do repent: but heaven hath pleas'd it so,
To punish me with this and this with me,

138–139 *ecstasy is very cunning in,* madness is very skilful in.   **145** *flattering unction,* soothing salve.
153 *pursy,* corpulent.   **155** *curb,* bow the knee.   **162** *Of habits devil,* the wicked attendant on
habits.   **165** *aptly is put on,* is easily donned.   **168** *use,* habit.

That I must be their scourge and minister.   175
I will bestow him, and will answer well
The death I gave him. So, again, good night.
I must be cruel, only to be kind:
Thus bad begins and worse remains behind.
One word more, good lady.

QUEEN: What shall I do?   180

HAMLET: Not this, by no means, that I bid you do:
Let the bloat king tempt you again to bed;
Pinch wanton on your cheek; call you his mouse;
And let him, for a pair of reechy kisses,
Of paddling in your neck with his damn'd fingers,   185
Make you to ravel all this matter out,
That I essentially am not in madness,
But mad in craft. 'Twere good you let him know;
For who, that's but a queen, fair, sober, wise,
Would from a paddock, from a bat, a gib,   190
Such dear concernings hide? Who would do so?
No, in despite of sense and secrecy,
Unpeg the basket on the house's top,
Let the birds fly, and, like the famous ape
To try conclusions, in the basket creep,   195
And break your own neck down.

QUEEN: Be thou assur'd, if words be made of breath,
And breath of life, I have no life to breathe
What thou hast said to me.

HAMLET: I must to England; you know that?

QUEEN: Alack,   200
I had forgot: 'tis so concluded on.

HAMLET: There's letters seal'd; and my two schoolfellows,
Whom I will trust as I will adders fang'd,
They bear the mandate; they must sweep my way,
And marshal me to knavery. Let it work,   205
For 'tis the sport to have the enginer
Hoist with his own petar: and 't shall go hard
But I will delve one yard below their mines,
And blow them at the moon. O, 'tis most sweet,

---

175 *minister,* Hamlet begins to acknowledge God's control.   176 *bestow,* dispose of; *answer well,*
willingly be held responsible for.   181 *Not . . . do,* at least avoid doing the things I bid you not to
do.   184 *reechy,* reeking.   186 *ravel . . . out,* unravel, give away.   189 *that's but,* except.
190 *paddock,* toad; *gib,* tomcat.   191 *dear concernings,* matters of such deep importance.
193–194 *Unpeg . . . ape,* an ape who opened a basket of birds on the house top and, after watching
them fly, tried to imitate them and jumped to his death.   195 *try conclusions,* repeat the experiment.
205 *knavery,* the treachery to be done to Hamlet.   206 *engineer,* engineer, the tunneler under
fortifications.   207 *Hoist,* blown up; *petar,* bomb.

When in one line two crafts directly meet.   210
This man shall set me packing:
I'll lug the guts into the neighbour room.
Mother, good night. Indeed this counsellor
Is now most still, most secret, and most grave,
Who was in life a foolish prating knave.   215
Come, sir, to draw toward an end with you.
Good night, mother.

(Exeunt severally; Hamlet dragging in Polonius.)

Act IV

Scene I

A room in the castle. Enter King, Queen, Rosencrantz, and Guildenstern.

KING: There's matter in these sighs, these profound heaves,
    You must translate; 'tis fit we understand them.
    Where is your son?
QUEEN: Bestow this place on us a little while.

(Exeunt Rosencrantz and Guildenstern.)

Ah, mine own lord, what have I seen to-night!   5
KING: What, Gertrude? How does Hamlet?
QUEEN: Mad as the sea and wind, when both contend
    Which is the mightier. In his lawless fit,
    Behind the arras hearing something stir,
    Whips out his rapier, cries, "A rat, a rat!"   10
    And, in this brainish apprehension, kills
    The unseen good old man.
KING: O heavy deed!
    It had been so with us, had we been there.
    His liberty is full of threats to all;
    To you yourself, to us, to every one.   15
    Alas, how shall this bloody deed be answer'd?
    It will be laid to us, whose providence
    Should have kept short, restrain'd, and out of haunt,
    This mad young man: but so much was our love,
    We would not understand what was most fit,   20
    But, like the owner of a foul disease,
    To keep it from divulging, let it feed
    Even on the pith of life. Where is he gone?

210 *crafts,* crafty schemes.   211 *packing,* a pun on three meanings: (1) loading, (2) plotting, (3)
hurrying off.   1 *matter,* meaning.   2 *translate,* explain.   13 *us,* me, the King.   17 *providence,*
foresight.   18 *short,* on short tether; *haunt,* company.   22 *divulging,* coming to light.

QUEEN: To draw apart the body he hath kill'd;
O'er whom his very madness, like some ore   25
Among a mineral of metals base,
Shows itself pure; he weeps for what is done.

KING: O Gertrude, come away!
The sun no sooner shall the mountains touch,
But we will ship him hence; and this vile deed   30
We must, with all our majesty and skill,
Both countenance and excuse. Ho, Guildenstern!

(Re-enter Rosencrantz and Guildenstern.)

Friends both, go join you with some further aid.
Hamlet in madness hath Polonius slain,
And from his mother's closet hath he dragg'd him.   35
Go seek him out; speak fair, and bring the body
Into the chapel. I pray you, haste in this.

(Exeunt Rosencrantz and Guildenstern.)

Come, Gertrude, we'll call up our wisest friends;
And let them know, both what we mean to do,
And what's untimely done, so, haply, slander   40
Whose whisper o'er the world's diameter,
As level as the cannon to his blank,
Transports his poison'd shot, may miss our name,
And hit the woundless air. O, come away!
My soul is full of discord and dismay.   45

(Exeunt.)

Act IV

Scene II

Another room in the castle. Enter Hamlet.

HAMLET: Safely stowed.

ROSENCRANTZ: }
GUILDENSTERN: }   *(Within)* Hamlet! Lord Hamlet!

HAMLET: But soft, what noise? who calls on Hamlet? O, here they come.

(Enter Rosencrantz and Guildenstern.)

ROSENCRANTZ: What have you done, my lord, with the dead body?

HAMLET: Compounded it with dust, whereto 'tis kin.   5

ROSENCRANTZ: Tell us where 'tis, that we may take it thence
And bear it to the chapel.

---

26 *mineral,* mine.   **42** *level,* straight; *blank,* the center of the target.   **44** *woundless,* invulnerable.
5 *Compounded,* mixed.

HAMLET: Do not believe it.

ROSENCRANTZ: Believe what?

HAMLET: That I can keep your counsel and not mine own. Besides, to
be demanded of a sponge! What replication should be made by the
son of a king?   10

ROSENCRANTZ: Take you me for a sponge, my lord?

HAMLET: Ay, sir, that soaks up the king's countenance, his rewards, his
authorities. But such officers do the king best service in the end: he
keeps them, like an ape, in the corner of his jaw; first mouthed, to
be last swallowed. When he needs what you have gleaned, it is but   15
squeezing you, and, sponge, you shall be dry again.

ROSENCRANTZ: I understand you not, my lord.

HAMLET: I am glad of it: a knavish speech sleeps in a foolish ear.

ROSENCRANTZ: My lord, you must tell us where the body is, and go with
us to the king.

HAMLET: The body is with the king, but the king is not with the body.
The king is a thing—   20

GUILDENSTERN: A thing, my lord!

HAMLET: Of nothing: bring me to him. Hide fox, and all after.

(Exeunt.)

Act IV

Scene III

Another room in the castle. Enter King, attended.

KING: I have sent to seek him, and to find the body.
How dangerous is it that this man goes loose!
Yet must not we put the strong law on him:
He's lov'd of the distracted multitude,
Who like not in their judgement, but their eyes;   5
And where 'tis so, the offender's scourge is weigh'd,
But never the offence. To bear all smooth and even,
This sudden sending him away must seem
Deliberate pause. Diseases desperate grown
By desperate appliance are reliev'd,   10
Or not at all.

(Enter Rosencrantz.)

How now! what hath befall'n?

10 *counsel,* secrets, that you are spying on me.   10 *demanded of,* questioned by.   10 *replication,*
reply.   20 *The body is with the king,* perhaps body politic, the state.   22 *Hide fox,* the cry used
in hide and seek.   5 *in,* in accordance with.   6 *scourge,* punishment; *weigh'd,* taken into consideration.   9 *Deliberate pause,* a planned rest.

ROSENCRANTZ: Where the dead body is bestow'd, my lord,
We cannot get from him.

KING: But where is he?

ROSENCRANTZ: Without, my lord; guarded, to know your pleasure.   15

KING: Bring him before us.

ROSENCRANTZ: Ho, Guildenstern! bring in my lord.

(Enter Hamlet and Guildenstern.)

KING: Now, Hamlet, where's Polonius?

HAMLET: At supper.

KING: At supper! where?   20

HAMLET: Not where he eats, but where he is eaten: a certain convocation
of politic worms are e'en at him. Your worm is your only emperor
for diet: we fat all creatures else to fat us, and we fat ourselves for
maggots: your fat king and your lean beggar is but variable service,
two dishes, but to one table: that's the end.   25

KING: Alas, alas!

HAMLET: A man may fish with the worm that hath eat of a king, and
eat of the fish that hath fed of that worm.

KING: What dost thou mean by this?

HAMLET: Nothing but to show you how a king may go a progress
through the guts of a beggar.

KING: Where is Polonius?   30

HAMLET: In heaven; send thither to see: if your messenger find him not
there, seek him i' th' other place yourself. But indeed, if you find
him not within this month, you shall nose him as you go up the
stairs into the lobby.

KING: Go seek him there.   35

(To some Attendants.)

HAMLET: He will stay till you come.

(Exeunt Attendants.)

KING: Hamlet, this deed, for thine especial safety,—
Which we do tender, as we dearly grieve
For that which thou hast done,—must send thee hence
With fiery quickness: therefore prepare thy-self;   40
The bark is ready, and the wind at help,
The associates tend, and everything is bent
For England.

HAMLET: For England!

KING: Ay, Hamlet.

HAMLET: Good.

---

22 *e'en,* right now.   **25** *variable service,* variety of food.   **29** *go a progress,* make a royal journey.
38 *Which . . . grieve,* which we hold as dearly as we grieve.

KING: So is it, if thou knew'st our purposes.

HAMLET: I see a cherub that sees them. But, come; for England! Farewell, dear mother.   45

KING: Thy loving father, Hamlet.

HAMLET: My mother: father and mother is man and wife, man and wife is one flesh, and so, my mother. Come, for England!

(Exit.)

KING: Follow him at foot; tempt him with speed aboard;
Delay it not; I'll have him hence to-night.
Away! For every thing is seal'd and done   50
That else leans on the affair. Pray you, make haste.

(Exeunt Rosencrantz and Guildenstern.)

And, England, if my love thou hold'st at aught—
As my great power thereof may give thee sense,
Since yet thy cicatrice looks raw and red
After the Danish sword, and thy free awe   55
Pays homage to us—thou mayst not coldly set
Our sovereign process; which imports at full,
By letters congruing to that effect,
The present death of Hamlet. Do it, England!
For like the hectic in my blood he rages,   60
And thou must cure me. Till I know 'tis done,
Howe'er my haps, my joys were ne'er begun.   *(Exit.)*

Act IV

Scene IV

Near Elsinore. Enter Fortinbras, a Captain, and Soldiers, marching.

FORTINBRAS: Go, captain, from me greet the Danish king.
Tell him that, by his license, Fortinbras
Craves the conveyance of a promis'd march
Over his kingdom. You know the rendezvous.
If that his majesty would aught with us,   5
We shall express our duty in his eye,
And let him know so.

CAPTAIN: I will do 't, my lord.

FORTINBRAS: Go softly on.

---

45 *cherub,* angel who sees everything.   **48** *at foot,* at his heels.   **51** *else . . . affair,* has anything
else to do with the business.   **52** *England,* the King of England.   **54** *cicatrice,* scar.   **55** *free,* no
longer forced by arms.   **56** *coldly set,* estimate lightly   **57** *process,* behest; *imports at full,* fully
implies.   **60** *hectic,* fever.   **62** *Howe'er my haps,* whatever my lot.   **3** *conveyance,* official escort.
6 *in his eye,* in his presence.   **8** *softly,* slowly.

(Exeunt Fortinbras and Soldiers.)

(Enter Hamlet, Rosencrantz, Guildenstern, and others.)

HAMLET: Good sir, whose powers are these?
CAPTAIN: They are of Norway, sir.   10
HAMLET: How purpos'd, sir, I pray you?
CAPTAIN: Against some part of Poland.
HAMLET: Who commands them, sir?
CAPTAIN: The nephew to old Norway, Fortinbras.
HAMLET: Goes it against the main of Poland, sir,   15
    Or for some frontier?
CAPTAIN: Truly to speak, and with no addition,
    We go to gain a little patch of ground
    That hath in it no profit but the name.
    To pay five ducats, five, I would not farm it;   20
    Nor will it yield to Norway or the Pole
    A ranker rate, should it be sold in fee.
HAMLET: Why, then the Polack never will defend it.
CAPTAIN: Yes, it is already garrison'd.
HAMLET: Two thousand souls and twenty thousand ducats   25
    Will not debate the question of this straw:
    This is the imposthume of much wealth and peace,
    That inward breaks, and shows no cause without
    Why the man dies. I humbly thank you, sir.
CAPTAIN: God be wi' you, sir.   *(Exit.)*
ROSENCRANTZ: Will 't please you go, my lord?   30
HAMLET: I'll be with you straight. Go a little before.
                              (Exeunt all except Hamlet.)
    How all occasions do inform against me,
    And spur my dull revenge! What is a man,
    If his chief good and market of his time
    Be but to sleep and feed? A beast, no more.   35
    Sure, he that made us with such large discourse,
    Looking before and after, gave us not
    That capability and god-like reason
    To fust in us unus'd. Now, whether it be
    Bestial oblivion, or some craven scruple   40
    Of thinking too precisely on the event,
    A thought which, quarter'd, hath but one part wisdom
    And ever three parts coward, I do not know

---

15 *the main,* the whole.   **20** *five ducats,* as an annual rental.   **22** *ranker,* larger; *sold in fee,* sold outright.   **26** *not debate,* not begin to settle.   **27** *imposthume,* hidden abscess.   **36** *large discourse,* broad comprehension.   **39** *fust,* grow moldy.   **40** *Bestial oblivion,* animal forgetfulness.
41 *event,* outcome.

Why yet I live to say "This thing's to do,"
Sith I have cause and will and strength and means   45
To do 't. Examples gross as earth exhort me.
Witness this army of such mass and charge
Led by a delicate and tender prince,
Whose spirit with divine ambition puff'd
Makes mouths at the invisible event,   50
Exposing what is mortal and unsure
To all that fortune, death, and danger dare,
Even for an egg-shell. Rightly to be great
Is not to stir without great argument,
But greatly to find quarrel in a straw   55
When honour's at the stake. How stand I then,
That have a father kill'd, a mother stain'd,
Excitements of my reason and my blood,
And let all sleep? While, to my shame, I see
The imminent death of twenty thousand men,   60
That, for a fantasy and trick of fame,
Go to their graves like beds, fight for a plot
Whereon the numbers cannot try the cause,
Which is not tomb enough and continent
To hide the slain? O, from this time forth,   65
My thoughts be bloody, or be nothing worth!

(Exit.)

Act IV

Scene V

Elsinore. A room in the castle. Enter Queen, Horatio, and a Gentleman.

QUEEN: I will not speak with her.
GENTLEMAN: She is importunate, indeed distract:
    Her mood will needs be pitied.
QUEEN: What would she have?
GENTLEMAN: She speaks much of her father; says she hears
    There's tricks i' the world; and hems, and beats her heart;   5
    Spurns enviously at straws; speaks things in doubt,
    That carry but half sense. Her speech is nothing,
    Yet the unshapèd use of it doth move
    The hearers to collection; they aim at it,
    And botch the words up fit to their own thoughts;   10

---

46 *gross,* obvious.   **47** *charge,* expense.   **48** *delicate and tender,* gentle and refined.   **50** *invisible event,* unknown outcome.   **54** *argument,* cause.   **63** *try the cause,* fight the battle.   **64** *continent,* receptacle.   **5** *heart,* breast.   **6** *Spurns,* kicks; *in doubt,* ambiguous.   **7** *is nothing,* makes no sense.   **9** *collection,* inference; *aim,* guess.

Which, as her winks, and nods, and gestures yield them,
Indeed would make one think there might be thought,
Though nothing sure, yet much unhappily.

HORATIO: 'Twere good she were spoken with, for she may strew
Dangerous conjectures in ill-breeding minds.   15

QUEEN: Let her come in. *(Exit Gentleman.)*
To my sick soul, as sin's true nature is,
Each toy seems prologue to some great amiss:
So full of artless jealousy is guilt,
It spills itself in fearing to be spilt.   20

(Enter Ophelia distracted.)

OPHELIA: Where is the beauteous Majesty of Denmark?

QUEEN: How now, Ophelia!

OPHELIA: *(Sings)* How should I your true love know
          From another one?
        By his cockle hat and staff,   25
          And his sandal shoon.

QUEEN: Alas, sweet lady, what imports this song?

OPHELIA: Say you? nay, pray you, mark.
   (Sings)   He is dead and gone, lady,
                He is dead and gone;   30
             At his head a grass-green turf,
                At his heels a stone.
        O, ho!

QUEEN: Nay, but, Ophelia,—

OPHELIA: Pray you, mark
   (Sings) White his shroud as the mountain snow,—   35

(Enter King.)

QUEEN: Alas, look here, my lord.

OPHELIA: *(Sings)* Larded with sweet flowers;
        Which bewept to the grave did go
          With true-love showers.

KING: How do you, pretty lady?   40

OPHELIA: Well, God 'ild you! They say the owl was a baker's daughter.
        Lord, we know what we are, but know not what we may be. God
        be at your table!

15 *ill-breeding,* that breed evil.   18 *toy,* trifle; *amiss,* disaster.   19 *jealousy,* suspicion.   20 *spills itself,* gives itself away.   25 *cockle hat,* pilgrim's hat, with cockle shell on it, the sign of a visit to the shrine of St. James of Compostella in Spain. The metaphor of the lover as pilgrim and his beloved as the saint whose shrine he visited was common. Romeo puts on a pilgrim's costume and enacts the metaphor at the masquerade where he meets Juliet.   41 *'ild,* yield or reward; *owl . . . daughter,* a medieval legend has a baker's daughter turned into an owl for refusing bread to Christ.

KING: Conceit upon her father.

OPHELIA: Pray you, let's have no words of this; but when they ask you   45
what it means, say you this:
> *(Sings)* To-morrow is Saint Valentine's day,
>   All in the morning betime,
> And I a maid at your window,
>   To be your Valentine.   50
> Then up he rose, and donn'd his clothes,
>   And dupp'd the chamber-door;
> Let in the maid, that out a maid
>   Never departed more.

KING: Pretty Ophelia!   55

OPHELIA: Indeed, la, without an oath, I'll make an end on 't:
> *(Sings)* By Gis and by Saint Charity,
>   Alack, and fie for shame!
> Young men will do 't, if they come to 't;
>   By cock, they are to blame.   60
> Quoth she, before you tumbled me,
>   You promis'd me to wed.
> So would I ha' done, by yonder sun,
>   An thou hadst not come to my bed.

KING: How long hath she been thus?   65

OPHELIA: I hope all will be well. We must be patient; but I cannot choose
but weep, to think they should lay him i' the cold ground. My
brother shall know of it; and so I thank you for your good counsel.
Come, my coach! Good night, ladies; good night, sweet ladies; good
night, good night.   *(Exit)*   70

KING: Follow her close; give her good watch, I pray you.

(Exit Horatio.)

> O, this is the poison of deep grief; it springs
> All from her father's death. O Gertrude, Gertrude,
> When sorrows come, they come not single spies,
> But in battalions. First, her father slain;   75
> Next, your son gone; and he most violent author
> Of his own just remove; the people muddied,
> Thick and unwholesome in their thoughts and whispers,
> For good Polonius' death; and we have done but greenly,
> In hugger-mugger to inter him; poor Ophelia   80
> Divided from herself and her fair judgement,

---

44 *Conceit upon,* thinking about.   **45** *let's . . . this,* don't mention this to anyone.   **48** *in the morning,* the first girl a man saw on Valentine's day would be his true love.   **52** *dupp'd,* opened. **57** *Gis,* Jesus.   **60** *By cock,* "By God."   **77** *muddied,* stirred up, like a pool.   **79** *greenly,* foolishly.   **80** *hugger-mugger,* hastily and secretly.

Without the which we are pictures, or mere beasts;
Last, and as much containing as all these,
Her brother is in secret come from France,
Feeds on his wonder, keeps himself in clouds,   85
And wants not buzzers to infect his ear
With pestilent speeches of his father's death;
Wherein necessity, of matter beggar'd,
Will nothing stick our person to arraign
In ear and ear. O my dear Gertrude, this,   90
Like to a murdering-piece, in many places
Gives me superfluous death. *(A noise within.)*

QUEEN: Alack, what noise is this?
KING: Where are my Switzers? Let them guard the door.

(Enter a Messenger.)

What is the matter?
MESSENGER: Save yourself, my lord;
The ocean, overpeering of his list,   95
Eats not the flats with more impetuous haste
Than young Laertes, in a riotous head,
O'erbears your officers. The rabble call him lord;
And, as the world were now but to begin,
Antiquity forgot, custom not known,   100
The ratifiers and props of every word,
They cry "Choose we; Laertes shall be king!"
Caps, hands, and tongues, applaud it to the clouds,
"Laertes shall be king, Laertes king!"
QUEEN: How cheerfully on the false trail they cry!   105
O, this is counter, you false Danish dogs!
KING: The doors are broke.

(Noise within.)

(Enter Laertes with others.)

LAERTES: Where is this king? Sirs, stand you all without.
ALL: No, let's come in.
LAERTES: I pray you, give me leave.
ALL: We will, we will.   110

(They retire without the door.)

---

85 *in clouds,* invisible.   **86** *buzzers,* scandal mongers.   **88** *matter,* facts.   **89** *nothing stick,* stick at nothing.   **91** *murdering-piece,* a mortar firing shot.   **92** *superfluous,* more than enough.
93 *Switzers,* Swiss guards.   **95** *overpeering of his list,* rising above its usual limit.   **96** *flats,* lowlands.   **97** *head,* armed force.   **106** *counter,* following the scent in the wrong direction.

LAERTES: I thank you. Keep the door. O thou vile king,
 Give me my father!

QUEEN: Calmly, good Laertes.

LAERTES: That drop of blood that's calm proclaims me bastard,
 Cries cuckold to my father, brands the harlot
 Even here, between the chaste unsmirchèd brows   115
 Of my true mother.

KING: What is the cause, Laertes,
 That thy rebellion looks so giant-like?
 Let him go, Gertrude; do not fear our person:
 There's such divinity doth hedge a king,
 That treason can but peep to what it would,   120
 Acts little of his will. Tell me, Laertes,
 Why thou art thus incens'd. Let him go, Gertrude.
 Speak, man.

LAERTES: Where is my father?

KING: Dead.

QUEEN: But not by him.

KING: Let him demand his fill.   125

LAERTES: How came he dead? I'll not be juggled with.
 To hell, allegiance! Vows, to the blackest devil!
 Conscience and grace, to the profoundest pit!
 I dare damnation. To this point I stand,
 That both the worlds I give to negligence,   130
 Let come what comes; only I'll be reveng'd
 Most throughly for my father.

KING: Who shall stay you?

LAERTES: My will, not all the world!
 And for my means, I'll husband them so well,
 They shall go far with little.

KING: Good Laertes,   135
 If you desire to know the certainty
 Of your dear father's death, is 't writ in your revenge,
 That, swoopstake, you will draw both friend and foe,
 Winner and loser?

LAERTES: None but his enemies.

KING: Will you know them then?   140

LAERTES: To his good friends thus wide I'll ope my arms;
 And like the kind life-rendering pelican,
 Repast them with my blood.

KING: Why, now you speak

---

118 *fear,* fear for. **130** *both the worlds* heaven and hell. **138** *swoopstake,* sweeping up all the stakes on the table. **142** *life-rendering pelican,* the female pelican was supposed to feed her young with her own blood.

Like a good child and a true gentleman.
That I am guiltless of your father's death,   145
And am most sensibly in grief for it,
It shall as level to your judgement pierce
As day does to your eye.
(A noise within). Let her come in.
LAERTES: How now! What noise is that?   150

(Enter Ophelia.)

O heat, dry up my brains! Tears seven times salt,
Burn out the sense and virtue of mine eye.
By heaven, thy madness shall be paid with weight,
Till our scale turn the beam. O rose of May!
Dear maid, kind sister, sweet Ophelia!   155
O heavens! Is't possible, a young maid's wits
Should be as mortal as an old man's life?
Nature is fine in love, and where 'tis fine,
It sends some precious instance of itself
After the thing it loves.   160
OPHELIA: *(Sings)*
    They bore him barefac'd on the bier;
    Hey non nonny, nonny, hey nonny;
    And in his grave rain'd many a tear;—
Fare you well, my dove!
LAERTES: Hadst thou thy wits, and didst persuade revenge,   165
It could not move thus.
OPHELIA: *(Sings)*
    You must sing a-down a-down,
      An you call him a-down-a.
O, how the wheel becomes it! It is the false steward, that stole his
master's daughter.   170
LAERTES: This nothing's more than matter.
OPHELIA: There's rosemary, that's for remembrance; pray, love, remem-
ber: and there is pansies, that's for thoughts.
LAERTES: A document in madness, thoughts and remembrance fitted.
OPHELIA: There's fennel for you, and columbines: there's rue for you;   175
and here's some for me: we may call it herb-grace o' Sundays. O,
you must wear your rue with a difference. There's a daisy; I would

---

146 *sensibly,* feelingly.   **158** *fine* delicate.   **169** *wheel,* refrain.   **171** *This . . . matter,* this nonsense is more revealing than sensible talk.   **172** *rosemary,* Cf. *The Handfull of Pleasant Delights*
(1584): *Rosemarie* is for remembrance,/ betweene us daie and night:/ Wishing that I might alwaies
have/ you present in my sight. Rosemary was also strewn on biers.   **173** *pansies,* pensées for
"thoughts."   **175** *fennel,* for flattery.   **175** *columbines,* ingratitude.   **176** *herb-grace,* rue when
mixed with holy water.   **177** *rue,* for sorrow; *difference,* heraldic term for the distinction between
two coats of arms of different members of the same family.   **177** *daisy,* for faithlessness.

give you some violets, but they withered all when my father died.
They say he made a good end,—
(Sings) For bonny sweet Robin is all my joy.   180
LAERTES: Thought and affliction, passion, hell itself,
She turns to favour and to prettiness.
OPHELIA: *(Sings)*

And will he not come again?
And will he not come again?
No, no, he is dead;   185
Go to thy death-bed;
He never will come again.

His beard was as white as snow,
All flaxen was his poll.
He is gone, he is gone,   190
And we cast away moan.
God ha' mercy on his soul!

And of all Christian souls, I pray God. God be wi' ye.   *(Exit.)*
LAERTES: Do you see this, O God?
KING: Laertes, I must commune with your grief,   195
Or you deny me right. Go but apart,
Make choice of whom your wisest friends you will,
And they shall hear and judge 'twixt you and me:
If by direct or by collateral hand
They find us touch'd, we will our kingdom give,   200
Our crown, our life, and all that we call ours,
To you in satisfaction; but if not,
Be you content to lend your patience to us,
And we shall jointly labour with your soul
To give it due content.
LAERTES: Let this be so;   205
His means of death, his obscure funeral—
No trophy, sword, nor hatchment o'er his bones,
No noble rite nor formal ostentation—
Cry to be heard, as 'twere from heaven to earth,
That I must call 't in question.
KING: So you shall;   210
And where th' offence is let the great axe fall.
I pray you, go with me.   *(Exeunt.)*

Act IV

Scene VI

Another room in the castle. Enter Horatio and a Servant.

191 *cast away,* castaways.   200 *touch'd,* implicated.   207 *trophy,* memorial; *hatchment,* tablet
bearing the coat of arms of the deceased.   208 *ostentation,* ceremony.

HORATIO: What are they that would speak with me?

SERVANT: Sailors, sir. They say they have letters for you.

HORATIO: Let them come in.   *(Exit Servant.)*

I do not know from what part of the world I should be greeted, if not
from lord Hamlet.

(Enter Sailors.)

SAILOR: God bless you, sir.   5

HORATIO: Let him bless thee too.

SAILOR: He shall, sir, an 't please him. There's a letter for you, sir; it
comes from the ambassador that was bound for England; if your
name be Horatio, as I am let to know it is.

HORATIO: *(Reads)* "Horatio, when thou shalt have overlooked this, give
these fellows some means to the king: they have letters for him. Ere
we were two days old at sea, a pirate of very warlike appointment   10
gave us chase. Finding ourselves too slow of sail, we put on a
compelled valour, and in the grapple I boarded them. On the instant
they got clear of our ship; so I alone became their prisoner. They
have dealt with me like thieves of mercy; but they knew what they
did; I am to do a good turn for them. Let the king have the letters   15
I have sent; and repair thou to me with as much speed as thou
wouldst fly death. I have words to speak in thine ear will make thee
dumb; yet are they much too light for the bore of the matter. These
good fellows will bring thee where I am. Rozencrantz and Guildenstern hold their course for England: of them I have much to tell   20
thee. Farewell.

       "He that thou knowest thine, HAMLET."

Come, I will give you way for these your letters;
And do 't the speedier, that you may direct me
To him from whom you brought them.   25

(Exeunt.)

Act IV

Scene VII

Another room in the castle. Enter King and Laertes.

KING: Now must your conscience my acquittance seal,
 And you must put me in your heart for friend,
 Sith you have heard, and with a knowing ear,
 That he which hath your noble father slain
 Pursu'd my life.

LAERTES: It well appears; but tell me   5

---

8 *overlooked,* looked over. **10** *appointment,* equipment. **12** *in the grapple,* when the ships were
grappled together. **14** *thieves of mercy,* merciful thieves. **18** *bore,* caliber, importance.
1 *conscience,* knowledge of the facts. **5** *Pursu'd,* sought.

Why you proceeded not against these feats,
So crimeful and so capital in nature,
As by your safety, wisdom, all things else,
You mainly were stirr'd up.

KING: O, for two special reasons;
Which may to you, perhaps, seem much unsinew'd,   10
But yet to me they are strong. The queen his mother
Lives almost by his looks; and for myself—
My virtue or my plague, be it either which—
She's so conjunctive to my life and soul,
That, as the star moves not but in his sphere,   15
I could not but by her. The other motive,
Why to a public count I might not go,
Is the great love the general gender bear him;
Who, dipping all his faults in their affection,
Would, like the spring that turneth wood to stone,   20
Convert his gyves to graces; so that my arrows,
Too slightly timber'd for so loud a wind,
Would have reverted to my bow again,
And not where I had aim'd them.

LAERTES: And so have I a noble father lost;   25
A sister driven into desperate terms,
Whose worth, if praises may go back again,
Stood challenger on mount of all the age
For her perfections. But my revenge will come.

KING: Break not your sleeps for that; you must not think 30
That we are made of stuff so flat and dull
That we can let our beard be shook with danger
And think it pastime. You shortly shall hear more.
I lov'd your father, and we love ourself,
And that, I hope, will teach you to imagine—   35

(Enter a Messenger.)

How now! What news?
MESSENGER: Letters, my lord, from Hamlet:
This to your majesty; this to the queen.
KING: From Hamlet! Who brought them?
MESSENGER: Sailors, my lord, they say; I saw them not.
They were given me by Claudio; he receiv'd them   40
Of him that brought them.

---

7 *capital,* punishable by death.   17 *count,* reckoning.   18 *general gender,* common people.
20 *the spring,* a famous spring in Yorkshire.   21 *gyves,* fetters.   22 *loud,* violent.   26 *terms,*
conditions.   27 *if praises ... again,* if I may praise her former self.   29 *Stood ... perfections,* Stood
challenger of all the age, mounted to defend her claim to perfection.

KING: Laertes, you shall hear them.
Leave us.   *(Exit Messenger.)*
(Reads) "High and mighty, You shall know I am set naked on your
    kingdom. To-morrow shall I beg leave to see your kingly eyes; when
    I shall, first asking your pardon thereunto, recount the occasion of
    my sudden and more strange return.

                                                                "HAMLET."

What should this mean? Are all the rest come back?   45
Or is it some abuse, and no such thing?
LAERTES: Know you the hand?
KING: 'Tis Hamlet's character. "Naked!"
    And in a postscript here, he says "alone."
    Can you advise me?   50
LAERTES: I'm lost in it, my lord. But let him come;
    It warms the very sickness in my heart,
    That I shall live and tell him to his teeth,
    "Thus didst thou."
KING: If it be so, Laertes—
    As how should it be so? how otherwise?—   55
    Will you be rul'd by me?
LAERTES: Ay, my lord,
    So you will not o'errule me to a peace.
KING: To thine own peace. If he be now return'd,
    As checking at his voyage, and that he means
    No more to undertake it, I will work him   60
    To an exploit, now ripe in my device,
    Under the which he shall not choose but fall;
    And for his death no wind of blame shall breathe,
    But even his mother shall uncharge the practice
    And call it accident.
LAERTES: My lord, I will be rul'd;   65
    The rather, if you could devise it so
    That I might be the organ.
KING: It falls right.
    You have been talk'd of since your travel much,
    And that in Hamlet's hearing, for a quality
    Wherein, they say, you shine; your sum of parts   70
    Did not together pluck such envy from him
    As did that one, and that, in my regard,
    Of the unworthiest siege.
LAERTES: What part is that, my lord?

---

43 *naked,* destitute.   **46** *abuse,* deception.   **48** *character,* handwriting.   **59** *checking,* balking.
A falcon "checked" when stopping flight to veer at another target.   **61** *ripe in my device,* completely
planned.   **73** *siege,* rank.

KING: A very riband in the cap of youth,
    Yet needful too; for youth no less becomes   **75**
    The light and careless livery that it wears
    Than settled age his sables and his weeds,
    Importing health and graveness. Two months since
    Here was a gentleman of Normandy.
    I've seen myself, and serv'd against, the French,   **80**
    And they can well on horseback; but this gallant
    Had witchcraft in 't; he grew unto his seat;
    And to such wondrous doing brought his horse,
    As had he been incorps'd and demi-natur'd
    With the brave beast; so far he topp'd my thought,   **85**
    That I, in forgery of shapes and tricks,
    Come short of what he did.
LAERTES: A Norman was 't?
KING: A Norman.
LAERTES: Upon my life, Lamond.
KING: The very same.
LAERTES: I know him well; he is the brooch indeed   **90**
    And gem of all the nation.
KING: He made confession of you,
    And gave you such a masterly report
    For art and exercise in your defence
    And for your rapier most especial,   **95**
    That he cried out, 'twould be a sight indeed,
    If one could match you; the scrimers of their nation,
    He swore, had neither motion, guard, nor eye,
    If you oppos'd them. Sir, this report of his
    Did Hamlet so envenom with his envy   **100**
    That he could nothing do but wish and beg
    Your sudden coming o'er, to play with him.
    Now, out of this,—
LAERTES: What out of this, my lord?
KING: Laertes, was your father dear to you?
    Or are you like the painting of a sorrow,   **105**
    A face without a heart?
LAERTES: Why ask you this?
KING: Not that I think you did not love your father,
    But that I know love is begun by time;
    And that I see, in passages of proof,
    Time qualifies the spark and fire of it.   **110**

---

81 *can well,* are skillful.   **85** *thought,* expectations.   **86** *in forgery,* in imagining.   **89** *Lamond,* perhaps Pietro Monte (La Mont) a famous French horseman.   **92** *confession,* full report. **97** *scrimers,* fencers.   **102** *play,* fence.   **109** *passages of proof,* well-authenticated examples. **110** *qualifies,* diminishes.

There lives within the very flame of love
A kind of wick or snuff that will abate it;
And nothing is at a like goodness still;
For goodness, growing to a plurisy,
Dies in his own too much. That we would do,   115
We should do when we would; for this "would" changes
And hath abatements and delays as many
As there are tongues, are hands, are accidents;
And then this "should" is like a spendthrift sigh,
That hurts by easing. But, to the quick o' the ulcer:—   120
Hamlet comes back; what would you undertake,
To show yourself your father's son in deed
More than in words?
LAERTES: To cut his throat i' the church.
KING: No place, indeed, should murder sanctuarize;
Revenge should have no bounds. But, good Laertes,   125
Will you do this, keep close within your chamber.
Hamlet return'd shall know you are come home.
We'll put on those shall praise your excellence
And set a double varnish on the fame
The Frenchman gave you, bring you, in fine, together   130
And wager on your heads. He, being remiss,
Most generous and free from all contriving,
Will not peruse the foils; so that, with ease,
Or with a little shuffling, you may choose
A sword unbated, and in a pass of practice   135
Requite him for your father.
LAERTES: I will do 't:
And, for that purpose, I'll anoint my sword.
I bought an unction of a mountebank,
So mortal that, but dip a knife in it,
Where it draws blood no cataplasm so rare,   140
Collected from all simples that have virtue
Under the moon, can save the thing from death
That is but scratch'd withal; I'll touch my point
With this contagion, that, if I gall him slightly,
It may be death.
KING: Let's further think of this,   145
Weigh what convenience both of time and means
May fit us to our shape. If this should fail,
And that our drift look through our bad performance,
'Twere better not assay'd; therefore this project

---

113 *still,* always.   **114** *plurisy,* plethora, excess.   **135** *unbated,* unblunted; *pass of practice,* treacherous thrust   **140** *cataplasm,* poultice.   **141** *simples,* herbs; *virtue,* medicinal property.
147 *shape,* plan.   **148** *drift look through,* scheme show through.

Should have a back or second, that might hold,   150
If this should blast in proof. Soft! Let me see;
We'll make a solemn wager on your cunnings:
I ha 't:
When in your motion you are hot and dry—
As make your bouts more violent to that end—   155
And that he calls for drink, I'll have prepar'd him
A chalice for the nonce, whereon but sipping,
If he by chance escape your venom'd stuck,
Our purpose may hold there.

(Enter QUEEN.*)*

                                        How now, sweet queen!
QUEEN: One woe doth tread upon another's heel,   160
    So fast they follow: your sister's drown'd, Laertes.
LAERTES: Drown'd! O, where?
QUEEN: There is a willow grows aslant a brook,
    That shows his hoar leaves in the glassy stream;
    There with fantastic garlands did she come   165
    Of crow-flowers, nettles, daisies, and long purples
    That liberal shepherds give a grosser name,
    But our cold maids do dead men's fingers call them;
    There, on the pendent boughs her coronet weeds
    Clambering to hang, an envious sliver broke;   170
    When down her weedy trophies and herself
    Fell in the weeping brook. Her clothes spread wide,
    And, mermaid-like, awhile they bore her up;
    Which time she chanted snatches of old tunes,
    As one incapable of her own distress,   175
    Or like a creature native and indu'd
    Unto that element; but long it could not be
    Till that her garments, heavy with their drink,
    Pull'd the poor wretch from her melodious lay
    To muddy death.
LAERTES: Alas, then, she is drown'd?   180
QUEEN: Drown'd, drown'd.
LAERTES: Too much of water hast thou, poor Ophelia,
    And therefore I forbid my tears; but yet
    It is our trick, nature her custom holds,
    Let shame say what it will; when these are gone,   185

---

152 *solemn,* formal; *cunnings,* skills.   **157** *nonce,* occasion.   **158** *stuck,* thrust.   **164** *hoar,* gray.
166 *crow-flowers,* buttercups; *long purples,* a kind of orchid, *orchis mascula,* a popular phallic symbol.
167 *liberal,* licentious.   **170** *envious sliver,* spiteful branch.   **175** *incapable,* not understanding.
176 *indu'd,* suited.   **177** *that element,* the water.

The woman will be out. Adieu, my lord.
I have a speech of fire, that fain would blaze,
But that this folly douts it.   *(Exit.)*
KING: Let's follow, Gertrude:
How much I had to do to calm his rage!
Now fear I this will give it start again;   190
Therefore let's follow.   *(Exeunt.)*

Act V

Scene I

A churchyard. Enter two Clowns, with spades, etc.

CLOWN: Is she to be buried in Christian burial that willfully seeks her
    own salvation?

OTHER: I tell thee she is; and therefore make her grave straight: the
    crowner hath sat on her, and finds it Christian burial.

CLOWN: How can that be, unless she drowned herself in her own de-
    fence?

OTHER: Why, 'tis found so.

CLOWN: It must be *se offendendo*, it cannot be else. For here lies the   5
    point: if I drown myself wittingly, it argues an act; and an act hath
    three branches; it is, to act, to do, and to perform: argal, she
    drowned herself wittingly.

OTHER: Nay, but hear you, goodman delver,—

CLOWN: Give me leave. Here lies the water; good: here stands the man;   10
    good: if the man go to this water, and drown himself, it is, will he,
    nill he, he goes,—mark you that? But if the water come to him and
    drown him, he drowns not himself: argal, he that is not guilty of his
    own death shortens not his own life.

OTHER: But is this law?   15

CLOWN: Ay, marry, is 't; crowner's quest law.

OTHER: Will you ha' the truth on 't? If this had not been a gentlewoman,
    she should have been buried out o' Christian burial.

CLOWN: Why, there thou say'st; and the more pity that great folk should
    have countenance in this world to drown or hang themselves, more
    than their even Christian. Come, my spade. There is no ancient   20
    gentlemen but gardeners, ditchers, and grave-makers; they hold up
    Adam's profession.

---

186 *woman will be out,* my womanly softness will be gone.   **188** *douts it,* puts it out. s.d., *Clowns,*
country bumpkins, played by the company's comic actors.   **1** *Christian burial,* within the churchyard—suicides were denied burial in consecrated ground.   **2** *straight,* at once.   **2** *crowner . . . her,*
the coroner has rendered his decision about her.   **5** *se offendendo,* he means "se defendendo," in
self-defense.   **7** *argal,* the bumpkin's version of *ergo,* therefore.   **16** *quest,* inquest.   **20** *even,*
fellow.

OTHER: Was he a gentleman?

CLOWN: 'A was the first that ever bore arms.

OTHER: Why, he had none.   25

CLOWN: What! Art a heathen? How dost thou understand the Scripture?
      The Scripture says "Adam digg'd." Could he dig without arms? I'll
      put another question to thee; if thou answerest me not to the pur-
      pose, confess thyself—

OTHER: Go to.   30

CLOWN: What is he that builds stronger than either the mason, the
      shipwright, or the carpenter?

OTHER: The gallows-maker, for that frame outlives a thousand tenants.

CLOWN: I like thy wit well, in good faith; the gallows does well; but how
      does it well? it does well to those that do ill; now thou dost ill to
      say the gallows is built stronger than the church: argal, the gallows
      may do well to thee. To 't again, come.

OTHER: Who builds stronger than a mason, a shipwright, or a carpenter?

CLOWN: Ay, tell me that, and unyoke.   35

OTHER: Marry, now I can tell.

CLOWN: To 't.

OTHER: Mass, I cannot tell.

(Enter Hamlet and Horatio afar off.)

CLOWN: Cudgel thy brains no more about it, for your dull ass will not
      mend his pace with beating; and, when you are asked this question   40
      next, say "a grave-maker:" the houses that he makes last till dooms-
      day. Go, get thee to Yaughan; fetch me a stoup of liquor.

                                                        (Exit other Clown.)

(He digs, and sings.)

      In youth, when I did love, did love,
         Methought it was very sweet,
      To contract, Oh, the time, for, ah, my behove,   45
         Oh, methought, there was nothing meet.

HAMLET: Has this fellow no feeling of his business, that he sings at
      grave-making?

HORATIO: Custom hath made it in him a property of easiness.

HAMLET: 'Tis e'en so; the hand of little employment hath the daintier   50
      sense.

CLOWN: *(Sings)*

      But age, with his stealing steps,
         Hath claw'd me in his clutch,

---

24 *bore arms.* a pun on a gentleman's coat of arms, his armorial bearing, and being a soldier.
29 *confess thyself,* "and be hanged" is the rest of the proverb.   35 *unyoke,* your team—your job
is done.   42 *Yaughan,* probably an actual alehouse keeper near the Globe theater; *stoup,* a two-quart
mug.   45 *contract,* shorten; *behove,* advantage.

And hath shipped me intil the land,
    As if I had never been such.   55

(Throws up a skull.)

HAMLET: That skull had a tongue in it, and could sing once. How the
    knave jowls it to the ground, as if it were Cain's jaw-bone, that did
    the first murder! It might be the pate of a politician, which this ass
    now o'er-reaches; one that would circumvent God, might it not?

HORATIO: It might, my lord.   60

HAMLET: Or of a courtier; which could say "Good morrow, sweet lord!
    How dost thou, good lord?" This might be my lord such-a-one, that
    praised my lord such-a-one's horse, when he meant to beg it; might
    it not?

HORATIO: Ay, my lord.   65

HAMLET: Why, e'en so; and now my Lady Worm's; chapless, and
    knocked about the mazzard with a sexton's spade. Here's fine revo-
    lution, an we had the trick to see 't. Did these bones cost no more
    the breeding, but to play at loggats with 'em? Mine ache to think
    on 't.   70

CLOWN: *(Sings)*
    A pick-axe, and a spade, a spade,
        For and a shrouding sheet:
    O, a pit of clay for to be made
        For such a guest is meet.

(Throws up another skull.)

HAMLET: There's another; why may not that be the skull of a lawyer?   75
    Where be his quiddities now, his quillets, his cases, his tenures, and
    his tricks? Why does he suffer this rude knave now to knock him
    about the sconce with a dirty shovel, and will not tell him of his
    action of battery? Hum! This fellow might be in 's time a great buyer
    of land, with his statutes, his recognizances, his fines, his double   80
    vouchers, his recoveries; is this the fine of his fines, and the recovery
    of his recoveries, to have his fine pate full of fine dirt? Will his
    vouchers vouch him no more of his purchases, and double ones too,
    than the length and breadth of a pair of indentures? The very
    conveyances of his lands will hardly lie in this box, and must the   85
    inheritor himself have no more, ha?

HORATIO: Not a jot more, my lord.

HAMLET: Is not parchment made of sheepskins?

HORATIO: Ay, my lord, and of calf-skins too.

54 *intil,* into.   **57** *jowls,* hurls; *jaw-bone,* in popular belief, Cain killed Abel with the jawbone of an
ass.   **66** *chapless,* jawless.   **67** *mazzard,* head.   **68** *trick,* knack.   **69** *play at loggats,* game in
which skull-shaped pieces of wood (loggats) were thrown to lie near a stake.   **76** *quiddities,* quibbles.
quillets, hair-splittings; *tenures,* leases.   **78** *sconce,* head.   **81** *fine,* "end."   **84** *pair of indentures,*
contracts in duplicate.   **85** *conveyances,* deeds.

HAMLET: They are sheep and calves which seek out assurance in that.   90
    I will speak to this fellow. Whose grave's this, sirrah?

CLOWN: Mine sir.

    (Sings) O, a pit of clay for to be made
           For such a guest is meet.

HAMLET: I think it be thine, indeed; for thou liest in 't.   95

CLOWN: You lie out on 't, sir, and therefor it is not yours; for my part,
    I do not lie in 't, and yet it is mine.

HAMLET: Thou dost lie in 't, to be in 't and say it is thine: 'tis for the
    dead, not for the quick; therefore thou liest.

CLOWN: 'Tis a quick lie, sir; 'twill away again, from me to you.   100

HAMLET: What man dost thou dig it for?

CLOWN: For no man, sir.

HAMLET: What woman, then?

CLOWN: For none, neither.

HAMLET: Who is to be buried in 't?   105

CLOWN: One that was a woman, sir; but, rest her soul, she's dead.

HAMLET: How absolute the knave is! We must speak by the card, or
    equivocation will undo us. By the Lord, Horatio, these three years
    I have taken note of it; the age is grown so picked that the toe of
    the peasant comes so near the heel of the courtier, he galls his kibe.   110
    How long hast thou been a grave-maker?

CLOWN: Of all the days i' the year, I came to 't that day that our last
    king Hamlet overcame Fortinbras.

HAMLET: How long is that since?

CLOWN: Cannot you tell that? Every fool can tell that; it was the very   115
    day that young Hamlet was born, he that is mad, and sent into
    England.

HAMLET: Ay, marry, why was he sent into England?

CLOWN: Why, because 'a was mad. 'A shall recover his wits there; or,
    if 'a do not, it 's no great matter there.   120

HAMLET: Why?

CLOWN: 'Twill not be seen in him there. There the men are as mad as
    he.

HAMLET: How came he mad?

CLOWN: Very strangely, they say.   125

HAMLET: How strangely?

CLOWN: Faith, e'en with losing his wits.

HAMLET: Upon what ground?

CLOWN: Why, here in Denmark. I have been sexton here, man and boy,
    thirty years.   130

HAMLET: How long will a man lie i' the earth ere he rot?

---

90 *assurance in that,* safety in legal documents.   107 *absolute,* meticulous.   107 *card,* compass,
considering every point.   109 *picked,* fastidious.   110 *galls his kibe,* chafes his chilblain.

CLOWN: I' faith, if 'a be not rotten before 'a die—as we have many pocky
  corses now-a-days, that will scarce hold the laying in—'a will last
  you some eight year or nine year; a tanner will last you nine year.

HAMLET: Why he more than another?   135

CLOWN: Why, sir, his hide is so tann'd with his trade, that 'a will keep
  out water a great while; and your water is a sore decayer of your
  whoreson dead body. Here's a skull now; this skull has lain i' the
  earth three and twenty years.

HAMLET: Whose was it?   140

CLOWN: A whoreson mad fellow's it was: whose do you think it was?

HAMLET: Nay, I know not.

CLOWN: A pestilence on him for a mad rogue! 'a pour'd a flagon of
  Rhenish on my head once. This same skull, sir, was Yorick's skull,
  the king's jester.   145

HAMLET: This?

CLOWN: E'en that.

HAMLET: Let me see. *(Takes the skull.)* Alas, poor Yorick! I knew him,
  Horatio: a fellow of infinite jest, of most excellent fancy; he hath
  borne me on his back a thousand times; and now, how abhorred in   150
  my imagination it is! my gorge rises at it. Here hung those lips that
  I have kissed I know not how oft. Where be your gibes now? Your
  gambols? Your songs? Your flashes of merriment, that were wont
  to set the table on a roar? Not one now, to mock your own grinning?
  Quite chap-fallen? Now get you to my lady's chamber, and tell her, 155
  let her paint an inch thick, to this favour she must come; make her
  laugh at that. Prithee, Horatio, tell me one thing.

HORATIO: What's that, my lord?

HAMLET: Dost thou think Alexander looked o' this fashion i' the
  earth?   160

HORATIO: E'en so.

HAMLET: And smelt so? Pah!

(Puts down the skull.)

HORATIO: E'en so, my lord.

HAMLET: To what base uses we may return, Horatio! Why may not
  imagination trace the noble dust of Alexander, till he find it stopping 165
  a bung-hole?

HORATIO: 'Twere to consider too curiously, to consider so.

HAMLET: No, faith, not a jot; but to follow him thither with modesty
  enough, and likelihood to lead it; as thus: Alexander died, Alexander was buried, Alexander returneth into dust; the dust is earth; of 170
  earth we make loam; and why of that loam, whereto he was con-
  verted, might they not stop a beer-barrel?

---

132 *pocky,* rotten with syphilis, the pox.   **155** *chap-fallen,* a pun (1) down in the mouth, (2) having
no lower jaw.   **156** *favour,* appearance.   **167** *curiously,* minutely.

Imperious Cæsar, dead and turn'd to clay,
Might stop a hole to keep the wind away:
O, that that earth, which kept the world in awe,   175
Should patch a wall to expel the winter's flaw!
But soft! but soft! aside: here comes the king,

(Enter Priests, etc., with a coffin, King, Queen, Laertes, with Lords attendant.)

The queen, the courtiers: who is this they follow?
And with such maimèd rites? This doth betoken
The corse they follow did with desperate hand   180
Fordo it own life; 'twas of some estate.
Couch we awhile, and mark.

(Retiring with Horatio)

LAERTES: What ceremony else?
HAMLET: That is Laertes,
A very noble youth: mark.   185
LAERTES: What ceremony else?
PRIEST: Her obsequies have been as far enlarg'd
As we have warranty: her death was doubtful;
And, but that great command o'ersways the order,
She should in ground unsanctified have lodg'd   190
Till the last trumpet; for charitable prayers,
Shards, flints, and pebbles should be thrown on her;
Yet here she is allow'd her virgin crants,
Her maiden strewments and the bringing home
Of bell and burial.   195
LAERTES: Must there no more be done?
PRIEST: No more be done:
We should profane the service of the dead
To sing a requiem and such rest to her
As to peace-parted souls.
LAERTES: Lay her i' the earth:
And from her fair and unpolluted flesh   200
May violets spring! I tell thee, churlish priest,
A ministering angel shall my sister be,
When thou liest howling.
HAMLET: What! The fair Ophelia?
QUEEN: Sweets to the sweet: farewell!

---

176 *flaw,* gust of wind.   **179** *maimèd,* incomplete.   **193** *crants,* garlands.   **194** *strewments,* the
strewing of flowers; *bringing home,* (1) bringing home a bride after a wedding, (2) bringing Ophelia
to her eternal home.

(Scattering flowers.)

I hop'd thou shouldst have been my Hamlet's wife;   205
I thought thy bride-bed to have deck'd, sweet maid,
And not have strew'd thy grave.

LAERTES: O! Treble woe
Fall ten times treble on that cursèd head,
Whose wicked deed thy most ingenious sense
Depriv'd thee of! Hold off the earth awhile,   210
Till I have caught her once more in mine arms.

(Leaps into the grave.)

Now pile your dust upon the quick and dead,
Till of this flat a mountain you have made,
To o'ertop old Pelion, or the skyish head
Of blue Olympus.   215

HAMLET: *(Advancing)* What is he whose grief
Bears such an emphasis? whose phrase of sorrow
Conjures the wandering stars, and makes them stand
Like wonder-wounded hearers? This is I,
Hamlet the Dane.   *(Leaps into the grave.)*

LAERTES: The devil take thy soul!   220

(Grappling with him.)

HAMLET: Thou pray'st not well.
I prithee, take thy fingers from my throat;
For, though I am not splenitive and rash,
Yet have I something in me dangerous,
Which let thy wisdom fear. Hold off thy hand!   225

KING: Pluck them asunder.

QUEEN: Hamlet! Hamlet!

ALL: Gentlemen,—

HORATIO: Good my lord, be quiet.

(The Attendants part them, and they come out of the grave.)

HAMLET: Why, I will fight with him upon this theme
Until my eyelids will no longer wag.

QUEEN: O my son, what theme?   230

HAMLET: I lov'd Ophelia: forty thousand brothers
Could not, with all their quantity of love,
Make up my sum. What wilt thou do for her?

KING: O, he is mad, Laertes.

QUEEN: For love of God, forbear him.   235

HAMLET: 'Swounds, show me what thou'lt do:

214 *Pelion,* The Titans, at war with the gods, tried to pile Mt. Pelion on Mt. Ossa to reach Olympus.
218 *wandering stars,* planets.   **223** *splenitive,* hot-tempered.   **235** *forbear,* have patience with.

Woo 't weep? woo 't fight? woo 't fast? woo 't tear thyself?
Woo 't drink up eisel? eat a crocodile?
I'll do 't. Dost thou come here to whine?
To outface me with leaping in her grave?   240
Be buried quick with her, and so will I.
And, if thou prate of mountains, let them throw
Millions of acres on us, till our ground
Singeing his pate against the burning zone,
Make Ossa like a wart! Nay, an thou'lt mouth,   245
I'll rant as well as thou.

QUEEN: This is mere madness;
And thus awhile the fit will work on him;
Anon, as patient as the female dove,
When that her golden couplets are disclos'd,
His silence will sit dropping.

HAMLET: Hear you, sir;   250
What is the reason that you use me thus?
I lov'd you ever: but it is no matter;
Let Hercules himself do what he may,
The cat will mew and dog will have his day.

(Exit.)

KING: I pray you, good Horatio, wait upon him.   *(Exit Horatio.)*   255
(To Laertes) Strengthen your patience in our last night's speech;
We'll put the matter to the present push.
Good Gertrude, set some watch over your son.
This grave shall have a living monument:
An hour of quiet shortly shall we see;   260
Till then, in patience our proceeding be.

(Exeunt.)

Act V

Scene II

A hall in the castle. Enter Hamlet and Horatio.

HAMLET: So much for this, sir: now shall you see the other;
     You do remember all the circumstance?
HORATIO: Remember it, my lord!
HAMLET: Sir, in my heart there was a kind of fighting,

---

237 *Woo 't,* wilt, an illiterate form and thus insulting.   **238** *eisel,* vinegar, a supposed antidote to anger.   **244** *burning zone,* the sun's orbit.   **246** *mere,* complete.   **249** *golden couplets,* the dove lays only two eggs, and the chicks are covered with golden down; *disclos'd,* hatched.   **256** *in,* by remembering.   **257** *present push,* immediate test.   **259** *living,* lasting.

That would not let me sleep. Methought I lay   5
Worse than the mutines in the bilboes. Rashly,
And prais'd be rashness for it, let us know,
Our indiscretion sometimes serves us well,
When our deep plots do pall; and that should teach us
There's a divinity that shapes our ends,   10
Rough-hew them how we will,—

HORATIO: That is most certain.

HAMLET: Up from my cabin,
My sea-gown scarf'd about me, in the dark
Grop'd I to find out them; had my desire,
Finger'd their packet, and in fine withdrew   15
To mine own room again; making so bold,
My fears forgetting manners, to unseal
Their grand commission; where I found, Horatio,—
O royal knavery!—an exact command,
Larded with many several sorts of reasons   20
Importing Denmark's health and England's too,
With, ho! such bugs and goblins in my life,
That, on the supervise, no leisure bated,
No, not to stay the grinding of the axe,
My head should be struck off.

HORATIO: Is 't possible?   25

HAMLET: Here's the commission: read it at more leisure.
But wilt thou hear me how I did proceed?

HORATIO: I beseech you.

HAMLET: Being thus be-netted round with villanies,—
Ere I could make a prologue to my brains,   30
They had begun the play—I sat me down,
Devis'd a new commission, wrote it fair;
I once did hold it, as our statists do,
A baseness to write fair and labour'd much
How to forget that learning, but, sir, now   35
It did me yeoman's service. Wilt thou know
The effect of what I wrote?

HORATIO: Ay, good my lord.

HAMLET: An earnest conjuration from the king,
As England was his faithful tributary,
As love between them like the palm might flourish,   40
As peace should still her wheaten garland wear

---

6 *mutines,* mutineers; *bilboes,* fetters.   **11** *That is most certain,* As in I.iv. 91, Horatio underlines Shakespeare's thesis that God is in control after all.   **13** *sea-gown,* short-sleeved gown reaching to the calf.   **15** *Finger'd,* stole.   **23** *on the supervise,* upon looking it over; *leisure bated,* delay allowed.   **24** *stay,* wait for.   **32** *fair,* legibly.   **41** *wheaten garland,* symbol of peace.

And stand a comma 'tween their amities,
And many such-like "As"es of great charge,
That, on the view and knowing of these contents,
Without debatement further, more or less,   45
He should the bearers put to sudden death,
Not shriving-time allow'd.

HORATIO: How was this seal'd?

HAMLET: Why, even in that was heaven ordinant.
I had my father's signet in my purse,
Which was the model of that Danish seal;   50
Folded the writ up in form of the other,
Subscrib'd it, gave 't the impression, plac'd it safely,
The changeling never known. Now, the next day
Was our sea-fight, and what to this was sequent
Thou know'st already.   55

HORATIO: So Guildenstern and Rosencrantz go to 't.

HAMLET: Why, man, they did make love to this employment;
They are not near my conscience; their defeat
Does by their own insinuation grow.
'Tis dangerous when the baser nature comes   60
Between the pass and fell incensèd points
Of mighty opposites.

HORATIO: Why, what a king is this!

HAMLET: Does it not, thinks't thee, stand me now upon—
He that hath kill'd my king and whor'd my mother,
Popp'd in between the election and my hopes,   65
Thrown out his angle for my proper life,
And with such cozenage—is't not perfect conscience,
To quit him with this arm? and is 't not to be damn'd,
To let this canker of our nature come
In further evil?   70

HORATIO: It must be shortly known to him from England
What is the issue of the business there.

HAMLET: It will be short; the interim is mine;
And a man's life's no more than to say "One."
But I am very sorry, good Horatio,   75
That to Laertes I forgot myself;
For, by the image of my cause, I see

42 *comma,* connecting link.   43 *"As" es,* pun on "asses"; *charge,* burden.   45 *debatement,* discussion.   46 *sudden,* immediate.   47 *shriving-time,* time for absolution.   48 *ordinant,* ordering events.   52 *Subscrib'd,* signed; *gave . . . impression,* stamped it with the King's seal.   53 *changeling,* substitution.   57 *make . . . employment,* wooed this kind of treatment.   59 *insinuation,* meddling.   61 *pass,* thrust; *fell,* cruel.   62 *opposites,* opponents.   63 *stand . . . upon,* become my duty.   65 *election,* the Danish monarch was elective.   66 *angle,* fishing hook; *proper,* very.   67 *cozenage,* deceit.   68 *quit,* get even with.   69 *canker of,* cankerworm in.   74 *to say "One,"* life is short.

The portraiture of his: I'll court his favours.
But, sure, the bravery of his grief did put me
Into a towering passion.

HORATIO: Peace! who comes here?   80

(Enter Osric.)

OSRIC: Your lordship is right welcome back to Denmark.

HAMLET: I humbly thank you, sir. Dost know this water-fly?

HORATIO: No, my good lord.

HAMLET: Thy state is the more gracious; for 'tis a vice to know him. He
   hath much land, and fertile: let a beast be lord of beasts, and his crib   85
   shall stand at the king's mess. 'Tis a chough; but, as I say, spacious
   in the possession of dirt.

OSRIC: Sweet lord, if your lordship were at leisure, I should impart a
   thing to you from his majesty.

HAMLET: I will receive it, sir, with all diligence of spirit. Put your bonnet
   to his right use; 'tis for the head.

OSRIC: I thank your lordship, it is very hot.   90

HAMLET: No, believe me, 'tis very cold; the wind is northerly.

OSRIC: It is indifferent cold, my lord, indeed.

HAMLET: But yet methinks it is very sultry and hot for my complexion.

OSRIC: Exceedingly, my lord; it is very sultry, as 'twere, I cannot tell
   how. But, my lord, his majesty bade me signify to you that he has
   laid a great wager on your head. Sir, this is the matter,—

HAMLET: I beseech you, remember—   95

(Hamlet moves him to put on his hat.)

OSRIC: Nay, good my lord; for mine ease, in good faith. Sir, here is newly
   come to court Laertes; believe me, an absolute gentleman, full of
   most excellent differences, of very soft society and great showing.
   Indeed, to speak feelingly of him, he is the card or calendar of
   gentry, for you shall find in him the continent of what part a   100
   gentleman would see.

HAMLET: Sir, his definement suffers no perdition in you; though, I know,
   to divide him inventorially would dizzy the arithmetic of memory,
   and yet but yaw neither, in respect of his quick sail. But, in the verity
   of extolment, I take him to be a soul of great article; and his infusion
   of such dearth and rareness, as, to make true diction of him, his   105
   semblable in his mirror; and who else would trace him, his umbrage,
   nothing more.

---

79 *bravery,* ostentation.   **86** *mess,* table.   **86** *chough,* a crow, a chatterer.   **93** *complexion,*
temperament.   **98** *differences,* distinguishing qualities, soft, refined; *great showing,* fine appearance.
99 *card,* chart.   **100** *continent,* summary.   **105** *of such dearth,* so exceptional.   **106** *semblable,*
no one is like him but his image in the mirror; *trace,* imitate; umbrage, shadow.

OSRIC: Your lordship speaks most infallibly of him.

HAMLET: The concernancy, sir? why do we wrap the gentleman in our
more rawer breath?   110

OSRIC: Sir?

HORATIO: Is 't not possible to understand in another tongue? You will
do't, sir, really.

HAMLET: What imports the nomination of this gentleman?

OSRIC: Of Laertes?   115

HORATIO: His purse is empty already; all's golden words are spent.

HAMLET: Of him, sir.

OSRIC: I know you are not ignorant—

HAMLET: I would you did, sir; yet, in faith, if you did, it would not much
approve me. Well, sir?   120

OSRIC: You are not ignorant of what excellence Laertes is—

HAMLET: I dare not confess that, lest I should compare with him in
excellence; but, to know a man well, were to know himself.

OSRIC: I mean, sir, for his weapon; but in the imputation laid on him by
them, in his meed he's unfellowed.   125

HAMLET: What's his weapon?

OSRIC: Rapier and dagger.

HAMLET: That's two of his weapons: but, well.

OSRIC: The king, sir, hath wagered with him six Barbary horses; against
the which he has imponed, as I take it, six French rapiers and   130
poniards, with their assigns, as girdle, hangers, and so. Three of the
carriages, in faith, are very dear to fancy, very responsive to the
hilts, most delicate carriages, and of very liberal conceit.

HAMLET: What call you the carriages?

HORATIO: I knew you must be edified by the margent ere you had
done.   135

OSRIC: The carriages, sir, are the hangers.

HAMLET: The phrase would be more german to the matter, if we could
carry cannon by our sides. I would it might be hangers till then. But,
on: six Barbary horses against six French swords, their assigns, and
three liberal-conceited carriages; that's the French bet against the   140
Danish. Why is this "imponed," as you call it?

OSRIC: The king, sir, hath laid, that in a dozen passes between yourself
and him, he shall not exceed you three hits; he hath laid on twelve
for nine, and it would come to immediate trial, if your lordship
would vouchsafe the answer.   145

HAMLET: How if I answer "no"?

---

109 *concernancy,* meaning.   **112** *Is't . . . tongue?* Can't you understand your own jargon in another
man's mouth?   **114** *nomination,* naming.   **125** *meed,* merits.   **132** *carriages,* straps and scab-
bards.   **132** *very responsive,* corresponding exactly   **133** *liberal conceit,* elaborate design.
135 *margent,* marginal comment.   **137** *german,* germane, appropriate.

OSRIC: I mean, my lord, the opposition of your person in trial.

HAMLET: Sir, I will walk here in the hall. If it please his majesty, 't is
the breathing time of day with me; let the foils be brought, the
gentleman willing, and the king hold his purpose, I will win for him   150
an I can; if not, I will gain nothing but my shame and the odd hits.

OSRIC: Shall I re-deliver you e'en so?

HAMLET: To this effect, sir; after what flourish your nature will.

OSRIC: I commend my duty to your lordship.

HAMLET: Yours, yours. *(Exit Osric.)* He does well to commend it him-   155
self; there are no tongues else for's turn.

HORATIO: This lapwing runs away with the shell on his head.

HAMLET: He did comply with his dug, before he sucked it. Thus has he
—and many more of the same breed that I know the drossy age
dotes on—only got the tune of the time and outward habit of   160
encounter; a kind of yesty collection, which carries them through
and through the most fond and winnowed opinions; and do but blow
them to their trial, the bubbles are out.

(Enter a Lord.)

LORD: My lord, his majesty commended him to you by young Osric, who
brings back to him, that you attend him in the hall; he sends to know   165
if your pleasure hold to play with Laertes, or that you will take
longer time.

HAMLET: I am constant to my purposes; they follow the king's pleasure:
if his fitness speaks, mine is ready; now or whensoever, provided I
be so able as now.   170

LORD: The king and queen and all are coming down.

HAMLET: In happy time.

LORD: The queen desires you to use some gentle entertainment to Laertes
before you fall to play.

HAMLET: She well instructs me. *(Exit Lord.)*   175

HORATIO: You will lose this wager, my lord.

HAMLET: I do not think so; since he went into France, I have been in
continual practice; I shall win at the odds. But thou wouldst not
think how ill all's here about my heart; but it is no matter.

HORATIO: Nay, good my lord,—   180

HAMLET: It is but foolery; but it is such a kind of gain-giving, as would
perhaps trouble a woman.

HORATIO: If your mind dislike any thing, obey it; I will forestall their
repair hither, and say you are not fit.

---

149 *breathing time,* time for exercise.   **157** *lapwing . . . head,* English sandpiper supposed to start
running before completely hatched.   **158** *comply . . . dug,* bowed to his mother's breast.
159 *drossy,* worthless.   **161** *yesty collection,* frothy anthology.   **162** *blow . . . are* out, blow on them
and their bubbles burst.   **173** *use . . . entertainment,* give a friendly welcome.   **181** *gain-giving,*
misgiving.

HAMLET: Not a whit, we defy augury; there's a special providence in the   185
    fall of a sparrow. If it be now, 'tis not to come; if it be not to come,
    it will be now; if it be not now, yet it will come: the readiness is all.
    Since no man has aught of what he leaves, what is't to leave betimes?
    Let be.

(Enter King, Queen, Laertes, Lords, Osric, and Attendants with foils, etc.)

    KING: Come, Hamlet, come, and take this hand from me.   190

(The King puts Laertes's hand into Hamlet's.)

HAMLET: Give me your pardon, sir; I've done you wrong;
    But pardon 't, as you are a gentleman.
    This presence knows,
    And you must needs have heard, how I am punish'd
    With sore distraction. What I have done,   195
    That might your nature, honour, and exception
    Roughly awake, I here proclaim was madness.
    Was 't Hamlet wrong'd Laertes? Never Hamlet:
    If Hamlet from himself be ta'en away,
    And when he's not himself does wrong Laertes,   200
    Then Hamlet does it not, Hamlet denies it.
    Who does it, then? His madness. If 't be so,
    Hamlet is of the faction that is wrong'd;
    His madness is poor Hamlet's enemy.
    Sir, in this audience,   205
    Let my disclaiming from a purpos'd evil
    Free me so far in your most generous thoughts,
    That I have shot mine arrow o'er the house,
    And hurt my brother.
LAERTES: I am satisfied in nature,
    Whose motive, in this case, should stir me most   210
    To my revenge: but in my terms of honour
    I stand aloof; and will no reconcilement,
    Till by some elder masters, of known honour,
    I have a voice and precedent of peace,
    To keep my name ungor'd. But till that time,   215
    I do receive your offer'd love like love,
    And will not wrong it.
HAMLET: I embrace it freely;
    And will this brother's wager frankly play.
    Give us the foils. Come on.
LAERTES: Come, one for me.
HAMLET: I'll be your foil, Laertes; in mine ignorance   220

188 *betimes,* soon.   **193** *presence,* royal assembly.   **205** *audience,* royal presence.   **218** *frankly*
play, fence without bitterness.   **219** *foil,* punning to mean the background of a jewel.

Your skill shall, like a star i' the darkest night,
Stick fiery off indeed.

LAERTES: You mock me, sir.

HAMLET: No, by this hand.

KING: Give them the foils, young Osric. Cousin Hamlet,
You know the wager?

HAMLET: Very well, my lord;   225
Your grace hath laid the odds o' the weaker side.

KING: I do not fear it; I have seen you both;
But since he is better'd, we have therefore odds.

LAERTES: This is too heavy, let me see another.

HAMLET: This likes me well. These foils have all a length?

(They prepare to play.)   230

OSRIC: Ay, my good lord.

KING: Set me the stoups of wine upon that table.
If Hamlet give the first or second hit,
Or quit in answer of the third exchange,
Let all the battlements their ordinance fire;   235
The king shall drink to Hamlet's better breath;
And in the cup an union shall he throw,
Richer than that which four successive kings
In Denmark's crown have worn. Give me the cups;
And let the kettle to the trumpet speak,   240
The trumpet to the cannoneer without,
The cannons to the heavens, the heavens to earth,
"Now the king drinks to Hamlet." Come, begin;
And you, the judges, bear a wary eye.

HAMLET: Come on, sir.

LAERTES: Come, my lord.

(They play.)

HAMLET: One.

LAERTES: No.

HAMLET: Judgement.   245

OSRIC: A hit, a very palpable hit.

LAERTES: Well; again.

KING: Stay; give me drink. Hamlet, this pearl is thine;
Here's to thy health.

(Trumpets sound, and cannon shot off within.)

                          Give him the cup.

HAMLET: I'll play this bout first; see it by awhile.   250
Come. *(They play.)* Another hit; what say you?

LAERTES: A touch, a touch, I do confess.

---

228 *better'd,* considered superior.   **234** *quit,* scores a draw.   **237** *union,* an onion, a large pearl.
240 *kettle,* kettle drum.

KING: Our son shall win.

QUEEN: He's fat, and scant of breath.
Here, Hamlet, take my napkin, rub thy brows;
The queen carouses to thy fortune, Hamlet. 255

HAMLET: Good madam!

KING: Gertrude, do not drink.

QUEEN: I will, my lord; I pray you, pardon me.

KING: *(Aside)* It is the poison'd cup; it is too late.

HAMLET: I dare not drink yet, madam; by and by.

QUEEN: Come, let me wipe thy face. 260

LAERTES: My lord, I'll hit him now.

KING: I do not think 't.

LAERTES: *(Aside)* And yet 'tis almost 'gainst my conscience.

HAMLET: Come, for the third, Laertes. You but dally,
I pray you, pass with your best violence;
I am afeard you make a wanton of me. 265

LAERTES: Say you so? Come on. *(They play.)*

OSRIC: Nothing, neither way.

LAERTES: Have at you now!

(Laertes wounds Hamlet; then, in scuffling, they change rapiers, and Hamlet wounds Laertes.)

KING: Part them! They are incens'd.

HAMLET: Nay, come, again. *(The Queen falls.)*

OSRIC: Look to the queen there, ho!

HORATIO: They bleed on both sides. How is it, my lord? 270

OSRIC: How is 't, Laertes?

LAERTES: Why, as a woodcock to mine own springe, Osric;
I am justly kill'd with mine own treachery.

HAMLET: How does the queen?

KING: She swounds to see them bleed.

QUEEN: No, no, the drink, the drink,—O my dear Hamlet,— 275
The drink, the drink! I am poison'd. *(Dies.)*

HAMLET: O villany! Ho! Let the door be lock'd.
Treachery! Seek it out.

LAERTES: It is here, Hamlet: Hamlet, thou art slain;
No medicine in the world can do thee good; 280
In thee there is not half an hour of life;
The treacherous instrument is in thy hand,
Unbated and envenom'd. The foul practice
Hath turn'd itself on me; lo! here I lie,
Never to rise again. Thy mother's poison'd. 285
I can no more. The king, the king's to blame.

---

265 *wanton,* a child.   **272** *springe,* snare.   **283** *Unbated,* not blunted; *practice,* plot.

HAMLET: The point envenom'd too!
   Then, venom, to thy work. *(Stabs the King.)*
ALL: Treason! treason!
KING: O, yet defend me, friends; I am but hurt.   290
HAMLET: Here, thou incestuous, murderous, damnèd Dane,
   Drink off this potion. Is thy union here?
   Follow my mother.   *(King dies.)*
LAERTES: He is justly serv'd;
   It is a poison temper'd by himself.
   Exchange forgiveness with me, noble Hamlet: 295
   Mine and my father's death come not upon thee,
   Nor thine on me!   *(Dies.)*
HAMLET: Heaven make thee free of it! I follow thee.
   I am dead, Horatio. Wretched queen, adieu!
   You that look pale and tremble at this chance,   300
   That are but mutes or audience to this act,
   Had I but time—as this fell sergeant, death,
   Is strict in his arrest—O, I could tell you—
   But let it be. Horatio, I am dead;
   Thou liv'st; report me and my cause aright   305
   To the unsatisfied.
HORATID: Never believe it;
   I am more an antique Roman than a Dane:
   Here's yet some liquor left.
HAMLET: As thou'rt a man,
   Give me the cup: let go; by heaven, I'll have't.
   O good Horatio, what a wounded name,   310
   Things standing thus unknown, shall live behind me!
   If thou didst ever hold me in thy heart,
   Absent thee from felicity awhile,
   And in this harsh world draw thy breath in pain,
   To tell my story.   *(March afar off, and shot within.)*
         What warlike noise is this?   315
OSRIC: Young Fortinbras, with conquest come from Poland,
   To the ambassadors of England gives
   This warlike volley.
HAMLET: O, I die, Horatio;
   The potent poison quite o'er-crows my spirit:
   I cannot live to hear the news from England;   320
   But I do prophesy the election lights
   On Fortinbras: he has my dying voice;
   So tell him, with the occurrents, more and less,
   Which have solicited. The rest is silence.   *(Dies.)*

292 *union,* punning on the pearl and Claudius's marriage. 294 *temper'd,* concocted. 301 *mutes,*
actors without speaking parts.

HORATIO: Now cracks a noble heart. Good night, sweet prince,   325
And flights of angels sing thee to thy rest!
Why does the drum come hither?

(March within.)

(Enter Fortinbras, the English Ambassadors, and others.)

FORTINBRAS: Where is this sight?
HORATIO: What is it ye would see?
If aught of woe or wonder, cease your search.
FORTINBRAS: This quarry cries on havoc. O proud death,   330
What feast is toward in thine eternal cell,
That thou so many princes at a shot
So bloodily hast struck?
AMBASSADOR: The sight is dismal;
And our affairs from England come too late:
The ears are senseless that should give us hearing,   335
To tell him his commandment is fulfill'd,
That Rosencrantz and Guildenstern are dead.
Where should we have our thanks?
HORATIO: Not from his mouth,
Had it the ability of life to thank you:
He never gave commandment for their death.   340
But since, so jump upon this bloody question,
You from the Polack wars, and you from England,
Are here arriv'd, give order that these bodies
High on a stage be placed to the view;
And let me speak to the yet unknowing world   345
How these things came about: so shall you hear
Of carnal, bloody, and unnatural acts,
Of accidental judgements, casual slaughters,
Of deaths put on by cunning and forc'd cause,
And, in this upshot, purposes mistook   350
Fall'n on the inventors' heads; all this can I
Truly deliver.
FORTINBRAS: Let us haste to hear it,
And call the noblest to the audience.
For me, with sorrow I embrace my fortune;
I have some rights of memory in this kingdom,   355
Which now to claim my vantage doth invite me.
HORATIO: Of that I shall have also cause to speak,
And from his mouth whose voice will draw on more.

341 *so jump upon,* following so close upon; *question,* quarrel.   358 *voice ... more,* vote will influence
more votes.

But let this same be presently perform'd,
Even while men's minds are wild; lest more mischance,   360
On plots and errors, happen.
FORTINBRAS: Let four captains
Bear Hamlet, like a soldier, to the stage;
For he was likely, had he been put on,
To have prov'd most royally: and, for his passage,
The soldiers' music and the rites of war   365
Speak loudly for him.
Take up the bodies: such a sight as this
Becomes the field, but here shows much amiss.
Go, bid the soldiers shoot.

(A dead march. Exeunt, bearing off the dead bodies; after which a peal of ordnance is shot off.)

QUESTIONS

1. In what ways does the opening scene set the tone for the play and set it in motion?
2. In Act I, Scene ii, Hamlet replies to his mother, "Seems, madam! nay, it is; I know not 'seems.' " What are some of the major instances of "seems" and "is" in the play, of appearance and reality?
3. Where does Hamlet apparently derive his idea of playing the madman?
4. Why doesn't Hamlet "sweep to his revenge"?
5. How do Laertes and Fortinbras function in establishing Hamlet's character? What do Horatio and Ophelia contribute to our picture of him?
6. How guilty is Gertrude? What is she guilty of? How does the "Mousetrap" scene (Act III, Scene ii) help to define her character?
7. Hamlet describes his state of mind to Rosencrantz and Guildenstern (Act II, Scene ii, 264–277). In what way does this description reflect the view of reality later to be proclaimed by Descartes? What other passages reflect this view?
8. At the end of Act I, Hamlet curses his plight "that ever I was born" to set the disjointed world aright. How does his sense of the world and his place in it evolve from there?
9. What role does accident or chance play, including the flurry of accidents at the end?

363 *put on,* promoted to the throne.

CHAPTER 2

COMEDY, SATIRE, AND ROMANCE

Diametrically opposed to tragedy is comedy, the upturned mirth of the comic mask as opposed to tragedy's downturned mouth. As tragedies provoke tears, comedies provoke laughter. In both tragedy and comedy we see ourselves, made slightly more noble or slightly more ridiculous than in real life, but recognizable all the same. This fundamental reality of vision binds the two together around the twin poles of emotion and intellect. On the tragic side, the tug is toward emotion, on the comic toward intellect. But in the end, we are both moved and rendered thoughtful about the human predicament.

In comedy the emphasis on laughter sometimes complicates plot at the expense of character, or, alternatively, stresses character at the expense of plot. Frequently, however, the interplay between plot and character is as important as it is in tragedy. The comic hero, only a little less noble than ourselves, is embroiled in comic entanglements that are in large degree self-made, the result of choices arising from his or her personality. Like the tragic hero, he or she is buffeted by incidents that suggest an unkind Fate, but the uninvolved bystander is not so sure that they were not self-engendered. Whereas in tragedy the hero is at the end removed from society through death or exile, the comic hero is at the end embraced by a society that has threatened to cast him or her out.

Below the horizontal axis of tragedy and comedy, lies the realm of *satire*. Herein the fundamental reality of the tragic-comic vision is subordinated to the desire to expose humanity and its institutions to ridicule and contempt. Both tragedy and comedy move sometimes in this direction, becoming *satiric tragedy* or *satiric comedy*. Above the tragic-comic axis lies *romance*. Herein the fundamental reality of the tragic-comic vision is subordinated to sentimental wish fulfillment. Moving in this direction, tragedy and comedy become *romantic tragedy* and *romantic comedy*. Just as the common element binding tragedy and comedy is a vision of the real, so the common element binding satire and romance is a vision of the ideal, either directly or ironically expressed. When the characters of a comedy or tragedy seem abstractions of human types, rather than rounded, individualized human beings, we begin to suspect elements either of romance or satire. When the play denigrates these human abstractions as falling ironically short of the ideal that we hope for in this world, we have satire. When it elevates them toward an ideal that in this world we only aspire to, we have romance. Adopting the mythic vision of the Bible, we may say that satire directs our attention toward humanity's demonic potential, and romance toward humanity's angelic potential.

Both comedy and satire tend to provoke bawdy laughter to whatever extent current society allows. Both present humanity as a cosmic joke, half-angel, half-beast, necessarily disguised in social hypocrisies. We laugh at the comic predicament we try to conceal: that we are sexual, smelly, alimentary animals cunningly clothed in velvet and virtue. And the laughter humbles us, as all comedy does, as we acknowledge the reality of our common lot beneath our pride and pretension.

Comedy engages two opposite impulses, affirmation and hostility. The plot is affirmative, with the lovers, immune to the rough comedy outside, fulfilling our wishes and ultimately celebrating life's central energy and good luck in marriage, a dance, and social approval. Around this center, we satisfy and purge our hostilities, laughing in elevated detachment as we pass off our pains, humiliations, and aggressions on the bumbling victims of banana peels. The comic character is blind, with an idée fixe that he is a master mechanic or she a ravishing siren. We, the superior normals, laugh at their dramatic ironies—until, with a sly kick, comedy reminds us that we too are fallible. Comedy depends on intellectual detachment, but the best comedy also contains the tragic element that would destroy it, as we momentarily sympathize with the benighted even as we laugh.

Because tragedy and comedy reside with us in the world that nestles between the unrealized ideal above and its ironic alternative below, they have throughout history seemed more central to the human experience than either romance or satire. Comedy, indeed, has always taken to itself large elements of romance and satire. The great classics of comedy, however, are constructed around a central core of realistic truth.

LYSISTRATA

Aristophanes was the undisputed master of Greek Old Comedy, a form that flourished in Athens for about a century, beginning a generation before his birth and ending with his death. Like Greek tragedy, Old Comedy was performed before thousands in the huge theater of Dionysus during the annual Dionysian festivals. It was shaped by the physical theater as well as by the festive ritual. The actors wore grotesque comic masks and ludicrously padded costumes,

including large leather phalluses for the male characters. All parts, male and
female, were played by men, with the women distinguished by their masks and
long gowns. Within these conventions, Aristophanes commented astutely on the
human situation. *Lysistrata* was especially timely when first performed in 411
B.C. After twenty years of war between Athens and Sparta, broken only by one
short truce, Aristophanes imagined the women of both sides conspiring for the
peace that had eluded the politicians.

LYSISTRATA*

Aristophanes   (CA. *447–380* B.C.)

Characters

LYSISTRATA ⎫	OLD MARKET-WOMEN
KALONIKE ⎬ Athenian women	CINESIAS, an Athenian, husband
MYRRHINA ⎭	of Myrrhina
LAMPITO, a Spartan woman	SPARTAN HERALD
CHORUS OF OLD MEN	SPARTAN AMBASSADORS
CHORUS OF WOMEN	ATHENIAN AMBASSADORS
ATHENIAN COMMISSIONER	

A street in Athens before daylight.

LYSISTRATA: If anyone had asked them to a festival
   of Aphrodite[1] or of Bacchus[2] or of Pan,[3]
   you couldn't get through Athens for the tambourines,
   but now there's not one solitary woman here.
   Except my next-door neighbor. Here she's coming out.   5
   Hello, Kalonike.
KALONIKE: Hello, Lysistrata.
   What are you so upset about? Don't scowl so, dear.
   You're less attractive when you knit your brows and glare.
LYSISTRATA: I know, Kalonike, but I am smoldering
   with indignation at the way we women act.   10
   Men think we are so gifted for all sorts of crime
   that we will stop at nothing—
KALONIKE: Well, we are, by Zeus!
LYSISTRATA: —but when it comes to an appointment here with me
   to plot and plan for something really serious
   they lie in bed and do not come.
KALONIKE: They'll come, my dear.   15
   You know what trouble women have in going out:

*Translated by Donald Sutherland.

[1]Goddess of love and beauty. [2]God of wine and revelry. [3]God of fields and forests.

one of us will be wrapped up in her husband still,
another waking up the maid, or with a child
to put to sleep, or give its bath, or feed its pap.
LYSISTRATA: But they had other more important things to do than
those.   20
KALONIKE: What ever is it, dear Lysistrata?
What have you called us women all together for?
How much of a thing is it?
LYSISTRATA: Very big.
KALONIKE: And thick?
LYSISTRATA: Oh very thick indeed.
KALONIKE: Then *how* can we be late?
LYSISTRATA: That's not the way it is. Or we would all be here.   25
But it is something I have figured out myself
and turned and tossed upon for many a sleepless night.
KALONIKE: It must be something slick you've turned and tossed
upon!
LYSISTRATA: So slick that the survival of all Greece depends upon the
women.
KALONIKE: On the women? In that case poor Greece has next to noth-
ing to depend upon.
LYSISTRATA: Since now it's we who must decide affairs of state: 30
either there is to be no Spartan left alive—
KALONIKE: A very good thing too, if none were left, by Zeus!
LYSISTRATA: —and every living soul in Thebes to be destroyed—
KALONIKE: Except the eels![4] Spare the delicious eels of Thebes!
LYSISTRATA: —and as for Athens—I can't bring myself to say   35
the like of that for us. But just think what I mean!
Yet if the women meet here as I told them to
from Sparta, Thebes, and all of their allies,
and we of Athens, all together we'll save Greece.
KALONIKE: What reasonable thing could women ever do,   40
or glorious, we who sit around all prettied up
in flowers and scandalous saffron-yellow gowns,
groomed and draped to the ground in oriental stuffs
and fancy pumps?
LYSISTRATA: And those are just the very things
I count upon to save us—wicked saffron gowns,   45
perfumes and pumps and rouge and sheer transparent frocks.
KALONIKE: But what use can they be?
LYSISTRATA: So no man in our time
will raise a spear against another man again—
KALONIKE: I'll get a dress dyed saffron-yellow, come what may!

[4]Considered a delicacy.

LYSISTRATA: —nor touch a shield—

KALONIKE: I'll slip into the sheerest gown!   50

LYSISTRATA: —nor so much as a dagger—

KALONIKE: I'll buy a pair of pumps!

LYSISTRATA: So don't you think the women should be here by now?

KALONIKE: I don't. They should have *flown* and got here long ago.

LYSISTRATA: You'll see, my dear. They will, like good Athenians,
do everything too late. But from the coastal towns   55
no woman is here either, nor from Salamis.

KALONIKE: I'm certain those from Salamis have crossed the strait:
they're always straddling *something* at this time of night.

LYSISTRATA: Not even those I was expecting would be first
to get here, from Acharnae, from so close to town,   60
not even they are here.

KALONIKE: But one of them, I know,
is under way, and three sheets to the wind, by now.
But look—some women are approaching over there.

LYSISTRATA: And over here are some, coming this way—

KALONIKE: Phew! Phew!   65
Where are they from?

LYSISTRATA: Down by the marshes.

KALONIKE: Yes, by Zeus!
It smells as if the bottoms had been all churned up!

(Enter Myrrhina, and others)

MYRRHINA: Hello Lysistrata. Are we a little late?
What's that? Why don't you speak?

LYSISTRATA: I don't think much of you,
Myrrhina, coming to this business only now.   70

MYRRHINA: Well, I could hardly find my girdle in the dark.
If it's so urgent, tell us what it is. We're here.

KALONIKE: Oh no. Let's wait for just a little while until
the delegates from Sparta and from Thebes arrive.

LYSISTRATA: You show much better judgment.

(Enter Lampito, and others)

                           Here comes Lampito!

LYSISTRATA: Well, darling Lampito! My dearest Spartan friend!   75
How very sweet, how beautiful you look! That fresh
complexion! How magnificent your figure is!
Enough to crush a bull!

LAMPITO: Ah shorely think Ah could.[5]
Ah take mah exacise. Ah jump and thump mah butt.

KALONIKE: And really, what a handsome set of tits you have!   80

---

[5] A comic southern accent here represents the Doric of the original. Other translators have
tried Northern British, Scots, and American hillbilly.

LAMPITO: You feel me ovah lahk a cow of sacrafahce!

LYSISTRATA: And this other young thing—where ever is *she* from?

LAMPITO: She's prominent, Ah sweah, in Thebes—a delegate
   ample enough.

LYSISTRATA: By Zeus, she represents Thebes well,
   having so trim a ploughland.

KALONIKE: Yes, by Zeus, she does!   85
   There's not a weed of all her field she hasn't plucked.

LYSISTRATA: And who's the other girl?

LAMPITO: Theah's nothing small, Ah sweah,
   or tahght about her folks in Corinth.

KALONIKE: No, by Zeus!—   90
   to judge by this side of her, nothing small or tight.

LAMPITO: But who has called togethah such a regiment
   of all us women?

LYSISTRATA: Here I am. I did.

LAMPITO: Speak up,
   just tell us what you want.

KALONIKE: Oh yes, by Zeus, my dear,
   do let us know what the important business is!   95

LYSISTRATA: Let me explain it, then. And yet . . . before I do . . .
   I have one little question.

KALONIKE: Anything you like.

LYSISTRATA: Don't you all miss the fathers of your little ones,
   your husbands who have gone away to war? I'm sure
   you all have husbands in the armies far from home.   100

KALONIKE: Mine's been away five months in Thrace—a general's guard,
   posted to see his general does not desert.

MYRRHINA: And mine has been away in Pylos seven whole months.

LAMPITO: And mahn, though he does get back home on leave some-
      tahms,
   no soonah has he come than he is gone again.   105

LYSISTRATA: No lovers either. Not a sign of one is left.
   For since our eastern allies have deserted us
   they haven't sent a single six-inch substitute
   to serve as leatherware replacement for our men.
   Would you be willing, then, if I thought out a scheme,   110
   to join with me to end the war?

KALONIKE: Indeed I would,
   even if I had to pawn this very wrap-around
   and drink up all the money in one day, I would!

MYRRHINA: And so would I, even if I had to see myself
   split like a flounder, and give half of me away!   115

LAMPITO: And so would Ah! Ah'd climb up Mount Taÿgetos
   if Ah just had a chance of seeing peace from theah!

LYSISTRATA: Then I will tell you. I may now divulge my plan.

Women of Greece!—if we intend to force the men
to make a peace, we must abstain . . .
KALONIKE: From what? Speak out!   120
LYSISTRATA: But will you do it?
KALONIKE: We will, though death should be the price!
LYSISTRATA: Well then, we must abstain utterly from the prick.
   Why do you turn your backs? Where are you off to now?
   And you—why pout and make such faces, shake your heads?   125
   Why has your color changed? Why do you shed those tears?
   Will you do it or will you not? Why hesitate?
KALONIKE: I will not do it. Never. Let the war go on!
MYRRHINA: Neither will I. By Zeus, no! Let the war go on!
LYSISTRATA: How can you say so, Madam Flounder, when just now   130
   you were declaiming you would split yourself in half?
KALONIKE: Anything else you like, anything! If I must
   I'll gladly walk through fire. That, rather than the prick!
   Because there's nothing like it, dear Lysistrata.
LYSISTRATA: How about you?
MYRRHINA: I too would gladly walk through fire.   135
LYSISTRATA: Oh the complete depravity of our whole sex!
   It is no wonder tragedies are made of us,
   we have such unrelenting unity of mind!
   But you, my friend from Sparta, dear, if you alone
   stand by me, only you, we still might save the cause.   140
   Vote on my side!
LAMPITO: They'ah hahd conditions, mahty hahd,
   to sleep without so much as the fo'skin of one . . .
   but all the same . . . well . . . yes. We need peace just as bad.
LYSISTRATA: Oh dearest friend!—the one real woman of them all!
KALONIKE: And if we really should abstain from what you say—   145
   which Heaven forbid!—do you suppose on that account
   that peace might come to be?
LYSISTRATA: I'm absolutely sure.
   If we should sit around, rouged and with skins well creamed,
   with nothing on but a transparent negligé,
   and come up to them with our deltas plucked quite smooth,   150
   and, once our men get stiff and want to come to grips,
   we do not yield to them at all but just hold off,
   they'll make a truce in no time. There's no doubt of that.
LAMPITO: We say in Spahta that when Menelaos[6] saw
   Helen's ba'e apples he just tossed away his swo'd.   155
KALONIKE: And what, please, if our husbands just toss *us* away?
LYSISTRATA: Well, you have heard the good old saying: Know
   Thyself.

[6]Husband of Helen of Troy.

KALONIKE: It isn't worth the candle. I hate cheap substitutes.
But what if they should seize and drag us by brute force
into the bedroom?

LYSISTRATA: Hang onto the doors!

KALONIKE: And if—   160
they beat us?

LYSISTRATA: Then you must give in, but nastily,
and do it badly. There's no fun in it by force.
And then, just keep them straining. They will give it up
in no time—don't you worry. For never will a man   165
enjoy himself unless the woman coincides.

KALONIKE: If both of you are for this plan, then so are we.

LAMPITO: And we of Spahta shall persuade ouah men to keep
the peace sinceahly and with honah in all ways,
but how could anyone pe'suade the vulgah mob   170
of Athens not to deviate from discipline?

LYSISTRATA: Don't worry, we'll persuade our men. They'll keep the
peace.

LAMPITO: They won't, so long as they have battleships afloat
and endless money sto'ed up in the Pahthenon.[7]

LYSISTRATA: But that too has been carefully provided for: 175
we shall take over the Acropolis[8] today.
The oldest women have their orders to do that:
while we meet here, they go as if to sacrifice
up there, but really seizing the Acropolis.

LAMPITO: All should go well. What you say theah is very smaht.   180

LYSISTRATA: In that case, Lampito, what are we waiting for?
Let's take an oath, to bind us indissolubly.

LAMPITO: Well, just you show us what the oath is. Then we'll
sweah.

LYSISTRATA: You're right. Where is that lady cop?

(To the armed Lady Cop looking around for a Lady Cop)

                                  What do you think
you're looking for? Put down your shield in front of us,
there, on its back, and someone get some scraps of gut.   185

KALONIKE: Lysistrata, what in the world do you intend
to make us take an oath on?

LYSISTRATA: What? Why, on a shield,
just as they tell me some insurgents in a play
by Aeschylus[9] once did, with a sheep's blood and guts.

KALONIKE: Oh *don't,* Lysistrata, don't swear upon a *shield,*   190
not if the oath has anything to do with peace!

[7]A war reserve fund had been kept for years in the Parthenon.   [8]The fortified upper part of
Athens, including the Parthenon.   [9]A Greek tragic playwright (525–456 B.C.).

LYSISTRATA: Well then, what *will* we swear on? Maybe we should
  get
    a white horse somewhere, like the Amazons, and cut
    some bits of gut from it.
KALONIKE: *Where* would we get a horse?
LYSISTRATA: But what kind of an oath *is* suitable for us?
KALONIKE: By Zeus, I'll tell you if you like. First we put down   195
    a big black drinking-cup, face up, and then we let
    the neck of a good jug of wine bleed into it,
    and take a solemn oath to—add no water in.
LAMPITO: Bah Zeus, Ah jest can't tell you how Ah lahk that oath!
LYSISTRATA: Someone go get a cup and winejug from inside.   200

(Kalonike goes and is back in a flash)

KALONIKE: My dears, my dearest dears—how's *this* for pottery?
    You feel good right away, just laying hold of it.
LYSISTRATA: Well, set it down, and lay your right hand on this pig.
    O goddess of Persuasion, and O Loving-cup,
    accept this victim's blood! Be gracious unto us.   205
KALONIKE: It's not anaemic, and flows clear. Those are good signs.
LAMPITO: What an aroma, too! Bah Castah[10] it *is* sweet!
KALONIKE: My dears, if you don't mind—I'll be the first to swear.
LYSISTRATA: By Aphrodite, no! If you had drawn first place
    by lot—but now let all lay hands upon the cup.   210
    Yes, Lampito—and now, let one of you repeat
    for all of you what I shall say. You will be sworn
    by every word she says, and bound to keep this oath:
    No lover and no husband and no man on earth—
KALONIKE: No lover and no husband and no man on earth—   215
LYSISTRATA: *shall e'er approach me with his penis up.* Repeat.
KALONIKE: shall e'er approach me with his penis up. Oh dear,
    my knees are buckling under me, Lysistrata!
LYSISTRATA: *and I shall lead an unlaid life alone at home,*
KALONIKE: and I shall lead an unlaid life alone at home,   220
LYSISTRATA: *wearing a saffron gown and groomed and beautified*
KALONIKE: wearing a saffron gown and groomed and beautified
LYSISTRATA: *so that my husband will be all on fire for me*
KALONIKE: so that my husband will be all on fire for me
LYSISTRATA: *but I will never willingly give in to him*   225
KALONIKE: but I will never willingly give in to him
LYSISTRATA: *and if he tries to force me to against my will*
KALONIKE: and if he tries to force me to against my will
LYSISTRATA: *I'll do it badly and not wiggle in response*

---

[10]Castor, son of Leda and Zeus.

KALONIKE: I'll do it badly and not wiggle in response   230
LYSISTRATA: *nor toward the ceiling will I lift my Persian pumps*
KALONIKE: nor toward the ceiling will I lift my Persian pumps
LYSISTRATA: *nor crouch down as the lions on cheese-graters do*
KALONIKE: nor crouch down as the lions on cheese-graters do
LYSISTRATA: *and if I keep my promise, may I drink of this—*   235
KALONIKE: and if I keep my promise, may I drink of this—
LYSISTRATA: *but if I break it, then may water fill the cup!*
KALONIKE: but if I break it, then may water fill the cup!
LYSISTRATA: Do you all swear to this with her?
ALL: We do, by Zeus!
LYSISTRATA: I'll consecrate our oath now.
KALONIKE: Share alike, my dear,   240
    so we'll be friendly to each other from the start.
LAMPITO: What was that screaming?
LYSISTRATA: That's what I was telling you:
    the women have already seized the Parthenon
    and the Acropolis. But now, dear Lampito
    return to Sparta and set things in order there—   245
    but leave these friends of yours as hostages with us—
    And let *us* join the others in the citadel
    and help them bar the gates.
KALONIKE: But don't you think the men
    will rally to the rescue of the citadel,
    attacking us at once?
LYSISTRATA: They don't worry me much: 250
    they'll never bring against us threats or fire enough
    to force open the gates, except upon our terms.
KALONIKE: Never by Aphrodite! Or we'd lose our name
    for being battle-axes and unbearable!

(Exeunt. The scene changes to the Propylaea[11] *of the Acropolis. A chorus of very
old men struggles slowly in, carrying logs and firepots.)*

ONE OLD MAN: Lead on! O Drakēs, step by step, although your   255
                    shoulder's aching
               and under this green olive log's great weight
                    your back be breaking!
    ANOTHER: Eh, life is long but always has
                    more surprises for us!   260
               Now who'd have thought we'd live to hear
                    this, O Strymodorus?—
               The wives we fed and looked upon
                    as helpless liabilities

[11]The roofed gateway on the west side of the Acropolis.

now dare to occupy the Parthenon,   265
    our whole Acropolis, for once they seize
    the Propylaea, straightway
    they lock and bar the gateway.

CHORUS: Let's rush to the Acropolis with due precipitation
and lay these logs down circlewise, till presently we turn them   270
into one mighty pyre to make a general cremation
of all the women up there—eh! with our own hands we'll burn them,
the leaders and the followers, without discrimination!

AN OLD MAN: They'll never have the laugh on me!
                    Though I may not look it,   275
            I rescued the Acropolis
                when the Spartans took it
            about a hundred years ago.
            We laid a siege that kept their king
                six years unwashed, so when I made him throw   280
                his armor off, for all his blustering,
            in nothing but his shirt he
            looked very very dirty.

CHORUS: How strictly I besieged the man! These gates were all invested
with seventeen ranks of armored men all equally ferocious!   285
Shall women—by Euripides[12] and all the gods detested—
not be restrained—with me on hand—from something so atrocious?
They shall!—or may our trophies won at Marathon[13] be bested!
                But we must go a long way yet
                up that steep and winding road   290
            before we reach the fortress where we want to get.
                How shall we ever drag this load,
                lacking pack-mules, way up there?
            I can tell you that my shoulder has caved in beyond repair!
                Yet we must trudge ever higher,   295
                ever blowing on the fire,
            so its coals will still be glowing when we get where we are going
                Fooh! Fooh!
                Whoo! I choke!
                What a smoke!   300

            Lord Herakles![14] How fierce it flies
            out against me from the pot!

---

[12]A Greek tragic playwright (c. 485–406 B.C.).   [13]Where the Athenians defeated the Persians
in 490 B.C., almost eighty years before the first performance of *Lysistrata*.   [14]Hercules, son of
Zeus and Alcmene.

and like a rabid bitch it bites me in the eyes!
  It's female fire, or it would not
  scratch my poor old eyes like this.   305
Yet undaunted we must onward, up the high Acropolis
  where Athena's temple stands
  fallen into hostile hands.
O my comrades! shall we ever have a greater need to save her?
  Fooh! Fooh!   310
  Whoo! I choke!
  What a smoke!

FIRST OLD MAN: Well, thank the gods, I see the fire is yet alive and
  waking!
SECOND OLD MAN: Why don't we set our lumber down right here in
  handy batches,
then stick a branch of grape-vine in the pot until it catches   315
THIRD OLD MAN: and hurl ourselves against the gate with battering and
  shaking?
FIRST OLD MAN: and if the women won't unbar at such an ultimatum
  we'll set the gate on fire and then the smoke will suffocate 'em.
SECOND OLD MAN: Well, let's put down our load. Fooh fooh, what
  smoke! But blow as needed!   320
THIRD OLD MAN: Your ablest generals *these* days would not carry
  wood like *we* did.
SECOND OLD MAN: At last the lumber ceases grinding my poor back to
  pieces!
THIRD OLD MAN: These are your orders, Colonel Pot: wake up the coals
  and bid them
report here and present to me a torch lit up and flaring.   325
FIRST OLD MAN: O Victory, be with us! If you quell the women's daring
  we'll raise a splendid trophy of how you and we undid them!

(A Chorus of middle-aged women appears in the offing)

A WOMAN: I think that I perceive a smoke in which appears a flurry
  of sparks as of a lighted fire. Women, we'll have to hurry!

CHORUS OF WOMEN: 330
  Oh fleetly fly, oh swiftly flit,
  my dears, e'er Kalykë be lit
  and with Kritylla swallowed up alive
    in flames which the gales dreadfully drive
    and deadly old men fiercely inflate!   335
  Yet one thing I'm afraid of: will I not arrive too late?
  for filling up my water-jug has been no easy matter
  what with the crowd at the spring in the dusk and the

clamor and pottery clatter.
Pushed as I was, jostled by slave-   340
women and sluts marked with a brand
yet with my jug firmly in hand
here I have come, hoping to save
      my burning friends and brave,

for certain windy, witless, old,   345
and wheezy fools, so I was told,
with wood some tons in weight crept up this path,
      not having in mind heating a bath
      but uttering threats, vowing they will
consume those nasty women into cinders on grill!   350
But O Athena! never may I see my friends igniting!
Nay!—let them save all the cities of Greece and their
      people from folly and fighting!
      Goddess whose crest flashes with gold,
      they were so bold taking your shrine   355
only for this—Goddess who hold
Athens—for *this* noble design,
      braving the flames, calling on you
      to carry water too!

(One of the old men urinates noisily)

CHORUS OF WOMEN: Be still! What was that noise? Aha! Oh, wicked and
      degraded!   360
Would any good religious men have ever done what *they* did?
CHORUS OF MEN: Just look! It's a surprise-attack! Oh, dear, we're being
      raided
by swarms of them below us when we've got a swarm above us!
CHORUS OF WOMEN: Why panic at the sight of us? This is not many of
      us.
We number tens of thousands but you've hardly seen a fraction.   365
CHORUS OF MEN: O Phaidrias, shall they talk so big and we not take
      some action?
Oh, should we not be bashing them and splintering our lumber?

(The old men begin to strip for combat)

CHORUS OF WOMEN: Let us, too, set our pitchers down, so they will not
      encumber
our movements if these gentlemen should care to offer battle.
CHORUS OF MEN: Oh someone should have clipped their jaws—twice,
      thrice, until they rattle—   370
(as once the poet put it)—then we wouldn't hear their prating.

CHORUS OF WOMEN: Well, here's your chance. Won't someone hit me? Here I stand, just waiting!

No other bitch will ever grab your balls, the way I'll treat you!

CHORUS OF MEN: Shut up—or I will drub you so old age will never reach you!

CHORUS OF WOMEN: Won't anyone step and lay one finger on Stratyllis?   375

CHORUS OF MEN: And if we pulverize her with our knuckles, will you kill us?

CHORUS OF WOMEN: No, only chew your lungs out and your innards and your eyes, sir.

CHORUS OF MEN: How clever is Euripides! There is no poet wiser: he says indeed that women are the worst of living creatures.

CHORUS OF WOMEN: Now is the time, Rhodippe: let us raise our brimming pitchers.   380

CHORUS OF MEN: Why come up here with water, you, the gods' abomination?

CHORUS OF WOMEN: And why come here with fire, you tomb? To give yourself cremation?

CHORUS OF MEN: To set your friends alight upon a pyre erected for them.

CHORUS OF WOMEN: And so we brought our water-jugs. Upon your pyre we'll pour them.

CHORUS OF MEN: *You'll* put my fire out?   385

CHORUS OF WOMEN: Any time! You'll see there's nothing to it.

CHORUS OF MEN: I think I'll grill you right away, with just this torch to do it!

CHORUS OF WOMEN: Have you some dusting-powder? Here's your wedding-bath all ready.

CHORUS OF MEN: *You'll* bathe me, garbage that you are?

CHORUS OF WOMEN: Yes, bridegroom, just hold steady!   390

CHORUS OF MEN: Friends, you have heard her insolence—

CHORUS OF WOMEN: I'm free-born, not your slave, sir.

CHORUS OF MEN: I'll have this noise of yours restrained—

CHORUS OF WOMEN: Court's out—so be less grave, sir.

CHORUS OF MEN: Why don't you set her hair on fire!   395

CHORUS OF WOMEN: Oh, Water, be of service!

CHORUS OF MEN: Oh woe is me!

CHORUS OF WOMEN: Was it too hot?

CHORUS OF MEN: Oh, stop! What *is* this? Hot? Oh no!

CHORUS OF WOMEN: I'm watering you to make you grow.

CHORUS OF MEN: I'm withered from this chill I got!   400

CHORUS OF WOMEN: You've got a fire, so warm yourself. You're trembling: are you nervous?

(Enter a Commissioner, escorted by four Scythian policemen with bows and quivers slung on their backs)

> COMMISSIONER: Has the extravagance of women broken out
> into full fury, with their banging tambourines
> and constant wailings for their oriental gods,
> and on the roof-tops their Adonis[15] festival,   405
> which I could hear myself from the Assembly once?
> For while Demostratos—that numbskull—had the floor,
> urging an expedition against Sicily,
> his wife was dancing and we heard her crying out
> "Weep for Adonis!"—so the expedition failed   410
> with such an omen. When the same Demostratos
> was urging that we levy troops from our allies
> his wife was on the roof again, a little drunk:
> "Weep for Adonis! Beat your breast!" says she. At that,
> he gets more bellicose, that god-Damn-ox-tratos.   415
> To this has the incontinence of women come!
>
> CHORUS OF MEN: You haven't *yet* heard how outrageous they can be!
> With other acts of violence, these women here
> have showered us from their jugs, so now we are reduced
> to shaking out our shirts as if we'd pissed in them.   420
>
> COMMISSIONER: Well, by the God of Waters, what do you expect?
> When we ourselves conspire with them in waywardness
> and give them good examples of perversity
> such wicked notions naturally sprout in them.
> We go into a shop and say something like this: 425
> "Goldsmith, about that necklace you repaired: last night
> my wife was dancing, when the peg that bolts the catch
> fell from its hole. I have to sail for Salamis,
> but if you have the time, by all means try to come
> towards evening, and put in the peg she needs."   430
> Another man says to a cobbler who is young
> and has no child's-play of a prick, "Cobbler," he says,
> "her sandal-strap is pinching my wife's little toe,
> which is quite delicate. So please come by at noon
> and stretch it for her so it has a wider play."   435
> Such things as that result of course in things like this:
> when I, as a Commissioner, have made a deal
> to fit the fleet with oars and need the money now,
> I'm locked out by these women from the very gates.
> But it's no use just standing here. Bring on the bars, 440
> so I can keep these women in their proper place.
> What are *you* gaping at, you poor unfortunate?

[15] A handsome young man of myth, loved by Aphrodite. He was killed by a wild boar.

Where are *you* looking? Only seeing if a bar
is open yet downtown? Come, drive these crowbars in
under the gates on that side, pry away, and I   **445**
will pry away on this.

(Lysistrata comes out)

LYSISTRATA: No need to pry at all.
I'm coming out, of my own will. What use are bars?
It isn't bolts and bars we need so much as brains.
COMMISSIONER: Really, you dirty slut? Where is that officer?
Arrest her, and tie both her hands behind her back.   **450**
LYSISTRATA: By Artemis,[16] just let him lift a hand at me
and, public officer or not, you'll hear him howl.
COMMISSIONER: You let her scare you? Grab her round the middle, you.
Then *you* go help him and between you get her tied.

(Kalonike comes out)

KALONIKE: By Artemis, if you just lay one hand on her   **455**
I have a mind to trample the shit out of you.
COMMISSIONER: It's out already! Look! Now where's the other one?
Tie up *that* woman first. She babbles, with it all.

(Myrrhina comes out)

MYRRHINA: By Hecatë,[17] if you just lay a hand on her
you'll soon ask for a cup—to get your swellings down!   **460**

(The policeman dashes behind the Commissioner and clings to him for protection)

COMMISSIONER: What happened? Where's that bowman, now? Hold
onto *her!*

(He moves quickly away downhill)

I'll see that none of you can get away through here!
LYSISTRATA: By Artemis, you come near her and I'll bereave
your head of every hair! You'll weep for each one, too.
COMMISSIONER: What a calamity! This one has failed me too.   **465**
But never must we let ourselves be overcome
by women. All together now, O Scythians!—
let's march against them in formation!
LYSISTRATA: You'll find out
that inside there we have four companies
of fighting women perfectly equipped for war.   **470**
COMMISSIONER: Charge! Turn their flanks, O Scythians! and tie their
hands!

[16]Goddess of the moon and hunting.   [17]Goddess of the moon and witchcraft.

LYSISTRATA: O allies—comrades—women! Sally forth and fight!
O vegetable vendors, O green-grocery-
grain-garlic-bread-bean-dealers and inn-keepers all!

(A group of fierce Old Market-Women, carrying baskets of vegetables, spindles, etc. emerges. There is a volley of vegetables. The Scythians are soon routed.)

Come pull them, push them, smite them, smash them into bits!   475
Rail and abuse them in the strongest words you know!
Halt, Halt! Retire in order! We'll forego the spoils!
COMMISSIONER: *(tragically, like say Xerxes[18])* Oh what reverses have
my bowmen undergone!
LYSISTRATA: But what did you imagine? Did you think you came   480
against a pack of slaves? Perhaps you didn't know
that women can be resolute?
COMMISSIONER: I know they can—
above all when they spot a bar across the way.
CHORUS OF MEN: Commissioner of Athens, you are spending words
unduly,
to argue with these animals, who only roar the louder,   485
or don't you know they showered us so coldly and so cruelly,
and in our undershirts at that, and furnished us no powder?
CHORUS OF WOMEN: But beating up your neighbor is inevitably bringing
a beating on yourself, sir, with your own eyes black and bloody.
I'd rather sit securely like a little girl demurely   490
not stirring up a single straw nor harming anybody,
So long as no one robs my hive and rouses me to stinging.
CHORUS OF MEN: How shall we ever tame these brutes? We cannot
tolerate
the situation further, so we must investigate   495
this occurrence and find
with what purpose in mind
they profane the Acropolis, seize it, and lock
the approach to this huge and prohibited rock,
to our holiest ground!   500
Cross-examine them! Never believe one word
they tell you—refute them, confound them!
We must get to the bottom of things like this
and the circumstances around them.
COMMISSIONER: Yes indeed! and I want to know first one thing: 505
just *why* you committed this treason,
barricading the fortress with locks and bars—
I insist on knowing the reason.

[18]A king of Persia, defeated by the Greeks at the decisive naval battle at Salamis in 480 B.C.

LYSISTRATA: To protect all the money up there from you— 510
    you'll have nothing to fight for without it.
COMMISSIONER: You think it is *money* we're fighting for?
LYSISTRATA: All the troubles we have are about it.
  It was so Peisander[19] and those in power
    of his kind could embezzle the treasure
  that they cooked up emergencies all the time. 515
      Well, let them, if such is their pleasure,
  but they'll never get into this money again,
    though you men should elect them to spend it.
COMMISSIONER: And just what will *you* do with it?
LYSISTRATA: Can you ask?
    Of course we shall superintend it. 520
COMMISSIONER: You will superintend the treasury, *you!?*
LYSISTRATA: And why should it strike you so funny?
  when we manage our houses in everything
    and it's we who look after your money.
COMMISSIONER: But it's not the same thing!
LYSISTRATA: Why not?
COMMISSIONER: It's war, 525
  and *this* money must pay the expenses.
LYSISTRATA: To begin with, you needn't be waging war.
COMMISSIONER: To survive, we don't need our defenses?
LYSISTRATA: You'll survive: we shall save you.
COMMISSIONER: Who? You?
LYSISTRATA: Yes, we.
COMMISSIONER: You absolutely disgust me. 530
LYSISTRATA: You may like it or not, but you *shall* be saved.
COMMISSIONER: I protest!
LYSISTRATA: If you care to, but, trust me,
  this has got to be done all the same.
COMMISSIONER: It has?
    It's illegal, unjust, and outrageous!
LYSISTRATA: We must save you, sir.
COMMISSIONER: Yes? And if I refuse? 535
LYSISTRATA: You will much the more grimly engage us.
COMMISSIONER: And whence does it happen that war and peace
    are fit matters for women to mention?
LYSISTRATA: I will gladly explain—
COMMISSIONER: And be quick, or else
    you'll be howling!
LYSISTRATA: Now, just pay attention 540
  and keep your hands to yourself, if you can!

---

[19]A contemporary politician, frequently attacked for corruption.

COMMISSIONER: But I can't. You can't think how I suffer
from holding them back in my anger!
AN OLD WOMAN: Sir—
if you don't you will have it much rougher.
COMMISSIONER: You may croak that remark to yourself, you hag!   545
     Will *you* do the explaining?
LYSISTRATA: I'll do it.
Heretofore we women in time of war
     have endured very patiently through it,
putting up with whatever you men might do,
     for never a peep would you let us   550
deliver on your unstatesmanly acts
     no matter how much they upset us,
but we knew very well, while we sat at home,
     when you'd handled a big issue poorly,
and we'd ask you then, with a pretty smile   555
     though our heart would be grieving us sorely,
"And what were the terms for a truce, my dear,
     you drew up in assembly this morning?"
"And what's it to you?" says our husband, "Shut up!"
     —so, as ever, at this gentle warning   560
I of course would discreetly shut up.
KALONIKE: Not me!
     You can bet I would never be quiet!
COMMISSIONER: I'll bet, if you weren't, you were beaten up.
LYSISTRATA: *I'd* shut up, and I do not deny it,
but when plan after plan was decided on,   565
     so bad we could scarcely believe it,
I would say "This last is so mindless, dear,
     I cannot think how you achieve it!"
And then he would say, with a dirty look,
     "Just you think what your spindle is for, dear,   570
or your head will be spinning for days on end—
     let the *men* attend to the war, dear."
COMMISSIONER: By Zeus, *he* had the right idea!
LYSISTRATA: You fool!
     Right ideas were quite out of the question,
when your reckless policies failed, and yet   575
     we never could make a suggestion.
And lately we heard you say so yourselves:
     in the streets there'd be someone lamenting:
"There's not one man in the country now!"
     —and we heard many others assenting.   580
After that, we conferred through our deputies
     and agreed, having briefly debated,

to act in common to save all Greece
 at once—for why should we have waited?
So now, when we women are talking sense,   585
 if you'll only agree to be quiet
and to listen to us as we did to you,
 you'll be very much edified by it.
COMMISSIONER: *You* will edify *us!* I protest!
LYSISTRATA: Shut up!
COMMISSIONER: *I'm* to shut up and listen, you scum, you?!   590
 Sooner death! And a veil on your head at that!
LYSISTRATA: We'll fix that. It may really become you:
 do accept this veil as a present from me.
 Drape it modestly—so—round your head, do you see?
 And now—*not* a word more, sir.   595
KALONIKE: Do accept this dear little wool-basket, too!
 Hitch your girdle and card! Here are beans you may chew
 the way all of the nicest Athenians do—
 and the *women* will see to the war, sir!

CHORUS OF WOMEN: Oh women, set your jugs aside and keep a   600
 closer distance:
 our friends may need from us as well some resolute assistance.

  Since never shall I weary of the stepping of the dance
 nor will my knees of treading, for these ladies I'll advance
  anywhere they may lead,   605
  and they're daring indeed,
 they have wit, a fine figure, and boldness of heart,
 they are prudent and charming, efficient and smart,
  patriotic and brave!
But, O manliest grandmothers, onward now!   610
 And you matronly nettles, don't waver!
but continue to bristle and rage, my dears,
 for you've still got the wind in your favor!

(The Chorus of Women and the Old Market-Women join)

LYSISTRATA: But if only the spirit of tender Love
 and the power of sweet Aphrodite   615
were to breathe down over our breasts and thighs
 an attraction both melting and mighty,
and infuse a pleasanter rigor in men,
 raising only their cudgels of passion,
then I think we'd be known throughout all of Greece   620
 as makers of peace and good fashion.
COMMISSIONER: Having done just what?

LYSISTRATA: Well, first of all
   we shall certainly make it unlawful
   to go madly to market in armor.
AN OLD MARKET-WOMAN: Yes!
   By dear Aphrodite, it's awful!   625
LYSISTRATA: For now, in the midst of the pottery-stalls
   and the greens and the beans and the garlic,
   men go charging all over the market-place
   in full armor and beetling and warlike.
COMMISSIONER: They must do as their valor impels them to!   630
LYSISTRATA: But it makes a man only look funny
   to be wearing a shield with a Gorgon's[20] head
   and be wanting sardines for less money.
OLD MARKET-WOMEN: Well, I saw a huge cavalry-captain once
   on a stallion that scarcely could hold him,   635
   pouring into his helmet of bronze a pint
   of pea-soup an old woman had sold him,
   and a Thracian who, brandishing shield and spear
   like some savage Euripides staged once,
   when he'd frightened a vendor of figs to death,   640
   gobbled up all her ripest and aged ones.
COMMISSIONER: And how, on the international scale,
   can you straighten out the enormous
   confusion among all the states of Greece?
LYSISTRATA: Very easily.
COMMISSIONER: How? Do inform us.   645
LYSISTRATA: When our skein's in a tangle we take it thus
   on our spindles, or haven't you seen us?—
   one on this side and one on the other side,
   and we work out the tangles between us.
   And that is the way we'll undo this war,   650
   by exchanging ambassadors, whether
   you like it or not, one from either side,
   and we'll work out the tangles together.
COMMISSIONER: Do you really think that with wools and skeins
   and just being able to spin you   655
   can end these momentous affairs, you fools?
LYSISTRATA: With any intelligence in you
   you statesmen would govern as we work wool,
   and in everything Athens would profit.
COMMISSIONER: How so? Do tell.
LYSISTRATA: First, you take raw fleece   660
   and you wash the beshittedness off it:

---

[20]The Gorgons of Greek myth were three sisters with snakes for hair. Medusa was the most
famous of them.

just so, you should first lay the city out
    on a washboard and beat out the rotters
and pluck out the sharpers like burrs, and when
    you find tight knots of schemers and plotters   665
who are out for key offices, card them loose,
    but best tear off their heads in addition.
Then into one basket together card
    all those of a good disposition
be they citizens, resident aliens, friends,   670
    an ally or an absolute stranger,
even people in debt to the commonwealth,
    you can mix them all in with no danger.
And the cities which Athens has colonized—
    by Zeus, you should try to conceive them   675
as so many shreddings and tufts of wool
    that are scattered about and not leave them
to lie around loose, but from all of them
    draw the threads in here, and collect them
into one big ball and then weave a coat   680
    for the people, to warm and protect them.
COMMISSIONER: Now, isn't this awful? They treat the state
    like wool to be beaten and carded,
who have nothing at all to do with war!
LYSISTRATA: Yes we do, you damnable hard-head!   685
We have none of your honors but we have more
    then double your sufferings by it.
First of all, we bear sons whom you send to war.
COMMISSIONER: Don't bring up our old sorrows! Be quiet!
LYSISTRATA: And now, when we ought to enjoy ourselves,   690
    making much of our prime and our beauty,
we are sleeping alone because all the men
    are away on their soldierly duty.
But never mind *us*—when young girls grow old
    in their bedrooms with no men to share them.   695
COMMISSIONER: You seem to forget that men, too, grow old.
LYSISTRATA: By Zeus, but you cannot compare them!
When a man gets back, though he be quite gray,
    he can wed a young girl in a minute,
but the season of woman is very short: 700
    she must take what she can while she's in it.
And you know she must, for when it's past,
    although you're not awfully astute, you're
aware that no man will marry her then
    and she sits staring into the future.   705
COMMISSIONER: But he who can raise an erection still—
LYSISTRATA: Is there some good reason you don't drop dead?

We'll sell you a coffin if you but will.
Here's a string of onions to crown your head
and I'll make a honey-cake large and round   710
you can feed to Cerberus[21] underground!

FIRST OLD MARKET-WOMAN: Accept these few fillets of leek from
     me!

SECOND OLD MARKET-WOMAN: Let me offer you these for your garland,
     sir!

LYSISTRATA: What now? Do you want something else you see?
     Listen! Charon's[22] calling his passenger—   715
     will you catch the ferry or still delay
     when his other dead want to sail away?

COMMISSIONER: Is it not downright monstrous to treat *me* like
     this?
     By Zeus, I'll go right now to the Commissioners
     and show myself in evidence, just as I am!   720

(He begins to withdraw with dignity and his four Scythian policemen)

LYSISTRATA: Will you accuse us of not giving you a wake?
     But your departed spirit will receive from us
     burnt offerings in due form, two days from now at dawn!

*(Lysistrata with the other women goes into the Acropolis. The Commissioner etc.
have left. The male chorus and the mixed female chorus are alone.)*

CHORUS OF MEN: No man now dare fall to drowsing, if he wishes
     to stay free!   725
     Men, let's strip and gird ourselves for this eventuality!
          To me this all begins to have a smell
          of bigger things and larger things as well:
     most of all I sniff a tyranny afoot. I'm much afraid
          certain secret agents of the Spartans may have come, 730
          meeting under cover here, in Cleisthenes's home,
     instigating those damned women by deceit to make a raid
          upon our treasury and that great sum
          the city paid my pension from.
     Sinister events already!—think of lecturing the state,   735
     women as they are, and prattling on of things like shields of
     bronze,
     even trying hard to get us reconciled to those we hate—
     those of Sparta, to be trusted like a lean wolf when it yawns!
     All of this is just a pretext, men, for a dictatorship—   740

[21]The three-headed dog guarding the gate of Hades.   [22]Charon ferried the dead across the
River Styx to Hades.

but to me they shall not dictate! Watch and ward! A sword I'll
hide
underneath a branch of myrtle; through the agora[23] I'll slip,
following Aristogeiton, backing the tyrannicide!

*(The Old Men pair off to imitate the gestures of the famous group statue of the
tyrannicides Harmodius and Aristogeiton[24])*

Thus I'll take my stand beside him! Now my rage is goaded raw   745
I'm as like as not to clip this damned old woman on the jaw!
CHORUS OF WOMEN: Your own mother will not know you when
   you come home, if you do!
Let us first, though, lay our things down, O my dear old friends
   and true.   750
      For now, O fellow-citizens, we would
      consider what will do our city good.
Well I may, because it bred me up in wealth and elegance:
      letting me at seven help with the embroidering
      of Athena's mantle, and at ten with offering   755
cakes and flowers. When I was grown and beautiful I had my
   chance
      to bear her baskets, at my neck a string
      of figs, and proud as anything.

Must I not, then, give my city any good advice I can?
Need you hold the fact against me that I was not born a man,   760
when I offer better methods than the present ones, and when
I've a share in this economy, for I contribute men?
But, you sad old codgers, *yours* is forfeited on many scores:
you have drawn upon our treasure dating from the Persian wars,
what they call grampatrimony, and you've paid no taxes back.   765
Worse, you've run it nearly bankrupt, and the prospect's pretty
   black.
Have you anything to answer? Say you were within the law
and I'll take this rawhide boot and clip you one across the jaw!
CHORUS OF MEN: Greater insolence than ever!—   770
      that's the method that she calls
      "better"—if you would believe her.
But this threat must be prevented! Every man with both his balls
must make ready—take our shirts off, for a man must reek of   775
   male
outright—not wrapped up in leafage like an omelet for sale!

---

[23]Assembly place.   [24]Memorialized for their part in overthrowing the tyrant Hippias, who
ruled from 527 to 510 B.C.

Forward and barefoot: we'll do it again
to the death, just as when we resisted
tyranny out at Leipsydrion, when
we really existed!

Now or never we must grow   780
young again and, sprouting wings
over all our bodies, throw
off this heaviness age brings!

For if any of us give them even just a little hold
nothing will be safe from their tenacious grasp. They are so bold
they will soon build ships of war and, with exorbitant intent,   785
send such navies out against us as Queen Artemisia[25] sent.
But if they attack with horse, our knights we might as well delete:
nothing rides so well as woman, with so marvelous a seat,
never slipping at the gallop. Just look at those Amazons
in that picture in the Stoa, from their horses bringing bronze   790
axes down on men. We'd better grab *these* members of the sex
one and all, arrest them, get some wooden collars on their necks!
CHORUS OF WOMEN: By the gods, if you chagrin me
                             or annoy me, if you dare,   795
                             I'll turn loose the sow that's in me
till you rouse the town to help you with the way I've done your
hair!
Let us too make ready, women, and our garments quickly doff
so we'll smell like women angered fit to bite our fingers off!

Now I am ready: let one of the men   800
come against me, and *he'll* never hanker
after a black bean or garlic again:
no woman smells ranker!

Say a single unkind word,
I'll pursue you till you drop,
as the beetle did the bird.   805
My revenge will never stop!

Yet you will not worry me so long as Lampito's alive
and my noble friends in Thebes and other cities still survive.
You'll not overpower us, even passing seven decrees or eight,
you, poor brutes, whom everyone and everybody's neighbors hate.
Only yesterday I gave a party, honoring Hecatë,   810

[25]Artemisia fought with the Persians against the Greeks at Salamis in 480 B.C.

but when I invited in the neighbor's child to come and play,
such a pretty thing from Thebes, as nice and quiet as you please,
just an eel, they said she couldn't, on account of your decrees.
You'll go on forever passing such decrees without a check
till somebody takes you firmly by the leg and breaks your neck!   815

(Lysistrata comes out. The Chorus of Women addresses her in the manner of tragedy.)

Oh Queen of this our enterprise and all our hopes,
   wherefore in baleful brooding hast thou issued forth?
LYSISTRATA: The deeds of wicked women and the female mind discour-
   age me and set me pacing up and down.
CHORUS OF WOMEN: What's that? What's that you say?
LYSISTRATA: The truth, alas, the truth!   820
CHORUS OF WOMEN: What is it that's so dreadful? Tell it to your friends.
LYSISTRATA: A shameful thing to tell and heavy not to tell.
CHORUS OF WOMEN: Oh, never hide from me misfortune that is ours!
LYSISTRATA: To put it briefly as I can, we are in heat.
CHORUS OF WOMEN: Oh Zeus!   825
LYSISTRATA: Why call on Zeus? This is the way things are.
   At least it seems I am no longer capable
   of keeping them from men. They are deserting me.
   This morning I caught one of them digging away
   to make a tunnel to Pan's grotto down the slope,   830
   another letting herself down the parapet
   with rope and pulley, and another climbing down
   its sheerest face, and yesterday was one I found
   sitting upon a sparrow with a mind to fly
   down to some well-equipped whoremaster's place in town.   835
   Just as she swooped I pulled her backward by the hair.
   They think of every far-fetched excuse they can
   for going home. And here comes one deserter now.
   You there, where are you running?
FIRST WOMAN: I want to go home,
   because I left some fine Milesian wools at home   840
   that must be riddled now with moths.
LYSISTRATA: Oh, damn your moths!
   Go back inside.
FIRST WOMAN: But I shall come back right away,
   just time enough to stretch them out upon my bed.
LYSISTRATA: Stretch nothing out, and don't you go away at all.   845
FIRST WOMAN: But shall I let my wools be ruined?
LYSISTRATA: If you must.
SECOND WOMAN: Oh miserable me! I sorrow for the flax
   I left at home unbeaten and unstripped!

LYSISTRATA: One more—
wanting to leave for stalks of flax she hasn't stripped.
Come back here! 850
SECOND WOMAN: But, by Artemis, I only want
to strip my flax. Then I'll come right back here again.
LYSISTRATA: Strip me no strippings! If you start this kind of thing
some other woman soon will want to do the same.
THIRD WOMAN: O lady Artemis, hold back this birth until 855
I can get safe to some unconsecrated place!
LYSISTRATA: What is this raving?
THIRD WOMAN: I'm about to have a child.
LYSISTRATA: But you weren't pregnant yesterday.
THIRD WOMAN: I am today.
Oh, send me home this instant, dear Lysistrata,
so I can find a midwife.
LYSISTRATA: What strange tale is this? 860
What is this hard thing you have here?
THIRD WOMAN: The child is male.
LYSISTRATA: By Aphrodite, no! You obviously have
some hollow thing of bronze. I'll find out what it is.
You silly thing!—you have Athena's helmet here—
and claiming to be pregnant!
THIRD WOMAN: So I am, by Zeus! 865
LYSISTRATA: In that case, what's the helmet for?
THIRD WOMAN: So if the pains
came on me while I'm still up here, I might give birth
inside the helmet, as I've seen the pigeons do.
LYSISTRATA: What an excuse! The case is obvious. Wait here.
I want to show this bouncing baby helmet off. 870

(She passes the huge helmet around the Chorus of Women)

SECOND WOMAN: But I can't even sleep in the Acropolis,
not for an instant since I saw the sacred snake!
FOURTH WOMAN: The owls are what are killing *me.* How can I sleep
with their eternal whit-to-whoo-to-whit-to-whoo?
LYSISTRATA: You're crazy! Will you stop this hocus-pocus now? 875
No doubt you miss your husbands: don't you think that they
are missing us as much? I'm sure the nights they pass
are just as hard. But, gallant comrades, do bear up,
and face these gruelling hardships yet a little while.
There is an oracle that says we'll win, if we 880
only will stick together. Here's the oracle.
CHORUS OF WOMEN: Oh, read us what it says!
LYSISTRATA: Keep silence, then and hear:

"Now when to one high place are gathered the fluttering swallows,
Fleeing the Hawk and the Cock however hotly it follows, 885
Then will their miseries end, and that which is over be under:
Thundering Zeus will decide.

A WOMAN: Will *we* lie on top now, I wonder?
LYSISTRATA: *But if the Swallows go fighting each other and springing and*
winging
Out of the holy and high sanctuary, then people will never
Say there was any more dissolute bitch of a bird whatsoever. 890
A WOMAN: The oracle is clear, by Zeus!
LYSISTRATA: By *all* the gods!
So let us not renounce the hardships we endure.
But let us go back in. Indeed, my dearest friends,
it would be shameful to betray the oracle.

(Exeunt into the Acropolis)

CHORUS OF MEN: Let me tell you a story I heard one day 895
                          when I was a child:
There was once a young fellow Melanion by name
who refused to get married and ran away
                          to the wild.
                          To the mountains he came 900
                          and inhabited there
                               in a grove
                          and hunted the hare
                          both early and late
                          with nets that he wove 905
                          and also a hound
and he never came home again, such was his hate,
                          all women he found
                          so nasty, and we
                          quite wisely agree. 910
           Let us kiss you, dear old dears!
CHORUS OF WOMEN: With no onions, you'll shed tears!
CHORUS OF MEN: I mean, lift my leg and *kick.*
CHORUS OF WOMEN: My, you wear your thicket thick!
CHORUS OF MEN: Great Myronides[26] was rough 915
                          at the front and black enough
                          in the ass to scare his foes.
                               Just ask anyone who knows:
                               it's with hair that wars are won—
                               take for instance Phormion.[27] 920

[26]An Athenian general, fifth century B.C.   [27]Athenian admiral, fifth century B.C.

CHORUS OF WOMEN: Let me tell you a story in answer to
                                Melanion's case.
    There is now a man, Timon,²⁸ who wanders around
    in the wilderness, hiding his face from view
                        in a place   925
                where the brambles abound
                so he looks like a chip
                        off a Fury,²⁹
                        curling his lip.
    Now Timon retired   930
    in hatred and pure
    contempt of all men
    and he cursed them in words that were truly inspired
        again and again
        but women he found   935
        delightful and sound.
    Would you like your jaw repaired?
CHORUS OF MEN: Thank you, no. You've got me scared.
CHORUS OF WOMEN: Let me jump and kick it though.
CHORUS OF MEN: You will let your man-sack show.   940
CHORUS OF WOMEN: All the same you wouldn't see,
                old and gray as I may be,
                any superfluity
                    of unbarbered hair on me:
                    it is plucked and more, you scamp,   945
                    since I singe it with a lamp!

(Enter Lysistrata on the wall)

LYSISTRATA: Women, O women, come here quickly, here to me!
WOMEN: Whatever is it? Tell me! What's the shouting for?
LYSISTRATA: I see a man approaching, shaken and possessed,
    seized and inspired by Aphrodite's power.   950
    O thou, of Cyprus, Paphos, and Cythera, queen!
    continue straight along this way you have begun!
A WOMAN: Whoever he is, where is he?
LYSISTRATA: Near Demeter's³⁰ shrine.
A WOMAN: Why yes, by Zeus, he is. Who ever can he be?
LYSISTRATA: Well, look at him. Do any of you know him?
MYRRHINA: Yes.   955
    I do. He's my own husband, too, Cinesias.
LYSISTRATA: Then it's your duty now to turn him on a spit,
    cajole him and make love to him and not make love,

---

²⁸A semilegendary character, the original of Shakespeare's *Timon of Athens*.   ²⁹The Furies
were female avengers, with snakelike hair, who punished evildoers.   ³⁰Goddess of agriculture.

to offer everything, short of those things of which
the wine-cup knows.

MYRRHINA: I'll do it, don't you fear.

LYSISTRATA: And I   960

will help you tantalize him. I will stay up here
and help you roast him slowly. But now, disappear!

(Enter Cinesias)

CINESIAS: Oh how unfortunate I am, gripped by what spasms,
   stretched tight like being tortured on a wheel!

LYSISTRATA: Who's there? Who has got this far past the sentries?

CINESIAS: I.   965

LYSISTRATA: A man?

CINESIAS: A man, for sure.

LYSISTRATA: Then clear away from here.

CINESIAS: Who're you, to throw me out?

LYSISTRATA: The look-out for the day.

CINESIAS: Then, for the gods' sake, call Myrrhina out for me.

LYSISTRATA: You don't say! Call Myrrhina out! And who are you?

CINESIAS: Her husband. I'm Cinesias Paionides.   970

LYSISTRATA: Well, my dear man, hello! Your name is not unknown
   among us here and not without a certain fame,
   because your wife has it forever on her lips.
   She can't pick up an egg or quince but she must say:
   Cinesias would enjoy it so!

CINESIAS: How wonderful!   975

LYSISTRATA: By Aphrodite, yes. And if we chance to talk
   of husbands, your wife interrupts and says the rest
   are nothing much compared to her Cinesias.

CINESIAS: Go call her.

LYSISTRATA: Will you give me something if I do?

CINESIAS: Indeed I will, by Zeus, if it is what you want.   980
   I can but offer what I have, and I have this.

LYSISTRATA: Wait there. I will go down and call her.

CINESIAS: Hurry up!

because I find no charm whatever left in life
since she departed from the house. I get depressed
whenever I go into it, and everything   985
seems lonely to me now, and when I eat my food
I find no taste in it at all—because I'm stiff.

MYRRHINA *(offstage)*: I love him, how I love him! But he doesn't want
   my love! *(on wall)* So what's the use of calling me to him?

CINESIAS: My sweet little Myrrhina, why do you act like that?   990
   Come down here.

MYRRHINA: There? By Zeus, I certainly will not.

CINESIAS: Won't you come down, Myrrhina, when I'm calling you?
MYRRHINA: Not when you call me without needing anything.
CINESIAS: Not needing anything? I'm desperate with need.
MYRRHINA: I'm going now.
CINESIAS: Oh, no! No, don't go yet! At least   995
       you'll listen to the baby. Call your mammy, you.
BABY: Mammy mammy mammy!
CINESIAS: What's wrong with you? Have you no pity on your child
       when it is six days now since he was washed or nursed?
MYRRHINA: Oh, *I* have pity. But his father takes no care   1000
       of him.
CINESIAS: Come down, you flighty creature, for the child.
MYRRHINA: Oh, what it is to be a mother! I'll come down,
       for what else can I do?

(Myrrhina exits to reenter below)

CINESIAS: It seems to me she's grown
       much younger, and her eyes have a more tender look.   1005
       Even her being angry with me and her scorn
       are just the things that pain me with the more desire.
MYRRHINA: Come let me kiss you, dear sweet little baby mine,
       with such a horrid father. Mammy loves you, though.
CINESIAS: But why are you so mean? Why do you listen to   1010
       those other women, giving me such pain?—And you,
       you're suffering yourself.
MYRRHINA: Take your hands off of me!
CINESIAS: But everything we have at home, my things and yours,
       you're letting go to pieces.
MYRRHINA: Little do I care!
CINESIAS: Little you care even if your weaving's pecked apart and   1015
       carried off by chickens?
MYRRHINA *(bravely)*:   Little I care, by Zeus!
CINESIAS: You have neglected Aphrodite's rituals
       for such a long time now. Won't you come back again?
MYRRHINA: Not I, unless you men negotiate a truce
       and make an end of war.
CINESIAS: Well, if it's so decreed,   1020
       we will do even that.
MYRRHINA: Well, if it's so decreed,
       I will come home again. Not now. I've sworn I won't.
CINESIAS: All right, all right. But now lie down with me once more.
MYRRHINA: No! No!—yet I don't say I'm not in love with you.
CINESIAS: You love me? Then why not lie down, Myrrhina dear?   1025
MYRRHINA: Don't be ridiculous! Not right before the child!

CINESIAS: By Zeus, of course not. Manes, carry him back home.
There now. You see the baby isn't in your way.
Won't you lie down?
MYRRHINA: But *where,* you rogue, just where
is one to do it?
CINESIAS: Where? Pan's grotto's a fine place. 1030
MYRRHINA: But how could I come back to the Acropolis
in proper purity?
CINESIAS: Well, there's a spring below
the grotto—you can very nicely bathe in that.

(Ekkyklema[31] *or inset-scene with grotto)*

MYRRHINA: And then I'm under oath. What if I break my vows?
CINESIAS: Let me bear all the blame. Don't worry about your oath. 1035
MYRRHINA: Wait here, and I'll go get a cot for us.
CINESIAS: No no,
the ground will do.
MYRRHINA: No, by Apollo! Though you *are*
so horrid, I can't have you lying on the ground. *(Leaves)*
CINESIAS: You know, the woman loves me—*that's* as plain as day.
MYRRHINA: There. Get yourself in bed and I'll take off my clothes. 1040
Oh, what a nuisance! I must go and get a mat.
CINESIAS: What for? I don't need one
MYRRHINA: Oh yes, by Artemis!
On the bare cords? How ghastly!
CINESIAS: Let me kiss you now.
MYRRHINA: Oh, very well.
CINESIAS: Wow! Hurry, hurry and come back.

(Myrrhina leaves. A long wait.)

MYRRHINA: Here is the mat. Lie down now, while I get undressed. 1045
Oh, what a nuisance! You don't have a pillow, dear.
CINESIAS: But I don't need one, not one bit!
MYRRHINA: By Zeus, *I* do!

(Leaves)

CINESIAS: Poor prick, the service around here is terrible!
MYRRHINA: Sit up, my dear, jump up! Now I've got everything.
CINESIAS: Indeed you have. And now, my golden girl, come here. 1050
MYRRHINA: I'm just untying my brassiere. Now don't forget:
about that treaty—you won't disappoint me, dear?

[31]A movable or revolving platform sometimes used as a supplement to the more famous stage
machine, the *mēchanē*, or derrick.

CINESIAS: By Zeus, no! On my life!

MYRRHINA: You have no blanket, dear.

CINESIAS: By Zeus, I do not need one. I just want to screw.

MYRRHINA: Don't worry, dear, you will. I'll be back right away.   1055

(Leaves)

CINESIAS: This number, with her bedding, means to murder me.

MYRRHINA: Now raise yourself upright.

CINESIAS: But *this* is upright now!

MYRRHINA: Wouldn't you like some perfume?

CINESIAS: By Apollo, no!

MYRRHINA: By Aphrodite, yes! You must—like it or not.

(Leaves)

CINESIAS: Lord Zeus! Just let the perfume spill! That's all I ask!   1060

MYRRHINA: Hold out your hand. Take some of this and rub it on.

CINESIAS: This perfume, by Apollo, isn't sweet at all.
   It smells a bit of stalling—not of wedding nights!

MYRRHINA: I brought the *Rhodian* perfume! How absurd of me!

CINESIAS: It's fine! Let's keep it.

MYRRHINA: You *will* have your little joke.   1065

(Leaves)

CINESIAS: Just let me at the man who first distilled perfumes!

MYRRHINA: Try this, in the long vial.

CINESIAS: I've got one like it, dear.
   But don't be tedious. Lie down. And please don't bring
   anything more.

MYRRHINA *(going):* That's what I'll do, by Artemis!   1070
   I'm taking off my shoes. But dearest, don't forget
   you're going to vote for peace.

CINESIAS: I will consider it.
   She has destroyed me, murdered me, that woman has!
   On top of which she's got me skinned and gone away!
   What shall I do? Oh, whom shall I screw,   1075
   cheated of dear Myrrhina, the first
   beauty of all, a creature divine?
   How shall I tend this infant of mine?
   Find me a pimp: it has to be nursed!

CHORUS OF MEN: *(in tragic style, as if to Prometheus or*
                           Andromeda [32] *bound)*   1080
                   In what dire woe, how heavy-hearted
                   I see thee languishing, outsmarted!
                   I pity thee, alas I do.

---

[32]The mythical hero and heroine, respectively, of Aeschylus's *Prometheus Bound* and Euripides's
lost play *Andromeda*.

What kidney could endure such pain,
what spirit could, what balls, what back, 1085
what loins, what sacroiliac,
if they came under such a strain
and never had a morning screw?

CINESIAS: O Zeus! the twinges! Oh, the twitches!

CHORUS OF MEN: And this is what she did to you, 1090
that vilest, hatefullest of bitches!

CINESIAS: Oh nay, by Zeus, she's dear and sweet!

CHORUS OF MEN: How can she be? She's vile, O Zeus, she's vile!
Oh treat her, Zeus, like so much wheat—
O God of Weather, hear my prayer— 1095
and raise a whirlwind's mighty blast
to roll her up into a pile
and carry her into the sky
far up and up and then at last
drop her and land her suddenly 1100
astride that pointed penis there!

(The ekkyklema turns, closing the inset-scene. Enter, from opposite sides, a Spartan and an Athenian official.)

SPARTAN: Wheah is the Senate-house of the Athenians?
Ah wish to see the chaihman. Ah have news of him.

ATHENIAN: And who are you? Are you a Satyr or a man?

SPARTAN: Ah am a herald, mah young friend, yes, by the gods, 1105
and Ah have come from Sparta to negotiate.

ATHENIAN: And yet you come here with a spear under your arm?

SPARTAN: Not Ah, bah Zeus, not Ah!

ATHENIAN: Why do you turn around?
Why throw your cloak out so in front? Has the long trip
given you a swelling?

SPARTAN: Ah do think the man is queah! 1110

ATHENIAN: But you have an erection, oh you reprobate!

SPARTAN: Bah Zeus, Ah've no sech thing! And don't you fool around!

ATHENIAN: And what have you got there?

SPARTAN: A Spahtan scroll-stick, suh.

ATHENIAN: Well, if it is, *this* is a Spartan scroll-stick, too.
But look, I know what's up; you can tell *me* the truth. 1115
Just how are things with you in Sparta: tell me that.

SPARTAN: Theah is uprising in all Spahta. Ouah allies
are all erect as well. We need ouah milkin'-pails.

ATHENIAN: From where has this great scourge of frenzy fallen on
you?
From Pan? 1120

SPARTAN: No, Ah think Lampito began it all,
and then, the othah women throughout Spahta joined

togethah, just lahk at a signal fo a race,
and fought theah husbands off and drove them from theah cunts.
ATHENIAN: So, how're you getting on?
SPARTAN: We suffah. Through the town 1125
we walk bent ovah as if we were carrying
lamps in the wind. The women will not let us touch
even theah berries, till we all with one acco'd
have made a peace among the cities of all Greece.
ATHENIAN: This is an international conspiracy 1130
launched by the women! Now I comprehend it all!
Return at once to Sparta. Tell them they must send
ambassadors fully empowered to make peace.
And our Assembly will elect ambassadors
from our side, when I say so, showing them this prick. 1135
SPARTAN: Ah'll run! Ah'll flah! Fo all you say is excellent!
CHORUS OF MEN: No wild beast is more impossible than woman is to
fight,
nor is fire, nor has the panther such unbridled appetite!
CHORUS OF WOMEN: Well you know it, yet you go on warring with me
without end,
when you might, you cross-grained creature, have me as a trusty
friend. 1140
CHORUS OF MEN: Listen: I will never cease from hating women till I die!
CHORUS OF WOMEN: Any time you like. But meanwhile is there any
reason why
I should let you stand there naked, looking so ridiculous?
I am only coming near you, now, to slip your coat on, thus.
CHORUS OF MEN: That was very civil of you, very kind to treat me
so, 1145
when in such uncivil rage I took it off a while ago.
CHORUS OF WOMEN: Now you're looking like a man again, and not
ridiculous.
If you hadn't hurt my feelings, I would not have made a fuss,
I would even have removed that little beast that's in your eye.
CHORUS OF MEN: *That* is what was hurting me! Well, won't you take
my ring to pry 1150
back my eyelid? Rake the beast out. When you have it, let me see,
for some time now it's been in my eye and irritating me.
CHORUS OF WOMEN: Very well, I will—though you were *born* an irrita-
ble man.
What a monster of a gnat, by Zeus! Look at it if you can.
Don't you see it? It's a native of great marshes, can't you tell? 1155
CHORUS OF MEN: Much obliged, by Zeus! The brute's been digging at
me like a well!
So that now you have removed it, streams of tears come welling out.

CHORUS OF WOMEN: I will dry them. You're the meanest man alive, beyond a doubt,
   yet I will, and kiss you, too.
CHORUS OF MEN: Don't kiss me!
CHORUS OF WOMEN: If you will or not!
CHORUS OF MEN: Damn you! Oh, what wheedling flatterers you all are,
   born and bred!   1160
That old proverb is quite right and not inelegantly said:
"There's no living *with* the bitches and, without them, even *less*"—
so I might as well make peace with you, and from now on, I guess,
I'll do nothing mean to you and, from you, suffer nothing wrong.
So let's draw our ranks together now and start a little song: 1165
      For a change, we're not preparing
      any mean remark or daring
      aimed at any man in town,
   but the very opposite: we plan to do and say
   only good to everyone   1170
   when the ills we have already are sufficient anyway.
      Any man or woman who
      wants a little money, oh
      say three minas, maybe two,
      kindly let us know.   1175
      What we have is right in here.
      (Notice we have purses, too!)
      And if ever peace appear,
      he who takes our loan today
   never need repay.   1180
      We are having guests for supper,
      allies asked in by our upper
      classes to improve the town.
   There's pea-soup, and I had killed a sucking-pig of mine:
   I shall see it is well done,   1185
   so you will be tasting something very succulent and fine.
      Come to see us, then, tonight
      early, just as soon as you
      have a bath and dress up right:
      bring your children, too.   1190
      Enter boldly, never mind
      asking anyone in sight.
      Go straight in and you will find
      you are quite at home there, but
      all the doors are shut.

And here come the Spartan ambassadors,   1195
   dragging beards that are really the biggest I

have ever beheld, and around their thighs
    they are wearing some sort of a pig-sty.

Oh men of Sparta, let me bid you welcome first,
    and then you tell us how you are and why you come.

SPARTAN: What need is theah to speak to you in many words?   **1200**
    Fo you may see youahself in what a fix we come.
CHORUS OF MEN: Too bad! Your situation has become terribly hard and
    seems to be at fever-pitch.
SPARTAN: Unutterably so! And what is theah to say?
    Let someone bring us peace on any tuhms he will!
CHORUS OF MEN: And here I see some natives of Athenian soil,   **1205**
    holding their cloaks far off their bellies, like the best
    wrestlers, who sicken at the touch of cloth. It seems
    that overtraining may bring on this strange disease.
ATHENIAN: Will someone tell us where to find Lysistrata?
    We're men, and here we are, in this capacity.   **1210**
CHORUS OF MEN: This symptom and that other one sound much alike.
    Toward morning I expect convulsions do occur?
ATHENIAN: By Zeus, we are exhausted with just doing that,
    so, if somebody doesn't reconcile us quick,
    there's nothing for it: we'll be screwing Cleisthenes.[33]   **1215**
CHORUS OF MEN: Be careful—put your cloaks on, or you might be seen
    by some young blade who knocks the phalluses off herms.
ATHENIAN: By Zeus, an excellent idea!
SPARTAN *(having overheard):* Yes, bah the gods!
    It altogethah is. Quick, let's put on our cloaks.   **1220**

(Both groups cover quick and then recognize each other with full diplomatic pomp)

ATHENIAN: Greetings, O men of Sparta! *(to his group)* We have been
    disgraced!
SPARTAN *(to one of his group):* Mah dearest fellah, what a dreadful thing
    fo *us,*
    if these Athenians had seen ouah wo'st defeat!
ATHENIAN: Come now, O Spartans: one must specify each point.
    Why have you come here?
SPARTAN: To negotiate a peace.   **1225**
    We ah ambassadahs.
ATHENIAN: Well put. And so are we.
    Therefore, why do we not call in Lysistrata,
    she who alone might get us to agree on terms?
SPARTAN: Call her or any man, even a Lysistratus!

---

[33] A famous Athenian homosexual.

CHORUS OF MEN: But you will have no need, it seems, to call her
    now,   **1230**
  for here she is. She heard you and is coming out.
CHORUS OF MEN *and* CHORUS OF WOMEN: All hail, O manliest woman
    of all!
        It is time for you now to be turning
  into something still better, more dreadful, mean,
        unapproachable, charming, discerning,   **1235**
  for here are the foremost nations of Greece,
        bewitched by your spells like a lover,
  who have come to you, bringing you all their claims,
        and to *you* turning everything over.
LYSISTRATA: The work's not difficult, if one can catch them now   **1240**
  while they're excited and not making passes at
  each other. I will soon find out. Where's *HARMONY?*

(A naked maid, perhaps wearing a large ribbon reading HARMONY, appears from inside)

  Go take the Spartans first, and lead them over here,
  not with a rough hand nor an overbearing one,
  nor, as our husbands used to do this, clumsily,   **1245**
  but like a woman, in our most familiar style:
  If he won't give his hand, then lead him by the prick.
  And now, go bring me those Athenians as well,
  leading them by whatever they will offer you.
  O men of Sparta, stand right here, close by my side,   **1250**
  and *you* stand over there, and listen to my words.
  I am a woman, yes, but there is mind in me.
  In native judgment I am not so badly off,
  and, having heard my father and my elders talk
  often enough, I have some cultivation, too.   **1255**
  And so, I want to take and scold you, on both sides,
  as you deserve, for though you use a lustral[34] urn
  in common at the altars, like blood-relatives,
  when at Olympia, Delphi, or Thermopylae—
  how many others I might name if I took time!—   **1260**
  yet, with barbarian hordes of enemies at hand,
  it is Greek men, it is Greek cities, you destroy.
  That is one argument so far, and it is done.
ATHENIAN: My prick is skinned alive—that's what's destroying *me.*
LYSISTRATA: Now, men of Sparta—for I shall address you first—   **1265**
  do you not know that once one of your kings came here
  and as a suppliant of the Athenians

[34]Ceremonial; used for purification.

sat by our altars, death-pale, in his purple robe,
and begged us for an army? For Messenë then
oppressed you[35] and an earthquake from the gods as well.   1270
Then Cimon[36] went, taking four thousand infantry,
and saved the whole of Lacedaemon for your state.
That is the way Athenians once treated you:
you ravage their land now, which once received you well.
ATHENIAN: By Zeus, these men are in the wrong, Lysistrata!   1275
SPARTAN *(with his eyes on Harmony):* We'ah wrong . . . What
an unutterably lovely ass!
LYSISTRATA: Do you suppose I'm letting you Athenians off?
Do you not know that once the Spartans in their turn,
when you were wearing the hide-skirts of slavery,   1280
came with their spears and slew many Thessalians,
many companions and allies of Hippias?[37]
They were the only ones who fought for you that day,
freed you from tyranny and, for the skirt of hide,
gave back your people the wool mantle of free men.   1285
SPARTAN: Ah nevah saw a woman broadah—in her views.
ATHENIAN: And I have never seen a lovelier little nook.
LYSISTRATA: So why, when you have done each other so much good,
go on fighting with no end of malevolence?
Why don't you make a peace? Tell me, what's in your way?   1290
SPARTAN: Whah, *we* ah willin', if *they* will give up to us
that very temptin' cuhve.   *(of Harmony, as hereafter)*
LYSISTRATA: What curve, my friend?
SPARTAN: The bay
of Pylos,[38] which we've wanted and felt out so long.
ATHENIAN: No, by Poseidon,[39] you will not get into that!
LYSISTRATA: Good friend, do let them have it.
ATHENIAN: No! What other town   1295
can we manipulate so well?
LYSISTRATA: Ask them for one.
ATHENIAN: Damn, let me think! Now first suppose you cede to us
that bristling tip of land, Echinos, behind which
the gulf of Malia recedes, and those long walls,
the legs on which Megara reaches to the sea.   1300
SPARTAN: No, mah deah man, not *everything,* bah Castah, no!
LYSISTRATA: Oh, give them up. Why quarrel for a pair of legs?
ATHENIAN: I'd like to strip and get to plowing right away.
SPARTAN: And *Ah* would lahk to push manuah, still earliah.

---

[35]In the Messenian revolt of 464 B.C.   [36]An Athenian general (d. 449 B.C.).   [37]An Athenian tyrant expelled in 510 B.C.   [38]Pylos had formerly been Sparta's but at the time of the play belonged to Athens.   [39]God of the sea.

LYSISTRATA: When you have made a peace, then you will do all
    that.   1305
  But if you want to do it, first deliberate,
  go and inform your allies and consult with them.
ATHENIAN: Oh, damn our allies, my good woman! We are stiff.
  Will all of our allies not stand resolved with us—
  namely, to screw?
SPARTAN: And so will ouahs, Ah'll guarantee.   1310
ATHENIAN: Our mercenaries, even, will agree with us.
LYSISTRATA: Excellent. Now to get you washed and purified
  so you may enter the Acropolis, where we
  women will entertain you out of our supplies.
  You will exchange your pledges there and vows for peace.   1315
  And after that each one of you will take his wife,
  departing then for home.
ATHENIAN: Let's go in right away.
SPARTAN: Lead on, ma'am, anywheah you lahk.
ATHENIAN: Yes, and be quick.

(Exeunt into Acropolis)

CHORUS OF MEN *and* CHORUS OF WOMEN: 1320
    All the rich embroideries, the
    scarves, the gold accessories, the
    trailing gowns, the robes I own
I begrudge to no man: let him take what things he will
for his children or a grown   1325
daughter who must dress for the procession up Athena's hill.
    Freely of my present stocks
    I invite you all to take.
    There are here no seals nor locks
    very hard to break.   1330
    Search through every bag and box,
    look—you will find nothing there
    if your eyesight isn't fine—
    sharper far than mine!

    Are there any of you needing   1335
    food for all the slaves you're feeding,
    all your little children, too?
I have wheat in tiny grains for you, the finest sort,
and I also offer you
plenty of the handsome strapping grains that slaves get by the quart. 1340
    So let any of the poor
    visit me with bag or sack
    which my slave will fill with more

wheat than they can pack,
giving each his ample share.   1345
Might I add that at my door
I have watch-dogs?—so beware.
Come too close by day or night,
you will find they bite.

(Voice of drunken Athenians from inside)

FIRST ATHENIAN: Open the door! *(shoves the porter aside)*   1350
                            And will you get out of my way?

(A second drunken Athenian follows. The first sees the chorus.)

What are you sitting *there* for? Shall I, with this torch,
burn you alive? *(drop character)*
                            How vulgar! Oh, how commonplace!
I can not do it!   1355

(Starts back in. The second Athenian stops him and remonstrates with him in a whisper. The first turns and addresses the audience.)

            Well, if it really must be done
to please you, we shall face it and go through with it.

CHORUS OF MEN *and* CHORUS OF WOMEN:
    And *we* shall face it and go through with it with you.

FIRST ATHENIAN *(in character again, extravagantly):*   1360
    Clear out of here! Or you'll be wailing for your hair!

(Chorus of Woman scours away in mock terror)

    Clear out of here! so that the Spartans can come out
    and have no trouble leaving, after they have dined.

(Chorus of Men scours away in mock terror)

SECOND ATHENIAN: I never saw a drinking-party like this one:
    even the Spartans were quite charming, and of course   1365
    we make the cleverest company, when in our cups.
FIRST ATHENIAN: You're right, because when sober we are not quite
        sane.
    If I can only talk the Athenians into it,
    we'll always go on any embassy quite drunk,
    for now, going to Sparta sober, we're so quick   1370
    to look around and see what trouble we can make
    that we don't listen to a single word they say—
    instead we think we hear them say what they do not—
    and none of our reports on anything agree.
    But just now everything was pleasant. If a man   1375

got singing words belonging to another song,
we all applauded and swore falsely it was fine!
But here are those same people coming back again
to the same spot! Go and be damned, the pack of you!

(The Chorus, having thrown off their masks, put on other cloaks, and rushed back on stage, stays put)

SECOND ATHENIAN: Yes, damn them, Zeus! Just when the party's com-
    ing out!   1380

(The party comes rolling out)

A SPARTAN *(to another)*:
Mah very chahmin friend, will you take up youah flutes?
Ah'll dance the dipody[40] and sing a lovely song
of us and the Athenians, of both at once!
FIRST ATHENIAN *(as pleasantly as he can):*   1385
Oh yes, take up your little reeds, by all the gods:
I very much enjoy seeing you people dance.
SPARTAN: Memory, come,
    come inspiah thah young
    votaries to song,   1390
    come inspiah theah dance!

(Other Spartans join)

Bring thah daughtah, bring the sweet
    Muse, fo well she knows
us and the Athenians,
    how at Ahtemisium[41]   1395
they in godlike onslaught rose
hahd against the Puhsian fleet,
    drove it to defeat!
Well she knows the Spartan waws,
    how Leonidas[42]   1400
    in the deadly pass
    led us on lahk baws
whettin' shahp theah tusks, how sweat
on ouah cheeks in thick foam flowahed,
off ouah legs how thick it showahed,   1405
    fo the Puhsian men were mo'
    than the sands along the sho'.
Goddess, huntress, Ahtemis,
slayeh of the beasts, descend:

---

[40]Two-foot verse. [41]Artemesium, where the Greeks and Persians fought a sea battle in 480 B.C.
prior to the decisive Greek victory at Salamis. [42]Leonidas, King of Sparta, died with all his men
defending the pass at Thermopylae against the Persians in 480 B.C.

vuhgin goddess, come to this   1410
feast of truce to bind us fast
so ouah peace may nevah end.
Now let friendship, love, and wealth
come with ouah acco'd at last.
May we stop ouah villainous   1415
wahly foxy stealth!
    Come, O huntress, heah to us,
    heah, O vuhgin, neah to us!

LYSISTRATA: Come, now that all the rest has been so well arranged,
  you Spartans take these women home; these others, you.   1420
  Let husband stand beside his wife, and let each wife
  stand by her husband: then, when we have danced a dance
  to thank the gods for our good fortune, let's take care
  hereafter not to make the same mistakes again.

ATHENIAN: Bring on the chorus! Invite the three Graces to follow,   1425
  and then call on Artemis, call her twin brother,
  the leader of choruses, healer Apollo!

CHORUS *(joins):* Pray for their friendliest favor, the one and the
    other.
  Call Dionysus,[43] his tender eyes casting
flame in the midst of his Maenads[44] ecstatic with dancing.   1430
    Call upon Zeus, the resplendent in fire,
    call on his wife, rich in honor and ire,
  call on the powers who possess everlasting
  memory, call them to aid,
  call them to witness the kindly, entrancing   1435
  peace Aphrodite has made!
      Alalai!
      Bound, and leap high! Alalai!
      Cry, as for victory, cry
      Alalai!   1440

LYSISTRATA: Sing us a new song, Spartans, capping our new song.

SPARTANS: Leave thah favohed mountain's height,
  Spahtan Muse, come celebrate
  Amyclae's lord[45] with us and great
  Athena housed in bronze;   1445
  praise Tyndareus' paih of sons,[46]
  gods who pass the days in spoht
  wheah the cold Eurotas[47] runs.

(General dancing)

---

[43]God of wine and revelry (Bacchus).   [44]Female followers of Dionysus.   [45]Apollo (there was a
temple to him in the town of Amyclae).   [46]Castor and Pollux, twin sons of Tyndareus, King of
Sparta, and Leda.   [47]A river flowing by Sparta.

Now to tread the dance,
now to tread it light,   1450
praising Spahta, wheah you find
  love of singing quickened bah the pounding beat
    of dancing feet,
when ouah guhls lahk foals cavoht
wheah the cold Eurotas runs,   1455
when they fleetly bound and prance
  till theah haih unfilleted shakes in the wind,
as of Maenads brandishin'
ahvied wands and revelin',
  Leda's daughtah, puah and faiah,   1460
  leads the holy dances theah.
FULL CHORUS *(as everyone leaves dancing):* So come bind up youah haih
  with youah hand,
    with youah feet make a bound
lahk a deeah; fo the chorus clap out
  an encouragin' sound,   1465
singin' praise of the temple of bronze
  housin' her we adaw:
sing the praise of Athena: the goddess unvanquished in waw!

Women in Athens in the time of Aristophanes had no vote and no business outside the household. Although they were certainly in the audience, they were probably relegated to the back rows, apart from the men. Basic to the comedy of *Lysistrata* is the spectacle of powerless creatures using their one overmastering power. But there is more to it. Consider the following questions.

QUESTIONS

1. How would you characterize Lysistrata? Is she a person worth listening to?
2. Do Kalonike and Myrrhina have individualized characters? How would you describe each? In what scenes or lines do they exist most memorably?
3. Characterize Cinesias. What is the function of his scene with Myrrhina?
4. Do the men generally show themselves more capable of managing the affairs of state than the women?
5. Does the play embody any serious suggestions for settling the war?
6. One theme is the power of sex. Are there others? In what ways are the themes made memorable?
7. This play leans much more heavily on the satiric side of comedy than on the romantic. Which individuals, classes, or institutions are most effectively satirized?

8. What do the meters and rhyming do for the comedy? What is the effect of the southern dialect? Could this play be staged, as written, in your community?

THE WAY OF THE WORLD

Congreve wrote for a relatively small and sophisticated audience. Whereas *Oedipus Rex* and *Lysistrata* played before as many as 14,000 spectators and *Hamlet* before 2,000 or 3,000, *The Way of the World* (1700) played in the Drury Lane theater designed by Christopher Wren, which seated an estimated 663. Wren had kept part of the Elizabethan stage for most of the acting—seventeen feet deep with boxes for spectators at each side—with an almost equal stage behind the proscenium opening, which eventually became the modern picture-frame stage, behind the curtain. Scenery was economically suggested.

Congreve's play culminated his and the Restoration's comedy of manners. He softens its cynicism as he heightens its comedy, purveying a kind of sophisticated playing at life to contain its shocks and emotions, like the real love of Mirabell and Millamant in his playful proviso scene in Act IV. Lady Wishfort is one of the world's great comic characters—her name is a stroke of genius—especially in the comic dramatic irony of her preparations for Sir Rowland in Act III. Congreve's plot, unmatched and even maddening in its perplexity—a kind of comic satire on all plotting—is nevertheless flawlessly motivated by character.

THE WAY OF THE WORLD

William Congreve   *(1670–1729)*

Dramatis Personae

MEN

FAINALL, in love with MRS. MARWOOD
MIRABELL, in love with MRS. MILLAMANT
WITWOUD,
PETULANT,   Followers of MRS. MILLAMANT
SIR WILFULL WITWOUD, Half-brother to WITWOUD, and Nephew to LADY WISHFORT
WAITWELL, Servant to MIRABELL

WOMEN

LADY WISHFORT, Enemy to MIRABELL, for having falsely pretended love to her
MRS. MILLAMANT, A fine Lady, Niece to LADY WISHFORT, and loves MIRABELL
MRS. MARWOOD, Friend to MR. FAINALL, and likes MIRABELL
MRS. FAINALL, Daughter to LADY WISHFORT, and Wife to FAINALL, formerly Friend
  to MIRABELL

FOIBLE, Woman to LADY WISHFORT
MINCING, Woman to MRS. MILLAMANT
Dancers, Footmen, and Attendants

Scene—London

Act I

A Chocolate-house. Mirabell and Fainall, rising from cards; Betty waiting.

MIRABELL: You are a fortunate man, Mr. Fainall.

FAINALL: Have we done?

MIRABELL: What you please. I'll play on to entertain you.

FAINALL: No, I'll give you your revenge another time, when you are not so indifferent; you are thinking of something else now, and play too negligently. The coldness of a losing gamester lessens the pleasure of the winner. I'd no more play with a man that slighted his ill fortune than I'd make love to a woman who undervalued the loss of her reputation.

MIRABELL: You have a taste extremely delicate and are for refining on your pleasures.

FAINALL: Prithee, why so reserved? Something has put you out of humor.

MIRABELL: Not at all; I happen to be grave today, and you are gay; that's all.

FAINALL: Confess, Millamant and you quarreled last night, after I left you; my fair cousin has some humors that would tempt the patience of a stoic. What, some coxcomb came in, and was well received by her, while you were by.

MIRABELL: Witwoud and Petulant, and what was worse, her aunt, your wife's mother, my evil genius; or to sum up all in her own name, my old Lady Wishfort came in.

FAINALL: Oh, there it is then! She has a lasting passion for you, and with reason. What, then my wife was there?

MIRABELL: Yes, and Mrs. Marwood and three or four more, whom I never saw before. Seeing me, they all put on their grave faces, whispered one another; then complained aloud of the vapors,[1] and after fell into a profound silence.

FAINALL: They had a mind to be rid of you.

MIRABELL: For which reason I resolved not to stir. At last the good old lady broke through her painful taciturnity, with an invective against long visits. I would not have understood her, but Millamant joining in the argument, I rose and with a constrained smile told her, I thought nothing was so easy as to know when a visit began to be troublesome. She reddened and I withdrew, without expecting her reply.

FAINALL: You were to blame to resent what she spoke only in compliance with her aunt.

---

[1] Fashionable fit of female melancholy.

MIRABELL: She is more mistress of herself than to be under the necessity of such a resignation.

FAINALL: What? Though half her fortune depends upon her marrying with my lady's approbation?

MIRABELL: I was then in such a humor, that I should have been better pleased if she had been less discreet.

FAINALL: Now I remember, I wonder not they were weary of you. Last night was one of their cabal-nights; they have 'em three times a week, and meet by turns, at one another's apartments, where they come together like the coroner's inquest, to sit upon the murdered reputations of the week. You and I are excluded; and it was once proposed that all the male sex should be excepted; but somebody moved that, to avoid scandal, there might be one man of the community; upon which motion Witwoud and Petulant were enrolled members.

MIRABELL: And who may have been the foundress of this sect? My Lady Wishfort, I warrant, who publishes her detestation of mankind, and full of the vigor of fifty-five, declares for a friend and ratafia;[2] and let posterity shift for itself, she'll breed no more.

FAINALL: The discovery of your sham addresses to her, to conceal your love to her niece, has provoked this separation. Had you dissembled better, things might have continued in the state of nature.

MIRABELL: I did as much as man could, with any reasonable conscience. I proceeded to the very last act of flattery with her, and was guilty of a song in her commendation. Nay, I got a friend to put her into a lampoon, and compliment her with the imputation of an affair with a young fellow, which I carried so far, that I told her the malicious town took notice that she was grown fat of a sudden; and when she lay in of a dropsy, persuaded her she was reported to be in labor. The devil's in't, if an old woman is to be flattered further, unless a man should endeavor downright personally to debauch her; and that my virtue forbade me. But for the discovery of that amour, I am indebted to your friend, or your wife's friend, Mrs. Marwood.

FAINALL: What should provoke her to be your enemy, unless she has made you advances, which you have slighted? Women do not easily forgive omissions of that nature.

MIRABELL: She was always civil to me, till of late. I confess I am not one of those coxcombs who are apt to interpret a woman's good manners to her prejudice, and think that she who does not refuse 'em everything can refuse 'em nothing.

FAINALL: You are a gallant man, Mirabell; and though you may have cruelty enough not to satisfy a lady's longing, you have too much generosity not to be tender of her honor. Yet you speak with an indifference which seems to be affected, and confesses you are conscious of a negligence.

[2]Fruit-flavored liqueur.

MIRABELL: You pursue the argument with a distrust that seems to be un-affected, and confesses you are conscious of a concern for which the lady is more indebted to you than your wife.

FAINALL: Fie, fie, friend! If you grow censorious, I must leave you. I'll look upon the gamesters in the next room.

MIRABELL: Who are they?

FAINALL: Petulant and Witwoud. *(To Betty.)* Bring me some chocolate.

(Exit.)

MIRABELL: Betty, what says your clock?

BETTY: Turned of the last canonical hour,[3] sir.   *(Exit.)*

MIRABELL: How pertinently the jade answers me! *(Looking on his watch.)* Ha? almost one o'clock! Oh, y'are come!

(Enter a Servant.)

Well, is the grand affair over? You have been something tedious.

SERVANT: Sir, there's such coupling at Pancras,[4] that they stand behind one another, as 'twere in a country dance. Ours was the last couple to lead up; and no hopes appearing of dispatch, besides the parson growing hoarse, we were afraid his lungs would have failed before it came to our turn; so we drove round to Duke's Place, and there they were riveted in a trice.

MIRABELL: So, so, you are sure they are married.

SERVANT: Married and bedded, sir; I am witness.

MIRABELL: Have you the certificate?

SERVANT: Here it is, sir.

MIRABELL: Has the tailor brought Waitwell's clothes home, and the new liveries?

SERVANT: Yes, sir.

MIRABELL: That's well. Do you go home again, d'ye hear, and adjourn the consummation till farther order; bid Waitwell shake his ears, and Dame Partlet[5] rustle up her feathers, and meet me at one o'clock by Rosamond's Pond,[6] that I may see her before she returns to her lady; and as you tender your ears, be secret.   *(Exit Servant.)*

(Re-enter Fainall and Betty.)

FAINALL: Joy of your success, Mirabell; you look pleased.

MIRABELL: Aye, I have been engaged in a matter of some sort of mirth, which is not yet ripe for discovery. I am glad this is not a cabal-night. I wonder, Fainall, that you who are married, and of consequence should be discreet, will suffer your wife to be of such a party.

---

[3]Twelve noon. Marriages were legal only in the morning, from eight to twelve.   [4]St. Pancras Church, where couples could marry without a license, as they also could at "Duke's Place," St. James' Church in Aldgate.   [5]Pertelote, the hen in Chaucer's *Nun's Priest's Tale.*   [6]A lake in St. James's Park associated with disastrous love.

FAINALL: Faith, I am not jealous. Besides, most who are engaged are women and relations; and for the men, they are of a kind too contemptible to give scandal.

MIRABELL: I am of another opinion. The greater the coxcomb, always the more scandal; for a woman who is not a fool can have but one reason for associating with a man that is.

FAINALL: Are you jealous as often as you see Witwoud entertained by Millamant?

MIRABELL: Of her understanding I am, if not of her person.

FAINALL: You do her wrong; for, to give her her due, she has wit.

MIRABELL: She has beauty enough to make any man think so, and complaisance enough not to contradict him who shall tell her so.

FAINALL: For a passionate lover, methinks you are a man somewhat too discerning in the failings of your mistress.

MIRABELL: And for a discerning man, somewhat too passionate a lover; for I like her with all her faults; nay, like her for her faults. Her follies are so natural, or so artful, that they become her; and those affectations which in another woman would be odious, serve but to make her more agreeable. I'll tell thee, Fainall, she once used me with that insolence, that in revenge I took her to pieces; sifted her and separated her failings; I studied 'em, and got 'em by rote. The catalogue was so large that I was not without hopes one day or other to hate her heartily: to which end I so used myself to think of 'em that at length, contrary to my design and expectation, they gave me every hour less and less disturbance; till in a few days it became habitual to me to remember 'em without being displeased. They are now grown as familiar to me as my own frailties; and in all probability, in a little time longer I shall like 'em as well.

FAINALL: Marry her, marry her! Be half as well acquainted with her charms as you are with her defects, and my life on't, you are your own man again.

MIRABELL: Say you so?

FAINALL: Aye, aye, I have experience: I have a wife, and so forth.

(Enter Messenger.)

MESSENGER: Is one Squire Witwoud here?

BETTY: Yes; what's your business?

MESSENGER: I have a letter for him, from his brother Sir Wilfull, which I am charged to deliver into his own hands.

BETTY: He's in the next room, friend; that way.   *(Exit Messenger.)*

MIRABELL: What, is the chief of that noble family in town, Sir Wilfull Witwoud?

FAINALL: He is expected today. Do you know him?

MIRABELL: I have seen him. He promises to be an extraordinary person; I think you have the honor to be related to him.

FAINALL: Yes, he is half brother to this Witwoud by a former wife, who was sister to my Lady Wishfort, my wife's mother. If you marry Millamant, you must call cousins too.

MIRABELL: I had rather be his relation than his acquaintance.

FAINALL: He comes to town in order to equip himself for travel.

MIRABELL: For travel! Why the man I mean is above forty.

FAINALL: No matter for that; 'tis for the honor of England that all Europe should know we have blockheads of all ages.

MIRABELL: I wonder there is not an act of parliament to save the credit of the nation, and prohibit the exportation of fools.

FAINALL: By no means; 'tis better as 'tis. 'Tis better to trade with a little loss, than to be quite eaten up with being overstocked.

MIRABELL: Pray, are the follies of this knight-errant and those of the squire his brother anything related?

FAINALL: Not at all; Witwoud grows by the knight, like a medlar grafted on a crab.[7] One will melt in your mouth, and t'other set your teeth on edge; one is all pulp, and the other all core.

MIRABELL: So one will be rotten before he be ripe, and the other will be rotten without ever being ripe at all.

FAINALL: Sir Wilfull is an odd mixture of bashfulness and obstinacy. But when he's drunk, he's as loving as the monster in *The Tempest,* and much after the same manner. To give t'other his due, he has something of good nature and does not always want[8] wit.

MIRABELL: Not always; but as often as his memory fails him, and his commonplace of comparisons.[9] He is a fool with a good memory and some few scraps of other folks' wit. He is one whose conversation can never be approved, yet it is now and then to be endured. He has indeed one good quality, he is not exceptious;[10] for he so passionately affects the reputation of understanding raillery, that he will construe an affront into a jest, and call downright rudeness and ill language satire and fire.

FAINALL: If you have a mind to finish his picture, you have an opportunity to do it at full length. Behold the original!

(Enter Witwoud.)

WITWOUD: Afford me your compassion, my dears! Pity me, Fainall! Mirabell, pity me!

MIRABELL: I do from my soul.

FAINALL: Why, what's the matter?

WITWOUD: No letters for me, Betty?

BETTY: Did not the messenger bring you one but now, sir?

WITWOUD: Aye, but no other?

BETTY: No, sir.

WITWOUD: That's hard, that's very hard. A messenger, a mule, a beast of

---

[7]A fruit, resembling the crab apple ("a crab"), traditionally rotten before it's ripe. [8]Lack. [9]Commonplace book, diary. [10]Picking arguments.

burden! He has brought me a letter from the fool my brother, as heavy as a panegyric in a funeral sermon, or a copy of commendatory verses from one poet to another. And what's worse, 'tis as sure a forerunner of the author as an epistle dedicatory.

MIRABELL: A fool, and your brother Witwoud!

WITWOUD: Aye, aye, my half brother. My half brother he is, no nearer upon honor.

MIRABELL: Then 'tis possible he may be but half a fool.

WITWOUD: Good, good, Mirabell, *le drôle!*[11] Good, good; hang him, don't let's talk of him. Fainall, how does your lady? Gad, I say anything in the world to get this fellow out of my head. I beg pardon that I should ask a man of pleasure, and the town, a question at once so foreign and domestic. But I talk like an old maid at a marriage, I don't know what I say; but she's the best woman in the world.

FAINALL: 'Tis well you don't know what you say, or else your commendation would go near to make me either vain or jealous.

WITWOUD: No man in town lives well with a wife but Fainall. Your judgment, Mirabell.

MIRABELL: You had better step and ask his wife, if you would be credibly informed.

WITWOUD: Mirabell

MIRABELL: Aye.

WITWOUD: My dear, I ask ten thousand pardons. Gad, I have forgot what I was going to say to you!

MIRABELL: I thank you heartily, heartily.

WITWOUD: No, but prithee excuse me: my memory is such a memory.

MIRABELL: Have a care of such apologies, Witwoud; for I never knew a fool but he affected to complain, either of the spleen[12] or his memory.

FAINALL: What have you done with Petulant?

WITWOUD: He's reckoning his money, my money it was. I have no luck today.

FAINALL: You may allow him to win of you at play, for you are sure to be too hard for him at repartee; since you monopolize the wit that is between you, the fortune must be his of course.

MIRABELL: I don't find that Petulant confesses the superiority of wit to be your talent, Witwoud.

WITWOUD: Come, come, you are malicious now, and would breed debates. Petulant's my friend, and a very honest fellow, and a very pretty fellow, and has a smattering—faith and froth, a pretty deal of an odd sort of a small wit; nay, I'll do him justice. I'm his friend, I won't wrong him neither. And if he had but any judgment in the world, he would not be altogether contemptible. Come, come, don't detract from the merits of my friend.

FAINALL: You don't take your friend to be over-nicely bred?

[11]Comic. [12]Melancholy.

WITWOUD: No, no, hang him, the rogue has no manners at all, that I must own. No more breeding than a bum-baily,[13] that I grant you. 'Tis pity, faith; the fellow has fire and life.

MIRABELL: What, courage?

WITWOUD: Hum, faith, I don't know as to that, I can't say as to that. Yes, faith, in a controversy he'll contradict anybody.

MIRABELL: Though 'twere a man whom he feared, or a woman whom he loved.

WITWOUD: Well, well, he does not always think before he speaks; we have all our failings. You're too hard upon him, you are, faith. Let me excuse him. I can defend most of his faults, except one or two. One he has, that's the truth on't; if he were my brother, I could not acquit him. That, indeed, I could wish were otherwise.

MIRABELL: Aye, marry, what's that, Witwoud?

WITWOUD: Oh, pardon me! Expose the infirmities of my friend! No, my dear, excuse me there.

FAINALL: What, I warrant he's unsincere, or 'tis some such trifle.

WITWOUD: No, no, what if he be? 'Tis no matter for that, his wit will excuse that. A wit should no more be sincere than a woman constant; one argues a decay of parts,[14] as t'other of beauty.

MIRABELL: Maybe you think him too positive?

WITWOUD: No, no, his being positive is an incentive to argument, and keeps up conversation.

FAINALL: Too illiterate?

WITWOUD: That! that's his happiness; his want of learning gives him the more opportunities to show his natural parts.

MIRABELL: He wants words?

WITWOUD: Aye, but I like him for that now; for his want of words gives me the pleasure very often to explain his meaning.

FAINALL: He's impudent?

WITWOUD: No, that's not it.

MIRABELL: Vain?

WITWOUD: No.

MIRABELL: What! He speaks unseasonable truths sometimes, because he has not wit enough to invent an evasion?

WITWOUD: Truths! Ha! Ha! Ha! No, no, since you will have it, I mean he never speaks truth at all, that's all. He will be like a chambermaid, or a woman of quality's porter. Now that is a fault.

(Enter Coachman.)

COACHMAN: Is Master Petulant here, mistress?

BETTY: Yes.

COACHMAN: Three gentlewoman in the coach would speak with him.

FAINALL: Oh brave Petulant! Three!

[13]Bailiff. [14]Abilities.

BETTY: I'll tell him.

COACHMAN: You must bring two dishes of chocolate and a glass of cinnamon-water.   *(Exeunt Betty and Coachman.)*

WITWOUD: That should be for two fasting strumpets, and a bawd troubled with wind. Now you may know what the three are.

MIRABELL: You are very free with your friend's acquaintance.

WITWOUD: Aye, aye, friendship without freedom is as dull as love without enjoyment, or wine without toasting; but to tell you a secret, these are trulls that he allows coach-hire, and something more, by the week, to call on him once a day at public places.

MIRABELL: How!

WITWOUD: You shall see he won't go to 'em because there's no more company here to take notice of him. Why, this is nothing to what he used to do: before he found out this way, I have known him call for himself.

FAINALL: Call for himself? What dost thou mean?

WITWOUD: Mean! Why, he would slip you out of this chocolate-house, just when you had been talking to him. As soon as your back was turned, whip, he was gone! Then trip to his lodging, clap on a hood and scarf, and mask, slap into a hackney-coach, and drive hither to the door again in a trice, where he would send in for himself; that I mean, call for himself, wait for himself; nay, and what's more, not finding himself, sometimes leave a letter for himself.

MIRABELL: I confess this is something extraordinary. I believe he waits for himself now, he is so long a-coming. Oh! I ask his pardon.

(Enter Petulant and Betty)

BETTY: Sir, the coach stays.

PETULANT: Well, well; I come. 'Sbud, a man had as good be a professed midwife as a professed whoremaster, at this rate! To be knocked up and raised at all hours, and in all places! Pox on 'em, I won't come! D'ye hear, tell 'em I won't come. Let 'em snivel and cry their hearts out.

FAINALL: You are very cruel, Petulant.

PETULANT: All's one, let it pass. I have a humor to be cruel.

MIRABELL: I hope they are not persons of condition that you use at this rate.

PETULANT: Condition! Condition's a dried fig, if I am not in humor! By this hand, if they were your—a—a—your what-d'ye-call'-ems themselves, they must wait or rub off,[15] if I want appetite.

MIRABELL: What-d'ye-call-'ems! What are they, Witwoud?

WITWOUD: Empresses, my dear; by your what-d'ye-call-'ems he means sultana queens.

PETULANT: Aye, Roxolanas.[16]

MIRABELL: Cry you mercy.

---

[15]Clear out.   [16]Roxolana, the queen in William D'Avenant's *The Siege of Rhodes* (1661), now an epithet for prostitute.

FAINALL: Witwoud says they are—

PETULANT: What does he say th'are?

WITWOUD: I? Fine ladies, I say.

PETULANT: Pass on, Witwoud. Harkee, by this light his relations: two co-heiresses his cousins, and an old aunt, that loves caterwauling better than a conventicle.[17]

WITWOUD: Ha! Ha! Ha! I had a mind to see how the rogue would come off. Ha! Ha! Ha! Gad, I can't be angry with him, if he had said they were my mother and my sisters.

MIRABELL: No!

WITWOUD: No; the rogue's wit and readiness of invention charm me. Dear Petulant!

BETTY: They are gone, sir, in great anger.

PETULANT: Enough, let 'em trundle. Anger helps complexion, saves paint.

FAINALL: This continence is all dissembled; this is in order to have something to brag of the next time he makes court to Millamant, and swear he has abandoned the whole sex for her sake.

MIRABELL: Have you not left off your impudent pretensions there yet? I shall cut your throat some time or other, Petulant, about that business.

PETULANT: Aye, aye, let that pass. There are other throats to be cut.

MIRABELL: Meaning mine, sir?

PETULANT: Not I. I mean nobody; I know nothing. But there are uncles and nephews in the world, and they may be rivals. What then? All's one for that.

MIRABELL: How! Harkee Petulant, come hither. Explain, or I shall call your interpreter.

PETULANT: Explain! I know nothing. Why, you have an uncle, have you not, lately come to town, and lodges by my Lady Wishfort's?

MIRABELL: True.

PETULANT: Why, that's enough. You and he are not friends; and if he should marry and have a child, you may be disinherited, ha?

MIRABELL: Where hast thou stumbled upon all this truth?

PETULANT: All's one for that; why, then say I know something.

MIRABELL: Come, thou art an honest fellow, Petulant, and shalt make love to my mistress, thou sha't, faith. What hast thou heard of my uncle?

PETULANT: I? Nothing I. If throats are to be cut, let swords clash! Snug's the word; I shrug and am silent.

MIRABELL: Oh, raillery, raillery! Come, I know thou art in the women's secrets. What, you're a cabalist; I know you stayed at Millamant's last night, after I went. Was there any mention made of my uncle or me? Tell me. If thou hadst but good nature equal to thy wit, Petulant, Tony Witwoud, who is now thy competitor in fame, would show as dim by thee as a dead whiting's eye by a pearl of orient; he would no

[17]Gathering of fundamentalist Protestants.

more be seen by thee than Mercury is by the sun. Come, I'm sure thou wo't tell me.

PETULANT: If I do, will you grant me common sense then for the future?

MIRABELL: Faith, I'll do what I can for thee; and I'll pray that Heaven may grant it thee in the meantime.

PETULANT: Well, harkee.   *Mirabell and Petulant talk apart.*

FAINALL: Petulant and you both will find Mirabell as warm a rival as a lover.

WITWOUD: Pshaw! pshaw! That she laughs at Petulant is plain. And for my part, but that it is almost a fashion to admire her, I should—harkee, to tell you a secret, but let it go no further; between friends, I shall never break my heart for her.

FAINALL: How!

WITWOUD: She's handsome; but she's a sort of an uncertain woman.

FAINALL: I thought you had died for her.

WITWOUD: Umh—no—

FAINALL: She has wit.

WITWOUD: 'Tis what she will hardly allow anybody else. Now, demme, I should hate that, if she were as handsome as Cleopatra. Mirabell is not so sure of her as he thinks for.

FAINALL: Why do you think so?

WITWOUD: We stayed pretty late there last night, and heard something of an uncle to Mirabell, who is lately come to town, and is between him and the best part of his estate. Mirabell and he are at some distance, as my Lady Wishfort has been told; and you know she hates Mirabell worse than a Quaker hates a parrot, or than a fishmonger hates a hard frost. Whether this uncle has seen Mrs. Millamant or not, I cannot say; but there were items of such a treaty being in embryo, and if it should come to life, poor Mirabell would be in some sort unfortunately fobbed, i'faith.

FAINALL: 'Tis impossible Millamant should hearken to it.

WITWOUD: Faith, my dear, I can't tell; she's a woman and a kind of a humorist.[18]

MIRABELL: And is this the sum of what you could collect last night?

PETULANT: The quintessence. Maybe Witwoud knows more; he stayed longer. Besides, they never mind him; they say anything before him.

MIRABELL: I thought you had been the greatest favorite.

PETULANT: Aye, *tête à tête,* but not in public, because I make remarks.

MIRABELL: You do?

PETULANT: Aye, aye, pox, I'm malicious, man! Now he's soft, you know, they are not in awe of him. The fellow's well-bred, he's what you call a—what-d'ye-call—'em, a fine gentleman, but he's silly withal.

MIRABELL: I thank you. I know as much as my curiosity requires Fainall, are you for the Mall?

FAINALL: Aye, I'll take a turn before dinner.

---

[18]A whimsical fellow.

WITWOUD: Aye, we'll all walk in the park; the ladies talked of being there.

MIRABELL: I thought you were obliged to watch for your brother Sir Wilfull's arrival.

WITWOUD: No, no, he comes to his aunt's, my Lady Wishfort. Pox on him! I shall be troubled with him too; what shall I do with the fool?

PETULANT: Beg him for his estate, that I may beg you afterwards; and so have but one trouble with you both.

WITWOUD: Oh, rare Petulant! Thou art as quick as a fire in a frosty morning; thou shalt to the Mall with us, and we'll be very severe.

PETULANT: Enough, I'm in a humor to be severe.

MIRABELL: Are you? Pray then walk by yourselves. Let not us be accessory to your putting the ladies out of countenance with your senseless ribaldry, which you roar out aloud as often as they pass by you; and when you have made a handsome woman blush, then you think you have been severe.

PETULANT: What, what? Then let 'em show their innocence by not understanding what they hear, or else show their discretion by not hearing what they would not be thought to understand.

MIRABELL: But hast not thou then sense enough to know that thou ought'st to be most ashamed thyself, when thou hast put another out of countenance?

PETULANT: Not I, by this hand! I always take blushing either for a sign of guilt or ill-breeding.

MIRABELL: I confess you ought to think so. You are in the right, that you may plead the error of your judgment in defense of your practice.

Where modesty's ill manners, 'tis but fit

That impudence and malice pass for wit.   *(Exeunt.)*

Act II

St. James's Park. Enter Mrs. Fainall and Mrs. Marwood.

MRS. FAINALL: Aye, aye, dear Marwood, if we will be happy, we must find the means in ourselves, and among ourselves. Men are ever in extremes, either doting or averse. While they are lovers, if they have fire and sense, their jealousies are insupportable. And when they cease to love (we ought to think at least) they loathe; they look upon us with horror and distaste; they meet us like the ghosts of what we were, and as such, fly from us.

MRS. MARWOOD: True, 'tis an unhappy circumstance of life, that love should ever die before us; and that the man so often should outlive the lover. But say what you will, 'tis better to be left than never to have been loved. To pass our youth in dull indifference, to refuse the sweets of life because they once must leave us, is as preposterous as to wish to have been born old, because we one day must be old. For my part, my youth may wear and waste, but it shall never rust in my possession.

MRS. FAINALL: Then it seems you dissemble an aversion to mankind, only in compliance with my mother's humor.

MRS. MARWOOD: Certainly. To be free,[19] I have no taste of those insipid
  dry discourses with which our sex of force must entertain themselves,
  apart from men. We may affect endearments to each other, profess
  eternal friendships, and seem to dote like lovers; but 'tis not in our
  natures long to persevere. Love will resume his empire in our breasts;
  and every heart, or soon or late, receive and readmit him as its lawful
  tyrant.

MRS. FAINALL: Bless me, how have I been deceived! Why you profess a
  libertine!

MRS. MARWOOD: You see my friendship by my freedom. Come, be as sincere,
  acknowledge that your sentiments agree with mine.

MRS. FAINALL: Never!

MRS. MARWOOD: You hate mankind?

MRS. FAINALL: Heartily, inveterately.

MRS. MARWOOD: Your husband?

MRS. FAINALL: Most transcendently; aye, though I say it, meritoriously.

MRS. MARWOOD: Give me your hand upon it.

MRS. FAINALL: There.

MRS. MARWOOD: I join with you; what I have said has been to try you.

MRS. FAINALL: It is possible? Dost thou hate those vipers, men?

MRS. MARWOOD: I have done hating 'em, and am now come to despise 'em;
  the next thing I have to do, is eternally to forget 'em.

MRS. FAINALL: There spoke the spirit of an Amazon, a Penthesilea.[20]

MRS. MARWOOD: And yet I am thinking sometimes to carry my aversion
  further.

MRS. FAINALL: How?

MRS. MARWOOD: Faith, by marrying; if I could but find one that loved me very
  well and would be thoroughly sensible of ill usage, I think I should do
  myself the violence of undergoing the ceremony.

MRS. FAINALL: You would not make him a cuckold?

MRS. MARWOOD: No, but I'd make him believe I did, and that's as bad.

MRS. FAINALL: Why had not you as good do it?

MRS. MARWOOD: Oh, if he should ever discover it, he would then know the
  worst, and be out of his pain; but I would have him ever to continue upon
  the rack of fear and jealousy.

MRS. FAINALL: Ingenious mischief! Would thou wert married to Mirabell.

MRS. MARWOOD: Would I were!

MRS. FAINALL: You change color.

MRS. MARWOOD: Because I hate him.

MRS. FAINALL: So do I; but I can hear him named. But what reason have you
  to hate him in particular?

MRS. MARWOOD: I never loved him; he is, and always was, insufferably proud.

MRS. FAINALL: By the reason you give for your aversion, one would think it

---

[19]Frank.   [20]Queen of the Amazons.

dissembled; for you have laid a fault to his charge of which his enemies must acquit him.

MRS. MARWOOD: Oh, then it seems you are one of his favorable enemies! Methinks you look a little pale, and now you flush again.

MRS. FAINALL: Do I? I think I am a little sick o' the sudden.

MRS. MARWOOD: What ails you?

MRS. FAINALL: My husband. Don't you see him? He turned short upon me unawares, and has almost overcome me.

(Enter Fainall and Mirabell.)

MRS. MARWOOD: Ha! Ha! Ha! He comes opportunely for you.

MRS. FAINALL: For you, for he has brought Mirabell with him.

FAINALL: My dear!

MRS. FAINALL: My soul!

FAINALL: You don't look well today, child.

MRS. FAINALL: D'ye think so?

MIRABELL: He is the only man that does, madam.

MRS. FAINALL: The only man that I would tell me so at least, and the only man from whom I could hear it without mortification.

FAINALL: Oh my dear, I am satisfied of your tenderness; I know you cannot resent anything from me, especially what is an effect of my concern.

MRS. FAINALL: Mr. Mirabell, my mother interrupted you in a pleasant relation last night; I would fain hear it out.

MIRABELL: The persons concerned in that affair have yet a tolerable reputation. I am afraid Mr. Fainall will be censorious.

MRS. FAINALL: He has a humor more prevailing than his curiosity, and will willingly dispense with the hearing of one scandalous story, to avoid giving an occasion to make another by being seen to walk with his wife. This way, Mr. Mirabell, and I dare promise you will oblige us both.

(Exeunt Mrs. Fainall and Mirabell.)

FAINALL: Excellent creature! Well, sure if I should live to be rid of my wife, I should be a miserable man.

MRS. MARWOOD: Aye!

FAINALL: For having only that one hope, the accomplishment of it, of consequence must put an end to all my hopes; and what a wretch is he who must survive his hopes! Nothing remains when that day comes, but to sit down and weep like Alexander, when he wanted other worlds to conquer.

MRS. MARWOOD: Will you not follow 'em?

FAINALL: Faith, I think not.

MRS. MARWOOD: Pray let us; I have a reason.

FAINALL: You are not jealous?

MRS. MARWOOD: Of whom?

FAINALL: Of Mirabell.

MRS. MARWOOD: If I am, is it inconsistent with my love to you that I am tender of your honor?

FAINALL: You would intimate then, as if there were a fellow-feeling between my wife and him.

MRS. MARWOOD: I think she does not hate him to that degree she would be thought.

FAINALL: But he, I fear, is too insensible.

MRS. MARWOOD: It may be you are deceived.

FAINALL: It may be so. I do now begin to apprehend it.

MRS. MARWOOD: What?

FAINALL: That I have been deceived, madam, and you are false.

MRS. MARWOOD: That I am false! What mean you?

FAINALL: To let you know I see through all your little arts. Come, you both love him; and both have equally dissembled your aversion. Your mutual jealousies of one another have made you clash till you have both struck fire. I have seen the warm confession reddening on your cheeks, and sparkling from your eyes.

MRS. MARWOOD: You do me wrong.

FAINALL: I do not. 'Twas for my ease to oversee²¹ and wilfully neglect the gross advances made him by my wife; that by permitting her to be engaged, I might continue unsuspected in my pleasures, and take you oftener to my arms in full security. But could you think, because the nodding husband would not wake, that e'er the watchful lover slept?

MRS. MARWOOD: And wherewithal can you reproach me?

FAINALL: With infidelity, with loving of another, with love of Mirabell.

MRS. MARWOOD: 'Tis false. I challenge you to show an instance that can confirm your groundless accusation. I hate him.

FAINALL: And wherefore do you hate him? He is insensible, and your resentment follows his neglect. An instance? The injuries you have done him are a proof, your interposing in his love. What cause had you to make discoveries of his pretended passion? To undeceive the credulous aunt, and be the officious obstacle of his match with Millamant?

MRS. MARWOOD: My obligations to my lady urged me; I had professed a friendship to her, and could not see her easy nature so abused by that dissembler.

FAINALL: What, was it conscience then? Professed a friendship! Oh, the pious friendships of the female sex!

MRS. MARWOOD: More tender, more sincere, and more enduring, than all the vain and empty vows of men, whether professing love to us, or mutual faith to one another.

FAINALL: Ha! ha! ha! you are my wife's friend too.

MRS. MARWOOD: Shame and ingratitude! Do you reproach me? You, you

²¹Overlook.

upbraid me! Have I been false to her, through strict fidelity to you, and sacrificed my friendship to keep my love inviolate? And have you the baseness to charge me with the guilt, unmindful of the merit! To you it should be meritorious, that I have been vicious; and do you reflect that guilt upon me, which should lie buried in your bosom?

FAINALL: You misinterpret my reproof. I meant but to remind you of the slight account you once could make of strictest ties, when set in comparison with your love to me.

MRS. MARWOOD: 'Tis false; you urged it with deliberate malice! 'Twas spoke in scorn, and I never will forgive it.

FAINALL: Your guilt, not your resentment, begets your rage. If yet you loved, you could forgive a jealousy; but you are stung to find you are discovered.

MRS. MARWOOD: It shall be all discovered. You too shall be discovered; be sure you shall. I can but be exposed. If I do it myself, I shall prevent[22] your baseness.

FAINALL: Why, what will you do?

MRS. MARWOOD: Disclose it to your wife; own what has passed between us.

FAINALL: Frenzy!

MRS. MARWOOD: By all my wrongs I'll do't! I'll publish to the world the injuries you have done me, both in my fame and fortune! With both I trusted you, you bankrupt in honor, as indigent of wealth.

FAINALL: Your fame I have preserved. Your fortune has been bestowed as the prodigality of your love would have it, in pleasures which we both have shared. Yet had not you been false, I had ere this repaid it. 'Tis true, had you permitted Mirabell with Millamant to have stolen their marriage, my lady been incensed beyond all means of reconcilement; Millamant had forfeited the moiety[23] of her fortune, which then would have descended to my wife. And wherefore did I marry, but to make lawful prize of a rich widow's wealth, and squander it on love and you?

MRS. MARWOOD: Deceit and frivolous pretense!

FAINALL: Death, am I not married? What's pretense? Am I not imprisoned, fettered? Have I not a wife? Nay a wife that was a widow, a young widow, a handsome widow; and would be again a widow, but that I have a heart of proof,[24] and something of a constitution to bustle through the ways of wedlock and this world. Will you yet be reconciled to truth and me?

MRS. MARWOOD: Impossible. Truth and you are inconsistent. I hate you, and shall for ever.

FAINALL: For loving you?

MRS. MARWOOD: I loathe the name of love after such usage; and next to the guilt with which you would asperse me, I scorn you most. Farewell!

FAINALL: Nay, we must not part thus.

MRS. MARWOOD: Let me go.

---

[22]Anticipate.   [23]Half.   [24]Tested.

FAINALL: Come, I'm sorry.

MRS. MARWOOD: I care not, let me go. Break my hands, do! I'd leave 'em to get loose.

FAINALL: I would not hurt you for the world. Have I no other hold to keep you here?

MRS. MARWOOD: Well, I have deserved it all.

FAINALL: You know I love you.

MRS. MARWOOD: Poor dissembling! Oh, that—Well, it is not yet—.

FAINALL: What? What is it not? What is it not yet? It is not yet too late—.

MRS. MARWOOD: No, it is not yet too late; I have that comfort.

FAINALL: It is, to love another.

MRS. MARWOOD: But not to loathe, detest, abhor mankind, myself, and the whole treacherous world.

FAINALL: Nay, this is extravagance. Come, I ask your pardon. No tears. I was to blame; I could not love you and be easy in my doubts. Pray, forbear. I believe you. I'm convinced I've done you wrong; and any way, every way will make amends. I'll hate my wife yet more, damn her! I'll part with her, rob her of all she's worth, and we'll retire somewhere, anywhere, to another world. I'll marry thee; be pacified. 'Sdeath, they come; hide your face, your tears. You have a mask; wear it a moment. This way, this way. Be persuaded. *(Exeunt.)*

(Enter Mirabell and Mrs. Fainall.)

MRS. FAINALL: They are here yet.

MIRABELL: They are turning into the other walk.

MRS. FAINALL: While I only hated my husband, I could bear to see him; but since I have despised him, he's too offensive.

MIRABELL: Oh, you should hate with prudence.

MRS. FAINALL: Yes, for I have loved with indiscretion.

MIRABELL: You should have just so much disgust for your husband as may be sufficient to make you relish your lover.

MRS. FAINALL: You have been the cause that I have loved without bounds, and would you set limits to that aversion of which you have been the occasion? Why did you make me marry this man?

MIRABELL: Why do we daily commit disagreeable and dangerous actions? To save that idol, reputation. If the familiarities of our loves had produced that consequence of which you were apprehensive, where could you have fixed a father's name with credit, but on a husband? I knew Fainall to be a man lavish of his morals, an interested[25] and professing friend, a false and a designing lover; yet one whose wit and outward fair behavior have gained a reputation with the town enough to make that woman stand excused who has suffered herself to be won by his addresses. A better man

---

[25]Self-interested.

ought not to have been sacrificed to the occasion; a worse had not answered to the purpose. When you are weary of him, you know your remedy.

MRS. FAINALL: I ought to stand in some degree of credit with you, Mirabell.

MIRABELL: In justice to you, I have made you privy to my whole design, and put it in your power to ruin or advance my fortune.

MRS. FAINALL: Whom have you instructed to represent your pretended uncle?

MIRABELL: Waitwell, my servant.

MRS. FAINALL: He is an humble servant to Foible, my mother's woman, and may win her to your interest.

MIRABELL: Care is taken for that. She is won and worn by this time. They were married this morning.

MRS. FAINALL: Who?

MIRABELL: Waitwell and Foible. I would not tempt my servant to betray me by trusting him too far. If your mother, in hopes to ruin me, should consent to marry my pretended uncle, he might, like Mosca in *The Fox,* stand upon terms;[26] so I made him sure beforehand.

MRS. FAINALL: So, if my poor mother is caught in a contract, you will discover the imposture betimes, and release her by producing a certificate of her gallant's former marriage.

MIRABELL: Yes, upon condition she consent to my marriage with her niece, and surrender the moiety of her fortune in her possession.

MRS. FAINALL: She talked last night of endeavoring at a match between Millamant and your uncle.

MIRABELL: That was by Foible's direction, and my instruction, that she might seem to carry it more privately.

MRS. FAINALL: Well, I have an opinion of your success, for I believe my lady will do anything to get a husband; and when she has this, which you have provided for her, I suppose she will submit to anything to get rid of him.

MIRABELL: Yes, I think the good lady would marry anything that resembled a man, though 'twere no more than what a butler could pinch out of a napkin.

MRS. FAINALL: Female frailty! We must all come to it, if we live to be old and feel the craving of a false appetite when the true is decayed.

MIRABELL: An old woman's appetite is depraved like that of a girl. 'Tis the green sickness[27] of a second childhood; and like the faint offer of a latter spring, serves but to usher in the fall, and withers in an affected bloom.

MRS. FAINALL: Here's your mistress.

(Enter Mrs. Millamant, Witwoud, and Mincing.)

MIRABELL: Here she comes, i'faith, full said, and with her fan spread and her streamers out, and a shoal of fools for tenders. Ha, no, I cry her mercy!

[26]Mosca, in Ben Jonson's *Volpone, or The Fox,* threatens blackmail.   [27]Anemia.

MRS. FAINALL: I see but one poor empty sculler; and he tows her woman after him.

MIRABELL: You seem to be unattended, madam. You used to have the beau monde throng after you, and a flock of gay fine perukes hovering round you.

WITWOUD: Like moths about a candle. I had like to have lost my comparison for want of breath.

MILLAMANT: Oh, I have denied myself airs today. I have walked as fast through the crowd—

WITWOUD: As a favorite in disgrace, and with as few followers.

MILLAMANT: Dear Mr. Witwoud, truce with your similitudes; for I am as sick of 'em—

WITWOUD: As a physician of a good air. I cannot help it, madam, though 'tis against myself.

MILLAMANT: Yet again! Mincing, stand between me and his wit.

WITWOUD: Do, Mrs. Mincing, like a screen before a great fire. I confess I do blaze today; I am too bright.

MRS. FAINALL: But, dear Millamant, why were you so long?

MILLAMANT: Long! Lord, have I not made violent haste? I have asked every living thing I met for you; I have inquired after you, as after a new fashion.

WITWOUD: Madam, truce with your similitudes. No, you met her husband, and did not ask him for her.

MIRABELL: By your leave, Witwoud, that were like inquiring after an old fashion, to ask a husband for his wife.

WITWOUD: Hum, a hit! A hit! A palpable hit![28] I confess it.

MRS. FAINALL: You were dressed before I came abroad.

MILLAMANT: Aye, that's true. Oh, but then I had—Mincing, what had I? Why was I so long?

MINCING: O mem, your la'ship stayed to peruse a pecquet of letters.

MILLAMANT: Oh, aye, letters; I had letters. I am persecuted with letters. I hate letters. Nobody knows how to write letters; and yet one has 'em, one does not know why. They serve one to pin up one's hair.

WITWOUD: Is that the way? Pray, madam, do you pin up your hair with all your letters? I find I must keep copies.

MILLAMANT: Only with those in verse, Mr. Witwoud. I never pin up my hair with prose. I fancy one's hair would not curl if it were pinned up with prose. I think I tried once, Mincing.

MINCING: O mem, I shall never forget it.

MILLAMANT: Aye, poor Mincing tift and tift[29] all the morning.

MINCING: 'Till I had the cremp in my fingers, I'll vow, mem. And all to no purpose. But when your la'ship pins it up with poetry, it sits so pleasant the next day as anything, and is so pure and so crips.

WITWOUD: Indeed, so crips?

MINCING: You're such a critic, Mr. Witwoud.

---

[28]See *Hamlet,* p. 955.   [29]Did and redid her hair.

MILLAMANT: Mirabell, did not you take exceptions last night? Oh, aye, and went away. Now I think on't, I'm angry. No, now I think on't, I'm pleased; for I believe I gave you some pain.

MIRABELL: Does that please you?

MILLAMANT: Infinitely; I love to give pain.

MIRABELL: You would affect a cruelty which is not in your nature; your true vanity is in the power of pleasing.

MILLAMANT: Oh, I ask your pardon for that. One's cruelty is one's power; and when one parts with one's cruelty, one parts with one's power; and when one has parted with that, I fancy one's old and ugly.

MIRABELL: Aye, aye, suffer your cruelty to ruin the object of your power, to destroy your lover, and then how vain, how lost a thing you'll be! Nay, 'tis true: you are no longer handsome when you've lost your lover; your beauty dies upon the instant. For beauty is the lover's gift; 'tis he bestows your charms, your glass is all a cheat. The ugly and the old, whom the looking glass mortifies, yet after commendation can be flattered by it, and discover beauties in it; for that reflects our praises, rather than your face.

MILLAMANT: Oh, the vanity of these men! Fainall, d'ye hear him? If they did not commend us, we were not handsome! Now you must know they could not commend one, if one was not handsome. Beauty the lover's gift! Lord, what is a lover, that it can give? Why, one makes lovers as fast as one pleases, and they live as long as one pleases, and they die as soon as one pleases; and then, if one pleases, one makes more.

WITWOUD: Very pretty. Why, you make no more of making of lovers, madam, than of making so many card-matches.[30]

MILLAMANT: One no more owes one's beauty to a lover than one's wit to an echo. They can but reflect what we look and say; vain empty things if we are silent or unseen, and want a being.

MIRABELL: Yet to those two vain empty things you owe two [of] the greatest pleasures of your life.

MILLAMANT: How so?

MIRABELL: To your lover you owe the pleasure of hearing yourselves praised; and to an echo the pleasure of hearing yourselves talk.

WITWOUD: But I know a lady that loves talking so incessantly, she won't give an echo fair play; she has that everlasting rotation of tongue, that an echo must wait till she dies, before it can catch her last words.

MILLAMANT: Oh, fiction! Fainall, let us leave these men.

MIRABELL: Draw off Witwoud. *(Aside to Mrs. Fainall.)*

MRS. FAINALL: Immediately. I have as word or two for Mr. Witwoud.

(Exeunt Witwoud and Mrs. Fainall.)

MIRABELL: I would beg a little private audience too. You had the tyranny to deny me last night, though you knew I came to impart a secret to you that concerned my love.

---

[30]Matches made of cardboard dipped in melted sulphur.

MILLAMANT: You saw I was engaged.

MIRABELL: Unkind! You had the leisure to entertain a herd of fools; things who visit you from their excessive idleness, bestowing on your easiness that time which is the incumbrance of their lives. How can you find delight in such society? It is impossible they should admire you; they are not capable. Or if they were, it should be to you as a mortification, for sure to please a fool is some degree of folly.

MILLAMANT: I please myself. Besides, sometimes to converse with fools is for my health.

MIRABELL: Your health! Is there a worse disease than the conversation of fools?

MILLAMANT: Yes, the vapors; fools are physic for it, next to assafoetida.[31]

MIRABELL: You are not in a course of fools?

MILLAMANT: Mirabell, if you persist in this offensive freedom, you'll displease me. I think I must resolve, after all, not to have you; we shan't agree.

MIRABELL: Not in our physic, it may be.

MILLAMANT: And yet our distemper, in all likelihood, will be the same; for we shall be sick of one another. I shan't endure to be reprimanded nor instructed; 'tis so dull to act always by advice, and so tedious to be told of one's faults—I can't bear it. Well, I won't have you, Mirabell—I'm resolved—I think—you may go.—Ha! Ha! Ha! What would you give that you could help loving me?

MIRABELL: I would give something that you did not know I could not help it.

MILLAMANT: Come, don't look grave then. Well, what do you say to me?

MIRABELL: I say that a man may as soon make a friend by his wit, or a fortune by his honesty, as win a woman with plain dealing and sincerity.

MILLAMANT: Sententious Mirabell! Prithee, don't look with that violent and inflexible wise face, like Solomon at the dividing of the child in an old tapestry hanging.

MIRABELL: You are merry, madam, but I would persuade you for one moment to be serious.

MILLAMANT: What, with that face? No, if you keep your countenance, 'tis impossible I should hold mine. Well, after all, there is something very moving in a love-sick face. Ha! Ha! Ha!—Well, I won't laugh, don't be peevish—Heighho! Now I'll be melancholy, as melancholy as a watch-light.[32] Well, Mirabell, if ever you will win me, woo me now.—Nay, if you are so tedious, fare you well.—I see they are walking away.

MIRABELL: Can you not find in the variety of your disposition one moment—

MILLAMANT: To hear you tell me Foible's married, and your plot like to speed?—No.

MIRABELL: But how came you to know it?

---

[31]Persian resin, smelling like garlic, widely used as a smelling salt in faintings.   [32]Night-light.

MILLAMANT: Unless by the help of the devil, you can't imagine; unless she
    should tell me herself. Which of the two it may have been, I will leave
    you to consider; and when you have done thinking of that, think of me.

                                                     (Exit with Mincing.)

MIRABELL: I have something more—Gone! Think of you! To think of a whirl-
    wind, though 'twere in a whirlwind, were a case of more steady contem-
    plation; a very tranquility of mind and mansion. A fellow that lives in a
    windmill has not a more whimsical dwelling than the heart of a man that
    is lodged in a woman. There is no point of the compass to which they
    cannot turn, and by which they are not turned; and by one as well as
    another, for motion, not method, is their occupation. To know this, and
    yet continue to be in love, is to be made wise from the dictates of reason,
    and yet persevere to play the fool by the force of instinct.—Oh, here come
    my pair of turtles![33]—What, billing so sweetly! Is not Valentine's Day over
    with you yet?

(Enter Waitwell and Foible.)

    Sirrah, Waitwell, why sure you think you were married for your own
    recreation, and not for my conveniency.

WAITWELL: Your pardon, sir. With submission, we have indeed been solacing
    in lawful delights; but still with an eye to business, sir. I have instructed
    her as well as I could. If she can take your directions as readily as my
    instructions, sir, your affairs are in a prosperous way.

MIRABELL: Give you joy, Mrs. Foible.

FOIBLE: O las, sir, I'm so ashamed! I'm afraid my lady has been in a thousand
    inquietudes for me. But I protest, sir, I made as much haste as I could.

WAITWELL: That she did indeed, sir. It was my fault that she did not make
    more.

MIRABELL: That I believe.

FOIBLE: But I told my lady as you instructed me, sir, that I had a prospect
    of seeing Sir Rowland, your uncle; and that I would put her ladyship's
    picture in my pocket to show him, which I'll be sure to say has made him
    so enamored of her beauty, that he burns with impatience to lie at her
    ladyship's feet and worship the original.

MIRABELL: Excellent Foible! Matrimony has made you eloquent in love.

WAITWELL: I think she has profited, sir. I think so.

FOIBLE: You have seen Madam Millamant, sir?

MIRABELL: Yes.

FOIBLE: I told her, sir, because I did not know that you might find an opportu-
    nity; she had so much company last night.

MIRABELL: Your diligence will merit more. In the meantime—

                                                     (Gives money.)

---

[33]Turtle doves.

FOIBLE: O dear sir, your humble servant.

WAITWELL: Spouse.[34]

MIRABELL: Stand off, sir, not a penny! Go on and prosper, Foible; the lease shall be made good and the farm stocked, if we succeed.

FOIBLE: I don't question your generosity, sir; and you need not doubt of success. If you have no more commands, sir, I'll be gone; I'm sure my lady is at her toilet and can't dress till I come.—Oh dear, I'm sure that *(looking out)* was Mrs. Marwood that went by in a mask; if she has seen me with you I'm sure she'll tell my lady. I'll make haste home and prevent her. Your servant, sir. B'w'y, Waitwell. *(Exit.)*

WAITWELL: Sir Rowland, if you please. The jade's so pert upon her preferment she forgets herself.

MIRABELL: Come, sir, will you endeavor to forget yourself, and transform into Sir Rowland?

WAITWELL: Why, sir, it will be impossible I should remember myself. Married, knighted, and attended all in one day! 'Tis enough to make any man forget himself. The difficulty will be how to recover my acquaintance and familiarity with my former self, and fall from my transformation to a reformation into Waitwell. Nay, I shan't be quite the same Waitwell neither; for now I remember me, I am married and can't be my own man again.

Aye, there's the grief; that's the sad change of life,

To lose my title, and yet keep my wife. *(Exeunt.)*

Act III

A Room in Lady Wishfort's House. Lady Wishfort at her toilet, Peg waiting.

LADY WISHFORT: Merciful! No news of Foible yet?

PEG: No, madam.

LADY WISHFORT: I have no more patience. If I have not fretted myself till I am pale again, there's no veracity in me! Fetch me the red; the red, do you hear, sweetheart? An arrant ash-color, as I'm a person! Look you how this wench stirs! Why dost thou not fetch me a little red? Didst thou not hear me, mopus?

PEG: The red ratafia does your ladyship mean, or the cherry brandy?

LADY WISHFORT: Ratafia, fool! No, fool! Not the ratafia, fool. Grant me patience! I mean the Spanish paper,[35] idiot; complexion, darling. Paint, paint, paint, dost thou understand that, changeling, dangling thy hands like bobbins before thee? Why dost thou not stir, puppet? thou wooden thing upon wires!

PEG: Lord, madam, your ladyship is so impatient! I cannot come at the paint, madam; Mrs. Foible has locked it up and carried the key with her.

LADY WISHFORT: A pox take you both! Fetch me the cherry brandy then. *(Exit Peg.)* I'm as pale and as faint, I look like Mrs. Qualmsick, the curate's

---

[34]Waitwell tries to take the money Mirabell has given to Foible.   [35]Rouge.

wife, that's always breeding. Wench, come, come, wench, what art thou doing? sipping? tasting? Save thee, dost thou not know the bottle?

(Re-enter Peg with a bottle and china cup.)

PEG: Madam, I was looking for a cup.

LADY WISHFORT: A cup, save thee! and what a cup hast thou brought! Dost thou take me for a fairy, to drink out of an acorn? Why didst thou not bring thy thimble? Hast thou ne'er a brass thimble clinking in thy pocket with a bit of nutmeg?[36] I warrant thee. Come, fill, fill! So; again. *(One knocks.)* See who that is. Set down the bottle first. Here, here, under the table. What, wouldst thou go with the bottle in thy hand, like a tapster? As I'm a person, this wench has lived in an inn upon the road, before she came to me, like Maritornes the Asturian in *Don Quixote!* No Foible yet?

PEG: No, madam, Mrs. Marwood.

LADY WISHFORT: Oh, Marwood, let her come in. Come in, good Marwood.

(Enter Mrs. Marwood.)

MRS. MARWOOD: I'm surprised to find your ladyship in dishabillé at this time of day.

LADY WISHFORT: Foible's a lost thing; has been abroad since morning, and never heard of since.

MRS. MARWOOD: I saw her but now, as I came masked through the park, in conference with Mirabell.

LADY WISHFORT: With Mirabell! You call my blood into my face with mentioning that traitor. She durst not have the confidence! I sent her to negotiate an affair in which, if I'm detected, I'm undone. If that wheedling villain has wrought upon Foible to detect me, I'm ruined. Oh my dear friend, I'm a wretch of wretches if I'm detected.

MRS. MARWOOD: O madam, you cannot suspect Mrs. Foible's integrity.

LADY WISHFORT: Oh, he carries poison in his tongue that would corrupt integrity itself! If she has given him an opportunity, she has as good as put her integrity into his hands. Ah, dear Marwood, what's integrity to an opportunity? Hark! I hear her! Go, you thing, and send her in. *(Exit Peg.)* Dear friend, retire into my closet,[37] that I may examine her with more freedom. You'll pardon me, dear friend; I can make bold with you. There are books over the chimney. Quarles and Prynne, and the *Short View of the Stage,* with Bunyan's works,[38] to entertain you.

(Exit Mrs. Marwood.)

(Enter Foible.)

O Foible, where hast thou been? What hast thou been doing?

FOIBLE: Madam, I have seen the party.

[36]Good luck charms.   [37]Private room, off the bedchamber.   [38]Righteous Puritan works. Jeremy Collier's *Short View of the Immorality and Profaneness of the English Stage* (1698) had attacked Congreve.

LADY WISHFORT: But what hast thou done?

FOIBLE: Nay, 'tis your ladyship has done, and are to do; I have only promised.
  But a man so enamored, so transported! Well, here it is, all that is left;
  all that is not kissed away. Well, if worshiping of pictures be a sin,[39] poor
  Sir Rowland, I say.

LADY WISHFORT: The miniature has been counted like. But hast thou not
  betrayed me, Foible? Hast thou not detected me to that faithless Mirabell?
  What hadst thou to do with him in the Park? Answer me, has he got
  nothing out of thee?

FOIBLE *(aside):* So the devil has been beforehand with me. What shall I say?
  —Alas, madam, could I help it, if I met that confident thing? Was I in
  fault? If you had heard how he used me, and all upon your ladyship's
  account, I'm sure you would not suspect my fidelity. Nay, if that had been
  the worst, I could have borne; but he had a fling at your ladyship too. And
  then I could not hold; but i'faith I gave him his own.

LADY WISHFORT: Me? What did the filthy fellow say?

FOIBLE: O madam! 'Tis a shame to say what he said, with his taunts and his
  fleers, tossing up his nose. Humph! (says he), what, you are a hatching
  some plot (says he), you are so early abroad, or catering (says he), ferreting for some disbanded officer, I warrant. Half-pay is but thin subsistence
  (says he). Well, what pension does your lady propose? Let me see (says
  he), what, she must come down pretty deep now, she's superannuated
  (says he) and—

LADY WISHFORT: Ods my life, I'll have him, I'll have him murdered. I'll have
  him poisoned. Where does he eat? I'll marry a drawer[40] to have him
  poisoned in his wine. I'll send for Robin from Locket's[41] immediately.

FOIBLE: Poison him? Poisoning's too good for him. Starve him, madam, starve
  him; marry Sir Rowland and get him disinherited. Oh, you would bless
  yourself to hear what he said!

LADY WISHFORT: A villain! Superannuated!

FOIBLE: Humph! (says he), I hear you are laying designs against me too (says
  he), and Mrs. Millamant is to marry my uncle (he does not suspect a word
  of your ladyship); but (says he) I'll fit you for that. I warrant you (says
  he), I'll hamper you for that (says he), you and your old frippery[42] too
  (says he), I'll handle you—

LADY WISHFORT: Audacious villain! Handle me! would he durst! Frippery?
  Old frippery! Was there ever such a foulmouthed fellow? I'll be married
  tomorrow; I'll be contracted tonight.

FOIBLE: The sooner the better, madam.

LADY WISHFORT: Will Sir Rowland be here, say'st thou? When, Foible?

FOIBLE: Incontinently, madam. No new sheriff's wife expects the return of
  her husband after knighthood with that impatience in which Sir Row-

---

[39]Foible reflects Lady Wishfort's superficial Puritanism by alluding to Catholic reverence for
religious images.   [40]Bartender.   [41]A fashionable tavern in Charing Cross.   [42]Cast-off clothes.

land burns for the dear hour of kissing your ladyship's hands after dinner.

LADY WISHFORT: Frippery? Superannuated frippery! I'll frippery the villain; I'll reduce him to frippery and rags! A tatterdemalion! I hope to see him hung with tatters, like a Long Lane penthouse[43] or a gibbet thief. A slander-mouthed railer! I warrant the spendthrift prodigal's in debt as much as the million lottery,[44] or the whole court upon a birthday. I'll spoil his credit with his tailor. Yes, he shall have my niece with her fortune, he shall!

FOIBLE: He! I hope to see him lodge in Ludgate first, and angle into Blackfriars for brass farthings with an old mitten.[45]

LADY WISHFORT: Aye, dear Foible; thank thee for that, dear Foible. He has put me out of all patience. I shall never recompose my features to receive Sir Rowland with any economy of face. This wretch has fretted me that I am absolutely decayed. Look, Foible.

FOIBLE: Your ladyship has frowned a little too rashly, indeed, madam. There are some cracks discernible in the white varnish.

LADY WISHFORT: Let me see the glass. Cracks, say'st thou? Why I am arrantly flayed; I look like an old peeled wall. Thou must repair me, Foible, before Sir Rowland comes, or I shall never keep up to my picture.

FOIBLE: I warrant you, madam, a little art once made your picture like you; and now a little of the same art must make you like your picture. Your picture must sit for you, madam.

LADY WISHFORT: But art thou sure Sir Rowland will not fail to come? Or will he not fail when he does come? Will he be importunate, Foible, and push? For if he should not be importunate, I shall never break decorums. I shall die with confusion, if I am forced to advance. Oh no, I can never advance! I shall swoon if he should expect advances. No, I hope Sir Rowland is better bred than to put a lady to the necessity of breaking her forms. I won't be too coy neither. I won't give him despair; but a little disdain is not amiss, a little scorn is alluring.

FOIBLE: A little scorn becomes your ladyship.

LADY WISHFORT: Yes, but tenderness becomes me best, a sort of a dyingness. You see that picture has a sort of a—ha, Foible? A swimmingness in the eyes. Yes, I'll look so. My niece affects it; but she wants features. Is Sir Rowland handsome? Let my toilet be removed. I'll dress above. I'll receive Sir Rowland here. Is he handsome? Don't answer me. I won't know; I'll be surprised, I'll be taken by surprise.

FOIBLE: By storm, madam. Sir Rowland's a brisk man.

LADY WISHFORT: Is he! Oh, then he'll importune, if he's a brisk man. I shall save decorums if Sir Rowland importunes. I have a mortal terror at the

---

[43]A stall under an overhanging roof in Long Lane, Smithfield, selling old clothes and rags.
[44]A government lottery in 1694 to raise a million pounds.   [45]Old debtors in Ludgate Prison begged by lowering a mitten on a string into Blackfriars Road.

apprehension of offending against decorums. Nothing but importunity can surmount decorums. Oh, I'm glad he's a brisk man. Let my things be removed, good Foible.   *(Exit.)*

(Enter Mrs. Fainall.)

MRS. FAINALL: O Foible, I have been in a fright, lest I should come too late! That devil Marwood saw you in the Park with Mirabell, and I'm afraid will discover it to my lady.[46]

FOIBLE: Discover what, madam?

MRS. FAINALL: Nay, nay, put not on that strange face. I am privy to the whole design, and know that Waitwell, to whom thou wert this morning married, is to personate Mirabell's uncle, and as such, winning my lady, to involve her in those difficulties from which Mirabell only must release her, by his making his conditions to have my cousin and her fortune left to her own disposal.

FOIBLE: O dear madam, I beg your pardon. It was not my confidence in your ladyship that was deficient; but I thought the former good correspondence between your ladyship and Mr. Mirabell might have hindered his communicating this secret.

MRS. FAINALL: Dear Foible, forget that.

FOIBLE: O dear madam, Mr. Mirabell is such a sweet, winning gentleman, but your ladyship is the pattern of generosity. Sweet lady, to be so good! Mr. Mirabell cannot choose but be grateful. I find your ladyship has his heart still. Now, madam, I can safely tell your ladyship our success. Mrs. Marwood had told my lady; but I warrant I managed myself. I turned it all for the better. I told my lady that Mr. Mirabell railed at her. I laid horrid things to his charge, I'll vow; and my lady is so incensed that she'll be contracted to Sir Rowland tonight, she says. I warrant I worked her up, that he may have her for asking for, as they say of a Welsh maidenhead.

MRS. FAINALL: O rare Foible!

FOIBLE: Madam, I beg your ladyship to acquaint Mr. Mirabell of his success. I would be seen as little as possible to speak to him; besides, I believe Madame Marwood watches me. She has a month's mind;[47] but I know Mr. Mirabell can't abide her. *(Enter Footman.)* John, remove my lady's toilet. Madam, your servant. My lady is so impatient, I fear she'll come for me, if I stay.

MRS. FAINALL: I'll go with you up the backstairs, lest I should meet her.
                                                                  (Exeunt.)

(Enter Mrs. Marwood.)

MRS. MARWOOD: Indeed, Mrs. Engine, is it thus with you? Are you become a go-between of this importance? Yes, I shall watch you. Why this wench

[46]This scene sometimes stages Mrs. Marwood at one of the doors overhearing the dialogue.
[47]Fixed determination.

is the *passe-partout,* a very master key to everybody's strongbox. My friend Fainall, have you carried it so swimmingly? I thought there was something in it; but it seems it's over with you. Your loathing is not from a want of appetite then, but from a surfeit. Else you could never be so cool to fall from a principal to be an assistant; to procure for him! A pattern of generosity, that I confess. Well, Mr. Fainall, you have met with your match. O man, man! woman, woman! The devil's an ass; if I were a painter, I would draw him like an idiot, a driveler with a bib and bells. Man should have his head and horns, and woman the rest of him. Poor simple fiend! Madam. Marwood has a month's mind, but he can't abide her. 'Twere better for him you had not been his confessor in that affair, without you could have kept his counsel closer. I shall not prove another pattern of generosity and stalk for him, till he takes his stand to aim at a fortune. He has not obliged me to that, with those excesses of himself; and now I'll have none of him. Here comes the good lady, panting ripe; with a heart full of hope, and a head full of care, like any chemist upon the day of projection.[48]

(Enter Lady Wishfort.)

LADY WISHFORT: O dear Marwood, what shall I say, for this rude forgetfulness? But my dear friend is all goodness.

MRS. MARWOOD: No apologies, dear madam. I have been very well entertained.

LADY WISHFORT: As I'm a person, I am in a very chaos to think I should so forget myself; but I have such an olio of affairs, really I know not what to do.—[*Calls.*] Foible!—I expect my nephew, Sir Wilfull, every moment too.—Why, Foible!—He means to travel for improvement.

MRS. MARWOOD: Methinks Sir Wilfull should rather think of marrying than traveling at his years. I hear he is turned of forty.

LADY WISHFORT: Oh, he's in less danger of being spoiled by his travels. I am against my nephew's marrying too young. It will be time enough when he comes back and has acquired discretion to choose for himself.

MRS. MARWOOD: Methinks Mrs. Millamant and he would make a very fit match. He may travel afterwards. 'Tis a thing very usual with young gentlemen.

LADY WISHFORT: I promise you I have thought on't; and since 'tis your judgment, I'll think on't again. I assure you I will; I value your judgment extremely. On my word, I'll propose it.

(Enter Foible.)

Come, come, Foible, I had forgot my nephew will be here before dinner. I must make haste.

FOIBLE: Mr. Witwoud and Mr. Petulant are come to dine with your ladyship.

---

[48]When his process will change lead into gold.

LADY WISHFORT: Oh dear, I can't appear till I'm dressed. Dear Marwood, shall I be free with you again, and beg you to entertain 'em? I'll make all imaginable haste. Dear friend, excuse me.

(Exeunt Lady Wishfort and Foible.)

(Enter Mrs. Millamant and Mincing.)

MILLAMANT: Sure never anything was so unbred as that odious man! Marwood, your servant.

MRS. MARWOOD: You have a color, what's the matter?

MILLAMANT: That horrid fellow, Petulant, has provoked me into a flame. I have broke my fan. Mincing, lend me yours; is not all the powder out of my hair?

MRS. MARWOOD: No, what has he done?

MILLAMANT: Nay, he has done nothing; he has only talked. Nay, he has said nothing neither; but he has contradicted everything that has been said. For my part, I thought Witwoud and he would have quarreled.

MINCING: I vow, mem, I thought once they would have fit.

MILLAMANT: Well, 'tis a lamentable thing, I'll swear, that one has not the liberty of choosing one's acquaintance as one does one's clothes.

MRS. MARWOOD: If we had the liberty, we should be as weary of one set of acquaintance, though never so good, as we are of one suit, though never so fine. A fool and a doily stuff[49] would now and then find days of grace, and be worn for variety.

MILLAMANT: I could consent to wear 'em, if they would wear alike; but fools never wear out—they are such *drap-de-Berry*[50] things without one could give 'em to one's chambermaid after a day or two!

MRS. MARWOOD: 'Twere better so indeed. Or what think you of the playhouse? A fine, gay, glossy fool should be given there, like a new masking habit, after the masquerade is over, and we have done with the disguise. For a fool's visit is always a disguise, and never admitted by a woman of wit, but to blind her affair with a lover of sense. If you would but appear barefaced now, and own Mirabell, you might as easily put off Petulant and Witwoud as your hood and scarf. And indeed 'tis time, for the town has found it; the secret is grown too big for the pretense. 'Tis like Mrs. Primly's great belly; she may lace it down before, but it burnishes on her hips. Indeed, Millamant, you can no more conceal it than my Lady Strammel can her face, that goodly face, which, in defiance of her Rhenish wine tea,[51] will not be comprehended in a mask.

MILLAMANT: I'll take my death, Marwood, you are more censorious than a decayed beauty, or a discarded toast.[52] Mincing, tell the men they may come up. My aunt is not dressing [here].—Their folly is less provoking than your malice. *(Exit Mincing.)* The town has found it! What has it

---

[49]Cheap woollen.   [50]Coarse woollen.   [51]Rhine wine to promote a slim figure and reduce a ruddy complexion.   [52]Lady no longer toasted.

found? That Mirabell loves me is no more a secret than it is a secret that you discovered it to my aunt, or than the reason why you discovered it is a secret.

MRS. MARWOOD: You are nettled.

MILLAMANT: You're mistaken. Ridiculous!

MRS. MARWOOD: Indeed, my dear, you'll tear another fan, if you don't mitigate those violent airs.

MILLAMANT: O silly! Ha! Ha! Ha! I could laugh immoderately. Poor Mirabell! His constancy to me has quite destroyed his complaisance for all the world beside. I swear, I never enjoined it him to be so coy. If I had the vanity to think he would obey me, I would command him to show more gallantry. 'Tis hardly well-bred to be so particular on one hand, and so insensible on the other. But I despair to prevail, and so let him follow his own way. Ha! Ha! Ha! Pardon me, dear creature, I must laugh, ha! Ha! Ha!—though I grant you 'tis a little barbarous, ha! Ha! Ha!

MRS. MARWOOD: What pity 'tis, so much fine raillery, and delivered with so significant gesture, should be so unhappily directed to miscarry.

MILLAMANT: Ha? Dear creature, I ask your pardon. I swear I did not mind you.

MRS. MARWOOD: Mr. Mirabell and you both may think it a thing impossible, when I shall tell him by telling you—

MILLAMANT: Oh dear, what? For it is the same thing, if I hear it, ha! Ha! Ha!

MRS. MARWOOD: That I detest him, hate him, madam.

MILLAMANT: O madam, why so do I—and yet the creature loves me, ha! Ha! Ha! How can one forbear laughing to think of it! I am a sybil if I am not amazed to think what he can see in me. I'll take my death, I think you are handsomer—and within a year or two as young. If you could but stay for me, I should overtake you—but that cannot be.—Well, that thought makes me melancholy.—Now I'll be sad.

MRS. MARWOOD: Your merry note may be changed sooner than you think.

MILLAMANT: D'ye say so? Then I'm resolved to have a song to keep up my spirits.

(Enter Mincing.)

MINCING: The gentlemen stay but to comb, madam, and will wait on you.

MILLAMANT: Desire Mrs. ——, that is in the next room, to sing the song I would have learned yesterday. You shall hear it, madam, not that there's any great matter in it, but 'tis agreeable to my humor.

Song

I

> Love's but the frailty of the mind,
> When 'tis not with ambition joined;
> A sickly flame, which, if not fed, expires,
> And feeding, wastes in self-consuming fires.

II

'Tis not to wound a wanton boy
Or amorous youth, that gives the joy;
But 'tis the glory to have pierced a swain,
For whom inferior beauties sighed in vain.

III

Then I alone the conquest prize,
When I insult a rival's eyes;
If there's delight in love, 'tis when I see
That heart, which others bleed for, bleed for me.

(Enter Petulant and Witwoud.)

MILLAMANT: Is your animosity composed, gentlemen?

WITWOUD: Raillery, raillery, madam; we have no animosity. We hit off a little wit now and then, but no animosity. The falling-out of wits is like the falling-out of lovers; we agree in the main,[53] like treble and bass. Ha, Petulant?

PETULANT: Aye, in the main, but when I have a humor to contradict.

WITWOUD: Aye, when he has a humor to contradict, then I contradict too. What, I know my cue. Then we contradict one another like two battledores; for contradictions beget one another like Jews.

PETULANT: If he says black's black, if I have a humor to say 'tis blue, let that pass; all's one for that. If I have a humor to prove it, it must be granted.

WITWOUD: Not positively must, but it may, it may.

PETULANT: Yes, it positively must, upon proof positive.

WITWOUD: Aye, upon proof positive it must; but upon proof presumptive it only may. That's a logical distinction now, madam.

MRS. MARWOOD: I perceive your debates are of importance and very learnedly handled.

PETULANT: Importance is one thing, and learning's another; but a debate's a debate, that I assert.

WITWOUD: Petulant's an enemy to learning; he relies altogether on his parts.

PETULANT: No, I'm no enemy to learning, it hurts not me.

MRS. MARWOOD: That's a sign indeed it's no enemy to you.

PETULANT: No, no, it's no enemy to anybody but them that have it.

MILLAMANT: Well, an illiterate man's my aversion. I wonder at the impudence of any illiterate man to offer to make love.

WITWOUD: That I confess I wonder at too.

MILLAMANT: Ah! To marry an ignorant that can hardly read or write!

PETULANT: Why should a man be ever the further from being married, though he can't read, any more than he is from being hanged? The ordinary's[54]

---

[53]A pun on *mainly* and the *main* (mean, middle), the tenor part on which the other two harmonize.
[54]The clergy assigned to a prison.

paid for setting the psalm, and the parish priest for reading the ceremony. And for the rest which is to follow in both cases, a man may do it without book; so all's one for that.

MILLAMANT: D'ye hear the creature? Lord, here's company, I'll be gone.

(Exeunt Millamant and Mincing.)

WITWOUD: In the name of Bartlemew and his fair,[55] what have we here?

MRS. MARWOOD: 'Tis your brother, I fancy. Don't you know him?

WITWOUD: Not I. Yes, I think it is he. I've almost forgot him; I have not seen him since the Revolution.[56]

(Enter Sir Wilfull Witwoud in a country riding habit, and a Servant to Lady Wishfort.)

SERVANT: Sir, my lady's dressing. Here's company; if you please to walk in, in the meantime.

SIR WILFULL: Dressing! What, it's but morning here, I warrant, with you in London; we should count it towards afternoon in our parts, down in Shropshire. Why then, belike my aunt han't dined yet, ha, friend?

SERVANT: Your aunt, sir?

SIR WILFULL: My aunt, sir! Yes, my aunt, sir, and your lady, sir; your lady is my aunt, sir. Why, what, dost thou not know me, friend? Why then, send somebody here that does. How long hast thou lived with thy lady, fellow, ha?

SERVANT: A week, sir; longer than anybody in the house, except my lady's woman.

SIR WILFULL: Why then, belike thou dost not know thy lady, if thou seest her, ha, friend?

SERVANT: Why truly, sir, I cannot safely swear to her face in a morning, before she is dressed. 'Tis like I may give a shrewd guess at her by this time.

SIR WILFULL: Well, prithee try what thou canst do; if thou can'st not guess, inquire her out, dost hear, fellow? And tell her, her nephew, Sir Wilfull Witwoud, is in the house.

SERVANT: I shall, sir.

SIR WILFULL: Hold ye, hear me, friend; a word with you in your ear. Prithee who are these gallants?

SERVANT: Really, sir, I can't tell; here come so many here, 'tis hard to know 'em all.   *(Exit Servant.)*

SIR WILFULL: Oons, this fellow knows less than a starling; I don't think a' knows his own name.

MRS. MARWOOD: Mr. Witwoud, your brother is not behindhand in forgetfulness; I fancy he has forgot you too.

WITWOUD: I hope so. The devil take him that remembers first, I say.

SIR WILFULL: Save you, gentlemen and lady!

---

[55]Bartholomew Fair, held annually in Smithfield around August 24, St. Bartholomew's Day.
[56]The Bloodless Revolution of 1688.

MRS. MARWOOD: For shame, Mr. Witwoud; why won't you speak to him? And
you sir.

WITWOUD: Petulant, speak.

PETULANT: And you, sir.

SIR WILFULL: No offense, I hope.   *(Salutes Marwood.)*

MRS. MARWOOD: No sure, sir.

WITWOUD: This is a vile dog, I see that already. No offense! Ha! Ha! Ha! Ha!
To him; to him, Petulant, smoke him.[57]

PETULANT: It seems as if you had come a journey, sir; hem, hem.

(Surveying him round.)

SIR WILFULL: Very likely, sir, that it may seem so.

PETULANT: No offense, I hope, sir.

WITWOUD: Smoke the boots, the boots; Petulant, the boots, ha! Ha! Ha!

SIR WILFULL: May be not, sir; thereafter as 'tis meant, sir.

PETULANT: Sir, I presume upon the information of your boots.

SIR WILFULL: Why, 'tis like you may, sir. If you are not satisfied with the
information of my boots, sir, if you will step to the stable, you may inquire
further of my horse, sir.

PETULANT: Your horse, sir! Your horse is an ass, sir!

SIR WILFULL: Do you speak by way of offense, sir?

MRS. MARWOOD: The gentleman's merry, that's all, sir. —*(Aside.)* 'Slife, we
shall have a quarrel betwixt an horse and an ass, before they find one
another out.—*(Aloud.)* You must not take anything amiss from your
friends, sir. You are among your friends here, though it may be you don't
know it. If I am not mistaken, you are Sir Wilfull Witwoud.

SIR WILFULL: Right, lady; I am Sir Wilfull Witwoud, so I write myself; no
offense to anybody, I hope; and nephew to the Lady Wishfort of this
mansion.

MRS. MARWOOD: Don't you know this gentleman, sir?

SIR WILFULL: Hum! What, sure 'tis not—yea by'r Lady, but 'tis. 'Sheart, I
know not whether 'tis or no. Yea, but 'tis by the Wrekin.[58] Brother
Anthony! What, Tony, i'faith! What, dost thou not know me? By'r Lady,
nor I thee, thou art so be-cravated and be-periwigged. 'Sheart, why dost
not speak? Art thou o'erjoyed?

WITWOUD: Odso, brother, is it you? Your servant, brother.

SIR WILLFULL: Your servant! Why, yours, sir. Your servant again, 'sheart, and
your friend and servant to that, and a—*(puff)* and a flapdragon[59] for your
service, sir! And a hare's foot, and a hare's scut[60] for your service, sir, an
you be so cold and so courtly!

[57]Make fun of him.   [58]A hill in Shropshire. "All friends round the Wrekin" is still a Shropshire
toast.   [59]A raisin snatched from burning brandy, popped in the mouth, and swallowed; hence,
no real dragon.   [60]A hare's tail.

WITWOUD: No offense, I hope, brother.

SIR WILFULL: 'Sheart, sir, but there is, and much offense! A pox, is this your Inns o'Court[61] breeding, not to know your friends and your relations, your elders and your betters?

WITWOUD: Why, brother Wilfull of Salop,[62] you may be as short as a Shrewsbury cake,[63] if you please. But I tell you, 'tis not modish to know relations in town. You think you're in the country, where great lubberly brothers slabber and kiss one another when they meet, like a call of sergeants.[64] 'Tis not the fashion here; 'tis not indeed, dear brother.

SIR WILFULL: The fashion's a fool; and you're a fop, dear brother. 'Sheart, I've suspected this. By'r Lady, I conjectured you were a fop, since you began to change the style of your letters and write in a scrap of paper, gilt round the edges, no broader than a subpoena. I might expect this when you left off Honored Brother, and hoping you are in good health, and so forth— to begin with a Rat me, knight, I'm so sick of a last night's debauch— ods heart, and then tell a familiar tale of a cock and a bull, and a whore and a bottle, and so conclude. You could write news before you were out of your time,[65] when you lived with honest Pumple[66] Nose, the attorney of Furnival's Inn;[67] you could entreat to be remembered then to your friends round the Wrekin. We could have gazettes then, and *Dawks's Letter,*[68] and the *Weekly Bill,* till of late days.

PETULANT: 'Slife, Witwoud, were you ever an attorney's clerk? Of the family of the Furnivals? Ha! Ha! Ha!

WITWOUD: Aye, aye, but that was for a while, not long, not long. Pshaw! I was not in my own power then; an orphan, and this fellow was my guardian. Aye, aye, I was glad to consent to that man to come to London. He had the disposal of me then. If I had not agreed to that, I might have been bound prentice to a felt-maker in Shrewsbury; this fellow would have bound me to a maker of felts.

SIR WILFULL: 'Sheart, and better than to be bound to a maker of fops, where, I suppose, you have served your time; and now you may set up for yourself.

MRS. MARWOOD: You intend to travel, sir, as I'm informed.

SIR WILFULL: Belike I may, madam. I may chance to sail upon the salt seas, if my mind hold.

PETULANT: And the wind serve.

SIR WILFULL: Serve or not serve, I shan't ask license of you, sir; nor the weathercock your companion. I direct my discourse to the lady, sir. 'Tis like my aunt may have told you, madam. Yes, I have settled my concerns,

---

[61]London's legal societies, in which lawyers were trained.   [62]Shropshire.   [63]A cake without shortening. Shrewsbury is the county town of Shropshire.   [64]A group of law students made sergeants-at-law at the same time.   [65]While you were still apprentice to an attorney.   [66]Pimple.   [67]A lesser inn of court attached to Lincoln's Inn.   [68]*Dawks's* was a weekly sheet; the *Weekly Bill* listed deaths.

I may say now, and am minded to see foreign parts. If an how that the peace holds,[69] whereby, that is, taxes abate.

MRS. MARWOOD: I thought you had designed for France at all adventures.

SIR WILFULL: I can't tell that; 'tis like I may, and 'tis like I may not. I am somewhat dainty in making a resolution, because when I make it, I keep it. I don't stand shill I, shall I, then; if I say't, I'll do't. But I have thoughts to tarry a small matter in town, to learn somewhat of your lingo first, before I cross the seas. I'd gladly have a spice of your French, as they say, whereby to hold discourse in foreign countries.

MRS. MARWOOD: Here is an academy in town for that use.

SIR WILFULL: There is? 'Tis like there may.

MRS. MARWOOD: No doubt you will return very much improved.

WITWOUD: Yes, refined, like a Dutch skipper from a whale-fishing.

(Enter Lady Wishfort and Fainall.)

LADY WISHFORT: Nephew, you are welcome.

SIR WILFULL: Aunt, your servant.

FAINALL: Sir Wilfull, your most faithful servant.

SIR WILFULL: Cousin Fainall, give me your hand.

LADY WISHFORT: Cousin Witwoud, your servant; Mr. Petulant, your servant. Nephew, you are welcome again. Will you drink anything after your journey, nephew, before you eat? Dinner's almost ready.

SIR WILFULL: I'm very well, I thank you, aunt; however, I thank you for your courteous offer. 'Sheart, I was afraid you would have been in the fashion too, and have remembered to have forgot your relations. Here's your cousin Tony; belike I mayn't call him brother for fear of offense.

LADY WISHFORT: Oh, he's a rallier, nephew. My cousin's a wit; and your great wits always rally their best friends to choose.[70] When you have been abroad, nephew, you'll understand raillery better.

(Fainall and Mrs. Marwood talk apart.)

SIR WILFULL: Why, then, let him hold his tongue in the meantime, and rail when that day comes.

(Enter Mincing.)

MINCING: Mem, I come to acquaint your la'ship that dinner is impatient.

SIR WILFULL: Impatient? Why then, belike it won't stay till I pull off my boots. Sweetheart, can you help me to a pair of slippers? My man's with his horses, I warrant.

LADY WISHFORT: Fie, fie, nephew, you would not pull off your boots here. Go

---

[69]The Peace of Ryswick (1697) stopped the war with France, which broke out again in 1701, the year after Congreve's play.   [70]Make as much fun of them as they like.

down into the hall; dinner shall stay for you. My nephew's a little unbred; you'll pardon him, madam. Gentlemen, will you walk? Marwood?

MRS. MARWOOD: I'll follow you, madam, before Sir Wilfull is ready.

(Exeunt all but Mrs. Marwood and Fainfall.)

FAINALL: Why then, Foible's a bawd, an arrant, rank, matchmaking bawd. And I, it seems, am a husband, a rank husband; and my wife a very arrant, rank wife, all in the way of the world. 'Sdeath, to be an anticipated cuckold, a cuckold in embryo! Sure I was born with budding antlers, like a young satyr, or a citizen's child.[71] 'Sdeath, to be out-witted, to be out-jilted, out-matrimonied! If I had kept my speed like a stag, 'twere somewhat; but to crawl after, with my horns like a snail, and outstripped by my wife, 'tis scurvy wedlock.

MRS. MARWOOD: Then shake it off. You have often wished for an opportunity to part; and now you have it. But first prevent their plot; the half of Millamant's fortune is too considerable to be parted with, to a foe, to Mirabell.

FAINALL: Damn him! That had been mine, had you not made that fond discovery. That had been forfeited, had they been married. My wife had added luster to my horns by that increase of fortune; I could have worn 'em tipt with gold, though my forehead had been furnished like a deputy lieutenant's hall.[72]

MRS. MARWOOD: They may prove a cap of maintenance[73] to you still, if you can away with[74] your wife. And she's no worse than when you had her. I dare swear she had given up her game before she was married.

FAINALL: Hum! That may be. She might throw up her cards; but I'll be hanged if she did not put Pam in her pocket.[75]

MRS. MARWOOD: You married her to keep you; and if you can contrive to have her keep you better than you expected, why should you not keep her longer than you intended?

FAINALL: The means, the means.

MRS. MARWOOD: Discover to my lady your wife's conduct; threaten to part with her. My lady loves her, and will come to any composition to save her reputation. Take the opportunity of breaking it, just upon the discovery of this imposture. My lady will be enraged beyond bounds, and sacrifice niece and fortune and all, at that conjuncture. And let me alone to keep her warm; if she should flag in her part, I will not fail to prompt her.

FAINALL: Faith, this has an appearance.

MRS. MARWOOD: I'm sorry I hinted to my lady to endeavor a match between Millamant and Sir Wilfull; that may be an obstacle.

---

[71]Offspring of merchants cuckolded by their gentleman customers. [72]With many antlers mounted. [73]In heraldry, a cap with two points, here suggesting both the cuckold's horns and his financial compensation from his wife's seducer. [74]Put up with. [75]Pam, the jack of clubs, is the highest card in the game of loo. Fainall implies that his wife has an ace up her sleeve in Mirabell.

FAINALL: Oh, for that matter leave me to manage him; I'll disable him for that. He will drink like a Dane; after dinner, I'll set his hand in.

MRS. MARWOOD: Well, how do you stand affected towards your lady?

FAINALL: Why, faith, I'm thinking of it. Let me see. I am married already, so that's over. My wife has played the jade with me; well, that's over too. I never loved her, or if I had, why that would have been over too by this time. Jealous[76] of her I cannot be, for I am certain; so there's an end of jealousy. Weary of her I am, and shall be. No, there's no end of that; no, no, that were too much to hope. Thus far concerning my repose; now for my reputation. As to my own, I married not for it; so that's out of the question. And as to my part in my wife's, why she had parted with hers before; so bringing none to me, she can take none from me. 'Tis against all rule of play that I should lose to one who has not wherewithal to stake.

MRS. MARWOOD: Besides, you forget, marriage is honorable.

FAINALL: Hum! Faith, and that's well thought on. Marriage is honorable, as you say; and if so, wherefore should cuckoldom be a discredit, being derived from so honorable a root?

MRS. MARWOOD: Nay, I know not; if the root be honorable, why not the branches?[77]

FAINALL: So, so; why this point's clear. Well, how do we proceed?

MRS. MARWOOD: I will contrive a letter which shall be delivered to my lady at the time when that rascal who is to act Sir Rowland is with her. It shall come as from an unknown hand, for the less I appear to know of the truth, the better I can play the incendiary. Besides, I would not have Foible provoked if I could help it, because you know she knows some passages. Nay, I expect all will come out; but let the mine be sprung first, and then I care not if I'm discovered.

FAINALL: If the worst come to the worst, I'll turn my wife to grass.[78] I have already a deed of settlement of the best part of her estate, which I have wheedled out of her; and that you shall partake at least.

MRS. MARWOOD: I hope you are convinced that I hate Mirabell; now you'll be no more jealous.

FAINALL: Jealous! No, by this kiss. Let husbands be jealous; but let the lover still believe. Or if he doubt, let it be only to endear his pleasure, and prepare the joy that follows, when he proves his mistress true. But let husbands' doubts convert to endless jealousy; or if they have belief, let it corrupt to superstition and blind credulity. I am single, and will herd no more with 'em. True, I wear the badge, but I'll disown the order. And since I take my leave of 'em, I care not if I leave 'em a common motto to their common crest:

All husbands must or pain or shame endure;

The wise too jealous are, fools too secure.   (*Exeunt.*)

---

[76]Suspicious.   [77]The cuckold's horns.   [78]Turn her out to pasture.

Act IV

Scene continues. Enter Lady Wishfort and Foible.

LADY WISHFORT: Is Sir Rowland coming, say'st thou, Foible? and are things in order?

FOIBLE: Yes, madam, I have put wax lights in the sconces, and placed the footmen in a row in the hall, in their best liveries, with the coachman and postilion to fill up the equipage.

LADY WISHFORT: Have you pulvilled[79] the coachman and postilion that they may not stink of the stable when Sir Rowland comes by?

FOIBLE: Yes, madam.

LADY WISHFORT: And are the dancers and the music ready, that he may be entertained in all points with correspondence to his passion?

FOIBLE: All is ready, madam.

LADY WISHFORT: And—well—and how do I look, Foible?

FOIBLE: Most killing well, madam.

LADY WISHFORT: Well, and how shall I receive him? In what figure shall I give his heart the first impression? There is a great deal in the first impression. Shall I sit?—No, I won't sit—I'll walk—aye, I'll walk from the door upon his entrance; and then turn full upon him.—No, that will be too sudden. I'll lie—aye, I'll lie down—I'll receive him in my little dressing-room; there's a couch—yes, yes, I'll give the first impression on a couch.—I won't lie neither, but loll and lean upon one elbow, with one foot a little dangling off, jogging in a thoughtful way—yes—and then as soon as he appears, start, aye, start and be surprised, and rise to meet him in a pretty disorder—yes—oh, nothing is more alluring than a levee[80] from a couch in some confusion.—It shows the foot to advantage, and furnishes with blushes, and recomposing airs beyond comparison. Hark! There's a coach.

FOIBLE: 'Tis he, madam.

LADY WISHFORT: Oh dear, has my nephew made his addresses to Millamant? I ordered him.

FOIBLE: Sir Wilfull is set in to drinking, madam, in the parlor.

LADY WISHFORT: Ods my life, I'll send him to her. Call her down, Foible; bring her hither. I'll send him as I go. When they are together, then come to me, Foible, that I may not be too long alone with Sir Rowland. *(Exit.)*

(Enter Mrs. Millamant and Mrs. Fainall.)

FOIBLE: Madam, I stayed here, to tell your ladyship that Mr. Mirabell has waited this half hour for an opportunity to talk with you, though my lady's orders were to leave you and Sir Wilfull together. Shall I tell Mr. Mirabell that you are at leisure?

MILLAMANT: No—what would the dear man have? I am thoughtful and would amuse myself—bid him come another time.

[79]Powdered.   [80]Rising.

There never yet was woman made,
Nor shall, but to be cursed.[81]   *(Repeating and walking about.)*
That's hard!

MRS. FAINALL: You are very fond of Sir John Suckling today, Millamant, and
the poets.

MILLAMANT: He? Aye, and filthy verses; so I am.

FOIBLE: Sir Wilfull is coming, madam. Shall I send Mr. Mirabell away?

MILLAMANT: Aye, if you please, Foible, send him away—or send him hither
—just as you will, dear Foible.—I think I'll see him—shall I? Aye, let the
wretch come.   *(Exit* Foible.)
Thyrsis, a youth of the inspired train.[82]   *(Repeating.)*
Dear Fainall, entertain Sir Wilfull. Thou hast philosophy to undergo a fool;
thou art married and hast patience. I would confer with my own thoughts.

MRS. FAINALL: I am obliged to you, that you would make me your proxy in
this affair; but I have business of my own.

(Enter Sir Wilfull.)

O Sir Wilfull, you are come at the critical instant. There's your mistress up
to the ears in love and contemplation; pursue your point, now or never.

SIR WILFULL: Yes; my aunt would have it so. I would gladly have been
encouraged with a bottle or two, because I'm somewhat wary at first,
before I am acquainted. *(This while Millamant walks about repeating to
herself.)* But I hope, after a time, I shall break my mind; that is, upon
further acquaintance. So for the present, cousin, I'll take my leave. If so
be you'll be so kind to make my excuse, I'll return to my company.

MRS. FAINALL: Oh, fie, Sir Wilfull! What, you must not be daunted.

SIR WILFULL: Daunted! No, that's not it. It is not so much for that; for if so
be that I set on't, I'll do't. But only for the present; 'tis sufficient till
further acquaintance, that's all. Your servant.

MRS. FAINALL: Nay, I'll swear you shall never lose so favorable an opportunity, if I can help it. I'll leave you together and lock the door. *(Exit.)*

SIR WILFULL: Nay, nay, cousin. I have forgot my gloves. What d'ye do?
'Sheart, 'a has locked the door indeed, I think. Nay, Cousin Fainall, open
the door! Pshaw, what a vixen trick is this? Nay, now 'a has seen me too.
Cousin, I made bold to pass through as it were. I think this door's
enchanted!

MILLAMANT *(repeating):* I prithee spare me, gentle boy,
Press me no more for that slight toy—[83]

SIR WILFULL: Anan?[84] Cousin, your servant.

MILLAMANT *(repeating):* That foolish trifle of a heart—
Sir Wilfull!

SIR WILFULL: Yes. Your servant. No offense, I hope, cousin.

---

[81]The first lines of an untitled poem by Sir John Suckling.   [82]The first line of Edmund Waller's
The Story of Phoebus and Daphne, Applied. Millamant recalls poems about love's brevity and fickle
man.   [83]These two lines and the next three Millamant recites are the first stanza of another
untitled poem by Suckling.   [84]A rustic expression for "How's that?"

MILLAMANT *(repeating):* I swear it will not do its part,
    Though thou dost thine, employ'st thy power and art.
    Natural, easy Suckling!
SIR WILFULL: Anan? Suckling? No such suckling neither, cousin, nor stripling;
    I thank heaven, I'm no minor.
MILLAMANT: Ah, rustic! Ruder than Gothic!
SIR WILFULL: Well, well, I shall understand your lingo one of these days,
    cousin; in the meanwhile, I must answer in plain English.
MILLAMANT: Have you any business with me, Sir Wilfull?
SIR WILFULL: Not at present, cousin. Yes, I made bold to see, to come and
    know if that how you were disposed to fetch a walk this evening, if so be
    that I might not be troublesome, I would have fought[85] a walk with you.
MILLAMANT: A walk! What then?
SIR WILFULL: Nay, nothing. Only for the walk's sake, that's all.
MILLAMANT: I nauseate walking; 'tis a country diversion. I loathe the country
    and everything that relates to it.
SIR WILFULL: Indeed! Ha! Look ye, look ye, you do? Nay, 'tis like you may.
    Here are choice of pastimes here in town, as plays and the like; that must
    be confessed indeed.
MILLAMANT: Ah, *l'étourdie!*[86] I hate the town too.
SIR WILFULL: Dear heart, that's much. Ha! That you should hate 'em both!
    Ha! 'Tis like you may; there are some can't relish the town, and others
    can't away with the country. 'Tis like you may be one of those, cousin.
MILLAMANT: Ha! Ha! Ha! Yes, 'tis like I may. You have nothing further to
    say to me?
SIR WILFULL: Not at present, cousin. 'Tis like when I have an opportunity to
    be more private, I may break my mind in some measure. I conjecture you
    partly guess.—However, that's as time shall try; but spare to speak and
    spare to speed, as they say.
MILLAMANT: If it is of no great importance, Sir Wilfull, you will oblige me
    to leave me; I have just now a little business—
SIR WILFULL: Enough, enough, cousin, yes, yes, all a case; when you're dis-
    posed, when you're disposed. Now's as well as another time; and another
    time as well as now. All's one for that. Yes, yes, if your concerns call you,
    there's no haste; it will keep cold, as they say. Cousin, your servant. I
    think this door's locked.
MILLAMANT: You may go this way, sir.
SIR WILFULL: Your servant; then with your leave I'll return to my company.
                                         (Exit)
MILLAMANT: Aye, aye; ha! Ha! Ha!
    Like Phoebus sung the no less amorous boy.[87]

(Enter Mirabell.)

---

[85]A rustic form of *fetched.*   [86]"Ah, the giddy town!"   [87]The third line of Waller's *Phoebus and Daphne.* Mirabell completes the couplet.

MIRABELL:
  Like Daphne she, as lovely and as coy.
  Do you lock yourself up from me, to make my search more curious?[88] Or
  is this pretty artifice contrived, to signify that here the chase must end and
  my pursuit be crowned, for you can fly no further?

MILLAMANT: Vanity! No. I'll fly and be followed to the last moment.
  Though I am upon the very verge of matrimony, I expect you should
  solicit me as much as if I were wavering at the grate of a monastery,
  with one foot over the threshold. I'll be solicited to the very last, nay
  and afterwards.

MIRABELL: What, after the last?

MILLAMANT: Oh, I should think I was poor and had nothing to bestow, if I
  were reduced to an inglorious ease and freed from the agreeable fatigues
  of solicitation.

MIRABELL: But do not you know that when favors are conferred upon instant
  and tedious solicitation, that they diminish in their value, and that both
  the giver loses the grace, and the receiver lessens his pleasure?

MILLAMANT: It may be in things of common application; but never sure in
  love. Oh, I hate a lover that can dare to think he draws a moment's air
  independent on the bounty of his mistress. There is not so impudent a
  thing in nature as the saucy look of an assured man, confident of success.
  The pedantic arrogance of a very husband has not so pragmatical an air.
  Ah! I'll never marry, unless I am first made sure of my will and pleasure.

MIRABELL: Would you have 'em both before marriage? Or will you be contented with the first now, and stay for the other till after grace?

MILLAMANT: Ah! Don't be impertinent.—My dear liberty, shall I leave thee?
  My faithful solitude, my darling contemplation, must I bid you then
  adieu? Ay-h adieu—my morning thoughts, agreeable wakings, indolent
  slumbers, all ye *douceurs,* ye *sommeils du matin,* [89] adieu?—I can't do't,
  'tis more than impossible. Positively, Mirabell, I'll lie abed in a morning
  as long as I please.

MIRABELL: Then I'll get up in a morning as early as I please.

MILLAMANT: Ah! Idle creature, get up when you will.—And d'ye hear, I won't
  be called names after I'm married; positively I won't be called names.

MIRABELL: Names!

MILLAMANT: Aye, as wife, spouse, my dear, joy, jewel, love, sweetheart, and
  the rest of that nauseous cant, in which men and their wives are so
  fulsomely familiar—I shall never bear that.—Good Mirabell, don't let us
  be familiar or fond, nor kiss before folks, like my Lady Fadler[90] and Sir
  Francis; nor go to Hyde Park together the first Sunday in a new chariot,
  to provoke eyes and whispers; and then never to be seen there together
  again; as if we were proud of one another the first week, and ashamed of
  one another ever after. Let us never visit together, nor go to a play
  together. But let us be very strange and well-bred; let us be as strange[91]

---

[88]Complicated. [89]Sweetnesses and morning naps. [90]To faddle is to fondle. [91]Reserved.

as if we had been married a great while, and as well-bred as if we were not married at all.

MIRABELL: Have you any more conditions to offer? Hitherto your demands are pretty reasonable.

MILLAMANT: Trifles!—As liberty to pay and receive visits to and from whom I please; to write and receive letters, without interrogatories or wry faces on your part; to wear what I please; and choose conversation with regard only to my own taste; to have no obligation upon me to converse with wits that I don't like, because they are your acquaintance; or to be intimate with fools, because they may be your relations. Come to dinner when I please; dine in my dressing room when I'm out of humor, without giving a reason. To have my closet inviolate; to be sole empress of my tea table, which you must never presume to approach without first asking leave. And lastly, wherever I am, you shall always knock at the door before you come in. These articles subscribed, if I continue to endure you a little longer, I may by degrees dwindle into a wife.

MIRABELL: Your bill of fare is something advanced in this latter account. Well, have I liberty to offer conditions—that when you are dwindled into a wife, I may not be beyond measure enlarged into a husband?

MILLAMANT: You have free leave. Propose your utmost; speak and spare not.

MIRABELL: I thank you. *Imprimis*[92] then, I covenant that your acquaintance be general; that you admit no sworn confidante, or intimate of your own sex; no she-friend to screen her affairs under your countenance, and tempt you to make trial of a mutual secrecy. No decoy-duck to wheedle you a fop, scrambling to the play in a mask; then bring you home in a pretended fright, when you think you shall be found out, and rail at me for missing the play, and disappointing the frolic which you had, to pick me up and prove my constancy.

MILLAMANT: Detestable *imprimis!* I go to the play in a mask!

MIRABELL: *Item,* I article that you continue to like your own face as long as I shall; and while it passes current with me, that you endeavor not to new-coin it. To which end, together with all vizards[93] for the day, I prohibit all masks for the night, made of oiled skins and I know now what —hog's bones, hare's gall, pig-water, and the marrow of a roasted cat. In short, I forbid all commerce with the gentlewoman in What-d'ye-call-it Court. *Item,* I shut my doors against all bawds with baskets, and penny-worths of muslin, china, fans, atlases,[94] etc.—*Item,* when you shall be breeding—

MILLAMANT: Ah! Name it not.

MIRABELL: Which may be presumed, with a blessing on our endeavors—

MILLAMANT: Odious endeavors!

MIRABELL: I denounce against all strait-lacing, squeezing for a shape, till you mold my boy's head like a sugar loaf, and instead of a man-child, make me the father to a crooked billet.[95] Lastly, to the dominion of the tea table

[92]"In the first place," the phrasing of legal documents.   [93]Masks.   [94]Oriental satins.   [95]A stick of firewood.

I submit, but with proviso, that you exceed not in your province, but restrain yourself to native and simple tea-table drinks, as tea, chocolate, and coffee. As likewise to genuine and authorized tea-table talk—such as mending of fashions, spoiling reputations, railing at absent friends, and so forth; but that on no account you encroach upon the men's prerogative, and presume to drink healths, or toast fellows; for prevention of which, I banish all foreign forces, all auxiliaries to the tea table, as orange brandy, all aniseed, cinnamon, citron, and Barbadoes waters, together with ratafia and the most noble spirit of clary.[96] But for cowslip-wine, poppy-water, and all dormitives, those I allow. These provisos admitted, in other things I may prove a tractable and complying husband.

MILLAMANT: Oh, horrid provisos! filthy strong waters! I toast fellows, odious men! I hate your odious provisos.

MIRABELL: Then we're agreed. Shall I kiss your hand upon the contract? And here comes one to be a witness to the sealing of the deed.

(Enter Mrs. Fainfall.)

MILLAMANT: Fainall, what shall I do? Shall I have him? I think I must have him.

MRS. FAINALL: Aye, aye, take him, take him, what should you do?

MILLAMANT: Well then—I'll take my death I'm in a horrid fright—Fainall, I shall never say it—well—I think—I'll endure you.

MRS. FAINALL: Fie, fie! Have him, have him, and tell him so in plain terms; for I am sure you have a mind to him.

MILLAMANT: Are you? I think I have—and the horrid man looks as if he thought so too.—Well, you ridiculous thing you, I'll have you—I won't be kissed, nor I won't be thanked—here, kiss my hand though.—So, hold your tongue now, and don't say a word.

MRS. FAINALL: Mirabell, there's a necessity for your obedience; you have neither time to talk nor stay. My mother is coming; and in my conscience, if she should see you, would fall into fits and maybe not recover, time enough to return to Sir Rowland, who, as Foible tells me, is in a fair way to succeed. Therefore spare your ecstasies for another occasion, and slip down the backstairs, where Foible waits to consult you.

MILLAMANT: Aye, go, go. In the meantime I suppose you have said something to please me.

MIRABELL: I am all obedience.   *(Exit.)*

MRS. FAINALL: Yonder Sir Wilfull's drunk, and so noisy that my mother has been forced to leave Sir Rowland to appease him; but he answers her only with singing and drinking. What they have done by this time I know not; but Petulant and he were quarreling as I came by.

MILLAMANT: Well, if Mirabell should not make a good husband, I am a lost thing—for I find I love him violently.

[96]All of these are spiced liqueurs.

MRS. FAINALL: So it seems, when you mind not what's said to you. If you doubt him, you had best take up with Sir Wilfull.

MILLAMANT: How can you name that superannuated lubber? Foh!

(Enter Witwoud from drinking.)

MRS. FAINALL: So, is the fray made up, that you have left 'em?

WITWOUD: Left 'em? I could stay no longer. I have laughed like ten christenings; I am tipsy with laughing. If I had stayed any longer I should have burst; I must have been let out and pieced in the sides like an unsized camlet.[97] Yes, yes, the fray is composed; my lady came in like a *nolle prosequi*[98] and stopped their proceedings.

MILLAMANT: What was the dispute?

WITWOUD: That's the jest; there was no dispute. They could neither of 'em speak for rage, and so fell a-sputtering at one another like two roasting apples.

(Enter Petulant drunk.)

Now Petulant, all's over, all's well. Gad, my head begins to whim it about. Why dost thou not speak? Thou art both as drunk and as mute as a fish.

PETULANT: Look you, Mrs. Millamant, if you can love me, dear nymph, say it, and that's the conclusion. Pass on, or pass off; that's all.

WITWOUD: Thou hast uttered volumes, folios, in less than *decimo sexto,*[99] my dear Lacedemonian.[100] Sirrah Petulant, thou art an epitomizer of words.

PETULANT: Witwoud, you are an annihilator of sense.

WITWOUD: Thou art a retailer of phrases and dost deal in remnants of remnants, like a maker of pincushions; thou art in truth (metaphorically speaking) a speaker of shorthand.

PETULANT: Thou art (without a figure) just one half of an ass, and Baldwin[101] yonder, thy half brother, is the rest. A gemini of asses split would make just four of you.

WITWOUD: Thou dost bite, my dear mustard seed; kiss me for that.

PETULANT: Stand off! I'll kiss no more males. I have kissed your twin yonder in a humor of reconciliation, till he *(hiccup)* rises upon my stomach like a radish.

MILLAMANT: Eh! Filthy creature! What was the quarrel?

PETULANT: There was no quarrel; there might have been a quarrel.

WITWOUD: If there had been words enow between 'em to have expressed provocation, they had gone together by the ears like a pair of castanets.

PETULANT: You were the quarrel.

MILLAMANT: Me!

PETULANT: If I have a humor to quarrel, I can make less matters conclude

---

[97] An unstiffened oriental fabric.   [98] A legal phrase for ending a lawsuit.   [99] A "sixteen-mo," a very small book.   [100] Spartan, men of very few words.   [101] The ass in the beast epic *Reynard the Fox.*

premises. If you are not handsome, what then, if I have a humor to prove it? If I shall have my reward, say so; if not, fight for your face the next time yourself. I'll go sleep.

WITWOUD: Do, wrap thyself up like a wood louse, and dream revenge; and hear me, if thou canst learn to write by tomorrow morning, pen me a challenge. I'll carry it for thee.

PETULANT: Carry your mistress's monkey a spider! Go flea dogs, and read romances! I'll go to bed to my maid. *(Exit.)*

MRS. FAINALL: He's horridly drunk. How came you all in this pickle?

WITWOUD: A plot! a plot! to get rid of the knight. Your husband's advice; but he sneaked off.

(Enter Lady Wishfort, and Sir Wilfull drunk.)

LADY WISHFORT: Out upon't, out upon't! At years of discretion, and comport yourself at this rantipole[102] rate!

SIR WILFULL: No offense, aunt.

LADY WISHFORT: Offense? As I'm a person, I'm ashamed of you—foh! how you stink of wine! D'ye think my niece will ever endure such a borachio![103] you're an absolute borachio.

SIR WILFULL: Borachio!

LADY WISHFORT: At a time when you should commence an amour and put your best foot foremost—

SIR WILFULL: 'Sheart, an you grutch me your liquor, make a bill. Give me more drink, and take my purse. *(Sings.)*

> Prithee fill me the glass,
> Till it laugh in my face,
> With ale that is potent and mellow;
> He that whines for a lass
> Is an ignorant ass,
> For a bumper has not its fellow.

But if you would have me marry my cousin, say the word, and I'll do't. Wilfull will do't; that's the word. Wilfull will do't; that's my crest. My motto I have forgot.

LADY WISHFORT: My nephew's a little overtaken, cousin, but 'tis with drinking your health. O' my word you are obliged to him.

SIR WILFULL: *In vino veritas,*[104] aunt. If I drunk your health today, cousin, I am a borachio. But if you have a mind to be married, say the word, and send for the piper; Wilful will do't. If not, dust it away, and let's have t'other round.—Tony!—Odsheart, where's Tony?—Tony's an honest fellow; but he spits after a bumper, and that's a fault. *(Sings.)*

> We'll drink, and we'll never ha' done, boys,
> Put the glass then around with the sun, boys;
> Let Apollo's example invite us;

---

[102]Ill-mannered.　[103]Winebeg.　[104]"In wine there is truth."

For he's drunk every night,
And that makes him so bright,
That he's able next morning to light us.

The sun's a good pimple,[105] an honest soaker; he has a cellar at your Antipodes. If I travel, aunt, I touch at your Antipodes; your Antipodes are a good, rascally sort of topsy-turvy fellows. If I had a bumper, I'd stand upon my head and drink a health to 'em. A match, or no match, cousin with the hard name? Aunt, Wilfull will do't. If she has her maidenhead, let her look to't; if she has not, let her keep her own counsel in the meantime, and cry out at the nine months' end.

MILLAMANT: Your pardon, madam, I can stay no longer. Sir Wilfull grows very powerful. Egh! How he smells! I shall be overcome if I stay. Come, cousin.

(Exeunt Millamant and Mrs. Fainall.)

LADY WISHFORT: Smells! He would poison a tallow chandler[106] and his family. Beastly creature, I know not what to do with him! Travel, quotha! Aye, travel, travel, get thee gone, get thee but far enough, to the Saracens, or the Tartars, or the Turks, for thou art not fit to live in a Christian commonwealth, thou beastly pagan!

SIR WILFULL: Turks, no; no Turks, aunt; your Turks are infidels, and believe not in the grape. Your Mahometan, your Mussulman, is a dry stinkard. No offense, aunt. My map says that your Turk is not so honest a man as your Christian. I cannot find by the map that your Mufti[107] is orthodox; whereby it is a plain case that orthodox is a hard word, aunt, and *(hiccup)* Greek for claret.   *(Sings.)*

To drink is a Christian diversion,
Unknown to the Turk and the Persian:
    Let Mahometan fools
    Live by heathenish rules,
And be damned over tea cups and coffee!
    But let British lads sing,
    Crown a health to the king,
And a fig for your sultan and sophy![108]
Ah, Tony!

(Enter Foible, and whispers Lady Wishfort.)

LADY WISHFORT *(aside to Foible):* Sir Rowland impatient? Good lack! what shall I do with this beastly tumbril?[109] *(Aloud.)* Go lie down and sleep, you sot! Or, as I'm a person, I'll have you bastinadoed[110] with broomsticks. Call up the wenches.   *(Exit Foible.)*

SIR WILFULL: Ahey! Wenches, where are the wenches?

[105]Boon companion.   [106]A maker or seller of candles.   [107]Moslem priest.   [108]The Shah of Persia.
[109]Dung cart.   [110]Beaten on the soles of the feet.

LADY WISHFORT: Dear Cousin Witwoud, get him away, and you will bind me to you inviolably. I have an affair of moment that invades me with some precipitation. You will oblige me to all futurity.

WITWOUD: Come, knight. Pox on him, I don't know what to say to him. Will you go to a cock-match?

SIR WILFULL: With a wench, Tony? Is she a shake-bag,[111] Sirrah? Let me bite your cheek for that.

WITWOUD: Horrible! He has a breath like a bagpipe! Aye, aye, come, will you march, my Salopian?[112]

SIR WILFULL: Lead on, little Tony; I'll follow thee, my Anthony, my Tantony. Sirrah, thou shalt be my Tantony,[113] and I'll be thy pig.
And a fig for your sultan and sophy.

(Exit singing with Witwoud.)

LADY WISHFORT: This will never do. It will never make a match—at least before he has been abroad.

(Enter Waitwell, disguised as for Sir Rowland.)

Dear Sir Rowland, I am confounded with confusion at the retrospection of my own rudeness! I have more pardons to ask than the Pope distributes in the Year of Jubilee.[114] But I hope, where there is likely to be so near an alliance, we may unbend the severity of decorum and dispense with a little ceremony.

WAITWELL: My impatience, madam, is the effect of my transport; and till I have the possession of your adorable person, I am tantalized on a rack, and do but hang, madam, on the tenter of expectation.

LADY WISHFORT: You have an excess of gallantry, Sir Rowland, and press things to a conclusion with a most prevailing vehemence. But a day or two for decency of marriage—

WAITWELL: For decency of funeral, madam! The delay will break my heart; or, if that should fail, I shall be poisoned. My nephew will get an inkling of my designs and poison me; and I would willingly starve him before I die; I would gladly go out of the world with that satisfaction. That would be some comfort to me, if I could but live so long as to be revenged on that unnatural viper.

LADY WISHFORT: Is he so unnatural, say you? Truly I would contribute much both to the saving of your life, and the accomplishment of your revenge. Not that I respect[115] myself, though he has been a perfidious wretch to me.

WAITWELL: Perfidious to you!

LADY WISHFORT: O Sir Rowland, the hours that he has died away at my feet, the tears that he has shed, the oaths that he has sworn, the palpitations that he has felt, the trances and the tremblings, the ardors and the ecsta-

---

[111]Large gamecock.   [112]Native of Shropshire   [113]St. Anthony, patron of swineherds.   [114]1700, the year of this play, was a jubilee year.   [115]Consider.

sies, the kneelings and the risings, the heart-heavings, and the hand-grippings, the pangs and the pathetic regards of his protesting eyes! Oh, no memory can register.

WAITWELL: What, my rival! Is the rebel my rival? 'A dies.

LADY WISHFORT: No, don't kill him at once, Sir Rowland; starve him gradually, inch by inch.

WAITWELL: I'll do't. In three weeks he shall be barefoot; in a month out at knees with begging an alms. He shall starve upward and upward, till he has nothing living but his head, and then go out in a stink like a candle's end upon a save-all.[116]

LADY WISHFORT: Well, Sir Rowland, you have the way. You are no novice in the labyrinth of love; you have the clue. But as I am a person, Sir Rowland, you must not attribute my yielding to any sinister appetite, or indigestion of widowhood; nor impute my complacency to any lethargy of continence. I hope you do not think me prone to any iteration of nuptials.

WAITWELL: Far be it from me—

LADY WISHFORT: If you do, I protest I must recede, or think that I have made a prostitution of decorums; but in the vehemence of compassion, and to save the life of a person of so much importance—

WAITWELL: I esteem it so.

LADY WISHFORT: Or else you wrong my condescension.

WAITWELL: I do not, I do not!

LADY WISHFORT: Indeed you do.

WAITWELL: I do not, fair shrine of virtue!

LADY WISHFORT: If you think the least scruple of carnality was an ingredient—

WAITWELL: Dear madam, no. You are all camphire[117] and frankincense, all chastity and odor.

LADY WISHFORT: Or that—

(Enter Foible.)

FOIBLE: Madam, the dancers are ready, and there's one with a letter, who must deliver it into your own hands.

LADY WISHFORT: Sir Rowland, will you give me leave? Think favorably, judge candidly, and conclude you have found a person who would suffer racks in honor's cause, dear Sir Rowland, and will wait on you incessantly.[118]

(Exit.)

WAITWELL: Fie, fie! What a slavery have I undergone! Spouse, hast thou any cordial? I want spirits.

FOIBLE: What a washy rogue art thou, to pant thus for a quarter of an hour's lying and swearing to a fine lady!

[116]A device for burning candles to the end.   [117]Camphor, supposed to lessen sexual desire.
[118]Instantly.

WAITWELL: Oh, she is the antidote to desire! Spouse, thou wilt fare the worse for't. I shall have no appetite to iteration of nuptials this eight-and-forty hours. By this hand I'd rather be a chairman in the dog-days[119] than act Sir Rowland till this time tomorrow!

(Enter Lady Wishfort, with a letter.)

LADY WISHFORT: Call in the dancers. Sir Rowland, we'll sit, if you please, and see the entertainment.

(Dance.)

> Now, with your permission, Sir Rowland, I will peruse my letter. I would open it in your presence, because I would not make you uneasy. If it should make you uneasy, I would burn it. Speak, if it does. But you may see by the superscription it is like a woman's hand.

FOIBLE *(aside to Waitwell):* By heaven! Mrs. Marwood's; I know it. My heart aches. Get it from her.

WAITWELL: A woman's hand? No, madam, that's no woman's hand; I see that already. That's somebody whose throat must be cut.

LADY WISHFORT: Nay, Sir Rowland, since you give me a proof of your passion by your jealousy, I promise you I'll make you a return, by a frank communication. You shall see it; we'll open it together. Look you here. *(Reads.)* "Madam, though unknown to you"—Look you there, 'tis from nobody that I know—"I have that honor for your character, that I think myself obliged to let you know you are abused. He who pretends to be Sir Rowland is a cheat and a rascal."—Oh, heavens! what's this?

FOIBLE *(aside):* Unfortunate! all's ruined!

WAITWELL: How, how, let me see, let me see! *(Reading.)* "A rascal, and disguised and suborned for that imposture."—O villainy! O villainy—"by the contrivance of—"

LADY WISHFORT: I shall faint, I shall die, I shall die, oh!

FOIBLE *(aside to Waitwell):* Say 'tis your nephew's hand. Quickly, his plot, swear, swear it!

WAITWELL: Here's a villain! Madam, don't you perceive it? don't you see it?

LADY WISHFORT: Too well, too well! I have seen too much.

WAITWELL: I told you at first I knew the hand. A woman's hand? The rascal writes a sort of a large hand, your Roman hand. I saw there was a throat to be cut presently. If he were my son, as he is my nephew, I'd pistol him!

FOIBLE: Oh, treachery! But are you sure, Sir Rowland, it is his writing?

WAITWELL: Sure? Am I here? Do I live? Do I love this pearl of India? I have twenty letters in my pocket from him in the same character.

LADY WISHFORT: How!

FOIBLE: Oh, what luck it is, Sir Rowland, that you were present at this juncture! This was the business that brought Mr. Mirabell disguised to

---

[119]Bearer of a sedan chair in the hottest part of summer.

Madam Millamant this afternoon. I thought something was contriving, when he stole by me and would have hid his face.

LADY WISHFORT: How, how! I heard the villain was in the house indeed; and now I remember, my niece went away abruptly, when Sir Wilfull was to have made his addresses.

FOIBLE: Then, then, madam, Mr. Mirabell waited for her in her chamber, but I would not tell your ladyship to discompose you when you were to receive Sir Rowland.

WAITWELL: Enough, his date is short.

FOIBLE: No, good Sir Rowland, don't incur the law.

WAITWELL: Law? I care not for law. I can but die, and 'tis in a good cause. My lady shall be satisfied of my truth and innocence, though it cost me my life.

LADY WISHFORT: No, dear Sir Rowland, don't fight; if you should be killed, I must never show my face; or hanged—oh, consider my reputation, Sir Rowland! No, you shan't fight. I'll go in and examine my niece; I'll make her confess. I conjure you, Sir Rowland, by all your love, not to fight.

WAITWELL: I am charmed, madam; I obey. But some proof you must let me give you; I'll go for a black box, which contains the writings of my whole estate, and deliver that into your hands.

LADY WISHFORT: Aye, dear Sir Rowland, that will be some comfort; bring the black box.

WAITWELL: And may I presume to bring a contract to be signed this night? May I hope so far?

LADY WISHFORT: Bring what you will; but come alive, pray come alive. Oh, this is a happy discovery!

WAITWELL: Dead or alive I'll come, and married we will be in spite of treachery; aye, and get an heir that shall defeat the last remaining glimpse of hope in my abandoned nephew. Come, my buxom widow.
Ere long you shall substantial proof receive
That I'm an arrant knight—

FOIBLE *(aside).*   Or arrant knave.[120] *(Exeunt.)*

Act V

Scene continues. Enter Lady Wishfort and Foible.

LADY WISHFORT: Out of my house, out of my house, thou viper! thou serpent, that I have fostered! thou bosom traitress that I raised from nothing! Begone! begone! begone! go! go! That I took from washing of old gauze and weaving of dead hair,[121] with a bleak blue nose, over a chafing dish of starved embers, and dining behind a traverse rag, in a shop no bigger than a birdcage! Go, go! starve again, do, do!

FOIBLE: Dear madam, I'll beg pardon on my knees.

LADY WISHFORT: Away! out! out! Go set up for yourself again! Do, drive a

---

[120]*Arrant knave,* knight errant, downright knave.   [121]Making wigs.

trade, do, with your three-pennyworth of small ware, flaunting upon a pack-thread, under a brandy-seller's bulk,[122] or against a dead wall by a ballad-monger! Go, hang out an old frisoneer gorget,[123] with a yard of yellow colberteen[124] again. Do! an old gnawed mask, two rows of pins, and a child's fiddle; a glass necklace with the beads broken, and a quilted nightcap with one ear. Go, go, drive a trade! These were your commodities, you treacherous trull! This was your merchandise you dealt in, when I took you into my house, placed you next myself, and made you governante of my whole family! You have forgot this, have you, now you have feathered your nest?

FOIBLE: No, no, dear madam. Do but hear me; have but a moment's patience. I'll confess all. Mr. Mirabell seduced me; I am not the first that he has wheedled with his dissembling tongue. Your ladyship's own wisdom has been deluded by him; then how should I, a poor ignorant, defend myself? O madam, if you knew but what he promised me, and how he assured me your ladyship should come to no damage! Or else the wealth of the Indies should not have bribed me to conspire against so good, so sweet, so kind a lady as you have been to me.

LADY WISHFORT: No damage? What, to betray me, to marry me to a cast servingman?[125] to make me a receptacle, an hospital for a decayed pimp? No damage? O thou frontless[126] impudence, more than a big-bellied actress.

FOIBLE: Pray do but hear me, madam; he could not marry your ladyship, madam. No indeed; his marriage was to have been void in law, for he was married to me first, to secure your ladyship. He could not have bedded your ladyship; for if he had consummated with your ladyship, he must have run the risk of the law and been put upon his clergy.[127] Yes indeed; I inquired of the law in that case before I would meddle or make.

LADY WISHFORT: What, then I have been your property, have I? I have been convenient to you, it seems! While you were catering for Mirabell, I have been broker[128] for you? What, have you made a passive bawd of me? This exceeds all precedent; I am brought to fine uses, to become a botcher[129] of secondhand marriages between Abigails and Andrews![130] I'll couple you! Yes, I'll baste you together, you and your Philander![131] I'll Duke's Place you,[132] as I'm a person! Your turtle is in custody already; you shall coo in the same cage, if there be constable or warrant in the parish.   *(Exit.)*

FOIBLE: Oh, that ever I was born! Oh, that I was ever married! A bride! Aye, I shall be a Bridewell-bride.[133] Oh!

(Enter Mrs. Fainall.)

[122]Stall.   [123]Woollen neckpiece.   [124]Cheap lace.   [125]Discharged servant.   [126]Shameless.   [127]First offenders who could read and write might escape death by showing they could read and write, thus claiming "benefit of clergy," an immunity formerly limited to clergymen.   [128]Marriage broker.   [129]Mender of old clothes.   [130]Maids and servants.   [131]Lover.   [132]See footnote 4, p. 1007.   [133]Bridewell was London's women's prison.

MRS. FAINALL: Poor Foible, what's the matter?

FOIBLE: O madam, my lady's gone for a constable. I shall be had to a justice, and put to Bridewell to beat hemp. Poor Waitwell's gone to prison already.

MRS. FAINALL: Have a good heart, Foible; Mirabell's gone to give security for him. This is all Marwood's and my husband's doing.

FOIBLE: Yes, yes, I know it, madam; she was in my lady's closet, and overheard all that you said to me before dinner. She sent the letter to my lady; and that missing effect, Mr. Fainall laid this plot to arrest Waitwell, when he pretended to go for the papers; and in the meantime Mrs. Marwood declared all to my lady.

MRS. FAINALL: Was there no mention made of me in the letter? My mother does not suspect my being in the confederacy? I fancy Marwood has not told her, though she has told my husband.

FOIBLE: Yes, madam; but my lady did not see that part. We stifled the letter before she read so far. Has that mischievous devil told Mr. Fainall of your ladyship then?

MRS. FAINALL: Aye, all's out, my affair with Mirabell, everything discovered. This is the last day of our living together; that's my comfort.

FOIBLE: Indeed, madam, and so 'tis a comfort if you knew all. He has been even with your ladyship; which I could have told you long enough since, but I love to keep peace and quietness by my good will. I had rather bring friends together than set 'em at distance. But Mrs. Marwood and he are nearer related than ever their parents thought for.

MRS. FAINALL: Say'st thou so, Foible? Canst thou prove this?

FOIBLE: I can take my oath of it, madam; so can Mrs. Mincing. We have had many a fair word from Madam Marwood, to conceal something that passed in our chamber one evening when you were at Hyde Park and we were thought to have gone a-walking; but we went up unawares, though we were sworn to secrecy too. Madam Marwood took a book and swore us upon it, but it was a book of verses and poems. So as long as it was not a Bible-oath, we may break it with a safe conscience.

MRS. FAINALL: This discovery is the most opportune thing I could wish. Now, Mincing?

(Enter Mincing)

MINCING: My lady would speak with Mrs. Foible, mem. Mr. Mirabell is with her; he has set your spouse at liberty, Mrs. Foible, and would have you hide yourself in my lady's closet till my old lady's anger is abated. Oh, my old lady is in a perilous passion at something Mr. Fainall has said; he swears, and my old lady cries. There's a fearful hurricane, I vow. He says, mem, how that he'll have my lady's fortune made over to him, or he'll be divorced.

MRS. FAINALL: Does your lady or Mirabell know that?

MINCING: Yes, mem; they have sent me to see if Sir Wilfull be sober and to bring him to them. My lady is resolved to have him, I think, rather than lose such a vast sum as six thousand pounds. Oh, come, Mrs. Foible, I hear my old lady.

MRS. FAINALL: Foible, you must tell Mincing that she must prepare to vouch when I call her.

FOIBLE: Yes, yes, madam.

MINCING: O yes, mem, I'll vouch anything for your ladyship's service, be what it will.   (*Exeunt Mincing and Foible.*)

(*Enter Lady Wishfort and Marwood.*)

LADY WISHFORT: O my dear friend, how can I enumerate the benefits that I have received from your goodness? To you I owe the timely discovery of the false vows of Mirabell; to you the detection of the imposter Sir Rowland. And now you are become an intercessor with my son-in-law, to save the honor of my house, and compound[134] for the frailties of my daughter. Well, friend, you are enough to reconcile me to the bad world, or else I would retire to deserts and solitudes, and feed harmless sheep by groves and purling streams. Dear Marwood, let us leave the world, and retire by ourselves and be shepherdesses.

MRS. MARWOOD: Let us first dispatch the affair in hand, madam. We shall have leisure to think of retirement afterwards. Here is one who is concerned in the treaty.

LADY WISHFORT: O daughter, daughter, is it possible thou shouldst be my child, bone of my bone, and flesh of my flesh, and, as I may say, another me, and yet transgress the most minute particle of severe virtue? It is possible you should lean aside to iniquity, who have been cast in the direct mold of virtue? I have not only been a mold but a pattern for you, and a model for you, after you were brought into the world.

MRS. FAINALL: I don't understand your ladyship.

LADY WISHFORT: Not understand? Why, have you not been naught?[135] Have you not been sophisticated?[136] Not understand? Here I am ruined to compound for your caprices and your cuckoldoms. I must pawn my plate and my jewels, and ruin my niece, and all little enough.

MRS. FAINALL: I am wronged and abused, and so are you. 'Tis a false accusation, as false as hell, as false as your friend there, aye, or your friend's friend, my false husband.

MRS. MARWOOD: My friend, Mrs. Fainall? Your husband my friend? What do you mean?

MRS. FAINALL: I know what I mean, madam, and so do you; and so shall the world at a time convenient.

MRS. MARWOOD: I am sorry to see you so passionate, madam. More temper[137] would look more like innocence. But I have done. I am sorry my zeal to serve your ladyship and family should admit of misconstruction, or make

---

[134]Settled for money.   [135]Naughty.   [136]Corrupted.   [137]Moderation.

me liable to affronts. You will pardon me, madam, if I meddle no more
with an affair in which I am not personally concerned.

LADY WISHFORT: O dear friend, I am so ashamed that you should meet with
such returns! *(To Mrs. Fainall.)* You ought to ask pardon on your knees,
ungrateful creature; she deserves more from you than all your life can
accomplish. *(To Mrs. Marwood.)* Oh, don't leave me destitute in this
perplexity! No, stick to me, my good genius.

MRS. FAINALL: I tell you, madam, you're abused. Stick to you? Aye, like a
leech, to suck your best blood; she'll drop off when she's full. Madam, you
shan't pawn a bodkin,[138] nor part with a brass counter,[139] in composition
for me. I defy 'em all. Let 'em prove their aspersions; I know my own
innocence, and dare stand by a trial.   *(Exit.)*

LADY WISHFORT: Why, if she should be innocent, if she should be wronged
after all, ha? I don't know what to think—and, I promise you, her education has been unexceptionable. I may say it; for I chiefly made it my own
care to initiate her very infancy in the rudiments of virtue, and to impress
upon her tender years a young odium and aversion to the very sight of
men—aye, friend, she would ha' shrieked if she had but seen a man, till
she was in her teens. As I'm a person, 'tis true. She was never suffered
to play with a male child, though but in coats; nay, her very babies[140] were
of the feminine gender. Oh, she never looked a man in the face but her
own father, or the chaplain, and him we made a shift to put upon her for
a woman, by the help of his long garments and his sleek face, till she was
going in her fifteen.

MRS. MARWOOD: 'Twas much she should be deceived so long.

LADY WISHFORT: I warrant you, or she would never have borne to have been
catechized by him; and have heard his long lectures against singing and
dancing, and such debaucheries; and going to filthy plays, and profane
music-meetings, where the lewd trebles squeak nothing but bawdy, and
the basses roar blasphemy. Oh, she would have swooned at the sight or
name of an obscene playbook! And can I think, after all this, that my
daughter can be naught? What, a whore? And thought it excommunica-
tion to set her foot within the door of a playhouse! O my dear friend, I
can't believe it, no, no! As she says, let him prove it, let him prove it.

MRS. MARWOOD: Prove it, madam? What, and have your name prostituted in
a public court! Yours and your daughter's reputation worried at the bar
by a pack of bawling lawyers! To be ushered in with an *Oyez*[141] of scandal,
and have your case opened by an old fumbling lecher in a quoif[142] like a
man midwife; to bring your daughter's infamy to light; to be a theme for
legal punsters and quibblers by the statute, and become a jest against a
rule of court, where there is no precedent for a jest in any record, not even
in Doomsday Book;[143] to discompose the gravity of the bench, and pro-

[138]Hairpin.   [139]A token coin.   [140]Dolls.   [141]"Hear ye," the court cry (from old French) for silence.   [142]White cap then worn by a serjeant-at-law.   [143]The record of a survey of English lands
made in 1085–1086.

voke naughty interrogatories in more naughty law Latin, while the good judge, tickled with the proceeding, simpers under a gray beard, and fidges[144] off and on his cushion as if he had swallowed cantharides,[145] or sat upon cow-itch.[146]

LADY WISHFORT: Oh, 'tis very hard!

MRS. MARWOOD: And then to have my young revelers of the Temple[147] take notes, like prentices at a conventicle;[148] and after, talk it all over again in commons, or before drawers in an eating house.

LADY WISHFORT: Worse and worse!

MRS. MARWOOD: Nay, this is nothing; if it would end here, 'twere well. But it must, after this, be consigned by the shorthand writers to the public press; and from thence be transferred to the hands, nay into the throats and lungs of hawkers, with voices more licentious than the loud flounder-man's,[149] or the woman that cries gray peas. And this you must hear till you are stunned; nay, you must hear nothing else for some days.

LADY WISHFORT: Oh, 'tis insupportable! No, no, dear friend; make it up, make it up; aye, aye, I'll compound. I'll give up all, myself and my all, my niece and her all, anything, everything for composition.

MRS. MARWOOD: Nay, madam, I advise nothing; I only lay before you, as a friend, the inconveniences which perhaps you have overseen.[150] Here comes Mr. Fainall. If he will be satisfied to huddle up all in silence, I shall be glad. You must think I would rather congratulate than condole with you.

(Enter Fainall.)

LADY WISHFORT: Aye, aye, I do not doubt it, dear Marwood; no, no, I do not doubt it.

FAINALL: Well, madam, I have suffered myself to be overcome by the importunity of this lady your friend, and am content that you shall enjoy your own proper estate during life, on condition you oblige yourself never to marry, under such penalty as I think convenient.

LADY WISHFORT: Never to marry?

FAINALL: No more Sir Rowlands; the next imposture may not be so timely detected.

MRS. MARWOOD: That condition, I dare answer, my lady will consent to, without difficulty; she has already but too much experienced the perfidiousness of men. Besides, madam, when we retire to our pastoral solitude, we shall bid adieu to all other thoughts.

LADY WISHFORT: Aye, that's true; but in case of necessity, as of health, or some such emergency—

---

[144]Fidgets.   [145]Spanish fly, an aphrodisiac.   [146]Cowhage, a tropical vine, with pods covered with fine bristles.   [147]Law students. The Inner and Middle Temples were two of the Inns of Court. [148]Apprentices of dissenting tradesmen were required to take notes on sermons.   [149]A certain street vendor had long made himself famous by his loud crying of flounders.   [150]Overlooked.

FAINALL: Oh, if you are prescribed marriage, you shall be considered; I will only reserve to myself the power to choose for you. If your physic be wholesome, it matters not who is your apothecary. Next, my wife shall settle on me the remainder of her fortune, not made over already; and for her maintenance depend entirely on my discretion.

LADY WISHFORT: This is most inhumanly savage, exceeding the barbarity of a Muscovite husband.

FAINALL: I learned it from his Czarish majesty's retinue,[151] in a winter evening's conference over brandy and pepper, amongst other secrets of matrimony and policy, as they are at present practiced in the northern hemisphere. But this must be agreed unto, and that positively. Lastly, I will be endowed, in right of my wife, with that six thousand pound, which is the moiety of Mrs. Millamant's fortune in your possession; and which she has forfeited (as will appear by the last will and testament of your deceased husband, Sir Jonathan Wishfort) by her disobedience in contracting herself against your consent or knowledge, and by refusing the offered match with Sir Wilfull Witwoud, which you, like a careful aunt, had provided for her.

LADY WISHFORT: My nephew was *non compos,*[152] and could not make his addresses.

FAINALL: I come to make demands. I'll hear no objections.

LADY WISHFORT: You will grant me time to consider?

FAINALL: Yes, while the instrument is drawing,[153] to which you must set your hand till more sufficient deeds can be perfected; which I will take care shall be done with all possible speed. In the meanwhile, I will go for the said instrument, and till my return you may balance this matter in your own discretion. *(Exit.)*

LADY WISHFORT: This insolence is beyond all precedent, all parallel. Must I be subject to this merciless villain?

MRS. MARWOOD: 'Tis severe indeed, madam, that you should smart for your daughter's wantonness.

LADY WISHFORT: 'Twas against my consent that she married this barbarian, but she would have him, though her year was not out.[154]—Ah! her first husband, my son Languish, would not have carried it thus. Well, that was my choice, this is hers; she is matched now with a witness.[155] I shall be mad! Dear friend, is there no comfort for me? Must I live to be confiscated at this rebel rate?—Here come two more of my Egyptian plagues, too.

(Enter Millamant and Sir Wilfull Witwoud.)

SIR WILFULL: Aunt, your servant.

LADY WISHFORT: Out, caterpillar, call me not aunt! I know thee not!

---

[151]Peter the Great had visited England in 1698, two years before.   [152]Legal term, *non compos mentis,* "not of sound mind."   [153]While the agreement is being drafted.   [154]Her first year of widowhood, the traditional period of mourning.   [155]With a vengeance.

SIR WILFULL: I confess I have been a little in disguise,[156] as they say. 'Sheart! And I'm sorry for't. What would you have? I hope I committed no offense, aunt, and, if I did, I am willing to make satisfaction; and what can a man say fairer? If I have broke anything, I'll pay for't, an it cost a pound. And so let that content for what's past, and make no more words. For what's to come, to pleasure you I'm willing to marry my cousin. So pray let's all be friends; she and I are agreed upon the matter before a witness.

LADY WISHFORT: How's this, dear niece? Have I any comfort? Can this be true?

MILLAMANT: I am content to be a sacrifice to your repose, madam; and to convince you that I had no hand in the plot, as you were misinformed, I have laid my commands on Mirabell to come in person, and be a witness that I give my hand to this flower of knighthood; and for the contract that passed between Mirabell and me, I have obliged him to make a resignation of it in your ladyship's presence. He is without, and waits your leave for admittance.

LADY WISHFORT: Well, I'll swear I am something revived at this testimony of your obedience; but I cannot admit that traitor. I fear I cannot fortify myself to support his appearance. He is as terrible to me as a Gorgon; if I see him, I fear I shall turn to stone, petrify incessantly.

MILLAMANT: If you disoblige him, he may resent your refusal and insist upon the contract still. Then 'tis the last time he will be offensive to you.

LADY WISHFORT: Are you sure it will be the last time? If I were sure of that! Shall I never see him again?

MILLAMANT: Sir Willfull, you and he are to travel together, are you not?

SIR WILFULL: 'Sheart, the gentleman's a civil gentleman, aunt; let him come in. Why, we are sworn brothers and fellow travelers. We are to be Pylades and Orestes,[157] he and I. He is to be my interpreter in foreign parts. He has been overseas once already; and with proviso that I marry my cousin, will cross 'em once again, only to bear me company. 'Sheart, I'll call him in. An I set on't once, he shall come in; and see who'll hinder him.   *(Exit.)*

MRS. MARWOOD: This is precious fooling, if it would pass; but I'll know the bottom of it.

LADY WISHFORT: O dear Marwood, you are not going?

MRS. MARWOOD: Not far, madam; I'll return immediately.   *(Exit.)*

(Re-enter Sir Wilfull and Mirabell.)

SIR WILFULL: Look up, man, I'll stand by you; 'sbud an she do frown, she can't kill you; besides—harkee, she dare not frown desperately, because her face is none of her own. 'Sheart, an she should, her forehead would wrinkle like the coat of a cream cheese; but mum for that, fellow traveler.

MIRABELL: If a deep sense of the many injuries I have offered to so good a lady, with a sincere remorse and a hearty contrition, can but obtain the least

---

[156]Drunk.   [157]Devoted traveling companions.

glance of compassion, I am too happy. Ah, madam, there was a time! But let it be forgotten. I confess I have deservedly forfeited the high place I once held, of sighing at your feet. Nay, kill me not, by turning from me in disdain. I come not to plead for favor; nay, not for pardon. I am a suppliant only for your pity. I am going where I never shall behold you more.

SIR WILFULL: How, fellow traveler! You shall go by yourself then.

MIRABELL: Let me be pitied first, and afterwards forgotten—I ask no more.

SIR WILFULL: By'r Lady, a very reasonable request, and will cost you nothing, aunt. Come, come, forgive and forget, aunt; why you must, an you are a Christian.

MIRABELL: Consider, madam, in reality you could not receive much prejudice; it was an innocent device, though I confess it had a face of guiltiness. It was at most an artifice which love contrived, and errors which love produces have ever been accounted venial. At least think it is punishment enough that I have lost what in my heart I hold most dear, that to your cruel indignation I have offered up this beauty, and with her my peace and quiet; nay, all my hopes of future comfort.

SIR WILFULL: An he does not move me, would I might never be o' the quorum![158] An it were not as good a deed as to drink, to give her to him again, I would I might never take shipping! Aunt, if you don't forgive quickly, I shall melt, I can tell you that. My contract went no farther than a little mouth-glue, and that's hardly dry; one doleful sigh more from my fellow traveler, and 'tis dissolved.

LADY WISHFORT: Well, nephew, upon your account—ah, he has a false insinuating tongue! Well, sir, I will stifle my just resentment at my nephew's request. I will endeavor what I can to forget, but on proviso that you resign the contract with my niece immediately.

MIRABELL: It is in writing and with papers of concern; but I have sent my servant for it, and will deliver it to you, with all acknowledgments for your transcendent goodness.

LADY WISHFORT (aside): Oh, he has witchcraft in his eyes and tongue! When I did not see him, I could have bribed a villain to his assassination; but his appearance rakes the embers which have so long lain smothered in my breast.

(Enter Fainall and Mrs. Marwood.)

FAINALL: Your date of deliberation, madam, is expired. Here is the instrument; are you prepared to sign?

LADY WISHFORT: If I were prepared, I am not empowered. My niece exerts a lawful claim, having matched herself by my direction to Sir Wilfull.

FAINALL: That sham is too gross to pass on me, though 'tis imposed on you, madam.

MILLAMANT: Sir, I have given my consent.

---

[158] A justice of the peace.

MIRABELL: And, sir, I have resigned my pretensions.

SIR WILFULL: And, sir, I assert my right; and will maintain it in defiance of you, sir, and of your instrument. 'Sheart, an you talk of an instrument, sir, I have an old fox[159] by my thigh shall hack your instrument of ram vellum to shreds, sir! It shall not be sufficient for a mittimus[160] or a tailor's measure.[161] Therefore, withdraw your instrument, sir, or by'r Lady, I shall draw mine.

LADY WISHFORT: Hold, nephew, hold!

MILLAMANT: Good Sir Wilfull, respite your valor.

FAINALL: Indeed? Are you provided of a guard, with your single beefeater there? But I'm prepared for you, and insist upon my first proposal. You shall submit your own estate to my management and absolutely make over my wife's to my sole use, as pursuant to the purport and tenor of this other covenant. *(To Millamant.)* I suppose, madam, your consent is not requisite in this case; nor, Mr. Mirabell, your resignation; nor, Sir Wilfull, your right. You may draw your fox if you please, sir, and make a bear-garden flourish somewhere else; for here it will not avail. This, my Lady Wishfort, must be subscribed, or your darling daughter's turned adrift, like a leaky hulk, to sink or swim, as she and the current of this lewd town can agree.

LADY WISHFORT: Is there no means, no remedy to stop my ruin? Ungrateful wretch! Dost thou not owe thy being, thy subsistence, to my daughter's fortune?

FAINALL: I'll answer you when I have the rest of it in my possession.

MIRABELL: But that you would not accept of a remedy from my hands—I own I have not deserved you should owe any obligation to me; or else perhaps I could advise—

LADY WISHFORT: Oh, what? what? to save me and my child from ruin, from want, I'll forgive all that's past; nay, I'll consent to anything to come, to be delivered from this tyranny.

MIRABELL: Aye, madam, but that is too late; my reward is intercepted. You have disposed of her who only could have made me a compensation for all my services. But be it as it may, I am resolved I'll serve you; you shall not be wronged in this savage manner.

LADY WISHFORT: How! Dear Mr. Mirabell, can you be so generous at last? But it is not possible. Harkee, I'll break my nephew's match; you shall have my niece yet, and all her fortune, if you can but save me from this imminent danger.

MIRABELL: Will you? I take you at your word. I ask no more. I must have leave for two criminals to appear.

LADY WISHFORT: Aye, aye; anybody, anybody!

MIRABELL: Foible is one, and a penitent.

(Enter Mrs. Fainall, Foible, and Mincing.)

---

[159]Sword.   [160]Warrant of arrest.   [161]A tailor's parchment measuring tape.

MRS. MARWOOD *(to Fainall):* Oh, my shame! These corrupt things are bought and brought hither to expose me.

(Mirabell and Lady Wishfort go to Mrs. Fainall and Foible.)

FAINALL: If it must all come out, why let 'em know it; 'tis but the way of the world. That shall not urge me to relinquish or abate one tittle of my terms; no, I will insist the more.

FOIBLE: Yes indeed, madam; I'll take my Bible oath of it.

MINCING: And so will I, mem.

LADY WISHFORT: O Marwood, Marwood, art thou false? My friend deceive me? Hast thou been a wicked accomplice with that profligate man?

MRS. MARWOOD: Have you so much ingratitude and injustice, to give credit against your friend to the aspersions of two such mercenary trulls?

MINCING: Mercenary, mem? I scorn your words. 'Tis true we found you and Mr. Fainall in the blue garret; by the same token, you swore us to secrecy upon Messalina's poems.[162] Mercenary? No, if we would have been mercenary, we should have held our tongues; you would have bribed us sufficiently.

FAINALL: Go, you are an insignificant thing! Well, what are you the better for this? Is this Mr. Mirabell's expedient? I'll be put off no longer. You thing, that was a wife, shall smart for this! I will not leave thee wherewithal to hide thy shame; your body shall be as naked as your reputation.

MRS. FAINALL: I despise you, and defy your malice! You have aspersed me wrongfully. I have proved your falsehood. Go you and your treacherous —I will not name it, but starve together, perish!

FAINALL: Not while you are worth a groat, indeed, my dear. Madam, I'll be fooled no longer.

LADY WISHFORT: Ah, Mr. Mirabell, this is small comfort, the detection of this affair.

MIRABELL: Oh, in good time. Your leave for the other offender and penitent to appear, madam.

(Enter Waitwell with a box of writings.)

LADY WISHFORT: O Sir Rowland! Well, rascal?

WAITWELL: What your ladyship pleases. I have brought the black box at last, madam.

MIRABELL: Give it to me. Madam, you remember your promise.

LADY WISHFORT: Aye, dear sir.

MIRABELL: Where are the gentlemen?

WAITWELL: At hand, sir, rubbing their eyes; just risen from sleep.

FAINALL: 'Sdeath, what's this to me? I'll not wait your private concerns.

(Enter Petulant and Witwoud.)

[162]Mincing, something of a malapropist, seems to mean "miscellaneous poems."

PETULANT: How now? What's the matter? Whose hand's out?

WITWOUD: Heyday! What, are you all got together, like players at the end of the last act?

MIRABELL: You may remember, gentlemen, I once requested your hands as witnesses to a certain parchment.

WITWOUD: Aye, I do; my hand I remember. Petulant set his mark.

MIRABELL: You wrong him; his name is fairly written, as shall appear. You do not remember, gentlemen, anything of what that parchment contained? *(Undoing the box.)*

WITWOUD: No.

PETULANT: Not I. I writ. I read nothing.

MIRABELL: Very well; now you shall know. Madam, your promise

LADY WISHFORT: Aye, aye, sir, upon my honor.

MIRABELL: Mr. Fainall, it is now time that you should know that your lady, while she was at her own disposal, and before you had by your insinuations wheedled her out of a pretended settlement of the greatest part of her fortune—

FAINALL: Sir! Pretended!

MIRABELL: Yes, sir. I say that this lady, while a widow, having, it seems, received some cautions respecting your inconstancy and tyranny of temper, which from her own partial opinion and fondness of you she could never have suspected—she did, I say, by the wholesome advice of friends and of sages learned in the laws of this land, deliver this same as her act and deed to me in trust, and to the uses within mentioned. You may read if you please *(Holding out the parchment.)*—though perhaps what is inscribed on the back may serve your occasions.

FAINALL: Very likely, sir. What's here? Damnation! *(Reads.)* "A deed of conveyance of the whole estate real of Arabella Languish, widow, in trust to Edward Mirabell." Confusion!

MIRABELL: Even so, sir; 'tis the way of the world, sir, of the widows of the world. I suppose this deed may bear an elder date than what you have obtained from your lady.

FAINALL: Perfidious fiend! then thus I'll be revenged.

(Offers to run at Mrs. Fainall.)

SIR WILFULL: Hold, sir! Now you may make your bear-garden flourish somewhere else, sir.

FAINALL: Mirabell, you shall hear of this, sir; be sure you shall. Let me pass, oaf!   *(Exit.)*

MRS. FAINALL: Madam, you seem to stifle your resentment; you had better give it vent.

MRS. MARWOOD: Yes, it shall have vent, and to your confusion; or I'll perish in the attempt.   *(Exit.)*

LADY WISHFORT: O daughter, daughter, 'tis plain thou hast inherited thy mother's prudence.

MRS. FAINALL: Thank Mr. Mirabell, a cautious friend, to whose advice all is owing.

LADY WISHFORT: Well, Mr. Mirabell, you have kept your promise, and I must perform mine. First, I pardon, for your sake, Sir Rowland there and Foible. The next thing is to break the matter to my nephew, and how to do that—

MIRABELL: For that, madam, give yourself no trouble; let me have your consent. Sir Wilfull is my friend; he has had compassion upon lovers, and generously engaged a volunteer in this action for our service, and now designs to prosecute his travels.

SIR WILFULL: 'Sheart, aunt, I have no mind to marry. My cousin's a fine lady, and the gentleman loves her, and she loves him, and they deserve one another; my resolution is to see foreign parts. I have set on't, and when I'm set on't, I must do't. And if these two gentlemen would travel too, I think they may be spared.

PETULANT: For my part, I say little; I think things are best off or on.

WITWOUD: I gad, I understand nothing of the matter; I'm in a maze yet, like a dog in a dancing school.

LADY WISHFORT: Well, sir, take her, and with her all the joy I can give you.

MILLAMANT: Why does not the man take me? Would you have me give myself to you over again?

MIRABELL: Aye, and over and over again; for I would have you as often as possibly I can. *(Kisses her hand.)* Well, heaven grant I love you not too well; that's all my fear.

SIR WILFULL: 'Sheart, you'll have time enough to toy after you're married; or if you will toy now, let us have a dance in the meantime, that we who are not lovers may have some other employment besides looking on.

MIRABELL: With all my heart, dear Sir Wilfull. What shall we do for music?

FOIBLE: Oh, sir, some that were provided for Sir Rowland's entertainment are yet within call.

(A dance.)

LADY WISHFORT: As I am a person, I can hold out no longer. I have wasted my spirits so today already that I am ready to sink under the fatigue; and I cannot but have some fears upon me yet that my son Fainall will pursue some desperate course.

MIRABELL: Madam, disquiet not yourself on that account; to my knowledge his circumstances are such, he must of force comply. For my part, I will contribute all that in me lies to a reunion. In the meantime, madam *(to Mrs. Fainall),* let me before these witnesses restore to you this deed of trust; it may be a means, well-managed, to make you live easily together. From hence let those be warned, who mean to wed, Lest mutual falsehood stain the bridal bed; For each deceiver to his cost may find, That marriage frauds too oft are paid in kind.

(Exeunt omnes.)

QUESTIONS

1. To appreciate Congreve's ingenuity, write a summary of the plot. What motivates Mrs. Marwood? What is Mirabell's relationship with Mrs. Fainall?
2. What is the romantic element in the play?
3. Which characters and what impulses does Congreve satirize?
4. Where do sincere emotion and integrity show through the comic surface?
5. What does Fainall represent? How does Congreve treat him in the end, and why?
6. What is the significance of the dance—probably a minuet—in the last act?
7. What is the effect of Congreve's style? "Let us be as strange as if we had been married a great while, and as well-bred as if we were not married at all." Comment on some other examples.
8. What is "the way of the world"?

THE TEMPEST

In the first collected edition of Shakespeare's plays, the First Folio of 1623, *The Tempest* stood first. Probably the last play written entirely by Shakespeare, it is also one of his greatest. In it he combined the wisdom of maturity with a poetic and dramatic skill perfected through thirty-five earlier plays. Listed in the First Folio among the comedies, *The Tempest* has in some recent editions been designated a romance (a category not used in the First Folio). As is true with other romances, or with comedies reaching toward romance, laughter here is not as important as the genial good spirit that in the end prevails. The atmosphere is far removed from the satiric thrusts of *Lysistrata* or the high comedy of *The Way of the World*.

A play this rich invites a number of approaches. We may consider it as the court entertainment that it was in its first recorded productions (not in the Globe theater, but in Whitehall before King James in 1611 and again in the winter of 1612–1613 to celebrate the marriage of Princess Elizabeth). In its New World imagery it is a topical play exploiting the interest of the audience in a recent English shipwreck and survival on the coast of Bermuda, in an area that according to a contemporary account was "supposed to be enchanted and inhabited with witches and devils, which grew by reason of accustomed monstrous thunder, storm, and tempest, near unto those islands." Living today in an age far less credulous in some respects than the seventeenth century, we may wish to see the magic as more allegoric than literal and the play itself as a universal drama of appearance and reality. Remembering that it came at the end of Shakespeare's career, we may see in it the author's conjuring once more with the magic of his art, before, in the character of Prospero, he bids it farewell forever. Rejecting alike historical and biographical connections and deep-seated allegories, we may find in it that particular enchantment of the world of fairy tales and romance which is always and never present for all times and places.

THE TEMPEST*

William Shakespeare   (1564–1616)

Names of the Actors

ALONSO, King of Naples	MASTER of a ship
SEBASTIAN, his brother	BOATSWAIN
PROSPERO, the right Duke of Milan	MARINERS
ANTONIO, his brother, the usurping	MIRANDA, daughter to Prospero
Duke of Milan	ARIEL, an airy spirit
FERDINAND, son to the King of Naples	IRIS
GONZALO, an honest old councillor	CERES
ADRIAN AND FRANCISCO, lords	JUNO (presented by) spirits
CALIBAN, a savage and deformed slave	NYMPHS
TRINCULO, a jester	REAPERS
STEPHANO, a drunken butler	**(Other spirits attending on PROSPERO)**

The Scene: An uninhabited Island

Act I

Scene I

The deck of a ship. A tempestuous noise of thunder and lightning heard. Enter a Shipmaster and a Boatswain.

> MASTER: Boatswain!
> BOATSWAIN: Here, master. What cheer?
> MASTER: Good, speak to th' mariners; fall to't yarely, or we run our-   **3**
>   selves aground. Bestir, bestir!   *(Exit)*

(Enter Mariners)

> BOATSWAIN: Heigh, my hearts! Cheerly, cheerly, my hearts! Yare, yare!
>   Take in the topsail! Tend to th' master's whistle! Blow till thou burst   **6**
>   thy wind, if room enough!   **7**

(Enter Alonso, Sebastian, Antonio, Ferdinand, Gonzalo, and others)

> ALONSO: Good boatswain, have care. Where's the master? Play the men.   **8**
> BOATSWAIN: I pray now, keep below.

---

*Edited, with notes, by Northrop Frye.
3 *yarely*, briskly.   **6** *Tend*, attend; *Blow . . . wind*, addressed to the storm.   **7** *if room enough*, i.e. so long as we have searoom.   **8** *Play*, perhaps "ply," keep the men busy.

ANTONIO: Where is the master, bos'n?

BOATSWAIN: Do you not hear him? You mar our labor. Keep your cabins: you do assist the storm.

GONZALO: Nay, good, be patient.

BOATSWAIN: When the sea is. Hence! What cares these roarers for the   14
name of king? To cabin! Silence! Trouble us not!

GONZALO: Good, yet remember whom thou hast aboard.

BOATSWAIN: None that I more love than myself. You are a councillor: if you can command these elements to silence and work the peace of the present, we will not hand a rope more; use your authority.   19
If you cannot, give thanks you have lived so long, and make yourself ready in your cabin for the mischance of the hour, if it so hap.— Cheerly, good hearts!—Out of our way, I say.   *(Exit)*

GONZALO: I have great comfort from this fellow: me thinks he hath no drowning mark upon him; his complexion is perfect gallows. Stand   24
fast, good Fate, to his hanging! Make the rope of his destiny our cable, our own doth little advantage. If he be not born to be hanged,   26
our case is miserable.

(Exeunt)

(Enter Boatswain)

BOATSWAIN: Down with the topmast! Yare! Lower, lower! Bring her to try with main-course! *(A cry within)* A plague upon this howling!   29
They are louder than the weather or our office.   30

(Enter Sebastian, Antonio, and Gonzalo)

Yet again? What do you here? Shall we give o'er and drown? Have you a mind to sink?

SEBASTIAN: A pox o' your throat, you bawling, blasphemous, incharitable dog!

BOATSWAIN: Work you, then.

ANTONIO: Hang, cur, hang, you whoreson, insolent noisemaker! We are less afraid to be drowned than thou art.

GONZALO: I'll warrant him for drowning, though the ship were no   38
stronger than a nutshell and as leaky as an unstanched wench.   39

BOATSWAIN: Lay her ahold, ahold! Set her two courses! Off to sea again!   40
Lay her off!

14 *roarers,* (1) waves, (2) blusterers or bullies.   19 *hand,* handle.   24 *complexion,* indication of character in appearance of face.   24 *gallows,* alluding to the proverb "He that's born to be hanged need fear no drowning."   26 *doth little advantage,* doesn't help us much.   29 *try with main-course,* lie hove-to with only the mainsail.   29 *plague,* followed by a dash in F; possibly the boatswain's language was more profane than the text indicates; cf.1. 38, and V, i, 218–19.   30 *our office,* the noise we make at, our work.   38 *warrant . . . for* guarantee . . . against.   39 *unstanched,* i.e. loose.   40 *ahold,* perhaps "a-hull," without any sail. As the ship drifts to the rocks, the order is reversed and the *two courses,* foresail and mainsail, are set up again in an effort to clear the shore.

(Enter Mariners wet)

MARINERS: All lost! To prayers, to prayers! All lost!

(Exeunt)

BOATSWAIN: What, must our mouths be cold?
GONZALO: The King and Prince at prayers! Let's assist them,
    For our case is as theirs.
SEBASTIAN: I am out of patience.
ANTONIO: We are merely cheated of our lives by drunkards.   46
    This wide-chopped rascal—would thou mightst lie drowning   47
    The washing of ten tides!   48
GONZALO: He'll be hanged yet,
    Though every drop of water swear against it
    And gape at wid'st to glut him.   50

(A confused noise within)

                'Mercy on us!—
    We split, we split!—Farewell, my wife and children!—
    Farewell, brother!—We split, we split, we split!'

(Exit Boatswain)

ANTONIO: Let's all sink with th' King.
SEBASTIAN: Let's take leave of him.

(Exit with Antonio)

GONZALO: Now would I give a thousand furlongs of sea for an acre of
    barren ground—long heath, brown furze, anything.   55
    The wills above be done, but I would fain die a dry death.

(Exit)

Act I

Scene II

Before Prospero's cell. Enter Prospero and Miranda.

MIRANDA: If by your art, my dearest father, you have
    Put the wild waters in this roar, allay them.
    The sky, it seems, would pour down stinking pitch
    But that the sea, mounting to th' welkin's cheek,   4
    Dashes the fire out. O, I have suffered

46 *merely,* completely.   **47** *wide-chopped,* wide-jawed.   **48** *ten tides,* pirates were hanged on shore
and left until three tides washed over them.   **50** *glut,* gobble.   **55** *long heath, brown furze,* heather
and gorse (sometimes emended to "ling, heath, broom, furze").   **4** *cheek,* face (with perhaps a
secondary meaning of "side of a grate").

With those that I saw suffer! a brave vessel   6
(Who had no doubt some noble creature in her)
Dashed all to pieces! O, the cry did knock
Against my very heart! Poor souls, they perished!
Had I been any god of power, I would
Have sunk the sea within the earth or ere   11
It should the good ship so have swallowed and
The fraughting souls within her.

PROSPERO: Be collected.   13
No more amazement. Tell your piteous heart   14
There's no harm done.

MIRANDA: O, woe the day!

PROSPERO: No harm.
I have done nothing but in care of thee,
Of thee my dear one, thee my daughter, who
Art ignorant of what thou art, naught knowing
Of whence I am; nor that I am more better
Than Prospero, master of a full poor cell,
And thy no greater father.

MIRANDA: More to know
Did never meddle with my thoughts.   22

PROSPERO: 'Tis time
I should inform thee farther. Lend thy hand
And pluck my magic garment from me. So,
Lie there, my art. Wipe thou thine eyes; have comfort.   25
The direful spectacle of the wrack, which touched
The very virtue of compassion in thee,   27
I have with such provision in mine art   28
So safely ordered that there is no soul—
No, not so much perdition as an hair   30
Betid to any creature in the vessel   31
Which thou heard'st cry, which thou saw'st sink. Sit down;
For thou must now know farther.

MIRANDA: You have often
Begun to tell me what I am; but stopped
And left me to a bootless inquisition,   35
Concluding, 'Stay: not yet.'

PROSPERO: The hour's now come;
The very minute bids thee ope thine ear.
Obey, and be attentive. Canst thou remember   38

---

6 *brave*, fine, handsome (and so elsewhere throughout the play).   **11** *or ere*, before.   **13** *fraughting*, forming the cargo; *collected*, composed.   **14** *amazement*, distraction; *piteous*, pitying   **22** *meddle*, mingle.   **25** *art*, i.e., his robe.   **27** *virtue*, essence.   **28** *provision*, foresight.   **30** *perdition*, loss.   **31** *Betid*, happened.   **35** *bootless inquisition*, fruitless inquiry.   **38** *Obey*, listen.

A time before we came unto this cell?
I do not think thou canst, for then thou wast not
Out three years old.   41
MIRANDA: Certainly, sir, I can.
PROSPERO: By what? By any other house or person?
Of any thing the image tell me that   43
Hath kept with thy remembrance.
MIRANDA: 'Tis far off,
And rather like a dream than an assurance
That my remembrance warrants. Had I not   46
Four or five women once that tended me?
PROSPERO: Thou hadst, and more, Miranda. But how is it
That this lives in thy mind? What seest thou else
In the dark backward and abysm of time?   50
If thou rememb'rest aught ere thou cam'st here,
How thou cam'st here thou mayst.
MIRANDA: But that I do not.
PROSPERO: Twelve year since, Miranda, twelve year since,
Thy father was the Duke of Milan and
A prince of power.
MIRANDA: Sir, are not you my father?
PROSPERO: Thy mother was a piece of virtue, and   56
She said thou wast my daughter; and thy father
Was Duke of Milan; and his only heir
A princess—no worse issuèd.   59
MIRANDA: O the heavens!
What foul play had we that we came from thence?
Or blessed was't we did?
PROSPERO: Both, both, my girl!
By foul play, as thou say'st, were we heaved thence,
But blessedly holp hither.   63
MIRANDA: O, my heart bleeds
To think o'th' teen that I have turned you to,   64
Which is from my remembrance! Please you, farther.   65
PROSPERO: My brother and thy uncle, called Antonio—
I pray thee mark me—that a brother should
Be so perfidious!—he whom next thyself
Of all the world I loved, and to him put
The manage of my state, as at that time   70
Through all the signories it was the first   71

---

41 *Out,* fully.   **43** *tell me,* i.e., describe for me.   **46** *remembrance warrants,* memory guarantees.
50 *backward,* past; *abysm,* abyss.   **56** *piece,* masterpiece.   **59** *no worse issuèd,* no meaner in
descent.   **63** *blessedly holp,* providentially helped.   **64** *teen,* trouble; *turned you to,* put you in
mind of.   **65** *from,* out of.   **70** *put . . . state,* entrusted the control of my administration.
71 *signories,* states of northern Italy.

And Prospero the prime duke, being so reputed
In dignity, and for the liberal arts
Without a parallel; those being all my study,
The government I cast upon my brother
And to my state grew stranger, being transported
And rapt in secret studies. Thy false uncle—
Dost thou attend me?

MIRANDA: Sir, most heedfully.

PROSPERO: Being once perfected how to grant suits,   79
How to deny them, who t' advance, and who
To trash for over-topping, new-created   81
The creatures that were mine, I say, or changed 'em,   82
Or else new-formed 'em; having both the key   83
Of officer and office, set all hearts i' th' state
To what tune pleased his ear, that now he was
The ivy which had hid my princely trunk
And sucked my verdure out on't. Thou attend'st not?

MIRANDA: O, good sir, I do.

PROSPERO: I pray thee mark me.
I thus neglecting worldly ends, all dedicated
To closeness, and the bettering of my mind   90
With that which, but by being so retired,
O'er-prized all popular rate, in my false brother   92
Awaked an evil nature, and my trust,
Like a good parent, did beget of him   94
A falsehood in its contrary as great
As my trust was, which had indeed no limit,
A confidence sans bound. He being thus lorded,   97
Not only with what my revenue yielded   98
But what my power might else exact, like one
Who having unto truth, by telling of it,   100
Made such a sinner of his memory
To credit his own lie, he did believe   102
He was indeed the Duke, out o' th' substitution   103
And executing th' outward face of royalty
With all prerogative. Hence his ambition growing—
Dost thou hear?

79 *perfected,* grown skillful.   **81** *trash for over-topping,* (1) check, as hounds, for going too fast, (2) cut branches, as of over-tall trees.   **82** *or,* either.   **83** *key,* (used with pun on its musical sense, leading to the metaphor of *tune*).   **90** *closeness,* seclusion (?), secret studies (?).   **92** *O'er-prized,* overvalued; *rate,* estimation.   **94** *good parent,* (alluding to the same proverb cited by Miranda in 1. 120).   **97–99** *He . . . exact,* the senses is that Antonio had the prerogatives as well as the income of the Duke.   **97** *sans bound,* unlimited.   **98** *revenue,* (accent second syllable).   **100** *it,* i. e., the lie.   **102** *To,* as to.   **103** *out,* as a result.

MIRANDA: Your tale, sir, would cure deafness.

PROSPERO: To have no screen between this part he played
    And him he played it for, he needs will be
    Absolute Milan. Me (poor man) my library   109
    Was dukedom large enough. Of temporal royalties
    He thinks me now incapable; confederates   111
    (So dry he was for sway) with th' King of Naples   112
    To give him annual tribute, do him homage,
    Subject his coronet to his crown, and bend
    The dukedom yet unbowed (alas, poor Milan!)
    To most ignoble stooping

MIRANDA: O the heavens!

PROSPERO: Mark his condition, and th' event; then tell me   117
    If this might be a brother.

MIRANDA: I should sin
    To think but nobly of my grandmother.
    Good wombs have borne bad sons.

PROSPERO: Now the condition.
    This King of Naples, being an enemy
    To me inveterate, hearkens my brother's suit;
    Which was, that he, in lieu o' th' premises   123
    Of homage and I know not how much tribute,
    Should presently extirpate me and mine   125
    Out of the dukedom and confer fair Milan,
    With all the honors, on my brother. Whereon,
    A treacherous army levied, one midnight
    Fated to th' purpose, did Antonio open   129
    The gates of Milan; and i' th' dead of darkness,
    The ministers for th' purpose hurrièd thence   131
    Me and thy crying self.

MIRANDA: Alack, for pity!
    I, not rememb'ring how I cried out then,
    Will cry it o'er again; it is a hint   134
    That wrings mine eyes to't.   135

PROSPERO: Hear a little further,
    And then I'll bring thee to the present business
    Which now's upon's; without the which this story
    Were most impertinent.   138

---

109 *Absolute Milan,* Duke of Milan in fact.   **111** *confederates,* joins in league with.   **112** *dry,* thirsty, eager.   **117** *condition,* pact; *event,* outcome.   **123** *in lieu o' th' premises,* in return for the guarantees.   **125** *presently,* immediately; *extirpate,* remove (accent second syllable).   **129** *Fated,* devoted.   **131** *ministers,* agents.   **134** *hint,* occasion.   **135** *wrings,* constrains.   **138** *impertinent,* irrelevant.

MIRANDA: Wherefore did they not
  That hour destroy us?
PROSPERO: Well demanded, wench.
  My tale provokes that question. Dear, they durst not,
  So dear the love my people bore me; nor set
  A mark so bloody on the business; but
  With colors fairer painted their foul ends.
  In few, they hurried us aboard a bark,   **144**
  Bore us some leagues to sea; where they prepared
  A rotten carcass of a butt, not rigged,   **146**
  Nor tackle, sail, nor mast; the very rats
  Instinctively have quit it. There they hoist us,
  To cry to th' sea that roared to us; to sigh
  To th' winds, whose pity, sighing back again,
  Did us but loving wrong.
MIRANDA: Alack, what trouble
  Was I then to you!
PROSPERO: O, a cherubin
  Thou wast that did preserve me! Thou didst smile,
  Infusèd with a fortitude from heaven,
  When I have decked the sea with drops full salt,
  Under my burden groaned: which raised in me
  An undergoing stomach, to bear up   **157**
  Against what should ensue.
MIRANDA: How came we ashore?
PROSPERO: By providence divine.
  Some food we had, and some fresh water, that
  A noble Neapolitan, Gonzalo,
  Out of his charity, who being then appointed
  Master of this design, did give us, with
  Rich garments, linens, stuffs, and necessaries
  Which since have steaded much. So, of his gentleness,   **165**
  Knowing I loved my books, he furnished me
  From mine own library with volumes that
  I prize above my dukedom.
MIRANDA: Would I might
  But ever see that man!
PROSPERO: Now I arise.
  Sit still, and hear the last of our sea-sorrow.
  Here in this island we arrived; and here
  Have I, thy schoolmaster, made thee more profit   **172**

---

144 *few,* few words. **146** *butt,* tub. **157** *undergoing stomach,* resolution to endure.
165 *steaded,* been of use. **172** *more profit,* profit more.

Than other princess can, that have more time 173
For vainer hours, and tutors not so careful.
MIRANDA: Heavens thank for for't! And now I pray you, 'sir,—
For still 'tis beating in my mind,—your reason
For raising this sea-storm?
PROSPERO: Know thus far forth.
By accident most strange, bountiful Fortune
(Now, my dear lady) hath mine enemies
Brought to this shore; and by my prescience
I find my zenith doth depend upon 181
A most auspicious star, whose influence
If now I court not, but omit, my fortunes 183
Will ever after droop. Here cease more questions.
Thou art inclined to sleep. 'Tis a good dulness,
And give it way. I know thou canst not choose.

(Miranda sleeps)

Come away, servant, come! I am ready now. 187
Approach, my Ariel: come!

(Enter Ariel)

ARIEL: All hail, great master! Grave sir, hail! I come
To answer thy best pleasure; be't to fly,
To swim, to dive into the fire, to ride
On the curled clouds. To thy strong bidding task 192
Ariel and all his quality. 193
PROSPERO: Hast thou, spirit,
Performed to point the tempest that I bade thee? 194
ARIEL: To every article.
I boarded the King's ship: now on the beak, 196
Now in the waist, the deck, in every cabin, 197
I flamed amazement: sometime I'ld divide 198
And burn in many places; on the topmast,
The yards, and boresprit would I flame distinctly, 200
Then meet and join. Jove's lightnings, the precursors
O' th' dreadful thunderclaps, more momentary
And sight-outrunning were not. The fire and cracks
Of sulphurous roaring the most mighty Neptune
Seem to besiege and make his bold waves tremble;
Yea, his dread trident shake.

173 *princess,* princesses.   181 *zenith,* apex of fortune.   183 *omit,* neglect.   187 *Come away,* come here.   192 *task,* supply "come".   193 *quality,* cohorts (Ariel is leader of a band of elemental spirits).   194 *to point,* in detail.   196 *beak,* prow.   197 *waist,* middle; *deck,* poop.   198 *flamed amazement,* struck terror by appearing as (St Elmo's) fire.   200 *boresprit,* bowsprit; *distinctly,* in different places.

PROSPERO: My brave spirit!
Who was so firm, so constant, that this coil   207
Would not infect his reason?
ARIEL: Not a soul
But felt a fever of the mad and played   209
Some tricks of desperation. All but mariners
Plunged in the foaming brine and quit the vessel;
Then all afire with me the King's son Ferdinand,   212
With hair up-staring (then like reeds; not hair),   213
Was the first man that leapt; cried 'Hell is empty,
And all the devils are here!'
PROSPERO: Why, that's my spirit!
But was not this nigh shore?
ARIEL: Close by, my master.
PROSPERO: But are they, Ariel, safe?
ARIEL: Not a hair perished.
On their sustaining garments not a blemish,   218
But fresher than before; and as thou bad'st me,
In troops I have dispersed them 'bout the isle.
The King's son have I landed by himself,
Whom I left cooling of the air with sighs
In an odd angle of the isle, and sitting,
His arms in this sad knot.   224
PROSPERO: Of the King's ship
The mariners say how thou hast disposed,
And all the rest o' th' fleet.
ARIEL: Safely in harbor
Is the King's ship; in the deep nook where once
Thou call'dst me up at midnight to fetch dew
From the still-vexed Bermoothes, there she's hid;   229
The mariners all under hatches stowed,
Who, with a charm joined to their suff'red labor,   231
I have left asleep; and for the rest o' th' fleet,
Which I dispersed, they all have met again,
And are upon the Mediterranean flote   234
Bound sadly home for Naples,
Supposing that they saw the King's ship wracked
And his great person perish.
PROSPERO: Ariel, thy charge

---

207 *coil,* uproar.   **209** *of the mad,* such as madmen have.   **212** *afire with me,* (refers either to the vessel or to Ferdinand, depending on the punctuation; F suggests the latter).   **213** *up-staring,* standing on end.   **218** *sustaining,* buoying them up in the water.   **224** *this,* illustrated by a gesture. **229** *still-vexed Bermoothes,* constantly agitated Bermudas.   **231** *suff'red,* undergone.   **234** *flote,* sea.

Exactly is performed; but there's more work.
What is the time o' the' day?

ARIEL: Past the mid season.   239

PROSPERO: At least two glasses. The time 'twixt six and now   240
Must by us both be spent most preciously.

ARIEL: Is there more toil? Since thou dost give me pains,
Let me remember thee what thou hast promised,   243
Which is not yet performed me.

PROSPERO: How now? moody?
What is't thou canst demand?

ARIEL: My liberty.

PROSPERO: Before the time be out? No more!   246

ARIEL: I prithee,
Remember I have done thee worthy service,
Told thee no lies, made no mistakings, served
Without or grudge or grumblings. Thou did promise
To bate me a full year.   250

PROSPERO: Dost thou forget
From what a torment I did free thee?

ARIEL: No.

PROSPERO: Thou dost; and think'st it much to tread the ooze
Of the salt deep,
To run upon the sharp wind of the North,
To do me business in the veins o' th' earth   255
When it is baked with frost.   256

ARIEL: I do not, sir.

PROSPERO: Thou liest, malignant thing! Hast thou forgot
The foul witch Sycorax, who with age and envy   258
Was grown into a hoop? Hast thou forgot her?

ARIEL: No, sir.

PROSPERO: Thou hast. Where was she born? Speak!
Tell me!

ARIEL: Sir, in Argier.   261

PROSPERO: O, was she so? I must
Once in a month recount what thou hast been,
Which thou forget'st. This damned witch Sycorax,
For mischiefs manifold, and sorceries terrible
To enter human hearing, from Argier,
Thou know'st, was banished. For one thing she did   266
They would not take her life. Is not this true?

239 *mid season,* noon.   **240** *glasses,* hours.   **243** *remember,* remind.   **246** *time,* period of service.
250 *bate me,* shorten my term of service.   **255** *veins,* streams.   **256** *baked,* hardened.
258 *Sycorax,* (name not found elsewhere; usually connected with Greek *'sys',* sow, and *'korax',* which
means both raven—cf. 1.322—and curved, hence perhaps *hoop*); *envy,* malice.   **261** *Argier,* Algiers.
266 *one thing she did,* being pregnant, her sentence was commuted from death to exile.

ARIEL: Ay, sir.

PROSPERO: This blue-eyed hag was hither brought with child
And here was left by th' sailors. Thou, my slave,
As thou report'st thyself, wast then her servant;
And, for thou wast a spirit too delicate
To act her earthy and abhorred commands,
Refusing her grand hests, she did confine thee,　　274
By help of her more potent ministers,
And in her most unmitigable rage,
Into a cloven pine; within which rift
Imprisoned thou didst painfully remain
A dozen years; within which space she died
And left thee there, where thou didst vent thy groans
As fast as millwheels strike. Then was this island　　281
(Save for the son that she did litter here,
A freckled whelp, hag-born) not honored with
A human shape.

ARIEL:　　　　　　　Yes, Caliban her son.

PROSPERO: Dull thing, I say so: he, that Caliban
Whom now I keep in service. Thou best know'st
What torment I did find thee in: thy groans
Did make wolves howl and penetrate the breasts
Of ever-angry bears. It was a torment
To lay upon the damned, which Sycorax
Could not again undo. It was mine art,
When I arrived and heard thee, that made gape
The pine, and let thee out.

ARIEL:　　　　　　　　I thank thee, master.

PROSPERO: If thou more murmur'st, I will rend an oak
And peg thee in his knotty entrails till　　295
Thou hast howled away twelve winters.　　296

ARIEL:　　　　　　　　　Pardon, master.
I will be correspondent to command　　297
And do my spriting gently.　　298

PROSPERO:　　　　　　Do so; and after two days
I will discharge thee.

ARIEL:　　　　　　That's my noble master!
What shall I do? Say what? What shall I do?

PROSPERO: Go make thyself like a nymph o' th' sea. Be subject
To no sight but thine and mine; invisible
To every eyeball else. Go take this shape
And hither come in't. Go! Hence with diligence!

274 *hests,* commands.　281 *millwheels,* i.e., the clappers on the millwheels.　295 *his,* its.
296 *twelve,* the same length of time that Ariel has been released.　297 *correspondent,* obedient.
298 *spriting gently,* office as a spirit graciously.

(Exit Ariel)

    Awake, dear heart, awake! Thou hast slept well.
    Awake!

MIRANDA: The strangeness of your story put
    Heaviness in me.

PROSPERO: Shake it off. Come on.
    We'll visit Caliban, my slave, who never
    Yields us kind answer.

MIRANDA: 'Tis a villain, sir,
    I do not love to look on.

PROSPERO: But as 'tis,
    We cannot miss him: he does make our fire,   311
    Fetch in our wood, and serves in offices
    That profit us. What, ho! slave! Caliban!
    Thou earth, thou! Speak!

CALIBAN *(within):*   There's wood enough within.

PROSPERO: Come forth, I say! There's other business for thee.
    Come, thou tortoise! When?   316

(Enter Ariel like a water nymph)

    Fine apparition! My quaint Ariel,   317
    Hark in thine ear.

ARIEL: My lord, it shall be done.   *(Exit)*

PROSPERO: Thou poisonous slave, got by the devil himself
    Upon thy wicked dam, come forth!

(Enter Caliban)

CALIBAN: As wicked dew as e'er my mother brushed
    With raven's feather from unwholesome fen
    Drop on you both! A south-west blow on ye
    And blister you all o'er!

PROSPERO: For this, be sure, to-night thou shalt have cramps,
    Side-stitches that shall pen thy breath up; urchins   326
    Shall, for that vast of night that they may work,   327
    All exercise on thee; thou shalt be pinched
    As thick as honeycomb, each pinch more stinging
    Than bees that made 'em.

CALIBAN: I must eat my dinner.
    This island's mine by Sycorax my mother,
    Which thou tak'st from me. When thou cam'st first,
    Thou strok'st me and made much of me; wouldst give me
    Water with berries in't; and teach me how

---

311 *miss,* do without.   **316** *When,* expression of impatience.   **317** *quaint,* ingenious.   **326** *ur-chins,* hedgehogs (i.e., goblins in that shape).   **327** *vast,* void; *that they may work,* referring to the belief that malignant spirits had power only during darkness.

To name the bigger light, and how the less,
That burn by day and night; and then I loved thee
And showed thee all the qualities o' th' isle,   337
The fresh springs, brine-pits, barren place and fertile.
Cursed be I that did so! All the charms
Of Sycorax—toads, beetles, bats, light on you!
For I am all the subjects that you have,
Which first was mine own king; and here you sty me
In this hard rock, whiles you do keep from me
The rest o' th' island.

PROSPERO: Thou most lying slave,
Whom stripes may move, not kindness! I have used thee   345
(Filth as thou art) with humane care, and lodged thee
In mine own cell till thou didst seek to violate
The honor of my child.

CALIBAN: O ho, O ho! Wouldn't had been done!
Thou didst prevent me; I had peopled else
This isle with Calibans.

MIRANDA: Abhorrèd slave,   351
Which any print of goodness wilt not take,
Being capable of all ill! I pitied thee,
Took pains to make thee speak, taught thee each hour
One thing or other: when thou didst not, savage,
Know thine own meaning, but wouldst gabble like
A thing most brutish, I endowed thy purposes   357
With words that made them known. But thy vile race,   358
Though thou didst learn, had that in't which good natures   359
Could not abide to be with; therefore wast thou
Deservedly confined into this rock, who hadst
Deserved more than a prison.

CALIBAN: You taught me language, and my profit on't
Is, I know how to curse. The red plague rid you   364
For learning me your language!

PROSPERO: Hag-seed, hence!
Fetch us in fuel; and be quick, thou'rt best,   366
To answer other business. Shrug'st thou, malice?
If thou neglect'st or dost unwillingly
What I command, I'll rack thee with old cramps,   369
Fill all thy bones with aches, make thee roar   370
That beasts shall tremble at thy din.

CALIBAN: No, pray thee.

---

337 *qualities,* resources. **345** *stripes,* lashes. **351** *Miranda,* so F; some editors have given the speech to Prospero. **357** *purposes,* meanings. **358** *race,* nature. **359** *good natures,* natural virtues. **364** *red plague,* bubonic plague; *rid,* destroy. **366** *thou'rt best,* you'd be well advised. **369** *old,* i.e., such as old people have. **370** *aches,* pronounced "aitches."

(Aside)

    I must obey. His art is of such pow'r
    It would control my dam's god, Setebos,
    And make a vassal of him.

PROSPERO: So, slave; hence!

(Exit Caliban)

(Enter Ferdinand; and Ariel [invisible], playing and singing)

ARIEL'S SONG.

    Come unto these yellow sands,
        And then take hands.
    Curtsied when you have and kissed,
        The wild waves whist,
        Foot it featly here and there;
    And, sweet sprites, the burden bear.
        Hark, hark!
Burden, dispersedly. Bowgh, wawgh!
    The watchdogs bark.
Burden, dispersedly. Bowgh, wawgh!
    Hark, hark! I hear
    The strain of strutting chanticleer
        Cry cock-a-diddle-dowe.

FERDINAND: Where should this music be! I' th' air or th' earth?
    It sounds no more; and sure it waits upon
    Some god o' th' island. Sitting on a bank,
    Weeping again the King my father's wrack,
    This music crept by me upon the waters,
    Allaying both their fury and my passion
    With its sweet air. Thence I have followed it,
    Or it hath drawn me rather; but 'tis gone.
    No, it begins again.

ARIEL'S SONG.

    Full fathom five thy father lies;
        Of his bones are coral made;
    Those are pearls that were his eyes;
        Nothing of him that doth fade
        But doth suffer a sea-change
        Into something rich and strange.
    Sea nymphs hourly ring his knell:
Burden.   Ding-dong.
    Hark! now I hear them—Ding-dong bell.

378 *whist,* being hushed.   **379** *featly,* nimbly.   **380** *burden,* undersong, refrain.   **393** *passion,* lamentation.

FERDINAND: The ditty does remember my drowned father.   406
This is no mortal business, nor no sound
That the earth owes. I hear it now above me.   408
PROSPERO: The fringèd curtains of thine eye advance   409
And say what thou seest yond.
MIRANDA: What is't? a spirit?
Lord, how it looks about! Believe me, sir,
It carries a brave form. But 'tis a spirit.
PROSPERO: No, wench: it eats, and sleeps, and hath such
     senses
As we have, such. This gallant which thou seest
Was in the wrack; and, but he's something stained   415
With grief (that's beauty's canker), thou mightst call him
A goodly person. He hath lost his fellows
And strays about to find 'em.
MIRANDA: I might call him
A thing divine; for nothing natural
I ever saw so noble.
PROSPERO (aside): It goes on, I see,
As my soul prompts it. Spirit, fine spirit, I'll free thee   421
Within two days for this.
FERDINAND: Most sure, the goddess   422
On whom these airs attend! Vouchsafe my prayer
May know if you remain upon this island,   424
And that you will some good instruction give
How I may bear me here. My prime request,   426
Which I do last pronounce, is (O you wonder!)
If you be maid or no?
MIRANDA: No wonder, sir,
But certainly a maid.
FERDINAND: My language? Heavens!
I am the best of them that speak this speech,
Were I but where 'tis spoken.
PROSPERO: How? the best?
What wert thou if the King of Naples heard thee?
FERDINAND: A single thing, as I am now, that wonders   433
To hear thee speak of Naples. He does hear me;
And that he does I weep. Myself am Naples,   435
Who with mine eyes, never since at ebb, beheld
The King my father wracked.
MIRANDA: Alack, for mercy!

---

406 *remember*, allude to.   **408** *owes*, owns.   **409** *advance*, raise.   **415** *stained*, disfigured.
421 *prompts*, would like.   **422** *Most sure*, this is certainly.   **424** *remain*, dwell.   **426** *bear me*,
conduct myself.   **433** *single*, (1) solitary, (2) weak or helpless.   **435** *Naples*, King of Naples.

FERDINAND: Yes, faith, and all his lords, the Duke of Milan
  And his brave son being twain.   **439**
PROSPERO *(aside):*   The Duke of Milan
  And his more braver daughter could control thee,   **440**
  If now 'twere fit to do't. At the first sight
  They have changed eyes. Delicate Ariel,   **442**
  I'll set thee free for this.—A word, good sir.
  I fear you have done yourself some wrong. A word!   **444**
MIRANDA: Why speaks my father so ungently? This
  Is the third man that e'er I saw; the first
  That e'er I sighed for. Pity move my father
  To be inclined my way!
FERDINAND: O, if a virgin,
  And your affection not gone forth, I'll make you
  The Queen of Naples.
PROSPERO: Soft, sir! one word more.

(Aside)

  They are both in either's pow'rs. But this swift business
  I must uneasy make, lest too light winning
  Make the prize light.—One word more! I charge thee
  That thou attend me. Thou dost here usurp
  The name thou ow'st not, and hast put thyself   **455**
  Upon this island as a spy, to win it
  From me, the lord on't.
FERDINAND: No, as I am a man!
MIRANDA: There's nothing ill can dwell in such a temple.
  If the ill spirit have so fair a house,
  Good things will strive to dwell with't.
PROSPERO: Follow me.—
  Speak not you for him; he's a traitor.—Come!
  I'll manacle thy neck and feet together;
  Sea water shalt thou drink; thy food shall be
  The fresh-brook mussels, withered roots, and husks
  Wherein the acorn cradled. Follow!
FERDINAND: No.
  I will resist such entertainment till   **466**
  Mine enemy has more pow'r.

(He draws, and is charmed from moving)

439 *son,* Antonio's son is not elsewhere mentioned.   **440** *control,* refute.   **442** *changed eyes,*
exchanged love looks.   **444** *done . . . wrong,* told a lie.   **455** *ow'st,* ownest.   **466** *entertainment,*
treatment.

MIRANDA: O dear father,
Make not too rash a trial of him, for   **468**
He's gentle, and not fearful.   **469**
PROSPERO: What, I say,
My foot my tutor?—Put thy sword up, traitor!   **470**
Who mak'st a show but dar'st not strike, thy conscience
Is so possessed with guilt. Come, from thy ward!   **472**
For I can here disarm thee with this stick
And make thy weapon drop.
MIRANDA: Beseech you, father!
PROSPERO: Hence! Hang not on my garments.
MIRANDA: Sir, have pity.
I'll be his surety.
PROSPERO: Silence! One word more
Shall make me chide thee, if not hate thee. What,
An advocate for an impostor? Hush!
Thou think'st there is no more such shapes as he,
Having seen but him and Caliban. Foolish wench!
To th' most of men this is a Caliban,
And they to him are angels.
MIRANDA: My affections   **482**
Are then most humble. I have no ambition
To see a goodlier man.
PROSPERO: Come on, obey!   **484**
Thy nerves are in their infancy again   **485**
And have no vigor in them.
FERDINAND: So they are.
My spirits, as in a dream, are all bound up.
My father's loss, the weakness which I feel,
The wrack of all my friends, nor this man's threats
To whom I am subdued, are but light to me,
Might I but through my prison once a day
Behold this maid. All corners else o' th' earth
Let liberty make use of. Space enough
Have I in such a prison.
PROSPERO *(aside):* It works. *(to Ferdinand)* Come on.—
Thou hast done well, fine Ariel!
(To Ferdinand)   Follow me.

(To Ariel)

Hark what thou else shalt do me.

468 *trial,* judgment.   469 *gentle,* noble; *fearful,* cowardly.   470 *My . . . tutor,* i.e., instructed by
my underling.   472 *ward,* fighting posture.   482 *affections,* inclinations.   484 *obey,* follow.
485 *nerves,* sinews, tendons.

MIRANDA: Be of comfort.
My father's of a better nature, sir,
Than he appears by speech. This is unwonted
Which now came from him.
PROSPERO: Thou shalt be as free
As mountain winds; but then exactly do   500
All points of my command.
ARIEL: To th' syllable.
PROSPERO: Come, follow.—Speak not for him.   *(Exeunt)*

Act II

Scene I

Another part of the island. Enter Alonso, Sebastian, Antonio, Gonzalo, Adrian,
Francisco, and others.

GONZALO: Beseech you, sir, be merry. You have cause
   (So have we all) of joy; for our escape
   Is much beyond our loss. Our hint of woe   3
   Is common: every day some sailor's wife,
   The master of some merchant, and the merchant,   5
   Have just our theme of woe; but for the miracle,
   I mean our preservation, few in millions
   Can speak like us. Then wisely, good sir, weigh
   Our sorrow with our comfort.
ALONSO: Prithee peace.
SEBASTIAN: He receives comfort like cold porridge.   10
ANTONIO: The visitor will not give him o'er so.   11
SEBASTIAN: Look, he's winding up the watch of his wit; by and by it will
   strike.
GONZALO: Sir—
SEBASTIAN: One. Tell.   15
GONZALO: When every grief is entertained, that's offered 16
   Comes to th' entertainer—   17
SEBASTIAN: A dollar.
GONZALO: Dolor comes to him, indeed. You have spoken truer than you   19
   purposed.
SEBASTIAN: You have taken it wiselier than I meant you should.
GONZALO: Therefore, my lord—
ANTONIO: Fie, what a spendthrift is he of his tongue!   23

500 *then,* till then.   **3** *hint,* occasion.   **5** *master of some merchant,* master of a merchant ship;
the merchant, the owner of the ship.   **10** *porridge,* pun on *peace* (pease).   **11** *visitor,* spiritual
adviser; *give him o'er,* let him alone.   **15** *Tell,* count.   **16** *that's,* that which is.   **17** *entertainer,*
taken by Sebastian to mean "innkeeper."   **19** *Dolor,* grief (with pun on *dollar,* a continental coin).
23 *spendthrift,* Antonio labors the pun.

ALONSO: I prithee spare.

GONZALO: Well, I have done. But yet—

SEBASTIAN: He will be talking.

ANTONIO: Which, of he or Adrian, for a good wager, first begins to crow?

SEBASTIAN: The old cock.   28

ANTONIO: The cock'rel.   29

SEBASTIAN: Done! The wager?

ANTONIO: A laughter.   31

SEBASTIAN: A match!

ADRIAN: Though this island seem to be desert—

ANTONIO: Ha, ha, ha!

SEBASTIAN: So, you're paid.

ADRIAN: Uninhabitable and almost inaccessible—

SEBASTIAN: Yet—

ADRIAN: Yet—

ANTONIO: He could not miss't.

ADRIAN: It must needs be of subtle, tender, and delicate temperance.   40

ANTONIO: Temperance was a delicate wench.   41

SEBASTIAN: Ay, and a subtle, as he most learnedly delivered.

ADRIAN: The air breathes upon us here most sweetly.

SEBASTIAN: As if it had lungs, and rotten ones.

ANTONIO: Or as 'twere perfumed by a fen.

GONZALO: Here is everything advantageous to life.

ANTONIO: True; save means to live.

SEBASTIAN: Of that there's none, or little.

GONZALO: How lush and lusty the grass looks! how green!

ANTONIO: The ground indeed is tawny.

SEBASTIAN: With an eye of green in't.   51

ANTONIO: He misses not much.

SEBASTIAN: No; he doth but mistake the truth totally.

GONZALO: But the rarity of it is—which is indeed almost beyond
   credit—

SEBASTIAN: As many vouched rarities are.   56

GONZALO: That our garments, being, as they were, drenched in the sea,
   hold, notwithstanding, their freshness and gloss, being rather new-
   dyed than stained with salt water.

ANTONIO: If but one of his pockets could speak, would it not say he lies?

SEBASTIAN: Ay, or very falsely pocket up his report.

GONZALO: Methinks our garments are now as fresh as when we put them
   on first in Afric, at the marriage of the King's fair daughter Claribel
   to the King of Tunis.

---

28 *old cock,* i.e., Gonzalo.   29 *cock'rel,* i.e., Adrian.   31 *laughter,* the winner laughs.
40 *temperance,* climate.   41 *Temperance,* a girl's name.   51 *eye,* spot (or perhaps Gonzalo's eye).
56 *vouched rarities,* wonders guaranteed to be true.

SEBASTIAN: 'Twas a sweet marriage, and we prosper well in our
    return.

ADRIAN: Tunis was never graced before with such a paragon to their   66
    queen.

GONZALO: Not since widow Dido's time.   68

ANTONIO: Widow? A pox o' that! How came that 'widow' in? Widow
    Dido!

SEBASTIAN: What if he had said 'widower Aeneas' too? Good Lord, how
    you take it!

ADRIAN: 'Widow Dido,' said you? You make me study of that. She was
    of Carthage, not of Tunis.

GONZALO: This Tunis, sir, was Carthage.

ADRIAN: Carthage?

GONZALO: I assure you, Carthage.

ANTONIO: His word is more than the miraculous harp.   78

SEBASTIAN: He hath raised the wall and houses too.

ANTONIO: What impossible matter will he make easy next?

SEBASTIAN: I think he will carry this island home in his pocket and give
    it his son for an apple.

ANTONIO: And, sowing the kernels of it in the sea, bring forth more
    islands.

GONZALO: Ay!   85

ANTONIO: Why, in good time.

GONZALO: Sir, we were talking that our garments seem now as fresh as
    when we were at Tunis at the marriage of your daughter, who is now
    Queen.

ANTONIO: And the rarest that e'er came there.

SEBASTIAN: Bate, I beseech you, widow Dido.   91

ANTONIO: O, widow Dido? Ay, widow Dido!

GONZALO: Is not, sir, my doublet as fresh as the first day I wore it? I
    mean, in a sort.   94

ANTONIO: That 'sort' was well fished for.

GONZALO: When I wore it at your daughter's marriage.

ALONSO: You cram these words into mine ears against
    The stomach of my sense. Would I had never   98
    Married my daughter there! for, coming thence,
    My son is lost; and, in my rate, she too,   100
    Who is so far from Italy removed
    I ne'er again shall see her. O thou mine heir

---

66 *to,* for.   **68** *widow Dido,* Dido was the widow of Sychaeus; Aeneas was a widower, having lost his wife in the fall of Troy. The reasons for Antonio's amusement, if that is what it is, have not been explained.   **78** *miraculous harp,* of Amphion, which raised the walls of Thebes; Tunis and Carthage were near each other, but not the same city.   **85** *Ay,* F reads "I"; this and Antonio's rejoinder have not been satisfactorily explained.   **91** *Bate,* except.   **94** *in a sort,* i.e., comparatively.   **98** *stomach . . . sense,* i.e., inclination of my mind.   **100** *rate,* opinion.

Of Naples and of Milan, what strange fish
Hath made his meal on thee?
FRANCISCO: Sir, he may live.
I saw him beat the surges under him
And ride upon their backs. He trod the water,
Whose enmity he flung aside, and breasted
The surge most swol'n that met him. His bold head
'Bove the contentious waves he kept, and oared
Himself with his good arms in lusty stroke
To th' shore, that o'er his wave-worn basis bowed,   111
As stooping to relieve him. I not doubt
He came alive to land.
ALONSO: No, no, he's gone.
SEBASTIAN: Sir, you may thank yourself for this great loss,
That would not bless our Europe with your daughter,
But rather loose her to an African,
Where she, at least, is banished from your eye
Who hath cause to wet the grief on't.
ALONSO: Prithee peace.
SEBASTIAN: You were kneeled to and importuned otherwise
By all of us; and the fair soul herself
Weighed, between loathness and obedience, at
Which end o' th' beam should bow. We have lost your son,   122
I fear, for ever. Milan and Naples have
Moe widows in them of this business' making   124
Than we bring men to comfort them:
The fault's your own.
ALONSO: So is the dear'st o' th' loss.   126
GONZALO: My Lord Sebastian,
The truth you speak doth lack some gentleness,
And time to speak it in. You rub the sore
When you should bring the plaster.
SEBASTIAN: Very well.
ANTONIO: And most chirurgeonly.   131
GONZALO: It is foul weather in us all, good sir,
When you are cloudy.
SEBASTIAN: Foul weather?
ANTONIO: Very foul.
GONZALO: Had I plantation of this isle, my lord—   134
ANTONIO: He'd sow't with nettle seed.
SEBASTIAN: Or docks, or mallows.

---

111 *his,* its; *basis,* i.e., the sand.   122 *the fair . . . bow,* the sense is that Claribel hated the marriage,
and only obedience to her father turned the scale.   124 *Moe,* more.   126 *dear'st,* heaviest.
131 *chirurgeonly,* like a surgeon.   134 *plantation,* colonization (taken by Antonio in its other sense).

GONZALO: And were the king on't, what would I do?

SEBASTIAN: Scape being drunk for want of wine.

GONZALO: I' th' commonwealth I would by contraries   138
    Execute all things; for no kind of traffic   139
    Would I admit; no name of magistrate;
    Letters should not be known; riches, poverty,
    And use of service, none; contract, succession,   142
    Bourn, bound of land, tilth, vineyard, none;   143
    No use of metal, corn, or wine, or oil;
    No occupation; all men idle, all;
    And women too, but innocent and pure;
    No sovereignty.

SEBASTIAN: Yet he would be king on't.

ANTONIO: The latter end of his commonwealth forgets the beginning.

GONZALO: All things in common nature should produce
    Without sweat or endeavor. Treason, felony,
    Sword, pike, knife, gun, or need of any engine   151
    Would I not have; but nature should bring forth,
    Of it own kind, all foison, all abundance,   153
    To feed my innocent people.

SEBASTIAN: No marrying 'mong his subjects?

ANTONIO: None, man, all idle—whores and knaves.

GONZALO: I would with such perfection govern, sir,
    T' excel the golden age.

SEBASTIAN: Save his Majesty!

ANTONIO: Long live Gonzalo!

GONZALO: And—do you mark me, sir?

ALONSO: Prithee no more. Thou dost talk nothing to me.

GONZALO: I do well believe your Highness; and did it to minister occasion to these gentlemen, who are of such sensible and nimble lungs   162
that they always use to laugh at nothing.

ANTONIO: 'Twas you we laughed at.

GONZALO: Who in this kind of merry fooling am nothing to you: so you may continue, and laugh at nothing still.

ANTONIO: What a blow was there given!

SEBASTIAN: An it had not fall'n flatlong.   168

GONZALO: You are gentlemen of brave mettle; you would lift the moon out of her sphere if she would continue in it five weeks without changing.

(Enter Ariel, [invisible,] playing solemn music)

---

138 *by contraries*, in contrast to usual customs.   **139** *traffic*, trade.   **142** *use of service*, having a servant class; *succession*, inheritance.   **143** *Bourn*, limits of private property.   **151** *engine*, weapon.   **153** *it*, its; *foison*, abundance.   **162** *minister occasion*, afford opportunity.   **162** *sensible*, sensitive.   **168** *An*, if; *flatlong*, struck with the flat of a sword.

SEBASTIAN: We would so, and then go a-batfowling.   172
ANTONIO: Nay, good my lord, be not angry.
GONZALO: No, I warrant you: I will not adventure my discretion so   174
    weakly. Will you laugh me asleep, for I am very heavy?
ANTONIO: Go sleep, and hear us.

(All sleep except Alonso, Sebastian, and Antonio)

ALONSO: What, all so soon asleep? I wish mine eyes
    Would, with themselves, shut up my thoughts. I find
    They are inclined to do so.
SEBASTIAN: Please you, sir,
    Do not omit the heavy offer of it.   180
    It seldom visits sorrow; when it doth,
    It is a comforter.
ANTONIO: We two, my lord,
    Will guard your person while you take your rest,
    And watch your safety.
ALONSO: Thank you. Wondrous heavy.

(Alonso sleeps. Exit Ariel)

SEBASTIAN: What a strange drowsiness possesses them!
ANTONIO: It is the quality o' th' climate.
SEBASTIAN: Why
    Doth it not then our eyelids sink? I find not
    Myself disposed to sleep.
ANTONIO: Nor I: my spirits are nimble.
    They fell together all, as by consent.
    They dropped as by a thunder-stroke. What might,
    Worthy Sebastian—O, what might?—No more!
    And yet methinks I see it in thy face,
    What thou shouldst be. Th' occasion speaks thee, and   193
    My strong imagination sees a crown
    Dropping upon thy head.
SEBASTIAN: What? Art thou waking?
ANTONIO: Do you not hear me speak?
SEBASTIAN: I do; and surely
    It is a sleepy language, and thou speak'st
    Out of thy sleep. What is it thou didst say?
    This is a strange repose, to be asleep

172 *a-batfowling,* hunting birds with sticks "bats" at night (using the moon for a lantern).
174 *adventure,* risk (Gonzalo is saying, very politely, that their wit is too feeble for him to take offense
at it).   **180** *omit,* neglect; *heavy offer,* opportunity its heaviness affords.   **193** *speaks,* speaks to,
summons.

With eyes wide open; standing, speaking, moving,
And yet so fast asleep.
ANTONIO: Noble Sebastian,
Thou let'st thy fortune sleep—die, rather; wink'st   202
Whiles thou art waking.
SEBASTIAN: Thou dost snore distinctly;
There's meaning in thy snores.
ANTONIO: I am more serious than my custom. You
Must be so too, if heed me; which to do
Trebles thee o'er.   207
SEBASTIAN: Well, I am standing water.
ANTONIO: I'll teach you how to flow.
SEBASTIAN: Do so. To ebb
Hereditary sloth instructs me.   209
ANTONIO: O,
If you but knew how you the purpose cherish   210
Whiles thus you mock it! how, in stripping it,
You more invest it! Ebbing men indeed   212
(Most often) do so near the bottom run
By their own fear or sloth.
SEBASTIAN: Prithee say on.
The setting of thine eye and cheek proclaim
A matter from thee; and a birth, indeed,
Which throes thee much to yield.   217
ANTONIO: Thus, sir:
Although this lord of weak remembrance, this   218
Who shall be of as little memory   219
When he is earthed, hath here almost persuaded   220
(For he's a spirit of persuasion, only
Professes to persuade) the King his son's alive,   222
'Tis as impossible that he's undrowned
As he that sleeps here swims.
SEBASTIAN: I have no hope
That he's undrowned.
ANTONIO: O, out of that no hope
What great hope have you! No hope that way is
Another way so high a hope that even
Ambition cannot pierce a wink beyond,   228
But doubt discovery there. Will you grant with me   229
That Ferdinand is drowned?

---

202 *wink'st,* dost sleep.   **207** *Trebles thee o'er,* increases thy status threefold; *standing water,* at slack tide.   **209** *Hereditary sloth,* natural laziness.   **210** *cherish,* enrich.   **212** *invest,* clothe. **217** *throes thee much,* costs thee much pain, like a birth.   **218** *remembrance,* memory.   **219** *of . . . memory,* as little remembered.   **220** *earthed,* buried.   **222** *Professes,* has the function. **228** *wink,* glimpse.   **229** *doubt discovery there,* is uncertain of seeing accurately.

SEBASTIAN: He's gone.

ANTONIO: Then tell me,
Who's the next heir of Naples?

SEBASTIAN: Claribel.

ANTONIO: She that is Queen of Tunis; she that dwells
 Ten leagues beyond man's life; she that from Naples   233
 Can have no note, unless the sun were post—   234
 The man i' th' moon's too slow—till new-born chins
 Be rough and razorable; she that from whom
 We all were sea-swallowed, though some cast again,   237
 And, by that destiny, to perform an act
 Whereof what's past is prologue, what to come,
 In yours and my discharge.   240

SEBASTIAN: What stuff is this? How say you?
 'Tis true my brother's daughter's Queen of Tunis;
 So is she heir of Naples; 'twixt which regions
 There is some space.

ANTONIO: A space whose ev'ry cubit
 Seems to cry out 'How shall that Claribel
 Measure us back to Naples? Keep in Tunis,   245
 And let Sebastian wake!' Say this were death
 That now hath seized them, why, they were no worse
 Than now they are. There be that can rule Naples
 As well as he that sleeps; lords that can prate
 As amply and unnecessarily
 As this Gonzalo; I myself could make
 A chough of as deep chat. O, that you bore   252
 The mind that I do! What a sleep were this
 For your advancement! Do you understand me?

SEBASTIAN: Methinks I do.

ANTONIO: And how does your content   255
 Tender your own good fortune?

SEBASTIAN: I remember
 You did supplant your brother Prospero.

ANTONIO: True.
 And look how well my garments sit upon me,
 Much feater than before. My brother's servants   259
 Were then my fellows; now they are my men.   260

SEBASTIAN: But, for your conscience—

ANTONIO: Ay, sir, where lies that? If 'twere a kibe,   262

---

233 *Ten . . . life,* i.e., thirty miles from nowhere. **234** *note,* communication; *post,* messenger.
237 *cast,* thrown up (with a suggestion of its theatrical meaning which introduces the next metaphor).
240 *discharge,* business. **245** *us,* i.e., the cubits. **252** *chough,* jackdaw (a bird sometimes taught
to speak). **255** *content Tender,* inclination estimate. **259** *feater,* more suitable. **260** *fellows,*
equals; *men,* servants. **262** *kibe,* chilblain.

'Twould put me to my slipper; but I feel not   263
This deity in my bosom. Twenty consciences
That stand 'twixt me and Milan, candied be they   265
And melt, ere they molest! Here lies your brother,
No better than the earth he lies upon
If he were that which now he's like—that's dead;
Whom I with this obedient steel (three inches of it)
Can lay to bed for ever; whiles you, doing thus,
To the perpetual wink for aye might put   271
This ancient morsel, this Sir Prudence, who
Should not upbraid our course. For all the rest,
They'll take suggestion as a cat laps milk;
They'll tell the clock to any business that   275
We say befits the hour.
SEBASTIAN: Thy case, dear friend,
  Shall be my precedent. As thou got'st Milan,
  I'll come by Naples. Draw thy sword. One stroke
  Shall free thee from the tribute which thou payest,
  And I the King shall love thee.
ANTONIO: Draw together;
  And when I rear my hand, do you the like,
  To fall it on Gonzalo.   282

(They draw)

SEBASTIAN: O, but one word!

(Enter Ariel, [invisible,] with music and song)

ARIEL: My master through his art foresees the danger
  That you, his friend, are in, and sends me forth
  (For else his project dies) to keep them living.

(Sings in Gonzalo's ear)

> While you here do snoring lie,
> Open-eyed conspiracy
>   His time doth take.
> If of life you keep a care,
> Shake off slumber and beware.
>   Awake, awake!

ANTONIO: Then let us both be sudden.
GONZALO *(wakes):*   Now good angels
  Preserve the King!

263 *put me to,* make me wear.   265 *candied,* frozen.   271 *wink,* sleep.   275 *tell the clock,* answer
appropriately.   282 *fall it,* let it fall.

ALONSO: Why, how now?—Ho, awake!—Why are you drawn?
   Wherefore this ghastly looking?
GONZALO: What's the matter?
SEBASTIAN: Whiles we stood here securing your repose,   297
   Even now, we heard a hollow burst of bellowing
   Like bulls, or rather lions. Did't not wake you?
   It stuck mine ear most terribly.
ALONSO: I heard nothing.
ANTONIO: O, 'twas a din to fright a monster's ear,
   To make an earthquake! Sure it was the roar
   Of a whole herd of lions.
ALONSO: Heard you this, Gonzalo?
GONZALO: Upon mine honor, sir, I heard a humming,
   And that a strange one too, which did awake me.
   I shaked you, sir, and cried. As mine eyes opened,
   I saw their weapons drawn. There was a noise,
   That's verily. 'Tis best we stand upon our guard,
   Or that we quit this place. Let's draw our weapons.
ALONSO: Lead off this ground, and let's make further search
   For my poor son.
GONZALO: Heavens keep him from these beasts!
   For he is sure i' th' island.
ALONSO: Lead away.
ARIEL: Prospero my lord shall know what I have done.
   So, King, go safely on to seek thy son.   *(Exeunt)*

Act II

Scene II

A place near Prospero's cell. Enter Caliban with a burden of wood. A noise of thunder heard.

CALIBAN: All the infections that the sun sucks up
   From bogs, fens, flats, on Prosper fall, and make him
   By inchmeal a disease! His spirits hear me,   3
   And yet I needs must curse. But they'll nor pinch,   4
   Fright me with urchin-shows, pitch me i' th' mire,   5
   Nor lead me, like a firebrand, in the dark   6
   Out of my way, unless he bid 'em; but
   For every trifle are they set upon me;
   Sometime like apes that mow and chatter at me,   9
   And after bite me; then like hedgehogs which

---

297 *securing,* keeping watch over.   3 *By inchmeal,* inch by inch.   4 *nor,* neither.   5 *urchin-shows,* apparitions in the form of hedgehogs.   6 *like a firebrand,* in the form of a will-o'-the-wisp. 9 *mow,* make faces.

Lie tumbling in my barefoot way and mount
Their pricks at my footfall; sometime am I
All wound with adders, who with cloven tongues
Do hiss me into madness.
(Enter Trinculo)   Lo, now, lo!
Here comes a spirit of his, and to torment me
For bringing wood in slowly. I'll fall flat.
Perchance he will not mind me.

(Lies down)

TRINCULO: Here's neither bush nor shrub to bear off any weather at all,   18
and another storm brewing: I hear it sing i' the' wind. Yond same
black cloud, yond huge one, looks like a foul bombard that would   20
shed his liquor. If it should thunder as it did before, I know not
where to hide my head. Yond same cloud cannot choose but fall by
pailfuls. What have we here? a man or a fish? dead or alive? A fish:
he smells like a fish; a very ancient and fishlike smell; a kind of not
of the newest poor-John. A strange fish! Were I in England now, as   25
once I was, and had but this fish painted, not a holiday fool there   26
but would give a piece of silver. There would this monster make a
man: any strange beast there makes a man. When they will not give   28
a doit to relieve a lame beggar, they will lay out ten to see a dead   29
Indian. Legged like a man! and his fins like arms! Warm, o' my
troth! I do now let loose my opinion, hold it no longer: this is no
fish, but an islander, that hath lately suffered by a thunderbolt.
(Thunder) Alas, the storm is come again! My best way is to creep
under his gaberdine: there is no other shelter hereabout. Misery   34
acquaints a man with strange bed-fellows. I will here shroud till the
dregs of the storm be past.

(Creeps under Caliban's garment)

(Enter Stephano, singing [with a bottle in his hand])

STEPHANO: I shall no more to sea, to sea;
                        Here shall I die ashore.
This is a very scurvy tune to sing at a man's funeral. Well, here's my
comfort.

(Drinks)

The master, the swabber, the boatswain, and I,
   The gunner, and his mate,
Loved Mall, Meg, and Marian, and Margery,

18 *bear off,* ward off.   20 *bombard,* leather bottle; *his,* its.   25 *poor-John,* dried hake.
26 *painted,* i.e., on a signboard outside a booth at a fair.   28 *make a man,* also with sense of "make
a man's fortune."   29 *doit,* small coin.   34 *gaberdine,* cloak.

But none of us cared for Kate.
For she had a tongue with a tang,
Would cry to a sailor 'Go hang!'
She loved not the savor of tar nor of pitch;
Yet a tailor might scratch her where'er she did itch.
Then to sea, boys, and let her go hang!

This is a scurvy tune too; but here's my comfort.

(Drinks)

CALIBAN: Do not torment me! O!

STEPHANO: What's the matter? Have we devils here? Do you put tricks
upon's with savages and men of Inde, ha? I have not scaped drowning to be afeard now of your four legs; for it hath been said, 'As
proper a man as ever went on four legs cannot make him give
ground'; and it shall be said so again, while Stephano breathes at
nostrils.

CALIBAN: The spirit torments me. O!

STEPHANO: This is some monster of the isle, with four legs, who hath
got, as I take it, an ague. Where the devil should he learn our
language? I will give him some relief, if it be but for that. If I can
recover him, and keep him tame, and get to Naples with him, he's
a present for any emperor that ever trod on neat's leather.   63

CALIBAN: Do not torment me, prithee; I'll bring my wood home faster.

STEPHANO: He's in his fit now and does not talk after the wisest. He shall
taste of my bottle: if he have never drunk wine afore, it will go near
to remove his fit. If I can recover him and keep him tame, I will not
take too much for him; he shall pay for him that hath him, and that   68
soundly.

CALIBAN: Thou dost me yet but little hurt.
Thou wilt anon; I know it by thy trembling.   71
Now Prosper works upon thee.

STEPHANO: Come on your ways: open your mouth: here is that which
will give language to you, cat. Open your mouth. This will shake   74
your shaking, I can tell you, and that soundly. *(Gives Caliban drink)*
You cannot tell who's your friend. Open your chaps again.   76

TRINCULO: I should know that voice. It should be—but he is drowned;
and these are devils. O, defend me!

STEPHANO: Four legs and two voices—a most delicate monster! His
forward voice now is to speak well of his friend; his backward voice
is to utter foul speeches and to detract. If all the wine in my bottle
will recover him, I will help his ague. Come! *(Gives drink)* Amen!
I will pour some in thy other mouth.

---

63 *neat's leather,* cowhide.   **68** *not take too much,* i.e., take all I can get.   **71** *anon,* soon.
74 *cat,* alluding to the proverb "Liquor will make a cat talk".   **76** *chaps,* jaws.

TRINCULO: Stephano!

STEPHANO: Doth thy other mouth call me? Mercy, mercy! This is a devil,
and no monster. I will leave him; I have no long spoon.   86

TRINCULO: Stephano! If thou beest Stephano, touch me and speak to me;
for I am Trinculo—be not afeard—thy good friend Trinculo.

STEPHANO: If thou beest Trinculo, come forth. I'll pull thee by the lesser
legs. If any be Trinculo's legs, these are they. *(Draws him out from
under Caliban's garment)* Thou art very Trinculo indeed: how
cam'st thou to be the siege of this mooncalf? Can he vent Trinculos?   92

TRINCULO: I took him to be killed with a thunder-stroke. But art thou
not drowned, Stephano? I hope now thou art not drowned. Is the
storm overblown? I hid me under the dead mooncalf's gaberdine for
fear of the storm. And art thou living, Stephano? O Stephano, two
Neapolitans scaped!

STEPHANO: Prithee do not turn me about: my stomach is not constant.

CALIBAN *(aside)*: These be fine things, an if they be not sprites.   99
That's a brave god and bears celestial liquor.
I will kneel to him.

STEPHANO: How didst thou scape? How cam'st thou hither? Swear by
this bottle how thou cam'st hither. I escaped upon a butt of sack
which the sailors heaved o'erboard, by this bottle, which I made of
the bark of a tree with mine own hands since I was cast ashore.

CALIBAN: I'll swear upon that bottle to be thy true subject, for the liquor
is not earthly.

STEPHANO: Here! Swear then how thou escapedst.

TRINCULO: Swum ashore, man, like a duck. I can swim like a duck, I'll
be sworn.

STEPHANO: Here, kiss the book. *(Gives him drink)* Though thou canst   111
swim like a duck, thou art made like a goose.   112

TRINCULO: O Stephano, hast any more of this?

STEPHANO: The whole butt, man: my cellar is in a rock by th' seaside,
where my wine is hid. How now, moon-calf? How does thine ague?

CALIBAN: Hast thou not dropped from heaven?

STEPHANO: Out o' th' moon, I do assure thee. I was the Man i' th' Moon
when time was.   118

CALIBAN: I have seen thee in her, and I do adore thee.
My mistress showed me thee, and thy dog, and thy bush.

STEPHANO: Come, swear to that; kiss the book. I will furnish it anon with
new contents. Swear.

(Caliban drinks)

---

86 *spoon,* alluding to the proverb "He who sups with the devil must have a long spoon."   **92** *siege,*
excrement; *mooncalf,* monstrosity.   **99** *an if,* if.   **111** *book,* i.e., bottle.   **112** *like a goose,* i.e.,
with a long neck.   **118** *when time was,* once upon a time.

TRINCULO: By this good light, this is a very shallow monster! I afeard
of him? A very weak monster! The Man i' th' Moon? A most poor
credulous monster!—Well drawn, monster, in good sooth!

CALIBAN: I'll show thee every fertile inch o' th' island;
And I will kiss thy foot. I prithee be my god.

TRINCULO: By this light, a most perfidious and drunken monster! When's
god's asleep, he'll rob his bottle.

CALIBAN: I'll kiss thy foot. I'll swear myself thy subject.

STEPHANO: Come on then. Down, and swear!

TRINCULO: I shall laugh myself to death at this puppyheaded monster. A most scurvy monster! I could find in my heart to beat
him—

STEPHANO: Come, kiss.

TRINCULO: But that the poor monster's in drink. An abominable
monster!

CALIBAN: I'll show thee the best springs; I'll pluck thee berries;
I'll fish for thee, and get thee wood enough.
A plague upon the tyrant that I serve!
I'll bear him no more sticks, but follow thee,
Thou wondrous man.

TRINCULO: A most ridiculous monster, to make a wonder of a poor
drunkard!

CALIBAN: I prithee let me bring thee where crabs grow;   143
And I with my long nails will dig thee pignuts,   144
Show thee a jay's nest, and instruct thee how
To snare the nimble marmoset; I'll bring thee
To clust'ring filberts, and sometimes I'll get thee
Young scamels from the rock. Wilt thou go with me?   148

STEPHANO: I prithee now, lead the way without any more talking.
Trinculo, the King and all our company else being drowned, we will
inherit here. Here, bear my bottle. Fellow Trinculo, we'll fill him by 151
and by again.   152

(Caliban sings drunkenly)

CALIBAN: Farewell, master; farewell, farewell!

TRINCULO: A howling monster! a drunken monster!

CALIBAN: No more dams I'll make for fish,
        Nor fetch in firing
        At requiring,
        Nor scrape trenchering, nor wash dish.   158

---

143 *crabs,* crab apples.   **144** *pignuts,* peanuts.   **148** *scamels,* unexplained, but clearly either a
shellfish or a rock-nesting bird; perhaps a misprint for "seamels," sea mews.   **151** *inherit,* take
possession.   **152** *by and by,* soon.   **158** *trenchering,* trenchers, wooden plates.

'Ban, 'Ban, Ca—Caliban
Has a new master: get a new man.

Freedom, high-day! high-day, freedom! freedom, high-day, freedom!
STEPHANO: O brave monster! lead the way. *(Exeunt)*

Act III

Scene I

Before Prospero's cell. Enter Ferdinand, bearing a log.

FERDINAND: There be some sports are painful, and their labor	1
Delight in them sets off; some kinds of baseness	2
Are nobly undergone, and most poor matters	3
Point to rich ends. This my mean task	
Would be as heavy to me as odious, but	
The mistress which I serve quickens what's dead	6
And makes my labors pleasures. O, she is	
Ten times more gentle than her father's crabbèd;	
And he's composed of harshness! I must remove	
Some thousands of these logs and pile them up,	
Upon a sore injunction. My sweet mistress	11
Weeps when she sees me work, and says such baseness	
Had never like executor. I forget;	
But these sweet thoughts do even refresh my labors	
Most busy least, when I do it.	15

(Enter Miranda; and Prospero [behind, unseen])

MIRANDA: Alas, now pray you	
Work not so hard! I would the lightning had	
Burnt up those logs that you are enjoined to pile!	
Pray set it down and rest you. When this burns,	
'Twill weep for having wearied you. My father	19
Is hard at study: pray now rest yourself.	
He's safe for these three hours.	
FERDINAND: O most dear mistress,	
The sun will set before I shall discharge	
What I must strive to do.	
MIRANDA: If you'll sit down.	
I'll bear your logs the while. Pray give me that:	
I'll carry it to the pile.	
FERDINAND: No, precious creature:	

---

1 *painful,* strenuous.   **2** *sets off,* makes greater by contrast.   **3** *matters,* affairs.   **6** *quickens,*
brings to life.   **11** *sore injunction,* grievous command.   **15** *least,* i.e., least conscious of being busy
(F reads "lest").   **19** *weep,* i.e., exude resin.

I had rather crack my sinews, break my back,
Than you should such dishonor undergo
While I sit lazy by.

MIRANDA: It would become me
As well as it does you; and I should do it
With much more ease; for my good will is to it,
And yours it is against.

PROSPERO *(aside):*   Poor worm, thou art infected!
This visitation shows it.   32

MIRANDA: You look wearily.

FERDINAND: No, noble mistress: 'tis fresh morning with me
When you are by at night. I do beseech you,
Chiefly that I might set it in my prayers,
What is your name?

MIRANDA: Miranda. O my father,
I have broke your hest to say so!   37

FERDINAND: Admired Miranda!
Indeed the top of admiration, worth   38
What's dearest to the world! Full many a lady
I have eyed with best regard, and many a time   40
Th' harmony of their tongues hath into bondage
Brought my too diligent ear; for several virtues   42
Have I liked several women; never any
With so full soul but some defect in her   44
Did quarrel with the noblest grace she owed,   45
And put it to the foil. But you, O you,   46
So perfect and so peerless, are created
Of every creature's best.

MIRANDA: I do not know
One of my sex; no woman's face remember,
Save, from my glass, mine own; nor have I seen
More that I may call men than you, good friend,
And my dear father. How features are abroad   52
I am skilless of; but, by my modesty   53
(The jewel in my dower), I would not wish
Any companion in the world but you;
Nor can imagination form a shape,
Besides yourself, to like of. But I prattle   57
Something too wildly, and my father's precepts
I therein do forget.

---

32 *visitation*, (1) visit, (2) attack of plague (in the metaphor of *infected*).   **37** *hest*, command.
38 *admiration*, wonder, astonishment (the name Miranda means wonderful woman; cf. I, ii, 427).
40 *best regard*, highest approval.   **42** *several*, different.   **44** *With . . . soul*, i.e., so wholeheartedly.
45 *owed*, owned.   **46** *foil*, (1) overthrow, (2) contrast.   **52** *abroad*, elsewhere.   **53** *skilless*,
ignorant.   **57** *like of*, compare to.

FERDINAND: I am, in my condition,   59
A prince, Miranda; I do think, a king
(I would not so), and would no more endure
This wooden slavery than to suffer
The fleshfly blow my mouth. Hear my soul speak!
The very instant that I saw you, did
My heart fly to your service; there resides,
To make me slave to it; and for your sake
Am I this patient log-man.
MIRANDA: Do you love me?
FERDINAND: O heaven, O earth, bear witness to this sound,
And crown what I profess with kind event   69
If I speak true! if hollowly, invert
What best is boded me to mischief! I,
Beyond all limit of what else i' th' world,
Do love, prize, honor you.
MIRANDA: I am a fool
To weep at what I am glad of.
PROSPERO *(aside):*   Fair encounter
Of two most rare affections! Heavens rain grace
On that which breeds between 'em!
FERDINAND: Wherefore weep you?
MIRANDA: At mine unworthiness, that dare not offer
What I desire to give, and much less take
What I shall die to want. But this is trifling;   79
And all the more it seeks to hide itself,
The bigger bulk it shows. Hence, bashful cunning,   81
And prompt me, plain and holy innocence!
I am your wife, if you will marry me;
If not, I'll die your maid. To be your fellow   84
You may deny me; but I'll be your servant,
Whether you will or no.
FERDINAND: My mistress, dearest,
And I thus humble ever.
MIRANDA: My husband then?
FERDINAND: Ay, with a heart as willing
As bondage e'er of freedom. Here's my hand.   89
MIRANDA: And mine, with my heart in't; and now farewell
Till half an hour hence.
FERDINAND: A thousand thousand!

(Exeunt Ferdinand and Miranda severally)

---

59 *condition,* situation in the world.   **69** *kind event,* favorable outcome.   **79** *want,* lack.
81 *bashful cunning,* i.e. coyness.   **84** *fellow,* equal.   **89** *of freedom,* i.e., to win freedom.

PROSPERO: So glad of this as they I cannot be,
Who are surprised withal; but my rejoicing   93
At nothing can be more. I'll to my book;
For yet ere supper time must I perform
Much business appertaining.   96

(Exit)

Act III

Scene II

Another part of the island. Enter Caliban, Stephano, and Trinculo.

STEPHANO: Tell not me! When the butt is out, we will drink water; not
 a drop before. Therefore bear up and board 'em! Servant monster,   2
 drink to me.

TRINCULO: Servant monster? The folly of this island! They say there's
 but five upon this isle: we are three of them. If th' other two be
 brained like us, the state totters.

STEPHANO: Drink, servant monster, when I bid thee: thy eyes are almost
 set in thy head.

TRINCULO: Where should they be set else? He were a brave monster
 indeed if they were set in his tail.

STEPHANO: My man-monster hath drowned his tongue in sack. For my
 part, the sea cannot drown me. I swam, ere I could recover the   12
 shore, five-and-thirty leagues off and on, by this light. Thou shalt
 be my lieutenant, monster, or my standard.   14

TRINCULO: Your lieutenant, if you list; he's no standard.   15

STEPHANO: We'll not run, Monsieur Monster.   16

TRINCULO: Nor go neither; but you'll lie like dogs, and yet say nothing 17
 neither.

STEPHANO: Mooncalf, speak once in thy life, if thou beest a good mooncalf.

CALIBAN: How does thy honor? Let me lick thy shoe.
 I'll not serve him; he is not valiant.

TRINCULO: Thou liest, most ignorant monster: I am in case to justle a   23
 constable. Why, thou deboshed fish thou, was there ever man a   24
 coward that hath drunk so much sack as I to-day? Wilt thou tell
 a monstrous lie, being but half a fish and half a monster?

CALIBAN: Lo, how he mocks me! Wilt thou let him, my lord?

TRINCULO: 'Lord' quoth he? That a monster should be such a natural!   28

---

93 *surprised withal,* taken unaware by it.   **96** *appertaining,* relevant.   **2** *bear . . . 'em,* i.e. drink
up (Caliban has almost "passed out").   **12** *recover,* reach.   **14** *standard,* ensign.   **15** *no standard,*
i.e., incapable of standing up.   **16, 17** *run, lie,* (secondary meanings of) make water and excrete.
17 *go,* walk.   **23** *case,* fit condition.   **24** *deboshed,* debauched.   **28** *natural,* fool.

CALIBAN: Lo, lo, again! Bite him to death, I prithee.

STEPHANO: Trinculo, keep a good tongue in your head. If you prove a
mutineer—the next tree! The poor monster's my subject, and he
shall not suffer indignity.

CALIBAN: I thank my noble lord. Wilt thou be pleased
To hearken once again to the suit I made to thee?

STEPHANO: Marry, will I. Kneel and repeat it; I will stand, and so shall
Trinculo.　　　　　　　　　　　　　　　　　　　　　　　　　　36

(Enter Ariel, invisible)

CALIBAN: As I told thee before, I am subject to a tyrant,
A sorcerer, that by his cunning hath
Cheated me of the island.

ARIEL:　　　　　　　　　　　Thou liest.

CALIBAN: Thou liest, thou jesting monkey thou!
I would my valiant master would destroy thee.
I do not lie.

STEPHANO: Trinculo, if you trouble him any more in's tale, by this hand,
I will supplant some of your teeth.

TRINCULO: Why, I said nothing.

STEPHANO: Mum then, and no more.—Proceed.

CALIBAN: I say by sorcery he got this isle;
From me he got it. If thy greatness will
Revenge it on him—for I know thou dar'st,
But this thing dare not—　　　　　　　　　　　　　　　　　　50

STEPHANO: That's most certain.

CALIBAN: Thou shalt be lord of it, and I'll serve thee.

STEPHANO: How now shall this be compassed?
Canst thou bring me to the party?　　　　　　　　　　　　　54

CALIBAN: Yea, yea, my lord! I'll yield him thee asleep,
Where thou mayst knock a nail into his head.

ARIEL: Thou liest; thou canst not.

CALIBAN: What a pied ninny's this! Thou scurvy patch!　　　　58
I do beseech thy greatness give him blows
And take his bottle from him. When that's gone,
He shall drink naught but brine, for I'll not show him
Where the quick freshes are.　　　　　　　　　　　　　　62

STEPHANO: Trinculo, run into no further danger: interrupt the monster
one word further and, by this hand, I'll turn my mercy out o' doors
and make a stockfish of thee.　　　　　　　　　　　　　　65

---

36 s.d. (stage directions) *invisible,* "a robe for to go invisible" is listed in an Elizabethan stage account.
50 *this thing,* i.e., himself (or perhaps Trinculo).　　**54** *party,* person.　　**58** *pied ninny,* motley fool
(Trinculo wears a jester's costume); *patch,* clown.　　**62** *quick freshes,* fresh-water springs.
65 *stockfish,* dried cod, prepared by beating.

TRINCULO: Why, what did I? I did nothing. I'll go farther off.

STEPHANO: Didst thou not say he lied?

ARIEL: Thou liest.

STEPHANO: Do I so? Take thou that! *(Strikes Trinculo)* As you like this,
    give me the lie another time.

TRINCULO: I did not give the lie. Out o' your wits, and hearing too? A
    pox o' your bottle! This can sack and drinking do. A murrain on   72
    your monster, and the devil take your fingers!

CALIBAN: Ha, ha, ha!

STEPHANO: Now forward with your tale.—Prithee stand further off.

CALIBAN: Beat him enough. After a little time
    I'll beat him too.

STEPHANO: Stand farther.—Come, proceed.

CALIBAN: Why as I told thee, 'tis a custom with him
    I' th' afternoon to sleep; there thou mayst brain him,
    Having first seized his books, or with a log
    Batter his skull, or paunch him with a stake,   **81**
    Or cut his wesand with thy knife. Remember   **82**
    First to possess his books; for without them
    He's but a sot, as I am, nor hath not   **84**
    One spirit to command. They all do hate him
    As rootedly as I. Burn but his books.
    He has brave utensils (for so he calls them)   **87**
    Which, when he has a house, he'll deck withal.
    And that most deeply to consider is
    The beauty of his daughter. He himself
    Calls her a nonpareil. I never saw a woman
    But only Sycorax my dam and she;
    But she as far surpasseth Sycorax
    As great'st does least.

STEPHANO: Is it so brave a lass?

CALIBAN: Ay, lord. She will become thy bed, I warrant,
    And bring thee forth brave brood.

STEPHANO: Monster, I will kill this man: his daughter and I will be king
    and queen, save our Graces! and Trinculo and thyself shall be viceroys.
    Dost thou like the plot, Trinculo?

TRINCULO: Excellent.

STEPHANO: Give me thy hand. I am sorry I beat thee; but while thou
    liv'st, keep a good tongue in thy head.

CALIBAN: Within this half hour will he be asleep.
    Wilt thou destroy him then?

---

72 *murrain,* cattle disease.   **81** *paunch,* stab in the belly.   **82** *wesand,* windpipe.   **84** *sot,* fool.
87 *utensils,* furnishings.

STEPHANO: Ay, on mine honor.

ARIEL: This will I tell my master.

CALIBAN: Thou mak'st me merry; I am full of pleasure.
    Let us be jocund. Will you troll the catch   108
    You taught me but whilere?   109

STEPHANO: At thy request, monster, I will do reason, any reason. Come
    on, Trinculo, let us sing.

(Sings)

            Flout 'em and scout em
            And scout 'em and flout 'em!
            Thought is free.

CALIBAN: That's not the tune.

(Ariel plays the tune on a tabor and pipe)

STEPHANO: What is this same?   116

TRINCULO: This is the tune of our catch, played by the picture of
    Nobody.   118

STEPHANO: If thou beest a man, show thyself in thy likeness. If thou
    beest a devil, take't as thou list.   120

TRINCULO: O, forgive me my sins!

STEPHANO: He that dies pays all debts. I defy thee. Mercy upon us!

CALIBAN: Art thou afeard?

STEPHANO: No, monster, not I.

CALIBAN: Be not afeard: the isle is full of noises,
    Sounds and sweet airs that give delight and hurt not.
    Sometimes a thousand twangling instruments
    Will hum about mine ears; and sometime voices
    That, if I then had waked after long sleep,
    Will make me sleep again; and then, in dreaming,
    The clouds methought would open and show riches
    Ready to drop upon me, that, when I waked,
    I cried to dream again.

STEPHANO: This will prove a brave kingdom to me, where I shall have
    my music for nothing.

CALIBAN: When Prospero is destroyed.

STEPHANO: That shall be by and by: I remember the story.   137

TRINCULO: The sound is going away: let's follow it, and after do our
    work.

108 *troll the catch,* sing the part-song.   **109** *whilere,* just now.   **116 s.d.** *tabor,* small drum worn
at the side.   **118** *Nobody,* referring to pictures of figures with arms and legs but no trunk, used on
signs and elsewhere.   **120** *take't as thou list,* i.e., suit yourself.   **137** *by and by,* right away.

STEPHANO: Lead, monster; we'll follow. I would I could see this taborer:
he lays it on. Wilt come?

TRINCULO: I'll follow, Stephano.   *(Exeunt)*

Act III

Scene III

*Another part of the island. Enter Alonso, Sebastian, Antonio, Gonzalo, Adrian,
Francisco, etc.*

GONZALO: By'r Lakin, I can go no further, sir: 1
My old bones ache: here's a maze trod indeed
Through forthrights and meanders. By your patience,   3
I needs must rest me.

ALONSO: Old lord, I cannot blame thee,
Who am myself attached with weariness   5
To th' dulling of my spirits. Sit down and rest.
Even here I will put off my hope, and keep it
No longer for my flatterer: he is drowned
Whom thus we stray to find; and the sea mocks
Our frustrate search on land. Well, let him go.

ANTONIO *(aside to Sebastian):*
I am right glad that he's so out of hope.
Do not for one repulse forgo the purpose
That you resolved t' effect.

SEBASTIAN *(aside to Antonio):* The next advantage
Will we take throughly.   14

ANTONIO *(aside to Sebastian):* Let it be to-night;
For, now they are oppressed with travel, they
Will not nor cannot use such vigilance
As when they are fresh.

SEBASTIAN *(aside to Antonio):* I say to-night. No more.   17

*(Solemn and strange music; and Prospero on the top [invisible]. Enter several
strange Shapes, bringing in a banquet; and dance about it with gentle actions of
salutations; and, inviting the King etc. to eat, they depart.)*

ALONSO: What harmony is this? My good friends, hark!
GONZALO: Marvellous sweet music!
ALONSO: Give us kind keepers, heavens! What were these?   20
SEBASTIAN: A living drollery. Now I will believe   21
That there are unicorns; that in Arabia
There is one tree, the phoenix' throne; one phoenix
At this hour reigning there.

---

1 *By'r Lakin,* by our Ladykin (Virgin Mary).   3 *forthrights,* straight paths.   5 *attached,* seized.
14 *throughly,* thoroughly.   17 **s.d.** *on the top,* this may refer to an upper level of the tiring-house
of the theatre.   20 *kind keepers,* guardian angels.   21 *living drollery,* puppet show with live figures.

ANTONIO: I'll believe both;
And what does else want credit, come to me,   25
And I'll be sworn 'tis true. Travellers ne'er did lie,
Though fools at home condemn 'em.
GONZALO: If in Naples
I should report this now, would they believe me
If I should say I saw such islanders?
(For certes these are people of the island)
Who, though they are of monstrous shape, yet note,
Their manners are more gentle, kind, than of
Our human generation you shall find
Many—nay, almost any.
PROSPERO *(aside):*   Honest lord,
Thou has said well; for some of you there present
Are worse than devils.
ALONSO: I cannot too much muse   36
Such shapes, such gesture, and such sound, expressing
(Although they want the use of tongue) a kind
Of excellent dumb discourse.
PROSPERO *(aside):*   Praise in departing.   39
FRANCISCO: They vanished strangely.
SEBASTIAN: No matter, since
They have left their viands behind; for we have stomachs.
Will't please you taste of what is here?
ALONSO: Not I.
GONZALO: Faith, sir, you need not fear. When we were boys,
Who would believe that there were mountaineers
Dewlapped like bulls, whose throats had hanging at 'em   45
Wallets of flesh? or that there were such men
Whose heads stood in their breasts? which now we find   47
Each putter-out of five for one will bring us   48
Good warrant of.
ALONSO: I will stand to, and feed;
Although my last, no matter, since I feel
The best is past. Brother, my lord the Duke,
Stand to, and do as we.   52

*(Thunder and lightning. Enter Ariel, like a harpy: claps his wings upon the table;
and with a quaint device the banquet vanishes.)*

---

25 *want credit,* lack credibility.   **36** *muse,* wonder at.   **39** *Praise in departing,* save your praise
for the end.   **45** *Dewlapped,* with skin hanging from the neck (like the goitrous Swiss *mountaineers*).   **47** *in their breasts,* an ancient travellers' tale; cf. *Othello* I, iii, 144–45.   **48** *putter-out
. . . one,* traveler depositing a sum for insurance in London, to be repaid fivefold if he returned safely
and proved he had gone to his destination.   **52 s.d.** *quaint,* ingenious.

ARIEL: You are three men of sin, whom destiny—
That hath to instrument this lower world   54
And what is in't—the never-surfeited sea
Hath caused to belch up you, and on this island,
Where man doth not inhabit, you 'mongst men
Being most unfit to live, I have made you mad;
And even with such-like valor men hang and drown
Their proper selves.

(Alonso, Sebastian, etc. draw their swords)

              You fools: I and my fellows
Are ministers of Fate. The elements,
Of whom your swords are tempered, may as well
Wound the loud winds, or with bemocked-at stabs
Kill the still-closing waters, as diminish   64
One dowle that's in my plume. My fellow ministers   65
Are like invulnerable. If you could hurt,   66
Your swords are now too massy for your strengths   67
And will not be uplifted. But remember
(For that's my business to you) that you three
From Milan did supplant good Prospero;
Exposed unto the sea, which hath requit it,   71
Him and his innocent child; for which foul deed
The pow'rs, delaying, not forgetting, have
Incensed the seas and shores, yea, all the creatures,
Against your peace. Thee of thy son, Alonso,
They have bereft; and do pronounce by me
Ling'ring perdition (worse than any death   77
Can be at once) shall step by step attend
You and your ways; whose wraths to guard you from,
Which here, in this most desolate isle, else falls
Upon your heads, is nothing but heart's sorrow   81
And a clear life ensuing.   82

*(He vanishes in thunder; then, to soft music, enter the Shapes again, and dance
with mocks and mows, and carrying out the table)*

PROSPERO: Bravely the figure of this harpy has thou
Performed, my Ariel; a grace it had, devouring.   84
Of my instruction hast thou nothing bated   85

---

54 *to*, i.e., as its.   **64** *still*, constantly.   **65** *dowle*, fibre of feather-down.   **66** *like*, also.
67 *massy*, massive.   **71** *requit*, avenged; *it*, i.e., the usurpation.   **77** *perdition*, ruin.   **81** *heart's*
sorrow, repentance.   **82** *clear*, innocent; **s.d.** *mocks and mows*, grimaces and gestures.   **84** *devour-*
ing, i.e., making the banquet disappear.   **85** *bated*, omitted.

In what thou hadst to say. So, with good life   86
And observation strange, my meaner ministers   87
Their several kinds have done. My high charms work,   88
And these, mine enemies, are all knit up
In their distractions: they now are in my pow'r;
And in these fits I leave them, while I visit
Young Ferdinand, whom they suppose is drowned,
And his and mine loved darling.   *(Exit above)*
GONZALO: I' th' name of something holy, sir, why stand you   94
In this strange stare?
ALONSO: O, it is monstrous, monstrous!   95
Me thought the billows spoke and told me of it;
The winds did sing it to me; and the thunder,
That deep and dreadful organ pipe, pronounced
The name of Prosper; it did bass my trespass.   99
Therefore my son i' th' ooze is bedded; and
I'll seek him deeper than e'er plummet sounded
And with him there lie mudded.   *(Exit)*
SEBASTIAN: But one fiend at a time,
I'll fight their legions o'er!
ANTONIO: I'll be thy second.

(Exeunt Sebastian and Antonio)

GONZALO: All three of them are desperate: their great guilt,
Like poison given to work a great time after,
Now gins to bite the spirits. I do beseech you,
That are of suppler joints, follow them swiftly
And hinder them from what this ecstasy   108
May now provoke them to.
ADRIAN: Follow, I pray you   *(Exeunt omnes)*

Act IV

Scene I

Before Prospero's cell. Enter Prospero, Ferdinand, and Miranda.

PROSPERO: If I have too austerely punished you,
Your compensation makes amends; for I
Have given you here a third of mine own life,   3
Or that for which I live; who once again
I tender to thy hand. All thy vexations

---

86 *good life,* realistic acting.   **87** *observation strange,* wonderfully close attention.   **88** *several kinds,* separate parts.   **94** *why,* Gonzalo has not heard Ariel's speech.   **95** *it,* i.e., my sin.   **99** *bass,* proclaim in deep tones (literally, provide the bass part for).   **108** *ecstasy,* madness.   **3** *third,* Prospero's love, his knowledge and his power being the other two-thirds?

Were but my trials of thy love, and thou
Hast strangely stood the test. Here, afore heaven,   7
I ratify this my rich gift. O Ferdinand,
Do not smile at me that I boast her off,   9
For thou shalt find she will outstrip all praise
And make it halt behind her.   11

FERDINAND: I do believe it
Against an oracle.   12

PROSPERO: Then, as my gift, and thine own acquisition
Worthily purchased, take my daughter. But
If thou dost break her virgin-knot before
All sanctimonious ceremonies may   16
With full and holt rite be minist'red,
No sweet aspersion shall the heavens let fall   18
To make this contract grow; but barren hate,   19
Sour-eyed disdain, and discord shall bestrew
The union of your bed with weeds so loathly
That you shall hate it both. Therefore take heed,
As Hymen's lamp shall light you.

FERDINAND: As I hope
For quiet days, fair issue, and long life,
With such love as 'tis now, the murkiest den,
The most opportune place, the strong'st suggestion   26
Our worser genius can, shall never melt   27
Mine honor into lust, to take away
The edge of that day's celebration
When I shall think or Phoebus' steeds are foundered   30
Or Night kept chained below.

PROSPERO: Fairly spoke.
Sit then and talk with her; she is thine own.
What, Ariel! My industrious servant, Ariel!

(Enter Ariel)

ARIEL: What would my potent master? Here I am.
PROSPERO: Thou and thy meaner fellows your last service
Did worthily perform; and I must use you
In such another trick. Go bring the rabble,   37
O'er whom I give thee pow'r, here to this place.
Incite them to quick motion; for I must
Bestow upon the eyes of this young couple

7 *strangely,* in a rare fashion.   9 *boast her off,* boast about her.   11 *halt,* limp.   12 *Against an oracle,* even if an oracle denied it.   16 *sanctimonious,* holy.   18 *aspersion,* blessing, like rain on crops.   19 *grow,* become fruitful.   26 *opportune,* accent second syllable.   27 *worser genius can,* bad angel can make.   30 *or . . . foundered,* either the sun-god's horses are lame.   37 *rabble,* rank and file.

Some vanity of mine art; it is my promise,   41
And they expect it from me.
ARIEL: Presently?
PROSPERO: Ay, with a twink.
ARIEL: Before you can say 'Come' and 'Go,'
  And breathe twice and cry, 'So, so,'
  Each one, tripping on his toe,
  Will be here with mop and mow.   47
  Do you love me, master? No?
PROSPERO: Dearly, my delicate Ariel. Do not approach
  Till thou dost hear me call.
ARIEL: Well: I conceive.   *(Exit)*   50
PROSPERO: Look thou be true: do not give dalliance   51
  Too much the rein: the strongest oaths are straw
  To th' fire i' the' blood. Be more abstemious,
  Or else good night your vow!
FERDINAND: I warrant you, sir.
  The white cold virgin snow upon my heart
  Abates the ardor of my liver.   56
PROSPERO: Well.
  Now come, my Ariel: bring a corollary   57
  Rather than want a spirit. Appear, and pertly!   58
  No tongue! All eyes! Be silent.

(Soft music. Enter Iris)

IRIS: Ceres, most bounteous lady, thy rich leas   60
  Of wheat, rye, barley, fetches, oats, and pease;   61
  Thy turfy mountains, where live nibbling sheep,
  And flat meads thatched with stover, them to keep;   63
  Thy banks with pionèd and twillèd brims,   64
  Which spongy April at thy hest betrims
  To make cold nymphs chaste crowns; and thy broom groves,   66
  Whose shadow the dismissed bachelor loves,
  Being lasslorn; thy pole-clipt vineyard;   68
  And thy sea-marge, sterile and rocky-hard,   69
  Where thou thyself dost air—the queen o' th' sky,   70
  Whose wat'ry arch and messenger am I,

41 *vanity,* show.   **47** *mop and mow,* antics and gestures.   **50** *conceive,* understand.   **51** *be true,*
Prospero appears to have caught the lovers in an embrace.   **56** *liver,* supposed seat of sexual passion.
57 *corollary,* surplus.   **58** *want,* lack; *pertly,* briskly.   **60** *Iris,* goddess of the rainbow and female
messenger of the gods.   **61** *fetches,* vetch.   **63** *stover,* winter food for stock.   **64** *pionèd and
twillèd,* dug under by the current and protected by woven layers of branches (sometimes emended
to "peonied and lilied").   **66** *broom groves,* clumps of gorse.   **68** *pole-clipt,* pruned; *vineyard,*
probably a trisyllable.   **69** *sea-marge,* shore.   **70** *queen,* i.e., Juno.

Bids thee leave these, and with her sovereign grace,
Here on this grass-plot, in this very place,   73
To come and sport: her peacocks fly amain.   74
Approach, rich Ceres, her to entertain.

(Enter Ceres)

CERES: Hail, many-colored messenger, that ne'eer
Dost disobey the wife of Jupiter,
Who, with thy saffron wings, upon my flow'rs
Diffusest honey drops, refreshing show'rs,
And with each end of thy blue bow dost crown
My bosky acres and my unshrubbed down,   81
Rich scarf to my proud earth—why hath thy queen
Summoned me hither to this short-grassed green?

IRIS: A contract of true love to celebrate
And some donation freely to estate   85
On the blessed lovers.

CERES: Tell me, heavenly bow,
If Venus or her son, as thou dost know,   87
Do now attend the queen? Since they did plot
The means that dusky Dis my daughter got,   89
Her and her blind boy's scandalled company   90
I have forsworn.

IRIS: Of her society
Be not afraid: I met her Deity   92
Cutting the clouds towards Paphos, and her son   93
Dove-drawn with her. Here thought they to have done
Some wanton charm upon this man and maid,
Whose vows are, that no bed-right shall be paid
Till Hymen's torch be lighted; but in vain.
Mars's hot minion is returned again;   98
Her waspish-headed son has broke his arrows,   99
Swears he will shoot no more, but play with sparrows
And be a boy right out.   101

(Enter Juno)

---

73 *Here . . . place,* in F a stage direction at this point reads "Juno descends."   **74** *peacocks,* these
were sacred to Juno, as doves were to Venus (1.94) and drew her chariot.   **81** *bosky,* wooded.
85 *estate,* bestow.   **87** *her son,* Cupid, often represented a blind or blindfolded.   **89** *means,* i.e.,
the abduction of Proserpine, Ceres' daughter, by Pluto (Dis), god of the lower *(dusky)* world.
90 *scandalled,* disgraceful.   **92** *her Deity,* i.e., her Divine Majesty.   **93** *Paphos,* in Cyprus, center
of Venus's cult.   **98** *Mars's . . . again,* the lustful mistress of Mars (Venus) has gone back to where
she came from.   **99** *waspish-headed,* spiteful and inclined to sting (with his arrows).   **101** *right
out,* outright.

CERES: Highest queen of state,
  Great Juno, comes; I know her by her gait.
JUNO: How does my bounteous sister? Go with me
  To bless this twain, that they may prosperous be
  And honored in their issue.

(They sing)

  JUNO: Honor, riches, marriage blessing,
    Long continuance, and increasing,
    Hourly joys be still upon you!   108
    Juno sings her blessings on you.
  (CERES) Earth's increase, foison plenty,   110
    Barns and garners never empty,
    Vines with clust'ring bunches growing,
    Plants with goodly burden bowing;
    Spring come to you at the farthest
    In the very end of harvest.
    Scarcity and want shall shun you,
    Ceres' blessing so is on you.
FERDINAND: This is a most majestic vision, and
  Harmonious charmingly. May I be bold
  To think these spirits?
PROSPERO: Spirits, which by mine art
  I have from their confines called to enact
  My present fancies.
FERDINAND: Let me live here ever!
  So rare a wond'red father and a wise   123
  Makes this place Paradise.

(Juno and Ceres whisper, and send Iris on employment)

  PROSPERO: Sweet now, silence!
  Juno and Ceres whisper seriously.
  There's something else to do. Hush and be mute,
  Or else our spell is marred.
IRIS: You nymphs, called Naiades, of the windring brooks,   128
  With your sedged crowns and ever-harmless looks,
  Leave your crisp channels, and on this green land   130
  Answer your summons; Juno does command.
  Come, temperature nymphs, and help to celebrate
  A contract of true love: be not too late.

(Enter certain Nymphs)

108 *still,* constantly.   **110** *foison,* abundance.   **123** *wond'red,* wonderful.   **128** *windring,* winding and wandering.   **130** *crisp,* rippling.

You sunburned sicklemen, of August weary,
Come hither from the furrow and be merry.
Make holiday: your rye-straw hats put on,
And these fresh nymphs encounter every one
In country footing.   138

(Enter certain Reapers, properly habited. They join with the Nymphs in a graceful dance; towards the end whereof Prospero starts suddenly and speaks; after which, to a strange, hollow, and confused noise, they heavily vanish.)

PROSPERO *(aside):* I had forgot that foul conspiracy
Of the beast Caliban and his confederates
Against my life: The minute of their plot
Is almost come.
(To the Spirits) Well done! Avoid! No more!   142
FERDINAND: This is strange. Your father's in some passion
That works him strongly.
MIRANDA: Never till this day
Saw I him touched with anger so distempered.
PROSPERO: You do look, my son, in a moved sort,   146
As if you were dismayed: be cheerful, sir.
Our revels now are ended. These our actors,   148
As I foretold you, were all spirits and
Are melted into air, into thin air;
And, like the baseless fabric of this vision,   151
The cloud-capped tow'rs, the gorgeous palaces,
The solemn temples, the great globe itself,
Yea, all which it inherit, shall dissolve,   154
And, like this insubstantial pageant faded,
Leave not a rack behind. We are such stuff   156
As dreams are made on, and our little life   157
Is rounded with a sleep. Sir, I am vexed.
Bear with my weakness: my old brain is troubled.
Be not disturbed with my infirmity.
If you be pleased, retire into my cell
And there repose. A turn or two I'll walk
To still my beating mind.
FERDINAND, MIRANDA: We wish your peace.

(Exit Ferdinand with Miranda)

(Enter Ariel)

138 s.d. *speaks,* thereby dissolving the scene, which depended on silence.   **142** *Avoid,* be off.
146 *moved sort,* troubled state.   **148** *revels,* pageants.   **151** *baseless,* insubstantial, non—material.
154 *it inherit,* occupy it.   **156** *rack,* wisp of cloud.   **157** *on,* of.

PROSPERO: Come with a thought! I thank thee, Ariel. Come.
ARIEL: Thy thoughts I cleave to. What's thy pleasure?
PROSPERO: Spirit,
  We must prepare to meet with Caliban.
ARIEL: Ay, my commander: when I presented Ceres,   167
  I thought to have told thee of it, but I feared
  Lest I might anger thee.
PROSPERO: Say again, where didst thou leave these varlets?   170
ARIEL: I told you, sir, they were redhot with drinking;
  So full of valor that they smote the air
  For breathing in their faces, beat the ground
  For kissing of their feet; yet always bending
  Towards their project. Then I beat my tabor;
  At which like unbacked colts they pricked their ears,   176
  Advanced their eyelids, lifted up their noses   177
  As they smelt music. So I charmed their ears
  That calf-like they my lowing followed through
  Toothed briers, sharp furzes, pricking goss, and thorns,   180
  Which ent'red their frail shins. At last I left them
  I' th' filthy mantled pool beyond your cell,   182
  There dancing up to th' chins, that the foul lake
  O'erstunk their feet.
PROSPERO: This was well done, my bird.
  Thy shape invisible retain thou still.
  The trumpery in my house, go bring it hither
  For stale to catch these thieves.   187
ARIEL: I go, I go.   *(Exit)*
PROSPERO: A devil, a born devil, on whose nature
  Nurture can never stick: on whom my pains,
  Humanely taken, all, all lost, quite lost!
  And as with age his body uglier grows,
  So his mind cankers. I will plague them all,   192
  Even to roaring.

(Enter Ariel, loaden with glistering apparel, etc.)

        Come, hang them on this line.   193

(Prospero and Ariel remain, invisible. Enter Caliban, Stephano, and Trinculo, all wet.)

CALIBAN: Pray you tread softly, that the blind mole may not
  Hear a foot fall. We now are near his cell.

---

167 *presented,* acted the part of (?), introduced (?).   **170** *varlets,* ruffians.   **176** *unbacked,* unbroken.   **177** *Advanced,* lifted up.   **180** *goss,* gorse.   **182** *mantled,* scummed.   **187** *stale,* decoy.   **192** *cankers,* festers.   **193** *line,* lime or linden-tree, or perhaps a clothesline made of hair.

STEPHANO: Monster, your fairy, which you say is a harmless fairy, has
    done little better than played the Jack with us.   197

TRINCULO: Monster, I do smell all horse-piss, at which my nose is in
    great indignation.

STEPHANO: So is mine. Do you hear, monster? If I should take a displeas-
    ure against you, look you—

TRINCULO: Thou wert but a lost monster.

CALIBAN: Good my lord, give me thy favor still.
    Be patient, for the prize I'll bring thee to
    Shall hoodwink this mischance. Therefore speak softly.   205
    All's hushed as midnight yet.

TRINCULO: Ay, but to lose our bottles in the pool—

STEPHANO: There is not only disgrace and dishonor in that, monster, but
    an infinite loss.

TRINCULO: That's more to me than my wetting. Yet this is your harmless
    fairy monster.

STEPHANO: I will fetch off my bottle, though I be o'er ears for my labor.

CALIBAN: Prithee, my king, be quiet. Seest thou here?
    This is the mouth o' th' cell. No noise, and enter.
    Do that good mischief which may make this island
    Thine own for ever, and I, thy Caliban,
    For aye thy foot-licker.

STEPHANO: Give me thy hand. I do begin to have bloody thoughts.

TRINCULO: O King Stephano! O peer! O worthy Stephano, look what a   219
    wardrobe here is for thee!

CALIBAN: Let it alone, thou fool! It is but trash.

TRINCULO: O, ho, monster! we know what belongs to a frippery. O King   222
    Stephano!

STEPHANO: Put off that gown, Trinculo; by this hand, I'll have that
    gown!

TRINCULO: Thy Grace shall have it.

CALIBAN: The dropsy drown this fool! What do you mean
    To dote thus on such luggage? Let't alone,   228
    And do the murder first. If he awake,
    From toe to crown he'll fill our skins with pinches,
    Make us strange stuff.

STEPHANO: Be you quiet, monster. Mistress line, is not this my jerkin?
    (Takes it down) Now is the jerkin under the line. Now, jerkin, you   233
    are like to lose your hair and prove a bald jerkin.

TRINCULO: Do, do! We steal by line and level, an' like your Grace.   235

---

197 *Jack,* (1) knave, (2) jack-o'-lantern, will-o'-the-wisp.   **205** *hoodwink,* cover over.   **219** *peer,*
referring to the song "King Stephen was a worthy peer," quoted in *Othello* II, iii, 84–91.
222 *frippery,* old-clothes shop.   **228** *luggage,* junk.   **233 ff.** the jokes are probably obscene, but
their point is lost; sailors crossing the *line* or equator proverbially lost their hair from scurvy.
235 *by line and level,* according to rule (with pun on *line*); *an't like,* if it please.

STEPHANO: I thank thee for that jest. Here's a garment for't. Wit shall
 not go unrewarded while I am king of this country. 'Steal by line
 and level' is an excellent pass of pate. There's another garment for't. 239

TRINCULO: Monster, come put some lime upon your fingers, and away, 240
 with the rest.

CALIBAN: I will have none on't. We shall lose our time
 And all be turned to barnacles, or to apes   243
 With foreheads villainous low.

STEPHANO: Monster, lay-to your fingers: help to bear this away where
 my hogshead of wine is, or I'll turn you out of my kingdom. Go to,
 carry this.

STEPHANO: Ay, and this.

*(A noise of hunters heard. Enter divers Spirits in shape of dogs and hounds, hunting
them about, Prospero and Ariel setting them on.)*

PROSPERO: Hey, Mountain, hey!

ARIEL: Silver! there it goes, Silver!

PROSPERO: Fury, Fury! There, Tyrant, there! Hark, hark!

(Caliban, Stephano, and Trinculo are driven out)

 Go, charge my goblins that they grind their joints
 With dry convulsions, shorten up their sinews   254
 With agèd cramps, and more pinch-spotted make them 255
 Than pard or cat o' mountain.   256

ARIEL: Hark, they roar!

PROSPERO: Let them be hunted soundly. At this hour
 Lie at my mercy all mine enemies.
 Shortly shall all my labors end, and thou
 Shalt have the air at freedom. For a little,
 Follow, and do me service. *(Exeunt)*

Act V

Scene I

Before Prospero's cell. Enter Prospero in his magic robes, and Ariel.

PROSPERO: Now does my project gather to a head.
 My charms crack not, my spirits obey, and time
 Goes upright with his carriage. How's the day?   3

ARIEL: On the sixth hour, at which time, my lord,
 You said our work should cease.

---

239 *pass of pate,* sally of wit. **240** *lime,* bird-lime (sticky, hence appropriate for stealing).
243 *barnacles,* geese. **254** *dry,* resulting from deficiency of "humors" or bodily liquids. **255** *aged,*
i.e., such as old people have. **256** *pard or cat o' mountain,* leopard or catamount. **3** *time . . .
carriage,* time's burden is light.

PROSPERO: I did say so
When first I raised the tempest. Say, my spirit,
How fares the King and's followers?

ARIEL: Confined together
In the same fashion as you gave in charge,
Just as you left them—all prisoners, sir,
In the line grove which weather-fends your cell.   10
They cannot budge till your release. The King,   11
His brother, and yours abide all three distracted,
And the remainder mourning over them,
Brimful of sorrow and dismay; but chiefly
Him that you termed, sir, the good old Lord Gonzalo.
His tears run down his beard like winter's drops
From eaves of reeds. Your charm so strongly works 'em,   17
That if you now beheld them, your affections
Would become tender.

PROSPERO: Dost thou think so, spirit?

ARIEL: Mine would, sir, were I human.

PROSPERO: And mine shall.
Hast thou, which are but air, a touch, a feeling
Of their afflictions, and shall not myself,
One of their kind, that relish all as sharply   23
Passion as they, be kindlier moved than thou art?
Though with their high wrongs I am struck to th' quick,
Yet with my nobler reason 'gainst my fury
Do I take part. The rarer action is
In virtue than in vengeance. They being penitent,
The sole drift of my purpose doth extend
Not a frown further. Go, release them, Ariel.
My charms I'll break, their senses I'll restore,
And they shall be themselves.

ARIEL: I'll fetch them, sir.   *(Exit)*

PROSPERO: Ye elves of hills, brooks, standing lakes, and groves,
And ye that on the sands with printless foot
Do chase the ebbing Neptune, and do fly him
When he comes back; you demi-puppets that   36
By moonshine do the green sour ringlets make,
Whereof the ewe not bites; and you whose pastime
Is to make midnight mushrumps, that rejoice   39
To hear the solemn curfew; by whose aid
(Weak masters though ye be) I have bedimmed   41

---

10 *weather-fends,* protects from the weather.   **11** *till your release,* until you release them.
17 *eaves of reeds,* i.e., a thatched roof.   **23** *relish,* feel; *all,* quite.   **36** *demi-puppets,* i.e., fairies.
39 *mushrumps,* mushrooms.   **41** *masters,* forces.

The noontide sun, called forth the mutinous winds,
And 'twixt the green sea and the azured vault
Set roaring war; to the dread rattling thunder
Have I given fire and rifted Jove's stout oak   45
With his own bolt; the strong-based promontory
Have I made shake and by the spurs plucked up   47
The pine and cedar; graves at my command
Have waked their sleepers, oped, and let 'em forth
By my so potent art. But this rough magic
I here abjure; and when I have required   51
Some heavenly music (which even now I do)
To work mine end upon their senses that   53
This airy charm is for, I'll break my staff,
Bury it certain fathoms in the earth,
And deeper than did ever plummet sound
I'll drown my book.

*(Solemn music. Here enters Ariel before; then Alonso, with a frantic gesture,
attended by Gonzalo; Sebastian and Antonio in like manner, attended by Adrian
and Francisco. They all enter the circle which Prospero had made, and there stand
charmed; which Prospero observing, speaks.)*

A solemn air, and the best comforter   58
To an unsettled fancy, cure thy brains,
Now useless, boiled within thy skull! There stand,
For you are spell-stopped.
Holy Gonzalo, honorable man,
Mine eyes, ev'n sociable to the show of thine,   63
Fall fellowly drops. The charm dissolves apace;   64
And as the morning steals upon the night,
Melting the darkness, so their rising senses
Begin to chase the ignorant fumes that mantle
Their clearer reason. I good Gonzalo,
My true preserver, and a loyal sir
To him thou follow'st, I will pay thy graces   70
Home both in word and deed. Most cruelly
Didst thou, Alonso, use me and my daughter.
Thy brother was a furtherer in the act.
Thou art pinched for't now, Sebastian. Flesh and blood,
You, brother mine, that entertained ambition,
Expelled remorse and nature; who, with Sebastian   76
(Whose inward pinches therefore are most strong),

45 *rifted,* split.   47 *spurs,* roots.   51 *required,* asked for.   53 *their senses that,* the senses of those
whom.   58 *and,* i.e., which is.   63 *sociable,* sympathetic; *show,* sight.   64 *Fall,* let fall.
70 *graces,* favors.   76 *remorse,* pity; *nature,* natural feeling.

Would here have killed your king, I do forgive thee,
Unnatural though thou art. Their understanding
Begins to swell, and the approaching tide
Will shortly fill the reasonable shore,
That now lies foul and muddy. Not one of them
That yet looks on me or would know me. Ariel,
Fetch me the hat and rapier in my cell.
I will discase me, and myself present   85
As I was sometime Milan. Quickly, spirit!   86
Thou shalt ere long be free.

(Exit Ariel and returns immediately)

(Ariel sings and helps to attire him)

        Where the bee sucks, there suck I;
        In a cowslip's bell I lie;
        There I couch when owls do cry.
        On the bat's back I do fly
        After summer merrily.
Merrily, merrily shall I live now
Under the blossom that hangs on the bough.
PROSPERO: Why, that's my dainty Ariel! I shall miss thee,
But yet thou shalt have freedom; so, so, so.
To the King's ship, invisible as thou art!
There shalt thou find the mariners asleep
Under the hatches. The master and the boatswain
Being awake, enforce them to this place,
And presently, I prithee.   101
ARIEL: I drink the air before me, and return   102
Or ere your pulse twice beat.   *(Exit)*
GONZALO: All torment, trouble, wonder, and amazement
Inhabits here. Some heavenly power guide us
Out of this fearful country!
PROSPERO: Behold, sir King,
The wronged Duke of Milan, Prospero.
For more assurance that a living prince
Does now speak to thee, I embrace thy body,
And to thee and thy company I bid
A hearty welcome.
ALONSO: Whe'r thou be'st he or no.
Or some enchanted trifle to abuse me,   112
As late I have been, I not know. Thy pulse
Beats, as of flesh and blood; and, since I saw thee,

---

85 *discase,* undress.   86 *sometime Milan,* when I was Duke of Milan.   101 *presently,* right away.
102 *drink the air,* i.e., consume space.   112 *trifle,* trick; *abuse,* deceive.

Th' affliction of my mind amends, with which,
I fear, a madness held me. This must crave   116
(An if this be at all) a most strange story.   117
Thy dukedom I resign and do entreat
Thou pardon me my wrongs. But how should Prospero
Be living and be here?

PROSPERO: First, noble friend,
Let me embrace thine age, whose honor cannot
Be measured or confined.

GONZALO: Whether this be
Or be not, I'll not swear.

PROSPERO: You do yet taste
Some subtleties o' th' isle, that will not let you   124
Believe things certain. Welcome, my friends all.

(Aside to Sebastian and Antonio)

But you, my brace of lords, were I so minded,
I here could pluck his Highness' frown upon you,   127
And justify you traitors. At this time,   128
I will tell no tales.

SEBASTIAN *(aside):* The devil speaks in him.

PROSPERO: No.
For you, most wicked sir, whom to call brother
Would even infect my mouth, I do forgive
Thy rankest fault—all of them; and require
My dukedom of thee, which perforce I know
Thou must restore.

ALONSO: If thou beest Prospero,
Give us particulars of thy preservation;
How thou hast met us here, who three hours since
Were wracked upon this shore, where I have lost
(How sharp the point of this remembrance is!)
My dear son Ferdinand.

PROSPERO: I am woe for't, sir.   139

ALONSO: Irreparable is the loss, and patience
Says it is past her cure.

PROSPERO: I rather think
You have not sought her help, of whose soft grace
For the like loss I have her sovereign aid
And rest myself content.

ALONSO: You the like loss?

---

116 *crave,* require.   **117** *An if . . . all,* if this is really happening.   **124** *subtleties,* (secondary
meaning is) elaborate pastries representing allegorical figures, used in banquets and pageants.
127 *pluck,* pull down.   **128** *justify,* prove.   **139** *woe,* sorry.

PROSPERO: As great to me as late; and, supportable   145
     To make the dear loss, have I means much weaker   146
     Than you may call to comfort you; for I
     Have lost my daughter.
ALONSO: A daughter?
     O heavens, that they were living both in Naples.
     The King and Queen there! That they were, I wish
     Myself were mudded in that oozy bed
     Where my son lies. When did you lose your daughter?
PROSPERO: In this last tempest. I perceive these lords
     At this encounter do so much admire   154
     That they devour their reason, and scarce think
     Their eyes do offices of truth, their words   156
     Are natural breath. But, howsoev'r you have
     Been justled from your senses, know for certain
     That I am Prospero, and that very duke
     Which was thrust forth of Milan, who most strangely
     Upon this shore, where you were wracked, was landed
     To be the lord on't. No more yet of this;
     For 'tis a chronicle of day by day,
     Not a relation for a breakfast, nor
     Befitting this first meeting. Welcome, sir;
     This cell's my court. Here have I few attendants,
     And subjects none abroad. Pray you look in.
     My dukedom since you have given me again,
     I will requite you with as good a thing,
     At least bring forth a wonder to content ye
     As much as me my dukedom.   171

(Here Prospero discovers Ferdinand and Miranda playing at chess)

MIRANDA: Sweet lord, you play me false.
FERDINAND: No, my dearest love,
     I would not for the world.
MIRANDA: Yes, for a score of kingdoms, you should wrangle, 174
     And I would call it fair play.
ALONSO: If this prove
     A vision of the island, one dear son
     Shall I twice lose.
SEBASTIAN: A most high miracle!
FERDINAND: Though the seas threaten, they are merciful.
     I have cursed them without cause.

---

145 *late*, recent.   **146** *dear*, grievous.   **154** *admire*, wonder.   **156** *do offices*, perform services.
171 s.d. *discovers*, discloses.   **174** *should wrangle*, i.e., playing fair, as Ferdinand is doing, is not a
test of Miranda's love for him.

(Kneels)

ALONSO: Now all the blessings
Of a glad father compass thee about!
Arise, and say how thou cam'st here.

MIRANDA: O, wonder!
How many goodly creatures are there here!
How beauteous mankind is! O brave new world
That has such people in't!

PROSPERO: 'Tis new to thee.

ALONSO: What is this maid with whom thou wast at play?
Your eld'st acquaintance cannot be three hours.   186
Is she the goddess that hath severed us
And brought us thus together?

FERDINAND: Sir, she is mortal;
But by immortal providence she's mine.
I chose her when I could not ask my father
For his advice, nor thought I had one. She
Is daughter to this famous Duke of Milan,
Of whom so often I have heard renown
But never saw before; of whom I have
Received a second life; and second father
This lady makes him to me.

ALONSO: I am hers.
But, O, how oddly will it sound that I
Must ask my child forgiveness!

PROSPERO: There, sir, stop.
Let us not burden our remembrance with
A heaviness that's gone.

GONZALO: I have inly wept,
Or should have spoke ere this. Look down, you gods,
And on this couple drop a blessèd crown!
For it is you that have chalked forth the way
Which brought us hither.

ALONSO: I say amen, Gonzalo.

GONZALO: Was Milan thrust from Milan that his issue
Should become kings of Naples? O, rejoice
Beyond a common joy, and set it down
With gold on lasting pillars: in one voyage
Did Claribel her husband find at Tunis,
And Ferdinand her brother found a wife
Where he himself was lost; Prospero his dukedom
In a poor isle; and all of us ourselves
When no man was his own.

186 *eld'st,* i.e., longest period of.

ALONSO *(to Ferdinand and Miranda):*
                              Give me your hands.
Let grief and sorrow still embrace his heart   214
That doth not wish you joy.
GONZALO: Be it so! Amen!

(Enter Ariel, with the Master and Boatswain amazedly following)

O, look, sir; look, sir! Here is more of us!
I prophesied, if a gallows were on land,
This fellow could not drown. Now, blasphemy,
That swear'st grace o'erboard, not an oath on shore?
Hast thou no mouth by land? What is the news?
BOATSWAIN: The best news is that we have safely found
Our king and company; the next, our ship,
Which, but three glasses since, we gave out split,
Is tight and yare and bravely rigged as when   224
We first put out to sea.
ARIEL *(aside to Prospero):* Sir, all this service
Have I done since I went.
PROSPERO *(aside to Ariel):* My tricksy spirit!   226
ALONSO: These are not natural events; they strengthen
From strange to stranger. Say, how came you hither?
BOATSWAIN: If I did think, sir, I were well awake,
I'ld strive to tell you. We were dead of sleep
And (how we know not) all clapped under hatches;
Where, but even now, with strange and several noises   232
Of roaring, shrieking, howling, jingling chains,
And moe, diversity of sounds, all horrible,   234
We were awaked; straightway at liberty;
Where we, in all her trim, freshly beheld   236
Our royal, good, and gallant ship, our master
Cap'ring to eye her. On a trice, so please you,   238
Even in a dream, were we divided from them
And were brought moping hither.   240
ARIEL *(aside to Prospero):*   Was't well done?
PROSPERO *(aside to Ariel):* Bravely, my diligence. Thou shalt be free.
ALONSO: This is as strange a maze as e'er men trod,
And there is in this business more than nature
Was ever conduct of. Some oracle   244
Must rectify our knowledge.
PROSPERO: Sir, my liege,

---

214 *still,* forever.   224 *yare,* shipshape.   226 *tricksy,* i.e., ingenious.   232 *several,* various.
234 *moe,* more.   236 *trim,* sale.   238 *Cap'ring,* dancing for joy; *eye,* see.   240 *moping,* in a daze.
244 *conduct,* conductor.

Do not infest your mind with beating on   246
The strangeness of this business: at picked leisure,
Which shall be shortly, single I'll resolve you   248
(Which to you shall seem probable) of every   249
These happened accidents; till when, be cheerful   250
And think of each thing well.
(Aside to Ariel)   Come hither, spirit.
Set Caliban and his companions free.
Untie the spell.   *(Exit Ariel)*
                                 How fares my gracious sir?
There are yet missing of your company
Some few odd lads that you remember not.

(Enter Ariel, driving in Caliban, Stephano, and Trinculo, in their stolen apparel)

STEPHANO: Every man shift for all the rest, and let no man take care for
  himself; for all is but fortune. Coragio, bully-monster, coragio!
TRINCULO: If these be true spies which I wear in my head, here's a goodly   258
  sight.
CALIBAN: O Setebos, these be brave spirits indeed!
  How fine my master is! I am afraid
  He will chastise me.
SEBASTIAN: Ha, ha!
  What things are these, my Lord Antonio?
  Will money buy 'em?
ANTONIO: Very like. One of them
  Is a plain fish and no doubt marketable.
PROSPERO: Mark but the badges of these men, my lords,   266
  Then say if they be true. This misshapen knave,   267
  His mother was a witch, and one so strong
  That could control the moon, make flows and ebbs,
  And deal in her command without her power.   270
  These three have robbed me, and this demi-devil
  (For he's a bastard one) had plotted with them
  To take my life. Two of these fellows you
  Must know and own; this thing of darkness I
  Acknowledge mine.
CALIBAN: I shall be pinched to death.
ALONSO: Is not this Stephano, my drunken butler?
SEBASTIAN: He is drunk now: where had he wine?
ALONSO: And Trinculo is reeling ripe: where should they

246 *infest*, tease.   248 *single*, privately; *resolve*, explain.   249 *every*, every one of.   250 *accidents*,
incidents.   258 *spies*, eyes.   266 *badges of these men*, signs of these servants.   267 *true*, honest.
270 *her*, i.e., the moon's; *without*, beyond.

Find this grand liquor that hath gilded 'em?
How cam'st thou in this pickle?

TRINCULO: I have been in such a pickle, since I saw you last, that I fear   281
    me will never out of my bones. I shall not fear fly-blowing.

SEBASTIAN: Why, how now, Stephano?

STEPHANO: O, touch me not! I am not Stephano, but a cramp.   284

PROSPERO: You'ld be king o' the isle, sirrah?

STEPHANO: I should have been a sore one then.   286

ALONSO: This is a strange thing as e'er I looked on.

PROSPERO: He is as disproportioned in his manners
    As in his shape. Go, sirrah, to my cell;
    Take with you your companions. As you look
    To have my pardon, trim it handsomely.

CALIBAN: Ay, that I will; and I'll be wise hereafter,
    And seek for grace. What a thrice-double ass
    Was I to take this drunkard for a god
    And worship this dull fool!

PROSPERO: Go to! Away!

ALONSO: Hence, and bestow your luggage where you found it.

SEBASTIAN: Or stole it rather.

(Exeunt Caliban, Stephano, and Trinculo)

PROSPERO: Sir, I invite your Highness and your train
    To my poor cell, where you shall take your rest
    For this one night; which, part of it, I'll waste   300
    With such discourse as, I not doubt, shall make it
    Go quick away—the story of my life,
    And the particular accidents gone by
    Since I came to this isle; and in the morn
    I'll bring you to your ship, and so to Naples,
    Where I have hope to see the nuptial
    Of these our dear-beloved solemnizèd;   307
    And thence retire me to my Milan, where
    Every third thought shall be my grave.

ALONSO: I long
    To hear the story of your life, which must
    Take the ear strangely.   311

PROSPERO: I'll deliver all;
    And promise you calm seas, auspicious gales,

---

281 *pickle,* (1) predicament, (2) preservative (from the horse-pond; hence insects will let him alone).
284 *Stephano,* this name is said to be a slang Neapolitan term for stomach.   **286** *sore,* (1) tyrannical,
(2) aching.   **300** *waste,* spend.   **307** *solemnizèd,* accent second syllable.   **311** *Take,* captivate;
deliver, tell.

And sail so expeditious that shall catch   313
Your royal fleet far off.—My Ariel, chick,
That is thy charge. Then to the elements
Be free, and fare thou well!—Please you draw near.

(Exeunt omnes)

Epilogue

Spoken by Prospero.

> Now my charms are all o'erthrown,
> And what strength I have's mine own,
> Which is most faint. Now 'tis true
> I must be here confined by you,
> Or sent to Naples. Let me not,
> Since I have my dukedom got
> And pardoned the deceiver, dwell
> In this bare island by your spell;   8
> But release me from my bands   9
> With the help of your good hands.   10
> Gentle breath of yours my sails
> Must fill, or else my project fails,
> Which was to please. Now I want   13
> Spirits to enforce, art to enchant;
> And my ending is despair
> Unless I be relieved by prayer,
> Which pierces so that it assaults
> Mercy itself and frees all faults.
> As you from crimes would pardoned be,
> Let your indulgence set me free.   *(Exit)*

QUESTIONS

1. What elements of the play are romantic?
2. In what way are the comic episodes comic? In what way satiric?
3. How does emotion enter and qualify the comic atmosphere?
4. What function does the masque of Ceres serve?
5. What is Gonzalo's function? What is he trying to accomplish as Act II opens and Alonso and Sebastian mock him?
6. How do you account for Prospero's harshness to Miranda, Ferdinand, Ariel, Caliban?

313 *sail,* sailing.   **8** *spell,* i.e., silence.   **9** *bands,* bonds.   **10** *hands,* i.e., applause to break the spell.   **13** *want,* lack.

7. Prospero assures Miranda at the outset, "I have done nothing but in care of thee." Is this entirely true? What can you surmise about his original plans for his enemies? Why does he change?

8. Aside from young love, what does Miranda represent? Explain the irony in her "O brave new world" speech (Act V, Scene I, 181–4).

CHAPTER 3

SOCIAL DRAMA

Tragedy and comedy present life's enduring subjects—love, marriage, death, ambition, and revenge. Romance and satire embody them less concretely in individualized human beings and more abstractly as ideals (the four cardinal virtues) or vices (the seven deadly sins). Tragedy and comedy, as well as romance and satire, are, in a sense, varied containers into which the same contents are poured. Playwrights are sometimes not so interested in the shape of the container as its contents, the material of life. This is especially true when the theme, the idea upon which the play is built, forces our attention upon the world outside the play.

The plays in this section stress that social world. They mute or blend comedy and tragedy within a social context. They move from individual fortune to tell us something about society at large. *An Enemy of the People* raises questions about individual responsibilities to self and neighbors and to one's vision of the truth. *The Cherry Orchard,* which Chekhov considered comic, gives a dissonant and ambiguous picture of society characteristic of much modern drama. *Suppressed Desires* spoofs early understandings of Freudian psychology, exploring the possible effects on marriage of new ideas about the rights and mental health of men and women.

AN ENEMY OF THE PEOPLE

An Enemy of the People examines the social, economic, and political relationships within a small town threatened with closing of the baths that are its chief municipal pride and the source of its economic well-being. Grafting a personal drama on a political one by making the "enemy" the brother to the mayor, Ibsen

1129

depicted society's large and impersonal forces in sharply defined human dimensions.

AN ENEMY OF THE PEOPLE*

Henrik Ibsen   (1828–1906)

Characters

DR. THOMAS STOCKMANN, doctor at the Baths

MRS. KATHERINE STOCKMANN, his wife

PETRA, their daughter, a teacher

EJLIF
MORTEN ⎱ their sons, 13 and 10 years old

PETER STOCKMANN, the doctor's elder brother, Mayor, Chief of Police, Chairman of the Board of the Baths, &c.

MORTEN KIIL, owner of a tannery, Mrs. Stockmann's foster-father

HOVSTAD, editor of the *People's Herald*

BILLING, a journalist

CAPTAIN HORSTER

ASLAKSEN, a printer

Attending a public meeting are: men of all classes, some women and a group of schoolboys

The action takes place in a coastal town in Southern Norway

Act I

Evening. Dr. Stockmann's living-room, simply but tastefully furnished. In the side-wall, right, are two doors, one of which upstage leads to the hall, and the other to the doctor's study. On the opposite wall and directly facing the hall door, another door leads to the rest of the house. In the middle of this wall stands a stove; downstage of it is a sofa; above it hangs a mirror and in front of it is an oval table covered with a cloth. On the table, a shaded lamp is burning. In the back wall, the door to the dining-room stands open. Within, the table is laid for supper; a lighted lamp stands on the table.

Billing, a napkin tucked under his chin, is seated within at the supper table. Mrs. Stockmann stands by the table and hands him a serving dish on which is a large joint of beef. The other places at table are empty, and the table is in disarray as though after a meal.

> MRS. STOCKMANN: Well, if you will arrive an hour late, Mr. Billing, you'll have to put up with everything being cold.
>
> BILLING *(eating):* It's absolutely delicious, really excellent.

*Translated by James Walter McFarlane.

MRS. STOCKMANN: You know how strict my husband is about keeping punctually to his mealtimes. . . .

BILLING: It doesn't matter to me in the least. In fact I almost believe it tastes better, sitting down like this to it, alone and undisturbed.

MRS. STOCKMANN: Ah well, as long as you enjoy it. . . . *(Turns to the hall door and listens.)* That's probably Hovstad.

BILLING: Quite likely.

(Peter Stockmann, the Mayor, enters; he is wearing an overcoat and his mayor's hat, and he carries a stick)

MAYOR: A very good evening to you, Katherine.

MRS. STOCKMANN *(coming into the living-room):* Oh. It's you! Good evening. How nice of you to drop in like this.

MAYOR: I happened to be passing, so . . . *(With a glance towards the dining-room)* Oh, but it seems you have company.

MRS. STOCKMANN *(rather embarrassed):* No, not really. He just happened to drop in. *(Quickly)* Wouldn't you like to join him and let me get you something to eat?

MAYOR: Who, me? No thank you. Heavens above! A cooked meal in the evening! Not with my digestion.

MRS. STOCKMANN: Oh, couldn't you just for once . . . ?

MAYOR: Bless you, no. I stick to my tea and bread and butter. It's better for one's health in the long run . . . as well as being more economical.

MRS. STOCKMANN *(smiles):* Now you mustn't get the idea that Thomas and I are terribly extravagant, either.

MAYOR: Not *you,* Katherine. I'd never think that of you. *(Points to the doctor's study)* Isn't he at home?

MRS. STOCKMANN: No, he's gone for a little walk after his supper . . . with the boys.

MAYOR: I wonder if that really does one any good? *(Listens)* That's him now.

MRS. STOCKMANN: No, I don't think it's him. *(There is a knock on the door.)* Come in!

(Hovstad comes in from the hall)

MRS. STOCKMANN: Oh, it's Mr. Hovstad.

HOVSTAD: Yes, you must excuse me, but I got held up at the printer's. Good evening, Mr. Mayor.

MAYOR *(bowing rather stiffly):* Good evening! A business call, no doubt?

HOVSTAD: Partly. It's in connection with something for the paper.

MAYOR: That I can imagine. From all accounts, my brother is a prolific contributor to the *People's Herald.*

HOVSTAD: Yes, whenever he wants to get any particular home-truths off his chest, he writes a piece for the *Herald.*

MRS. STOCKMANN *(to Hovstad):* But won't you . . . ? *(She points to the dining-room)*

MAYOR: Indeed, and why not? Who am I to blame him if he decides to write for the class of reader he can expect the greatest response from! And in any case, there's no reason for me to feel any personal animosity towards your paper, Mr. Hovstad.

HOVSTAD: No, I don't think there is.

MAYOR: All in all, there is an admirable spirit of tolerance in our little town ... a sense of civic pride. That's what comes of having a great communal undertaking to unite us ... an undertaking which concerns all right-thinking citizens in equal measure. ...

HOVSTAD: The Baths, you mean.

MAYOR: Exactly. We have our splendid new Baths. Mark my words! The prosperity of the town will come to depend more and more on the Baths, Mr. Hovstad. No doubt about it!

MRS. STOCKMANN: Thomas says the same.

MAYOR: Just look at the quite extraordinary way things have improved, even in the last year or two. People have more money! There's more life, more things going on. Land and property are going up in value every day.

HOVSTAD: And unemployment falling.

MAYOR: Yes, that too. The burden of the poor-rate on the propertied classes has, I am happy to say, been considerably reduced—and it will be even less if only we have a really good summer this year ... with plenty of visitors, and lots of convalescents to help to give the place a reputation.

HOVSTAD: And things are looking pretty promising in that way, they tell me.

MAYOR: The prospects are very encouraging. Every day we receive more inquiries about accommodation and things like that.

HOVSTAD: Well then, I suppose the doctor's article will just come in nicely.

MAYOR: Has he been writing something else?

HOVSTAD: This is something he wrote during the winter, giving an account of the Baths and recommending the place generally as a very healthy spot. But I didn't use the article at the time.

MAYOR: Aha! I expect there was a snag in it somewhere.

HOVSTAD: No, it wasn't that. But I thought it might be better to hold it over till the spring; now's the time when people start thinking about their summer holidays. ...

MAYOR: Very sensible, very sensible indeed, Mr. Hovstad.

MRS. STOCKMANN: Yes, Thomas is quite indefatigable if it's anything to do with the Baths.

MAYOR: Well, as he's one of its officials it's only natural.

HOVSTAD: Besides, he was the one who started the whole thing.

MAYOR: *He* was! Indeed! Yes, this isn't the first time I've heard of people getting that idea. But I rather imagined *I* too had had a modest part in this enterprise.

MRS. STOCKMANN: Yes, that's what Thomas is always saying.

HOVSTAD: Of course, who would want to deny that, Mr. Mayor. It was you who got things moving, got it going as a practical concern, we all know

that, of course. All I meant was that the idea came first from Dr. Stockmann.

MAYOR: Yes, my brother's always had plenty of ideas—more's the pity. But
when it's a matter of getting things done, you have to look round for a
different type of man, Mr. Hovstad. I should at least have thought that
the members of *this* household would . . .

MRS. STOCKMANN: My dear Peter . . .

HOVSTAD: But Mr. Mayor, how can you . . . ?

MRS. STOCKMANN: You go and get yourself something to eat, Mr. Hovstad.
My husband is sure to be back by the time you're finished.

HOVSTAD: Thanks. Perhaps just a bite.

(He goes into the dining-room)

MAYOR *(lowering his voice):* Funny, these people from peasant stock! They
never have any tact.

MRS. STOCKMANN: But there's no point in upsetting yourself about it! Can't
you and Thomas share the credit like brothers!

MAYOR: Yes, one would have thought so. But apparently it isn't everybody
who is content to share.

MRS. STOCKMANN: Oh, nonsense. You and Thomas get on perfectly well
together on this point. *(Listens)* That's him now, I think.

(She goes over and opens the door into the hall)

DR. STOCKMANN *(laughing and talking outside):* Here we are, another visitor
for you, Katherine. Isn't this fun, eh! Come in, Captain Horster. Hang
your coat on that peg there. You don't bother with an overcoat, eh? You
know, Katherine, I ran into him on the street. . . . Had a terrible job
persuading him to come along.

(Captain Horster enters and bows to Mrs. Stockmann)

DR. STOCKMANN *(in the doorway):* In you go, lads. They are absolutely ravenous again, my dear. Come along, Captain Horster, what do you say to a
bit of roast beef . . . ?

(He urges Horster into the dining-room; Ejlif and Morten go in also)

MRS. STOCKMANN: But Thomas, don't you see . . . ?

DR. STOCKMANN *(turns in the doorway):* Oh, it's you, Peter. *(Walks across and
shakes hands.)* Well, this is very pleasant.

MAYOR: Unfortunately I can only stay a minute or two. . . .

DR. STOCKMANN: Rubbish! There'll be some hot toddy coming up soon. You
haven't forgotten the toddy, Katherine, have you?

MRS. STOCKMANN: Of course not! I've got the kettle on.

(She goes into the dining-room)

MAYOR: Toddy as well!

DR. STOCKMANN: Yes, sit yourself down and we'll make an evening of it.

MAYOR: Thanks, but I don't care for drinking parties.

DR. STOCKMANN: This isn't a drinking party.

MAYOR: It seems to me . . . *(He looks into the dining-room)* It's incredible the amount of food they manage to put away.

DR. STOCKMANN *(rubbing his hands):* Yes, isn't it grand to see young people eating well? Such an appetite they've got! That's as it ought to be. They need food . . . need to build up their strength. They'll be the ones to stir things up a bit in the coming years, Peter.

MAYOR: And what, if I may ask, is it that requires 'stirring up', as you put it?

DR. STOCKMANN: Ah, you'll have to ask the younger generation about that— when the time comes. We just can't see it, of course. Stands to reason! A couple of old fogies like you and me . . . !

MAYOR: Well, really! That's a most extraordinary description. . . .

DR. STOCKMANN: Oh, you mustn't take me too seriously, Peter. Thing is, I feel so full of the joy of everything, you see. I can't tell you how happy I feel, surrounded by all this growing, vigorous life. What a glorious age this is to live in! It's as if a whole new world were springing up all around.

MAYOR: Do you really think so?

DR. STOCKMANN: Well, you can't see it as clearly as I can, of course. All your life you've lived amongst this kind of thing, and it doesn't make the same sharp impression on you. But think of me, living all those years in the North, cut off from everything, hardly ever seeing a new face, never the chance of any decent conversation . . . for me it's like coming to some great throbbing metropolis.

MAYOR: Huh! Metropolis . . . !

DR. STOCKMANN: Well, I know everything's on a small scale compared with a lot of other places. But there's life here . . . and promise . . . and innumerable things to work and strive for. *That's* what counts. *(Shouts)* Katherine, has the postman been?

MRS. STOCKMANN *(in the dining-room):* No, nobody's been.

DR. STOCKMANN: And then what it is to have a decent income, Peter! That's something one learns to appreciate after living on a starvation wage as we did. . . .

MAYOR: Surely now . . .

DR. STOCKMANN: Oh yes we did. Let me tell you, things were often pretty tight up there. But now I can live like a gentleman. Today, for instance, we had a joint of beef for dinner; it did us for supper, too. Wouldn't you like a taste? Or let me show it to you, anyway. Come here. . . .

MAYOR: No, no, it's not necessary. . . .

DR. STOCKMANN: Well, come here then. Look, we've got a new table-cloth.

MAYOR: So I noticed.

DR. STOCKMANN: And we've got a lampshade. See? Katherine managed to save all that. Don't you think it makes the room look cosy? Just stand over here—no, no, not there—here, that's right! See? How it directs the light down like that . . . ? I think it looks really elegant, don't you?

MAYOR: Yes, for those who can afford such luxuries. . . .

DR. STOCKMANN: Oh, yes! Of course I can afford it. Katherine says I earn very nearly as much as we spend.

MAYOR: Nearly . . . yes!

DR. STOCKMANN: But a man of science ought to have a decent standard of living. I bet you there's many a civil servant spends more in a year than I do.

MAYOR: Well, I dare say there is. A civil servant, a senior executive. . . .

DR. STOCKMANN: Well, an ordinary businessman then. I'm sure that sort of person spends very much more. . . .

MAYOR: That depends on circumstances.

DR. STOCKMANN: Anyway, I don't go throwing my money away on any old thing, Peter. But I feel I can't deny myself the pleasure of having people in. I need something like that, you see, after being out of things for so long. For me it's like one of the necessities of life—to enjoy the company of eager young people, with initiative and minds of their own. That's the kind of person you'll find sitting at my table, enjoying their food. I wish you knew Hovstad a bit better. . . .

MAYOR: Ah, Hovstad, that's right. He was telling me he's going to print another one of your articles.

DR. STOCKMANN: One of my articles?

MAYOR: Yes, about the Baths. An article you'd apparently written during the winter.

DR. STOCKMANN: Oh, that one! Well, I don't want that one in just now.

MAYOR: Don't you? This seems to me to be exactly the right time for it.

DR. STOCKMANN: Yes, that's right . . . in ordinary circumstances. . . .

(He walks about the room)

MAYOR *(watching him):* And what's so extraordinary about the present circumstances?

DR. STOCKMANN *(halts):* In point of fact, Peter, that's something I can't tell you for the moment. Not this evening, anyway. There might be quite a lot that's unusual about the present state of affairs; on the other hand, it might be nothing at all. It might very well be just my imagination.

MAYOR: I must admit it all sounds very mysterious. What's going on? Why am I being kept out of it? I would remind you that, as Chairman of the Board of the Baths, I . . .

DR. STOCKMANN: And I would remind you that I . . . Oh, let's not jump down each other's throats, Peter.

MAYOR: Heaven forbid! I'm not in the habit of jumping down people's throats, as you put it. But I must insist most emphatically that all matters be considered and dealt with through the proper channels and by the appropriate authorities. I cannot permit any dubious or underhand methods.

DR. STOCKMANN: Since when have *I* used dubious or underhand methods?

MAYOR: You have a chronic disposition to take things into your own hands, at least. And in a well-ordered community, that can be equally reprehensible. The individual must be ready to subordinate himself to the community as a whole; or, more precisely, to the authorities charged with the welfare of that community.

DR. STOCKMANN: That may well be. But what the devil has that got to do with me?

MAYOR: Everything. Because, my dear Thomas, that's just the thing you don't seem to want to learn. But mark my words; one of these days you'll pay for it . . . sooner or later. I'm telling you. Goodbye.

DR. STOCKMANN: Have you gone stark, staring mad? You are barking up the wrong tree altogether. . . .

MAYOR: I'm not in the habit of doing that. And now if I may be excused. . . . *(He calls into the dining-room.)* Goodbye, Katherine. Goodbye, gentlemen.

(He leaves)

MRS. STOCKMANN *(comes into the living-room):* Has he gone?

DR. STOCKMANN: Yes, he has; and in high dudgeon.

MRS. STOCKMANN: Thomas, my dear, what have you been doing to him this time?

DR. STOCKMANN: Absolutely nothing. He can't expect an account from me before the proper time.

MRS. STOCKMANN: What are you expected to give him an account of?

DR. STOCKMANN: Hm! Don't bother me about that now, Katherine.—Funny the postman doesn't come.

(Hovstad, Billing and Horster have risen from the table and come into the living-room. Ejlif and Morten follow them after a while.)

BILLING *(stretches himself):* Ah! A supper like that and, damn me, if it doesn't make you feel like a new man!

HOVSTAD: Our Mayor wasn't in the best of moods this evening.

DR. STOCKMANN: It's his stomach. Digestion's none too good.

HOVSTAD: It was mainly us two from the *Herald* he couldn't stomach, I reckon.

MRS. STOCKMANN: I thought you seemed to be getting on quite nicely with him.

HOVSTAD: Oh yes, but it's only a kind of armistice.

BILLING: That's it. That describes it exactly.

DR. STOCKMANN: We mustn't forget that Peter's a lonely person, poor chap. He hasn't any proper home where he can relax. Business, nothing but business! And all that damned weak tea he keeps pouring into himself.

Now then, lads, pull your chairs up to the table. Katherine, don't we get any toddy?

MRS. STOCKMANN *(makes for the dining-room):* I'm just going to get it.

DR. STOCKMANN: Come and sit beside me on the sofa, Captain Horster. It's so rarely we see you. Do sit down, my friends.

(The men seat themselves round the table. Mrs. Stockmann enters with a tray on which there is a kettle, glasses, decanters and so on.)

MRS. STOCKMANN: There we are. This is Arrack, and this is rum, and this is cognac. Everybody just help themselves.

DR. STOCKMANN *(takes a glass):* Ah, we will that! *(Whilst the toddy is being mixed.)* Let's have the cigars out, too. Ejlif, you know where the box is kept. And you, Morten, can bring my pipe. *(The boys go into the room on the right.)* I have a suspicion Ejlif helps himself to a cigar now and then, but I don't let on I know. *(Calls.)* My smoking-cap as well, Morten! Katherine, could you tell him where I've put it. Ah! he's got it. *(The boys bring the various articles)* Help yourselves, my friends. I'll stick to my pipe. Many's the time this one's done the rounds with me, fair weather and foul, up there in the North. *(They clink glasses.)* Your health! Ah, it's much better to be sitting nice and snug in here.

MRS. STOCKMANN *(sits knitting):* Will you be sailing soon, Captain Horster?

HORSTER: I reckon we'll be ready by next week.

MRS. STOCKMANN: And then you're off to America?

HORSTER: That's the intention.

BILLING: Then you won't be able to vote in the municipal election.

HORSTER: Is there going to be an election?

BILLING: Didn't you know?

HORSTER: No, I don't bother about things like that.

BILLING: But you take an interest in public affairs, I suppose?

HORSTER: No, I don't know the first thing about them.

BILLING: I think people ought to vote, all the same.

HORSTER: Even those who have no idea what it's all about?

BILLING: No idea? What do you mean? Society's like a ship; everybody must help to steer it.

HORSTER: That might be all very well on dry land; but it wouldn't work very well at sea.

HOVSTAD: It's strange how little most seafaring people care about what goes on ashore.

BILLING: Quite remarkable.

DR. STOCKMANN: Sailors are like birds of passage, equally at home in the north or in the south. All the more reason for the rest of us to be even more active, Mr. Hovstad. Is there anything of public interest in the *Herald* tomorrow?

HOVSTAD: Nothing about municipal affairs. But I thought of putting in your article the day after. . . .

DR. STOCKMANN: Oh damn it, yes! That article. Listen, you must hold it over for a while.

HOVSTAD: Really! It just happens we have room for it now, and it seemed to be the right time for it. . . .

DR. STOCKMANN: Yes, yes, maybe you are right; but you'll have to wait all the same. I'll explain later. . . .

(Petra, wearing a hat and a cloak, comes in from the hall, a pile of exercise books under her arm)

PETRA: Good evening.

DR. STOCKMANN: Is that you, Petra? Good evening!

(Greetings all round. Petra takes off her things and puts them, along with the exercise books, on a chair beside the door.)

PETRA: So you've all been sitting here enjoying yourselves while I've been out slaving.

DR. STOCKMANN: Now *you* come and enjoy yourself too, then.

BILLING: Can I get you something to drink?

PETRA *(comes over to the table):* Thanks. But I'd rather do it myself. You always make it too strong. But I'm forgetting, Father, I have a letter for you.

(Goes over to the chair where her things are)

DR. STOCKMANN: A letter? Who from?

PETRA *(feels in her coat pocket):* The postman gave me it just as I was going out. . . .

DR. STOCKMANN *(gets up and goes across to her):* And you haven't brought it out before now!

PETRA: I hadn't time to run back again with it. Here it is.

DR. STOCKMANN *(seizing the letter):* Let me see it. Let me see it, child. *(Looks at the address)* Yes, that's it. . . .

MRS. STOCKMANN: Is *that* the one you have been waiting for, Thomas?

DR. STOCKMANN: Yes, that's the one. Excuse me if I take it straight into . . . Where can I find a light, Katherine? Is there still no lamp in my study!

MRS. STOCKMANN: Yes, of course. There's a lamp already lit on your desk.

DR. STOCKMANN: Good, good. Excuse me a minute. . . .

(He goes into his room, right)

PETRA: What can that be, Mother?

MRS. STOCKMANN: I don't know. He's done nothing else these last few days but ask whether the postman's been.

BILLING: Presumably some country patient.

PETRA: Poor Father! All this work, it's getting too much for him. *(She mixes her drink.)* Ah, I'm going to enjoy this!

HOVSTAD: Have you been taking Evening Classes again today?

PETRA *(sipping her glass):* Two hours.

BILLING: And four hours this morning at the Institute.

PETRA *(sits at the table):* Five hours.

MRS. STOCKMANN: And tonight I see you have essays to correct.

PETRA: A whole bundle of them.

HORSTER: You've got plenty of work to do yourself, it seems.

PETRA: Yes, but that's all right. It makes you feel so gloriously tired afterwards.

BILLING: Do you like that?

PETRA: Yes, it makes you sleep so well.

MORTEN: You must be a dreadful sinner, Petra!

PETRA: Sinner?

MORTEN: Working as hard as you do. Mr. Rörlund says that work is a punishment for our sins.

EJLIF: Puh! You must be stupid, believing a thing like that!

MRS. STOCKMANN: Now, now, Ejlif!

BILLING *(laughs):* Oh, that's good, that is!

HOVSTAD: Don't you want to work as hard as that, Morten?

MORTEN: No, I don't.

HOVSTAD: Well, what *do* you want to be when you grow up?

MORTEN: I want to be a Viking.

EJLIF: Well, you'd have to be a heathen.

MORTEN: All right, I'll be a heathen.

BILLING: I'm with you there, Morten. I say exactly the same.

MRS. STOCKMANN *(making signs):* I'm sure you wouldn't really do anything of the kind.

BILLING: Yes I would, so help me! I *am* a heathen, and proud of it. You watch, we'll all be heathens before long.

MORTEN: And *then* can we do exactly what we like?

BILLING: Well, you see, Morten . . .

MRS. STOCKMANN: Now, boys, off you go now; I'm sure you've got some homework for tomorrow.

EJLIF: Couldn't *I* just stay on a little bit longer . . . ?

MRS. STOCKMANN: No. Off you go now, both of you.

(The boys say good night and go into the room, left)

HOVSTAD: Do you really think it's bad for the boys to listen to things like that?

MRS. STOCKMANN: Oh, I don't know. But I don't much like it.

PETRA: Oh, Mother! I think you're quite mistaken there.

MRS. STOCKMANN: Yes, that's quite possible. But I *don't* like it, not in my own home.

PETRA: All this hypocrisy, both at home and at school. At home one mustn't say anything; and at school we have to stand there and lie to the children.

HORSTER: Lie to them?

PETRA: Yes. Can't you see we have to teach all sorts of things we don't even believe in ourselves?

BILLING: That's only too true.

PETRA: If only I had the money, I'd start a school myself, where things would be run very differently.

BILLING: Huh! The money!

HORSTER: Well, if you've got anything like that in mind, Miss Stockmann, I'd be glad to offer you the necessary accommodation. My father's big old house is standing there practically empty; there's an enormous dining-room on the ground floor. . . .

PETRA *(laughs):* Thanks, thanks very much. But nothing's likely to come of it.

HOVSTAD: No, I think Miss Petra's much more likely to join the ranks of the journalists. By the way, have you had any time to look at that English story you promised to translate for us?

PETRA: No, not yet. But you'll have it in good time.

(Doctor Stockmann comes out of his room, with the open letter in his hand)

DR. STOCKMANN *(waving the letter):* Well! Here's a bit of news that will set a few tongues wagging about the town!

BILLING: News?

MRS. STOCKMANN: What news?

DR. STOCKMANN: A great discovery, Katherine!

HOVSTAD: Really?

MRS. STOCKMANN: Which you've made?

DR. STOCKMANN: Which I've made, yes. *(Walks up and down)* Now let them come as they always do, and say it's some madman's crazy idea! Ah, but they'll watch their step this time! They'll watch out this time, I'll bet.

PETRA: But, Father, tell us what this is all about.

DR. STOCKMANN: Yes, yes, just give me time and you'll hear all about it. Ah, if only I had Peter here! Yes, it lets you see how we men go about our affairs as blind as bats. . . .

HOVSTAD: What do you mean, Doctor?

DR. STOCKMANN *(stands by the table):* Is it not generally believed that our town is a healthy place?

HOVSTAD: Yes, of course.

DR. STOCKMANN: A quite exceptionally healthy place, in fact . . . a place highly commended on this score both for the sick and for the healthy. . . .

MRS. STOCKMANN: Yes, but my dear Thomas . . .

DR. STOCKMANN: And have we not recommended it and acclaimed it? I myself have written repeatedly, both in the *Herald* and in a number of pamphlets. . . .

HOVSTAD: Well, what of it?

DR. STOCKMANN: And then these Baths—the so-called 'artery' of the town, or the 'nerve centre', and the devil only knows what else they've been called. . . .

BILLING: 'The throbbing heart of the town', as I was once, in a festive moment, moved to call it.

DR. STOCKMANN: Quite so. But do you know what they are in reality, these great and splendid and glorious Baths that have cost such a lot of money —do you know what they are?

HOVSTAD: No, what are they?

MRS. STOCKMANN: Yes, what are they?

DR. STOCKMANN: The Baths are nothing but a cesspool.

PETRA: The Baths, Father!

MRS. STOCKMANN (at the same time): Our Baths!

HOVSTAD (likewise): But, Doctor . . . !

BILLING: Absolutely incredible!

DR. STOCKMANN: The whole establishment is a whited poisoned sepulchre, I tell you! A most serious danger to health! All that filth up at Mölledal, where there's such an awful stench—it's all seeping into the pipes that lead to the pump-room! And that same damned, poisonous muck is seeping out on the beach as well!

HORSTER: Where the bathing place is, you mean?

DR. STOCKMANN: Exactly.

HOVSTAD: How are you so certain about all this, Doctor?

DR. STOCKMANN: I have investigated the position with scrupulous thoroughness. Oh, I've had my suspicions long enough. Last year there were a number of curious cases of sickness among the visitors . . . typhoid and gastric fever. . . .

MRS. STOCKMANN: Yes, so there were.

DR. STOCKMANN: It was thought at the time that the visitors had brought their infections with them. But afterwards . . . during the winter . . . I began to have other ideas. So I carried out a few tests on the water, as far as I could.

MRS. STOCKMANN: So *that's* what's been keeping you so busy!

DR. STOCKMANN: Yes, you may well say I've been busy, Katherine. But of course I didn't have all the necessary scientific equipment. So I sent some samples—drinking water as well as sea-water—up to the university to get an exact chemical analysis.

HOVSTAD: Which you have now received?

DR. STOCKMANN (shows the letter): Here it is! It testifies to the presence in the water of putrefied organic matter . . . it's full of bacteria. It is extremely dangerous to health, internally and externally.

MRS. STOCKMANN: What a mercy you found out in time!

DR. STOCKMANN: You may well say so.

HOVSTAD: And what do you intend to do now, Doctor?

DR. STOCKMANN: To see the matter put right, of course.

HOVSTAD: Can that be done?

DR. STOCKMANN: It must be done. Otherwise the whole establishment is useless, ruined. But there's no need for that. It's quite clear to me what must now be done.

MRS. STOCKMANN: But, my dear Thomas, what made you keep all this so secret?

DR. STOCKMANN: Did you expect me to run all round town gossiping about it before I was absolutely certain? No thank you! I'm not such a fool as all that.

PETRA: Still, your own family . . .

DR. STOCKMANN: No, not a living soul. Still, you can run round in the morning to the old 'Badger'. . . .

MRS. STOCKMANN: Please, Thomas!

DR. STOCKMANN: All right, to your grandfather, then. Yes, now we'll give that old boy something that will really open his eyes. He's another one who thinks I'm a bit cracked—oh yes, there are plenty more with the same idea, I can see. But now these good people are going to see something— they're certainly going to see something, this time. *(He walks round rubbing his hands.)* What a commotion this is going to cause in the town, Katherine! You've no idea! All the pipes will have to be re-laid.

HOVSTAD *(rising):* All the pipes . . . ?

DR. STOCKMANN: Naturally. The intake is sited too low down; it will have to be moved much higher up.

PETRA: So you were right after all.

DR. STOCKMANN: Ah, you remember, Petra? I wrote in opposing it, when they were drawing up the plans. But at that time nobody would listen to me. Well, now I'm going to let them have it. Naturally I've written a report for the Board—it's been lying there all ready for the past week. I was only waiting for this to come. *(He points to the letter.)* But now we'll get this off at once. *(He goes into his room and comes back with a sheaf of papers.)* Look! Four closely written sheets! And the letter attached. A newspaper, Katherine! Something to wrap it in. Good! There we are! Give it to . . . to . . . *(Stamps his foot)* . . . what the devil's her name again? Anyway, give it to that girl, and tell her to take it straight down to the Mayor.

(Mrs. Stockmann takes the packet and goes out through the dining-room)

PETRA: What do you think Uncle Peter's going to say, Father?

DR. STOCKMANN: What do you expect him to say? He can't help but be pleased that an important matter like this has been brought to light, surely.

HOVSTAD: Do you mind if we put a little paragraph in the *Herald* about your discovery?

DR. STOCKMANN: I should be extremely grateful if you would.

HOVSTAD: The sooner the public hears about this, the better.

DR. STOCKMANN: Certainly.

MRS. STOCKMANN *(returning):* She's just gone with it now.

BILLING: You'll be the leading light of the town, Dr. Stockmann, damn me if you won't!

DR. STOCKMANN *(walks happily up and down):* Oh, don't be silly! I've only done my duty. It just happened to be a lucky strike, that's all. All the same . . .

BILLING: Hovstad, don't you think the town ought to organize something to show its appreciation to Dr. Stockmann?

HOVSTAD: I'll certainly put it forward.

BILLING: And I'll talk it over with Aslaksen.

DR. STOCKMANN: Please, please, my dear friends! Let's have no more of this nonsense. I won't hear of it. And if the Board starts getting any ideas about increasing my salary, I shall refuse. Do you hear me, Katherine? —I won't take it.

MRS. STOCKMANN: Quite right, Thomas.

PETRA *(raising her glass):* Your health, Father!

HOVSTAD: ⎫
BILLING: ⎬ Your health, Dr. Stockmann!

HORSTER *(clinking glasses with him):* Here's wishing you joy of it!

DR. STOCKMANN: Thank you, my dear friends, thank you! I am extremely happy. . . . What a wonderful thing it is to feel that one's been of some service to one's home town and fellow citizens. Hurrah, Katherine!

(He puts his arms round her and whirls her round and round; she screams and tries to resist. Laughter, applause, and cheering for the Doctor. The boys poke their heads in at the door.)

Act II

The Doctor's living-room; the door to the dining-room is shut. It is morning. Mrs. Stockmann comes out of the dining-room, carrying in her hand a sealed letter; she crosses to the door of the Doctor's study, right, and peeps in.

MRS. STOCKMANN: Are you there, Thomas?

DR. STOCKMANN *(within):* Yes, I've just got back. *(Comes in)* What is it?

MRS. STOCKMANN: A letter from your brother.

(She hands him the letter)

DR. STOCKMANN: Aha, let us see. *(He opens the envelope and reads)* 'Your manuscript is herewith returned. . . .' *(He reads on to himself in a low murmur)* Hm!

MRS. STOCKMANN: What does he say?

DR. STOCKMANN: Oh, just that he'll look in about midday.

MRS. STOCKMANN: You mustn't forget to be at home this time.

DR. STOCKMANN: I'll manage that all right; I've finished all my morning calls.

MRS. STOCKMANN: I'm awfully curious to know how he's taking it.

DR. STOCKMANN: He'll not be very pleased that I was the one to make the discovery and not he, you'll see.

MRS. STOCKMANN: Doesn't that worry you a little?

DR. STOCKMANN: Oh, he'll be glad enough really, you know. It's just that Peter can't bear to see anybody other than himself doing things for the town.

MRS. STOCKMANN: Well, you know what I think, Thomas? I think you should be a dear and share the credit with him. Couldn't you drop a hint that it was he who first put you on the track . . . ?

DR. STOCKMANN: Certainly, for all it matters to me. I only want to see that something gets done about it. . . .

(Old Morten Kiil puts his head round the hall door, looks round inquiringly, and chuckles to himself)

MORTEN KIIL *(slyly):* This thing . . . is it true?

MRS. STOCKMANN *(crosses towards him):* Father! What are you doing here!

DR. STOCKMANN: Well, well! Good morning, Father-in-law!

MRS. STOCKMANN: Do come in.

KIIL: I will if it's true; if it isn't, I'm off again.

DR. STOCKMANN: If what's true?

KIIL: This queer business about the water-works. Well, is it true?

DR. STOCKMANN: Certainly it's true. But how did you get to know about it?

KIIL *(comes in):* Petra dashed in on her way to school. . . .

DR. STOCKMANN: Oh, did she?

KIIL: Yes, and from what she says . . . I thought she was just pulling my leg; but it isn't like Petra to do that.

DR. STOCKMANN: No, what made you think a thing like that!

KIIL: Oh, you should never trust anybody. You can be taken in almost before you know where you are. But it really is true, then?

DR. STOCKMANN: Definitely. Just you sit down now. *(Urges him to sit on the sofa)* Isn't this a real stroke of luck for the town . . . ?

KIIL *(fighting his laughter):* A stroke of luck for the town?

DR. STOCKMANN: Yes, the fact that I found out in time. . . .

KIIL *(as before):* Oh, yes, of course! But I never thought you would try any monkey tricks on your own brother.

DR. STOCKMANN: Monkey tricks?

MRS. STOCKMANN: Really, Father!

KIIL *(resting his hands and his chin on the handle of his stick and winking slyly at the Doctor):* Let me see, how was it now? Wasn't it something about some little creatures that had got into the water pipes?

DR. STOCKMANN: That's right. Bacteria.

KIIL: And from what Petra said, a whole lot of these animals had got in. An enormous number.

DR. STOCKMANN: That's right. Hundreds of thousands of them!

KIIL: And yet nobody can see them—isn't that what they say?

DR. STOCKMANN: Of course. Nobody can *see* them.

KIIL (*quietly chuckling*): Damn me if this isn't the best you've managed yet.

DR. STOCKMANN: I don't know what you mean!

KIIL: But you'll never get the Mayor to believe a thing like this.

DR. STOCKMANN: We'll see about that.

KIIL: You don't think he's such a fool as all that!

DR. STOCKMANN: I hope the whole town's going to be such fools as all that.

KIIL: The whole town. Well, that's not such a bad idea, after all. It'll serve them right . . . do them good. They all think they're so much smarter than us older men. They hounded me off the Council, they did, I tell you. Treated me like a dog, they did. But now they'll get what's coming to them. You just carry on with your little tricks, Stockmann.

DR. STOCKMANN: But really . . .

KIIL: You just keep it up, I say. (*Gets up*) If you can manage to put a thing like this across on the Mayor and his lot, I'll give a hundred crowns to charity on the spot.

DR. STOCKMANN: That's very good of you.

KIIL: Yes, I haven't all that much money to throw about, I'll have you know, but if you pull this off, I'll give fifty crowns to charity next Christmas.

(*Hovstad comes in from the hall*)

HOVSTAD: Good morning! (*Stops*) Oh, I beg your pardon. . . .

DR. STOCKMANN: No, come in, come in.

KIIL (*chuckles again*): Him! Is he in on this as well?

HOVSTAD: What do you mean?

DR. STOCKMANN: Of course he's in on it.

KIIL: I might have known! It has to get into the papers. Ah! You're a right one, Stockmann. I'll leave you to talk it over; and now I'll be off.

DR. STOCKMANN: Oh, can't you stay a bit longer?

KIIL: No, I must be off now. Keep it up and bring out all the tricks you can think of. I'm damned sure you won't lose by it.

(*He goes, accompanied by Mrs. Stockmann*)

DR. STOCKMANN (*laughs*): Fancy—the old man doesn't believe a word about this business of the water-works!

HOVSTAD: Ah, so that was what you . . . !

DR. STOCKMANN: Yes, that was what we were talking about. And you've probably come about the same thing, eh?

HOVSTAD: Yes, I have. Can you spare me a moment or two, Doctor?

DR. STOCKMANN: As long as you like, my dear fellow.

HOVSTAD: Have you heard anything from the Mayor?

DR. STOCKMANN: Not yet. He's coming round here later.

HOVSTAD: I've been thinking a lot about this thing since last night.

DR. STOCKMANN: Well?

HOVSTAD: As a doctor and a man of science, you regard this matter of the water-supply as something quite on its own, no doubt. What I mean is

—it probably hasn't struck you that it's tied up with a lot of other things?

DR. STOCKMANN: In what way . . . ? Come and sit down, my dear fellow. No, on the sofa there.

(Hovstad sits down on the sofa, the doctor in an armchair on the other side of the table)

DR. STOCKMANN: Now, what was it you were saying . . . ?

HOVSTAD: You said yesterday that the water was contaminated by impurities in the soil.

DR. STOCKMANN: Yes, there's no doubt it all comes from that poisonous swamp up at Mölledal.

HOVSTAD: You'll forgive me, Doctor, but I think it comes from a very different swamp.

DR. STOCKMANN: What swamp?

HOVSTAD: The swamp that our whole community is standing rotting in.

DR. STOCKMANN: What kind of damned nonsense is this you're talking, Mr. Hovstad?

HOVSTAD: Everything in this town has gradually found its way into the hands of a certain group of officials. . . .

DR. STOCKMANN: Come now, not every one of them is an official.

HOVSTAD: No, but those that aren't officials are friends and hangers-on of those that are—the wealthy ones of the town, and the well-connected. These are the people in control.

DR. STOCKMANN: Yes, but you mustn't forget these are people of ability and insight.

HOVSTAD: How much ability and insight did they show when they laid the water pipes where they are now?

DR. STOCKMANN: *That,* of course, was a tremendous piece of stupidity. But that's going to be put right now.

HOVSTAD: Do you think it will be as easy as all that?

DR. STOCKMANN: Easy or not, it's going to be done.

HOVSTAD: Yes, as long as the press takes a hand.

DR. STOCKMANN: That won't be necessary, my dear fellow. I am sure my brother . . .

HOVSTAD: Excuse me, Doctor, but what I'm trying to tell you is that I intend taking the matter up.

DR. STOCKMANN: In the paper?

HOVSTAD: Yes. When I took over the *Herald* it was with the express intention of breaking up this ring of obstinate old buffers who'd got hold of all the power.

DR. STOCKMANN: But you told me yourself what the outcome of that was; it nearly ruined the paper.

HOVSTAD: Yes, it's true we had to pipe down on that occasion. Only because there was a danger that the whole business about the Baths might have fallen through if those men had been turned out then. But now we've got the Baths, and now these fine gentlemen can be dispensed with.

DR. STOCKMANN: Dispensed with, perhaps. But we have much to thank them for.

HOVSTAD: Full acknowledgement will be given, with all punctiliousness. But no popular journalist, such as I am, can afford to let an opportunity like this go by. This myth of official infallibility must be destroyed. A thing like this has to be rooted out just like any other superstition.

DR. STOCKMANN: I agree with you whole-heartedly, Mr. Hovstad! If there is any superstition, then away with it!

HOVSTAD: I should be most reluctant to implicate the Mayor, seeing that he's your brother. But I'm sure you agree with me that truth must come first.

DR. STOCKMANN: That goes without saying. *(Vehemently)* Yes, but . . . but . . .

HOVSTAD: You mustn't think so badly of me. I am no more egotistical or ambitious than most.

DR. STOCKMANN: But, my dear fellow, who's suggesting you are?

HOVSTAD: I came from a fairly poor home, as you know. And I've had plenty of opportunity of seeing what's needed most among the working classes. And it's this: to have some say in the control of public affairs, Dr. Stockmann. *That's* the thing for developing people's ability and knowledge and confidence. . . .

DR. STOCKMANN: I can understand that very well. . . .

HOVSTAD: Yes . . . and that's why I think it's a terrible responsibility for a journalist if he neglects any opportunity that might bring some measure of freedom to the humble and the oppressed masses. Oh, I realize all the big noises will just call it 'agitation' and so on. Well, let them say what they like! As long as my conscience is clear . . .

DR. STOCKMANN: Absolutely! Absolutely, my dear Mr. Hovstad. All the same . . . damn it . . . ! *(There is a knock at the door)* Come in!

(Aslaksen, the printer, appears at the hall door. He is poorly but decently dressed in a black suit, with a slightly crumpled white necktie; he carries in his hand a felt hat and gloves.)

ASLAKSEN *(bows):* Excuse me, Doctor, intruding like this . . .

DR. STOCKMANN *(rises):* Well, well, here's Mr. Aslaksen!

ASLAKSEN: Yes, Doctor.

HOVSTAD *(stands):* Is it me you're looking for, Aslaksen?

ASLAKSEN: No, it isn't. I didn't know I'd be seeing you here. No, actually it was the Doctor himself. . . .

DR. STOCKMANN: Well, and what can I do for you?

ASLAKSEN: Is it true what Mr. Billing tells me—that you are thinking of trying to get the water-supply improved?

DR. STOCKMANN: Yes, for the Baths.

ASLAKSEN: Well then, I've just called to say that I am ready to give every support to a thing like that.

HOVSTAD *(to the Doctor):* There you are, you see!

DR. STOCKMANN: That's extremely kind of you, thank you very much; but . . .

ASLAKSEN: Because you might easily find you need some middle-class support to back you up. We now form what you might call a compact majority here in town—when we really *want* to, that is. And it's always a good thing to have the majority on your side, Dr. Stockmann.

DR. STOCKMANN: That is undoubtedly true. It's just that I don't quite understand why it should be necessary to take any special measures of that kind here. When it's such an ordinary straightforward thing, it seems to me . . .

ASLAKSEN: Ah, you never know but what it mightn't be a good thing anyway. I know well enough what the local authorities are like. Those in charge are never very keen on any kind of proposal that *other* people put forward. And that's why I think it wouldn't be a bad thing if we made a bit of a demonstration.

HOVSTAD: Yes, exactly.

DR. STOCKMANN: Demonstration, do you say? Well, what way did you think of demonstrating?

ASLAKSEN: Well, with great moderation, of course, Doctor. I try for moderation, in all things. For moderation is the first attribute of a good citizen . . . in my own opinion, that is.

DR. STOCKMANN: That's something that you yourself are well-known for, too, Mr. Aslaksen.

ASLAKSEN: Yes, I think I may say it is. And this matter of the water-supply is an extremely important one for us of the middle classes. The Baths show every sign of becoming a little goldmine for the town, as you might say; it's to them that many of us are looking for a means of livelihood, especially those of us who are house-holders. That's why we want to give the Baths all the support we can. And I happen to be the chairman of the Ratepayers Association . . .

DR. STOCKMANN: Yes?

ASLAKSEN: . . . and as I am moreover the local representative of the Temperance Society—you know, of course, that I take an active part in Temperance affairs?

DR. STOCKMANN: Yes, of course, of course.

ASLAKSEN: Well . . . you can see I meet quite a lot of people one way and another. And as I have the reputation of being a prudent and law-abiding citizen, as the Doctor himself said, it means that I have a certain influence in the town—a kind of little position of power, even though I say it myself.

DR. STOCKMANN: That I know very well, Mr. Aslaksen.

ASLAKSEN: And so, you see, it would be quite a simple matter for me to prepare an address, if such appeared necessary.

DR. STOCKMANN: An address?

ASLAKSEN: Yes, a kind of vote of thanks from the townspeople in appreciation of the way you have dealt with this matter of public interest. It goes without saying that the address would have to be drafted with proper moderation so as not to give offence to the authorities and those in power. And as long as we are careful about *that,* I don't really see that anybody can object, do you?

HOVSTAD: Well, even if they didn't like it very much . . .

ASLAKSEN: No, no, no! Nothing to give offence to the authorities, Mr. Hovstad. Nothing that might antagonize people with so much say in things. I've had quite enough of that sort of thing in my time, and no good ever comes of it, either. But the honest expression of a man's considered opinion surely cannot offend anybody.

DR. STOCKMANN *(shaking his hand):* I just can't tell you, my dear Mr. Aslaksen, how delighted I am to find this support among my fellow citizens. It gives me great pleasure . . . great pleasure! I tell you what! What about a little glass of sherry, eh?

ASLAKSEN: No, thank you very much. I never touch spirits.

DR. STOCKMANN: What do you say to a glass of beer, then?

ASLAKSEN: No thank you again, Doctor. I never take anything as early in the day as this. I am going into town now to talk to some of the ratepayers to see if I can prepare public opinion.

DR. STOCKMANN: Well, it really is extremely kind of you, Mr. Aslaksen. But I just cannot see all these arrangements being necessary. I think surely this matter can be managed on its own.

ASLAKSEN: The authorities sometimes take a bit of moving, Dr. Stockmann. Not that I'm trying to blame anybody, of course! Dear me, no!

HOVSTAD: We'll have a go at them in the paper tomorrow, Aslaksen.

ASLAKSEN: Please, Mr. Hovstad, no violence. Proceed with moderation, otherwise you'll get nowhere. You can take my word for it, because my experience was acquired in the school of life.—Well, I'll say goodbye now, Doctor. You now know that we of the middle classes stand solidly behind you. You have the compact majority on your side, Dr. Stockmann.

DR. STOCKMANN: Thank you very much, my dear Mr. Aslaksen. *(Holds out his hand)* Goodbye, goodbye!

ASLAKSEN: Are you coming with me as far as the office, Mr. Hovstad?

HOVSTAD: I'll be along soon. I still have one or two things to see to.

ASLAKSEN: Very good.

(He bows and goes. Dr. Stockmann accompanies him out into the hall)

HOVSTAD *(as the Doctor returns):* Well, Doctor, what d'you think of that? Don't you think it's about time we did a bit of shaking up and clearing out of all this weary, cowardly fiddle-faddle?

DR. STOCKMANN: Are you referring to Mr. Aslaksen?

HOVSTAD: Yes, I am. He's one of the ones in the swamp—decent enough sort though he may be in other ways. Most of them are like that round here, teetering along, wobbling one way then the other; they are so damned cautious and scrupulous that they never dare commit themselves to any proper step forward.

DR. STOCKMANN: Yes, but Aslaksen seemed so genuinely anxious to help.

HOVSTAD: There's something I value more than that; and that is to stand firm, like a man with confidence in himself.

DR. STOCKMANN: Yes, I think you are absolutely right there.

HOVSTAD: That's why I'm going to take this opportunity to see if I can't get these well-intentioned people to show a bit of backbone. This worship of authority must be wiped out in this town. The real significance of this tremendous and unforgivable blunder about the water-supply must be brought home to every single person with a vote.

DR. STOCKMANN: Very well. If you think it is for the public good, so be it. But not till I've had a word with my brother about it.

HOVSTAD: In the meantime I'll be drafting a leading article. And if the Mayor refuses to go on with things . . .

DR. STOCKMANN: Oh, but how could you possibly think that?

HOVSTAD: It's not impossible. And if so . . . ?

DR. STOCKMANN: In that case, I promise you. . . . Listen, in that case you can print my article; every word of it.

HOVSTAD: May I? Is that a promise?

DR. STOCKMANN (hands him the manuscript): Here it is, take it with you. There's no harm in your reading it through; you can give it back to me afterwards.

HOVSTAD: Good! I'll do that. Well then goodbye, Doctor!

DR. STOCKMANN: Goodbye, goodbye! You'll see, Mr. Hovstad, it'll be all plain sailing . . . nothing but plain sailing!

HOVSTAD: Hm! We'll see.

(He bows and goes out through the door)

DR. STOCKMANN (crosses and looks into the dining-room): Katherine . . . ! Ah, are you back, Petra?

PETRA (comes in): Yes, I've just come from school.

MRS. STOCKMANN (comes in): Hasn't he been yet?

DR. STOCKMANN: Peter? No. But I've had a long talk with Hovstad. He's quite worked up about this discovery I've made. It seems there's more in it than I'd first imagined, you know. He's put his paper at my disposal, if it's ever needed.

MRS. STOCKMANN: Do you think it will be needed?

DR. STOCKMANN: No, of course not. But it makes one very proud to think that one has the progressive and independent press on one's side. And what else do you think! I've also had the chairman of the Ratepayers Association here to see me.

MRS. STOCKMANN: Really? What did he want?

DR. STOCKMANN: Also to offer his support. They are all going to support me, if need be. Katherine—do you know what I've got backing me?

MRS. STOCKMANN: Backing you? No. What?

DR. STOCKMANN: The compact majority.

MRS. STOCKMANN: Oh, have you! And is that a good thing, then, Thomas?

DR. STOCKMANN: I should jolly well think it is! *(He walks up and down, rubbing his hands.)* Lord! How wonderful it is to stand, as it were, shoulder to shoulder in the brotherhood of one's fellow citizens!

PETRA: And to be doing such good and useful work, Father!

DR. STOCKMANN: Yes, not to mention that it's for one's own birthplace, too.

MRS. STOCKMANN: There's the bell.

DR. STOCKMANN: That must be him. *(There is a knock on the door.)* Come in!

MAYOR *(comes from the hall):* Good morning.

DR. STOCKMANN: Glad to see you, Peter!

MRS. STOCKMANN: Good morning, Peter! How are things with you?

MAYOR: Oh, so-so, thank you. *(To the Doctor)* I received from you yesterday, after office hours, a report concerning the state of the water at the Baths.

DR. STOCKMANN: Yes. Have you read it?

MAYOR: Yes, I have.

DR. STOCKMANN: And what have you got to say about it?

MAYOR *(with a sidelong glance):* Hm . . .

MRS. STOCKMANN: Come along, Petra.

(Mrs. Stockmann and Petra go into the room on the left)

MAYOR *(after a pause):* Was it necessary to make all these investigations behind my back?

DR. STOCKMANN: Yes, because until I knew with absolute certainty . . .

MAYOR: And now you do, you mean?

DR. STOCKMANN: Yes. Surely you are also convinced yourself by now!

MAYOR: Is it your intention to present this document to the Board as an official report?

DR. STOCKMANN: Of course. Something will have to be done about this thing. And quick.

MAYOR: As usual, you use some rather emphatic expressions in your report. Among other things, you say that what we offer our summer visitors is sheer poison.

DR. STOCKMANN: Well, Peter, what else can you call it? Just think! That water's poison whether you drink it or bathe in it! And this is what we offer those poor invalids who come to us in good faith and pay good money hoping to get their health back!

MAYOR: And then you conclude by stating we must build a sewer to deal with these alleged impurities from Mölledal, and that the present water pipes must be re-laid.

DR. STOCKMANN: Well, can you suggest any other solution? I can't.

MAYOR: This morning I made it my business to look in on the town engineer.

And—half as a joke, as it might be—I brought up these measures as something we might give consideration to at some future date.

DR. STOCKMANN: Some future date!

MAYOR: He smiled at what he took to be my extravagance—of course. Have you taken the trouble to think what these proposed alterations would cost? According to the information I received, the cost would very probably be several hundred thousand crowns.

DR. STOCKMANN: As much as that?

MAYOR: Yes. But that's not the worst. The work would take at least two years.

DR. STOCKMANN: Two years, eh? Two whole years?

MAYOR: At least. And what's to be done with the Baths in the meantime? Shall we shut them? We'll have to. You don't think people are going to come all the way here if the rumour got about that the water was polluted?

DR. STOCKMANN: But, Peter, that's just what it is.

MAYOR: And all this has to come out just when the Baths were beginning to pay their way. A lot of other places in the district could equally well develop into health resorts. Can't you see they would set to work at once to divert all our tourist traffic to themselves. Of course they would; no doubt whatever. And we'd be left sitting there with all that expensive plant on our hands; we'd probably have to abandon the entire project. The whole town would be ruined, thanks to you!

DR. STOCKMANN: Me . . . ? Ruined . . . ?

MAYOR: The whole future prosperity of the town is tied up with the Baths. You can see that as well as I can.

DR. STOCKMANN: Then what should be done, do you think?

MAYOR: I am not entirely convinced by your report that the state of the Baths is as serious as you make out.

DR. STOCKMANN: If anything it is worse. At least, it will be in the summer, when the warm weather comes.

MAYOR: As I said before, I think you exaggerate considerably. Any competent doctor would surely be able to meet this situation . . . take some suitable precautionary measures and treat any noticeable injurious effects, if there actually turned out to be any.

DR. STOCKMANN: Well? And what then?

MAYOR: The existing water-supply for the Baths is now an established fact, and must be treated as such. But it is reasonable to suppose that in time the Directors might not be disinclined to consider how far, in the light of the prevailing financial situation, it would be possible to initiate certain improvements.

DR. STOCKMANN: Do you honestly think I would lend myself to that sort of sharp practice?

MAYOR: Sharp practice?

DR. STOCKMANN: Sharp practice, yes! That's what it would be. A swindle, a fraud, an absolute crime against the public and against society!

MAYOR: As I remarked earlier, I have not been able to persuade myself that there is any actual imminent danger.

DR. STOCKMANN: Oh yes, you have! You couldn't help it. My report is absolutely correct and clear, I know that! And you know it too, Peter, but you won't admit it. You were the one responsible for having the Baths and the water-supply sited where they are now. And it's *this*—this damned blunder of yours—that you won't admit. Puh! Do you think I can't see right through you?

MAYOR: And even if that were so? Even if I may seem to guard my reputation somewhat jealously, it's all for the good of the town. Without some measure of moral authority, I should not be able to guide and direct public affairs in the way I consider best serves the common weal. Therefore— and for various other reasons—I consider it imperative that your report should not be presented to the Board. In the public interest, it must be withheld. Then I shall bring the matter up later, and we'll do all we can privately. But nothing, not a single word, of this disastrous business must be made public.

DR. STOCKMANN: My dear Peter, I doubt if we can prevent that now.

MAYOR: It must and shall be prevented.

DR. STOCKMANN: It's no use, I tell you. Too many people know about it already.

MAYOR: Know about it already! Who? I only hope it's not those people on the *Herald* . . . ?

DR. STOCKMANN: Oh yes, they know already. The progressive and independent press will see to it that you do your duty.

MAYOR *(after a short pause):* You are an astonishingly indiscreet man, Thomas! Did you never think what consequences this might have for you personally?

DR. STOCKMANN: Consequences? For me?

MAYOR: For you and your family.

DR. STOCKMANN: What the devil do you mean by *that?*

MAYOR: Would you agree I've always been a decent brother to you, always ready to help?

DR. STOCKMANN: Yes, you have. And I'm grateful to you for it.

MAYOR: There's no need to be. In a way I had to be . . . in my own interests. It was always my hope that, by helping to improve your position economically, I might be able to some extent to hold you in check.

DR. STOCKMANN: What's that? It was only in your own interests . . . !

MAYOR: In a way, I said. It is distressing for a public figure to have his nearest relative forever compromising himself.

DR. STOCKMANN: You mean that's what I do?

MAYOR: Yes, I'm afraid you do, without realizing it. You have a restless, pugnacious, aggressive temperament. And then there's this unfortunate habit of yours of rushing into print about everything under the sun. No sooner do you get some idea or other into your head than you've got to write an article for the papers about it . . . or even a whole pamphlet.

DR. STOCKMANN: But don't you think if a man's got hold of some new idea he has a duty to bring it to the notice of the public?

MAYOR: Oh, the public doesn't need new ideas. The public is best served by the good old, accepted ideas it already has.

DR. STOCKMANN: That's putting it pretty bluntly, anyway!

MAYOR: Yes, for once I'm going to be blunt with you. I've always tried to avoid that hitherto, knowing how irritable you are. But now, Thomas, I'm going to tell you the truth. You have no idea what harm you do yourself by this recklessness of yours. You complain about the authorities . . . about the government, even . . . you are always going on about them. Then you try to insist that you've been passed over, or been badly treated. But what do you expect, when you are so difficult?

DR. STOCKMANN: So I'm difficult too, am I?

MAYOR: Yes, Thomas, you are an extremely difficult man to work with, as I know from experience. You show absolutely no consideration. You seem to forget that it's me you have to thank for your appointment here as medical officer to the Baths. . . .

DR. STOCKMANN: I was the only possible man for the job! I, and nobody else! Wasn't I the first to see that the town could be made into a flourishing health resort? And wasn't I the only one to realize it at the time? Alone and single-handed I fought for the idea, year after year, writing and writing. . . .

MAYOR: Undoubtedly. But the time wasn't ripe for it then. Of course, you couldn't very well be any judge of that, living up there at the back of beyond. But when a more appropriate time came, then I—and some of the others—took the matter in hand. . . .

DR. STOCKMANN: Yes, and messed up the whole issue! My lovely plans! Oh yes, it's clear enough now all right what a brainy lot you turned out to be!

MAYOR: The only thing that's clear in my opinion is that you are simply trying to pick a quarrel again. You must find some outlet, so you go for your superiors—that's an old habit of yours. You just can't bear to submit to authority; you take a jaundiced view of anybody holding a superior appointment, regard him as a personal enemy. And straightway any weapon that happens to come to hand is good enough to attack him with. But now I've made it clear to you what other interests are at stake for the town as a whole—and consequently also for me personally. And that's why I'm telling you, Thomas, that I intend to be quite ruthless in demanding of you certain things.

DR. STOCKMANN: And what is it you demand?

MAYOR: Since you have been so indiscreet as to discuss this delicate matter with certain unauthorized persons—despite the fact that it should have been treated as a matter confidential to the Board—things can of course no longer be hushed up. All sorts of rumours will spread, and the more spiteful ones among us can be relied on to embellish them with all sorts of extras. It will therefore be necessary for you to make a public denial of these rumours.

DR. STOCKMANN: For me! How? I don't understand you.

MAYOR: We shall expect you, after making further investigations, to come to the conclusion that the matter is not by any means as dangerous or as serious as you in the first instance imagined it to be.

DR. STOCKMANN: Aha! So that's what you expect, is it?

MAYOR: Furthermore we shall expect you to make public declaration of your confidence in the Board, in its efficiency and its integrity, and in its readiness to take all necessary steps to remedy such defects as may arise.

DR. STOCKMANN: Yes, but don't you see, you'll never do anything just by fiddling with the problem, hoping to patch things up. I'm telling you straight, Peter, and I'm absolutely and utterly convinced . . .

MAYOR: As an employee you have no right to any private opinion.

DR. STOCKMANN *(falters):* No right. . . ?

MAYOR: As an employee, I mean. As a private individual—good Lord, yes, that's quite different. But as a subordinate member of the staff of the Baths, you have no right to express any opinion that conflicts with that of your superiors.

DR. STOCKMANN: That's going too far! Are you trying to say that a doctor, a man of science, has no right. . . !

MAYOR: The matter in this instance is by no means a purely scientific one; it is a combination of technical and economic factors.

DR. STOCKMANN: It can be what the hell it likes, as far as I'm concerned. What matters to me is the right to speak my mind about any damn' thing under the sun.

MAYOR: Certainly! Anything at all—except the Baths. That we forbid.

DR. STOCKMANN *(shouts):* Forbid! You lot!

MAYOR: *I* forbid you. I personally, your superior. And when I give you an order, it's up to you to obey.

DR. STOCKMANN *(controlling himself):* Peter . . . if it wasn't that you were my brother. . . !

PETRA *(flings the door open):* Don't stand for it, Father!

MRS. STOCKMANN *(following her):* Petra! Petra!

MAYOR: Aha! You've been listening!

MRS. STOCKMANN: You were talking so loud, we just couldn't help . . .

PETRA: No! I stood there and listened.

MAYOR: Actually, I'm just as well pleased . . .

DR. STOCKMANN *(approaches him):* You were saying something to me about ordering and obeying. . . ?

MAYOR: You compelled me to speak to you like that.

DR. STOCKMANN: And you expect me to get up in public and eat my own words?

MAYOR: We consider it absolutely necessary that you issue some sort of statement along the lines I laid down.

DR. STOCKMANN: And supposing I don't . . . obey?

MAYOR: Then we shall ourselves issue a statement to reassure the public.

DR. STOCKMANN: Indeed. Well, then I shall contradict you in the newspapers. I shall stand up for myself. I shall prove that I'm right and you're wrong. And then what will you do?

MAYOR: Then I shall not be able to prevent you from being dismissed.

DR. STOCKMANN: What!

PETRA: Father! Dismissed!

MRS. STOCKMANN: Dismissed!

MAYOR: Dismissed from the Baths. I shall be obliged to arrange for you to be given notice and to see that you sever all connection with the Baths.

DR. STOCKMANN: You wouldn't dare!

MAYOR: Blame your own recklessness.

PETRA: Uncle, this is a disgraceful way to treat a man like Father!

MRS. STOCKMANN: Do be quiet, Petra!

MAYOR (looks at Petra): Ah! So we can't wait to express our opinions, eh? Naturally. (To Mrs. Stockmann) Katherine, you are probably the most sensible one in this house. Please use whatever influence you have with your husband. Get him to see what this will mean both for his family . . .

DR. STOCKMANN: My family's got nothing to do with anybody but me!

MAYOR: . . . as I was saying, both for his family, and for the town he lives in.

DR. STOCKMANN: I'm the one with the real welfare of the town at heart. All I want to do is expose certain things that are bound to come out sooner or later anyway. Oh, I'll show them whether I love this town or not.

MAYOR: All you are really doing, by your sheer blind obstinacy, is cutting off the main source of the town's prosperity.

DR. STOCKMANN: That source is poisoned, man! Are you mad! We live by peddling filth and corruption! The whole of the town's prosperity is rooted in a lie!

MAYOR: Fantastic nonsense—or worse! Any man who can cast such aspersions against his own birthplace is nothing but a public enemy.

DR. STOCKMANN (goes up to him): You dare. . . !

MRS. STOCKMANN (throws herself between them): Thomas!

PETRA (seizes her father by the arm): Steady, Father!

MAYOR: I am not going to wait to be assaulted. You've had your warning. Try to realize what you owe to yourself and to your family. Goodbye.

(He goes)

DR. STOCKMANN (walks up and down): Have I to stand for this? In my own house, Katherine! What do you think?

MRS. STOCKMANN: I agree it's shameful and disgraceful, Thomas. . . .

PETRA: If only I could get my hands on that uncle of mine . . . !

DR. STOCKMANN: It's my own fault, I should have had it out with them long ago . . . bared my teeth . . . bit back! Calling me a public enemy! Me! By God, I'm not going to stand for that!

MRS. STOCKMANN: But, Thomas my dear, your brother has a lot of power on his side. . . .

DR. STOCKMANN: Yes, but I have *right* on mine!

MRS. STOCKMANN: Right! Yes, of course. But what's the use of right without might?

PETRA: Oh, Mother! How can you say such a thing?

DR. STOCKMANN: So you think having right on your side in a free country doesn't count for anything? You are just being stupid, Katherine. And anyway, haven't I the progressive and independent press to look to, and the compact majority behind me. There's enough might there, surely, isn't there?

MRS. STOCKMANN: But heavens, Thomas! You surely aren't thinking of . . .

DR. STOCKMANN: Not thinking of what?

MRS. STOCKMANN: . . . of setting yourself up against your brother, I mean.

DR. STOCKMANN: What the devil do you expect me to do? What else is there if I'm going to hold to what's right and proper.

PETRA: Yes, that's what I'm wondering too.

MRS. STOCKMANN: But you know very well it won't do a scrap of good. If they won't, they won't.

DR. STOCKMANN: Aha, Katherine, just give me time. I'll fight this thing to a finish, you watch.

MRS. STOCKMANN: Yes, and while you are fighting, you'll lose your job, that's what!

DR. STOCKMANN: Then at least I shall have done my duty by the public . . . and by society. Calling me a public enemy, indeed!

MRS. STOCKMANN: But what about your family, Thomas? What about us at home? Will you be doing your duty by the ones you should provide for first?

PETRA: Oh, stop thinking always about us, Mother!

MRS. STOCKMANN: Yes, it's easy for *you* to talk. You can stand on your own feet, if need be. But don't forget the boys, Thomas. And think a little of yourself too, and of me. . . .

DR. STOCKMANN: You must be absolutely mad, Katherine! If I were to be such a miserable coward as to go groveling to Peter and his blasted pals, do you think I'd ever be happy again as long as I lived?

MRS. STOCKMANN: I'm sure I don't know. But God preserve us from the kind of happiness we'll have if you insist on carrying on like this. We'll be just where we were before—no job, no regular income. I thought we had enough of that in the old days. Don't forget that, Thomas, and think what all this is going to lead to.

DR. STOCKMANN *(squirming and clenching his fists):* Oh, the things that a free

and decent man has to put up with at the hands of these damned bureau-
crats! Isn't it terrible, Katherine?

MRS. STOCKMANN: Yes, they've treated you disgracefully, I will say that. But
heavens! Once you start thinking of all the injustices in this world people
have to put up with . . . ! There's the boys, Thomas! Look at them! What's
going to become of them? Oh no, you'd never have the heart. . . .

(Meanwhile Ejlif and Morten have come in, carrying their schoolbooks)

DR. STOCKMANN: The boys . . . ! *(Suddenly stops with a determined look)* No!
Even if it meant the end of the world, I'm not knuckling under.

(He walks over to his study)

MRS. STOCKMANN *(following him):* Thomas! What are you going to do?

DR. STOCKMANN *(at the door):* I want to be able to look my boys in the face
when they grow up into free men.

(He goes in)

MRS. STOCKMANN *(bursts into tears):* Oh, God help us.

PETRA: Father's grand! He'll never give in.

*(The boys, in amazement, begin to ask what is happening; Petra signs to them to
be silent)*

Act III

The editorial office of the People's Herald. *The entrance door is on the back wall,
left; on the same wall, right, is a glazed door, through which the printing shop can
be seen. On the right wall is another door. A large table stands in the middle of
the room covered with papers, newspapers, and books. Downstage, left, is a window,
near which is a writing desk with high stool. A couple of armchairs by the table,
other chairs along the walls. The room is gloomy and cheerless; the furniture is old,
the armchairs dirty and torn. Within the printing shop, a few compositors are at
work; further back a hand press is being worked.*

*Hovstad is sitting at the desk, writing. After a moment or two, Billing comes in
from the right with the doctor's manuscript in his hand.*

BILLING: Well, I must say . . . !

HOVSTAD *(writing):* Have you read it through?

BILLING *(puts the manuscript on the desk):* Yes, I have that.

HOVSTAD: Pretty scathing, isn't he?

BILLING: Scathing! Damn it, it's absolutely devastating! Every word lands—
what shall I say?—like a blow from a sledge-hammer.

HOVSTAD: Yes, but they're not the sort you can knock down with one blow.

BILLING: That's true! But then we'll just keep on hitting them . . . time and
time again until the whole set-up collapses. Sitting in there reading it, I
just felt as though I could see the revolution coming.

HOVSTAD *(turning):* Hush! Don't let Aslaksen hear that.

BILLING *(lowering his voice):* Aslaksen is a chicken-hearted little coward. He's got no backbone. But I hope this time you're going to insist? Eh? The Doctor's article will go in?

HOVSTAD: Yes, as long as the Mayor doesn't give in without a fight. . . .

BILLING: Make things damned dull if he does.

HOVSTAD: Well, fortunately we can make something of the situation whatever happens. If the Mayor doesn't accept the Doctor's proposal, then he'll have all the middle class on to him . . . all the Ratepayers Association and and the rest. And if he does accept it, then he's got to face a pack of the bigger shareholders in the Baths who have so far been his strongest supporters. . . .

BILLING: Yes, that's right. I dare say it'll cost them a pretty penny. . . .

HOVSTAD: You can be damn' sure it will. Then, you see, once the ring is broken, we can keep pegging away day after day in the paper, pointing out to the public how completely incompetent the Mayor is, and how all the positions of responsibility, in fact the whole council, ought to be handed over to the Liberals.

BILLING: By God, that's good, that is! I can see it . . . I can see it! We're on the brink of revolution!

(There is a knock on the door)

HOVSTAD: Hush! *(Shouts)* Come in!

(Dr. Stockmann comes through the entrance door, back, left)

HOVSTAD *(crosses to him):* Ah, it's you, Doctor. Well?

DR. STOCKMANN: Print it, Mr. Hovstad!

HOVSTAD: Has it come to that?

BILLING: Hurrah!

DR. STOCKMANN: Print away, I tell you. Yes, it *has* come to that. Now they're going to get what's coming to them. This is war, Mr. Billing!

BILLING: War to the knife, I hope! Go ahead and slaughter them, Doctor!

DR. STOCKMANN: This article is only the beginning. Already I've got enough ideas for another four or five of them. Where's Aslaksen?

BILLING *(shouts into the printing shop):* Can you come here a minute, Aslaksen?

HOVSTAD: Another four or five articles, d'you say? About the same thing?

DR. STOCKMANN: Oh, no! Far from it, my dear fellow. No, they're about quite different things. But they're all bound up with the question of the water-supply and the sewers. You know how one thing leads to another. It's just like what happens when you start tinkering with an old building—just like that.

BILLING: By God, that's true. You pretty soon realize it's all such a shambles that you'll never finish the job properly until you've pulled the whole thing down.

ASLAKSEN *(from the printing shop):* Pulled the whole thing down! Surely, Doctor, you are not thinking of pulling the Baths down?

HOVSTAD: No, of course not! Don't get alarmed!

DR. STOCKMANN: No, we were referring to something quite different. Well, Mr. Hovstad, what have you got to say about my article?

HOVSTAD: I think it's an absolute masterpiece. . . .

DR. STOCKMANN: Yes, isn't it . . . ? Well, I'm very pleased, very pleased.

HOVSTAD: It's so clear and to the point. You don't need to be an expert to follow it; anybody can understand from it what it's all about. I bet you get every progressively-minded man on your side.

ASLAKSEN: And all the sensible ones as well, I hope.

BILLING: The sensible ones and the other sort too. . . . What I mean is, practically the whole town.

ASLAKSEN: In that case, I think we might venture to print it.

DR. STOCKMANN: I jolly well think so!

HOVSTAD: It will be in tomorrow morning.

DR. STOCKMANN: Yes, by heavens! We mustn't waste any time. By the way, Mr. Aslaksen, that was something I was going to ask you: you'll give the manuscript your own personal attention, won't you?

ASLAKSEN: I will indeed.

DR. STOCKMANN: Take care of it as though it were gold. No misprints, every word is important. I'll look in again later on; perhaps I could check some of the proofs.—Yes, I can't tell you how I'm longing to get this thing in print . . . slam it down . . .

BILLING: Slam it down, that's right! Like a thunderbolt!

DR. STOCKMANN: . . . to submit it to the scrutiny of every intelligent citizen. Oh, you can't imagine what I've had to put up with today. They've threatened me with all sorts of things; to deprive me of my most basic human rights . . .

BILLING: What! Your human rights!

DR. STOCKMANN: . . . They tried to degrade me, to rob me of my self-respect, tried to force me to put personal advantage before my most sacred convictions. . . .

BILLING: Damn it, that's going too far!

HOVSTAD: Ah, you can expect anything from that lot.

DR. STOCKMANN: But I'm not going to let them get away with it—I'll make that plain in black and white. Every blessed day I'll be in the *Herald*— lying at anchor, so to speak, and bombarding them with one high-explosive article after another . . .

ASLAKSEN: Oh but, come now. . . .

BILLING: Hurrah! It's war, it's war!

DR. STOCKMANN: . . . I'll batter them to the ground, I'll smash them, I'll blast their defences wide open for all right-thinking men to see! That's what I'll do!

ASLAKSEN: But you will act with moderation, Doctor! Shoot . . . but with moderation. . . .

BILLING: No, no! Don't spare the dynamite!

DR. STOCKMANN *(continues unbashed):* Because, you see, it's no longer just the water-supply and the sewers now. No, the whole community needs cleaning up, disinfecting. . . .

BILLING: That's what I like to hear!

DR. STOCKMANN: All these dodderers have got to be chucked out! Wherever they are! My eyes have been opened to a lot of things today. I haven't quite got everything sorted out yet, but I will in time. My friends, what we must look for is young and vigorous men to be our standard-bearers. We must have new men in command in all our forward positions.

BILLING: Hear, hear!

DR. STOCKMANN: And if only we hold together, things can't help but go smoothly! We'll launch this whole revolution as smoothly as a ship off the stocks. Don't you think so?

HOVSTAD: For my own part, I think we now have every prospect of placing the control of the council in the proper hands.

ASLAKSEN: And as long as we proceed with moderation, I can't see that there should be any risk.

DR. STOCKMANN: Who the devil cares whether it's risky or not? What I do, I do in the name of truth and in obedience to my conscience.

HOVSTAD: You deserve every support, Doctor.

ASLAKSEN: Yes, it's quite obvious that the Doctor is a true benefactor to the town, a real benefactor to society.

BILLING: By God, Aslaksen, Dr. Stockmann is the people's friend!

ASLAKSEN: I rather think the Ratepayers Association might soon be wanting to use that phrase.

DR. STOCKMANN *(greatly moved, grasps their hands):* Thank you, thank you, my good friends, for being so loyal. How gratifying it is to hear you say that. That brother of mine called me something quite different. Well, he'll get it all back again, with interest! Well, I must be off now to see a patient of mine, poor devil. But I'll be back, as I promised. Be sure you take good care of that manuscript, Mr. Aslaksen—and, whatever you do, don't go leaving out any of my exclamation marks! If anything, put a few more in! Well, Well! Goodbye for now, goodbye!

(As they show him out, they take leave of each other; he goes)

HOVSTAD: There's a man who could be extremely useful to us.

ASLAKSEN: Yes, as long as he keeps to this business of the Baths. But if he gets going on other things, it might not be very wise to follow him.

HOVSTAD: Hm! That all depends on . . .

BILLING: Don't be so damned frightened, Aslaksen.

ASLAKSEN: Frightened? Yes, Mr. Billing, I *am* frightened—when it's a question of local politics. That's something I've learnt in the hard school of experience, you see. But you just put me in high-level politics, even in opposition to the government itself, and you'll see then whether I'm frightened.

BILLING: No, I'm sure you wouldn't be. But that's just what makes you so inconsistent.

ASLAKSEN: It's because I'm a man with a conscience. That's what it is. You can attack the government without really doing society any harm, because you see people like that just don't take any notice—they stay in power as if nothing had happened. But the *local* leaders, they *can* be turned out; and then you might easily get a lot of inexperienced men at the helm, doing immense harm to the interests of the ratepayers and other people.

HOVSTAD: But what about self-government as a factor in the people's education—haven't you thought about *that?*

ASLAKSEN: When a man has acquired a vested interest in something, you can't always expect him to think of everything, Mr. Hovstad.

HOVSTAD: Then I hope to God I never have any vested interests.

BILLING: Hear, hear!

ASLAKSEN *(smiles):* Hm! *(He points to the desk.)* Your predecessor in that editorial chair was Mr. Steensgaard. He used to be sheriff.

BILLING *(spits):* Pah! That turncoat.

HOVSTAD: I'm no time-server—and never will be, either.

ASLAKSEN: A politician should never be too certain about anything, Mr. Hovstad. And you, Mr. Billing, hadn't you better draw your horns in just a little these days—seeing you've applied for the post of Secretary to the council?

BILLING: I . . . !

HOVSTAD: *Have* you, Billing?

BILLING: Well . . . Can't you see I'm only doing it to annoy our local bigwigs, damn them.

ASLAKSEN: Well, it's nothing whatever to do with me. But when people accuse me of being cowardly or inconsistent, there's one thing I want to stress: the political record of Aslaksen the printer is an open book. I haven't changed in any way except to become more moderate in my ways. My heart is still with the people. But I'll not deny that my head rather inclines me to support the authorities—the local ones, I mean.

(He goes into the printing shop)

BILLING: Don't you think we'd better finish with him, Hovstad?

HOVSTAD: Do you know anybody else who'd agree to let us have our paper and printing on credit?

BILLING: It's a damned nuisance not having the necessary capital.

HOVSTAD *(sits down at the desk):* Yes, if only we had *that* . . . *!*

BILLING: What about approaching Dr. Stockmann?

HOVSTAD *(turning over some papers):* Oh, what's the use of that? He hasn't anything.

BILLING: No, but he's got a good man up his sleeve—Old Morten Kiil, 'the Badger', as he is called.

HOVSTAD *(writing):* What makes you so sure *he's* got anything?

BILLING: By God, he's got money all right! And some of it is bound to come to the Stockmanns. Then he'll have to think of providing for . . . for the children, at any rate.

HOVSTAD *(half turning):* Are you counting on *that?*

BILLING: Counting? I'm not counting on anything.

HOVSTAD: You're right there. And you'd better not count on that job with the council, either. Because I can tell you now—you won't get it.

BILLING: Do you think I don't know that? That's just what I want—not to get it. To be rejected like that is just like adding fuel to the flames— it's like getting a new supply of fresh gall, and you need something like that in a dump like this where nothing really stimulating ever happens.

HOVSTAD *(writing):* Yes, yes, I know.

BILLING: Well . . . it won't be long now before they hear from me! Now I'm going to sit down and write that appeal to the Ratepayers.

(He goes into the room, right)

HOVSTAD *(sits at his desk, bites his pen shank and says slowly):* Hm! Aha, so that's it . . . *(There is a knock at the door)* Come in!

(Petra comes in by entrance door, back, left)

HOVSTAD *(rises):* Well, look who it is! What are you doing here?

PETRA: You must excuse me, but . . .

HOVSTAD *(pulling an armchair forward):* Won't you have a seat?

PETRA: No, thanks. I can't stay.

HOVSTAD: Is it something from your father, perhaps . . . ?

PETRA: No, it's something from me. *(She takes a book out of her coat pocket)* Here's that English story.

HOVSTAD: Why have you brought it back?

PETRA: Because I'm not going to translate it.

HOVSTAD: But you promised me faithfully . . .

PETRA: I hadn't read it then. And you haven't either, have you?

HOVSTAD: No, you know I don't know any English. But . . .

PETRA: Quite. That's why I wanted to tell you that you'll have to look round for something else. *(She puts the book on the table)* You can never use a thing like this for the *Herald.*

HOVSTAD: Why not?

PETRA: Because it runs completely contrary to everything you believe in.

HOVSTAD: Well, what does that matter . . . ?

PETRA: You don't quite understand. It's all about some supernatural power that's supposed to watch over all the so-called good people, and how everything is for the best . . . and how all the so-called wicked people get punished in the end. . . .

HOVSTAD: Yes, but that's just fine. That's exactly what people want.

PETRA: Can you honestly put stuff like that in front of people? When you yourself don't believe a word of it? You know very well that's not what happens in reality.

HOVSTAD: You're absolutely right, of course. But an editor cannot always do what he wants. You often have to give way to public opinion, in minor things. After all, politics is the most important thing in life—at least, for a newspaper, it is. And if I want to win people over to certain liberal and progressive ideas, it's no good scaring them all off. If they find a nice moral story like this on the back pages of the paper, they are much more ready to accept what we print on the front page—it gives them a sort of feeling of security.

PETRA: Oh, no! Not you, surely! I just can't picture you as a spider spinning a kind of web to trap unwary readers.

HOVSTAD (smiling): Thank you for those few kind words. No, in fact you are right—it was all Billing's idea, not mine.

PETRA: Billing's!

HOVSTAD: Yes, at least he was talking about it just the other day. Billing's really the one who is keen to get that story in. I don't know the book at all.

PETRA: Mr. Billing? A man with all his progressive ideas . . . ?

HOVSTAD: Oh, Billing is a man of parts. I've heard he's also applied for the post of Secretary to the council.

PETRA: I don't believe it, Mr. Hovstad. Whatever makes him think he could stand a job like that?

HOVSTAD: You'd better ask him yourself.

PETRA: I'd never have thought a thing like that of Mr. Billing.

HOVSTAD (looks at her intently): Wouldn't you? Does it come as such a surprise to you?

PETRA: Yes. Or perhaps not. Oh, I don't really know . . .

HOVSTAD: Journalists like us are not really up to much, Miss Stockmann.

PETRA: Do you really mean that?

HOVSTAD: Now and again I think it.

PETRA: In the ordinary daily routine, perhaps; that I could understand. But when you've taken on something big . . .

HOVSTAD: You mean this business about your father?

PETRA: Yes, exactly. I imagine you must feel like a man with a more worthwhile job than most people.

HOVSTAD: Yes, I do feel a bit like that today.

PETRA: I'm sure you must! Oh, what a splendid calling you have chosen. Blazing a trail for the advancement of truth, and of new and bold ideas . . . ! Or even just to step up and give your support, without fear or favour, to a man who has suffered a great wrong . . .

HOVSTAD: Especially when this unfortunate man happens to be . . . hm! . . . I don't really know how to put it . . .

PETRA: Happens to be so decent and honest, you mean?

HOVSTAD (quietly): Especially when he happens to be your father, is what I meant.

PETRA *(suddenly struck):* What?

HOVSTAD: Yes, Petra—Miss Petra.

PETRA: Is *that* what you are thinking of first? You're not concerned about the thing itself? Not about truth? Not about Father's public-spirited action?

HOVSTAD: Oh yes, that too, naturally!

PETRA: No thank you, Mr. Hovstad! You have given yourself away this time. And I can never trust you again about anything.

HOVSTAD: I don't see why you want to take it like this when it was mainly for your sake. . . !

PETRA: What makes me cross is that you haven't played straight with Father. You talked to him as though all you cared about was truth and the common good. You made fools of us both. You are not the man you pretended to be. I'll never forgive you . . . never!

HOVSTAD: I shouldn't be too outspoken actually, Miss Petra. Especially not now.

PETRA: Why not now, particularly?

HOVSTAD: Because your father cannot manage without my help.

PETRA *(looking down at him):* So you're one of those, are you? Pah!

HOVSTAD: No, no, I'm not. I don't know what came over me, saying a thing like that. You mustn't believe a word of it.

PETRA: I know what to believe. Goodbye!

ASLAKSEN *(comes in from the printing shop urgently and with an air of secrecy):* In Heaven's name, Mr. Hovstad . . . *(He sees Petra)* Oh, I'm sorry. I shouldn't . . .

PETRA: There's the book. You'd better give it to somebody else.

(She walks across to the main door)

HOVSTAD *(following her):* But, Miss Petra . . .

PETRA: Goodbye.

(She goes)

ASLAKSEN: I say, Mr. Hovstad!

HOVSTAD: Well, well . . . what is it?

ASLAKSEN: The Mayor's out there in the printing shop.

HOVSTAD: The Mayor, did you say?

ASLAKSEN: Yes, he wants a word with you. He came in the back way—didn't want to be seen, I suppose.

HOVSTAD: What does he want, I wonder? No, wait here, I'll go myself . . .

(He goes over to the door into the printing shop, opens it and invites the Mayor in)

HOVSTAD: Aslaksen, keep an eye open to see that nobody . . .

ASLAKSEN: I understand.

(He goes into the printing shop)

MAYOR: I don't suppose you were expecting me here, Mr. Hovstad.

HOVSTAD: No, as a matter of fact I wasn't.

MAYOR *(looking about him):* You've settled yourself in here nice and comfortably. Very nice.

HOVSTAD: Oh . . .

MAYOR: And here I come without any appointment, and proceed to take up all your precious time.

HOVSTAD: *Please,* Mr. Mayor, I'm only too delighted to be of service. Let me take your things. *(He puts the Mayor's hat and stick on a chair)* Now, won't you sit down?

MAYOR *(sits at the table):* Thank you.

(Hovstad also sits down at the table)

MAYOR: I have had an extremely disagreeable matter to deal with today, Mr. Hovstad.

HOVSTAD: Really? Of course, with so many things to see to . . .

MAYOR: This particular matter has been raised by the Medical Officer of the Baths.

HOVSTAD: By the Doctor?

MAYOR: He's written a kind of report about a number of alleged shortcomings at the Baths, and sent it to the Board.

HOVSTAD: Has he?

MAYOR: Yes, hasn't he told you? I thought he said . . .

HOVSTAD: Oh yes, that's right! He did mention something about . . .

ASLAKSEN *(coming from the printing shop):* I'd better have that manuscript. . . .

HOVSTAD *(angrily):* It's on the desk there.

ASLAKSEN *(finds it):* Good.

MAYOR: But I say, surely *that's* . . .

ASLAKSEN: Yes, that's the Doctor's article, Mr. Mayor.

HOVSTAD: Oh, is *that* what you were talking about?

MAYOR: Precisely. What do you think of it?

HOVSTAD: I'm no expert, of course, and I've only just glanced at it.

MAYOR: Yet you are printing it?

HOVSTAD: I can't very well refuse a man in his position. . . .

ASLAKSEN: I've got no say in what goes into the paper, Mr. Mayor. . . .

MAYOR: Of course not.

ASLAKSEN: I just print what I'm given.

MAYOR: Quite so.

ASLAKSEN: So if you'll excuse me . . .

(He walks across towards the printing shop)

MAYOR: Just a moment, please, Mr. Aslaksen. With your permission, Mr. Hovstad . . .

HOVSTAD: Please.

MAYOR: Now you are a wise and sensible sort of man, Mr. Aslaksen.

ASLAKSEN: I am very pleased you should think so, Mr. Mayor.

MAYOR: And a man of considerable influence in some circles.

ASLAKSEN: Mainly among the people of moderate means.

MAYOR: The small ratepayers are in the majority—here as everywhere else.

ASLAKSEN: That's right.

MAYOR: And I've no doubt you know what most of them think about things in general. Isn't that so?

ASLAKSEN: Yes, I think I can safely say I do, Mr. Mayor.

MAYOR: Well . . . the fact that this admirable spirit of self-sacrifice is to be found in our town among its less well-endowed citizens . . .

ASLAKSEN: How do you mean?

HOVSTAD: Self-sacrifice?

MAYOR: . . . This shows an admirable public spirit, most admirable. I almost said unexpected, too. But of course you know better than I what people's attitudes are.

ASLAKSEN: But, Mr. Mayor . . .

MAYOR: And in fact it's no small sacrifice that the town will have to make.

HOVSTAD: The town?

ASLAKSEN: But I don't understand. . . . You mean the Baths, surely. . . .

MAYOR: At a rough estimate, the alterations which the Medical Officer considers desirable will come to something like a couple of hundred thousand crowns.

ASLAKSEN: That's a lot of money, but . . .

MAYOR: Of course it will be necessary to raise a municipal loan.

HOVSTAD *(rises):* Surely it's not the idea that the town. . . ?

ASLAKSEN: It's not going to come out of the rates! Not out of the people's pockets!

MAYOR: My dear Mr. Aslaksen, where else do you see the money coming from?

ASLAKSEN: I think the owners ought to take care of that.

MAYOR: The owners do not see themselves in a position to provide any additional capital.

ASLAKSEN: Is that absolutely certain, Mr. Mayor?

MAYOR: I am assured on that point. If all these extensive alterations are considered desirable, the town itself must pay for them.

ASLAKSEN: But God damn it all—I beg your pardon!—but this puts a completely different light on things, Mr. Hovstad!

HOVSTAD: Yes, it does indeed.

MAYOR: The most ruinous thing is that we'll be forced to close the Baths for a couple of years.

HOVSTAD: Close them? Completely?

ASLAKSEN: For two years?

MAYOR: Yes, the work will take all that long—at least.

ASLAKSEN: Yes, but Heavens! We could never last out that long, Mr. Mayor. What would people like us live on in the meantime?

MAYOR: I regret to say that is an extremely difficult question to answer, Mr.

Aslaksen. But what do you expect us to do? Do you think anybody is going to come here if you get people going round making up these stories about the water being polluted, and about the place being a cesspool, and the whole town . . .

ASLAKSEN: Do you think the whole thing might just be imagination?

MAYOR: With the best will in the world, I cannot come to any other conclusion.

ASLAKSEN: Then I must say Dr. Stockmann is being most irresponsible in all this. You must forgive me, Mr. Mayor, but . . .

MAYOR: I regret what you say is quite true, Mr. Aslaksen. My brother has always been rather impetuous, unfortunately.

ASLAKSEN: Are you still prepared to support him after this, Mr. Hovstad?

HOVSTAD: But who would have thought. . . ?

MAYOR: I have drawn up a short statement of the facts, putting a rather more sober interpretation on them; and in it I have suggested some ways in which such defects as may come to light could reasonably be dealt with without going beyond the present resources of the Baths.

HOVSTAD: Have you this statement with you, Mr. Mayor?

MAYOR *(fumbling in his pocket):* Yes, I brought it with me on the off chance that . . .

ASLAKSEN *(hastily):* Heavens above, there he is!

MAYOR: Who? My brother?

HOVSTAD: Where?

ASLAKSEN: He's coming in through the printing shop.

MAYOR: It *would* happen. I don't want to bump into him here, and there was still a lot more I wanted to talk to you about.

HOVSTAD *(points to the door on the right):* In there for the present.

MAYOR: But . . . !

HOVSTAD: There's only Billing in there.

ASLAKSEN: Quick, quick! He's coming now.

MAYOR: All right. But see if you can't get rid of him quickly.

(He goes out through the door, right, which Aslaksen opens, and shuts again behind him)

HOVSTAD: Pretend you are doing something, Aslaksen.

(He sits down and begins to write. Aslaksen rummages through a pile of newspapers on a chair, right.)

DR. STOCKMANN *(entering from the printing shop):* Back again!

(He puts down his hat and stick)

HOVSTAD *(writing):* Already, Doctor? Hurry up with what we were talking about, Aslaksen. We haven't got a lot of time to spare today.

DR. STOCKMANN: No proofs yet, they tell me.

ASLAKSEN *(without turning around):* You could hardly expect them yet, Doctor.

DR. STOCKMANN: Well, well, it's just that I'm impatient—as you can well imagine. I can't settle to anything until I've seen the thing in print.

HOVSTAD: Hm! It'll be a good while yet, I fancy. Don't you think so, Aslaksen?

ASLAKSEN: Yes, I'm rather afraid so.

DR. STOCKMANN: Never mind, my dear fellows. I'll look in again. I don't mind coming twice if need be. An important thing like this . . . the welfare of the whole town . . . this is no time for dawdling on. *(About to go, but stops and comes back)* Actually . . . there was something else I wanted to talk to you about.

HOVSTAD: Excuse me, but couldn't we perhaps make it some other time. . . ?

DR. STOCKMANN: It won't take a second. You see it's just that . . . when people read my article in the paper tomorrow morning, and realize that all through the winter I have been quietly working away in the interests of the town . . .

HOVSTAD: Yes, but Doctor . . .

DR. STOCKMANN: I know what you are going to say. You think I was only damn' well doing my duty . . . my simple duty as a citizen. Of course! I know that as well as you do. But my fellow citizens, you know. . . . Well, I mean, they think rather highly of me, actually, these good people. . . .

ASLAKSEN: Yes, the people have thought very highly of you up to now, Dr. Stockmann.

DR. STOCKMANN: Yes, and that's just what I'm a little bit afraid of. . . . What I mean is . . . a thing like this comes along, and they—especially the underprivileged classes—take it as a rousing call to take the affairs of the town into their own hands in future.

HOVSTAD *(rising):* Hm! Dr. Stockmann, I don't think I ought to conceal from you . . .

DR. STOCKMANN: Aha! I might have guessed there'd be something in the wind. But I won't hear of it! If anybody's thinking of organizing anything like that . . .

HOVSTAD: Like what?

DR. STOCKMANN: Well, anything at all—a parade or a banquet or a presentation—whatever it is, you must promise me faithfully to put a stop to it. And you too, Mr. Aslaksen! I insist!

HOVSTAD: Excuse me, Doctor, but sooner or later you've got to hear the real truth . . .

(Mrs. Stockmann, in hat and coat, enters by the main door, back, left)

MRS. STOCKMANN *(sees the Doctor):* Just as I thought!

HOVSTAD *(goes over to her):* You here too, Mrs. Stockmann?

DR. STOCKMANN: What the devil do you want here, Katherine?

MRS. STOCKMANN: You know very well what I want.

HOVSTAD: Won't you take a seat? Or perhaps . . .

MRS. STOCKMANN: Thanks, but don't you bother about me. And you must forgive me coming here to fetch my husband; for I'm the mother of three children, I'll have you know.

DR. STOCKMANN: What's all this rubbish! We all know that!

MRS. STOCKMANN: But it doesn't look as if you care very much these days about your wife and children; otherwise you wouldn't be carrying on as you are, bringing us all to rack and ruin.

DR. STOCKMANN: Have you gone stark, staring mad, Katherine? Are you trying to say a man with wife and children has no right to proclaim the truth—has no right to be a useful and active citizen—has no right to be of service to the town he lives in?

MRS. STOCKMANN: Do be reasonable, Thomas!

ASLAKSEN: Just what I say. Moderation in all things.

MRS. STOCKMANN: That's why it's very wrong of you, Mr. Hovstad, to lure my husband away from house and home and fool him into getting mixed up in all this.

HOVSTAD: I don't go about fooling people. . . .

DR. STOCKMANN: Fool me! Do you think I'd let anybody make a fool of *me!*

MRS. STOCKMANN: Yes, you would. I know, I know, you are the cleverest man in town. But you're too easily fooled, Thomas. *(To Hovstad)* Remember, if you print what he's written he loses his job at the Baths. . . .

ASLAKSEN: What!

HOVSTAD: You know, Doctor . . .

DR. STOCKMANN *(laughs):* Ha ha! Just let them try! Oh no, they wouldn't dare. You see, I have the compact majority behind me.

MRS. STOCKMANN: Yes, worse luck! Fancy having a nasty thing like that behind you.

DR. STOCKMANN: Fiddlesticks, Katherine! Go home and look to your house and let me look to society. Why should you be so afraid; I'm quite confident, and really rather pleased with things. *(Walks up and down, rubbing his hands)* Truth and the People will prevail, you can take your oath on that. Oh, I see the massed ranks of a great citizen army marching on to victory. . . ! *(Stops by a chair)* What the devil is *that?*

ASLAKSEN *(turns to look):* Oh!

HOVSTAD *(similarly):* Hm!

DR. STOCKMANN: There lies the highest mark of authority.

(He picks the Mayor's hat up carefully by the tips of his fingers and holds it aloft)

MRS. STOCKMANN: The Mayor's hat!

DR. STOCKMANN: And here the baton of office, too. How in the name of glory. . . ?

HOVSTAD: Well . . .

DR. STOCKMANN: Ah, I see! He's been here trying to talk you over. Ha ha!

Came to the right man, eh? Then he must have seen me in the printing shop. *(Bursts into laughter)* Did he run away, Mr. Aslaksen?

ASLAKSEN *(hurriedly):* Yes, Doctor, he ran away.

DR. STOCKMANN: Ran away without either his stick or . . . Rubbish, Peter never runs away from anything. But what the devil have you done with him? Ah . . . in there, of course. Now I'll show you something, Katherine!

MRS. STOCKMANN: Thomas . . . please!

ASLAKSEN: Have a care, Doctor!

(Dr. Stockmann puts the Mayor's hat on, takes his stick, walks over and throws open the door, and stands there saluting. The Mayor comes in, red with anger; behind him comes Billing.)

MAYOR: What's the meaning of all this tomfoolery?

DR. STOCKMANN: Show some respect, my dear Peter. I'm the one in authority here now.

(He walks up and down)

MRS. STOCKMANN *(near to tears):* Oh, Thomas, really!

MAYOR *(following him about):* Give me my hat and my stick!

DR. STOCKMANN *(as before):* You might be chief constable, but I am the Mayor—I'm head of the whole town, can't you see!

MAYOR: Take that hat off, I tell you. Don't forget it's an official badge of office!

DR. STOCKMANN: Pooh! When a people rises from its slumber like a giant refreshed, do you think anybody's going to be scared by a hat? Because you might as well know, we are having a revolution in town tomorrow. You threatened to dismiss me; well now I'm dismissing you, relieving you of all your official positions. . . . Perhaps you think I can't? Oh yes, I can. Because I can bring irresistible social pressure to bear. Hovstad and Billing will put down a barrage in the *People's Herald,* and Aslaksen will sally forth at the head of the entire Ratepayers Association.. . .

ASLAKSEN: Not me, Doctor.

DR. STOCKMANN: Yes of course you will. . . .

MAYOR: Aha! Then perhaps Mr. Hovstad has decided to associate himself with this agitation after all?

HOVSTAD: No, Mr. Mayor.

ASLAKSEN: No, Mr. Hovstad is not so stupid as to go and ruin both the paper and himself for the sake of some wild idea.

DR. STOCKMANN *(looks round):* What does this mean?

HOVSTAD: You have represented your case in a false light, Dr. Stockmann; consequently I cannot give it my support.

BILLING: And after what the Mayor was kind enough to tell me in there . . .

DR. STOCKMANN: A false light! You leave that side of things to me. You just print my article—I'm quite ready to stand by everything I say.

HOVSTAD: I'm not going to print it. I cannot and will not and dare not print it.

DR. STOCKMANN: Dare not? What sort of talk is that? You are the editor, aren't you? And it's the editors who control the press, surely?

ASLAKSEN: No, it's the readers.

MAYOR: Fortunately, yes.

ASLAKSEN: It's public opinion, the educated public, the ratepayers and all the others—these are the people who control the press.

DR. STOCKMANN *(calmly):* And all these forces are against me?

ASLAKSEN: Yes, they are. It would mean total ruin for the town if your article were printed.

DR. STOCKMANN: Indeed.

MAYOR: My hat and my stick!

(Dr. Stockmann takes the hat off and puts it on the table, along with the stick)

MAYOR *(collecting them both):* Your term as mayor has come to an abrupt end.

DR. STOCKMANN: This is not the end yet. *(To Hovstad)* So it's quite impossible to get my article in the *Herald?*

HOVSTAD: Quite impossible. And I'm thinking partly also of your family. . . .

MRS. STOCKMANN: Oh, you needn't start worrying about his family, Mr. Hovstad.

MAYOR *(takes a sheet of paper out of his pocket):* For the guidance of the public, it will be sufficient to print this. It is an official statement.

HOVSTAD *(takes it):* Good. I'll see that it goes in.

DR. STOCKMANN: But not mine! You think you can gag me and silence the truth! You'll not get away with this so easily. Mr. Aslaksen, will you please take my manuscript and print it for me at once as a pamphlet— at my own expense, and on my authority. I want four hundred copies— no, five . . . six hundred, I want.

ASLAKSEN: Not if you offered me its weight in gold could I let my printing press be used for a thing like that. I daren't offend public opinion. You'll not get anybody in town to print it, I shouldn't think.

DR. STOCKMANN: Give it back to me then.

HOVSTAD *(hands him the manuscript):* There you are.

DR. STOCKMANN *(takes his hat and stick):* I'll get it out somehow. I'll call a mass meeting and read it out! All my fellow citizens shall hear the voice of truth!

MAYOR: You'll never get anybody to hire you a hall.

ASLAKSEN: Absolutely nobody, I'm quite certain.

BILLING: No, I'm dammed if they will.

MRS. STOCKMANN: But that would be outrageous! Why is everybody against you all of a sudden?

DR. STOCKMANN *(angrily):* I'll tell you why. It's because all the men in this town are nothing but a lot of old women—like you. All they can think about is their families; they never think about the rest of the community.

MRS. STOCKMANN *(taking his arm):* Then I'll show them one . . . old woman at least who can be a man . . . for once. I'll stick by you, Thomas!

DR. STOCKMANN: Well said, Katherine. And I *will* have my say, by Heaven! If I can't book a hall, I'll hire a man with a drum to march round town with me, and I'll proclaim it at every street corner.

MAYOR: I can't believe you'd be so absolutely crazy.

DR. STOCKMANN: Oh yes, I would!

ASLAKSEN: You'll not get a single man in the whole of the town to go with you!

BILLING: No, I'm dammed if you will!

MRS. STOCKMANN: Don't you give in now, Thomas. I'll get the boys to go with you.

DR. STOCKMANN: That's a wonderful idea!

MRS. STOCKMANN: Morten will love to go; and Ejlif's sure to come along as well.

DR. STOCKMANN: Yes, and then what about Petra! And you too, Katherine?

MRS. STOCKMANN: No, no, not me. But I'll stand in the window and watch, that's what I'll do.

DR. STOCKMANN *(puts his arms around her and kisses her):* Thank you for that! And now, gentlemen, the gloves are off. We'll see whether you and your shabby tricks can stop an honest citizen who wants to clean up the town.

(He and his wife go out through the door, back, left)

MAYOR *(shakes his head thoughtfully):* Now he's sent her mad, too.

Act IV

A large, old-fashioned room in the house of Captain Horster. At the back of the room, double doors open on to an anteroom. On the wall, left, are three windows; against the opposite wall is a dais, on which is a small table, and on it two candles, a water carafe, a glass, and a bell.

The room is additionally lit by wall lamps between the windows. Downstage left, a table with candles and a chair. Down right is a door, and beside it a couple of chairs.

There is a big crowd of townspeople of all classes. A few women and one or two schoolboys can be seen among them. More and more people keep coming in through the door at the back, filling up the room.

FIRST MAN *(bumping into another man):* Hello, Lamstad! You here as well?

SECOND MAN: I never miss a public meeting.

THIRD MAN: I expect you've brought your whistle?

SECOND MAN: You bet I have. Haven't you?

THIRD MAN: I'll say I have. Skipper Evensen said he was going to bring his great big cow-horn.

SECOND MAN: Good old Evensen!

(Laughter in the group)

FOURTH MAN *(joining them):* Here, I say, what's going on here tonight?

SECOND MAN: It's Dr. Stockmann. He's holding a protest meeting against the Mayor.

FOURTH MAN: But the Mayor's his brother!

FIRST MAN: That doesn't matter. Dr. Stockmann's not frightened.

THIRD MAN: But he's got it all wrong. It said so in the *Herald.*

SECOND MAN: Yes, he must be wrong this time, because nobody would let him have a hall for his meeting—Ratepayers Association, Men's Club, nobody!

FIRST MAN: He couldn't even get the Baths Hall.

SECOND MAN: I should think not.

A MAN *(in another group):* Whose side are we on here, eh?

A SECOND MAN *(in the same group):* Just you keep an eye on Aslaksen, and do what *he* does.

BILLING *(with a briefcase under his arm, pushing his way through the crowd):* Excuse me, gentlemen! May I come through, please? I'm reporting for the *Herald.* Thank you . . . thank you!

(He sits at the table, left)

A WORKMAN: Who's he?

SECOND WORKMAN: Don't you know *him?* That's Billing, he's on Aslaksen's paper.

(Captain Horster conducts Mrs. Stockmann and Petra in through the door, right front. Ejlif and Morten are with them.)

HORSTER: I thought perhaps the family might like to sit here. You can easily slip out there if anything happens.

MRS. STOCKMANN: Do you really think things might get out of hand?

HORSTER: You never know . . . with all these people here. But you sit here, and don't worry.

MRS. STOCKMANN *(sits down):* It was very kind of you to offer my husband this room.

HORSTER: Well, since nobody else would . . .

PETRA *(who has also sat down):* And it was brave of you too, Captain Horster.

HORSTER: Oh, I can't see there was anything particularly brave about it.

(Hovstad and Aslaksen arrive simultaneously but separately, and make their way through the crowd)

ASLAKSEN *(walks over to Horster):* Hasn't Dr. Stockmann arrived yet?

HORSTER: He's waiting in there.

(Movement in the crowd near the door at the back)

HOVSTAD *(to Billing):* Look! Here's the Mayor.

BILLING: Yes, damn me if he hasn't turned up after all!

(The Mayor eases his way through the crowd, bowing politely, and takes up a position by the wall, left. A moment later, Dr. Stockmann enters by the door, right front. He wears a black frock coat and a white cravat. Some people clap uncertainly, which is met by subdued hissing. Then there is silence.)

DR. STOCKMANN *(in an undertone):* How do you feel, Katherine?

MRS. STOCKMANN: I'm all right, thanks. *(Lowers her voice)* Try not to lose your temper, Thomas.

DR. STOCKMANN: Oh, I can control myself. *(Looks at his watch, steps up on the dais, and bows)* It's now quarter past . . . so I think we can begin. . . .

(He produces his manuscript)

ASLAKSEN: First I think we ought to elect a chairman.

DR. STOCKMANN: No. That's not necessary.

SEVERAL VOICES *(shouting):* Yes, yes it is!

MAYOR: I should also have thought that we should elect a chairman.

DR. STOCKMANN: But I've called this meeting to deliver a lecture, Peter.

MAYOR: Your lecture might just possibly lead to divergent expressions of opinion.

MANY VOICES *(from the crowd):* A Chairman! A chairman!

HOVSTAD: The consensus of opinion seems to be that we should have a chairman.

DR. STOCKMANN *(controlling himself):* Very well! Let the 'consensus of opinion' have its way.

ASLAKSEN: Wouldn't the Mayor accept nomination?

THREE MEN *(applauding):* Bravo! Bravo!

MAYOR: For a number of obvious reasons, I must decline. But fortunately we have here with us a man whom I think we can all accept. I refer, of course, to the chairman of the Ratepayers Association, Mr. Aslaksen.

MANY VOICES: Yes, yes. Good old Aslaksen! Bravo!

(Dr. Stockmann gathers up his manuscript and steps down from the dais)

ASLAKSEN: If it is the wish of my fellow citizens, I can hardly refuse. . . .

(Clapping and cheers. Aslaksen mounts the dais.)

BILLING *(writing):* Let's see—'Mr. Aslaksen elected by acclamation . . .'

ASLAKSEN: And now, perhaps I may be allowed, in this present capacity, to take the opportunity of saying a few brief words. I am a quiet and peace-loving man, who believes in discreet moderation and in . . . and in moderate discretion. Everyone who knows me is aware of that.

MANY VOICES: That's right! That's right, Aslaksen!

ASLAKSEN: I have learnt from long experience in the school of life that modera-
    tion is the quality that best befits a citizen . . .

MAYOR: Hear, hear!

ASLAKSEN: . . . and that discretion and moderation are the things whereby
    society is best served. I might perhaps, therefore, suggest to the honoura-
    ble gentleman who has called this meeting that he endeavour to keep
    within the bounds of moderation.

A MAN *(near the door):* Up the Moderates!

A VOICE: Shut up there!

MANY VOICES: Sh! Sh!

ASLAKSEN: No interruptions, gentlemen, please! Has anybody any comment
    to make?

MAYOR: Mr. Chairman!

ASLAKSEN: Yes, Mr. Mayor.

MAYOR: In view of the close relationship which, as is doubtless well known,
    exists between me and the present Medical Officer of the Baths, I should
    have much preferred not to speak this evening. But my connections with
    the Baths, to say nothing of my concern for the vital interests of the town,
    compel me to put forward some sort of proposal. I think I may safely
    assume that not a single one of us present here today wants to see irre-
    sponsible and exaggerated accounts put about concerning the sanitary
    conditions at the Baths and in the town generally.

MANY VOICES: No, no! Certainly not! We protest!

MAYOR: I should like to propose, therefore, that the Medical Officer be not
    permitted by this meeting to present his account of the matter.

DR. STOCKMANN *(flaring up):* Not permitted! What is this . . . ?

MRS. STOCKMANN *(coughing):* Hm! Hm!

DR. STOCKMANN *(composing himself):* Ah! Not permitted, eh!

MAYOR: In my communication to the *People's Herald,* I acquainted the public
    with the relevant facts, and every right-thinking person can quite well
    form his own opinion. It clearly shows that the Doctor's proposal—apart
    from being a vote of censure on the leading citizens of the town—simply
    means saddling the ratepayers with an unnecessary expenditure of at least
    several hundred thousand crowns.

(Cries of disapproval, and whistles)

ASLAKSEN *(ringing the bell):* Order please, gentlemen! I should like to support
    the Mayor's proposal. I too believe there is some ulterior motive behind
    the Doctor's agitation. He talks about the Baths, but what he's really after
    is revolution. He wants to see the control of the council pass into other
    hands. Nobody doubts but what the Doctor is sincere in his intentions—
    nobody can be in two minds about that, surely. I too am in favour of
    self-government by the people, as long as it doesn't fall too heavily on the
    ratepayers. But that's just what *would* happen here. And that's why I'm

damned . . . excuse me, gentlemen . . . why I just can't bring myself to agree with Dr. Stockmann this time. You can pay too dearly even for the best of things sometimes. That's *my* opinion.

(Animated applause on all sides)

HOVSTAD: I feel I ought to make my position clear, too. Dr. Stockmann's agitation seemed in the early stages to be attracting a certain measure of approval and I supported it as impartially as I was able. But then we got wind of the fact that we had allowed ourselves to be misled by an incorrect account. . . .

DR. STOCKMANN: Incorrect. . . !

HOVSTAD: A not wholly reliable account, then. The Mayor's statement has proved that. I trust nobody here doubts my liberal convictions. The policy of the *People's Herald* on the more important political questions must surely be known to everybody. But I have profited from the advice of experienced and thoughtful men that, when it comes to local affairs, a paper should proceed with a certain caution.

ASLAKSEN: I entirely agree with the speaker.

HOVSTAD: And in the matter under discussion it is now undeniably true that Dr. Stockmann has public opinion against him. But what is the first and foremost duty of an editor, gentlemen? Is it not to work in harmony with his readers? Has he not been given, as it were, a tacit mandate to work loyally and unremittingly for the welfare of his fellows? Or am I perhaps mistaken?

MANY VOICES: No, no! Hovstad is right!

HOVSTAD: It has been a sad thing for me to break with a man in whose house I have of late been a frequent guest—a man who until today has enjoyed the undivided goodwill of his fellow citizens—a man whose only . . . or should we say, whose most characteristic failing is to be guided more by his heart than by his head.

A FEW SCATTERED VOICES: That's true! Good old Dr. Stockmann!

HOVSTAD: But my duty to the community compelled me to break with him. There is also one further consideration that impels me to oppose him and, if possible, to prevent him from going any further along this fateful course he has taken. And that is consideration for his family . . .

DR. STOCKMANN: You stick to the water-supply and the sewers!

HOVSTAD: . . . Consideration for his wife and his helpless children.

MORTEN: Is that us he means, Mother?

MRS. STOCKMANN: Hush!

ASLAKSEN: I shall now put the Mayor's proposal to the vote.

DR. STOCKMANN: You needn't bother! I don't intend speaking about all the dirty business at the Baths tonight. No! You are going to hear about something quite different.

MAYOR *(in an undertone):* Now what's he up to?

A DRUNKEN MAN *(beside the entrance door):* If I'm entitled to pay rates, I'm also entitled to my own opinion. And it's my entire . . . firm . . . incomprehensible opinion that . . .

SEVERAL VOICES: Be quiet over there!

OTHERS: He's drunk. Chuck him out.

(The drunken man is put out)

DR. STOCKMANN: May I speak?

ASLAKSEN *(rings the bell):* Dr. Stockmann has the floor!

DR. STOCKMANN: If anybody, even a few days ago, had tried gagging me as they've tried tonight . . . they'd have seen me leaping like a lion to the defence of my sacred rights as an individual. But that hardly matters to me now. Now I have more important things to speak about.

(The crowd presses closer around him. Morten Kiil can be seen in the crowd.)

DR. STOCKMANN *(continues):* I've been doing a lot of thinking in the last few days . . . turning so many things over in my mind that in the end my head was buzzing . . .

MAYOR *(coughs):* Hm!

DR. STOCKMANN: . . . but I sorted things out in the finish. Then I saw the whole situation very clearly. That's why I am here this evening. I am going to make a great exposure, gentlemen! And the revelation I am going to make to you is incomparably bigger than this petty business about the water-supply being polluted and the Baths standing over a cesspool.

SEVERAL VOICES *(shouting):* Don't talk about the Baths! We don't want to hear it! None of that!

DR. STOCKMANN: I have said I am going to speak about the tremendous discovery I have made in the last few days . . . the discovery that all our *spiritual* sources are polluted and that our whole civic community is built over a cesspool of lies.

DISCONCERTED VOICES *(subdued):* What's he saying?

MAYOR: Making insinuations. . . !

ASLAKSEN *(his hand on the bell):* I call upon the speaker to moderate his language.

DR. STOCKMANN: I love my native town as much as ever a man can. I wasn't very old when I left here; and distance and longing and memory lent a kind of enchantment to both the place and the people. *(Some clapping and cheers)* Then for many a long year I sat up there in the far North, in a miserable hole of a place. Coming across some of the people living here and there in that rocky wilderness, I often used to think they would have been better served, poor half-starved creatures that they were, if they had sent for a vet instead of somebody like me.

(There is a murmuring in the room)

BILLING *(putting his pen down):* Damn me if I've ever heard. . . !

HOVSTAD: That's a slander on a respectable people!

DR. STOCKMANN: Just be patient a little!—I don't think anybody would want to accuse me of having forgotten my home town up there. I sat brooding —rather like an eider duck—and the thing I hatched out . . . was the plan for the Baths. *(Applause and protests)* And when fate at long last smiled on me, and it turned out I could come home again—yes, my friends, there didn't seem to be very much more I wanted from life. Just one thing I wanted: to be able to work—eagerly, tirelessly, ardently—for the common good and for the good of the town.

MAYOR *(looking away):* You choose rather a peculiar way of . . . hm!

DR. STOCKMANN: So there I was—deliriously, blindly happy. Then, yesterday morning—no, actually, it was the evening before—my eyes were opened wide, and the first thing I saw was the colossal stupidity of the authorities. . . .

(Noises, shouts and laughter. Mrs. Stockmann coughs earnestly.)

MAYOR: Mr. Chairman!

ASLAKSEN *(rings the bell):* By virtue of my position. . . !

DR. STOCKMANN: Let's not be too fussy about a word here and there, Mr. Aslaksen! All I mean is I got wind of the colossal botch-up our so-called leaders had managed to make of things down at the Baths. If there's anything I just can't stand at any price—it's leaders! I've just about had enough of them. They are just like a lot of goats in a young forest—there's damage everywhere they go. Any decent man and they just get in his way, they're under his feet wherever he turns. If I had my way I'd like to see them exterminated like any other pest. . . .

(Uproar in the room)

MAYOR: Mr. Chairman, is it in order to make remarks like this?

ASLAKSEN *(his hand on the bell):* Dr. Stockmann. . . !

DR. STOCKMANN: I can't understand why it has taken me till now to wake up to what these gentlemen really are, when practically every day I've had a perfect specimen of them right in front of my very eyes—my brother Peter—slow on the uptake and set in his ideas.. . .

(Laughter, noise and whistles. Mrs. Stockmann sits coughing. Aslaksen rings his bell violently.)

THE DRUNKEN MAN *(who has come in again):* Are you referring to me? Because they do call me Petersen . . . but I'll be damned if . . .

ANGRY VOICES: Throw that drunk out! Get rid of him!

(The man is again thrown out)

MAYOR: Who was that person?

A BYSTANDER: Don't know him, sir.

A SECOND MAN: He doesn't belong here.

A THIRD MAN: It must be that timber merchant over from . . . *(The rest is inaudible)*

ASLAKSEN: The man had obviously had too much to drink. Proceed, Doctor, but do please remember—with moderation.

DR. STOCKMANN: Very well, gentlemen, I shall say no more about our leaders. If anyone imagines from what I've just said that I'm out after these gentlemen's blood this evening, then he's wrong—quite definitely wrong! Because I am happily convinced that all these old dodderers, these relics of a dying age, are managing very nicely to see themselves off—they don't need to call in a doctor to hasten the end. And besides they are not the people who constitute the greatest danger to society. *They* are not the ones who do most to pollute our spiritual life, or to infect the ground beneath us. *They* are not the ones who are the worst enemies of truth and freedom in our society.

SHOUTS FROM ALL SIDES: Who then? Who is, then? Name them!

DR. STOCKMANN: Yes, I'll name them, don't you fret! Because *that's* precisely the great discovery I made yesterday. *(Raises his voice)* The worst enemy of truth and freedom in our society is the compact majority. Yes, the damned, compact, liberal majority. *That's* what! Now you know.

(Tremendous commotion in the room. Most of the crowd are shouting, stamping and whistling. Some of the more elderly men exchange glances, and seem to be enjoying things. Mrs. Stockmann anxiously gets to her feet. Ejlif and Morten advance threateningly on some schoolboys who are misbehaving. Aslaksen rings his bell and shouts for order. Hovstad and Billing are both trying to speak, but cannot be heard above the noise. At last quiet is restored.)

ASLAKSEN: As Chairman, I must request the speaker to withdraw his wild remarks.

DR. STOCKMANN: Not on your life, Mr. Aslaksen. It is that majority here which is robbing me of my freedom and is trying to prevent me from speaking the truth.

HOVSTAD: The majority is always right!

BILLING: And it damn' well always stands for the truth too!

DR. STOCKMANN: The majority is never right. Never, I tell you! That's one of these lies in society that no free and intelligent man can help rebelling against. Who are the people that make up the biggest proportion of the population—the intelligent ones or the fools? I think we can agree it's the fools, no matter where you go in this world, it's the fools that form the overwhelming majority. But I'll be damned if that means it's right that the fools should dominate the intelligent. *(Uproar and shouting)* Yes, yes, shout me down if you like but you can't deny it! The majority has the *might*—more's the pity—but it hasn't *right*. *I* am right—I and one or two other individuals like me. The minority is always right.

(Renewed uproar)

HOVSTAD: Ha! Ha! In the last day or two Dr. Stockmann has turned aristocrat!

DR. STOCKMANN: I've already said I'm not going to waste any words on that bunch of narrow-chested, short-winded old has-beens. They've no longer anything to give to the red-blooded life of today. I'm thinking of the few, the genuine individuals in our midst, with their new and vigorous ideas. These men stand in the very forefront of our advance, so far ahead that the compact majority hasn't even begun to approach them—and it's *there* they fight for truths too newly-born to have won any support from the majority.

HOVSTAD: Aha! So now he's a revolutionary.

DR. STOCKMANN: Yes, by God, I am, Mr. Hovstad! I'm plotting revolution against this lie that the majority has a monopoly of the truth. What are these truths that always bring the majority rallying round? Truths so elderly they are practically senile. And when a truth is as old as that, gentlemen, you can hardly tell it from a lie. *(Laughter and jeers)* All right, believe it or not! But truths are not by any means the tough old Methuselahs people imagine. The life of a normally constituted truth is generally, say, about seventeen or eighteen years, at most twenty; rarely longer. But truths as elderly as that have always worn terribly then. But it's only *then* that the majority will have anything to do with them; then it will recommend them as wholesome food for thought. But there's no great food-value in that sort of diet, I can tell you—as a doctor, I know what I'm talking about. All these majority truths are just like salt meat that's been kept too long and gone bad and mouldy. That's at the root of all this moral scurvy that's going about.

ASLAKSEN: It appears to me that the honourable gentleman is straying rather a long way from his subject.

MAYOR: I concur very much with what the Chairman says.

DR. STOCKMANN: You must be mad, Peter. I'm sticking as close to my subject as I can. For that's just what I'm trying to say: that the masses, this damned compact majority—*this* is the thing that's polluting the sources of our spiritual life and infecting the very ground we stand on.

HOVSTAD: And this is what happens, you say, just because the great majority of thinking people are sensible enough to keep their approval for recognized and well-founded truths?

DR. STOCKMANN: My dear Mr. Hovstad, don't talk to me about well-founded truths. The truths the masses recognize today are the same truths as were held by advanced thinkers in our grandfathers' day. We who man the advanced outposts today, we don't recognize them any more. In my opinion, only one thing is certain: and that is that no society can live a healthy life on the old dry bones of that kind of truth.

HOVSTAD: But instead of you standing there and giving us all this airy talk, it would be interesting to hear a bit more about these old, dry bones of truth we are supposed to be living on.

(Approval from several quarters)

DR. STOCKMANN: Oh, I could draw up a whole list of these horrors. But for the moment I'll restrict myself to *one* recognized truth, which is actually a rotten lie but which nevertheless Mr. Hovstad and the *People's Herald* and all the *Herald's* supporters live by.

HOVSTAD: And that is?

DR. STOCKMANN: A doctrine inherited from your forefathers which you fatuously go on spreading far and wide—the doctrine that the general public, the common herd, the masses are the very essence of the people—that they *are* the people—that the common man, and all the ignorant and immature elements in society have the same right to criticize and to approve, to govern and to counsel as the few intellectually distinguished people.

BILLING: Well I'll be damned. . . .

HOVSTAD *(shouting at the same time):* Citizens, take note of this!

ANGRY VOICES: So we are not the people, eh? Only the top people are to have any say, eh?

A WORKMAN: Chuck him out, saying things like that!

OTHERS: Out with him!

A MAN *(shouting):* Let's have a blast of it now, Evensen!

(Great blasts on a horn, along with whistles and tremendous uproar)

DR. STOCKMANN *(after the noise has died down somewhat):* Be reasonable! Can't you bear to hear the voice of truth just for once? I don't expect you all to agree with me straight off. But I must say I expected Mr. Hovstad to admit I was right when he'd got over his first shock. Mr. Hovstad claims to be a free-thinker. . . .

VOICES *(in astonished undertones):* Free-thinker, did he say? What? Mr. Hovstad a free-thinker?

HOVSTAD *(shouting):* Prove it, Dr. Stockmann! Have I ever said so in black and white?

DR. STOCKMANN *(reflectively):* No, damn it, you are right. You've never had the guts. Well, I don't want to embarrass you, Mr. Hovstad. Let's say it's me who's the free-thinker, then. What I'm going to do is prove to you, scientifically, that when the *People's Herald* tells you that you—the general public, the masses—are the real essence of the people, it's just a lot of bunkum. Don't you see it's just a journalistic lie? The public is only the raw material from which a people is made. *(Murmurs, laughter and general disturbance in the room)* Well, isn't that the way it is with life generally. Look at the difference between pedigree and cross-bred animals. Look at an ordinary barnyard hen, for instance—fat lot of meat you get off a scraggy old thing like that! And what about the eggs it lays? Any decent, self-respecting crow could do as well. But take a purebred Spanish or Japanese hen, or take a pheasant or a turkey—ah! what a difference!

Or I might mention dogs, which are so like humans in many ways. Think first of an ordinary mongrel—I mean one of those filthy, shaggy rough dogs that do nothing but run about the streets and cock their legs against all the walls. Compare a mongrel like that with a poodle whose pedigree goes back many generations, who has been properly fed and has grown up among quiet voices and soft music. Don't you think the poodle's brain will have developed quite differently from the mongrel's? You bet it will! That kind of pedigree dog can be trained to do the most fantastic tricks —things an ordinary mongrel could never learn even if it stood on its head.

(Uproar and laughter)

A MAN *(shouts):* Are you trying to make out we are dogs now?

ANOTHER MAN: We're not animals, Doctor!

DR. STOCKMANN: Ah, but that's just exactly what we *are,* my friend! We are as good animals as any man could wish for. But you don't find all that many really outstanding ones. Oh, there's a tremendous difference between the poodles and the mongrels amongst us men. And the funny thing is that Mr. Hovstad fully agrees with me as long as we are talking about four-footed animals. . . .

HOVSTAD: Yes, it's all right for *them.*

DR. STOCKMANN: All right. But as soon as I apply the principle to two-legged creatures, that's the end of it for Mr. Hovstad. He hasn't the courage of his convictions, he doesn't take things to their logical conclusion. So he turns the whole theory upside down and proclaims in the *Herald* that the barnyard hen and the street-corner mongrel—that these are the finest exhibits in the menagerie. But that's always the way, and always will be as long as a man still remains infected by the mass mind, and hasn't worked his way free to some kind of intellectual distinction.

HOVSTAD: I make no claim to any kind of distinction. I came from simple peasant stock, and I am proud that my roots go deep into that common people he is insulting.

SOME WORKMEN: Good old Hovstad! Hurrah! Hurrah!

DR. STOCKMANN: The sort of common people I'm talking about are not found simply among the lower classes; they are crawling and swarming all round us—right up to the highest social level. You've only got to look at that nice, pretty Mayor of yours. My brother Peter is as mass-minded a person as anything you'll find on two legs. . . .

(Laughter and hisses)

MAYOR: I must protest against these personal remarks.

DR. STOCKMANN *(imperturbably):* . . . and that's not because he's descended, like me, from some awful old Pomeranian pirate or something—because that's what we are . . .

MAYOR: An absurd story. I deny it!

DR. STOCKMANN: . . . but because he thinks what his superiors think, and believes what his superiors believe. And anybody who does that is just one of the masses in spirit. You see, that's why my magnificent brother Peter is so terribly lacking in natural distinction—and consequently has so little independence of mind.

MAYOR: Mr. Chairman . . . !

HOVSTAD: So in this country it seems it's the distinguished people who are the liberals! That's a new one!

(Laughter)

DR. STOCKMANN: Yes, that's another part of my discovery. And along with that goes the fact that free-thinking is almost exactly the same as morality. That's why I call it downright irresponsible of the *Herald* to keep putting out this distorted idea, day in day out, that it's the masses, the compact majority that has the monopoly of morality and liberal principles—and that vice and corruption and every kind of depraved idea are an overflow from culture, just as all the filth in our Baths is an overflow from the tannery up at Mölledal! *(Uproar and interruptions. Dr. Stockmann, unperturbed, smiles in his eagerness.)* And yet this same *Herald* can preach about raising the standards of the masses! Good Lord, if what the *Herald* says is right, raising the level of the masses would amount precisely to toppling them straight over the edge to perdition. But fortunately it's just one of those old lies we've had handed down—this idea that culture is demoralizing. No, stupidity and poverty and ugliness are the things that do the devil's work! A house that isn't aired and swept every day—and my wife Katherine says it ought to be scrubbed as well, but that's a debatable point—anybody living for more than two or three years in *that* kind of house will end up by having no moral sense left whatsoever. No oxygen, no conscience! And there must be an awful lot of houses in this town short of oxygen, it seems, if the entire compact majority is so irresponsible as to want to build the prosperity of the town on a quagmire of lies and deceit.

ASLAKSEN: I cannot allow such abusive remarks to be directed at the entire community.

A MAN: I move that the Chairman rule the speaker out of order!

ANGRY VOICES: Yes, yes! That's right. Out of order!

DR. STOCKMANN *(flaring up)*: Then I'll shout the truth on every street corner! I'll write to all the other newspapers! I'll see that the whole country gets to know what's going on here!

HOVSTAD: It might almost seem that Dr. Stockmann is set on ruining the town.

DR. STOCKMANN: I love this town so much that I'd rather destroy it than see it prosper on a lie.

ASLAKSEN: That's putting it pretty strongly.

(Uproar and whistles. Mrs. Stockmann coughs in vain; the Doctor no longer hears her.)

HOVSTAD *(shouting above the din):* Any man who wants to destroy a whole community must be a public enemy.

DR. STOCKMANN *(with rising temper):* When a place has become riddled with lies, who cares if it's destroyed? I say it should simply be razed to the ground! And all the people living by these lies should be wiped out, like vermin! You'll have the whole country infested in the end, so that eventually the whole country deserves to be destroyed. And if it ever comes to that, then I'd say with all my heart: let it all be destroyed, let all its people be wiped out!

A MAN *(in the crowd):* That's the talk of an enemy of the people!

BILLING: That, God damn me, was the voice of the people!

THE WHOLE CROWD *(shouting):* Yes! Yes! He's an enemy of the people. He hates his country. He hates his people.

ASLAKSEN: As a citizen of this country, and as an individual, I am profoundly shocked by what I have just had to listen to. Dr. Stockmann has betrayed himself in a way I should never have dreamt possible. I must therefore, with great regret, associate myself with the opinion that has just been expressed by my honourable fellow citizens, and I propose we embody that opinion in the form of a resolution. I suggest something like this: 'This meeting declares that it considers Dr. Thomas Stockmann, Medical Officer to the Baths, to be an enemy of the people.'

(A storm of applause and cheers. A number of people crowd round Dr. Stockmann, cat-calling. Mrs. Stockmann and Petra have risen. Morten and Ejlif fight with the other schoolboys who have also been booing. Some of the grown-ups separate them.)

DR. STOCKMANN *(to those whistling):* You fools! I tell you that . . .

ASLAKSEN *(ringing his bell):* Dr. Stockmann is out of order. A formal vote must be taken; but so as not to hurt anybody's feelings, we will do it by secret ballot. Have you any paper, Mr. Billing?

BILLING: There's both blue and white.. . .

ASLAKSEN *(stepping down):* That's fine. We can do it quicker that way. Cut it into strips . . . there we are, now. *(To the meeting)* Blue means no, white means yes. I'll come round myself to collect the votes.

(The Mayor leaves the room. Aslaksen and one or two others carry round the slips of paper in their hats.)

ONE MAN *(to Hovstad):* What's come over the Doctor? What are you to make of it?

HOVSTAD: Well, you know how impetuous he is.

SECOND MAN *(to Billing):* Tell me—you've been in their house quite a bit. Does the man drink, have you noticed?

BILLING: I'm damned if I know really what to say. They always bring the toddy out when anybody calls.

THIRD MAN: No, I think it's more likely he's a bit crazy.

FIRST MAN: Ah, I wonder if there's insanity in the family.

BILLING: Could very well be.

FOURTH MAN: No, it's just spite, that's what it is. Wants to get his own back about something.

BILLING: He did say something secretly about wanting a raise; but he didn't get it.

ALL THE MEN TOGETHER: Well, there you are then!

THE DRUNKEN MAN *(in the crowd):* I want a blue one. And I want a white one an' all.

VOICES: Is that that drunk again? Chuck him out!

MORTEN KIIL *(approaches the Doctor):* Well, Stockmann, now you see where these monkey tricks of yours have landed you!

DR. STOCKMANN: I have simply done my duty.

KIIL: What was that you said about the tanneries at Mölledal?

DR. STOCKMANN: You heard. I said that was where all the muck came from.

KIIL: From *my* tannery as well?

DR. STOCKMANN: I'm afraid so. Yours is the worst.

KIIL: Are you going to print *that* in the papers?

DR. STOCKMANN: I'm not hiding anything.

KIIL: You might find that costly, Stockmann.

(He leaves)

A FAT MAN *(goes up to Horster, ignoring the ladies):* So, Captain Horster, so you lend your house to enemies of the people, eh?

HORSTER: I think I can do what I like with my own property, Mr. Vik.

THE FAT MAN: So you won't mind if I do the same with mine.

HORSTER: What do you mean?

THE FAT MAN: You'll hear from me in the morning.

(He turns and goes)

PETRA: Isn't he the owner of your ship, Captain Horster?

HORSTER: Yes, that's Mr. Vik.

ASLAKSEN *(mounts the platform with the ballot papers; he rings the bell):* Gentlemen, let me announce the result. With only one vote to the contrary.. . .

A YOUNG MAN: That's the drunk!

ASLAKSEN: With only one drunken man's vote to the contrary, the resolution of this meeting was carried unanimously: that Dr. Thomas Stockmann is an enemy of the people. *(Shouting and applause)* Three cheers for our ancient and honourable community! *(More cheers)* Three cheers for our able and efficient Mayor, for putting duty before family! *(Cheers)* The meeting is adjourned.

(He steps down)

BILLING: Three cheers for the chairman!

THE WHOLE CROWD: Good old Aslaksen!

DR. STOCKMANN: My hat and coat, Petra! Captain, have you any room aboard for passengers for the New World?

HORSTER: For you and your family we'll make room, Doctor.

DR. STOCKMANN *(as Petra helps him on with his coat):* Good! Come on, Katherine! Come along, lads!

(He takes his wife by the arm)

MRS. STOCKMANN *(in a low voice):* Thomas dear, let's go out by the back way.

DR. STOCKMANN: No back way for me, Katherine. *(Raises his voice)* You'll hear again from this enemy of the people before he shakes the dust off his feet. I'm not as sweet-tempered as a certain person I could mention. I'm not saying: 'I forgive you, for you know not what you do.'

ASLAKSEN *(shouts):* That comparison is blasphemous, Dr. Stockmann!

BILLING: Well I'll be . . . ! What dreadful things to say in the presence of decent people.

A COARSE VOICE: And what about those threats he made!

ANGRY SHOUTS: Let's go and break his windows! Duck him in the fjord!

A MAN *(in the crowd):* Give us another blast, Evensen! Blow! Blow!

(The sound of a horn and whistles and wild shouts. The Doctor and his family make for the exit, and Horster clears a way for them.)

THE WHOLE CROWD *(howling after them):* Enemy of the people! Enemy of the people! Enemy of the people!

BILLING *(tidying his papers):* Well I'm damned if I would want to drink toddy at the Stockmanns' tonight!

(The crowd makes for the exit; the noise is continued outside; shouts from the street of 'Enemy of the people! Enemy of the people!')

Act V

Dr. Stockmann's study. Along the walls are bookcases and medicine cupboards. On the back wall is the door to the hall; left front is the door to the living-room. On the right wall are two windows, all the glass panes of which are smashed. In the centre of the room is the Doctor's desk; covered with books and papers. The room is in disorder. It is morning.

Dr. Stockmann, in dressing-gown, slippers and skull-cap, is bending down and raking under one of the cupboards with an umbrella. Finally he manages to rake out a stone.

DR. STOCKMANN *(calling through the open door into the sitting-room):* I've found another one, Katherine.

MRS. STOCKMANN *(from the living-room):* Oh, you'll find a lot more yet, I'm sure.

DR. STOCKMANN *(adding the stone to a pile of others on the table):* I'm going to keep these stones—like relics. Ejlif and Morten must see them every day, and when they grow up, they'll inherit them. *(Rakes under a bookcase)* Hasn't—what the devil's her name again—you know, that girl—hasn't she gone for the glazier yet?

MRS. STOCKMANN *(comes in):* Yes, but he said he didn't know if he could come today.

DR. STOCKMANN: He daren't—you'll see.

MRS. STOCKMANN: Yes, that's what Randina thought too—he was afraid of what the neighbours might say. *(Calls into the living-room.)* What's that you want, Radina? I see. *(She goes out and comes back at once.)* It's a letter for you, Thomas.

DR. STOCKMANN: Let me see. *(He opens it and reads)* Aha!

MRS. STOCKMANN: Who's it from?

DR. STOCKMANN: From the landlord. He's given us notice.

MRS. STOCKMANN: Has he really? But he was such a nice man. . . .

DR. STOCKMANN *(looking at the letter):* He daren't do anything else, he says. He's very sorry, but he daren't do anything else . . . because of the others . . . public opinion . . . not his own master . . . dare not risk putting certain people's backs up. . . .

MRS. STOCKMANN: There you see, Thomas.

DR. STOCKMANN: Yes, yes, I see all right. They are all cowards, the whole lot of them here. Nobody dares do anything because of all the others. *(Flings the letter on the table)* But that doesn't make any difference to us, Katherine. We are leaving for the New World, and then . . .

MRS. STOCKMANN: But, Thomas, have you really thought about it properly, this business about leaving . . . ?

DR. STOCKMANN: You wouldn't want me to stay here, would you? Not after the way they've taken it out of me, branding me as an enemy of the people, and smashing all my windows! And look here, Katherine! I've even got a tear in my black trousers through them.

MRS. STOCKMANN: So you have! And they are the best pair you've got!

DR. STOCKMANN: You should never have your best trousers on when you turn out to fight for freedom and truth. Well, it's not that I care all that much about the trousers—you can always put a stitch in them for me. But what gets me is the idea of that mob going for me as though they were my equals —*that's* what I can't stomach, damn it!

MRS. STOCKMANN: Yes, they've really been horrid to you here, Thomas. But do we have to go so far as to leave the country for *that?*

DR. STOCKMANN: Don't you think you would get the same insolence from the masses in the other towns as you do here? Of course you would! They're all the same! Oh, to hell! Let them yap! That's not the worst; the worst thing is that all over the country everybody's got to toe the party line. Not that it's likely to be very much better out West either; it will be the same there too, with your liberal public opinions and your compact majorities and all the rest of the rigmarole. But things are on a bigger scale there, you see. They might kill, but they don't torture. They don't take a free man and put the screws on his soul, as they do here. And if the worst comes to the worst, you can get away from it all. *(Walks up and down)* If only I knew where there was a primeval forest or a little South Sea island going cheap. . . .

MRS. STOCKMANN: But, Thomas, what about the boys?

DR. STOCKMANN *(halts):* You are funny, Katherine! Would you rather the boys grew up in a society like this? You saw yourself last night how half the population is absolutely mad; and if the other half haven't lost their wits, it's only because they are such thickheads they haven't any wits to lose.

MRS. STOCKMANN: Now then, Thomas dear, you ought to watch what you are saying.

DR. STOCKMANN: Hah! You don't think I'm telling you the truth? Don't they turn every single idea upside down? Don't they make a complete hotchpotch of what's right and what's wrong? Don't they go and call lies what I know perfectly well is the truth? But the craziest thing of the lot is to see all these grown-up men going round calling themselves liberals and imagining they are men of independent minds! Have you ever heard anything like it, Katherine?

MRS. STOCKMANN: Yes, yes, of course that's quite stupid, but . . . *(Petra comes in from the living-room)* Back from school already?

PETRA: Yes. I've been given my notice.

MRS. STOCKMANN: Your notice?

DR. STOCKMANN: You too!

PETRA: Mrs. Busk gave me notice. And I thought it was better to leave at once.

DR. STOCKMANN: How right you were!

MRS. STOCKMANN: Who would have thought Mrs. Busk was that sort!

PETRA: Oh, Mother, Mrs. Busk isn't bad, really. I could see quite well she didn't like doing it. But she daren't do anything else, she said. So I have to leave.

DR. STOCKMANN *(laughs and rubs his hands):* So she didn't dare do anything else, either! That's great!

MRS. STOCKMANN: Oh well, I dare say after that awful scene last night . . .

PETRA: It wasn't just *that.* Listen, Father!

DR. STOCKMANN: Well?

PETRA: Mrs. Busk showed me no less than three letters she'd had this morning. . . .

DR. STOCKMANN: Anonymous, of course?

PETRA: Yes.

DR. STOCKMANN: You see they *daren't* put their names to them, Katherine!

PETRA: And in two of them it said that a certain gentleman, who has been a frequent visitor here, had been talking in the club last night and saying that I had extremely advanced ideas about all sorts of things. . . .

DR. STOCKMANN: Which I hope you didn't deny?

PETRA: You know very well I wouldn't. Mrs. Busk has got one or two pretty advanced ideas herself, when she talks to me privately. But now that this has come out about me, she daren't keep me.

MRS. STOCKMANN: Fancy! A frequent visitor here! You see what you get for your hospitality, Thomas.

DR. STOCKMANN: We are not going to live in this stinking hole any longer. Pack up as quick as you can, Katherine. The sooner we get away the better.

MRS. STOCKMANN: Be quiet—I think there's somebody in the hall. Go and see, Petra.

PETRA *(opens the door):* Oh, it's you, Captain Horster? Do come in.

HORSTER *(from the hall):* Good morning. I thought I'd just look in to see how things were.

DR. STOCKMANN *(shaking his hand):* Thank you. That's very kind of you.

MRS. STOCKMANN: And thank you for your help last night, Captain Horster.

PETRA: But how did you get back home again?

HORSTER: Oh, I managed. I'm pretty tough, you know. The only thing those people are good for is shooting off their mouths.

DR. STOCKMANN: Yes, isn't it astonishing, this sickening cowardice? Here, I want to show you something! Look, here are all the stones they chucked at us last night. Just look at them! Not more than a couple of honest-to-goodness lumps in the whole lot—the rest are just pebbles, bits of gravel! And yet they went on standing out there, shouting and yelling and swearing they were going to beat me up. But as for *doing* anything—no, there isn't much of that in this town.

HORSTER: It was just as well this time, Doctor.

DR. STOCKMANN: I dare say you're right. But it makes you angry all the same. Because if it ever comes to the point where the country really *has* to fight in earnest, then you'll see how public opinion is all for clearing out fast, and the whole of the compact majority will make for the woods like a great flock of sheep, Captain Horster. That's the saddening thing; that's what really upsets me. . . . Oh, what the hell . . . it's all just a lot of nonsense, really. If they've called me an enemy of the people, I might as well be an enemy of the people.

MRS. STOCKMANN: That's something you'll never be, Thomas.

DR. STOCKMANN: I shouldn't bet on it if I were you, Katherine. To be called some nasty name is just like getting a pinprick in the lung. And this blasted name they've called me—it's lodged here under the heart, embedded deep, griping me as if it were acid. And it's no use taking magnesia for *that!*

PETRA: Puh! I should just laugh at them, Father!

HORSTER: They'll come round to other ways of thinking in time, Doctor.

MRS. STOCKMANN: They will, you know, Thomas, as sure as you're standing here.

DR. STOCKMANN: When it's too late, perhaps. Well, serve them right! Then, as they wallow in their filth, they'll wish they hadn't been so ready to drive a patriot into exile. When do you sail, Captain Horster?

HORSTER: Well, actually that was what I came to talk to you about. . . .

DR. STOCKMANN: Well? Something wrong with the ship?

HORSTER: No, only that I'm not sailing with her.

PETRA: Surely you haven't been given notice?

HORSTER *(smiles):* Yes, I have.

PETRA: You too.

MRS. STOCKMANN: There you are, you see, Thomas.

DR. STOCKMANN: And all in the cause of truth! Oh, if I'd thought for one moment that . . .

HORSTER: Don't you worry about that! I'll get a job all right with some company away from here.

DR. STOCKMANN: So that's our Mr. Vik . . . a man of means, beholden to nobody . . . ! It's a damned shame!

HORSTER: He's very decent otherwise. And he said himself he would have liked to keep me on, if only he dared. . . .

DR. STOCKMANN: But he didn't dare? No, of course not.

HORSTER: He said it wasn't so easy when you belonged to a party. . . .

DR. STOCKMANN: He never spoke a truer word, that fine friend of ours! A party's just like a mincing machine, grinding people's brains up into a kind of hash, and churning out a lot of thickheaded clots.

MRS. STOCKMANN: Oh, Thomas, really!

PETRA *(to Horster):* If only you hadn't walked home with us, things might not have gone so far.

HORSTER: I don't regret it.

PETRA *(holds out her hand):* Thank you!

HORSTER *(to the Doctor):* What I really wanted to say was this: that if you are set on leaving, I've another idea. . . .

DR. STOCKMANN: Fine! As long as we can get away quickly.

MRS. STOCKMANN: Hush! Wasn't that a knock?

PETRA: That'll be Uncle, for sure.

DR. STOCKMANN: Aha! *(Shouts)* Come in!

MRS. STOCKMANN: Thomas, dear, promise me . . .

(The Mayor comes in from the hall)

MAYOR *(in the doorway):* Oh, you are busy. In that case I'd better . . .

DR. STOCKMANN: No, no! Come in.

MAYOR: But I wanted to speak to you alone.

MRS. STOCKMANN: We'll go into the living-room for the time being.

HORSTER: And I'll look in again later.

DR. STOCKMANN: No, you just go next door with them, Captain Horster. I want to know a bit more about . . .

HORSTER: Very well, I'll wait then.

(He goes with Mrs. Stockmann and Petra into the living-room. The Mayor says nothing but glances at the windows.)

DR. STOCKMANN: Perhaps it's a bit draughty for you in here today. Put your hat on.

MAYOR: Thank you, if I may. *(Does so)* I think I must have caught a cold yesterday. I stood there shivering. . . .

DR. STOCKMANN: Really? Things seemed warm enough to me.

MAYOR: I regret I was unable to prevent the excesses of last night.

DR. STOCKMANN: Is there anything particular you want to tell me besides that?

MAYOR *(produces a big envelope):* I have this document for you, from the directors.

DR. STOCKMANN: My notice?

MAYOR: Yes, from today. *(Lays the letter on the table.)* We don't like doing this, but—to be perfectly frank—we daren't do anything else, in the light of public opinion.

DR. STOCKMANN *(smiles):* Daren't? I seem to have heard that word before, today.

MAYOR: I want you to realize your position. You can't count on any kind of practice in this town in future.

DR. STOCKMANN: To hell with the practice! But what makes you so certain?

MAYOR: The Ratepayers Association is circulating a list, urging all respectable citizens to have nothing to do with you. And I am pretty confident that not a single man will dare refuse to sign it. They simply wouldn't *dare.*

DR. STOCKMANN: I don't doubt. But what then?

MAYOR: If I may give you some advice, it's this: go away for a while. . . .

DR. STOCKMANN: Yes, I had actually been thinking of going away.

MAYOR: Good. And after you'd had six months or so to think things over, and if after mature consideration you then felt you were ready to write a few words of apology, admitting your mistake . . .

DR. STOCKMANN: Then I might perhaps get my job back again, you mean?

MAYOR: Perhaps. It's not altogether impossible.

DR. STOCKMANN: But what about public opinion? Surely you won't dare, in the light of public opinion.

MAYOR: Opinion is an extremely variable thing. And, in point of fact, it's rather important that we get some sort of admission from you along those lines.

DR. STOCKMANN: Yes, I can see how you'd come slobbering after that. But, by God, surely you haven't forgotten already what I've told you before about dirty tricks like this!

MAYOR: At that time your position was quite different. At that time you had reason to suppose you had the whole town at your back. . . .

DR. STOCKMANN: Yes, and now I'm supposed to feel as though I had the whole town *on* my back.... *(Flares up)* I wouldn't care if I had the devil himself *and* his old woman on my back. . . . Never, I tell you! Never!

MAYOR: A man with a family has no right to be carrying on as you are. You have no right, Thomas.

DR. STOCKMANN: Haven't I? There's only one thing in this world a free man has no right to do. Do you know what that is?

MAYOR: No.

DR. STOCKMANN: Of course not. But *I'll* tell you. A free man has no right to get messed up with filth; things should never reach the stage where he feels like spitting in his own eye.

MAYOR: This all sounds extremely plausible. And if there weren't some other explanation for your obstinacy . . . But then, of course, there is. . . .

DR. STOCKMANN: What do you mean by *that?*

MAYOR: You know perfectly well what I mean. Speaking as your brother and as one who understands these things, let me give you some advice: don't build too much on certain expectations or prospects that might so terribly easily fall through.

DR. STOCKMANN: What on earth are you getting at?

MAYOR: You don't really expect me to believe that you are ignorant of the terms of Morten Kiil's will?

DR. STOCKMANN: I know that what little he has is to go to an Old People's Home. But what's that got to do with me?

MAYOR: In the first place, it's not so little. Morten Kiil is a pretty wealthy man.

DR. STOCKMANN: I had absolutely no idea . . .

MAYOR: Hm . . . really? And you have no idea, I suppose, that a not inconsiderable part of his fortune is to be left to your children, and that you and your wife are to have the interest on this money during your lifetime? Did he never tell you that?

DR. STOCKMANN: Blessed if he did! On the contrary, he's done nothing the whole time but grouse about the impossibly high taxes he had to pay. Are you quite sure about this, Peter?

MAYOR: I have it from a completely reliable source.

DR. STOCKMANN: But, Heavens, that means Katherine's taken care of—and the children too! I must tell them. . . . *(Shouts)* Katherine, Katherine!

MAYOR *(holds him back):* Hush! Don't say anything yet!

MRS. STOCKMANN *(opens the door):* What is the matter?

DR. STOCKMANN: Nothing, my dear. Just go back in again. *(Mrs. Stockmann shuts the door; he walks up and down.)* Provided for! To think they're all provided for! And for life! It's a wonderful feeling to know that one has that security!

MAYOR: Yes, but that's just it! You can't be sure. Morten Kiil can alter his will any time he likes.

DR. STOCKMANN: But he won't, my dear Peter. The old boy is tickled to death at the way I've gone for you and your precious friends.

MAYOR *(starts, and looks intently at him):* Aha, that puts a lot of things in a different light.

DR. STOCKMANN: What things?

MAYOR: So the whole thing has been a combined operation. These violent, ruthless attacks you have made—all in the name of truth—against the leading men of the town. . . .

DR. STOCKMANN: What about them?

MAYOR: Just your part of the bargain in exchange for being included in that vindictive old man's will.

DR. STOCKMANN *(almost speechless):* Peter . . . of all the scum I ever met, you are the worst.

MAYOR: Things are finished now between us. Your dismissal is final . . . for now we have a weapon against you.

(He goes)

DR. STOCKMANN: Well I'll be. . . ! Of all the. . . ! *(Shouts)* Katherine! I want the floor swilled down after him. Get her to bring her bucket in . . . what's her name . . . damn it, you know . . . that girl who's always got a dirty nose. . . .

MRS. STOCKMANN *(in the living-room doorway):* Hush, Thomas, please!

PETRA *(also in doorway):* Father, Grandfather's here. He wants to know if he can have a word with you alone.

DR. STOCKMANN: Yes, of course he can. *(At the door)* Come in, Father-in-law. *(Morten Kiil comes in; the Doctor shuts the door after him.)* Well now, what can I do for you? Do sit down.

MORTEN KIIL: I won't sit. *(Looks round him)* It's looking very nice in here today, Stockmann.

DR. STOCKMANN: It is, isn't it?

KIIL: Very nice indeed it looks. And lots of fresh air too; plenty of that oxygen stuff you were talking about yesterday. Your conscience must be in pretty good shape today, I imagine.

DR. STOCKMANN: Yes, it is.

KIIL: I imagined it would be. *(Tapping his breast pocket)* Do you know what I've got here?

DR. STOCKMANN: A good conscience too, I should hope.

KIIL: Puh! Something much better than that.

(He brings out a fat wallet, opens it, and produces a bundle of papers)

DR. STOCKMANN *(looks at him in amazement):* Shares in the Baths?

KIIL: They weren't difficult to come by today.

DR. STOCKMANN: You mean to say you've gone and bought. . . ?

KIIL: As many as I could afford.

DR. STOCKMANN: But, my dear Father-in-law—with things at the Baths in the state they are in now. . . !

KIIL: If only you behave like a sensible man, you'll soon have the place on its feet again.

DR. STOCKMANN: Well, you can see for yourself, I'm doing all I can, but . . . The people in this town are mad!

KIIL: You said yesterday that the worst of the filth came from my works. But if this happened to be true, then my grandfather, and my father before me, to say nothing of myself, have been slowly poisoning the town all these years—like three unclean spirits. You don't think I'm going to take this lying down, do you?

DR. STOCKMANN: I'm afraid you can't help it.

KIIL: No thank you. My good name means a lot to me. I'm told people call me an old badger; and a badger's a kind of pig, isn't it? But I'm not going to let them say 'I told you so'. I want to live and die with my reputation clear.

DR. STOCKMANN: And how are you going to manage that?

KIIL: You are going to clear me, Stockmann.

DR. STOCKMANN: *I* am!

KIIL: Do you know where I got the money to buy all these shares? No, how could you? But I'll tell you. This is the money that Katherine and Petra and the boys are to inherit from me. Because, you see, I've managed to put quite a bit aside, after all.

DR. STOCKMANN *(flaring up):* You mean you've gone and taken Katherine's money for *this?*

KIIL: Yes, every bit of the money is tied up now in the Baths. And I just want to see now if you really are completely and absolutely stark raving mad, Stockmann. If you are still going to have it that creepy, crawly things are coming from my works, you might as well be flaying Katherine alive, for all the difference it makes—*and* Petra, *and* the boys as well. But then no decent father would do that—not unless he was a madman.

DR. STOCKMANN *(pacing up and down):* But I *am* a madman! I *am* a madman!

KIIL: But you couldn't be so stark, staring mad as all that, not when it affects your wife and children.

DR. STOCKMANN *(halts in front of him):* Why couldn't you have talked to me first before going and buying all that trash!

KIIL: What's done can't be undone—it's got to be faced.

DR. STOCKMANN *(walks about restlessly):* If only I wasn't so certain. . . ! But I'm absolutely convinced I'm right.

KIIL *(weighing his wallet in his hand):* If you persist with these stupid ideas, then these things will not be worth much, you know.

(He puts his wallet in his pocket)

DR. STOCKMANN: Damn it, surely science could find *some* sort of prophylactic, some preventive or other. . . .

KIIL: You mean something to kill off the animals?

DR. STOCKMANN: Yes, or to render them harmless, at least.

KIIL: Couldn't you try with a bit of rat poison?

DR. STOCKMANN: Oh, don't talk rubbish! But then everybody keeps telling me it's just my imagination. Well, let's make it that then! Let them have it the way they want it! These ignorant little mongrels—calling me an enemy of the people! And tearing the very clothes off my back!

KIIL: And smashing all your windows!

DR. STOCKMANN: And then there's this business of my duty towards my family. I'll have to talk to Katherine about it. She's better than I am at things like that.

KIIL: Fine! She's a sensible woman—and just you pay attention to what she says.

DR. STOCKMANN (turning on him): You're a fine one, too, behaving in this stupid way! Fancy gambling with Katherine's money—and putting me in this dreadful dilemma! When I look at you, it's just like looking at the devil himself. . . !

KIIL: I think I'd better go. But I want to hear from you by two o'clock at the latest. Yes or no. If it's no, the shares go to charity—this very day.

DR. STOCKMANN: And what does Katherine get then?

KIIL: Not a penny. (The hall door opens; Hovstad and Aslaksen can be seen outside.) Well, look who's here!

DR. STOCKMANN (stares at them): What's this! You dare come to my house?

HOVSTAD: Yes, we do.

ASLAKSEN: You see, we want to talk to you about something.

KIIL (whispers): Yes or no—by two o'clock.

ASLAKSEN (with a glance at Hovstad): Aha!

(Morten Kiil leaves)

DR. STOCKMANN: Well! What do you want with me? Make it snappy!

HOVSTAD: I can well understand that you are not very well disposed towards us as a result of our attitude at the meeting yesterday. . . .

DR. STOCKMANN: Attitude, you call it! A fine attitude that was! Of all the spineless exhibitions. . . ! Like a couple of old women! God damn it!

HOVSTAD: Call it what you like; but we couldn't do anything else.

DR. STOCKMANN: You daren't do anything else, you mean! Well?

HOVSTAD: Yes, if you like.

ASLAKSEN: But why didn't you drop us a hint beforehand? All it needed was a word to Mr. Hovstad or me.

DR. STOCKMANN: A hint? What about?

ASLAKSEN: About what was behind it all.

DR. STOCKMANN: I don't understand you at all.

ASLAKSEN (nods confidentially): Oh yes you do, Dr. Stockmann.

HOVSTAD: There's no need to make a mystery of it any longer.

DR. STOCKMANN (looks from one to the other): For God's sake, won't somebody tell me. . . !

ASLAKSEN: If you don't mind my asking—isn't it true that your father-in-law is going round town buying up all the shares in the Baths.

DR. STOCKMANN: Yes, he's been and bought some shares today. But. . . ?

ASLAKSEN: It might have been wise if you had picked somebody else to do that —somebody not quite so closely related.

HOVSTAD: And you shouldn't have done all this in your own name, either. There wasn't any need for people to know that the attack on the Baths came from you. You should have approached me, Dr. Stockmann.

DR. STOCKMANN (*looks fixedly ahead; the truth seems to dawn on him, and he says as though thunderstruck*): But this is incredible! Are such things possible?

ASLAKSEN (*smiles*): Evidently they are. But they ought preferably to be done with finesse, you know.

HOVSTAD: And it's best to have one or two others in on it, too. Because then the individual responsibility is always reduced if there are several people.

DR. STOCKMANN (*composedly*): Come to the point, gentlemen. What is it you want?

ASLAKSEN: Perhaps Mr. Hovstad had better . . .

HOVSTAD: No, you do it, Aslaksen.

ASLAKSEN: Well, the thing is that—now that we know how things really are —we think we might venture to put the *People's Herald* at your disposal.

DR. STOCKMANN: So *now* you dare do it? But what about public opinion? Aren't you afraid of having to face a storm of protest.

HOVSTAD: We must try to ride that storm.

ASLAKSEN: And then you must be ready to change your tack quickly, Doctor. As soon as your campaign has had its effect. . . .

DR. STOCKMANN: You mean as soon as my father-in-law and I have bought the shares up cheap. . . ?

HOVSTAD: I suppose it's mainly for research purposes you are anxious to get control of the Baths.

DR. STOCKMANN: Of course. It was with an eye on my research that I managed to get the old Badger to come in on it with me. Then we'll patch up the pipes a bit, and dig up a bit of the beach, and it won't cost the town a penny. Don't you think that'll work? Eh?

HOVSTAD: I think so—if you've got the *Herald* with you.

ASLAKSEN: In a free society, the press has great power, you know, Doctor.

DR. STOCKMANN: Yes, indeed. And so has public opinion. And you, Mr. Aslaksen, will take responsibility for the Ratepayers Association, I suppose?

ASLAKSEN: The Ratepayers Association *and* the Temperance Society. You may depend on that.

DR. STOCKMANN: But, gentlemen—I feel ashamed putting a question like this —but . . . what do *you* get out of this. . . ?

HOVSTAD: Actually, we'd rather not take anything at all for our help, really. But in fact the *Herald* is a bit shaky at the moment; it just can't quite make ends meet, and I should be most reluctant to wind the paper up now, just when there's such a lot of political work to be done.

DR. STOCKMANN: Of course. That would be a sad blow for a friend of the people like yourself. *(Flares up)* But I am an enemy of the people. *(Rushes about the room)* Where's my stick? Where the devil's my stick?

HOVSTAD: What does this mean?

ASLAKSEN: Surely you don't. . . !

DR. STOCKMANN *(stops):* And what if I didn't give you a single brass farthing out of all my shares? It's not easy to get money out of us rich people, don't forget.

HOVSTAD: And *you* mustn't forget that this business about the shares can be presented in two very different ways.

DR. STOCKMANN: Yes, and you are just the man to do it. If I don't come to the aid of the *Herald,* then you'll take a pretty poor view of things. The hunt will be up, I dare say. . . . You'll be after my blood . . . you'll be on to me like a dog on to a hare!

HOVSTAD: That's the law of nature. Every animal must fight for survival.

ASLAKSEN: You've got to take your food where you find it, you know.

DR. STOCKMANN: Then let's see if you can find anything out in the gutter. *(Rushes about the room)* Because now we are damned well going to see who is the strongest animal amongst us three. *(Finds his umbrella and waves it)* Now, watch out. . . !

HOVSTAD: You wouldn't dare attack us!

ASLAKSEN: Watch what you are doing with that umbrella!

DR. STOCKMANN: Out of the window with you, Mr. Hovstad.

HOVSTAD *(near the hall door):* Have you gone completely mad?

DR. STOCKMANN: Out of the window, Mr. Aslaksen! Jump, I tell you. And quick about it!

ASLAKSEN *(running round the desk):* Moderation, Dr. Stockmann! I'm not very strong, I can't stand very much of this. . . . *(Shouts)* Help! Help!

(Mrs. Stockmann, Petra and Horster come in from the living-room)

MRS. STOCKMANN: Heavens above, Thomas, what's going on?

DR. STOCKMANN *(swinging the umbrella):* Jump! Down into the gutter!

HOVSTAD: Unprovoked assault! You're a witness of this, Captain Horster.

(He hurries out through the hall)

ASLAKSEN *(bewildered):* Anybody who knew the lie of the land about here . . .

(He slinks out through the living-room)

MRS. STOCKMANN *(clinging to her husband):* Control yourself, Thomas!

DR. STOCKMANN *(throws the umbrella down):* Damn them, they got away after all.

MRS. STOCKMANN: But what did they want with you?

DR. STOCKMANN: I'll tell you later. I've got other things to think about now. *(He goes to his desk and writes on a visiting card)* Look, Katherine, what does this say?

MRS. STOCKMANN: 'No', three times. What's that for?

DR. STOCKMANN: That's something else I'll tell you later. *(Hands the card to Petra) There,* Petra. Get little dirty-face to run over to the Badger's with it, as quick as she can. Hurry! *(Petra takes the card and goes out through the hall.)* Well, if this hasn't been a hell of a day for callers, I don't know what is. But now I'm going to sharpen up my pen; I'll impale them on it; I'll dip it in venom and gall; I'll chuck the inkpot right in their faces!

MRS. STOCKMANN: Yes, but we're leaving, aren't we, Thomas?

(Petra comes back)

DR. STOCKMANN: Well?

PETRA: She's taken it.

DR. STOCKMANN: Good! Leaving, did you say? No, I'm damned if we are. We're staying where we are, Katherine!

PETRA: We're staying?

MRS. STOCKMANN: In this town?

DR. STOCKMANN: Yes, just here. The battlefield is here; here the fight will be fought and here I shall triumph! As soon as I've had my trousers stitched, I'm off to town to look for somewhere to live. We've got to have a roof over our heads this winter.

HORSTER: You are welcome to share my house.

DR. STOCKMANN: Can I?

HORSTER: Yes, of course you can. I've plenty of room, and I'm hardly ever at home.

MRS. STOCKMANN: How very kind of you, Captain Horster.

PETRA: Thank you!

DR. STOCKMANN *(shaking his hand):* Thank you! Thank you! That's that worry off my mind. Now I can get straight down to work in real earnest. Oh, there's no end to the things here that need going into, Katherine! But it's grand that I can give all my time to this now. Because—I was going to tell you—I've got my notice from the Baths, you know. . . .

MRS. STOCKMANN *(sighing):* Yes, I was expecting that.

DR. STOCKMANN: . . . And they want to take my practice away as well. Well, let them! I won't lose the poor people anyway—those who don't pay anything. And, heavens, they are the ones who need me most. But, by God, they are going to listen to what I have to say. I'll read them a lesson, both in and out of season, as it says somewhere.

MRS. STOCKMANN: But, Thomas dear, surely you've seen now that reading them a lesson doesn't do much good.

DR. STOCKMANN: Don't be so ridiculous, Katherine. D'you think I'm going to let public opinion and the compact majority and all that rigmarole get the better of me? No, thank you! And anyway, what I want to do is so simple and clear and straightforward. I just want to take these mongrels and knock it into their heads that the Liberals are the worst enemies of freedom . . . that the party programmes grab hold of every young and promising idea and wring its neck . . . and that policies of expediency are turning all our standards of morality and justice upside down, so that life's just not going to be worth living. Surely I can make people understand that, Captain Horster? Don't you think so?

HORSTER: Very likely. I don't know very much about these things myself.

DR. STOCKMANN: Well, look here—I'll tell you what I mean! It's the party bosses you've got to get rid of. A party boss is just like a wolf, you see . . . a ravenous wolf who needs so and so many victims every year to keep him going. Just look at Hovstad and Aslaksen! How many do you think *they* haven't seen off in their time? Or else they worry them and maul them about so badly that they are no use for anything except to join the Ratepayers Association and subscribe to the *Herald! (Sits on the edge of the table)* Come over here, Katherine . . . look how beautifully the sun is shining in here today. And this glorious, fresh, spring air that's been let in.

MRS. STOCKMANN: If only we could live on sun and fresh air, Thomas.

DR. STOCKMANN: Well, you'll just have to skimp and scrape a bit on the side —we'll manage all right. That's my least worry. No, the worst thing is this: I don't know of anybody with enough independence of mind to feel like taking on my work after me.

PETRA: Oh, you mustn't think about that, Father. You've plenty of time yet. —Why, here are the boys already.

(Ejlif and Morten come in from the living-room)

MRS. STOCKMANN: Have you got a holiday today?

MORTEN: No, but we went for the others at playtime. . . .

EJLIF: That's not true. They started fighting us.

MORTEN: And then Mr. Rörlund said we'd better stay away for a few days.

DR. STOCKMANN *(snaps his fingers and jumps down from the table):* I've got it! I've got it, by Heaven! You are not going to set foot in that school again!

THE BOYS: No more school!

MRS. STOCKMANN: Thomas, really . . .!

DR. STOCKMANN: Never, I say! I'll teach you myself—what I mean is, you'll not learn a blessed thing. . . .

MORTEN: Hurrah!

DR. STOCKMANN: . . . but I'll make decent and independent-minded men of you both. . . . And you must help me, Petra.

PETRA: You can count on me, Father.

DR. STOCKMANN: And we'll have the school in the very room where they called me an enemy of the people. But there ought to be a few more of us. I must have at least a dozen boys to start with.

MRS. STOCKMANN: You're not likely to get them here, not in this town.

DR. STOCKMANN: We'll see about that. *(To the boys)* What about some of the streetcorner lads . . . the real guttersnipes. . . .?

MORTEN: Yes, Father. I know plenty of them!

DR. STOCKMANN: That's fine! Get hold of one or two for me, will you? Just for once, I'm going to try an experiment on these mongrels. You never know what you might find amongst them.

MORTEN: But what are you going to do, when we've grown up into decent and independent-minded men?

DR. STOCKMANN: Then you can drive all the wolves out, lads—make sure that they all go west!

(Ejlif looks rather doubtful; Morten jumps and shouts for joy)

MRS. STOCKMANN: Oh, just so long as it isn't the wolves who go chasing you, Thomas.

DR. STOCKMANN: You must be mad, Katherine! Chase *me! Now!* When I'm the strongest man in the town!

MRS. STOCKMANN: The strongest. . . .? *Now?*

DR. STOCKMANN: Yes, and I could even go so far as to say that *now* I'm one of the strongest men in the whole world.

MORTEN: Honestly?

DR. STOCKMANN *(dropping his voice):* Sh! You mustn't say anything about it yet. But I've made a great discovery.

MRS. STOCKMANN: What, again?

DR. STOCKMANN: Yes, I have. *(He gathers them about him and says confidentially)* The thing is, you see, that the strongest man in the world is the man who stands alone.

MRS. STOCKMANN *(smiles and shakes her head):* Oh, Thomas, Thomas. . . .!

PETRA *(bravely, grasping his hands):* Father!

QUESTIONS

1. What does this play reveal about life in a small nineteenth-century Norwegian town?
2. What ideas about the role of the press in society are expressed in the play? Which characters change their views about the press in the course of the play? Why?
3. Do the issues raised about the press still seem valid?
4. What ways has society developed to deal with the conflicts between environmental purity and economic development that are suggested by this play?

5. Characterize the Mayor, Aslaksen, and Hovstad. What are the major motivations of each?
6. What qualities of Dr. Stockmann do you admire? What are his faults? Is he an individualized or a type character?
7. Ibsen was only one of many nineteenth-century thinkers, including America's Henry David Thoreau, who were seriously concerned about conflicts between majority rule and individual rights. In your experience, is it true that the "compact majority" sometimes fails to recognize significant truths espoused by individuals or minorities? What are some exceptions to Stockmann's assertion in Act Four, that "the majority is never right"?

THE CHERRY ORCHARD

In observing the decline of a land-based aristocracy and the rise of a commercial class in prerevolutionary Russia, Chekhov found material for comedy (he thought the conception "funny, very funny," and subtitled the play "A Comedy in Four Acts"). Yet playgoers do not experience much laughter in this play. Occasionally, the spectacle of self-indulgent humans who cannot communicate is wryly amusing, but a sadness in promises misunderstood and ambitions frustrated seems even stronger.

The Cherry Orchard is a fine example of *realistic drama*. In it Chekhov avoided the exaggerations in plot and characterization traditional (and necessary) in plays more clearly either comic or tragic. These people are neither above us, so that we look up to them, or below us, so that we look down. If we find comedy in the scenes, for example, in which nobody seems to listen to anyone else or talk to anyone except him- or herself, we are amused because we recognize scenes in which we ourselves have participated. This kind of comedy is attractively quizzical: how precisely are we to take a speech or action as inept as some of our own, but not so pointedly exaggerated that we are sure we should laugh? Our involvement in that emotional puzzle itself makes the play engagingly realistic.

Much depends upon theater and actors. More than the earlier plays in this collection, *The Cherry Orchard* demands the realistic staging techniques developed in Chekhov's time at the Moscow Art Theater, under its director, Constantin Stanislavsky. The Moscow Art Theater was elaborately equipped to make possible the most accurately detailed stage settings. Tremendous care was taken with costuming and lighting to preserve the illusion of reality. Stanislavsky pioneered an acting style in which the players learned to live their parts, speaking and acting as though under the stress of real emotions. The stage curtain rose on a *fourth wall* as far as the players were concerned: they moved about as though in a room, playing to each other and not to the audience. As you read *The Cherry Orchard,* you will want to stage it that way in the theater of your mind. The effect is not at all like that of a play by Sophocles or Shakespeare.

THE CHERRY ORCHARD*

A Comedy in Four Acts

Anton Chekhov   *(1860–1904)*

LUBOV ANDREYEVNA RANEVSKAYA, a landowner.

ANYA, her seventeen-year-old daughter.

VARYA, her adopted daughter, twenty-two years old.

LEONID ANDREYEVICH GAYEV, MME. RANEVSKAYA'S brother.

YERMOLAY ALEXEYEVICH LOPAHIN, a merchant.

PYOTR SERGEYEVICH TROFIMOV, a student.

SIMEONOV-PISHCHIK, a landowner.

CHARLOTTA IVANOVNA, a governess.

SEMYON YEPIHODOV, a clerk.

DUNYASHA, a maid.

FIRS (pronounced *fierce*), a man-servant, aged eighty-seven.

YASHA, a young valet.

A TRAMP.

STATIONMASTER, POST OFFICE CLERK, GUESTS, SERVANTS.

The action takes place on Mme. Ranevskaya's estate.

Act I

A room that is still called the nursery. One of the doors leads into Anya's room. Dawn, the sun will soon rise. It is May, the cherry trees are in blossom, but it is cold in the orchard; there is a morning frost. The windows are shut. Enter Dunyasha with a candle, and Lopahin with a book in his hand.

LOPAHIN: The train is in, thank God. What time is it?

DUNYASHA: Nearly two. *(Puts out the candle)* It's light already.

LOPAHIN: How late is the train, anyway? Two hours at least. *(Yawns and stretches)* I'm a fine one! What a fool I've made of myself! I came here on purpose to meet them at the station, and then I went and overslept. I fell asleep in my chair. How annoying! You might have waked me . . .

DUNYASHA: I thought you'd left. *(Listens.)* I think they're coming!

LOPAHIN *(listens):* No, they've got to get the luggage, and one thing and another . . . *(Pause)* Lubov Andreyevna spent five years abroad, I don't know what she's like now . . . She's a fine person—lighthearted, simple. I remember when I was a boy of fifteen, my poor father—he had a shop here in the village then—punched me in the face with his fist and made my nose bleed. We'd come into the yard, I don't know what for, and he'd had a drop too much. Lubov Andreyevna, I remember her as if it were yesterday—she was still young and so slim—led

*Translated by Avrahm Yarmolinsky.

me to the wash-basin, in this very room . . . in the nursery. "Don't cry, little peasant," she said, "it'll heal in time for your wedding. . . ." *(Pause)* Little peasant . . . my father was a peasant, it's true, and here I am in a white waistcoat and yellow shoes. A pig in a pastry shop, you might say. It's true I'm rich, I've got a lot of money. . . . But when you look at it closely, I'm a peasant through and through. *(Pages the book)* Here I've been reading this book and I didn't understand a word of it. . . . Was reading it and fell asleep. . . . *(Pause)*

DUNYASHA: And the dogs were awake all night, they feel that their masters are coming.

LOPAHIN: Dunyasha, why are you so—

DUNYASHA: My hands are trembling. I'm going to faint.

LOPAHIN: You're too soft, Dunyasha. You dress like a lady, and look at the way you do your hair. That's not right. One should remember one's place.

(Enter Yepihodov with a bouquet; he wears a jacket and highly polished boots that squeak badly. He drops the bouquet as he comes in.)

YEPIHODOV *(picking up the bouquet):* Here, the gardener sent these, said you're to put them in the dining room. *(Hands the bouquet to Dunyasha)*

LOPAHIN: And bring me some *kvass.*[1]

DUNYASHA: Yes, sir. *(Exits)*

YEPIHODOV: There's a frost this morning—three degrees below—and yet the cherries are all in blossom. I cannot approve of our climate. *(Sighs)* I cannot. Our climate does not activate properly. And, Yermolay Alexeyevich, allow me to make a further remark. The other day I bought myself a pair of boots, and I make bold to assure you, they squeak so that it is really intolerable. What should I grease them with?

LOPAHIN: Oh, get out! I'm fed up with you.

YEPIHODOV: Every day I meet with misfortune. And I don't complain, I've got used to it, I even smile.

(Dunyasha enters, hands Lopahin the kvass)

YEPIHODOV: I am leaving. *(Stumbles against a chair, which falls over)* There! *(Triumphantly, as it were)* There again, you see what sort of circumstance, pardon the expression. . . . It is absolutely phenomenal! *(Exits)*

DUNYASHA: You know, Yermolay Alexeyevich, I must tell you, Yepihodov has proposed to me.

LOPAHIN: Ah!

DUNYASHA: I simply don't know . . . he's a quiet man, but sometimes when he starts talking, you can't make out what he means. He speaks nicely— and it's touching—but you can't understand it. I sort of like him though, and he is crazy about me. He's an unlucky man . . . every day something

---

[1]A beer made from rye or barley.

happens to him. They tease him about it here . . . they call him, Two-and-Twenty Troubles.

LOPAHIN *(listening):* There! I think they're coming.

DUNYASHA: They *are* coming! What's the matter with me? I feel cold all over.

LOPAHIN: They really are coming. Let's go and meet them. Will she recognize me? We haven't seen each other for five years.

DUNYASHA *(in a flutter):* I'm going to faint this minute. . . . Oh, I'm going to faint!

(Two carriages are heard driving up to the house. Lopahin and Dunyasha go out quickly. The stage is left empty. There is a noise in the adjoining rooms. Firs, who had driven to the station to meet Lubov Andreyevna Ranevskaya, crosses the stage hurriedly, leaning on a stick. He is wearing an old-fashioned livery and a tall hat. He mutters to himself indistinctly. The hubbub off-stage increases. A voice: "Come, let's go this way." Enter Lubov Andreyevna, Anya and Charlotta Ivanovna, with a pet dog on a leash, all in traveling dresses; Varya, wearing a coat and kerchief; Gayev, Simeonov-Pishchik, Lopahin, Dunyasha with a bag and an umbrella, servants with luggage. All walk across the room.)

ANYA: Let's go this way. Do you remember what room this is, mamma?

MME. RANEVSKAYA *(joyfully, through her tears):* The nursery!

VARYA: How cold it is! My hands are numb. *(To Mme. Ranevskaya)* Your rooms are just the same as they were mamma, the white one and the violet.

MME. RANEVSKAYA: The nursery! My darling, lovely room! I slept here when I was a child . . . *(Cries)* And here I am, like a child again! *(Kisses her brother and Varya, and then her brother again)* Varya's just the same as ever, like a nun. And I recognized Dunyasha. *(Kisses Dunyasha)*

GAYEV: The train was two hours late. What do you think of that? What a way to manage things!

CHARLOTTA *(to Pishchik):* My dog eats nuts, too.

PISHCHIK *(in amazement):* You don't say so! *(All go out, except Anya and Dunyasha)*

DUNYASHA: We've been waiting for you for hours. *(Takes Anya's hat and coat)*

ANYA: I didn't sleep on the train for four nights and now I'm frozen . . .

DUNYASHA: It was Lent when you left; there was snow and frost, and now . . . My darling! *(Laughs and kisses her)* I have been waiting for you, my sweet, my darling! But I must tell you something . . . I can't put it off another minute . . .

ANYA *(listlessly):* What now?

DUNYASHA: The clerk, Yepihodov, proposed to me, just after Easter.

ANYA: There you are, at it again . . . *(Straightening her hair)* I've lost all my hairpins . . . *(She is staggering with exhaustion)*

DUNYASHA: Really, I don't know what to think. He loves me—he loves me so!

ANYA *(looking towards the door of her room, tenderly):* My own room, my windows, just as though I'd never been away. I'm home! Tomorrow morning I'll get up and run into the orchard. Oh, if I could only get some sleep. I didn't close my eyes during the whole journey—I was so anxious.

DUNYASHA: Pyotr Sergeyevich came the day before yesterday.

ANYA *(joyfully):* Petya!

DUNYASHA: He's asleep in the bath-house. He has settled there. He said he was afraid of being in the way. *(Looks at her watch)* I should wake him, but Miss Varya told me not to. "Don't you wake him," she said.

(Enter Varya with a bunch of keys at her belt)

VARYA: Dunyasha, coffee, and be quick . . . Mamma's asking for coffee.

DUNYASHA: In a minute. *(Exits)*

VARYA: Well, thank God, you've come. You're home again. *(Fondling Anya)* My darling is here again. My pretty one is back.

ANYA: Oh, what I've been through!

VARYA: I can imagine.

ANYA: When we left, it was Holy Week, it was cold then, and all the way Charlotta chattered and did her tricks. Why did you have to saddle me with Charlotta?

VARYA: You couldn't have traveled all alone, darling—at seventeen!

ANYA: We got to Paris, it was cold there, snowing. My French is dreadful. Mamma lived on the fifth floor; I went up there, and found all kinds of Frenchmen, ladies, an old priest with a book. The place was full of tobacco smoke, and so bleak. Suddenly I felt sorry for mamma, so sorry, I took her head in my arms and hugged her and couldn't let go of her. Afterwards mamma kept fondling me and crying . . .

VARYA *(through tears):* Don't speak of it . . . don't.

ANYA: She had already sold her villa at Mentone, she had nothing left, nothing. I hadn't a kopeck[2] left either, we had only just enough to get home. And mamma wouldn't understand! When we had dinner at the stations, she always ordered the most expensive dishes, and tipped the waiters a whole ruble. Charlotta, too. And Yasha kept ordering, too—it was simply awful. You know Yasha's mamma's footman now, we brought him here with us.

VARYA: Yes, I've seen the blackguard.

ANYA: Well, tell me—have you paid the interest?

VARYA: How could we?

ANYA: Good heavens, good heavens!

VARYA: In August the estate will be put up for sale.

ANYA: My God!

LOPAHIN *(peeps in at the door and bleats):* Meh-h-h. *(Disappears)*

VARYA *(through tears):* What I couldn't do to him! *(Shakes her fist threateningly)*

ANYA *(embracing Varya, gently):* Varya, has he proposed to you? *(Varya*

[2]A small coin, 1/100 of a ruble.

shakes her head) But he loves you. Why don't you come to an understanding? What are you waiting for?

VARYA: Oh, I don't think anything will ever come of it. He's too busy, he has no time for me . . . pays no attention to me. I've washed my hands of him —I can't bear the sight of him. They all talk about our getting married, they all congratulate me—and all the time there's really nothing to it— it's all like a dream. *(In another tone)* You have a new brooch—like a bee.

ANYA *(sadly):* Mamma bought it. *(She goes into her own room and speaks gaily like a child)* And you know, in Paris I went up in a balloon.

VARYA: My darling's home, my pretty one is back! *(Dunyasha returns with the coffee-pot and prepares coffee. Varya stands at the door of Anya's room.)* All day long, darling, as I go about the house, I keep dreaming. If only we could marry you off to a rich man, I should feel at ease. Then I would go into a convent, and afterwards to Kiev, to Moscow . . . I would spend my life going from one holy place to another . . . I'd go on and on . . . What a blessing that would be!

ANYA: The birds are singing in the orchard. What time is it?

VARYA: It must be after two. Time you were asleep, darling. *(Goes into Anya's room)* What a blessing that would be!

(Yasha enters with a plaid and a traveling bag, crosses the stage)

YASHA *(finically):* May I pass this way, please?

DUNYASHA: A person could hardly recognize you, Yasha. Your stay abroad has certainly done wonders for you.

YASHA: Hm-m . . . and who are you?

DUNYASHA: When you went away I was that high— *(Indicating with her hand)* I'm Dunyasha—Fyodor Kozoyedev's daughter. Don't you remember?

YASHA: Hm! What a peach!

(He looks round and embraces her. She cries out and drops a saucer. Yasha leaves quickly)

VARYA *(in the doorway, in a tone of annoyance):* What's going on here?

DUNYASHA *(through tears):* I've broken a saucer.

VARYA: Well, that's good luck.

ANYA *(coming out of her room):* We ought to warn mamma that Petya's here.

VARYA: I left orders not to wake him.

ANYA *(musingly):* Six years ago father died. A month later brother Grisha was drowned in the river. . . . Such a pretty little boy he was—only seven. It was more than mamma could bear, so she went away, went away without looking back . . . *(Shudders)* How well I understand her, if she only knew! *(Pauses)* And Petya Trofimov was Grisha's tutor, he may remind her of it all. . . .

(Enter Firs, wearing a jacket and a white waistcoat. He goes up to the coffee-pot.)

FIRS *(anxiously):* The mistress will have her coffee here. *(Puts on white gloves)* Is the coffee ready? *(Sternly; to Dunyasha)* Here, you! And where's the cream?

DUNYASHA: Oh, my God! *(Exits quickly)*

FIRS *(fussing over the coffee-pot):* Hah! the addlehead! *(Mutters to himself)* Home from Paris. And the old master used to go to Paris too . . . by carriage. *(Laughs)*

VARYA: What is it, Firs?

FIRS: What is your pleasure, Miss? *(Joyfully)* My mistress has come home, and I've seen her at last! Now I can die. *(Weeps with joy)*

(Enter Mme. Ranevskaya, Gayev, and Simeonov-Pishchik. The latter is wearing a tight-waisted, pleated coat of fine cloth, and full trousers. Gayev, as he comes in, goes through the motions of a billiard player with his arms and body.)

MME. RANEVSKAYA: Let's see, how does it go? Yellow ball in the corner! Bank shot in the side pocket!

GAYEV: I'll tip it in the corner! There was a time, sister, when you and I used to sleep in this very room, and now I'm fifty-one, strange as it may seem.

LOPAHIN: Yes, time flies.

GAYEV: Who?

LOPAHIN: I say, time flies.

GAYEV: It smells of patchouli here.

ANYA: I'm going to bed. Good night, mamma. *(Kisses her mother)*

MME. RANEVSKAYA: My darling child! *(Kisses her hands)* Are you happy to be home? I can't come to my senses.

ANYA: Good night, uncle.

GAYEV *(kissing her face and hands):* God bless you, how like your mother you are! *(To his sister)* At her age, Luba, you were just like her.

(Anya shakes hands with Lopahin and Pishchik, then goes out, shutting the door behind her)

MME. RANEVSKAYA: She's very tired.

PISHCHIK: Well, it was a long journey.

VARYA *(to Lopahin and Pishchik):* How about it, gentlemen? It's past two o'clock—isn't it time for you to go?

MME. RANEVSKAYA *(laughs):* You're just the same as ever, Varya. *(Draws her close and kisses her)* I'll have my coffee and then we'll all go. *(Firs puts a small cushion under her feet)* Thank you, my dear. I've got used to coffee. I drink it day and night. Thanks, my dear old man. *(Kisses him)*

VARYA: I'd better see if all the luggage has been brought in. *(Exits)*

MME. RANEVSKAYA: Can it really be I sitting here? *(Laughs)* I feel like dancing, waving my arms about. *(Covers her face with her hands)* But maybe I am dreaming! God knows I love my country, I love it tenderly; I couldn't look out of the window in the train, I kept crying so. *(Through tears)* But I must have my coffee. Thank you, Firs, thank you, dear old man. I'm so happy that you're still alive.

FIRS: Day before yesterday.

GAYEV: He's hard of hearing.

LOPAHIN: I must go soon, I'm leaving for Kharkov about five o'clock. How annoying! I'd like to have a good look at you, talk to you . . . You're just as splendid as ever.

PISHCHIK *(breathing heavily):* She's even better-looking . . . Dressed in the latest Paris fashion . . . Perish my carriage and all its four wheels . . .

LOPAHIN: Your brother, Leonid Andreyevich, says I'm a vulgarian and an exploiter. But it's all the same to me—let him talk. I only want you to trust me as you used to. I want you to look at me with your touching, wonderful eyes, as you used to. Dear God! My father was a serf of your father's and grandfather's, but you, you yourself, did so much for me once . . . so much . . . that I've forgotten all about that; I love you as though you were my sister—even more.

MME. RANEVSKAYA: I can't sit still, I simply can't. *(Jumps up and walks about in violent agitation)* This joy is too much for me . . . Laugh at me, I'm silly! My own darling bookcase! My darling table! *(Kisses it)*

GAYEV: While you were away, nurse died.

MME. RANEVSKAYA *(sits down and takes her coffee):* Yes, God rest her soul; they wrote me about it.

GAYEV: And Anastasy is dead. Petrushka Kossoy has left me and has gone into town to work for the police inspector. *(Takes a box of sweets out of his pocket and begins to suck one)*

PISHCHIK: My daughter Dashenka sends her regards.

LOPAHIN: I'd like to tell you something very pleasant—cheering. *(Glancing at his watch)* I am leaving directly. There isn't much time to talk. But I will put it in a few words. As you know, your cherry orchard is to be sold to pay your debts. The sale is to be on the twenty-second of August; but don't you worry, my dear, you may sleep in peace; there is a way out. Here is my plan. Give me your attention! Your estate is only fifteen miles from the town; the railway runs close by it; and if the cherry orchard and the land along the river bank were cut up into lots and these leased for summer cottages, you would have an income of at least 25,000 rubles a year out of it.

GAYEV: Excuse me . . . What nonsense.

MME. RANEVSKAYA: I don't quite understand you, Yermolay Alexeyevich.

LOPAHIN: You will get an annual rent of at least ten rubles per acre, and if you advertise at once, I'll give you any guarantee you like that you won't have a square foot of ground left by autumn, all the lots will be snapped up. In short, congratulations, you're saved. The location is splendid—by that deep river. . . . Only, of course the ground must be cleared . . . all the old buildings, for instance, must be torn down, and this house, too, which is useless, and of course, the old cherry orchard must be cut down.

MME. RANEVSKAYA: Cut down? My dear, forgive me, but you don't know what you're talking about. If there's one thing that's interesting—indeed, remarkable—in the whole province, it's precisely our cherry orchard.

LOPAHIN: The only remarkable thing about this orchard is that it's a very large one. There's a crop of cherries every other year, and you can't do anything with them; no one buys them.

GAYEV: This orchard is even mentioned in the Encyclopedia.

LOPAHIN *(glancing at his watch)*: If we can't think of a way out, if we don't come to a decision, on the twenty-second of August the cherry orchard and the whole estate will be sold at auction. Make up your minds! There's no other way out—I swear. None, none.

FIRS: In the old days, forty or fifty years ago, the cherries were dried, soaked, pickled, and made into jam, and we used to—

GAYEV: Keep still, Firs.

FIRS: And the dried cherries would be shipped by the cartload. It meant a lot of money! And in those days the dried cherries were soft and juicy, sweet, fragrant . . . They knew the way to do it, then.

MME. RANEVSKAYA: And why don't they do it that way now?

FIRS: They've forgotten. Nobody remembers it.

PISHCHIK *(to Mme. Ranevskaya)*: What's doing in Paris? Eh? Did you eat frogs there?

MME. RANEVSKAYA: I ate crocodiles.

PISHCHIK: Just imagine!

LOPAHIN: There used to be only landowners and peasants in the country, but now these summer people have appeared on the scene . . . All the towns, even the small ones, are surrounded by these summer cottages; and in another twenty years, no doubt, the summer population will have grown enormously. Now the summer resident only drinks tea on his porch, but maybe he'll take to working his acre, too, and then your cherry orchard will be a rich, happy, luxuriant place.

GAYEV *(indignantly)*: Poppycock!

(Enter Varya and Yasha)

VARYA: There are two telegrams for you, mamma dear. *(Picks a key from the bunch at her belt and noisily opens an old-fashioned bookcase)* Here they are.

MME. RANEVSKAYA: They're from Paris. *(Tears them up without reading them)* I'm through with Paris.

GAYEV: Do you know, Luba, how old this bookcase is? Last week I pulled out the bottom drawer and there I found the date burnt in it. It was made exactly a hundred years ago. Think of that! We could celebrate its centenary. True, it's an inanimate object, but nevertheless, a bookcase . . . .

PISHCHIK *(amazed)*: A hundred years! Just imagine!

GAYEV: Yes. *(Tapping it)* That's something. . . . Dear, honored bookcase, hail to you who for more than a century have served the glorious ideals of goodness and justice! Your silent summons to fruitful toil has never weakened in all those hundred years *(through tears)* sustaining, through successive generations of our family, courage and faith in a better future, and fostering in us ideals of goodness and social consciousness . . . *(Pauses)*

LOPAHIN: Yes . . .

MME. RANEVSKAYA: You haven't changed a bit, Leonid.

GAYEV *(somewhat embarrassed)*: I'll play it off the red in the corner! Tip it in the side pocket!

LOPAHIN *(looking at his watch)*: Well it's time for me to go . . .

YASHA *(handing a pill box to Mme. Ranevskaya)*: Perhaps you'll take your pills now.

PISHCHIK: One shouldn't take medicines, dearest lady, they do neither harm nor good. . . . Give them here, my valued friend. *(Takes the pill box, pours the pills into his palm, blows on them, puts them in his mouth, and washes them down with some kvass)* There!

MME. RANEVSKAYA *(frightened)*: You must be mad!

PISHCHIK: I've taken all the pills.

LOPAHIN: What a glutton!

(All laugh)

FIRS: The gentleman visited us in Easter week, ate half a bucket of pickles, he did . . . *(Mumbles)*

MME. RANEVSKAYA: What's he saying?

VARYA: He's been mumbling like that for the last three years—we're used to it.

YASHA: His declining years!

(Charlotta Ivanovna, very thin, tightly laced, dressed in white, a lorgnette at her waist, crosses the stage)

LOPAHIN: Forgive me, Charlotta Ivanovna, I've not had time to greet you. *(Tries to kiss her hand)*

CHARLOTTA *(pulling away her hand)*: If I let you kiss my hand, you'll be wanting to kiss my elbow next, and then my shoulder.

LOPAHIN: I've no luck today. *(All laugh)* Charlotta Ivanovna, show us a trick.

MME. RANEVSKAYA: Yes, Charlotta, do a trick for us.

CHARLOTTA: I don't see the need. I want to sleep.

(Exits)

LOPAHIN: In three weeks we'll meet again. *(Kisses Mme. Ranevskaya's hand)* Good-by till then. Time's up. *(To Gayev)* Bye-bye. *(Kisses Pishchik)* Bye-bye. *(Shakes hands with Varya, then with Firs and Yasha)* I hate to leave. *(To Mme. Ranevskaya)* If you make up your mind about the cottages, let me know; I'll get you a loan of 50,000 rubles. Think it over seriously.

VARYA *(crossly)*: Will you never go!

LOPAHIN: I'm going, I'm going. *(Exits)*

GAYEV: The vulgarian. But, excuse me . . . Varya's going to marry him, he's Varya's fiancé.

VARYA: You talk too much, uncle dear.

MME. RANEVSKAYA: Well, Varya, it would make me happy. He's a good man.

PISHCHIK: Yes, one must admit, he's a most estimable man. And my Dashenka . . . she too says that . . . she says . . . lots of things. *(Snores; but wakes up at once)* All the same, my valued friend, could you oblige me . . . with a loan of 240 rubles? I must pay the interest on the mortgage tomorrow.

VARYA *(alarmed):* We can't, we can't!

MME. RANEVSKAYA: I really haven't any money.

PISHCHIK: It'll turn up. *(Laughs)* I never lose hope, I thought everything was lost, that I was done for, when lo and behold, the railway ran through my land . . . and I was paid for it . . . And something else will turn up again, if not today, then tomorrow . . . Dashenka will win two hundred thousand . . . she's got a lottery ticket.

MME. RANEVSKAYA: I've had my coffee, now let's go to bed.

FIRS *(brushes off Gayev; admonishingly):* You've got the wrong trousers on again. What am I to do with you?

VARYA *(softly):* Anya's asleep. *(Gently opens the window)* The sun's up now, it's not a bit cold. Look, mamma dear, what wonderful trees. And heavens, what air! The starlings are singing!

GAYEV *(opens the other window):* The orchard is all white. You've not forgotten it? Luba? That's the long alley that runs straight, straight as an arrow; how it shines on moonlight nights, do you remember? You've not forgotten?

MME. RANEVSKAYA *(looking out of the window into the orchard):* Oh, my childhood, my innocent childhood. I used to sleep in this nursery—I used to look out into the orchard, happiness waked with me every morning, the orchard was just the same then . . . nothing has changed. *(Laughs with joy)* All, all white! Oh, my orchard! After the dark, rainy autumn and the cold winter, you are young again, and full of happiness, the heavenly angels have not left you . . . If I could free my chest and my shoulders from this rock that weighs on me, if I could only forget the past!

GAYEV: Yes, and the orchard will be sold to pay our debts, strange as it may seem. . . .

MME. RANEVSKAYA: Look! There is our poor mother walking in the orchard . . . all in white . . . *(Laughs with joy)* It is she!

GAYEV: Where?

VARYA: What are you saying, mamma dear!

MME. RANEVSKAYA: There's no one there, I just imagined it. To the right, where the path turns towards the arbor, there's a little white tree, leaning over, that looks like a woman . . .

(Trofimov enters, wearing a shabby student's uniform and spectacles)

MME. RANEVSKAYA: What an amazing orchard! White masses of blossom, the blue sky . . .

TROFIMOV: Lubov Andreyevna! *(She looks round at him)* I just want to pay my respects to you, then I'll leave at once. *(Kisses her hand ardently)* I was told to wait until morning, but I hadn't the patience . . . *(Mme. Ranevskaya looks at him, perplexed)*

VARYA *(through tears):* This is Petya Trofimov.

TROFIMOV: Petya Trofimov, formerly your Grisha's tutor. . . . Can I have changed so much? *(Mme. Ranevskaya embraces him and weeps quietly)*

GAYEV *(embarrassed):* Don't, don't, Luba.

VARYA *(crying):* I told you, Petya, to wait until tomorrow.

MME. RANEVSKAYA: My Grisha . . . my little boy . . . Grisha . . . my son.

VARYA: What can one do, mamma dear, it's God's will.

TROFIMOV *(softly, through tears):* There . . . there.

MME. RANEVSKAYA *(weeping quietly):* My little boy was lost . . . drowned. Why? Why, my friend? *(More quietly)* Anya's asleep in there, and here I am talking so loudly . . . making all this noise. . . . But tell me, Petya, why do you look so badly? Why have you aged so?

TROFIMOV: A mangy master, a peasant woman in the train called me.

MME. RANEVSKAYA: You were just a boy then, a dear little student, and now your hair's thin—and you're wearing glasses! Is it possible you're still a student? *(Goes towards the door)*

TROFIMOV: I suppose I'm a perpetual student.

MME. RANEVSKAYA *(kisses her brother, then Varya):* Now, go to bed . . . You have aged, too, Leonid.

PISHCHIK *(follows her):* So now we turn in. Oh, my gout! I'm staying the night here . . . Lubov Andreyevna, my angel, tomorrow morning. . . . I do need 240 rubles.

GAYEV: He keeps at it.

PISHCHIK: I'll pay it back, dear . . . it's a trifling sum.

MME. RANEVSKAYA: All right, Leonid will give it to you. Give it to him, Leonid.

GAYEV: Me give it to him! That's a good one!

MME. RANEVSKAYA: It can't be helped. Give it to him! He needs it. He'll pay it back.

(Mme. Ranevskaya, Trofimov, Pishchik, and Firs go out; Gayev, Varya, and Yasha remain)

GAYEV: Sister hasn't got out of the habit of throwing money around. *(To Yasha)* Go away, my good fellow, you smell of the barnyard.

YASHA *(with a grin):* And you, Leonid Andreyevich, are just the same as ever.

GAYEV: Who? *(To Varya)* What did he say?

VARYA *(to Yasha):* Your mother's come from the village; she's been sitting in the servants' room since yesterday, waiting to see you.

YASHA: Botheration!

VARYA: You should be ashamed of yourself!

YASHA: She's all I needed! She could have come tomorrow. *(Exit)*

VARYA: Mamma is just the same as ever; she hasn't changed a bit. If she had her own way, she'd keep nothing for herself.

GAYEV: Yes . . . *(Pauses)* If a great many remedies are offered for some disease, it means it is incurable; I keep thinking and racking my brains; I have many remedies, ever so many, and that really means none. It would be fine if we came in for a legacy; it would be fine if we married off our Anya to a very rich man; or we might go to Yaroslavl and try our luck with our aunt, the Countess. She's very, very rich, you know . . .

VARYA *(weeping):* If only God would help us!

GAYEV: Stop bawling. Aunt's very rich, but she doesn't like us. In the first place, sister married a lawyer who was no nobleman . . . *(Anya appears in the doorway)* She married beneath her, and it can't be said that her behavior has been very exemplary. She's good, kind, sweet, and I love her, but no matter what extenuating circumstances you may adduce, there's no denying that she has no morals. You sense it in her least gesture.

VARYA *(in a whisper):* Anya's in the doorway.

GAYEV: Who? *(Pauses)* It's queer, something got into my right eye—my eyes are going back on me. . . . And on Thursday, when I was in the circuit court—

(Enter Anya)

VARYA: Why aren't you asleep, Anya?

ANYA: I can't get to sleep, I just can't.

GAYEV: My little pet! *(Kisses Anya's face and hands)* My child! *(Weeps)* You are not my niece, you're my angel! You're everything to me. Believe me, believe—

ANYA: I believe you, uncle. Everyone loves you and respects you . . . but, uncle dear, you must keep still. . . . You must. What were you saying just now about my mother? Your own sister? What made you say that?

GAYEV: Yes, yes . . . *(Covers his face with her hand)* Really, that was awful! Good God! Heaven help me! Just now I made a speech to the bookcase . . . so stupid! And only after I was through, I saw how stupid it was.

VARYA: It's true, uncle dear, you ought to keep still. Just don't talk, that's all.

ANYA: If you could only keep still, it would make things easier for you too.

GAYEV: I'll keep still. *(Kisses Anya's and Varya's hands)* I will. But now about business. On Thursday I was in court; well, there were a number of us there, and we began talking of one thing and another, and this and that, and do you know, I believe it will be possible to raise a loan on a promissory note, to pay the interest at the bank.

VARYA: If only God would help us!

GAYEV: On Tuesday I'll go and see about it again. *(To Varya)* Stop bawling. *(To Anya)* Your mamma will talk to Lopahin, and he, of course, will not refuse her . . . and as soon as you're rested, you'll go to Yaroslavl to the Countess, your great-aunt. So we'll be working in three directions at once, and the thing is in the bag. We'll pay the interest—I'm sure of it. *(Puts a candy in his mouth)* I swear on my honor, I swear by anything you like, the estate shan't be sold. *(Excitedly)* I swear by my own happiness! Here's my hand on it, you can call me a swindler and a scoundrel if I let it come to an auction! I swear by my whole being.

ANYA *(relieved and quite happy again):* How good you are, uncle, and how clever! *(Embraces him)* Now I'm at peace, quite at peace, I'm happy.

FIRS *(reproachfully):* Leonid Andreyevich, have you no fear of God? When are you going to bed?

GAYEV: Directly, directly. Go away. Firs, I'll . . . yes, I will undress myself. Now, children, 'nightie-'nightie. We'll consider details tomorrow, but now go to sleep. *(Kisses Anya and Varya)* I am a man of the 'Eighties; they have nothing good to say of that period nowadays. Nevertheless, in the course of my life I have suffered not a little for my convictions. It's not for nothing that the peasant loves me; one should know the peasant; one should know from which—

ANYA: There you go again, uncle.

VARYA: Uncle dear, be quiet.

FIRS *(angrily):* Leonid Andreyevich!

GAYEV: I'm coming, I'm coming! Go to bed! Double bank shot in the side pocket! Here goes a clean shot . . .

(Exits, Firs hobbling after him)

ANYA: I am at peace now. I don't want to go to Yaroslavl—I don't like my great-aunt, but still, I am at peace, thanks to uncle. *(Sits down)*

VARYA: We must get some sleep. I'm going now. While you were away something unpleasant happened. In the old servants' quarters there are only the old people, as you know; Yefim, Polya, Yevstigney, and Karp, too. They began letting all sorts of rascals in to spend the night. . . . I didn't say anything. Then I heard they'd been spreading a report that I gave them nothing but dried peas to eat—out of stinginess, you know . . . and it was all Yevstigney's doing. . . . All right, I thought, if that's how it is, I thought, just wait. I sent for Yevstigney. . . . *(Yawns)* He comes. . . . "How's this, Yevstigney?" I say, "You fool . . ." *(Looking at Anya)* Anichka! *(Pauses)* She's asleep. *(Puts her arm around Anya)* Come to your little bed. . . . Come . . . *(Leads her)* My darling has fallen asleep. . . . Come.

(They go out. Far away beyond the orchard a shepherd is piping. Trofimov crosses the stage and, seeing Varya and Anya, stands still.)

VARYA: Sh! She's asleep . . . asleep . . . Come, darling.

ANYA *(softly, half-asleep):* I'm so tired. Those bells . . . uncle . . . dear. . . . Mamma and uncle . . .

VARYA: Come, my precious, come along. *(They go into Anya's room)*

TROFIMOV *(with emotion):* My sunshine, my spring!

Act II

A meadow. An old, long-abandoned, lopsided little chapel; near it, a well, large slabs, which had apparently once served as tombstones, and an old bench. In the background, the road to the Gayev estate. To one side poplars loom darkly, where the cherry orchard begins. In the distance a row of telegraph poles, and far off, on the horizon, the faint outline of a large city which is seen only in fine, clear weather. The sun will soon be setting. Charlotta, Yasha, and Dunyasha are seated on the bench. Yepihodov stands near and plays a guitar. All are pensive. Charlotta wears an old peaked cap. She has taken a gun from her shoulder and is straightening the buckle on the strap.

CHARLOTTA *(musingly):* I haven't a real passport, I don't know how old I am, and I always feel that I am very young. When I was a little girl, my father and mother used to go from fair to fair and give performances, very good ones. And I used to do the *salto mortale,* [3] and all sorts of other tricks. And when papa and mamma died, a German lady adopted me and began to educate me. Very good. I grew up and became a governess. But where I come from and who I am, I don't know. . . . Who were my parents? Perhaps they weren't even married. . . . I don't know. . . . *(Takes a cucumber out of her pocket and eats it)* I don't know a thing. *(Pause)* One wants so much to talk, and there isn't anyone to talk to. . . . I haven't anybody.

YEPIHODOV *(plays the guitar and sings):* "What care I for the jarring world? What's friend or foe to me? . . ." How agreeable it is to play the mandolin.

DUNYASHA: That's a guitar, not a mandolin. *(Looks in a hand mirror and powders her face)*

YEPIHODOV: To a madman in love it's a mandolin. *(Sings)* "Would that the heart were warmed by the fire of mutual love!" *(Yasha joins in)*

CHARLOTTA: How abominably these people sing. Pfui! Like jackals!

DUNYASHA *(to Yasha):* How wonderful it must be though to have stayed abroad!

YASHA: Ah, yes, of course, I cannot but agree with you there. *(Yawns and lights a cigar)*

YEPIHODOV: Naturally. Abroad, everything has long since achieved full perplexion.

YASHA: That goes without saying.

YEPIHODOV: I'm a cultivated man, I read all kinds of remarkable books. And yet I can never make out what direction I should take, what is it that I want, properly speaking. Should I live, or should I shoot myself, properly speaking? Nevertheless, I always carry a revolver about me. . . . Here it is . . . *(Shows revolver)*

CHARLOTTA: I've finished. I'm going. *(Puts the gun over her shoulder)* You are a very clever man, Yepihodov, and a very terrible one; women must be

[3] A standing somersault.

crazy about you. Br-r-r! *(Starts to go)* These clever men are all so stupid; there's no one for me to talk to . . . always alone, alone, I haven't a soul . . . and who I am, and why I am, nobody knows. *(Exits unhurriedly)*

YEPIHODOV: Properly speaking and letting other subjects alone, I must say regarding myself, among other things, that fate treats me mercilessly, like a storm treats a small boat. If I am mistaken, let us say, why then do I wake up this morning, and there on my chest is a spider of enormous dimensions . . . like this . . . *(indicates with both hands)* Again, I take up a pitcher of kvass to have a drink, and in it there is something unseemly to the highest degree, something like a cockroach. *(Pause)* Have you read Buckle?[4] *(Pause)* I wish to have a word with you, Avdotya Fyodorovna, if I may trouble you.

DUNYASHA: Well, go ahead.

YEPIHODOV: I wish to speak with you alone. *(Sighs)*

DUNYASHA, *(embarrassed):* Very well. Only first bring me my little cape. You'll find it near the wardrobe. It's rather damp here.

YEPIHODOV: Certainly, ma'am; I will fetch it, ma'am. Now I know what to do with my revolver. *(Takes the guitar and goes off playing it)*

YASHA: Two-and-Twenty Troubles! An awful fool, between you and me. *(Yawns)*

DUNYASHA: I hope to God he doesn't shoot himself! *(Pause)* I've become so nervous, I'm always fretting. I was still a little girl when I was taken into the big house. I am quite unused to the simple life now, and my hands are white, as white as a lady's. I've become so soft, so delicate, so refined, I'm afraid of everything. It's so terrifying; and if you deceive me, Yasha, I don't know what will happen to my nerves. *(Yasha kisses her)*

YASHA: You're a peach! Of course, a girl should never forget herself; and what I dislike more than anything is when a girl don't behave properly.

DUNYASHA: I've fallen passionately in love with you; you're educated—you have something to say about everything *(Pause)*

YASHA *(yawns):* Yes, ma'am. Now the way I look at it, if a girl loves someone, it means she is immoral. *(Pause)* It's agreeable smoking a cigar in the fresh air. *(Listens)* Someone's coming this way . . . It's our madam and the others. *(Dunyasha embraces him impulsively)* You go home, as though you'd been to the river to bathe; go by the little path, or else they'll run into you and suspect me of having arranged to meet you here. I can't stand that sort of thing.

DUNYASHA *(coughing softly):* Your cigar's made my head ache.

(Exits. Yasha standing near the chapel. Enter Mme. Ranevskaya, Gayev, and Lopahin.)

LOPAHIN: You must make up your mind once and for all—there's no time to lose. It's quite a simple question, you know. Do you agree to lease your

---

[4]Henry Thomas Buckle (1821–1862), an English historian.

land for summer cottages or not? Answer in one word, yes or no; only one word!

MME. RANEVSKAYA: Who's been smoking such abominable cigars here? *(Sits down)*

GAYEV: Now that the railway line is so near, it's made things very convenient. *(Sits down)* Here we've been able to have lunch in town. Yellow ball in the side pocket! I feel like going into the house and playing just one game.

MME. RANEVSKAYA: You can do that later.

LOPAHIN: Only one word! *(Imploringly)* Do give me an answer!

GAYEV *(yawning):* Who?

MME. RANEVSKAYA *(looks into her purse):* Yesterday I had a lot of money and now my purse is almost empty. My poor Varya tries to economize by feeding us just milk soup; in the kitchen the old people get nothing but dried peas to eat, while I squander money thoughtlessly *(Drops the purse, scattering gold pieces)* You see there they go . . . *(Shows vexation)*

YASHA: Allow me—I'll pick them up. *(Picks up the money)*

MME. RANEVSKAYA: Be so kind, Yasha. And why did I go to lunch in town? That nasty restaurant, with its music and the tablecloth smelling of soap . . . Why drink so much, Leonid? Why eat so much? Why talk so much? Today again you talked a lot, and all so inappropriately about the 'Seventies, about the decadents. And to whom? Talking to waiters about decadents!

LOPAHIN: Yes.

GAYEV *(Waving his hand):* I'm incorrigible; that's obvious. *(Irritably, to Yasha)* Why do you keep dancing about in front of me?

YASHA *(laughs):* I can't hear your voice without laughing—

GAYEV: Either he or I—

MME. RANEVSKAYA: Go away, Yasha; run along.

YASHA *(handing Mme. Ranevskaya her purse):* I'm going, at once. *(Hardly able to suppress his laughter)* This minute. *(Exits)*

LOPAHIN: That rich man, Deriganov, wants to buy your estate. They say he's coming to the auction himself.

MME. RANEVSKAYA: Where did you hear that?

LOPAHIN: That's what they are saying in town.

GAYEV: Our aunt in Yaroslavl has promised to help; but when she will send the money, and how much, no one knows.

LOPAHIN: How much will she send? A hundred thousand? Two hundred?

MME. RANEVSKAYA: Oh, well, ten or fifteen thousand; and we'll have to be grateful for that.

LOPAHIN: Forgive me, but such frivolous people as you are, so queer and unbusinesslike—I never met in my life. One tells you in plain language that your estate is up for sale, and you don't seem to take it in.

MME. RANEVSKAYA: What are we to do? Tell us what to do.

LOPAHIN: I do tell you, every day; every day I say the same thing! You must lease the cherry orchard and the land for summer cottages, you must do it and as soon as possible—right away. The auction is close at hand. Please understand! Once you've decided to have the cottages, you can raise as much money as you like, and you're saved.

MME. RANEVSKAYA: Cottages—summer people—forgive me, but it's all so vulgar.

GAYEV: I agree with you absolutely.

LOPAHIN: I shall either burst into tears or scream or faint! I can't stand it! You've worn me out! *(To Gayev)* You're an old woman!

GAYEV: Who?

LOPAHIN: An old woman! *(Gets up to go)*

MME. RANEVSKAYA *(alarmed):* No, don't go! Please stay, I beg you, my dear. Perhaps we shall think of something.

LOPAHIN: What is there to think of?

MME. RANEVSKAYA: Don't go, I beg you. With you here it's more cheerful anyway. *(Pause)* I keep expecting something to happen, it's as though the house were going to crash about our ears.

GAYEV *(in deep thought):* Bank shot in the corner. . . . Three cushions in the side pocket. . . .

MME. RANEVSKAYA: We have been great sinners . . .

LOPAHIN: What sins could you have committed?

GAYEV *(putting a candy in his mouth):* They say I've eaten up my fortune in candy! *(Laughs)*

MME. RANEVSKAYA: Oh, my sins! I've squandered money away recklessly, like a lunatic, and I married a man who made nothing but debts. My husband drank himself to death on champagne, he was a terrific drinker. And then, to my sorrow, I fell in love with another man, and I lived with him. And just then—that was my first punishment—a blow on the head: my little boy was drowned here in the river. And I went abroad, went away forever . . . never to come back, never to see this river again . . . I closed my eyes and ran, out of my mind. . . . But he followed me, pitiless, brutal. I bought a villa near Mentone, because he fell ill there; and for three years, day and night, I knew no peace, no rest. The sick man wore me out, he sucked my soul dry. Then last year, when the villa was sold to pay my debts, I went to Paris, and there he robbed me, abandoned me, took up with another woman, I tried to poison myself—it was stupid, so shameful— and then suddenly I felt drawn back to Russia, back to my own country, to my little girl. *(Wipes her tears away)* Lord, Lord! Be merciful, forgive me my sins—don't punish me any more! *(Takes a telegram out of her pocket)* This came today from Paris—he begs me to forgive him, implores me to go back . . . *(Tears up the telegram)* Do I hear music? *(Listens)*

GAYEV: That's our famous Jewish band, you remember? Four violins, a flute, and a double bass.

MME. RANEVSKAYA: Does it still exist? We ought to send for them some evening and have a party.

LOPAHIN *(listens):* I don't hear anything. *(Hums softly)* "The Germans for a fee will Frenchify a Russian." *(Laughs)* I saw a play at the theater yesterday—awfully funny.

MME. RANEVSKAYA: There was probably nothing funny about it. You shouldn't go to see plays, you should look at yourselves more often. How drab your lives are—how full of unnecessary talk.

LOPAHIN: That's true; come to think of it, we do live like fools. *(Pause)* My pop was a peasant, an idiot; he understood nothing, never taught me anything, all he did was beat me when he was drunk, and always with a stick. Fundamentally, I'm just the same kind of blockhead and idiot. I was never taught anything—I have a terrible handwriting, I write so that I feel ashamed before people, like a pig.

MME. RANEVSKAYA: You should get married, my friend.

LOPAHIN: Yes . . . that's true.

MME. RANEVSKAYA: To our Varya, she's a good girl.

LOPAHIN: Yes.

MME. RANEVSKAYA: She's a girl who comes of simple people, she works all day long; and above all, she loves you. Besides, you've liked her for a long time now.

LOPAHIN: Well, I've nothing against it. She's a good girl. *(Pause)*

GAYEV: I've been offered a place in the bank—6,000 a year. Have you heard?

MME. RANEVSKAYA: You're not up to it. Stay where you are.

(Firs enters, carrying an overcoat)

FIRS *(to Gayev):* Please put this on, sir, it's damp.

GAYEV *(putting it on):* I'm fed up with you, brother.

FIRS: Never mind. This morning you drove off without saying a word. *(Looks him over)*

MME. RANEVSKAYA: How you've aged, Firs.

FIRS: I beg your pardon?

LOPAHIN: The lady says you've aged.

FIRS: I've lived a long time; they were arranging my wedding and your papa wasn't born yet. *(Laughs)* When freedom[5] came I was already head footman. I wouldn't consent to be set free then; I stayed on with the master . . . *(Pause)* I remember they were all very happy, but why they were happy, they didn't know themselves.

LOPAHIN: It was fine in the old days! At least there was flogging!

FIRS *(not hearing):* Of course. The peasants kept to the masters, the masters kept to the peasants; but now they've all gone their own ways, and there's no making out anything.

GAYEV: Be quiet, Firs. I must go to town tomorrow. They've promised to introduce me to a general who might let us have a loan.

LOPAHIN: Nothing will come of that. You won't even be able to pay the interest, you can be certain of that.

---

[5]The serfs were emancipated in 1861.

MME. RANEVSKAYA: He's raving, there isn't any general. *(Enter Trofimov, Anya, and Varya)*

GAYEV: Here come our young people.

ANYA: There's mamma, on the bench.

MME. RANEVSKAYA *(tenderly):* Come here, come along, my darlings. *(Embraces Anya and Varya)* If you only knew how I love you both! Sit beside me—there, like that. *(All sit down)*

LOPAHIN: Our perpetual student is always with the young ladies.

TROFIMOV: That's not any of your business.

LOPAHIN: He'll soon be fifty, and he's still a student!

TROFIMOV: Stop your silly jokes.

LOPAHIN: What are you so cross about, you queer bird?

TROFIMOV: Oh, leave me alone.

LOPAHIN *(laughs):* Allow me to ask you, what do you think of me?

TROFIMOV: What I think of you, Yermolay Alexeyevich, is this: you are a rich man who will soon be a millionaire. Well, just as a beast of prey, which devours everything that comes in its way, is necessary for the process of metabolism to go on, so you too are necessary. *(All laugh)*

VARYA: Better tell us something about the planets, Petya.

MME. RANEVSKAYA: No, let's go on with yesterday's conversation.

TROFIMOV: What was it about?

GAYEV: About man's pride.

TROFIMOV: Yesterday we talked a long time, but we came to no conclusion. There is something mystical about man's pride in your sense of the word. Perhaps you're right, from your own point of view. But if you reason simply, without going into subtleties, then what call is there for pride? Is there any sense in it, if man is so poor a thing physiologically, and if, in the great majority of cases, he is coarse, stupid, and profoundly unhappy? We should stop admiring ourselves. We should work, and that's all.

GAYEV: You die, anyway.

TROFIMOV: Who knows? And what does it mean—to die? Perhaps man has a hundred senses, and at his death only the five we know perish, while the other ninety-five remain alive.

MME. RANEVSKAYA: How clever you are, Petya!

LOPAHIN *(ironically):* Awfully clever!

TROFIMOV: Mankind goes forward, developing its powers. Everything that is now unattainable for it will one day come within man's reach and be clear to him; only we must work, helping with all our might those who seek the truth. Here among us in Russia only the very few work as yet. The great majority of the intelligentsia, as far as I can see, seek nothing, do nothing, are totally unfit for work of any kind. They call themselves the intelligentsia, yet they are uncivil to their servants, treat the peasants like animals, are poor students, never read anything serious, do absolutely nothing at all, only talk about science, and have little appreciation of the arts. They are all solemn, have grim faces, they all philosophize and talk of weighty matters. And meanwhile the vast majority of us, ninety-nine out of a hundred, live like savages. At the least provocation—a punch in the jaw, and curses. They eat disgustingly, sleep in filth and stuffiness, bedbugs everywhere, stench and damp and moral slovenliness. And obviously, the only purpose of all our fine talk is to hoodwink ourselves and others. Show me where the public nurseries are that we've heard so much about, and the libraries. We read about them in novels, but in reality they don't exist, there is nothing but dirt, vulgarity, and Asiatic backwardness. I don't like very solemn faces, I'm afraid of them, I'm afraid of serious conversations. We'd do better to keep quiet for a while.

LOPAHIN: Do you know, I get up at five o'clock in the morning, and I work from morning till night; and I'm always handling money, my own and other people's, and I see what people around me are really like. You've only to start doing anything to see how few honest, decent people there are. Sometimes when I lie awake at night, I think: "Oh, Lord, thou hast given us immense forests, boundless fields, the widest horizons, and living in their midst, we ourselves ought really to be giants."

MME. RANEVSKAYA: Now you want giants! They're only good in fairy tales; otherwise they're frightening.

(Yepihodov crosses the stage at the rear, playing the guitar)

MME. RANEVSKAYA *(pensively):* There goes Yepihodov.

ANYA *(pensively):* There goes Yepihodov.

GAYEV: Ladies and gentlemen, the sun has set.

TROFIMOV: Yes.

GAYEV *(in a low voice, declaiming as it were):* Oh, Nature, wondrous Nature, you shine with eternal radiance, beautiful and indifferent! You, whom we call our mother, unite within yourself life and death! You animate and destroy!

VARYA *(pleadingly):* Uncle dear!

ANYA: Uncle, again!

TROFIMOV: You'd better bank the yellow ball in the side pocket.

GAYEV: I'm silent, I'm silent . . .

(All sit plunged in thought. Stillness reigns. Only Firs's muttering is audible. Suddenly a distant sound is heard, coming from the sky as it were, the sound of a snapping string, mournfully dying away.)

MME. RANEVSKAYA: What was that?

LOPAHIN: I don't know. Somewhere far away, in the pits, a bucket's broken loose; but somewhere very far away.

GAYEV: Or it might be some sort of bird, perhaps a heron.

TROFIMOV: Or an owl . . .

MME. RANEVSKAYA *(shudders):* It's weird, somehow. *(Pause)*

FIRS: Before the calamity the same thing happened—the owl screeched, and the samovar hummed all the time.

GAYEV: Before what calamity?

FIRS: Before the Freedom. *(Pause)*

MME. RANEVSKAYA: Come, my friends, let's be going. It's getting dark. *(To Anya)* You have tears in your eyes. What is it, my little one? *(Embraces her)*

ANYA: I don't know, mamma; it's nothing.

TROFIMOV: Somebody's coming.

(A tramp appears, wearing a shabby white cap and an overcoat. He is slightly drunk.)

TRAMP: Allow me to inquire, will this short-cut take me to the station?

GAYEV: It will. Just follow that road.

TRAMP: My heartfelt thanks. *(Coughing)* The weather is glorious. *(Recites)* "My brother, my suffering brother . . . Go down to the Volga! Whose groans . . . ?" *(To Varya)* Mademoiselle, won't you spare 30 kopecks for a hungry Russian?

(Varya, frightened, cries out)

LOPAHIN *(angrily):* Even panhandling has its proprieties.

MME. RANEVSKAYA *(scared):* Here, take this. *(Fumbles in her purse)* I haven't any silver . . . never mind, here's a gold piece.

TRAMP: My heartfelt thanks. *(Exits. Laughter)*

VARYA *(frightened):* I'm leaving. I'm leaving . . . Oh, mamma dear, at home the servants have nothing to eat, and you gave him a gold piece!

MME. RANEVSKAYA: What are you going to do with me? I'm such a fool. When we get home, I'll give you everything I have. Yermolay Alexeyevich, you'll lend me some more . . .

LOPAHIN: Yes, ma'am.

MME. RANEVSKAYA: Come, ladies and gentlemen, it's time to be going. Oh! Varya, we've settled all about your marriage. Congratulations!

VARYA *(through tears):* Really, mamma, that's not a joking matter.

LOPAHIN: "Aurelia, get thee to a nunnery, go . . ."[6]

GAYEV: And do you know, my hands are trembling: I haven't played billiards in a long time.

LOPAHIN: "Aurelia, nymph, in your orisons, remember me!"[7]

MME. RANEVSKAYA: Let's go, it's almost suppertime.

VARYA: He frightened me! My heart's pounding.

LOPAHIN: Let me remind you, ladies and gentlemen, on the twenty-second of August the cherry orchard will be up for sale. Think about that! Think!

(All except Trofimov and Anya go out)

ANYA *(laughs):* I'm grateful to that tramp, he frightened Varya and so we're alone.

TROFIMOV: Varya's afraid we'll fall in love with each other all of a sudden.

[6]Translating Hamlet to Ophelia, Shakespeare's *Hamlet,* III, i, 137. [7]The end of Hamlet's "To be, or not to be" speech, *Hamlet,* III, i, 89–90.

She hasn't left us alone for days. Her narrow mind can't grasp that we're above love. To avoid the petty and illusory, everything that prevents us from being free and happy—that is the goal and meaning of our life. Forward! Do not fall behind, friends!

ANYA *(strikes her hands together):* How well you speak! *(Pause)* It's wonderful here today.

TROFIMOV: Yes, the weather's glorious.

ANYA: What have you done to me, Petya? Why don't I love the cherry orchard as I used to? I loved it so tenderly. It seemed to me there was no spot on earth lovelier than our orchard.

TROFIMOV: All Russia is our orchard. Our land is vast and beautiful, there are many wonderful places in it. *(Pause)* Think of it, Anya, your grandfather, your great-grandfather and all your ancestors were serf-owners, owners of living souls, and aren't human beings looking at you from every tree in the orchard, from every leaf, from every trunk? Don't you hear voices? Oh, it's terrifying! Your orchard is a fearful place, and when you pass through it in the evening or at night, the old bark on the trees gleams faintly, and the cherry trees seem to be dreaming of things that happened a hundred, two hundred years ago and to be tormented by painful visions. What is there to say? We're at least two hundred years behind, we've really achieved nothing yet, we have no definite attitude to the past, we only philosophize, complain of the blues, or drink vodka. It's all so clear: in order to live in the present, we should first redeem our past, finish with it, and we can expiate it only by suffering, only by extraordinary, unceasing labor. Realize that, Anya.

ANYA: The house in which we live has long ceased to be our own, and I will leave it, I give you my word.

TROFIMOV: If you have the keys, fling them into the well and go away. Be free as the wind.

ANYA *(in ecstasy):* How well you put that!

TROFIMOV: Believe me, Anya, believe me! I'm not yet thirty, I'm young, I'm still a student—but I've already suffered so much. In winter I'm hungry, sick, harassed, poor as a beggar, and where hasn't Fate driven me? Where haven't I been? And yet always, every moment of the day and night, my soul is filled with inexplicable premonitions. . . . I have a premonition of happiness, Anya. . . . I see it already!

ANYA *(pensively):* The moon is rising.

(Yepihodov is heard playing the same mournful tune on the guitar. The moon rises. Somewhere near the poplars Varya is looking for Anya and calling "Anya, where are you.")

TROFIMOV: Yes, the moon is rising. *(Pause)* There it is, happiness, it's approaching, it's coming nearer and nearer, I can already hear its footsteps. And if we don't see it, if we don't know it, what does it matter? Others will!

VARYA *(offstage):* Anya! Where are you?

TROFIMOV: That Varya again! *(Angrily)* It's revolting!

ANYA: Never mind, let's go down to the river. It's lovely there.

TROFIMOV: Come on. *(They go)*

VARYA *(offstage):* Anya! Anya!

Act III

A drawing-room separated by an arch from a ballroom. Evening. Chandelier burning. The Jewish band is heard playing in the anteroom. In the ballroom they are dancing the Grand Rond. Pishchik is heard calling, "Promenade à une paire." *Pishchik and Charlotta, Trofimov and Mme. Ranevskaya, Anya and the Post Office Clerk, Varya and the Station-master, and others, enter the drawing-room in couples. Dunyasha is in the last couple. Varya weeps quietly, wiping her tears as she dances. All parade through drawing-room. Pishchik calling "Grand rond, balancez!" and "Les cavaliers à genoux et remerciez vox dames!" Firs wearing a dress-coat, brings in soda-water on a tray. Pishchik and Trofimov enter the drawing-room.*

PISHCHIK: I'm a full-blooded man; I've already had two strokes. Dancing's hard work for me; but as they say, "If you run with the pack, you can bark or not, but at least wag your tail." Still, I'm as strong as a horse. My late lamented father, who would have his joke, God rest his soul, used to say, talking about our origin, that the ancient line of the Simeonov-Pishchiks was descended from the very horse that Caligula had made a senator. *(Sits down)* But the trouble is, I have no money. A hungry dog believes in nothing but meat. *(Snores and wakes up at once)* It's the same with me—I can think of nothing but money.

TROFIMOV: You know, there *is* something equine about your figure.

PISHCHIK: Well, a horse is a fine animal—one can sell a horse.

(Sound of billiards being played in an adjoining room. Varya appears in the archway.)

TROFIMOV *(teasing her):* Madam Lopahina! Madam Lopahina!

VARYA *(angrily):* Mangy master!

TROFIMOV: Yes, I am a mangy master and I'm proud of it.

VARYA *(reflecting bitterly):* Here we've hired musicians, and what shall we pay them with? *(Exits)*

TROFIMOV *(to Pishchik):* If the energy you have spent during your lifetime looking for money to pay interest had gone into something else, in the end you could have turned the world upside down.

PISHCHIK: Nietzsche, the philosopher, the greatest, most famous of men, that colossal intellect, says in his works, that it is permissible to forge banknotes.

TROFIMOV: Have you read Nietzsche?

PISHCHIK: Well . . . Dashenka told me . . . And now I've got to the point where forging banknotes is about the only way out for me. . . . The day after tomorrow I have to pay 310 rubles—I already have 130 (. . . *Feels in his pockets. In alarm)* The money's gone! I've lost my money! *(Through tears)* Where's my money? *(Joyfully)* Here it is! Inside the lining . . . I'm all in a sweat . . .

(Enter Mme. Ranevskaya and Charlotta)

MME. RANEVSKAYA *(hums the "Lezginka"):* Why isn't Leonid back yet? What is he doing in town? *(To Dunyasha)* Dunyasha, offer the musicians tea.

TROFIMOV: The auction hasn't taken place, most likely.

MME. RANEVSKAYA: It's the wrong time to have the band, and the wrong time to give a dance. Well, never mind. *(Sits down and hums softly)*

CHARLOTTA *(hands Pishchik a pack of cards):* Here is a pack of cards. Think of any card you like.

PISHCHIK: I've thought of one.

CHARLOTTA: Shuffle the pack now. That's right. Give it here, my dear Mr. Pishchik. *Ein, zwei, drei.* Now look for it—it's in your side pocket.

PISHCHIK *(taking the card out of his pocket):* The eight of spades! Perfectly right! Just imagine!

CHARLOTTA *(holding pack of cards in her hands. To Trofimov):* Quickly, name the top card.

TROFIMOV: Well, let's see—the queen of spades.

CHARLOTTA: Right! *(To Pishchik)* Now name the top card.

PISHCHIK: The ace of hearts.

CHARLOTTA: Right! *(Claps her hands and the pack of cards disappears)* Ah, what lovely weather it is today! *(A mysterious feminine voice which seems to come from under the floor, answers her)* "Oh, yes, it's magnificent weather, madam."

CHARLOTTA: You are my best ideal.

VOICE: "And I find you pleasing too, madam."

STATIONMASTER *(applauding):* The lady ventriloquist, bravo!

PISHCHIK *(amazed):* Just imagine! Enchanting Charlotta Ivanovna, I'm simply in love with you.

CHARLOTTA: In love? *(Shrugs her shoulders)* Are you capable of love? *Guter Mensch, aber schlechter Musikant.*[8]

TROFIMOV *(claps Pishchik on the shoulder):* You old horse, you!

CHARLOTTA: Attention please! One more trick! *(Takes a plaid from a chair)* Here is a very good plaid; I want to sell it. *(Shaking it out)* Does anyone want to buy it?

PISHCHIK *(in amazement):* Just imagine!

CHARLOTTA: *Ein, zwei, drei!*

(Raises the plaid quickly, behind it stands Anya. She curtsies, runs to her mother, embraces her, and runs back into the ballroom, amidst general enthusiasm.)

---

[8]A good man, but a bad musician.

MME. RANEVSKAYA *(applauds):* Bravo! Bravo!

CHARLOTTA: Now again! *Ein, zwei, drei! (Lifts the plaid; behind it stands Varya bowing)*

PISHCHIK *(running after her):* The rascal! What a woman, what a woman! *(Exits)*

MME. RANEVSKAYA: And Leonid still isn't here. What is he doing in town so long? I don't understand. It must be all over by now. Either the estate has been sold, or the auction hasn't taken place. Why keep us in suspense so long?

VARYA *(trying to console her):* Uncle's bought it, I feel sure of that.

TROFIMOV *(mockingly):* Oh, yes!

VARYA: Great-aunt sent him an authorization to buy it in her name, and to transfer the debt. She's doing it for Anya's sake. And I'm sure that God will help us, and uncle will buy it.

MME. RANEVSKAYA: Great-aunt sent fifteen thousand to buy the estate in her name, she doesn't trust us, but that's not even enough to pay the interest. *(Covers her face with her hands)* Today my fate will be decided, my fate—

TROFIMOV *(teasing Varya):* Madam Lopahina!

VARYA *(angrily):* Perpetual student! Twice already you've been expelled from the university.

MME. RANEVSKAYA: Why are you so cross, Varya? He's teasing you about Lopahin. Well, what of it? If you want to marry Lopahin, go ahead. He's a good man, and interesting; if you don't want to, don't. Nobody's compelling you, my pet!

VARYA: Frankly, mamma dear, I take this thing seriously; he's a good man and I like him.

MME. RANEVSKAYA: All right then, marry him. I don't know what you're waiting for.

VARYA: But, mamma, I can't propose to him myself. For the last two years everyone's been talking to me about him—talking. But he either keeps silent, or else cracks jokes. I understand; he's growing rich, he's absorbed in business—he has no time for me. If I had money, even a little, say, 100 rubles, I'd throw everything up and go far away—I'd go into a nunnery.

TROFIMOV: What a blessing . . .

VARYA: A student ought to be intelligent *(Softly, with tears in her voice)* How homely you've grown, Petya! How old you look! *(To Mme. Ranevskaya, with dry eyes)* But I can't live without work, mamma dear; I must keep busy every minute.

(Enter Yasha)

YASHA *(hardly restraining his laughter):* Yepihodov has broken a billiard cue! *(Exits)*

VARYA: Why is Yepihodov here? Who allowed him to play billiards? I don't understand these people! *(Exits)*

MME. RANEVSKAYA: Don't tease her, Petya. She's unhappy enough without that.

TROFIMOV: She bustles so—and meddles in other people's business. All summer long she's given Anya and me no peace. She's afraid of a love-affair between us. What business is it of hers? Besides, I've given no grounds for it, and I'm far from such vulgarity. We are above love.

MME. RANEVSKAYA: And I suppose I'm beneath love? *(Anxiously)* What can be keeping Leonid. If I only knew whether the estate has been sold or not. Such a calamity seems so incredible to me that I don't know what to think —I feel lost. . . . I could scream. . . . I could do something stupid. . . . Save me, Petya, tell me something, talk to me!

TROFIMOV: Whether the estate is sold today or not, isn't it all one? That's all done with long ago—there's no turning back, the path is overgrown. Calm yourself, my dear. You mustn't deceive yourself. For once in your life you must face the truth.

MME. RANEVSKAYA: What truth? You can see the truth, you can tell it from falsehood, but I seem to have lost my eyesight, I see nothing. You settle every great problem so boldly, but tell me, my dear boy, isn't it because you're young, because you don't yet know what one of your problems means in terms of suffering? You look ahead fearlessly, but isn't it because you don't see and don't expect anything dreadful, because life is still hidden from your young eyes? You're bolder, more honest, more profound than we are, but think hard, show just a bit of magnanimity, spare me. After all, I was born here, my father and mother lived here, and my grandfather; I love this house. Without the cherry orchard, my life has no meaning for me, and if it really must be sold, then sell me with the orchard. *(Embraces Trofimov, kisses him on the forehead)* My son was drowned here. *(Weeps)* Pity me, you good, kind fellow!

TROFIMOV: You know, I feel for you with all my heart.

MME. RANEVSKAYA: But that should have been said differently, so differently! *(Takes out her handkerchief—a telegram falls on the floor)* My heart is so heavy today—you can't imagine! The noise here upsets me—my inmost being trembles at every sound—I'm shaking all over. But I can't go into my own room; I'm afraid to be alone. Don't condemn me, Petya. . . . I love you as though you were one of us, I would gladly let you marry Anya —I swear I would—only, my dear boy, you must study—you must take your degree—you do nothing, you let yourself be tossed by Fate from place to place—it's so strange. It's true, isn't it? And you should do something about your beard, to make it grow somehow! *(Laughs)* You're so funny!

TROFIMOV *(picks up the telegram)*: I've no wish to be a dandy.

MME. RANEVSKAYA: That's a telegram from Paris. I get one every day. One yesterday and one today. That savage is ill again—he's in trouble again.

He begs forgiveness, implores me to go to him, and really I ought to go to Paris to be near him. Your face is stern, Petya; but what is there to do, my dear boy? What am I to do? He's ill, he's alone and unhappy, and who is to look after him, who is to keep him from doing the wrong thing, who is to give him his medicine on time? And why hide it or keep still about it—I love him! That's clear. I love him, love him! He's a millstone round my neck, he'll drag me to the bottom, but I love that stone. I can't live without it. *(Presses Trofimov's hand)* Don't think badly of me, Petya, and don't say anything, don't say . . .

TROFIMOV *(through tears):* Forgive me my frankness in heaven's name; but, you know, he robbed you!

MME. RANEVSKAYA: No, no, no, you mustn't say such things! *(Covers her ears)*

TROFIMOV: But he's a scoundrel! You're the only one who doesn't know it. He's a petty scoundrel—a nonentity!

MME. RANEVSKAYA *(controlling her anger):* You are twenty-six or twenty-seven years old, but you're still a schoolboy.

TROFIMOV: That may be.

MME. RANEVSKAYA: You should be a man at your age. You should understand people who love—and ought to be in love yourself. You ought to fall in love! *(Angrily)* Yes, yes! And it's not purity in you, it's prudishness, you're simply a queer fish, a comical freak!

TROFIMOV *(horrified):* What is she saying!

MME. RANEVSKAYA: "I am above love!" You're not above love, but simply, as our Firs says, you're an addlehead. At your age not to have a mistress!

TROFIMOV *(horrified):* This is frightful! What is she saying! *(Goes rapidly into the ballroom, clutching his head)* It's frightful—I can't stand it, I won't stay! *(Exits, but returns at once)* All is over between us! *(Exits into anteroom)*

MME. RANEVSKAYA *(shouts after him):* Petya! Wait! You absurd fellow, I was joking. Petya!

(Sound of somebody running quickly downstairs and suddenly falling down with a crash. Anya and Varya scream. Sound of laughter a moment later.)

MME. RANEVSKAYA: What's happened? *(Anya runs in)*

ANYA *(laughing):* Petya's fallen downstairs! *(Runs out)*

MME. RANEVSKAYA: What a queer bird that Petya is!

(Stationmaster, standing in the middle of the ballroom, recites Alexey Tolstoy's "Magdalene,"[9] to which all listen, but after a few lines, the sound of a waltz is heard from the anteroom and the reading breaks off. All dance. Trofimov, Anya, Varya, and Mme. Ranevskaya enter from the anteroom.)

MME. RANEVSKAYA: Petya, you pure soul, please forgive me. . . . Let's dance.

---

[9]A poem in which Christ appears at a society banquet.

(Dances with Petya. Anya and Varya dance. Firs enters, puts his stick down by the side door. Yasha enters from the drawing-room and watches the dancers.)

YASHA: Well, grandfather?

FIRS: I'm not feeling well. In the old days it was generals, barons, and admirals that were dancing at our balls, and now we have to send for the Post Office clerk and the Stationmaster, and even they aren't too glad to come. I feel kind of shaky. The old master that's gone, their grandfather, dosed everyone with sealing-wax, whatever ailed 'em. I've been taking sealing-wax every day for twenty years or more. Perhaps that's what's kept me alive.

YASHA: I'm fed up with you, grandpop. *(Yawns)* It's time you croaked.

FIRS: Oh, you addlehead! *(Mumbles)*

(Trofimov and Mme. Ranevskaya dance from the ballroom into the drawing-room)

MME. RANEVSKAYA: *Merci.* I'll sit down a while. *(Sits down)* I'm tired.

(Enter Anya)

ANYA *(excitedly):* There was a man in the kitchen just now who said the cherry orchard was sold today.

MME. RANEVSKAYA: Sold to whom?

ANYA: He didn't say. He's gone. *(Dances off with Trofimov)*

YASHA: It was some old man gabbing, a stranger.

FIRS: And Leonid Andreyevich isn't back yet, he hasn't come. And he's wearing his lightweight between-season overcoat; like enough, he'll catch cold. Ah, when they're young they're green.

MME. RANEVSKAYA: This is killing me. Go, Yasha, find out to whom it has been sold.

YASHA: But the old man left long ago. *(Laughs)*

MME. RANEVSKAYA: What are you laughing at? What are you pleased about?

YASHA: That Yepihodov is such a funny one. A funny fellow, Two-and-Twenty Troubles!

MME. RANEVSKAYA: Firs, if the estate is sold, where will you go?

FIRS: I'll go where you tell me.

MME. RANEVSKAYA: Why do you look like that? Are you ill? You ought to go to bed.

FIRS: Yes! *(With a snigger)* Me go to bed, and who's to hand things round? Who's to see to things? I'm the only one in the whole house.

YASHA *(to Mme. Ranevskaya):* Lubov Andreyevna, allow me to ask a favor of you, be so kind! If you go back to Paris, take me with you, I beg you. It's positively impossible for me to stay here. *(Looking around; sotto voce*[10]*)* What's the use of talking? You see for yourself, it's an uncivilized country, the people have no morals, and then the boredom! The food in the kitchen's revolting, and besides there's this Firs wand-

[10]In an undertone.

ers about mumbling all sorts of inappropriate words. Take me with you, be so kind!

(Enter Pishchik)

PISHCHIK: May I have the pleasure of a waltz with you, charming lady? *(Mme. Ranevskaya accepts)* All the same, enchanting lady, you must let me have 180 rubles. . . . You must let me have *(dancing)* just one hundred and eighty rubles. *(They pass into the ballroom)*

YASHA *(hums softly):* "Oh, wilt thou understand the tumult in my soul?"

(In the ballroom a figure in a gray top hat and checked trousers is jumping about and waving its arms; shouts: "Bravo, Charlotta Ivanovna!")

DUNYASHA *(stopping to powder her face; to Firs):* The young miss has ordered me to dance. There are so many gentlemen and not enough ladies. But dancing makes me dizzy, my heart begins to beat fast, Firs Nikolayevich. The Post Office clerk said something to me just now that quite took my breath away. *(Music stops)*

FIRS: What did he say?

DUNYASHA: "You're like a flower," he said.

YASHA *(yawns):* What ignorance. *(Exits)*

DUNYASHA: "Like a flower!" I'm such a delicate girl. I simply adore pretty speeches.

FIRS: You'll come to a bad end.

(Enter Yepihodov)

YEPIHODOV *(to Dunyasha):* You have no wish to see me, Avdotya Fyodorovna . . . as though I was some sort of insect. *(Sighs)* Ah, life!

DUNYASHA: What is it you want?

YEPIHODOV: Indubitably you may be right. *(Sighs)* But of course, if one looks at it from the point of view, if I may be allowed to say so, and apologizing for my frankness, you have completely reduced me to a state of mind. I know my fate. Every day some calamity befalls me, and I grew used to it long ago, so that I look upon my fate with a smile. You gave me your word, and though I—

DUNYASHA: Let's talk about it later, please. But just now leave me alone, I am daydreaming. *(Plays with a fan)*

YEPIHODOV: A misfortune befalls me every day; and if I may be allowed to say so, I merely smile, I even laugh.

(Enter Varya)

VARYA *(to Yepihodov):* Are you still here? What an impertinent fellow you are really! Run along, Dunyasha. *(To Yepihodov)* Either you're playing billiards and breaking a cue, or you're wandering about the drawing-room as though you were a guest.

YEPIHODOV: You cannot, permit me to remark, penalize me.

VARYA: I'm not penalizing you. I'm just telling you. You merely wander from place to place, and don't do your work. We keep you as a clerk, but Heaven knows what for.

YEPIHODOV *(offended):* Whether I work or whether I walk, whether I eat or whether I play billiards, is a matter to be discussed only by persons of understanding and of mature years.

VARYA *(enraged):* You dare say that to me—you dare? You mean to say I've no understanding? Get out of here at once! This minute!

YEPIHODOV *(scared):* I beg you to express yourself delicately.

VARYA *(beside herself):* Clear out this minute! Out with you!

(Yepihodov goes towards the door, Varya following)

VARYA: Two-and-Twenty Troubles! Get out—don't let me set eyes on you! *(Exit Yepihodov. His voice is heard behind the door):* "I shall lodge a complaint against you!"

VARYA: Oh, you're coming back? *(She seizes the stick left near door by Firs)* Well, come then . . . come . . . I'll show you . . . Ah, you're coming? You're coming? . . . Come . . . *(Swings the stick just as Lopahin enters)*

LOPAHIN: Thank you kindly.

VARYA *(angrily and mockingly):* I'm sorry.

LOPAHIN: It's nothing. Thank you kindly for your charming reception.

VARYA: Don't mention it. *(Walks away, looks back and asks softly)* I didn't hurt you, did I?

LOPAHIN: Oh, no, not at all. I shall have a large bump, though. *(Voices from the ballroom):* "Lopahin is here! Lopahin!"

(Enter Pishchik)

PISHCHIK: My eyes do see, my ears do hear! *(Kisses Lopahin)*

LOPAHIN: You smell of cognac, my dear friends. And we've been celebrating here, too. *(Enter Mme. Ranevskaya)*

MME. RANEVSKAYA: Is that you, Yermolay Alexeyevich? What kept you so long? Where's Leonid?

LOPAHIN: Leonid Andreyevich arrived with me. He's coming.

MME. RANEVSKAYA: Well, what happened? Did the sale take place? Speak!

LOPAHIN *(embarrassed, fearful of revealing his joy):* The sale was over at four o'clock. We missed the train—had to wait till half past nine. *(Sighing heavily)* Ugh. I'm a little dizzy.

(Enter Gayev. In his right hand he holds parcels, with his left he is wiping away his tears)

MME. RANEVSKAYA: Well, Leonid? What news? *(Impatiently, through tears)* Be quick, for God's sake!

GAYEV *(not answering, simply waves his hand. Weeping, to Firs):* Here, take these; anchovies, Kerch herrings . . . I haven't eaten all day. What I've been through! *(The click of billiard balls comes through the open door of the billiard room and Yasha's voice is heard)* "Seven and eighteen!" *(Gayev's expression changes, he no longer weeps)* I'm terribly tired. Firs, help me change. *(Exits, followed by Firs)*

PISHCHIK: How about the sale? Tell us what happened.

MME. RANEVSKAYA: Is the cherry orchard sold?

LOPAHIN: Sold.

MME. RANEVSKAYA: Who bought it?

LOPAHIN: I bought it.

(Pause. Mme. Ranevskaya is overcome. She would fall to the floor, were it not for the chair and table near which she stands. Varya takes the keys from her belt, flings them on the floor in the middle of the drawing-room and goes out.)

LOPAHIN: I bought it. Wait a bit, ladies and gentlemen, please, my head is swimming. I can't talk. *(Laughs)* We got to the auction and Deriganov was there already. Leonid Andreyevich had only 15,000 and straight off Deriganov bid 30,000 over and above the mortgage. I saw how the land lay, got into the fight, bid 40,000. He bid 45,000. I bid fifty-five. He kept adding five thousands, I ten. Well . . . it came to an end. I bid ninety above the mortgage and the estate was knocked down to me. Now the cherry orchard's mine! Mine! *(Laughs uproariously)* Lord! God in Heaven! The cherry orchard's mine! Tell me that I'm drunk—out of my mind—that it's all a dream. *(Stamps his feet)* Don't laugh at me! If my father and my grandfather could rise from their graves and see all that has happened— how their Yermolay, who used to be flogged, their half-literate Yermolay, who used to run about barefoot in winter, how that very Yermolay has bought the most magnificent estate in the world. I bought the estate where my father and grandfather were slaves, where they weren't even allowed to enter the kitchen. I'm asleep—it's only a dream—I only imagine it . . . It's the fruit of your imagination, wrapped in the darkness of the unknown! *(Picks up the keys, smiling genially)* She threw down the keys, wants to show she's no longer mistress here. *(Jingles keys)* Well, no matter. *(The band is heard tuning up)* Hey, musicians! Strike up! I want to hear you! Come, everybody, and see how Yermolay Lopahin will lay the ax to the cherry orchard and how the trees will fall to the ground. We will build summer cottages there, and our grandsons and great-grandsons will see a new life here. Music! Strike up!

(The band starts to play. Mme. Ranevskaya has sunk into a chair and is weeping bitterly.)

LOPAHIN *(reproachfully):* Why, why didn't you listen to me? My dear friend, my poor friend, you can't bring it back now. *(Tearfully)* Oh, if only this were over quickly! Oh, if only our wretched, disordered life were changed!

PISHCHIK *(takes him by the arm; sotto voce):* She's crying. Let's go into the ballroom. Let her be alone. Come. *(Takes his arm and leads him into the ballroom)*

LOPAHIN: What's the matter? Musicians, play so I can hear you! Let me have things the way I want them. *(Ironically)* Here comes the new master, the owner of the cherry orchard. *(Accidentally he trips over a little table, almost upsetting the candelabra)* I can pay for everything. *(Exits with Pishchik. Mme. Ranevskaya, alone, sits huddled up, weeping bitterly. Music plays softly. Enter Anya and Trofimov quickly. Anya goes to her mother and falls on her knees before her. Trofimov stands in the doorway.)*

ANYA: Mamma, mamma, you're crying! Dear, kind, good mamma, my precious, I love you. I bless you! The cherry orchard is sold, it's gone, that's true, quite true. But don't cry, mamma, life is still before you, you still have your kind, pure heart. Let us go, let us go away from here, darling. We will plant a new orchard, even more luxuriant than this one. You will see it, you will understand, and like the sun at evening, joy—deep, tranquil joy—will sink into your soul, and you will smile, mamma. Come, darling, let us go.

Act IV

Scene as in Act I. No window curtains or pictures, only a little furniture, piled up in a corner, as if for sale. A sense of emptiness. Near the outer door and at the back, suitcases, bundles, etc., are piled up. A door open on the left and the voices of Varya and Anya are heard. Lopahin stands waiting. Yasha holds a tray with glasses full of champagne. Yepihodov in the anteroom is tying up a box. Behind the scene a hum of voices: peasants have come to say good-by. Voice of Gayev: "Thanks, brothers, thank you."

YASHA: The country folk have come to say good-by. In my opinion, Yermolay Alexeyevich, they are kindly souls, but there's nothing in their heads.

(The hum dies away. Enter Mme. Ranevskaya and Gayev. She is not crying, but is pale, her face twitches and she cannot speak.)

GAYEV: You gave them your purse, Luba. That won't do! That won't do!

MME. RANEVSKAYA: I couldn't help it! I couldn't! *(They go out)*

LOPAHIN *(calls after them)*: Please, I beg you, have a glass at parting. I didn't think of bringing any champagne from town and at the station I could find only one bottle. Please, won't you? *(Pause)* What's the matter, ladies and gentlemen, don't you want any? *(Moves away from the door)* If I'd known, I wouldn't have bought it. Well, then I won't drink any, either. *(Yasha carefully sets the tray down on a chair)* At least you have a glass, Yasha.

YASHA: Here's to the travelers! And good luck to those that stay! *(Drinks)* This champagne isn't the real stuff, I can assure you.

LOPAHIN: Eight rubles a bottle. *(Pause)* It's devilishly cold here.

YASHA: They didn't light the stoves today—it wasn't worth it, since we're leaving. *(Laughs)*

LOPAHIN: Why are you laughing?

YASHA: It's just that I'm pleased.

LOPAHIN: It's October, yet it's as still and sunny as though it were summer. Good weather for building. *(Looks at his watch, and speaks off)* Bear in mind, ladies and gentlemen, the train goes in forty-seven minutes, so you ought to start for the station in twenty minutes. Better hurry up!

(Enter Trofimov wearing an overcoat)

TROFIMOV: I think it's time to start. The carriages are at the door. The devil only knows what's become of my rubbers; they've disappeared. *(Calling off)* Anya! My rubbers are gone. I can't find them.

LOPAHIN: I've got to go to Kharkov. I'll take the same train you do. I'll spend the winter in Kharkov. I've been hanging round here with you, till I'm worn out with loafing. I can't live without work—I don't know what to do with my hands, they dangle as if they didn't belong to me.

TROFIMOV: Well, we'll soon be gone, then you can go on with your useful labors again.

LOPAHIN: Have a glass.

TROFIMOV: No, I won't.

LOPAHIN: So you're going to Moscow now?

TROFIMOV: Yes. I'll see them into town, and tomorrow I'll go on to Moscow.

LOPAHIN: Well, I'll wager the professors aren't giving any lectures, they're waiting for you to come.

TROFIMOV: That's none of your business.

LOPAHIN: Just how many years have you been at the university?

TROFIMOV: Can't you think of something new? Your joke's stale and flat. *(Looking for his rubbers)* We'll probably never see each other again, so allow me to give you a piece of advice at parting: don't wave your hands about! Get out of the habit. And another thing: building bungalows, figuring that summer residents will eventually become small farmers, figuring like that is just another form of waving your hands about. . . . Never mind, I love you anyway; you have fine, delicate fingers, like an artist; you have a fine, delicate soul.

LOPAHIN *(embracing him)*: Good-by, my dear fellow. Thank you for everything. Let me give you some money for the journey, if you need it.

TROFIMOV: What for? I don't need it.

LOPAHIN: But you haven't any.

TROFIMOV: Yes, I have, thank you. I got some money for a translation—here it is in my pocket. *(Anxiously)* But where are my rubbers?

VARYA *(from the next room)*: Here! Take the nasty things. *(Flings a pair of rubbers onto the stage)*

TROFIMOV: What are you so cross about, Varya? Hm . . . and these are not my rubbers.

LOPAHIN: I sowed three thousand acres of poppies in the spring, and now I've made 40,000 on them, clear profit; and when my poppies were in bloom, what a picture it was! So, as I say, I made 40,000; and I am offering you a loan because I can afford it. Why turn up your nose at it? I'm a peasant —I speak bluntly.

TROFIMOV: Your father was a peasant, mine was a druggist—that proves absolutely nothing whatever. *(Lopahin takes out his wallet)* Don't, put that away! If you were to offer me two hundred thousand I wouldn't take it. I'm a free man. And everything that all of you, rich and poor alike, value so highly and hold so dear, hasn't the slightest power over me. It's like so much fluff floating in the air. I can get on without you, I can pass you by, I'm strong and proud. Mankind is moving towards the highest truth, towards the highest happiness possible on earth, and I am in the front ranks.

LOPAHIN: Will you get there?

TROFIMOV: I will. *(Pause)* I will get there, or I will show others the way to get there.

(The sound of axes chopping down trees is heard in the distance)

LOPAHIN: Well, good-by, my dear fellow. It's time to leave. We turn up our noses at one another, but life goes on just the same. When I'm working hard, without resting, my mind is easier, and it seems to me that I too know why I exist. But how many people are there in Russia, brother, who exist nobody knows why? Well, it doesn't matter. That's not what makes the wheels go round. They say Leonid Andreyevich has taken a position in the bank, 6,000 rubles a year. Only, of course, he won't stick to it, he's too lazy. . . .

ANYA *(in the doorway)*: Mamma begs you not to start cutting down the cherry-trees until she's gone.

TROFIMOV: Really, you should have more tact! *(Exits)*

LOPAHIN: Right away—right away! Those men . . . *(Exits)*

ANYA: Has Firs been taken to the hospital?

YASHA: I told them this morning. They must have taken him.

ANYA *(to Yepihodov who crosses the room)*: Yepihodov, please find out if Firs has been taken to the hospital.

YASHA *(offended)*: I told Yegor this morning. Why ask a dozen times?

YEPIHODOV: The aged Firs, in my definitive opinion, is beyond mending. It's time he was gathered to his fathers. And I can only envy him. *(Puts a suitcase down on a hat-box and crushes it)* There now, of course. I knew it! *(Exits)*

YASHA *(mockingly)*: Two-and-Twenty Troubles!

VARYA *(through the door)*: Has Firs been taken to the hospital?

ANYA: Yes.

VARYA: Then why wasn't the note for the doctor taken too?

ANYA: Oh! Then someone must take it to him. *(Exits)*

VARYA *(from adjoining room)*: Where's Yasha? Tell him his mother's come and wants to say good-by.

YASHA *(waves his hand)*: She tries my patience.

(Dunyasha has been occupied with the luggage. Seeing Yasha alone, she goes up to him.)

DUNYASHA: You might just give me one little look, Yasha. You're going away
. . . You're leaving me . . . *(weeps and throws herself on his neck)*

YASHA: What's there to cry about? *(Drinks champagne)* In six days I shall be
in Paris again. Tomorrow we get into an express train and off we go, that's
the last you'll see of us. . . . I can scarcely believe it. *Vive la France!* It
don't suit me here, I just can't live here. That's all there is to it. I'm fed
up with the ignorance here. I've had enough of it. *(Drinks champagne)*
What's there to cry about? Behave yourself properly, and you'll have no
cause to cry.

DUNYASHA *(powders her face, looking in pocket mirror):* Do send me a letter
from Paris. You know I loved you, Yasha, how I loved you! I'm a delicate
creature, Yasha.

YASHA: Somebody's coming! *(Busies himself with the luggage, hums softly)*

(Enter Mme. Ranevskaya, Gayev, Anya, and Charlotta)

GAYEV: We ought to be leaving. We haven't much time. *(Looks at Yasha)* Who
smells of herring?

MME. RANEVSKAYA: In about ten minutes we should be getting into the
carriages. *(Looks around the room)* Good-by, dear old home, good-by,
grandfather. Winter will pass, spring will come, you will no longer be
here, they will have torn you down. How much these walls have seen!
(Kisses Anya warmly) My treasure, how radiant you look! Your eyes are
sparkling like diamonds. Are you glad? Very?

ANYA *(gaily):* Very glad. A new life is beginning, mamma.

GAYEV: Well, really, everything is all right now. Before the cherry orchard was
sold, we all fretted and suffered; but afterwards, when the question was
settled finally and irrevocably, we all calmed down, and even felt quite
cheerful. I'm a bank employee now, a financier. The yellow ball in the side
pocket! And anyhow, you are looking better Luba, there's no doubt of
that.

MME. RANEVSKAYA: Yes, my nerves are better, that's true. *(She is handed her
hat and coat)* I sleep well. Carry out my things, Yasha. It's time. *(To
Anya)* We shall soon see each other again, my little girl. I'm going to
Paris, I'll live there on the money your great-aunt sent us to buy the estate
with—long live Auntie! But that money won't last long.

ANYA: You'll come back soon, soon, mamma, won't you? Meanwhile I'll
study, I'll pass my high school examination, and then I'll go to work and
help you. We'll read all kinds of books together, mamma, won't we?
(Kisses her mother's hands) We'll read in the autumn evenings, we'll read
lots of books, and a new wonderful world will open up before us. *(Falls
into a revery)* Mamma, do come back.

MME. RANEVSKAYA: I will come back, my precious.

(Embraces her daughter. Enter Lopahin and Charlotta who is humming softly.)

GAYEV: Charlotta's happy: she's singing.

CHARLOTTA *(picks up a bundle and holds it like a baby in swaddling-clothes):* Bye, baby, bye. *(A baby is heard crying)* "Wah! Wah!" Hush, hush, my pet, my little one. "Wah! Wah!" I'm so sorry for you! *(Throws the bundle down)* You will find me a position, won't you? I can't go on like this.

LOPAHIN: We'll find one for you, Charlotta Ivanovna, don't worry.

GAYEV: Everyone's leaving us. Varya's going away. We've suddenly become of no use.

CHARLOTTA: There's no place for me to live in town, I must go away. *(Hums)*

(Enter Pishchik)

LOPAHIN: There's nature's masterpiece!

PISHCHIK *(gasping):* Oh . . . let me get my breath . . . I'm in agony. . . . Esteemed friends . . . Give me a drink of water. . . .

GAYEV: Wants some money, I suppose. No, thank you. . . . I'll keep out of harm's way. *(Exits)*

PISHCHIK: It's a long while since I've been to see you, most charming lady. *(To Lopahin)* So you are here . . . glad to see you, you intellectual giant. . . . There . . . *(Gives Lopahin money)* Here's 400 rubles, and I still owe you 840.

LOPAHIN *(shrugging his shoulders in bewilderment):* I must be dreaming . . . Where did you get it?

PISHCHIK: Wait a minute . . . It's hot . . . A most extraordinary event! Some Englishmen came to my place and found some sort of white clay on my land . . . *(To Mme. Ranevskaya)* And 400 for you . . . most lovely . . . most wonderful . . . *(Hands her the money)* The rest later. *(Drinks water)* A young man in the train was telling me just now that a great philosopher recommends jumping off roofs. "Jump!" says he; "that's the long and the short of it!" *(In amazement)* Just imagine! Some more water!

LOPAHIN: What Englishmen?

PISHCHIK: I leased them the tract with the clay on it for twenty-four hours. . . . And now, forgive me, I can't stay. . . . I must be dashing on. . . . I'm going over to Znoikov . . . to Kardamanov . . . I owe them all money . . . *(Drinks water)* Good-by, everybody . . . I'll look in on Thursday . . .

MME. RANEVSKAYA: We're just moving into town; and tomorrow I go abroad.

PISHCHIK *(upset):* What? Why into town? That's why the furniture is like that . . . and the suitcases . . . Well, never mind! *(Through tears)* Never mind . . . Men of colossal intellect, these Englishmen . . . Never mind . . . Be happy. God will come to your help. . . . Never mind. . . . Everything in this world comes to an end. *(Kisses Mme. Ranevskaya's hand)* If the rumor reaches you that it's all up with me, remember this old . . . horse, and say: Once there lived a certain . . . Simeonov-Pishchik . . . the kingdom of Heaven be his . . . Glorious weather . . . Yes . . . *(Exits, in great confusion, but at once returns and says in the doorway)* My daughter Dashenka sends her regards. *(Exit)*

MME. RANEVSKAYA: Now we can go. I leave with two cares weighing on me. The first is poor old Firs. *(Glancing at her watch)* We still have about five minutes.

ANYA: Mamma, Firs has already been taken to the hospital. Yasha sent him there this morning.

MME. RANEVSKAYA: My other worry is Varya. She's used to getting up early and working; and now, with no work to do, she is like a fish out of water. She has grown thin and pale, and keeps crying, poor soul. *(Pause)* You know this very well, Yermolay Alexeyevich; I dreamed of seeing her married to you, and it looked as though that's how it would be. *(Whispers to Anya, who nods to Charlotta and both go out)* She loves you. You find her attractive. I don't know, I don't know why it is you seem to avoid each other; I can't understand it.

LOPAHIN: To tell you the truth, I don't understand it myself. It's all a puzzle. If there's still time, I'm ready now, at once. Let's settle it straight off, and have done with it! Without you, I feel I'll never be able to propose.

MME. RANEVSKAYA: That's splendid. After all, it will only take a minute. I'll call her at once. . . .

LOPAHIN: And luckily, here's champagne too. *(Looks at the glasses)* Empty! Somebody's drunk it all. *(Yasha coughs)* That's what you might call guzzling. . . .

MME. RANEVSKAYA *(animatedly):* Excellent! We'll go and leave you alone. Yasha, *allez!* I'll call her. *(At the door)* Varya, leave everything and come here. Come! *(Exits with Yasha)*

LOPAHIN *(looking at his watch):* Yes . . .

(Pause behind the door, smothered laughter and whispering; at last, enter Varya)

VARYA *(looking over the luggage in leisurely fashion):* Strange, I can't find it . . .

LOPAHIN: What are you looking for?

VARYA: Packed it myself, and I don't remember . . . *(Pause)*

LOPAHIN: Where are you going now, Varya?

VARYA: I? To the Ragulins'. I've arranged to take charge there—as housekeeper, if you like.

LOPAHIN: At Yashnevo? About fifty miles from here. *(Pause)* Well, life in this house is ended!

VARYA *(examining luggage):* Where is it? Perhaps I put it in the chest. Yes, life in this house is ended. . . . There will be no more of it.

LOPAHIN: And I'm just off to Kharkov—by this next train. I've a lot to do there. I'm leaving Yepihodov here . . . I've taken him on.

VARYA: Oh!

LOPAHIN: Last year at this time it was snowing, if you remember, but now it's sunny and there's no wind. It's cold, though. . . . It must be three below.

VARYA: I didn't look. *(Pause)* And besides, our thermometer's broken. *(Pause. Voice from the yard)* "Yermolay Alexeyevich!"

LOPAHIN *(as if he had been waiting for the call):* This minute!

(Exit quickly. Varya sits on the floor and sobs quietly, her head on a bundle of clothes. Enter Mme. Ranevskaya cautiously.)

MME. RANEVSKAYA: Well? *(Pause)* We must be going.

VARYA *(wiping her eyes):* Yes, it's time, mamma dear. I'll be able to get to the Ragulins' today, if only we don't miss the train.

MME. RANEVSKAYA *(at the door):* Anya, put your things on.

(Enter Anya, Gayev, Charlotta. Gayev wears a heavy overcoat with a hood. Enter servants and coachmen. Yepihodov bustles about the luggage.)

MME. RANEVSKAYA: Now we can start on our journey.

ANYA *(joyfully):* On our journey!

GAYEV: My friends, my dear, cherished friends, leaving this house forever, can I be silent? Can I at leave-taking refrain from giving utterance to those emotions that now fill my being?

ANYA *(imploringly):* Uncle!

VARYA: Uncle, uncle dear, don't.

GAYEV *(Forlornly):* I'll bank the yellow in the side pocket . . . I'll be silent . . .

(Enter Trofimov, then Lopahin)

TROFIMOV: Well, ladies and gentlemen, it's time to leave.

LOPAHIN: Yepihodov, my coat.

MME. RANEVSKAYA: I'll sit down just a minute. It seems as though I'd never before seen what the walls of this house were like, the ceilings, and now I look at them hungrily, with such tender affection.

GAYEV: I remember when I was six years old sitting on that window sill on Whitsunday, watching my father going to church.

MME. RANEVSKAYA: Has everything been taken?

LOPAHIN: I think so. *(Putting on his overcoat)* Yepihodov, see that everything's in order.

YEPIHODOV *(in a husky voice):* You needn't worry, Yermolay Alexeyevich.

LOPAHIN: What's the matter with your voice?

YEPIHODOV: I just had a drink of water. I must have swallowed something.

YASHA *(contemptuously):* What ignorance!

MME. RANEVSKAYA: When we're gone, not a soul will be left here.

LOPAHIN: Until the spring.

(Varya pulls an umbrella out of a bundle, as though about to hit someone with it. Lopahin pretends to be frightened.)

VARYA: Come, come, I had no such idea!

TROFIMOV: Ladies and gentlemen, let's get into the carriages—it's time. The train will be in directly.

VARYA: Petya, there they are, your rubbers, by that trunk. *(Tearfully)* And what dirty old things they are!

TROFIMOV *(puts on rubbers):* Let's go, ladies and gentlemen.

GAYEV *(greatly upset, afraid of breaking down):* The train . . . the station . . . Three cushions in the side pocket, I'll bank this one in the corner . . .

MME. RANEVSKAYA: Let's go.

LOPAHIN: Are we all here? No one in there? *(Locks the side door on the left)* There are some things stored here, better lock up. Let us go!

ANYA: Good-by, old house! Good-by, old life!

TROFIMOV: Hail to you, new life!

(Exit with Anya. Varya looks round the room and goes out slowly. Yasha and Charlotta with her dog go out.)

LOPAHIN: And so, until the spring. Go along, friends . . . 'Bye-'bye! *(Exits)*

(Mme. Ranevskaya and Gayev remain alone. As though they had been waiting for this, they throw themselves on each other's necks, and break into subdued, restrained sobs, afraid of being overheard.)

GAYEV *(in despair):* My sister! My sister!

MME. RANEVSKAYA: Oh, my orchard—my dear, sweet, beautiful orchard! My life, my youth, my happiness—good-by! Good-by! *(Voice of Anya, gay and summoning)* "Mamma!" *(Voice of Trofimov, gay and excited)* "Halloo!"

MME. RANEVSKAYA: One last look at the walls, at the windows . . . Our poor mother loved to walk about this room . . .

GAYEV: My sister, my sister! *(Voice of Anya)* "Mamma!" *(Voice of Trofimov)* "Halloo!"

MME. RANEVSKAYA: We're coming.

(They go out. The stage is empty. The sound of doors being locked, of carriages driving away. Then silence. In the stillness is heard the muffled sound of the ax striking a tree, a mournful, lonely sound.

Footsteps are heard. Firs appears in the doorway on the right. He is dressed as usual in a jacket and white waistcoat and wears slippers. He is ill.)

FIRS *(goes to the door, tries the handle):* Locked! They've gone . . . *(Sits down on the sofa)* They've forgotten me . . . Never mind . . . I'll sit here a bit . . . I'll wager Leonid Andreyevich hasn't put his fur coat on, he's gone off in his light overcoat . . . *(Sighs anxiously)* I didn't keep an eye on him . . . Ah, when they're young, they're green . . . *(Mumbles something indistinguishable)* Life has gone by as if I had never lived. *(Lies down)* I'll lie down a while . . . There's no strength left in you, old fellow; nothing is left, nothing. Ah, you addlehead!

(Lies motionless. A distant sound is heard coming from the sky as it were, the sound of a snapping string mournfully dying away. All is still again, and nothing is heard but the strokes of the ax against a tree far away in the orchard.)

QUESTIONS

1. Why is the cherry orchard so important to Madame Ranevskaya?
2. The Russian Revolution did not happen until after this play was written and produced. Where within the play can you find evidence that a revolution is on the way?
3. What does Leonid's endless billiard game communicate about his character?
4. What elements of the play suggest most forcibly that its characters do not really interact or change?
5. What clues to Lopahin's character in Acts One and Two prepare the audience for what he does at the auction described in Act Three?
6. What specific things do you learn from Firs about the lives and values of aristocrats and serfs and the relationships between them under the old feudal system?
7. What offstage sounds intrude at the end of each act and in the middle of Act Two? What tone or mood does each communicate?
8. What elements of description, action, or speech serve to individualize each major character? To what extent does each seem representative of a type? What type?
9. Why did Chekhov call this a comedy? Why not a tragedy?

SUPPRESSED DESIRES

Suppressed Desires, like *The Cherry Orchard,* was part of a new chapter in the history of the theater. It was among the first productions of The Provincetown Players, a "little theater" group founded to counter the commercialism of Broadway and to support American playwrights, most notably Eugene O'Neill. Susan Glaspell and her husband George Cram Cook first acted the roles of Henrietta and Stephen in a friend's Cape Cod home and then in a ramshackle fish house at the end of a Provincetown wharf, bringing it later to the group's new Playwright's Theater in Greenwich Village. Because of its considerable success in mocking a misguided enthusiasm for Freudian psychoanalysis, its simple staging, and its ease of casting, *Suppressed Desires* became a longtime favorite of amateur theater groups. After the length and thematic weight of *An Enemy of the People* and *The Cherry Orchard,* this play shows us that social drama can also be brief, light, and pointed.

SUPPRESSED DESIRES

Susan Glaspell   (1882–1948)
and George Cram Cook   (1873–1924)

Scene I

A studio apartment in an upper story, Washington Square South. Through an immense north window in the back wall appear tree tops and the upper part of the Washington Arch. Beyond it you look up Fifth Avenue. Near the window is a big table, loaded at one end with serious-looking books and austere scientific periodicals. At the other end are architect's drawings, blue prints, dividing compasses, square, ruler, etc. At the left is a door leading to the rest of the apartment; at the right the outer door. A breakfast table is set for three, but only two are seated at it—Henrietta and Stephen Brewster. As the curtains withdraw Steve pushes back his coffee cup and sits dejected.

HENRIETTA: It isn't the coffee, Steve dear. There's nothing the matter with the coffee. There's something the matter with *you.*
STEVE: *(Doggedly.)* There may be something the matter with my stomach.
HENRIETTA: *(Scornfully)* Your stomach! The trouble is not with your stomach but in your subconscious mind.
STEVE: Subconscious piffle!

(Takes morning paper and tries to read.)

HENRIETTA: Steve, you never used to be so disagreeable. You certainly have got some sort of a complex. You're all inhibited. You're no longer open to new ideas. You won't listen to a word about psychoanalysis.
STEVE: A word! I've listened to volumes!
HENRIETTA: You've ceased to be creative in architecture—your work isn't going well. You're not sleeping well—
STEVE: How can I sleep, Henrietta, when you're always waking me up to find out what I'm dreaming?
HENRIETTA: But dreams are so important, Steve. If you'd tell yours to Dr. Russell he'd find out exactly what's wrong with you.
STEVE: There's nothing wrong with me.
HENRIETTA: You don't even talk as well as you used to.
STEVE: Talk? I can't say a thing without you looking at me in that dark fashion you have when you're on the trail of a complex.
HENRIETTA: This very irritability indicates that you're suffering from some suppressed desire.
STEVE: I'm suffering from a suppressed desire for a little peace.
HENRIETTA: Dr. Russell is doing simply wonderful things with nervous cases. Won't you go to him, Steve?

STEVE: *(Slamming down his newspaper.)* No, Henrietta, I won't!

HENRIETTA: But, Stephen—!

STEVE: Tst! I hear Mabel coming. Let's not be at each other's throats the first day of her visit.

(He takes out cigarettes. Mabel comes in from door left, the side opposite Steve, so that he is facing her. She is wearing a rather fussy negligee in contrast to Henrietta, who wears "radical" clothes. Mabel is what is called plump.)

MABEL: Good morning.

HENRIETTA: Oh, here you are, little sister.

STEVE: Good morning, Mabel.

(Mabel nods to him and turns, her face lighting up, to Henrietta.)

HENRIETTA: *(Giving Mabel a hug as she leans against her.)* It's so good to have you here. I was going to let you sleep, thinking you'd be tired after the long trip. Sit down. There'll be fresh toast in a minute and *(Rising)* will you have—

MABEL: Oh, I ought to have told you, Henrietta. Don't get anything for me. I'm not eating breakfast.

HENRIETTA: *(At first in mere surprise.)* Not eating breakfast?

(She sits down, then leans toward Mabel who is seated now, and scrutinizes her.)

STEVE: *(Half to himself.)* The psychoanalytical look!

HENRIETTA: Mabel, why are you not eating breakfast?

MABEL: *(A little startled.)* Why, no particular reason. I just don't care much for breakfast, and they say it keeps down—*(A hand on her hip—the gesture of one who is "reducing")* that is, it's a good thing to go without it.

HENRIETTA: Don't you sleep well? Did you sleep well last night?

MABEL: Oh, yes, I slept all right. Yes, I slept fine last night, only *(Laughing)* I did have the funniest dream!

STEVE: S-h! S-t!

HENRIETTA: *(Moving closer.)* And what did you dream, Mabel?

STEVE: Look-a-here, Mabel, I feel it's my duty to put you on. Don't tell Henrietta your dreams. If you do she'll find out that you have an underground desire to kill your father and marry your mother—

HENRIETTA: Don't be absurd, Stephen Brewster. *(Sweetly to Mabel.)* What was your dream, dear?

MABEL: *(Laughing.)* Well, I dreamed I was a hen.

HENRIETTA: A hen?

MABEL: Yes; and I was pushing along through a crowd as fast as I could, but being a hen I couldn't walk very fast—it was like having a tight skirt, you know; and there was some sort of creature in a blue cap—you know how mixed up dreams are—and it kept shouting after me, "Step, Hen! Step, Hen!" until I got all excited and just couldn't move at all.

HENRIETTA: *(Resting chin in palm and peering.)* You say you became much excited?

MABEL: *(Laughing.)* Oh, yes; I was in a terrible state.

HENRIETTA: *(Leaning back, murmurs.)* This is significant.

STEVE: She dreams she's a hen. She is told to step lively. She becomes violently agitated. What can it mean?

HENRIETTA: *(Turning impatiently from him.)* Mabel, do you know anything about psychoanalysis?

MABEL: *(Feebly.)* Oh—not much. No—I—*(Brightening.)* It's something about the war, isn't it?

STEVE: Not that kind of war.

MABEL: *(Abashed.)* I thought it might be the name of a new explosive.

STEVE: It *is.*

MABEL: *(Apologetically to Henrietta, who is frowning.)* You see, Henrietta, I —we do not live in touch with intellectual things, as you do. Bob being a dentist—somehow our friends—

STEVE: *(Softly.)* Oh, to be a dentist!

(Goes to window and stands looking out.)

HENRIETTA: Don't you see anything more of that editorial writer—what was his name?

MABEL: Lyman Eggleston?

HENRIETTA: Yes, Eggleston. He was in touch with things. Don't you see him?

MABEL: Yes, I see him once in a while. Bob doesn't like him very well.

HENRIETTA: Your husband does not like Lyman Eggleston? *(Mysteriously.)* Mabel, are you perfectly happy with your husband?

STEVE: *(Sharply.)* Oh, come now, Henrietta—that's going a little strong!

HENRIETTA: Are you perfectly happy with him, Mabel?

(Steve goes to work-table.)

MABEL: Why—yes—I guess so. Why—of course I am!

HENRIETTA: Are you happy? Or do you only think you are? Or do you only think you *ought* to be?

MABEL: Why, Henrietta, I don't know what you mean!

STEVE: *(Seizes stack of books and magazines and dumps them on the breakfast table.)* This is what she means, Mabel. Psychoanalysis. My work-table groans with it. Books by Freud, the new Messiah; books by Jung, the new St. Paul; the Psychoanalytical Review—back numbers two-fifty per.

MABEL: But what's it all about?

STEVE: All about your sub-un-non-conscious mind and desires you know not of. They may be doing you a great deal of harm. You may go crazy with them. Oh, yes! People are doing it right and left. Your dreaming you're a hen—

(Shakes his head darkly.)

HENRIETTA: Any fool can ridicule anything.

MABEL: *(Hastily, to avert a quarrel.)* But what do you say it is, Henrietta?

STEVE: *(Looking at his watch.)* Oh, if Henrietta's going to start that!

(During Henrietta's next speech settles himself at work-table and sharpens a lead pencil.)

HENRIETTA: It's like this, Mabel. You want something. You think you can't have it. You think it's wrong. So you try to think you don't want it. Your mind protects you—avoids pain—by refusing to think the forbidden thing. But it's there just the same. It stays there shut up in your unconscious mind, and it festers.

STEVE: Sort of an ingrowing mental toenail.

HENRIETTA: Precisely. The forbidden impulse is there full of energy which has simply got to do something. It breaks into your consciousness in disguise, masks itself in dreams, makes all sorts of trouble. In extreme cases it drives you insane.

MABEL: *(With a gesture of horror.)* Oh!

HENRIETTA: *(Reassuring.)* But psychoanalysis has found out how to save us from that. It brings into consciousness the suppressed desire that was making all the trouble. Psychoanalysis is simply the latest scientific method of preventing and curing insanity.

STEVE: *(From his table.)* It is also the latest scientific method of separating families.

HENRIETTA: *(Mildly.)* Families that ought to be separated.

STEVE: The Dwights, for instance. You must have met them, Mabel, when you were here before. Helen was living, apparently, in peace and happiness with good old Joe. Well—she went to this psychoanalyzer—she was "psyched," and biff!—bang!—home she comes with an unsuppressed desire to leave her husband.

(He starts work, drawing lines on a drawing board with a T-square.)

MABEL: How terrible! Yes, I remember Helen Dwight. But—but did she have such a desire?

STEVE: First she'd known of it.

MABEL: And she *left* him?

HENRIETTA: *(Coolly.)* Yes, she did.

MABEL: Wasn't he good to her?

HENRIETTA: Why yes, good enough.

MABEL: Wasn't he kind to her?

HENRIETTA: Oh, yes—kind to her.

MABEL: And she left her good kind husband—!

HENRIETTA: Oh, Mabel! "Left her good, kind husband!" How naïve—forgive me, dear, but how bourgeoise you are! She came to know herself. And she had the courage!

MABEL: I may be very naïve and—bourgeoise—but I don't see the good of a new science that breaks up homes.

(Steve applauds.)

STEVE: In enlightening Mabel, we mustn't neglect to mention the case of Art Holden's private secretary, Mary Snow, who has just been informed of her suppressed desire for her employer.

MABEL: Why, I think it is terrible, Henrietta! It would be better if we didn't know such things about ourselves.

HENRIETTA: No, Mabel, that is the old way.

MABEL: But—but her employer? Is he married?

STEVE: *(Grunts.)* Wife and four children.

MABEL: Well, then, what good does it do the girl to be told she has a desire for him? There's nothing can be done about it.

HENRIETTA: Old institutions will have to be reshaped so that something can be done in such cases. It happens, Mabel, that this suppressed desire was on the point of landing Mary Snow in the insane asylum. Are you so tight-minded that you'd rather have her in the insane asylum than break the conventions?

MABEL: But—but have people always had these awful suppressed desires?

HENRIETTA: Always.

STEVE: But they've just been discovered.

HENRIETTA: The harm they do has just been discovered. And free, sane people must face the fact that they have to be dealt with.

MABEL: *(Stoutly.)* I don't believe they have them in Chicago.

HENRIETTA: *(Business of giving Mabel up.)* People "have them" wherever the living Libido—the center of the soul's energy—is in conflict with petrified moral codes. That means everywhere in civilization. Psychoanalysis—

STEVE: Good God! I've got the roof in the cellar!

HENRIETTA: The roof in the cellar!

STEVE: *(Holding plan at arm's length.)* That's what psychoanalysis does!

HENRIETTA: That's what psychoanalysis could *un-*do. Is it any wonder I'm concerned about Steve? He dreamed the other night that the walls of his room melted away and he found himself alone in a forest. Don't you see how significant it is for an architect to have *walls* slip away from him? It symbolizes his loss of grip in his work. There's some suppressed desire—

STEVE: *(Hurling his ruined plan viciously to the floor.)* Suppressed hell!

HENRIETTA: You speak more truly than you know. It is through suppressions that hells are formed in us.

MABEL: *(Looking at Steve, who is tearing his hair.)* Don't you think it would be a good thing, Henrietta, if we went somewhere else? *(They rise and begin to pick up the dishes. Mabel drops a plate which breaks. Henrietta draws up short and looks at her—the psychoanalytic look.)* I'm sorry, Henrietta. One of the Spode plates, too. *(Surprised and re-*

sentful as Henrietta continues to peer at her.) Don't take it so to heart, Henrietta.

HENRIETTA: I can't help taking it to heart.

MABEL: I'll get you another. *(Pause. More sharply as Henrietta does not answer.)* I said I'll get you another plate, Henrietta.

HENRIETTA: It's not the plate.

MABEL: For heaven's sake, what is it then?

HENRIETTA: It's the significant little false movement that made you drop it.

MABEL: Well, I suppose everyone makes a false movement once in a while.

HENRIETTA: Yes, Mabel, but these false movements all mean something.

MABEL: *(About to cry.)* I don't think that's very nice! It was just because I happened to think of that Mabel Snow you were talking about—

HENRIETTA: *Mabel* Snow!

MABEL: Snow—Snow—well, what was her name, then?

HENRIETTA: Her name is Mary. You substituted *your own* name for hers.

MABEL: Well, *Mary* Snow, then; *Mary* Snow. I never heard her name but once. I don't see anything to make such a fuss about.

HENRIETTA: *(Gently.)* Mabel dear—mistakes like that in names—

MABEL: *(Desperately.)* They don't mean something, too, do they?

HENRIETTA: *(Gently.)* I am sorry, dear, but they do.

MABEL: But I'm always doing that!

HENRIETTA: *(After a start of horror.)* My poor little sister, tell me about it.

MABEL: About what?

HENRIETTA: About your not being happy. About your longing for another sort of life.

MABEL: But I *don't.*

HENRIETTA: Ah, I understand these things, dear. You feel Bob is limiting you to a life in which you do not feel free—

MABEL: Henrietta! When did I ever say such a thing?

HENRIETTA: You said you are not in touch with things intellectual. You showed your feeling that it is Bob's profession—that has engendered a resentment which has colored your whole life with him.

MABEL: Why—Henri*et*ta!

HENRIETTA: Don't be afraid of me, little sister. There's nothing can shock me or turn me from you. I am not like that. I wanted you to come for this visit because I had a feeling that you needed more from life than you were getting. No one of these things I have seen would excite my suspicion. It's the combination. You don't eat breakfast *(Enumerating on her fingers);* you make false moves; you substitute your own name for the name of another *whose love is misdirected.* You're nervous; you *look* queer; in your eyes there's a frightened look that is most unlike you. And this dream. A *hen.* Come with me this afternoon to Dr. Russell! Your whole life may be at stake, Mabel.

MABEL: *(Gasping.)* Henrietta, I—you—you always were the smartest in the family, and all that, but—this is terrible! I don't think we *ought* to think such things. *(Brightening.)* Why, I'll tell you why I dreamed I was a hen. It was because last night, telling about that time in Chicago, you said I was as mad as a wet hen.

HENRIETTA: *(Superior.)* Did you dream you were a *wet* hen?

MABEL: *(Forced to admit it.)* No.

HENRIETTA: No. You dreamed you were a *dry* hen. And why, being a hen, were you urged to step?

MABEL: Maybe it's because when I am getting on a street car it always irritates me to have them call "Step lively."

HENRIETTA: No, Mabel, that is only a child's view of it—if you will forgive me. You see merely the elements used in the dream. You do not see into the dream; you do not see its meaning. This dream of the hen—

STEVE: Hen—hen—wet hen—dry hen—mad hen! *(Jumps up in a rage.)* Let me out of this!

HENRIETTA: *(Hastily picking up dishes, speaks soothingly.)* Just a minute, dear, and we'll have things so you can work in quiet. Mabel and I are going to sit in my room.

(She goes out left, carrying dishes.)

STEVE: *(Seizing hat and coat from an alcove near the outside door.)* I'm going to be psychoanalyzed. I'm going now! I'm going straight to that infallible doctor of hers—that priest of this new religion. If he's got honesty enough to tell Henrietta there's nothing the matter with my unconscious mind, perhaps I can be let alone about it, and then I *will* be all right. *(From the door in a low voice.)* Don't tell Henrietta I'm going. It might take weeks, and I couldn't stand all the talk.

(He hurries out.)

HENRIETTA: *(Returning.)* Where's Steve? Gone? *(With a hopeless gesture.)* You see how impatient he is—how unlike himself! I tell you, Mabel, I'm nearly distracted about Steve.

MABEL: I think he's a little distracted, too.

HENRIETTA: Well, if he's gone—you might as well stay here. I have a committee meeting at the book-shop, and will have to leave you to yourself for an hour or two. *(As she puts her hat on, taking it from the alcove where Steve found his, her eye, lighting up almost carnivorously, falls on an enormous volume on the floor beside the work table. The book has been half hidden by the wastebasket. She picks it up and carries it around the table toward Mabel.)* Here, dear, is one of the simplest statements of psychoanalysis. You just read this and then we can talk more intelligently. *(Mabel takes volume and staggers back under its weight to chair rear center, Henrietta goes to outer door, stops and asks abruptly.)* How old is Lyman Eggleston?

MABEL: *(Promptly.)* He isn't forty yet. Why, what made you ask that, Henrietta?

(As she turns her head to look at Henrietta her hands move toward the upper corners of the book balanced on her knees.)

HENRIETTA: Oh, nothing. Au revoir.

(She goes out. Mabel stares at the ceiling. The book slides to the floor. She starts; looks at the book, then at the broken plate on the table.) The plate! The book! *(She lifts her eyes, leans forward elbow on knee, chin on knuckles and plaintively queries)* Am I unhappy?

(Curtain)

Scene II

Two weeks later. The stage is as in Scene I, except that the breakfast table has been removed. During the first few minutes the dusk of a winter afternoon deepens. Out of the darkness spring rows of double street-lights almost meeting in the distance. Henrietta is at the psychoanalytical end of Steve's work-table, surrounded by open books and periodicals, writing. Steve enters briskly.

STEVE: What are you doing, my dear?

HENRIETTA: My paper for the Liberal Club.

STEVE: Your paper on—?

HENRIETTA: On a subject which does not have your sympathy.

STEVE: Oh, I'm not sure I'm wholly out of sympathy with psychoanalysis, Henrietta. You worked it so hard. I couldn't even take a bath without it's meaning something.

HENRIETTA: *(Loftily.)* I talked it because I knew you needed it.

STEVE: You haven't said much about it these last two weeks. Uh—your faith in it hasn't weakened any?

HENRIETTA: Weakened? It's grown stronger with each new thing I've come to know. And Mabel. She is with Dr. Russell now. Dr. Russell is wonderful! From what Mabel tells me I believe his analysis is going to prove that I was right. Today I discovered a remarkable confirmation of my theory in the hen-dream.

STEVE: What is your theory?

HENRIETTA: Well, you know about Lyman Eggleston. I've wondered about him. I've never seen him, but I know he's less bourgeois than Mabel's other friends—more intellectual—and [*Significantly*] she doesn't see much of him because Bob doesn't like him.

STEVE: But what's the confirmation?

HENRIETTA: Today I noticed the first syllable of his name.

STEVE: Ly?

HENRIETTA: No—egg.

STEVE: Egg?

HENRIETTA: *(Patiently.)* Mabel dreamed she was a *hen*. *(Steve laughs.)* You wouldn't laugh if you knew how important names are in interpreting dreams. Freud is full of just such cases in which a whole hidden complex is revealed by a single significant syllable—like this egg.

STEVE: Doesn't the traditional relation of hen and egg suggest rather a maternal feeling?

HENRIETTA: There is something maternal in Mabel's love, of course, but that's only one element.

STEVE: Well, suppose Mabel hasn't a suppressed desire to be this gentleman's mother, but his beloved. What's to be done about it? What about Bob? Don't you think it's going to be a little rough on him?

HENRIETTA: That can't be helped. Bob, like everyone else, must face the facts of life. If Dr. Russell should arrive independently at this same interpretation I shall not hesitate to advise Mabel to leave her present husband.

STEVE: Um—hum! *(The lights go up on Fifth Avenue. Steve goes to the window and looks out.)* How long is it we've lived here, Henrietta?

HENRIETTA: Why, this is the third year, Steve.

STEVE: I—we—one would miss this view if one went away, wouldn't one?

HENRIETTA: How strangely you speak! Oh, Stephen, I *wish* you'd go to Dr. Russell. Don't think my fears have abated because I've been able to restrain myself. I had to on account of Mabel. But now, dear—won't you go?

STEVE: I—*(He breaks off, turns on the light, then comes and sits beside Henrietta.)* How long have we been married, Henrietta?

HENRIETTA: Stephen, I don't understand you! You *must* go to Dr. Russell.

STEVE: I have gone.

HENRIETTA: You—what?

STEVE: *(Jauntily.)* Yes, Henrietta, I've been psyched.

HENRIETTA: You went to Dr. Russell?

STEVE: The same.

HENRIETTA: And what did he say?

STEVE: He said—I—I was a little surprised by what he said, Henrietta.

HENRIETTA: *(Breathlessly.)* Of course—one can so seldom anticipate. But tell me—your dream, Stephen? It means—?

STEVE: It means—I was considerably surprised by what it means.

HENRIETTA: *Don't* be so exasperating!

STEVE: It means—you really want to know, Henrietta?

HENRIETTA: Stephen, you'll drive me mad!

STEVE: He said—of course he may be wrong in what he said.

HENRIETTA: He *isn't* wrong. *Tell* me!

STEVE: He said my dream of the walls receding and leaving me alone in a forest indicates a suppressed desire—

HENRIETTA: Yes—yes!

STEVE: To be freed from—

HENRIETTA: Yes—freed from—?

STEVE: Marriage.

HENRIETTA: *(Crumples. Stares.)* Marriage!

STEVE: He—he may be mistaken, you know.

HENRIETTA: *May* be mistaken?

STEVE: I—well, of course, I hadn't taken any stock in it myself. It was only your great confidence—

HENRIETTA: Stephen, are you telling me that Dr. Russell—Dr. A. E. Russell —told you this? *(Steve nods.)* Told you you have a suppressed desire to separate from *me?*

STEVE: That's what he said.

HENRIETTA: Did he know who you were?

STEVE: Yes.

HENRIETTA: That you were married to me?

STEVE: Yes, he knew that.

HENRIETTA: And he told you to leave me?

STEVE: It seems he must be wrong, Henrietta.

HENRIETTA: *(Rising.)* And I've sent him more patients—I *(Catches herself and resumes coldly.)* What reason did he give for this analysis?

STEVE: He says the confining walls are a symbol of my feeling about marriage and that their fading away is a wish-fulfillment.

HENRIETTA: *(Gulping.)* Well, is it? Do you want our marriage to end?

STEVE: It was a great surprise to me that I did. You see I hadn't known what was in my unconscious mind.

HENRIETTA: *(Flaming.)* What did you tell Dr. Russell about me to make him think you weren't happy?

STEVE: I never told him a thing, Henrietta. He got it all from his confounded clever inferences. I—I tried to refute them, but he said that was only part of my self-protective lying.

HENRIETTA: And that's why you were so—happy—when you came in just now!

STEVE: Why, Henrietta, how can you say such a thing? I was *sad.* Didn't I speak sadly of—of the view? Didn't I ask how long we had been married?

HENRIETTA: Stephen Brewster, have you no sense of the seriousness of this? Dr. Russell doesn't know what our marriage has been. You do. You should have laughed him down! Confined—in life with me? Did you tell him that I *believe* in freedom?

STEVE: I very emphatically told him that his results were a great surprise to me.

HENRIETTA: But you accepted them.

STEVE: Oh, not at all. I merely couldn't refute his arguments. I'm not a psychologist. I came home to talk it over with you. You being a disciple of psychoanalysis—

HENRIETTA: If you are going, I wish you would go tonight!

STEVE: Oh, my dear! I—surely I couldn't do that! Think of my feelings. And my laundry hasn't come home.

HENRIETTA: I ask you to go tonight. Some women would falter at this, Steve, but I am not such a woman. I leave you free. I do not repudiate psychoanalysis; I say again that it has done great things. It has also made mistakes, of course. But since you accept this analysis—*(She sits down and pretends to begin work.)* I have to finish this paper. I wish you would leave me.

STEVE: *(Scratches his head, goes to the inner door.)* I'm sorry, Henrietta, about my unconscious mind.

(Alone, Henrietta's face betrays her outraged state of mind—disconcerted, resentful, trying to pull herself together. She attains an air of bravely bearing an outrageous thing.—The outer door opens and Mabel enters in great excitement.)

MABEL: *(Breathless.)* Henrietta, I'm so glad you're here. And alone? *(Looks toward the inner door.)* Are you alone, Henrietta?

HENRIETTA: *(With reproving dignity.)* Very much so.

MABEL: *(Rushing to her.)* Henrietta, he's found it!

HENRIETTA: *(Aloof.)* Who has found what?

MABEL: Who has found what? Dr. Russell has found my suppressed desire!

HENRIETTA: That is interesting.

MABEL: He finished with me today—he got hold of my complex—in the most amazing way! But, oh, Henrietta—it is so terrible!

HENRIETTA: Do calm yourself, Mabel. Surely there's no occasion for all this agitation.

MABEL: But there is! And when you think of the lives that are affected—the readjustments that must be made in order to bring the suppressed hell out of me and save me from the insane asylum—!

HENRIETTA: The insane asylum!

MABEL: You said that's where these complexes brought people!

HENRIETTA: What did the doctor tell you, Mabel?

MABEL: Oh, I don't know how I can tell you—it is so awful—so unbelievable.

HENRIETTA: I rather have my hand in at hearing the unbelievable.

MABEL: Henrietta, who would ever have thought it? How can it be true? But the doctor is perfectly certain that I have a suppressed desire for—

(Looks at Henrietta, is unable to continue.)

HENRIETTA: Oh, go on, Mabel. I'm not unprepared for what you have to say.

MABEL: Not unprepared? You mean you have suspected it?

HENRIETTA: From the first. It's been my theory all along.

MABEL: But, Henrietta, I didn't know myself that I had this secret desire for Stephen.

HENRIETTA: *(Jumps up.)* Stephen!

MABEL: My brother-in-law! My own sister's husband!

HENRIETTA: *You* have a suppressed desire for *Stephen!*

MABEL: Oh, Henrietta, aren't these unconscious selves terrible? They seem so unlike *us!*

HENRIETTA: What insane thing are you driving at?

MABEL: *(Blubbering.)* Henrietta, don't you use that word to me. I don't *want* to go to the insane asylum.

HENRIETTA: What did Dr. Russell say?

MABEL: Well, you see—oh, it's the strangest thing! But you know the voice in my dream that called "Step, Hen!" Dr. Russell found out today that when I was a little girl I had a story-book in words of one syllable and I read the name Stephen wrong. I used to read it S-t-e-p, step, h-e-n, hen. *(Dramatically.)* Step Hen is Stephen. *(Enter Stephen, his head bent over a time-table.)* Stephen is Step Hen!

STEVE: I? Step Hen?

MABEL: *(Triumphantly.)* S-t-e-p, step, H-e-n, hen, Stephen!

HENRIETTA: *(Exploding.)* Well, what if Stephen is Step Hen? *(Scornfully.)* Step Hen! Step Hen! For that ridiculous coincidence—

MABEL: Coincidence! But it's childish to look at the mere elements of a dream. You have to look *into* it—you have to see what it *means!*

HENRIETTA: On account of that trivial, meaningless play on syllables—on that flimsy basis—you are ready—*(Wails.)* O-h!

STEVE: What on earth's the matter? What has happened? Suppose I *am* Step Hen? What about it? What does it mean?

MABEL: *(Crying.)* It means—that I—have a suppressed desire for *you!*

STEVE: For me! The deuce you have! *(Feebly.)* What—er—makes you think so?

MABEL: Dr. Russell has worked it out scientifically.

HENRIETTA: Yes. Through the amazing discovery that Step Hen equals Stephen!

MABEL: *(Tearfully.)* Oh, that isn't all—that isn't near all. Henrietta won't give me a chance to tell it. She'd rather I'd go to the insane asylum than be unconventional.

HENRIETTA: We'll all go there if you can't control yourself. We are still waiting for some rational report.

MABEL: *(Drying her eyes.)* Oh, there's such a lot about names. *(With some pride.)* I don't see how I ever did it. It all works in together. I dreamed I was a hen because that's the first syllable of *Hen-* rietta's name, and when I dreamed I was a hen, I was putting myself in Henrietta's place.

HENRIETTA: With Stephen?

MABEL: With Stephen.

HENRIETTA: *(Outraged.)* Oh! *(Turns in rage upon Stephen, who is fanning himself with the time-table.)* What are you doing with that time-table?

STEVE: Why—I thought—you were so keen to have me go tonight—I thought I'd just take a run up to Canada, and join Billy—a little shooting—but—

MABEL: But there's more about the names.

HENRIETTA: Mabel, have you thought of Bob—dear old Bob—your good, kind husband?

MABEL: Oh, Henrietta, "my good, kind husband!"

HENRIETTA: Think of him, Mabel, out there alone in Chicago, working his head off, fixing people's *teeth*—for you!

MABEL: Yes, but think of the living Libido—in conflict with petrified moral codes! And think of the perfectly wonderful way the names all prove it. Dr. Russell said he's never seen anything more convincing. Just look at Stephen's last name—Brewster. I dream I'm a hen, and the name Brewster—you have to say its first letter by itself—and then the hen, that's me, she says to him: "Stephen, Be Rooster!"

(Henrietta and Stephen collapse into the nearest chairs.)

MABEL: I think it's perfectly wonderful! Why, if it wasn't for psychoanalysis you'd never find out how wonderful your own mind is!

STEVE: *(Begins to chuckle.)* Be Rooster! Stephen, Be Rooster!

HENRIETTA: You think it's funny, do you?

STEVE: Well, what's to be done about it? Does Mabel have to go away with me?

HENRIETTA: Do you want Mabel to go away with you?

STEVE: Well, but Mabel herself—her complex—her suppressed desire—!

HENRIETTA: *(Going to her.)* Mabel, are you going to insist on going away with Stephen?

MABEL: I'd rather go with Stephen than go to the insane asylum!

HENRIETTA: For heaven's sake, Mabel, drop that insane asylum! If you *did* have a suppressed desire for Stephen hidden away in you—God knows it isn't hidden now. Dr. Russell has brought it into your consciousness —with a vengeance. That's all that's necessary to break up a complex. Psychoanalysis doesn't say you have to *gratify* every suppressed desire.

STEVE: *(Softly.)* Unless it's for Lyman Eggleston.

HENRIETTA: *(Turning on him.)* Well, if it comes to that, Stephen Brewster, I'd like to know why that interpretation of mine isn't as good as this one? Step, Hen!

STEVE: But Be Rooster! *(He pauses, chuckling to himself.)* Step-Hen B-rooster. And *Hen*rietta. Pshaw, my dear, Doc Russell's got you beat a mile! *(He turns away and chuckles.)* Be rooster!

MABEL: What has Lyman Eggleston got to do with it?

STEVE: According to Henrietta, you, the hen, have a suppressed desire for *Egg*-leston, the egg.

MABEL: Henrietta, I think that's indecent of you! He is bald as an egg and little and fat—the idea of you thinking such a thing of me!

HENRIETTA: Well, Bob isn't little and bald and fat! Why don't you stick to your own husband? *(To Stephen.)* What if Dr. Russell's interpretation has got mine "beat a mile"? *(Resentful look at him.)* It would only mean that Mabel doesn't want Eggleston and does want you. Does that mean she has to have you?

MABEL: But you said Mabel Snow—

HENRIETTA: *Mary* Snow! You're not as much like her as you think—substituting your name for hers! The cases are entirely different. Oh, I wouldn't have *believed* this of you, Mabel. *(Beginning to cry.)* I brought you here for a pleasant visit—thought you needed brightening *up*—wanted to be *nice* to you—and now you—my husband—you insist—

(In fumbling her way to her chair she brushes to the floor some sheets from the psychoanalytical table.)

STEVE: *(With solicitude.)* Careful, dear. Your paper on psychoanalysis!

(Gathers up sheets and offers them to her.)

HENRIETTA: I don't want my paper on psychoanalysis! I'm sick of psychoanalysis!

STEVE: *(Eagerly.)* Do you mean that, Henrietta?

HENRIETTA: Why shouldn't I mean it? Look at all I've done for psychoanalysis —and—*(Raising a tear-stained face)* what has psychoanalysis done for me?

STEVE: Do you mean, Henrietta, that you're going to stop *talking* psychoanalysis?

HENRIETTA: Why shouldn't I stop talking it? Haven't I seen what it does to people? Mabel has gone crazy about psychoanalysis!

(At the word "crazy" with a moan Mabel sinks to chair and buries her face in her hands.)

STEVE: *(Solemnly.)* Do you swear never to wake me up in the night to find out what I'm dreaming?

HENRIETTA: Dream what you please—I don't care what you're dreaming.

STEVE: Will you clear off my work-table so the Journal of Morbid Psychology doesn't stare me in the face when I'm trying to plan a house?

HENRIETTA: *(Pushing a stack of periodicals off the table.)* I'll *burn* the Journal of Morbid Psychology!

STEVE: My dear Henrietta, if you're going to separate from psychoanalysis, there's no reason why I should separate from *you.*

(They embrace ardently. Mabel lifts her head and looks at them woefully.)

MABEL: *(Jumping up and going toward them.)* But what about me? What am I to do with my suppressed desire?

STEVE: *(With one arm still around Henrietta, gives Mabel a brotherly hug.)* Mabel, you just keep right on suppressing it!

(Curtain)

QUESTIONS

1. What are the psychoanalytic terms in Henrietta's speeches before Mabel's first entrance? What symptoms has she observed in Steve?
2. How would you characterize Mabel? What kinds of information individualize her? What kinds suggest she is a type?

3. To what extent are Henrietta and Steve individuals? To what extent types?
4. How is it significant that Henrietta and Steve live in New York, in Greenwich Village, while Mabel lives in Chicago?
5. What signs of psychic disturbance does Henrietta find in Mabel's behavior?
6. How would you describe Henrietta's relationship with Mabel? With Steve? What significant changes in the relationships are suggested at the end of the play?

CHAPTER 4

PLAYS FOR STUDY

In this final chapter, we present three plays by modern masters. All begin with the essential dramatic impulse of enactment, creating spectacles where in prose fiction and poetry there are only words. All draw upon the long traditions of the theater, stretching back to the ancient Greeks. All reflect their origins in the twentieth century, from the literal spotlights, shadows, and illuminations of contemporary stagecraft to the metaphorical illuminations of modern psychology.

Our first play, Samuel Beckett's mysterious *Not I,* is nothing more than a scene, strangely puzzling to an audience. We will approach it by reminding ourselves once again that a play is meant to be seen. Reading it in a book, we must struggle to envision the impact of the staging, the lighting, the spatial arrangement, and the concentration on pause and gesture. But because it is in a book, we experience the great advantage of literature—letters formed into words on pages. They are there permanently to ponder, to take in at pleasure, to read and to turn back to and read yet again.

After you read the play, we will give you an interpretation, to suggest the kinds of things you can say about drama and to help you to check your own impressions. If you disagree, so much the better. You will already have something to discuss or to write about. But to get there well primed, give a simple zenlike flick of your mental switches. Imagine yourself in a theater. You know the title. Wonder about it a little. Then read the stage directions slowly, perhaps more than once, until you *see* the darkened theater, and its curtained stage, in your mind's eye and hear the murmuring voice, and watch the curtain draw to reveal the stage's strange display. *Upstage* is back; *downstage* is front, toward the audience. Here we go.

NOT I

Samuel Beckett   (1906–   )

Characters

MOUTH
AUDITOR

Note

Movement: this consists in simple sideways raising of arms from sides and their falling back, in a gesture of helpless compassion. It lessens with each recurrence till scarcely perceptible at third. There is just enough pause to contain it as MOUTH recovers from vehement refusal to relinquish third person.

Stage in darkness but for Mouth, upstage audience right, about 8' above stage level, faintly lit from close-up and below, rest of face in shadow. Invisible microphone. Auditor, downstage audience left, tall standing figure, sex undeterminable, enveloped from head to foot in loose black djellaba, with hood, fully faintly lit, standing on invisible podium about 4' high, shown by attitude alone to be facing diagonally across stage intent on Mouth, dead still throughout but for four brief movements where indicated. See Note.

As house lights down Mouth's voice unintelligible behind curtain. House lights out. Voice continues unintelligible behind curtain, 10 seconds. With rise of curtain ad-libbing from text as required leading when curtain fully up and attention sufficient into:

MOUTH: . . . out . . . into this world . . . this world . . . tiny little thing . . . before its time . . . in a godfor- . . . what? . . . girl? . . . yes . . . tiny little girl . . . into this . . . out into this . . . before her time . . . godforsaken hole called . . . called . . . no matter . . . parents unknown . . . unheard of . . . he having vanished . . . thin air . . . no sooner buttoned up his breeches . . . she similarly . . . eight months later . . . almost to the tick . . . so no love . . . spared that . . . no love such as normally vented on the . . . speechless infant . . . in the home . . . no . . . nor indeed for that matter any of any kind . . . no love of any kind . . . at any subsequent stage . . . so typical affair . . . nothing of any note till coming up to sixty when— . . . what? . . . seventy? . . . good God! . . . coming up to seventy . . . wandering in a field . . . looking aimlessly for cowslips . . . to make a ball . . . a few steps then stop . . . stare into space . . . then on . . . a few more . . . stop and stare again . . . so on . . . drifting around . . . when suddenly . . . gradually . . . all went out . . . all that early April morning light . . . and she found herself in the— . . . what? . . . who? . . . no! . . . she! . . . *(pause and movement 1)* . . . found herself in the dark . . . and if not exactly . . . insentient . . . insentient . . . for she could still hear the buzzing . . . so-called . . . in the ears . . . and a ray of light came

and went . . . came and went . . . such as the moon might cast . . . drifting
. . . in and out of cloud . . . but so dulled . . . feeling . . . feeling so dulled
. . . she did not know . . . what position she was in . . . imagine! . . . what
position she was in! . . . whether standing . . . or sitting . . . but the
brain— . . . what? . . . kneeling? . . . yes . . . whether standing . . . or sitting
. . . or kneeling . . . but the brain— . . . what? . . . lying? . . . yes . . . whether
standing . . . or sitting . . . or kneeling . . . or lying . . . but the brain still
. . . in a way . . . for her first thought was . . . oh long after . . . sudden
flash . . . brought up as she had been to believe . . . with the other waifs
. . . in a merciful . . . *(brief laugh)* . . . God . . . *(good laugh)* . . . first
thought was . . . oh long after . . . sudden flash . . . she was being punished
. . . for her sins . . . a number of which then . . . further proof if proof
were needed . . . flashed through her mind . . . one after another . . . then
dismissed as foolish . . . oh long after . . . this thought dismissed . . . as
she suddenly realized . . . gradually realized . . . she was not suffering
. . . imagine! . . . not suffering! . . . indeed could not remember . . . off-hand
. . . when she had suffered less . . . unless of course she was . . . *meant*
to be suffering . . . ha! . . . *thought* to be suffering . . . just as the odd time
. . . in her life . . . when clearly intended to be having pleasure . . . she
was in fact . . . having none . . . not the slightest . . . in which case of course
. . . that notion of punishment . . . for some sin or other . . . or for the
lot . . . or no particular reason . . . for its own sake . . . thing she understood
perfectly . . . that notion of punishment . . . which had first occurred to
her . . . brought up as she had been to believe . . . with the other waifs
. . . in a merciful . . . *(brief laugh)* . . . God . . . *(good laugh)* . . . first
occurred to her . . . then dismissed . . . as foolish . . . was perhaps not
so foolish . . . after all . . . so on . . . all that . . . vain reasonings . . . till
another thought . . . oh long after . . . sudden flash . . . very foolish really
but— . . . what? . . . the buzzing? . . . yes . . . all the time the buzzing
. . . so-called . . . in the ears . . . though of course actually . . . not in the
ears at all . . . in the skull . . . dull roar in the skull . . . and all the time
this ray or beam . . . like moonbeam . . . but probably not . . . certainly
not . . . always the same spot . . . now bright . . . now shrouded . . . but
always the same spot . . . as no moon could . . . no . . . no moon . . . just
all part of the same wish to . . . torment . . . though actually in point of
fact . . . not in the least . . . not a twinge . . . so far . . . ha! . . . so far
. . . this other thought then . . . oh long after . . . sudden flash . . . very
foolish really but so like her . . . in a way . . . that she might do well to
. . . groan . . . on and off . . . writhe she could not . . . as if in actual
. . . agony . . . but could not . . . could not bring herself . . . some flaw
in her make-up . . . incapable of deceit . . . or the machine . . . more likely
the machine . . . so disconnected . . . never got the message . . . or powerless
to respond . . . like numbed . . . couldn't make the sound . . . not any sound
. . . no sound of any kind . . . no screaming for help for example . . . should
she feel so inclined . . . scream . . . *(screams)* . . . then listen . . . *(silence)*

. . . scream again . . . *(screams again)* . . . then listen again . . . *(silence)*
. . . no . . . spared that . . . all silent as the grave . . . no part— . . . what?
. . . the buzzing? . . . yes . . . all silent but for the buzzing . . . so-called
. . . no part of her moving . . . that she could feel . . . just the eyelids
. . . presumably . . . on and off . . . shut out the light . . . reflex they call
it . . . no feeling of any kind . . . but the lids . . . even best of times
. . . who feels them? . . . opening . . . shutting . . . all that moisture
. . . but the brain still . . . still sufficiently . . . oh very much so! . . . at
this stage . . . in control . . . under control . . . to question even this
. . . for on that April morning . . . so it reasoned . . . that April morning
. . . she fixing with her eye . . . a distant bell . . . as she hastened towards
it . . . fixing it with her eye . . . lest it elude her . . . had not all gone out
. . . all that light . . . of itself . . . without any . . . any . . . on her part
. . . so on . . . so on it reasoned . . . vain questionings . . . and all dead
still . . . sweet silent as the grave . . . when suddenly . . . gradually
. . . she realiz— . . . what? . . . the buzzing? . . . yes . . . all dead still but
for the buzzing . . . when suddenly she realized . . . words were— . . . what?
. . . who? . . . no! . . . she! . . . *(pause and movement 2)* . . . realized
. . . words were coming . . . imagine! . . . words were coming . . . a voice
she did not recognize . . . at first . . . so long since it had sounded . . .
then finally had to admit . . . could be none other . . . than her own
. . . certain vowel sounds . . . she had never heard . . . elsewhere . . . so
that people would stare . . . the rare occasions . . . once or twice a year
. . . always winter some strange reason . . . stare at her uncomprehending
. . . and now this stream . . . steady stream . . . she who had never
. . . on the contrary . . . practically speechless . . . all her days . . . how
she survived! . . . even shopping . . . out shopping . . . busy shopping centre
. . . supermart . . . just hand in the list . . . with the bag . . . old black
shopping bag . . . then stand there waiting . . . any length of time . . .
middle of the throng . . . motionless . . . staring into space . . . mouth half
open as usual . . . till it was back in her hand . . . the bag back in her hand
. . . then pay and go . . . not as much as goodbye . . . how she survived!
. . . and now this stream . . . not catching the half of it . . . not the quarter
. . . no idea . . . what she was saying . . . imagine! . . . no idea what she
was saying! . . . till she began trying to . . . delude herself . . . it was not
hers at all . . . not her voice at all . . . and no doubt would have . . . vital
she should . . . was on the point . . . after long efforts . . . when suddenly
she felt . . . gradually she felt . . . her lips moving . . . imagine! . . . her
lips moving! . . . as of course till then she had not . . . and not alone the
lips . . . the cheeks . . . the jaws . . . the whole face . . . all those—
. . . what? . . . the tongue? . . . yes . . . the tongue in the mouth . . . all
those contortions without which . . . no speech possible . . . and yet in
the ordinary way . . . not felt at all . . . so intent one is . . . on what one
is saying . . . the whole being . . . hanging on its words . . . so that not
only she had . . . had she . . . not only had she . . . to give up . . . admit

hers alone . . . her voice alone . . . but this other awful thought . . . oh long after . . . sudden flash . . . even more awful if possible . . . that feeling was coming back . . . imagine! . . . feeling coming back! . . . starting at the top . . . then working down . . . the whole machine . . . but no . . . spared that . . . the mouth alone . . . so far . . . ha! . . . so far . . . then thinking . . . oh long after . . . sudden flash . . . it can't go on . . . all this . . . all that . . . steady stream . . . straining to hear . . . make something of it . . . and her own thoughts . . . make something of them . . . all— . . . what? . . . the buzzing? . . . yes . . . all the time the buzzing . . . so-called . . . all that together . . . imagine! . . . whole body like gone . . . just the mouth . . . lips . . . cheeks . . . jaws . . . never— . . . what? . . . tongue? . . . yes . . . lips . . . cheeks . . . jaws . . . tongue . . . never still a second . . . mouth on fire . . . stream of words . . . in her ear . . . practically in her ear . . . not catching the half . . . not the quarter . . . no idea what she's saying! . . . imagine! . . . no idea what she's saying! . . . and can't stop . . . no stopping it . . . she who but a moment before . . . but a moment! . . . could not make a sound . . . no sound of any kind . . . now can't stop . . . imagine! . . . can't stop the stream . . . and the whole brain begging . . . something begging in the brain . . . begging the mouth to stop . . . pause a moment . . . if only for a moment . . . and no response . . . as if it hadn't heard . . . or couldn't . . . couldn't pause a second . . . like maddened . . . all that together . . . straining to hear . . . piece it together . . . and the brain . . . raving away on its own . . . trying to make sense of it . . . or make it stop . . . or in the past . . . dragging up the past . . . flashes from all over . . . walks mostly . . . walking all her days . . . day after day . . . a few steps then stop . . . stare into space . . . then on . . . a few more . . . stop and stare again . . . so on . . . drifting around . . . day after day . . . or that time she cried . . . the one time she could remember . . . since she was a baby . . . must have cried as a baby . . . perhaps not . . . not essential to life . . . just the birth cry to get her going . . . breathing . . . then no more till this . . . old hag already . . . sitting staring at her hand . . . where was it? . . . Croker's Acres . . . one evening on the way home . . . home! . . . a little mound in Croker's Acres . . . dusk . . . sitting staring at her hand . . . there in her lap . . . palm upward . . . suddenly saw it wet . . . the palm . . . tears presumably . . . hers presumably . . . no one else for miles . . . no sound . . . just the tears . . . sat and watched them dry . . . all over in a second . . . or grabbing at the straw . . . the brain . . . flickering away on its own . . . quick grab and on . . . nothing there . . . on to the next . . . bad as the voice . . . worse . . . as little sense . . . all that together . . . can't— . . . what? . . . the buzzing . . . yes . . . all the time the buzzing . . . dull roar like falls . . . and the beam . . . flickering on and off . . . starting to move around . . . like moonbeam but not . . . all part of the same . . . keep an eye on that too . . . corner of the eye . . . all that together . . . can't go on . . . God is love . . . she'll be purged . . . back in the field

. . . morning sun . . . April . . . sink face down in the grass . . . nothing but the larks . . . so on . . . grabbing at the straw . . . straining to hear . . . the odd word . . . make some sense of it . . . whole body like gone . . . just the mouth . . . like maddened . . . and can't stop . . . no stopping it . . . something she— . . . something she had to— . . . what? . . . who? . . . no! . . . she! . . . *(pause and movement 3)* . . . something she had to— . . . what? . . . the buzzing? . . . yes . . . all the time the buzzing . . . dull roar . . . in the skull . . . and the beam . . . ferreting around . . . painless . . . so far . . . ha! . . . so far . . . then thinking . . . oh long after . . . sudden flash . . . perhaps something she had to . . . had to . . . tell . . . could that be it? . . . something she had to . . . tell . . . tiny little thing . . . before its time . . . godforsaken hole . . . no love . . . spared that . . . speechless all her days . . . practically speechless . . . how she survived! . . . that time in court . . . what had she to say for herself . . . guilty or not guilty . . . stand up woman . . . speak up woman . . . stood there staring into space . . . mouth half open as usual . . . waiting to be led away . . . glad of the hand on her arm . . . now this . . . something she had to tell . . . could that be it? . . . something that would tell . . . how it was . . . how she— . . . what? . . . had been? . . . yes . . . something that would tell how it had been . . . how she had lived . . . lived on and on . . . guilty or not . . . on and on . . . to be sixty . . . something she— . . . what? . . . seventy? . . . good God! . . . on and on to be seventy . . . something she didn't know herself . . . wouldn't know if she heard . . . then forgiven . . . God is love . . . tender mercies . . . new every morning . . . back in the field . . . April morning . . . face in the grass . . . nothing but the larks . . . pick it up there . . . get on with it from there . . . another few— . . . what? . . . not that? . . . nothing to do with that? . . . nothing she could tell? . . . all right . . . nothing she could tell . . . try something else . . . think of something else . . . oh long after . . . sudden flash . . . not that either . . . all right . . . something else again . . . so on . . . hit on it in the end . . . think everything keep on long enough . . . then forgiven . . . back in the— . . . what? . . . not that either? . . . nothing to do with that either? . . . nothing she could think? . . . all right . . . nothing she could tell . . . nothing she could think . . . nothing she— . . . what? . . . who? . . . no! . . . she! . . . *(pause and movement 4)* . . . tiny little thing . . . out before its time . . . godforsaken hole . . . no love . . . spared that . . . speechless all her days . . . practically speechless . . . even to herself . . . never out loud . . . but not completely . . . sometimes sudden urge . . . once or twice a year . . . always winter some strange reason . . . the long evenings . . . hours of darkness . . . sudden urge to . . . tell . . . then rush out stop the first she saw . . . nearest lavatory . . . start pouring it out . . . steady stream . . . mad stuff . . . half the vowels wrong . . . no one could follow . . . till she saw the stare she was getting . . . then die of shame . . . crawl back in . . . once or twice a year . . . always winter some strange reason . . . long hours of darkness . . . now this . . . this

. . . quicker and quicker . . . the words . . . the brain . . . flickering away like mad . . . quick grab and on . . . nothing there . . . on somewhere else . . . try somewhere else . . . all the time something begging . . . something in her begging . . . begging it all to stop . . . unanswered . . . prayer unanswered . . . or unheard . . . too faint . . . so on . . . keep on . . . trying . . . not knowing what . . . what she was trying . . . what to try . . . whole body like gone . . . just the mouth . . . like maddened . . . so on . . . keep— . . . what? . . . the buzzing? . . . yes . . . all the time the buzzing . . . dull roar like falls . . . in the skull . . . and the beam . . . poking around . . . painless . . . so far . . . ha! . . . so far . . . all that . . . keep on . . . not knowing what . . . what she was— . . . what? . . . who? . . . no! . . . she! . . . SHE! . . . *(pause)* . . . what she was trying . . . what to try . . . no matter . . . keep on . . . *(curtain starts down)* . . . hit on it in the end . . . then back . . . God is love . . . tender mercies . . . new every morning . . . back in the field . . . April morning . . . face in the grass . . . nothing but the larks . . . pick it up—

(Curtain fully down. House dark. Voice continues behind curtain, unintelligible, 10 seconds, ceases as house lights up.)

Now, as you leave your mental theater, somewhat dazed, and wander up your mind's aisle into daylight, you begin to ask again the questions that have nudged you in the dark. Why "not I," with such growing insistence? Why only a "MOUTH," eight feet in the air, like a spot of light in the darkness? Why such unintelligibility? Why an "AUDITOR" who never speaks? Or does he? Though AUDITOR's sex is "undeterminable," and MOUTH's unspecified, which sex does each seem to project?—and in what way?—and why? How have you cast the two roles in your mental staging? What significance do the four "movements" have? What *is* the story, so sparsely and brokenly conveyed? And finally, for a gauge of the author's skill, what is typical of the drama and what not typical?

Well, here is how we would put these thoughts together, in a kind of written meditation from which we might draft an essay. The play's visual impact comes across the darkened footlights as the very essence of lighting, staging, and choreographic gesture pared down to simplest terms. The play has no action, no movement except the lips moving in the faint circle of light and AUDITOR's single repeated "gesture of helpless compassion," which diminishes each time until it disappears and impresses us by its absence. The play has no dialogue. This is a dramatic monologue, broken by eloquent silences, with all the AUDITOR's remarks silent, implied only in MOUTH's responses.

The darkness of the theater and the indistinctness of the figures communicate immediately the mystery that haunts us throughout the play and afterwards, as we try to find meaning in this soul-shaking theatrical experience, itself a search for meaning. Before the curtain rises, we hear unintelligible words coming from total darkness. The curtain rises, and the words grow haltingly distinct. First we notice the mouth, suspended in air, in its dim circle of light, eight feet above the stage, seemingly detached from any body whatsoever—a human being reduced to mouth and words alone. As our eyes accustom to the darkness, we notice the AUDITOR, who is nearer us and to the left, facing MOUTH diagonally across the stage, motionless, but intent, looming over MOUTH from the podium. He seems masculine from his extra height—a "tall standing figure" on a four-foot podium, his nearness to us making him seem even still taller than MOUTH, who, from her story, is distinctly feminine. This tall, motionless, hooded figure suggests the supernatural, as if it were an idol or a god, or a judge, or perhaps even God Himself. It is vaguely phallic, across from the female orifice speaking of copulation and birth. AUDITOR and MOUTH also suggest psychiatrist and patient. These wordless effects, together with the running silences, heighten tremendously the mystery of life, the subject of this incoherent tale of barren existence from the accident of birth to the accident of death toward the age of seventy, the Biblical span of life—but an unnatural life from its prematurity onward. The one circle of dim light concentrates our attention on this simultaneous search for identity and meaning in one's life, through the discovery of language, which makes meaning intelligible. The title says, "This is not I," but the play seems to imply "This *is* I," not only the forlorn mute but all who search for meaning and identity, as do all of us in our lives, however different.

A girl, an illegitimate waif, is born prematurely from a chance copulation and abandoned to some godforsaken hole of an orphanage. The "godforsaken hole" at first seems also to refer to the passageway of insemination and birth. First the mother, then the baby, are forsaken, and the MOUTH, moving in its circle of dim light, a visible hole, conveys an uncanny and slightly obscene impression as it discusses copulation and birth. No love was "vented" on the child, which MOUTH seems to regret even as it assumes that parental love is usually bad— "spared that"—being excessively poured out, almost like excrement. Again, the visual mouth and the words convey a vaguely obscene effect.

The person experienced no love of any kind throughout life. Her prematurity evidently left her moronic and speechless, except that sometimes, in the dark of winter, she would rush out to find the first person, in the nearest public lavatory, and pour out an unintelligible gibberish, trying to express something about herself to someone. Again, with *lavatory* and the outpouring, we have a flicker of obscenity. The darkness of winter and the darkness of the stage, from which words pour out, haltingly seeking expression, seem a psychic inner darkness, a darkness of the soul. The woman has been convicted of some crime, perhaps accosting people in lavatories, and has been unable to speak to defend herself.

Opposite the urge for expression amid winter darkness is the urge of spring, of April light, to find cowslips to form into a ball—natural beauty shaped into coherence, like a world—and to stare into space and wonder. She has cried only once in her life, while sitting on a little mound at dusk in Croker's Acres. The name suggests death and pain: a "croaker" is a killer, and *acres* sounds like things that ache. With this, the little mound suggests a mounded grave. But the crying had been totally silent; evident only from the tears in her hand, and she reaches for some meaning: "grabbing at a straw." The dusk and the search for meaning clearly relate to the dark winter that urges her to find words. The tears seem to flow from some pity for the unfulfillment in death, from some self-pity for a life so lost and meaningless that it seems somehow to represent those qualities in every life, in which we seek for meaning, expression, and communication with others and seem to find little. AUDITOR's four gestures also indicate this "helpless compassion."

Then suddenly in the full light of an April morning, in the bounty of nature that affirms rebirth, she finds herself in the dark, her whole body gone, with no pain, reduced to nothing but a mouth and a dull buzzing in her brain, in the darkness of which a tiny beam of light, like moonlight, flickers and searches, begging for meaning, for a prayer to be answered. Certainly this is death itself: "silent as the grave," the distant bell, "dead still." The MOUTH we see is the woman's mouth, after death, endlessly piecing together the words and meanings she could not find in life, "not knowing what . . . what she was . . . ," but endlessly trying to find out, in our universal search for identity and meaning within the mystery of existence. MOUTH is now her own inner identity, now rejecting yet pitying her former helpless and speechless self, now obsessed with words and meaning and the problem of self, and, contrarily, also begging the words and the search to stop, wanting oblivion. AUDITOR from the first has asked questions, in supernatural silence, to help her get the identity clear, as we see from her answers: " . . . what? . . . girl? . . . yes . . . tiny little girl." AUDITOR seems to want her to affirm the "I" of identity rather than the "Not I" of the title. MOUTH resists identifying herself with the helpless, wordless woman she has risen above in death. From the first, AUDITOR has evidently asked the crucial question as to whether "she" isn't really "I," as we infer from MOUTH's response: " . . . what? . . . who? . . . no! . . . she! . . . ." And this series is always followed by a pause, filled only with the AUDITOR's silent gesture. The pause, as the "Note" tells us, is just enough to allow MOUTH to recover "from a vehement refusal to relinquish third person": she evidently refuses to shift from "she" to "I" (shifting to "you" would be meaningless). With each pause, the "gesture of helpless compassion" diminishes, until no gesture fills the last pause after the last and most vehement denial: ". . . what? . . . who? . . . no! . . . she! . . . SHE! . . . ." The helpless pity has subsided into a resigned helplessness. But MOUTH keeps talking compulsively on and on. Will she ever find the meaning her words seek? Will she ever accept identity with her helpless former self, as "I," with the defensive "Not" erased? The play leaves us wondering.

Yet MOUTH does move from negative to positive. She has laughed at the idea of mercy and God, in telling how the woman, having been brought up in a religious orphanage, had illogically thought that a merciful God punished sins, and that this sudden April darkness was her punishment. MOUTH ends affirming "God is love . . . tender mercies . . . new every morning . . . face in the grass . . . nothing but larks. . . ." The final "pick it up—," as the curtain falls and the words continue on into eternity, is also affirmative, referring to the meaning, the straw, she is picking up continually in her search for identity and meaning, with the voice she has found only in death.

It is a strange and moving play, and strangely affirmative. Or so it seems. It is cryptic enough to admit many other interpretations, but perhaps this summary will help you to ask the questions and suggest the answers. The play arouses our own unexpressed searchings for identity and for answers to the overwhelming questions of why and what life is, and of who we are, really. One is surprised to find Beckett, the puckish nihilist of the modern world, suddenly in company with St. Augustine, affirming, apparently, that one's inner being grows toward the spiritual, in this world and beyond, and the more wonderfully so because we are born in the extremes of the physical, in sin and obscenity—*inter faeces et urinam* ("between, and amid, feces and urine"), in Augustine's starkly accurate physiology.

Beckett's sad and wistful dramatic monologue, with its stunning theatrical impact, does seem to affirm that life has meaning, toward which the soul progresses, even though we cannot now comprehend nor express it, that God is merciful in giving even such a life as this, that in this totally loveless life, beginning in a godforsaken hole, God is love, even if people are not, with mercy new every morning in all the Aprils filled with larks (which sing at heaven's gate, according to Shakespeare and Shelley), Aprils that follow the dark nights of winter where the soul yearns for expression and spring.

Or are we overreading? What *does* Beckett mean? Some ominous hints—no pain, *so far;* the brain's prayer for oblivion, to stop the flow of meaning and agony of knowing; a God omniscient, compassionate, but progressively more helpless—may suggest a darker interpretation that you may wish to explore in class discussion. Or perhaps you can clarify your thoughts by expressing them in writing. Make yourself a thesis asserting what all this does seem to mean. "In spite of obscurity and ambiguity, Beckett's *Not I* seems to suggest that. . . ." And now write an essay to demonstrate it.

THE GLASS MENAGERIE

Although *The Glass Menagerie* is less immediately puzzling than *Not I,* it, too, draws upon the technical possibilities of twentieth-century stagecraft to create a drama remarkably fluid and dreamlike. Again we will want to consider the nonverbal elements of the play—the physical setting, the words projected on a screen, the lighting, the music. The playwright's mind, we may observe, seems cinematic, as his characters talk about the movies and his scenes fade in and out as though they were all projected in the flickering images of a movie theater. The play is not a movie, of course, but it seems to strive in that direction. None of this, we are told, is real. "The play is memory," says Tom in his opening monologue, ". . . it is not realistic." And Tennessee Williams, in implicit acknowledgment of how often these days we sit down to read plays instead of going to the theater to experience them on stage, starts us off with a careful description of what we should visualize when the curtain goes up.

THE GLASS MENAGERIE

Tennessee Williams   (1911–1983)

Nobody, not even the rain, has such small hands.
                                        E. E. Cummings

Scene: An Alley in St. Louis

   Part I. Preparation for a Gentleman Caller.
   Part II. The Gentleman calls.

Time: Now and the Past.

The Characters

AMANDA WINGFIELD *(the mother)* A little woman of great but confused vitality clinging frantically to another time and place. Her characterization must be carefully created, not copied from type. She is not paranoiac, but her life is paranoia. There is much to admire in Amanda, and as much to love and pity as there is to laugh at. Certainly she has endurance and a kind of heroism, and though her foolishness makes her unwittingly cruel at times, there is tenderness in her slight person.

LAURA WINGFIELD *(her daughter)* Amanda, having failed to establish contact with reality, continues to live vitally in her illusions, but Laura's situation is even graver. A childhood illness has left her crippled, one leg slightly shorter than the other, and held in a brace. This defect need not be more than suggested on the stage. Stemming from this, Laura's separation increases till she is like a piece of her own glass collection, too exquisitely fragile to move from the shelf.

TOM WINGFIELD *(her son)* And the narrator of the play. A poet with a job in a warehouse. His nature is not remorseless, but to escape from a trap he has to act without pity.

JIM O'CONNOR *(the gentleman caller)* A nice, ordinary, young man.

Scene I

   The Wingfield apartment is in the rear of the building, one of those vast hive-like conglomerations of cellular living-units that flower as warty growths in overcrowded urban centers of lower middle-class population and are symptomatic of the impulse of this largest and fundamentally enslaved section of American society to avoid fluidity and differentiation and to exist and function as one interfused mass of automatism.
   The apartment faces an alley and is entered by a fire escape, a structure whose name is a touch of accidental poetic truth, for all of these huge buildings are always burning with the slow and implacable fires of human desperation. The fire escape is part of what we see—that is, the landing of it and steps descending from it.
   The scene is memory and is therefore nonrealistic. Memory takes a lot of poetic license. It omits some details; others are exaggerated, according to the emotional

value of the articles it touches, for memory is seated predominantly in the heart.
The interior is therefore rather dim and poetic.

At the rise of the curtain, the audience is faced with the dark, grim rear wall
of the Wingfield tenement. This building is flanked on both sides by dark, narrow
alleys which run into murky canyons of tangled clotheslines, garbage cans, and the
sinister latticework of neighboring fire escapes. It is up and down these side alleys
that exterior entrances and exits are made during the play. At the end of Tom's
opening commentary, the dark tenement wall slowly becomes transparent and
reveals the interior of the ground-floor Wingfield apartment.

Nearest the audience is the living room, which also serves as a sleeping room for
Laura, the sofa unfolding to make her bed. Just beyond, separated from the living
room by a wide arch or second proscenium with transparent faded portieres (or
second curtain), is the dining room. In an old-fashioned whatnot in the living room
are seen scores of transparent glass animals. A blown-up photograph of the father
hangs on the wall of the living room, to the left of the archway. It is the face of
a very handsome young man in a doughboy's First World War cap. He is gallantly
smiling, ineluctably smiling, as if to say "I will be smiling forever."

Also hanging on the wall, near the photograph, are a typewriter keyboard chart
and a Gregg shorthand diagram. An upright typewriter on a small table stands
beneath the charts.

The audience hears and sees the opening scene in the dining room through both
the transparent fourth wall of the building and the transparent gauze portieres of
the dining-room arch. It is during this revealing scene that the fourth wall slowly
ascends, out of sight. This transparent exterior wall is not brought down again until
the very end of the play, during Tom's final speech.

The narrator is an undisguised convention of the play. He takes whatever license
with dramatic convention is convenient to his purposes.

Tom enters, dressed as a merchant sailor, and strolls across to the fire escape.
There he stops and lights a cigarette. He addresses the audience.

TOM: Yes, I have tricks in my pocket, I have things up my sleeve. But I am
the opposite of a stage magician. He gives you illusion that has the
appearance of truth. I give you truth in the pleasant disguise of illusion.

To begin with, I turn back time. I reverse it to that quaint period, the
thirties, when the huge middle class of America was matriculating in a
school for the blind. Their eyes had failed them, or they had failed their
eyes, and so they were having their fingers pressed forcibly down on the
fiery Braille alphabet of a dissolving economy. In Spain there was revolution. Here there was only shouting and confusion. In Spain there was
Guernica. Here there were disturbances of labor, sometimes pretty violent, in otherwise peaceful cities such as Chicago, Cleveland, Saint Louis
. . . This is the social background of the play.

(Music begins to play.)

The play is memory. Being a memory play, it is dimly lighted, it is sentimental, it is not realistic. In memory everything seems to happen to music. That explains the fiddle in the wings. I am the narrator of the play, and also a character in it. The other characters are my mother, Amanda, my sister, Laura, and a gentleman caller who appears in the final scenes. He is the most realistic character in the play, being an emissary from a world of reality that we were somehow set apart from. But since I have a poet's weakness for symbols, I am using this character also as a symbol; he is the long-delayed but always expected something that we live for. There is a fifth character in the play who doesn't appear except in this larger-than-life-size photograph over the mantel. This is our father who left us a long time ago. He was a telephone man who fell in love with long distances; he gave up his job with the telephone company and skipped the light fantastic out of town . . . The last we heard of him was a picture postcard from Mazatlan, on the Pacific coast of Mexico, containing a message of two words: "Hello—Goodbye!" and no address. I think the rest of the play will explain itself. . . .

(Amanda's voice becomes audible through the portieres.)
(Legend on screen: "Où sont les neiges."[1])
(Tom divides the portieres and enters the dining room. Amanda and Laura are seated at a drop-leaf table. Eating is indicated by gestures without food or utensils. Amanda faces the audience. Tom and Laura are seated in profile. The interior has lit up softly and through the scrim we see Amanda and Laura seated at the table.)

AMANDA: *(Calling.)* Tom?

TOM: Yes, Mother.

AMANDA: We can't say grace until you come to the table!

TOM: Coming, Mother. *(He bows slightly and withdraws, reappearing a few moments later in his place at the table.)*

AMANDA: *(To her son.)* Honey, don't *push* with your *fingers.* If you have to push with something, the thing to push with is a crust of bread. And chew —chew! Animals have secretions in their stomachs which enable them to digest food without mastication, but human beings are supposed to chew their food before they swallow it down. Eat food leisurely, son, and really enjoy it. A well-cooked meal has lots of delicious flavors that have to be held in the mouth for appreciation. So chew your food and give your salivary glands a chance to function!

(Tom deliberately lays his imaginary fork down and pushes his chair back from the table.)

[1]From the refrain, "Mais où sont les neiges d'antan?" ("But where are the snows of yesteryear?") from the "Ballade des dames du temps jadis" ("Ballade of the Ladies of Bygone Times") by François Villon (1431–?).

TOM: I haven't enjoyed one bite of this dinner because of your constant directions on how to eat it. It's you that make me rush through meals with your hawklike attention to every bite I take. Sickening—spoils my appetite—all this discussion of—animals' secretion—salivary glands—mastication!

AMANDA: *(Lightly.)* Temperament like a Metropolitan star!

(Tom rises and walks toward the living room.)

You're not excused from the table.

TOM: I'm getting a cigarette.

AMANDA: You smoke too much.

(Laura rises.)

LAURA: I'll bring in the blanc mange.

(Tom remains standing with his cigarette by the portieres.)

AMANDA: *(Rising.)* No, sister, no, sister—you be the lady this time and I'll be the darky.

LAURA: I'm already up.

AMANDA: Resume your seat, little sister—I want you to stay fresh and pretty —for gentlemen callers!

LAURA: *(Sitting down.)* I'm not expecting any gentlemen callers.

AMANDA: *(Crossing out to the kitchenette, airily.)* Sometimes they come when they are least expected! Why, I remember one Sunday afternoon in Blue Mountain—

(She enters the kitchenette.)

TOM: I know what's coming!

LAURA: Yes. But let her tell it.

TOM: Again?

LAURA: She loves to tell it.

(Amanda returns with a bowl of dessert.)

AMANDA: One Sunday afternoon in Blue Mountain—your mother received— *seventeen!*—gentlemen callers! Why, sometimes there weren't chairs enough to accommodate them all. We had to send the nigger over to bring in folding chairs from the parish house.

TOM: *(Remaining at the portieres.)* How did you entertain those gentlemen callers?

AMANDA: I understood the art of conversation!

TOM: I bet you could talk.

AMANDA: Girls in those days *knew* how to talk, I can tell you.

TOM: Yes?

(Image on screen: Amanda as a girl on a porch, greeting callers.)

AMANDA: They knew how to entertain their gentlemen callers. It wasn't enough for a girl to be possessed of a pretty face and a graceful figure—although I wasn't slighted in either respect. She also needed to have a nimble wit and a tongue to meet all occasions.

TOM: What did you talk about?

AMANDA: Things of importance going on in the world! Never anything coarse or common or vulgar.

(She addresses Tom as though he were seated in the vacant chair at the table though he remains by the portieres. He plays this scene as though reading from a script.)

My callers were gentlemen—all! Among my callers were some of the most prominent young planters of the Mississippi Delta—planters and sons of planters!

(Tom motions for music and a spot of light on Amanda. Her eyes lift, her face glows, her voice becomes rich and elegiac.)

(Screen legend: "Où sont les neiges d'antan?")

There was young Champ Laughlin who later became vice-president of the Delta Planters Bank. Hadley Stevenson who was drowned in Moon Lake and left his widow one hundred and fifty thousand in Government bonds. There were the Cutrere brothers, Wesley and Bates. Bates was one of my bright particular beaux! He got in a quarrel with that wild Wainwright boy. They shot it out on the floor of Moon Lake Casino. Bates was shot through the stomach. Died in the ambulance on his way to Memphis. His widow was also well provided-for, came into eight or ten thousand acres, that's all. She married him on the rebound—never loved her—carried my picture on him the night he died! And there was that boy that every girl in the Delta had set her cap for! That beautiful, brilliant young Fitzhugh boy from Greene County!

TOM: What did he leave his widow?

AMANDA: He never married! Gracious, you talk as though all of my old admirers had turned up their toes to the daisies!

TOM: Isn't this the first you've mentioned that still survives?

AMANDA: That Fitzhugh boy went North and made a fortune—came to be known as the Wolf of Wall Street! He had the Midas touch, whatever he touched turned to gold! And I could have been Mrs. Duncan J. Fitzhugh, mind you! But—I picked your *father!*

LAURA: *(Rising.)* Mother, let me clear the table.

AMANDA: No, dear, you go in front and study your typewriter chart. Or practice your shorthand a little. Stay fresh and pretty!—It's almost time for our gentlemen callers to start arriving. *(She flounces girlishly toward the kitchenette.)* How many do you suppose we're going to entertain this afternoon?

(Tom throws down the paper and jumps up with a groan.)

LAURA: *(Alone in the dining room.)* I don't believe we're going to receive any, Mother.

AMANDA: *(Reappearing, airily.)* What? No one—not one? You must be joking!

(Laura nervously echoes her laugh. She slips in a fugitive manner through the half-open portieres and draws them gently behind her. A shaft of very clear light is thrown on her face against the faded tapestry of the curtains. Faintly the music of "The Glass Menagerie" is heard as she continues, lightly.)

Not one gentleman caller? It can't be true! There must be a flood, there must have been a tornado!

LAURA: It isn't a flood, it's not a tornado, Mother. I'm just not popular like you were in Blue Mountain. . . .

(Tom utters another groan. Laura glances at him with a faint, apologetic smile. Her voice catches a little.)

Mother's afraid I'm going to be an old maid.

(The scene dims out with the "Glass Menagerie" music.)

Scene II

On the dark stage the screen is lighted with the image of blue roses. Gradually Laura's figure becomes apparent and the screen goes out. The music subsides.

Laura is seated in the delicate ivory chair at the small claw-foot table. She wears a dress of soft violet material for a kimono—her hair is tied back from her forehead with a ribbon. She is washing and polishing her collection of glass. Amanda appears on the fire escape steps. At the sound of her ascent, Laura catches her breath, thrusts the bowl of ornaments away, and seats herself stiffly before the diagram of the typewriter keyboard as though it held her spellbound. Something has happened to Amanda. It is written in her face as she climbs to the landing: a look that is grim and hopeless and a little absurd. She has on one of those cheap or imitation velvety-looking cloth coats with imitation fur collar. Her hat is five or six years old, one of those dreadful cloche hats that were worn in the late Twenties, and she is clutching an enormous black patent-leather pocketbook with nickel clasps and initials. This is her full-dress outfit, the one she usually wears to the D.A.R. Before entering she looks through the door. She purses her lips, opens her eyes very wide, rolls them upward and shakes her head. Then she slowly lets herself in the door. Seeing her mother's expression Laura touches her lips with a nervous gesture.

LAURA: Hello, Mother, I was—*(She makes a nervous gesture toward the chart on the wall. Amanda leans against the shut door and stares at Laura with a martyred look.)*

AMANDA: Deception? Deception? *(She slowly removes her hat and gloves, continuing the sweet suffering stare. She lets the hat and gloves fall on the floor—a bit of acting.)*

LAURA: *(Shakily.)* How was the D.A.R. meeting?

(Amanda slowly opens her purse and removes a dainty white handkerchief which she shakes out delicately and delicately touches to her lips and nostrils.)

Didn't you go to the D.A.R. meeting, Mother?

AMANDA: *(Faintly, almost inaudibly.)*—No.—No. *(Then more forcibly.)* I did not have the strength—to go to the D.A.R. In fact, I did not have the courage! I wanted to find a hole in the ground and hide myself in it forever! *(She crosses slowly to the wall and removes the diagram of the typewriter keyboard. She holds it in front of her for a second, staring at it sweetly and sorrowfully—then bites her lips and tears it in two pieces.)*

LAURA: *(Faintly.)* Why did you do that, Mother?

(Amanda repeats the same procedure with the chart of the Gregg Alphabet.)

Why are you—

AMANDA: Why? Why? How old are you, Laura?

LAURA: Mother, you know my age.

AMANDA: I thought that you were an adult; it seems that I was mistaken. *(She crosses slowly to the sofa and sinks down and stares at Laura.)*

LAURA: Please don't stare at me, Mother.

(Amanda closes her eyes and lowers her head. There is a ten-second pause.)

AMANDA: What are we going to do, what is going to become of us, what is the future?

(There is another pause.)

LAURA: Has something happened, Mother?

(Amanda draws a long breath, takes out the handkerchief again, goes through the dabbing process.)

Mother, has—something happened?

AMANDA: I'll be all right in a minute, I'm just bewildered—*(She hesitates.)*—by life. . . .

LAURA: Mother, I wish that you would tell me what's happened!

AMANDA: As you know, I was supposed to be inducted into my office at the D.A.R. this afternoon.

(Screen image: A swarm of typewriters.*)*

But I stopped off at Rubicam's Business College to speak to your teachers about your having a cold and ask them what progress they thought you were making down there.

LAURA: Oh. . . .

AMANDA: I went to the typing instructor and introduced myself as your mother. She didn't know who you were. "Wingfield," she said, "We don't have any such student enrolled at the school!" I assured her she did, that you had been going to classes since early in January. "I wonder," she said, "If you could be talking about that terribly shy little girl who dropped out of school after only a few days' attendance?" "No," I said, "Laura, my daughter, has been going to school every day for the past six weeks!" "Excuse me," she said. She took the attendance book out and there was your name, unmistakably printed, and all the dates you were absent until they decided that you had dropped out of school. I still said, "No, there must have been some mistake! There must have been some mix-up in the records!" And she said, "No—I remember her perfectly now. Her hands shook so that she couldn't hit the right keys! The first time we gave a speed test, she broke down completely—was sick at the stomach and almost had to be carried into the wash room! After that morning she never showed up any more. We phoned the house but never got any answer"—While I was working at Famous-Barr, I suppose, demonstrating those—

(She indicates a brassiere with her hands.)

Oh! I felt so weak I could barely keep on my feet! I had to sit down while they got me a glass of water! Fifty dollars' tuition, all of our plans—my hopes and ambitions for you—just gone up the spout, just gone up the spout like that.

(Laura draws a long breath and gets awkwardly to her feet. She crosses to the Victrola and winds it up.)

What are you doing?

LAURA: Oh! *(She releases the handle and returns to her seat.)*

AMANDA: Laura, where have you been going when you've gone out pretending that you were going to business college?

LAURA: I've just been going out walking.

AMANDA: That's not true.

LAURA: It is. I just went walking.

AMANDA: Walking? Walking? In winter? Deliberately courting pneumonia in that light coat? Where did you walk to, Laura?

LAURA: All sorts of places—mostly in the park.

AMANDA: Even after you'd started catching that cold?

LAURA: It was the lesser of two evils, Mother.

(Screen image: Winter scene in a park.*)*

I couldn't go back there. I—threw up—on the floor!

AMANDA: From half past seven till after five every day you mean to tell me you walked around in the park, because you wanted to make me think that you were still going to Rubicam's Business College?

LAURA: It wasn't as bad as it sounds. I went inside places to get warmed up.

AMANDA: Inside where?

LAURA: I went in the art museum and the bird houses at the Zoo. I visited the penguins every day! Sometimes I did without lunch and went to the movies. Lately I've been spending most of my afternoons in the Jewel Box, that big glass house where they raise the tropical flowers.

AMANDA: You did all this to deceive me, just for deception? *(Laura looks down.)* Why?

LAURA: Mother, when you're disappointed, you get that awful suffering look on your face, like the picture of Jesus' mother in the museum!

AMANDA: Hush!

LAURA: I couldn't face it.

(There is a pause. A whisper of strings is heard. Legend on screen: "The Crust of Humility.")

AMANDA: *(Hopelessly fingering the huge pocketbook.)* So what are we going to do the rest of our lives? Stay home and watch the parades go by? Amuse ourselves with the glass menagerie, darling? Eternally play those worn-out phonograph records your father left as a painful reminder of him? We won't have a business career—we've given that up because it gave us nervous indigestion! *(She laughs wearily.)* What is there left but dependency all our lives? I know so well what becomes of unmarried women who aren't prepared to occupy a position. I've seen such pitiful cases in the South—barely tolerated spinsters living upon the grudging patronage of sister's husband or brother's wife!—stuck away in some little mouse-trap of a room—encouraged by one in-law to visit another—little birdlike women without any nest—eating the crust of humility all their life!
Is that the future that we've mapped out for ourselves? I swear it's the only alternative I can think of! *(She pauses.)* It isn't a very pleasant alternative, is it? *(She pauses again.)* Of course—some girls *do marry.*

(Laura twists her hands nervously.)

Haven't you ever liked some boy?

LAURA: Yes. I liked one once. *(She rises.)* I came across his picture a while ago.

AMANDA: *(With some interest.)* He gave you his picture?

LAURA: No, it's in the yearbook.

AMANDA: *(Disappointed.)* Oh—a high school boy.

(Screen image: Jim as the high school hero bearing a silver cup.)

LAURA: Yes. His name was Jim. *(She lifts the heavy annual from the claw-foot table.)* Here he is in *The Pirates of Penzance.*

AMANDA: *(Absently.)* The what?

LAURA: The operetta the senior class put on. He had a wonderful voice and we sat across the aisle from each other Mondays, Wednesdays and Fridays in the Aud. Here he is with the silver cup for debating! See his grin?

AMANDA: *(Absently.)* He must have had a jolly disposition.

LAURA: He used to call me—Blue Roses.

(Screen image: Blue roses*)*

AMANDA: Why did he call you such a name as that?

LAURA: When I had that attack of pleurosis—he asked me what was the matter when I came back. I said pleurosis—he thought that I said Blue Roses! So that's what he always called me after that. Whenever he saw me, he'd holler, "Hello, Blue Roses!" I didn't care for the girl that he went out with. Emily Meisenbach. Emily was the best-dressed girl at Soldan. She never struck me, though, as being sincere . . . It says in the Personal Section—they're engaged. That's—six years ago! They must be married by now.

AMANDA: Girls that aren't cut out for business careers usually wind up married to some nice man. *(She gets up with a spark of revival.)* Sister, that's what you'll do!

(Laura utters a startled, doubtful laugh. She reaches quickly for a piece of glass.)

LAURA: But, Mother—

AMANDA: Yes? *(She goes over to the photograph.)*

LAURA: *(In a tone of frightened apology.)* I'm—crippled!

AMANDA: Nonsense! Laura, I've told you never, never to use that word. Why, you're not crippled, you just have a little defect—hardly noticeable, even! When people have some slight disadvantage like that, they cultivate other things to make up for it—develop charm—and vivacity—and—*charm!* That's all you have to do! *(She turns again to the photograph.)* One thing your father had *plenty of*—was *charm!*

(The scene fades out with music.)

Scene III

Legend on screen: "After the fiasco—"
Tom speaks from the fire escape landing.

TOM: After the fiasco at Rubicam's Business College, the idea of getting a gentleman caller for Laura began to play a more and more important part in Mother's calculations. It became an obsession. Like some archetype of the universal unconscious, the image of the gentleman caller haunted our small apartment. . . .

(Screen image: A young man at the door of a house with flowers.*)*

An evening at home rarely passed without some allusion to this image, this specter, this hope. . . . Even when he wasn't mentioned, his presence hung in Mother's preoccupied look and in my sister's frightened, apologetic manner—hung like a sentence passed upon the Wingfields!

Mother was a woman of action as well as words. She began to take logical steps in the planned direction. Late that winter and in the early spring—realizing that extra money would be needed to properly feather the nest and plume the bird—she conducted a vigorous campaign on the telephone, roping in subscribers to one of those magazines for matrons called *The Homemaker's Companion,* the type of journal that features the serialized sublimations of ladies of letters who think in terms of delicate cuplike breasts, slim, tapering waists, rich, creamy thighs, eyes like wood smoke in autumn, fingers that soothe and caress like strains of music, bodies as powerful as Etruscan sculpture.

(Screen image: The cover of a glamor magazine.*)*
(Amanda enters with the telephone on a long extension cord. She is spotlighted in the dim stage.)

AMANDA: Ida Scott? This is Amanda Wingfield! We *missed* you at the D.A.R. last Monday! I said to myself: She's probably suffering with that sinus condition!

How is that sinus condition?

Horrors! Heaven have mercy!—You're a Christian martyr, yes, that's what you are, a Christian martyr!

Well, I just now happened to notice that your subscription to the *Companion*'s about to expire! Yes, it expires with the next issue, honey! —just when that wonderful new serial by Bessie Mae Hopper is getting off to such an exciting start. Oh, honey, it's something that you can't miss! You remember how *Gone with the Wind* took everybody by storm! You simply couldn't go out if you hadn't read it. All everybody *talked* was Scarlett O'Hara. Well, this is a book that critics already compare to *Gone with the Wind.* It's the *Gone with the Wind* of the post-World-War generation!—What?—Burning?—Oh, honey, don't let them burn, go take a look in the oven and I'll hold the wire! Heavens—I think she's hung up!

(The scene dims out.)
(Legend on screen: "You think I'm in love with Continental Shoemakers?"*)*
(Before the lights come up again, the violent voices of Tom and Amanda are heard. They are quarreling behind the portieres. In front of them stands Laura with clenched hands and panicky expression. A clear pool of light on her figure throughout this scene.)

TOM: What in Christ's name am I—
AMANDA: *(Shrilly.)* Don't you use that—
TOM: —supposed to do?
AMANDA: —expression! Not in my—
TOM: Ohhh!
AMANDA: —presence! Have you gone out of your senses?

TOM: I have, that's true, *driven* out!

AMANDA: What is the matter with you, you—big—big—IDIOT!

TOM: Look!—I've got *no thing,* no single thing—

AMANDA: Lower your voice!

TOM: —in my life here that I can call my OWN! Everything is—

AMANDA: Stop that shouting!

TOM: Yesterday you confiscated my books! You had the nerve to—

AMANDA: I took that horrible novel back to the library—yes! That hideous book by that insane Mr. Lawrence.

(Tom laughs wildly.)

I cannot control the output of diseased minds or people who cater to them—

(Tom laughs still more wildly.)

BUT I WON'T ALLOW SUCH FILTH BROUGHT INTO MY HOUSE! No, no, no, no, no!

TOM: House, house! Who pays rent on it, who makes a slave of himself to—

AMANDA: *(Fairly screeching.)* Don't you DARE to—

TOM: No, no, *I* mustn't say things! *I've* got to just—

AMANDA: Let me tell you—

TOM: I don't want to hear any more!

(He tears the portieres open. The dining-room area is lit with a turgid smoky red glow. Now we see Amanda; her hair is in metal curlers and she is wearing a very old bathrobe, much too large for her slight figure, a relic of the faithless Mr. Wingfield. The upright typewriter now stands on the drop-leaf table, along with a wild disarray of manuscripts. The quarrel was probably precipitated by Amanda's interruption of Tom's creative labor. A chair lies overthrown on the floor. Their gesticulating shadows are cast on the ceiling by the fiery glow.)

AMANDA: You *will* hear more, you—

TOM: No, I won't hear more, I'm going out!

AMANDA: You come right back in—

TOM: Out, out, out! Because I'm—

AMANDA: Come back here, Tom Wingfield! I'm not through talking to you!

TOM: Oh, go—

LAURA: *(Desperately.)*—Tom!

AMANDA: You're going to listen, and no more insolence from you! I'm at the end of my patience!

(He comes back toward her.)

TOM: What do you think I'm at? Aren't I supposed to have any patience to reach the end of, Mother? I know, I know. It seems unimportant to you, what I'm *doing*—what I *want* to do—having a little *difference* between them! You don't think that—

AMANDA: I think you've been doing things that you're ashamed of. That's why you act like this. I don't believe that you go every night to the movies. Nobody goes to the movies night after night. Nobody in their right mind goes to the movies as often as you pretend to. People don't go to the movies at nearly midnight, and movies don't let out at two A.M. Come in stumbling. Muttering to yourself like a maniac! You get three hours' sleep and then go to work. Oh, I can picture the way you're doing down there. Moping, doping, because you're in no condition!

TOM: *(Wildly.)* No, I'm in no condition!

AMANDA: What right have you got to jeopardize your job? Jeopardize the security of us all? How do you think we'd manage if you were—

TOM: Listen! You think I'm crazy about the *warehouse?* *(He bends fiercely toward her slight figure.)* You think I'm in love with the Continental Shoemakers? You think I want to spend fifty-five *years* down there in that —*celotex interior!* with—*fluorescent—tubes!* Look! I'd rather somebody picked up a crowbar and battered out my brains—than go back mornings! I *go!* Every time you come in yelling that Goddamn *"Rise and Shine!"* *"Rise and Shine!"* I say to myself, "How *lucky dead* people are!" But I get up. I *go!* For sixty-five dollars a month I give up all that I dream of doing and being *ever!* And you say self—*self's* all I ever think of. Why, listen, if self is what I thought of, Mother, I'd be where he is—GONE! *(He points to his father's picture.)* As far as the system of transportation reaches! *(He starts past her. She grabs his arm.)* Don't grab at me, Mother!

AMANDA: Where are you going?

TOM: I'm going to the *movies!*

AMANDA: I don't believe that lie!

(Tom crouches toward her, overtowering her tiny figure. She backs away, gasping.)

TOM: I'm going to opium dens! Yes, opium dens, dens of vice and criminals' hangouts, Mother. I've joined the Hogan Gang, I'm a hired assassin, I carry a tommy gun in a violin case! I run a string of cat houses in the Valley! They call me Killer, Killer Wingfield, I'm leading a double-life, a simple, honest warehouse worker by day, by night a dynamic *czar* of the *underworld, Mother.* I go to gambling casinos, I spin away fortunes on the roulette table! I wear a patch over one eye and a false mustache, sometimes I put on green whiskers. On those occasions they call me—*El Diablo!* Oh, I could tell you many things to make you sleepless! My enemies plan to dynamite this place. They're going to blow us all sky-high some night! I'll be glad, very happy, and so will you! You'll go up, up on a broomstick, over Blue Mountain with seventeen gentlemen callers! You ugly—babbling old—*witch.* . . . *(He goes through a series of violent, clumsy movements, seizing his overcoat, lunging to the door, pulling it fiercely open. The women watch him, aghast. His arm catches in the sleeve of the coat as he struggles to pull it on. For a moment he is pinioned by the bulky garment. With an outraged groan he tears the coat off again, splitting the*

shoulder of it, and hurls it across the room. It strikes against the shelf of Laura's glass collection, and there is a tinkle of shattering glass. Laura cries out as if wounded.)
(Music.)
(Screen legend: "The Glass Menagerie.")

LAURA: *(Shrilly.)* My glass!—menagerie. . . . *(She covers her face and turns away.)*

(But Amanda is still stunned and stupefied by the "ugly witch" so that she barely notices this occurrence. Now she recovers her speech.)

AMANDA: *(In an awful voice.)* I won't speak to you—until you apologize!

(She crosses through the portieres and draws them together behind her. Tom is left with Laura. Laura clings weakly to the mantel with her face averted. Tom stares at her stupidly for a moment. Then he crosses to the shelf. He drops awkwardly on his knees to collect the fallen glass, glancing at Laura as if he would speak but couldn't.)
("The Glass Menagerie" music steals in as the scene dims out.)

Scene IV

The interior of the apartment is dark. There is a faint light in the alley. A deep-voiced bell in a church is tolling the hour of five.

Tom appears at the top of the alley. After each solemn boom of the bell in the tower, he shakes a little noisemaker or rattle as if to express the tiny spasm of man in contrast to the sustained power and dignity of the Almighty. This and the unsteadiness of his advance make it evident that he has been drinking. As he climbs the few steps to the fire escape landing light steals up inside. Laura appears in the front room in a nightdress. She notices that Tom's bed is empty. Tom fishes in his pockets for his door key, removing a motley assortment of articles in the search, including a shower of movie ticket stubs and an empty bottle. At last he finds the key, but just as he is about to insert it, it slips from his fingers. He strikes a match and crouches below the door.

TOM: *(Bitterly.)* One crack—and it falls through!

(Laura opens the door.)

LAURA: Tom! Tom, what are you doing?
TOM: Looking for a door key.
LAURA: Where have you been all this time?
TOM: I have been to the movies.
LAURA: All this time at the movies?
TOM: There was a very long program. There was a Garbo picture and a Mickey Mouse and a travelogue and a newsreel and a preview of coming attractions. And there was an organ solo and a collection for the Milk Fund

—simultaneously—which ended up in a terrible fight between a fat lady and an usher!

LAURA: *(Innocently.)* Did you have to stay through everything?

TOM: Of course! And, oh, I forgot! There was a big stage show! The headliner on this stage show was Malvolio the Magician. He performed wonderful tricks, many of them, such as pouring water back and forth between pitchers. First it turned to wine and then it turned to beer and then it turned to whisky. I know it was whisky it finally turned into because he needed somebody to come up out of the audience to help him, and I came up—both shows! It was Kentucky Straight Bourbon. A very generous fellow, he gave souvenirs. *(He pulls from his back pocket a shimmering rainbow-colored scarf.)* He gave me this. This is his magic scarf. You can have it, Laura. You wave it over a canary cage and you get a bowl of goldfish. You wave it over the goldfish bowl and they fly away canaries. . . . But the wonderfullest trick of all was the coffin trick. We nailed him into a coffin and he got out of the coffin without removing one nail. *(He has come inside.)* There is a trick that would come in handy for me—get me out of this two-by-four situation! *(He flops onto the bed and starts removing his shoes.)*

LAURA: Tom—shhh!

TOM: What're you shushing me for?

LAURA: You'll wake up Mother.

TOM: Goody, goody! Pay 'er back for all those "Rise an' Shines." *(He lies down, groaning.)* You know it don't take much intelligence to get yourself into a nailed-up coffin, Laura. But who in hell ever got himself out of one without removing one nail?

(As if in answer, the father's grinning photograph lights up. The scene dims out.) (Immediately following, the church bell is heard striking six. At the sixth stroke the alarm clock goes off in Amanda's room, and after a few moments we hear her calling: "Rise and Shine! Rise and Shine! Laura, go tell your brother to rise and shine!")

TOM: *(Sitting up slowly.)* I'll rise—but I won't shine.

(The light increases.)

AMANDA: Laura, tell your brother his coffee is ready.

(Laura slips into the front room.)

LAURA: Tom!—It's nearly seven. Don't make Mother nervous.

(He stares at her stupidly.)

(Beseechingly.) Tom, speak to Mother this morning. Make up with her, apologize, speak to her!

TOM: She won't to me. It's her that started not speaking.

LAURA: If you just say you're sorry she'll start speaking.

TOM: Her not speaking—is that such a tragedy?

LAURA: Please—please!

AMANDA: *(Calling from the kitchenette.)* Laura, are you going to do what I asked you to do, or do I have to get dressed and go out myself?

LAURA: Going, going—soon as I get on my coat!

(She pulls on a shapeless felt hat with a nervous, jerky movement, pleadingly glancing at Tom. She rushes awkwardly for her coat. The coat is one of Amanda's, inaccurately made-over, the sleeves too short for Laura.)

Butter and what else?

AMANDA: *(Entering from the kitchenette.)* Just butter. Tell them to charge it.

LAURA: Mother, they make such faces when I do that.

AMANDA: Sticks and stones can break our bones, but the expression on Mr. Garfinkel's face won't harm us! Tell your brother his coffee is getting cold.

LAURA: *(At the door.)* Do what I asked you, will you, will you, Tom?

(He looks sullenly away.)

AMANDA: Laura, go now or just don't go at all!

LAURA: *(Rushing out.)* Going—going!

(A second later she cries out. Tom springs up and crosses to the door. Tom opens the door.)

TOM: Laura?

LAURA: I'm all right. I slipped, but I'm all right.

AMANDA: *(Peering anxiously after her.)* If anyone breaks a leg on those fire-escape steps, the landlord ought to be sued for every cent he possesses!

(She shuts the door. Now she remembers she isn't speaking to Tom and returns to the other room.)
(As Tom comes listlessly for his coffee, she turns her back to him and stands rigidly facing the window on the gloomy gray vault of the areaway. Its light on her face with its aged but childish features is cruelly sharp, satirical as a Daumier print.)
(The music of "Ave Maria," is heard softly.)
(Tom glances sheepishly but sullenly at her averted figure and slumps at the table. The coffee is scalding hot; he sips it and gasps and spits it back in the cup. At his gasp, Amanda catches her breath and half turns. Then she catches herself and turns back to the window. Tom blows on his coffee, glancing sidewise at his mother. She clears her throat. Tom clears his. He starts to rise, sinks back down again, scratches his head, clears his throat again. Amanda coughs. Tom raises his cup in both hands to blow on it, his eyes staring over the rim of it at his mother for several moments. Then he slowly sets the cup down and awkwardly and hesitantly rises from the chair.)

TOM: *(Hoarsely.)* Mother. I—I apologize, Mother.

(Amanda draws a quick, shuddering breath. Her face works grotesquely. She breaks into childlike tears.)

> I'm sorry for what I said, for everything that I said, I didn't mean it.

AMANDA: *(Sobbingly.)* My devotion has made me a witch and so I make myself hateful to my children!

TOM: *No,* you *don't.*

AMANDA: I worry so much, don't sleep, it makes me nervous!

TOM: *(Gently.)* I understand that.

AMANDA: I've had to put up a solitary battle all these years. But you're my right-hand bower! Don't fall down, don't fail!

TOM: *(Gently.)* I try, Mother.

AMANDA: *(With great enthusiasm.)* Try and you will *succeed!* *(The notion makes her breathless.)* Why, you—you're just *full* of natural endowments! Both of my children—they're *unusual* children! Don't you think I know it? I'm so—*proud!* Happy and—feel I've—so much to be thankful for but —promise me one thing, son!

TOM: What, Mother?

AMANDA: Promise, son, you'll—never be a drunkard!

TOM: *(Turns to her grinning.)* I will never be a drunkard, Mother.

AMANDA: That's what frightened me so, that you'd be drinking! Eat a bowl of Purina!

TOM: Just coffee, Mother.

AMANDA: Shredded wheat biscuit?

TOM: No. No, Mother, just coffee.

AMANDA: You can't put in a day's work on an empty stomach. You've got ten minutes—don't gulp! Drinking too-hot liquids makes cancer of the stomach. . . . Put cream in.

TOM: No, thank you.

AMANDA: To cool it.

TOM: No! No, thank you, I want it black.

AMANDA: I know, but it's not good for you. We have to do all that we can do to build ourselves up. In these trying times we live in, all that we have to cling to is—each other. . . . That's why it's so important to—Tom, I —I sent out your sister so I could discuss something with you. If you hadn't spoken I would have spoken to you. *(She sits down.)*

TOM: *(Gently.)* What is it, Mother, that you want to discuss?

AMANDA: *Laura!*

(Tom puts his cup down slowly.)
(Legend on screen: "Laura." Music: "The Glass Menagerie.")

TOM: —Oh.—Laura. . . .

AMANDA: *(Touching his sleeve.)* You know how Laura is. So quiet but—still water runs deep! She notices things and I think she—broods about them.

(Tom looks up.)

A few days ago I came in and she was crying.

TOM: What about?

AMANDA: You.

TOM: Me?

AMANDA: She has an idea that you're not happy here.

TOM: What gave her that idea?

AMANDA: What gives her any idea? However, you do act strangely. I—I'm not criticizing, understand *that!* I know your ambitions do not lie in the warehouse, that like everybody in the whole wide world—you've had to —make sacrifices, but—Tom—Tom—life's not easy, it calls for—Spartan endurance! There's so many things in my heart that I cannot describe to you! I've never told you but I—*loved* your father. . . .

TOM: *(Gently.)* I know that, Mother.

AMANDA: And you—when I see you taking after his ways! Staying out late— and—well, you *had* been drinking the night you were in that—terrifying condition! Laura says that you hate the apartment and that you go out nights to get away from it! Is that true, Tom?

TOM: No. You say there's so much in your heart that you can't describe to me. That's true of me, too. There's so much in my heart that I can't describe to *you!* So let's respect each other's—

AMANDA: But, why—*why,* Tom—are you always so *restless?* Where do you *go* to, nights?

TOM: I—go to the movies.

AMANDA: Why do you go to the movies so much, Tom?

TOM: I go to the movies because—I like adventure. Adventure is something I don't have much of at work, so I go to the movies.

AMANDA: But, Tom, you go to the movies *entirely* too *much!*

TOM: I like a lot of adventure.

(Amanda looks baffled, then hurt. As the familiar inquisition resumes, Tom becomes hard and impatient again. Amanda slips back into her querulous attitude toward him.)
(Image on screen: A sailing vessel with Jolly Roger.)

AMANDA: Most young men find adventure in their careers.

TOM: Then most young men are not employed in a warehouse.

AMANDA: The world is full of young men employed in warehouses and offices and factories.

TOM: Do all of them find adventure in their careers?

AMANDA: They do or they do without it! Not everybody has a craze for adventure.

TOM: Man is by instinct a lover, a hunter, a fighter, and none of those instincts are given much play at the warehouse!

AMANDA: Man is by instinct! Don't quote instinct to me! Instinct is something that people have got away from! It belongs to animals! Christian adults don't want it!

TOM: What do Christian adults want, then, Mother?

AMANDA: Superior things! Things of the mind and the spirit! Only animals have to satisfy instincts! Surely your aims are somewhat higher than theirs! Than monkeys—pigs—

TOM: I reckon they're not.

AMANDA: You're joking. However, that isn't what I wanted to discuss.

TOM: *(Rising.)* I haven't much time.

AMANDA: *(Pushing his shoulders.)* Sit down.

TOM: You want me to punch in red at the warehouse, Mother?

AMANDA: You have five minutes. I want to talk about Laura.

(Screen legend: "Plans and Provisions."*)*

TOM: All right! What about Laura?

AMANDA: We have to be making some plans and provisions for her. She's older than you, two years, and nothing has happened. She just drifts along doing nothing. It frightens me terribly how she just drifts along.

TOM: I guess she's the type that people call home girls.

AMANDA: There's no such type, and if there is, it's a pity! That is unless the home is hers, with a husband!

TOM: What?

AMANDA: Oh, I can see the handwriting on the wall as plain as I see the nose in front of my face! It's terrifying! More and more you remind me of your father! He was out all hours without explanation!—Then *left! Goodbye!* And me with the bag to hold. I saw that letter you got from the Merchant Marine. I know what you're dreaming of. I'm not standing here blindfolded. *(She pauses.)* Very well, then. Then *do* it! But not till there's somebody to take your place.

TOM: What do you mean?

AMANDA: I mean that as soon as Laura has got somebody to take care of her, married, a home of her own, independent—why, then you'll be free to go wherever you please, on land, on sea, whichever way the wind blows you! But until that time you've got to look out for your sister. I don't say me because I'm old and don't matter! I say for your sister because she's young and dependent.

I put her in business college—a dismal failure! Frightened her so it made her sick at the stomach. I took her over to the Young People's League at the church. Another fiasco. She spoke to nobody, nobody spoke to her. Now all she does is fool with those pieces of glass and play those worn-out records. What kind of a life is that for a girl to lead?

TOM: What can I do about it?

AMANDA: Overcome selfishness! Self, self, self is all that you think of!

(Tom springs up and crosses to get his coat. It is ugly and bulky. He pulls on a cap with earmuffs.)

Where is your muffler? Put your wool muffler on!

(He snatches it angrily from the closet, tosses it around his neck and pulls both ends tight.)

Tom! I haven't said what I had in mind to ask you.

TOM: I'm too late to—

AMANDA: *(Catching his arm—very importunately; then shyly.)* Down at the warehouse, aren't there some—nice young men?

TOM: No!

AMANDA: There *must* be—*some* . . .

TOM: Mother—*(He gestures.)*

AMANDA: Find out one that's clean-living—doesn't drink and ask him out for sister!

TOM: What?

AMANDA: For *sister!* To *meet!* Get *acquainted!*

TOM: *(Stamping to the door.)* Oh, my *go-osh!*

AMANDA: Will you?

(He opens the door. She says, imploringly.)

Will you?

(He starts down the fire escape.)

Will you? *Will* you, dear?

TOM: *(Calling back.)* Yes!

(Amanda closes the door hesitantly and with a troubled but faintly hopeful expression.)
(Screen image: The cover of a glamor magazine.)
(The spotlight picks up Amanda at the phone.)

AMANDA: Ella Cartwright? This is Amanda Wingfield! How are you, honey? How is that kidney condition?

(There is a five-second pause.)

Horrors!

(There is another pause.)

You're a Christian martyr, yes, honey, that's what you are, a Christian martyr! Well, I just now happened to notice in my little red book that your subscription to the *Companion* has just run out! I knew that you wouldn't want to miss out on the wonderful serial starting in this new issue. It's by Bessie Mae Hopper, the first thing she's written since *Honeymoon for Three.* Wasn't that a strange and interesting story? Well, this one is even lovelier, I believe. It has a sophisticated, society background. It's all about the horsey set on Long Island!

(The light fades out.)

Scene V

Legend on the screen: "Annunciation."
Music is heard as the light slowly comes on.

It is early dusk of a spring evening. Supper has just been finished in the Wingfield apartment. Amanda and Laura, in light-colored dresses, are removing dishes from the table in the dining room, which is shadowy, their movements formalized almost as a dance or ritual, their moving forms as pale and silent as moths. Tom, in white shirt and trousers, rises from the table and crosses toward the fire escape.

AMANDA: *(As he passes her.)* Son, will you do me a favor?
TOM: What?
AMANDA: Comb your hair! You look so pretty when your hair is combed!

(Tom slouches on the sofa with the evening paper. Its enormous headline reads: "Franco Triumphs.")

There is only one respect in which I would like you to emulate your father.
TOM: What respect is that?
AMANDA: The care he always took of his appearance. He never allowed himself to look untidy.

(He throws down the paper and crosses to the fire escape.)

Where are you going?
TOM: I'm going out to smoke.
AMANDA: You smoke too much. A pack a day at fifteen cents a pack. How much would that amount to in a month? Thirty times fifteen is how much, Tom? Figure it out and you will be astounded at what you could save. Enough to give you a night-school course in accounting at Washington U.! Just think what a wonderful thing that would be for you, son!

(Tom is unmoved by the thought.)

TOM: I'd rather smoke. *(He steps out on the landing, letting the screen door slam.)*
AMANDA: *(Sharply.)* I know! That's the tragedy of it. . . . *(Alone, she turns to look at her husband's picture.)*

(Dance music: "The World Is Waiting for the Sunrise!")

TOM: *(To the audience.)* Across the alley from us was the Paradise Dance Hall. On evenings in spring the windows and doors were open and the music came outdoors. Sometimes the lights were turned out except for a large glass sphere that hung from the ceiling. It would turn slowly about and filter the dusk with delicate rainbow colors. Then the orchestra played a waltz or a tango, something that had a slow and sensuous rhythm. Couples would come outside, to the relative privacy of the alley. You could see them kissing behind ash pits and telephone poles. This was the compensation for lives that passed like mine, without any change or adventure. Adventure and change were imminent in this year. They were waiting around the corner for all these kids. Suspended in the mist over Berchtesgaden, caught in the folds of Chamberlain's umbrella. In Spain there was Guernica! But here there was only hot swing music and liquor, dance halls, bars, and movies, and sex that hung in the gloom like a chandelier and flooded the world with brief, deceptive rainbows. . . . All the world was waiting for bombardments!

(Amanda turns from the picture and comes outside.)

AMANDA: *(Sighing.)* A fire escape landing's a poor excuse for a porch. *(She spreads a newspaper on a step and sits down, gracefully and demurely as if she were settling into a swing on a Mississippi veranda.)* What are you looking at?

TOM: The moon.

AMANDA: Is there a moon this evening?

TOM: It's rising over Garfinkel's Delicatessen.

AMANDA: So it is! A little silver slipper of a moon. Have you made a wish on it yet?

TOM: Um-hum.

AMANDA: What did you wish for?

TOM: That's a secret.

AMANDA: A secret, huh? Well, I won't tell mine either. I will be just as mysterious as you.

TOM: I bet I can guess what yours is.

AMANDA: Is my head so transparent?

TOM: You're not a sphinx.

AMANDA: No, I don't have secrets. I'll tell you what I wished for on the moon. Success and happiness for my precious children! I wish for that whenever there's a moon, and when there isn't a moon, I wish for it, too.

TOM: I thought perhaps you wished for a gentleman caller.

AMANDA: Why do you say that?

TOM: Don't you remember asking me to fetch one?

AMANDA: I remember suggesting that it would be nice for your sister if you brought home some nice young man from the warehouse. I think that I've made that suggestion more than once.

TOM: Yes, you have made it repeatedly.

AMANDA: Well?

TOM: We are going to have one.

AMANDA: *What?*

TOM: A gentleman caller!

(The annunciation is celebrated with music.)
(Amanda rises.)

(Image on screen: A caller with a bouquet.*)*

AMANDA: You mean you have asked some nice young man to come over?

TOM: Yep. I've asked him to dinner.

AMANDA: You really did?

TOM: I did!

AMANDA: You did, and did he—*accept?*

TOM: He did!

AMANDA: Well, well—well, well! That's—lovely!

TOM: I thought that you would be pleased.

AMANDA: It's definite then?

TOM: Very definite.

AMANDA: Soon?

TOM: Very soon.

AMANDA: For heaven's sake, stop putting on and tell me some things, will you?

TOM: What things do you want me to tell you?

AMANDA: *Naturally* I would like to know when he's *coming!*

TOM: He's coming tomorrow.

AMANDA: *Tomorrow?*

TOM: Yep. Tomorrow.

AMANDA: But, Tom!

TOM: Yes, Mother?

AMANDA: Tomorrow gives me no time!

TOM: Time for what?

AMANDA: Preparations! Why didn't you phone me at once, as soon as you asked him, the minute that he accepted? Then, don't you see, I could have been getting ready!

TOM: You don't have to make any fuss.

AMANDA: Oh, Tom, Tom, Tom, of course I have to make a fuss! I want things nice, not sloppy! Not thrown together. I'll certainly have to do some fast thinking, won't I?

TOM: I don't see why you have to think at all.

AMANDA: You just don't know. We can't have a gentleman caller in a pigsty! All my wedding silver has to be polished, the monogrammed table linen ought to be laundered! The windows have to be washed and fresh curtains put up. And how about clothes? We have to *wear* something, don't we?

TOM: Mother, this boy is no one to make a fuss over!

AMANDA: Do you realize he's the first young man we've introduced to your sister? It's terrible, dreadful, disgraceful that poor little sister has never received a single gentleman caller! Tom, come inside! *(She opens the screen door.)*

TOM: What for?

AMANDA: I want to ask you some things.

TOM: If you're going to make such a fuss, I'll call it off, I'll tell him not to come!

AMANDA: You certainly won't do anything of the kind. Nothing offends people worse than broken engagements. It simply means I'll have to work like a Turk! We won't be brilliant, but we will pass inspection. Come on inside.

(Tom follows her inside, groaning.)

Sit down.

TOM: Any particular place you would like me to sit?

AMANDA: Thank heavens I've got that new sofa! I'm also making payments on a floor lamp I'll have sent out! And put the chintz covers on, they'll brighten things up! Of course I'd hoped to have these walls re-papered. . . . What is the young man's name?

TOM: His name is O'Connor.

AMANDA: That, of course, means fish—tomorrow is Friday! I'll have that salmon loaf—with Durkee's dressing! What does he do? He works at the warehouse?

TOM: Of course! How else would I—

AMANDA: Tom, he—doesn't drink?

TOM: Why do you ask me that?

AMANDA: Your father *did!*

TOM: Don't get started on that!

AMANDA: He *does* drink, then?

TOM: Not that I know of!

AMANDA: Make sure, be certain! The last thing I want for my daughter's a boy who drinks!

TOM: Aren't you being a little bit premature? Mr. O'Connor has not yet appeared on the scene!

AMANDA: But will tomorrow. To meet your sister, and what do I know about his character? Nothing! Old maids are better off than wives of drunkards!

TOM: Oh, my God!

AMANDA: Be still!

TOM: *(Leaning forward to whisper.)* Lots of fellows meet girls whom they don't marry!

AMANDA: Oh, talk sensibly, Tom—and don't be sarcastic! *(She has gotten a hairbrush.)*

TOM: What are you doing?

AMANDA: I'm brushing that cowlick down! *(She attacks his hair with the brush.)* What is this young man's position at the warehouse?

TOM: *(Submitting grimly to the brush and the interrogation.)* This young man's position is that of a shipping clerk, Mother.

AMANDA: Sounds to me like a fairly responsible job, the sort of job *you* would be in if you had more *get-up.* What is his salary? Have you any idea?

TOM: I would judge it to be approximately eighty-five dollars a month.

AMANDA: Well—not princely, but—

TOM: Twenty more than I make.

AMANDA: Yes, how well I know! But for a family man, eighty-five dollars a month is not much more than you can just get by on. . . .

TOM: Yes, but Mr. O'Connor is not a family man.

AMANDA: He might be, mightn't he? Some time in the future?

TOM: I see. Plans and provisions.

AMANDA: You are the only young man that I know of who ignores the fact that the future becomes the present, the present the past, and the past turns into everlasting regret if you don't plan for it!

TOM: I will think that over and see what I can make of it.

AMANDA: Don't be supercilious with your mother! Tell me some more about this—what do you call him?

TOM: James D. O'Connor. The D. is for Delaney.

AMANDA: Irish on *both* sides! *Gracious!* And doesn't drink?

TOM: Shall I call him up and ask him right this minute?

AMANDA: The only way to find out about those things is to make discreet inquiries at the proper moment. When I was a girl in Blue Mountain and it was suspected that a young man drank, the girl whose attentions he had been receiving, if any girl *was,* would sometimes speak to the minister of his church, or rather her father would if her father was living, and sort of feel him out on the young man's character. That is the way such things are discreetly handled to keep a young woman from making a tragic mistake!

TOM: Then how did you happen to make a tragic mistake?

AMANDA: That innocent look of your father's had everyone fooled! He *smiled* — the world was *enchanted!* No girl can do worse than put herself at the mercy of a handsome appearance! I hope that Mr. O'Connor is not too good-looking.

TOM: No, he's not too good-looking. He's covered with freckles and hasn't too much of a nose.

AMANDA: He's not right-down homely, though?

TOM: Not right-down homely. Just medium homely, I'd say.

AMANDA: Character's what to look for in a man.

TOM: That's what I've always said, Mother.

AMANDA: You've never said anything of the kind and I suspect you would never give it a thought.

TOM: Don't be suspicious of me.

AMANDA: At least I hope he's the type that's up and coming.

TOM: I think he really goes in for self-improvement.

AMANDA: What reason have you to think so?

TOM: He goes to night school.

AMANDA: *(Beaming.)* Splendid! What does he do, I mean study?

TOM: Radio engineering and public speaking!

AMANDA: Then he has visions of being advanced in the world! Any young man who studies public speaking is aiming to have an executive job some day! And radio engineering? A thing for the future! Both of these facts are very illuminating. Those are the sort of things that a mother should know concerning any young man who comes to call on her daughter. Seriously or—not.

TOM: One little warning. He doesn't know about Laura. I didn't let on that we had dark ulterior motives. I just said, why don't you come and have dinner with us? He said okay and that was the whole conversation.

AMANDA: I bet it was! You're eloquent as an oyster. However, he'll know about Laura when he gets here. When he sees how lovely and sweet and pretty she is, he'll thank his lucky stars he was asked to dinner.

TOM: Mother, you mustn't expect too much of Laura.

AMANDA: What do you mean?

TOM: Laura seems all those things to you and me because she's ours and we love her. We don't even notice she's crippled any more.

AMANDA: Don't say crippled! You know that I never allow that word to be used!

TOM: But face facts, Mother. She is and—that's not all—

AMANDA: What do you mean "not all"?

TOM: Laura is very different from other girls.

AMANDA: I think the difference is all to her advantage.

TOM: Not quite all—in the eyes of others—strangers—she's terribly shy and lives in a world of her own and those things make her seem a little peculiar to people outside the house.

AMANDA: Don't say peculiar.

TOM: Face the facts. She is.

(The dance hall music changes to a tango that has a minor and somewhat ominous tone.)

AMANDA: In what way is she peculiar—may I ask?

TOM: *(Gently.)* She lives in a world of her own—a world of little glass ornaments, Mother. . . .

(He gets up. Amanda remains holding the brush, looking at him, troubled.)

She plays old phonograph records and—that's about all—*(He glances at himself in the mirror and crosses to the door.)*

AMANDA: *(Sharply.)* Where are you going?

TOM: I'm going to the movies. *(He goes out the screen door.)*

AMANDA: Not to the movies, every night to the movies! *(She follows quickly to the screen door.)* I don't believe you always go to the movies!

(He is gone. Amanda looks worriedly after him for a moment. Then vitality and optimism return and she turns from the door, crossing to the portieres.)

Laura! Laura!

(Laura answers from the kitchenette.)

LAURA: Yes, Mother.

AMANDA: Let those dishes go and come in front!

(Laura appears with a dish towel. Amanda speaks to her gaily.)

Laura, come here and make a wish on the moon!

(Screen image: The Moon.*)*

LAURA: *(Entering.)* Moon—moon?

AMANDA: A little silver slipper of a moon. Look over your left shoulder, Laura, and make a wish!

(Laura looks faintly puzzled as if called out of sleep. Amanda seizes her shoulders and turns her at an angle by the door.)

Now! Now, darling, *wish!*

LAURA: What shall I wish for, Mother?

AMANDA: *(Her voice trembling and her eyes suddenly filling with tears.)* Happiness! Good fortune!

(The sound of the violin rises and the stage dims out.)

Scene VI

The light comes up on the fire escape landing. Tom is leaning against the grill, smoking.

(Screen image: The high school hero.*)*

TOM: And so the following evening I brought Jim home to dinner. I had known Jim slightly in high school. In high school Jim was a hero. He had tremendous Irish good nature and vitality with the scrubbed and polished look of white chinaware. He seemed to move in a continual spotlight. He was a star in basketball, captain of the debating club, president of the senior class and the glee club and he sang the male lead in the annual light operas. He was always running or bounding, never just walking. He seemed always at the point of defeating the law of gravity. He was shooting with such velocity through his adolescence that you would logically expect him to arrive at nothing short of the White House by the time he was thirty. But Jim apparently ran into more interference after his graduation from Soldan. His speed had definitely slowed. Six years after he left high school he was holding a job that wasn't much better than mine.

(Screen image: The Clerk.*)*

He was the only one at the warehouse with whom I was on friendly terms. I was valuable to him as someone who could remember his former glory, who had seen him win basketball games and the silver cup in debating. He knew of my secret practice of retiring to a cabinet of the washroom to work on poems when business was slack in the warehouse. He called

me Shakespeare. And while the other boys in the warehouse regarded me
with suspicious hostility, Jim took a humorous attitude toward me. Gradually his attitude affected the others, their hostility wore off and they also
began to smile at me as people smile at an oddly fashioned dog who trots
across their path at some distance.

I knew that Jim and Laura had known each other at Soldan, and I had
heard Laura speak admiringly of his voice. I didn't know if Jim remembered her or not. In high school Laura had been as unobtrusive as Jim
had been astonishing. If he did remember Laura, it was not as my sister,
for when I asked him to dinner, he grinned and said, "You know, Shakespeare, I never thought of you as having folks!"

He was about to discover that I did. . . .

(Legend on screen: "The accent of a coming foot.")
*(The light dims out on Tom and comes up in the Wingfield living room—a delicate
lemony light. It is about five on a Friday evening of late spring which comes
"scattering poems in the sky.")*
*(Amanda has worked like a Turk in preparation for the gentleman caller. The
results are astonishing. The new floor lamp with its rose silk shade is in place, a
colored paper lantern conceals the broken light fixture in the ceiling, new billowing
white curtains are at the windows, chintz covers are on the chairs and sofa, a pair
of new sofa pillows make their initial appearance. Open boxes and tissue paper are
scattered on the floor.)*
*(Laura stands in the middle of the room with lifted arms while Amanda crouches
before her, adjusting the hem of a new dress, devout and ritualistic. The dress is
colored and designed by memory. The arrangement of Laura's hair is changed; it
is softer and more becoming. A fragile, unearthly prettiness has come out in Laura:
she is like a piece of translucent glass touched by light, given a momentary radiance,
not actual, not lasting.)*

AMANDA: *(Impatiently.)* Why are you trembling?
LAURA: Mother, you've made me so nervous!
AMANDA: How have I made you nervous?
LAURA: By all this fuss! You make it seem so important!
AMANDA: I don't understand you, Laura. You couldn't be satisfied with just
    sitting home, and yet whenever I try to arrange something for you, you
    seem to resist it. *(She gets up.)* Now take a look at yourself. No, wait! Wait
    just a moment—I have an idea!
LAURA: What is it now?

*(Amanda produces two powder puffs which she wraps in handkerchiefs and stuffs
in Laura's bosom.)*

LAURA: Mother, what are you doing?
AMANDA: They call them "Gay Deceivers"!
LAURA: I won't wear them!
AMANDA: You will!

LAURA: Why should I?

AMANDA: Because, to be painfully honest, your chest is flat.

LAURA: You make it seem like we were setting a trap.

AMANDA: All pretty girls are a trap, a pretty trap, and men expect them to be.

(Legend on screen: "A pretty trap.")

> Now look at yourself, young lady. This is the prettiest you will ever be! *(She stands back to admire Laura.)* I've got to fix myself now! You're going to be surprised by your mother's appearance!

(Amanda crosses through the portieres, humming gaily. Laura moves slowly to the long mirror and stares solemnly at herself. A wind blows the white curtains inward in a slow, graceful motion and with a faint, sorrowful sighing.)

> AMANDA: *(From somewhere behind the portieres.)* It isn't dark enough yet.

(Laura turns slowly before the mirror with a troubled look.)
(Legend on screen: "This is my sister: Celebrate her with strings!" Music plays.)

> AMANDA: *(Laughing, still not visible.)* I'm going to show you something. I'm going to make a spectacular appearance!

LAURA: What is it, Mother?

AMANDA: Possess your soul in patience—you will see! Something I've resurrected from that old trunk! Styles haven't changed so terribly much after all. . . . *(She parts the portieres.)* Now just look at your mother! *(She wears a girlish frock of yellowed voile with a blue silk sash. She carries a bunch of jonquils—the legend of her youth is nearly revived. Now she speaks feverishly.)* This is the dress in which I led the cotillion. Won the cakewalk twice at Sunset Hill, wore one Spring to the Governor's Ball in Jackson! See how I sashayed around the ballroom, Laura? *(She raises her skirt and does a mincing step around the room.)* I wore it on Sundays for my gentlemen callers! I had it on the day I met your father. . . . I had malaria fever all that Spring. The change of climate from East Tennessee to the Delta—weakened resistance. I had a little temperature all the time—not enough to be serious—just enough to make me restless and giddy! Invitations poured in—parties all over the Delta! "Stay in bed," said Mother, "you have a fever!"—but I just wouldn't. I took quinine but kept on going, going! Evenings, dances! Afternoons, long, long rides! Picnics—lovely! So lovely, that country in May—all lacy with dogwood, literally flooded with jonquils! That was the spring I had the craze for jonquils. Jonquils became an absolute obsession. Mother said, "Honey, there's no more room for jonquils." And still I kept on bringing in more jonquils. Whenever, wherever I saw them, I'd say, "Stop! Stop! I see jonquils!" I made the young men help me gather the jonquils! It was a joke, Amanda and her jonquils! Finally there were no more vases to hold them, every available space was filled with jonquils. No vases to hold them? All right, I'll hold them myself! And then I—*(She stops in front of the picture. Music plays.)* met your father! Malaria fever and jonquils and then—this—boy. . . . *(She switches on the rose-colored lamp.)* I hope they get here before it starts to rain. *(She crosses the room and places the jonquils in a bowl on the table.)* I gave your brother a little extra change so he and Mr. O'Connor could take the service car home.

LAURA: *(With an altered look.)* What did you say his name was?

AMANDA: O'Connor.

LAURA: What is his first name?

AMANDA: I don't remember. Oh, yes, I do. It was—Jim!

(Laura sways slightly and catches hold of a chair.)
(Legend on screen: "Not Jim!")

LAURA: *(Faintly)* Not—Jim!

AMANDA: Yes, that was it, it was Jim! I've never known a Jim that wasn't nice!

(The music becomes ominous.)

LAURA: Are you sure his name is Jim O'Connor?

AMANDA: Yes. Why?

LAURA: Is he the one that Tom used to know in high school?

AMANDA: He didn't say so. I think he just got to know him at the warehouse.

LAURA: There was a Jim O'Connor we both knew in high school—*(Then, with effort.)* If that is the one that Tom is bringing to dinner—you'll have to excuse me, I won't come to the table.

AMANDA: What sort of nonsense is this?

LAURA: You asked me once if I ever liked a boy. Don't you remember I showed you this boy's picture?

AMANDA: You mean the boy you showed me in the yearbook?

LAURA: Yes, that boy.

AMANDA: Laura, Laura, were you in love with that boy?

LAURA: I don't know, Mother. All I know is I couldn't sit at the table if it was him!

AMANDA: It won't be him! It isn't the least bit likely. But whether it is or not, you will come to the table. You will not be excused.

LAURA: I'll have to be, Mother.

AMANDA: I don't intend to humor your silliness, Laura. I've had too much from you and your brother, both! So just sit down and compose yourself till they come. Tom has forgotten his key so you'll have to let them in, when they arrive.

LAURA: *(Panicky.)* Oh, Mother—*you* answer the door!

AMANDA: *(Lightly.)* I'll be busy in the kitchen—busy!

LAURA: Oh, Mother, please answer the door, don't make me do it!

AMANDA: *(Crossing into the kitchenette.)* I've got to fix the dressing for the salmon. Fuss, fuss—silliness!—over a gentleman caller!

(The door swings shut. Laura is left alone.)
(Legend on screen: "Terror!")
(She utters a low moan and turns off the lamp—sits stiffly on the edge of the sofa, knotting her fingers together.)
(Legend on screen: "The Opening of a Door!")
(Tom and Jim appear on the fire escape steps and climb to the landing. Hearing their approach, Laura rises with a panicky gesture. She retreats to the portieres. The doorbell rings. Laura catches her breath and touches her throat. Low drums sound.)

AMANDA: *(Calling.)* Laura, sweetheart! The door!

(Laura stares at it without moving.)

JIM: I think we just beat the rain.
TOM: Uh-huh. *(He rings again, nervously. Jim whistles and fishes for a cigarette.)*
AMANDA: *(Very, very gaily.)* Laura, that is your brother and Mr. O'Connor! Will you let them in, darling?

(Laura crosses toward the kitchenette door.)

LAURA: *(Breathlessly.)* Mother—you go to the door!

(Amanda steps out of the kitchenette and stares furiously at Laura. She points imperiously at the door.)

LAURA: Please, please!
AMANDA: *(In a fierce whisper.)* What is the matter with you, you silly thing?
LAURA: *(Desperately.)* Please, you answer it, *please!*
AMANDA: I told you I wasn't going to humor you, Laura. Why have you chosen this moment to lose your mind?
LAURA: Please, please, please, you go!
AMANDA: You'll have to go to the door because I can't!
LAURA: *(Despairingly.)* I can't either!
AMANDA: *Why?*
LAURA: I'm *sick!*
AMANDA: I'm sick, too—of your nonsense! Why can't you and your brother be normal people? Fantastic whims and behavior!

(Tom gives a long ring.)

Preposterous goings on! Can you give me one reason—*(She calls out lyrically.) Coming! Just one second!*—why you should be afraid to open a door? Now you answer it, Laura!
LAURA: Oh, oh, oh . . . *(She returns through the portieres, darts to the Victrola, winds it frantically and turns it on.)*
AMANDA: Laura Wingfield, you march right to that door!
LAURA: Yes—yes, Mother!

(A faraway, scratchy rendition of "Dardanella" softens the air and gives her strength to move through it. She slips to the door and draws it cautiously open. Tom enters with the caller, Jim O'Connor.)

TOM: Laura, this is Jim. Jim, this is my sister, Laura.

JIM: *(Stepping inside.)* I didn't know that Shakespeare had a sister!

LAURA: *(Retreating, stiff and trembling, from the door.)* How—how do you do?

JIM: *(Heartily, extending his hand.)* Okay!

(Laura touches it hesitantly with hers.)

JIM: Your hand's *cold*, Laura!

LAURA: Yes, well—I've been playing the Victrola. . . .

JIM: Must have been playing classical music on it! You ought to play a little hot swing music to warm you up!

LAURA: Excuse me—I haven't finished playing the Victrola. . . .

(She turns awkwardly and hurries into the front room. She pauses a second by the Victrola. Then she catches her breath and darts through the portieres like a frightened deer.)

JIM: *(Grinning.)* What was the matter?

TOM: Oh—with Laura? Laura is—terribly shy.

JIM: Shy, huh? It's unusual to meet a shy girl nowadays. I don't believe you ever mentioned you had a sister.

TOM: Well, now you know. I have one. Here is the *Post Dispatch.* You want a piece of it?

JIM: Uh-huh.

TOM: What piece? The comics?

JIM: Sports! *(He glances at it.)* Ole Dizzy Dean is on his bad behavior.

TOM: *(Uninterested.)* Yeah? *(He lights a cigarette and goes over to the fire-escape door.)*

JIM: Where are *you* going?

TOM: I'm going out on the terrace.

JIM: *(Going after him.)* You know, Shakespeare—I'm going to sell you a bill of goods!

TOM: What goods?

JIM: A course I'm taking.

TOM: Huh?

JIM: In public speaking! You and me, we're not the warehouse type.

TOM: Thanks—that's good news. But what has public speaking got to do with it?

JIM: It fits you for—executive positions!

TOM: Awww.

JIM: I tell you it's done a helluva lot for me.

(Image on screen: Executive at his desk.)

TOM: In what respect?

JIM: In every! Ask yourself what is the difference between you an' me and men in the office down front? Brains?—No!—Ability?—No! Then what? Just one little thing—

TOM: What is that one little thing?

JIM: Primarily it amounts to—social poise! Being able to square up to people and hold your own on any social level!

AMANDA: *(From the kitchenette.)* Tom?

TOM: Yes, Mother?

AMANDA: Is that you and Mr. O'Connor?

TOM: Yes, Mother.

AMANDA: Well, you just make yourselves comfortable in there.

TOM: Yes, Mother.

AMANDA: Ask Mr. O'Connor if he would like to wash his hands.

JIM: Aw, no—no—thank you—I took care of that at the warehouse. Tom—

TOM: Yes?

JIM: Mr. Mendoza was speaking to me about you.

TOM: Favorably?

JIM: What do you think?

TOM: Well—

JIM: You're going to be out of a job if you don't wake up.

TOM: I am waking up—

JIM: You show no signs.

TOM: The signs are interior.

(Image on screen: The sailing vessel with the Jolly Roger again.*)*

TOM: I'm planning to change. *(He leans over the fire-escape rail, speaking with quiet exhilaration. The incandescent marquees and signs of the first-run movie houses light his face from across the alley. He looks like a voyager.)* I'm right at the point of committing myself to a future that doesn't include the warehouse and Mr. Mendoza or even a night-school course in public speaking.

JIM: What are you gassing about?

TOM: I'm tired of the movies.

JIM: Movies!

TOM: Yes, movies! Look at them—*(A wave toward the marvels of Grand Avenue.)* All of those glamorous people—having adventures—hogging it all, gobbling the whole thing up! You know what happens? People go to the *movies* instead of *moving!* Hollywood characters are supposed to have all the adventures for everybody in America, while everybody in America sits in a dark room and watches them have them! Yes, until there's a war. That's when adventure becomes available to the masses! *Everyone's* dish, not only Gable's! Then the people in the dark room come out of the dark room to have some adventures themselves—goody, goody! It's our turn now, to go to the South Sea Island—to make a safari—to be exotic, far-off!

But I'm not patient. I don't want to wait till then. I'm tired of the *movies*
and I am *about* to *move!*

JIM: *(Incredulously.)* Move?

TOM: Yes.

JIM: When?

TOM: Soon!

JIM: Where? Where?

(The music seems to answer the question, while Tom thinks it over. He searches in his pockets.)

TOM: I'm starting to boil inside. I know I seem dreamy, but inside—well, I'm boiling! Whenever I pick up a shoe, I shudder a little thinking how short life is and what I am doing! Whatever that means, I know it doesn't mean shoes—except as something to wear on a traveler's feet! *(He finds what he has been searching for in his pockets and holds out a paper to Jim.)* Look—

JIM: What?

TOM: I'm a member.

JIM: *(Reading.)* The Union of Merchant Seamen.

TOM: I paid my dues this month, instead of the light bill.

JIM: You will regret it when they turn the lights off.

TOM: I won't be here.

JIM: How about your mother?

TOM: I'm like my father. The bastard son of a bastard! Did you notice how he's grinning in his picture in there? And he's been absent going on sixteen years!

JIM: You're just talking, you drip. How does your mother feel about it?

TOM: Shhh! Here comes Mother! Mother is not acquainted with my plans!

AMANDA: *(Coming through the portieres.)* Where are you all?

TOM: On the terrace, Mother.

(They start inside. She advances to them. Tom is distinctly shocked at her appearance. Even Jim blinks a little. He is making his first contact with girlish Southern vivacity and in spite of the night-school course in public speaking is somewhat thrown off the beam by the unexpected outlay of social charm. Certain responses are attempted by Jim but are swept aside by Amanda's gay laughter and chatter. Tom is embarrassed but after the first shock Jim reacts very warmly. He grins and chuckles, is altogether won over.)

(Image on screen: Amanda as a girl.*)*

AMANDA: *(Coyly smiling, shaking her girlish ringlets.)* Well, well, well, so this is Mr. O'Connor. Introductions entirely unnecessary. I've heard so much about you from my boy. I finally said to him, Tom—good gracious!—why don't you bring this paragon to supper? I'd like to meet this nice young man at the warehouse!—instead of just hearing him sing your praises so much! I don't know why my son is so stand-offish—that's not Southern behavior!

Let's sit down and—I think we could stand a little more air in here! Tom, leave the door open. I felt a nice fresh breeze a moment ago. Where has it gone to? Mmm, so warm already! And not quite summer, even. We're going to burn up when summer really gets started. However, we're having —we're having a very light supper. I think light things are better fo' this time of year. The same as light clothes are. Light clothes an' light food are what warm weather calls fo'. You know our blood gets so thick during th' winter—it takes a while fo' us to *adjust* ou'selves!—when the season changes . . . It's come so quick this year. I wasn't prepared. All of a sudden —heavens! Already summer! I ran to the trunk an' pulled out this light dress—terribly old! Historical almost! But feels so good—so good an' co-ol, y' know. . . .

TOM: Mother—

AMANDA: Yes, honey?

TOM: How about—supper?

AMANDA: Honey, you go ask Sister if supper is ready! You know Sister is in full charge of supper! Tell her you hungry boys are waiting for it. *(To Jim.)* Have you met Laura?

JIM: She—

AMANDA: Let you in? Oh, good, you've met already! It's rare for a girl as sweet an' pretty as Laura to be domestic! But Laura is, thank heavens, not only pretty but also very domestic. I'm not at all. I never was a bit. I never could make a thing but angel-food cake. Well, in the South we had so many servants. Gone, gone, gone. All vestige of gracious living! Gone completely! I wasn't prepared for what the future brought me. All of my gentlemen callers were sons of planters and so of course I assumed that I would be married to one and raise my family on a large piece of land with plenty of servants. But man proposes—and woman accepts the proposal! To vary that old, old saying a little bit—I married no planter! I married a man who worked for the telephone company! That gallantly smiling gentleman over there! *(She points to the picture.)* A telephone man who—fell in love with long-distance! Now he travels and I don't even know where! But what am I going on for about my—tribulations? Tell me yours—I hope you don't have any! Tom?

TOM: *(Returning.)* Yes, Mother?

AMANDA: Is supper nearly ready?

TOM: It looks to me like supper is on the table.

AMANDA: Let me look—*(She rises prettily and looks through the portieres.)* Oh, lovely! But where is Sister?

TOM: Laura is not feeling well and she says that she thinks she'd better not come to the table.

AMANDA: What? Nonsense! Laura? Oh, Laura!

LAURA: *(From the kitchenette, faintly.)* Yes, Mother.

AMANDA: You really must come to the table. We won't be seated until you come to the table! Come in, Mr. O'Connor. You sit over there, and I'll. . . . Laura? Laura Wingfield! You're keeping us waiting, honey! We can't say grace until you come to the table!

(The kitchenette door is pushed weakly open and Laura comes in. She is obviously quite faint, her lips trembling, her eyes wide and staring. She moves unsteadily toward the table.)
(Screen legend: "Terror!")
(Outside a summer storm is coming on abruptly. The white curtains billow inward at the windows and there is a sorrowful murmur from the deep blue dusk.)
(Laura suddenly stumbles; she catches at a chair with a faint moan.)

TOM: Laura!
AMANDA: Laura!

(There is a clap of thunder.)
(Screen legend: "Ah!")

(Despairingly.) Why, Laura, you *are* ill, darling! Tom, help your sister into the living room, dear! Sit in the living room, Laura—rest on the sofa. Well! *(To Jim as Tom helps his sister to the sofa in the living room.)* Standing over the hot stove made her ill! I told her that it was just too warm this evening, but—

(Tom comes back to the table.)

Is Laura all right now?
TOM: Yes.
AMANDA: What *is* that? Rain? A nice cool rain has come up! *(She gives Jim a frightened look.)* I think we may—have grace—now. . . .
(Tom looks at her stupidly.) Tom, honey—you say grace!
TOM: Oh . . . "For these and all thy mercies—"

(They bow their heads, Amanda stealing a nervous glance at Jim. In the living room Laura, stretched on the sofa, clenches her hand to her lips, to hold back a shuddering sob.)

God's Holy Name be praised—

(The scene dims out.)

Scene VII

It is half an hour later. Dinner is just being finished in the dining room, Laura is still huddled upon the sofa, her feet drawn under her, her head resting on a pale blue pillow, her eyes wide and mysteriously watchful. The new floor lamp with its shade of rose-colored silk gives a soft, becoming light to her face, bringing out the fragile, unearthly prettiness which usually escapes attention. From outside there is a steady murmur of rain, but it is slackening and soon stops; the air outside becomes pale and luminous as the moon breaks through the clouds. A moment after the curtain rises, the lights in both rooms flicker and go out.

JIM: Hey, there, Mr. Light Bulb!

(Amanda laughs nervously.)

(Legend on screen: "Suspension of a public service.")

AMANDA: Where was Moses when the lights went out? Ha-ha. Do you know the answer to that one, Mr. O'Connor?

JIM: No, Ma'am, what's the answer?

AMANDA: In the dark!

(Jim laughs appreciatively.)

Everybody sit still. I'll light the candles. Isn't it lucky we have them on the table? Where's a match? Which of you gentlemen can provide a match?

JIM: Here.

AMANDA: Thank you, Sir.

JIM: Not at all, Ma'am!

AMANDA: *(As she lights the candles.)* I guess the fuse has burnt out. Mr. O'Connor, can you tell a burnt-out fuse? I know I can't and Tom is a total loss when it comes to mechanics.

(They rise from the table and go into the kitchenette, from where their voices are heard.)

Oh, be careful you don't bump into something. We don't want our gentle-man caller to break his neck. Now wouldn't that be a fine howdy-do?

JIM: Ha-ha! Where is the fuse-box?

AMANDA: Right here next to the stove. Can you see anything?

JIM: Just a minute.

AMANDA: Isn't electricity a mysterious thing? Wasn't it Benjamin Franklin who tied a key to a kite? We live in such a mysterious universe, don't we? Some people say that science clears up all the mysteries for us. In my opinion it only creates more! Have you found it yet?

JIM: No, Ma'am. All these fuses look okay to me.

AMANDA: Tom!

TOM: Yes, Mother?

AMANDA: That light bill I gave you several days ago. The one I told you we got the notices about?

(Legend on screen: "Ha!")

TOM: Oh—yeah.

AMANDA: You didn't neglect to pay it by any chance?

TOM: Why, I—

AMANDA: Didn't! I might have known it!

JIM: Shakespeare probably wrote a poem on that light bill, Mrs. Wingfield.

AMANDA: I might have known better than to trust him with it! There's such a high price for negligence in this world!

JIM: Maybe the poem will win a ten-dollar prize.

AMANDA: We'll just have to spend the remainder of the evening in the nineteenth century, before Mr. Edison made the Mazda lamp!

JIM: Candlelight is my favorite kind of light.

AMANDA: That shows you're romantic! But that's no excuse for Tom. Well, we got through dinner. Very considerate of them to let us get through dinner before they plunged us into everlasting darkness, wasn't it, Mr. O'Connor?

JIM: Ha-ha!

AMANDA: Tom, as a penalty for your carelessness you can help me with the dishes.

JIM: Let me give you a hand.

AMANDA: Indeed you will not!

JIM: I ought to be good for something.

AMANDA: Good for something? *(Her tone is rhapsodic.) You?* Why, Mr. O'-Connor, nobody, *nobody's* given me this much entertainment in years— as you have!

JIM: Aw, now, Mrs. Wingfield!

AMANDA: I'm not exaggerating, not one bit! But Sister is all by her lonesome. You go keep her company in the parlor! I'll give you this lovely old candelabrum that used to be on the altar at the Church of the Heavenly Rest. It was melted a little out of shape when the church burnt down. Lightning struck it one spring. Gypsy Jones was holding a revival at the time and he intimated that the church was destroyed because the Episcopalians gave card parties.

JIM: Ha-ha.

AMANDA: And how about you coaxing Sister to drink a little wine? I think it would be good for her! Can you carry both at once?

JIM: Sure. I'm Superman!

AMANDA: Now, Thomas, get into this apron!

(Jim comes into the dining room, carrying the candelabrum, its candles lighted, in one hand and a glass of wine in the other. The door of the kitchenette swings closed on Amanda's gay laughter; the flickering light approaches the portieres. Laura sits up nervously as Jim enters. She can hardly speak from the almost intolerable strain of being alone with a stranger.)

(Screen legend: "I don't suppose you remember me at all!")

(At first, before Jim's warmth overcomes her paralyzing shyness, Laura's voice is thin and breathless, as though she had just run up a steep flight of stairs. Jim's attitude is gently humorous. While the incident is apparently unimportant, it is to Laura the climax of her secret life.)

JIM: Hello there, Laura.

LAURA: *(Faintly.)* Hello.

(She clears her throat.)

> JIM: How are you feeling now? Better?
> LAURA: Yes. Yes, thank you.
> JIM: This is for you. A little dandelion wine. *(He extends the glass toward her
> with extravagant gallantry.)*
> LAURA: Thank you.
> JIM: Drink it—but don't get drunk!

(He laughs heartily. Laura takes the glass uncertainly; she laughs shyly.)

> Where shall I set the candles?
> LAURA: Oh—oh, anywhere. . . .
> JIM: How about here on the floor? Any objections?
> LAURA: No.
> JIM: I'll spread a newspaper under to catch the drippings. I like to sit on the
> floor. Mind if I do?
> LAURA: Oh, no.
> JIM: Give me a pillow?
> LAURA: What?
> JIM: A pillow!
> LAURA: Oh . . . *(She hands him one quickly.)*
> JIM: How about you? Don't you like to sit on the floor?
> LAURA: Oh—yes.
> JIM: Why don't you, then?
> LAURA: I—will.
> JIM: Take a pillow!

*(Laura does. She sits on the floor on the other side of the candelabrum. Jim crosses
his legs and smiles engagingly at her.)*

> I can't hardly see you sitting way over there.
> LAURA: I can—see you.
> JIM: I know, but that's not fair, I'm in the limelight.

(Laura moves her pillow closer.)

> Good! Now I can see you! Comfortable?
> LAURA: Yes.
> JIM: So am I. Comfortable as a cow! Will you have some gum?
> LAURA: No, thank you.
> JIM: I think that I will indulge, with your permission. *(He musingly unwraps
> a stick of gum and holds it up.)* Think of the fortune made by the guy that
> invented the first piece of chewing gum. Amazing, huh? The Wrigley
> Building is one of the sights of Chicago—I saw it when I went up to the
> Century of Progress. Did you take in the Century of Progress?
> LAURA: No, I didn't.
> JIM: Well, it was quite a wonderful exposition. What impressed me most was

the Hall of Science. Gives you an idea of what the future will be in America, even more wonderful than the present time is! *(There is a pause. Jim smiles at her.)* Your brother tells me you're shy. Is that right, Laura?

LAURA: I—don't know.

JIM: I judge you to be an old-fashioned type of girl. Well, I think that's a pretty good type to be. Hope you don't think I'm being too personal—do you?

LAURA: *(Hastily, out of embarrassment.)* I believe I *will* take a piece of gum, if you—don't mind. *(Clearing her throat.)* Mr. O'Connor, have you—kept up with your singing?

JIM: Singing? Me?

LAURA: Yes. I remember what a beautiful voice you had.

JIM: When did you hear me sing?

(Laura does not answer, and in the long pause which follows a man's voice is heard singing offstage.)

> VOICE:
> O blow, ye winds, heigh-ho,
> A-roving I will go!
>   I'm off to my love
>   With a boxing glove—
> Ten thousand miles away!

JIM: You say you've heard me sing?

LAURA: Oh, yes! Yes, very often . . . I—don't suppose—you remember me—at all?

JIM: *(Smiling doubtfully.)* You know I have an idea I've seen you before. I had that idea soon as you opened the door. It seemed almost like I was about to remember your name. But the name that I started to call you—wasn't a name! And so I stopped myself before I said it.

LAURA: Wasn't it—Blue Roses?

JIM: *(Springing up, grinning.)* Blue Roses! My gosh, yes—Blue Roses! That's what I had on my tongue when you opened the door! Isn't it funny what tricks your memory plays? I didn't connect you with high school some-how or other. But that's where it was; it was high school. I didn't even know you were Shakespeare's sister! Gosh, I'm sorry.

LAURA: I didn't expect you to. You—barely knew me!

JIM: But we did have a speaking acquaintance, huh?

LAURA: Yes, we—spoke to each other.

JIM: When did you recognize me?

LAURA: Oh, right away!

JIM: Soon as I came in the door?

LAURA: When I heard your name I thought it was probably you. I knew that Tom used to know you a little in high school. So when you came in the door—well, then I was—sure.

JIM: Why didn't you *say* something, then?

LAURA: *(Breathlessly.)* I didn't know what to say, I was—too surprised!

JIM: For goodness' sakes! You know, this sure is funny!

LAURA: Yes! Yes, isn't it, though . . .

JIM: Didn't we have a class in something together?

LAURA: Yes, we did.

JIM: What class was that?

LAURA: It was—singing—chorus!

JIM: Aw!

LAURA: I sat across the aisle from you in the Aud.

JIM: Aw.

LAURA: Mondays, Wednesdays, and Fridays.

JIM: Now I remember—you always came in late.

LAURA: Yes, it was so hard for me, getting upstairs. I had that brace on my leg—it clumped so loud!

JIM: I never heard any clumping.

LAURA: *(Wincing at the recollection.)* To me it sounded like—thunder!

JIM: Well, well, well, I never even noticed.

LAURA: And everybody was seated before I came in. I had to walk in front of all those people. My seat was in the back row. I had to go clumping all the way up the aisle with everyone watching!

JIM: You shouldn't have been self-conscious.

LAURA: I know, but I was. It was always such a relief when the singing started.

JIM: Aw, yes, I've placed you now! I used to call you Blue Roses. How was it that I got started calling you that?

LAURA: I was out of school a little while with pleurosis. When I came back you asked me what was the matter. I said I had pleurosis—you thought I said *Blue Roses*. That's what you always called me after that!

JIM: I hope you didn't mind.

LAURA: Oh, no—I liked it. You see, I wasn't acquainted with many—people. . . .

JIM: As I remember you sort of stuck by yourself.

LAURA: I—I—never have had much luck at—making friends.

JIM: I don't see why you wouldn't.

LAURA: Well, I—started out badly.

JIM: You mean being—

LAURA: Yes, it sort of—stood between me—

JIM: You shouldn't have let it!

LAURA: I know, but it did, and—

JIM: You were shy with people!

LAURA: I tried not to be but never could—

JIM: Overcome it?

LAURA: No, I—I never could!

JIM: I guess being shy is something you have to work out of kind of gradually.

LAURA: *(Sorrowfully.)* Yes—I guess it—

JIM: Takes time!

LAURA: Yes—

JIM: People are not so dreadful when you know them. That's what you have to remember! And everybody has problems, not just you, but practically everybody has got some problems. You think of yourself as having the only problems, as being the only one who is disappointed. But just look around you and you will see lots of people as disappointed as you are. For instance, I hoped when I was going to high school that I would be further along at this time, six years later, than I am now. You remember that wonderful write-up I had in *The Torch?*

LAURA: Yes! *(She rises and crosses to the table.)*

JIM: It said I was bound to succeed in anything I went into!

(Laura returns with the high school yearbook.)

Holy Jeez! *The Torch!*

(He accepts it reverently. They smile across the book with mutual wonder. Laura crouches beside him and they begin to turn the pages. Laura's shyness is dissolving in his warmth.)

LAURA: Here you are in *The Pirates of Penzance!*

JIM: *(Wistfully.)* I sang the baritone lead in that operetta.

LAURA: *(Raptly.)* So—*beautifully!*

JIM: *(Protesting.)* Aw—

LAURA: Yes, yes—beautifully—beautifully!

JIM: You heard me?

LAURA: All three times!

JIM: No!

LAURA: Yes!

JIM: All three performances?

LAURA: *(Looking down.)* Yes.

JIM: Why?

LAURA: I—wanted to ask you to—autograph my program. *(She takes the program from the back of the yearbook and shows it to him.)*

JIM: Why didn't you ask me to?

LAURA: You were always surrounded by your own friends so much that I never had a chance to.

JIM: You should have just—

LAURA: Well, I—thought you might think I was—

JIM: Thought I might think you was—what?

LAURA: Oh—

JIM: *(With reflective relish.)* I was beleaguered by females in those days.

LAURA: You were terribly popular!

JIM: Yeah—

LAURA: You had such a—friendly way—

JIM: I was spoiled in high school.

LAURA: Everybody—liked you!

JIM: Including you?

LAURA: I—yes, I—did, too— *(She gently closes the book in her lap.)*

JIM: Well, well, well! Give me that program, Laura.

(She hands it to him. He signs it with a flourish.)

There you are—better late than never!

LAURA: Oh, I—what a—surprise!

JIM: My signature isn't worth very much right now. But some day—maybe —it will increase in value! Being disappointed is one thing and being discouraged is something else. I am disappointed but I am not discouraged. I'm twenty-three years old. How old are you?

LAURA: I'll be twenty-four in June.

JIM: That's not old age!

LAURA: No, but—

JIM: You finished high school?

LAURA: *(With difficulty.)* I didn't go back.

JIM: You mean you dropped out?

LAURA: I made bad grades in my final examinations. *(She rises and replaces the book and the program on the table. Her voice is strained.)* How is— Emily Meisenbach getting along?

JIM: Oh, that kraut-head!

LAURA: Why do you call her that?

JIM: That's what she was.

LAURA: You're not still—going with her?

JIM: I never see her.

LAURA: It said in the "Personal" section that you were—engaged!

JIM: I know, but I wasn't impressed by that—propaganda!

LAURA: It wasn't—the truth?

JIM: Only in Emily's optimistic opinion!

LAURA: Oh—

(Legend: "What have you done since high school?")
(Jim lights a cigarette and leans indolently back on his elbows smiling at Laura with a warmth and charm which lights her inwardly with altar candles. She remains by the table, picks up a piece from the glass menagerie collection, and turns it in her hands to cover her tumult.)

JIM: *(After several reflective puffs on his cigarette.)* What have you done since high school?

(She seems not to hear him.)

Huh?

(Laura looks up.)

I said what have you done since high school, Laura?

LAURA: Nothing much.

JIM: You must have been doing something these six long years.

LAURA: Yes.

JIM: Well, then, such as what?

LAURA: I took a business course at business college—

JIM: How did that work out?

LAURA: Well, not very—well—I had to drop out, it gave me—indigestion—

(Jim laughs gently.)

JIM: What are you doing now?

LAURA: I don't do anything—much. Oh, please don't think I sit around doing nothing! My glass collection takes up a good deal of time. Glass is something you have to take good care of.

JIM: What did you say—about glass?

LAURA: Collection I said—I have one— *(She clears her throat and turns away again, acutely shy.)*

JIM: *(Abruptly.)* You know what I judge to be the trouble with you? Inferiority complex! Know what that is? That's what they call it when someone low-rates himself! I understand it because I had it, too. Although my case was not so aggravated as yours seems to be. I had it until I took up public speaking, developed my voice, and learned that I had an aptitude for science. Before that time I never thought of myself as being outstanding in any way whatsoever! Now I've never made a regular study of it, but I have a friend who says I can analyze people better than doctors that make a profession of it. I don't claim that to be necessarily true, but I can sure guess a person's psychology, Laura! *(He takes out his gum.)* Excuse me, Laura. I always take it out when the flavor is gone. I'll use this scrap of paper to wrap it in. I know how it is to get it stuck on a shoe. *(He wraps the gum in paper and puts it in his pocket.)* Yep—that's what I judge to be your principal trouble. A lack of confidence in yourself as a person. You don't have the proper amount of faith in yourself. I'm basing that fact on a number of your remarks and also on certain observations I've made. For instance that clumping you thought was so awful in high school. You say that you even dreaded to walk into class. You see what you did? You dropped out of school, you gave up an education because of a clump, which as far as I know was practically non-existent! A little physical defect is what you have. Hardly noticeable even! Magnified thousands of times by imagination! You know what my strong advice to you is? Think of yourself as *superior* in some way!

LAURA: In what way would I think?

JIM: Why, man alive, Laura! Just look about you a little. What do you see? A world full of common people! All of 'em born and all of 'em going to die! Which of them has one-tenth of your good points! Or mine! Or anyone else's, as far as that goes—gosh! Everybody excels in some one thing. Some in many! *(He unconsciously glances at himself in the mirror.)* All you've got to do is discover in *what!* Take me, for instance. *(He adjusts his tie at the mirror.)* My interest happens to lie in electrodynamics. I'm taking a course in radio engineering at night school, Laura, on top of a fairly responsible job at the warehouse. I'm taking that course and studying public speaking.

LAURA: Ohhhh.

JIM: Because I believe in the future of television! *(Turning his back to her.)* I wish to be ready to go up right along with it. Therefore I'm planning to get in on the ground floor. In fact I've already made the right connections and all that remains is for the industry itself to get under way! Full steam — *(His eyes are starry.) Knowledge—*Zzzzzp! *Money—*Zzzzzzp!*—Power!* That's the cycle democracy is built on!

(His attitude is convincingly dynamic. Laura stares at him, even her shyness eclipsed in her absolute wonder. He suddenly grins.)

I guess you think I think a lot of myself!

LAURA: No—o-o-o, I—

JIM: Now how about you? Isn't there something you take more interest in than anything else?

LAURA: Well, I do—as I said—have my—glass collection—

(A peal of girlish laughter rings from the kitchenette.)

JIM: I'm not right sure I know what you're talking about. What kind of glass is it?

LAURA: Little articles of it, they're ornaments mostly! Most of them are little animals made out of glass, the tiniest little animals in the world. Mother calls them a glass menagerie! Here's an example of one, if you'd like to see it! This one is one of the oldest. It's nearly thirteen.

(Music: "The Glass Menagerie.")
(He stretches out his hand.)

Oh, be careful—if you breathe, it breaks!

JIM: I'd better not take it. I'm pretty clumsy with things.

LAURA: Go on, I trust you with him! *(She places the piece in his palm.)* There now—you're holding him gently! Hold him over the light, he loves the light! You see how the light shines through him?

JIM: It sure does shine!

LAURA: I shouldn't be partial, but he is my favorite one.

JIM: What kind of a thing is this one supposed to be?

LAURA: Haven't you noticed the single horn on his forehead?

JIM: A unicorn, huh?

LAURA: Mmmm-hmmm!

JIM: Unicorns—aren't they extinct in the modern world?

LAURA: I know!

JIM: Poor little fellow, he must feel sort of lonesome.

LAURA: *(Smiling.)* Well, if he does, he doesn't complain about it. He stays on a shelf with some horses that don't have horns and all of them seem to get along nicely together.

JIM: How do you know?

LAURA: *(Lightly.)* I haven't heard any arguments among them!

JIM: *(Grinning.)* No arguments, huh? Well, that's a pretty good sign! Where shall I set him?

LAURA: Put him on the table. They all like a change of scenery once in a while!

JIM: Well, well, well, well— *(He places the glass piece on the table, then raises his arms and stretches.)* Look how big my shadow is when I stretch!

LAURA: Oh, oh, yes—it stretches across the ceiling!

JIM: *(Crossing to the door.)* I think it's stopped raining. *(He opens the fire-escape door and the background music changes to a dance tune.)* Where does the music come from?

LAURA: From the Paradise Dance Hall across the alley.

JIM: How about cutting the rug a little, Miss Wingfield?

LAURA: Oh, I—

JIM: Or is your program filled up? Let me have a look at it. *(He grasps an imaginary card.)* Why, every dance is taken! I'll just have to scratch some out.

(Waltz music: "La Golondrina.")

Ahhh, a waltz! *(He executes some sweeping turns by himself, then holds his arms toward Laura.)*

LAURA: *(Breathlessly.)* I—can't dance!

JIM: There you go, that inferiority stuff!

LAURA: I've never danced in my life!

JIM: Come on, try!

LAURA: Oh, but I'd step on you!

JIM: I'm not made out of glass.

LAURA: How—how—how do we start?

JIM: Just leave it to me. You hold your arms out a little.

LAURA: Like this?

JIM: *(Taking her in his arms)* A little bit higher. Right. Now don't tighten up, that's the main thing about it—relax.

LAURA: *(Laughing breathlessly.)* It's hard not to.

JIM: Okay.

LAURA: I'm afraid you can't budge me.

JIM: What do you bet I can't? *(He swings her into motion.)*

LAURA: Goodness, yes, you can!

JIM: Let yourself go, now, Laura, just let yourself go.

LAURA: I'm—

JIM: Come on!

LAURA: —trying!

JIM: Not so stiff—easy does it!

LAURA: I know but I'm—

JIM: Loosen th' backbone! There now, that's a lot better.

LAURA: Am I?

JIM: Lots, lots better! *(He moves her about the room in a clumsy waltz.)*

LAURA: Oh, my!

JIM: Ha-ha!

LAURA: Oh, my goodness!

JIM: Ha-ha-ha!

(They suddenly bump into the table, and the glass piece on it falls to the floor. Jim stops the dance.)

What did we hit on?

LAURA: Table.

JIM: Did something fall off it? I think—

LAURA: Yes.

JIM: I hope that it wasn't the little glass horse with the horn!

LAURA: Yes. *(She stoops to pick it up.)*

JIM: Aw, aw, aw. Is it broken?

LAURA: Now it is just like all the other horses.

JIM: It's lost its—

LAURA: Horn! It doesn't matter. Maybe it's a blessing in disguise.

JIM: You'll never forgive me. I bet that that was your favorite piece of glass.

LAURA: I don't have favorites much. It's no tragedy, Freckles. Glass breaks so easily. No matter how careful you are. The traffic jars the shelves and things fall off them.

JIM: Still I'm awfully sorry that I was the cause.

LAURA: *(Smiling.)* I'll just imagine he had an operation. The horn was removed to make him feel less—freakish!

(They both laugh.)

Now he will feel more at home with the other horses, the ones that don't have horns. . . .

JIM: Ha-ha, that's very funny! *(Suddenly he is serious.)* I'm glad to see that you have a sense of humor. You know—you're—well—very different! Surprisingly different from anyone else I know! *(His voice becomes soft and hesitant with a genuine feeling.)* Do you mind me telling you that?

(Laura is abashed beyond speech.)

I mean it in a nice way—

(Laura nods shyly, looking away.)

You make me feel sort of—I don't know how to put it! I'm usually pretty good at expressing things, but—this is something that I don't know how to say!

(Laura touches her throat and clears it—turns the broken unicorn in her hands. His voice becomes softer.)

Has anyone ever told you that you were pretty?

(There is a pause, and the music rises slightly. Laura looks up slowly, with wonder, and shakes her head.)

Well, you are! In a very different way from anyone else. And all the nicer because of the difference, too.

(His voice becomes low and husky. Laura turns away, nearly faint with the novelty of her emotions.)

I wish that you were my sister. I'd teach you to have some confidence in yourself. The different people are not like other people, but being different is nothing to be ashamed of. Because other people are not such wonderful people. They're one hundred times one thousand. You're one times one! They walk all over the earth. You just stay here. They're common as— weeds, but—you—well, you're—*Blue Roses!*

(Image on screen: Blue Roses.*)*
(The music changes.)

LAURA: But blue is wrong for—roses. . . .
JIM: It's right for you! You're—pretty!
LAURA: In what respect am I pretty?
JIM: In all respects—believe me! Your eyes—your hair—are pretty! Your hands are pretty! *(He catches hold of her hand.)* You think I'm making this up because I'm invited to dinner and have to be nice. Oh, I could do that! I could put on an act for you, Laura, and say lots of things without being very sincere. But this time I am. I'm talking to you sincerely. I happened to notice you had this inferiority complex that keeps you from feeling comfortable with people. Somebody needs to build your confidence up and make you proud instead of shy and turning away and—blushing. Somebody—ought to—*kiss* you, Laura!

(His hand slips slowly up her arm to her shoulder as the music swells tumultuously. He suddenly turns her about and kisses her on the lips. When he releases her, Laura sinks on the sofa with a bright, dazed look. Jim backs away and fishes in his pocket for a cigarette.)
(Legend on screen: "A souvenir.")

Stumblejohn!

(He lights the cigarette, avoiding her look. There is a peal of girlish laughter from Amanda in the kitchenette. Laura slowly raises and opens her hand. It still contains the little broken glass animal. She looks at it with a tender, bewildered expression.)

Stumblejohn! I shouldn't have done that—that was way off the beam. You don't smoke, do you?

(She looks up, smiling, not hearing the question. He sits beside her rather gingerly. She looks at him speechlessly—waiting. He coughs decorously and moves a little farther aside as he considers the situation and senses her feelings, dimly, with perturbation. He speaks gently.)

Would you—care for a—mint?

(She doesn't seem to hear him but her look grows brighter even.)

Peppermint? Life Saver? My pocket's a regular drugstore—wherever I go. . . .

(He pops a mint in his mouth. Then he gulps and decides to make a clean breast of it. He speaks slowly and gingerly.) Laura, you know, if I had a sister like you, I'd do the same thing as Tom. I'd bring out fellows and —introduce her to them. The right type of boys—of a type to—appreciate her. Only—well—he made a mistake about me. Maybe I've got no call to be saying this. That may not have been the idea in having me over. But what if it was? There's nothing wrong about that. The only trouble is that in my case—I'm not in a situation to—do the right thing. I can't take down your number and say I'll phone. I can't call up next week and— ask for a date. I thought I had better explain the situation in case you— misunderstood it and—I hurt your feelings. . . .

(There is a pause. Slowly, very slowly, Laura's look changes, her eyes returning slowly from his to the glass figure in her palm. Amanda utters another gay laugh in the kitchenette.)

LAURA: *(Faintly.)* You—won't—call again?

JIM: No, Laura, I can't. *(He rises from the sofa.)* As I was just explaining, I've —got strings on me, Laura, I've—been going steady! I go out all the time with a girl named Betty. She's a home-girl like you, and Catholic, and Irish, and in a great many ways we—get along fine. I met her last summer on a moonlight boat trip up the river to Alton, on the *Majestic.* Well— right away from the start it was—love!

(Legend: Love!)
(Laura sways slightly forward and grips the arm of the sofa. He fails to notice, now enrapt in his own comfortable being.)

Being in love has made a new man of me!

(Leaning stiffly forward, clutching the arm of the sofa, Laura struggles visibly with her storm. But Jim is oblivious; she is a long way off.)

The power of love is really pretty tremendous! Love is something that— changes the whole world, Laura!

(The storm abates a little and Laura leans back. He notices her again.)

It happened that Betty's aunt took sick, she got a wire and had to go to Centralia. So Tom—when he asked me to dinner—I naturally just accepted the invitation, not knowing that you—that he—that I— *(He stops awkwardly.)* Huh—I'm a stumblejohn!

(He flops back on the sofa. The holy candles on the altar of Laura's face have been snuffed out. There is a look of almost infinite desolation. Jim glances at her uneasily.)

I wish that you would—say something.

(She bites her lip which was trembling and then bravely smiles. She opens her hand again on the broken glass figure. Then she gently takes his hand and raises it level with her own. She carefully places the unicorn in the palm of his hand, then pushes his fingers closed upon it.)

What are you—doing that for? You want me to have him? Laura?

(She nods.)

What for?

LAURA: A—souvenir. . . .

(She rises unsteadily and crouches beside the Victrola to wind it up.)
(Legend on screen: "Things have a way of turning out so badly!" Or image: "Gentleman caller waving goodbye—gaily.")
(At this moment Amanda rushes brightly back into the living room. She bears a pitcher of fruit punch in an old-fashioned cut-glass pitcher, and a plate of macaroons. The plate has a gold border and poppies painted on it.)

AMANDA: Well, well, well! Isn't the air delightful after the shower? I've made you children a little liquid refreshment.

(She turns gaily to Jim.) Jim, do you know that song about lemonade?

"Lemonade, lemonade
Made in the shade and stirred with a spade—
Good enough for any old maid!"

JIM: *(Uneasily.)* Ha-ha! No—I never heard it.
AMANDA: Why, Laura! You look so serious!
JIM: We were having a serious conversation.
AMANDA: Good! Now you're better acquainted!
JIM: *(Uncertainly.)* Ha-ha! Yes.
AMANDA: You modern young people are much more serious-minded than my generation. I was so gay as a girl!
JIM: You haven't changed, Mrs. Wingfield.
AMANDA: Tonight I'm rejuvenated! The gaiety of the occasion, Mr. O'Connor!
(She tosses her head with a peal of laughter, spilling some lemonade.) Oooo! I'm baptizing myself!

JIM: Here—let me—

AMANDA: *(Setting the pitcher down.)* There now. I discovered we had some maraschino cherries. I dumped them in, juice and all!

JIM: You shouldn't have gone to that trouble, Mrs. Wingfield.

AMANDA: Trouble, trouble? Why it was loads of fun! Didn't you hear me cutting up in the kitchen? I bet your ears were burning! I told Tom how outdone with him I was for keeping you to himself so long a time! He should have brought you over much, much sooner! Well, now that you've found your way, I want you to be a very frequent caller! Not just occasional but all the time. Oh, we're going to have a lot of gay times together! I see them coming! Mmm, just breathe that air! So fresh, and the moon's so pretty! I'll skip back out—I know where my place is when young folks are having a—serious conversation!

JIM: Oh, don't go out, Mrs. Wingfield. The fact of the matter is I've got to be going.

AMANDA: Going, now? You're joking! Why, it's only the shank of the evening, Mr. O'Connor!

JIM: Well, you know how it is.

AMANDA: You mean you're a young workingman and have to keep working-men's hours. We'll let you off early tonight. But only on the condition that next time you stay later. What's the best night for you? Isn't Saturday night the best night for you workingmen?

JIM: I have a couple of time-clocks to punch, Mrs. Wingfield. One at morning, another one at night!

AMANDA: My, but you *are* ambitious! You work at night, too?

JIM: No, Ma'am, not work but—Betty!

(He crosses deliberately to pick up his hat. The band at the Paradise Dance Hall goes into a tender waltz.)

AMANDA: Betty? Betty? Who's—Betty!

(There is an ominous cracking sound in the sky.)

JIM: Oh, just a girl. The girl I go steady with!

(He smiles charmingly. The sky falls.)
(Legend: "The Sky Falls.")

AMANDA: *(A long-drawn exhalation.)* Ohhhh . . . Is it a serious romance, Mr. O'Connor?

JIM: We're going to be married the second Sunday in June.

AMANDA: Ohhhh—how nice! Tom didn't mention that you were engaged to be married.

JIM: The cat's not out of the bag at the warehouse yet. You know how they are. They call you Romeo and stuff like that. *(He stops at the oval mirror to put on his hat. He carefully shapes the brim and the crown to give a*

discreetly dashing effect.) It's been a wonderful evening, Mrs. Wingfield.
  I guess this is what they mean by Southern hospitality.

AMANDA: It really wasn't anything at all.

JIM: I hope it don't seem like I'm rushing off. But I promised Betty I'd pick
  her up at the Wabash depot, an' by the time I get my jalopy down there
  her train'll be in. Some women are pretty upset if you keep 'em waiting.

AMANDA: Yes, I know—the tyranny of women! *(She extends her hand.)* Goodbye, Mr. O'Connor. I wish you luck—and happiness—and success! All
  three of them, and so does Laura! Don't you, Laura?

LAURA: Yes!

JIM: *(Taking Laura's hand.)* Goodbye, Laura. I'm certainly going to treasure
  that souvenir. And don't you forget the good advice I gave you. *(He raises
  his voice to a cheery shout.)* So long, Shakespeare! Thanks again, ladies.
  Good night!

*(He grins and ducks jauntily out. Still bravely grimacing, Amanda closes the door
on the gentleman caller. Then she turns back to the room with a puzzled expression.
She and Laura don't dare to face each other. Laura crouches beside the Victrola
to wind it.)*

AMANDA: *(Faintly.)* Things have a way of turning out so badly. I don't believe
  that I would play the Victrola. Well, well—well! Our gentleman caller was
  engaged to be married! *(She raises her voice.)* Tom!

TOM: *(From the kitchenette.)* Yes, Mother?

AMANDA: Come in here a minute. I want to tell you something awfully funny.

TOM: *(Entering with a macaroon and a glass of the lemonade.)* Has the gentleman caller gotten away already?

AMANDA: The gentleman caller has made an early departure. What a wonderful joke you played on us!

TOM: How do you mean?

AMANDA: You didn't mention that he was engaged to be married.

TOM: Jim? Engaged?

AMANDA: That's what he just informed us.

TOM: I'll be jiggered! I didn't know about that.

AMANDA: That seems very peculiar.

TOM: What's peculiar about it?

AMANDA: Didn't you call him your best friend down at the warehouse?

TOM: He is, but how did I know?

AMANDA: It seems extremely peculiar that you wouldn't know your best friend
  was going to be married!

TOM: The warehouse is where I work, not where I know things about people!

AMANDA: You don't know things anywhere! You live in a dream; you manufacture illusions!

(He crosses to the door.)

  Where are you going?

TOM: I'm going to the movies.

AMANDA: That's right, now that you've had us make such fools of ourselves. The effort, the preparations, all the expense! The new floor lamp, the rug, the clothes for Laura! All for what? To entertain some other girl's fiancé! Go to the movies, go! Don't think about us, a mother deserted, an unmarried sister who's crippled and has no job! Don't let anything interfere with your selfish pleasure! Just go, go, go—to the movies!

TOM: All right, I will! The more you shout about my selfishness to me the quicker I'll go, and I won't go to the movies!

AMANDA: Go, then! Go to the moon—you selfish dreamer!

(Tom smashes his glass on the floor. He plunges out on the fire escape, slamming the door. Laura screams in fright. The dance-hall music becomes louder. Tom stands on the fire escape, gripping the rail. The moon breaks through the storm clouds, illuminating his face.)

(Legend on screen: "And so goodbye . . .")

(Tom's closing speech is timed with what is happening inside the house. We see, as though through soundproof glass, that Amanda appears to be making a comforting speech to Laura, who is huddled upon the sofa. Now that we cannot hear the mother's speech, her silliness is gone and she has dignity and tragic beauty. Laura's hair hides her face until, at the end of the speech, she lifts her head to smile at her mother. Amanda's gestures are slow and graceful, almost dancelike, as she comforts her daughter. At the end of her speech she glances a moment at the father's picture—then withdraws through the portieres. At the close of Tom's speech, Laura blows out the candles, ending the play.)

TOM: I didn't go to the moon, I went much further—for time is the longest distance between two places. Not long after that I was fired for writing a poem on the lid of a shoe-box. I left Saint Louis. I descended the steps of this fire escape for a last time and followed, from then on, in my father's footsteps, attempting to find in motion what was lost in space. I traveled around a great deal. The cities swept about me like dead leaves, leaves that were brightly colored but torn away from the branches. I would have stopped, but I was pursued by something. It always came upon me unawares, taking me altogether by surprise. Perhaps it was a familiar bit of music. Perhaps it was only a piece of transparent glass. Perhaps I am walking along a street at night, in some strange city, before I have found companions. I pass the lighted window of a shop where perfume is sold. The window is filled with pieces of colored glass, tiny transparent bottles in delicate colors, like bits of a shattered rainbow. Then all at once my sister touches my shoulder. I turn around and look into her eyes. Oh, Laura, Laura, I tried to leave you behind me, but I am more faithful than I intended to be! I reach for a cigarette, I cross the street, I run into the movies or a bar, I buy a drink, I speak to the nearest stranger—anything that can blow your candles out!

(Laura bends over the candles.)

For nowadays the world is lit by lightning! Blow out your candles, Laura
—and so goodbye. . . .

(She blows the candles out.)

QUESTIONS

1. What stage settings and props serve as reminders that this is "a
   memory play"? How does the lighting serve the same purpose? The
   music? The dialogue? The actions of the characters?
2. What seem to be the major effects of the box set, with most of the
   action confined to the living room and dining room of the Wingfield
   apartment?
3. Characterize Amanda. What speeches and actions do most to help
   you understand her?
4. Using their most important speeches and actions as evidence, how
   would you characterize Tom and Laura?
5. Why is Jim O'Connor, "a nice, ordinary, young man," important to
   the play?
6. What importance can you suggest for the father, who never appears?
7. Beginning with the fire escape—"a structure whose name is a touch
   of accidental poetic truth"—what symbols seem important? Why?
8. What is the symbolism in the breaking of the horn on the glass
   unicorn? How is the impression immediately after the horn breaks
   changed or qualified by the end of the play?
9. When Amanda dismisses Tom and characterizes him in her last
   speech ("Go then! Go to the moon—you selfish dreamer!"), how
   fully are we supposed to accept her summation?
10. Why did Tom leave home? Where did he go?
11. Considering especially Tom's last speech, and the simultaneous
    scene in memory within the house, what is symbolized when Laura
    "blows the candles out"?

DEATH OF A SALESMAN

Death of a Salesman takes brilliant advantage of the conventions and physical
possibilities of the twentieth-century theater. The audience now sits in a darkened auditorium to watch a play strikingly enhanced in light and sound by the
magic of electricity, played upon a multilevel set by actors schooled in the
realistic techniques common in America and Europe since the days of the
Moscow Art Theater. Like Tennessee Williams and other twentieth-century
playwrights, Miller has tried to make full use of the technical possibilities of his

time by writing elaborate directions to guide the technicians and give the actors a sense of the lives they are trying to lead (rather than merely the lines they are supposed to speak). Reading the play, we must be careful to absorb the stage directions, so that we see the action unfold in the way the author intended. Producing it, we may want to make some changes (as we would with Shakespeare) to adapt it to the technical possibilities of the stage we have available.

Much of the realism is interior; we see Willy's thoughts and dreams as well as his speeches and actions. The exposition of the present situation blends with the exposition of past events that have placed the Loman family where it is. Miller thought of the play as a tragedy of a common man attempting, like Oedipus, to confront a fate that in the end destroys and does not destroy him.

DEATH OF A SALESMAN

Certain private conversations in two acts and a requiem

Arthur Miller   (1915–   )

The Characters

WILLY LOMAN	UNCLE BEN
LINDA	HOWARD WAGNER
BIFF	JENNY
HAPPY	STANLEY
BERNARD	MISS FORSYTHE
THE WOMAN	LETTA
CHARLEY	

The action takes place in Willy Loman's house and yard and in various places he visits in the New York and Boston of today.

Act I

A melody is heard, played upon a flute. It is small and fine, telling of grass and trees and the horizon. The curtain rises.

Before us is the Salesman's house. We are aware of towering, angular shapes behind it, surrounding it on all sides. Only the blue light of the sky falls upon the house and forestage; the surrounding area shows an angry glow of orange. As more light appears, we see a solid vault of apartment houses around the small, fragile-seeming home. An air of the dream clings to the place, a dream rising out of reality. The kitchen at center seems actual enough, for there is a kitchen table with three chairs, and a refrigerator. But no other fixtures are seen. At the back of the kitchen there is a draped entrance, which leads to the living-room. To the right of the kitchen, on a level raised two feet, is a bedroom furnished only with a brass bedstead and a straight chair. On a shelf over the bed a silver athletic trophy stands. A window opens onto the apartment house at the side.

Behind the kitchen, on a level raised six and a half feet, is the boys' bedroom, at present barely visible. Two beds are dimly seen, and at the back of the room a dormer window. (This bedroom is above the unseen living-room.) At the left a stairway curves up to it from the kitchen.

The entire setting is wholly or, in some places, partially transparent. The roof-line of the house is one-dimensional; under and over it we see the apartment buildings. Before the house lies an apron, curving beyond the forestage into the orchestra. This forward area serves as the back yard as well as the locale of all Willy's imaginings and of his city scenes. Whenever the action is in the present the actors observe the imaginary wall-lines, entering the house only through its door at the left. But in the scenes of the past these boundaries are broken, and characters enter or leave a room by stepping "through" a wall onto the forestage.

From the right, Willy Loman, the Salesman, enters, carrying two large sample cases. The flute plays on. He hears but is not aware of it. He is past sixty years of age, dressed quietly. Even as he crosses the stage to the doorway of the house, his exhaustion is apparent. He unlocks the door, comes into the kitchen, and thankfully lets his burden down, feeling the soreness of his palms. A word-sigh escapes his lips—it might be "Oh, boy, oh, boy." He closes the door, then carries his cases out into the living-room, through the draped kitchen doorway.

Linda, his wife, has stirred in her bed at the right. She gets out and puts on a robe, listening. Most often jovial, she has developed an iron repression of her exceptions to Willy's behavior—she more than loves him, she admires him, as though his mercurial nature, his temper, his massive dreams and little cruelties, served her only as sharp reminders of the turbulent longings within him, longings which she shares but lacks the temperament to utter and follow to their end.

LINDA *(hearing Willy outside the bedroom, calls with some trepidation):* Willy!

WILLY: It's all right. I came back.

LINDA: Why? What happened? *(Slight pause)* Did something happen, Willy?

WILLY: No, nothing happened.

LINDA: You didn't smash the car, did you?

WILLY *(with casual irritation):* I said nothing happened. Didn't you hear me?

LINDA: Don't you feel well?

WILLY: I'm tired to the death. *(The flute has faded away. He sits on the bed beside her, a little numb)* I couldn't make it. I just couldn't make it, Linda.

LINDA *(very carefully, delicately):* Where were you all day? You look terrible.

WILLY: I got as far as a little above Yonkers. I stopped for a cup of coffee. Maybe it was the coffee.

LINDA: What?

WILLY *(after a pause):* I suddenly couldn't drive any more. The car kept going off onto the shoulder, y'know?

LINDA *(helpfully):* Oh. Maybe it was the steering again. I don't think Angelo knows the Studebaker.

WILLY: No, it's me, it's me. Suddenly I realize I'm goin' sixty miles an hour and I don't remember the last five minutes. I'm—I can't seem to—keep my mind to it.

LINDA: Maybe it's your glasses. You never went for your new glasses.

WILLY: No, I see everything. I came back ten miles an hour. It took me nearly four hours from Yonkers.

LINDA *(resigned):* Well, you'll just have to take a rest, Willy, you can't continue this way.

WILLY: I just got back from Florida.

LINDA: But you didn't rest your mind. Your mind is overactive, and the mind is what counts, dear.

WILLY: I'll start out in the morning. Maybe I'll feel better in the morning. *(She is taking off his shoes)* These goddam arch supports are killing me.

LINDA: Take an aspirin. Should I get you an aspirin? It'll soothe you.

WILLY *(with wonder):* I was driving along, you understand? And I was fine. I was even observing the scenery. You can imagine, me looking at scenery, on the road every week of my life. But it's so beautiful up there, Linda, the trees are so thick, and the sun is warm. I opened the windshield and just let the warm air bathe over me. And then all of a sudden I'm goin' off the road! I'm tellin' ya, I absolutely forgot I was driving. If I'd've gone the other way over the white line I might've killed somebody. So I went on again—and five minutes later I'm dreamin' again, and I nearly— *(He presses two fingers against his eyes)* I have such thoughts, I have such strange thoughts.

LINDA: Willy, dear. Talk to them again. There's no reason why you can't work in New York.

WILLY: They don't need me in New York. I'm the New England man. I'm vital in New England.

LINDA: But you're sixty years old. They can't expect you to keep traveling every week.

WILLY: I'll have to send a wire to Portland. I'm supposed to see Brown and Morrison tomorrow morning at ten o'clock to show the line. Goddammit, I could sell them! *(He starts putting on his jacket)*

LINDA *(taking the jacket from him):* Why don't you go down to the place tomorrow and tell Howard you've simply got to work in New York? You're too accommodating, dear.

WILLY: If old man Wagner was alive, I'd a been in charge of New York now! That man was a prince, he was a masterful man. But that boy of his, that Howard, he don't appreciate. When I went north the first time, the Wagner Company didn't know where New England was!

LINDA: Why don't you tell those things to Howard, dear?

WILLY *(encouraged):* I will, I definitely will. Is there any cheese?

LINDA: I'll make you a sandwich.

WILLY: No, go to sleep. I'll take some milk. I'll be up right away. The boys in?

LINDA: They're sleeping. Happy took Biff on a date tonight.

WILLY *(interested):* That so?

LINDA: It was so nice to see them shaving together, one behind the other, in the bathroom. And going out together. You notice? The whole house smells of shaving lotion.

WILLY: Figure it out. Work a lifetime to pay off a house. You finally own it, and there's nobody to live in it.

LINDA: Well, dear, life is a casting off. It's always that way.

WILLY: No, no, some people—some people accomplish something. Did Biff say anything after I went this morning?

LINDA: You shouldn't have criticized him, Willy, especially after he just got off the train. You mustn't lose your temper with him.

WILLY: When the hell did I lose my temper? I simply asked him if he was making any money. Is that a criticism?

LINDA: But, dear, how could he make any money?

WILLY *(worried and angered):* There's such an undercurrent in him. He became a moody man. Did he apologize when I left this morning?

LINDA: He was crestfallen, Willy. You know how he admires you. I think if he finds himself, then you'll both be happier and not fight any more.

WILLY: How can he find himself on a farm? Is that a life? A farmhand? In the beginning, when he was young, I thought, well, a young man, it's good for him to tramp around, take a lot of different jobs. But it's more than ten years now and he has yet to make thirty-five dollars a week!

LINDA: He's finding himself, Willy.

WILLY: Not finding yourself at the age of thirty-four is a disgrace!

LINDA: Shh!

WILLY: The trouble is he's lazy, goddammit!

LINDA: Willy, please!

WILLY: Biff is a lazy bum!

LINDA: They're sleeping. Get something to eat. Go on down.

WILLY: Why did he come home? I would like to know what brought him home.

LINDA: I don't know. I think he's still lost, Willy. I think he's very lost.

WILLY: Biff Loman is lost. In the greatest country in the world a young man with such—personal attractiveness, gets lost. And such a hard worker. There's one thing about Biff—he's not lazy.

LINDA: Never.

WILLY *(with pity and resolve):* I'll see him in the morning; I'll have a nice talk with him. I'll get him a job selling. He could be big in no time. My God! Remember how they used to follow him around in high school? When he smiled at one of them their faces lit up. When he walked down the street . . . *(He loses himself in reminiscences)*

LINDA *(trying to bring him out of it):* Willy, dear, I got a new kind of American-type cheese today. It's whipped.

WILLY: Why do you get American when I like Swiss?

LINDA: I just thought you'd like a change—

WILLY: I don't want a change! I want Swiss cheese. Why am I always being contradicted?

LINDA *(with a covering laugh):* I thought it would be a surprise.

WILLY: Why don't you open a window in here, for God's sake?

LINDA *(with infinite patience):* They're all open, dear.

WILLY: The way they boxed us in here. Bricks and windows, windows and bricks.

LINDA: We should've bought the land next door.

WILLY: The street is lined with cars. There's not a breath of fresh air in the neighborhood. The grass don't grow any more, you can't raise a carrot in the back yard. They should've had a law against apartment houses. Remember those two beautiful elm trees out there? When I and Biff hung the swing between them?

LINDA: Yeah, like being a million miles from the city.

WILLY: They should've arrested the builder for cutting those down. They massacred the neighborhood. *(Lost)* More and more I think of those days, Linda. This time of year it was lilac and wisteria. And then the peonies would come out, and the daffodils. What fragrance in this room!

LINDA: Well, after all, people had to move somewhere.

WILLY: No, there's more people now.

LINDA: I don't think there's more people. I think—

WILLY: There's more people! That's what ruining this country! Population is getting out of control. The competition is maddening! Smell the stink from that apartment house! And another one on the other side . . . How can they whip cheese?

(On Willy's last line, Biff and Happy raise themselves up in their beds, listening)

LINDA: Go down, try it. And be quiet.

WILLY *(turning to Linda, guiltily):* You're not worried about me, are you, sweetheart?

BIFF: What's the matter?

HAPPY: Listen!

LINDA: You've got too much on the ball to worry about.

WILLY: You're my foundation and my support, Linda.

LINDA: Just try to relax, dear. You make mountains out of molehills.

WILLY: I won't fight with him any more. If he wants to go back to Texas, let him go.

LINDA: He'll find his way.

WILLY: Sure. Certain men just don't get started till later in life. Like Thomas Edison, I think. Or B. F. Goodrich. One of them was deaf. *(He starts for the bedroom doorway)* I'll put my money on Biff.

LINDA: And Willy—if it's warm Sunday we'll drive in the country. And we'll open the windshield, and take lunch.

WILLY: No, the windshields don't open on the new cars.

LINDA: But you opened it today.

WILLY: Me? I didn't. *(He stops)* Now isn't that peculiar! Isn't that a remarkable — *(He breaks off in amazement and fright as the flute is heard distantly)*

LINDA: What, darling?

WILLY: That is the most remarkable thing.

LINDA: What, dear?

WILLY: I was thinking of the Chevvy. *(Slight pause)* Nineteen twenty-eight
. . . when I had that red Chevvy— *(Breaks off)* That funny? I coulda
sworn I was driving that Chevvy today.

LINDA: Well, that's nothing. Something must've reminded you.

WILLY: Remarkable. Ts. Remember those days? The way Biff used to simonize
that car? The dealer refused to believe there was eighty thousand miles
on it. *(He shakes his head)* Heh! *(To Linda)* Close your eyes, I'll be right
up. *(He walks out of the bedroom)*

HAPPY *(To Biff):* Jesus, maybe he smashed up the car again!

LINDA *(calling after Willy):* Be careful on the stairs, dear! The cheese is on the
middle shelf! *(She turns, goes over to the bed, takes his jacket, and goes out
of the bedroom)*

*(Light has risen on the boys' room. Unseen, Willy is heard talking to himself,
"Eighty thousand miles," and a little laugh. Biff gets out of bed, comes downstage
a bit, and stands attentively. Biff is two years older than his brother Happy, well
built, but in these days bears a worn air and seems less self-assured. He has
succeeded less, and his dreams are stronger and less acceptable than Happy's.
Happy is tall, powerfully made. Sexuality is like a visible color on him, or a scent
that many women have discovered. He, like his brother, is lost, but in a different
way, for he has never allowed himself to turn his face toward defeat and is thus
more confused and hard-skinned, although seemingly more content.)*

HAPPY *(getting out of bed):* He's going to get his license taken away if he keeps
that up. I'm getting nervous about him, y'know, Biff?

BIFF: His eyes are going.

HAPPY: No, I've driven with him. He sees all right. He just doesn't keep his
mind on it. I drove into the city with him last week. He stops at a green
light and then it turns red and he goes. *(He laughs)*

BIFF: Maybe he's color-blind.

HAPPY: Pop? Why he's got the finest eye for color in the business. You know
that.

BIFF *(sitting down on his bed):* I'm going to sleep.

HAPPY: You're not still sour on Dad, are you, Biff?

BIFF: He's all right, I guess.

WILLY *(underneath them, in the living-room):* Yes, sir, eighty thousand miles
—eighty-two thousand!

BIFF: You smoking?

HAPPY *(holding out a pack of cigarettes):* Want one?

BIFF *(taking a cigarette):* I can never sleep when I smell it.

WILLY: What a simonizing job, heh!

HAPPY *(with deep sentiment):* Funny, Biff, y'know? Us sleeping in here again?
The old beds. *(He pats his bed affectionately)* All the talk that went across
those two beds, huh? Our whole lives.

BIFF: Yeah. Lotta dreams and plans.

HAPPY *(with a deep and masculine laugh):* About five hundred women would like to know what was said in this room.

(They share a soft laugh)

BIFF: Remember that big Betsy something—what the hell was her name—over on Bushwick Avenue?

HAPPY *(combing his hair):* With the collie dog!

BIFF: That's the one. I got you in there, remember?

HAPPY: Yeah, that was my first time—I think. Boy, there was a pig! *(They laugh, almost crudely)* You taught me everything I know about women. Don't forget that.

BIFF: I bet you forgot how bashful you used to be. Especially with girls.

HAPPY: Oh, I still am, Biff.

BIFF: Oh, go on.

HAPPY: I just control it, that's all. I think I got less bashful and you got more so. What happened, Biff? Where's the old humor, the old confidence? *(He shakes Biff's knee. Biff gets up and moves restlessly about the room)* What's the matter?

BIFF: Why does Dad mock me all the time?

HAPPY: He's not mocking you, he—

BIFF: Everything I say there's a twist of mockery on his face. I can't get near him.

HAPPY: He just wants you to make good, that's all. I wanted to talk to you about Dad for a long time, Biff. Something's—happening to him. He—talks to himself.

BIFF: I noticed that this morning. But he always mumbled.

HAPPY: But not so noticeable. It got so embarrassing I sent him to Florida. And you know something? Most of the time he's talking to you.

BIFF: What's he say about me?

HAPPY: I can't make it out.

BIFF: What's he say about me?

HAPPY: I think the fact that you're not settled, that you're still kind of up in the air . . .

BIFF: There's one or two other things depressing him, Happy.

HAPPY: What do you mean?

BIFF: Never mind. Just don't lay it all to me.

HAPPY: But I think if you just got started—I mean—is there any future for you out there?

BIFF: I tell ya, Hap, I don't know what the future is. I don't know—what I'm supposed to want.

HAPPY: What do you mean?

BIFF: Well, I spent six or seven years after high school trying to work myself up. Shipping clerk, salesman, business of one kind or another. And it's a measly manner of existence. To get on that subway on the hot mornings in summer. To devote your whole life to keeping stock, or making phone calls, or selling or buying. To suffer fifty weeks of the year for the sake of a two-week vacation, when all you really desire is to be outdoors, with your shirt off. And always to have to get ahead of the next fella. And still —that's how you build a future.

HAPPY: Well, you really enjoy it on a farm? Are you content out there?

BIFF *(with rising agitation):* Hap, I've had twenty or thirty different kinds of jobs since I left home before the war, and it always turns out the same. I just realized it lately. In Nebraska when I herded cattle, and the Dakotas, and Arizona, and now in Texas. It's why I came home now, I guess, because I realized it. This farm I work on, it's spring there now, see? And they've got about fifteen new colts. There's nothing more inspiring or— beautiful than the sight of a mare and a new colt. And it's cool there now, see? Texas is cool now, and it's spring. And whenever spring comes to where I am, I suddenly get the feeling, my God, I'm not gettin' anywhere! What the hell am I doing, playing around with horses, twenty-eight dollars a week! I'm thirty-four years old, I oughta be makin' my future. That's when I come running home. And now, I get here, and I don't know what to do with myself. *(After a pause)* I've always made a point of not wasting my life, and everytime I come back here I know that all I've done is to waste my life.

HAPPY: You're a poet, you know that, Biff? You're a—you're an idealist!

BIFF: No, I'm mixed up very bad. Maybe I oughta get married. Maybe I oughta get stuck into something. Maybe that's my trouble. I'm like a boy. I'm not married, I'm not in business, I just—I'm like a boy. Are you content, Hap? You're a success, aren't you? Are you content?

HAPPY: Hell, no!

BIFF: Why? You're making money, aren't you?

HAPPY *(moving about with energy, expressiveness):* All I can do now is wait for the merchandise manager to die. And suppose I get to be merchandise manager? He's a good friend of mine, and he just built a terrific estate on Long Island. And he lived there about two months and sold it, and now he's building another one. He can't enjoy it once it's finished. And I know that's just what I would do. I don't know what the hell I'm workin' for. Sometimes I sit in my apartment—all alone. And I think of the rent I'm paying. And it's crazy. But then, it's what I always wanted. My own apartment, a car, and plenty of women. And still, goddammit, I'm lonely.

BIFF *(with enthusiasm):* Listen, why don't you come out West with me?

HAPPY: You and I, heh?

BIFF: Sure, maybe we could buy a ranch. Raise cattle, use our muscles. Men built like we are should be working out in the open.

HAPPY *(avidly):* The Loman Brothers, heh?

BIFF *(with vast affection):* Sure, we'd be known all over the counties!

HAPPY *(enthralled):* That's what I dream about, Biff. Sometimes I want to just rip my clothes off in the middle of the store and outbox that goddam merchandise manager. I mean I can outbox, outrun, and outlift anybody in that store, and I have to take orders from those common, petty sons-of-bitches till I can't stand it any more.

BIFF: I'm tellin' you, kid, if you were with me I'd be happy out there.

HAPPY *(enthused):* See, Biff, everybody around me is so false that I'm constantly lowering my ideals . . .

BIFF: Baby, together we'd stand up for one another, we'd have someone to trust.

HAPPY: If I were around you—

BIFF: Hap, the trouble is we weren't brought up to grub for money. I don't know how to do it.

HAPPY: Neither can I!

BIFF: Then let's go!

HAPPY: The only thing is—what can you make out there?

BIFF: But look at your friend. Builds an estate and then hasn't the peace of mind to live in it.

HAPPY: Yeah, but when he walks into the store the waves part in front of him. That's fifty-two thousand dollars a year coming through the revolving door, and I got more in my pinky finger than he's got in his head.

BIFF: Yeah, but you just said—

HAPPY: I gotta show some of those pompous, self-important executives over there that Hap Loman can make the grade. I want to walk into the store the way he walks in. Then I'll go with you, Biff. We'll be together yet, I swear. But take those two we had tonight. Now weren't they gorgeous creatures?

BIFF: Yeah, yeah, most gorgeous I've had in years.

HAPPY: I get that any time I want, Biff. Whenever I feel disgusted. The only trouble is, it gets like bowling or something. I just keep knockin' them over and it doesn't mean anything. You still run around a lot?

BIFF: Naa. I'd like to find a girl—steady, somebody with substance.

HAPPY: That's what I long for.

BIFF: Go on! You'd never come home.

HAPPY: I would! Somebody with character, with resistance! Like Mom, y'know? You're gonna call me a bastard when I tell you this. That girl Charlotte I was with tonight is engaged to be married in five weeks. *(He tries on his new hat)*

BIFF: No kiddin'!

HAPPY: Sure, the guy's in line for the vice-presidency of the store. I don't know what gets into me, maybe I just have an overdeveloped sense of competition or something, but I went and ruined her, and furthermore I can't get rid of her. And he's the third executive I've done that to. Isn't that a crummy characteristic? And to top it all, I go to their weddings! *(Indignantly, but laughing)* Like I'm not supposed to take bribes. Manufacturers offer me a hundred-dollar bill now and then to throw an order their way. You know how honest I am, but it's like this girl, see. I hate myself for it. Because I don't want the girl, and, still, I take it and—I love it!

BIFF: Let's go to sleep.

HAPPY: I guess we didn't settle anything, heh?

BIFF: I just got one idea that I think I'm going to try.

HAPPY: What's that?

BIFF: Remember Bill Oliver?

HAPPY: Sure, Oliver is very big now. You want to work for him again?

BIFF: No, but when I quit he said something to me. He put his arm on my shoulder, and he said, "Biff, if you ever need anything, come to me."

HAPPY: I remember that. That sounds good.

BIFF: I think I'll go to see him. If I could get ten thousand or even seven or eight thousand dollars I could buy a beautiful ranch.

HAPPY: I bet he'd back you. 'Cause he thought highly of you, Biff. I mean, they all do. You're well liked, Biff. That's why I say to come back here, and we both have the apartment. And I'm tellin' you, Biff, any babe you want . . .

BIFF: No, with a ranch I could do the work I like and still be something. I just wonder though. I wonder if Oliver still thinks I stole that carton of basketballs.

HAPPY: Oh, he probably forgot that long ago. It's almost ten years. You're too sensitive. Anyway, he didn't really fire you.

BIFF: Well, I think he was going to. I think that's why I quit. I was never sure whether he knew or not. I know he thought the world of me, though. I was the only one he'd let lock up the place.

WILLY (below): You gonna wash the engine, Biff?

HAPPY: Shh!

(Biff looks at Happy, who is gazing down, listening. Willy is mumbling in the parlor.)

HAPPY: You hear that?

(They listen. Willy laughs warmly)

BIFF (growing angry): Doesn't he know Mom can hear that?

WILLY: Don't get your sweater dirty, Biff!

(A look of pain crosses Biff's face)

HAPPY: Isn't that terrible? Don't leave again, will you? You'll find a job here. You gotta stick around. I don't know what to do about him, it's getting embarrassing.

WILLY: What a simonizing job!

BIFF: Mom's hearing that!

WILLY: No kiddin', Biff, you got a date? Wonderful!

HAPPY: Go on to sleep. But talk to him in the morning, will you?

BIFF *(reluctantly getting into bed):* With her in the house. Brother!
HAPPY *(getting into bed):* I wish you'd have a good talk with him.

(The light on their room begins to fade)

BIFF *(to himself in bed):* That selfish, stupid . . .
HAPPY: Sh . . . Sleep, Biff.

Their light is out. Well before they have finished speaking, Willy's form is dimly seen below in the darkened kitchen. He opens the refrigerator, searches in there, and takes out a bottle of milk. The apartment houses are fading out, and the entire house and surroundings become covered with leaves. Music insinuates itself as the leaves appear.

WILLY: Just wanna be careful with those girls, Biff, that's all. Don't make any promises. No promises of any kind. Because a girl, y'know, they always believe what you tell 'em, and you're very young, Biff, you're too young to be talking seriously to girls.

(Light rises on the kitchen. Willy, talking, shuts the refrigerator door and comes downstage to the kitchen table. He pours milk into a glass. He is totally immersed in himself, smiling faintly)

WILLY: Too young entirely, Biff. You want to watch your schooling first. Then when you're all set, there'll be plenty of girls for a boy like you. *(He smiles broadly at a kitchen chair)* That so? The girls pay for you? *(He laughs)* Boy, you must really be makin' a hit.

(Willy is gradually addressing—physically—a point offstage, speaking through the wall of the kitchen, and his voice has been rising in volume to that of a normal conversation.)

WILLY: I been wondering why you polish the car so careful. Ha! Don't leave the hubcaps, boys. Get the chamois to the hubcaps. Happy, use newspaper on the windows, it's the easiest thing. Show him how to do it, Biff! You see, Happy? Pad it up, use it like a pad. That's it, that's it, good work. You're doin' all right, Hap. *(He pauses, then nods in approbation for a few seconds, then looks upward)* Biff, first thing we gotta do when we get time is clip that big branch over the house. Afraid it's gonna fall in a storm and hit the roof. Tell you what. We get a rope and sling her around, then we climb up there with a couple of saws and take her down. Soon as you finish the car, boys, I wanna see ya. I got a surprise for you, boys.
BIFF *(offstage):* Whatta ya got, Dad?
WILLY: No, you finish first. Never leave a job till you're finished—remember that. *(Looking toward the "big trees")* Biff, up in Albany I saw a beautiful hammock. I think I'll buy it next trip, and we'll hang it right between those two elms. Wouldn't that be something? Just swingin' there under those branches. Boy, that would be . . .

(Young Biff and Young Happy appear from the direction Willy was addressing. Happy carries rags and a pail of water. Biff, wearing a sweater with a block "S," carries a football.)

BIFF *(pointing in the direction of the car offstage):* How's that, Pop, professional?

WILLY: Terrific. Terrific job, boys. Good work, Biff.

HAPPY: Where's the surprise, Pop?

WILLY: In the back seat of the car.

HAPPY: Boy! *(He runs off)*

BIFF: What is it, Dad? Tell me, what'd you buy?

WILLY *(laughing, cuffs him):* Never mind, something I want you to have.

BIFF *(turns and starts off):* What is it, Hap?

HAPPY *(offstage):* It's a punching bag!

BIFF: Oh, Pop!

WILLY: It's got Gene Tunney's signature on it!

(Happy runs onstage with a punching bag)

BIFF: Gee, how'd you know we wanted a punching bag?

WILLY: Well, it's the finest thing for the timing.

HAPPY *(lies down on his back and pedals with his feet):* I'm losing weight, you notice. Pop?

WILLY *(to Happy):* Jumping rope is good too.

BIFF: Did you see the new football I got?

WILLY *(examining the ball):* Where'd you get a new ball?

BIFF: The coach told me to practice my passing.

WILLY: That so? And he gave you the ball, heh?

BIFF: Well, I borrowed it from the locker room. *(He laughs confidentially)*

WILLY *(laughing with him at the theft):* I want you to return that.

HAPPY: I told you he wouldn't like it!

BIFF *(angrily):* Well, I'm bringing it back!

WILLY *(stopping the incipient argument, to Happy):* Sure, he's gotta practice with a regulation ball, doesn't he? *(To Biff)* Coach'll probably congratulate you on your initiative!

BIFF: Oh, he keeps congratulating my initiative all the time, Pop.

WILLY: That's because he likes you. If somebody else took that ball there'd be an uproar. So what's the report, boys, what's the report?

BIFF: Where'd you go this time, Dad? Gee we were lonesome for you.

WILLY *(pleased, puts an arm around each boy and they come down to the apron):* Lonesome, heh?

BIFF: Missed you every minute.

WILLY: Don't say? Tell you a secret, boys. Don't breathe it to a soul. Someday I'll have my own business, and I'll never have to leave home any more.

HAPPY: Like Uncle Charley, heh?

WILLY: Bigger than Uncle Charley! Because Charley is not—liked. He's liked, but he's not—well liked.

BIFF: Where'd you go this time, Dad?

WILLY: Well, I got on the road, and I went north to Providence. Met the Mayor.

BIFF: The Mayor of Providence!

WILLY: He was sitting in the hotel lobby.

BIFF: What'd he say?

WILLY: He said, "Morning!" And I said, "You got a fine city here, Mayor." And then he had coffee with me. And then I went to Waterbury. Waterbury is a fine city. Big clock city, the famous Waterbury clock. Sold a nice bill there. And then Boston—Boston is the cradle of the Revolution. A fine city. And a couple of other towns in Mass., and on to Portland and Bangor and straight home!

BIFF: Gee, I'd love to go with you sometime, Dad.

WILLY: Soon as summer comes.

HAPPY: Promise?

WILLY: You and Hap and I, and I'll show you all the towns. America is full of beautiful towns and fine, upstanding people. And they know me, boys, they know me up and down New England. The finest people. And when I bring you fellas up, there'll be open sesame for all of us, 'cause one thing, boys: I have friends. I can park my car in any street in New England, and the cops protect it like their own. This summer, heh?

BIFF and HAPPY *(together):* Yeah! You bet!

WILLY: We'll take our bathing suits.

HAPPY: We'll carry your bags, Pop!

WILLY: Oh, won't that be something! Me comin' into the Boston stores with you boys carryin' my bags. What a sensation!

(Biff is prancing around, practicing passing the ball)

WILLY: You nervous, Biff, about the game?

BIFF: Not if you're gonna be there.

WILLY: What do they say about you in school, now that they made you captain?

HAPPY: There's a crowd of girls behind him everytime the classes change.

BIFF *(taking Willy's hand):* This Saturday, Pop, this Saturday—just for you, I'm going to break through for a touchdown.

HAPPY: You're supposed to pass.

BIFF: I'm takin' one play for Pop. You watch me, Pop, and when I take off my helmet, that means I'm breakin' out. Then you watch me crash through that line!

WILLY *(kisses Biff):* Oh, wait'll I tell this in Boston!

(Bernard enters in knickers. He is younger than Biff, earnest and loyal, a worried boy.)

BERNARD: Biff, where are you? You're supposed to study with me today.

WILLY: Hey, looka Bernard. What're you lookin' so anemic about, Bernard?

BERNARD: He's gotta study, Uncle Willy. He's got Regents[1] next week.

HAPPY *(tauntingly, spinning Bernard around):* Let's box, Bernard!

BERNARD: Biff! *(He gets away from Happy)* Listen, Biff, I heard Mr. Birnbaum say that if you don't start studyin' math he's gonna flunk you, and you won't graduate. I heard him!

WILLY: You better study with him, Biff. Go ahead now.

BERNARD: I heard him!

BIFF: Oh, Pop, you didn't see my sneakers! *(He holds up a foot for Willy to look at)*

WILLY: Hey, that's a beautiful job of printing!

BERNARD *(wiping his glasses):* Just because he printed University of Virginia on his sneakers doesn't mean they've got to graduate him, Uncle Willy!

WILLY *(angrily):* What're you talking about? With scholarships to three universities they're gonna flunk him?

BERNARD: But I heard Mr. Birnbaum say—

WILLY: Don't be a pest, Bernard! *(To his boys)* What an anemic!

BERNARD: Okay, I'm waiting for you in my house, Biff.

(Bernard goes off. The Lomans laugh.)

WILLY: Bernard is not well liked, is he?

BIFF: He's liked, but he's not well liked.

HAPPY: That's right, Pop.

WILLY: That's just what I mean. Bernard can get the best marks in school, y'understand, but when he gets out in the business world, y'understand, you are going to be five times ahead of him. That's why I thank Almighty God you're both built like Adonises.[2] Because the man who makes an appearance in the business world, the man who creates personal interest, is the man who gets ahead. Be liked and you will never want. You take me, for instance. I never have to wait in line to see a buyer. "Willy Loman is here!" That's all they have to know, and I go right through.

BIFF: Did you know them dead, Pop?

WILLY: Knocked 'em cold in Providence, slaughtered 'em in Boston.

HAPPY *(on his back, pedaling again):* I'm losing weight, you notice, Pop?

(Linda enters, as of old, a ribbon in her hair, carrying a basket of washing)

LINDA *(with youthful energy):* Hello, dear!

WILLY: Sweetheart!

LINDA: How'd the Chevvy run?

WILLY: Chevrolet, Linda, is the greatest car ever built. *(To the boys)* Since when do you let your mother carry wash up the stairs?

---

[1]A New York State high school proficiency examination.   [2]Adonis, in Greek myth, was a handsome human beloved by Aphrodite, goddess of love and beauty.

BIFF: Grab hold there, boy!

HAPPY: Where to, Mom?

LINDA: Hang them up on the line. And you better go down to your friends, Biff. The cellar is full of boys. They don't know what to do with themselves.

BIFF: Ah, when Pop comes home they can wait!

WILLY *(laughs appreciatively):* You better go down and tell them what to do, Biff.

BIFF: I think I'll have them sweep out the furnace room.

WILLY: Good work, Biff.

BIFF *(goes through wall-line of kitchen to doorway at back and calls down):* Fellas! Everybody sweep out the furnace room! I'll be right down!

VOICES: All right! Okay, Biff.

BIFF: George and Sam and Frank, come out back! We're hangin' up the wash! Come on, Hap, on the double! *(He and Happy carry out the basket)*

LINDA: The way they obey him!

WILLY: Well, that's training, the training. I'm tellin' you, I was sellin' thousands and thousands, but I had to come home.

LINDA: Oh, the whole block'll be at that game. Did you sell anything?

WILLY: I did five hundred gross in Providence and seven hundred gross in Boston.

LINDA: No! Wait a minute, I've got a pencil. *(She pulls pencil and paper out of her apron pocket)* That makes your commission . . . Two hundred— my God! Two hundred and twelve dollars!

WILLY: Well, I—I did—about a hundred and eighty gross in Providence. Well, no—it came to—roughly two hundred gross on the whole trip.

LINDA *(without hesitation):* Two hundred gross. That's . . . *(She figures)*

WILLY: The trouble was that three of the stores were half closed for inventory in Boston. Otherwise I woulda broke records.

LINDA: Well, it makes seventy dollars and some pennies. That's very good.

WILLY: What do we owe?

LINDA: Well, on the first there's sixteen dollars on the refrigerator—

WILLY: Why sixteen?

LINDA: Well, the fan belt broke, so it was a dollar eighty.

WILLY: But it's brand new.

LINDA: Well, the man said that's the way it is. Till they work themselves in, y'know.

(They move through the wall-line into the kitchen)

WILLY: I hope we didn't get stuck on that machine.

LINDA: They got the biggest ads of any of them!

WILLY: I know, it's a fine machine. What else?

LINDA: Well, there's nine-sixty for the washing machine. And for the vacuum cleaner, there's three and a half due on the fifteenth. Then the roof, you got twenty-one dollars remaining.

WILLY: It don't leak, does it?

LINDA: No, they did a wonderful job. Then you owe Frank for the carburetor.

WILLY: I'm not going to pay that man! That goddam Chevrolet, they ought to prohibit the manufacture of that car!

LINDA: Well, you owe him three and a half. And odds and ends, comes to around a hundred and twenty dollars by the fifteenth.

WILLY: A hundred and twenty dollars! My God, if business don't pick up I don't know what I'm gonna do!

LINDA: Well, next week you'll do better.

WILLY: Oh, I'll knock 'em dead next week. I'll go to Hartford. I'm very well liked in Hartford. You know, the trouble is, Linda, people don't seem to take to me.

(They move onto the forestage)

LINDA: Oh, don't be foolish.

WILLY: I know it when I walk in. They seem to laugh at me.

LINDA: Why? Why would they laugh at you? Don't talk that way, Willy.

(Willy moves to the edge of the stage. Linda goes into the kitchen and starts to darn stockings.)

WILLY: I don't know the reason for it, but they just pass me by. I'm not noticed.

LINDA: But you're doing wonderful, dear. You're making seventy to a hundred dollars a week.

WILLY: But I gotta be at it ten, twelve hours a day. Other men—I don't know —they do it easier. I don't know why—I can't stop myself—I talk too much. A man oughta come in with a few words. One thing about Charley. He's a man of few words, and they respect him.

LINDA: You don't talk too much, you're just lively.

WILLY *(smiling):* Well, I figure, what the hell, life is short, a couple of jokes. *(To himself)* I joke too much! *(The smile goes)*

LINDA: Why? You're—

WILLY: I'm fat. I'm very—foolish to look at, Linda. I didn't tell you, but Christmas time I happened to be calling on F. H. Stewarts, and a salesman I know, as I was going in to see the buyer I heard him say something about —walrus. And I—I cracked him right across the face. I won't take that. I simply will not take that. But they do laugh at me. I know that.

LINDA: Darling . . .

WILLY: I gotta overcome it. I know I gotta overcome it. I'm not dressing to advantage, maybe.

LINDA: Willy, darling, you're the handsomest man in the world—

WILLY: Oh, no, Linda.

LINDA: To me you are. *(Slight pause)* The handsomest.

(From the darkness is heard the laughter of a woman. Willy doesn't turn to it, but it continues through Linda's lines.)

LINDA: And the boys, Willy. Few men are idolized by their children the way you are.

(Music is heard as behind a scrim,[3] *to the left of the house. The Woman, dimly seen, is dressing.)*

WILLY *(with great feeling):* You're the best there is, Linda, you're a pal, you know that? On the road—on the road I want to grab you sometimes and just kiss the life outa you.

(The laughter is loud now, and he moves into a brightening area at the left, where The Woman has come from behind the scrim and is standing, putting on her hat, looking into a "mirror" and laughing.)

WILLY: 'Cause I get so lonely—especially when business is bad and there's nobody to talk to. I get the feeling that I'll never sell anything again, that I won't make a living for you, or a business, a business for the boys. *(He talks through The Woman's subsiding laughter! The Woman primps at the "mirror.")* There's so much I want to make for—

THE WOMAN: Me? You didn't make me, Willy. I picked you.

WILLY *(pleased):* You picked me?

THE WOMAN *(who is quite proper-looking, Willy's age):* I did. I've been sitting at that desk watching all the salesmen go by, day in, day out. But you've got such a sense of humor, and we do have such a good time together, don't we?

WILLY: Sure, sure. *(He takes her in his arms)* Why do you have to go now?

THE WOMAN: It's two o'clock . . .

WILLY: No, come on in! *(He pulls her)*

THE WOMAN: . . . my sister'll be scandalized. When'll you be back?

WILLY: Oh, two weeks about. Will you come up again?

THE WOMAN: Sure thing. You do make me laugh. It's good for me. *(She squeezes his arm, kisses him)* And I think you're a wonderful man.

WILLY: You picked me, heh?

THE WOMAN: Sure. Because you're so sweet. And such a kidder.

WILLY: Well, I'll see you next time I'm in Boston.

THE WOMAN: I'll put you right through to the buyers.

WILLY *(slapping her bottom):* Right. Well, bottoms up!

THE WOMAN *(slaps him gently and laughs):* You just kill me, Willy. *(He suddenly grabs her and kisses her roughly)* You kill me. And thanks for the stockings. I love a lot of stockings. Well, good night.

WILLY: Good night. And keep your pores open!

THE WOMAN: Oh, Willy!

(The Woman bursts out laughing, and Linda's laughter blends in. The Woman disappears into the dark. Now the area at the kitchen table brightens. Linda is

---

[3] A painted gauze cloth, opaque when illuminated from the front but becoming nearly transparent as the lights come on from behind.

sitting where she was at the kitchen table, but now is mending a pair of her silk stockings.)

LINDA: You are, Willy. The handsomest man. You've got no reason to feel that—

WILLY *(coming out of The Woman's dimming area and going over to Linda):* I'll make it all up to you, Linda, I'll—

LINDA: There's nothing to make up, dear. You're doing fine, better than—

WILLY *(noticing her mending):* What's that?

LINDA: Just mending my stockings. They're so expensive—

WILLY *(angrily, taking them from her):* I won't have you mending stockings in this house! Now throw them out!

(Linda puts the stockings in her pocket)

BERNARD *(entering on the run):* Where is he? If he doesn't study!

WILLY *(moving to the forestage, with great agitation):* You'll give him the answers!

BERNARD: I do, but I can't on a Regents! That's a state exam! They're liable to arrest me!

WILLY: Where is he? I'll whip him, I'll whip him!

LINDA: And he'd better give back that football, Willy, it's not nice.

WILLY: Biff! Where is he? Why is he taking everything?

LINDA: He's too rough with the girls, Willy. All the mothers are afraid of him!

WILLY: I'll whip him!

BERNARD: He's driving the car without a license!

(The Woman's laugh is heard)

WILLY: Shut up!

LINDA: All the mothers—

WILLY: Shut up!

BERNARD *(backing quietly away and out):* Mr. Birnbaum says he's stuck up.

WILLY: Get outa here!

BERNARD: If he doesn't buckle down he'll flunk math! *(He goes off)*

LINDA: He's right, Willy, you've gotta—

WILLY *(exploding at her):* There's nothing the matter with him! You want him to be a worm like Bernard? He's got spirit, personality . . .

(As he speaks, Linda, almost in tears, exits into the livingroom. Willy is alone in the kitchen, wilting and staring. The leaves are gone. It is night again, and the apartment houses look down from behind.)

WILLY: Loaded with it. Loaded! What is he stealing? He's giving it back, isn't he? Why is he stealing? What did I tell him? I never in my life told him anything but decent things.

(Happy in pajamas has come down the stairs; Willy suddenly becomes aware of Happy's presence)

HAPPY: Let's go now, come on.

WILLY (*sitting down at the kitchen table*): Huh! Why did she have to wax the floors herself? Everytime she waxes the floors she keels over. She knows that!

HAPPY: Shh! Take it easy. What brought you back tonight?

WILLY: I got an awful scare. Nearly hit a kid in Yonkers. God! Why didn't I go to Alaska with my brother Ben that time! Ben! That man was a genius, that man was success incarnate! What a mistake! He begged me to go.

HAPPY: Well, there's no use in—

WILLY: You guys! There was a man started with the clothes on his back and ended up with diamond mines!

HAPPY: Boy, someday I'd like to know how he did it.

WILLY: What's the mystery? The man knew what he wanted and went out and got it! Walked into a jungle, and comes out, the age of twenty-one, and he's rich! The world is an oyster, but you don't crack it open on a mattress!

HAPPY: Pop, I told you I'm gonna retire you for life.

WILLY: You'll retire me for life on seventy goddam dollars a week? And your women and your car and your apartment, and you'll retire me for life! Christ's sake, I couldn't get past Yonkers today! Where are you guys, where are you? The woods are burning! I can't drive a car!

(*Charley has appeared in the doorway. He is a large man, slow of speech, laconic, immovable. In all he says, despite what he says, there is pity, and, now, trepidation. He has a robe over pajamas, slippers on his feet. He enters the kitchen.*)

CHARLEY: Everything all right?

HAPPY: Yeah, Charley, everything's . . .

WILLY: What's the matter?

CHARLEY: I heard some noise. I thought something happened. Can't we do something about the walls? You sneeze in here, and in my house hats blow off.

HAPPY: Let's go to bed, Dad. Come on.

(*Charley signals to Happy to go*)

WILLY: You go ahead, I'm not tired at the moment.

HAPPY (*to Willy*): Take it easy, huh? (*He exits*)

WILLY: What're you doin' up?

CHARLEY (*sitting down at the kitchen table opposite Willy*): Couldn't sleep good. I had a heartburn.

WILLY: Well, you don't know how to eat.

CHARLEY: I eat with my mouth.

WILLY: No, you're ignorant. You gotta know about vitamins and things like that.

CHARLEY: Come on, let's shoot. Tire you out a little.

WILLY (*hesitantly*): All right. You got cards?

CHARLEY *(taking a deck from his pocket):* Yeah, I got them. Someplace. What is it with those vitamins?

WILLY *(dealing):* They build up your bones. Chemistry.

CHARLEY: Yeah, but there's no bones in a heartburn.

WILLY: What are you talkin' about? Do you know the first thing about it?

CHARLEY: Don't get insulted.

WILLY: Don't talk about something you don't know anything about.

(They are playing. Pause)

CHARLEY: What're you doin' home?

WILLY: A little trouble with the car.

CHARLEY: Oh. *(Pause)* I'd like to take a trip to California.

WILLY: Don't say.

CHARLEY: You want a job?

WILLY: I got a job, I told you that. *(After a slight pause)* What the hell are you offering me a job for?

CHARLEY: Don't get insulted.

WILLY: Don't insult me.

CHARLEY: I don't see no sense in it. You don't have to go on this way.

WILLY: I got a good job. *(Slight pause)* What do you keep comin' in here for?

CHARLEY: You want me to go?

WILLY *(after a pause, withering):* I can't understand it. He's going back to Texas again. What the hell is that?

CHARLEY: Let him go.

WILLY: I got nothin' to give him, Charley, I'm clean, I'm clean.

CHARLEY: He won't starve. None of them starve. Forget about him.

WILLY: Then what have I got to remember?

CHARLEY: You take it too hard. To hell with it. When a deposit bottle is broken you don't get your nickel back.

WILLY: That's easy enough for you to say.

CHARLEY: That ain't easy for me to say.

WILLY: Did you see the ceiling I put up in the living-room?

CHARLEY: Yeah, that's a piece of work. To put up a ceiling is a mystery to me. How do you do it?

WILLY: What's the difference?

CHARLEY: Well, talk about it.

WILLY: You gonna put up a ceiling?

CHARLEY: How could I put up a ceiling?

WILLY: Then what the hell are you bothering me for?

CHARLEY: You're insulted again.

WILLY: A man who can't handle tools is not a man. You're disgusting.

CHARLEY: Don't call me disgusting, Willy.

(Uncle Ben, carrying a valise and an umbrella, enters the forestage from around the right corner of the house. He is a stolid man, in his sixties, with a mustache

and an authoritative air. He is utterly certain of his destiny, and there is an aura of far places about him. He enters exactly as Willy speaks.)

WILLY: I'm getting awfully tired, Ben.

(Ben's music is heard. Ben looks around at everything.)

CHARLEY: Good, keep playing; you'll sleep better. Did you call me Ben?

(Ben looks at his watch)

WILLY: That's funny. For a second there you reminded me of my brother Ben.

BEN: I only have a few minutes. *(He strolls, inspecting the place. Willy and Charley continue playing.)*

CHARLEY: You never heard from him again, heh? Since that time?

WILLY: Didn't Linda tell you? Couple of weeks ago we got a letter from his wife in Africa. He died.

CHARLEY: That so.

BEN *(chuckling):* So this is Brooklyn, eh?

CHARLEY: Maybe you're in for some of his money.

WILLY: Naa, he had seven sons. There's just one opportunity I had with that man . . .

BEN: I must make a train, William. There are several properties I'm looking at in Alaska.

WILLY: Sure, sure! If I'd gone with him to Alaska that time, everything would've been totally different.

CHARLEY: Go on, you'd froze to death up there.

WILLY: What're you talking about?

BEN: Opportunity is tremendous in Alaska, William. Surprised you're not up there.

WILLY: Sure, tremendous.

CHARLEY: Heh?

WILLY: There was the only man I ever met who knew the answers.

CHARLEY: Who?

BEN: How are you all?

WILLY *(taking a pot, smiling):* Fine, fine.

CHARLEY: Pretty sharp tonight.

BEN: Is Mother living with you?

WILLY: No, she died a long time ago.

CHARLEY: Who?

BEN: That's too bad. Fine specimen of a lady, Mother.

WILLY *(to Charley):* Heh?

BEN: I'd hoped to see the old girl.

CHARLEY: Who died?

BEN: Heard anything from Father, have you?

WILLY *(unnerved):* What do you mean, who died?

CHARLEY *(taking a pot):* What're you talkin' about?

BEN *(looking at his watch):* William, it's half-past eight!

WILLY *(as though to dispel his confusion he angrily stops Charley's hand):* That's my build!

CHARLEY: I put the ace—

WILLY: If you don't know how to play the game I'm not gonna throw my money away on you!

CHARLEY *(rising):* It was my ace, for God's sake!

WILLY: I'm through, I'm through!

BEN: When did Mother die?

WILLY: Long ago. Since the beginning you never knew how to play cards.

CHARLEY *(picks up the cards and goes to the door):* All right! Next time I'll bring a deck with five aces.

WILLY: I don't play that kind of game!

CHARLEY *(turning to him):* You ought to be ashamed of yourself!

WILLY: Yeah?

CHARLEY: Yeah! *(He goes out)*

WILLY *(slamming the door after him):* Ignoramus!

BEN *(as Willy comes toward him through the wall-line of the kitchen):* So you're William.

WILLY *(shaking Ben's hand):* Ben! I've been waiting for you so long! What's the answer? How did you do it?

BEN: Oh, there's a story in that.

(Linda enters the forestage, as of old, carrying the wash basket)

LINDA: Is this Ben?

BEN *(gallantly):* How do you do, my dear.

LINDA: Where've you been all these years? Willy's always wondered why you—

WILLY *(pulling Ben away from her impatiently):* Where is Dad? Didn't you follow him? How did you get started?

BEN: Well, I don't know how much you remember.

WILLY: Well, I was just a baby, of course, only three or four years old—

BEN: Three years and eleven months.

WILLY: What a memory, Ben!

BEN: I have many enterprises, William, and I have never kept books.

WILLY: I remember I was sitting under the wagon in—was it Nebraska?

BEN: It was South Dakota, and I gave you a bunch of wild flowers.

WILLY: I remember you walking away down some open road.

BEN *(laughing):* I was going to find Father in Alaska.

WILLY: Where is he?

BEN: At that age I had a very faulty view of geography, William. I discovered after a few days that I was heading due south, so instead of Alaska, I ended up in Africa.

LINDA: Africa!

WILLY: The Gold Coast!

BEN: Principally diamond mines.

LINDA: Diamond mines!

BEN: Yes, my dear. But I've only a few minutes—

WILLY: No! Boys! Boys! *(Young Biff and Happy appear)* Listen to this. This is your Uncle Ben, a great man! Tell my boys, Ben!

BEN: Why, boys, when I was seventeen I walked into the jungle, and when I was twenty-one I walked out. *(He laughs)* And by God I was rich.

WILLY *(to the boys):* You see what I been talking about? The greatest things can happen!

BEN *(glancing at his watch):* I have an appointment in Ketchikan Tuesday week.

WILLY: No, Ben! Please tell about Dad. I want my boys to hear. I want them to know the kind of stock they spring from. All I remember is a man with a big beard, and I was in Mamma's lap, sitting around a fire, and some kind of high music.

BEN: His flute. He played the flute.

WILLY: Sure, the flute, that's right!

(New music is heard, a high, rollicking tune)

BEN: Father was a very great and a very wild-hearted man. We would start in Boston, and he'd toss the whole family into the wagon, and then he'd drive the team right across the country; through Ohio, and Indiana, Michigan, Illinois, and all the Western states. And we'd stop in the towns and sell the flutes that he'd made on the way. Great inventor, Father. With one gadget he made more in a week than a man like you could make in a lifetime.

WILLY: That's just the way I'm bringing them up, Ben—rugged, well liked, all-around.

BEN: Yeah? *(To Biff)* Hit that, boy—hard as you can. *(He pounds his stomach)*

BIFF: Oh, no, sir!

BEN *(taking boxing stance):* Come on, get to me! *(He laughs)*

WILLY: Go to it, Biff! Go ahead, show him!

BIFF: Okay! *(He cocks his fist and starts in)*

LINDA *(to Willy):* Why must he fight, dear?

BEN *(sparring with Biff):* Good boy! Good boy!

WILLY: How's that, Ben, heh?

HAPPY: Give him the left, Biff!

LINDA: Why are you fighting?

BEN: Good boy! *(Suddenly comes in, trips Biff, and stands over him, the point of his umbrella poised over Biff's eye)*

LINDA: Look out, Biff!

BIFF: Gee!

BEN *(patting Biff's knee):* Never fight fair with a stranger, boy. You'll never get out of the jungle that way. *(Taking Linda's hand and bowing)* It was an honor and a pleasure to meet you, Linda.

LINDA *(withdrawing her hand coldly, frightened):* Have a nice—trip.

BEN *(to Willy):* And good luck with your—what do you do?

WILLY: Selling.

BEN: Yes. Well . . . *(He raises his hand in farewell to all)*

WILLY: No, Ben, I don't want you to think . . . *(He takes Ben's arm to show him)* It's Brooklyn, I know, but we hunt too.

BEN: Really, now.

WILLY: Oh, sure, there's snakes and rabbits and—that's why I moved out here. Why, Biff can fell any one of these trees in no time! Boys! Go right over to where they're building the apartment house and get some sand. We're gonna rebuild the entire front stoop right now! Watch this, Ben!

BIFF: Yes, sir! On the double, Hap!

HAPPY *(as he and Biff run off):* I lost weight, Pop, you notice?

(Charley enters in knickers, even before the boys are gone)

CHARLEY: Listen, if they steal any more from that building the watchman'll put the cops on them!

LINDA *(to Willy):* Don't let Biff . . .

(Ben laughs lustily)

WILLY: You shoulda seen the lumber they brought home last week. At least a dozen six-by-tens worth all kinds a money.

CHARLEY: Listen, if that watchman—

WILLY: I gave them hell, understand. But I got a couple of fearless characters there.

CHARLEY: Willy, the jails are full of fearless characters.

BEN *(clapping Willy on the back, with a laugh at Charley):* And the stock exchange, friend!

WILLY *(joining in Ben's laughter):* Where are the rest of your pants?

CHARLEY: My wife bought them.

WILLY: Now all you need is a golf club and you can go upstairs and go to sleep. *(To Ben):* Great athlete! Between him and his son Bernard they can't hammer a nail!

BERNARD *(rushing in):* The watchman's chasing Biff!

WILLY *(angrily):* Shut up! He's not stealing anything!

LINDA *(alarmed, hurrying off left):* Where is he? Biff, dear! *(She exits)*

WILLY *(moving toward the left, away from Ben):* There's nothing wrong. What's the matter with you?

BEN: Nervy boy. Good!

WILLY *(laughing):* Oh, nerves of iron, that Biff!

CHARLEY: Don't know what it is. My New England man comes back and he's bleedin', they murdered him up there.

WILLY: It's contacts, Charley, I got important contacts!

CHARLEY *(sarcastically):* Glad to hear it, Willy. Come in later, we'll shoot a little casino. I'll take some of your Portland money. *(He laughs at Willy and exits)*

WILLY *(turning to Ben):* Business is bad, it's murderous. But not for me, of course.

BEN: I'll stop by on my way back to Africa.

WILLY *(longingly):* Can't you stay a few days? You're just what I need, Ben, because I—I have a fine position here, but I—well, Dad left when I was such a baby and I never had a chance to talk to him and I still feel—kind of temporary about myself.

BEN: I'll be late for my train.

(They are at opposite ends of the stage)

WILLY: Ben, my boys—can't we talk? They'd go into the jaws of hell for me, see, but I—

BEN: William, you're being first-rate with your boys. Outstanding, manly chaps!

WILLY *(hanging on to his words):* Oh, Ben, that's good to hear! Because sometimes I'm afraid that I'm not teaching them the right kind of—Ben, how should I teach them?

BEN *(giving great weight to each word, and with a certain vicious audacity):* William, when I walked into the jungle, I was seventeen. When I walked out I was twenty-one. And, by God, I was rich! *(He goes off into darkness around the right corner of the house)*

WILLY: . . . was rich! That's just the spirit I want to imbue them with! To walk into a jungle! I was right! I was right! I was right!

(Ben is gone, but Willy is still speaking to him as Linda, in nightgown and robe, enters the kitchen, glances around for Willy, then goes to the door of the house, looks out and sees him. Comes down to his left. He looks at her.)

LINDA: Willy, dear? Willy?

WILLY: I was right!

LINDA: Did you have some cheese? *(He can't answer)* It's very late, darling. Come to bed, heh?

WILLY *(looking straight up):* Gotta break your neck to see a star in this yard.

LINDA: You coming in?

WILLY: Whatever happened to that diamond watch fob? Remember? When Ben came from Africa that time? Didn't he give me a watch fob with a diamond in it?

LINDA: You pawned it, dear. Twelve, thirteen years ago. For Biff's radio correspondence course.

WILLY: Gee, that was a beautiful thing. I'll take a walk.

LINDA: But you're in your slippers.

WILLY *(starting to go around the house at the left):* I was right! I was! *(Half to Linda, as he goes shaking his head)* What a man! There was a man worth talking to. I was right!

LINDA *(calling after Willy):* But in your slippers, Willy!

(Willy is almost gone when Biff, in his pajamas, comes down the stairs and enters the kitchen)

BIFF: What is he doing out there?

LINDA: Sh!

BIFF: God Almighty, Mom, how long has he been doing this?

LINDA: Don't, he'll hear you.

BIFF: What the hell is the matter with him?

LINDA: It'll pass by morning.

BIFF: Shouldn't we do anything?

LINDA: Oh, my dear, you should do a lot of things, but there's nothing to do, so go to sleep.

(Happy comes down the stair and sits on the steps)

HAPPY: I never heard him so loud, Mom.

LINDA: Well, come around more often; you'll hear him. *(She sits down at the table and mends the lining of Willy's jacket)*

BIFF: Why didn't you ever write me about this, Mom?

LINDA: How would I write to you? For over three months you had no address.

BIFF: I was on the move. But you know I thought of you all the time. You know that, don't you, pal?

LINDA: I know, dear, I know. But he likes to have a letter. Just to know that there's still a possibility for better things.

BIFF: He's not like this all the time, is he?

LINDA: It's when you come home he's always the worst.

BIFF: When I come home?

LINDA: When you write you're coming, he's all smiles, and talks about the future, and—he's just wonderful. And then the closer you seem to come, the more shaky he gets, and then, by the time you get here, he's arguing, and he seems angry at you. I think it's just that maybe he can't bring himself to—to open up to you. Why are you so hateful to each other? Why is that?

BIFF *(evasively):* I'm not hateful, Mom.

LINDA: But you no sooner come in the door than you're fighting!

BIFF: I don't know why. I mean to change. I'm tryin', Mom, you understand?

LINDA: Are you home to stay now?

BIFF: I don't know. I want to look around, see what's doin'.

LINDA: Biff, you can't look around all your life, can you?

BIFF: I just can't take hold, Mom. I can't take hold of some kind of a life.

LINDA: Biff, a man is not a bird, to come and go with the springtime.

BIFF: Your hair . . . . *(He touches her hair)* Your hair got so gray.

LINDA: Oh, it's been gray since you were in high school. I just stopped dyeing it, that's all.

BIFF: Dye it again, will ya? I don't want my pal looking old. *(He smiles)*

LINDA: You're such a boy! You think you can go away for a year and . . .

You've got to get it into your head now that one day you'll knock on this
door and there'll be strange people here—

BIFF: What are you talking about? You're not even sixty, Mom.

LINDA: But what about your father?

BIFF *(lamely):* Well, I meant him too.

HAPPY: He admires Pop.

LINDA: Biff, dear, if you don't have any feeling for him, then you can't have
any feeling for me.

BIFF: Sure I can, Mom.

LINDA: No. You can't just come to see me, because I love him. *(With a threat,
but only a threat, of tears)* He's the dearest man in the world to me, and
I won't have anyone making him feel unwanted and low and blue. You've
got to make up your mind now, darling, there's no leeway any more.
Either he's your father and you pay him that respect, or else you're not
to come here. I know he's not easy to get along with—nobody knows that
better than me—but . . .

WILLY *(from the left, with a laugh):* Hey, hey, Biffo!

BIFF *(starting to go out after Willy):* What the hell is the matter with him?
(Happy stops him)

LINDA: Don't—don't go near him!

BIFF: Stop making excuses for him! He always, always wiped the floor with
you. Never had an ounce of respect for you.

HAPPY: He's always had respect for—

BIFF: What the hell do you know about it?

HAPPY *(surlily):* Just don't call him crazy!

BIFF: He's got no character—Charley wouldn't do this. Not in his own house
—spewing out that vomit from his mind.

HAPPY: Charley never had to cope with what he's got to.

BIFF: People are worse off than Willy Loman. Believe me, I've seen them!

LINDA: Then make Charley your father, Biff. You can't do that, can you? I
don't say he's a great man. Willy Loman never made a lot of money. His
name was never in the paper. He's not the finest character that ever lived.
But he's a human being, and a terrible thing is happening to him. So
attention must be paid. He's not to be allowed to fall into his grave like
an old dog. Attention, attention must be finally paid to such a person. You
called him crazy—

BIFF: I didn't mean—

LINDA: No, a lot of people think he's lost his—balance. But you don't have
to be very smart to know what his trouble is. The man is exhausted.

HAPPY: Sure!

LINDA: A small man can be just as exhausted as a great man. He works
for a company thirty-six years this March, opens up unheard-of territories
to their trademark, and now in his old age they take his salary
away.

HAPPY *(indignantly):* I didn't know that, Mom.

LINDA: You never asked, my dear! Now that you get your spending money someplace else you don't trouble your mind with him.

HAPPY: But I gave you money last—

LINDA: Christmas time, fifty dollars! To fix the hot water it cost ninety-seven fifty! For five weeks he's been on straight commission, like a beginner, an unknown!

BIFF: Those ungrateful bastards!

LINDA: Are they any worse than his sons? When he brought them business, when he was young, they were glad to see him. But now his old friends, the old buyers that loved him so and always found some order to hand him in a pinch—they're all dead, retired. He used to be able to make six, seven calls a day in Boston. Now he takes his valises out of the car and puts them back and takes them out again and he's exhausted. Instead of walking he talks now. He drives seven hundred miles, and when he gets there no one knows him any more, no one welcomes him. And what goes through a man's mind, driving seven hundred miles home without having earned a cent? Why shouldn't he talk to himself? Why? When he has to go to Charley and borrow fifty dollars a week and pretend to me that it's his pay? How long can that go on? How long? You see what I'm sitting here and waiting for? And you tell me he has no character? The man who never worked a day but for your benefit? When does he get the medal for that? Is this his reward—to turn around at the age of sixty-three and find his sons, who he loved better than his life, one a philandering bum—

HAPPY: Mom!

LINDA: That's all you are, my baby! *(To Biff)* And you! What happened to the love you had for him? You were such pals! How you used to talk to him on the phone every night! How lonely he was till he could come home to you!

BIFF: All right, Mom. I'll live here in my room, and I'll get a job. I'll keep away from him, that's all.

LINDA: No, Biff. You can't stay here and fight all the time.

BIFF: He threw me out of this house, remember that.

LINDA: Why did he do that? I never knew why?

BIFF: Because I know he's a fake and he doesn't like anybody around who knows!

LINDA: Why a fake? In what way? What do you mean?

BIFF: Just don't lay it all at my feet. It's between me and him—that's all I have to say. I'll chip in from now on. He'll settle for half my pay check. He'll be all right. I'm going to bed. *(He starts for the stairs)*

LINDA: He won't be all right.

BIFF *(turning on the stairs, furiously):* I hate this city and I'll stay here. Now what do you want?

LINDA: He's dying, Biff.

(Happy turns quickly to her)

BIFF *(after a pause):* Why is he dying?

LINDA: He's been trying to kill himself.

BIFF *(with great horror):* How?

LINDA: I live from day to day.

BIFF: What're you talking about?

LINDA: Remember I wrote you that he smashed up the car again? In February?

BIFF: Well?

LINDA: The insurance inspector came. He said that they have evidence. That all these accidents in the last year—weren't—weren't—accidents.

HAPPY: How can they tell that? That's a lie.

LINDA: It seems there's a woman . . . *(She takes a breath as)*

BIFF *(sharply but contained):* What woman?

LINDA *(simultaneously):* . . . and this woman . . .

LINDA: What?

BIFF: Nothing. Go ahead.

LINDA: What did you say?

BIFF: Nothing. I just said what woman?

HAPPY: What about her?

LINDA: Well, it seems she was walking down the road and saw his car. She says that he wasn't driving fast at all, and that he didn't skid. She says he came to that little bridge, and then deliberately smashed into the railing, and it was only the shallowness of the water that saved him.

BIFF: Oh, no, he probably just fell asleep again.

LINDA: I don't think he fell asleep.

BIFF: Why not?

LINDA: Last month . . . *(With great difficulty)* Oh, boys, it's so hard to say a thing like this! He's just a big stupid man to you, but I tell you there's more good in him than in many other people. *(She chokes, wipes her eyes)* I was looking for a fuse. The lights blew out, and I went down the cellar. And behind the fuse box—it happened to fall out—was a length of rubber pipe—just short.

HAPPY: No kidding?

LINDA: There's a little attachment on the end of it. I knew right away. And sure enough, on the bottom of the water heater there's a new little nipple on the gas pipe.

HAPPY *(angrily):* That—jerk.

BIFF: Did you have it taken off?

LINDA: I'm—I'm ashamed to. How can I mention it to him? Every day I go down and take away that little rubber pipe. But, when he comes home, I put it back where it was. How can I insult him that way? I don't know what to do. I live from day to day, boys. I tell you, I know every thought in his mind. It sounds so old-fashioned and silly, but I tell you he put his whole life into you and you've turned your backs on him. *(She is bent over in the chair, weeping, her face in her hands)* Biff, I swear to God! Biff, his life is in your hands!

HAPPY *(to Biff):* How do you like that damned fool!

BIFF *(kissing her):* All right, pal, all right. It's all settled now. I've been remiss. I know that, Mom. But now I'll stay, and I swear to you, I'll apply myself. *(Kneeling in front of her, in a fever of self-reproach)* It's just—you see, Mom, I don't fit in business. Not that I won't try. I'll try, and I'll make good.

HAPPY: Sure you will. The trouble with you in business was you never tried to please people.

BIFF: I know, I—

HAPPY: Like when you worked for Harrison's. Bob Harrison said you were tops, and then you go and do some damn fool thing like whistling whole songs in the elevator like a comedian.

BIFF *(against Happy):* So what? I like to whistle sometimes.

HAPPY: You don't raise a guy to a responsible job who whistles in the elevator!

LINDA: Well, don't argue about it now.

HAPPY: Like when you'd go off and swim in the middle of the day instead of taking the line around.

BIFF *(his resentment rising):* Well, don't you run off? You take off sometimes, don't you? On a nice summer day?

HAPPY: Yeah, but I cover myself!

LINDA: Boys!

HAPPY: If I'm going to take a fade the boss can call any number where I'm supposed to be and they'll swear to him that I just left. I'll tell you something that I hate to say, Biff, but in the business world some of them think you're crazy.

BIFF *(angered):* Screw the business world!

HAPPY: All right, screw it! Great, but cover yourself!

LINDA: Hap, Hap!

BIFF: I don't care what they think! They've laughed at Dad for years, and you know why? Because we don't belong in this nuthouse of a city! We should be mixing cement on some open plain, or—or carpenters. A carpenter is allowed to whistle!

(Willy walks in from the entrance of the house, at left)

WILLY: Even your grandfather was better than a carpenter. *(Pause. They watch him)* You never grew up. Bernard does not whistle in the elevator, I assure you.

BIFF *(as though to laugh Willy out of it):* Yeah, but you do, Pop.

WILLY: I never in my life whistled in an elevator! And who in the business world thinks I'm crazy?

BIFF: I didn't mean it like that, Pop. Now don't make a whole thing out of it, will ya?

WILLY: Go back to the West! Be a carpenter, a cowboy, enjoy yourself!

LINDA: Willy, he was just saying—

WILLY: I heard what he said!

HAPPY *(trying to quiet Willy):* Hey, Pop, come on now . . .

WILLY *(continuing over Happy's line):* They laugh at me, heh? Go to Filene's, go to the Hub, go to Slattery's, Boston. Call out the name Willy Loman and see what happens! Big shot!

BIFF: All right, Pop.

WILLY: Big!

BIFF: All right!

WILLY: Why do you always insult me?

BIFF: I didn't say a word. *(To Linda)* Did I say a word?

LINDA: He didn't say anything, Willy.

WILLY *(going to the doorway of the living-room):* All right, good night, good night.

LINDA: Willy, dear, he just decided . . .

WILLY *(to Biff):* If you get tired hanging around tomorrow, paint the ceiling I put up in the living-room.

BIFF: I'm leaving early tomorrow.

HAPPY: He's going to see Bill Oliver, Pop.

WILLY *(interestedly):* Oliver? For what?

BIFF *(with reserve, but trying, trying):* He always said he'd stake me. I'd like to go into business, so maybe I can take him up on it.

LINDA: Isn't that wonderful?

WILLY: Don't interrupt. What's wonderful about it? There's fifty men in the City of New York who'd stake him. *(To Biff)* Sporting goods?

BIFF: I guess so. I know something about it and—

WILLY: He knows something about it! You know sporting goods better than Spalding, for God's sake! How much is he giving you?

BIFF: I don't know, I didn't even see him yet, but—

WILLY: Then what're you talkin' about?

BIFF *(getting angry):* Well, all I said was I'm gonna see him, that's all!

WILLY *(turning away):* Ah, you're counting your chickens again.

BIFF *(starting left for the stairs):* Oh, Jesus, I'm going to sleep!

WILLY *(calling after him):* Don't curse in this house!

BIFF *(turning):* Since when did you get so clean?

HAPPY *(trying to stop them):* Wait a . . .

WILLY: Don't use that language to me! I won't have it!

HAPPY *(grabbing Biff, shouts):* Wait a minute! I got an idea. I got a feasible idea. Come here, Biff, let's talk this over now, let's talk some sense here. When I was down in Florida last time, I thought of a great idea to sell sporting goods. It just came back to me. You and I, Biff—we have a line, the Loman Line. We train a couple of weeks, and put on a couple of exhibitions, see?

WILLY: That's an idea!

HAPPY: Wait! We form two basketball teams, see? Two waterpolo teams. We play each other. It's a million dollars' worth of publicity. Two brothers, see? The Loman Brothers. Displays in the Royal Palms—all the hotels.

And banners over the ring and the basketball court: "Loman Brothers."
Baby, we could sell sporting goods!

WILLY: That is a one-million-dollar idea!

LINDA: Marvelous!

BIFF: I'm in great shape as far as that's concerned.

HAPPY: And the beauty of it is, Biff, it wouldn't be like a business. We'd be
out playin' ball again . . .

BIFF *(enthused):* Yeah, that's . . .

WILLY: Million-dollar . . .

HAPPY: And you wouldn't get fed up with it, Biff. It'd be the family again.
There'd be the old honor, and comradeship, and if you wanted to go off
for a swim or somethin'—well, you'd do it! Without some smart cooky
gettin' up ahead of you!

WILLY: Lick the world! You guys together could absolutely lick the civilized
world.

BIFF: I'll see Oliver tomorrow. Hap, if we could work that out . . .

LINDA: Maybe things are beginning to—

WILLY *(wildly enthused, to Linda):* Stop interrupting! *(To Biff)* But don't wear
sport jacket and slacks when you see Oliver.

BIFF: No, I'll—

WILLY: A business suit, and talk as little as possible, and don't crack any jokes.

BIFF: He did like me. Always liked me.

LINDA: He loved you!

WILLY *(to Linda):* Will you stop! *(To Biff)* Walk in very serious. You are not
applying for a boy's job. Money is to pass. Be quiet, fine, and serious.
Everybody likes a kidder, but nobody lends him money.

HAPPY: I'll try to get some myself, Biff. I'm sure I can.

WILLY: I see great things for you kids, I think your troubles are over. But
remember, start big and you'll end big. Ask for fifteen. How much you
gonna ask for?

BIFF: Gee, I don't know—

WILLY: And don't say "Gee." "Gee" is a boy's word. A man walking in for
fifteen thousand dollars does not say "Gee!"

BIFF: Ten, I think, would be top though.

WILLY: Don't be so modest. You always started too low. Walk in with a big
laugh. Don't look worried. Start off with a couple of your good stories to
lighten things up. It's not what you say, it's how you say it—because
personality always wins the day.

LINDA: Oliver always thought the highest of him—

WILLY: Will you let me talk?

BIFF: Don't yell at her, Pop, will ya?

WILLY *(angrily):* I was talking, wasn't I?

BIFF: I don't like you yelling at her all the time, and I'm tellin' you, that's all.

WILLY: What're you, takin' over this house?

LINDA: Willy—

WILLY *(turning on her):* Don't take his side all the time, goddammit!

BIFF *(furiously):* Stop yelling at her!

WILLY *(suddenly pulling on his cheek, beaten down, guilt ridden):* Give my best to Bill Oliver—he may remember me. *(He exits through the living-room doorway)*

LINDA *(her voice subdued):* What'd you have to start that for? *(Biff turns away)* You see how sweet he was as soon as you talked hopefully? *(She goes over to Biff)* Come up and say good night to him. Don't let him go to bed that way.

HAPPY: Come on, Biff, let's buck him up.

LINDA: Please, dear. Just say good night. It takes so little to make him happy. Come. *(She goes through the living-room doorway, calling upstairs from within the living-room)* Your pajamas are hanging in the bathroom, Willy!

HAPPY *(looking toward where Linda went out):* What a woman! They broke the mold when they made her. You know that, Biff?

BIFF: He's off salary. My God, working on commission!

HAPPY: Well, let's face it: he's no hot-shot selling man. Except that sometimes, you have to admit, he's a sweet personality.

BIFF *(deciding):* Lend me ten bucks, will ya? I want to buy some new ties.

HAPPY: I'll take you to a place I know. Beautiful stuff. Wear one of my striped shirts tomorrow.

BIFF: She got gray. Mom got awful old. Gee, I'm gonna go in to Oliver tomorrow and knock him for a—

HAPPY: Come on up. Tell that to Dad. Let's give him a whirl. Come on.

BIFF *(steamed up):* You know, with ten thousand bucks, boy!

HAPPY *(as they go into the living-room):* That's the talk, Biff, that's the first time I've heard the old confidence out of you! *(From within the living-room, fading off)* You're gonna live with me, kid, and any babe you want just say the word . . . *(The last lines are hardly heard. They are mounting the stairs to their parents' bedroom.)*

LINDA *(entering her bedroom and addressing Willy, who is in the bathroom. She is straightening the bed for him.)* Can you do anything about the shower? It drips.

WILLY *(from the bathroom):* All of a sudden everything falls to pieces! Goddam plumbing, oughta be sued, those people. I hardly finished putting it in and the thing . . . *(His words rumble off)*

LINDA: I'm just wondering if Oliver will remember him. You think he might?

WILLY *(coming out of the bathroom in his pajamas):* Remember him? What's the matter with you, you crazy? If he'd've stayed with Oliver he'd be on top by now! Wait'll Oliver gets a look at him. You don't know the average caliber any more. The average young man today—*(he is getting into bed)*—is got a caliber of zero. Greatest thing in the world for him was to bum around.

(Biff and Happy enter the bedroom. Slight pause.)

WILLY *(stops short, looking at Biff):* Glad to hear it, boy.

HAPPY: He wanted to say good night to you, sport.

WILLY *(to Biff):* Yeah. Knock him dead, boy. What'd you want to tell me?

BIFF: Just take it easy, Pop. Good night. *(He turns to go)*

WILLY *(unable to resist):* And if anything falls off the desk while you're talking to him—like a package or something—don't you pick it up. They have office boys for that.

LINDA: I'll make a big breakfast—

WILLY: Will you let me finish? *(To Biff)* Tell him you were in the business in the West. Not farm work.

BIFF: All right, Dad.

LINDA: I think everything—

WILLY *(going right through her speech):* And don't undersell yourself. No less than fifteen thousand dollars.

BIFF *(unable to bear him):* Okay. Good night, Mom. *(He starts moving)*

WILLY: Because you got a greatness in you, Biff, remember that. You got all kinds a greatness . . . *(He lies back, exhausted. Biff walks out.)*

LINDA *(calling after Biff):* Sleep well, darling!

HAPPY: I'm gonna get married, Mom. I wanted to tell you.

LINDA: Go to sleep, dear.

HAPPY *(going):* I just wanted to tell you.

WILLY: Keep up the good work. *(Happy exits)* God . . . remember that Ebbets Field game? The championship of the city?

LINDA: Just rest. Should I sing to you?

WILLY: Yeah. Sing to me. *(Linda hums a soft lullaby)* When that team came out—he was the tallest, remember?

LINDA: Oh, yes. And in gold.

(Biff enters the darkened kitchen, takes a cigarette, and leaves the house. He comes downstage into a golden pool of light. He smokes, staring at the night.)

WILLY: Like a young god. Hercules—something like that. And the sun, the sun all around him. Remember how he waved to me? Right up from the field, with the representatives of three colleges standing by? And the buyers I brought, and the cheers when he came out—Loman, Loman, Loman! God Almighty, he'll be great yet. A star like that, magnificent, can never really fade away!

(The light on Willy is fading. The gas heater begins to glow through the kitchen wall, near the stairs, a blue flame beneath red coils.)

LINDA *(timidly):* Willy dear, what has he got against you?

WILLY: I'm so tired. Don't talk any more.

(Biff slowly returns to the kitchen. He stops, stares toward the heater.)

LINDA: Will you ask Howard to let you work in New York?

WILLY: First thing in the morning. Everything'll be all right.

(Biff reaches behind the heater and draws out a length of rubber tubing. He is horrified and turns his head toward Willy's room, still dimly lit, from which the strains of Linda's desperate but monotonous humming rise.)

WILLY *(staring through the window into the moonlight):* Gee, look at the moon moving between the buildings!

(Biff wraps the tubing around his hand and quickly goes up the stairs)
(Curtain)

Act II

Music is heard, gay and bright. The curtain rises as the music fades away. Willy, in shirt sleeves, is sitting at the kitchen table, sipping coffee, his hat in his lap. Linda is filling his cup when she can.

WILLY: Wonderful coffee. Meal in itself.

LINDA: Can I make you some eggs?

WILLY: No. Take a breath.

LINDA: You look so rested, dear.

WILLY: I slept like a dead one. First time in months. Imagine, sleeping till ten on a Tuesday morning. Boys left nice and early, heh?

LINDA: They were out of here by eight o'clock.

WILLY: Good work!

LINDA: It was so thrilling to see them leaving together. I can't get over the shaving lotion in this house!

WILLY *(smiling):* Mmm—

LINDA: Biff was very changed this morning. His whole attitude seemed to be hopeful. He couldn't wait to get downtown to see Oliver.

WILLY: He's heading for a change. There's no question, there simply are certain men that take longer to get—solidified. How did he dress?

LINDA: His blue suit. He's so handsome in that suit. He could be a—anything in that suit!

(Willy gets up from the table. Linda holds his jacket for him.)

WILLY: There's no question, no question at all. Gee, on the way home tonight I'd like to buy some seeds.

LINDA *(laughing):* That'd be wonderful. But not enough sun gets back there. Nothing'll grow any more.

WILLY: You wait, kid, before it's all over we're gonna get a little place out in the country, and I'll raise some vegetables, a couple of chickens . . .

LINDA: You'll do it yet, dear.

(Willy walks out of his jacket. Linda follows him.)

WILLY: And they'll get married, and come for a weekend. I'd build a little guest house. 'Cause I got so many fine tools, all I'd need would be a little lumber and some peace of mind.

LINDA *(joyfully):* I sewed the lining . . .

WILLY: I could build two guest houses, so they'd both come. Did he decide how much he's going to ask Oliver for?

LINDA *(getting him into the jacket):* He didn't mention it, but I imagine ten or fifteen thousand. You going to talk to Howard today?

WILLY: Yeah. I'll put it to him straight and simple. He'll just have to take me off the road.

LINDA: And Willy, don't forget to ask for a little advance, because we've got the insurance premium. It's the grace period now.

WILLY: That's a hundred . . .?

LINDA: A hundred and eight, sixty-eight. Because we're a little short again.

WILLY: Why are we short?

LINDA: Well, you had the motor job on the car . . .

WILLY: That goddam Studebaker!

LINDA: And you got one more payment on the refrigerator . . .

WILLY: But it just broke again!

LINDA: Well, it's old, dear.

WILLY: I told you we should've bought a well-advertised machine. Charley bought a General Electric and it's twenty years old and it's still good, that son-of-a-bitch.

LINDA: But, Willy—

WILLY: Whoever heard of a Hastings refrigerator? Once in my life I would like to own something outright before it's broken! I'm always in a race with the junkyard! I just finished paying for the car and it's on its last legs. The refrigerator consumes belts like a goddam maniac. They time those things. They time them so when you finally paid for them, they're used up.

LINDA *(buttoning up his jacket as he unbuttons it):* All told, about two hundred dollars would carry us, dear. But that includes the last payment on the mortgage. After this payment, Willy, the house belongs to us.

WILLY: It's twenty-five years!

LINDA: Biff was nine years old when we bought it.

WILLY: Well, that's a great thing. To weather a twenty-five year mortgage is—

LINDA: It's an accomplishment.

WILLY: All the cement, the lumber, the reconstruction I put in this house! There ain't a crack to be found in it any more.

LINDA: Well, it served its purpose.

WILLY: What purpose? Some stranger'll come along, move in, and that's that. If only Biff would take this house, and raise a family . . . *(He starts to go)* Good-by, I'm late.

LINDA *(suddenly remembering):* Oh, I forgot! You're supposed to meet them for dinner.

WILLY: Me?

LINDA: At Frank's Chop House on Forty-eighth near Sixth Avenue.

WILLY: Is that so! How about you?

LINDA: No, just the three of you. They're gonna blow you to a big meal!

WILLY: Don't say! Who thought of that?

LINDA: Biff came to me this morning, Willy, and he said, "Tell Dad, we want to blow him to a big meal." Be there six o'clock. You and your two boys are going to have dinner.

WILLY: Gee whiz! That's really somethin'. I'm gonna knock Howard for a loop, kid. I'll get an advance, and I'll come home with a New York job. Goddammit, now I'm gonna do it!

LINDA: Oh, that's the spirit, Willy!

WILLY: I will never get behind a wheel the rest of my life.

LINDA: It's changing, Willy, I can feel it changing!

WILLY: Beyond a question. G'by, I'm late. *(He starts to go again)*

LINDA *(calling after him as she runs to the kitchen table for a handkerchief)*: You got your glasses?

WILLY *(feels for them, then comes back in)*: Yeah, yeah, got my glasses.

LINDA *(giving him the handkerchief)*: And a handkerchief.

WILLY: Yeah, handkerchief.

LINDA: And your saccharine?

WILLY: Yeah, my saccharine.

LINDA: Be careful on the subway stairs.

(She kisses him, and a silk stocking is seen hanging from her hand. Willy notices it.)

WILLY: Will you stop mending stockings? At least while I'm in the house. It gets me nervous. I can't tell you. Please.

(Linda hides the stocking in her hand as she follows Willy across the forestage in front of the house)

LINDA: Remember, Frank's Chop House.

WILLY *(passing the apron)*: Maybe beets would grow out there.

LINDA *(laughing)*: But you tried so many times.

WILLY: Yeah. Well, don't work hard today. *(He disappears around the right corner of the house)*

LINDA: Be careful!

(As Willy vanishes, Linda waves to him. Suddenly the phone rings. She runs across the stage and into the kitchen and lifts it.)

LINDA: Hello? Oh, Biff? I'm so glad you called, I just . . . Yes, sure, I just told him. Yes, he'll be there for dinner at six o'clock, I didn't forget. Listen, I was just dying to tell you. You know that little rubber pipe I told you about? That he connected to the gas heater? I finally decided to go down the cellar this morning and take it away and destroy it. But it's gone! Imagine? He took it away himself, it isn't there! *(She listens)* When? Oh, then you took it. Oh—nothing, it's just that I'd hoped he'd taken it away

himself. Oh, I'm not worried, darling, because this morning he left in such
high spirits, it was like the old days! I'm not afraid any more. Did Mr.
Oliver see you? . . . Well, you wait there then. And make a nice impression
on him, darling. Just don't perspire too much before you see him. And
have a nice time with Dad. He may have big news too! . . . That's right,
a New York job. And be sweet to him tonight, dear. Be loving to him.
Because he's only a little boat looking for a harbor. *(She is trembling with
sorrow and joy)* Oh, that's wonderful, Biff, you'll save his life. Thanks,
darling. Just put your arm around him when he comes into the restaurant.
Give him a smile. That's the boy . . . Good-by, dear. . . . You got your
comb? . . . That's fine. Good-by, Biff dear.

*(In the middle of her speech, Howard Wagner, thirty-six, wheels on a small
typewriter table on which is a wire-recording machine and proceeds to plug it in.
This is on the left forestage. Light slowly fades on Linda as it rises on Howard.
Howard is intent on threading the machine and only glances over his shoulder as
Willy appears.)*

WILLY: Pst! Pst!
HOWARD: Hello, Willy, come in.
WILLY: Like to have a little talk with you, Howard.
HOWARD: Sorry to keep you waiting. I'll be with you in a minute.
WILLY: What's that Howard?
HOWARD: Didn't you ever see one of these? Wire recorder.
WILLY: Oh. Can we talk a minute?
HOWARD: Records things. Just got delivery yesterday. Been driving me crazy,
    the most terrific machine I ever saw in my life. I was up all night with
    it.
WILLY: What do you do with it?
HOWARD: I bought it for dictation, but you can do anything with it. Listen to
    this. I had it home last night. Listen to what I picked up. The first one
    is my daughter. Get this. *(He flicks the switch and "Roll out the Barrel"
    is heard being whistled)* Listen to that kid whistle.
WILLY: That is lifelike, isn't it?
HOWARD: Seven years old. Get that tone.
WILLY: Ts, ts. Like to ask a little favor if you . . .

(The whistling breaks off, and the voice of Howard's daughter is heard)

HIS DAUGHTER: "Now you, Daddy."
HOWARD: She's crazy for me! *(Again the same song is whistled)* That's me! Ha!
    (He winks)
WILLY: You're very good!

(The whistling breaks off again. The machine runs silent for a moment.)

HOWARD: Sh! Get this now, this is my son.
HIS SON: "The capital of Alabama is Montgomery; the capital of Arizona is

Phoenix; the capital of Arkansas is Little Rock; the capital of California is Sacramento . . ." *(and on, and on)*

HOWARD *(holding up five fingers):* Five years old, Willy!

WILLY: He'll make an announcer some day!

HIS SON *(continuing):* "The capital . . ."

HOWARD: Get that—alphabetical order! *(The machine breaks off suddenly)* Wait a minute. The maid kicked the plug out.

WILLY: It certainly is a—

HOWARD: Sh, for God's sake!

HIS SON: "It's nine o'clock, Bulova watch time. So I have to go to sleep."

WILLY: That really is—

HOWARD: Wait a minute! The next is my wife.

(They wait)

HOWARD'S VOICE: "Go on, say something," *(Pause)* "Well, you gonna talk?"

HIS WIFE: "I can't think of anything."

HOWARD'S VOICE: "Well, talk—it's turning."

HIS WIFE *(shyly, beaten):* "Hello." *(Silence)* "Oh, Howard, I can't talk into this . . ."

HOWARD *(snapping the machine off):* That was my wife.

WILLY: That is a wonderful machine. Can we—

HOWARD: I tell you, Willy, I'm gonna take my camera, and my bandsaw, and all my hobbies, and out they go. This is the most fascinating relaxation I ever found.

WILLY: I think I'll get one myself.

HOWARD: Sure, they're only a hundred and a half. You can't do without it. Supposing you wanna hear Jack Benny, see? But you can't be at home at that hour. So you tell the maid to turn the radio on when Jack Benny comes on, and this automatically goes on with the radio . . .

WILLY: And when you come home you . . .

HOWARD: You can come home twelve o'clock, one o'clock, any time you like, and you get yourself a Coke and sit yourself down, throw the switch, and there's Jack Benny's program in the middle of the night!

WILLY: I'm definitely going to get one. Because lots of time I'm on the road, and I think to myself, what I must be missing on the radio!

HOWARD: Don't you have a radio in the car?

WILLY: Well, yeah, but who ever thinks of turning it on?

HOWARD: Say, aren't you supposed to be in Boston?

WILLY: That's what I want to talk to you about, Howard. You got a minute? *(He draws a chair in from the wing)*

HOWARD: What happened? What're you doing here?

WILLY: Well . . .

HOWARD: You didn't crack up again, did you?

WILLY: Oh, no. No . . .

HOWARD: Geez, you had me worried there for a minute. What's the trouble?

WILLY: Well, tell you the truth, Howard. I've come to the decision that I'd rather not travel anymore.

HOWARD: Not travel! Well, what'll you do?

WILLY: Remember, Christmas time, when you had the party here? You said you'd try to think of some spot for me here in town.

HOWARD: With us?

WILLY: Well, sure.

HOWARD: Oh, yeah, yeah. I remember. Well, I couldn't think of anything for you, Willy.

WILLY: I tell ya, Howard. The kids are all grown up, y'know. I don't need much any more. If I could take home—well, sixty-five dollars a week, I could swing it.

HOWARD: Yeah, but Willy, see I—

WILLY: I tell ya why, Howard. Speaking frankly and between the two of us, y'know—I'm just a little tired.

HOWARD: Oh, I could understand that, Willy. But you're a road man, Willy, and we do a road business. We've only got a half-dozen salesmen on the floor here.

WILLY: God knows, Howard, I never asked a favor of any man. But I was with the firm when your father used to carry you in here in his arms.

HOWARD: I know that, Willy, but—

WILLY: Your father came to me the day you were born and asked me what I thought of the name of Howard, may he rest in peace.

HOWARD: I appreciate that, Willy, but there just is no spot here for you. If I had a spot I'd slam you right in, but I just don't have a single solitary spot.

(He looks for his lighter. Willy has picked it up and gives it to him. Pause.)

WILLY *(with increasing anger):* Howard, all I need to set my table is fifty dollars a week.

HOWARD: But where am I going to put you, kid?

WILLY: Look, it isn't a question of whether I can sell merchandise, is it?

HOWARD: No, but it's a business, kid, and everybody's gotta pull his own weight.

WILLY *(desperately):* Just let me tell you a story, Howard—

HOWARD: 'Cause you gotta admit, business is business.

WILLY *(angrily):* Business is definitely business, but just listen for a minute. You don't understand this. When I was a boy—eighteen, nineteen—I was already on the road. And there was a question in my mind as to whether selling had a future for me. Because in those days I had a yearning to go to Alaska. See, there were three gold strikes in one month in Alaska, and I felt like going out. Just for the ride, you might say.

HOWARD *(barely interested):* Don't say.

WILLY: Oh, yeah, my father lived many years in Alaska. He was an adventurous man. We've got quite a little streak of self-reliance in our family. I thought I'd go out with my older brother and try to locate him, and maybe settle in the North with the old man. And I was almost decided to go, when I met a salesman in the Parker House. His name was Dave Single-man. And he was eighty-four years old, and he'd drummed merchandise in thirty-one states. And old Dave, he'd go up to his room, y'understand, put on his green velvet slippers—I'll never forget—and pick up his phone and call the buyers, and without ever leaving his room, at the age of eighty-four, he made his living. And when I saw that, I realized that selling was the greatest career a man could want. 'Cause what could be more satisfying than to be able to go, at the age of eighty-four, into twenty or thirty different cities, and pick up a phone, and be remembered and loved and helped by so many different people? Do you know? when he died—and by the way he died the death of a salesman, in his green velvet slippers in the smoker of the New York, New Haven and Hartford, going into Boston—when he died, hundreds of salesmen and buyers were at his funeral. Things were sad on a lotta trains for months after that. *(He stands up. Howard has not looked at him)* In those days there was personality in it, Howard. There was respect, and comradeship, and gratitude in it. Today, it's all cut and dried, and there's no chance for bringing friendship to bear—or personality. You see what I mean? They don't know me any more.

HOWARD *(moving away, toward the right):* That's just the thing, Willy.

WILLY: If I had forty dollars a week—that's all I'd need. Forty dollars, How-ard.

HOWARD: Kid, I can't take blood from a stone, I—

WILLY *(desperation is on him now):* Howard, the year Al Smith[4] was nomi-nated, your father came to me and—

HOWARD *(starting to go off):* I've got to see some people, kid.

WILLY *(stopping him):* I'm talking about your father! There were promises made across this desk! You mustn't tell me you've got people to see—I put thirty-four years into this firm, Howard, and now I can't pay my insurance! You can't eat the orange and throw the peel away—a man is not a piece of fruit! *(After a pause)* Now pay attention. Your father—in 1928 I had a big year. I averaged a hundred and seventy dollars a week in commissions.

HOWARD *(impatiently):* Now, Willy, you never averaged—

WILLY *(banging his hand on the desk):* I averaged a hundred and seventy dollars a week in the year of 1928! And your father came to me—or rather, I was in the office here—it was right over this desk—and he put his hand on my shoulder—

HOWARD *(getting up):* You'll have to excuse me, Willy, I gotta see some people. Pull yourself together. *(Going out)* I'll be back in a little while.

(On Howard's exit, the light on his chair grows very bright and strange)

---

[4]Alfred E. Smith (1873–1944) was the Democratic candidate for president running against Herbert Hoover in 1928.

WILLY: Pull myself together! What the hell did I say to him? My God, I was yelling at him! How could I! *(Willy breaks off, staring at the light, which occupies the chair, animating it. He approaches this chair, standing across the desk from it.)* Frank, Frank, don't you remember what you told me that time? How you put your hand on my shoulder, and Frank . . . *(He leans on the desk and as he speaks the dead man's name he accidentally switches on the recorder, and instantly)*

HOWARD'S SON: ". . . of New York is Albany. The capital of Ohio is Cincinnati, the capital of Rhode Island is . . ." *(The recitation continues)*

WILLY *(leaping away with fright, shouting):* Ha! Howard! Howard! Howard!

HOWARD *(rushing in):* What happened?

WILLY *(pointing at the machine, which continues nasally, childishly, with the capital cities):* Shut it off! Shut it off!

HOWARD *(pulling the plug out):* Look, Willy . . .

WILLY *(pressing his hands to his eyes):* I gotta get myself some coffee. I'll get some coffee . . .

(Willy starts to walk out. Howard stops him.)

HOWARD *(rolling up the cord):* Willy, look . . .

WILLY: I'll go to Boston.

HOWARD: Willy, you can't go to Boston for us.

WILLY: Why can't I go?

HOWARD: I don't want you to represent us. I've been meaning to tell you for a long time now.

WILLY: Howard, are you firing me?

HOWARD: I think you need a good long rest, Willy.

WILLY: Howard—

HOWARD: And when you feel better, come back, and we'll see if we can work something out.

WILLY: But I gotta earn money, Howard. I'm in no position to—

HOWARD: Where are your sons? Why don't your sons give you a hand?

WILLY: They're working on a very big deal.

HOWARD: This is no time for false pride, Willy. You go to your sons and you tell them that you're tired. You've got two great boys, haven't you?

WILLY: Oh, no question, no question, but in the meantime . . .

HOWARD: Then that's that, heh?

WILLY: All right, I'll go to Boston tomorrow.

HOWARD: No, no.

WILLY: I can't throw myself on my sons. I'm not a cripple!

HOWARD: Look, kid, I'm busy this morning.

WILLY *(grasping Howard's arm):* Howard, you've got to let me go to Boston!

HOWARD *(hard, keeping himself under control):* I've got a line of people to see this morning. Sit down, take five minutes, and pull yourself together, and then go home, will ya? I need the office, Willy. *(He starts to go, turns, remembering the recorder, starts to push off the table holding the recorder)*

Oh, yeah. Whenever you can this week, stop by and drop off the samples. You'll feel better, Willy, and then come back and we'll talk. Pull yourself together, kid, there's people outside.

(Howard exits, pushing the table off left. Willy stares into space, exhausted. Now the music is heard—Ben's music—first distantly, then closer, closer. As Willy speaks, Ben enters from the right. He carries valise and umbrella.)

WILLY: Oh, Ben, how did you do it? What is the answer? Did you wind up the Alaska deal already?

BEN: Doesn't take much time if you know what you're doing. Just a short business trip. Boarding ship in an hour. Wanted to say good-by.

WILLY: Ben, I've got to talk to you.

BEN *(glancing at his watch):* Haven't the time, William.

WILLY *(crossing the apron to Ben):* Ben, nothing's working out. I don't know what to do.

BEN: Now, look here, William. I've bought timberland in Alaska and I need a man to look after things for me.

WILLY: God, timberland! Me and my boys in those grand outdoors!

BEN: You've a new continent at your doorstep, William. Get out of these cities, they're full of talk and time payments and courts of law. Screw on your fists and you can fight for a fortune up there.

WILLY: Yes, yes! Linda, Linda!

(Linda enters as of old, with the wash)

LINDA: Oh, you're back?

BEN: I haven't much time.

WILLY: No, wait! Linda, he's got a proposition for me in Alaska.

LINDA: But you've got— *(To Ben)* He's got a beautiful job here.

WILLY: But in Alaska, kid, I could—

LINDA: You're doing well enough, Willy!

BEN *(to Linda):* Enough for what, my dear?

LINDA *(frightened of Ben and angry at him):* Don't say those things to him! Enough to be happy right here, right now. *(To Willy, while Ben laughs)* Why must everybody conquer the world? You're well liked, and the boys love you, and someday— *(to Ben)* —why, old man Wagner told him just the other day that if he keeps it up he'll be a member of the firm, didn't he, Willy?

WILLY: Sure, sure. I am building something with this firm, Ben, and if a man is building something he must be on the right track, mustn't he?

BEN: What are you building? Lay your hand on it. Where is it?

WILLY *(hesitantly):* That's true, Linda, there's nothing.

LINDA: Why? *(To Ben)* There's a man eighty-four years old—

WILLY: That's right, Ben, that's right. When I look at that man I say, what is there to worry about?

BEN: Bah!

WILLY: It's true, Ben. All he has to do is go into any city, pick up the phone, and he's making his living and you know why?

BEN *(picking up his valise):* I've got to go.

WILLY *(holding Ben back):* Look at this boy!

(Biff, in his high school sweater, enters carrying suitcase. Happy carries Biff's shoulder guards, gold helmet, and football pants.)

WILLY: Without a penny to his name, three great universities are begging for him, and from there the sky's the limit, because it's not what you do, Ben. It's who you know and the smile on your face! It's contacts, Ben, contacts! The whole wealth of Alaska passes over the lunch table at the Commodore Hotel, and that's the wonder, the wonder of this country, that a man can end with diamonds here on the basis of being liked! *(He turns to Biff)* And that's why when you get out on that field today it's important. Because thousands of people will be rooting for you and loving you. *(To Ben, who has again begun to leave)* And Ben! when he walks into a business office his name will sound out like a bell and all the doors will open to him! I've seen it, Ben, I've seen it a thousand times! You can't feel it with your hand like timber, but it's there!

BEN: Good-by, William.

WILLY: Ben, am I right? Don't you think I'm right? I value your advice.

BEN: There's a new continent at your doorstep, William. You could walk out rich. Rich! *(He is gone)*

WILLY: We'll do it here, Ben! You hear me? We're gonna do it here!

(Young Bernard rushes in. The gay music of the Boys is heard.)

BERNARD: Oh, gee, I was afraid you left already!

WILLY: Why? What time is it?

BERNARD: It's half-past one!

WILLY: Well, come on, everybody! Ebbets Field next stop! Where's the pennants? *(He rushes through the wall-line of the kitchen and out into the living-room)*

LINDA *(to Biff):* Did you pack fresh underwear?

BIFF *(who has been limbering up):* I want to go!

BERNARD: Biff, I'm carrying your helmet, ain't I?

HAPPY: No, I'm carrying the helmet.

BERNARD: Oh, Biff, you promised me.

HAPPY: I'm carrying the helmet.

BERNARD: How am I going to get in the locker room?

LINDA: Let him carry the shoulder guards. *(She puts her coat and hat on in the kitchen)*

BERNARD: Can I, Biff? 'Cause I told everybody I'm going to be in the locker room.

HAPPY: In Ebbets Field it's the clubhouse.

BERNARD: I meant the clubhouse. Biff!

HAPPY: Biff!

BIFF *(grandly, after a slight pause):* Let him carry the shoulder guards.

HAPPY *(as he gives Bernard the shoulder guards):* Stay close to us now.

(Willy rushes in with the pennants)

WILLY *(handing them out):* Everybody wave when Biff comes out on the field. *(Happy and Bernard run off)* You set now, boy?

(The music has died away)

BIFF: Ready to go, Pop. Every muscle is ready.

WILLY *(at the edge of the apron):* You realize what this means?

BIFF: That's right Pop.

WILLY *(feeling Biff's muscles):* You're comin' home this afternoon captain of the All-Scholastic Championship Team of the City of New York.

BIFF: I got it, Pop. And remember, pal, when I take off my helmet, the touchdown is for you.

WILLY: Let's go! *(He is starting out, with his arm around Biff, when Charley enters, as of old, in knickers)* I got no room for you, Charley.

CHARLEY: Room? For what?

WILLY: In the car.

CHARLEY: You goin' for a ride? I wanted to shoot some casino.

WILLY *(furiously):* Casino! *(Incredulously)* Don't you realize what today is?

LINDA: Oh, he knows, Willy. He's just kidding you.

WILLY: That's nothing to kid about!

CHARLEY: No, Linda, what's goin' on?

LINDA: He's playing in Ebbets Field.

CHARLEY: Baseball in this weather?

WILLY: Don't talk to him. Come on, come on! *(He is pushing them out)*

CHARLEY: Wait a minute, didn't you hear the news?

WILLY: What?

CHARLEY: Don't you listen to the radio? Ebbets Field just blew up.

WILLY: You go to hell! *(Charley laughs. Pushing them out)* Come on, come on! We're late.

CHARLEY *(as they go):* Knock a homer, Biff, knock a homer!

WILLY *(the last to leave, turning to Charley):* I don't think that was funny, Charley. This is the greatest day of his life.

CHARLEY: Willy, when are you going to grow up?

WILLY: Yeah, heh? When this game is over, Charley, you'll be laughing out the other side of your face. They'll be calling him another Red Grange.[5] Twenty-five thousand a year.

CHARLEY *(kidding):* Is that so?

WILLY: Yeah, that's so.

[5]Harold Edward Grange, an All-American football player at the University of Illinois, 1923–1925.

CHARLEY: Well, then, I'm sorry, Willy. But tell me something.

WILLY: What?

CHARLEY: Who is Red Grange?

WILLY: Put up your hands. Goddam you, put up your hands!

(Charley, chuckling, shakes his head and walks away, around the left corner of the stage. Willy follows him. The music rises to a mocking frenzy.)

WILLY: Who the hell do you think you are, better than everybody else? You don't know everything, you big, ignorant, stupid . . . Put up your hands!

(Light rises, on the right side of the forestage, on a small table in the reception room of Charley's office. Traffic sounds are heard. Bernard, now mature, sits whistling to himself. A pair of tennis rackets and an overnight bag are on the floor beside him.)

WILLY *(offstage):* What are you walking away for? Don't walk away! If you're going to say something say it to my face! I know you laugh at me behind my back. You'll laugh out of the other side of your goddam face after this game. Touchdown! Touchdown! Eighty thousand people! Touchdown! Right between the goal posts.

(Bernard is a quiet, earnest, but self-assured young man. Willy's voice is coming from right upstage now. Bernard lowers his feet off the table and listens. Jenny, his father's secretary, enters.)

JENNY *(distressed):* Say, Bernard, will you go out in the hall?

BERNARD: What is that noise? Who is it?

JENNY: Mr. Loman. He just got off the elevator.

BERNARD *(Getting up):* Who's he arguing with?

JENNY: Nobody. There's nobody with him. I can't deal with him any more, and your father gets all upset everytime he comes. I've got a lot of typing to do, and your father's waiting to sign it. Will you see him?

WILLY *(entering):* Touchdown! Touch— *(He sees Jenny)* Jenny, Jenny, good to see you. How're ya? Workin'? Or still honest?

JENNY: Fine. How've you been feeling?

WILLY: Not much any more, Jenny. Ha, ha! *(He is surprised to see the rackets)*

BERNARD: Hello, Uncle Willy.

WILLY *(almost shocked):* Bernard! Well, look who's here! *(He comes quickly, guiltily, to Bernard and warmly shakes his hand)*

BERNARD: How are you? Good to see you.

WILLY: What are you doing here?

BERNARD: Oh, just stopped by to see Pop. Get off my feet till my train leaves. I'm going to Washington in a few minutes.

WILLY: Is he in?

BERNARD: Yes, he's in his office with the accountant. Sit down.

WILLY *(sitting down):* What're you going to do in Washington?

BERNARD: Oh, just a case I've got there, Willy.

WILLY: That so? *(Indicating the rackets)* You going to play tennis there?

BERNARD: I'm staying with a friend who's got a court.

WILLY: Don't say. His own tennis court. Must be fine people, I bet.

BERNARD: They are, very nice. Dad tells me Biff's in town.

WILLY *(with a big smile):* Yeah, Biff's in. Working on a very big deal, Bernard.

BERNARD: What's Biff doing?

WILLY: Well, he's been doing very big things in the West. But he decided to establish himself here. Very big. We're having dinner. Did I hear your wife had a boy?

BERNARD: That's right. Our second.

WILLY: Two boys! What do you know!

BERNARD: What kind of a deal has Biff got?

WILLY: Well, Bill Oliver—very big sporting-goods man—he wants Biff very badly. Called him in from the West. Long distance, carte blanche, special deliveries. Your friends have their own private tennis court?

BERNARD: You still with the old firm, Willy?

WILLY *(after a pause):* I'm—I'm overjoyed to see how you made the grade, Bernard, overjoyed. It's an encouraging thing to see a young man really —really—Looks very good for Biff—very—*(He breaks off, then)* Bernard —*(He is so full of emotion, he breaks off again)*

BERNARD: What is it, Willy?

WILLY *(small and alone):* What—what's the secret?

BERNARD: What secret?

WILLY: How—how did you? Why didn't he ever catch on?

BERNARD: I wouldn't know that, Willy.

WILLY *(confidentially, desperately):* You were his friend, his boyhood friend. There's something I don't understand about it. His life ended after that Ebbets Field game. From the age of seventeen nothing good ever happened to him.

BERNARD: He never trained himself for anything.

WILLY: But he did, he did. After high school he took so many correspondence courses. Radio mechanics; television; God knows what, and never made the slightest mark.

BERNARD *(taking off his glasses):* Willy, do you want to talk candidly?

WILLY *(rising, faces Bernard):* I regard you as a very brilliant man, Bernard. I value your advice.

BERNARD: Oh, the hell with advice, Willy. I couldn't advise you. There's just one thing I've always wanted to ask you. When he was supposed to graduate, and the math teacher flunked him—

WILLY: Oh, that son-of-a-bitch ruined his life.

BERNARD: Yeah, but, Willy, all he had to do was go to summer school and make up that subject.

WILLY: That's right, that's right.

BERNARD: Did you tell him not to go to summer school?

WILLY: Me? I begged him to go. I ordered him to go!

BERNARD: Then why wouldn't he go?

WILLY: Why? Why! Bernard, that question has been trailing me like a ghost for the last fifteen years. He flunked the subject, and laid down and died like a hammer hit him!

BERNARD: Take it easy, kid.

WILLY: Let me talk to you—I got nobody to talk to. Bernard, Bernard, was it my fault? Y'see? It keeps going around in my mind, maybe I did something to him. I got nothing to give him.

BERNARD: Don't take it so hard.

WILLY: Why did he lay down? What is the story there? You were his friend!

BERNARD: Willy, I remember, it was June, and our grades came out. And he'd flunked math.

WILLY: That son-of-a-bitch!

BERNARD: No, it wasn't right then. Biff just got very angry, I remember, and he was ready to enroll in summer school.

WILLY (surprised): He was?

BERNARD: He wasn't beaten by it at all. But then, Willy, he disappeared from the block for almost a month. And I got the idea that he'd gone up to New England to see you. Did he have a talk with you then?

(Willy stares in silence)

BERNARD: Willy?

WILLY (with a strong edge of resentment in his voice): Yeah, he came to Boston. What about it?

BERNARD: Well, just that when he came back—I'll never forget this, it always mystifies me. Because I'd thought so well of Biff, even though he'd always taken advantage of me. I loved him, Willy, y'know? And he came back after that month and took his sneakers—remember those sneakers with "University of Virginia" printed on them? He was so proud of those, wore them every day. And he took them down in the cellar, and burned them up in the furnace. We had a fist fight. It lasted at least half an hour. Just the two of us, punching each other down the cellar, and crying right through it. I've often thought of how strange it was that I knew he'd given up his life. What happened in Boston, Willy?

(Willy looks at him as at an intruder)

BERNARD: I just bring it up because you asked me.

WILLY (angrily): Nothing. What do you mean, "What happened?" What's that got to do with anything?

BERNARD: Well, don't get sore.

WILLY: What are you trying to do, blame it on me? If a boy lays down is that my fault?

BERNARD: Now, Willy, don't get—

WILLY: Well, don't—don't talk to me that way! What does that mean, "What happened?"

(Charley enters. He is in his vest, and he carries a bottle of bourbon.)

CHARLEY: Hey, you're going to miss that train. *(He waves the bottle)*

BERNARD: Yeah, I'm going. *(He takes the bottle)* Thanks, Pop. *(He picks up his rackets and bag)* Good-by, Willy, and don't worry about it. You know, "If at first you don't succeed . . ."

WILLY: Yes, I believe in that.

BERNARD: But sometimes, Willy, it's better for a man just to walk away.

WILLY: Walk away?

BERNARD: That's right.

WILLY: But if you can't walk away?

BERNARD *(after a slight pause):* I guess that's when it's tough. *(Extending his hand)* Good-by, Willy.

WILLY *(shaking Bernard's hand):* Good-by, boy.

CHARLEY: *(an arm on Bernard's shoulder):* How do you like this kid? Gonna argue a case in front of the Supreme Court.

BERNARD *(protesting):* Pop!

WILLY *(genuinely shocked, pained, and happy):* No! The Supreme Court!

BERNARD: I gotta run. 'By, Dad!

CHARLEY: Knock 'em dead, Bernard!

(Bernard goes off)

WILLY *(as Charley takes out his wallet):* The Supreme Court! And he didn't even mention it!

CHARLEY *(counting out money on the desk):* He don't have to—he's gonna do it.

WILLY: And you never told him what to do, did you? You never took any interest in him.

CHARLEY: My salvation is that I never took any interest in anything. There's some money—fifty dollars. I got an accountant inside.

WILLY: Charley, look . . . *(With difficulty)* I got my insurance to pay. If you can manage it—I need a hundred and ten dollars.

(Charley doesn't reply for a moment; merely stops moving)

WILLY: I'd draw it from my bank but Linda would know, and I . . .

CHARLEY: Sit down, Willy.

WILLY *(moving toward the chair):* I'm keeping an account of everything, remember. I'll pay every penny back. *(He sits)*

CHARLEY: Now listen to me, Willy.

WILLY: I want you to know I appreciate . . .

CHARLEY *(sitting down on the table):* Willy, what're you doin'? What the hell is goin' on in your head?

WILLY: Why? I'm simply . . .

CHARLEY: I offered you a job. You can make fifty dollars a week. And I won't send you on the road.

WILLY: I've got a job.

CHARLEY: Without pay? What kind of a job is a job without pay? *(He rises)* Now, look, kid, enough is enough. I'm no genius but I know when I'm being insulted.

WILLY: Insulted!

CHARLEY: Why don't you want to work for me?

WILLY: What's the matter with you? I've got a job.

CHARLEY: Then what're you walkin' in here every week for?

WILLY *(getting up):* Well, if you don't want me to walk in here—

CHARLEY: I am offering you a job.

WILLY: I don't want your goddam job!

CHARLEY: When the hell are you going to grow up?

WILLY *(furiously):* You big ignoramus, if you say that to me again I'll rap you one! I don't care how big you are!

(He's ready to fight. Pause)

CHARLEY *(kindly, going to him):* How much do you need, Willy?

WILLY: Charley, I'm strapped, I'm strapped. I don't know what to do. I was just fired.

CHARLEY: Howard fired you?

WILLY: That snotnose. Imagine that? I named him. I named him Howard.

CHARLEY: Willy, when're you gonna realize that them things don't mean anything? You named him Howard, but you can't sell that. The only thing you got in this world is what you can sell. And the funny thing is that you're a salesman, and you don't know that.

WILLY: I've always tried to think otherwise, I guess. I always felt that if a man was impressive, and well liked, that nothing—

CHARLEY: Why must everybody like you? Who liked J. P. Morgan?[6] Was he impressive? In a Turkish bath he'd look like a butcher. But with his pockets on he was very well liked. Now listen, Willy, I know you don't like me, and nobody can say I'm in love with you, but I'll give you a job because—just for the hell of it, put it that way. Now what do you say?

WILLY: I—I just can't work for you, Charley.

CHARLEY: What're you, jealous of me?

WILLY: I can't work for you, that's all, don't ask me why.

CHARLEY *(angered, takes out more bills):* You been jealous of me all your life, you damned fool! Here, pay your insurance. *(He puts the money in Willy's hand)*

WILLY: I'm keeping strict accounts.

CHARLEY: I've got some work to do. Take care of yourself. And pay your insurance.

WILLY *(moving to the right):* Funny, y'know? After all the highways, and the

---

[6]John Pierpont Morgan (1837–1913) established the Morgan financial empire. His son, also J. P. Morgan (1867–1943), carried on the tradition.

trains, and the appointments, and the years, you end up worth more dead than alive.

CHARLEY: Willy, nobody's worth nothin' dead. *(After a slight pause)* Did you hear what I said?

(Willy stands still, dreaming)

CHARLEY: Willy!

WILLY: Apologize to Bernard for me when you see him. I didn't mean to argue with him. He's a fine boy. They're all fine boys, and they'll end up big— all of them. Someday they'll all play tennis together. Wish me luck, Charley. He saw Bill Oliver today.

CHARLEY: Good luck.

WILLY *(on the verge of tears)*: Charley, you're the only friend I got. Isn't that a remarkable thing? *(He goes out)*

CHARLEY: Jesus!

(Charley stares after him a moment and follows. All light blacks out. Suddenly raucous music is heard, and a red glow rises behind the screen at right. Stanley, a young waiter, appears, carrying a table, followed by Happy, who is carrying two chairs.)

STANLEY *(putting the table down)*: That's all right, Mr. Loman, I can handle it myself. *(He turns and takes the chairs from Happy and places them at the table)*

HAPPY *(glancing around)*: Oh, this is better.

STANLEY: Sure, in the front there you're in the middle of all kinds a noise. Whenever you got a party, Mr. Loman, you just tell me and I'll put you back here. Y'know, there's a lotta people they don't like it private, because when they go out they like to see a lotta action around them because they're sick and tired to stay in the house by theirself. But I know you, you ain't from Hackensack. You know what I mean?

HAPPY *(sitting down)*: So how's it coming, Stanley?

STANLEY: Ah, it's a dog's life. I only wish during the war they'd a took me in the Army. I coulda been dead by now.

HAPPY: My brother's back, Stanley.

STANLEY: Oh, he come back, heh? From the Far West.

HAPPY: Yeah, big cattle man, my brother, so treat him right. And my father's coming too.

STANLEY: Oh, your father too!

HAPPY: You got a couple of nice lobsters?

STANLEY: Hundred per cent, big.

HAPPY: I want them with the claws.

STANLEY: Don't worry, I don't give you no mice. *(Happy laughs)* How about some wine? It'll put a head on the meal.

HAPPY: No, You remember, Stanley, that recipe I brought you from overseas? With the champagne in it?

STANLEY: Oh, yeah, sure. I still got it tacked up yet in the kitchen. But that'll have to cost a buck apiece anyways.

HAPPY: That's all right.

STANLEY: What'd you, hit a number or somethin'?

HAPPY: No, it's a little celebration. My brother is—I think he pulled off a big deal today. I think we're going into business together.

STANLEY: Great! That's the best for you. Because a family business, you know what I mean?—that's the best.

HAPPY: That's what I think.

STANLEY: 'Cause what's the difference? Somebody steals? It's in the family. Know what I mean? *(Sotto voce)*[7] Like this bartender here. The boss is goin' crazy what kinda leak he's got in the cash register. You put it in but it don't come out.

HAPPY *(raising his head):* Sh!

STANLEY: What?

HAPPY: You notice I wasn't lookin' right or left, was I?

STANLEY: No.

HAPPY: And my eyes are closed.

STANLEY: So what's the—?

HAPPY: Strudel's comin'.

STANLEY *(catching on, looks around):* Ah, no, there's no—

(He breaks off as a furred, lavishly dressed girl enters and sits at the next table. Both follow her with their eyes.)

STANLEY: Geez, how'd ya know?

HAPPY: I got radar or something. *(Staring directly at her profile):* Oooooooo . . . Stanley.

STANLEY: I think that's for you, Mr. Loman.

HAPPY: Look at that mouth. Oh, God. And the binoculars.

STANLEY: Geez, you got a life, Mr. Loman.

HAPPY: Wait on her.

STANLEY *(going to the girl's table):* Would you like a menu, ma'am?

GIRL: I'm expecting someone, but I'd like a—

HAPPY: Why don't you bring her—excuse me, miss, do you mind? I sell champagne, and I'd like you to try my brand. Bring her a champagne, Stanley.

GIRL: That's awfully nice of you.

HAPPY: Don't mention it. It's all company money. *(He laughs)*

GIRL: That's a charming product to be selling, isn't it?

HAPPY: Oh, gets to be like everything else. Selling is selling, y'know.

GIRL: I suppose.

HAPPY: You don't happen to sell, do you?

GIRL: No, I don't sell.

[7]In an undertone.

HAPPY: Would you object to a compliment from a stranger? You ought to be on a magazine cover.

GIRL *(looking at him a little archly):* I have been.

(Stanley comes in with a glass of champagne)

HAPPY: What'd I say before, Stanley? You see? She's a cover girl.

STANLEY: Oh, I could see, I could see.

HAPPY *(to the Girl):* What magazine?

GIRL: Oh, a lot of them. *(She takes the drink)* Thank you.

HAPPY: You know what they say in France, don't you? "Champagne is the drink of the complexion"—Hya, Biff!

(Biff has entered and sits with Happy)

BIFF: Hello, kid. Sorry I'm late.

HAPPY: I just got here. Uh, Miss—?

GIRL: Forsythe.

HAPPY: Miss Forsythe, this is my brother.

BIFF: Is Dad here?

HAPPY: His name is Biff. You might've heard of him. Great football player.

GIRL: Really? What team?

HAPPY: Are you familiar with football?

GIRL: No, I'm afraid I'm not.

HAPPY: Biff is quarterback with the New York Giants.

GIRL: Well, that is nice, isn't it? *(She drinks)*

HAPPY: Good health.

GIRL: I'm happy to meet you.

HAPPY: That's my name. Hap. It's really Harold, but at West Point they called me Happy.

GIRL *(now really impressed):* Oh, I see. How do you do? *(She turns her profile)*

BIFF: Isn't Dad coming?

HAPPY: You want her?

BIFF: Oh, I could never make that.

HAPPY: I remember the time that idea would never come into your head. Where's the old confidence, Biff?

BIFF: I just saw Oliver—

HAPPY: Wait a minute. I've got to see that old confidence again. Do you want her? She's on call.

BIFF: Oh, no. *(He turns to look at the Girl)*

HAPPY: I'm telling you. Watch this. *(Turning to the Girl.)* Honey? *(She turns to him)* Are you busy?

GIRL: Well, I am . . . but I could make a phone call.

HAPPY: Do that, will you, honey? And see if you can get a friend. We'll be here for a while. Biff is one of the greatest football players in the country.

GIRL *(standing up):* Well, I'm certainly happy to meet you.

HAPPY: Come back soon.

GIRL: I'll try.

HAPPY: Don't try, honey, try hard.

(The Girl exits. Stanley follows, shaking his head in bewildered admiration.)

HAPPY: Isn't that a shame now? A beautiful girl like that? That's why I can't get married. There's not a good woman in a thousand. New York is loaded with them, kid!

BIFF: Hap, look—

HAPPY: I told you she was on call!

BIFF *(strangely unnerved):* Cut it out, will ya? I want to say something to you.

HAPPY: Did you see Oliver?

BIFF: I saw him all right. Now look, I want to tell Dad a couple of things and I want you to help me.

HAPPY: What? Is he going to back you?

BIFF: Are you crazy? You're out of your goddam head, you know that?

HAPPY: Why? What happened?

BIFF *(breathlessly):* I did a terrible thing today, Hap. It's been the strangest day I ever went through. I'm all numb, I swear.

HAPPY: You mean he wouldn't see you?

BIFF: Well, I waited six hours for him, see? All day. Kept sending my name in. Even tried to date his secretary so she'd get me to him, but no soap.

HAPPY: Because you're not showin' the old confidence, Biff. He remembered you, didn't he?

BIFF *(stopping Happy with a gesture):* Finally, about five o'clock, he comes out. Didn't remember who I was or anything. I felt like such an idiot, Hap.

HAPPY: Did you tell him my Florida idea?

BIFF: He walked away. I saw him for one minute. I got so mad I could've torn the walls down! How the hell did I ever get the idea I was a salesman there? I even believed myself that I'd been a salesman for him! And then he gave me one look and—I realized what a ridiculous lie my whole life has been! We've been talking in a dream for fifteen years. I was a shipping clerk.

HAPPY: What'd you do?

BIFF *(with great tension and wonder):* Well, he left, see. And the secretary went out. I was all alone in the waiting-room. I don't know what came over me, Hap. The next thing I know I'm in his office—paneled walls, everything. I can't explain it. I—Hap, I took his fountain pen.

HAPPY: Geez, did he catch you?

BIFF: I ran out. I ran down all eleven flights. I ran and ran and ran.

HAPPY: That was an awful dumb—what'd you do that for?

BIFF *(agonized):* I don't know, I just—wanted to take something, I don't know. You gotta help me, Hap, I'm gonna tell Pop.

HAPPY: You crazy? What for?

BIFF: Hap, he's got to understand that I'm not the man somebody lends that kind of money to. He thinks I've been spiting him all these years and it's eating him up.

HAPPY: That's just it. You tell him something nice.

BIFF: I can't.

HAPPY: Say you got a lunch date with Oliver tomorrow.

BIFF: So what do I do tomorrow?

HAPPY: You leave the house tomorrow and come back at night and say Oliver is thinking it over. And he thinks it over for a couple of weeks, and gradually it fades away and nobody's the worse.

BIFF: But it'll go on forever!

HAPPY: Dad is never so happy as when he's looking forward to something!

(Willy enters)

HAPPY: Hello, scout!

WILLY: Gee, I haven't been here in years!

(Stanley has followed Willy in and sets a chair for him. Stanley starts off but Happy stops him.)

HAPPY: Stanley!

(Stanley stands by, waiting for an order)

BIFF *(going to Willy with guilt, as to an invalid):* Sit down, Pop. You want a drink?

WILLY: Sure, I don't mind.

BIFF: Let's get a load on.

WILLY: You look worried.

BIFF: N-no. *(To Stanley)* Scotch all around. Make it doubles.

STANLEY: Doubles, right. *(He goes)*

WILLY: You had a couple already, didn't you?

BIFF: Just a couple, yeah.

WILLY: Well, what happened, boy? *(Nodding affirmatively, with a smile)* Everything go all right?

BIFF *(takes a breath, then reaches out and grasps Willy's hand):* Pal . . . *(He is smiling bravely, and Willy is smiling too)* I had an experience today.

HAPPY: Terrific, Pop.

WILLY: That so? What happened?

BIFF *(high, slightly alcoholic, above the earth):* I'm going to tell you everything from first to last. It's been a strange day. *(Silence. He looks around, composes himself as best he can, but his breath keeps breaking the rhythm of his voice.)* I had to wait quite a while for him, and—

WILLY: Oliver?

BIFF: Yeah, Oliver. All day, as a matter of cold fact. And a lot of—instances —facts, Pop, facts about my life came back to me. Who was it, Pop? Who ever said I was a salesman with Oliver?

WILLY: Well, you were.

BIFF: No, Dad, I was a shipping clerk.

WILLY: But you were practically—

BIFF *(with determination):* Dad, I don't know who said it first, but I was never a salesman for Bill Oliver.

WILLY: What're you talking about?

BIFF: Let's hold on to the facts tonight, Pop. We're not going to get anywhere bullin' around. I was a shipping clerk.

WILLY *(angrily):* All right, now listen to me—

BIFF: Why don't you let me finish?

WILLY: I'm not interested in stories about the past or any crap of that kind because the woods are burning, boys, you understand? There's a big blaze going on all around. I was fired today.

BIFF *(shocked):* How could you be?

WILLY: I was fired, and I'm looking for a little good news to tell your mother, because the woman has waited and the woman has suffered. The gist of it is that I haven't got a story left in my head, Biff. So don't give me a lecture about facts and aspects. I am not interested. Now what've you got to say to me?

(Stanley enters with three drinks. They wait until he leaves.)

WILLY: Did you see Oliver?

BIFF: Jesus, Dad!

WILLY: You mean you didn't go up there?

HAPPY: Sure he went up there.

BIFF: I did. I—saw him. How could they fire you?

WILLY *(on the edge of his chair):* What kind of a welcome did he give you?

BIFF: He won't even let you work on commission?

WILLY: I'm out! *(Driving)* So tell me, he gave you a warm welcome?

HAPPY: Sure, Pop, sure!

BIFF *(driven):* Well, it was kind of—

WILLY: I was wondering if he'd remember you. *(To Happy)* Imagine, man doesn't see him for ten, twelve years and gives him that kind of a welcome!

HAPPY: Damn right!

BIFF *(trying to return to the offensive):* Pop, look—

WILLY: You know why he remembered you, don't you? Because you impressed him in those days.

BIFF: Let's talk quietly and get this down to the facts, huh?

WILLY *(as though Biff had been interrupting):* Well, what happened? It's great news, Biff. Did he take you into his office or'd you talk in the waiting-room?

BIFF: Well, he came in, see, and—

WILLY *(with a big smile):* What'd he say? Betcha he threw his arm around you.

BIFF: Well, he kinda—

WILLY: He's a fine man. *(To Happy)* Very hard man to see, y'know.

HAPPY *(agreeing):* Oh, I know.

WILLY *(to Biff):* Is that where you had the drinks?

BIFF: Yeah, he gave me a couple of—no, no!

HAPPY *(cutting in):* He told him my Florida idea.

WILLY: Don't interrupt. *(To Biff)* How'd he react to the Florida idea?

BIFF: Dad, will you give me a minute to explain?

WILLY: I've been waiting for you to explain since I sat down here! What happened? He took you into his office and what?

BIFF: Well—I talked. And—and he listened, see.

WILLY: Famous for the way he listens, y'know. What was his answer?

BIFF: His answer was—*(He breaks off, suddenly angry)* Dad, you're not letting me tell you what I want to tell you!

WILLY *(accusing, angered):* You didn't see him, did you?

BIFF: I did see him!

WILLY: What'd you insult him or something? You insulted him, didn't you?

BIFF: Listen, will you let me out of it, will you just let me out of it!

HAPPY: What the hell!

WILLY: Tell me what happened!

BIFF *(to Happy):* I can't talk to him!

(A single trumpet note jars the ear. The light of green leaves stains the house, which holds the air of night and a dream. Young Bernard enters and knocks on the door of the house.)

YOUNG BERNARD *(frantically):* Mrs. Loman, Mrs. Loman!

HAPPY: Tell him what happened!

BIFF *(to Happy):* Shut up and leave me alone!

WILLY: No, no! You had to go and flunk math!

BIFF: What math? What're you talking about?

YOUNG BERNARD: Mrs. Loman, Mrs. Loman!

(Linda appears in the house, as of old)

WILLY *(wildly):* Math, math, math!

BIFF: Take it easy, Pop!

YOUNG BERNARD: Mrs. Loman!

WILLY *(furiously):* If you hadn't flunked you'd've been set by now!

BIFF: Now, look, I'm gonna tell you what happened, and you're going to listen to me.

YOUNG BERNARD: Mrs. Loman!

BIFF: I waited six hours—

HAPPY: What the hell are you saying?

BIFF: I kept sending in my name but he wouldn't see me. So finally he . . .
    (He continues unheard as light fades low on the restaurant)

YOUNG BERNARD: Biff flunked math!

LINDA: No!

YOUNG BERNARD: Birnbaum flunked him! They won't graduate him!

LINDA: But they have to. He's gotta go to the university. Where is he? Biff! Biff!

YOUNG BERNARD: No, he left. He went to Grand Central.

LINDA: Grand—You mean he went to Boston!

YOUNG BERNARD: Is Uncle Willy in Boston?

LINDA: Oh, maybe Willy can talk to the teacher. Oh, the poor, poor boy!

(Light on house area snaps out)

BIFF *(at the table, now audible, holding up a gold fountain pen):* . . . so I'm washed up with Oliver, you understand? Are you listening to me?

WILLY *(at a loss):* Yeah, sure. If you hadn't flunked—

BIFF: Flunked what? What're you talking about?

WILLY: Don't blame everything on me! I didn't flunk math—you did! What pen?

HAPPY: That was awful dumb, Biff, a pen like that is worth—

WILLY *(seeing the pen for the first time):* You took Oliver's pen?

BIFF *(weakening):* Dad, I just explained it to you.

WILLY: You stole Bill Oliver's fountain pen?

BIFF: I didn't exactly steal it! That's just what I've been explaining to you!

HAPPY: He had it in his hand and just then Oliver walked in, so he got nervous and stuck it in his pocket!

WILLY: My God, Biff!

BIFF: I never intended to do it, Dad!

OPERATOR'S VOICE: Standish Arms, good evening!

WILLY *(shouting):* I'm not in my room!

BIFF *(frightened):* Dad, what's the matter? *(He and Happy stand up)*

OPERATOR: Ringing Mr. Loman for you!

WILLY: I'm not there, stop it!

BIFF *(horrified, gets down on one knee before Willy):* Dad I'll make good, I'll make good. *(Willy tries to get to his feet. Biff holds him down)* Sit down now.

WILLY: No, you're no good, you're no good for anything.

BIFF: I am, Dad, I'll find something else, you understand? Now don't worry about anything. *(He holds up Willy's face)* Talk to me, Dad.

OPERATOR: Mr. Loman does not answer. Shall I page him?

WILLY *(attempting to stand as though to rush and silence the Operator):* No, no, no!

HAPPY: He'll strike something, Pop.

WILLY: No, no . . .

BIFF *(desperately standing over Willy):* Pop, listen! Listen to me! I'm telling you something good. Oliver talked to his partner about the Florida idea. You listening? He—he talked to his partner and he came to me . . . I'm going to be all right, you hear? Dad, listen to me, he said it was just a question of the amount?

WILLY: Then you . . . got it?

HAPPY: He's gonna be terrific, Pop!

WILLY *(trying to stand):* Then you got it, haven't you? You got it! You got it!

BIFF *(agonized holds Willy down):* No, no. Look, Pop. I'm supposed to have lunch with them tomorrow. I'm just telling you this so you'll know that I can still make an impression, Pop. And I'll make good somewhere, but I can't go tomorrow, see?

WILLY: Why not? You simply—

BIFF: But the pen, Pop!

WILLY: You give it to him and tell him it was an oversight!

HAPPY: Sure, have lunch tomorrow!

BIFF: I can't say that—

WILLY: You were doing a crossword puzzle and accidentally used his pen!

BIFF: Listen, kid, I took those balls years ago, now I walk in with his fountain pen? That clinches it, don't you see? I can't face him like that! I'll try elsewhere.

PAGE'S VOICE: Paging Mr. Loman!

WILLY: Don't you want to be anything?

BIFF: Pop, how can I go back?

WILLY: You don't want to be anything, is that what's behind it?

BIFF *(now angry at Willy for not crediting his sympathy):* Don't take it that way! You think it was easy walking into that office after what I'd done to him? A team of horses couldn't have dragged me back to Bill Oliver!

WILLY: Then why'd you go?

BIFF: Why did I go? Why did I go! Look at you! Look at what's become of you!

(Off left, The Woman laughs)

WILLY: Biff, you're going to go to that lunch tomorrow, or—

BIFF: I can't go. I've got no appointment!

HAPPY: Biff, for . . . !

WILLY: Are you spiting me?

BIFF: Don't take it that way! Goddammit!

WILLY *(strikes Biff and falters away from the table):* You rotten little louse! Are you spiting me?

THE WOMAN: Someone's at the door, Willy!

BIFF: I'm no good, can't you see what I am?

HAPPY *(separating them):* Hey, you're in a restaurant! Now cut it out, both of you? *(The girls enter)* Hello, girls, sit down.

(The Woman laughs, off left)

MISS FORSYTHE: I guess we might as well. This is Letta.

THE WOMAN: Willy, are you going to wake up?

BIFF *(ignoring Willy):* How're ya, miss, sit down. What do you drink?

MISS FORSYTHE: Letta might not be able to stay long.

LETTA: I gotta get up very early tomorrow. I got jury duty. I'm so excited! Were you fellows ever on a jury?

BIFF: No, but I been in front of them! *(The girls laugh)* This is my father.

LETTA: Isn't he cute? Sit down with us, Pop.

HAPPY: Sit him down, Biff!

BIFF *(going to him):* Come on, slugger, drink us under the table. To hell with it! Come on, sit down pal.

(On Biff's last insistence, Willy is about to sit)

THE WOMAN *(now urgently):* Willy, are you going to answer the door!

(The Woman's call pulls Willy back. He starts right, befuddled.)

BIFF: Hey, where are you going?

WILLY: Open the door.

BIFF: The door?

WILLY: The washroom . . . the door . . . where's the door?

BIFF *(leading Willy to the left):* Just go straight down.

(Willy moves left)

THE WOMAN: Willy, Willy, are you going to get up, get up, get up, get up?

(Willy exits left)

LETTA: I think it's sweet you bring your daddy along.

MISS FORSYTHE: Oh, he isn't really your father!

BIFF *(at left, turning to her resentfully):* Miss Forsythe, you've just seen a prince walk by. A fine troubled prince. A hardworking, unappreciated prince. A pal, you understand? A good companion. Always for his boys.

LETTA: That's so sweet.

HAPPY: Well, girls, what's the program? We're wasting time. Come on, Biff. Gather round. Where would you like to go?

BIFF: Why don't you do something for him?

HAPPY: Me!

BIFF: Don't you give a damn for him, Hap?

HAPPY: What're you talking about? I'm the one who—

BIFF: I sense it, you don't give a good goddam about him. *(He takes the rolled-up hose from his pocket and puts it on the table in front of Happy)* Look what I found in the cellar, for Christ's sake. How can you bear to let it go on?

HAPPY: Me? Who goes away? Who runs off and—

BIFF: Yeah but he doesn't mean anything to you. You could help him—I can't! Don't you understand what I'm talking about? He's going to kill himself, don't you know that?

HAPPY: Don't I know it! Me!

BIFF: Hap, help him! Jesus . . . help him . . . Help me, help me, I can't bear to look at his face! *(Ready to weep, he hurries out, up right)*

HAPPY *(starting after him):* Where are you going?

MISS FORSYTHE: What's he so mad about?

HAPPY: Come on, girls, we'll catch up with him.

MISS FORSYTHE *(as Happy pushes her out):* Say, I don't like that temper of his!

HAPPY: He's just a little overstrung, he'll be all right!

WILLY *(off left, as The Woman laughs):* Don't answer! Don't answer!

LETTA: Don't you want to tell your father—

HAPPY: No, that's not my father. He's just a guy. Come on, we'll catch Biff, and honey, we're going to paint this town! Stanley, where's the check! Hey, Stanley!

(They exit. Stanley looks toward left)

STANLEY *(calling to Happy indignantly):* Mr. Loman! Mr. Loman!

(Stanley picks up a chair and follows them off. Knocking is heard off left. The Woman enters, laughing. Willy follows her. She is in a black slip; he is buttoning his shirt. Raw, sensuous music accompanies their speech.)

WILLY: Will you stop laughing? Will you stop?

THE WOMAN: Aren't you going to answer the door? He'll wake the whole hotel.

WILLY: I'm not expecting anybody.

THE WOMAN: Whyn't you have another drink, honey, and stop being so damn self-centered?

WILLY: I'm so lonely.

THE WOMAN: You know you ruined me, Willy? From now on, whenever you come to the office, I'll see that you go right through to the buyers. No waiting at my desk any more, Willy. You ruined me.

WILLY: That's nice of you to say that.

THE WOMAN: Gee, you are self-centered! Why so sad? You are the saddest self-centeredest soul I ever did see-saw. *(She laughs. He kisses her.)* Come on inside, drummer boy. It's silly to be dressing in the middle of the night. *(As knocking is heard)* Aren't you going to answer the door?

WILLY: They're knocking on the wrong door.

THE WOMAN: But I felt the knocking. And he heard us talking in here. Maybe the hotel's on fire!

WILLY *(his terror rising):* It's a mistake.

THE WOMAN: Then tell him to go away!

WILLY: There's nobody there.

THE WOMAN: It's getting on my nerves, Willy. There's somebody standing out there and it's getting on my nerves!

WILLY *(pushing her away from him):* All right, stay in the bathroom here, and don't come out. I think there's a law in Massachusetts about it, so don't come out. It may be that new room clerk. He looked very mean. So don't come out. It's a mistake, there's no fire.

(The knocking is heard again. He takes a few steps away from her, and she vanishes into the wing. The light follows him and now he is facing Young Biff, who carries a suitcase. Biff steps toward him. The music is gone.)

BIFF: Why didn't you answer?

WILLY: Biff! What are you doing in Boston?

BIFF: Why didn't you answer? I've been knocking for five minutes, I called you on the phone—

WILLY: I just heard you. I was in the bathroom and had the door shut. Did anything happen home?

BIFF: Dad—I let you down.

WILLY: What do you mean?

BIFF: Dad . . .

WILLY: Biffo, what's this about. *(Putting his arm around Biff)* Come on, let's go downstairs and get you a malted.

BIFF: Dad, I flunked math.

WILLY: Not for the term?

BIFF: The term. I haven't got enough credits to graduate.

WILLY: You mean to say Bernard wouldn't give you the answers?

BIFF: He did, he tried, but I only got a sixty-one.

WILLY: And they wouldn't give you four points?

BIFF: Birnbaum refused absolutely. I begged him, Pop, but he won't give me those points. You gotta talk to him before they close the school. Because if he saw the kind of man you are, and you just talked to him in your way, I'm sure he'd come through for me. The class came right before practice, see, and I didn't go enough. Would you talk to him? He'd like you, Pop. You know the way you could talk.

WILLY: You're on. We'll drive right back.

BIFF: Oh, Dad, good work! I'm sure he'll change it for you!

WILLY: Go downstairs and tell the clerk I'm checkin' out. Go right down.

BIFF: Yes, sir! See the reason he hates me, Pop—one day he was late for class so I got up at the blackboard and imitated him. I crossed my eyes and talked with a lithp.

WILLY *(laughing):* You did? The kids like it?

BIFF: They nearly died laughing!

WILLY: Yeah? What'd you do?

BIFF: The thquare root of thixthy twee is . . . *(Willy bursts out laughing; Biff joins him)* And in the middle of it he walked in!

(Willy laughs and The Woman joins in offstage)

WILLY *(without hesitation):* Hurry downstairs and—

BIFF: Somebody in there?

WILLY: No, that was next door.

(The Woman laughs offstage)

BIFF: Somebody got in your bathroom!

WILLY: No, it's the next room, there's a party—

THE WOMAN *(enters laughing. She lisps this):* Can I come in? There's something in the bathtub, Willy, and it's moving!

(Willy looks at Biff, who is staring open-mouthed and horrified at The Woman)

WILLY: Ah—you better go back to your room. They must be finished painting by now. They're painting her room so I let her take a shower here. Go back, go back . . . *(He pushes her)*

THE WOMAN *(resisting):* But I've got to get dressed, Willy, I can't—

WILLY: Get out of here! Go back, go back . . . *(Suddenly striving for the ordinary)* This is Miss Francis, Biff, she's a buyer. They're painting her room. Go back, Miss Francis, go back . . .

THE WOMAN: But my clothes, I can't go out naked in the hall!

WILLY *(pushing her offstage):* Get outa here! Go back, go back!

(Biff slowly sits down on his suitcase as the argument continues offstage)

THE WOMAN: Where's my stockings? You promised me stockings, Willy!

WILLY: I have no stockings here!

THE WOMAN: You had two boxes of size nine sheers for me, and I want them!

WILLY: Here, for God's sake, will you get outa here!

THE WOMAN *(enters holding a box of stockings):* I just hope there's nobody in the hall. That's all I hope. *(To Biff)* Are you football or baseball?

BIFF: Football.

THE WOMAN *(angry, humiliated):* That's me too. G'night. *(She snatches her clothes from Willy, and walks out)*

WILLY *(after a pause):* Well, better get going. I want to get to the school first thing in the morning. Get my suits out of the closet. I'll get my valise. *(Biff doesn't move)* What's the matter? *(Biff remains motionless, tears falling)* She's a buyer. Buys for J. H. Simmons. She lives down the hall —they're painting. You don't imagine— *(He breaks off. After a pause)* Now listen, pal, she's just a buyer. She sees merchandise in her room and they have to keep it looking just so . . . *(Pause. Assuming command)* All right, get my suits. *(Biff doesn't move)* Now stop crying and do as I say. I gave you an order. Biff, I gave you an order! Is that what you do when I give you an order? How dare you cry! *(Putting his arm around Biff)* Now look, Biff, when you grow up you'll understand about these things. You mustn't—you mustn't overemphasize a thing like this. I'll see Birnbaum first thing in the morning.

BIFF: Never mind.

WILLY *(getting down beside Biff):* Never mind! He's going to give you those points. I'll see to it.

BIFF: He wouldn't listen to you.

WILLY: He certainly will listen to me. You need those points for the U. of Virginia.

BIFF: I'm not going there.

WILLY: Heh? If I can't get him to change that mark you'll make it up in summer school. You've got all summer to—

BIFF *(his weeping breaking from him):* Dad . . .

WILLY *(infected by it):* Oh, my boy . . .

BIFF: Dad . . .

WILLY: She's nothing to me, Biff. I was lonely, I was terribly lonely.

BIFF: You—you gave her Mama's stockings! *(His tears break through and he rises to go)*

WILLY *(grabbing for Biff):* I gave you an order!

BIFF: Don't touch me, you—liar!

WILLY: Apologize for that!

BIFF: You fake! You phony little fake! You fake! *(Overcome, he turns quickly and weeping fully goes out with his suitcase. Willy is left on the floor on his knees)*

WILLY: I gave you an order! Biff, come back here or I'll beat you! Come back here! I'll whip you!

(Stanley comes quickly in from the right and stands in front of Willy)

WILLY *(shouts at Stanley):* I gave you an order . . .

STANLEY: Hey, let's pick it up, pick it up, Mr. Loman. *(He helps Willy to his feet)* Your boys left with the chippies. They said they'll see you home.

(A second waiter watches some distance away)

WILLY: But we were supposed to have dinner together.

(Music is heard, Willy's theme)

STANLEY: Can you make it?

WILLY: I'll—sure, I can make it. *(Suddenly concerned about his clothes)* Do I—I look all right?

STANLEY: Sure, you look all right. *(He flicks a speck off Willy's lapel)*

WILLY: Here—here's a dollar.

STANLEY: Oh, your son paid me. It's all right.

WILLY *(putting it in Stanley's hand):* No, take it. You're a good boy.

STANLEY: Oh, no, you don't have to . . .

WILLY: Here—here's some more, I don't need it any more. *(After a slight pause)* Tell me—is there a seed store in the neighborhood?

STANLEY: Seeds? You mean like to plant?

(As Willy turns, Stanley slips the money back into his jacket pocket)

WILLY: Yes. Carrots, peas . . .

STANLEY: Well, there's hardware stores on Sixth Avenue, but it may be too late now.

WILLY *(anxiously):* Oh, I'd better hurry. I've got to get some seeds. *(He starts*

off to the right) I've got to get some seeds, right away. Nothing's planted.
I don't have a thing in the ground.

(Willy hurries out as the light goes down. Stanley moves over to the right after him, watches him off. The other waiter has been staring at Willy.)

STANLEY *(to the waiter):* Well, whatta you looking at?

(The waiter picks up the chairs and moves off right. Stanley takes the table and follows him. The light fades on this area. There is a long pause, the sound of the flute coming over. The light gradually rises on the kitchen, which is empty. Happy appears at the door of the house, followed by Biff. Happy is carrying a large bunch of long-stemmed roses. He enters the kitchen, looks around for Linda. Not seeing her, he turns to Biff, who is just outside the house door, and makes a gesture with his hands, indicating "Not here, I guess." He looks into the living-room and freezes. Inside, Linda, unseen, is seated, Willy's coat on her lap. She rises ominously and quietly and moves toward Happy, who backs up into the kitchen, afraid.)

HAPPY: Hey, what're you doing up? *(Linda says nothing but moves toward him implacably)* Where's Pop? *(He keeps backing to the right, and now Linda is in full view in the doorway to the living-room)* Is he sleeping?

LINDA: Where were you?

HAPPY *(trying to laugh it off):* We met two girls, Mom, very fine types. Here, we brought you some flowers. *(Offering them to her)* Put them in your room, Ma.

(She knocks them to the floor at Biff's feet. He has now come inside and closed the door behind him. She stares at Biff, silent.)

HAPPY: Now what'd you do that for? Mom, I want you to have some flowers—

LINDA *(cutting Happy off, violently to Biff):* Don't you care whether he lives or dies?

HAPPY *(going to the stairs):* Come upstairs, Biff.

BIFF *(with a flare of disgust, to Happy):* Go away from me! *(To Linda)* What do you mean, lives or dies? Nobody's dying around here, pal.

LINDA: Get out of my sight! Get out of here!

BIFF: I wanna see the boss.

LINDA: You're not going near him!

BIFF: Where is he? *(He moves into the living-room and Linda follows)*

LINDA *(shouting after Biff):* You invite him for dinner. He looks forward to it all day— *(Biff appears in his parents' bedroom, looks around, and exits)* —and then you desert him there. There's no stranger you'd do that to!

HAPPY: Why? He had a swell time with us. Listen, when I— *(Linda comes back into the kitchen)*—desert him I hope I don't outlive the day!

LINDA: Get out of here!

HAPPY: Now look, Mom . . .

LINDA: Did you have to go to women tonight? You and your lousy rotten whores!

(Biff re-enters the kitchen)

HAPPY: Mom, all we did was follow Biff around trying to cheer him up! *(To Biff)* Boy, what a night you gave me!

LINDA: Get out of here, both of you, and don't come back! I don't want you tormenting him any more. Go on now, get your things together! *(To Biff)* You can sleep in his apartment. *(She starts to pick up the flowers and stops herself)* Pick up this stuff, I'm not your maid any more. Pick it up, you bum, you!

(Happy turns his back to her in refusal. Biff slowly moves over and gets down on his knees, picking up the flowers.)

LINDA: You're a pair of animals! Not one, not another living soul would have had the cruelty to walk out on that man in a restaurant!

BIFF *(not looking at her):* Is that what he said?

LINDA: He didn't have to say anything. He was so humiliated he nearly limped when he came in.

HAPPY: But, Mom, he had a great time with us—

BIFF *(cutting him off violently):* Shut up!

(Without another word, Happy goes upstairs)

LINDA: You! You didn't even go in to see if he was all right!

BIFF *(still on the floor in front of Linda, the flowers in his hand; with self-loathing):* No. Didn't. Didn't do a damned thing. How do you like that, heh? Left him babbling in a toilet.

LINDA: You louse. You . . .

BIFF: Now you hit it on the nose! *(He gets up, throws the flowers in the wastebasket)* The scum of the earth, and you're looking at him!

LINDA: Get out of here!

BIFF: I gotta talk to the boss, Mom. Where is he?

LINDA: You're not going near him. Get out of this house!

BIFF *(with absolute assurance, determination):* No. We're gonna have an abrupt conversation, him and me.

LINDA: You're not talking to him!

(Hammering is heard from outside the house, off right. Biff turns toward the noise.)

LINDA *(suddenly pleading):* Will you please leave him alone?

BIFF: What's he doing out there?

LINDA: He's planting the garden!

BIFF *(quietly):* Now? Oh, my God!

(Biff moves outside, Linda following. The light dies down on them and comes up on the center of the apron as Willy walks into it. He is carrying a flashlight, a hoe,

and a handful of seed packets. He raps the top of the hoe sharply to fix it firmly, and then moves to the left, measuring off the distance with his foot. He holds the flashlight to look at the seed packets, reading off the instructions. He is in the blue of night.)

WILLY: Carrots . . . quarter-inch apart. Rows . . . one-foot rows. *(He measures it off)* One foot. *(He puts down a package and measures off)* Beets. *(He puts down another package and measures again)* Lettuce. *(He reads the package, puts it down)* One foot— *(He breaks off as Ben appears at the right and moves slowly down to him)* What a proposition, ts, ts. Terrific, terrific. 'Cause she's suffered, Ben, the woman has suffered. You understand me? A man can't go out the way he came in, Ben, a man has got to add up to something. You can't, you can't—*(Ben moves toward him as though to interrupt)* You gotta consider, now. Don't answer so quick. Remember, it's a guaranteed twenty-thousand-dollar proposition. Now look, Ben, I want you to go through the ins and outs of this thing with me. I've got nobody to talk to, Ben, and the woman has suffered, you hear me?

BEN *(standing still, considering):* What's the proposition?

WILLY: It's twenty thousand dollars on the barrelhead. Guaranteed, gilt-edged, you understand?

BEN: You don't want to make a fool of yourself. They might not honor the policy.

WILLY: How can they dare refuse? Didn't I work like a coolie to meet every premium on the nose? And now they don't pay off! Impossible!

BEN: It's called a cowardly thing, William.

WILLY: Why? Does it take more guts to stand here the rest of my life ringing up a zero?

BEN *(yielding):* That's a point, William. *(He moves, thinking, turns)* And twenty thousand—that *is* something one can feel with the hand, it is there.

WILLY *(now assured, with rising power):* Oh, Ben, that's the whole beauty of it! I see it like a diamond, shining in the dark, hard and rough, that I can pick up and touch in my hand. Not like—like an appointment! This would not be another damned-fool appointment, Ben, and it changes all the aspects. Because he thinks I'm nothing, see, and so he spites me. But the funeral— *(Straightening up)* Ben, that funeral will be massive! They'll come from Maine, Massachusetts, Vermont, New Hampshire! All the old-timers with the strange license plates—that boy will be thunderstruck, Ben, because he never realized—I am known! Rhode Island, New York, New Jersey—I am known, Ben, and he'll see it with his eyes once and for all. He'll see what I am, Ben! He's in for a shock, that boy!

BEN *(coming down to the edge of the garden):* He'll call you a coward.

WILLY *(suddenly fearful):* No, that would be terrible.

BEN: Yes. And a damned fool.

WILLY: No, no, he mustn't, I won't have that! *(He is broken and desperate)*

BEN: He'll hate you, William.

(The gay music of the Boys is heard)

WILLY: Oh Ben, how do we get back to all the great times! Used to be so full of light, and comradeship, the sleigh-riding in winter, and the ruddiness on his cheeks. And always some kind of good news coming up, always something nice coming up ahead. And never even let me carry the valises in the house, and simonizing, simonizing that little red car! Why, why can't I give him something and not have him hate me?

BEN: Let me think about it. *(He glances at his watch).* I still have a little time. Remarkable proposition but you've got to be sure you're not making a fool of yourself.

(Ben drifts off upstage and goes out of sight. Biff comes down from the left.)

WILLY *(suddenly conscious of Biff, turns and looks up at him, then begins picking up the packages of seeds in confusion):* Where the hell is that seed? *(Indignantly)* You can't see nothing out here! They boxed in the whole goddam neighborhood!

BIFF: There are people all around here. Don't you realize that?

WILLY: I'm busy. Don't bother me.

BIFF *(taking the hoe from Willy):* I'm saying good-by to you Pop. *(Willy looks at him silent unable to move)* I'm not coming back any more.

WILLY: You're not going to see Oliver tomorrow?

BIFF: I've got no appointment Dad.

WILLY: He put his arm around you, and you've got no appointment?

BIFF: Pop get this now, will you? Everytime I've left it's been a fight that sent me out of here. Today I realized something about myself and I tried to explain it to you and I—I think I'm just not smart enough to make any sense out of it for you. To hell with whose fault it is or anything like that. *(He takes Willy's arm)* Let's just wrap it up, heh? Come on in, we'll tell Mom. *(He gently tries to pull Willy to left)*

WILLY *(frozen immobile with guilt in his voice):* No, I don't want to see her.

BIFF: Come on! *(He pulls again, and Willy tries to pull away)*

WILLY *(highly nervous):* No, no, I don't want to see her.

BIFF *(tries to look into Willy's face, as if to find the answer there):* Why don't you want to see her?

WILLY *(more harshly now):* Don't bother me, will you?

BIFF: What do you mean, you don't want to see her? You don't want them calling you yellow, do you? This isn't your fault; it's me, I'm a bum. Now come inside! *(Willy strains to get away)* Did you hear what I said to you?

(Willy pulls away and quickly goes by himself into the house. Biff follows)

LINDA *(to Willy):* Did you plant dear?

BIFF *(at the door to Linda):* All right, we had it out. I'm going and I'm not writing any more.

LINDA *(going to Willy in the kitchen):* I think that's the best way, dear. 'Cause there's no use drawing it out, you'll just never get along.

(Willy doesn't respond)

BIFF: People ask where I am and what I'm doing, you don't know, and you don't care. That way it'll be off your mind and you can start brightening up again. All right? That clears it, doesn't it? *(Willy is silent, and Biff goes to him)* You gonna wish me luck, scout? *(He extends his hand)* What do you say?

LINDA: Shake his hand, Willy.

WILLY *(turning to her, seething with hurt):* There's no necessity to mention the pen at all, y'know.

BIFF *(gently):* I've got no appointment, Dad.

WILLY *(erupting fiercely):* He put his arm around . . .?

BIFF: Dad you're never going to see what I am, so what's the use of arguing? If I strike oil I'll send you a check. Meantime forget I'm alive.

WILLY *(to Linda):* Spite, see?

BIFF: Shake hands, Dad.

WILLY: Not my hand.

BIFF: I was hoping not to go this way.

WILLY: Well this is the way you're going. Good-by.

(Biff looks at him a moment, then turns sharply and goes to the stairs)

WILLY *(stops him with):* May you rot in hell if you leave this house!

BIFF *(turning):* Exactly what is it that you want from me?

WILLY: I want you to know, on the train, in the mountains, in the valleys, wherever you go, that you cut down your life for spite!

BIFF: No, no.

WILLY: Spite, spite, is the word of your undoing! And when you're down and out, remember what did it. When you're rotting somewhere beside the railroad tracks, remember, and don't you dare blame it on me!

BIFF: I'm not blaming it on you!

WILLY: I won't take the rap for this, you hear?

(Happy comes down the stairs and stands on the bottom step, watching)

BIFF: That's just what I'm telling you!

WILLY *(sinking into a chair at the table, with full accusation):* You're trying to put a knife in me—don't think I don't know what you're doing!

BIFF: All right, phony! Then let's lay it on the line. *(He whips the rubber tube out of his pocket and puts it on the table)*

HAPPY: You crazy—

LINDA: Biff! *(She moves to grab the hose, but Biff holds it down with his hand)*

BIFF: Leave it there! Don't move it!

WILLY *(not looking at it):* What is that?

BIFF: You know goddam well what that is.

WILLY *(caged wanting to escape):* I never saw that.

BIFF: You saw it. The mice didn't bring it into the cellar! What is this supposed to do, make a hero out of you? This supposed to make me sorry for you?

WILLY: Never heard of it.

BIFF: There'll be no pity for you, you hear it? No pity!

WILLY *(to Linda):* You hear the spite!

BIFF: No, you're going to hear the truth—what you are and what I am!

LINDA: Stop it!

WILLY: Spite!

HAPPY *(coming down toward Biff):* You cut it now!

BIFF *(to Happy):* The man don't know who we are! The man is gonna know! *(To Willy)* We never told the truth for ten minutes in this house!

HAPPY: We always told the truth!

BIFF *(turning on him):* You big blow, are you the assistant buyer? You're one of the two assistants to the assistant, aren't you?

HAPPY: Well I'm practically—

BIFF: You're practically full of it! We all are! And I'm through with it. *(To Willy)* Now hear this, Willy, this is me.

WILLY: I know you!

BIFF: You know why I had no address for three months? I stole a suit in Kansas City and I was in jail. *(To Linda who is sobbing)* Stop crying. I'm through with it.

(Linda turns away from them, her hands covering her face)

WILLY: I suppose that's my fault!

BIFF: I stole myself out of every good job since high school!

WILLY: And whose fault is that?

BIFF: And I never got anywhere because you blew me so full of hot air I could never stand taking orders from anybody! That's whose fault it is!

WILLY: I hear that!

LINDA: Don't Biff!

BIFF: It's goddam time you heard that! I had to be boss big shot in two weeks, and I'm through with it!

WILLY: Then hang yourself! For spite, hang yourself!

BIFF: No! Nobody's hanging himself, Willy! I ran down eleven flights with a pen in my hand today. And suddenly I stopped, you hear me? And in the middle of that office building, do you hear this? I stopped in the middle of that building and I saw—the sky. I saw the things that I love in this world. The work and the food and time to sit and smoke. And I looked at the pen and said to myself, what the hell am I grabbing this for? Why am I trying to become what I don't want to be? What am I doing in an office, making a contemptuous, begging fool of myself, when all I want is out there, waiting for me the minute I say I know who I am! Why can't I say that Willy? *(He tries to make Willy face him, but Willy pulls away and moves to the left)*

WILLY *(with hatred, threateningly):* The door of your life is wide open!

BIFF: Pop! I'm a dime a dozen, and so are you!

WILLY *(turning on him now in an uncontrolled outburst):* I am not a dime a dozen! I am Willy Loman, and you are Biff Loman!

(Biff starts for Willy, but is blocked by Happy. In his fury, Biff seems on the verge of attacking his father.)

BIFF: I am not a leader of men, Willy, and neither are you. You were never anything but a hard-working drummer who landed in the ash can like all the rest of them! I'm one dollar an hour, Willy! I tried seven states and couldn't raise it. A buck an hour! Do you gather my meaning? I'm not bringing home any prizes any more, and you're going to stop waiting for me to bring them home!

WILLY *(directly to Biff):* You vengeful spiteful mutt!

(Biff breaks from Happy. Willy, in fright, starts up the stairs. Biff grabs him.)

BIFF *(at the peak of his fury):* Pop I'm nothing! I'm nothing Pop. Can't you understand that? There's no spite in it any more. I'm just what I am, that's all.

(Biff's fury has spent itself, and he breaks down, sobbing, holding on to Willy, who dumbly fumbles for Biff's face)

WILLY *(astonished):* What're you doing? What're you doing? *(To Linda)* Why is he crying?

BIFF *(crying, broken):* Will you let me go, for Christ's sake? Will you take that phony dream and burn it before something happens? *(Struggling to contain himself, he pulls away and moves to the stairs)* I'll go in the morning. Put him—put him to bed. *(Exhausted, Biff moves up the stairs to his room)*

WILLY *(after a long pause, astonished, elevated):* Isn't that—isn't that remarkable? Biff—he likes me!

LINDA: He loves you Willy!

HAPPY *(deeply moved):* Always did, Pop.

WILLY: Oh Biff! *(Staring wildly)* He cried! Cried to me. *(He is choking with his love, and now cries out his promise)* That boy—that boy is going to be magnificent!

(Ben appears in the light just outside the kitchen)

BEN: Yes, outstanding, with twenty thousand behind him.

LINDA *(sensing the racing of his mind, fearfully, carefully):* Now come to bed, Willy. It's all settled now.

WILLY *(finding it difficult not to rush out of the house):* Yes, we'll sleep. Come on. Go to sleep, Hap.

BEN: And it does take a great kind of a man to crack the jungle.

(In accents of dread, Ben's idyllic music starts up)

HAPPY *(his arm around Linda):* I'm getting married, Pop, don't forget it. I'm changing everything. I'm gonna run that department before the year is up. You'll see, Mom. *(He kisses her)*

BEN: The jungle is dark but full of diamonds, Willy.

(Willy turns, moves, listening to Ben)

LINDA: Be good. You're both good boys, just act that way, that's all.

HAPPY: 'Night Pop. *(He goes upstairs)*

LINDA *(to Willy):* Come dear.

BEN *(with greater force):* One must go in to fetch a diamond out.

WILLY *(to Linda, as he moves slowly along the edge of the kitchen, toward the door):* I just want to get settled down, Linda. Let me sit alone for a little.

LINDA *(almost uttering her fear):* I want you upstairs.

WILLY *(taking her in his arms):* In a few minutes, Linda. I couldn't sleep right now. Go on, you look awful tired. *(He kisses her)*

BEN: Not like an appointment at all. A diamond is rough and hard to the touch.

WILLY: Go on now. I'll be right up.

LINDA: I think this is the only way, Willy.

WILLY: Sure it's the best thing.

BEN: Best thing!

WILLY: The only way. Everything is gonna be—go on kid, get to bed. You look so tired.

LINDA: Come right up.

WILLY: Two minutes.

(Linda goes into the living-room, then reappears in her bedroom. Willy moves just outside the kitchen door.)

WILLY: Loves me. *(Wonderingly)* Always loved me. Isn't that a remarkable thing? Ben, he'll worship me for it!

BEN *(with promise):* It's dark there, but full of diamonds.

WILLY: Can you imagine that magnificence with twenty thousand dollars in his pocket?

LINDA *(calling from her room):* Willy! Come up!

WILLY *(calling into the kitchen):* Yes! Yes. Coming! It's very smart, you realize that, don't you, sweetheart? Even Ben sees it. I gotta go baby. 'By! 'By! *(Going over to Ben almost dancing)* Imagine? When the mail comes he'll be ahead of Bernard again!

BEN: A perfect proposition all around.

WILLY: Did you see how he cried to me? Oh, if I could kiss him, Ben!

BEN: Time, William, time!

WILLY: Oh, Ben, I always knew one way or another we were gonna make it, Biff and I!

BEN *(looking at his watch):* The boat. We'll be late. *(He moves slowly off into the darkness)*

WILLY *(elegiacally, turning to the house):* Now when you kick off, boy, I want a seventy-yard boot, and get right down the field under the ball, and when you hit, hit low and hit hard, because it's important, boy. *(He swings around and faces the audience)* There's all kinds of important people in the stands, and the first thing you know... *(Suddenly realizing he is alone)* Ben! Ben, where do I...? *(He makes a sudden movement of search)* Ben, how do I...?

LINDA *(calling):* Willy, you coming up?

WILLY *(uttering a gasp of fear, whirling about as if to quiet her):* Sh! *(He turns around as if to find his way; sounds, faces, voices, seem to be swarming in upon him and he flicks at them, crying)* Sh! Sh! *(Suddenly music, faint and high, stops him. It rises in intensity, almost to an unbearable scream. He goes up and down on his toes, and rushes off around the house.)* Shhh!

LINDA: Willy?

(There is no answer. Linda waits. Biff gets up off his bed. He is still in his clothes. Happy sits up. Biff stands listening.)

LINDA *(with real fear):* Willy, answer me! Willy!

(There is the sound of a car starting and moving away at full speed)

LINDA: No!

BIFF *(rushing down the stairs):* Pop!

(As the car speeds off, the music crashes down in a frenzy of sound, which becomes the soft pulsation of a single cello string. Biff slowly returns to his bedroom. He and Happy gravely don their jackets. Linda slowly walks out of her room. The music has developed into a dead march. The leaves of day are appearing over everything. Charley and Bernard, somberly dressed, appear and knock on the kitchen door. Biff and Happy slowly descend the stairs to the kitchen as Charley and Bernard enter. All stop a moment when Linda, in clothes of mourning, bearing a little bunch of roses, comes through the draped doorway into the kitchen. She goes to Charley and takes his arm. Now all move toward the audience, through the wall-line of the kitchen. At the limit of the apron, Linda lays down the flowers, kneels, and sits back on her heels. All stare down at the grave.)

Requiem

CHARLEY: It's getting dark, Linda.

(Linda doesn't react. She stares at the grave.)

BIFF: How about it, Mom? Better get some rest, heh? They'll be closing the gate soon.

(Linda makes no move. Pause.)

HAPPY *(deeply angered):* He had no right to do that. There was no necessity for it. We would've helped him.

CHARLEY *(grunting):* Hmmm.

BIFF: Come along, Mom.

LINDA: Why didn't anybody come?

CHARLEY: It was a very nice funeral.

LINDA: But where are all the people he knew? Maybe they blame him.

CHARLEY: Naa. It's a rough world, Linda. They wouldn't blame him.

LINDA: I can't understand it. At this time especially. First time in thirty-five years we were just about free and clear. He only needed a little salary. He was even finished with the dentist.

CHARLEY: No man only needs a little salary.

LINDA: I can't understand it.

BIFF: There were a lot of nice days. When he'd come home from a trip; or on Sundays, making the stoop; finishing the cellar; putting on the new porch; when he built the extra bathroom; and put up the garage. You know something, Charley, there's more of him in that front stoop than in all the sales he ever made.

CHARLEY: Yeah. He was a happy man with a batch of cement.

LINDA: He was so wonderful with his hands.

BIFF: He had the wrong dreams. All, all, wrong.

HAPPY *(almost ready to fight Biff):* Don't say that!

BIFF: He never knew who he was.

CHARLEY *(stopping Happy's movement and reply. To Biff):* Nobody dast blame this man. You don't understand: Willy was a salesman. And for a salesman, there is no rock bottom to the life. He don't put a bolt to a nut, he don't tell you the law or give you medicine. He's a man way out there in the blue, riding on a smile and a shoeshine. And when they start not smiling back—that's an earthquake. And then you get yourself a couple of spots on your hat, and you're finished. Nobody dast blame this man. A salesman is got to dream, boy. It comes with the territory.

BIFF: Charley, the man didn't know who he was.

HAPPY *(infuriated):* Don't say that!

BIFF: Why don't you come with me, Happy?

HAPPY: I'm not licked that easily. I'm staying right in this city, and I'm gonna beat this racket! *(He looks at Biff, his chin set)* The Loman Brothers!

BIFF: I know who I am, kid.

HAPPY: All right, boy. I'm gonna show you and everybody else that Willy Loman did not die in vain. He had a good dream. It's the only dream you can have—to come out number-one man. He fought it out here, and this is where I'm gonna win it for him.

BIFF *(with a hopeless glance at Happy, bends toward his mother):* Let's go, Mom.

LINDA: I'll be with you in a minute. Go on, Charley. *(He hesitates)* I want to, just for a minute. I never had a chance to say good-by.

(Charley moves away, followed by Happy. Biff remains a slight distance up and left of Linda. She sits there, summoning herself. The flute begins, not for away, playing behind her speech.)

LINDA: Forgive me, dear. I can't cry. I don't know what it is, but I can't cry. I don't understand it. Why did you ever do that? Help me, Willy, I can't cry. It seems to me that you're just on another trip. I keep expecting you. Willy, dear, I can't cry. Why did you do it? I search and search and I search, and I can't understand it, Willy. I made the last payment on the house today. Today, dear. And there'll be nobody home. *(A sob rises in her throat)* We're free and clear. *(Sobbing more fully, released)* We're free. *(Biff comes slowly toward her)* We're free . . . We're free . . .

(Biff lifts her to her feet and moves out up right with her in his arms. Linda sobs quietly. Bernard and Charley come together and follow them, followed by Happy. Only the music of the flute is left on the darkening stage as over the house the hard towers of the apartment buildings rise into sharp focus.)
(Curtain)

Questions

1. How do the setting and opening stage directions prepare you for the play?
2. What lines in the opening dialogue best reveal Willy's state of mind?
3. What lines in the first act best illuminate the relationship between Biff and Willy?
4. What attitudes toward women do Willy, Biff, and Happy share? What ideas about the role of men in society do they share?
5. What kind of a person is Ben? How do Ben's appearances in the play help to illuminate Willy's character?
6. What signals indicate which scenes occur in the present, which in Willy's past, and which in his imagination?
7. Why is a garden important to Willy?
8. What "guaranteed proposition" is Willy discussing with Ben as he works in the garden in Act II?
9. How accurate is Biff's assertion that "We never told the truth for ten minutes in this house"? What does Biff think is the truth about Willy? About Happy? About himself?
10. What importance does Bernard have in the play?
11. In the Requiem, what does Charley mean by "No man only needs a little salary?"
12. In Act I, Linda makes clear that even for her Willy is not a hero in the classic sense, ". . . But he's a human being, and a terrible thing is happening to him. So attention must be paid." What details underline the "human being"? What terrible thing is happening?
13. Why should an audience care about an essentially personal tragedy that affects only one family?

GLOSSARY AND INDEX OF TERMS

The following definitions are adapted from Northrop Frye, Sheridan Baker, and George Perkins, The Harper Handbook to Literature, *where many of these terms are more fully treated. Words in SMALL CAPITALS refer to other entries in this index. Page numbers in italics refer to discussions in this text.*

Allegory. *(242, 537)* A story that suggests another story. The first part of this word comes from the Greek *allos,* "other," and an allegory is present in literature whenever it is clear that the author is saying, "By this I also mean that." Allegory is normally a continuous technique, like counterpoint in music, and a work of literature that seems to have a continuous parallel between its narrative and conceptual or moral ideas, or historical events looked at as illustrations of moral precepts, may be called an allegory. Examples in English literature would include Spenser's *Faerie Queene* and Bunyan's *Pilgrim's Progress;* in American literature, some of Hawthorne's stories, such as "The Birthmark."

The simplest form of allegory is usually conveyed by personification: thus in the *Pilgrim's Progress* the hero, Christian, with his companion Hopeful, is imprisoned in the castle of Giant Despair, but they escape by means of a key to the prison door called Promise.

Alliteration. *(544)* "Adding letters" (Latin *ad* + *littera,* "letter"). Two or more words, or accented syllables, chime on the same initial letter: *l*ost *l*ove a*l*one; a*f*ter *a*pple-picking, or repeat the same consonant, as in Tennyson's lines:

The *m*oan of doves in i*mm*em*m*orial el*m*s,
And *m*ur*m*uring of innu*m*erable bees.

1397

Allusion. *(479)* A meaningful reference, direct or indirect, as when Yeats writes, "Another Troy must rise and set," calling to the reader's mind the whole tragic history of Troy; or when Shakespeare's Falstaff alludes to the biblical "Dives who lived in purple" to describe the color of Bardolf's face; or when T. S. Eliot in *The Waste Land,* with a cryptic "To Carthage then I came / Burning," calls up the young St. Augustine's wayward life.

Anagnorisis. *(849)* The Greek term for DISCOVERY or RECOGNITION used by Aristotle in his *Poetics;* from the *anagnorisis* comes the PERIPETEIA, or REVERSAL of fortune. See PLOT; TRAGEDY.

Anapest. A metrical foot going ∪ ∪ —. See METER.

Antagonist. In Greek drama, the CHARACTER who opposes the PROTAGONIST, or hero: therefore, any character who opposes another. In some works, the antagonist is clearly the villain (Iago in *Othello;* Claggart in *Billy Budd*), but in strict terminology an antagonist is merely an opponent, and may be in the right, like Creon in *Oedipus Rex.*

Antistrophe. (1) The second choral movement and song in Greek tragedy, matching the STROPHE, which preceded it in form and movement. While singing the strophe, the chorus moved from left to right. The antistrophe then reversed the movement back to the starting point. (2) The second part of the triad (strophe, antistrophe, epode) constituting a section of a Pindaric ode. (3) The second STANZA, and those like it, in poems that alternate stanzaic forms.

Apostrophe. *(453)* An address to an imaginary or absent person (or as if the person were absent), a thing, or a personified abstraction:

O wild West Wind, thou breath of Autumn's being

Milton: thou shouldst be living at this hour

Ebb, ocean of life, (the flow will return,)
Cease not your moaning you fierce old mother

See PERSONIFICATION.

Approximate Rhyme. See SLANT RHYME.

Assonance. *(545)* Repetition of middle vowel sounds: *fight, hive; pane, make.* Assonance, most effective on stressed syllables, is often found within a line of poetry; less frequently it substitutes for END RHYME. Like other sounds of poetry, it is sometimes a useful effect in prose. See ALLITERATION; CONSONANCE; RHYME.

Auditory Imagery. *(503)* Imagery that appeals to the ear, mimicking sounds: bacon *sizzles* in a pan.

Author's Voice. (1) The passages in which an author speaks directly, in his or her own person, as distinct from those in which the writer adopts a role or speaks through a PERSONA. In an autobiography, essay, and letters, the author's voice is generally undisguised. In fiction, too, authors sometimes speak directly, as when Fielding and Thackeray address the reader in voices we assume to be their own. (2) The characteristic style of a writer, evident in many works even when there is no direct address to the reader. In this sense, Henry James and Ernest Hemingway, although they seldom speak directly to the reader in their fictions, may both be said to have characteristic voices.

In either sense, the author's voice may change, just as a speaking voice may, for different circumstances; it may not represent the author's permanent self, but only the self of the occasion. Terminology useful to qualify the voice in a given work includes IMPLIED AUTHOR and NARRATOR.

Balanced Couplet. Another name for the CLOSED COUPLET.

Ballad. *(587)* A narrative poem in short stanzas, with or without music. The term derives by way of French *ballade* from Latin *ballare,* "to dance," and once meant a simple song of any kind, lyric or narrative, especially one to accompany a dance. As ballads evolved, most lost their direct association with dance, although they kept their strong rhythms. Modern usage distinguishes three major kinds: the *traditional ballad (popular ballad* or *folk ballad),* a song of anonymous authorship, transmitted orally; the *broadside ballad,* printed and sold on single sheets; and the *literary ballad,* a sophisticated imitation of the traditional ballad.

Ballad Stanza. *(587)* The name for COMMON METER as found in ballads: a QUATRAIN in iambic METER, alternating tetrameter and trimeter lines, usually rhyming *abcb* (see RHYME SCHEME):

> There lived a wife at Usher's Well,
> > And a wealthy wife was she;
> She had three stout and stalwart sons,
> > And sent them o'er the sea.

In the traditional BALLAD, essentially a song, the musical structure allows considerable freedom with syllable count, since an underlying and fundamental four beats to the line is carried by the music. Thus the music provides the fourth beat at the end of lines two and four in the 4/3/4/3 pattern given above and is accompanied by the lyrics in the 4/4/4/4 pattern of *long meter.* Against this musical four beats, the iambics of standard metrical SCANSION frequently appear very irregular in folk songs. Occasionally in the stanzas of folk songs, and frequently in more sophisticated poems, the basic rhyme scheme is complicated by the addition of rhyme in the first and third lines in an *abab* pattern. A shorter version of the same stanza is known as *short meter.*

Blank Verse. *(560)* Unrhymed iambic pentameter. See METER.

Broadside Ballad. *(587)* A BALLAD printed and sold on single sheets.

Burlesque. (1) A ridicule, especially on the stage, treating the lofty in low style and absurd episode, or the low in grandiose style. (2) A bawdy vaudeville, with obscene clowning and stripteasing.

Cacophony. *(554)* "Bad-sounding." The opposite of EUPHONY, the term signifies discordant, jarring, unharmonious language.

Caesura. *(550)* A pause in a metrical line, indicated by punctuation, momentarily suspending the beat (from Latin "a cutting off"). Caesuras are *masculine* at the end of a foot, and *feminine* in midfoot. Pope's opening lines in "An Epistle to Dr. Arbuthnot," spaced out to indicate the foot pause, have five feminine caesuras and three masculines, all marked ‖ :

> Shut, ‖ shut | the door, ‖ good *John:* ‖ fatigu'd | I said,
> Tye up | the knock- | er, ‖ say | I'm sick, ‖ I'm dead,
> The Dog- | star rage- | s: ‖ nay | 'tis past | a doubt,
> All *Bed-* | *lam,* ‖ or | *Parnas-* | *sus,* ‖ is | let out.

See FEMININE CAESURA; MASCULINE CAESURA.

Carpe Diem. *(662)* "Seize the day"—the theme of poems urging a young woman to live and love, since time is short and youth fleeting. The expression comes from the concluding line of Horace's ode to Leuconoë (I.xi): *". . . carpe diem, quam minimum credula postero":* "seize the day; trust tomorrow as little as possible," since envious time will have fled even as we talk.

Catharsis. *(850)* Purification, purgation, cleansing, specifically of the bowels, metaphorically of emotions. Aristotle introduced *catharsis* as essential to tragedy in the *Poetics* (1449b.28): "incidents arousing pity and terror to achieve a catharsis of these emotions." Critics have interpreted this differently: as (1) a discovery that pity and terror destroy, and thus should be disciplined; (2) a vicarious experience that unloads pity and terror on the hero as scapegoat; (3) a detached pity and an involved terror that leave the spectator, like Milton's Samson, with "calm of mind all passion spent." Plato, Aristotle's teacher, had several times called catharsis the soul's collection from the body's senses to be "alone by itself, freed from the body as from fetters."

Character. *(849)* (1) A person in a work of fiction. See CHARACTERS. (2) The moral qualities, personality traits, or other distinctive attributes of a real or fictional person.

Characterization. *(165, 462)* The delineation of a real person or the creation of an imaginary one. Among the methods of characterization are summary (in the words of author, narrator, or another character), naming (Squire Allworthy in *Tom Jones*), and dramatic illustration of character through action and speech.

Characters. *(164, 849)* The people in a work of literature. The hero and heroine are central to the PLOT and generally, though not always, to be admired by the reader. The villain is set in evil opposition. The Greek terms PROTAGONIST, for the principal actor in a drama, and ANTAGONIST, for a second actor opposing the first, are also useful for nondramatic works and carry less of a connotative burden than "hero" and "villain." A CHORUS CHARACTER, originally a member of the chorus in a Greek play, is now any character in fiction who stands apart from the central action, commenting on it with a wisdom that is presumably the author's or is representative of the best moral standards of the community. A *ficelle* is a character whose primary function in a narrative is to manipulate other characters for the purposes of the author, like a string on a puppet. A *confidant* serves a similar purpose, accepting the confidences of a more central character at least partially so the reader may overhear.

Characters may also be classified by the degree or quality of their resemblance to real people. E. M. Forster distinguishes the *flat* from the *round*. *Flat characters,* often vivid in outline, are *two-dimensional,* like cardboard cutouts, lacking the depth and complexity of living humans. *Round characters,* sometimes called *three-dimensional,* have the depths and complexities of real life. Flat characters are sometimes called *black and white,* as opposed to *grayed* for more rounded characters. *Individualized characters* stand out as individuals; *type characters* represent a class—the lawyer; the preacher; the salesman—or, in allegories, abstractions like Truth and Falsehood.

Chorus. In Greek drama, the group of singers and dancers that appears at intervals within a play to comment on the action or the antagonists, or sing the praises of the gods. Generally, the chorus expresses the judgment of objective bystanders, compassionate and intelligent, representative of the best morality of the community, but not directly involved in the passions of the PROTAGONIST and the other major CHARACTERS. In later times, the chorus is sometimes one person, as in Shakespeare's *Henry V,* where the chorus introduces and concludes the play.

Chorus Character. *(850)* A CHARACTER that functions as a CHORUS in a literary work, without necessarily being named as such. Standing apart from the central action, the chorus character observes and comments on it. A common device in the construction of a NOVEL, the chorus character provides a guide to interpretation, especially when the author's choice of NARRATIVE PERSPECTIVE has diminished or eliminated the writer's own direct commentary from without.

Climax. (1) A point of high emotional intensity, the CRISIS or turning point in a drama or STORY. In the tightly constructed PLOT of a TRAGEDY, there is often one major climax, but in an episodic structure there may be a series of climaxes of varying intensities. (2) A rhetorical FIGURE OF SPEECH repeating the same word or sound in each succeeding phrase or clause: "Knowing that tribulation works patience, and patience experience, and experience hope" (Rom. 5.3–4).

Closed Couplet. *(584)* The HEROIC COUPLET, especially when the thought and grammar are complete in the two iambic pentameter lines, as in Pope's:

A *little Learning* is a dang'rous Thing;
Drink deep, or taste not the *Pierian* Spring.

Comedy. *(803, 960)* One of the typical literary structures, originating as a form of drama and later extending into prose fiction and other genres as well. Comedy has preserved throughout its history the sense of two levels of existence, one an absurd reversal of the normal order, the other pragmatically more sensible. The first comedies extant are those of Aristophanes (438?—380? B.C.); they belong mainly to what is called *Old Comedy,* a highly conventionalized form that included personal attacks, Socrates and Euripides being among the targets. Later came *New Comedy,* of which the best-known Greek practitioner was Menander (342?–291 B.C.), whose work is known only by fragments except for one complete play recently discovered. The Greek New Comedy dramatists were imitated and adapted by Plautus (c. 254—184 B.C.) and Terence in Rome, and about two dozen plays from them survive. When drama revived in the Renaissance period, these plays served as the main classical models for comedy.

What frequently happens in a New Comedy is that a young man wants to marry or become sexually allied to a young woman; that other characters with more money, influence, pretenses, or social position are opposed to this; and that toward the end of the story some device in the plot reverses the current of the action and allows hero and heroine to be united. A tricky or resourceful servant is often the hero's ally; the hero's father or a rival supported by his father is often in the opposition. Thus in New Comedy an absurd or obviously unjust situation forms most of the comic action, and a more sensible order of things is reached at the end. In comic drama there is, as a rule, a final scene in which everyone is assembled on the stage, forming a new society that crystalizes around the united pair.

The characterization of New Comedy fits the plot. The hero and heroine are usually likable but not very interesting people, because their real lives are assumed to begin just after the play stops. The chief character interest thus falls on the blocking characters. In Molière, for example, the central blocking character—a miser, a hypochondriac, a snob, or a hypocrite—usually has the play named after him. Earlier than Molière, Ben Jonson's theory of "humors" had described the character appropriate to a New Comedy plot. A humor, Jonson, said, is a person dominated by a single obsession, and is thus confined to a simple repetitive and mechanical behavior, which is the source of the amusement caused by the character.

Comedy often develops in either a romantic or an ironic direction. A mystery of birth, affecting either hero or heroine, is often the means of bringing about the comic resolution. This theme is central in *Tom Jones* and is frequent in Dickens. In Shakespeare's comedies a symbolic representation of the freer world reached at the end is often hidden within the action, where it takes the form of a forest or enchanted island or a world connected with mystery, magic, fairies, identical twins, dreams, or wish fulfillment.

The other direction is the ironic or realistic direction, in which the blocking activities of stupid or obsessed characters are triumphant and the hero's efforts are crushed in frustation and despair. In the twentieth century, when writers became weary of the rigidities of New Comedy plots with their compulsory happy endings, this ironic structure has predominated. The darker comedies that begin with Ibsen, Strindberg, and Chekhov present anything from farce to brutal-ity or terror, but remain within the general comic area because the dominant impression they leave is one of absurdity—in fact, many such black comedies belong explicitly to the *theater of the absurd.*

Common Meter. *(585)* The BALLAD STANZA as found in hymns (abbreviated *C.M.* in hymn books) and other poems: a quatrain (four-line stanza) in iambic METER, alternating tetrameter and trimeter, rhyming *abcb* or *abab.*

Connotation. *(473)* The ideas, attitudes, or emotions associated with a word in the mind of speaker or listener, writer or reader. It is contrasted with the DENOTATION, the thing the word stands for, the dictionary definition, an objective concept without emotional coloring.

Consonance. *(545)* Repetition of inner or end consonant sounds, as, for example, the *r* and *s* sounds in this phrase from Gerard Manley Hopkins's "God's Grandeur": "broods with warm breast."

Convention. An unwritten but widely accepted agreement about the terms of communication.

Couplet. *(584)* A pair of rhymed metrical lines, usually in iambic tetrameter or pentameter. Sometimes the two lines are of different length. See CLOSED COUPLET; HEROIC COUPLET; METER.

Crisis. In a play or novel, the "turning point" for better or worse. *Crisis* refers to the episode or events where the protagonist's choices go right or wrong; CLIMAX, to the peak of the audience's emotional response. The two do not always coincide, since the PROTAGONIST may choose quite casually in innocuous circumstances.

Dactyl. A three-syllable metrical foot: — ∪ ∪. See METER.

Dead Metaphor. *(520)* A METAPHOR accepted without its figurative picture: "a jacket," for the paper around a book, with no mental picture of the human coat that prompted the original metaphor; "a tie," for a business or social relationship, with no picture of a knot under the collar nor of two teams bound equally in rope.

Denotation. *(473)* The thing a word stands for, the dictionary definition, an objective concept without emotional coloring. It is contrasted with the CONNOTATION, the ideas, attitudes, or emotions associated with the word in the mind of user or hearer.

Denouement. French for "unknotting": the unraveling of PLOT threads toward the end of a play, NOVEL, or other narrative.

Deus Ex Machina. *(850)* Latin for "god out of the machine." The term refers to the practice in the Greek theater of lowering a god from the heavens by a crane or other mechanical device when the play required his or her presence on stage. More generally, it is a term for any unlikely PLOT contrivance or solution to a narrative problem, as though the author had called upon the gods for assistance.

Dimeter. Metrical lines of two feet. See METER.

Dipodic Verse. *(546)* "Two-footed." Surviving from Old English poetry, dipodic verse is a lighthearted rocking meter in two half-lines, each with two stresses falling among scattered light syllables.

Discovery. *(849)* Revelation of the truth toward the end of a play, Aristotle's ANAGNORISIS, a discovery, like Oedipus's discovery of the awful truth that he has murdered his father and slept with his mother, or the happy discovery in comedy of the orphan's true identity.

Double rhyme.   See FEMININE RHYME.

Downstage.   Toward the front part of the stage; the opposite of UPSTAGE.

Dramatic Irony. *(12, 467, 492)* A situation in which a character in drama or fiction unknowingly says or does something in ironic contrast to an awareness possessed by an audience or reader.

Dramatic Method. *(118)* A technique of writing a NOVEL or SHORT STORY in a manner that provides the reader with only the information available to the viewer of a realistic play: SETTING, CHARACTER description, action, and dialogue. All other elements usual in narrations are eliminated—as, for example, the author's commentaries and summaries, and the thoughts of the characters, except as they express them aloud. See NARRATIVE PERSPECTIVE.

Dramatic Monologue. *(466)* A monologue in verse. A speaker addresses a silent listener, revealing, in DRAMATIC IRONY, things about himself or herself of which the speaker is unaware.

Dramatic Situation. *(452)* A situation inherently dramatic, as is frequently the case even with LYRIC poems. In assessing the dramatic situation, a critic considers who is speaking, to whom, and in what circumstances.

Dramatis Personae.   "The persons of the drama." (1) The list of characters in a play, printed under this Latin heading before the text and in program notes, frequently with phrases describing each role: "a tyrannical father"; "Malwit's daughter, in love with Goodbody." (2) Any listing of characters in a short story, novel, poem, or play. (3) A metaphorical reference to "all the characters."

Effect.   The impression made by a literary work on a reader or on society. Effect in either sense is difficult to measure, its use as a tool of criticism much debated. As an indication of the effect of literature on society, President Lincoln is reported to have greeted Harriet Beecher Stowe, author of *Uncle Tom's Cabin*, with the words "So, this is the little lady who made this big war!" A phrase from W. H. Auden's "In Memory of W. B. Yeats," however, says that "poetry makes nothing happen." Effect on an individual is an equally slippery concept, since a reader must be aware that the effect on one person, either intellectual or emotional, may be different for others, or for the same person at another time.

From the perspective of the writer, however, effect remains a necessary consideration, as the writer must assume that the work will impress someone in some way. Edgar Allan Poe is much cited for his concept of the *single effect* that should govern the construction of a poem or SHORT STORY. For Poe, there is no such thing as a long poem, but only short poems, each organized around one effect, a long poem like *Paradise Lost* being but a succession of shorter poems. For the short story, his idea is condensed in the following passage from his review of Hawthorne's *Twice-Told Tales:*

> A skilful literary artist has constructed a tale. If wise, he has not fashioned his thoughts to accommodate his incidents; but having conceived, with deliberate care, a certain unique or single *effect* to be wrought out, he then invents such incidents—he then combines such events as may best aid him in establishing this preconceived effect. If his very initial sentence tend not to the outbringing of this effect, then he has failed in his first step. In the whole composition there should be no word written, of which the tendency, direct or indirect, is not to the one pre-established design. And by such means, with such care and skill, a picture is at length painted which leaves in the mind of him who contemplates it with a kindred art, a sense of the fullest satisfaction.

End Rhyme.   RHYME at the end of a line of verse (the usual placement), as distinguished from *initial rhyme,* at the beginning, or INTERNAL RHYME, within the line.

End-Stopped Line.   *(550)* A line marked with a grammatical pause at the end. It is the opposite of a RUN-ON LINE, or ENJAMBMENT, where the grammatical phrase runs from one line of poetry onto the next, without pause (i.e., no punctuation).

Enjambment.   *(550)* RUN-ON LINES. The opposite of END-STOPPED LINE. In enjambment the grammatical sense runs from one line of poetry to the next without pause or punctuation.

Envoy (or **Envoi**).   *(608)* A concluding STANZA, generally shorter than the earlier stanzas of a poem, normally linked to them by rhyme, and bringing about a formal conclusion in brief summary of theme, address to a prince or patron, or return to a refrain. The ballade and SESTINA are verse forms employing envoys.

Epic.   A long narrative poem, typically a recounting of history or legend or of the deeds of a national hero.

Episodic Plot.   In narration, the incidental stringing of one *episode* upon another, as in *Don Quixote* or *Moll Flanders,* where one episode follows another with no necessary causal connection.

Ethos.   *(197)* Greek for "character": the prevailing or characteristic TONE or sentiment of a people or community. In criticism, ethos is the prevailing tone or character of a work considered in its social context or as a reflection of the character of the author. It is manifested in fiction primarily through CHARACTERIZATION and SETTING. Contrasted with *pathos,* ethos suggests the stable, ideal, or permanent truths of a narrative or dramatic work, as opposed to the temporary passions expressed in the PLOT. In discussions of rhetoric, ethos may be thought of, simply, as the character the author projects through the work, the IMPLIED AUTHOR.

Euphony. *(554)* Melodious sound, the opposite of CACOPHONY.

Exact Rhyme. Also called *full, true, perfect, complete, whole:* RHYME that repeats the sound precisely (except for the initial consonant), as *fine, dine; heather, weather.*

Explication. A detailed explanation or interpretation.

Exposition. In drama or narration, the unfolding or explanation of present events or past history necessary to understand the PLOT development.

Eye Rhyme. A RHYME of words that look but do not sound the same: *one, stone; word, lord; teak, break.* Sometimes eye rhyme is intentional, sometimes the result of dialect or of a change in pronunciation, as with *proved* and *loved* (rhyming in sound for Shakespeare but not for modern readers).

Fable. A short, allegorical story in verse or prose, frequently of animals, told to illustrate a moral. Loosely, any legendary or fabulous account.

Falling Meter. A meter beginning with a stress, running from heavy to light, as Coleridge described it:

> Trochee is in falling duple,
>   Dactyl is falling, like—Tripoli.

Farce. A wildly comic play, mocking dramatic and social conventions, frequently with satiric intent.

Fear. See PITY AND FEAR.

Feminine Caesura. A syntactic pause (‖) in the middle of a metrical foot, or one following an unstressed syllable within a line:

> Ĭ knew | ă wom- | ăn, ‖ love- | lў ĭn | her bones
> Dáddy, ‖ Ĭ have | had tŏ | kill yŏu.

Feminine Rhyme. *(545)* A rhyme of both the stressed and unstressed syllables of one feminine ending with another:

> Yet in these thoughts myself almost *despising,*
> Haply I think on thee,—and then my state,
> Like to the lark at break of day *arising*
> From sullen earth, sings hymns at heaven's gate.

Also called *double rhyme.*

Figurative Language. *(527)* Language that is not literal, being either metaphorical or rhetorically patterned. See also FIGURE OF SPEECH; IMAGERY; METAPHOR.

Figure of Speech. *(527)* An expression extending language beyond its literal meaning, either pictorially through METAPHOR, SIMILE, ALLUSION, and the like, or rhetorically through repetition, balance, antithesis, and the like. A figure of speech is also called a *trope.* The most common pictorial figures are metaphor, simile, METONYMY, SYNECDOCHE, and PERSONIFICATION. The most common rhetorical figures are simple repetition, PARALLELISM, antithesis, CLIMAX, HYPERBOLE, and IRONY. APOSTROPHE is a rhetorical figure very nearly a metaphor. See IMAGERY.

First-Person Narration. *(40, 86, 116)* Narration by a CHARACTER involved in a STORY. See NARRATIVE PERSPECTIVE.

Flat Character. *(849)* In a literary work, a character that is two-dimensional, without the depth and complexity of a living person; the opposite of a ROUND CHARACTER. See CHARACTERS.

Folk Ballad. *(587)* Another name for the *traditional ballad* or *popular ballad,* a song of anonymous authorship, transmitted orally. See BALLAD.

Form. The shape or structure of a literary work, or of a part of one. Form is frequently distinguished from content, the point being that the writer's idea has no shape until the work is written, in the form, say, of a short story, a novel, a poem, or a play. Form, in this first sense, is synonymous with genre, but the term is also used to suggest the distinction between works in verse and prose (in the form of verse or the form of prose), as well as to describe the smaller units of a work (as the form of its lines—metrical or free verse; or of its stanzas—the ballad stanza, for example).

Coleridge originated the useful distinction between *organic form,* a shape arising naturally out of the writer's conception, and mechanical (conventional, or fixed) form, a shape imposed from without.

Fourth Wall. *(1202)* The area of the PROSCENIUM arch on a picture frame stage, treated by the actors as an invisible fourth wall through which the audience views the action in a room.

Free Verse. *(613)* French *vers libre;* poetry free of traditional metrical and stanzaic patterns.

Groundlings. Spectators in the Elizabethan theater who stood on the ground in the pit, or orchestra, where there were no seats, for the cheapest price.

Hamartia. *(850)* The *tragic flaw* or *error of judgment* considered by Aristotle to form a necessary part of the CHARACTER of a tragic hero. The hero must be good, but not perfect: "a man who is not eminently good and just, yet whose misfortune is brought about not by vice or depravity, but by some error or frailty."

Heptameter. Seven-foot lines. See METER.

Heroic Couplet. *(565, 584)* The closed and balanced iambic pentameter couplet typical of the heroic play of Dryden; hence, any CLOSED COUPLET.

Hexameter. Six-foot lines. See METER.

Humors. CHARACTERS exhibiting single traits in their actions and speeches. The name comes from the *cardinal humors* of ancient medical theory: blood, phlegm, yellow bile (choler), and black bile (melancholy). Galen (c. A.D. 130–200) suggested that character types are produced by dominance of fluids: *san-*

guine, or kindly, cheerful, amorous; *phlegmatic,* or sluggish, unresponsive; *choleric,* or quick tempered; *melancholic,* or brooding, dejected. In literature, especially in the Renaissance, characters were portrayed according to the humors that dominated them.

Hyperbole. *(527)* OVERSTATEMENT to make a point, either direct or ironical.

Hypercatalectic. Having an extra metrical syllable at the end; also called a *hypermetrical* line. See FEMININE RHYME.

Hypermetrical. See HYPERCATALECTIC.

Iambus (or **Iamb**). A metrical foot going ∪ —. See METER.

Image. *(503)* A concrete picture, either literally descriptive, as in "Red roses covered the white wall," or figurative, as in "She is a rose," each carrying a sensual and emotive connotation.

Imagery. *(503)* Collectively, the images of a literary work (see IMAGE). The images, taken individually, are representative of things accessible to the five senses: sight, hearing, touch, taste, and smell. Thus, the water imagery of a work may be *visual,* suggesting a picture; *auditory,* representing the sounds of a running brook; *tactile,* if wetness or temperature is brought to mind; or even *gustatory* or *olfactory,* if the water is given a taste or smell.

Images standing for single things in nature tend to represent the world in simple, primary terms. When an image is made to stand for two things, as when a rose represents itself and also the color in a young woman's cheeks, the image turns into a METAPHOR, SIMILE, or other form of FIGURATIVE LANGUAGE. When an image is used so as to suggest complex or multiple meanings, as when a rose represents itself, young women generally, and also beauty and fragility, it becomes a SYMBOL.

Within many works and for many writers, patterns of imagery are important, as when Shakespeare in *Macbeth* and Hawthorne in *The Scarlet Letter* bring the reader back repeatedly to patterns of light and dark, with an occasional flash of red.

Imagination. *(505)* The forming of mental images. Francis Bacon associated it with literature ("History has reference to the memory, poetry to the imagination, philosophy to the reason") as did Shakespeare in *A Midsummer Night's Dream:*

> And as imagination bodies forth
> The forms of things unknown, the poet's pen
> Turns them to shapes, and gives to airy nothing
> A local habitation and a name.

For the eighteenth century, particularly under Locke's influence, the term imagination referred to the picturing of objects from the physical world: "When we speak of Justice or Gratitude, we frame to ourselves no Imagination of any thing" *(Essay Concerning Human Understanding).* In the *Spectator* papers, Addison asserted that we "cannot, indeed, have a single image in the fancy that did not make its first entrance through the sight; but we have the power of retaining, altering, and compounding those images, which we have once received, into all the varieties of picture and vision that are agreeable to the imagination."

At the beginning of the nineteenth century, in *The Prelude,* Wordsworth suggested a higher power for the imagination, seeing it as a means of perceiving the divine Love at the heart of nature and the mind's experience:

> This spiritual Love acts not nor can exist
> Without Imagination, which, in truth,
> Is but another name for absolute power,
> And clearest insight, amplitude of mind,
> And Reason in her most exalted mood.

Coleridge followed, in his *Biographia Literaria* distinguishing Fancy as a mere "mode of Memory emancipated from the order of time and space" from Imagination, the "shaping and modifying" power that transcends the senses to an ultimate reality.

Imagination remains the higher power, giving literature and art authority. Fancy is lighter, associative, amusing, *fanciful,* as in reverie.

Implied Author. Wayne Booth's term for the Aristotelian ETHOS, the authorial PERSONA, of a novel—the authorial personality as gathered from the voice behind the words—distinct from the biographical person of the writer, which may inhere only partially, tangentially, or not at all (*The Rhetoric of Fiction,* 1961).

Initial Rhyme. RHYME at the beginnings of lines.

Interior Monologue. *(118)* A fictional presentation of unspoken thoughts as though delivered in monologue, typically characterized by stream of consciousness content and technique. James Joyce, Virginia Woolf, and William Faulkner are masters. *Direct interior monologue* presents thoughts in first-person narration directly to the reader, excluding any sense of participation by an author or external narrator, as in Faulkner's *As I Lay Dying. Indirect interior monologue,* a form of third-person limited omniscient narration, presents thoughts as seen from within the mind but expressed in the words of an external narrator, as frequently in Joyce's *Ulysses* and Woolf's *Mrs. Dalloway* and *To the Lighthouse.* See NARRATIVE PERSPECTIVE.

Internal Narrative Perspective. *(117)* A placement of a perspective within a mind that is communicated through interior monologue or by objectively reporting what the mind perceives.

Internal Rhyme. RHYME within a line, rather than at the beginning *(initial rhyme)* or end *(end rhyme);* also, rhyme matching sounds at the middle of a line with sounds at the end.

Inverted Foot. A trochee in an iambic line. See METER.

Ionic Foot.   A Greek and Latin foot going $\cup\cup - -$. In English iambics, the term refers to a *double* foot, one of the three recurrent substitutions, along with the *trochee* and the *spondee.* It is the farthest stretch of iambic meter, as in the second line of Marvell's couplet:

$$\overset{\cup}{\text{Anni-}} \mid \overset{-}{\text{hilat-}} \mid \overset{\cup}{\text{ing}} \overset{-}{\text{all}} \mid \overset{\cup}{\text{that's}} \overset{-}{\text{made}} \mid$$

$$\overset{\cup}{\text{To}} \overset{\cup}{\text{a}} \mid \overset{-}{\text{green}} \overset{-}{\text{thought}} \mid \overset{\cup}{\text{in}} \overset{\cup}{\text{a}} \mid \overset{-}{\text{green}} \overset{-}{\text{shade.}} \mid$$

Irony.   *(12, 23, 492, 802)* In general, irony is the perception of a clash between appearance and reality, between *seems* and *is,* or between *ought* and *is.* The myriad shadings of irony seem to fall into three categories: (1) verbal, (2) dramatic, (3) situational.

1. *Verbal irony*—saying something contrary to what it means. The appearance is what the words say; the reality, their contrary meaning. Both speaker and listener are aware of the contrast, mutually understanding the situation and each other. "A marvelous time" means a boring time. "A great guy" is a petty sniveler. "A truth universally acknowledged" is a self-interested opinion.
2. *Dramatic irony*—saying or doing something while unaware of its ironic contrast with the whole truth. Dramatic irony, named for its frequency in drama, is a verbal irony with the speaker's awareness erased. The speaker's, or doer's, assumptions are the appearance, to him or her; the true situation is the reality, which the audience knows. Someone says, "This is the happiest day of my life," and dances a jig, while members of the audience, and perhaps some of the people on stage, know that his mortgage has been foreclosed and his family wiped out at the intersection. When someone goes to open a door behind which the audience knows disaster awaits, the audience has dramatic irony in action alone.
3. *Situational irony*—events turning to the opposite of what is expected or what should be (also called *circumstantial irony* and the *irony of fate* or, in some circumstances, *cosmic irony*), as when it rains on the Weather Bureau's annual picnic. The ironic situation—the *ought* upended by the *is*—is integral to dramatic irony. The ironic situation turns the speaker's unknowing words ironic. Situational irony is the very essence of both comedy and tragedy. The young lovers run into the worst possible luck, until everything clears up happily. The most noble spirits go to their death, while the featherheads survive.

Italian Sonnet (or **Petrarchan Sonnet**).   *(599)* A SONNET composed of an OCTAVE and SESTET, rhyming *abbaabba cdecde* (or *cdcdcd* or some variant), without a closing couplet.

Kinetic Imagery.   *(509)* Imagery in the form of pictures that move, in contrast to STATIC IMAGERY.

Limited Omniscient Narration.   See THIRD-PERSON LIMITED OMNISCIENCE.

Literary Ballad.   A sophisticated imitation of the traditional BALLAD.

Litotes. *(527)* A kind of IRONY: the assertion of something by the denial of its opposite: "Not bad." "This is no small matter." "She was not supremely happy." "He was not unmindful of it."

Lyric. *(432)* A poem, brief and discontinuous, emphasizing sound and pictorial imagery rather than narrative or dramatic movement.

Masculine Caesura. A CAESURA (‖) following a stressed syllable at the end of a metrical foot. Three are in this line:

$$\overset{\cup}{\text{Came}}\ \overset{-}{\text{loud}}\!\!—\ \|\ \overset{\cup}{\text{and}}\ \overset{-}{\text{hark,}}\ \|\ \overset{\cup}{\text{again:}}\ \overset{-}{\|}\ \overset{-}{\text{loud}}\ \overset{\cup}{\text{as}}\ |\ \overset{\cup}{\text{be}}\overset{-}{\text{fore.}}\ |$$

Masculine Rhyme. *(545)* RHYME on the last syllable of a line, the most common rhyme in English. See FEMININE RHYME; TRIPLE RHYME.

Masque. An allegorical, poetic, and musical dramatic spectacle popular in the English courts and mansions of the sixteenth and early seventeenth centuries. Figures from mythology, history, and romance mingled in a pastoral fantasy with fairies, fauns, satyrs, and witches, as masked amateurs from the court (including kings and queens) participated in dances and scenes.

Metaphor. *(242, 518)* Greek for "transfer" (*meta* and *trans* meaning "across"; *phor* and *fer* meaning "carry"): to carry something across. Hence a metaphor treats something as if it were something else. Money becomes a *nest egg;* a person who fails, a *washout;* a sandwich, a *submarine.* I. A. Richards describes this metaphorical transfer as *tenor* and *vehicle,* the general idea and its pictorial image. Shakespeare wrote:

> That time of year thou mayst in me behold
> When yellow leaves, or none, or few, do hang
> Upon those boughs which shake against the cold. . . .

The *tenor* is the loneliness and loss of age. The *vehicle* is a tree (or trees) in autumn. A metaphor implies a comparison. If Shakespeare had written "I am like a tree losing its leaves," he would have stated the comparison and made a SIMILE.

Meter. *(546)* The measured pulse of poetry. English meters derive from four Greek and Roman quantitative meters, which English stresses more sharply, though the patterns are the same. The unit of each pattern is the *foot,* containing one stressed syllable and one or two light ones. RISING METER goes from light to heavy; FALLING METER, from heavy to light. One meter—iambic—has dominated English poetry, with the three others lending an occasional foot, for variety, and producing a few poems.

RISING METERS

Iambic: ∪ — (the iambus)
Anapestic: ∪ ∪ — (the anapest)

FALLING METERS

Trochaic: − ∪ (the trochee)

Dactylic: − ∪ ∪ (the dactyl)

The number of feet in a line also gives the verse a name:

1 foot: monometer

2 feet: dimeter

3 feet: trimeter

4 feet: tetrameter

5 feet: pentameter

6 feet: hexameter

7 feet: heptameter (rare)

All meters will show some variations, and substitutions of other kinds of feet, but three variations in iambic writing are virtually standard:

Inverted foot: − ∪ (a trochee)

Spondee: − −

Ionic double foot: ∪ ∪ | − −

The *pyrrhic foot* of classical meters, two light syllables (∪ ∪), lives in the English line only in the Ionic double foot (see IONIC FOOT), though some prosodists will scan a relatively light iambus as pyrrhic. See DIPODIC VERSE and SCANSION.

Metonymy.   *(527)* "Substitute naming." An associated idea names the item: *"Homer* is *hard"* for "Reading Homer's poems is difficult," or "The *pen* is mightier than the *sword"* for "Literature and propaganda accomplish more and survive longer than warfare," or "The *White House* announced" for "The President announced." See SYNECDOCHE.

Mixed Metaphor.   *(525)* A METAPHOR not consistent with the physical world: for instance, "The population explosion has paved the way for new intellectual growth." It looks good. But then we realize that explosions do not pave and that grass does not sprout through pavement. If the statement had said "cleared" instead of "paved," the picture would not have been scrambled and the metaphor would not have been mixed.

Monologue.   (1) A poem or story in the form of a SOLILOQUY. (2) Any extended speech. See DRAMATIC MONOLOGUE; INTERIOR MONOLOGUE.

Monometer.   A line containing one metrical foot. See METER.

Narrative Perspective.   *(40, 86, 116)* The standpoint from which a story is told. *Perspective,* from the Latin for "to look through," first meant in English an optical glass or telescope. The narrative perspective is the lens, or eye (and by extension the mind behind the eye), through which a story is presented. It is sometimes called *point of view,* a term useful to focus attention on the mental processes of the narrator rather than on the physical relation to the story, as "She narrates from a feminist point of view."

The *narrator,* or teller of the story, may stand within the story or outside it, narrating as it occurs, shortly after, or much later, providing in each instance a different narrative perspective in space and time. The reader sees the story through a narrative perspective close to the events or removed from them by various kinds and degrees of distance, examining, as it were, with a microscope, field glass, or telescope.

Narrative perspective in time is a question of how long after the events the narration occurs.

The two chief *narrative perspectives in space,* within the story or outside it, take their names from the grammatical stance employed by the narrator: *first-person narration* for a narrative perspective inside the story, *third-person narration* for one outside. The *first-person narrator* speaks as an "I" and may be identified in one of three roles: *first person as protagonist,* the hero or heroine of the story; *first person as participant,* a character in a subsidiary role; *first person as observer,* a character without essential function except to observe and record.

The third-person narrator came first, in the form of the anonymous storyteller who pretends no personal relation to the tale beyond the fact of knowing it and perhaps contributing to its shape. The narrative perspective in such tales is called THIRD-PERSON OMNISCIENCE, because the narrator assumes the privileges of omniscience, moving about in time and space, entering freely into the unverbalized thoughts and motives of the characters:

In THIRD-PERSON LIMITED OMNISCIENCE, the narrator frequently limits the revelation of thoughts to those of one character, presenting the other characters only externally. In another common form of limited omniscience, the narrator follows one character throughout a story, presenting only scenes involving the chosen character while ignoring the privileges of omniscience that would allow attention to other times and places.

The *objective method* or *objective point of view* is a form of third-person limited omniscience widely used by novelists from the late nineteenth-century onward. This narrative strategy rules out subjective commentary by the author but still allows the omniscient privileges of movement in time and space as well as into and out of the minds of the characters. Joyce's *Ulysses* is the most famous example. The term *self-effacing author* has frequently been applied to such a writer.

DRAMATIC METHOD is a term used to describe a severely limited form of third-person narration where the privileges of omniscience are sacrificed almost entirely. Using this method, a writer of fiction limits communication to the kind of evidence available to the viewers of a realistic stage play or to an invisible watcher positioned near the scene of the action. The dramatic method is sometimes called the scenic method, because it unfolds the story in scenes like a play, or the fly-on-the-wall technique, for its alert, observant detachment.

Narrative Poem. *(443)* A poem that tells a story.

Narrator. One who tells a STORY. See NARRATIVE PERSPECTIVE.

Novel. The extended prose fiction that arose in the eighteenth century in the work of Defoe, Richardson, Fielding, Sterne, and other writers to become the major literary expression of the modern world. The nineteenth century produced masterpieces on both sides of the Atlantic by a host of writers, including Austen, Scott, Dickens, Thackeray, Balzac, Hawthorne, the Brontës, Melville, Eliot, Flaubert, Dostoevsky, Tolstoy, Twain, James, and Hardy, as the novel became the leading international literary form. Major twentieth-century novelists in English have included Conrad, Joyce, Lawrence, Woolf, Hemingway, Faulkner, and many more recent. Longer and more complex than the SHORT STORY or NOVELETTE, the novel has embraced many styles, elements of content, and techniques.

Novelette. A short novel or long short story, like Stevenson's *Dr. Jekyll and Mr. Hyde,* Melville's *Billy Budd,* James's *Turn of the Screw,* Conrad's "Heart of Darkness," and Bellow's *Seize the Day.*

Objective Correlative. T. S. Eliot's term for the objective events in an artistic work that represent its essential emotion. Eliot found *Hamlet* a disquieting artistic failure because Shakespeare could find no *"objective correlative"* for the emotional significance he himself could not grasp:

> The only way of expressing emotion in the form of art is by finding an "objective correlative"; in other words, a set of objects, a situation, a chain of events which shall be the formula of that *particular* emotion; such that when the external facts, which must terminate in sensory experience, are given, the emotion is immediately evoked.

Octave. (1) The first unit in an Italian SONNET: eight lines of iambic pentameter, rhyming *abbaabba*. See METER. (2) A STANZA in eight lines.

Off Rhyme. See SLANT RHYME.

Omniscient Narrator. *(117)* See THIRD-PERSON OMNISCIENCE.

Onomatopoeia. *(555)* The use of words formed or sounding like what they signify—*buzz, crack, smack, whinny*—especially in an extensive capturing of sense by sound, as in Tennyson's frequently quoted lines from *The Princess:*

> The moan of doves in immemorial elms,
> And murmuring of innumerable bees.

Overstatement. *(527)* Exaggeration understood as such, to emphasize a point; also called HYPERBOLE.

Parallelism. From Greek roots meaning "beside one another," the comparison of things by placing them side by side. In poetry, parallelism is a fundamental aesthetic device, emphasizing similarities in content, and organizing sounds and rhythms through repetition of words, phrases, and patterns of stress and pronunciation. It has been a mainstay of many poets in FREE VERSE. In Walt Whitman's verse it is the single most obtrusive device:

> I am the poet of the Body and I am the poet of the Soul,
> The pleasures of heaven are with me and the pains of hell are with me,
> The first I graft and increase upon myself, the latter I translate into a new tongue.

Paraphrase.   A rendering in other words of the sense of a text or passage, as of a poem, essay, short story, or other writing.

Pentameter.   A line of five metrical feet. See METER.

Peripeteia (or **Peripetia, Peripety**).   *(849)* A sudden change in situation in a drama or fiction, a reversal of luck for good or ill. See PLOT.

Persona.   *(462)* A mask (in Latin); in poetry and fiction, the projected speaker or narrator of the work—that is, a mask for the actual author. It may be an IMPLIED AUTHOR, who is very similar to the author, or a completely different and ironic projection, like Swift's proposer in *A Modest Proposal* or Browning's duke in "My Last Duchess." Some poets, particularly, seem to speak directly for themselves, with no intervening personae, though critics may insist that even these are projected masks. See NARRATIVE PERSPECTIVE.

Personification.   *(48)* The technique of treating abstractions, things, or animals as persons. A kind of METAPHOR, personification turns abstract ideas, like love, into physical beauties named Venus, or conversely, makes dumb animals speak and act like humans: Mickey Mouse, Donald Duck, Reynard the Fox.

Petrarchan Sonnet.   Another name for an ITALIAN SONNET.

Pity and Fear.   *(850)* According to Aristotle, the essential tragic emotions. Pity is aroused when we witness undeserved misfortune, fear (or terror) when the misfortune happens to one like ourselves.

Plot.   *(26, 848)* The events of a story. The word that Aristotle used for plot in the *Poetics* is *mythos,* which is the origin also of the world myth. In its broadest sense *mythos* means narrative or sequential movement, such as any form of verbal structure designed to be read sequentially would possess. But in practice there is a rough distinction between fictions, or narratives that are stories, and thematic narratives, or arguments, as in essays. Aristotle appears to identify the *mythos,* or plot, with his central conception of drama as a *mimesis praxeos,* or imitation of action. The plot is thus the central form, or metaphorically the soul, of the drama.

Such a plot has, Aristotle said, a beginning, middle, and end. This distinguishes the plot from the type of narrative that is merely sequential, starting and stopping arbitrarily, as in a diary or in some of the more naïve forms of romance. If a plot begins and ends, the beginning must somehow suggest an end, and the end return to the beginning. Thus *Oedipus Rex* begins with the king determined to discover why his land is suffering from a drought: the reader or audience assumes that his discovery of the reason will end the play. He eventually discovers that *he* is the reason; he has killed his father and lives in incest with his mother. Two things are involved here: one is "reversal" *(peripeteia)*, or sudden change in fortune; the other is "discovery" *(anagnorisis)*.

The plot, then, is not simply an arrangement of events in a straight line. There is always something of a parabola shape about a story that ends in some kind of "recognition" that aligns the end with the beginning. Again, a plot has a shape that, to use a word appropriate to Aristotle's mode of thought, is teleological: it has a purpose in moving as it does, and its purpose is to illuminate the beginning by the end, and vice versa. Plot in this sense is not wholly disconnected from plot in the sense of a planned conspiracy; in fact, most comic and tragic plots include actual conspiracies of one kind or another.

Point of View.   See NARRATIVE PERSPECTIVE.

Proscenium.   Originally, in Greece, the whole acting area ("in front of the scenery"); now, that part of the stage projecting in front of the curtain, which hangs from the proscenium arch.

Protagonist.   The leading character in a play or story, originally the leader of the CHORUS in the agon ("contest") of Greek drama, faced with the ANTAGONIST, the opposition. See CHARACTERS.

Quatrain.   *(584)* A STANZA of four lines, rhymed or unrhymed.

Recognition.   *(849)* The moment at which a chief character recognizes the happy or awful truth, usually of his or her own or another's identity, of which the audience (or reader) is frequently aware. Aristotle, in his *Poetics,* first named it, and prized it, citing *Oedipus Rex* as the greatest instance. See PLOT.

Reversal.   *(849)* The thrilling change of luck for the PROTAGONIST at the last moment in comedy or tragedy—the *peripeteia,* which Aristotle first described in his *Poetics,* along with the DISCOVERY (or RECOGNITION) that usually sparks it. See PLOT.

Rhetorical Accent.   Emphasis for the sake of meaning, either where English naturally puts it ("The house is green") or where the speaker puts the meaning ("Are you going?" "Are you going?"), as distinct from *word accent,* which is fixed in polysyllabic words like *going* and *potentate.* The poet fits both word accent and rhetorical accent to the metrical frame, using the metrical accents to bring out the rhetorical ones.

Rhyme (sometimes **Rime,** an older spelling).   *(544)* The effect created by matching sounds at the end of words. Ordinarily, this includes the last accented vowel and the sounds that follow it, but not the sound of the preceding consonant. See END RHYME, EXACT RHYME, EYE RHYME, FEMININE RHYME, INITIAL RHYME, INTERNAL RHYME, MASCULINE RHYME, SLANT RHYME, TRIPLE RHYME.

Rhyme Scheme.   *(557)* The pattern created by the rhyming words of a STANZA or poem. In the most common method of describing end rhyme (at the end of lines), each ending sound is designated by a letter. For example, *abcb* is the rhyme scheme of the BALLAD STANZA, in which the second and fourth lines rhyme, but the first and third do not.

Riddle.   *(522)* An ingenious problem, puzzle, or conundrum, typically a META-PHOR with one element of the implied comparison expressed and the other left for guessing.

Rising Meter.   A METER beginning unstressed, running from light to heavy, as Coleridge describes it:

> Iambics march from short to long.
> With a leap and a bound the swift Anapests throng.

Romantic Comedy.   *(960)* A COMEDY with love as the primary theme. Shakespeare's *Midsummer Night's Dream, As You Like It,* and *Twelfth Night* are the classic examples.

Round Character.   *(849)* One possessing the depth and complexity of a living person, the opposite of a FLAT CHARACTER. See CHARACTERS.

Run-on Line.   *(550)* A line of poetry whose sense does not stop at the end, with punctuation, but runs on to the next line. The opposite of END-STOPPED LINE. See ENJAMBMENT.

Satire.   *(960)* Literature that ridicules vices and follies.

Scansion.   *(548)* A system for analyzing and marking poetical meters and feet. Two prevail: (1) marking short and long, light and accented, syllables thus ∪ —; (2) marking unstressed and stressed syllables so as to include secondary stress thus ∪ ´ | ∪ ` .

(1) Ă sŭn, | ă shăd- | ow ŏf | ă măg- | nĭtūde. |

(2) Ă sún, | ă shăd- | ow ŏf | ă măg- | nĭtùde. |

Other symbols are | (a vertical bar to mark feet) and ‖ (CAESURA).

Secondary Stress.   A stress lighter than the major stress, as in the second foot below:

The kĭng | sĭts ĭn | Dŭm fér- | lĭng Tŏwn |

See METER; SCANSION.

Sestet.   (1) the second unit of an Italian SONNET, following the OCTAVE. To the *abbaabba* rhyme of the octave, the sestet adds six lines rhyming *cdecde, cdcdcd,* or in some variant pattern. (2) A STANZA of six lines.

Sestina.   *(608)* A verse form from medieval France, consisting of six stanzas of six lines each, followed by a three-line ENVOY. In place of rhyme, ordinarily not used, six key words are selected for systematic repetition. In strict form, these six words, to which we may assign the order 1, 2, 3, 4, 5, 6 in the first stanza, are repeated in the second stanza, weaving back and forth from last to first to give a new order 6, 1, 5, 2, 4, 3. This pattern is repeated in stanzas 3 through 6, giving 3, 6, 4, 1, 2, 5; 5, 3, 2, 6, 1, 4; 4, 5, 1, 3, 6, 2; 2, 4, 6, 5, 3, 1. In the envoy the six key words appear again, three within the lines and three at line ends, in varying patterns, but most often 2, 4, 6 within the lines and 5, 3, 1 at the ends, repeating the order of the last stanza. Kipling's "Sestina of the Tramp-Royal" and John Ashbery's "The Painter" provide excellent examples.

Setting. *(197)* (1) The time and place of a STORY or play; its locale. In a broader sense, setting includes also such elements as the moral, intellectual, and social milieu in which the characters move. (2) Also, in the theater, the scenery and props used on stage.

Shakespearean Sonnet (or **English Sonnet**). *(599)* A SONNET in three quatrains and a COUPLET, rhyming *abab cdcd efef gg.*

Shaped Poem. *(513)* A poem constructed so that its shape on a page presents a picture of its subject. Examples include George Herbert's "The Altar" and "Easter Wings" (1633) and John Hollander's "Swan and Shadow" (1969).

Short Story. A fictional prose narrative read comfortably in a single sitting. In length, it falls between the short short story of under 2,000 words and the NOVELETTE of over 15,000. Although any brief narrative is by some definitions a short story, in common literary usage the term refers most often to fictions of the nineteenth and twentieth centuries.

Simile. *(242, 519)* A METAPHOR containing *like, as,* or *as if:*

> She swims *like* a fish.
> She swims *as* a fish swims.
> She swims *as if* she were a fish.

Situational Irony. *(23, 493)* See IRONY.

Slant Rhyme. *(545)* Also called *half, approximate, imperfect, near, off, oblique.* It provides an approximation of the sound: *up, step; peer, pare.*

Social Drama. Drama stressing the social world, with emphasis on the individual's place in the society of his or her time. Examples include Ibsen's *Enemy of the People,* Strindberg's *Miss Julie,* Chekhov's *Cherry Orchard,* and Miller's *Death of a Salesman.*

Soliloquy. "Talking alone" (from Latin *solus*) in a play, wherein the character reveals his or her thoughts and, frequently, informs the audience of attitudes and background.

Sonnet. *(599)* A verse form of fourteen lines, in English characteristically in iambic pentameter and most often in one of two rhyme schemes: the *Italian* (or *Petrarchan*) or *Shakespearean* (or *English*), described here under their respective entries.

Spondee. A metrical foot of two long, or stressed, syllables: — —. See METER.

Sprung Rhythm. Gerard Manley Hopkins's term to describe his variations of iambic METER to avoid the "same and tame." His feet, he said, vary from one to four syllables, with one stress per foot, on the first syllable. Hence "four sorts of feet, a monosyllable and the so-called accentual Trochee, Dactyl, and the First Paeon" (— | — ∪ | — ∪∪ | — ∪∪∪). Hopkins said that it is "the most natural of things."

Stanza. *(586)* Loosely, any grouping of lines in a separate unit in a poem: a verse paragraph. More strictly, a stanza is a grouping of a prescribed number of lines in a given METER, usually with a particular RHYME SCHEME, repeated as a unit of structure.

Static Imagery. *(509)* Imagery in the form of stationary pictures, in contrast to KINETIC IMAGERY.

Stock Characters. *(849)* Familiar types repeated in literature to become the stock in trade of a particular genre, like the strong, silent hero of the Western or the hard-boiled hero of the detective story.

Story. *(848)* A narrative, or sequence of events. Using the word in a specialized sense, critics sometimes distinguish a *story* from a PLOT, with the story defined as the sequence of events as they happened, or are imagined to have happened, in their proper chronological order, and the plot defined as the author's arrangement of the events of the story, which is sometimes quite different.

Strophe. Part of the choral ode in classical Greek drama. The strophe was chanted by the CHORUS, as it moved in one direction. An ANTISTROPHE, chanted while the chorus reversed the first movement, and an epode, chanted while the chorus stood still, completed the ode. Later, the term was applied to a STANZA of any ode and to stanzaic units of irregular length in other poems, as, for example, in poems in FREE VERSE.

Style. An author's personal manner of expression. This may be highly individualistic or idiosyncratic, so that we understand rather quickly by the manner, without much consideration, that we have come upon a passage, say, by Faulkner or Dickens—or at least that the passage was written by someone using a Faulknerian or Dickensian style. A style may also be without telltale marks of a strong personality—the *plain style* of much good expository prose.

Style is the result of the choices an author makes, with respect not to subject matter but to its presentation. A style may be abstract or concrete, heavy with CONNOTATION or essentially denotative, characterized by particular uses of FIGURATIVE LANGUAGE or largely free of them. Indeed, all elements of diction (word choice), syntax, paragraph construction, and organization are proper subjects for stylistic analysis in prose, as are, in verse, such elements as METER and RHYME.

A style is individual, personal to the writer, but it is also marked by characteristics derived from circumstances. Hence, it is possible to speak of period styles; of styles appropriate to a particular occasion, as formal, informal, or colloquial; of styles distinguished by their uses, as satiric, journalistic, literary, scientific.

Syllabic Verse. *(580)* Poetry in which METER has been set aside and the line is controlled by an arbitrary number of syllables, regardless of stress. Marianne Moore and other twentieth-century writers have preferred this form. It is standard in the unstressed Romance languages and in Japanese verse forms such as *Haiku.*

Symbol. *(242, 434)* Considered simply, the symbols of literature fall into three classes. (1) *Natural symbols* present things not for themselves, but for the ideas people commonly associate with them: a star for hope, a cloud for despair, night for death, a sunrise for a new beginning. (2) *Conventional symbols* present things for the meanings people within a particular group have agreed to give them: a national flag for the ideas of home or patriotism associated with it, or a Christian cross or star of David for the associations they evoke in people familiar with the appropriate religion. (3) *Literary symbols* sometimes build upon natural or conventional symbols, adding meanings appropriate primarily within the work at hand, but sometimes they also create meanings within a work for things that have no natural or conventional meaning outside it, as Melville does with his white whale, for instance.

Synecdoche. *(528)* The understanding of one thing by another—a kind of METAPHOR in which a part stands for the whole, or the whole for a part: *a hired hand* meaning "a laborer," or *the law* meaning "a police officer."

Technique. A systematic method, as in the following examples of literary analysis: "E. E. Cummings's technique of fracturing and spacing language to elicit meaning," or "The technique of merging fragmentary sentences to suggest the stream of consciousness."

Tercet (or **Triplet**). *(606)* A verse unit of three lines, sometimes rhymed, sometimes not.

Tetrameter. Four-foot lines. See METER.

Theme. *(302, 648)* (1) A central or recurring topic in a literary work, as, for example, love or death: the *thematic material* that helps to give the work focus. (2) A thought about a topic, suggested by a work, as, for example, that love ennobles or debases: the *thematic idea* that gives the work meaning.

Third-Person Limited Omniscience. *(117)* A method sometimes adopted in modern story telling whereby the omniscience of the traditional storyteller is constrained in some significant way. For instance, the narrator may present only the knowledge that is available to the protagonist, or main character, keeping other information hidden. See NARRATIVE PERSPECTIVE.

Third-Person Narration. *(117)* Method of story telling in which someone who is not involved in the story, but stands somewhere outside it in space and time, tells of the events. See NARRATIVE PERSPECTIVE.

Third-Person Omniscience. *(117)* The traditional way of telling a story by a THIRD-PERSON NARRATOR, who is not involved in the events. By story-telling CONVENTION, the narrator possesses the powers of omniscience, knowing all there is to know, but revealing it in the manner of Scheherazade in the *Thousand and One Nights*—in the way that will make the story most interesting. See NARRATIVE PERSPECTIVE.

Tone. The author's attitude toward subject and audience—playful, serious, ironic, formal, somber, and the like; a work's mood.

Traditional Ballad. *(587)* Another name for the *popular ballad* or *folk ballad,* a song of anonymous authorship, transmitted orally. See BALLAD.

Tragedy. *(803, 848)* Fundamentally a serious fiction involving the downfall of a hero or heroine. Greek tragedy was strongly influenced by the conception of a contract of order and stability in which gods, human society, and nature all participated. An act of aggression (Greek *hybris,* often spelled *hubris*) throws this cosmic machinery out of gear, and hence it must make a countermovement to right itself. This countermovement is usually called *nemesis,* and many words that are often translated as "fate" *(heimarmene, moira, ananke)* also refer to this recovery of order, which makes the tragic action seem inevitable. The conception of a contract is a moral conception, but the particular action called tragic that happens to the hero does not depend on moral status. Aristotle spoke of a tragic *hamartia,* usually translated "flaw," as essential to the hero, but this flaw, despite the fact that *hamartia* is the ordinary New Testament word for sin, is not necessarily a moral defect, but rather a matter of being exposed to a tragic action in a certain place.

Three main themes of tragedy are evident. One is the theme of isolation, in which a hero, a character of greater than ordinary human size, becomes isolated from the community. Then there is the theme of the violation and reestablishment of order, in which the neutralizing of the violent act may take the form of revenge. Finally, a character may embody a passion too great for the cosmic order to tolerate, such as the passion of sexual love.

In Shakespeare the theme of the social isolation of the hero appears at its most powerful and concentrated in *King Lear,* where the king's abdication of royal power leaves him exposed to the malignancy of the two of his three daughters who supplant him. Revenge tragedy, a common Elizabethan and Jacobean form, appears in *Hamlet,* with revenge being imposed on the hero as a moral obligation. The tragedy of passion, in its commonest form of sexual love, is the mode of *Romeo and Juliet.*

Prose fiction *(Crime and Punishment, Anna Karenina, Moby-Dick, Madame Bovary)* has been the genre of most of the really powerful modern tragedies. Here the ironic component of tragedy predominates over the heroic one, because of the difficulty of assuming the convention of a tragic hero who is larger than life size. Such a figure as Willy Loman in Arthur Miller's *Death of a Salesman,* for example, gains his heroic aura only through being a representative of a specific social development, the emphasis on hustling and hard-selling capitalism that at one time, at least, formed a prominent part of what is called the American dream. Loman's isolation in itself is simply ironic; it is the collapse of the dream he embodies that is tragic.

Tragic Flaw. *(850)* Greek *hamartia:* in a TRAGEDY, the defect in the hero that leads to a downfall.

Tragic Irony. The essence of TRAGEDY, in which the most noble and most deserving person, because of the very grounds of his or her excellence, dies in defeat. See IRONY.

Trimeter. Three-foot lines. See METER.

Triple Rhyme. The matching of three final syllables, the accented plus two unaccented: *listening / glistening; syllable / killable.* It is a variation of FEMININE RHYME.

Trochee. A metrical foot going — ∪. See METER.

Type Characters. *(164, 849)* Ones endowed with traits that mark them more distinctly as representatives of a type or class than as individuals standing apart from a type: the typical doctor or housewife, for example. Type characters are the opposite of individualized characters. They are common in romance, ALLE-GORY, and the various forms of popular literature. See CHARACTERS.

Unities. *(849)* With reference to drama, the three traditional unities: PLOT, time, and place. The idea stems from Aristotle's discussion of TRAGEDY in his *Poetics,* where he stresses the importance of unity of plot. Critics of the sixteenth and seventeenth centuries insisted also upon the importance of unity of time and place, which some assumed as necessary corollaries to the idea of a unified plot. Of time, Aristotle suggested only that the ideal tragedy should occur within "a single revolution of the sun," or little more. Of place, he said nothing. His definition of a unified plot emphasized continuous action, from beginning through middle to end, with each event the necessary or probable result of the one that preceded it, and with no irrelevant episode.

Unity. The quality of an artistic work that allows it to stand as a complete and independent whole, with each part related to each other part and no part irrelevant or superfluous.

Unreliable Narrator. *(41)* A narrator, or storyteller, who displays attitudes toward the story, or judgments about it, markedly different from those we know or assume to belong to the author.

Upstage. The rear of a stage. An actor "upstages" another by moving toward the rear and forcing the other actor to turn his or her back to the audience.

Variable Foot. In FREE VERSE, a unit with one primary stress, and a variable number of unstressed or lightly stressed syllables. William Carlos Williams used the term frequently, applying it especially to the stepped-down TERCET of *The*

Desert Music and Other Poems (1954) and *Journey to Love* (1955), as in the opening lines of "The Sparrow":

This sparrow
        who comes to sit at my window
                is a poetic truth
more than a natural one.
      His voice,
           his movements,

Count one beat (one foot) to each line.

Verbal Irony. *(23, 492)* See IRONY.

Verisimilitude. The appearance of actuality.

Villanelle. *(606)* One of the French verse forms, in five TERCETS, all rhyming *aba,* and a QUATRAIN, rhyming *abaa.* The entire first and third lines are repeated alternately as the final lines of tercets 2, 3, 4, and 5, and together to conclude the quatrain. Examples include E. A. Robinson's "The House on the Hill," William Empson's "Missing Dates," Theodore Roethke's "The Waking," and Dylan Thomas's "Do Not Go Gentle into That Good Night."

Visual Imagery. *(503)* Imagery that appeals to the eye, creating pictures.

ACKNOWLEDGMENTS

A. R. Ammons. "Kind" and "Corsons Inlet" are reprinted from *Collected Poems, 1951–1971* by A. R. Ammons, by permission of W. W. Norton & Company, Inc. Copyright © 1972 by A. R. Ammons.

Sherwood Anderson. "I'm a Fool," copyright 1922 by Dial Publishing Co.; copyright renewed 1949 by Eleanor Copenhaver Anderson. Reprinted by permission of Harold Ober Associates Incorporated.

Anonymous. "Barbry Ellen" from *The Ballad Tree* by Evelyn Kendrick Wells. Copyright renewed 1978. Reprinted by permission of John Wiley & Sons, Inc.

Anonymous. "Ho! Ye Sun, Moon Stars" reprinted by permission of Smithsonian Institution Press from the 27th Annual Report of the Bureau of American Ethnology, *The Omaha Tribe*, by Alice C. Fletcher and Francis LaFlesche. Pp. 115–116. Smithsonian Institution, Washington, D.C. 1911.

Anonymous. "Ruin" from *An Anthology of Old English Poetry*, translated by Charles Kennedy. Copyright © 1960 by Oxford University Press, Inc. Reprinted by permission.

Anonymous. "The Two Sisters," version C, from *Traditional Ballads of Virginia*, edited by Arthur K. Davis. Copyright 1929 by The President and Fellows of Harvard College. Reprinted by permission of University Press of Virginia.

Aristophanes. *Lysistrata* translated by Donald Sutherland. Copyright © 1959 by Donald Sutherland; copyright © 1961 by Harper & Row, Publishers, Inc.

John Ashbery. "The Desperado" from *Shadow Train* by John Ashbery. Copyright © 1980, 1981 by John Ashbery. Reprinted by permission of Viking Penguin Inc.

Margaret Atwood. "When It Happens" from the short story collection *Dancing Girls* published by McClelland & Stewart Limited in Canada, 1977, and by Simon & Schuster in the United States, 1982. "At First I Was Given Centuries" from *Power Politics* published by Oxford University Press in Canada and by Harper & Row, Publishers, Inc. in the United States. All reprinted by permission of the author.

W. H. Auden. "Musee des Beaux Arts" and "As I Walked Out One Evening" from *Collected Poems* by W. H. Auden, edited by Edward Mendelson. Copyright 1923 and renewed 1968 by W. H. Auden. "September 1, 1939" from *The English Auden: Poems, Essays and Dramatic Writings, 1927–1939* by W. H. Auden, edited by Edward Mendelson. Copyright 1940 by W. H. Auden. "In Memory of W. B. Yeats" from *Collected Poems* by W. H. Auden, edited by Edward Mendelson. All poems reprinted by permission of Random House, Inc. and Faber and Faber Ltd.

John Barth. "Lost in the Funhouse" from the book *Lost in the Funhouse* by John Barth. Copyright © 1968 by John Barth. Reprinted by permission of Doubleday & Company, Inc.

Ann Beattie. "Janus," copyright 1985 by Ann Beattie. Reprinted by permission of International Creative Management. Originally published in *The New Yorker*.

Samuel Beckett. *Not I* from *Ends and Odds*. Copyright © 1974, 1975, 1976, 1977 by Samuel Beckett. Reprinted by permission of Grove Press, Inc. and Faber and Faber Ltd.

John Berryman. "Dream Song #4" and "Dream Song #14" from *77 Dream Songs* by John Berryman. Copyright © 1959, 1962, 1963, 1964 by John Berryman. Reprinted by permission of Farrar, Straus & Giroux, Inc.

Earle Birney. "The Bear on the Delhi Road" from *The Collected Poems of Earle Birney*. Copyright © 1975 by Earle Birney. Used by permission of The Canadian Publishers, McClelland and Stewart Limited, Toronto.

Elizabeth Bishop. "Sestina" from *The Complete Poems* by Elizabeth Bishop. Copyright © 1956 by

J. V. Cunningham. "Montana Pastoral" and "Coffee" from *The Collected Poems and Epigrams of J. V. Cunningham,* Swallow Press. Copyright © 1971 by J. V. Cunningham. Reprinted by permission of Ohio University Press.

James Dickey. "Cherrylog Road" from *Poems 1957–1967.* Copyright © 1964 by James Dickey. Reprinted by permission of Wesleyan University Press.

Emily Dickinson. "After Great Pain, a Formal Feeling Comes" from *The Complete Poems of Emily Dickinson,* edited by Thomas H. Johnson. Copyright 1929 by Martha Dickinson Bianchi; copyright © renewed 1957 by Mary L. Hampson. Reprinted by permission of Little, Brown and Company. "After Great Pain, a Formal Feeling Comes", "I Like to See It Lap the Miles," and "The Heart Asks Pleasure—First" from *The Poems of Emily Dickinson,* edited by Thomas H. Johnson, Cambridge, Mass.: The Belknap Press of Harvard University Press. Copyright 1951, © 1955, 1979, 1983 by the President and Fellows of Harvard College.

E. L. Doctorow. "The Hunter" from *Lives of the Poets* by E. L. Doctorow. Copyright © 1984 by E. L. Doctorow. Reprinted by permission of Random House, Inc.

Hilda Doolittle. "Heat" from *Selected Poems of H.D.* Copyright © 1957 by Norman Holmes Pearson. Reprinted by permission of New Directions Publishing Corp.

George Draper. "Rink Keeper's Sestina," copyright © 1975 by The Atlantic Monthly Company, Boston, Mass. Reprinted with permission.

Richard Eberhart. "The Fury of Aerial Bombardment" from *Collected Poems: 1930–1976* by Richard Eberhart. Copyright © 1976 by Richard Eberhart. Reprinted by permission of Oxford University Press.

T. S. Eliot. "The Love Song of J. Alfred Prufrock" from *Collected Poems 1909–1962* by T. S. Eliot. Copyright 1936 by Harcourt Brace Jovanovich, Inc.; copyright © 1963, 1964 by T. S. Eliot. "Little Gidding" from *Four Quartets* by T. S. Eliot. Copyright 1943 by T. S. Eliot; renewed 1971 by Esme Valerie Eliot. All poems reprinted by permission of Harcourt Brace Jovanovich, Inc. and Faber and Faber Ltd.

Ralph Ellison. "Flying Home." Reprinted by permission of William Morris, Inc. on behalf of the author. Copyright 1944.

William Faulkner. "A Rose for Emily" from *Collected Stories of William Faulkner* by William Faulkner. Copyright 1930 and renewed 1958 by William Faulkner. Reprinted by permission of Random House, Inc.

Lawrence Ferlinghetti. "Constantly Risking Absurdity" from *A Coney Island of the Mind.* Copyright © 1958 by Lawrence Ferlinghetti. Reprinted by permission of New Directions Publishing Corp.

Thomas Hornsby Ferril. "Always Begin Where You Are" from *Words for Denver and Other Poems* by Thomas Hornsby Ferril. Copyright © 1966 by Thomas Hornsby Ferril. Reprinted by permission of William Morrow & Company.

F. Scott Fitzgerald. "Babylon Revisited" from *Taps At Reveille.* Copyright 1931 by The Curtis Publishing Company; copyright renewed © 1959 Frances Scott Fitzgerald Lanahan. Reprinted by permission of Charles Scribner's Sons.

Robert Frost. "Home Burial," "After Apple-Picking," "Stopping by Woods on a Snowy Evening," "Design," "Directive," "Mending Wall," "Dust of Snow," "Two Tramps in Mud Time," "Fire and Ice," and "Once by the Pacific," from *The Poetry of Robert Frost,* edited by Edward Connery Lathem. Copyright 1923, 1928, 1930, 1936, 1939, 1947, © 1969 by Holt, Rinehart and Winston; copyright 1951, 1956, © 1958 by Robert Frost; copyright © 1964, © 1967, © 1975 by Lesley Frost Ballantine. Reprinted by permission of Holt, Rinehart and Winston, Publishers.

George Garrett. "King of the Mountain" from *An Evening Performance.* Copyright © 1985 by George Garrett. Reprinted by permission of Doubleday & Company, Inc.

Allen Ginsberg. "A Supermarket in California" from *Collected Poems 1947–1980* by Allen Ginsberg. Copyright © 1955 by Allen Ginsberg. Reprinted by permission of Harper & Row, Publishers, Inc.

Susan Glaspell. *Suppressed Desires* from *Plays* by Susan Glaspell. Copyright 1920 by Dodd, Mead & Company, Inc.; copyright renewed 1948 by Susan Glaspell. Reprinted by permission of Dodd, Mead & Company, Inc.

Gail Godwin. "A Sorrowful Woman" from *Dream Children* by Gail Godwin. Copyright © 1976 by Gail Godwin. Reprinted by permission of Alfred A. Knopf, Inc.

Robert Graves. "Ulysses" and "The Cool Web" from *Robert Graves: Collected Poems 1975.* Reprinted by permission of The Executors of The Estate of Robert Graves.

Thomas Gray. "Elegy Written in a Country Churchyard" and "Ode: On a Distant Prospect of Eton College" from *The Complete Poems of Thomas Gray,* edited by H. W. Starr and J. R. Hendrickson. Copyright © 1966 by Oxford University Press, Inc. Reprinted by permission of Oxford University Press.

Thom Gunn. "Moly" from *Moly and My Sad Captains* by Thom Gunn. Copyright © 1961, 1971, 1973 by Thom Gunn. Reprinted by permission of Farrar, Straus & Giroux, Inc. and Faber and Faber Ltd.

Woody Guthrie. "Plane Wreck at Los Gatos," lyric by Woody Guthrie, music by Martin Hoffman. TRO © Copyright 1961 and 1963 Ludlow Music, Inc., New York, N.Y. Used by permission.

Thomas Hardy. "The Walk," "The Convergence of the Twain," "I Look into My Glass," "The Self-Unseeing," "In Tenebris," and "Channel Firing" from *Collected Poems* by Thomas Hardy. Reprinted by permission of Macmillan Publishing Co., Inc., The Macmillan Company of Canada Ltd., Macmillan London and Basingstoke, and the Trustees of the Hardy Estate.

Ernest Hemingway. "Hills Like White Elephants" from *Men Without Women.* Copyright 1927 by Charles Scribner's Sons; copyright renewed 1955 by Ernest Hemingway. Reprinted by permission of Charles Scribner's Sons.

William Heyen. "The Snapper" from *Long Island Light: Poems & a Memoir* by William Heyen. Reprinted by permission of the publisher, Vanguard Press, Inc. Copyright © 1967, 1968, 1969, 1970, 1971, 1972, 1973, 1974, 1979, by William Heyen.

Gerard Manley Hopkins. "God's Grandeur," "Felix Randal," "The Windhover," and "Pied Beauty" from *Poems of Gerard Manley Hopkins,* Fourth Edition, edited by W. H. Gardner and N. H. MacKenzie. Copyright © 1967 by The Society of Jesus. Reprinted by permission of Oxford University Press, Inc.

A. E. Housman. "Loveliest of Trees, the Cherry Now," "Terence, This Is Stupid Stuff," "1887," "With Rue My Heart Is Laden," "To an Athlete Dying Young," "On Wenlock Edge the Wood's in Trouble," "The Chestnut Casts His Flambeaux," and "The Night Is Freezing Fast," from "A Shropshire Lad"—Authorized Edition—from *The Collected Poems of A. E. Housman.* Copyright 1922, 1939, 1940, © 1965 by Holt, Rinehart and Winston. Copyright © 1967, 1968 by Robert F. Symons. Copyright 1950 by Barclays Bank Ltd. Reprinted by permission of The Society of Authors as the literary representative of the Estate of A. E. Housman, Jonathan Cape Ltd., publishers of A. E. Housman's *Collected Poems,* and Holt, Rinehart and Winston.

Langston Hughes. "Feet Live Their Own Life" from *The Best of Simple* by Langston Hughes. Copyright © 1961 by Langston Hughes. Reprinted by permission of Hill and Wang, a division of Farrar, Straus & Giroux, Inc.

Ted Hughes. "Second Glance at a Jaguar" from *New Selected Poems* by Ted Hughes. Copyright © 1967 by Ted Hughes. Reprinted by permission of Harper & Row, Publishers, Inc. Reprinted by permission of Faber and Faber Ltd. from *Wodwo* by Ted Hughes.

Henrik Ibsen. *An Enemy of the People* from *The Oxford Ibsen,* Vol. vi, translated and edited by James Walter McFarlane. Copyright © 1960 by Oxford University Press. Reprinted by permission of Oxford University Press.

David Ignatow. "Rescue the Dead" from *Rescue the Dead.* Copyright © 1968 by David Ignatow. Reprinted by permission of Wesleyan University Press.

W. W. Jacobs. "The Monkey's Paw" from *The Lady of the Barge.* Copyright © 1902. Reprinted by permission of The Society of Authors as the literary representative of the Estate of W. W. Jacobs.

Randall Jarrell. "The Death of the Ball-Turret Gunner" from *The Complete Poems* by Randall Jarrell. Copyright © 1973 by Mrs. Randall Jarrell. Reprinted by permission of Farrar, Straus & Giroux, Inc.

Robinson Jeffers. "Iona: The Graves of the Kings," copyright 1931 and renewed 1959 by Robinson Jeffers. "Shine, Perishing Republic," copyright 1925 and renewed 1953 by Robinson Jeffers. "The Purse-Seine," copyright 1937 and renewed 1965 by Donnan Jeffers and Garth Jeffers. "To the Stone-Cutters," copyright 1924 and renewed 1952 by Robinson Jeffers. "Hurt Hawks," copyright

1928 and renewed 1956 by Robinson Jeffers. Reprinted from *Selected Poetry of Robinson Jeffers* by permission of Random House, Inc.

James Joyce. "A Little Cloud" from *Dubliners* by James Joyce. Copyright 1918 by B. W. Huebsch; copyright © 1967 by the Estate of James Joyce. All Rights Reserved. Reprinted by permission of Viking Penguin Inc.

Galway Kinnell. "To Christ Our Lord" from *What A Kingdom It Was* by Galway Kinnell. Copyright © 1960 by Galway Kinnell. Reprinted by permission of Houghton Mifflin Company.

Rudyard Kipling. "Sestina of the Tramp-Royal" from *The Definitive Edition of Rudyard Kipling's Verse.* Reprinted by permission of The National Trust for Places of Historic Interest or Natural Beauty and Macmillan London Ltd.

Carolyn Kizer. "The Skein" from *Knock upon Silence* by Carolyn Kizer. Copyright © 1963, 1964, 1965, 1971 by Carolyn Kizer. Reprinted by permission of Doubleday & Company, Inc.

Kenneth Koch. "Down at the Docks" from *Thank You and Other Poems.* Copyright © 1962 by Kenneth Koch.

Ring Lardner. "Haircut" from *Roundup.* Copyright 1925 by Ellis A. Lardner; copyright renewed 1953. Reprinted with the permission of Charles Scribner's Sons.

Philip Larkin. "Cut Grass" from *High Windows* by Philip Larkin. Copyright © 1974 by Philip Larkin. Reprinted by permission of Faber and Faber Ltd. and Farrar, Straus & Giroux, Inc. "Church Going" and "Poetry of Departures" from *The Less Deceived.* Reprinted by permission of The Marvell Press, England.

D. H. Lawrence. "The Rocking-Horse Winner" from *The Complete Short Stories of D. H. Lawrence,* Volume III by D. H. Lawrence. Copyright 1933 by The Estate of D. H. Lawrence; renewed © 1961 by Angelo Ravagli and C. Montague Weekley, Executors of the Estate of Frieda Lawrence Ravagli. Reprinted by permission of Viking Penguin, Inc. "Mother and Daughter" from *The Complete Short Stories of D. H. Lawrence* by D. H. Lawrence. Copyright © 1933 by the Estate of D. H. Lawrence; renewed © 1961 by Angelo Ravagli and C. Montague Weekley, Executors of the Estate of Frieda Lawrence Ravagli. Reprinted by permission of Viking Penguin Inc.

Ursula K. Le Guin. "The Ones Who Walk Away from Omelas," copyright © 1973, 1974 by Ursula K. Le Guin. Reprinted by permission of the author and the author's agent, Virginia Kidd.

Stanislaw Lem. "The Seventh Sally" from *The Cyberiad* by Stanislaw Lem. English translation copyright © 1974 by The Seabury Press, Inc. Used by permission of the publishers.

John Lennon & Paul McCartney. "Eleanor Rigby," © 1966 Northern Songs LTD. All rights controlled & administered by Blackwood Music Inc. under license from ATV Music (MACLEN). All rights reserved. International copyright secured. Used by permission.

Doris Lessing. "The Old Chief Mshlanga" from *African Stories.* Copyright © 1951, 1953, 1954, 1957, 1958, 1962, 1963, 1964, 1965 by Doris Lessing. Reprinted by permission of Simon & Schuster, Inc. and Curtis Brown, Ltd.

Jack London. "To Build A Fire" from *The Best Short Stories of Jack London.* Copyright © 1945 by Doubleday. Reprinted by permission of the Estate of Irving Shepard.

Robert Lowell. "Skunk Hour" from *Life Studies* by Robert Lowell. Copyright © 1956, 1959 by Robert Lowell. "For the Union Dead" from *For the Union Dead* by Robert Lowell. Copyright © 1960, 1964 by Robert Lowell. Reprinted by permission of Farrar, Straus & Giroux, Inc.

Archibald MacLeish. "You, Andrew Marvell" and "Survivor" from *New and Collected Poems 1917–1976* by Archibald MacLeish. Copyright © 1976 by Archibald MacLeish. Reprinted by permission of Houghton Mifflin Company.

Katherine Mansfield. "Bliss" from *The Short Stories of Katherine Mansfield* by Katherine Mansfield. Copyright 1920 by Alfred A. Knopf, Inc.; renewed 1948 by John Middleton Murry. Reprinted by permission of Alfred A. Knopf, Inc.

James Merrill. "The Broken Home" from *Nights and Days.* Copyright © 1966 by James Merrill. Reprinted by permission of Atheneum Publishers, Inc.

W. S. Merwin. "Grandmother Watching at Her Window" from *The First Four Books of Poems* (published originally in *The Drunk in the Furnace*) by W. S. Merwin. Copyright © 1975 by W. S. Merwin. *The Drunk in the Furnace* © 1960 by W. S. Merwin. Reprinted by permission of Atheneum Publishers, Inc.

Robinson; renewed 1949 by Ruth Nivison. Reprinted from *Collected Poems* by permission of Macmillan Publishing Co., Inc. "The House on the Hill" from *The Children of the Night* (1897). Reprinted by permission of Charles Scribner's Sons. "The Mill," copyright 1920 by Edwin Arlington Robinson; renewed 1948 by Ruth Nivison. From *Collected Poems* by permission of Macmillan Publishing Co., Inc.

Theodore Roethke. "I Knew a Woman," copyright © 1954 by Theodore Roethke. "My Papa's Waltz," copyright 1942 by Hearst Magazines, Inc. "The Waking," copyright 1948 by Theodore Roethke. "The Far Field," copyright © 1962 by Beatrice Roethke as Administratix of the estate of Theodore Roethke. All from *The Collected Poems of Theodore Roethke.* Reprinted by permission of Doubleday & Company, Inc.

Delmore Schwartz. "Calmly We Walk Throught This April's Day" from *Selected Poems; Summer Knowledge.* Copyright 1938 by New Directions Publishing Corp. Reprinted by permission of New Directions.

William Shakespeare. *The Tempest,* edited by Northrop Frye. Copyright © 1956 by Penguin Books, Inc.; renewed © 1971 by Viking Penguin Inc. All Rights Reserved. Reprinted by permission of Viking Penguin Inc.

Louis Simpson. "Carentan O Carentan" from *A Dream of Governors.* Copyright © 1959 by Louis Simpson. Reprinted by permission of Wesleyan University Press.

L. E. Sissman. "Henley, July 4: 1914–1964" from *Dying: An Introduction* by L. E. Sissman. Copyright © 1964 by L. E. Sissman. Originally appeared in *The New Yorker.* Reprinted by permission of Little, Brown and Company, in association with The Atlantic Monthly Press.

Edith Sitwell. "Sir Beelzebub" from *The Collected Poems of Edith Sitwell.* Copyright © 1968 by The Vanguard Press, Inc.; copyright © 1949, 1953, 1954, 1962, 1963 by Dame Edith Sitwell. Reprinted by permission of Vanguard Press, Inc.

Stevie Smith. "Not Waving But Drowning" from *The Collected Poems of Stevie Smith.* Copyright © 1972 by Stevie Smith. Reprinted by permission of New Directions Publishing Corp.

W. D. Snodgrass. "April Inventory" from *Heart's Needle* by W. D. Snodgrass. Copyright © 1957 by W. D. Snodgrass. Reprinted by permission of Alfred A. Knopf. Inc.

Sophocles. *Oedipus Rex* from *The Oedipus Rex of Sophocles:* An English Version by Dudley Fitts and Robert Fitzgerald. Copyright 1949 by Harcourt Brace Jovanovich, Inc; renewed 1977 by Cornelia Fitts and Robert Fitzgerald. Reprinted by permission of the publisher. All rights, including professional, amateur, motion picture, recitation, lecturing, performance, public reading, radio broadcasting, and television are strictly reserved. Inquiries on all rights should be addressed to Harcourt Brace Jovanovich, Inc., Orlando, Florida 32887.

Stephen Spender. "Airman" from *Selected Poems* (U.S.A.) and *Collected Poems 1928–85* (Canada) by Stephen Spender. Copyright 1934 and renewed 1962 by Stephen Spender. Reprinted by permission of Random House, Inc. and Faber and Faber Ltd.

Wallace Stevens. "Anecdote of the Jar" and "The Snow Man," copyright 1923 and renewed 1951 by Wallace Stevens. "The Idea of Order at Key West," copyright 1936 by Wallace Stevens; renewed 1964 by Holly Stevens. "Of Modern Poetry," copyright 1942 by Wallace Stevens; renewed 1970 by Holly Stevens. Reprinted from *The Palm at the End of the Mind: Selected Poems and a Play* by Wallace Stevens, edited by Holly Stevens, by permission of Alfred A. Knopf, Inc.

May Swenson. "Question" from *Another Animal: Poems* by May Swenson. Copyright 1954 by May Swenson. Reprinted by permission of the author.

Dylan Thomas. "The Force That Through the Green Fuse Drives the Flower," "Poem in October," "Do Not Go Gentle into that Good Night," from *Collected Poems* by Dylan Thomas (Canada). Copyright © 1945 by J. M. Dent & Sons Ltd. and the Trustees for the copyrights of Dylan Thomas. Also from *Poems of Dylan Thomas* (U.S.A.). Copyright 1939 by New Directions Publishing Corp.; © 1952 by Dylan Thomas. Reprinted by permission of New Directions. "Poem in October" originally appeared in *Poetry.*

Leo Tolstoy. "The Death of Ivan Ilych" from *The Death of Ivan Ilych and Other Stories,* translated by Louise and Aylmer Maude. Reprinted by permission of Oxford University Press.

John Updike. "A & P" from *Pigeon Feathers and Other Stories* by John Updike. Copyright © 1962

INDEX OF AUTHORS, TITLES, AND FIRST LINES OF POEMS